STUDIA TRADITIONIS THEOLOGIAE

Explorations in Early and Medieval Theology

Theology continually engages with its past: the people, experience, Scriptures, liturgy, learning, and customs of Christians. The past is preserved, rejected, modified; but the legacy steadily evolves as Christians are never indifferent to history. Even when engaging the future, theology looks backwards: the next generation's training includes inheriting a canon of Scripture, doctrine, and controversy; while adapting the past is central in every confrontation with a modernity.

This is the dynamic realm of tradition, and this series's focus. Whether examining people, texts, or periods, its volumes are concerned with how the past evolved in the past, and the interplay of theology, culture, and tradition.

STUDIA TRADITIONIS THEOLOGIAE

Explorations in Early and Medieval Theology

14

Series Editor: Thomas O'Loughlin,
Professor of Historical Theology
in the University of Nottingham

EARLY MEDIEVAL IRELAND AND EUROPE: CHRONOLOGY, CONTACTS, SCHOLARSHIP

A Festschrift for Dáibhí Ó Cróinín

Edited by
Pádraic Moran
&
Immo Warntjes

BREPOLS

Cover illustration: *Tabula Peutingeriana* © ÖNB Vienna: Cod. 324, Segm. VIII + IX

D/2015/0095/100
ISBN 978-2-503-55313-9 (printed version)
ISBN 978-2-503-55420-4 (online version)

Printed on acid-free paper

CONTENTS

SCHOLARSHIP

ABBREVIATIONS

CCSL	*Corpus Christianorum, Series Latina*	
CLA	*Codices Latini Antiquiores*	
CSEL	*Corpus Scriptorum Ecclesiasticorum Latinorum*	
DIL	*Dictionary of the Irish language, based mainly on Old and Middle Irish materials*	
GCS	*Die griechischen christlichen Schriftsteller der ersten Jahrhunderte*	
HRG	*Handwörterbuch zur deutschen Rechtsgeschichte*	
MGH	*Monumenta Germaniae Historica*	
	Auct. ant.	*Auctores antiquissimi*
	Conc.	*Concilia*
	Epp. sel.	*Epistolae selectae*
	Poetae	*Poetae Latini medii aevi*
	SS	*Scriptores (in Folio)*
	SS rer. Germ.	*Scriptores rerum Germanicarum in usum scholarum separatim editi*
	SS rer. Merov.	*Scriptores rerum Merovingicarum*
ODNB	*Oxford Dictionary of National Biography*	
PL	*Patrologia Latina*	
PRIA	*Proceedings of the Royal Irish Academy*	

ACKNOWLEDGEMENTS

Editing a collection of articles is never straightforward, and we are extremely grateful to three individuals who helped shepherd the volume smoothly through the publication process: first, to Tom O'Loughlin, the series editor, for his unwavering support; second, to Bart Janssens at Brepols for seeing the volume through the press with patience and competence; and third, to Daniel Frisch, now a professional desk editor, for once again lending his expertise in preparing the pre-print layout.

By offering this volume to Dáibhí Ó Cróinín on his 60th birthday, we are following a time-honoured German tradition: students pay their respect to their mentor on this occasion (while colleagues have their turn five years later). As the first students of Dáibhí to complete their Ph.D.s (we enrolled on the same day in 2003 and were examined on the same day in 2007), we both felt that the gesture was appropriate. But merging the traditionally separate volumes by students and colleagues brought its own challenges. Well acquainted as we are with Dáibhí's activities over the past 15 years, we are less so for the previous two and a half decades. While we tried to include those who have been close to Dáibhí academically throughout his career, we feel we may inevitably have overlooked some potential contributors, and we would regret if any colleagues feel disappointed at their omission.

Many of those who originally subscribed to the project with great enthusiasm were eventually forced to pull out because of other commitments (notably several of Dáibhí's continental friends, where the academic circus is dancing to ever faster tunes). To all of those who were able to submit articles, however, we thank them sincerely here both for taking the time to contribute to what we believe is a very worthy enterprise and for their (sometimes willing, occasionally hesitant) co-operation.

It remains to thank those institutions that very kindly allowed us to print images of material under their copyright: Biblioteca Antoniana, Padua; Biblioteca Apostolica Vaticana; The Bodleian Library, University of Oxford; Canna House, National Trust for Scotland; Corpus Christi College, Cambridge; Department of the Environment for Northern Ireland; Düsseldorf, Universitätsbibliothek; National Folklore Collection, University College, Dublin; National Monuments Service (Ireland); St John's College, Cambridge; St Gallen, Stiftsbibliothek; Vatican Museums.

INTRODUCTION

The purpose of this volume is to honour Dáibhí Ó Cróinín as an outstanding mentor, colleague, and friend, but even more so to acknowledge his achievements in scholarship. Dáibhí's research interests are laudably wide, in both geographical and thematic terms, something quite exceptional in the often rather insular milieu of medieval Irish studies. The title of the collection reflects what we consider to be Dáibhí's greatest achievement: placing early medieval Ireland in its wider European perspective.

The editors each made contact with Dáibhí a few years before starting our Ph.D.s in 2003, and from the first we were very impressed by the easy and unpretentious manner of this eminent professor in Irish medieval studies. At the time, one of us had a career outside of academia, while the other was an undergraduate in the rigidly hierarchical German system, and so we took great encouragement in being taken seriously as potential researchers. Both of us being in our mid- to late twenties, we were about to take major decisions in our lives, and Dáibhí was extremely supportive, persuading us that the rocky road on which we were setting out was, against the odds, the right one to take. One left a secure job despite having a family to support, the other his social environment, continental comforts, and many shaking heads in order to study 'almost at the end of the earth', as Pope Honorius put it in the 7th century. And all this for the most impenetrable and exotic (some might say dullest) of research topics: early medieval glossaries and computistics, respectively. This would have been impossible without the steady support of our mentor. Even though neither of us had seen a manuscript before we started, Dáibhí always gave us the feeling that we could do it; his confidence (blind faith?) helped to allay our uncertainties.

The Foundations of Irish Culture project, which Dáibhí had established the previous year, was of enormous help. It provided financial support, but also two post-doctoral colleagues in Mark Stansbury and Eric Graff, who as mentors were extremely enthusiastic, generous, and patient. Many of our problems were solved collaboratively within the group (which came to include Jacopo Bisagni, at the time a Ph.D. student in the School of Irish, another liaison initiated by Dáibhí), whether over lunch, dinner, or in one of Galway's pubs. Dáibhí is not a man disposed to deadlines, and his approach instead was extremely liberal, always making himself available to discuss any text, manuscript or historical problem and unfailingly generous in supplying books and articles from his vast personal library. This left the initiative to us, and despite its dangers, his open approach gave us the freedom and space to *think* (and not just to produce), which is increasingly rare in 21st century academia. We hope we have used that freedom well.

Dáibhí enjoyed having a group of researchers around him, for two reasons. First, he is an engaging and enthusiastic teacher, known for his breadth of knowledge, his wit and rhetorical flourish. Our Friday afternoon Old Irish seminars invariably carried on into lengthy discussions over *Weissbier* in the College Bar. Second, we could sense that the project represented a departure from the relative isolation of his earlier career, focused on a specialism not exactly in the mainstream of medieval studies. What transcended any isolation, in those days, was his generosity. An expert especially in the transmission of early medieval computistica, he readily shared information and resources with other interested researchers. Neither did he hesitate in seeking out scholars who could bring their own expertise to specific problems, which drew, for example, Dan Mc Carthy into the field. But no doubt it was the First International Conference on the Science of Computus, held in Galway in 2006, which did most to open up new horizons. This first attempt at bringing into one room all scholars, worldwide, interested in medieval computus proved so successful that it has since become a biannual institution, with the fifth event occurring in 2014. 'The Irish town of Galway has become the world centre of research into the science of computus, especially in its early medieval and Insular traditions', as a recent review (by Philipp Nothaft) put it. It has created networks and produced an exchange of ideas, texts, and publications on a level previously unknown. The isolation is gone, not only for Dáibhí, but for other scholars in this field as well.

Arguably the most dramatic advances in scholarship made by Dáibhí were in the field known to the unacquainted as medieval chronology, to specialists as the science of computus: the reckoning of time and all related issues. His initial interest was triggered when introduced, in the late 1970s, to Charles W. Jones's 1943 edition of Bede's scientific works. Dáibhí was struck immediately by the erudition of the book, still unsurpassed. Furthermore, with his interest in the history of scholarship, he would have admired the circumstances in which the work was produced. In the 1930s Jones, an American in his late twenties, travelled the libraries of Europe unperturbed while the Continent heaved in the political turmoil brought on by fascism. With the outbreak of war, he broke off his tour and used the remainder of his stipend to produce his edition. Dáibhí likes to relate the story of his visit to the great man's home in California in the late 1970s, as a young Irish scholar yet without academic credentials, and of the gracious welcome with which Jones received him.

In Jones's 1943 edition, and in two earlier studies, he hinted at the Irish element in the development of early medieval science. He saw computistical studies reaching an early culmination in Visigothic Spain in the late 6th and early 7th centuries, before arriving in Ireland via a collection of texts towards the middle of the 7th century, from where it continued to Northumbria and served as a major source for Bede. It thus dawned on Dáibhí that computus must have been a central element in the Irish 'Golden Age' of the 7th and 8th centuries, on a par with biblical exegesis and grammar. The limitation of Jones's work, however, was that he stressed only the Irish role in the *transmission* of late antique texts; he did not specify whether Irish scholars made any *original* contribution to the field. Dáibhí therefore started working on the known Irish computistical texts of the period, while a student on the MPhil. in Medieval Studies programme at University College, Dublin. The obvious starting point was Cummian's Letter, which featured prominently in Jones's 1943 edition, though was less well known beyond that. Dáibhí's interest in this text was apparently reinforced by the fact that a charming fellow student from the United States, Maura Walsh, had also worked on it for her thesis; it became their joint project and the beginning of a lifetime alliance.

The next obvious text was the Munich Computus. It was introduced to modern scholarship by Bruno Krusch in 1880; its Irish background, however, was first identified by an Irish scholar, Bartholomew Mac Carthy in 1901. After his MPhil. on the Irish *Sex aetates mundi* (subsequently published by the Dublin Institute for Advanced Studies in 1983), Dáibhí took the prescient decision to travel to Munich to study under Bernhard Bischoff. While there, he learnt that Menso Folkerts had just moved his enormous microfilm collection of medieval mathematical texts to Munich from Oldenburg. Many of these microfilms (still the best such collection worldwide) also contained computistica, and Dáibhí continued to study them whenever he had a chance. The results are well known. First, he discovered a major Irish computistical textbook of the period, which he published under the title *De ratione conputandi* (Toronto, 1988). This, more than any other Irish text yet known, bears witness to the erudition and especially scientific sophistication of early medieval Irish scholars. Second, in 1985, he identified an Easter table transmitted in a 10th-century codex now in Padua as the one followed by the Christian people of Britain and Ireland before the introduction of the Victorian and Dionysiac reckonings respectively. Before Dáibhí's discovery, only speculations concerning the 'Irish' or 'Celtic' Easter dates could be advanced—all of them wrong, as Dan Mc Carthy's reconstruction of the *latercus* was to prove. In effect, this discovery made it possible, for the first time, not only to understand fully the vibrant early medieval Easter controversy, but also, and more important, to produce a reliable chronological framework for early Irish history.

If nothing else, the fact that Irish computistica are transmitted in continental manuscripts would have made Dáibhí aware of the inadequacy of studying Irish history in isolation, disconnected from its European contacts. His interest in transmission extended to other texts. Inspired by the famous 'Wendepunkte' article of his Munich mentor Bernhard Bischoff, he continues to chase Irish Gospel commentaries in continental manuscripts. And as an admirer (and cultivator) of rhetorical wit, he was naturally drawn to the transmission of Virgilius Maro Grammaticus, this Myles na gCopaleen (alias Flann O'Brien alias Brian O'Nolan) of the 7th century, as he used to term him.

Another early medieval Irish export was script, most notably to Northumbria, which had received Christianity, and with it literary culture, from the Irish monastery of Iona. This dependency certainly makes it extremely difficult, for the early period, to distinguish Anglo-Saxon from Irish in this insular contact zone. Still, responding to publications that since the early 20th century placed special emphasis on the Anglo-Saxon dimension, Dáibhí counter-balanced this with an Irish perspective. Most notably, he drew attention to the fact that a continental foundation like Echternach could hardly be viewed simply as Anglo-Saxon, in either script or culture, considering the fact that its founder, Willibrord, Northumbrian though he was, spent the twelve years prior to his mission to Frisia in Ireland. Dáibhí certainly profited from the opportunity to learn about script and scribes from Bernhard Bischoff, unrivalled in his knowledge of early medieval Latin palaeography. (Together with David Ganz, he translated Bischoff's handbook *Paläographie des Altertums und des abendländischen Mittelalters*, published as *Latin paleography, Antiquity and the Middle Ages* in 1990. Working with the German professor was not always easy, however—in fact, he sometimes compares it to the dental surgery he had to undergo at the time.)

Medieval Irish culture on the Continent revealed itself not only in the texts proper, but also in the glosses elaborating on their contents, and many of these were written in the vernacular. The Irish language is certainly dear to Dáibhí's heart. His father Donncha (1919–90), a native of Ballyvourney, Co. Cork, was a renowned scholar of modern Irish, and Dáibhí was exposed to the language and its literature from a very early age. Among his publications is a new edition of *Eachtra Phinocchio* (2003), an Irish translation of Carlo Collodi's classic, by Pádraig Ó Buachalla. The family connection is also prominent in relation to traditional Irish music. Dáibhí's grandmother, Elizabeth (Bess) Cronin was one of the most celebrated Irish folk singers of her generation. Dáibhí used his skills as a historian to honour her by editing a complete collection of her songs (*The songs of Elizabeth Cronin, Irish traditional singer*, Dublin, 2000).

There are areas of Dáibhí's research which could not or only inadequately be covered in the present volume. The most striking among these is historiography, or, more accurately, the biographies of scholars who worked in the fields of Dáibhí's interest over the past four hundred years. On entering Dáibhí's office, the visitor was struck by two aspects: first, the number of books crammed into such a small space (and Dáibhí's ability to rout out the most obscure article within seconds); and second, what Dáibhí calls his 'wall of fame'—photographs of distinguished scholars including Irish historians James Ussher and Eóin Mac Neill; early scholars of medieval chronology including Scaliger, Bucherius, Petavius, and lesser known figures such as Johannes van der Hagen, followed by Bruno Krusch, Bartholomew Mac Carthy, and Charles W. Jones; and the grand figures of medieval Latin palaeography, Ludwig Traube, Wallace M. Lindsay, and Bernhard Bischoff. A special place is reserved for Wilhelm Levison, as he embodies more than any other pre-World War II scholar the interconnectedness of early medieval Europe, with his interest in Irish and Anglo-Saxon contributions to Frankish culture and politics.

Most prominent among Dáibhí's heroes, however, are the Celticists. Through his own initiative, an Irish postal stamp was issued in 2006 to mark the 200th anniversary of the birth of Johann Kaspar Zeuss and at the same time the 150th anniversary of his death. Other pioneers cherished by Dáibhí include Kuno Meyer and Rudolf Thurneysen. In this field, Dáibhí's research has recently taken an interesting and fortuitous turn. While on sabbatical in the academic year 2006–7, Dáibhí spent a few weeks working in the Albertina Library of the University of Leipzig. The decision for Leipzig was four-fold (at least): he was interested in an early Gospel fragment housed there; he was hopeful that East German libraries, understudied in GDR days, might reveal new treasures, computistical or otherwise; the Albertina houses part of the *Nachlass* of the great Bernhard Bischoff; and Leipzig, of course, was where Ernst Windisch was Professor of Celtic for most of his career. The Windisch connection turned out to be the most rewarding. While working in the manuscript room of the Albertina, a librarian (Thomas Döring) came up to Dáibhí with some boxes of small sized booklets. The script in the books looked potentially Irish, as did Dáibhí's name, so he asked Dáibhí whether could he identify the contents. They turned out to be notebooks belonging to the pre-eminent Celticist Whitley Stokes, part of a larger collection bequeathed to his friend Windisch and long since forgotten. (Dáibhí's index of Stokes's 150 notebooks was published as *Whitley Stokes (1830–1909): the lost Celtic notebooks rediscovered*, Dublin, 2010.)

Like Stokes and other Celticists cherished by Dáibhí, he has devoted considerable efforts to editorial duties. One of Dáibhí's major contributions to the field of early Irish history was his sole editorship of the monumental (1200-page) Royal Irish Academy's *New History of Ireland, Vol. 1, Prehistoric & Early Medieval Ireland,* published finally in 2005 after a gestation of more than thirty years. His editorial service also includes his work on *Peritia*, the Journal of the Medieval Academy of Ireland, first published in 1982 and distinguished by its broad multi-disciplinary approach to Irish and insular studies in the context of the European Middle Ages; the journal was initiated by Donnchadh Ó Corráin, and the two DÓCs (the Elder and the Younger, as they would call themselves) were instrumental in promoting the study of early Irish history (through teaching and public talks) when the Celtic Tiger saw no use for the past in Ireland's future. Dáibhí, a devoted and charismatic teacher, also sought to engage more students by writing a textbook, *Early medieval Ireland, 400–1200* (London, 1995), the first work of its kind since the early 1970s.

* * *

It seems apt, then, to begin our volume with 'Early Irish history and chronology' (the title of Dáibhí's collection of articles, dubbed affectionately by him as his 'greatest hits'), and equally so to give first place to Dan Mc Carthy, Dáibhí's long-time collaborator, who deals with 6th century annals and the chronology of Saint Columba's life. Three other contributors deal with the Easter controversy beginning in the 7th century and its aftermath: Immo Warntjes presents a fresh perspective on how the conflict developed within Ireland; Eric Graff argues that the core of the Catalogue of the Saints of Ireland was composed within living memory of the controversy; while Masako Ohashi finds that this issue underlies Bede's letter On the Vernal Equinox.

Dáibhí's interest in early medieval Irish language, literature, and ideas, and their connections with Britain and the Continent is reflected in the second section of the book. We have divided the section 'Contacts' into three parts: Ireland in the insular world, continental influences in Ireland, and Irish influences on the Continent. In the first of these, Colin Ireland continues the Anglo-Saxon focus of the previous contribution, looking at the Irish features in the *Vita Gregorii*, roughly contemporary with Bede's Letter. Anthony Harvey draws on his work for the Dictionary of Medieval Latin from Celtic Sources (for which Dáibhí chairs the editorial board) to focus on the Latin of Celtic Britain. Three articles then foreground Welsh connections: Paul Russell looks at the interaction of Welsh and Irish glosses in the Cambridge Juvencus manuscript; Pierre-Yves Lambert begins with an Old Welsh gloss and the Irish *Collectio Canonum* to consider the significance of the phrase *pretium benedictionis*; and David Howlett's analysis of 'Two Irish jokes' treat a variety of Welsh connections, among others. Finally, Pádraig Ó Neill extends the time-frame by looking at Anglo-Irish relations in the 12th century, with a focus on a central genre of texts for the medieval ordering of time, the calendar tradition.

The second contacts section focuses on the continental influences in Ireland. Donnchadh Ó Corráin presents a hypothesis that the peculiar *h* abbreviation for *úa* ('grandson, descendant') in Irish genealogical texts derives from a Tironian abbreviation. Two contributions deal specifically with art-historical topics: Hayley Humphrey draws on continental iconography to offer a new reading for a scene on the high cross of Camus in Co. Derry, while Peter Harbison's reconsideration of the work of Tuotilo is set against a context of artists and craftsmen travelling from the court of Charles the Bald to Ireland and elsewhere. Jacopo Bisagni sets textual, linguistic, and iconographical evidence into a comparative framework with his study of the terminology of woodwinds in Irish sources, and organology recurs in Leofranc Holford-Strevens's collection of evidence for the knowledge of Aulus Gellius in early medieval Ireland, via the works of Virgilius Maro Grammaticus. Tom O'Loughlin analyzes the *capitula* to the Apocalypse in the Book of Armagh with reference to continental parallels, and Jean-Michel Picard find parallels between Irish and continental Saints' Lives in their assertion of apostolicity. Michael Clarke and Pádraic Moran both look at the construction of an international Irish identity, the former relating the Irish origin narrative to Carolingian global and national histories, the latter at how ideas about Greek dialects informed a scholarly perception of the Irish language.

The study of Greek provides a bridge to our third contacts section, where Michael Herren's assessment of Sedulius Scottus' knowledge of the language changes the focus to Irish activities on the Continent. Rob Meens traces the controversy between Boniface and the Irish bishop Clemens in the context of the Christianization of Frisia in the 8th century. The next two contributions deal with book culture: David Ganz analyses the script of fragments of Lathcen's *Eclogae Moralium Gregorii*, while Mark Stansbury analyses the books held by individual monks at Bobbio in the 9th or 10th centuries.

In the last section of the book, three contributions bridge medievalism and the modern world. Richard Sharpe chronicles the activities of Seán Ó Cléirigh in the early 19th century, and the intrigues surrounding the manuscripts passed down through generations of his family. Hans Ulrich Schmid analyses the adaptations by Scottish poet George Mackey Brown of the 13th-century *Orkneyinga Saga*. Finally, and perhaps fittingly, we close the volume with Nicholas Carolan's profile of A. Martin Freeman, a scholar who, like our honorand, was not only immersed in medieval Gaelic learning but also deeply engaged in the modern folksong tradition (and Ballyvourney in particular).

*

* *

Few historians make it into history. Some help shape the thought or outlook of their own peers, but are soon forgotten by subsequent generations. Dáibhí succeeded in opening up new avenues to Medieval Studies by showing the potential of somewhat exotic topics; certainly, the rise of interest in early medieval computistics at the turn of the 21st century will be connected with his name (as with that of Arno Borst). He has also created an awareness especially among a younger generation of scholars not only that medieval Ireland is a field worthy of research in itself, but that studying its connections is also essential for a fuller understanding of the culture of medieval Britain and the Continent. Most of all, his discoveries will influence medieval scholarship for generations to come.

Pádraic Moran & Immo Warntjes
Galway & Belfast
May 2014

BIOGRAPHICAL NOTE

When the editors asked me to write a biography of Dáibhí Ó Cróinín for this collection in his honour, I was a bit worried. Balancing the objective biography with subjective material was a bit of a daunting project. I hope that I have gotten the balance right, and that Dáibhí won't be dismayed by any of my personal recollections!

Dáibhí was born in Dublin, one of four brothers, but he cannot claim to be a true 'Dub' as neither of his parents were from the city. His mother, Margaret Honan, was from Cloughjordan, Co. Tipperary, and his father, Donncha Ó Cróinín, from Ballyvourney, Co. Cork. His father was a native Irish speaker from a home thoroughly immersed in a love of language, music, and song. Dáibhí's grandmother was the well-known traditional singer Bess Cronin and his uncle, Seán Ó Cróinín, a folklore collector with the Irish Folklore Commission. Dáibhí's father became Professor of Irish in Carysfort Teacher Training College, Blackrock. He was also a fiddler and, until work and family cares made it difficult, he enjoyed many a session with musicians such as Seamus Ennis, his brother Seán, and Denis Murphy. By the time Dáibhí came along, however, the sessions had ceased and one of Dáibhí's earliest memories is hearing his father play the lament *Caoineadh Uí Dhomhnail* alone in his darkened study, a sound that always seemed sad to his son.

Attempting to raise a family bilingually in Dublin at that time was not easy, and, after Dáibhí's eldest brother was teased by his playmates, Dáibhí's father gave up on the idea. However, he did send his children to the newly established Gaelscoil in Monkstown, Co. Dublin, Scoil Lorcáin. Dáibhí got his grounding in Irish there, but in preparation for attending Blackrock College, he was moved to Willow Park, Blackrock, Co. Dublin, for the last years of primary school.

Willow Park was where his rugby career began. Having been seen successfully escaping from the fastest sprinter in the school, the rugby coach gave him no choice but to join the team. Dáibhí enjoyed playing rugby for Willow and then for Blackrock College on the senior team, fearlessly tackling even the largest defender, since they all looked the same without his glasses (or so the story goes!). He hung up his boots when he graduated from Blackrock, but always maintains that he is ready to be called on to the Irish team at a moment's notice.

Dáibhí attended University College Dublin (UCD) for his undergraduate degree. His subjects were Irish and History. The undergraduate course in Irish gave not only a solid grounding in modern Irish, but also covered early modern and Old Irish. Both the language and the literature fascinated Dáibhí. He happily delved into Bardic poetry and Old Irish saga texts, appreciating not only the linguistic puzzles but also the literary richness of Ireland's early writing. His earliest publication (*Eriú*, 1975) was an edition of a bardic poem by Muircheartach Ó Cobhthaigh, beginning *Séd fine teisd Thoirrdhealbhaigh*. His study of Irish literature and, perhaps, especially grammar, inspired him to write his only work of fiction, *An cuigiú diochlaonadh*, published in 1994.

In history, Dáibhí's first love was Second World War military and intelligence history, with a special interest in Russian tanks and espionage. He had thought at one time to do his undergraduate degree in Edinburgh, where his favorite writer in this field, John Erikson, taught. But such was not to be, and early on in University College Dublin, he developed a keen interest in Irish and European early medieval history. Prof. Francis John Byrne and Mr Denis Bethel were sources of inspiration and example in this field.

On completion of his BA in 1975, Dáibhí began the two-year MPhil. in Medieval Studies at UCD, an interdisciplinary degree that attracted international as well as Irish students. Directed by Denis Bethel, the MPhil. was an outstanding opportunity to study languages alongside history and to learn the joy of discovering primary sources and weighing secondary sources. The group that Dáibhí joined was diverse, but became close-knit. Amongst Dáibhí's fellow students were Prof. Jean-Michel Picard, Frank McGuinness, and Eilís Ní Dhuibhne, amongst many other fine scholars. And it was as one of these students that I first met Dáibhí. Those two years of postgraduate study were halcyon. Puzzling out *Fled Bricrend* with Prof. Proinsias Mac Cana, reading *Egeria* with Prof. Ludwig Bieler, listening to Prof. Francis John Byrne elucidate a severely complicated genealogy—who could ask for more? But we had more. We had friends who enjoyed our academic pursuits as much as we did, who provided support when things got tough and with whom we had some great laughs. Dáibhí graduated with an MPhil. with distinction. His thesis, *The Irish Sex Aetates Mundi,* was subsequently published by the Dublin Institute of Advanced Studies.

It was during the MPhil. that Dáibhí made a proposal to me: 'Would you like to translate some Latin with me?'. The Latin in question was *Cummian's letter on the paschal controversy,* which became my MPhil. thesis, later published along with Dáibhí's first great discovery, *A computus from the circle of Cummian.* This co-operative venture had a very romantic outcome—we were engaged to be married.

After completing the MPhil., Dáibhí received a Deutscher Akademischer Austauschdienst (DAAD) scholarship to study at the Ludwig-Maximilians-Universität München, a baptism of fire in both German and Latin, but a wonderful experience and one that resulted in many life-long friends and colleagues. Access to the magnificent Staatsbibliothek in München and its collection of manuscripts gave Dáibhí his greatest enjoyment and confirmed him in his belief that there is so much still to be discovered, if one keeps looking and browsing. Also while in Munich, he immersed himself in German culture by standing through the whole of Wagner's Ring Cycle (student tickets were standing room only in 'the Gods').

On his return to Ireland from Germany, Dáibhí and I were married. I was working on the Royal Irish Academy *Dictionary of Latin from Insular Sources* project and Dáibhí became a Research Scholar at the Dublin Institute for Advanced Studies. We both went to the Celtic Congress in Galway in 1979, where Dáibhí gave his talk on 'The earliest Irish names for the days of the week', another one of his discoveries. The Galway Celtic Congress was a great occasion. It was the first time either of us had been in Galway, and we came away with a wonderful impression of the city and the university.

So we were very pleased when, in 1980, Dáibhí was appointed lecturer in History at University College Galway (now the National University of Ireland, Galway), where he has taught ever since. He also taught as a guest lecturer for two semesters (each separated by a number of years) in the Irish Studies programme at the University of Toronto. Along with the teaching, he has continued to research, write, and speak on a wide variety of topics.

In addition to his teaching and research, Dáibhí was co-editor (with Prof. Donnchadh Ó Corráin, University College Cork) of *Peritia,*

Journal of the Medieval Academy of Ireland since its foundation in 1982, and has now taken over responsibility of the journal together with Elva Johnston (University College Dublin). He is a Fellow of the Society of Antiquaries of London and a Member of the Royal Irish Academy (RIA) and Chairman of a number of RIA committees.

In 1985, Dáibhí received an Alexander von Humboldt scholarship, which allowed him (and the family) to live in Munich for a year, where he continued his intensive manuscript research. Here he also completed the translation of Prof. Bernhard Bischoff's *Latin palaeography: Antiquity and the Middle Ages*, going over it line by line with Prof. Bischoff himself—a daunting task!

The Alexander von Humboldt scholarship also allowed him to spend another semester in Munich in 1999 and to return to Germany again in 2010, this time to East Germany, to study particular manuscripts in Leipzig. It was in Leipzig that the Library staff brought a small copybook to him in the hopes that he could identify the language. He not only recognized the language as Irish, he also saw that the notebook was signed by Whitley Stokes. The notebook turned out to be only one of a large collection of Stokes's original notebooks. Dáibhí spent an extra week in Leipzig to catalogue the notebooks, which he subsequently published as *Whitley Stokes (1830–1909): the lost Celtic notebooks rediscovered*.

When he was awarded a substantial research grant in the 3rd round of the Programme for Research in Third Level Institutions (PRTLI), for a 5-year project under the umbrella title *Foundations of Irish Culture*, he gathered a team of post-doctoral researchers and doctoral students who established a wonderful comraderie, not only amongst themselves, but among all the young scholars working in the Moore Institute at the time. It gives Dáibhí a great deal of satisfaction that his core team (Dr Mark Stansbury, Dr Eric Graff, Dr Pádraic Moran, and Dr Immo Warntjes) have all gone on to permanent academic posts and continue to keep up with each other and to publish excellent new work in the field.

It was as a result of the work and research being done in the *Foundations of Irish Culture* that in 2006 he organized the First International Conference on the Science of Computus. The combination of Dáibhí's relaxed and welcoming approach to the conference, the hard work of students and colleagues, and Galway's inherent attractions made that first conference such a success that another was demanded by all. Each subsequent conference has included a wider group of scholars in the field of computus, where there is always something new to discuss and new manuscript discoveries made.

The growing circle of medievalists in Galway encouraged Dáibhí to initiate the MA in Medieval Studies, a multi-disciplinary degree, in NUI Galway. The MA was subsequently directed by Dr Mark Stansbury (Classics) and is currently directed by Dr Kimberley Lo Prete (History).

Dáibhí's past undergraduate students have often contacted him after years to say how much they enjoyed his lectures. His enthusiasm and his humour when lecturing on challenging and often unfamiliar material is always part of the positive feedback that he gets from students.

His postgraduate students and colleagues appreciate his generosity with his knowledge and discoveries. He doesn't mind being disagreed with, as long as the argument is well written and researched, something that has sometimes surprised his doctoral students.

Dáibhí is an inveterate bookshop browser and book buyer. His abilities as a browser are legend, and he often spots books for colleagues, friends, and family. Not surprisingly, he prefers a bookshop to the internet, and prefers a printed book to reading on-line. Thus, not only is his office book-lined, but much of his home is as well. Besides collecting volumes relating to his area of study, he has maintained his interest in espionage, several shelves full and growing. He has a strong interest in Irish traditional music and song. When his father died, he completed his father's work on Bess Cronin, a ground-breaking publication that included a CD along with a thorough study of the songs and their sources. For this project he amassed a large collection of books on traditional and folk music—a collection still growing. Then there is the literature collection...

These reflections on Dáibhí's life as a scholar have neglected his life as a husband and a father. Woven through the academic life is family life, especially the joys of three beautiful and talented daughters. He is a beloved husband and father who is supportive, encouraging, and engaged in all the interests of myself and our daughters, interests that range from early music to theatre, art, and politics. He takes great pleasure in having his family around him—amongst women!

In conclusion, Dáibhí's colleagues, family, and friends present this volume to Dáibhí on his 60th birthday with love.

Maura Walsh Ó Cróinín

EARLY IRISH HISTORY AND CHRONOLOGY

DANIEL P. MC CARTHY

THE CHRONOLOGY OF SAINT COLUMBA'S LIFE

Abstract

Between Adomnán's *Vita Columbae* and Bede's account in his *Historia ecclesiastica*, Saint Columba's life and missionary career are the best recorded of all early Irish ecclesiastics. Further, and in great contrast to his 5th-century British missionary predecessor, Saint Patrick, Columba's chronology has not been the subject of controversy in modern times. At least from the 17th-century scholarship has been almost unanimous that Columba died in AD 597, a date that derives from Adomnán's assertion that he died on Sunday, and that he left Ireland in AD 563, which likewise derives from Adomnán's statement that his mission had lasted 34 years. However, Dáibhí Ó Cróinín's identification in 1985 that Padua, Biblioteca Antoniana, I 27, 76r–77v preserves a copy of the paschal table followed by the early Irish church demonstrated that the *feria* of the kalends of January was the primary chronological criterion used by early insular Christian scholars to identify each successive year. It was this discovery that prompted examination of the ferial data preserved in the Clonmacnoise group of Irish annals, which in turn revealed that annals were compiled contemporaneously with Columba's life, and hence that the annalistic account of Columba predates those of Adomnán and Bede by a century. These ferial data locate Columba's obit unmistakeably at AD 593, and this four-year discrepancy raises serious doubt regarding the veracity and honesty of Adomnán's account of Columba's life.

Keywords

Columba/Colm Cille; Iona; chronology; kalends, *feriae*, *Annus Domini*; Irish annals, Adomnán's *Vita Columbae*, Bede's *Historia ecclesiastica*.

Early medieval Ireland and Europe: chronology, contacts, scholarship, ed. by Pádraic Moran and Immo Warntjes, Studia Traditionis Theologiae, 14 (Turnhout, 2015), pp. 3–32.

 10.1484/M.STT-EB.5.103115

Introduction[1]

Two early medieval documents have ensured that Saint Columba, founder of the monastery on Iona, has been regarded as an important historical figure of the 6th century by historians of early medieval insular Christianity. The earlier of these documents is Adomnán's *Vita Columbae*, written *c.*AD 697, and the later is Bede's account in his *Historia ecclesiastica* III 4, completed in *c.*AD 731.[2] Both of these represent Columba as an inspiring, accomplished Christian leader and monastic founder, and both provide brief chronological details regarding his departure from Ireland, mission in Britain, and death. These are not the only early medieval chronological details to have survived; the Calendar of Willibrord, dating from the early 8th century, registers the day of Columba's feast at *v idus iunii*, that is 9 June, and indeed this is the only day on which his feast is known to have been celebrated.[3] This day, together with the details given by Adomnán and Bede, have been carefully examined by numerous scholars down the centuries, and in *Figure 1* I summarize their conclusions concerning the year of Columba's birth, his departure from Ireland, the duration of his mission, and his death. In this table I have, when an author has provided the means to derive a further datum by a single addition or subtraction, included the resulting value in square brackets '[...]'. For example, Bede states that Columba departed from Ireland for Britain in AD 565, and that he died on Iona aged 77 years after *c.*32 years, implying thereby that Columba died in

[1] The annalistic chronology for Columba was first presented on 24 November 2001, as a paper entitled 'The Chronology of Colum Cille' to *An Tionól*, at the Dublin Institute for Advanced Studies, and the script and slides of that paper have been available online at www.celt.dias.ie/english/tionol/tionol01.html ever since. In the intervening decade, while Columba's annalistic chronology has remained unchanged, many of the chronological details of the relationship between the annalistic chronology and the accounts of Adomnán and Bede have been re-examined, so that this article supersedes that online account.

[2] The *Vita Columbae* is ed. and trans. by Anderson and Anderson (1961), 178–543, revised by Anderson (1991), 1–235; for the date of this text see Anderson and Anderson (1961), 96; Anderson (1991), xlii; Sharpe (1991), 55; Herbert (1996), 12. The edition of Bede's *Historia ecclesiastica* cited in the present article is Plummer (1896), with chapter III 4 on pp. i 133–5, a discussion of the date on pp. i x, xviii, xlv.

[3] The Calendar of Willibrord is ed. by Wilson (1918), with the relevant entry on p 8 (*v idus iunii sancti columcillae*) and a discussion of its date on p xi ('the original Calendar was written within the first few years of the cycle 703–721').

Author	Date	Birth AD	Departure AD/age	Mission years	Death AD/age
Adomnán's *Vita*	*c.*697	–	–/42	34	Sun./[76]
Calendar of Willibrord	*c.*708	–	–	–	9 June
Bede's *HE*	*c.*731	–	565/[*c.*45]	*c.*32	[*c.*597]/77
Ussher	1639	522	563/[41]	34	9 June 597/[75]
Colgan	1647	519–20	562	[34–5]	9 June 596–7/77
Reeves	1857	[521]	563/42	34	Sun. 9 June 597/76
O'Hanlon	*c.*1873	518–22	563	34	Sun. 9 June 597
Healy	1890	521	–	34	Sun. 9 June 597/77
Plummer	1896	–	565	[32]	9 June 597
Kenney	1929	–	563	[*c.*34]	*c.*597
O'Rahilly	1946	–	563	[34]	597
Grosjean	1960	[521–2]	563	34	9 June 597/76
Anderson & Anderson	1961	521–2	563	34	Sun. 9 June 597/75
Colgrave & Mynors	1969	–	*c.*565	–	*c.*597
Hughes	1972	–	–	–	597
Byrne	1973	–	–	–	597
Farmer	1978	*c.*521	563/[*c.*42]	[34]	597
Duncan	1981	[520–2]	563	34	Sun. 9 June 597/77
Anderson	1991	519–22	563	[34]	Sun. 9 June 597/*c.*75
Sharpe	1991	520–2	563	[34]	Sun. 9 June 597/*c.*76
Clancy & Márkus	1995	[522]	563	[34]	9 June 597/75
Herbert	1996	–	563	[34]	597
Ó Riain	2006	–	–	–	9 June 597

Figure 1 A conspectus of the chronological data for Columba's birth, departure, mission, and death, as provided by authors from medieval times to 2006.[4]

[4] Adomnán, *Vita Columbae* 2nd preface, III 22–23 (Anderson (1991), 6–7, 216–7, 218–27) (*navigatio* aged 42 years, mission of 34 years, death on Sunday); Willibrord's Calendar (Wilson (1918), 8) (*v idus iunii*); Bede, *Historia ecclesiastica* III 4 (Plummer (1896), i 133–4) (*navigatio* 565, mission *c.*32 years, died aged 77 years); Ussher (1639),

AD 565 + c.32 = c.AD 597, and that at the time of his departure from Ireland he was aged 77 – c.32 = c.45 years.[5]

Thus, from the 17th century to the 21st century the scholarly consensus has been that Columba died on Sunday, 9 June AD 597, aged 75–77, and that he departed from Ireland in AD 563. Some scholars have stated this date for his death very emphatically; for example, Marjorie Anderson wrote: 'There can be no doubt that Columba died on 9 June 597, a Sunday as Adomnán says.'[6] This obit date is the result of taking his feast day of 9 June together with Adomnán's assertion that Columba died on Sunday, for then the only year between 586 and 603 when 9 June falls on a Sunday is AD 597. This deduction then appears to be supported by Bede's assertions that he died about 32 years after AD 565. The year AD 563 has then been deduced for Columba's departure by subtracting Adomnán's 34 years for his mission from AD 597. From this it is clear that it has been Adomnán's chronological account that has determined the years of Columba's departure, mission, and death for the great majority of scholars. It is somewhat incongruent then that some of these same scholars have preferred Bede's figure of 77 years for Columba's age at death, rather than Adomnán's implied 76 years.

In these analyses the chronological evidence of the Irish annals for Columba's life has generally been only sporadically referenced. In most cases scholars provided no explanation as to why they preferred the witness of Adomnán or Bede, who both wrote a century or more after Columba's death, to that of the annals. Máire Herbert was one of the few who addressed the issue, writing: 'there is no consensus about the

692–4, 1131, 1143, 1151; Colgan (1647), 484–6; Reeves (1857), 310–2; O'Hanlon (c.1873), vi 281, 541–5; Healy (1890), 292, 326; Plummer (1896), ii xi, 130, 132; Kenney (1929), 423–5; O'Rahilly (1946), 508–9; Grosjean (1960), 388–9; Anderson and Anderson (1961), 66–7; Colgrave and Mynors (1969), 221 n 3; Hughes (1972), 226; Byrne (1973), 14, 258; Farmer (1978), 87; Duncan (1981), 5–6, 9; Anderson (1991), xxviii, xxxxv; Sharpe (1991), 1, 9, 11; Clancy and Márkus (1995), 9–10; Herbert (1996), 27; Ó Riain (2006), 58 n 10 (cf. idem (2011), 212–3). An absolutely precise chronology was given by Simpson (1963), 1 ('Saint Columba [...] was born on Thursday, 7th December 521'); 8 ('On the day of Pentecost 13th May 563, the exiled strife-monger [...] landed on Iona'); 74 ('So died Columba, in the very early minutes of Sunday, 9th June 597, and in the six-and-seventieth year of his age'); cf. Pochin Mould (1964), 94–5, 102.

[5] Bede, *Historia ecclesiastica* III 4 (Plummer (1896), i 133–4): *anno incarnationis dominicae D·LX·V·* [...] *uenit de Hibernia presbyter* [...] *nomine Columba Brittaniam* [...] *ipse sepultus est, cum esset annorum LXXVII, post annos circiter XXX et duos, ex quo ipse Brittaniam praedicturus adiit.*

[6] Anderson (1991), xxviii; cf. Sharpe (1991), 1: 'Columba died on Sunday, 9 June, 597'; Duncan (1981), 5: 'Columba died in his seventy-seventh year on Sunday, 9 June 597'.

date at which contemporary [annalistic] recording begins'. She then cited Alfred Smyth's conclusion, based on the first systematic assessment of the distribution of non-retrospective annalistic entries, that 'our earliest body of annals take their origins from the time of the saint himself [*sc.* Columba]'. Nevertheless, Herbert set aside Smyth's conclusion and instead offered the tentative view that there were grounds for holding 'that a systematic, year-by-year chronicle, varied in its scope, is in evidence in Iona at least from the early seventh century'.[7] Likewise, Richard Sharpe had earlier written:[8] 'the Irish annals are a series of different annal collections, of various dates, which for this period ultimately depend on year-by-year notes begun in Iona – perhaps in St Columba's time, but if not, then probably no later than the 630s'. Such starting dates placed contemporaneous chronicling in Iona long before the compilations of Adomnán and Bede, and should, therefore, have required that priority be given to the annalistic chronology, especially when the provenance of this chronicle was Columba's own foundation. But, as can be seen from *Figure 1*, Sharpe and Herbert instead chose to follow the scholarly consensus.

However, in 1985 Dáibhí Ó Cróinín identified the paschal table in Padua, Biblioteca Antoniana, I 27, 76r–77v as a full copy of the 84-year *latercus* that had been followed by the early churches in Britain and Ireland. Bede is our principal source for the information that Columba brought this paschal tradition from Ireland to Iona.[9] From there Columban missionaries brought the tradition to Northumbria where it was followed until the Synod of Whitby in AD 664, when it was decreed that the Northumbrian churches were to henceforth follow the 19-year Dionysiac paschal tradition supported by the Roman church, and in AD 716 Iona itself abandoned the *latercus*.[10] So effectively was the *latercus* displaced by the Dionysiac tradition that by the end of the 8th century there remained only very brief allusions to it, such as those recorded in the Munich Computus.[11] As a consequence, all of the modern

7 Smyth (1972), 4–30 (survey), 42 (conclusion); Herbert (1996), 22–3 (citations).

8 Sharpe (1991), 7.

9 Bede, *Historia ecclesiastica* III 4 (Plummer (1896), i 133–4).

10 For the Synod of Whitby, see Bede, *Historia ecclesiastica* III 25 (Plummer (1896), i 181–9); for Iona's paschal conversion in AD 716, see Bede, *Historia ecclesiastica* V 22, 24 (Plummer (1896), i 346, 356); AT 716.3 (Stokes (1895–7), i 185); AU 715.4 (Mac Airt and Mac Niocaill (1984), 172).

11 Warntjes (2007), 83–5 (Munich Computus *latercus* references); Warntjes (2010a), XVII–XX, XXXVI–VII, LXXII, LXXXIV, XCIV n 253, CXXII–IV (discussion); 184, 186, 194, 196, 232, 288 (*latercus* references).

reconstructions of the *latercus* inevitably incorporated a great deal of conjecture regarding its presentation and structural organization, and Ó Cróinín's discovery showed that many of these conjectures were incorrect. In particular it showed that it was the *feria* of the kalends of January that provided the primary sequencing mechanism for the table, and that this was written in the form *Kl* followed by the *feria* written either in Roman numerals *ii–vi* for Monday through to Friday, or *S* for *Sabbatum* or *D* for *Dominicus* (see *Plate 1*).

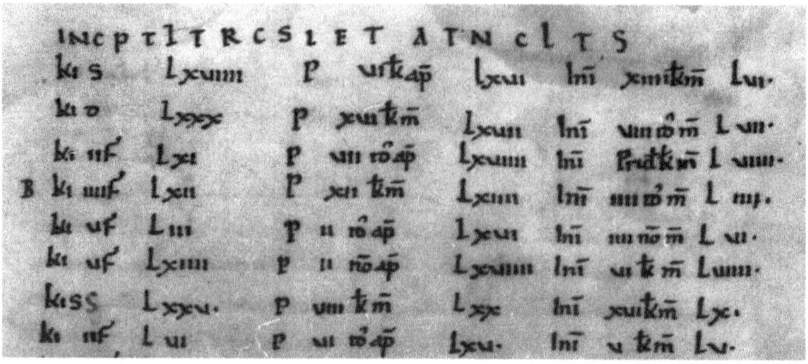

Plate 1 The heading and first eight years of the 84-year paschal table preserved in Padua, Biblioteca Antoniana, I 27, 76r, wherein each year is identified by the *feria* of the kalends of January. (Reproduced with permission.)

Ó Cróinín's discovery also had implications for our perception of the Irish annals for the early medieval period, which exist in various manuscripts dating from the 11th to the 17th centuries. Of these scholarship had concluded that, on the one hand, the late 15th-century edition known as the Annals of Ulster (AU) represented the oldest surviving and most trustworthy version of the annals.[12] On the other hand, scholarship considered that the three editions known as the Clonmacnoise group, the Annals of Tigernach (AT), the *Chronicum Scottorum* (CS) and the Annals of Roscrea (AR), represented later, inferior editions, despite the fact that the earliest manuscript for AT (Oxford, Bodleian Library, Rawlinson B. 502) is four centuries older than the earliest manuscript for AU (Dublin, Trinity College, 1282). Moreover, a feature common to all members of the Clonmacnoise group is that over the years AD 1–616 their primary sequencing mechanism is *Kl* followed by

[12] Mc Carthy (2008), 81–110 (annalistic scholarship from 1861), 85–7 (AU priority).

the *feria* expressed as a Roman numeral *i–vii*, and it thus corresponds very closely with that used in the *latercus*. In consequence, Ó Cróinín's discovery prompted me to embark upon the systematic collation and synchronization of all the chronological criteria in the early medieval Irish annals, and this revealed that the oldest elements are the kalends and *feriae* extending over AD 1–616 found in the Clonmacnoise group.[13] With regard to the period relevant to Columba's life, the 6th century, this collation has shown that AT, CS, and AR all preserve a cognate series of kalends and ferial data which, when correlated with the 28-year solar cycle, transpires to have been precisely synchronized to the Julian year for the years AD 524–540. For the remaining years AD 500–523, 541–599, three out of every four ferial data for successive years are precisely synchronized to the Julian year, while the feria of the fourth year, that immediately following the bissextile year, is systematically one less, modulo seven.[14] For example, for the years AD 500–503 AT preserves the successive *feriae* for the kalends of January as *uii*, *i*, *iii*, *iiii*, whereas the actual *feriae* for these years are *uii*, *ii*, *iii*, *iiii*. Thus, when critically analyzed almost eighty percent of the ferial data of the annals of this Clonmacnoise group for the 6th century is found to have been accurately synchronized to the Julian year, and the remainder to have been systematically decremented by one.[15]

Moreover, collation of this Clonmacnoise group kalend plus *feria* chronology for phenomenological events, such as meteorological extremes and social catastrophe, against the independent witness of dendrochronological and ice-core series, has shown that this annalistic chronology reliably records events as far back as the 5th century. For example, a series of annalistic records of profound social catastrophe in the years AD 538, 540, 550, and 552 synchronizes appropriately with

[13] Mc Carthy (1999–2005), *s.a.* 1–616 (collation and synchronization of the early Irish annals).

[14] Mc Carthy (1998a), 213 (the solar cycle), 213–31 (priority and analysis of the kalends and *feriae* of AT/CS); Mc Carthy (1999–2005), *s.a.* 1–616 (systematic collation and synchronization of chronological criteria); Mc Carthy (1998b), 98–152 (integrity of the pre- and post-Patrician annals); Mc Carthy (2001), 323–41; Mc Carthy (2008), 21–34 (Clonmacnoise group).

[15] Compare the repeated scholarly dismissals of ferial data: Mac Neill (1913), 101: '[the kalends and *feriae* of AT] afford no precise basis for dating year by year'; O'Rahilly (1946), 239: 'they [the *feriae* of AT] are often hopelessly confused. In the kindred Chron. Scot., likewise the ferials are noted, irregularly and incorrectly'; Walsh (1940–1), 359 n 1: 'they [the *feriae* of CS] are almost entirely wrong'; cf. Mc Carthy (1998a), 215.

the dendrochronological record for AD 534–552.[16] Regarding the ice-core record, Francis Ludlow has comprehensively documented over the years AD 431–1649 the persistent and statistically non-random chronological correlation between volcanic acid deposits found in Greenland ice-cores and annalistic records of extreme cold, when synchronized using the Clonmacnoise group chronology.[17] In particular, he has highlighted that the entry in the Annals of Inisfallen (AI) of *Nix magnus* at AD 436 synchronizes with the acid concentration found in the GISP2 ice-core at this year.[18] Similarly, he has pointed out that the entry *Nix maghna* found in AT, AU, and AI synchronized at AD 586, correlates closely with the acid concentration in further Greenland ice-cores, including the Dye 3 ice-core with a major acid concentration at AD 585.[19]

Thus there is substantial evidence that contemporaneous chronicling was well established in an Irish monastic context long before Herbert's estimate of 'the early seventh-century', or Sharpe's 'no later than the 630s'. Furthermore, ever since the studies on the compilation of early Irish annals published by John Bannerman and Alfred Smyth scholarship has accepted that the monastic annals for the latter 6th century to *c.*AD 740 were compiled in Columba's own monastery on Iona.[20] In these circumstances I submit that the annalistic kalend plus *feria* chronology of the later 6th-century should be regarded as a record compiled contemporaneously with Columba's life in his own monastery, and consequently their associated entries to represent a more authoritative account of events contemporaneous with his life than either Adomnán's *Vita Columbae* or Bede's *Historia ecclesiastica*. It is, therefore, the

[16] Mc Carthy (2008), 160–1 (social catastrophe AD 538–552 vs the dendrochronological record).

[17] Ludlow (2010), i 275–82 (summary account of the relationship between the Greenland ice-core chronology and the annalistic records of cold years when synchronized by the Clonmacnoise group chronology), 278 Figure 6.21 (GISP2 acid signals vs annalistic years of cold AD 431–1649).

[18] AI 435.2 (Mac Airt (1951), 56). Ludlow (2010), ii 2–3 (cold and ice-core acid at AD 436); Zielinski et al. (1994), 949 Table 1 *s.a.* AD 436.

[19] ATig 586.4 (Stokes (1895–7), i 117); AU 587.4 (Mac Airt and Mac Niocaill (1983), 94); AI 590.1 (Mac Airt (1951), 78). Ludlow (2010), i 281 (cold and ice-core acid at AD 585–586); Clausen et al. (1997), 26714 Table 3 *s.a.* AD 585 (acid concentration at AD 585). I am grateful to Dr Ludlow for his advice concerning the foregoing volcanic acid and ice-core references.

[20] Bannerman (1968), 149–70 (Iona annalistic compilation); Smyth (1972), 31–4 (Iona annalistic compilation).

purpose of this article to examine critically the annalistic chronology of Columba.

Annalistic references to Columba

A survey of all of the major annals discloses a total of eight events where at least some of these annals include a reference to Columba, and in *Figure 2* I comprehensively tabulate a concise summary of these entries, citing for each event the synchronized AD derived from the kalends and *feriae* of the Clonmacnoise group of annals.

This total of eight entries registering either significant events in Columba's life, or events in which he is represented to have played a significant role, is without parallel in the 6th-century annals. However, in only three of these entries does Columba form the primary subject, namely his *natus*, *navigatio*, and *quies*. In the remaining five entries the reference to Columba is subordinated to an event concerning others: the birth of Baithéne, the death of Cornáin, the battle of Cuil Dreimne, and the deaths of Conall and Aedh. Given the subsequent status accorded to the memory of Columba there must be some doubt concerning these subordinate references, especially when the reference to Columba is in Irish and contrasts with the primary entry in Latin.[21] Because of this uncertainty I intend in this article to confine my examination to the entries where Columba forms the primary subject, and these are collated in *Figures 3–5*.

Regarding first the *natus* (cf. *Figure 3*), textually AT and CS are virtually verbatim, and chronologically their kalend and *feria* synchronize at 520, with CS preserving the correct *feria* of *iiii*, while AT's datum of *uii* is the result of a typical scribal error of misreading two minims as *u*.[22] The entries of AT, CS, and AU 522.2–3 all place Buite's obit first, and there is no syntactic interconnection between it and Columba's *natus*, they are simply proximate entries. On the other hand, the quatrains of AT, CS, AB, and the entries of MB and AU 518.1 all emphasise the synchronism of Columba's birth with the day of Buite's death. Similarly, AI and AB

[21] For example, AU 588.2 (Mac Airt and Mac Niocaill (1984), 94): 'Aedh m. Brendain, *.i. as é ro edhbair Dermhaigh do Cholum Cille*, rex Tethba, mortuus est'; and similarly in AT 587.2 (Stokes (1895–7), i 118); CS 587.2 (Hennessy (1866), 62); AR § 70.2 (Gleeson and Mac Airt (1959), 149).

[22] Mc Carthy (1998a), 219 Table 4 (showing that in AT the *ii* to *u* corruption is by far the most frequent scribal error, accounting for 47% of ferial errors).

AD	Primary event	AT	CS	AR	AU	AI	AB	MB	FM
520	Colum Cille natus	**520.3**	**520.3**	–	**518.1**, *522.2–3*	**521.1**	**§169.1**	**76a**	–
534	Baithine natus	**534.3**	**534.2**	–	–	–	–	**78b**	–
559	Iugulatio Cornain	**559.4**	**559.4**	§30.2	–	560B.1	–	–	**554.4**
560	Bellum Cuile Dreimne	**560.1**	**560.1**	**§31.1**	559.3, **560.1**, *560.2*	561.1	**§180.1**	–	**555.2**
562	Navigatio Colum Cille	**562.1**	**562.1**	**§34.1**	*562.4*	**563.1**	**§181.1**	**88b**	**557.3**
573	Mors Conaill	**573.1**	**573.1**	**§55.1**	**573.2**	574.1	–	**89b**	**572.3**
587	Aedh m. Brendain mort.	**587.2**	**587.2**	**§70.2**	*588.2*	–	–	**91a**	**585.2**
593	Quies Coluim Cille	**593.1**	**593.1**	**§76.1**	**594.1**, ***600.4***	**597.1**	**§190.1**	**91d**	**592.2**

Figure 2 Annalistic entries referencing Columba, where those shown in bold explicitly reference him, while those in plain font do not but are cognate with those that do. AU entries shown in italic are subsequent additions by Ruaidhrí Ó Casaide.[23]

[23] For the AD dates see Mc Carthy (1999–2005), *s.a.* For these references see: AT – Stokes (1895–7), referenced using the synchronized AD concatenated with the entry number; CS – Hennessy (1866), referenced using the synchronized AD concatenated with the entry number; AR – Gleeson and Mac Airt (1959), referenced using the editors' paragraph numbers; AU – Mac Airt and Mac Niocaill (1983), referenced using the MS AD concatenated with the entry number; AI – Mac Airt (1951), referenced using the editor's marginal AD chronology concatenated with the entry number; AB – Freeman (1924–7), referenced using the editor's paragraph numbers concatenated with the entry number; MB – Murphy (1896), referenced using the page number followed by a quarter letter where a=1st quarter, b=2nd quarter, c=3rd quarter, d=4th quarter; FM – O'Donovan (1848–51), referenced using the MS AD concatenated with the entry number. For Ruaidhrí Ó Casaide see Mc Carthy (2008), 316–22, and Mc Carthy (2013), 444–59.

have both given priority to Columba's *natus*, and the editor of AI has inserted a syntactic coupling to Buite's obit. Based on this collation one would judge that this *natus* entry was originally an addition inserted immediately after the obit for Buite, as in AT and CS. It was evidently this proximity that precipitated the subsequent inference that the two events had occurred on the same day, and so a quatrain expressing this was added not long after *c.*AD 740.[24] Thus the versions in AU 518.1, AI and MB, and the quatrain all represent developments of the original obit and *natus* entries that were intended to shift the emphasis to Columba's birth. Of course it is not plausible that such a birth notice was entered contemporaneously into a monastic chronicle, and the question of when it was inserted will be discussed below following examination of the entries registering Columba's departure from Ireland and death.

Regarding entries registering Columba's departure from Ireland (cf. *Figure 4*), AT, CS, and AR agree closely as to their orthography and semantic content, all synchronize at AD 562, and AT and CS both preserve the correct *feria* of *i* for this year, and AR implicitly so.[25] Apropos Columba's age at this time, CS, AR, AU, and MB all agree that he was aged 42 years, which does indeed correspond precisely with the non-inclusive count of the kalends from AD 520 to 562.[26] On the other hand AT's *xlu* appears to be another instance of scribal misreading *ii* as *u*. Thus in the Clonmacnoise group this departure entry implicitly references and is synchronized to the *natus* entry and presupposes its existence, and

[23 cont.] I have omitted from this tabulation the secondary entry at AU 574.1 (Mac Airt and Mac Niocaill (1983), 86): *Magna con[ven]tio Droma Ceta, in qua erant Colum Cille ocus Aedh mc. Ainmirech*, because: a) the entry is unique to AU, and the kalend under which it appears is an interpolation (cf. Mc Carthy (1998a), 261); b) as Sharpe (1991), 313, has discussed in detail, numerous chronological problems arise from AU's date, and he concluded 'the conference at Druim Cett was entered retrospectively at the wrong date, and that we should rather date it to somewhere between 586 and Columba's death in 597'. While AU's explicit AD datum of 574 is commonly incremented to 575, when synchronized to the Clonmacnoise group the entry stands at AD 573 (cf. Mc Carthy (1999–2005), *s.a.* 573), and this exacerbates still further the chronological problems identified by Sharpe.

[24] Mc Carthy (2008), 175–8 (addition of quatrains to the annals post *c.*AD 740).

[25] Jaski and Mc Carthy (2012), xvi Table 1 (reconstruction of AR's ferial series for AD 550–567).

[26] The only way to reckon the number of years between two events registered in annals with only a kalend plus *feria* chronological apparatus is to count the number of kalends between their entries. A non-inclusive count omits the kalend preceding the initial entry, and consequently non-inclusive counts of consecutive intervals may be simply added together. These non-inclusive counts yield the same result as the subtraction of the initial AD from the final AD.

Source	AD 520 – *Natus*
AT 520.3	Buitte mac Bronaig obit. Colam cille natus est. De quibus dictum est: Gein chain Colaim ar cleirig indíu os Erinn eolaig for aenlíth, ní rad n-uabair, bas bain buadhaig maic Bronaigh.
CS 520.3	Buti mac Bronaigh obíít. Colam Cille natus est, de quibus dictum est: Gein caoin Cholaim ar ccleirigh Aniú ós Eirind ólaicch; For aon lith ní radh nuabaír Básban buadhaigh mic Bronaigh.
MB 76a	Boyhin m^cBroynn, dyed. St. Culumbkill was borne this yeare. He was born the night that St. Boyhinn dyed.
AU 518.1	Natiuitas Coluim Cille eodem die quo Bute mc. Bronaigh dormiuit.
AU 522.2–3	*Buithi mc. Bronaigh obiit. Colum Cille natus est.*
AI 521.1	Natiuitas Coluimb Chille (7) dormitatio Buti m. Bronaig.
AB §169.1	Colum Chilli natus est. ['In margin, in Irish script:'] Butti mac Bronaig obiit. F. Gein chain Coluim ar clerig. indiu os Erinn eoluigh. for oenlith ni ráth uabair. bas bán buadaig meic bronaig.

Figure 3 Collation of annalistic references to Columba's birth, which the kalends and *feriae* of AT and CS synchronize with the year AD 520. The entries AU 522.2–3 were added by Ruaidhrí Ó Casaide and so are shown in italic, and the sigla refer to the editions cited in n 23.

the entry in CS appears to be the earliest surviving version of it. For AU, Ó Casaide has subsequently added at the appropriate AD year an entry clearly cognate with the Clonmacnoise group entry. On the other hand AI's exceptional assertion that Columba was a pilgrim and that his first night in Scotland was on Penetecost is unique, while the entries in AB and MB are clearly paraphrases deriving from the Clonmacnoise entry. The celebratory inclusion of Columba's age in this Clonmacnoise

Source	AD 562 – *Navigatio*
AT 562.1	Navigacio Coluim cilli ad insolam Ie etatis sue ·xluº· [anno].
CS 562.1	Navigatio Coluim Cille ad insolam Iae .xliiº. anno aetatis suae.
AR §34.1	Nauigatio Coluim Cille ad Insolam Iae anno aetatis suae 42º.
AU 562.4	*Nauigatio Coluim Chille ad Insolam Iae anno etatis sue .xlº.iiº.*
AI 563.1	Colum Cille i n-ailithre. Prima nox eius i nAlbain in Pentecostén.
AB §181	Passatio Colim Chilli ad insulam Ia.
MB 88b	The sayleing of St. Columb Kill to Scotland in the 42nd yeare of his age.
FM 557.3	Colom Cille do dol i nd-Albain go ro fothaidh iarumh ecclus, & as uadh ainmnighter.

Figure 4 Collation of annalistic references to Columba's departure, which the kalends and *feriae* of AT and CS synchronize with the year AD 562. The entry AU 562.4 is an addition by Ruaidhrí Ó Casaide and so is shown in italics, and the sigla refer to the editions cited in n 23.

group entry suggests that the entry was inserted retrospectively into the chronicle, as shall be discussed further below. Finally, FM, having already abandoned Columba's *natus* entry, likewise abandons his age at departure and his destination, and instead registers his foundation of a church in Scotland that is named for him, at the same time advancing this departure by five years to AD 557.

Regarding the obits for Columba (cf. *Figure 5*), the Latin parts of AT, CS, and AR agree semantically, and their kalend plus *feria* synchronize at AD 593, and they all record the *feria* of *iiii*, which is one less than the actual *feria u* of 593. However, as discussed in the introduction this decrement is a regular feature of the annalistic ferial series between AD 541 and 613 for those years that immediately follow a bissextile year, as AD 593. Of greater chronological significance than this decrement is the fact that AT's *feria* for the three preceding and three succeeding years correspond precisely with the *feria* for the Julian years AD 590–592 and 594–596.[27] We further note that in every instance when the day of his death is given it is either the fifth day before the Ides of June, or its equivalent 9 June, and so accords with the day given in Willibrord's calendar of *c.*AD 708 and subsequent martyrologies.[28] Thus there is complete annalistic unanimity regarding the day of

[27] Mc Carthy (1999–2005), *s.a.* 590–596.

[28] Ó Riain (2006), 226, 238 (Columba in later martyrologies).

Source	AD 593 – *Quies*
AT 593.1	Quies Coluim cille in nocte dominica pentecostes, quintídh Iuin, anno perigrinacionis sue .xxxu. etatis uero .lxx.uii. Teora bliadna bai cen less, Colum ina duibregless, luid co haingliu asa chacht, iar [secht] mbliadna sechtmogad.
CS 593.1	Quies Coluim Cille in nocte Dominica Pentecostes, u. id. Iuin, anno perigrinationis suae .xxx°.u°., aetatis uero lxx°.uii°. ut dicitur: Tricha bliadhain baoí gan les, Colum Cille na dupregles, Luidh go hainglib asa cacht, Iar seacht mbliadhna seachtmogat.
AR §76.1	Quies Coluimbe Cille in nocte Dominica Penthecoste, v° idus Iunii, anno peregrinationis suae 35, aetatis vero 77. Teora bliadna bai cen less, Colum inna duibhreacles; Luid co aingliu as a chacht, iar shecht mbliadnaigh sechtmogat.
AU 594.1	Quies Coluim Cille .u. Id. Iuini anno ętatis sue .lxx.ui.
AU 600.4	*Uel hoc anno quies Choluim Chille in nocte Dominica.*
AI 597.1	Quies Coluimb Cille nocte Dominica hi .ú. Íd Iúin anno .xx°.x.u°. perigrinationis suae, aetate autem .lxxui.
AB §190.1	Colum Chilli in nocte Dominica etatis sue anno lxxvii quieuit in Christo.
MB 91d	Saint Columb Kill Dyed on Whitsunday eve the 5th of the Ides of June in the Island of Hugh in the 35th year of his pilgrimage in Scotland, & banished thither & in the 77 yeare of his age, as he was saying his prayers ... [5 pages of biography follow].
FM 592.2	Colum Cille, mac Feaidhlimidh, apstal Alban, ceann crabhaidh ermhoir Ereann, & Alban iar b-Pattraicc, d'écc ina ecclais fein i n h-I i nd-Albain, iarsan c-cúicceadh bliadhain triochad a oilithre, oidhce domhnaigh do shundradh an 9 lá Iunii. Seacht m-bliadhn a seachtmoghatt a aois uile an tan ro faoidh a spiorait dochum nimhe, amhail as-berar isin rann: Teora bliadhna bai gan lés, Colum ina Duibhreglés, Luidh go h-aingli asa chacht, iar seacht m-bliadhna seachtmoghat.

Figure 5 Collation of annalistic references to Columba's obit, which the kalends and *feriae* of AT, CS, and AR synchronize with the year AD 593. The entry AU 600.4 is an addition by Ruaidhrí Ó Casaide and so is shown in italics, and the sigla refer to the editions cited in n 23.

Columba's death. On the other hand, all of the remaining annalistic chronological data given by the Clonmacnoise group for his obit conflicts irreconcilably with their own kalend plus *feria* chronology of his *natus*, *navigatio*, and *quies*. For example, all Clonmacnoise group entries state that he died on Sunday, but 9 June AD 593 fell on Tuesday, so that this assertion is in conflict with both the annalistic *feria*, and with the true *feria* for AD 593. Furthermore, the year AD 593 is 31 years from AD 562, and 73 years from AD 520, both reckoned non-inclusively, so that none of the figures given for either his mission or age at death reconcile with the annalistic kalend counts. Finally, and inevitably, none of the paschal traditions of the *latercus*, Victorius, or Dionysius could celebrate Pentecost on 9 June AD 593, since it fell on a Tuesday. In AD 593 the *latercus* Easter was on 19 April, so Pentecost fell on 7 June, while the Victorian and Dionysiac Easters were both on 29 March, so their Pentecost fell on 17 May.[29] Thus, excepting only their day of 9 June, all of the remaining chronological data supplied by the entries of the Clonmacnoise group are in absolute conflict with their own kalend plus *feria* chronology. Furthermore, it is apparent that most of these anachronistic data represent later glosses that derive principally from Adomnán and Bede's accounts. For example, their *in nocte dominica* may be compared with Adomnán's *sanctus ad uespertinalem dominicae noctis misam ingreditur eclesiam.*[30] Regarding the assignments in AT, CS, AR, MB, and FM of an age at death of 77 years to Columba, this is the age allocated by Bede, and so I conclude that adjustment of his mission in these entries to 35 years was done in order that when added to the annalistic count of 42 years at his departure it would conform to Bede's 77 years.[31] On the other hand there is no obvious source for the annalistic reference to Pentecost, and none of Adomnán's temporal references in his account of Columba's death can be used to deduce Pentecost on 9 June. However, since this Pentecost reference is in every instance embedded in a series of anachronistic data (*in nocte Dominica Pentecostes* [...] *anno perigrinationis suae .xxx°.u°., aetatis uero lxx°.uii°.*), it seems most likely that it originated with a chronologically incompetent glossator wishing to further emphasize the sanctity of the day of Columba's death.[32]

When we turn to the Cuana group of AU, AI, and AB we find that they are all free of the 'Pentecost' reference, and that AU's entry in the

[29] Blackburn and Holford-Strevens (1999), 874 *s.a.* 593 (*latercus* Easter); Krusch (1938), 28 *s.a.* 593 (Victorian Easter), 73 *s.a. DLXLIII* (Dionysiac Easter); Cheney (2000), 8/8 (calendar for Easter on 29 March showing Pentecost on 17 May); 8/29 (calendar for Easter on 19 April showing Pentecost on 7 June).

[30] Adomnán, *Vita Columbae* III 23 (Anderson (1991), 222, 224).

[31] Since Bede originated the figure of 77 years for Columba's age at death, the hypothesis maintained in Ó Riain (2011), 211–2, that it derives from 'the numerologically 'perfect figure seven'', is not credible.

[32] Anscombe (1892), 516–9, insisting that Columba had died on Pentecost Sunday, 9 June, deduced the unique chronology: *natus* AD 504, *navigatio* AD 546, *quies* AD 580.

first hand, AU 594.1, is also free of the 'Sunday' reference, and simply asserts that Columba died on 9 June aged 76 years.[33] While it is tempting to think that this may be a fortunate survival of the original entry in which *lxxiii* became *lxxui* by scribal misreading of *ii*, I do not believe this to be the case for the following reasons. The reference in the last line of the quatrain to Bede's specification of Columba's age at death of 77 years found in the Clonmacnoise group entry suggests that this datum had been interpolated into the obit by the mid-8th century. The appearance of *nocte Dominica* and anachronistic years for Columba's life and mission in both AI and AB, the other two members of the Cuana group, suggest rather that AU's entry is the result of a computistically astute editor correcting the anachronistic 'Sunday', 'Pentecost', and 35-year mission by deleting them. Since I have dated the compilation of the *Liber Cuanach*, the common origin of the Cuana group, to *c.*AD 1022, this correction must postdate that compilation.[34] Notwithstanding this late date it is this AU entry that conforms best to the annalistic chronology for Columba's *natus* and *quies*. Thus examination of all of the annalistic entries for Columba's *natus*, *navigatio*, and *quies* leads to the conclusion that their earliest attested forms and chronology were as follows:[35]

[520] K.iiii. Coluim Cille natus est.
[562] K.i. Navigatio Coluim Cille ad insolam Iae .xliio. anno aetatis suae.
[593] K.u. Quies Coluim Cille .u. Id. Iuini anno ętatis sue .lxx.iii.

Here I do not intend to suggest that this reconstruction accurately represents the orthography of the original entries, for clearly Columba's name has undergone change influenced by its Irish form.

Turning to the question of when these entries were compiled, as mentioned above it is not plausible that the *natus* entry was made contemporaneously with his birth, and both the form and content of the *navigatio* entry likewise suggest it to be retrospective. Rather, since the *navigatio* and obit entries both reference the *natus* by citing Columba's age, it seems likely that all three entries were made into the Iona chronicle shortly after his death. While this means that both entries were ret-

33 Mc Carthy (2008), 11–2, 34–44 (Cuana group).

34 Mc Carthy (2008), 198–222 (*Liber Cuanach* and its date).

35 This chronology has been accepted by Warntjes (2010b), 211, and by Lacey (2013), 8, 22, 72–3, 83.

rospective, it should be borne in mind that the annalist making these additions had before him a chronicle that had been maintained from long before the time of Columba. This chronicle supplied a cryptic but accurate account of events, both ecclesiastic and secular, extending back over Columba's entire life, many of which events were surely known to the annalist and his colleagues. In these circumstances that annalist was in a far better position to accurately evaluate and record the years of Columba's *natus*, *navigatio*, and obit, than were Adomnán and Bede over a century later. On the one hand, Columba's departure from Ireland is inherently likely to have generated correspondence, some of which is likely to have been available to the annalist, and on the other, all Iona monks living at the time of Columba's death and aged fifty or more were in a position to have personally experienced some aspect of Columba's *navigatio*. For example, his cousin and disciple, Baithéne, was about fourteen years his junior, and, according to the appendix to Adomnán's *Vita*, had 'sailed over with Saint Columba from Ireland in his first crossing to Britain'.[36] Baithéne appears repeatedly in Adomnán's *Vita Columbae* in the role of confidant and supporter of Columba, and ultimately served as his successor as abbot until his own death in AD 596.[37] Thus Baithéne was uniquely placed to ensure that the record of Columba's *navigatio* was accurate; indeed, as his successor abbot he is the most likely person to have been the annalist responsible for making these additions.[38] Consequently, there are in my view good grounds for believing that the chronology of this *navigatio* entry is accurate. On the other hand, since Columba's *natus* occurred about seven decades earlier, there was a far lower possibility of the existence in AD 593 of surviving witnesses to that event, and correspondingly a greater probability of error, so that it would seem more prudent to consider the year AD 520 as approximating that of Columba's birth and likewise the ages that depend upon this year.

[36] Anderson (1991), 238: *Hec sunt xii. uirorum nomina, qui cum sancto Columba de Scotia primo eius transitu ad Brittanniam transnauigauerunt. Duo filii Brendin: Baithen, qui et Conin, sancti successor Columbe; et Cobthach frater eius.*

[37] Baithéne's obit appears at AD 596 with the correct *feria i* in AT, CS, and AR, e.g. AT 596.1 (Stokes (1895–7), i 121): *K.i. Quies Baithin abb Éa anno sexagesimo sexto etatis sue*; in AU it is *s.a.* 597 as AU 597.1 (Mac Airt and Mac Niocaill (1983), 98): *Quies Baeitheni, abb Iae.* For Adomnán's references to Baithéne see his *Vita Columbae* I 2, 19, 21, 22, 23, 30, 37, 41; II 15, 45; III 8, 18, 23 (Anderson (1991), 20–2, 44, 48, 50, 58, 68bis, 74, 114bis, 178, 194, 208, 222).

[38] Sharpe (1991), 256 n 55 (account of Baithéne).

Locating Columba's obit to AD 593 resolves the confusion that has prevailed amongst scholars regarding the chronology of Columba's abbatial successor at Iona, Baithéne, which is clearly summarized by Herbert:[39]

> 'In their dating of Baithéne's death, AU, ATig, and CS agree in placing it three years after the death of Colum Cille. However, there is some confusion in the dating of the latter event, as AU assigns it to the year 595 instead of 597. Should one take it, therefore, that Baithéne's death occurred in the year 600, three years after 597, the proper date for the obit of Colum Cille, or should one accept that Baithéne died in 598, the date which stands in AU?'

Here Herbert is divided between accepting AU's AD chronology for Columba's and Baithéne's obits, in each instance augmented by one, or the year 597 which she considers the 'proper date' for Columba's obit. The answer to her question is 'neither', because on the one hand all of the evidence shows AU's AD chronology to be unreliable from the 5th to the 11th century, and on the other it is the case that the Clonmacnoise group, AT, CS, and AR, all locate Baithéne's obit three years after that of Columba in a year they all identify as *K.i*, which is indeed the *feria* for the kalends of January in AD 596. Since these data and the obit itself were recorded in the annals of the monastery of which Baithéne was abbot they must be considered of far greater authority than deductions based upon Adomnán's restrospective, and, as we shall see, contrived account.

A re-assessment of Adomnán's and Bede's accounts of Columba's chronology

The introductory discussion of the scholarly consensus on Columba's chronology (cf. *Figure 1*) and the Clonmacnoise group entries for his obit (cf. *Figure 5*) demonstrate that Adomnán's account of Columba's chronology in his *Vita Columbae* has been the dominant influence on scholars from medieval times until the present. The foregoing also shows that Adomnán's *Vita Columbae* exhibits a complex relationship with the annalistic account, an account which, as abbot of Iona from AD 679

[39] Herbert (1996), 38 (citation); cf. Byrne (1973), 258; Ó Riain (2006), 58 n 10.

to 704, was surely available to him.[40] On the one hand, his chronology of Columba's *navigatio* aged 42 years corresponds precisely with the annalistic location of Columba's *natus* at 520 and his *navigatio* at 562 at the stated age of 42 years. Furthermore, Adomnán twice locates the *navigatio* two years after the battle of Cúl Drebene, alias Cuil Dreimne, which corresponds exactly with the annalistic chronology which places this battle in AD 560.[41] It seems very likely, therefore, that Adomnán did indeed use the Iona chronicle in the compilation of his *Vita*.[42] On the other hand, Adomnán's placing of Columba's death on a Sunday, 34 years after his *navigatio*, conflicts irreconcilably with the annalistic obit on 9 June AD 593. Consequently, I wish to scrutinize both of these details of Adomnán's account.

I begin with the observation that in his highly dramatic account of Columba's death, in the very last chapter of his *Vita*, Adomnán made his first reference to 'Sunday' in the context of 'the rites of the Mass were being celebrated on a Lord's-day according to the custom'. At this Mass he asserts of Columba that, having experienced a vision of an angel, 'the venerable man lifted up his eyes, and suddenly his face was seen to flush with a ruddy glow', and Adomnán explains this phenomenon with the words: 'because the calm and lovely sight of holy angels fills the hearts of the elect with joy and exultation, this was the cause of the sudden gladness that filled the blessed man'.[43] However, these words were not Adomnán's own, but rather words that derive from Evagrius' Latin translation of Athanasius' Life of St Antony of Egypt, as Gertrud Brüning demonstrated in 1917 with the following collation:[44]

[40] Mc Carthy (2008), 137, 150 (Adomnán's engagement with the Iona chronicle).

[41] Adomnán, *Vita Columbae* 2nd preface; I 7 (Anderson (1991), 6–7, 30–31); cf. Mc Carthy (1999–2005), *s.a.* 560.

[42] Smyth (1972), 38–40 (further annalistic references found also in Adomnán's *Vita*).

[43] Adomnán, *Vita Columbae* III 23 (Anderson (1991), 218–9): *dum misarum sollempnia ex more dominica celebrarentur die, subito susum eleuatis oculis facies uenerabilis uiri florido respersa rubore uidetur* [...] *quia sanctorum angelorum amabilis et tranquillus aspectus gaudium et exultationem electorum pectoribus infundit, haec fuit illius subitae causa laetitiae beato infusa<e> uiro.*

[44] Brüning (1915–7), 245–6.

Vita Antonii	Adamnan
Sanctorum angelorum amabilis et tranquillus aspectus est [...] *gaudium exultationem,* fiduciam *pectoribus infund*unt, siquidem cum illis est dominus, qui est fons et origo *laetitiae.*	et quia *sanctorum angelorum amabilis et tranquillus aspectus gaudium* et *exultationem* electorum *pectoribus infund*it, haec fuit illius subitae causa *laetititae*

Here all of the words shown in italic were taken by Adomnán from Evagrius, while his own addendum (*haec fuit illius subitae causa laetititae*) served to heighten the dramatic tension. Following this Adomnán introduced his second reference to 'Sunday' in the form of a prophecy of both the day and the time of Columba's death that he placed in Columba's own mouth, delivered under promise of secrecy to his servant Diormait. In translation it reads as follows:[45]

> 'the venerable man made a statement to this effect: 'This day is called in the sacred books 'Sabbath', which is interpreted as 'rest'. And truly this day is for me a Sabbath, because it is my last day of this present laborious life. In it after my toilsome labours I keep Sabbath; and at midnight of this following venerated Lord's-day, in the language of the Scriptures I shall go the way of the fathers. For now my Lord Jesus Christ deigns to invite me. To him I shall depart, I say, when he invites me, in the middle of this night. For so it has been revealed to me by the Lord himself'.'

Yet again Adomnán took part of this 'prophecy' from Evagrius, as Brüning's collation demonstrated:[46]

[45] Adomnán, *Vita Columbae* III 23 (Anderson (1991), 220–1): *uir uenerandus consequenter sic profatur: 'Haec in sacris uoluminibus dies sabbatum nuncupatur, quod interpraetatur requies. Et uere mihi est sabbatum haec hodierna, quia huius praesentis laboriosae uitae mihi ultima est, in qua post meas laborationum molestias sabatizo. Et hac sequenti media uenerabili dominica nocte, secundum eloquia scripturarum, patrum gradiar uiam. Iam enim dominus meus Iesus Christus me inuitare dignatur; ad quem inquam hac mediante nocte ipso me inuitatnte emigrabo. Sic enim mihi ab ipso domino reuelatum est'.*

[46] Brüning (1915–17), 246.

Vita Antonii	**Adamnan**
Ego quidem, filioli, *secundum eloquia scripturarum, patrum gradior uiam; iam enim Dominus me inuitat.*	"Et hac sequenti media uenerabili dominica nocte, *secundum eloquia scripturarum, patrum gradiar uiam. Iam enim dominus meus Iesus Christus me inuitare* dignatur; ad quem inquam hac mediante nocte ipso me inuitante emigrabo".

The words here in italic, which Adomnán attributed in direct speech to Columba, he took from Evagrius, and the additions to this made by him served to twice purport that Columba himself had prophesied that he would die 'at midnight of this following venerated Lord's-day' and 'I shall depart [...] in the middle of this night'. I submit that the sudden emergence, in a *Vita* which everywhere eschews chronological order, of this detailed, precise, and emphatic chronological data, juxtaposed to Adomnán's borrowings from Evagrius, raises a serious doubt regarding the veracity of these details. In fact, as Brüning documented, Adomnán drew seven citations from Evagrius when composing his account of Columba's death, as well as other citations from Sulpicius' *Vita Martini* and Pope Gregory's *Dialogi*. Consequently, it is virtually certain that in these passages Adomnán was inventing, not reporting. If the whole of Adomnán's protracted account of Columba's death is examined it will be seen that both the hour and the day play a major dramatic role in the narrative, and consequently these textual features of his introduction of 'Sunday' into this narrative certainly provide substantial grounds for distrust regarding both the honesty and accuracy of his account.

This suspicion is further strengthened when we turn to examine Adomnán's account of the chronology of Columba's *peregrinatio*, which account he first gives cryptically in his second preface simply as: 'Living as an island soldier for thirty-four years'.[47] However, in the penultimate chapter of the *Vita* this single datum is expanded into a substantial narrative, where, just as in the instance of the hour and day of his death, Columba is made to deliver a rationalization of it as a secret prophecy to two of his disciples. The gist of the account is that God had agreed to Columba's entreaty that he be allowed to die after he had spent exactly thirty years in Britain, but then his churches pray for him and so God

47 Adomnán, *Vita Columbae* 2nd preface (Anderson (1991), 6–7): *Per annos xxxiiii insulanus miles.*

grants them a precise four year extension to Columba's life. The chronological essentials read in translation as follows:[48]

> 'the venerable man thus spoke to them saying:
> 'Thirty years have been completed of my pilgrimage in Britain, down to *this present day*.
> Meanwhile, for many days past, I have earnestly requested my Lord that in the end of this present thirtieth year he would release me from my residence, and at once call me to the heavenly country. [...] the Lord granted me when I asked it with my whole strength, that I should pass to him from the world on *this day*, [but now] he has changed [...] answering in preference the prayers of many churches for me.
> And it has so been granted by the Lord to the prayers of those churches that [...] **four more years** from *this day* shall be added to my sojourn in the flesh [...]
> After the end of the **four coming years** in this life, by God's favour I shall [...] joyfully depart to the Lord [...]'
> In accordance with these words [...] he remained in the flesh for **four years** afterwards.
> [...] When the end was drawing near of the **four years** abovementioned, after the completion of which the foreteller of truth had long ago foreknown that his present life would come to a close, one day in the month of May' [Adomnán's account of Columba's last days and death follow.]

There are a number of aspects of this narrative which require comment. First, note the precision which Adomnán establishes for these separate intervals of thirty years and four years by means of his emphatic ref-

[48] Adomnán, *Vita Columbae* III 22–23 (Anderson (1991), 216–7): *uir uenerandus sic ad eos proloquitur: 'Vsque in hunc', inquiens, 'praesentem diem meae in Brittannia perigrinationis terdeni conpleti sunt anni. Interea multis ante diebus a domino meo deuote postulaui, ut in fine tricensimi huius praesentis anni me de meo absolueret inculatu, et ad caelestem patriam ilico aduocaret* [...] *Quia dominus quod mihi totis uiribus roganti donauit, ut hac in die ad ipsum de mundo transirem, multarum magis eclesiarum pro me orationes exaudiens dicto citius inmotauit. Quibus scilicet eclesiis exorantibus sic a domino donatum est ut* [...] *quatuor ab hac die mihi in carne manenti superaddantur anni* [...] *Quibus uidelicet iiii. futuris deo propitio terminatis in hac uita annis* [...] *ad dominum laetus emigrabo.' Secundum haec uerba* [...] *quatuor postea annis in carne mansit.* [...] *Annorvm supra iiii. memoratorum termino iam appropinquante, post quorum conpletionem finem prasentis uitae ueridicus praesagator sibi futurum fore multo ante praesciebat tempore, quadam die mense maio.*

erences to 'this present day' and 'this day', here shown in italic. Since Columba's feast day was celebrated on 9 June, Adomnán's references to 'this day' are implicitly to 9 June, as is indeed consistent with his reference to 'one day in the month of May' at the beginning in the following chapter, just weeks prior to Columba's death. Second, Adomnán's account gives Columba a *peregrinatio* of exactly 34 elapsed years in total, agreeing with the earlier reference in his 2nd preface, but here it is made up as a sum of a period of exactly 30 years, shown above as underscored, plus the four additional years here shown in bold. Third, in this account Adomnán introduces an ambiguity with respect to the year of Columba's death. The first such year he identifies is that in which Columba was granted by God to die, and the second such year is that in which, allegedly, as a result of the prayers of his churches, he actually does die, and Adomnán repeatedly emphasizes the precise four year interval between these two events. These are shown above in bold, and we see that twice Columba is made to repeat it in prophecy, and then twice Adomnán himself states it, as follows. Columba: 'four more years from this day shall be added to my sojourn in the flesh', and 'after the end of the four coming years [...] I shall [...] joyfully depart to the Lord'; then Adomnán: 'he remained in the flesh for four years afterwards' and 'the end was drawing near of the four years abovementioned'. Now four years is the precise interval by which Columba's death must be delayed from Tuesday 9 June AD 593, in order to ensure that it will fall on a Sunday, as Adomnán has insisted in the following chapter. That is, four elapsed years from Tuesday 9 June AD 593 brings one exactly to Sunday 9 June AD 597.

I conclude that these repeated emphases on a delay of his death by precisely four years betray an awareness by Adomnán that, if Columba were to die on a Sunday, as his following chapter so emphatically asserts, then the supposed year of his death had to be deferred by exactly four years from the actual year. In these circumstances I conclude that the four year extension and death on Sunday are both deliberate inventions by Adomnán and must be rejected.

This conclusion naturally prompts the further question as to what could have been Adomnán's motives for doing this? At a dramatic level it is easy to see that locating Columba's death on a Sunday gave him much greater scope for gathering pious and spiritual allusions about the event. Further, Adomnán's representation that it was after just 30 years of Columba's pilgrimage that the Lord had agreed to call him 'to the heavenly country', had the result that this interval then resonated with the chronology of Jesus' life, being commonly regarded as Jesus' age at baptism and the commencement of his divine ministry.[49] At a political level Adomnán's retardation of Columba's death to AD 597 meant that its supposed centenary synchronized not only with the successful promulgation of his *Lex Innocentium* in Birr in AD 697 but also with the time at which he compiled the *Vita*.[50] This synchronization may then possibly have provided him with some leverage in his campaign to coax the Iona community to abandon the *latercus* paschal tradition and adopt the Dionysiac tradition then promoted by the Roman church, as is recounted by Bede.[51] This motive is indeed suggested by the final paragaph of his *Vita Columbae* proper, in which Adomnán again drew upon Evagrius' *Vita Antonii* in order to explicitly connect Columba via Britain, Spain, Gaul, and Italy to 'the Roman city itself, which is the chief of all cities'.[52] This would appear to be an expression of Adomnán's own ecclesiastical polity.

Finally, I turn to consider briefly Bede's account of Columba's chronology and begin by noting that I have elsewhere presented the evidence that for the compilation of his chronicles in *De temporibus* and *De temporum ratione*, Bede employed a copy of the Iona chronicle.[53] This source then would give him ready access to the day of Columba's death, 9 June, and to his ages at *navigatio* and death, 42 and 73 years respectively. However, when we consider Bede's chronology for Columba's death, we find that his *c.*AD 597 and 77 years instead closely approximates the chronology derived from Adomnán's account. Now while Bede's statement that 'some written records of his life and teachings are said to have been preserved by his disciples',[54] ambivalently suggests that he had not seen Adomnán's *Vita Columbae*, it also makes clear that he had at least received some verbal account of that text. The only element of Adomnán's

[49] Cf. Lk 3:23.

[50] Ní Dhonnchadha (2001), 14–5 (promulgation in AD 697, and where she suggests that this took place 'shortly before St Columba's feast on 9 June'); cf. Adomnán, *Vita Columbae* II 45 (Anderson (1991), 176–9), where he describes his own hurried return to Iona 'in the summer season, after the meeting of the Irish synod' (*cum nos aestio tempore post euerniensis sinodi condictum*), just in time to celebrate Columba's feast.

[51] Bede, *Historia ecclesiastica* V 15 (Plummer (1896), i 315–7).

[52] Adomnán, *Vita Columbae* III 23 (Anderson (1991), 232–3): *ipsam quoque romanam ciuitatem, quae caput est omnium ciuitatum*; cf. Brüning (1915–7), 246.

[53] Mc Carthy (2008), 125–39; Mc Carthy (2010) (Bede's use of a copy of the Iona chronicle).

[54] Bede, *Historia ecclesiastica* III 4 (Plummer (1896), i 133–5; translation by Colgrave and Mynors (1969), 225): *de cuius uita et uerbis nonnulla a discipulis eius feruntur scripta haberi.*

account required by Bede to deduce the year AD 597 was his assertion that Columba had died on Sunday, and so I conclude that Bede had indeed received and used this detail in deriving his chronology for Columba's death. However, when we consider Bede's chronology for Columba's departure from Ireland we find that his figure of *c.* 32 years closely approximates the annalistic 31 years.[55] These details of Bede's treatment imply, therefore, that he derived his chronology for Columba from both the annals and Adomnán's *Vita Columbae*, and he was consequently confronted by the irreconcilable conflict between them and his solution was to conflate the two sources. It is important also to note the emphasis and prominence that Bede gives to the year AD 565, using the incarnation era to announce Columba's arrival in Britain is polemic in its purpose. For in commencing his account of the very start of Columba's mission with the words *Siquidem anno incarnationis dominicae D·LX·V·*, Bede was here employing the first datum of the fifteenth year of the second 19-year cycle of the paschal table compiled by Dionysius Exiguus in Rome in AD 525.[56] This was the paschal tradition promoted by the Roman church and adopted in Northumbria at the Synod of Whitby in AD 664, eclipsing thereby the 84-year *latercus* paschal tradition brought by Columba from Ireland to Iona, and from thence to Northumbria by Aidan. Thus Bede's emphasis on *anno incarnationis dominicae D·LX·V·*, while at first sight appearing to be of chronological significance, is rather polemical, asserting the triumph of the Dionysiac paschal tradition over Columba's *latercus* tradition even before his mission had commenced.

Conclusions

The foregoing examination of early sources providing a chronology for Columba's life has shown that the earliest of these is the annalistic chronology preserved in the Clonmacnoise group reconstructed as AD 520 *natus*, AD 562 *navigatio*, and AD 593 obit. While the details of the entries show that only the obit may be considered contemporaneous, the circumstances imply that the *navigatio* chronology is likely accurate, and the *natus* to be a good approximation. On the other hand it has emerged clearly that Adomnán's assertions that Columba died on Sun-

[55] Evans (2008) presents a protracted but inconclusive discussion of Bede's chronology of Columba's arrival in Britain.

[56] Bede, *Historia ecclesiastica* III 4 (Plummer (1896), i 133–5); Dionysius' paschal table is ed. by Krusch (1938), 69–74, with the relevant entry on p 71.

day, precisely 34 years after his *navigatio*, which data have dominated scholarly deductions regarding Columba's chronology from Bede to the present day, are untrustworthy. This in turn reveals that we need to re-assess the declaration of his *bona fides* that Adomnán made towards the end of his 2nd preface:[57]

> 'Let not any one suppose that I will write concerning this so memorable man either falsehood or things that might be doubtful or unsure; but let him understand that I shall relate what has come to my knowledge through the tradition passed on by our predecessors, and by trustworthy men who knew the facts, and that I shall set it down unequivocally, and either from among those things that we have been able to find put into writing before our time, or else from among those that we have learned, after diligent inquiry, by hearing them from the lips of certain informed and trustworthy aged men who related them without any hesitation.'

These assurances must be regarded as profoundly disingenuous, and it seems likely that it was Adomnán's campaign to reform the paschal tradition on Iona that occasioned his dishonesty.[58] Adomnán's silence regarding the *Liber de uirtutibus sancti Columbae* written by his predecessor Cumméne, abbot AD 656–669, has often been regarded as simply an instance of medieval reticence regarding sources. However, when Adomnán's minimalistic treatment of paschal matters in his *Vita Columbae* is considered, Archibald Duncan's conclusion concerning Cumméne's book, that 'it had reference to the Easter controversy is suggested by its disappearance and the circulation of a new Life written by Adomnan', seems much the more plausible view.[59]

The foregoing comparative analyses of annalistic entries have highlighted that it is essential to examine comprehensively all of the annalistic witnesses to any historical event. While the Clonmacnoise group has been shown to provide the most reliable chronology, this does not

57 Adomnán, *Vita Columbae* 2nd preface (Anderson (1991), 6–7): *Nemo itaque me de hoc tam praedicabili uiro aut mentitum estimet aut quasi quaedam dubia uel incerta scripturum; sed ea quae maiorum fideliumque uirorum tradita expertorum cognoui relatione narraturum et sine ulla ambiguitate craxaturum sciat, et uel ex hís quae auditu ab expertís quibusdam fidelibus antiquís sine ulla dubitatione narrantibus diligentius sciscitantes didicimus.*

58 Cf. Sharpe (1991), 55–6: 'Adomnán was concerned to make it clear that what he wrote could be relied upon, because he used only the best sources.'

59 Adomnán's use of Cumméne's book: Anderson (1991), lxv; Herbert (1996), 24–6; Sharpe (1991), 357 n 360; Duncan (1981), 6 (citation).

guarantee that members of this group will provide the earliest versions of the entries. In the present instance, while they do so for Columba's *natus* and *navigatio*, in the case of his obit it is AU that transmits the version conforming most closely with the annalistic chronology. Finally, these collations instructively demonstrate the way in which chronicle entries referencing prominent historical figures attract significant additions and modifications. In the case of Columba's *natus* entry, its proximity to Buite's obit resulted in the subsequent synchronization of Columba's birth day with Buite's feast day, and the celebration of this supposed synchronization in verse. In the case of Columba's obit, completely asynchronous elements from Adomnán's *Vita Columbae* and Bede's *Historia ecclesiastica* were subsequently interpolated into the annalistic entry, and these additions again celebrated in verse. This phenomenon of celebrated events and personages attracting subsequent addenda, which is a norm of all chronicle transmission, should not be allowed to determine judgement on the overall reliability of the annals. For the vast majority of annalistic entries refer to events and personages that are hardly otherwise known, and such entries do not attract subsequent addenda. Moreover, even in instances where they do, as has been demonstated for Columba, careful and comprehensive collation can reveal the effect of these addenda and an informed judgement made upon their significance.

Bibliography

Anderson, A.O. and M.O. Anderson (1961) *Adomnán's Life of Columba*, Edinburgh.

Anderson, M.O. (1991) *Adomnán's Life of Columba*, Oxford, a revision of Anderson and Anderson (1961).

Anscombe, A. (1892) 'The obit of St. Columba and the chronology of the early kings of Alban,' *English Historical Review* 7, 510–31.

Bannerman, J. (1968) 'Notes on the Scottish entries in the early Irish annals,' *Scottish Gaelic Studies* 11, 149–70.

Blackburn, B. and L. Holford-Strevens (1999) *The Oxford companion to the year: an exploration of calendar customs and time-reckoning*, Oxford.

Brüning, G. (1915–7) 'Adamnans Vita Columbae und ihre Ableitungen,' *Zeitschrift für celtische Philologie* 11, 213–304.

Byrne, F.J. (1973) *Irish kings and high-kings*, London.

Cheney, C.R. (2000) *A handbook of dates for students of British history*, revised by M. Jones, Cambridge.

Clausen, H.B. et al. (Nov 30, 1997) 'A comparison of the volcanic records over the past 4000 years from the Greenland Ice Core project and Dye 3 Greenland ice cores,' *Journal of Geophysical Research* 102:C12, 26707–23.

Clancy, T.O. and G. Márkus (1995) *Iona – Earliest poetry of a Celtic monastery*, Edinburgh.

Colgan, J. (1645) *Acta sanctorum veteris et maioris Scotiae seu Hiberniae, sanctorum insulae*, Louvain, repr. Dublin 1948.

Colgrave, B. and R.A.B. Mynors (1969) *Bede: Ecclesiastical History of the English People*, Oxford.

Duncan, A.A.M. (1981) 'Bede, Iona, and the Picts,' in R.H.C. Davis and J.M. Wallace-Hadrill, *The writing of history in the Middle Ages*, Oxford, 1–42.

Elrington, C.R. (1847–64) *The whole works of the most Rev. James Ussher, D.D.*, 17 vols., Dublin.

Evans, N. (2008) 'The calculation of Columba's arrival in Britain in Bede's *Ecclesiastical History* and the Pictish king lists,' *Scottish Historical Review* 87, 183–205.

Farmer, D.H. (1978) *The Oxford dictionary of saints*, Oxford.

Freeman, A.M. (1924–7) 'The annals in Cotton MS Titus A xxv,' *Revue Celtique* 41 (1924), 301–30; 42 (1925), 283–305; 43 (1926), 358–84; 44 (1927), 336–61.

Gleeson, D. and S. Mac Airt (1959) 'The Annals of Roscrea,' *PRIA* 59C, 137–80.

Grosjean, P. (1960) 'Notes d'hagiographie celtique,' *Analecta Bollandia* 78, 364–95.

Healy, J. (1890) *Insula sanctorum et doctorem*, Dublin.

Hennessy, W.M. (1866) *Chronicum Scotorum: a chronicle of Irish affairs from earliest times to A.D. 1135*, London, repr. Wiesbaden 1964.

Herbert, M. (1996) *Iona, Kells and Derry: the history and hagiography of the monastic familia of Columba*, Dublin.

Hughes, K. (1972) *Early Christian Ireland: introduction to the sources*, London.

Jaski, B. and D.P. Mc Carthy (2012) *A diplomatic edition of the Annals of Roscrea*, Roscrea, available online since November 2011 at www.irish-annals.cs.tcd.ie/editions.

Kenney, J. (1929) *The sources for the early history of Ireland*, New York, repr. Dublin 1966.

Krusch, B. (1938) 'Studien zur christlich-mittelalterlichen Chronologie: Die Entstehung unserer heutigen Zeitrechnung,' *Abhandlungen der Preußischen Akademie der Wissenschaften, Jahrgang 1937, phil.-hist. Klasse, Nr. 8*, Berlin.

Lacey, B. (2013) *Saint Columba: his life and legacy*, Dublin.

Ludlow, F.M. (2010) *The utility of the Irish annals as a source for the reconstruction of climate*, 2 vols., unpubl. Ph.D. thesis, Trinity College, Dublin.
Mac Airt, S. (1951) *The Annals of Inisfallen*, Dublin.
Mac Airt, S. and G. Mac Niocaill (1983) *The Annals of Ulster (to A.D. 1131)*, Dublin.
Mac Neill, E. (1913) 'The authorship and structure of the "Annals of Tigernach",' *Ériu* 7, 30–120.
Mc Carthy, D.P. (1998a) 'The chronology of the Irish annals,' *PRIA* 98C, 203–55.
— (1998b) 'The status of the pre-Patrician Irish annals,' *Peritia* 12, 98–152.
— (1999–2005) 'Chronological synchronisation of the Irish annals,' at www.irish-annals.cs.tcd.ie
— (2001) 'The chronology and sources of the early Irish annals,' *Early medieval Europe* 10, 323–41.
— (2008) *The Irish annals: their genesis, evolution and history*, Dublin, repr. 2010.
— (2010) 'Bede's primary source for the Vulgate chronology in his chronicles in *De temporibus* and *De temporum ratione*,' in I. Warntjes and D. Ó Cróinín, *Computus and its cultural context in the Latin West, AD 300–1200*, Turnhout, 159–89.
— (2013) 'Ruaidhrí Ua Caiside's contribution to the Annals of Ulster,' in S. Duffy, *Princes, prelates and poets in medieval Ireland: essays in honour of Katharine Simms*, Dublin, 444–59.
Murphy, D. (1896) *The Annals of Clonmacnoise, being Annals of Ireland from the earliest period to A.D. 1408, translated into English A.D. 1627 by Conell Mageoghagan and now for the first time printed*, Dublin, repr. Felinfach 1993.
Ní Dhonnchadha, M. (2001) 'Birr and the Law of the Innocents,' in T. O'Loughlin, *Adomnán at Birr – AD 697*, Dublin, 13–32.
O'Donovan, J. (1848–51) *Annala Rioghachta Eireann – Annals of the Kingdom of Ireland*, 8 vols., Dublin, repr. New York 1966.
O'Hanlon, J. (*c.*1873) *Lives of Irish saints*, 10 vols., Dublin.
O'Rahilly, T.F. (1946) *Early Irish history and mythology*, Dublin, repr. 1971.
Ó Riain, P. (2006) *Feastdays of the saints: a history of Irish martyrologies*, Brussels.
— (2011) *A dictionary of Irish saints*, Dublin.
Pochin Mould, D. (1964) *The Irish saints*, Dublin.
Plummer, C. (1896) *Venerabilis Baedae Historiam ecclesiasticam gentis Anglorum*, 2 vols., Oxford.
Reeves, W. (1857) *The Life of St. Columba*, Dublin.
Sharpe, R. (1991) *Adomnán of Iona – Life of St Columba*, London.
Simpson, W.D. (1963) *The historical Saint Columba*, Edinburgh.

Smyth, A.P. (1972) 'The earliest Irish annals – their first contemporary entries, and the earliest centres of recording,' *PRIA* 72C, 1–48.

Stokes, W. (1895–7) 'The Annals of Tigernach,' *Revue Celtique* 16 (1895), 374–419; 17 (1896), 6–33, 119–263, 337–420; 18 (1897), 9–59, 150–97, 267–303; repr. in 2 vols. Felinfach 1993, whose pagination is cited in this article.

Ussher, J. (1639) *Britannicarum ecclesiarum antiquitates*, Dublin, repr. in Elrington (1847–64), v–vi.

Walsh, P. (1940–1) 'The dating of the Irish annals,' *Irish Historical Studies* 2, 355–75.

Warntjes, I. (2007) 'The Munich Computus and the 84 (14)-year Easter reckoning,' *PRIA* 107C, 31–85.

— (2010a) *The Munich Computus: text and translation. Irish computistics between Isidore of Seville and the Venerable Bede and its reception in Carolingian times,* Stuttgart.

— (2010b) 'The role of the church in early Irish regnal succession – the case of Iona,' in *L'irlanda e gli irlandesi nell'alto medioevo*, Spoleto.

Wilson, H.A. (1918) *The Calendar of St. Willibrord*, London, repr. Woodbridge 1998.

Zielinski, G.A. et al. (May 13, 1994) 'Record of volcanism since 7000 B.C. from the GISP2 Greenland ice core and implications for the volcano-climate system,' *Science N.S.* 264:5161, 948–52.

IMMO WARNTJES

VICTORIUS VS DIONYSIUS: THE IRISH EASTER CONTROVERSY OF AD 689

Abstract

Over the past few decades, the early medieval Easter controversy has increasingly been portrayed as a conflict between the 'Celtic' and the 'Roman' churches, limiting the geographical extent of this most vibrant debate to Britain and Ireland (with the exception of the disputes caused by Columbanus' appearance on the Continent). Both are not the case. Before *c.*AD 800, there was no unanimity within the 'Roman' cause. Two 'Roman' Easter reckonings existed, which could not be reconciled, one invented by Victorius of Aquitaine in AD 457, the other being the Alexandrian system as translated into Latin by Dionysius Exiguus in AD 525. The conflict between followers of Victorius and adherents of Dionysius occurred in Visigothic Spain first, reached Ireland in the second half of the 7th century, and finally dominated the intellectual debate in Francia in the 8th century. This article will focus on the Irish dimension of this controversy. It is argued that the southern Irish clergy introduced the Victorian reckoning in the AD 630s and strictly adhered to that system until the end of the 7th century. When Adomnán, the abbot of Iona, converted to Dionysius in the late AD 680s and convinced most of the northern Irish churches to follow his example, this caused considerable tension with southern Irish followers of Victorius, as is impressively witnessed by the computistical literature of the time, especially the texts produced in AD 689. From this literature, the issues debated at the time are reconstructed. This analysis has serious consequences for how we read Irish history towards the end of the 7th century; rather than bringing the formerly 'Celtic' northern Irish clergy in line with southern Irish 'Roman' practise, Adomnán added a new dimension to the conflict.

Keywords

Anatolius, Dionysius Exiguus, Victorius of Aquitaine, Adomnán, Bede, Mo Sinu moccu Min, Cummian, Fintan (Munnu), Columbanus, Leo monachus, Braulio of Zaragossa, Pope John IV; Iona, Armagh; *latercus*; *De mirabilibus*

Early medieval Ireland and Europe: chronology, contacts, scholarship, ed. by Pádraic Moran and Immo Warntjes, Studia Traditionis Theologiae, 14 (Turnhout, 2015), pp. 33–97.

 10.1484/M.STT-EB.5.103116

sacrae scripturae, Victorian Computus of AD 689, *De comparatione epactarum Dionysii et Victorii*, *Computus Einsidlensis*, Munich Computus, *De ratione conputandi*, *De divisionibus temporum*, Sirmond collection, *Catalogus sanctorum Hiberniae.*

Introduction[1]

Throughout his career, the honorand of the present volume has made numerous groundbreaking discoveries, many of which will feature prominently in this article. Arguably the most important among these was the identification, in 1985, of an Easter table in Padua, Biblioteca Antoniana, I 27 as the 84-year Easter reckoning followed in the *regiones Scottorum*.[2] Before this discovery, many scholars had tried to reconstruct the system applied in Ireland and parts of Britain, all in vein. James Ussher's 17th-century views on this question provoked Johannes van der Hagen's response in the early 18th century, which in turn inspired Bruno Krusch's attempt at reconstruction in his seminal study of 1884 on 'Die Einführung des griechischen Paschalritus im Abendlande'.[3] Krusch was on the completely wrong track, though the latest edition of Grotefend's popular *Taschenbuch* of 2007, first published in 1898, still reproduces his wrong dates.[4] In the end, it was the Irish scholar Bartholomew Mac Carthy who first identified and assembled, in his *Introduction to the Annals of Ulster* of 1901, all known data for this central Easter reckoning.[5] Mac Carthy's discussion of the material laid the foundation for the

[1] I thank Leofranc Holford-Strevens and Philipp Nothaft for stimulating comments on the present article.

[2] For the story of discovery and reconstruction see Ó Cróinín (2003), 4; Mc Carthy (2008), xiii–xiv. The discovery was first announced in Mc Carthy and Ó Cróinín (1987–8); the table and underlying system has been reconstructed by Mc Carthy (1993); it is translated in Blackburn and Holford-Strevens (1999), 870–5; an excellent technical commentary can be found in Holford-Strevens (2008), 178–87; a full facsimile is printed in Warntjes (2007), 80–2.

[3] Ussher (1639), ii 491–7; van der Hagen (1733), 293–376, especially 336–49; Krusch (1884), 167–9.

[4] Grotefend (1898), 215.

[5] Mac Carthy (1901), lxvi–lxxxi; his main achievement was the identification of the *latercus* mentioned in the Munich Computus, which Krusch (1880), 5–19, had introduced into modern scholarship, with the Easter reckoning followed in Ireland in the early centuries of Christianity, a connection Krusch had failed to realize (but accepted in (1938), 58); the *latercus* data of the Munich Computus were thoroughly analyzed only a few years later by Schwartz (1905), 89–104.

subsequent studies by Daniel O'Connell in 1940 and Knut Schäferdiek in 1985, which corrected details and thereby maximized the degree of probability of the reconstructed data.[6] Still, probability it remained, as no Easter table of this reckoning was known before Ó Cróinín's discovery. The analysis of the Padua *latercus*, then, as executed by Daniel Mc Carthy in 1993, yielded some surprising results (especially the base-year of the table of AD 354 and the Julian calendar limits for Easter Sunday of 26 March to 23 April), as these had not been deducible from the data previously known. Only since 1993, then, is modern society equipped with the chronological framework that helps to explain its early medieval heritage.

Unsurprisingly, this had serious consequences and an immediate impact on medieval scholarship. Early medieval intellectual thought was dominated by one central issue, the Easter controversy. Three different systems for the calculation of Easter, the most important feast in Christianity, were known and competed with each other in the period *c.*AD 525 to 800. Traditionally, the conflict was between Alexandria and Rome.[7] While Alexandrian scholars managed to produce a solid system by the early 4th century, Romans found it difficult to follow suit. In the 5th century, two new attempts were made in the Latin West, one regional, the other authorized by Rome. The regional system is the one referred to above, the *latercus*, an 84-year Easter table with 14-year *saltus*, of which only one copy has survived, discovered by Ó Cróinín and reconstructed by Mc Carthy. Subsequent scholarship has revealed that this reckoning originated *c.*AD 410, with Sulpicius Severus its probable author.[8] Southern Gaul also saw the production of the second system,

6 O'Connell (1940); Schäferdiek (1985).

7 For the Easter controversy between Alexandria and Rome, East and West, and its underlying systems see now Mosshammer (2008), 109–316; and Nothaft (2012), 35–80, as a good introduction to the sources; among the older literature, see especially Hilgenfeld (1860); Duchesne (1880); Schwartz (1905), 3–88; Schmid (1907), 1–60; Chaîne (1925), 19–70; van de Vyver (1957); Grumel (1960); Strobel (1977).

8 Sulpicius Severus' authorship is claimed by Aldhelm, *Epistola ad Geruntium* (ed. by Rudolf Ehwald in MGH Auct. ant. 15, 483); it has been validated by Mc Carthy (1994), with a full discussion of older scholarship on the issue; further arguments are outlined in Warntjes (2007), 34, 36–7. Charles-Edwards (2000), 406–7; Holford-Strevens (2008), 179; Stancliffe (2010), 58 n 31; Pelteret (2011), 158 concur, but Wallis (1999), lvi n 116 does not (and neither does Woods (2011), 1 n 1), pointing to Columbanus' testimony in *Epistola* II 7 (ed. Walker (1957), 18) that the *latercus* dates from the time of St Martin, Jerome, and Pope Damasus, i.e. the second half of the 4th century. The two arguments are not exclusive, however. Sulpicius composed the *latercus* in *c.*AD 410, but started the Easter table proper in the year of St Martin's baptism (AD 354), and this is

invented by Victorius of Aquitaine in AD 457 on papal commission.[9] Victorius aimed at reconciliation of Roman and Alexandrian principles, and his table proved extremely popular especially in the Frankish kingdoms of later centuries, but failed to convince experts further afield. Finally, in AD 525, the Rome-based monk Dionysius Exiguus translated the traditional Alexandrian system into Latin and with this made its dates and intricacies known to the Latin West.[10] It was this so-called Dionysiac reckoning which was to become the unanimously accepted system from the early 9th century until the Gregorian Calendar Reform of AD 1582 (and still is in the Orthodox Church today).

Before the 9th century, however, i.e. roughly between AD 525 and 800, the three systems were bitter rivals. Three irreconcilable systems can obviously produce three different conflicts. In this case, these are:

1) *latercus* vs Victorian reckoning
2) *latercus* vs Dionysiac reckoning
3) Victorian reckoning vs Dionysiac reckoning

All three conflicts were prominent in the Latin West in different regions at different times of the early medieval period. A thorough analysis of these cultural battlegrounds on a European scale is a pressing desideratum of medieval scholarship which deserves a monograph-length study. The classics, by Bruno Krusch and Joseph Schmid, are outdated, though still worth consulting for their balanced approach.[11] Interest in the Easter controversy, particularly its insular dimension, has recently been revived by Ó Cróinín's discovery of the *latercus*. Thomas Charles-Edwards devotes an entire chapter to this issue in his *Early Christian Ireland* of 2000, while Caitlin Corning reassessed the insular paschal

what Columbanus refers to. Englisch (2011), 96–8, believes that Aldhelm's statement refers to Visigothic practice, but fails to disprove the more obvious connection to the Easter reckoning followed by the addressee of Aldhelm's letter, the Briton King Geraint. Sulpicius' authorship has been accepted by some scholars since the days of Ussher (1639), ii 497, but more vehemently rejected by others since van der Hagen (1733), 342–7; all discussions prior to the discovery of the *latercus* are obviously obsolete.

9 Victorius' computistica are edited by Krusch (1938), 4–52; literature on this Easter reckoning is conveniently listed in Warntjes (2010), XXXVIII n 82.

10 Dionysius' computistica are edited by Krusch (1938), 59–86; literature on this Easter reckoning is conveniently listed in Warntjes (2010), XXXIX n 85.

11 Krusch (1884); Schmid (1904); Schmid (1907). Rich in material are Mac Carthy (1901), xiv–clx; Jones (1943), 3–113; also worth consulting are Poole (1918); Betten (1928); Kenney (1929), 210–23; Gougaud (1932), 185–201; Jones (1934); O'Connell (1936); Grosjean (1946).

controversy for her Ph.D. thesis, published in 2006.[12] As these studies were at least stimulated by the spectacular *latercus* findings, the balance of earlier scholarship was somewhat lost. In these most recent publications, the conflict is simply presented as between the *latercus* on the one hand and the Victorian and Dionysiac reckoning on the other, as 'Celtic' vs 'Roman' tradition.[13]

The discovery of the *latercus* is, however, only one and a rather minor reason for this imbalance. Two important sources and a scholarly tradition established by one of the greatest computistical experts of the 20th century, Charles W. Jones, are more prominent:

First, there is the *Collectio Canonum Hibernensis*.[14] In this collection of canon law directives, the Irish church is portrayed as being divided into two principal parties, the *Romani* and the *Hibernenses*. Modern scholars have then projected this division into a Roman and an Irish party on the more specific Easter question.[15] The *Collectio* itself, however, does not deal with this issue.[16] Two main recensions of the *Collectio* have

[12] Charles-Edwards (2000), 391–415 (see also the following chapter, 416–40); Corning (2006). Stevens (1999), in his flawed summary of the Anglo-Saxon Easter controversy, fails to mention either Ó Cróinín's discovery of the *latercus* published in 1985 or Mc Carthy's 1993 reconstruction of that table. An exemplary recent study of one aspect of the 7th-century Easter controversy is Holford-Strevens (2010a).

[13] This view is pointedly expressed by Declercq (2000), 153–5, as well as in the title of Caitlin Corning's (2006) monograph: *The Celtic and Roman traditions: conflict and consensus in the early medieval church.*

[14] The standard edition still is Wasserschleben (1885); a new edition by Roy Flechner (Dublin) awaits publication.

[15] See, e.g., Richter (2000), 71.

[16] The other central issue of controversy in the 7th and early 8th centuries, the question of the tonsure (for which see James (1984); Mc Carthy (2003); McIlwain (2008)), receives an entire book, *Collectio Canonum Hibernensis* LII (Wasserschleben (1885), 211–3). Thus, one would expect at least the same for the more important issue of dating Easter, but in vein. Only two manuscripts of the B-recension (Rome, Biblioteca Vallicelliana, T 18; Oxford, Bodleian Library, Hatton 42; 9th and 10th century respectively) add in the tonsure book that the Britons celebrate Easter with the Jews on *luna* 14 (Wasserschleben (1885), 212, only notes the first of these two MSS; the second was pointed out to me by Roy Flechner): *pascha cum Judaeis quarta decima luna celebrantes*; the source for this information may be *Epistola Cyrilli* 5 (ed. Krusch (1880), 347, cited verbatim in *De ratione conputandi* 98 (ed. Ó Cróinín in Walsh and Ó Cróinín (1988), 203–4): *caelebremus pascha in sequenti dominico et non faciamus in luna XIIII cum Judaeis*; here possibly quoted through a computistical text like the Munich Computus 63 (ed. Warntjes (2010), 292): *Non faciamus pascha in XIII luna cum Iudaeis*; or *Dial. Neustr.* 13B (ed. Borst (2006), 394): *Non celebramus Pascha luna quarta decima cum Iudaeis.* It is telling that this information is added in a section dealing with the Britons (who followed the *latercus* right into the second half of the 8th century), therewith disconnecting it from the Irish conflict; also, this sentence may have been added

survived, labelled A and B. The latest authority cited in A is Theodore of Canterbury (†AD 690), in B Adomnán of Iona (†AD 704).[17] In a 9th-century Breton manuscript of the A recension, the text is ascribed to Ruben of Dairinis (†AD 725) and Cú Chuimne of Iona (†AD 747).[18] Written in the early decades of the 8th century by scholars from conflicting backgrounds (with disputes still ongoing or just solved), it seems that a cloak of silence was deliberately casted over the issue in the *Collectio*. Thus, this text is not an ideal witness for the Irish Easter question. Certainly, the projection on the paschal controversy of the *Collectio*'s division of the Irish church into a Roman and an Irish party is oversimplistic.

Second, there is Bede's *Historia ecclesiastica* of AD 731.[19] It is an extremely curious fact that Bede, in this work, makes no distinction between the Dionysiac and the Victorian reckoning. In his account, the controversy resulted from the introduction of Roman orthodoxy into Britain and Ireland, which was met by Celtic stubbornness, especially in the northern parts of both islands. He leaves no room for doubt that Celtic tradition favoured the *latercus*, while Roman orthodoxy meant Dionysiac principles, implying this to be the case since the Augustinian mission in the late 6th century. Bede here deliberately twisted the facts, or at least he cleverly avoids all references to the Victorian reckoning. From Columbanus' Letter to Pope Gregory, the person who initiated the Augustinian mission to Kent, we know that the papal curia followed

later on in England (Wasserschleben (1885), XXVI–XXVII, XXXIII–XXXIV) or by Cú Chuimne when he revised the text after Ruben's death in AD 725 (for the B recension being a revision of A see Sheehy (1982), 534–5; for this being executed by Cú Chuimne see Charles-Edwards (1998), 237), i.e. after the *latercus* had been abandoned in Iona, which left this now heretical practice a characteristic of the Britons only. For the Britons following misguided doctrine, see also *Collectio Canonum Hibernensis* XX (Wasserschleben (1885), 60–1); in the same book, a reminiscence of the late antique paschal dispute between Rome and Alexandria can be found, though in reconciliatory terms (Wasserschleben (1885), 61); I am grateful to Roy Flechner for pointing these two passages out to me. The absence of the Easter question in the *Collectio* was noted by Hughes (1966), 133 n 3, and others.

[17] This has been established by Henry Bradshaw, in a letter published in Wasserschleben (1885), lxx.

[18] The manuscript in question is Paris, Bibliothèque nationale de France, Lat. 12021; for this colophon ascribing the *Collectio* to Ruben and Cú Chuimne see especially Nicholson (1901); Thurneysen (1908). For Ruben and Cú Chuimne see especially Jaski (2000). A discussion of the date of compilation can be found in Davies (1997), 215–6; Howlett (2003–4), 149, dates the *Collectio* to AD 735.

[19] Plummer's 1896 edition is here prefered to later editions, especially Colgrave and Mynors (1969), as this does not rival Plummer's in erudition and manuscript analysis (though it includes the St Petersburg MS unknown to Plummer).

Victorius at the time, and this did not change before the AD 630s at the earliest, as Cummian's Letter reveals.[20] Bede himself certainly knew better; at least he was fully aware of the fundamental differences between the Victorian and the Dionysiac system, as he devotes two entire chapters of his earlier *De temporum ratione* of AD 725 to condemn Victorius' teaching.[21] The *Historia ecclesiastica* was of a different genre from his computistical works and he did not want his reader to become confused about what Roman orthodoxy meant, especially since Victorius appears still to have had some followers even in Anglo-Saxon England in Bede's own days. The solution was to ignore Victorius' teaching in the *Historia ecclesiastica*, and this silence turned the controversy into one between Dionysius and the *latercus*; Bede deliberately erased all disputes between adherents of Victorius and Dionysius from the records.[22] The Anglo-Saxons had become true followers of Roman orthodoxy against Celtic extravagance, and this is what modern scholarship too readily accepted.

Bede's tendency to downplay the conflict between the Victorian and the Dionysiac systems also influenced the greatest Bedan scholar, Charles W. Jones. Being the editor of Bede's computistica, he was fully aware of Bede's resentment towards Victorius. Still, in a seminal article on the Dionysiac and Victorian reckoning of 1934, he outlined the theory that 7th-century insular computists did not make much of a difference between the Victorian and the Dionysiac systems.[23] To be sure, the principles underlying these two reckonings differed considerably, but still the most important data for practical purposes, the Julian calendar dates for Easter Sunday, rarely did, so that the transition from the Victorian to the Dionysiac reckoning in the Ireland and Britain was a rather smooth process according to Jones.[24] In fact, Jones argues that insular

[20] Columbanus, *Epistola* I 3–5 (Walker (1957), 2, 4, 6, 8); cf. pp. 80–1, 82–3 below. Cummian, *De controversi paschali* ll. 10–11, 75–85, 275–288 (Walsh and Ó Cróinín (1988), 56, 66, 68, 92, 94).

[21] Bede, *De temporum ratione* 51, 62 (ed. Jones (1943), 270-3, 283–4). See below pp. 84–5.

[22] See especially the ground-breaking studies by Ohashi (2005); Ohashi (2011); cf. also Holford-Strevens (2010a), 149. Bede's deliberate neglect of the Victorian reckoning in his *Historia ecclesiastica* has already been noted by Kenney (1929), 222–3; Poole (1918), 59–60, argues that Bede deliberately twisted the facts when summarizing Pope-elect John's letter of AD 640 (see pp. 57–9 below), omitting references to the Victorian reckoning that Poole believed featured prominently in John's letter, and replacing this by a summary account promoting Dionysiac criteria; Poole was too harshly criticized for his argument by Jones (1934), 417–8; Harrison (1976), 61; more moderately by Harrison (1982), 227–9.

[23] Jones (1934).

[24] Already Mac Carthy (1901), cxliii–cxliv, had argued along these lines.

computists of the 'Roman' party in the 7th century would have followed a hybrid system reconciling Victorian and Dionysiac principles (or rather would have used both tables side-by-side), which is the ultimate antithesis to potential conflict between the two.[25] There are numerous flaws with Jones's theory, not the least being that no contemporary document of such a hybrid system has survived, neither a treatise nor an Easter table; other problems will become apparent in the following.

These are the reasons why the most recent writers on the subject paint an unbalanced, if not wrong picture of the Irish Easter controversy: According to this view, the Irish church split into two parties in the late AD 620s and early AD 630s, with the southern Irish following 'Roman', the northern Irish the traditional 'Celtic' customs. Order was restored when the northern Irish church, in a slow process between the AD 680 and AD 716, converted to Roman orthodoxy, first Armagh and the Iona Abbot Adomnán, with his community remaining the last stronghold; the 'Roman' Easter reckonings are the Victorian reckoning initially, then a hybrid Victorian-Dionysiac system, followed by Dionysius' table unaltered. What this scholarship has overlooked is the fact that the introduction of the Dionysiac reckoning in the north of Ireland marked a continuation or rather a new beginning, not the end of conflict. As this article will demonstrate, the southern Irish church followed Victorius throughout the 7th century and the introduction of the Dionysiac system in the north led to serious disputes between traditional adherents of Victorius in the south and the new converts to Dionysius in the north. The reasons for misinterpreting the Irish situation of the AD 680s lies in a fairly uncritical approach to historiographic sources (especially Bede) and the almost complete neglect of computistical evidence, which is difficult to understand given the fact that computistica deal, first and foremost, with the calculation of Easter. These neglected computistica will form the basis for the present analysis.

The Victorian reckoning in Ireland

Before we turn to the controversy of the AD 680s itself, the *Vorgeschichte* needs to be analyzed. It is obviously crucial for the argument

[25] Jones (1934), 418–9; Jones (1943), 91, 103. Jones's theory of a hybrid table (or both Victorius and Dionysius being used 'side-by-side', or Dionysius as a 'corrective' to Victorius) was accepted by Walsh and Ó Cróinín (1988), 46; Wallis (1999), lx, lxxviii; Declercq (2000), 153–5.

that, before the AD 680s, the Dionysiac reckoning was not followed in any part of the *regiones Scottorum*, either in its pure form or as part of a hybrid Victorian-Dionysiac system. Had that been the case, there obviously would not have been much outcry or debate among those following 'Roman' customs when the northern Irish clergy turned from *latercus* to Dionysius in the AD 680s.

To be sure, Dionysius' writings were known in Ireland since the early 7th century. There is no trace of them in Columbanus' letters, but Cummian, in the AD 630s, is fully aware of their existence.[26] Whether they came from Spain as part of a larger collection of computistical texts, as is traditionally believed, remains an open question, as very little is known about 6th- and 7th-century Visigothic developments.[27] It appears as likely that such a collection was first compiled in Ireland, maybe as part of the debate in the late AD 620s and early AD 630s so impressively witnessed by Cummian. The manuscript tradition of this collection of computistica, the so-called Sirmond group,[28] at least points to mid-7th century southern Ireland and not beyond, which fits the Cummian context quite well. For the present purpose, all that matters is that Dionysius' writings were known in Ireland by the AD 630s at the latest. This reception of Dionysiac computistica, however, should not be confused with the adoption of the Dionysiac reckoning.

Certainly, all datable computistical evidence from 7th-century Ireland is unanimous in its adherence to Victorius and Victorius only. The witnesses are the following texts, of which at least the first two are well known and often cited in this context:

Epistola Cummiani: The central document for the introduction of the Victorian reckoning in Ireland is Cummian's Letter, which has been masterfully edited and translated by the honorand and his wife. The

[26] Cummian, *De ratione paschali* ll. 212–213 (Walsh and Ó Cróinín (1988), 86).

[27] That a portfolio of all computistical texts available was first collected in 6th- or early 7th-century Spain and was from there exported to Ireland is the theory of Jones (1943), 75–7, 105. For Visigothic computistics, see especially the studies assembled in Gómez Pallarès (1999); none of the manuscripts analyzed there includes a collection of computistical classics and none is related to the Sirmond group of manuscripts discussed below; all these codices represent 9th-century and later computistical thought; an important witness for 7th-century Visigothic computistica (Paris, Bibliothèque nationale de France, Lat. 609) has, until now, been overlooked by modern scholarship (cf. Warntjes (2012), 77–8); Alden Mosshammer is currently investigating this MS in detail and more remains to be done to get a substantial picture of 6th- and 7th-century Iberian computistical thought and its sources.

[28] For the Sirmond group of manuscripts see pp. 52–3 below.

name of the author alone is clear proof of its Irish origin, as are the addressees, Ségéne *abbas, Columbae sancti et caeterorum sanctorum successor* and Béccán *solitarius*, with at least the former being identifiable as the abbot of Iona.[29] The date has to be inferred from internal evidence, as outlined below. The Augustinian mission to Anglo-Saxon England had not only introduced a different reckoning to Britain, the Victorian one, it also created an awareness at the papal see of the unconventional, if not heretical custom practised in Ireland and Britain. In a famous passage of his *Historia ecclesiastica* mentioned above, Bede relates that Pope Honorius wrote a letter to the Irish clergy, urging them to adopt orthodox practice.[30] Like the Augustinian mission, Columban monasticism may have played its part in creating a sense of urgency among the successors of Peter that the Irish had to conform if church unity was to be achieved.[31] Bede does not provide a date for this letter, but modern scholarship, quite plausibly, regards this document as the impetus for the debate outlined by Cummian.[32] There, it is argued that when the Victorian Easter table (*cyclus quingentorum XXX duorum annorum*) was introduced in southern Ireland, it caused considerable debate among monastic scholars in the area concerned.[33] According to his own testimony, Cummian himself studied the relevant literature (the Gospels, Church Fathers, computistical tracts and tables) for an entire year, at the end of which a synod was held in a place called Mag Léne. This synod approved the Victorian reckoning, but some southern Irish clergymen, particularly a person called allegorically *paries dealbatus*, did not consent. As a compromise, a delegation was sent to Rome to inquire about the correct method for the calculation of Easter. It returned in the third year after departure, having celebrated Easter in the Holy City on a date differing by an entire month (*mensis integer*) from traditional Irish customs. This news convinced everybody in the southern half of

[29] Cummian, *De ratione paschali* ll. 2–5 (Walsh and Ó Cróinín (1988), 56). For the identification of both author and addressees of this letter see especially Walsh and Ó Cróinín (1988), 7–15.

[30] Bede, *Historia ecclesiastica* II 19 (ed. Plummer (1896), i 122).

[31] Cf. Corning (2006), 84–5.

[32] Ussher (1639), ii 604; Krusch (1884), 148–9; Mac Carthy (1901), cxli; Schmid (1904), 35–6; Kenney (1929), 220; Gougaud (1932), 193; O'Connell (1936), 80–1; Jones (1934), 417; Jones (1943), 92; Walsh and Ó Cróinín (1988), 4; Blackburn and Holford-Strevens (1999), 795; Charles-Edwards (2000), 408; Corning (2006), 83–4. Cautious Plummer (1896), ii 125; Harrison (1976), 60.

[33] Cummian, *De ratione paschali* ll. 10–11 (Walsh and Ó Cróinín (1988), 56).

Ireland that the old ways had to be abandoned and Victorius was to be followed.[34]

The discrepancy of one month between the reckoning followed in Rome and that of Irish tradition is crucial for the dating of Cummian's Letter. After Dáibhí Ó Cróinín's discovery of the *latercus*, it can now be stated with certainty that such a discrepancy between the *latercus* and the Victorian reckoning of four weeks (Cummian's *mensis integer*) occurred only twice during the abbacy of Ségéne (*c.*AD 623–652), the addressee of Cummian's Letter, in AD 631 and AD 642, as *Figure 1* shows.

Which of the two dates is to be preferred remains a matter of interpretation. Bede, in another famous passage of his *Historia ecclesiastica*, relates that King Oswald of Northumbria had asked the community of Iona to send him a missionary to preach the faith to his people; the person chosen was Bishop Áedán, who, in accordance with the practice of Iona at the time, followed traditional Irish customs, i.e. the *latercus*, while the southern Irish 'had long before [*iamdudum*] learned to observe Easter according to canonical custom, through the teaching of the pope'.[35] Again, Bede avoids reference to Victorius in this statement. More important for the dating of Cummian's Letter, however, is the fact that Bede dates Áedán's mission to AD 635, which is confirmed by the Irish annals and the Annals of Lindisfarne.[36] Accordingly, if Bede

[34] Cummian, *De ratione paschali* ll. 15–17, 259–288 (Walsh and Ó Cróinín (1988), 58, 90, 92, 94).

[35] Bede, *Historia ecclesiastica* III 3 (Plummer (1896), i 131): *Porro gentes Scottorum, quae in australibus Hiberniae insulae partibus morabantur, iamdudum ad admonitionem apostolicae sedis antistitis, pascha canonico ritu obseruare didicerunt.* The translation is Colgrave's (Colgrave and Mynors (1969), 219); *iamdudum* may better be translated as 'some time before', as it does not necessarily convey an explicit chronology relative to the event in question, the foundation of Lindisfarne.

[36] In *Historia ecclesiastica* III 26, Bede argues that in AD 664 the Northumbrian bishophric had been in Irish hands for 30 years; likewise, in *Historia ecclesiastica* III 17, Bede states that Áedán died in his 17th year in office, and in V 24 he dates Áedán's obit to AD 651 (Plummer (1896), i 159–60, 189, 354). As mentioned in n 51, the dating of the Irish annals in the 7th century is not straightforward, so that the dates given in the modern editions of the various annals are often incorrect; in the following, reference will be made to the 'Irish annals' as a generic term followed by the date given in Daniel Mc Carthy's synchronization (www.irish-annals.cs.tcd.ie); as the dates presented there for the period AD 612–664 are approximate, they will be preceded by *c.*; this is then followed by explicit reference to the main two annals for this period, those of Ulster and of Tigernach; for the Annals of Ulster, the reference year is that of the 16th-century MS, while for the Annals of Tigernach the referencing system to parallel entries in the Annals of Ulster in rectangular brackets is adopted. Thus, the foundation of Lindisfarne can be found in the Irish annals *s.a.* *c.*AD 635 (Annals of Ulster *s.a.* 631 (ed. Mac Airt and Mac Niocaill (1983), 116); Annals of Tigernach *s.a.* [AU 631] (ed. Stokes

AD	Victorian Easter Sunday	Dionysiac Easter Sunday	*latercus* Easter Sunday
623	27 March	27 March	17 April
624	15 April	15 April	8 April
625	31 March	31 March	31 March
626	20 April	20 April	13 April
627	12 April	12 April	5 April
628	27 March	27 March	27 March
629	16 April	16 April	16 April
630	8 April	8 April	1 April
631	**24 March**	**24 March**	**21 April**
632	12 April	12 April	12 April
633	4 April	4 April	28 March
634	24 April	24 April	17 April
635	9 April	9 April	9 April
636	31 March	31 March	21 April
637	20 April	20 April	13 April
638	5 April	5 April	5 April
639	28 March	28 March	18 April
640	16 April	16 April	9 April
641	1 April / 8 April (L)	8 April	1 April
642	**24 March**	**24 March**	**21 April**
643	13 April	13 April	6 April
644	4 April	4 April	28 March
645	17 April / 24 April (G)	24 April	17 April
646	9 April	9 April	2 April
647	1 April	1 April	22 April
648	20 April	20 April	13 April
649	5 April	5 April	29 March
650	28 March	28 March	18 April
651	17 April	17 April	10 April
652	1 April	1 April	1 April

Figure 1 Comparison of the Julian calendar dates of Easter Sunday in the abbacy of Ségéne of Iona. The one-month differences between Victorius and Dionysius on the one hand and the *latercus* on the other, as mentioned in Cummian's Letter, are printed in bold. For the Victorian data see Krusch (1938), 30–1; for the Dionysiac data see Wallis (1999), 394; for the *latercus* data see Blackburn and Holford-Strevens (1999), 873–4; a similar comparative table can be found in Corning (2006), 184–5.

is trusted in this information, as modern scholarship almost unanimously does, the southern Irish church adopted the Victorian reckoning before AD 635, which leaves AD 631 as the only possible date for the discrepancy described in Cummian's Letter. Additionally, Zimmer has argued in 1902 that the *paries dealbatus*, the southern Irish dissenter who would not abandon the traditional ways, is best identified with Fintan (Munnu) of Tech Munnu, and this view was subsequently strengthened by further details introduced into the debate by O'Connell and the honorand of the present volume.[37] Certainly, the way Fintan is portrayed in the *Vita Sancti Munnu* fits Cummian's description of the *paries dealbatus* very well, the foremost defender of the old reckoning against the new order recently imported from Rome;[38] also, Fintan is variously portrayed as having influential links with Iona, Bangor, and other strongholds of the old ways.[39] If this identification of Fintan with

(1993), 182)). See also the *Annales Lindifarnenses s.a.* AD 635 (Levison (1961), 480, 492); for the importance of the *Annales Lindisfarnenses* as a historical source, see Story (2005).

[37] Zimmer (1902), 78; O'Connell (1936), 80–2; Walsh and Ó Cróinín (1988), 49–51. Butter (2010), 22, is not fully convinced by this identification, which is already at least implicit in Ussher (1639), ii 503–5, 604, who believed that the Synod of Mag Léne of Cummian's Letter (*in campo Lene*) was the same as the Synod of Mag nAilbe of the *Vita Sancti Munnu* (*in campo Albo* or rather *Ailbe*; cf. Dumville (1990), 148).

[38] *Vita Sancti Munnu* 26 (ed. Plummer (1910), ii 236): *Quodam tempore erat magnum consilium populorum Hibernie in campo Albo, inter quos erat contencio circa ordinem pasche. Lasreanus enim abbas monasterii Leighlinne, cui suberant mille quingenti monachi, nouum ordinem defendebat, qui nuper de Roma venit; alii vero veterem defendebant. Sanctus autem Munna ad hoc consilium statim non peruenit, et omnes expectabant eum; ipse iam veterem defendebat ordinem*. The Life survives in four recensions in manuscripts not older than the 14th century (Plummer (1910), i ix–xxiii, lxxxiv–lxxxvi; Kenney (1929), 450); Recension 2 is Plummer's *Leittext*; Recension 1 is more explicit about Fintan's role in the paschal controversy, as the last sentence just quoted reads thus there (Plummer (1910), ii 236 n 9): *ipse ... erat princeps et primus eorum qui uetus pascha defendebant*. Sharpe (1991), 297–337 (especially 329, 334–7), argues that what he calls the O'Donoghue group of saints' lives (which includes the *Vita Sancti Munnu*) was compiled in an archetype collection of *c*.AD 750–850 (see also Charles-Edwards (2003), 148–50, who fully endorses Sharpe's conclusions); the origin of the *Vita Sancti Munnu* would therefore predate this compilation; Plummer (1910), i lxxxv, pointed out that 'in the historical setting of the life there are no inconsistencies'; thus, I would be inclined to date the archetype of the *Vita Sancti Munnu* to the 7th century, certainly to a time when portraying Fintan as a champion of the *latercus* still was acceptable (i.e. pre-AD 716). For discussions of this chapter of the *Vita Sancti Munnu* in the context of the Easter controversy, see Mac Carthy (1901), cxlii; Schmid (1904), 36–8; Stevens (1981), 84; Sharpe (1984), 68; Corning (2006), 88–9.

[39] For these see now especially Butter (2010), who, however, avoids discussion of the Easter question. For biographical details of Fintan, see Jaski (2000), 56, 62.

the *paries dealbatus* is accepted, only the earlier date of AD 631 can apply, as the annals record Fintan's obit in *c.*AD 637.[40] The framework of conversion of the southern Irish church from the *latercus* to Victorius is, then, roughly the following:[41]

AD 628: Pope Honorius sent his paschal letter to the Irish clergy, urging them to convert to Roman practice. The only record of this document that has survived is a brief description in Bede's *Historia ecclesiastica*. Contrary to his usual practice, Bede does not provide verbatim excerpts or even the full text of this letter, which leaves the date of composition a matter of speculation. As mentioned above, most scholars have, quite rightly, regarded Honorius' letter as the stimulus for the controversy described in Cummian's Letter, so that the dating of the former depends on that of the latter.

AD 629: After the receipt of Honorius' letter, the southern Irish church decided to abandon the *latercus* and adopt the Victorian reckoning instead. This decision led Cummian to his study of the relevant literature for a whole year.

AD 630: At the end of Cummian's investigation, the southern Irish church met in Mag Léne to discuss the issue. Because of major dissension, a final decision was not reached. Instead, a delegation was sent to Rome to gather more information and directives.

AD 631: The delegation arrived in Rome early that year and celebrated Easter on the Victorian date, 24 March, which differed by a whole month from that listed in the *latercus*, 21 April.

[40] The obit of Fintan is recorded in the Irish annals *s.a.* *c.*AD 637 (Annals of Ulster *s.a.* 634 (Mac Airt and Mac Niocaill (1983), 118); Annals of Tigernach *s.a.* [AU 634] (Stokes (1993), 183)). Butter (2010), 21, trusts the traditional dating of Fintan's death to AD 635.

[41] For this chronological framework see especially Mac Carthy (1901), cxl–cxli; Schmid (1904), 38–43 (obviously with wrong 'Irish' Easter dates); O'Connell (1936), 80–3; Walsh and Ó Cróinín (1988), 3–7. It is generally accepted since the days of Ussher (1632), 432, 443; (1639), ii 505, 604–5, by scholars such as van der Hagen (1733), 336; Plummer (1896), ii 125; Mac Carthy (1901), cxl–cxli; Zimmer (1902), 77–8; Kenney (1929), 220–1; Gougaud (1932), 192–3; Jones (1934), 417; Jones (1943), 98; Harrison (1976), 58–9; Stevens (1981), 83–5; Sharpe (1984), 65–6; Blackburn and Holford-Strevens (1999), 795; Charles-Edwards (2000), 408–9; Richter (2000), 72; Corning (2006), 84–5.

AD 632: On the return of the delegation in the third year, the southern Irish clergy agreed on the Victorian system as the one to be followed for the calculation of Easter.

AD 633: Cummian composed his letter and the Victorian Easter of 4 April is unanimously celebrated among the southern Irish, differing from *latercus* practice by a week.

As mentioned, the preference for this date depends on Bede's random statement that the southern Irish had adopted Roman customs by the time of the foundation of Lindisfarne in AD 635 and the identification of the *paries dealbatus* with Fintan of Tech Munnu, whose death can be dated to *c.*AD 637. To be sure, this increases the degree of probability of the earlier dating, and therefore it remains the one to be preferred. Still, it is not hard evidence. One of Bede's major agendas in his *Historia ecclesiastica* is to promote Roman customs. He does not mind twisting the facts for that purpose; certainly, he is at pains trying to avoid any reference to dissension within the Roman cause, between followers of Dionysius and Victorius. Claiming an unhistorically early date for the conversion of the southern Irish church to Roman customs would fit this pattern well; or, he may simply not have been well informed about an event that took place a century before his time of writing. The identification of Fintan as the *paries dealbatus*, on the other hand, is extremely attractive and very plausible; still it cannot be proved beyond reasonable doubt. Therefore, the later date, though it appears less probable from the evidence available at present, cannot with good reason be ruled out completely.

Only one scholar, Bruno Krusch in his seminal article of 1884 already referred to above, has seriously considered a later option.[42] His theory, however, is based on wrong parameters. In the same article, Krusch reconstructed what he believed to represent the Easter reckoning followed in early medieval Ireland.[43] Even from the evidence known in his day, he should have done better, as Mac Carthy was to prove some 20 years later. Since the discovery of the *latercus*, his and all other pre-1993 attempts of reconstruction can be discarded, and with it Krusch's assumption of a month difference in the date of Easter between 'Roman' and 'Irish' practice in AD 636. Still, his reflex of a later date for Cummian's Let-

[42] Krusch (1884), 148–9. Kenney (1929), 221, mentions the alternative, but considers it too late.

[43] Krusch (1884), 167–9.

ter may have been right. Certainly, the place in the *Historia ecclesiastica* where Honorius' letter finds mention is worth noting. Generally, book 2 of this work is, more or less, structured chronologically. Chapter 18 cites verbatim a letter of Pope Honorius to the newly appointed archbishop of Canterbury of the same name, dated by Byzantine imperial customs which Bede correctly translates to AD 634.[44] Chapter 19 refers to Honorius' paschal letter and then outlines in considerable detail the paschal letter of pope-elect John to the northern Irish clergy of AD 640.[45] The chronological progression here may be from Honorius' letter of AD 634 to pope-elect John's of AD 640, with the reference to Honorius' paschal letter simply being included in Chapter 19 as a prelude to the more important document signed by John. Still, it cannot be ruled out that Bede here assigned the chronologically correct place to Honorius' letter, which would then have been composed between AD 634 and AD 638, the year in which Honorius died. Based on this interpretation and the year AD 642 for the divergence of one month between the *latercus* and the Victorian reckoning, the alternative chronological framework for Cummian's Letter is tentatively this:

AD 634–638: Honorius composed his letter to the Irish clergy.

AD 636?: A considerable number of southern Irish clergymen wanted to or did convert to the Victorian reckoning, but Fintan managed to convice them otherwise at the Synode of Mag nAilbe.

AD 639: With Fintan dead, a substantial part of the southern Irish church converted from the *latercus* to the Victorian reckoning and Cummian began his year-long study. This southern decision triggered a reaction by the northern Irish clergy, who sent a declaration to the pope outlining the reasons why they preferred the *latercus* over the Victorian system; the argumentation must very much have resembled that of Columbanus' Letter to Pope Gregory of four decades earlier.

AD 640: The news at the papal curia of the northern Irish continued adherence to the *latercus* prompted pope-elect

[44] Bede, *Historia ecclesiastica* II 18 (Plummer (1896), i 120–2; the phrase *id est anno dominicae incarnationis DCXXXIIII* at the very end of this chapter is Bede's translation of the date given in the letter proper and should therefore not be in italics).

[45] Bede, *Historia ecclesiastica* II 19 (Plummer (1896), i 122–4); pope-elect John's letter and its context are discussed below pp. 57–9.

John's reply. At the same time, presumably late in the year, the southern Irish clergy assembled at the synod of Mag Léne; one of the reasons for this synod was the terrifying prospect that the southern church would celebrate Easter in two years time on two dates a full month apart; the decision taken was to send a delegation to Rome to inquire about the correct method for the calculation of Easter.

AD 641: The delegation arrived in Rome.

AD 642: The delegation witnessed the discrepancy of a month between the Roman Easter date and the one prescribed by the *latercus.*

AD 643: The delegation returned to southern Ireland in the third year after its initial departure. On the basis of the delegates' experience, the southern Irish clergy unanimously adopted the Victorian system and Cummian composed his letter to Ségéne and Béccán.

To be sure, this interpretation stretches the timeframe to its limits, but not beyond the boundaries of possibility. Even the statements of Bede and the *Vita Sancti Munnu* can be vindicated by this later framework: Some (though not all) southern clerics may well have converted to Victorius before AD 635 and the Synod of Mag nAilbe then simply happened before, not after Mag Léne (with Fintan not the *paries dealbatus* of Cummian's Letter). Whether around AD 630 (which still has to be preferred on the evidence known at present) or AD 640, there can hardly be any doubt that it was the Victorian system that was adopted by the southern Irish clergy, as Cummian is very specific about its 532-year structure and lunar limits 16 to 22 for Easter Sunday, both being unique Victorian characteristics (the former at least until the Dionysiac Easter table was extended from its traditional 95-year period to a 532-year cycle in the early 8th century).[46]

[46] Cummian, *De paschali ratione* ll. 10–11, 75–85 (Walsh and Ó Cróinín (1988), 56, 66, 68). Ussher (1639), ii 501; Betten (1928), 488–9, believed that the Dionysiac reckoning was introduced into southern Ireland in the AD 630s, while Jones (1943), 91, and Walsh and Ó Cróinín (1988), 45–6, argue that Cummian made no real distinction between Victorius and Dionysius and that the southern Irish thereafter followed a hybrid Victorian-Dionysiac table (cf. n 25; in (1943a), 200, Jones simply states that the Dionysiac reckoning was introduced in southern Ireland at this time); Daniel Mc Carthy will publish a theory shortly arguing that the decision taken at Mag Léne was in favour of a modified Victorian table with Alexandrian lunar lim-

De mirabilibus sacrae scripturae of AD 654: Pope-elect John's letter to the northern Irish clergy of AD 640 mentioned above would be the next document in the line, but it does not provided explicit evidence for the reckoning followed by the southern party and is therefore discussed in the following section. The second direct witness, *De mirabilibus scripturae*, is not that frequently cited among modern computistical scholars (as its theme is rather exegetical and cosmological), but it is well-known otherwise. Irish authorship is undisputed, as especially the reference to the obit of a certain Manichaeus reveals, who died 'among other learned men of the Irish'; in fact, the Manichaeus in question can be identified with Manchéne of Min Droicht, a southern Irish churchman, so *De mirabilibus* certainly is a product of the southern Irish church.[47] The same passage also provides the date of composition by the following data:[48]

A. Three years after the death of Manichaeus.
B. Three years after the consuls Alia and Sparsa in *Anno Passionis* (AP) 92+532=624.
C. In *Anno Mundi* (AM) 11×532+3=5855.

Of these three dating clauses, only B is unambigious: The author of *De mirabilibus* obviously had a Victorian Easter table in front of him, in which the death of Manichaeus was noted in the margin to the year of the consuls Aviola and Sparsa, additionally defined as AP 92 in that table and by the author of *De mirabilibus*. Since Victorius

its for Easter Sunday (*luna* 15–21) attributed to Patrick. Stevens (1981), 83–4, avoids any commitment to which system the southern Irish clergy adopted; more recently, Blackburn and Holford-Strevens (1999), 795; Charles-Edwards (2000), 402; and Corning (2006), 87 (where it should read 'lunar range of 16–22'; see Holford-Strevens (2010), 321), more appropriately state that Cummian championed the Victorian reckoning in its pure format, and this is what most other scholars argued over the past 150 years; cf. Krusch (1884), 150–1; Mac Carthy (1901), cxliv–cxlv; Schmid (1904), 25–7; Poole (1918), 59–60; Kenney (1929), 221; Gougaud (1932), 190; Harrison (1976), 58–9, 64–5.

47 For the identification and critique, see especially Esposito (1918–20), 197–202; Grosjean (1955b), 73–5, 84–92; Simonetti (1979), 247–51; Ó Cróinín (1983), 180–3; Mac Ginty (1987), 72–9.

48 *De mirabilibus sacrae scripturae* II 4 (PL 35, 2175–6): *donec decimus inde oriens nonagesimo secundo anno post passionem Salvatoris, Alia et Sparso consulibus, peractis cursibus consummatur. Post quem undecimus a consulatu Paterni et Porquati ad nostra usque tempora decurrens, extremo anno Hibernensium moriente Manichaeo inter caeteros sapientes, peragitur. Et duodecimus nunc tertium annum agens ad futurorum scientiam se praestans, a nobis qualem finem sit habiturus ignoratur.*

had composed his 532-year Easter table of AP 1–532 in AD 457 (=AP 430), the author of *De mirabilius* obviously wrote in the second turn of this 532-year cycle, so that the year in question is AP 92+532=624, and the date of composition three years later, i.e. AP 627; Victorius set Christ's Passion in AD 28, so that AP 627 relates to AD 654; this is the year of compostion of *De mirabilibus*, without doubt or question.[49] Most recent scholars wrongly consider AD 655 as the date of composition by neglecting the only unambigious evidence B, citing A and C instead:[50] Most problematic is the use of A as a dating clause, linking the obit of Manichaeus mentioned in *De mirabilibus* to the evidence of the Irish annals, which do not provide secure dates for this period of Irish history.[51] The AM date C is ambigious, because translating this Eusebian-Victorian AM to AD depends on the context, with a) AD = AM–5200 or b) AD = AM–5201. Interestingly, a case can be made that a) was used by followers of Dionysius,[52] b) by followers of

[49] For this date, see especially Krusch (1884), 158–9 (only for the dating though, not the wrong identification of Manichaeus), and also Noris (1696), 180–2; Mommsen in MGH Auct. ant. 9, 694–5; Schmid (1904), 28–9. Smyth (2011), 137–8 n 3, remains doubtful whether this tract can be dated with certainty to AD 654 or 655; the reasoning above should make it clear that it can, AD 654 is the correct date; concerning her statement that Manichaeus did not die in the year of the consuls *Aviola et Pansa*: the year of the consuls Aviola and Pansa was AP 92 = AD 119; in this year Manichaeus did not die, correct; but the author of *De mirabilibus* used the Victorian Easter table in its second turn without updating either AP or the consul list, as was common in the 7th and 8th centuries; therefore, the obit of Manichaeus in this table was noted in AP 92, consuls *Aviola et Pansa*, which refers to the second turn of the table, AP 624 = AD 651, the year in which Manichaeus actually died.

[50] See the literature listed in Warntjes (2010), LXXVIII–LXXIX n 209.

[51] For the problems of the Irish annals chronology for mid-7th-century events see Mc Carthy (1998), 228–41; Mc Carthy (2008), especially 139–51; critique on Mc Carthy's reconstruction can be found in Charles-Edwards (2006), i 35–58; Evans (2010), 184–8. The dates between AD 612 and 664 have been heavily corrupted, and have to be reconstructed by external evidence; this is one such instance of external evidence, and Mc Carthy's synchonization has to be altered accordingly at this point, so that Manchéne's obit agrees with real-AD 654. In fact, the exact opposite to what Reeves (1861), 516, claimed ('This remarkable coincidence, which was observed by Archbishop Ussher, affords a wonderfully strong external testimony to the accuracy of our domestic annals.') is the case: The *De mirabilibus* dating clause proves the inaccuracy of the Irish annals at this point and provides vital evidence of correction.

[52] This is best illustrated by Dionysiac Easter tables listing Eusebian-Victorian AM, like Cologne, Dombibliothek, 83-II, 76v–79r, accessible online at: www.ceec.uni-koeln.de.

Victorius,[53] though a systematic study is needed. Here, option b) applies, the date of composition of *De mirabilibus* being 5855–5201= AD 654. This, and especially the apparent use of a Victorian Easter table is clear proof that the southern Irish author of *De mirabilibus*, writing in AD 654, was a follower of Victorius.

Sirmond material of AD 658: Direct computistical evidence for the Easter reckoning followed by the southern Irish church in the 7th century comes from a tract transmitted in the so-called Sirmond group of manuscripts. Modern scholarship of historical chronology began, at least if mainstream opinion is to be believed, with Joseph Justus Scaliger's *De emendatione temporum* of 1583. In Scaliger's tradition, the Jesuit Dionysius Petavius produced his masterful *De doctrina temporum* in 1627, which not only refined Scaliger's ideas, but which also provided the reader with editions (or rather transcriptions) of central texts. For many of the previously unknown documents, especially those of interest to the early history of Christian chronology, Petavius relied on a manuscript borrowed from his friend and fellow Jesuit Jacques Sirmond. All traces of this important codex were lost until it was rediscovered in the Bodleian Library of Oxford (with the shelf-mark Bodley 309) by Charles W. Jones on his tour through European libraries in the 1930s.[54] The greater part of this codex contains an almost complete (at least as known today) collection of computistical writings up to the early 7th century.[55] Jones himself asserted a Spanish origin of this collection,[56] but the Oxford codex, as well as most of the other manuscripts of this group, principally provide evidence for an Irish background; at least no broader Visigothic connection can be demonstrated. It appears likely that the debate about

[53] Examples are: the Sirmond dating clause of AD 658 (Ó Cróinín (1983), 177; see also p 53 below); the chronological note in the Bobbio Computus between Victorius' prologue and his Easter table (Milan, Biblioteca Ambrosiana, H 150 inf., 129v; printed in Krusch (1884), 132–3, not in PL 129); the Victorian Prologue of AD 699 (ed. Warntjes (2010a), 271–2; see also pp. 55–6 below); *Dial. Burg.* 17 (ed. Borst (2006), 374).

[54] Jones (1937).

[55] It is highly disputed which texts transmitted in the Sirmond manuscripts should be considered as part of the corpus termed 'Bede's Computus', as the origin and date of composition of some of the texts under discussion are controversial. Surely, all texts that can securely be dated pre-mid-7th century belong to this corpus, Dionysius' writings included. For the Sirmond group of manuscripts, see Jones (1943), 105–10; Ó Cróinín (1983); Ó Cróinín (2003a); Wallis (1999), lxxii–lxxix; Springsfeld (2002), 64–80; Graff (2010); Warntjes (2010), XXII n 37, XXVIIII–XXIX n 55; Warntjes (2010a); Warntjes (2011), 6–7.

[56] See especially Jones (1943), 75–7, 105.

the correct method of calculating Easter in southern Ireland in the AD 630s, as witnessed by Cummian who knew most of the texts assembled in the Sirmond codex, triggered this collection. Certainly, it was well known in southern Ireland by the AD 650s, as a dating clause discovered by the honorand of the present volume proves.[57] This dating clause states that there were 631 years from the passion of Christ to the Easter of Suibne mac Commáin. Ó Cróinín has identified this Suibne with a person of that name whose obit is recorded as an addition to the southern Irish Annals of Inisfallen in the year reconstructed as AD 658,[58] the very same year as independently recorded in the dating clause (AD = AP + 27); he appears to have been a leading member of the Déisi in east Munster. Only one conclusion can be drawn from this passage: its southern Irish author worked from (and followed) a Victorian Easter table with Suibne's obit noted in the margin. The rest of the tract incorporating this dating clause (fols 95v–95bisr in Oxford, Bodleian Library, Bodley 309) certainly corroborates this conclusion, as it is solely concerned with the Victorian reckoning.

Victorian Computus of AD 689: This brings us to three texts which will form the basis for the detailed analysis below, so it will suffice to briefly introduce them here. The first of these, a Victorian Computus of AD 689, has only survived in excerpts transmitted through the famous Munich Computus of AD 718/9. The Munich Computus has been well known among computistical scholars since Bruno Krusch introduced it into modern research in 1880, and its relevance for Irish culture and the Easter controversy has been variously stressed by the honorand of the present volume.[59] Still, the most recent commentators on the Easter controversy are ignorant of this central document, with the notable exception of Masako Ohashi's unpublished Ph.D. thesis, submitted to Nagoya University in 1999.[60] The reason for this neglect may lie in the fact that a modern edition and translation have only very recently been

[57] The discovery is announced and the context established in Ó Cróinín (1983), 176–81.

[58] Annals of Inisfallen *s.a.* 659 (ed. Mac Airt (1988), 94).

[59] The historiography of the Munich Computus is discussed in Warntjes (2010), XV–XXII; Ó Cróinín (1981) discovered an Irish term in the Munich Computus, and in (1982b), 107, 110–1, 118–9, 124–7, and in his edition of *De ratione conputandi* in Walsh and Ó Cróinín (1988), 23–4, 115–6, 134, 143–5, 156, 163, 165, 169, 172, 181, 204–5, 210, placed the Munich Computus solidly in its Irish computistical context.

[60] Ohashi (1999), especially 67–9 for the Munich Computus.

produced.[61] Its dating is, mathematically speaking, bijective, as the information given for the date of composition can precisely be translated to between Easter of AD 718 and that of AD 719; its Irish origin is equally beyond doubt given, among other characteristics, the inclusion of Old Irish terminology in the main text proper.[62] The Munich Computus is a compilation of numerous sources. Among these is a Victorian Computus of AD 689 now lost.[63] Which parts of the Munich Computus belong to the layer of AD 689 is difficult to establish: certainly those two passages of chapters 41 and 62 which contain the dating clauses.[64] As these dating clauses are based on the Victorian Easter table, there can be no doubt about the bias of the Computus of AD 689. The southern Irish origin of this now lost text is apparent through the parallels between the dating clauses and the southern Irish tract in the Sirmond manuscript just discussed, as well as the reliance on the southern Irish *De mirabilibus sacrae scripturae* in chapters 66 and 68.[65] Besides the two dating clauses, it has been argued that chapters 63 to 68, i.e. the entire final part of the Munich Computus, are direct copies from the Computus of AD 689, serving as addenda to the textbook proper.[66] Its contents will be analysed in detail below. All that matters here is that the Computus of AD 689 was written in southern Ireland and that its bias is strongly and solely Victorian.

De comparatione epactarum Dionysii et Victorii: The famous codex Cologne, Dombibliothek, 83-II contains an intriguing text which has until recently been passed over by modern scholarship.[67] Both date and

[61] Warntjes (2010), 1–317.

[62] For the date, see Warntjes (2010), LVII–LXI (with older literature); for the Irish origin of this text see ibidem, LXII–LXXVI (also with older literature); a full discussion of the Old Irish material in the Munich Computus can be found in Bisagni and Warntjes (2007).

[63] For the Victorian Computus of AD 689 see especially Warntjes (2010), LVII–LVIII, LXXX–LXXXII, CXXIV–CXXVI; and also Mac Carthy (1901), lxx–lxxi; Schwartz (1904), 101–2; Kenney (1929), 223; Warntjes (2007), 61, 74. A number of studies mention this Computus of AD 689 (or only its date) only in passing; these are conveniently listed in Warntjes (2010), LVII n 138.

[64] Munich Computus 41, 62 (Warntjes (2010), 140, 278); these dating clauses are discussed in Warntjes (2010), LVII–LVIII (with older literature).

[65] For the southern Irish origin of the Victorian Computus of AD 689 see Warntjes (2010), LVII–LVIII, LXXX–LXXXII, CXXV–CXXVI, 140, 278, 304–7, 314–7.

[66] Warntjes (2010), CXXIV–CXXV.

[67] *De comparatione epactarum Dionysii and Victorii* is now ed. by Warntjes (2010), 322–6, with discussion and facsimile of the table ibidem, CLII–CLVIII, 328; a facsim-

origin are difficult to establish. The content of this tract, to be outlined below, shows parallels to the Munich Computus, and in its details to the Munich Computus only,[68] so that it appears to have originated in close geographic proximity. The calendrical data of one example given in the text suggests that it may have been written in AD 689.[69] If both interpretations are accepted, this tract is the earliest computistical tract documenting the acceptance of the Dionysiac reckoning in Ireland. *De comparatione epactarum* was written by an adherent of Dionysius to counter certain accusations by his Victorian counterparts. It should be regarded as a northern Irish response of recent converts to Dionysius to southern Irish hardliners following Victorius.

Victorian Prologue of AD 699: Like *De comparatione epactarum*, the Victorian Prologue of AD 699 has only very recently been identified.[70] This text survives in a St Gall codex of *c.*AD 900 (now housed in the Universitäts- und Staatsbibliothek Bremen), which belongs to the Sirmond group of manuscripts discussed above. In this respect, this particular manuscript is extremely interesting in that it provides a pre-mid-7th century corpus of texts uncontaminated by later additions (contrary to Bodley 309, e.g.); only the Victorian Prologue under discussion here is of evidently later date. This manuscript context points to an Irish origin of the Victorian Prologue, as does the historical context, though it must be stressed that Irish authorship here is not as evident as it is for the other texts outlined above.[71] The date, on the other hand, is unambiguous: The present year is given as the 140th year of the Victorian Easter table (= AP 672 = AD 699), while the future year is, with some minor scribal errors, characterized in numerous ways, among these AP 673, AD 700, AM 5901; most importantly, the data provided for Easter Sunday of this future years agrees with Victorius, and with Victorius only. This fact demonstrates the bias of this text, as does the rest of its content, which reveals that this tract was originally designed to introduce an altered

ile of the entire text is readily accessible at www.ceec.uni-koeln.de. Previously, only the table incorporated in the text was briefly mentioned and inadequately characterized by Krusch (1880), 203; his view is repeated by von Euw (1998), 154; cf. Warntjes (2010), CLIII n 449.

68 Warntjes (2010), 194–203.

69 For details, see Warntjes (2010), CLVI.

70 The Victorian Prologue of AD 699 is ed. and trans. by Warntjes (2010a), 271–4, with a facsimile ibidem, 283–4.

71 Warntjes (2010a), 263–8.

Victorian Easter table covering the years AD 700–799. In southern Ireland, the Dionysiac reckoning had not won the day over the Victorian reckoning by AD 700.

These witnesses, because they are datable, must form the backbone for any assessment of the reckoning followed by the 'Roman' party in 7th-century Ireland. There are, however, other texts which have been variously interpreted to the extent that the Dionysiac system was adopted by either the northern Irish or the southern Irish church before the AD 680s, which runs counter to the two main arguments of the present article: First, the argument outlined above: the southern Irish clergy followed Victorius, and Victorius only, right until the end of the 7th century. Second, to be discussed below: in Ireland, the Dionysiac reckoning was first adopted in the AD 680s, and not by the southern Irish, but by a substantial part of the northern Irish clergy. The texts in question are the following:

Mo Sinu moccu Min: The first piece to be discussed here is a fragment bound in at the end of the codex Würzburg, Universitätsbibliothek, M.p.th.f. 61.[72] It argues that 'Mo Sinu maccu Min, scribe and abbot of Bangor, was the first of the Irish who learned the computation (*compotem*) by heart from a certain Greek'. Bartholomew Mac Carthy, in his admirable account of late antique and early medieval paschal literature, argues that the *compotem* in question was the Dionysiac system.[73] The implication obviously is that by *c.*AD 608 (the obit of the mentioned Mo Sinu[74]), Bangor, as the first among the Irish churches, had adopted the Dionysiac system. Charles W. Jones and, more vehemently, Paul Grosjean followed this interpretation.[75] It was the honorand of the present volume who corrected this mistaken assumption.[76] Mac Carthy had worked from a transcript which reproduced only three quarters of

72 This fragment has been printed in various publications, too often, however, under omission of the crucial final part. It can best be accessed in Ó Cróinín (1982a), 36–7 (edition, translation, and older literature); Ó Cróinín (2003), 214 (facsimile).

73 Mac Carthy (1901), cxxxiii–cxxxiv.

74 The obit of Mo Sinu is recorded in the Irish annals *s.a.* AD 608 (Annals of Ulster *s.a.* 609 (Mac Airt and Mac Niocaill (1983), 104); Annals of Tigernach *s.a.* [AU 609] (Stokes (1993), 169)).

75 Jones (1934), 419; Jones (1943), 81–2; Jones (1943a), 203–5; Grosjean (1946), 215–31, 244, especially 231. Likewise Kenney (1929), 218.

76 Ó Cróinín (1982a). Cf. Corning (2006), 82–3.

the text. The omitted crucial last quarter, which Ó Cróinín inspected *in situ*, made it apparent that the computation in question was simply the numerical values of the Greek alphabet, which became a common feature of computistical manuscripts in later centuries. The Dionysiac reckoning was not adopted in Bangor before the AD 680s.

The papal letter of AD 640: One of the most important documents for the 7th-century Irish Easter controversy, the letter of the northern Irish clergy to the papal curia of *c.*AD 639, is, unfortunately, lost. Its existence is attested by Bede, who, in chapter II 19 of his *Historia ecclesiastica*, reproduces excerpts and a summary of the papal response.[77] Thus, the information about the original letter is indirect and limited. A more or less general consensus existed in modern scholarship that northern Irish adherents of the *latercus* sent a letter of justification to the Holy See explaining the reasons why they remained faithful to the traditional method.[78] This view was challenged by Dáibhí Ó Cróinín in 1985, arguing that the addressees of the papal letter had converted to the Victorian reckoning which provided double dates for AD 640; the converts decided that they would follow the date designated as Greek in Victorius' Easter table and sent word to the pope about this decision; the papal see, however, had adopted Dionysius in the meantime and because of the differences in the lunar calendar of both systems, Victorius' Easter Sunday on *luna* 15 was *luna* 14 in the Dionysiac reckoning; consequently, the Victorian Greek date was considered unacceptable by the papal curia, prompting the harsh reply transmitted by Bede.[79]

Ó Cróinín's interpretation has since been rejected, principally on the ground that the Iona Abbot Ségéne featured prominently among the addressees of the papal letter.[80] Ségéne, as known from Cummian's Letter, had been a staunch supporter of the *latercus*, and, if Bede can be

77 Bede, *Historia ecclesiastica* II 19 (Plummer (1896), i 122–4).

78 Mac Carthy (1901), cxlviii; Kenney (1929), 222 (northern *latercus* adherents 'consulting' the papal see); O'Connell (1936), 83 (only arguing that the initial letter was sent from northern Ireland, not discussing its purpose); Gougaud (1932), 194; Jones (1943), 98–9. Wallis (1999), lxi, believes that the letter prompting the papal response was written by the southern rather than the northern Irish clergy; this view is at least as old as Zimmer (1901), 23–4, 137. Schmid (1904), 44, is undecided whether the initiative was northern or southern.

79 Ó Cróinín (1985).

80 See Warntjes (2010), LXXXII–LXXXVII; Ohashi (1999), 115–46, especially 124–30; Corning (2006), 89–92; Holford-Strevens (2003–4), 543. Ó Cróinín's theory is accepted by Charles-Edwards (2000), 409; Richter (2000), 72–3.

trusted in this aspect, Adomnán, almost 50 years later, was the first abbot of that monastic *familia* abandoning the traditional reckoning; the monastic community itself followed suit as late as AD 716.[81] Thus, Iona was a stronghold of traditionalists and therefore it is hardly conceivable that the northern Irish clergy led by the Iona Abbot Ségéne followed any reckoning other than the *latercus* in *c.*AD 639.

Still, Ó Cróinín introduced an important new dimension into the discussion, the question why the initial letter was written in *c.*AD 639. A justification of the *latercus* could have been composed at any time, so why in *c.*AD 639? The answer depends on the reading of Cummian's Letter. If the later chronological framework for this text is accepted, then the northern Irish clergy composed their initial Letter as a direct response to southern Irish conversion, which owed strongly to Roman initiative. If the earlier dating of Cummian's Letter is preferred, the question is more pressing. In this case, the answer lies in the Victorian reckoning. From Columbanus' letters we are very well informed about the issues which adherents of the *latercus* raised against Victorius: First, the celebration of Easter Sunday on *luna* 21 and *luna* 22;[82] second, the acceptance of the Easter full moon and/or Easter Sunday falling before the spring equinox;[83] third, the listing of double dates.[84] From the surviving manuscript evidence of Victorian Easter tables, it appears that double dates were not really an issue in the late AD 640s, as the southern Irish clergy had simply decreed, quite understandably, those labelled 'Roman' canonical.[85] The other two aspects, however,

[81] For Adomnán, see pp. 65–70 below; Iona's conversion is recorded in the Irish annals *s.a.* AD 716 (Annals of Ulster *s.a.* 715 (Mac Airt and Mac Niocaill (1983), 172); Annals of Tigernach *s.a.* [AU 715] (Stokes (1993), 185)); Bede, *Historia ecclesiastica* III 4, V 22, 24 (Plummer (1896), i 134–5, 346–8, 356); Woolf's suggestion (2013), 5 n 20, that the Annals of Ulster here refer to Mayo rather than Iona contradicts Bede's testimony and generally raises more questions than it solves.

[82] See pp. 79–82 below.

[83] See pp. 83–6 below.

[84] See pp. 86–7 below.

[85] See Warntjes (2010), LXXXIV–LXXXV n 228 with a discussion of all known manuscript evidence for the Victorian Easter table. One of these tables, transmitted in Paris, Bibliothèque nationale de France, Lat. 4860, 147v–148r and Vatican, Biblioteca Apostolica, Reg. lat. 586, 9r–10v, appears to have originated in Ireland and was then used in Francia; it invariably lists only Victorian Easter dates with *luna* 16–22, i.e. those ascribed to the *Latini* by Victorius; in certain years, however, it mentions that the *Greci* celebrate on a different date; these are not Victorian double dates, but rather the redactor of this table compared his Victorian 'Roman' table with a Dionysiac one, noting the years in which Dionysius differed from these Victorian 'Roman' dates; in

retained their potential of controversy. And both occurred in successive years in AD 641 and AD 642, with Easter Sunday falling on *luna* 22 in the first of these years, the Easter full moon on 20 March, i.e. before the 'Greek' equinox of 21 March, and Easter Sunday on 24 March, i.e. before the 'Roman' (and *latercus*) equinox, in the second.[86] This provided enough reason for the northern Irish clergy to send a letter of admonition to Rome; certainly, it was an ideal time for complaint, as this combination of unacceptable data would not recur for another 19 years.[87]

Whether directly connected to Cummian's Letter, to the Victorian lunar data of AD 641 and 642, or both, the northern Irish letter to Rome and its response of AD 640 do not call into question but rather confirm that, at this time, the northern Irish clergy followed the *latercus*, the southern Irish church Victorius.

Catalogus sanctorum Hiberniae: The text known as *Catalogus sanctorum Hiberniae* is a curious tract dealing with the state of the Irish church from the times of St Patrick to *mortalitatem magnam*, doubtless a reference to the great plague of AD 665.[88] It divides this period into three chronological sections or 'orders of saints', outlining the principal characteristics of the Irish church for each order, among which the Easter question features prominently. The orders of saints are portrayed to represent a natural decline in virtue, from the holiest first, to the holier second, to the holy third. This decline is reflected in their attitudes

the first such entry, for AD 740, the author argues that his Victorian 'Roman' table did not differ from the 'Greeks', i.e. Dionysius, for the past 50 years in the date of Easter Sunday, which is correct (and the discrepancy in AD 740 also triggered the famous comment in the *Continuationes Chronicarum Fredegarii* 24, ed. by Bruno Krusch in MGH SS rer. Merov. 2, 179). This table demonstrates, then, that also in Francia only the 'Roman' dates of Victorius were followed from at least the late 7th century and that this data was compared with Dionysius since the AD 690s. A detailed study of this and all other known Victorian Easter tables remains a pressing desideratum.

86 Victorius, *Cyclus* AP 82–83 (ed. Krusch (1938), 31).

87 In AD 661, both matters of complaint occurred in the same year, with the Easter full moon falling on 20 March, Easter Sunday on 28 March, *luna* 22; Victorius, *Cyclus* AP 102 (Krusch (1938), 32).

88 The various versions of the *Catalogus sanctorum Hiberniae* are ed. by Grosjean (1955a), 206–11, with the reference to *mortalitatem magnam* in § 3d pp. 207, 209–10; this reference to the great plague is to be identified with the Irish annals *s.a.* 664–5 (Annals of Ulster *s.a.* 663–4 (Mac Airt and Mac Niocaill (1983), 134, 136); Annals of Tigernach *s.a.* [AU 663–4] (Stokes (1992), 198–9)), which fully accords with the persons mentioned in the text (see the discussion in Grosjean (1955a), 301–16).

towards Easter, with the first two celebrating one and the same Pasch unanimously, while the third order differed in this crucial question, some following *luna* 14, others *luna* 16.[89]

The reliability of the *Catalogus* as a source for 7th-century Ireland has been severely questioned by Grosjean in his seminal study and edition of this text of 1955, considering it a production of the 9th or 10th century.[90] True, the manuscript transmission is late (the earliest MS is from the 14th century)[91] and the chronological framework outlined in the text is full of misconceptions, if modern standards of historical research are applied (which certainly was not the intention of the author). Still, certain elements speak for an early composition of this text, not least the Easter data provided, as Rick Graff has demonstrated in this volume.[92] The paschal information is especially interesting for the present study. If taken at face value, the *Catalogus* presents proof that at least until AD 664/5, only two Easter reckonings were followed in the *regiones Scottorum*, the *latercus* (*luna* 14–20) in the north, the Victorian reckoning (*luna* 16–22) in the south; the Dionysiac reckoning was yet to enter the scene.

89 I cite the version from London, British Library, Add. 30512 here, as it is the only one to transmit the numerals uncorrupted (note also that this is considered by Grosjean (1955a), 212, as the oldest recension): *Catalogus sanctorum Hiberniae* 1a–b, 2a–b, 3a–c (Grosjean (1955a), 208–9): *Primus ordo sanctorum* [...] *habebant* [...] *unam celebrationem* [...] *sufferebant unum pascha quarta decima luna post equinoctium vernale* [...] *Secundus ordo* [...] *celebrabant* [...] *unum pascha quarta decima luna* [...] *Tertius ordo sanctorum* [...] *diversam sollemnitatem resurrectionis quarta decima luna vel sexta decima cum duris intensionibus coelebrabant*. The *Salmanticensis* recension reads *luna xiii* instead of the correct *luna xvi* for the third order (Grosjean (1955a), 207), an obvious scribal error (Grosjean (1955a), 297). Grosjean's argument (1955a), 297–8, that the author of the *Catalogus* here believed that Easter in that period had been celebrated on *luna* 14 and *luna* 16 fixed irrespective of the weekday and that this reveals this text to be a late composition by an uninformed author, fails to convince; *luna* 14 and *luna* 16 was simply short-hand for the lunar terms starting with these lunar ages.

90 Grosjean (1955a), 213. Lapidge and Sharpe (1985), 106, are inclined to date this text to the 8th or 9th century; prior to Grosjean's study, the *Catalogus* was dated to the middle of the 8th century by scholars such as Todd (1864), 88–9 (who also provides a translation and a substantial discussion on the following pages); Haddan and Stubbs (1869–78), ii 292–4; Wasserscheben (1885), xxxix; Kenney (1929), 478–9.

91 The transmission of this text is summarized by Grosjean (1955a), 198–9.

92 See Graff's contribution pp. 99–117 of this volume, especially 109–13. It may be noted that the *Catalogus* was used by all three scholars who attempted to reconstruct the 'Irish' 84 (14)-year Easter reckoning prior to Ó Cróinín's discovery of the Padua *latercus*; Mac Carthy (1901), cxlix; O'Connell (1936), 83; Schäferdiek (1985), 360–1 n 13; note that Mac Carthy and O'Connell date this text towards the end of the 7th century.

De ratione conputandi: The honorand of the present volume fundamentally changed the study of Irish computistics principally through two major discoveries, the Padua *latercus* already mentioned and a computistical textbook which he termed *De ratione conputandi*. Jones had already referred to this text in his 1977 edition of Bede's scientifica, incorporating it in a list of potentially interesting texts of possibly pre-Bedan origin.[93] Independent of Jones's note, Ó Cróinín came across this text when studying computistical manuscripts in Menso Folkert's microfilm collection in Munich. Contrary to Jones, he immediately realized its Irish origin and, working at that time on an edition and translation of Cummian's Letter with his wife Maura Walsh, spotted substantial parallels between the two texts. This convinced him that *De ratione conputandi* must have been written in the circle of Cummian (i.e. in southern Ireland) *c*.AD 650.[94] The text itself presents a beautifully balanced and precise introduction to the Dionysiac reckoning.[95] Quintessentially, in this reading, *De ratione conputandi* bears witness to the adoption of the Dionysiac reckoning in southern Ireland by the mid-7th century.

The dating of this Irish textbook, however, is not straight forward, as it contains no explicit dating clause. Comparison with the other known Irish computistical textbooks, especially the datable Munich Computus of AD 719, demonstrates, in my opinion, that *De ratione conputandi* was composed in the AD 720s rather than the middle of the 7th century.[96] If this dating is accepted, then *De ratione conputandi* cannot be considered as an early witness to the adoption of the Dionysiac reckoning in southern Ireland.

[93] Jones in CCSL 123, 13.

[94] Ó Cróinín (1982b), especially 114 for the dating.

[95] *De ratione conputandi* is edited by Ó Cróinín in Walsh and Ó Cróinín (1988), 99–213.

[96] Warntjes (2010), LV n 134; CXCI–CCI. Before this publication, Ó Cróinín's date was generally accepted, especially by Borst (1995), 96–7; Borst (1998), 180–1; Borst (2006), 134–5; only Smyth (1987), 100, raised some doubts, favouring a date around AD 700. For Wesley Stevens's misguided attempt in (2010), 50–1, to place *De ratione conputandi* in a Frankish mid-9th-century context, see Warntjes (2012), 71–2 n 96. Gorman (2011), 39 n 57, likewise suggests a continental origin of this text, as he finds it unlikely that Virgilius Maro's *Epistola* 1 was known in Ireland; this interpretation is obviously directly linked to Gorman's opinion that Virgilius came from Gaul, which is not undisputed; the computistical evidence is more conclusive and it firmly places *De ratione conputandi* in the Irish intellectual milieu of the AD 720s.

De divisionibus temporum: Another intriguing and severely understudied text is the tract *De divisionibus temporum*.[97] As the title suggests, this text, at least in its original format, discussed fourteen divisions of time, progressing from the smallest to the largest unit. The original is lost. The recensions that have survived, the most important and earliest being listed in Graff's seminal article, incorporate a section on the Dionysiac *cyclus decemnovenalis* between the units *annus* and *aetas*.[98] Since the general concept of this tract is based on Isidore's *Etymologiae* and since its early reception and the manuscript transmission points to Ireland, the original appears to have been composed in mid-7th-century Ireland. Whether the insertion on the Dionysiac *cyclus decemnovenalis* was also incorporated there, remains an open question, but again the manuscript context suggests so. The date of this insertion is even more difficult to assess. Certainly, the dating clause of AD 658 discussed above, which can be found in two of the codices transmitting early recensions of *De divisionibus temporum* (Oxford, Bodleian Library, Bodley 309; Geneva, Bibliothèque publique et universitaire, 50), should not be regarded as a *terminus ante quem*, as this date has validity, until further research, for the tract incorporating the dating clause only; in the Oxford codex, e.g., *De divisionibus temporum* sits between Bede's *De temporum ratione* of AD 725 and an excerpt from this Bedan text.[99] It appears most likely to me that the section on the Dionysiac *cyclus decemnovenalis* was inserted into the original text in early 8th-century Ireland, but only a critical edition and detailed analysis of all recensions of this text can shed more light on this problem. Certainly, *De divisionibus temporum* in its earliest recensions cannot easily (and, in my opinion, should not at all) be considered a witness for the adoption of the Dionysiac reckoning in 7th-century Ireland.

7th-century Irish computistical literature, the most relevant evidence for the Easter question, therefore reveals that Victorius (and Victorius alone) was followed by the southern Irish clergy from the introduction of this reckoning in the AD 630s to the controversy of the AD 680s,

[97] One (8th-century) recension of this text is edited in PL 90, 653–64. The seminal studies of this text are Jones (1939), 48–51; Graff (2010), 117–25. For other, minor texts discussing the fourteen division of time see Warntjes (2010), CLIX–CLX (with further references).

[98] Graff (2010), 121–4.

[99] Cf. especially the descriptions of the content of this manuscript in Jones (1937), 213–4; Wallis (1999), lxxi–lxxix; Ó Cróinín (2003a), 202; Springsfeld (2002), 69 (where *De divisionibus temporum* is considered part of *Sententiae sancti Augustini et Isidori in laude compoti*).

while the northern Irish clergy strictly adhered to the *latercus* until this date.

The introduction of the Dionysiac reckoning in the AD 680s

Surely, it would have been odd had the southern Irish church abandoned Victorius shortly after introducing his system, especially considering the strife caused by its adoption, which had almost split the southern Irish church into rivalling factions; a second Mag Léne only a few years later certainly had to be avoided. Also, Merovingian Gaul, southern Ireland's neighbour and trade-partner in matters economical and cultural across the channel, was deeply routed in Victorian tradition since the Synod of Orléans in AD 541.[100] As so often, the religious divide was on land rather than marked by the sea; in this case, it went straight through the island of Ireland, with, since the AD 630s, followers of Victorius in the south, adherents of the *latercus* in the north. This opposition was not lifted with the introduction of the Dionysiac reckoning in the AD 680s. Quite the contrary, it rather led to a prolongation of the conflict for at least another decade.

How, when, and why the Dionysiac reckoning was introduced into Ireland remains speculative. A clear distinction needs to be drawn between the north and the south of Ireland. As mentioned earlier, since the seminal studies by Jones, most scholars believed in a smooth transitional period around the middle of the 7th century in which the Victorian and the Dionysiac reckoning were used side-by-side in the south, leading to a full adoption of Dionysius around the AD 660s. To be sure, Dionysius was known in Ireland since the AD 620s and both systems were certainly compared in southern Ireland around the middle of the 7th century, but, as has been demonstrated above, *only* the Victorian reckoning was *followed* right into the AD 680s and beyond. This is an extremely important observation and has serious consequence on how we read Irish history of the AD 680s.

[100] The Victorian reckoning was unanimously accepted by the Gallic church at the Synod of Orléans of AD 541 (CCSL 148A, 132); the gradual abandonment of Victorius in the Gallic church from the late 7th to the early 9th centuries, with all the controversies it must have caused, remains to be studied; still usefull but outdated are Krusch (1884), 122–41; Schmid (1907), 60–88; a step in the right direction is Declercq (2000), 169–88.

The introduction of the Dionysiac reckoning in the north, on the other hand, is usually ascribed to two influences, that of Armagh and the Iona Abbot Adomnán, both influenced by developments on the neighbouring island of Britain. Turning to Armagh first: The theory goes that the appointment of Theodore of Tharsus as archbishop of Canterbury in AD 669 triggered a debate on church organization in Britain and Ireland. First, there was the dispute between Theodore and Wilfrid about the status of York. Theodore was anxious to retain the primacy of Canterbury, while Wilfrid hoped for or worked towards an equal (if not superior) status of York, with York's influence covering the northern half of not only Britain, but also Ireland. This discourse was taken up by Kildare to claim supremacy of St Brigid's church, as an archbishopric, over all other ecclesiastical institutions of Ireland. Armagh, with its constantly growing cult of St Patrick, felt immediately challenged. In order to make similar claims, Armagh had to convert, as the first major church in the north, to Roman practices, which it did in the AD 680s.[101]

Plausible as this theory is, the evidence is scant, the chronological framework shaky, since, although all sources of relevance appear to have been written before AD 700, none can be dated with certainty.[102] The most central piece of evidence is the submission of Sleaty in south Leinster to Armagh's authority.[103] This must have occurred before AD 688, the year in which Bishop Ségéne of Armagh, the first of the two signatories, died.[104] For a southern Irish church turning to Armagh, the latter certainly would have to have embraced Roman customs before that date.[105] But what are the 'Roman' customs followed by the two rivals,

[101] See especially Charles-Edwards (2000), 416–40; Corning (2006), 108–9.

[102] A neat summary of the evidence can be found in Charles-Edwards (2000), 438–40.

[103] The passage in question, commonly called the Testament of Áed of Sleaty, is transmitted among the *Additamenta* (§16) of the early-9th-century Book of Armagh (ed. and trans. by Stokes and Strachan (1901–3), ii 242; Bieler (1979), 178–9; corr. trans. by Byrne (1982), 169). For the political background to this passage, see Ó Cróinín (1995), 156–8; Charles-Edwards (2000), 261–2; Doherty (1991), 75–8; for its traditional interpretation in the context of the Easter question, see Hughes (1966), 116; Sharpe (1984), 64; Charles-Edwards (2000), 428–9.

[104] Ségéne's obit is recorded in the Irish annals *s.a.* AD 688 (Annals of Ulster *s.a.* 687 (Mac Airt and Mac Niocaill (1983), 150); Annals of Tigernach *s.a.* [AU 687] (Stokes (1992), 210)).

[105] The texts transmitted in the early 9th-century Book of Armagh (Dublin, Trinity College, 52) are interesting in the context of Armagh's conversion to the Dionysiac reckoning, as they propagate pre-eminence of the church of Armagh over all other Irish churches by stressing a strong link to Rome, especially by reference to the relics of Peter

Kildare and Armagh? From the computistical evidence outlined above, Kildare, as one of the principal southern Irish churches, would still have followed Victorius, while Armagh, considering the developments in Anglo-Saxon England and in Rome, would have introduced Dionysius. This interpretation adds a new dimension to the conflict between Kildare and Armagh: Armagh did not simply outmaneuver Kildare by introducing the same reckoning as followed by St Brigid's church (i.e. Victorius' system), it even claimed supremacy by favouring Dionysius. After being accused of heresy by Kildare for decades for following the *latercus*, Armagh must have felt some satisfaction in turning the table by now being able to discredit Kildare on the same issue.

We are better informed about the second and more important influence, that of Adomnán, as here Bede again serves as witness. In chapter 15 of book 5 of his *Historia ecclesiastica*, Bede argues that Adomnán, abbot of Iona, visited the Northumbrian King Aldfrith on a mission from his own (that is the Irish) people; on this trip, he was converted to Roman customs and, even though unable to convince his own community off the coast of modern-day Scotland, was more successful on the island of Ireland, where almost all churches not under Iona jurisdiction followed his example.[106] There are numerous problems, particularly chronological ones, in Bede's story here, but these are of no immediate concern for the present purpose. Three aspects are important: First, Adomnán's conversion can, with relative certainty, be dated to the second half of the AD 680s:[107] Through Adomnán's own testimony,

and Paul; *Liber Angli* 19 (Bieler (1979), 186–9); Tírechán, prelude [II 3], *Collectanea* 48 (Bieler (1979), 122–3, 160–1). Accordingly, Armagh would have converted before the composition of the texts; unfortuantely, none of these texts provides hard chronological evidence and the dependency 'Easter controversy – date of these texts' invites circular arguments; cf. Sharpe (1984); Charles-Edwards (2000), 428–40; Doherty (2007), 279–83.

106 Bede, *Historia ecclesiastica* V 15 (Plummer (1896), i 315–6); the same information can be found in Ceolfrith's Letter to the Pictish King Nechtan, transmitted by Bede in *Historia ecclesiastica* V 21 (Plummer (1896), i 344–5).

107 The consensus of most scholars that Adomnán's conversion must have taken place in the second half of the AD 680s, has frequently been challenged by the theory that the abbot of Iona adopted the Dionysiac reckoning only shortly before his death in AD 704. Haddan and Stubbs (1869–78), ii 110, believed so, without further explanation, and Zimmer (1881–4), ii 198, argues that the story outlined in Bede, *Historia ecclesiastica* V 15, should be dated to *c.*AD 701; similarly O'Loughlin (2000), 71, repeating his argument verbatim twice in (2001), 46, and in (2007), 5, yet without reference or reasoning. The most detailed case for an early 8th-century conversion of Adomnán has very recently been outlined by Woods (2011); the main attraction of this theory lies in the fact that it provides a simple solution to the otherwise pressing question of

we know that the Iona abbot travelled to Northumbria twice, first *post bellum Ecfridi* (clearly the battle of Nechtansmere), and a second time two years later.[108] The battle of Nechtansmere can securely be dated to 20 May 685.[109] When exactly after this crucial event in Northumbrian history (for it made Adomnán's friend Aldfrith king) Adomnán visited Northumbria is difficult to assess. The abbot of Iona himself is silent about the purposes of his trips. Bede says that Adomnán was on a mission from his own people for the one trip he records. The Irish annals

how a monastic community could have functioned under a head following different practices than his nominal subjects for more than 15 years; but re-dating the process of conversion certainly is not the only possible explanation. Woods's main arguments are two: First, the relative chronology within Bede's *Historia ecclesiastica*, with the passage of Adomnán's conversion (V 15) being sandwiched between Willibrord's ordination in AD 696 (V 11) and Aldfrith's death in AD 705 (V 17); this is not conclusive: V 2–6 relate the life and miracles of John of Hexham, starting with his appointment to office in AD 685; V 7 narrates Caedwalla's trip to Rome in AD 688; V 8 Theodore of Tarsus's death in AD 690; V 9–11 record the beginning of the Frisian mission *eo tempore* (i.e. roughly around Theodore's death, and we know that Willibrord went to Frisia in AD 690) and its further development not until AD 696, but to Bede's present day; V 12–14 miracles happening *his temporibus*, in the reign of Cenred (AD 704–9), and *nuper*; V 15 Adomnán's conversion *quo tempore*; it is clear that this expression does not refer to Cenred's reign or *nuper*, and neither does it refer to Willibrord's consecration in AD 696, but to the time of Theodore's death and the Frisian mission, i.e. towards the end of the AD 680s. Second, Woods presents an unconventional reading of the *Vita Columbae*, regarding references to plagues as implicit statements of Adomnán's pro-*latercus* stand in the Easter debate when writing the *Vita* shortly before AD 700; this is highly speculative, certainly not hard evidence, and it fails to convince at the point when the British church comes into the picture (p 8): despite following the *latercus*, the Britons suffered from the plague; in Woods's theory, this is because they had no links to the Columban church, so only following the *latercus* and Columban protection was sufficient safeguard against disease; there is, however, no need for the parameter *latercus* in this equation, simply belonging to Columba's sphere of influence explains Adomnán's plague passages. Therefore, I consider the computistical evidence (not considered by Woods) and the following argument more substantial, especially the equation: Adomnán explicitly stating that he visited Northumbria after Nechtanesmere, i.e. in AD 685, and two years later, i.e. in AD 687 = the Irish annals stating for AD 687 that Adomnán returned to Ireland 60 prisoners of war = Bede arguing that Adomnán was converted when on a mission from his own people.

108 Adomnán, *Vita Columbae* II 46 (Anderson and Anderson (1961), 460, 462).

109 Bede, *Historia ecclesiastica* IV 26, V 24 (Plummer (1896), i 266–7, 355); Irish annals *s.a.* AD 686 (Annals of Ulster *s.a.* 685 (Mac Airt and Mac Niocaill (1983), 148); Annals of Tigernach *s.a.* [AU 685] (Stokes (1992), 209)). That the battle of Nechtanesmere took place on 20 May AD 685 is Bede's information, which is independently confirmed by the annals's record of the correct weekday, a Saturday; note, however, that the event is misplaced by a year in the annals, recording it in the year synchronized with AD 686; it seems that a layer of Northumbrian events was retrospectively introduced into the annals, presumably by Ecgberht in the early 8th century (cf. Mc Carthy, *Irish annals*, 151). I would like to thank Dan Mc Carthy for discussing this issue with me.

state for the year AD 687 that Adomnán 'brought back 60 captives to Ireland'.[110] The Northumbrian King Ecgfrith, who lost his life at Nechtansmere in AD 685, had raided Brega in Ireland only one year earlier.[111] Thus, the Irish prisoners of war quite certainly stemmed from this campaign and with the change of power from Ecgfrith to Adomnán's friend Aldfrith, the Brega people (southern Uí Néill) hoped that Adomnán would be able to negotiate their release. From this evidence, the chronological framework of Adomnán's trips to Northumbrian appears to be the following: After the battle of Nechtansmere in AD 685, Adomnán visited Northumbria, either accompanying his friend Aldfrith directly from Iona on his way to claim the Northumbrian throne[112] or immediately after Aldfrith was installed king. Aldfrith's accession changed Northumbrian-Irish relations, and the southern Uí Néill took advantage of this by asking Adomnán to negotiate the release of their kinsmen held hostage in Northumbria since AD 684. Following their request, the Iona abbot travelled to Northumbria in AD 687 and, having succeeded in his mission, continued to Ireland in the same year. Bede's account suggest that it was the second of these two visits, the one in AD 687, during which Adomnán converted to Roman customs.[113]

Second, it is obvious and central that the Roman customs Adomnán converted to included the Dionysiac, not the Victorian reckoning. Stephen of Ripon, in his *Vita Wilfridi*, is quite explicit that it was Dionysius who won the day over the *latercus* at the Synod of Whitby in AD 664 and there is no good reason to doubt his account.[114] This implies that from AD 664 onwards, the Dionysiac reckoning was considered the norm in Bede's Northumbria, where Adomnán was converted to

[110] Irish annals *s.a.* AD 687 (Annals of Ulster *s.a.* 686 (Mac Airt and Mac Niocaill (1983), 150–1); Annals of Tigernach *s.a.* [AU 686] (Stokes (1992), 210)).

[111] Bede, *Historia ecclesiastica* IV 26 (Plummer (1896), i 266); Irish annals *s.a.* AD 685 (Annals of Ulster *s.a.* 684 (Mac Airt and Mac Niocaill (1983), 148); Annals of Tigernach *s.a.* [AU 684] (Stokes (1992), 208)). For the misplacement of this entry by a year in the annals see n 109.

[112] For Iona's involvement in Aldfrith's coming to power see Warntjes (2010c), 176–82.

[113] See p 70 below.

[114] Stephen of Ripon, *Vita Wilfridi* 10 (ed. by Wilhelm Levison in MGH SS rer. Merov. 6, 203; ed. and trans. by Colgrave (1927), 20–1, with commentary 157–8); *pace* Levision and Colgrave, the reading in the Cottonian MS of lunar limits 14–22 being discredited by Wilfrid and his party is correct, conflating *latercus* with Victorian limits; cf. Corning (2006), 126; Ohashi (2011), 144–7.

Roman customs in the late AD 680s. Bede himself, when relating the story of Adomnán's conversion, is not that explicit. More revealing is the letter of Bede's Abbot Ceolfrith to the Pictish King Nechtan of AD 710.[115] Nechtan had decided slightly earlier that the Picts should abandon the *latercus* still followed by the dominant ecclesiastical force in the region, the monastery of Iona, and turn to Dionysius instead. In order to back his decision by authoritative writing, he approached Ceolfrith, abbot of Wearmouth and Jarrow. Ceolfrith's answer left no room for doubt that lunar limits of 15 to 21 had to be observed for Easter Sunday, which are Dionysiac (and Dionysiac only) criteria, and in the same explicit manner he rejected the limits of the other two systems, the *latercus*' 14 to 20 and Victorius' 16 to 22. Also, Ceolfrith tried to strengthen his argument by reference to traditional and recent authorities. Theophilus and Cyril of Alexandria had first outlined the methods of this system in successive Easter tables, Dionysius himself extended these for another 95 years; to be sure, the system became cyclic only after 532-years, and, according to Ceolfrith, many skilful computists of the time were able to compile Dionysiac Easter tables of this cyclic period. More important for Ceolfrith's cause of promoting Roman customs in tonsure (the Petrine one) and Easter reckoning (the Dionysiac one) to Nechtan was Adomnán's example. He relates in detail his personal conversation with the abbot of Iona, which convinced the latter to adopt catholic practices. The immediate implication obviously is that Roman tradition meant Dionysiac reckoning. And with Adomnán dead for only seven years at the time of composition of this letter and both the Northumbrians and the Picts being very well informed about Iona affairs, Ceolfrith could hardly have twisted the facts here.[116] Adomnán certainly had converted to Dionysius, and this in the late AD 680s.

Third, both Bede and Ceolfrith, in the letter just discussed, argue that Adomnán was the instrumental figure in winning large parts of the Irish church over to the Roman cause. Bede speaks of Adomnán restoring 'nearly all who were not under the dominion of Iona to Catholic unity, teaching them to observe Easter at the proper time', while Ceolfrith acknowledges that the abbot of Iona, 'when he had returned to Ireland, he led large numbers of that race to the Catholic observance of Easter by his preaching; nevertheless he could not bring the monks of Iona,

[115] Bede, *Historia ecclesiastica* V 21 (Plummer (1896), i 322–46).

[116] Cf. Corning (2006), 153.

over whom he presided as lawful head, to better ways'.[117] Surely, what both authors meant by these passages is that Adomnán convinced most of the northern Irish churches not under Iona jurisdiction to adopt the Dionysiac reckoning. Problematic as Bede's chronological details in this case may be, there is no good reason to doubt the veracity of these more general facts. Again, Ceolfrith, in AD 710, would have found it difficult to sell such bold statements to the Pictish King Nechtan had they not represented fact rather than fiction. More importantly, Adomnán developed, after his personal conversion, into the leading churchman of both Ireland and Britain. His reputation in Ireland is best highlighted by the promulgation of the law bearing his name, the *Cáin Adomnáin*. In AD 697, a synod was assembled in Birr in central Ireland by Adomnán and his relative, the king of Tara and most powerful ruler in the *regiones Scottorum*, Loingsech mac Óengusso. The resulting law-tract, dealing with the treatment in wartimes of the uninvolved, i.e. children, women, and clerics (therefore called *Lex innocentium* in Latin), was signed by 91 high standing representatives, both secular and ecclesiastical, of all parts of the *regiones Scottorum* and even Pictland.[118] Being a famous figure, the most influential and prominent churchman of the insular world, his biography was well known, especially when Ceolfrith wrote his letter to Nechtan in AD 710, but also at the time of Bede's composition of the *Historia ecclesiastica*.

On the basis of this evidence, the most likely scenario for the introduction of the Dionysiac reckoning in Ireland is the following: With the Synod of Whitby of AD 664, at the latest, Anglo-Saxon monasteries in Ireland, such as Rath Melsigi under Ecgberht's leadership, followed Dionysius and they were the first monastic communities on this island to do so. The major transition, however, came in the AD 680s, and not within the southern, but within the northern Irish church. Whether Armagh's acceptance of the Dionysiac system substantially predated

[117] Bede, *Historia ecclesiastica* V 15, 21 (Plummer (1896), i 316, 345): *Nauigauit Hiberniam, et praedicans eis, ac modesta exhortatione declarans legitimum paschae tempus, plurimos eorum, et pene omnes, qui ab Hiensium dominio erant liberi, ab errore auito correctos, ad unitatem reduxit catholicam, ac legitimum paschae tempus obseruare perdocuit.* [...] *cum reversus ad Scottiam, multas postea gentis eiusdem turbas ad catholicam temporis paschalis obseruantiam sua praedictatione correxit; tametsi eos, qui in Hii insula morabantur, monachos, quibusque speciali rectoris iure praeerat, necdum ad uiam statuti melioris reducere ualebat.*

[118] The *Cáin Adomnáin* has been printed (and translated) many times; the standard edition remains Meyer (1905); the 'guarantor list' is analyzed in detail by Ní Dhonnchadha (1982); for the context of this law, see Ní Dhonnchadha (1995); Ní Dhonnchadha (2001).

Adomnán's conversion, must remain speculative; I would be inclined to link the two. Adomnán himself outlines that he visited Northumbria twice, while Bede and Ceolfrith only speak of one visit. It is generally believed that these Anglo-Saxon churchmen conflated the two trips mentioned by Adomnán, with few scholars arguing for the first, most for the second trip as the one of conversion.[119] Still, there is no reason to assume a conflation of two of Adomnán's visits to Northumbria in these accounts. Ceolfrith, and Bede following him, were only concerned with the one trip that matter most to them, namely the one when Adomnán adopted Roman customs; they do not state that this was the only time Adomnán travelled to Northumbria; he may have done so twice or many more times as far as they were concerned, only the one trip that led to his conversion mattered to them. And they are quite specific about the occasion of this most important trip, Adomnán being 'on a mission from his own people', to be identified with the release of the Brega prisoners of war as documented in the Irish annals. Thus, Adomnán adopted the Dionysiac reckoning in AD 687 and when he returned to Ireland with the 60 former prisoners in the same year, his conversion must have aroused an enormous interest in the *regiones Scottorum* as a whole. Some churches may have followed his example immediately, others presumably remained more reluctant, like his own community of Iona. The ensuing debates, however, were not confined to *latercus* traditionalists and recent converts to Dionysius among the northern clergy, but featured more prominently between southern adherents to Victorius and the recent northern followers of Dionysius. Arguments were exchanged in AD 688 and then put into writing in AD 689, with the Victorian Computus of AD 689 and *De comparatione epactarum* being the central documents. Rather than pacifying Ireland on the Easter question by bringing all Irish churches save Iona dependencies into line with 'Roman' custom, Adomnán added a new dimension to the conflict: southern followers of Victorius disputed heavily with northern converts to Dionysius, while the northern Dionysiac party disagreed with the Iona traditionalists (which is not the concern of the present article).

[119] The following are obviously only examples of the more prominent scholarship. First trip: Plummer (1896), ii 301–2. Second trip: Reeves (1857), 187; Anderson and Anderson (1961), 94; Sharpe (1995), 46–51; Stancliffe (2010), 52–3.

The issues of controversy

The conflict between the Victorian and the Dionysiac system has been underestimated for three principal reasons: First, some historians working on the Easter controversy refuse to enter its technicalities, which must result in a misrepresentation of the problems involved. Second, crucial manuscript evidence has been neglected, as modern scholarship too often works on the premise that all important early medieval documents have appeared in print. Third, and most crucially, the leading computistical scholar of the 20th century, Charles W. Jones, considered the differences between the Victorian and the Dionysiac reckoning minor, and this is what subsequent scholars readily accepted. In his seminal article on 'The Victorian and the Dionysiac paschal tables in the West' of 1934, Jones is principally concerned with the Julian calendar dates of Easter Sunday. He first explains the three reasons why those could potentially differ between the two reckonings: A. different Julian calendar limits for the Easter full moon; B. different lunar limits for Easter Sunday; C. different placement of the *saltus* within the 19-year lunar cycle. Then, he demonstrates that these variations in construction do not necessarily result in differing Julian calendar dates for Easter Sunday, as, in many cases, two differing criteria occurring in the same year even out the differences and lead to agreement in the date of Easter. Accordingly, only on 23 occasions in the just over 200 years between AD 457 and 664 do the Julian calendar dates of Easter Sunday differ between these two reckonings, a rather negligible total.[120] Jones concludes:[121]

> 'The recurring errors necessitated a remedy, which was found in the Dionysiac tables. These tables did not, to our knowledge, receive the official sanction of Rome, but spread by a slow and natural circulation, perhaps from Italy through Africa and Spain into France and England, and gradually supplanted for practical purposes the Victorian tables, although *in theory there was no difference between them.*'

This statement has fundamentally shaped modern scholarship in two ways: First, it is commonly believed that the Dionysiac reckoning gradually and peacefully replaced the Victorian system, with neither debate nor conflict. Second, there was no substantial difference between these two Easter reckonings. Both views are mistaken. Jones certainly is right

[120] Jones (1934), 411.

[121] Jones (1934), 421 (the italics are Jones's).

to argue that the differences in the Julian calendar date for the celebration of Easter were minor. But this only suggests harmony on the surface and, more importantly, no contemporary document supports the view that both systems were considered virtually interchangeable. Quite the contrary, recently uncovered evidence as well as well-known documents paint the opposite picture, illustrating that numerous theological issues made an easy adoption of the Dionysiac reckoning by followers of Victorius impossible. These are discussed in turn in the following.

Passion and resurrection data: It may be appropriate to start with the most important issue, the passion and resurrection of Christ. One of the most appealing aspects of the Victorian reckoning was the fact that it was formally based on the year of Christ's passion.[122] Obviously, since the whole purpose of Easter reckonings was calculating the date of Christ's resurrection, starting a cyclic Easter table with the year of Christ's passion was as ingenious as it was natural. The lunar data presented by Victorius for this year (AD 28 in modern notation), with the passion on *luna* 14 and resurrection on *luna* 16, matched the information given in John's Gospel. The Holy Scripture presented only one alternative, *luna* 15 and 17 respectively as implied by the Synoptic Gospels.[123] Neither the Johannine nor the Synoptic tradition had an impact on the Dionysiac reckoning in this respect, as this system was in no way concerned with the historic year of Christ's passion. The Roman monk Dionysius had, in AD 525, simply translated a system invented by 4th-century Alexandrian scientists. And the Alexandrians were not concerned with past events, only with astronomical accuracy. For this reason, 7th-century computists found it difficult to establish Dionysiac resurrection data. They had, in effect, only two options: The first, counting the years from Christ's birth, is discussed in the following section. The second was to synchronize the Victorian year of the passion with the Dionysiac table. This was obviously the most natural approach for followers of Victorius' system. Paralleling both Easter (or rather lunar) tables to this effect was a complex task, demonstrating the skill of 7th-century Irish computists. It yielded surprising results: In the year designated as the *annus passionis* in the Victorian Easter table, the Dionysiac reckoning produced *luna* 13 for the passion, *luna* 15 for the resurrection! This data could not be

[122] Victorius' Easter table starts with the year of Christ's passion (Krusch (1938), 27), and Victorius explains this choice in his Prologue 10 (Krusch (1938), 25).

[123] For the lunar data of Christ's passion and resurrection as presented in the Gospels see the most recent study by Nothaft (2012), 23–5.

squared with any biblical passage. In fact, it must have appeared outright heretical to those studying Dionysius' system closely.

Certainly adherents of the Victorian reckoning did not take this point lightly. Victorius had demonstrated that an Easter reckoning can produce biblical lunar data for the passion and resurrection of Christ, so that his followers were extremely sensitive on this issue. When parts of the northern Irish clergy started to follow Dionysius in the AD 680s, they were immediately accused of heresy by the southern Irish adherents of Victorius. At least this is what the tract *De comparatione epactarum Dionysii et Victorii* of AD 689, introduced above, suggest.[124] Apparently under attack by followers of Victorius on this issue, the Dionysiac author of this tract invented a scientific argument to prove the opposite. In the 7th century, the standard method to compare the Victorian with the Dionysiac reckoning was by comparison not of full Easter tables, but only of their respective lunar data. Both reckonings were based on a 19-year lunar cycle. Dionysius had explained how these 19 years are to be divided into two parts, one of 8 years called *ogdoas*, the other of 11 years called *hendecas*. 7th-century computists adapted this division to the Victorian reckoning also, aligning Dionysiac *ogdoas* with Victorian *ogdoas*, and the *hendecades* likewise. In the 19-year cycle (*cyclus decemnovenalis*), the Victorian *annus passions* occurred in the second year of the *hendecas*, in which the Victorian lunar ages were one higher than the Dionysiac ones. Accordingly, this correct comparison produced *luna* 13 for the passion of Christ and *luna* 15 for his resurrection in the Dionysiac equivalent of the Victorian *annus passionis*. Now, the author of *De comparatione epactarum* had the ingenious idea of comparing Victorian *hendecas* with Dionysiac *ogdoas*. Even though this approach was simply a theoretical construct and bore no relation to reality, it produced the desired result: Now, the Victorian lunar data trailed the Dionysiac one by one, so that the passion of Christ occurred on *luna* 15, his resurrection on *luna* 17 in the Dionysiac equivalent to the Victorian *annus passionis* (second year of the Dionysiac *ogdoas* = second year of the Victorian *hendecas*), matching the information of the Synoptic Gospels.[125] Dionysius was vindicated!

[124] See pp. 53–5 above.

[125] For discussions of the content of *De comparatione epactarum Dionysii et Victorii* see Warntjes (2010), CLIII–CLIV; Nothaft (2012), 78–80; the tables in Schwartz (1905), 94, and Warntjes (2007), 67, may help to illustrate the argument (with the *latercus* data being irrelevant for the theory discussed above).

De comparatione epactarum can, cautiously, be dated to AD 689. The only other tract that deals in substantial detail with the same theory is the Irish Munich Computus of AD 719, the argumentation being less fervent than in the earlier tract.[126] Thus, it is apparent that the problem of Dionysius not providing acceptable lunar data for the *annus passionis* was a virulent issue among Irish scholars towards the end of the 7th century. The obvious conclusion is that when some northern Irish churches converted to Dionysius in the AD 680s, they were immediately accused of heresy by their southern Irish counterparts following Victorius. *De comparatione epactarum* was invented to counter this most disturbing accusation. By the time its contents were incorporated into the Munich Computus in AD 719, written by a southern Irish convert from Victorius to Dionysius, the issue was settled and merely repeated for scientific purposes. Dionysius had won the day, 30 years later, despite his highly problematic neglect of the biblical data for Christ's passion and resurrection.

AD chronology: The discussion of the passion and resurrection data immediately leads to the linear chronologies of the Victorian and the Dionysiac systems. Victorius chose the year of Christ's passion as the base year of his table, from which he started a linear count for the 532 years of his Easter cycle; in the 6th century, precisely in AP 532 = AD 559, when the cycle ended and had to be restarted from its beginning, the AP count had to be continued (or 532 had to be added to the AP dates listed in the original table).[127] Dionysius, for his part, used a linear count of years starting with the incarnation of Christ, which was known in the East

[126] Munich Computus 49, 52 (Warntjes (2010), 170–1, 194–203); the basic theory of *De comparatione epactarum* is also pressed in table format in the *Computus Einsidlensis* p 109, though without further comments (a facsimile is printed in Warntjes (2010), 321, and is also readily accessible online at www.e-codices.unifr.ch/de/sbe/0321/109). Traces of this theory can also be found in *Comp. Col.* V 4–5 of AD 805 (ed. Borst (2006), 929–33; cf. Warntjes (2010), CII, CLIV, CLXXX–CLXXXI, 194–200), transmitted in the same very early 9th-century Cologne codex as *De comparatione epactarum*; this proves that the problem in question also received some attention in the Carolingian Empire, where the late 7th-century Irish debate was repeated in the 8th century when the Dionysiac system introduced by Anglo-Saxon and Irish monks challenged the Frankish clergy traditionally following Victorius.

[127] In practice, 7th-century Irish computists referred to the AP dates of the original table rather than their 532-year equivalents representing the present AP date of those scholars (and often the consular names were given additionally or instead); cf. the Victorian Computus of AD 689 as cited in the Munich Computus 41, 62 (Warntjes (2010), 140, 278; cf. ibidem, LVII–LVIII); Victorian Prologue of AD 699, with translation of AP 141 to AP 673 (Warntjes (2010a), 271).

before his time.[128] Contrary to Victorius, his table did not commence with the first year of this count, but with the 532nd and covered only the following 95 years.[129] Not being presented with a full count of years from the base to the present year may have caused suspicion about the validity of this timeframe. Certainly, once the Dionysiac system began to be tested for its passion and resurrection data, suspicion turned to irritation if not outright rejection. One method of establishing Dionysiac passion and resurrection data has been outlined in the previous section. This, it must be noted, was the intuitive approach by followers of Victorius when testing the Dionysiac system. The alternative method was more natural, at least for followers of Dionysius, as no comparison with a different system was needed. 7th-century computists soon realised that Dionysius' 95-year period was not cyclic, *pace* Isidore, who had just made that claim.[130] Rather, Dionysius' system was based on the same cyclic principle as the Victorian one, the 532-year luni-solar cycle. With this information at hand, the Dionysiac data for the *annus passionis* could easily be established. The original Dionysiac Easter table (or at least its continuations which included Dionysius' original 95-year period of AD 532–626) circulated widely in Ireland and Britain.[131] It started with AD 532, which, according to the 532-year cyclic period, was equivalent to 1 BC, the year of Christ's incarnation. The Gospels suggest two chronologies for the period between Christ's birth and his crucifixion, either 30 years and a few month or 33 years and a few months.[132] Accordingly, Christ's passion took place either in AD 31 = AD 563 or AD 34 = AD 566. Both years, however, yielded unacceptable lunar data: In the Dionysiac reckoning,

[128] See especially Mc Carthy (2003); Mosshammer (2008), 339–56.

[129] Dioysius' Easter table is printed in Krusch (1938), 69–74; to his Easter table proper he prefixed the final 19 years of the preceeding 95-year table composed by Cyril of Alexandria.

[130] See below pp. 117–9.

[131] Note that of the manuscripts used by Krusch (1938), 60, for his edition of Dionysius' Easter table, none covers the period of the original, AD 532–626, almost all are extended to AD 1063; also, only Oxford, Bodleian Library, Digby 63 transmits the final 19 years of Cyrill's table which Dionysius prefixed to his own. Therefore, Dionysius' table in its orginal format has not survived. Many of the manuscripts used by Krusch show insular connections; also, Dionysius' computistica are prominently transmitted in the Sirmond group of manuscripts unknown to Krusch; this Sirmond collection of texts including Dionysius' computistica is known to have circulated in southern Ireland by the AD 650s (cf. pp. 52–3 above); but since this collection survives only in 9th-century or later manuscripts, the Dionysiac table found therein is generally extended to AD 532–1063.

[132] See the most recent discussion in Nothaft (2012), 22–3.

AD 31 had *luna* 13 for the passion, *luna* 15 for the resurrection, while AD 34 provided *luna* 19 for the passion, *luna* 21 for the resurrection.[133]

Accordingly, listing AD dates was one of the weaknesses of the Dionysiac Easter table, not one of its strengths. That it was a major issue in the Irish Easter controversy towards the end of the 7th century can be inferred from silence rather than *expressis verbis*. The three Irish computistical textbooks which have survived, the *Computus Einsidlensis*, the Munich Computus, and *De ratione conputandi*, were all composed by southern Irish converts from Victorius to Dionysius in the very early 8th century.[134] Their suspicion of AD manifested itself in silence. The principal purpose of these texts was to explain all details of the Dionysiac reckoning. The *Computus Einsidlensis* and the Munich Computus do not even mention AD, while *De ratione conputandi* refers to it only once, in a discussion of the columns of the Dionysiac Easter table.[135] No doubt, this behaviour can be explained by the preceding controversy. Adherents of Victorius ridiculed Dionysius for not providing acceptable data for *the* most important event, the foundation of Christianity. When they finally had to convert to the Dionysiac system, they cast a cloak of silence over this controversial aspect. AD was a problem, not a useful chronological tool.

The perception of AD in the insular world changed with Bede. The earlier to contemporary controversy about this issue is explicitly addressed by Bede in chapter 47 of his *De temporum ratione* of AD 725.[136] AD 34 = AD 566 features prominently, though his discussion focuses on the Julian calendar dates of the crucifixion and resurrection rather than the lunar data; in this, Bede outlines a different dimension of the same problem and bears witness to the prominence of the issue even in the AD 720s. Irish computists preferred to discard AD altogether, as it obviously was not an essential part of the reckoning proper. Bede wanted to use AD as a chronological framework, especially in his *Historia ecclesiastica*

133 For the Dionysiac data of these years see the handy table in Wallis (1999), 392.

134 For the southern Irish origin of these Irish computistical textbooks and their relative chronology see especially Warntjes (2010), LII–XCVI, CXXXIII–CLII, CXCI–CCI.

135 *De ratione conputandi* 103 (Walsh and Ó Cróinín (1988), 207); for the silence concerning AD of the other two Irish textbooks, but also its adoption by the author of the Victorian Prologue of AD 699, see Warntjes (2010b), 93; Warntjes (2010a), 275–6.

136 Bede, *De temporum ratione* 47 (Jones (1943), 265–8). For commentaries on this chapter see van der Hagen (1734), 301–5; Jones (1943), 381–2; Wallis (1999), 336–8 (read 566 for 556 on pp. 337–8); Pillonel-Wyrsch (2004), 312–8; Nothaft (2012), 80–8; as well as Leofranc Holford-Strevens's analysis of it, to be published in the proceedings of the fourth conference on the science of computus.

composed only six years later, so he could not avoid the subject. He tried to silence the critics by irony turning sarcasm, without lasting success. Already in the Carolingian period, various attempts have been made to find a suitable answer for dating the passion of Christ, most notably by Claudius of Turin.[137] By the end of the tenth century and then throughout the high medieval period, Dionysius' AD chronology was serious questions and variously rectified, by Abbo of Fleury, Marianus Scottus, Sigibert of Gembloux, and others.[138] The invention and introduction of AD reckoning into chronology have been lauded as a landmark by modern historians only because the system prevails to the present day. Abbo, Marianus, Sigibert, and certainly 7th- and 8th-century Irish computists were less convinced, especially those educated in Victorian principles.

Cyclic character: One of the beauties of Easter reckonings is their cyclic character. After a certain period of years, the exact same weekday and lunar data recur on any given Julian calendar date. Often, the Easter tables cover the entire cyclical period. At least this is what southern Irish computists were used to. The *latercus*, the presumably first Easter reckoning followed in this area, is transmitted for its entire 84-year cyclic period in the only known Easter table of this system,[139] and likewise the oldest witness of the Victorian table covers all 532 years.[140] The Dionysiac 95-year Easter table, therefore, must have come as a bit of a surprise.[141] Isidore had declared this table a true Easter cycle,[142] but when his *Etymologiae* arrived in Ireland towards the middle of the 7th century at the earliest, it was blatantly obvious that Dionysius' original was outdated.[143] From Ceolfrith's Letter to the Pictish King Nechtan of AD

137 See especially Nothaft (2012), 88–102, and also his article 'Chronologically confused: Claudius of Turin and the Date of Christ's passion' in the proceedings of the third conference on the science of computus, forthcoming.

138 See especially the recent study by Verbist (2010), and the additional information and corrections in Nothaft (2012), 103–12; Nothaft (2013).

139 Padua, Biblioteca Antoniana, I 27, 76r–77v. For this Easter table see n 2.

140 Gotha, Forschungsbibliothek, 75, 77v–106r; see especially Krusch (1884a).

141 Cf. Jones (1943), 47. For the manuscript evidence of Dionysius' Easter table see n 131.

142 Isidore, *Etymologiae* VI 17 (ed. Lindsay (1911), i), following the 95-year Easter table: *post cuius expletionem ad primum exordium recurrendum*.

143 For the continuations of Dionysius' Easter table see the evidence and literature discussed in Warntjes (2010), XC–XCI n 242; as the Dionysiac system is based on a 532-year luni-solar cycle, the Périgueux table there mentioned may, however, belong to the 12th rather than the 7th century (cf. Warntjes (2011a), 30 n 111).

710 as transmitted in Bede's *Historia ecclesiastica*, we are informed that by this time the 532-year cyclic period of this reckoning was well established and that some computists had even produced Easter tables for the entire 532 years.[144] Still, how computists in the intervening period, *c.*AD 650–710, dealt with Dionysius' 95-year period, is a different story.

Certainly, the 95-year period presented a special case to early medieval computists. Its construction was extremely sophisticated: After the expiration of one period, only the data of the bissextile years of the original had to be recalculated to establish the subsequent 95 years; thus, ¾ of the original table remained the same, only every fourth year had to be renewed. This clever device was invented in 5th-century Alexandria, and its principles were reported to the Latin West by Dionysius in his Letter to Petronius, which factually served as a prologue to his Easter table.[145] Even with this manual at hand, 7th-century computists found it counterintuitive to work with a 95-year period for a simple reason: a multiple of this period would not lead to a cyclic total, i.e. 532 was not a multiple of 95.

Two texts in particular demonstrate the way in which the 95-year period was tested. The first of these, briefly introduced into modern scholarship by Charles W. Jones and as yet not sufficiently studied, is not immediately relevant to the present study.[146] It may suffice here to note that the text dates to *c.*AD 703, that it may have been composed in the circle of Willibrord or under influence of the Willibrordian mission on the Continent, and that it compares three successive 95-year periods,

[144] Bede, *Historia ecclesiastica* V 21 (Plummer (1896), i 341): *Item successor eius Cyrillus seriem XC et V annorum in quinque decennouenalibus circulis conprehendit; post quem Dionysius Exiguus totidem alios ex ordine pari schemate subnexuit, qui ad nostra usque tempora pertingebant. Quibus termino adpropinquantibus, tanta hodie calculatorum exuberat copia, ut etiam in nostris per Britanniam ecclesiis plures sint, qui mandatis memoriae ueteribus illis Aegyptiorum argumentis, facillime possint in quotlibet spatia temporum paschales protendere circulos, etiamsi ad quingentos usque et XXX duos uoluerint annos; quibus expletis, omnia, quae ad solis et lunae, mensis et septimanae consequentiam spectant, eodem, quo prius, ordine recurrunt.* Cf. also Bede, *De temporum ratione* 65 (Jones (1943), 290–1; read *vidlxxx* for *vdlxx* in l. 9 p 290; the mistake is retained in Jones's re-edition in CCSL 123, 460, but corrected by Wallis (1999), 155). For comments on these two Bedan chapters see the literature listed in Warntjes (2010), XCI n 243.

[145] Dionyisus, *Epistola ad Petronium* (ed. Krusch (1938), 64). For commentaries on this passage see especially van der Hagen (1734), 68–71, 194–6; Declercq (2000), 101, 105–6; Declercq (2002), 192, 198–9.

[146] London, British Library, Cotton Caligula A XV, 110r–117v. This intriguing text was first discussed by Jones (1938); it awaits a modern critical edition. For its content and background, cf. Warntjes (2010), 311; Warntjes (2011b), 175 n 6, 183.

starting in AD 703, 798, and 893 respectively. More important for the present study are chapters 65 and 67 of the Munich Computus of AD 719 which the author copied from the southern Irish Victorian Computus of AD 689 introduced above. In chapter 65, it is outlined that the 95-year Easter table comprised of three 28-year solar cycles with a remainder of 11 years (3×28+11=95), of five 19-year lunar cycles with no remainder (5×19=95), and that it revolves five times in the 532 years of the Victorian cycle with 57 years remaining (5×95+57=532).[147] The argument, therefore, is that the 95-year table was cyclic only in its lunar data, not in its solar information, and even a multiple of this period would not turn it into the Victorian 532-year luni-solar Easter cycle, which was considered the ultimate calendrical construction. The reference to Victorius here and in the chapter discussed in the following is important, as it reveals the perspective of the author, who doubtlessly was an adherent of the Victorian system. His message, composed in southern Ireland in AD 689, is clear: The 95-year table (as advocated by Dionysius) could not rival Victorius' construction. Chapter 67 has to be read in the same way.[148] Here, the anonymous of AD 689 demonstrates that a 95-year period is not cyclic in its solar data. The method is by comparison of the *concurrentes* (weekday on 24 March) of blocks of four years in successive 95-year periods. From one period to the next, the *concurrentes* of three out of the four years agree; when the third period is compared to the first, the *concurrentes* of only two out of the four years agree; when the fourth period is compared to the first, the *concurrentes* of only one out of the four years; when the fifth period is compared to the first, there is no agreement and 'thenceforth it leads into contradiction'. The message, again, is clear: The Victorian 532-year cycle is superior to the 95-year table of the 'Greeks'.[149] Certainly, this was one of the aspects discussed in the Irish Easter controversy of the late AD 680s.

Lunar limits: The diligent reader will have noted that the three aspects outlined above are arguments expressed by adherents of Victorius against the Dionysiac system. For the present study, these issues certain-

[147] Munich Computus 65 (Warntjes (2010), 302); for the context see also Warntjes (2010), XCI–XCII, CXXIV–CXXV; cf. also the outdated accounts in Mac Carthy (1901), lxxi; Schwartz (1905), 101.

[148] Munich Computus 67 (Warntjes (2010), 310–3); for content and context cf. Warntjes (2010), LX, LXXIII, XCI–XCII, CXXIV–CXXV, 337–8; Mac Carthy (1901), lxxi, is confused in his analysis of this chapter.

[149] Cf. Jones (1938), 205.

ly are the more central ones, as they are the ones that have been generally overlooked by modern scholarship for the simple reason that the sources revealing their importance, principally *De comparatione epactarum Dionysii et Victorii* of AD 689 and the Munich Computus of AD 719 with its Victorian stratum of AD 689, have been severely understudied. We now turn to the Dionysiac side of the conflict and therewith enter a different set of sources, which are strictly speaking not contemporary with the time of crisis, while, at the same time, they are very well known to scholars of the Easter controversy. The sources in question are primarily Columbanus' letters of the very early 7th century and Bede's *De temporum ratione* of AD 725.

Famously, Columbanus provoked not only the Frankish clergy, but also Pope Gregory with the question of how to calculate Easter. Columbanus himself was a staunch supporter of the *latercus*, while the Frankish clergy, since AD 541, unanimously followed Victorius, as did Gregory. One of the aspects criticized by the Irishman was the Victorian lunar limits for Easter Sunday of *luna* 16–22.[150] These are the lunar limits traditionally followed in Rome since the 3rd century,[151] being based on John's Gospel, which implied *luna* 16 on the day of resurrection.[152] The *latercus* followed by Columbanus, on the other hand, prescribed *luna* 14 to 20,[153] equally based on John's Gospel, although here the starting point was provided by the crucifixion rather than the resurrection. Accordingly, Columbanus might have objected that Victorius was solely concerned with the resurrection and did not consider the crucifixion as an integral part of paschal festivities, contrary to the dogmatic unity of the three Easter days. Yet his critique focused on a different aspect, the allegorical dichotomy of light and shadow. For this, he cites Anatolius Latinus as authority, who, in chapter 4 of his *De ratione paschali*, explicitly condemns *luna* 21 and 22 as outright heretical:[154] In his theory, midnight marks the middle of the night; moons up to *luna* 20 rise before, those from *luna* 21 onwards after midnight. Consequently, moons from

150 Columbanus, *Epistolae* I 3–4, II 5 (Walker (1957), 2, 4, 6, 16).

151 See especially Schwartz (1904), 29–88 (especially 31); Mosshammer (2008), 116–29, 204–13; Holford-Strevens (2008), 167–78.

152 See n 123 above.

153 See the reconstructed *latercus* in Mc Carthy (1993), 218–9, and its translation in Blackburn and Holford-Strevens (1999), 873–5.

154 Anatolius Latinus, *De ratione paschali* 4 (ed. Mc Carthy and Breen (2003), 47, with translation and commentary 65, 88–9). For discussion of this quote of Anatolius Latinus by Columbanus see Charles-Edwards (2000), 404.

luna 21 onwards shine less than half of the night, therefore darkness prevails over light, which is not lawful for the resurrection of Christ which marks the victory of light over shadows.

Anatolius Latinus' reasoning could obviously not be sustained in full by northern Irish converts from the *latercus* to the Dionysiac reckoning with its lunar limits of 15 to 21. It is worth noting that all save one manuscript of *De ratione paschali* transmit this passage in corruption, changing the argument to *luna* 22 and 23 belonging to the shadows, with this vindicating *luna* 21.[155] It is highly likely that this corruption belongs to the Irish Easter controversy of the AD 680s. The northern Irish were trained in the *latercus*, and in lack of any explanatory text for this reckoning, Anatolius Latinus had become the canonical substitute. Columbanus' arguments against the Victorian reckoning were certainly repeated by the northern Irish traditionalists when the southern Irish clergy converted to Victorius. When the northern Irish themselves changed sides in the AD 680s, adopting Dionysius rather than Victorius, they altered their standard text against Victorian doctrine in a way that it would fit their new reckoning but still condemned Victorius.

In the end, there was no need for this redaction of a canonical text. The celebration of Easter Sunday on *luna* 22 could easily be criticized on other grounds, as Bede in chapter 59 of *De temporum ratione* demonstrates.[156] He argues that *luna* 22 is nowhere mentioned in the Scripture and is therefore unacceptable for the celebration of the most important Christian feast. *Luna* 15 to 21, on the other hand, marked the week of unleavened bread. Adomnán, the principal instigator of conversion of the northern Irish from the *latercus* to Dionyisus, may have learned this argumentation in Bede's native Northumbria, where he himself became convinced of Dionysiac principles. Or, he may have turned to more traditional texts available to him (not least the Holy Scripture itself, cited by Dionysius, the authority for this reckoning), which outlined *luna* 14 to 21 as the lunar range of the week of unleaven bread, therefore explicitly ruling out *luna* 22.[157] How to direct this argument against Victorius, similar to Bede but a hundred years earlier, was demonstrated in the

155 See the variant readings in Mc Carthy and Breen (2003), 47, and the discussion ibidem, 89.

156 Bede, *De temporum ratione* 59 (Jones (1943), 278–80). For discussions of this chapter see Wallis (1999), 346–7; Pillonel-Wyrsch (2004), 347–50.

157 Lev 23:5–6; Ex 12:18–19; Dt 16:2–3; Dionysius, *Epistola ad Petronium* (Krusch (1880), 65); and many more texts. Cf. Pelteret (2011), 151–3. Bede, in the chapter mentioned in the previous note, is at pains to exclude *luna* 14.

letter of Leo monachus to a certain Sesuldus of AD 627, which also lay within Adomnán's range.[158]

Also, converts from the *latercus* to Dionysius, used to condemning Victorius, could claim that both their old and their new reckoning honoured the three-day period of Easter starting with the crucifixion and ending with the resurrection, as *latercus* lunar limits starting with *luna* 14 mark John's date of the crucifixion, Dionysiac lunar limits starting with *luna* 15 the crucifixion according to the Synoptic Gospels, while Victorius' *luna* 16 by contrast violated the unity of the three days by commemorating the resurrection according to John. Though no written source arguing on these lines has survived, it is worth noting that Cummian made the opposite case for the Victorian reckoning:[159] Easter Sunday was about the resurrection, and only Victorius' lunar limits fully recognized this; celebrating Easter Sunday, the day of resurrection, on *luna* 14 (*latercus*) or *luna* 15 (*latercus* and Dionyisus) implies crucifixion on *luna* 12 and *luna* 13 respectively, which was uncanonical, if not outright heretical. Surely, the lunar limits of Easter Sunday, with their fundamental theological importance, were one of the central issues in the Irish Easter controversy of the AD 680s.

[158] Leo monachus, *Epistola ad Sesuldum* (ed. Krusch (1880), 299–300): *Et illud sane non minoris erroris esse arbitror, ut vicessimam secundam lunam festi paschalis adscribat, cum manifestum illut habeamus veritatis exemplar, quod per Moysen populo die divina lege mandatur: XIIIIma, inquiens, die mensis novorum celebrabitis pascha septem diebus azima comeditis, in quo et festum pasche consummare iubenter. Unde et nos non inmerito infra hunc – a quartadecima luna pascha Hebreorum – septenarium numerum rite salvatoris et domini nostri sacratissimam resurrectionem indagamus et, cum res exigit, in ipsius septenarii numeri plenitudine, id est vicissimam primam lunam, compotum paschalem perducimus, cuius termini finis excedere magnum erroris genus.* When compiling his edition, Krusch was only aware of one manuscript transmitting the full text of this letter (Cologne, Dombibliothek, 83-II) and another one containing an excerpt (Leiden, Universiteitsbibliotheek, Scaliger 28); both these codices are affiliated to the Sirmond group of manuscripts (for which see pp. 52–3 above); a second full copy can be found in another manuscript belonging to the Sirmond group, Bremen, Staats- und Universitätsbibliothek, msc 0046 (see Warntjes (2010a), 259); a new edition with discussion will be published in the proceedings of the fourth conference on the science of computus.

[159] Cummian, *De ratione paschali* ll. 80–85 (Walsh and Ó Cróinín (1988), 66, 68). Cummian here quotes the *Prologus paschae* 8 (ed. Krusch (1880), 232–3, which, like Victorius, favours lunar limits of Easter Sunday of *luna* 16–22; Jones (1943), 90–2, misinterprets this passage of Cummian's letter because of his theory of a hybrid Victorian-Dionysiac Easter table (cf. n 25, 46 above); Charles-Edwards (2000), 402–3, believes that Cummian justified *luna* 16–22 by an uncommon interpretation of the Synoptic Gospels, but reference to John's Gospel would have been more natural and straight forward. For the context of justifying the lunar limits of Easter Sunday, see also the Munich Computus 55 (Warntjes (2010), 214), where *luna* 15–21 are explicitly connected to the passion.

Vernal equinox: Not observing the vernal equinox was one of the most central criticisms directed against Victorius. The accusations were of two kinds, however, and a clear distinction needs to be drawn between them: a) Easter Sunday and b) the Easter full moon falling before the equinox.

In the *Supputatio Romana*, the 84-year Easter cycle which Victorius was commissioned to replace, observance of the equinox was not a *sine qua non*, for neither the Easter full moon nor Easter Sunday.[160] Therefore, Victorius must have felt some satisfaction in the fact that he managed to place all Easter Sundays after the Alexandrian equinox of 21 March, with this strictly following the prescription of Bishop Dionysius of Alexandria.[161] The *latercus*, designed a few decades before Victorius for the same purpose (replacing the increasingly inaccurate *Supputatio Romana*) but independent of Rome, followed the same rule of Easter Sunday after the equinox. The date of the equinox, however, was different, as Sulpicius Severus, the inventor of this Easter table, made all Easter Sundays fall after the old Roman equinox of 25 March from Caesar's days, which had received a theological foundation when associated, among other events, with the conception of Christ.[162]

When the Victorian reckoning reached the *regiones Scottorum* in the 6th century, this difference in the equinoctial date obviously was destined to stir debates. Columbanus, writing to Pope Gregory in AD 600 and to the Frankish clergy in AD 603, argued that the *sapientissimi componendi calculi computarii* of his homeland had analyzed Victorius' system in detail and found it worthy of 'ridicule and indulgence rather than authority'.[163] One of two major points of criticism was that Victorius allowed Easter to fall before the equinox (the other being the lunar

[160] See the references in n 151.

[161] Eusebius, *Historia ecclesiastica* VII 20 (ed. by Theodor Mommsen and Eduard Schwartz in GCS 9,2, 674). For the context and application of this rule in Rome see Mosshammer (2008), 52, 110; Holford-Strevens (2008), 173.

[162] Interestingly, the Easter full moons fall strictly on or after 21 March in the *latercus*; cf. Warntjes (2007), 57–8 n 85. With this, Sulpicius Severus, ingeniously or accidentally, squared the Alexandrian and the Roman equinoxes. As Leofranc Holford-Strevens kindly pointed out to me, with the Easter full moon not falling before 21 March, Sulpicius made sure that the Julian calendar date of Easter Sunday was bijective, i.e. the construction of the *latercus* left no room for two lawful Easter dates in the same year; cf. Holford-Strevens (2008), 179–80.

[163] Columbanus, *Epistola* I 4 (Walker (1957), 6–7): *Scias namque nostris magistris et Hibernicis antiquis philosophis et sapientissimis componendi calculi computariis Victorium non fuisse receptum, sed magis risu vel venia dignum quam auctoritate.*

limits, discussed in the previous section).[164] This, it will be noted, is Victorius interpreted from a *latercus* perspective. Victorius allowed Easter Sunday to fall on 22 to 24 March, i.e. before the *latercus* equinox of 25 March (not before Victorius' own of 21 March though). It may well be that the same argument was addressed by the northern Irish clergy in their letter to the papal see of *c.*AD 640.[165]

Bede, roughly a century later, formulated similar criticism, though he tried to challenge Victorius within the confines of the Aquitanian's own system. Bede followed Dionysius and in both the Dionysiac and the Victorian system the equinox was set on 21 March. In Victorius' Prologue, Bede read that the *Latini* allowed the Easter new moon (*luna* 1) to fall as early as 5 March, which meant Easter full moon (*luna* 14) on 18 March, the earliest possible Easter Sunday in that system (*luna* 16) therefore on 20 March, before the 21 March equinox![166]

The *Latini* of Victorius' Prologue, however, were the Romans of old. Their rules do not represent those applied by Victorius himself, who rather placed the earliest Easter new moon (*luna* 1) on 7 March, leading to the Easter full moon (*luna* 14) on 20 March and the earliest possible Easter Sunday (*luna* 16) on 22 March, i.e. after the equinox. Yet, there was another problem inherent in Victorius' treatment of this year: the Easter full moon fell before the equinox of 21 March. This aspect must have appeared minor to Victorius, especially since all previous Western Easter tables had not required the Easter full moon to fall strictly on or after the equinox. Constructing a 532-year Easter table was not a simple task, and there were other technicalities he found more difficult

[164] Columbanus, *Epistolae* I 3, II 5 (Walker (1957), 4, 16): *Nec non sancti dogmatis legimus libro: 'Pascha id est solemnitas dominicae resurrectionis ante transgressum vernalis aequinoctii, decimae quartae* [XVI MSS] *lunae initium, non potest celebrari', ut scilicet aequinoctium non antecedat. Quod utique Victorius in suo transgressus est cyclo et per hoc Galliae iamdudum invexit errorem, seu, ut humilius dicam, confirmavit inolitum.* [...] *Omnes enim ecclesiae totius Occidentis, sicut in tomo responsionis meae, quem vobis nunc misi, licet ante triennium scriptum, indicavi, non respiciunt fieri debere resurrectionem ante passionem, id est ante aequinoctium Pascha.* Interestingly, the quote from Gennadius' *De ecclesiasticis dogmatibus* in the first of these two passages appears to imply that the Easter full moon also was supposed to fall after the equinox; this, however, is only due to Walker's fiddling with the text; both manuscripts actually read XVI rather than XIIII, and this reading makes more sense; it is corroborated by Gennadius' orginal text (PL 58, 1000; note that the editor, Geverhard Elmenhorst, also corrects to XIIII, and Walker seems to have simply copied Elmenhorst's editorial intervention).

[165] See pp. 58–9 above.

[166] Bede, *De ratione temporum* 51 (Jones (1943), 270–3). For commentaries on this chapter, see Jones (1943), 385–6, 390; Wallis (1999), 340–1; Pillonel-Wyrsch (2004), 325–8.

to square.[167] Still, with the rise of the legend that the Nicene Council of AD 325 had decreed observing the equinox a necessary condition for the Easter full moon, as Dionysius claimed in AD 525,[168] this issue turned from a matter of compromise between Western and Eastern practice, as Victorius had perceived it, to dogma. In the Alexandrian reckoning, which became Dionysiac practice in the West, the equinox was strictly observed for the Easter full moon, as acknowledged by Victorius himself.[169] Bede attacks Victorius vehemently on this ground; in true schoolteacher fashion, he takes a year with Easter Sunday on 26 March, *luna* 20 as an example; this appears, at first sight, to meet the essential requirement of Easter Sunday falling after the equinox, only for Bede to lecture the reader that *luna* 20 on 26 March entails *luna* 14 on 20 March, before the equinox.[170] Also, it may be that the northern Irish followers of the *latercus* made this observation in their letter to the

[167] E.g., Victorius was unable to produce an Easter Sunday respecting his own rules in AD 577, which led to the confusion noted by Gregory of Tours, *Libri historiarum X* V 17 (ed. by Bruno Krusch in MGH SS. rer. Merov. 1,1, 215); cf. Krusch (1884), 127–8; Holford-Strevens (2008), 193 n 52.

[168] Dionysius, *Epistola ad Petronium* (Krusch (1938), 63–7) claimed Nicene authority for the 19-year cycle and is quite specific that at Nicaea the 21 March equinox was sanctioned for the reckoning of Easter (Krusch (1938), 65): *Sed quia mensis hic, unde sumat exordium vel ubi terminetur, evidenter ibi non legitur, praefati venerabiles CCCXVIII pontifices antiqui moris observantiam et exinde a sancto Moyse traditam, sicut in septimo libro ecclesiasticae refertur historiae, sollertius investigantes, ab VIII. Idus Martii usque in diem Nonarum Aprilis natam lunam facere dixerunt primi mensis exordium; et a XII. kl. april. usque in XIIII. Kalendas Mai lunam XIIII sollertius inquirendum; quae quia cum solis cursu non aequaliter volvitur, tantorum dierum spatiis occursum vernalis aequinoctii consequatur, qui a XII. kl. apr. die, cunctorum orientalium [spatii] sententiis et maxime Aegyptiorum, qui calculationis prae omnibus gnari sunt, specialiter adnotatur. In quo etiam si luna XIIII. sabbato contigerit (quod semel in XCV annis accidere manifestum est), sequenti die dominico, id est, XI. Kal. April. luna XV., celebrandum pascha eadem sancta synodus sine ambiguitate firmavit, hoc modis omnibus ammonens, ut ante XII. Kal. Apr. lunam XIIII. paschalis festi nullus inquireret; quae non primi mensis, sed ultimi esse constaret.* Dionysius was not the first to formulate this opinion (cf. Lejbowicz (2010) and Holford-Strevens (2011), 1–6, for the context), but it was popularized through his writings; for the early spread of this legend see Jones (1943a), 206–9. It has long been acknowledged that the Nicene Council took no such decisions; see the review of the literature in Mosshammer (2008), 50–2, who himself is more cautious.

[169] Victorius, *Epistola ad Hilarum* 4 (Krusch (1938), 20).

[170] Bede, *De ratione temporum* 62 (Jones (1943), 284). For commentaries on this chapter see Jones (1943), 389–90; Wallis (1999), 348–9; Pillonel-Wyrsch (2004), 357–9. Also, in *De ratione temporum* 50 (Jones (1943), 269) Bede is very specific that the Easter full moon was not to precede the equinox.

papal see in *c.*AD 640, as this problem was to feature in the Victorian table in AD 642.[171]

Thus, Victorius not observing the equinox was a major issue for both followers of the *latercus* and those adhering to Dionysius. Though there is no documentation of disputes over the equinox in the Irish Easter controversy of AD 689, with this tradition of heavy criticism on this point, it can hardly be doubted that the northern Irish converts from the *latercus* to Dionysius placed this issue at the heart of their attack against the southern Irish still following Victorius.

Double dates: Finally, it may be worth noting that one of the aspects criticized by Columbanus appears not to have played any part in the controversial debates of the AD 680s. At the turn to the 7th century, Columbanus had accused Victorius of 'writing in a doubtful manner, defining nothing where it was necessary',[172] clearly referring to the latter's policy of listing double dates when, according to his lunar calculation, Easter Sunday could fall either on *luna* 15 or *luna* 22. Slightly later, in AD 627, the Visigothic monk Leo is more explicit, complaining that Victorius 'ambigiously gives two opinions for the day of Easter in one and the same year'.[173] This critique is at least as old as the middle of the 6th century, when Victor of Capua considered this feature of Victorius' Easter table irritating at best, at least if Bede cites him correctly.[174]

Bede himself does not expand on this issue, though he is otherwise extremely critical of Victorius' principles. Likewise, there is no trace of this controversial issue in Irish computistical literature of the late 7th and early 8th centuries. If the surviving Victorian Easter tables are examined, only few of them contain the notorious double dates, all of continental origin. On the other hand, the Victorian Easter tables closest to insular thought present only one date in the years in question, almost

[171] See p 59 above.

[172] Columbanus, *Epistola* II 7 (Walker (1957), 18): *iuxta Victorium nuper dubie scribentem et, ubi necesse erat, nihil definientem.*

[173] Leo monachus, *Epistola ad Sesuldum* (Krusch (1880), 299; my translation): *Sed illud me inter cetera movet, ubi ambigue duas opiniones dies paschae uno eodemque anno prefixit.* That Victorian double dates were still an issue in Visigothic Spain in AD 641 is demonstrated by Braulio of Zaragossa's Letter to Bishop Eutropius (ed. and trans. into Spanish by Riesco Terrero (1975), 114–7; an English translation can be found in Barlow (1969), 57–60).

[174] Bede, *De temporum ratione* 51 (Jones (1943), 272–3). For Victor of Capua's lost paschal tract work see especially Jones (1943), 74 n 5; Ohashi (1999a).

exclusively the one designated *Latini* by Victorius.[175] Apparently, when adopting the Victorian system in the AD 630s, the southern Irish clergy decided to abandon the 'Greek' dates, hoping to achieve Roman conformity by this act. Thus, when southern Irish adherents of Victorius clashed with northern Irish converts to Dionyius in the AD 680s, only Victorian Easter tables listing a single date per year circulated in Ireland and therefore formed the basis of discussion. Victorius' notorious double dates presented no issue.

The end of the crisis

Apparent as the conflict between northern Irish converts to Dionysius and Victorian hardliners in the south towards the end of the AD 680s is in contemporary computistical literature, it is difficult to assess just when this crisis came to an end. As a possible indicator, the *Cáin Adomnáin* immediately springs to mind, as Adomnán managed to make 40 churchmen from all parts of the *regiones Scottorum* sign this legal document.[176] Does this indicate unity in the paschal question? Hardly so. In 21st place of the list of guarantors appears Bishop Coeddi, who died in AD 712, being entitled 'bishop of Iona' in his obit.[177] For him to hold this prestigious position within the community of Iona before its conversion to Dionysius in AD 716, he must have been a *latercus* traditionalist. In the end, the *Lex innocentium* was about the safety of noncombatants in wartime, not the Easter question. Paschal factionalism was subdued to achieve this grander goal.

Again, only the computistical literature outlined above can provide clues, and among this especially the securely datable texts. The Victorian Prologue of AD 699 suggests, if Irish authorship of this text is accepted, that at least some churches in southern Ireland still adhered to Victorius. On the other hand, the Munich Computus of AD 719 indicates that conversion to Dionysius had taken place at this stage. In general, the three Irish computistical textbooks known to date, the *Computus Einsidlensis*, the Munich Computus, and *De ratione conputandi*, are the principal documents of this conversion process. All of them favour

[175] See especially the discussion in Warntjes (2010), LXXXIV–LXXXV n 228.

[176] For *Cáin Adomnáin* see n 118 above.

[177] *Cáin Adomnáin* 18 (Meyer (1905), 16); Irish annals *s.a.* AD 712 (Annals of Ulster *s.a.* 711 (Mac Airt and Mac Niocaill (1983), 168–9); Annals of Tigernach *s.a.* [AU 711] (Stokes (1993), 182)); cf. Meyer (1905), 39; Ní Dhonnchadha (1982), 191.

Dionysius, but especially the earlier two, the *Computus Einsidlensis* and the Munich Computus, bear witness to earlier criticism of this reckoning and to substantial comparisons of the Victorian and the Dionysiac 19-year cycles which marked the scientific debates in Ireland in the final two decades of the 7th century or thereabouts. This underlying but abandoned Victorian bias, which is particularly obvious in the Munich Computus' excerpts from the Victorian Computus of AD 689, reveal that these textbooks were composed in southern Ireland, by recent converts from the Victorian to the Dionysiac system.[178] By the very early 8th century, Dionysius had won the day in the south, and the highly scholarly conversion process generated the earliest comprehensive textbooks on the reckoning of time in the Latin West.[179]

Conclusion

Even at the risk of oversimplification, the Easter controversy of 7th- and early 8th-century Ireland can best be schematized by the following pattern: Until the AD 630s, the Irish church as a whole unanimously followed the *latercus*. In that decade, the southern Irish clergy decided, on papal initiative, to convert to the Victorian system, as Cummian's Letter illustrates. From the AD 630s to the AD 680s, the southern churches adhered to Victorius while their northern counterparts stuck to the traditional *latercus*. Principally moved by Adomnán's adoption of the Dionysiac reckoning, most of the northern clergy followed his example, with only Iona (and dependencies) remaining a traditionalist stronghold. This situation, with Victorius being observed in the south, Dionysius in the north, and the *latercus* in Iona, only slowly changed towards the end of the 7th century, with southern Irish gradual conversion to Dionysius being presumably completed in the first decade of the 8th century, Iona's in AD 716.

These times of change were preceded and especially followed by debate and controversy, if not outright animosity. To the modern historian, they are interesting for two principal reasons. First, they provide very rare and detailed insights into the issues under discussion, the problems

[178] For the southern Irish origin of the three Irish computistical textbooks see Ó Cróinín (1982b), 111–27; Warntjes (2010), LXXVII–XCVI, CXXXIII–CLII, CXCI–CCI.

[179] For the early development of the genre of the computistical textbook see Warntjes (2010), LII–LVI.

and questions that moved the early medieval mind, both scientifically and theologically. Second, they had severe cultural and sometimes even political implications and are therefore of outmost importance for the way we read the history of a certain region. For Ireland, the controversy between southern Irish adherents of Victorius and northern Irish converts from the *latercus* to the Dionysiac system in the AD 680s and early AD 690s in particular has been underrated, if not completely neglected. Its full assessment will change the way in which we perceive relations between the southern and the northern Irish churches in this decade, as one of prolonged and newly incited conflict rather than reconciliation.

Bibliography

Anderson, A.O. and M.O. Anderson (1961) *Adomnan's Life of Columba*, London.

Barlow, C. (1969) *Braulio of Saragossa, Fructuosus of Braga*, Washington.

Betten, F.S. (1928) 'The adoption of the Roman Easter calculation by the island Celts,' *Catholic Historical Review* 14, 485–99.

Bieler, L. (1979) *The Patrician texts in the Book of Armagh*, Dublin.

Bisagni, J. and I. Warntjes (2007) 'Latin and Old Irish in the Munich Computus: a reassessment and further evidence,' *Ériu* 57, 1–33.

Blackburn, B. and L. Holford-Strevens (1999) *The Oxford companion to the year: an exploration of calendar customs and time-reckoning*, Oxford.

Borst, A. (1995) *Das Buch der Naturgeschichte. Plinius und seine Leser im Zeitalter des Pergaments*, 2nd ed., Heidelberg.

— (1998) *Die karolingische Kalenderreform*, Hannover.

— (2006) *Schriften zur Komputistik im Frankenreich von 721 bis 818*, 3 vols., Hannover.

Butter, R. (2010) 'St Munnu in Ireland and Scotland: an exploration of his cult,' in S. Boardman and E. Williamson, *The cult of saints and the Virgin Mary in medieval Scotland*, Woodbridge, 21–41.

Byrne, F.J. (1982) 'Varia III,' *Ériu* 33, 167–9.

Chaîne, M. (1925) *La chronologie des temps chrétiens de l'Égypte et de l'Éthiopie*, Paris.

Charles-Edwards, T.M. (1998) 'The contruction of the *Hibernensis*,' *Peritia* 12 (1998), 209–37.

— (2000) *Early Christian Ireland*, Cambridge.

— (2003) 'The Northern Lectionary: a source for the *Codex Salmanticensis*?,' in J. Cartwright, *Celtic hagiography and saints' cults*, Cardiff, 148–60.

— (2006) *The chronicle of Ireland*, 2 vols., Liverpool.

Colgrave, B. (1927) *The Life of Bishop Wilfrid by Eddius Stephanus*, Cambridge.

Colgrave, B. and R.A.B. Mynors (1969) *Bede's Ecclesiastical History of the English People*, Oxford.

Corning, C. (2006) *The Celtic and Roman traditions: conflict and consensus in the early medieval church*, New York.

Davies, M.L. (1997) 'Isidorian texts and the *Hibernensis*,' *Peritia* 11, 207–49.

Declercq, G. (2000) *Anno Domini: the origins of the Christian era*, Turnhout.

— (2002) 'Dionysius Exiguus and the introduction of the Christian era,' *Sacris Erudiri* 41, 165–246.

Doherty, C. (1991) 'The cult of St Patrick and the politics of Armagh in the seventh century,' in Jean-Michel Picard, *Ireland and northern France, AD 600–850*, Dublin.

— (2007) 'Ireland and Rome in the seventh century,' in Éamonn Ó Carragáin and Carol Neuman de Vegvar, *Roma felix – formation and reflections of medieval Rome*, Aldershot, 277–86.

Duchesne, L. (1880) 'La question de la paque au conile de Nicée,' *Revue des questions historiques* 14, 5–42.

Dumville, D. (1990) 'Two troublesome abbots,' *Celtica* 21, 146–52.

Englisch, B. (2011) 'Ostern zwischen Arianismus und Katholizismus: zur Komputistik in den Reichen der Westgoten im 6. und 7. Jh.,' in I. Warntjes and D. Ó Cróinín, *The Easter controversy of Late Antiquity and the early Middle Ages*, Turnhout, 76–109.

Esposito, M. (1918–20) 'On the pseudo-Augustinian treatise "De mirabilibus sanctae scripturae" written in Ireland in the year 655,' *PRIA* 35C, 189–207, repr. in M. Esposito, *Latin learning in medieval Ireland*, ed. by M. Lapidge, London 1988, XI.

Evans, N. (2010) *The present and the past in medieval Irish chronicles*, Woodbridge.

Gorman, M. (2011) 'Patristic and pseudo-patristic citations in the *Collectio Hibernensis*,' *Revue Bénédictine* 121, 18–93.

Gougaud, L. (1932) *Christianity in Celtic lands*, London, repr. Dublin 1992.

Graff, E. (2010) 'The recension of two Sirmond texts: *Disputatio Morini* and *De divisionibus temporum*,' in I. Warntjes and D. Ó Cróinín, *Computus and its cultural context in the Latin West, AD 300–1200*, Turnhout, 112–42.

Grosjean, P. (1946) 'Recherches sur les debuts de la controverse pascale chez les Celtes,' *Analecta Bollandiana* 64, 200–44.

— (1955a) 'Edition et commentaire de *Catalogus sanctorum Hiberniae secundum diuersa tempora* ou *De tribus ordinibus sanctorum Hiberniae*,' *Analecta Bollandiana* 73, 197–213, 289–322.

— (1955b) 'Sur quelques exégètes irlandais du VIIe siècle,' *Sacris Erudiri* 7, 67–98.

Grotefend, H. (1898) *Taschenbuch der Zeitrechnung des deutschen Mittelalters und der Neuzeit*, Hannover, 14th ed. 2007.

Grumel, V. (1960) 'Le problème de la date pascale aux IIIe et IVe siècles,' *Revue des études byzantines* 18, 163–78.

Haddan, A.W. and W. Stubbs (1869–78) *Councils and ecclesiastical documents relating to Great Britain and Ireland*, 2 vols., Oxford.

Harrison, K. (1976) *The framework of Anglo-Saxon history to A.D. 900*, Cambridge.

— (1984) 'A letter from Rome to the Irish clergy, AD 640,' *Peritia* 3, 222–9.

Hilgenfeld, A. (1860) *Der Paschastreit der alten Kirche nach seiner Bedeutung für die Kirchengeschichte und für die Evangelienforschung*, Halle.

Holford-Strevens, L. (2003–4) Review of Dáibhí Ó Cróinín, *Early Irish history and chronology*, *Peritia* 17–18, 539–44.

— (2008) 'Paschal lunar calendars up to Bede,' *Peritia* 20, 165–208.

— (2010) Review of Caitlin Corning, *The Celtic and Roman traditions: conflict and consensus in the early medieval church*, *Peritia* 21, 310–22.

— (2010a) 'Maritial discord in Northumbria: Lent and Easter, his and hers,' in I. Warntjes and D. Ó Cróinín, *Computus and its cultural context in the Latin West, AD 300–1200*, Turnhout, 143–58.

— (2011) 'Church politics and the computus: from Milan to the ends of the earth,' in I. Warntjes and D. Ó Cróinín, *The Easter controversy of Late Antiquity and the early Middle Ages*, Turnhout, 1–20.

Howlett, D. (2003–4) 'The prologue to the *Collectio Canonum Hibernensis*,' *Peritia* 17–18, 144–9.

Hughes, K. (1966) *The church in early Irish society*, London.

James, E. (1984) 'Bede and the tonsure question,' *Peritia* 3, 85–93.

Jaski, B. (2000) 'Cú Chuimne, Ruben and the compilation of the *Collectio Canonum Hibernensis*,' *Peritia* 14, 51–69

Jones, C.W. (1934) 'The Victorian and Dionysiac paschal tables in the West,' *Speculum* 9, 408–21, repr. in Jones (1994) VIII.

— (1937) 'The 'lost' Sirmond manuscript of Bede's 'computus',' *English Historical Review* 52, 204–19, repr. in Jones (1999) X, under omission of the crucial final pages.

— (1938) 'Two Easter tables,' *Speculum* 13, 204–5.

— (1939) *Bedae pseudepigrapha: scientific writings falsely attributed to Bede*, Ithaca.

— (1943) *Bedae opera de temporibus*, Cambridge.

— (1943a) 'A legend of St. Pachomius,' *Speculum* 18, 198–210, repr. in Jones (1994) VII.

— (1994) *Bede, the schools, and the computus*, ed. W.M. Stevens, Aldershot.

Kenney, J.F. (1929) *The sources for the early history of Ireland: ecclesiastical. An introduction and guide*, New York, 2nd ed. Dublin 1966, repr. Dublin 1997.

Krusch, B. (1880) *Studien zur christlich-mittelalterlichen Chronologie. Der 84jährige Ostercyclus und seine Quellen*, Leipzig.

— (1884) 'Die Einführung des griechischen Paschalritus im Abendlande,' *Neues Archiv der Gesellschaft für ältere deutsche Geschichtskunde* 9, 99–169.

— (1884a) 'Über eine Handschrift des Victurius,' *Neues Archiv der Gesellschaft für ältere deutsche Geschichtskunde* 9, 269–81.

— (1938) 'Studien zur christlich-mittelalterlichen Chronologie. Die Entstehung unserer heutigen Zeitrechnung,' *Abhandlungen der Preußischen Akademie der Wissenschaften, Jahrgang 1937, phil.-hist. Klasse, Nr. 8*, Berlin.

Levison, W. (1961) 'Die *Annales Lindisfarnenses et Dunelmenses*,' ed. by H.E. Mayer, *Deutsches Archiv für Erforschung des Mittelalters* 17, 447–506.

Lindsay, W.M. (1911) *Isidori Hispalensis episcopi etymologiarum sive originum libri XX*, 2 vols., Oxford.

Mac Airt, S. (1988) *The Annals of Inisfallen (MS. Rawlinson B. 503)*, Dublin.

Mac Airt, S. and G. Mac Niocaill (1993), *The Annals of Ulster (to A.D. 1131)*, Dublin.

Mac Carthy, B. (1901) *Annals of Ulster, vol. 4: introduction and sources*, Dublin.

MacGinty, G. (1987) 'The Irish Augustine: *De mirabilibus sacrae scripturae*,' in Próinséas Ní Chatháin and Michael Richter, *Irland und die Christenheit: Bibelstudien und Mission*, Tübingen, 70–83.

Mc Carthy, D.P. (1993) 'Easter principles and a fifth-century lunar cycle used in the British Isles,' *Journal for the History of Astronomy* 24, 204–24.

— (1994) 'The origin of the *Latercus* paschal cycle of the insular Celtic churches,' *Cambrian Medieval Celtic Studies* 28, 25–49.

— (1998) 'The chronology of the Irish annals,' *PRIA* 98C, 203–55.

— (2003) 'The emergence of Anno Domini,' in G. Moreno-Riaño and G. Jaritz, *Time and eternity: the medieval discourse*, Turnhout, 31–53.

— (2003) 'On the shape of the insular tonsure,' *Celtica* 24, 140–67.

— (2008) *The Irish annals: their genesis, evolution and history*, Dublin, repr. 2010.

Mc Carthy, D.P. and A. Breen (2003) *The ante-Nicene Christian Pasch: De ratione paschali, the paschal tract of Anatolius, bishop of Laodicea*, Dublin.

Mc Carthy, D.P. and D. Ó Cróinín (1987–8) 'The 'lost' Irish 84-year Easter table rediscovered,' *Peritia* 6–7, 227–42, repr. in Ó Cróinín (2003), 58–75.

McIlwain, J.T. (2008) 'The 'Celtic' tonsure revisited,' in J.-L. Deuffic, *La Bretagne carolingienne: entre influence insulaires et continentals*, Saint-Denis.

Meyer, K. (1905) *Cáin Adamnáin: an old-Irish treatise on the Law of Adamnan*, Oxford.

Mosshammer, A.A. (2008) *The Easter computus and the origins of the Christian era*, Oxford.

Nicholson, E.W.B. (1901) 'The origin of the 'Hibernian' collection of Canons,' *Zeitschrift für celtische Philologie* 3, 99–103.

Ní Dhonnchadha, M. (1982) 'The guarantor list of *Cáin Adomnáin*, 697,' *Peritia* 1, 178–215.

— (1995) 'The *Lex innocentium*: Adomnán's law for women, clerics and youths, 697 A.D.,' in Mary O'Dowd and Sabine Wichert, *Chattel, servant or citizen: women's status in church, state and society*, Belfast, 58–69.

— (2001) 'Birr and the law of the innocents,' in T. O'Loughlin, *Adomnán at Birr, AD 697: essays in commemoration of the law of the innocents*, Dublin, 13–32.

Noris, H. (1696) *Annus et epochae Syromachedonum* [...] *Additis fastis consularibus anonymi omnium optimis. Accesserunt nuper dissertations De paschali Latinorum cyclo annorum LXXXIV, ac Ravennate annorum XCV*, Leipzig.

Nothaft, C.P.E. (2012) *Dating the passion: the life of Jesus and the emergence of scientific chronology (200–1600)*, Leiden.

— (2013) 'An eleventh-century chronologer at work: Marianus and the quest for the missing 22 years,' *Speculum* 88, 457–82.

O'Connell, D.J. (1936) 'Easter cycles in the early Irish church,' *Journal of the Royal Society of Antiquaries of Ireland* 66, 67–106.

Ó Cróinín, D. (1981) 'An Old Irish gloss in the Munich Computus,' *Éigse* 18, 289–90, repr. in Ó Cróinín (2003), 131–2.

— (1982a) 'Mo Sinu maccu Min and the computus at Bangor,' *Peritia* 1 (1982), 281–92, repr. in Ó Cróinín (2003), 35–47.

— (1982b) 'A seventh-century Irish computus from the circle of Cummianus,' *PRIA* 82C, 405–30, repr. in Ó Cróinín (2003), 99–130.

— (1983) 'The Irish provenance of Bede's computus,' *Peritia* 2, 229–47, repr. in Ó Cróinín (2003), 173–90.

— (1985) "A new heresy for old': pelagianism in Ireland and the papal letter of 640,' *Speculum* 60, 505–16, repr. in Ó Cróinín (2003), 87–98.

— (1995) *Early medieval Ireland, 400–1200*, London.

— (2003) *Early Irish history and chronology*, Dublin.

— (2003a) 'Bede's Irish computus,' in Ó Cróinín (2003), 201–12.

Ohashi, M. (1999) *The impact of the paschal controversy: computus, exegesis and church history in early Britain and Ireland*, unpubl. Ph.D. thesis, Nagoya.

— (1999a) 'Victor of Capua, *De aequinoctio* – criticism of the identification of the work quoted in Bede's Letter to Wicthed by C.W. Jones,' *Kirisuto-kyo-shigaku: Journal of History of Christianity* 53, 123–56.

— (2005) 'Theory and history: an interpretation of the paschal controversy in Bede's *Historia ecclesiastica*,' in S. Lebecq, M. Perrin, and O. Szerwiniack, *Bède le Vénérable: entre tradition et postérité*, Lille, 177–85.

— (2011) 'The Easter table of Victorius of Aquitaine in early medieval England,' in I. Warntjes and D. Ó Cróinín, *The Easter controversy of Late Antiquity and the early Middle Ages*, Turnhout, 137–49.

O'Loughlin, T. (2000) *Celtic theology: humanity, world and God in early Irish writings*, London.

— (2001) 'Adomnán: a man of many parts,' in T. O'Loughlin, *Adomnán at Birr, AD 697: essays in commemoration of the Law of the Innocents*, Dublin 41–51.

— (2007) *Adomnán and the holy places: the perceptions of an insular monk on the locations of biblical drama*, London.

Pelteret, D. (2011) 'The issue of apostolic authority at the Synod of Whitby,' in I. Warntjes and D. Ó Cróinín, *The Easter controversy of Late Antiquity and the early Middle Ages*, Turnhout, 150–72.

Pillonel-Wyrsch, R.-P. (2004) *Le calcul de la date de pâque au moyen âge: analyse et commentaires sur* De temporum ratione *de Bède*, Fribourg.

Plummer, C. (1896) *Venerabilis Baedae opera historica*, 2 vols., Oxford.

— (1910) *Vitae sanctorum Hiberniae*, 2 vols., Oxford.

Poole, R. (1918) 'The earliest use of the Easter cycle of Dionysius,' *English Historical Review* 33 (1918), 57–62, 210–3.

Reeves, W. (1857) *The Life of St. Columba, founder of Hy, written by Adamnan, ninth abbot of that monastery*, Dublin.

— (1861) 'On Augustin, an Irish writer of the seventh century,' *PRIA* 7, 514–22.

Richter, M. (2000) 'Dating the Irish synods in the *Collectio Canonum Hibernensis*,' *Peritia* 14 (2000), 70–84.

Risco Terrero, L. (1975) *Epistolario de San Braulio: introducción, edición crítica y traducción*, Sevilla.

Schäferdiek, K. (1985) 'Der irische Osterzyklus des sechsten und siebten Jahrhunderts,' *Deutsches Archiv für Erforschung des Mittelalters* 39, 357–78.

Schmid, J. (1904) *Die Osterfestberechnung auf den britischen Inseln vom Anfang des vierten bis zum Ende des achten Jahrhunderts*, Regensburg.

— (1907) *Die Osterfestberechnung in der abendländischen Kirche*, Freiburg.

Schwarz, E. (1905) 'Christliche und jüdische Ostertafeln,' *Abhandlungen der königlichen Gesellschaft der Wissenschaften zu Göttingen, philologisch-historische Klasse, Bd. 8, Nr. 6*, Berlin.

Sharpe, R. (1984) 'Armagh and Rome in the seventh century,' in P. Ní Chatháin and M. Richter, *Irland und Europa: die Kirche im Frühmittelalter*, Tübingen, 58–72.

— (1991) *Medieval Irish saints' lives: an introduction to the Vitae sanctorum Hiberniae*, Oxford.

— (1995) *Adomnán of Iona, Life of St Columba*, London.

Sheehy, M.P. (1982) 'The *Collectio Canonum Hibernensis*: a Celtic phenomenon,' in H. Löwe, *Die Iren und Europa im früheren Mittelalter*, 2 vols., Stuttgart, 525–35.

Simonetti, M. (1979) '*De mirabilibus sacrae scripturae*: un trattato irlandese sui miracoli della Sacra Scrittura,' *Romanobabarica* 4, 225–51.

Smyth, M. (1987) 'Isidore of Seville and early Irish cosmography,' *Cambridge Medieval Celtic Studies* 14, 69–102.

— (2011) 'The seventh-century Hiberno-Latin treatise *Liber de ordine creaturarum*: a translation,' *Journal of Medieval Latin* 21, 137–222.

Springsfeld, K. (2002) *Alkuins Einfluß auf die Komputistik zur Zeit Karls des Großen*, Stuttgart.

Stancliffe, C. (2010) ''Charity with peace': Adomnán and the Easter question,' in J.M. Wooding et. al., *Adomnán of Iona: theologian, lawmaker, peacemaker*, Dublin.

Stevens, W.M. (1981) 'Scientific instruction in early insular schools,' in M.W. Herren, *Insular Latin studies: papers on Latin texts and manuscripts of the British Isles, 550–1066*, Toronto, 83–111, repr. in W.M. Stevens, *Cycles of time and scientific learning in medieval Europe*, Aldershot 1995, IV.

— (1999) 'Easter controversy,' in M. Lapidge, J. Blair, S. Keynes, and D. Scragg, *The Blackwell encyclopaedia of Anglo-Saxon England*, Oxford, 155–7.

— (2010) 'Ars compoti quomodo inventa est,' in R. Corradini, M. Diesenberger, and M. Niederkorn-Bruck, *Zwischen Niederschrift und Wiederschrift. Hagiographie und Historiographie im Spannungsfeld von Kompendienüberlieferung und Editionstechnik*, Wien, 29–65.

Stokes, W. (1993) *The Annals of Tigernach, vol. 1*, Felinfach.

Stokes, W. and J. Strachan (1901–3) *Thesaurus palaeohibernicus: a collection of Old-Irish glosses, scholia, prose and verse*, 2 vols., Cambridge.

Story, J. (2005) 'The Frankish Annals of Lindisfarne and Kent,' *Anglo-Saxon England* 34, 59–109.

Strobel, A. (1977) *Ursprung und Geschichte des frühchristlichen Osterkalenders*, Berlin.

Todd, J.H. (1864) *St. Patrick, Apostle of Ireland: a memoire of his life and mission*, Dublin.

Thurneysen, R. (1908) 'Zur irischen Kanonensammlung,' *Zeitschrift für celtische Philologie* 6, 1–5.

Ussher, J. (1632) *Veterum epistolarum hibernicarum sylloge*, Dublin, repr. in C.R. Elrington, *The whole works of the most rev. James Ussher*, vol. 4, Dublin 1830, 383–572.

— (1639) *Britannicarum ecclesiarum antiquitates*, 2 vols., Dublin, repr. in C.R. Elrington, *The whole works of the most rev. James Ussher*, vol. 5 (= i) and 6 (= ii), Dublin 1830–1.

van der Hagen, J. (1733) *Observationes in Prosperi Aquitani Chronicon integrum ejusque LXXXIV annorum cyclum et in Anonymi cyclum LXXXIV annorum, a Muratorio editum, nec non in Anonymi laterculum paschalem centum annorum, a Bucherio editum*, Amsterdam.

— (1734) *Observationes in veterum partum et pontificium, prologos et epistolas, aliosque antiquos de ratione paschali scriptores, accedit Dissertatio de cyclo lunari Dionysii et Bedae*, Amsterdam.

van de Vyver, A. (1957) 'L'évolution du comput alexandrin et romain du IIIe au Ve siècle,' *Revue d'histoire ecclésiastique* 52, 5–25.

Verbist, P. (2010) *Duelling with the past: medieval authors and the problem of the Christian eary (c. 990–1135)*, Turnhout.

von Euw, A. (1998) 'Kat. Nr. 24: Kompendium der Zeitrechnung, Naturlehre und Himmelskunde (Dom Hs. 83[II]),' in J.M. Plotzek and U. Surmann, *Glaube und Wissen im Mittelalter. Die Kölner Dombibliothek*, München, 136–56.

Walker, G.S.M. (1957) *Sancti Columbani opera*, Dublin, repr. 1997.

Wallis, F. (1999) *Bede: The reckoning of time*, Liverpool.

Walsh, M. and D. Ó Cróinín (1988) *Cummian's letter* De controversia paschali, *together with a related Irish computistical tract* De ratione conputandi, Toronto.

Warntjes, I. (2007) 'The Munich Computus and the 84 (14)-year Easter reckoning,' *PRIA* 107 C, 31–85.

— (2010) *The Munich Computus: text and translation. Irish computistics between Isidore of Seville and the Venerable Bede and its reception in Carolingian times*, Stuttgart.

— (2010a) 'A newly discovered prologue of AD 699 to the Easter table of Victorius of Aquitaine in an unknown Sirmond manuscript,' *Peritia* 21, 255–84.

— (2010b) 'The *Argumenta* of Dionysius Exiguus and their early recensions,' in I. Warntjes and D. Ó Cróinín, *Computus and its cultural context in the Latin West, AD 300–1200*, Turnhout, 40–111.

— (2010c) 'The role of the church in early Irish regnal succession – the case of Iona,' in *L'irlanda e gli irlandesi nell'alto medioevo*, Spoleto, 155–213.

— (2011a) 'Irische Komputistik zwischen Isidor von Sevilla und Beda Venerabilis: Ursprung, karolingische Rezeption und generelle Forschungsperspektiven,' *Viator* 42 multilingual, 1–31.

— (2011b) 'The Computus Cottonianus of AD 689: a computistical formulary written for Willibrord's Frisian mission,' in I. Warntjes and D. Ó Cróinín, *The Easter controversy of Late Antiquity and the early Middle Ages*, Turnhout, 173–212.

— (2012) 'Köln als naturwissenschaftliches Zentrum in der Karolingerzeit: die frühmittelalterliche Kölner Schule und der Beginn der fränkischen Komputistik,' in H. Finger and H. Horst, *Mittelalterliche Hand-*

schriften der Kölner Dombibliothek: Viertes Symposion der Diözesan- und Dombibliothek Köln zu den Dom-Manuskripten, Köln, 41–96.

Wasserschleben, H. (1885) *Die irische Kanonensammlung*, 2nd ed., Leipzig, repr. Aalen 1966.

Woods, D. (2011) 'Adomnán, plague and the Easter controversy,' *Anglo-Saxon England* 40, 1–13.

Woolf, A. (2013) 'The churches of Pictavia,' *Kathleen Hughes memorial lectures* 11, Cambridge.

Zimmer, H. (1881–4) *Keltische Studien*, 2 vols., Berlin.

— (1901) *Pelagius in Irland: Texte und Untersuchungen zur patristischen Litteratur*, Berlin.

— (1902) *The Celtic Church in Britain and Ireland*, trans. by A. Meyer, London.

ERIC GRAFF

A NOTE ON THE DIVISIONS OF TIME IN THE CATALOGUE OF THE SAINTS OF IRELAND

Abstract

The Catalogue of the Saints of Ireland has been a point of reference for scholars since its first printing by Ussher in 1639. It has been the *locus classicus* for many issues related to the identity of the early Irish church, including the paschal computus, the role of women in the church, the form of tonsure, the mass, and the traditions attending many of the major saints of the early period. Following Grosjean's edition and study in 1955, however, the reputation of the work suffered as it was re-dated to the 9th or 10th century. Scholars almost uniformly dismissed the work afterward as a narrative about the early period told in the service of later political and ecclesial concerns. This article demonstrates that Grosjean's study overlooked a key aspect of the text—its chronological structure—and that this structure depends on a detailed knowledge of the 'Irish' paschal computus. It therefore questions the grounds upon which Grosjean and others have disparaged the text, and asserts that at least the core of the work was written within the living memory of those who kept the 'Irish' Easter.

Keywords

Computus, paschal, saints, Irish, Celtic, tonsure, Easter, chronology, Easter controversy; Patrick, Victorius of Aquitaine; *Catalogus sanctorum Hiberniae*, *latercus*.

Introduction

The full title of this work as given by its modern editor is *Catalogus sanctorum Hiberniae secundum diversa tempora*, or alternatively *De tribus*

Early medieval Ireland and Europe: chronology, contacts, scholarship, ed. by Pádraic Moran and Immo Warntjes, Studia Traditionis Theologiae, 14 (Turnhout, 2015), pp. 99–117.

 10.1484/M.STT-EB.5.103117

ordinibus sanctorum Hiberniae.[1] Naturally, scholars of early Irish saints have made use of the text for studies of hagiography and the traditions surrounding major figures like St Finnian.[2] Special attention has also been paid to the role of St Patrick in this work as a figurehead of the early Irish church.[3] Numerous studies have touched upon the Catalogue for its mention of one or another favorite topic, such as the existence or non-existence of an early diocesan structure, the role of women and lay people in the early monasteries, the tonsure in the Irish style, or the Easter controversies between 'Roman' and 'Celtic' factions.[4] This study of the text will interrogate a part of the work that has been somewhat neglected, although its importance ought to be obvious: the *diversa tempora* themselves. What exactly forms the basis for the triple organization of these saints, and why are the periods divided in the way that they are? The conclusions offered here do not touch every aspect of this work, but they do suggest a general correction to the opinions of the text developed by critics over the last 60 years. Specifically, the date of the work and its relevance for topics unrelated to the figure of Patrick have been grossly misunderstood in the modern literature.

[1] This text is edited by Grosjean (1955). Previous editions include Ussher (1639), 913–5, repr. in Elrington (1829–64), vi 477–9; 2nd ed. (1687), 473–4; Fleming (1667), 430–1; O'Conor (1814–26), ii 162–5; Haddan and Stubbs (1869–78), ii,2 292–4; de Smedt and de Backer (1888), 161–4; Heist (1955), 81–3.

[2] For the recent résumé of notices, see CCSL, Clavis Patrum Latinorum, 3rd ed. (no. 2035) and Lapidge and Sharpe (1985), 106 (no. 363); prior to these, Kenney (1929), 478–9 (no. 271). The manuscript relationships to the Life of Finnian are noted by Grosjean (1955), 301, 316–22, and at least one copy, in the Codex Salmanticensis, appends a note on Finnian's disciples to the text itself (Brussels, Bibliothèque royale de Belgique/Koninklijke Bibliotheek van België, 7672–4, 79r).

[3] Bury (1905), 285–7; Ryan (1931), 96–8, 175–8, 220–1, *et passim*; Hughes (1966), 69–72; Coccia (1967), 379; Chadwick (1961), 71–87; Sharpe (1984), 247–51.

[4] The major discussions are by now quite dated, especially Bury (1905), 285–7, and Ryan (1931), 97–8. Both rely on the work as written around 'the first half of the eighth century' (Bury (1905), 285) and offering 'the only general account' of the history between Patrick's death and the rise of the great monasteries. Bury discussed the programmatic history in the account, from uniformity to division, while Ryan treated among other topics the role of women in the early monasteries. Grosjean (1955) himself discussed each of these issues in his commentary: the authority of the church, including the tonsure (291–2), the mass (292–6), monastic custom (296–7), Easter (297–8), lay men and women in the church (298–9), and the royal synchronisms (301–6). Hughes's 1966 treatment of the Catalogue, discussed further below, began with the assumption of authenticity, but ended by dismissing the witness of the text. One recent topical notice, by Mc Carthy (2003), 143, avoids any reliance on the text of the *Catalogus* and suggests that it repeats the language of the *Collectio Canonum Hibernensis*.

The content of the Catalogue

The Catalogue of the Saints of Ireland is a short text deriving from the tradition of Hiberno-Latin saints' lives. Its purpose—at least the minimum intention that can be agreed upon by readers of the text—is to provide a schematically simple view of the Christian history of Ireland until the time of the great plague in AD 665. To say more than this is to choose from a range of problems, because despite its brevity the Catalogue is remarkably dense in its thematic structure; in the space of two pages it presses together the issues of women in the Irish church, of the legacy of Patrick, of the diocesan organization in the years after Patrick, of liturgical uniformity in the mass, of the native form of tonsure, and of the proper celebration of Easter.

This complex of issues brought the Catalogue a period of historical fame beginning with Ussher's edition in 1639 and Fleming's in 1667. It was re-edited in the nineteenth century by O'Conor (1825), by Haddan and Stubbs (1888), and by de Smedt and de Backer for the *Acta Sanctorum Hiberniae* (1888), and again in the twentieth century by Heist and by Grosjean, both in 1955. It was Grosjean's thorough treatment of the text—and his commentary on its peculiarities—that would become the standard point of reference. All subsequent discussions rely on his collection of the text in four different versions. The text provided here in the Appendix is from Grosjean's transcription of Ussher's edition of 1639 (U), which is generally agreed to be the most primitive version.[5]

A brief look at the contents of the Catalogue will trace the outlines of its structure. The first order of saints was in the time of Patrick. The saints were all bishops and founders of churches. They had—in the formula that stands at the center of this text—one head in Christ and one leader in Patrick. They used one liturgy, wore one tonsure, held one Pasch on the full moon after the spring equinox. They agreed on what was to be excluded from their churches and did not reject the fellowship and ministration of women, for they did not fear the breeze of temptation. There are added the names of four kings whose reigns supposedly encompass this period.

The passage on the second order follows the format of the first, but the saints now are priests and bishops. They had one head in Christ, but now they used different liturgies and followed different rules. Yet they

[5] Grosjean (1955), 212: 'Nous conclurons donc que la recension AU de Catalogue est la plus ancienne qui subsiste.' The other representative of this version (A) is London, British Library, Add. 30512, 72r–73v.

still shared one Pasch on the 14th moon and one tonsure. In this period, they separated women from the monasteries. The attached list of four kings contains a curious repetition of the name of Tuathail Mael Garb, and is followed by a note on the introduction of the British mass from Saints David, Gildas, and Docco, or Kew. Then the names of the most prominent saintly figures are listed.

Again in the third order we can see the worsening condition of the Irish church. In this period there are few bishops among the priests, who seem to have taken to the wilds to live on herbs and water and alms. Gone is the reference to one head in Christ, and no longer is the same tonsure worn by everyone. There are of course different rules and liturgies, and—for the first time—different paschal sollemnities (or Easters, if you will, but there is an important distinction to be made here). Again the Catalogue names four kings as the rulers at this time, then adds the bishops and priests most known for their sanctity in separate lists.

Finally, in paragraph four, the first order is called holiest, the second holier, and the third holy, and the orders are likened to the sun, moon, and stars respectively. The note in §4(b) was added by Ussher from another manuscript and repeats §4(a), adding another analogy from the life of St Patrick. Such is the Catalogue in outline. There are other particulars—the numbers of priests or bishops attached to each order, the meaning of certain phrases like *mulierum administrationem*, etc.—that merit separate discussions, but it is clear already how this short piece could attract the notice of historians for its uniquely synthetic treatment of difficult historical themes. No other work of this length so efficiently reviews the topics that have become emblematic of the character of early Christian Ireland.

The direction of historical criticism

Unfortunately, the Catalogue has gone missing among recent historical assessments of the period; it does not appear anywhere in the sweeping discussions of the *New History of Ireland*.[6] The reason is to be found in the condition of the text's reputation following the edition and commentary by Grosjean. By virtue of the alchemy that is academic

6 It should be noted that owing to the long history of the first volume of the *New History* (Ó Cróinín (2005)), the new editor, without whom the work would never have appeared at all, was forced to print some legacy essays on topics that might have used the Catalogue as a source; see Hughes (2005).

controversy, the many topics of the Catalogue have been reduced to a single line of discussion, namely the importance of Patrick as a figurehead of the early Irish church. With little more than a modernist's suspicion of antique sources, Grosjean preferred to place the work in the 9th or even 10th century, and so to connect it with the view of Patrick as a centrepiece of Armagh's claim to authority. Without speculating about Grosjean's motives for reading the text in this way, it is certain that the effect of his interpretation was to diminish the stature of the text in the eyes of historians ever since.

Grosjean's commentary notwithstanding, this reduction has been happening for a long time. The gold that was for Ussher a precious witness to 8th-century historical thinking—a text capable of throwing light on the most obscure topics in the development of the native Irish church—was put to the test first by Todd, who translated the work and applied it to the question of St Patrick's chronology.[7] Meanwhile, O'Conor and Haddan and Stubbs offered divergent dates for the periodization of the orders, the difference being that Haddan and Stubbs rigorously followed the annals in assigning the first period to AD 440–543, the second to AD 543–599, the third to AD 599–665.[8] O'Conor had preferred AD 544 as the date of the first transition and AD 598 as the date of the second transition.[9] In this chronology O'Conor was joined by Bury, who also pushed the beginning date back to the year AD 432.[10] For all these scholars the assumed date of composition was in the early to mid-8th century; their discussion centered around the internal divisions of the text, but never reached a consensus about the rationale for this particular way of dividing the 'ages' or *diversa tempora* of the scheme.

When Bury summarized the Catalogue in his *Life of St. Patrick*, he noted that 'the artificiality of this arrangement [i.e., into three distinct orders] is emphasized by the circumstance that the author conceives each period to be coincident with exactly four reigns. This is contrary to

7 Both Ussher (1639) and Todd (1864), 88–9, assumed the chronology began with Patrick's arrival in Ireland. Ussher (1639), 913, first identified the complete timeframe of the text as AD 433 to 664.

8 Haddan and Stubbs (1878), 294. It was Todd's argument about the rise of monastic power which Sharpe (1984), 248, says formed the 'basis of twentieth century views'.

9 O'Conor (1825), 163.

10 Bury (1905), 286.

fact in the case of periods 1 and 3'.[11] He goes on to note the absence of Muichertach Mac Ercae in period one and of three kingships in period three. At the last, Bury put these down as 'examples of looseness' that told against the Catalogue as evidence for real history. Nevertheless, he thought the conception of growing diversity and a 'rise in individualism after the Patrician period' to be, as he said, 'in consonance with probability and with other evidence'. He judged the work to have been written not later than the middle of the 8th century.[12]

Among the historians after Bury, Ryan in his *Irish Monasticism* treated the Catalogue as a true witness to the pedigree of Irish monastic organization.[13] He thought that the influence of the named Britons in period two was the decisive factor in making the second half of the 6th century such a period of growth for the *paruchiae* that—in his view—came to dominate the country after the flourishing of Patrick's episcopate. In the third period, according to this view, the growth of coenobitic life was extended into the practice of solitaries who sought the desert in the Eastern fashion.

But if it looked like the *Catalogus* would thus be accepted as a whole in the circles of historians, the edition and commentary of the Bollandist Grosjean changed the reception of the text immediately. When Grosjean published four variations of the Catalogue from the separate witnesses (three manuscripts and Ussher's *Antiquitates*), the effect was like pouring acid over the material. Suddenly the weakness and inconsistency of the patchwork structure were revealed. Grosjean demonstrated that there had been interference by at least one later redactor. He re-dated the text to the 9th or even the 10th century.[14]

On the basis of this re-dating of the text, Nora Chadwick argued in 1961 that when we look for information regarding the early Irish church, especially its balance between bishops, monks, and anchorites, we must 'disabuse our minds of the spurious authority of the *Catalogus*'.[15] To

[11] Bury (1905), 286.

[12] Bury (1905), 285.

[13] Ryan (1931), 164–6.

[14] Grosjean became suspect especially about the author's knowledge of so-called 'third-age' figures, and suggested that the material could all have been supplied by historical records (Grosjean (1955), 213): 'Pourtant, l'impression générale qui se dégage d'un étude attentive est que le IXe ou même le Xe siècle conviendraient mieux que la première moitié du VIIIe, et que les renseignements fournis, loin d'être de premiere main, même pour la période la plus récente, sont puisés à des sources écrites.'

[15] Chadwick (1961), 73.

show how influential was the opinion of Grosjean, we may cite an especially candid footnote from Kathleen Hughes' book, *The Church in Early Irish Society*. When introducing our Catalogue as a source for the changeover from episcopal to monastic modes in the Irish church, she effectively strips the work of its respectability, writing:[16]

> 'I am afraid that, when I reviewed Père Grosjean's edition [...] I did not realize the implications of his redating, and accepted the *Catalogus* as substantially true. So have Dr. Kenney, Dom Louis Gougaud, and Professor Ryan, writing before Père Grosjean's commentary.'

With this footnote, it seems to me, Hughes substantially gutted the work. All that was left after the text had been moved into the 9th century was the shell of an historical narrative.

Finally, and it seems inevitably, at the end of this operation Richard Sharpe surveyed the textual precipitate and found nothing but ashes. In his 1984 *Peritia* article, Sharpe looked hard at both sides of the thesis that held that the early Irish church changed from a diocesan to a monastic mode. He argued that:[17]

> 'there is [, then,] no contemporary evidence for the early existence of dioceses, nor is there any reason to suppose the monastic federations such as that dependent on Iona were the common pattern of ecclesiastical organization in the seventh century. One must wonder, therefore, how it came to be that the change from one pattern to the other has formed the central question in the study of the early Irish church for well over a century.'

Sharpe followed the question back to our text. He continued:

> 'The ultimate source of this doctrine of change, however, is to hand: the *Catalogus sanctorum Hiberniae secundum diuersa tempora*. This worthless text was known to and used by archbishop Ussher, giving rise to a classification of the early years of the Irish church in three periods or 'orders' of saints.'

[16] Hughes (1966), 69.

[17] Sharpe (1984), 247.

In fact, Sharpe recommended abandoning even the shell of the Catalogue, that arbitrary structure that had continued to shape discussions of church organization over time.

As a result, even in the areas where the Catalogue was held to be an essential medieval resource, it has been dismissed. Patrick as the leader of the early church was a source of suspicion to Grosjean. Patrick's association with the Armagh diocese implicated the entire narrative governing an early ecclesial structure based on his episcopacy. Historians were now warned away from a text that had framed—perhaps even generated—many of the discussions of the distinctiveness of early Irish Christianity in the first place. Mc Carthy's recent article on the Celtic tonsure, for example, passes lightly by the very text which for a long time was taken as the *locus classicus* for the differentiation between the 'coronal' and 'caesarian' styles.[18] The king-lists were dismissed as loose or inaccurate, but also, somehow, as too pat or symmetrical to be believed. The additional testimony of the work regarding women in the monasteries, or the role of laymen, or the reform of the liturgy, or the practice of eremiticism: all these have been dissolved into a worthless mass on account of the dissatisfaction some historians have felt with its ability to support certain claims about ecclesiology. It is a secondary effect of this disregard that the older series of questions about the text—the questions that interested Todd, O'Conor, Haddan and Stubbs, and Bury—remain unsettled. This article makes no attempt to resolve all of these problems, but a review of a few recent developments will establish the grounds for taking a new look at the Catalogue, especially at its chronological conceit.

The pre-eminence of Patrick

It appears that the motion to dismiss this work was made in pursuit of a new narrative about the progress of Irish ecclesial organization. One of the oldest assumptions about this organization was that it coincided with Patrick's becoming a figurehead of the church at Armagh. The definitive collection of Patrician texts in the Book of Armagh dates from the early 9th century, but the interest in Patrick at Armagh has always been understood to have begun in the later 7th century. What was

[18] See Mc Carthy (2003), especially 143–4. In this otherwise very thorough article, the authority of the Catalogue is assumed to be very suspect, following modern received opinion. Unfortunately, this opinion, which originates with Grosjean, seems for many scholars to obviate the need to refer to his modern edition.

unknown to Grosjean, and only lightly considered in more recent work, is that Patrick's pre-eminence could be a shared historical idea as early as the AD 630s without any of the Armagh associations. As Walsh and Ó Cróinín point out, the first reference to Patrick in the 7th-century texts is in Cummian's Letter, a southern work that nevertheless uses the rare honorific *papa noster* for the founding saint.[19] If a letter on behalf of the 'Roman' party in the paschal controversy can so easily cite the champion of Armagh's pretensions, then perhaps the equation of 'Patrician' with 'episcopal' in arguments about ecclesial organization is too simple to bear credence.

Moreover, the attachment of Patrick's reputation to the status of the Catalogue rests on a series of tenuous connections. Grosjean's edition ought to have convinced researchers of the complexity and compositeness of the Catalogue; the many issues and several versions of the text suggest a recension history that is limited in distribution but susceptible to the introduction of new themes.[20] Instead, however, modern researchers have followed a single and misguided line of reasoning that begins with the editor's conjectural date and ends with an opinion of the work's pervasive depravity. None has seen the need to assess each thematic element separately, and none has been inclined even to query the date affixed to the work by Grosjean's educated guess.

My purpose here is to make it possible to reassess the themes offered in the narrative of the Catalogue, but the means of achieving this end are limited here to the chronology. If we were interested only in rehabilitating this poor work, it would be enough to say that despite its 'later' date it is still useful as a witness to *that* period's historical thinking. This would be true, and sufficient grounds for further work, *if* we could decide which later period should claim the Catalogue as its own.[21] But I suspect any thorough attempt to resituate the text in a later century (as opposed to the brief judgment of Grosjean) would merely repeat the process of delegitimation by documenting all over again the inconsistencies inherent in its structure. Instead, I focus here on one piece of the

[19] Walsh and Ó Cróinín (1988), 29–32.

[20] Grosjean's treatment of the disciples of Finnian, who are named in a list attached to the text in the Codex Salmanticensis, demonstrates this flexibility; see the Appendix in Grosjean (1955), 316–22.

[21] Such a reading is at least partly developed by Etchingham (1999), 88–9: 'While the text is clearly unreliable as a guide to the reality of the fifth century to the seventh, it may be an indirect indicator of the continued standing of bishops in the eyes of Irish churchmen at a later period.'

composition: the paschal theme. The results of a rather simple interrogation may indicate some further possibilities within the Catalogue.

The royal synchronisms

It has already been mentioned that the Catalogue's royal synchronisms do not directly match the assertion of the text that each age endured 'through four reigns'. The data in *Figure 1* show regnal succession throughout the extent of the Catalogue's chronology. The transitional kings are highlighted in boxes.

1. Niall Noígiallach	9. *Domnall mac Muirchertaig* (†c.566)	16. Máel Cobo mac Áedo (†614)
2. Nath Í mac Fiachrach	10. Ainmuire mac Sétnai (†c.569)	17. Suibne Menn mac Fiachnai (†628)
3. *Lóeguire mac Néill* (†463)	11. Báetán mac Muirchertaig (†c.572)	18. *Domnall mac Áedo* (†642)
4. *Ailill Molt mac Nath Í* (†c.482)	11. Eochaid mac Domnaill (†c.572)	19. *Cellach mac Máele Cobo* (†658)
5. *Lugaid mac Lóeguiri* (†c.507)	12. Báetán mac Ninnedo (†c.586)	19. *Conall Cáel mac Máele Cobo* (†654)
6. Muirchertach Mac Ercae (†c.536)	13. *Áed mac Ainmuirech* (†c.598)	20. *Diarmait mac Áedo Sláine* (†665)
7. *Tuathal Máelgarb* (†c.544)	14. *Áed Sláine mac Diarmato* (†604)	20. *Blathmac mac Áedo Sláine* (†665)
8. *Diarmait mac Cerbaill* (†c.565)	14. Colmán Rímid mac Báetáin (†604)	21. Sechnussach mac Blathmaic (†671)
9. *Forggus mac Muirchertaig* (†c.566)	15. *Áed Uaridnach mac Domnaill* (†612)	

Figure 1 High kings of Ireland during the period of the Catalogue (following Byrne (1973), 275; italics have been added to indicate those rulers specifically mentioned in the text).

The appearance of Tuathal Máelgarb in both ages one and two is marked by a curious precision: the transition is made, according to paragraph 2(d), 'in the last years' of Tuathal's reign. No explanation is given, but the break with the structural conceit of four reigns is clearly noted. *Figure 1* also contains the names of many kings who are not included in the synchronisms, and so demonstrates their incompleteness. As with Tuathal, there is no explanation given for the position of Áed mac Ainmuirech at the transitional moment, even though it appears that his reign ought to be read as being completely contained within the second age. The same typical omissions are made in age three, and with language to reinforce them, pointing out the turbulent times and the generic reach of the third age beyond four reigns up to the time of the plague. Thus the king-lists are specifically a failure for the purposes of that overarching scheme that ostensibly directs the Catalogue. But in this failure is the ground of another reading of the Catalogue in which the real motivation for its structure is unexpressed within the text.

To return at last to a concern left behind with Bury's use of the work, we must look again at the interior divisions of the offered chronology with an eye on the paschal theme in specific. For ease of reference, the paschal data for the years surrounding each transition period have been collated in *Figures 2* and *3* below.

There are two coincidences to note about these years. First, the change from the first to the second ages is coincident with (i.e., in the year after) the Fourth Council of Orleans in AD 541, a meeting of importance because it maintained Pope Victor's (†AD 199) Easter against quartodeciman practice. A user of any variety of Easter tables arranged in 84 years would have noticed that AD 541 is exactly a full cycle after AD 457, when Victorius' table was published. Secondly, the change from the second to the third ages, which is said to fall neatly after the death of Áed mac Ainmuirech in AD 598, is 57 years, or three times 19 years, later. The only thing to be said for such a coincidence is that it might afford the chance for administrators of the computus to revisit paschal controversies or modify their use of the calendar for Easter.

A third, more urgent, coincidence is found in the paschal terms of the transition years. The *latercus* paschal cycle (i.e., the cycle governing the early Irish Easter custom) indicates that in both of these years the Irish saints of the first age would be celebrating Easter on the 14th lune.[22] For reasons of brevity, let it suffice to say that celebrating Easter on the 14th lune had first become a matter of doctrinal dispute in the time of Pope Victor. Prior to that time, it had been known especially among early Christian communities under the patronage of St John. Variations were troublesome and impractical, but had never before been attached to questions about true faith. By the time of Columbanus, the

[22] The precise years of transition in this reading would mark the change in ages at AD 542 and 599, in the midst of Tuathal's last years and after the end of Áed mac Ainmuirech's reign. These years appear in bold in the tables.

AD	*latercus* (insular Easter table of 84 years)				Victorian table (532 years)				Dionysian table			
	cycle #	Easter moon	Easter day	epact	cycle #	Easter moon	Easter day	epact	lunar cycle #	Easter moon	Easter day	epact
537	16	18	12A	5	510	16	12A	4	3	16	12A	25
538	17	14	28M	16	511	20	4A	16	4	19	4A	6
539	18	16	17A	27	512	21/15	24A/17A	27	5	20	24A	17
540	19	17	8A	8	513	16	8A	8	6	15	8A	28
541	20	20	31M	19	514	19	31M	19	7	18	31M	9
542	**21**	**14**	**13A**	**30**	**515**	**20**	**20A**	**30**	**8**	**19**	**20A**	**20**
543	22	17	5A	11	516	16/23!	5A/12A	11	9	15	5A	1
544	23	19	27M	22	517	18	27M	22	10	17	27M	12
545	24	20	16A	3	518	19	16A	3	11	18	16A	23
546	25	16	1A	14	519	22	8A	14	12	21	8A	4

Figure 2 Comparison of Easter tables for transition from first to second order of saints (bold type indicates the proposed year of transition; the epacts of the *latercus* and of the Victorian table refer to the lunar age on 1 January, the epacts of the Dionysian table to the lunar age on 22 March; for the *latercus* data see Blackburn and Holford-Strevens (1999), 873; for the Victorian data see Krusch (1938), 51; for the Dionysian data see Wallis (1999), 392).

	latercus (insular Easter table of 84 years)				Victorian table (532 years)				Dionysian table			
AD	cycle #	Easter moon	Easter day	epact	cycle #	Easter moon	Easter day	epact	lunar cycle #	Easter moon	Easter day	epact
594	73	18	11A	6	35	15/22	11A/18A	4	3	15	11A	25
595	74	14	27M	17	36	19	3A	16	4	18	3A	6
596	75	14	15A	28	37	19	22A	27	5	18	22A	17
597	76	17	7A	9	38	15/22	7A/14A	8	6	21	14A	28
598	77	20	30M	20	39	18	30M	19	7	17	30M	9
599	**78**	**14**	**12A**	**1**	**40**	**19**	**19A**	**30**	**8**	**18**	**19A**	**20**
600	79	16	3A	12	41	21	10A	11	9	20	10A	1
601	80	19	26M	23	42	17	26M	22	10	16	26M	12
602	81	20	15A	4	43	18	15A	3	11	17	15A	23
603	82	16	31M	15	44	21	7A	14	12	20	7A	4

Figure 3 Comparison of Easter tables for transition from second to third order of saints (bold type indicates the proposed year of transition; the epacts of the *latercus* and of the Victorian table refer to the lunar age on 1 January, the epacts of the Dionysian table to the lunar age on 22 March; for the *latercus* data see Blackburn and Holford-Strevens (1999), 874–5; for the Victorian data see Krusch (1938), 28–9; for the Dionysian data see Wallis (1999), 393; a similar comparative table can be found in Corning (2006), 183).

celebration on the 14th would be connected also to an absurd accusation that this was to practice 'with the Jews'.[23] More and more, the ancient practice, which sometimes occurred in the *latercus* cycle, seemed out of step with more recent calendars whose Easter terms had been shifted so that the earliest possible Easter fell on the 16th rather than the 14th day of the paschal moon. This is the basis for the phrase in the text at §3(b) that some celebrated the new paschal terms 'with hard feelings'.

After noting that the Catalogue says some 'celebrated the Resurrection' on the 14th moon and some on the 16th, Grosjean continues:[24]

> 'Ceci est proprement monstreux, car jamais il n'a été question, chez les Celtes, d'en fixer la célèbration toujours au quatorzième jours de la lune, non plus qu'au seizième, quel que fût le jour de la semaine, mais bien au dimanche qui suivait ce terme pascal ou coincidait avec lui.'

But he seems especially careless on this matter because the third section of the Catalogue refers explicitly to the paschal terms. Thus, unless we are to posit separate authors for each of the paragraphs, we must read the reference to the 14th moon in sections one and two as an indication of the paschal term and not an indication that Easter was celebrated on the full moon regardless of the weekday (a much more ancient quartodeciman practice). Thus while it was possible in the *latercus* to have an Easter on the 14th moon, it was not the usual state of affairs.

It is perhaps more important to note that the tone of the Catalogue resolutely supports the ancient custom, not only where Easter is concerned but also about the mass, the tonsure, and the presence or absence of women and layfolk within the monasteries. The declining status of Irish sanctity is expressed with regard to its unity or fragmentation, and especially to its fortitude (*super petram Christum fundati*). Would it have been strange to read a 9th- or even 10th-century author who lionized the early centuries of the church in Ireland? Perhaps not, for the character of sweeping histories such as this one is often nostalgic. Here again, however, the data may show us something essential to any reconstructive reading.

The paschal data point to a clear conflict between the *latercus* and the Victorian calendar in the years of transition. This conflict was one of the most ancient and significant for the unity of church practice in

[23] For his refutation of the charge, see Columbanus, *Epistola* I 4 (ed. Walker (1970), 6–7).

[24] Grosjean (1955), 297.

the West: the persistence of a possible Easter on the 14th lune. Although the discussion of these problematic years is not explicit in the text, the third-age discussion of paschal terms directly describes the problem. By ascribing the hard feelings to the party of the innovators, the Catalogue takes a side in the conflict and thereby advocates a usage that, by Grosjean's reckoning, had been extinct for as many as two centuries. It then connects the innovators to the loss of other qualities from the age of Patrick: the unified liturgy, tonsure, and spirit among churchmen.

All the while, the computistical data remain hidden, and perhaps this is the most significant fact of all. If Grosjean were correct in moving the date of the Catalogue to a later century, then by what means is the sixth-century paschal data preserved, even by inference, in the work of a much later writer? Who might still know in the 9th or 10th century that quartodeciman Easters were proposed in the *latercus* for AD 542 and 599? Grosjean and others have been assuming that all the material in the Catalogue could have been assembled by a historian with a later frame of reference, but it seems to strain belief that these particular data could be reconstructed from the habitually impermanent computistical handbooks of the day. If they had been, why would the supposed historian not be explicit about these years, especially if he took such a partisan view of the fragmentation of an earlier unity in the Irish church? It seems much more likely that the years were remembered in a near-contemporary period, or fashioned into their cinctures closer to the time of the last named date in the middle of the 7th century. It is most probable that the knowledge to build the Catalogue's chronology, which depends upon the *latercus* conflicts of AD 542 and 599, died out with the living memory of the 84-year Easter cycle. Since the last adherents to that cycle abandoned it in AD 716, the Catalogue's chronology must have been crafted before the middle of the 8th century.

Conclusions and reservations

There are other possible objections to the late date proposed in Père Grosjean's edition; the one offered here is sufficient to show that the text depends on information that by the late eight century had become exceedingly difficult to extract. Since the catastrophic decline in this text's reputation was caused by its replacement into a later century, I hope that scholars will be encouraged by this to take another look at a very interesting text.[25] Its authenticity, if not its accuracy, may be defended, but no claims are made here to a complete rehabilitation of the work. It may remain 'worthless' for certain purposes even if the conclusion of this study is accepted. At the very least, the Catalogue of the Saints of Ireland might survive its disastrous attachment to a singular question so that its testimony regarding other issues may be heard.

APPENDIX[26]

Incipit catalogus sanctorum Hiberniae secundum diuersa tempora.

1. (**a**) Primus ordo catholicorum sanctorum erat in tempore Patricii. Et tunc erant episcopi omnes clari et sancti et Spiritu sancto pleni, CCCL numero, ecclesiarum fundatores. (**b**) Unum caput Christum, et unam ducem Patricium habebant: unam missam, unam celebrationem, unam tonsuram (ab aure usque ad aurem) sufferebant. Unum pascha, XIV luna post aequinoctium uernale, celebrabant: et quod excummunicatum esset ab una Ecclesia omnes excommunicabant. (**c**) Mulierum administrationem et consortia non respuebant: [*mg.* nec laicos nec feminas de ecclesiis repellebant] quia super petram Christum fundati, uentum tentationis non timebant. (**d**) Hic ordo sanctorum per quaterna durauit regna, hoc est pro tempore Laeogarii, et Aila Muilt, et Lugada filio Laogarii, et Tuathail. (**e**) Hi omnes episcopi de Romanis et Francis et Britonibus et Scotis exorti sunt.
2. (**a**) Secundus ordo catholicorum presbyterorum. In hoc enim ordine pauci erant episcopi et multi presbyteri, numero CCC. (**b**) Unum caput Dominum nostrum habebant, diuersas missas celebrabant et diuersas regulas, unum pascha quarta decima luna post aequinoctium, unam tonsuram ab aure ad aurem: (**c**) abnegabant mulierum administrationem, separantes eas a

[25] Perhaps the only tribute this paper can make to the work that Dáibhí Ó Cróinín has done over many years is to excite and encourage the interest of scholars in a subject that will reward their attention. I am grateful to Dáibhí for the subject as well as the encouragement. The greater effects of these are seen growing year by year, most notably in the wide circle of friends, collaborators, and admirers that have followed him into neglected fields of study.

[26] The text provided here is that printed by Grosjean (1955), 209–11, and derived from Ussher's 1639 edition.

monasteriis. (**d**) Hic ordo per quaterna adhuc regna durauit, hoc est, ab extremis Tuathail, et per totum Diarmata regis regnum, et duorum Muredaig nepotum et Aedo filii Ainmerech. (**e**) A Dauide et Gilla et a Doco Britonibus missam acceperunt. (**f**) Quorum nomina haec sunt: duo Finiani, duo Brendani, Iairlaithea Tuama, Comgallus, Coemgenus, Ciaranus, Columba, Cainecus, Eogenius mac Laisreus, Lugeus, Ludeus, Moditeus, Cormacus, Colmanus, Nesanus, Laisreanus, Barrindeus, Coemanus, Cemanus, Comanus, [Endeus, Aedeus, Byrchinus,] et alii multi.

3. (**a**) Tertius ordo sanctorum erat talis. Erant presbyteri sancti et pauci episcopi, numero centum, (**b**) qui in locis desertis habitabant, et oleribus et aqua et eleemosynis [fidelium] uiuebant [*mg.* omnia terrena contemnebant, et omnem susurrationem et detractionem penitus euitabant] propria deuitabant, (**c**) et diuersas regulas et missas habebant, et diuersam tonsuram, (alii enim habebant coronam, alii caesariem) et diuersam solemnitatem paschalem (alii enim resurrectionem XIIII luna uel XVI cum duris intentionibus celebrabant). (**d**) Hi per quaterna regna uixerunt, hoc est, Aeda Allain (qui tribus annis, pro cogitatione mala, tantum regnauit), et Domnail, et filiorum Mailcobi et Aeda Slaine permixta tempora; et usque ad mortalitatem illam magnam perdurauerunt. (**e**) Haec sunt nomina eorum. Petranus episcopus, Ultanus episcopus, Colmanus episcopus, Murgeus episcopus, Aedanus episcopus, Lomanus episcopus, Senachus episcopus. Hi sunt episcopi, et alii plures. (**f**) Hi uero presbyteri: Fechinus presbyter, Airendanus, Failanus, Comanus, Commianus, Colmanus, Ernanus, Cronanus, et alii plurimi presbyteri.

4. (**a**) Primus ordo sanctissimus, secundus ordo sanctior, tertius sanctus. Primus sicut sol ardescit, secundus sicut luna, tertius sicut stellae. (**b**) Nota quod primus ordo erat sanctissimus, secundus sanctus sanctorum, tertius sanctus. Primus sicut sol in feruore claritatis calescit, secundus sicut luna pallescit, tertius sicut aurora splendescit. Hos tres ordines B. Patricius superno oraculo edoctus intellexit, cum in uisione illa prophetica uidit totam Hiberniam flamma ignis repletam, deinde montes tantum ardere, postea lucernas ardere in uallibus conspexit.

Bibliography

Blackburn, B. and L. Holford-Strevens (1999) *The Oxford companion to the year: an exploration of calendar customs and time-reckoning*, Oxford.

Bury, J.B. (1905) *The life of St. Patrick and his place in history*, London.

Byrne, F.J. (1973) *Irish kings and high kings*, London.

Chadwick, N.K. (1961) *The age of the saints in the early Celtic church*, London.

Coccia, E. (1967) 'La cultura irlandese precarolingia: miracolo o mito?,' *Studi medievali ser. 3* 8, 257–420.

Corning, C. (2006) *The Celtic and Roman traditions: conflict and consensus in the early medieval church*, New York.

de Smedt, C. and J. de Backer (1888) *Acta sanctorum Hiberniae ex Codice Salmanticensi*, Edinburgh.

Elrington, C.R. (1829–64) *The whole works of the most rev. James Ussher*, 17 vols., Dublin.

Etchingham, C. (1999) *Church organisation in Ireland, AD 650–1000*, Maynooth.

Fleming, P. (1667) *Collectanea sacra*, Louvain.

Grosjean, P. (1955) 'Edition et commentaire de *Catalogus sanctorum Hiberniae secundum diuersa tempora* ou *De tribus ordinibus sanctorum Hiberniae*,' *Analecta Bollandiana* 73, 197–213, 289–322.

Haddan, A. and W. Stubbs (1869–78) *Councils and ecclesiastical documents relating to Great Britain and Ireland*, 3 vols., Oxford.

Heist, W. (1955) *Vitae Sanctorum Hiberniae ex Codice Salmanticensi*, Brussels.

Hughes, K. (1966) *The church in early Irish society*, London.

— (2005) 'The church in Irish society, 400–800,' in D. Ó Cróinín, *A new history of Ireland, vol. 1: prehistoric and early Ireland*, Oxford.

Kenney, J.F. (1929) *Sources for the early history of Ireland: ecclesiastical*, New York.

Krusch, B. (1938) 'Studien zur christlich-mittelalterlichen Chronologie. Die Entstehung unserer heutigen Zeitrechnung,' *Abhandlungen der Preußischen Akademie der Wissenschaften, Jahrgang 1937, phil.-hist. Klasse, Nr. 8*, Berlin.

Lapidge, M. and R. Sharpe (1985) *A bibliography of Celtic-Latin literature 400–1200*, Dublin.

Mc Carthy, D.P. (2003) 'On the shape of the insular tonsure,' *Celtica* 24, 140–67.

O'Conor, C. (1814–26) *Rerum Hibernicarum scriptores veteres*, 4 vols., London.

Ó Cróinín, D. (2005) *A new history of Ireland, vol. 1: prehistoric and early Ireland*, Oxford.

Ryan, J. (1931) *Irish monasticism*, Dublin.

Sharpe, R. (1984) 'Some problems concerning the organization of the church in early medieval Ireland,' *Peritia* 3, 230–70.

Todd, J.H. (1864) *St. Patrick, apostle of Ireland: a memoir of his life and mission, with an introductory dissertation on some early usages of the church in*

Ireland, and its historical position from the establishment of the English colony to the present day, Dublin.

Ussher, J. (1639) *Britannicarum ecclesiarum antiquitates*, Dublin, repr. in Elrington (1829–64), v–vi; 2nd ed. Dublin 1687.

Walker, G.S.M. (1957) *Sancti Columbani opera*, Dublin, repr. 1970.

Wallis, F. (1999) *Bede: The reckoning of time*, Liverpool.

Walsh, M. and D. Ó Cróinín (1988) *Cummian's letter* De controversia paschali, *together with a related Irish computistical tract* De ratione conputandi, Toronto.

MASAKO OHASHI

THE 'REAL' ADDRESSEE(S) OF BEDE'S LETTER TO WICTHED

Abstract

Bede's letter 'On the vernal equinox, after Anatolius' was written between AD 725 and 731. The letter is addressed to his friend Wicthed, but the study of both the letter and the *Historia ecclesiastica* implies that Bede had a different readership in his mind. It is argued in this article that the 'real' addressees were the Irish monks expelled from Pictland in AD 717, who had access to the letter of Abbot Ceolfrith, which included a problematic passage on the vernal equinox; this Bede tried to rectify in the Letter to Wicthed.

Keywords

Bede, Anatolius of Laodicea, Eusebius of Caesarea, Victor of Capua; *De temporum ratione*, *Historia ecclesiastica*, Ceolfrith's Letter to King Nechtan, Bede's Letter to Wicthed; vernal equinox.

Introduction

At the very end of the *Historia ecclesiastica gentis Anglorum*, Bede inserts a list of his writings including a collection of five letters: (1) 'On the six ages of the world', (2) 'On the resting-places of the children of Israel', (3) 'On the words of Isaiah: 'And they shall be shut up in the prison and after many days shall they be visited'', (4) 'On the reason for the leap year', and (5) 'On the equinox, after Anatolius'.[1] The first letter is the one sent to Plegwin in AD 708,[2] the fourth is the letter ad-

[1] Bede, *Historia ecclesiastica* V 24 (ed. and trans. by Colgrave and Mynors (1969), 568–9).

[2] Bede, *Epistola ad Pleguinam* (ed. by Charles W. Jones in CCSL 123C, 617–26; trans. by Wallis (1999), 405–15).

Early medieval Ireland and Europe: chronology, contacts, scholarship, ed. by Pádraic Moran and Immo Warntjes, Studia Traditionis Theologiae, 14 (Turnhout, 2015), pp. 119–35.

 10.1484/M.STT-EB.5.103118

dressed to Helmwald[3] before the composition of *De temporum ratione* (AD 725), and the last one, written between *De temporum ratione* and the *Historia ecclesiastica* (AD 725/731),[4] is the subject of the present article; it appears, therefore, that Bede lists those letters in chronological order (the other two letters were addressed to Acca, bishop of Hexham *c.*AD 710–732).[5] Some other letters survive as prefaces to his writings.[6] It is an obvious conclusion to consider Bede's collection of letters as outlined in the above-mentioned passage of the *Historia ecclesiastica* as a selection for a specific purpose. Three of the five letters deal with computistical/chronological issues, and all three of them are addressed to local, otherwise unknown friends. The issues discussed certainly must have been of some importance to the author and addressees. The Letter to Plegwin is a good example of how Bede used correspondence as an instrument of self-justification. Bede, filled with indignation, wrote an *apologia* addressed to Plegwin in the space of three days after having been informed by a messenger about certain accusations levelled against him. The Letter to Wicthed ('On the equinox, after Anatolius') attacks a certain group following a different tradition of Easter reckoning. Unlike the Letter to Plegwin, this document is largely ignored in more general studies of the early-medieval paschal controversy.[7] What has not been realized, in this context, is that a thorough analysis of this letter can shed some important light on the development of the controversy in the Britain and Ireland up to the early and even to the mid-8th century.

Contents of Bede's Letter to Wicthed

At the beginning of the letter, Bede refers to the reason for writing to his friend Wicthed: he, a monk of an unidentified monastery, had asked

3 Bede, *Epistola ad Helmwaldum* (ed. by Charles W. Jones in CCSL 123C, 629; trans. by Wallis (1999), 416, 105–9). The major part of the letter is incorporated in chapters 38–39 of *De temporum ratione* by Bede himself (ed. by Charles W. Jones in CCSL 123C, 399–404; trans. by Wallis (1999), 105–9).

4 Bede, *Epistola ad Wicthedum* (ed. by Charles W. Jones in CCSL 123C, 635–42; trans. by Wallis (1999), 417–24).

5 Bede, *De mansionibus filiorum Israel* (PL 94, 699–702) and *De eo quod ait Isaias* (PL 94, 702–10).

6 Sharpe (1997–2001), i 73.

7 For Bede's *Epistola ad Wicthedum* see especially Jones (1943), 138–9, 168–9. As for the more recent publications on the Easter Controversy, this Bedan letter does not feature, e.g., in Corning (2006).

Bede why the date of the vernal equinox given by Bishop Anatolius of Laodicea, an Egyptian by birth and education, differed from the date given by other Eastern Fathers—the former fixes the date on 22 March (*XI Kal. Apr.*), the latter establish the date as 21 March (*XII Kal. Apr.*).[8] The Anatolian date mentioned (22 March) is actually from a partial quotation of Anatolius' *Canon paschalis* (*De ratione paschali*) in Eusebius' *Historia ecclesiastica*.[9] Since the holy Fathers should have no disagreement in sacred issues including Easter calculation, the author of *De temporum ratione* felt obliged to answer this simple question.

Bede suggests that the Eastern Fathers such as Bishops Proterius and Cyril of Alexandria followed 21 March as the date of the vernal equinox and that Bishop Anatolius agreed, despite the one-day difference. In order to show agreement among those Fathers, Bede cites Bishop Victor of Capua (incumbency AD 541–554).[10] Bede suggests that the discrepancy of one day in the date of the equinox can be solved by using the theory of the *bissextus* (leap-year). In the Julian calendar, a year contains 365 ¼ days, so that a full day is inserted every four years. The equinox (when the sun reaches the equinoctial point of its cycle in the zodiac) moves forward by a quarter-day per year from dawn to midday, sunset, and midnight in the four-year cycle of the leap-year. When it 'happens at dawn or midday, it is on the 12th kalends of April [21 March], and when it happens at sunset or midnight, it pertains to the 11th kalends of April [22 March]'.[11] Bede argues, therefore, that the date of the equinox given by Anatolius (following the Egyptian manner) is, in fact, that which happens at sunset or midnight,[12] hence the bishop does not contradict the Eastern Fathers. According to Victor (in Bede's quotation):[13]

[8] Bede, *Epistola ad Wicthedum* 1 (CCSL 123C, 635; Wallis (1999), 417–8).

[9] Eusebius, *Historia ecclesiastica* VII 32 (VII 28 in the Latin translation by Rufinus of Aquileia) (ed. by Eduard Schwartz and Theodor Mommsen in GCS 9, 722–6); cf. Anatolius Latinus, *De ratione paschali* 2 (ed. and trans. by Mc Carthy and Breen (1993), 46, 64, with commentary 80–5, 126–41).

[10] Jones suggests that Bede quoted from a single work of Victor of Capua (*De Pascha*) in both *De temporum ratione* 17, 50, 51, 64 (CCSL 123B, 339, 436, 441, 459) and in the Letter to Wicthed (CCSL 123C, 639). It seems, however, possible that Bede worked from at least two writings of Victor; cf. Ohashi (1999), 132.

[11] Bede, *Epistola ad Wicthedum* 3 (CCSL 123C, 636; Wallis (1999), 419): *quoties mane uel meridie fieri aequinoctium contigerit, ad duodecimum kal. Aprilium, quoties autem uesperi uel media noctis ad undecimum kal. earundem diem pertinet.*

[12] Bede, *Epistola ad Wicthedum* 5 (CCSL 123C, 637; Wallis (1999), 419–20).

[13] Bede, *Epistola ad Wicthedum* 8 (CCSL 123C, 639; Wallis (1999), 421–2).

> *quod* [= *anni principium*] *fit a duodecimo kal. Aprilium die usque ad undecimum, saepe enim uespere, interdum nocte, nonnumquam ipso xi kal. Aprilium die prouenire deprehenditur. Vicesima igitur quinta aut sexta die Martii mensis secundum Alexandrinos, hoc est iuxta Latinos duodecimo uel undecimo kal. Aprilium die, fit iuxta solis cursum primi mensis initium.* [...] *Et cum sit xxv dies Martii mensis xii kal. Aprilium, si uespere eiusdem diei sol spatium primae partis illustret iam xxvi dies ascribitur Aegyptiaca, ut diximus, traditione subtili et sine dubitatione probabili.*

> 'and this [= the beginning of the year, i.e. the vernal equinox] happens from the 12th kalends of April [21 March] to the 11th [22 March]. [The equinox] is ascertained to take place at evening, sometimes at night, and occasionally on the day of 11th kalends of April [22 March] itself. On the 25th or 26th day of the month of March according to the Alexandrians—that is, according to the Latins, the 12th or 11th kalends of April—the beginning of the first month according to the course of the Sun takes place. [...] And although the 25th of March is the 12th kalends of April [21 March], if the Sun lights up the space of the first part on the evening of the same day, it is already ascribed to the 26th day, as we said, following the subtle and without doubt probable Egyptian tradition.'

Victor's statements above survived only as partial citations by John the Deacon of Rome (mid-6th century)[14] and Bede. John, in his *Expositum in Heptateuchum*, quotes a much longer excerpt from Victor's writings, and the date of the work suggests that the bishop of Capua played an important role as computist around the middle of the 6th century. Here, Victor includes 22 March in his discussion of the vernal equinox. This date, however, was considered irregular by Bede in his *De temporum ratione*. In chapter 38 ('The calculation of the leap-year day'), he states:[15]

> *Et hic ergo sciat, solem morulis suis et tarditate quotidiana quadrantis huius annui disponente opere creatoris esse ministrum, quem diligentior inquisitio declarat, non ad eandem horologii lineam per ccclxv dies posse plene reduci; sed si, uerbi gratia, praesenti anno in aequinoctio uernali quod, iuxta Aegyptios qui calculatorum tenent palmam, duodecimo kalendarum Aprilium die solet uenire, a medio orientis surrexerit, eodem die post annum aliquanto inferius oriri, et tertio, quarto, quintoque anno eandem diminutionem in tantum naturali sui cursus augere temperantia*

[14] John the Deacon, *Expositum in Heptateuchum* (ed. by J.-P. Pitra (1852–8), i 278–301, with the quotation from Victor of Capua on pp. 296–301).

[15] Bede, *De temporum ratione* 38 (ed. by Charles W. Jones in CCSL 123B, 401; trans. by Wallis (1999), 107).

> *ut, nisi dies bissextilis antea iuxta morem intercaletur, iam undecimo kalendarum Aprilium die facturus aequinoctium a medio surgat orientis, eandem nihilominus tarditatis suae constantiam in caeteris quoque per totum annum seruaturus exortibus simul et occasibus.*
>
> 'He [= anyone] should know, then, that the Sun supplies this quarter-day to the year by brief delays and daily retardation, according to the ordering work of the Creator. Closer inspection shows that the Sun cannot be completely carried back to the same line on the sundial in 365 days. But if this year, for instance, at the [time of the] spring equinox (which according to the Egyptians, who bear the palm as computists, ordinarily comes on the 12th kalends of April [21 March]), the Sun rises in the mid-point of the east, on the same day a year later it will rise a little lower down. In the third, fourth and fifth years, it will augment this diminution, according to the natural measure of its course, to such a degree that unless the bissextile day is inserted beforehand according to custom, [the Sun] will then rise at the mid-point of the east to make the equinox on the 11th kalends of April [22 March], while at the same time continuing a regular pattern of retardation in its other risings and settings throughout the whole year regardless.'

Comparison between *De temporum ratione* and the Letter to Wicthed reveals, therefore, that Bede recognized the necessity of changing his argumentation concerning the date of the vernal equinox. In an earlier chapter (*De temporum ratione* 14: 'The Greek months'), Bede mentions Anatolius' date (22 March), but, tellingly, does not refer to it as the vernal equinox.[16] The conclusion to be drawn here is that Bede, when writing *De temporum ratione*, felt not sufficiently informed to tackle the problem of Anatolius' date of 22 March for the vernal equinox; relief came with the 'writings' of Victor of Capua, and these he exploited to the fullest when solving the one-day discrepancy of the date of the vernal equinox between the Eastern Fathers and Anatolius.

Having 'solved' this problem, Bede turns his attention to another date of the equinox, 25 March (*VIII Kal. Apr.*) in his Letter to Wicthed. According to Bede, some people insist that Anatolius fixed the equinox on 25 March, not 22 March, and that Eusebius changed the figure in his *Historia ecclesiastica*.[17] Against this accusation, Bede, trying to restore the authority of the bishop of Caesarea, asserts the following:

[16] Bede, *De temporum ratione* 14 (CCSL 123B, 328; Wallis (1999), 52–3).

[17] Bede, *Epistola ad Wicthedum* 9 (CCSL 123C, 640; Wallis (1999), 422).

> *Itaque uerisimile uidetur Eusebium quidem quod in Graeca auctoritate inueniret fideliter suis indidisse historiis; ipsum uero libellum Anatolii postmodum in aliquibus Latinorum exemplaribus esse corruptum, eorum nimirum fraude qui uerum paschae tempus ignorantes erroneam suam obseruantiam tanti patris auctoritate defendere gestirent.*
>
> 'Therefore it seems likely that Eusebius faithfully inserted into his histories what he found in the Greek authority. But that same treatise by Anatolius afterwards became corrupted in certain Latin exemplars, by whose considerable fraud those who did not know the true time of Easter would eagerly desire to defend their erroneous observance with the authority of so great a Father.'[18]

The 'Latin exemplar' of the Anatolian tract has been considered an Irish (or British) forgery by many historians.[19] As far as Bede was concerned, the Anatolian text was genuine except for the problematic date of the vernal equinox (it seems probable that Bede, in *De temporum ratione* 35, quoted from the Anatolian treatise by replacing the vernal equinox of 25 March with that of 21 March).[20] *Historia ecclesiastica* III 3, dealing

[18] Bede, *Epistola ad Wicthedum* 11 (CCSL 123C, 641; Wallis (1999), 423). Interestingly, another quotation from Anatolius suggests that Bede used the problematic version, which he criticizes as 'corrupted' in the letter, as an 'authority' in his *De temporum ratione* 35 (CCSL 123B, 393–4; Wallis (1999), 101–2): *Sed et homo ecclesiae sanctus Anatolius in opere suo paschali, cum de aequinoctiis et solstitiis deque horarum ac momentorum crementis subtilissime disputasset, ita disputationem suam simul et ipsum libellum terminauit: 'Hoc autem non ignores, quod ipsa quattuor, quae praediximus temporum confinia, licet mensium sequentium kalendis approximentur, unumquodque tamen medium temporum, id est uerni et aestatis autumni et hiemis, teneat, et non exinde temporum principia inchoantur, unde mensium kalendae initiantur. Sed ita unumquodque tempus inchoandum est, ut a prima die ueris tempus aequinoctium diuidat, et aestatis viii kl. Iulii et autumni viii kl. Octobri et hiemis viii kl. Ianuarii similiter diuidat.'* ('But that man of the Church St Anatolius, in his work about Easter, when he argues with great subtlety about the solstices and equinoxes, and about the increments of hours and *momenta*, ends his disputation, and at the same time, his book, in this wise: 'But you ought not to be unaware of the fact that although these four aforementioned frontiers of the seasons are close to the kalends of the following month, nevertheless each one contains within itself the mid-point of the seasons, that is, spring, summer, autumn and winter, and the beginnings of the seasons do not occur where the kalends of the months begin. But each season is to begin at such a point that the equinox divides the spring season [in half, beginning] from the first day; summer is similarly divided at the 8th kalends of July [24 June], autumn at the 8th kalends of October [24 September], and winter at the 8th kalends of January [25 December].")

[19] Daniel Mc Carthy considers the text authentic: Mc Carthy and Breen (2003), 117–8. For the Anatolian text and further literature on this, see Mosshammer (2008), 136–45; Warntjes (2010), LXIV–LXVII (esp. n 168). For the so-called 'Irish forgeries', see most recently Mc Carthy (2011), 51–7.

[20] See n 18 above.

with Irish and Pictish customs, reflects his account in the letter. In this chapter, Bede, relating to the Easter practice observed by Bishop Aidan of Lindisfarne (incumbency AD 635–651), argues:[21]

> *diem paschae dominicum more suae gentis, cuius saepius mentionem fecimus, quarta decima luna usque ad uicesimam obseruare solebat. Hoc etenim ordine septentrionalis Scottorum prouincia et omnis natio Pictorum illo adhuc tempore pascha dominicum celebrabat, aestimans se in hac obseruantia sancti ac laude digni patris Anatolii scripta secutam. Quod an uerum sit, peritus quisque facillime cognoscit.*

> 'after the manner of his race, as we have very often mentioned, he was accustomed to celebrate Easter Sunday between the fourteenth and the twentieth day of the moon. The northern province of the Irish and the whole nation of the Picts were still celebrating Easter Sunday according to this rule right up to that time, thinking that in this observance they were following the writings of the esteemed and holy father, Anatolius. Every instructed person can very easily judge whether this is true or not.'

Although he never refers to the other criteria of Easter reckoning in the Letter to Wicthed except for the date of the equinox, those who read both the letter and the *Historia ecclesiastica* knew exactly who was criticized here. In *De temporum ratione*, on the other hand, Bede does not mention any details concerning the people who followed the so-called 'Celtic' Easter; he only presents some data of that reckoning, namely lunar limits XIIII–XX and the underlying luni-solar cycle of 84 years. The different attitude towards the 'erroneous' reckoning(s) and their followers between the computus and the historical text suggests that Bede had a different readership in mind: the computus was designed for the monastic teaching of the technicalities of this science, the history, on the other hand, was concerned with the people of Britain and their customs. At the end of the letter, Bede, with some irony, states:

> *Qui ergo viii kal. Aprilium putat esse aequinoctium, necesse est idem aut ante aequinoctium Pascha celebrari licitum dicat aut ante viii kal. Aprilium diem Pascha celebrari licitum neget. Ipsum quoque Pascha quod Dominus pridie quam pateretur cum discipulis fecit aut nona kal. Aprilium die non fuisse aut ante aequinoctium fuisse confirmet.*

[21] Bede, *Historia ecclesiastica* III 3 (Colgrave and Mynors (1969), 218–9). Note that the Britons are not mentioned here.

> 'Whoever thinks that the 8th kalends of April [25 March] is the equinox is either obliged to state that it is licit for Easter to be celebrated before the equinox, or to deny that it is licit for Easter to be celebrated before the 8th kalends of April. Also, he will confirm that the Passover which our Lord kept with His disciples either was not on the 9th kalends of April [24 March], or was before the equinox.'[22]

Almost the same sentence is found in *De temporum ratione* 30 ('Equinoxes and solstices').[23] Given the importance and the tension of the argument in the latter part, it seems that the real purpose of the Letter to Wicthed was not to explain the discrepancy between the Eastern Fathers, but to argue against those who were fixing the date of the vernal equinox on 25 March.

The background to the Letter to Wicthed: a hypothesis

Although Bede does not name the people whose customs he criticizes in the Letter to Wicthed, there can hardly be any doubt that they were followers of the so-called 'Celtic' Easter, which fixed the date of the vernal equinox on 25 March. The earliest extant sources for the paschal controversy between the Irish and other peoples are the letters of Columbanus who, criticizing the Victorian table used by the Franks, refers to Anatolius as his authority.[24] His arguments against Victorius include the accusations of allowing Easter to fall before the equinox and on a lunar age older than the twentieth day of the moon.[25] Although there is no clear reference to the date of the vernal equinox itself, the contents

22 Bede, *Epistola ad Wicthedum* 12 (CCSL 123C, 642; Wallis (1999), 424).

23 Bede, *De temporum ratione* 30 (CCSL 123B, 375; Wallis (1999), 88). There is a one-day discrepancy between *De temporum ratione* and the Letter to Wicthed. In *De temporum ratione* 30, Bede states (the underlining is mine): *Qui igitur viii kl. Aprilium die putat aequinoctium, necesse est idem aut ante aequinoctium pascha celebrari licitum dicat, aut ante septimum kl. Aprilium diem pascha celebrari licitum neget. Ipsum quoque pascha, quod dominus pridie quam pateretur cum discipulis fecit, aut viiii kl. Aprilium die non fuisse aut ante aequinoctium fuisse confirmet.* ('Therefore he who thinks that the 8th kalends of April [25 March] is the equinox is obliged either to declare that it is licit to celebrate Easter before the 7th kalends of April [26 March], and also to confirm that the Pasch which our Lord kept with his disciples on the night before he suffered was either not on the 9th kalends of April [24 March] or was before the equinox.')

24 Columbanus, *Epistolae* I 2; II 6 (ed. and trans. by Walker (1957), 2–3, 18–9).

25 Columbanus, *Epistola* II 4 (Walker (1957), 16–7).

of his letters imply that he was fixing the equinox on 25 March for the observance of Easter.

As the rediscovery and reconstruction by Dáibhí Ó Cróinín and Daniel Mc Carthy of a copy of an 84-year Easter table with base year in AD 354 and every 84 years thereafter (preserved in the early 10th-century manuscript Padua, Biblioteca Antoniana, I 27) shows, this reckoning fixes Easter Sunday between 26 March and 23 April, with lunar limits between XIIII and XX.[26] The table excludes 25 March as Easter Sunday, which was thought to be the traditional date for Jesus' Passion.[27] The data of the Padua table reveal this to represent the Easter reckoning followed in Ireland and Britain, and these data certainly support the assumption that those attacked by Bede were the Irish, or possibly the Britons who were following the same criteria until the mid-8th century. There is no doubt that Bede could have identified his opponents, had he wished to. His information about them he probably obtained through verbal communication or even from written sources.

In the *Historia ecclesiastica*, Bede clearly reveals his hostility towards the 'erroneous' Easter reckoning followed by the Irish and the Britons. He sometimes states that they celebrated Easter Sunday between the fourteenth and the twentieth day of the moon and that their system was based on an 84-year luni-solar cycle. It is, however, curious that Bede in this text never refers to the problematic date of the vernal equinox, which was the other major cause for the discrepancy of Easter dates. As mentioned above, Bede tackles the problem in *De temporum ratione*, and almost the same sentence is repeated in the Letter to Wicthed. Why, then, did Bede omit the problem of the 'Anatolian' equinox in his *Historia ecclesiastica*?

The only reference to the date of the equinox in the *Historia ecclesiastica* appears in book V, chapter 21, in Abbot Ceolfrith's Letter to the Pictish King Nechtan.[28] This letter, written between AD 706 (Nechtan's accession to the Pictish throne) and 716 (the departure and death

26 Mc Carthy and Ó Cróinín (1987–8); Mc Carthy (1993).

27 For the dating of Christ's Passion from late antiquity to the time of Bede, see now Nothaft (2012), 19–88.

28 Bede, *Historia ecclesiastica* V 21 (Colgrave and Mynors (1969), 532–53, esp. 542–5). In the two most prominent modern editions of the *Historia ecclesiastica* (Plummer (1896), ii 332, 392; Colgrave and Mynors (1969), 534 (note by Colgrave)), Bede is thought to be the real author of the letter, but it seems more likely that Bede was not directly involved in its composition.

of Ceolfrith) and quoted by Bede in full with additional explanations, posed some problems from Bede's point of view.[29]

The letter contains two issues: Easter and tonsure. Concerning Easter, theological explanations for the Dionysiac date are given, while two other reckonings are labelled as 'erroneous'. These 'erroneous' reckonings are referred to by their lunar limits for Easter Sunday, XIIII–XX and XVI–XXII, clearly denoting the so-called 'Celtic' Easter and the Victorian table respectively.[30] After criticizing those lunar limits, Ceolfrith continues by pointing out another problematic feature in these reckonings, the beginning of the first month (i.e. the Easter month). He argues:[31]

> *Qui utrique non solum in difinitione et computo lunaris aetatis, sed et in mensis primi nonnumquam inuentione falluntur. Quae disputatio maior est, quam epistula hac uel ualeat conprehendi uel debeat. Tantum hoc dicam, quod per aequinoctium uernale semper inerrabiliter possit inueniri, qui mensis iuxta computum lunae primus anni, qui esse debeat ultimus. Aequinoctium autem iuxta sententiam omnium Orientalium et maxime Aegyptiorum, qui prae ceteris doctoribus calculandi palmam tenet, duodecim kalendarum Aprilium die prouenire consueuit, ut etiam ipsi horologica inspectione probamus.*

> 'And not only are both parties sometimes mistaken in fixing and computing the age of the moon, but they sometimes make mistakes in finding the first month. This controversy, however, is a greater one than this letter can or ought to deal with. I will only say this that, by reference to the vernal equinox, it can always be decided infallibly which month is first, and which last, according to the lunar computation. Now the equinox, according to the opinion of all eastern nations, and especially of the Egyptians who took the palm from all other learned men in

[29] The letter was written at the request of King Nechtan himself. It is possible that Bishop Wilfrid (the victor at the Synod of Whitby) was dead at this stage; at least his death precedes Bede's citation of Ceolfrith's Letter to Nechtan in the *Historia ecclesiastica* (V 19 on Wilfrid's death, V 20 on the appointments made after his death; Colgrave and Mynors (1969), 528–33) and there is no mention of Wilfrid in the chapter dealing with the Letter to Nechtan itself. Although there is no clear reference to the date of Bishop Wilfrid's death in the contemporary sources (Stephen of Ripon's Life of Bishop Wilfrid and Bede's History), two dates (24 April and 12 October) are assigned to his commemoration. On this issue, recent studies tend to support the former date (24 April 710); Stancliffe (2013), 17–26. This would suggest that Ceolfrith's letter was written between *c.*AD 710 and 716.

[30] Bede, *Historia ecclesiastica* V 21 (Colgrave and Mynors (1969), 540–1).

[31] Bede, *Historia ecclesiastica* V 21 (Colgrave and Mynors (1969), 542–3).

> calculations, usually falls on the twenty-first of March, as we can also prove by inspecting a sundial.'

Ceolfrith then turns to the relationship between the vernal equinox and the paschal full moon, and denounces the paschal full moon before the equinox as Pelagian heresy:[32]

> *Qui ergo plenitudinem lunae paschalis ante aequinoctium prouenire posse contenderit, talis in mysteriorum celebratione maximorum a sanctarum quidem scripturarum doctrina discordat: concordat autem eis, qui sine praeueniente gratia Christi se saluari posse confidunt, qui et si uera lux tenebras mundi moriendo ac resurgendo numquam uicisset, perfectam se habere posse iustitiam dogmatizare praesumunt.*
>
> 'Whoever argues, therefore, that the full Paschal moon can fall before the equinox disagrees with the teaching of the holy Scriptures in the celebration of the greatest mysteries, and agrees with those who trust that they can be saved without the grace of Christ preventing them and who presume to teach that they could have attained to perfect righteousness even though the true Light had never conquered the darkness of the world by dying and rising again.'

This second account is not as clear as it should be, because Ceolfrith does not mention any date for the equinox. It seems improbable that Bede omitted such a reference originally included in Ceolfrith's letter, although Bede does not always reproduce his sources faithfully. The Letter to Nechtan is the latest source quoted by Bede in his *Historia ecclesiastica*, thus people with access to the letter (or its copies) must have been alive when Bede completed his work. Since the paschal controversy was still continuing in Britain (the Britons were the last to adopt the Dionysiac table in AD 768), it was quite risky for Bede to make a change in his quotation from the letter.

The omission of the equinoctial date must have resulted in the rejection of Ceolfrith's arguments by some, as the Irish/Picts/Britons, who considered 25 March as the date of the equinox, would never observe the paschal full moon before Ceolfrith's equinox of 21 March.[33] The

[32] Bede, *Historia ecclesiastica* V 21 (Colgrave and Mynors (1969), 544–5).

[33] The 'Celtic' 84-year Easter table with base year AD 354 (as reconstructed from the Padua table) reveals that the earliest date for Easter Sunday is 26 March, and the highest lunar age on this date (for AD 433 and every 84 years thereafter) is 19; in this case, *luna XIIII* falls on 21 March, which is thus the earliest date for the Easter full

accusation of Pelagianism would simply not apply to them. The other Easter reckoning criticized in the letter, the Victorian table, did have this theoretical defect, as Bede in *De temporum ratione* 51 clearly demonstrates.[34] Victorius of Aquitaine, in his Letter to Archbishop Hilarus (or Hilarius), explains that the *Latini* follow the traditional limits for *luna I* (1 Nisan) from 5 March to 2 April.[35] This criterion may lead to a paschal full moon as early as 18 March, three days before the vernal equinox (21 March). In his Easter table, Victorius avoids the earliest dates, but still allows *luna XIIII* (the Easter full moon) to fall on 20 March in every 19th year.[36] In *De temporum ratione* 6 ('The world's first day'), Bede, connecting the paschal full moon before the equinox with Pelagianism, states:[37]

> *in celebratione maximae solemnitatis Christus ecclesiae debuit anteponi, quae non nisi per illum luceret. Nam si qui plenilunium paschale ante aequinoctium fieri posse contenderit, ostendat uel ecclesiam sanctam priusquam saluator in carne ueniret extitisse perfectam, uel quemlibet fidelium ante praeuentum gratiae illius aliquid posse supernae lucis habere.*

> 'in the celebration of the supreme solemnity, it was necessary that Christ precede the Church, which cannot shine save through Him. For if anyone were to argue that the full Moon can come before the equinox, he would be stating either that Holy Church existed in its perfection before the Saviour came in the flesh, or that one of the faithful, before the bestowing of His grace, can have something of the supernal light.'

The statement is similar to that found in Ceolfrith's letter. The reckoning connected by Bede with the paschal full moon before the equinox is not the 'Celtic' method with its 25 March equinox, but the Victorian table.

moon in this table, which is the same as in the Dionysiac table; cf. Warntjes (2007), 57–8; Holford-Strevens (2008), 179–80. This means that the 'Irish' Easter as represented in the Padua table allowed *luna XIIII* before the 'Irish' equinoctial date (25 March), and therefore the connection between the paschal full moon before the equinox and Pelagian heresy appears justified on this very point. In his letter, Ceolfrith, however, only mentions 21 March as the date of the equinox, and since the 'Irish' Easter full moon always fell after that date, the accusation of Pelagianism does not apply in this case.

34 Bede, *De temporum ratione* 51 (CCSL 123B, 437–41; Wallis (1999), 132–5).

35 Victorius of Aquitaine, *Prologus* 4 (ed. by Krusch (1938), 19).

36 Victorius, *Cyclos* (ed. by Krusch (1938), 27–52). The years in question are those marked by epact 25. Since Victorius applied lunar limits XVI–XXII for Easter Sunday, he made sure that this event would fall after the equinox.

37 Bede, *De temporum ratione* 6 (CCSL 123B, 292; Wallis (1999), 25–6).

Ceolfrith's letter probably caused some sort of tension between the sender and those who were supporting the traditional 'Celtic' calculation. But the adoption of the Roman reckoning (the Dionysiac table) had already been decided by Nechtan before the messenger arrived in Northumbria,[38] so that traditionalists in Pictland (monks from the Iona community), who were finally expelled beyond *Dorsum Brittaniae* by the same king in AD 717,[39] had no real chance to respond to Ceolfrith's charges. On returning to Iona, they were to find that their home monastery had also changed its policy. Moreover, due to the sudden departure and death of the sender of the letter, Abbot Ceolfrith, in AD 716, the Irish traditionalists lost their immediate target.

It can generally be suggested that a treatise (or letter) discussing a specific technical aspect may have been written at a time when the issue under discussion featured in the existing Easter tables. In the year following the compilation of *De temporum ratione*, the paschal full moon (*luna XIIII*) fell on 22 March, and Easter Sunday on 24 March (*luna XVI*) according to the Dionysiac table. This would have been good timing for a lecture on the vernal equinox of 21 March to be strictly observed in Easter reckonings. But those following different practices must have been severely offended by Bede's ironical statements in *De temporum ratione* 30 discussed above. As Bede in the Letter to Wicthed suggests, his opponents criticize Eusebius for manipulating evidence—a fact not mentioned in *De temporum ratione*. Of course, such criticism could have been raised at any given time, that is also before Bede's *De temporum ratione*. But the repetition of the same ironic account in the Letter to Wicthed implies that Bede was aware that the 'real' addressee(s) of the letter knew the content of his computistical textbook written in AD 725. It is possible that Bede's irony in *De temporum ratione* re-invoked a dispute on the Anatolian date of the equinox, with Bede's opponents responding to Bede's textbook by pointing to the problem in Ceolfrith's letter: Followers of the 'Celtic' reckoning could hardly be accused by 'Romans' of not observing the 'Roman' equinox for the paschal full moon, as all paschal full moons in the 'Celtic' system fell on or after the 'Roman' equinox of 21 March; on the contrary, members of the 'Celtic' party could certainly, like Columbanus had done, accuse the 'Romans' for not observing the 'Celtic' equinox, as the Dionysiac reckoning allowed Easter Sunday to fall before 25 March. At this point, we may

[38] Bede, *Historia ecclesiastica* V 21 (Colgrave and Mynors (1969), 532–3, 546–7).

[39] Annals of Ulster *s.a.* 717 (ed. by Mac Airt and Mac Niocaill (1983), 172–3).

understand why Bede was so eager to show to the 'real' addressees that 21 March was the correct Anatolian (and therefore 'Celtic') date of the vernal equinox. In the letter Bede did so by using a sort of syllogism (Anatolius 'actually' fixed the vernal equinox on 21 March, therefore those who are following the authority of Anatolius must do the same), probably in order to emend the unsatisfactory reference to the equinox in Ceolfrith's letter. This was the reason for writing the Letter to Wicthed and his list of writings (including this letter) in the *Historia ecclesiastica*. Any knowledgeable person was to be pointed to Bede's Letter to Wicthed as a corrective to the copy of Ceolfrith's letter provided in the *Historia ecclesiastica*. Therefore, the reference to his collection of letters was quite important for Bede himself.

Conclusion: possible addressees of the Letter to Wicthed

Since the Irish monks of Iona had already adopted the Dionysiac table in AD 716 (through the effort of the Northumbrian Ecgberht),[40] it is improbable that Bede wrote the letter 'On the equinox' against them. Monks remaining faithful to 'Celtic' customs (possibly including those who had been expelled by Nechtan), would have had to leave Iona. One of the places where those exiles could have found refugee was, probably, Wales. According to Aldhelm's Letter to King Geraint of Dumnonia,[41] many Britons were observing Easter on the fourteenth day of the moon, following Anatolius or Sulpicius Severus. The reference to Anatolius in Aldhelm's letter is very suggestive.

When Bede finished his *Historia ecclesiastica* in AD 731, the Britons were the only people still following the traditional custom and refusing to adopt the 'canonical' reckoning of Easter.[42] Throughout the *Historia ecclesiastica*, Bede is very direct in his hostility against the Britons. His was a common Anglo-Saxon sentiment for a long time, and, to be sure, the enmity between the two *gentes* was mutual. Although Bede believed that the paschal controversy would be settled in the (near) future, it was more than fifty years after the reform at Iona that the whole

[40] Bede, *Historia ecclesiastica* V 22 (Colgrave and Mynors (1969), 553–5).

[41] Aldhelm, *Epistola* IV (ed. by Rudolf Ehwald in MGH Auct. ant. 15, 480–6, here especially 483; trans. by Lapidge and Herren (1979), 157).

[42] Bede, *Historia ecclesiastica* V 23 (Colgrave and Mynors (1969), 560–1).

Briton church accepted the Dionysiac table (AD 768).[43] In his *Historia ecclesiastica*, Bede tries to demonstrate the steady 'progress' in the Easter question from the late 6th to the early 8th centuries: first, the Anglo-Saxons escaped from 'error', then the Irish and the Picts followed suit, and finally it was the turn of the Britons to accept Roman customs, which they had not done at his time of writing. But Bede's narrative is obviously over-simplified for this very purpose.[44] Did all Anglo-Saxons and all ecclesiasts in Ireland abandon the traditional custom right after the Synod of Whitby and following Adomnán's instructions respectively, as Bede wants to make us believe?[45] From Bede's account it can be deduced that the Irish, whom he praises especially for their attitude to monasticism, had already abandoned the old way when the *Historia ecclesiastica* was written in AD 731. Certainly, they should have done so. But did all the Irish really abandon the 25 March equinox after AD 716? In his Letter to Wicthed, Bede is adamant that followers of Anatolius should accept 21 March as the vernal equinox. Bede's insistence on this issue stems from the fact that the 'real' addressees were aware of the problem in Ceolfrith's letter.

It is highly likely that Bede was in the process of writing the *Historia ecclesiastica* when he composed the Letter to Wicthed. The reference to the Irish and Picts as 'followers of Anatolius' in the *Historia eccelsiastica*,[46] the list of his writings (the collection of letters) at the end of this work, and the Letter to Wicthed itself are all interconnected by their underlying theme of providing additional data for the unsatisfactory reference to the vernal equinox in Ceolfrith's letter. With this evidence, we may now suppose that the 'real' addressees of Bede's Letter to Wicthed were the Irish expelled by Nechtan. There remains, however, another possibility. As the letter of Aldhelm reveals, the Britons knew the Anatolian text(s), and the Irish 'exiles' may have found exile among them. In that case, the Britons may have been instructed by those Irish

[43] *Annales Cambriae s.a.* 768 (ed. and trans. by Morris (1980), 47, 88): *Pasca commutatur apud Brittones super dominicam diem emendante Elbodugo homine Dei.* ('Easter is changed among the Britons on the Lord's day, Elfoddw, servant of God, emending it.')

[44] In his *Historia ecclesiastica*, Bede omits all references to the use of the Victorian table in Britain; Ohashi (2011), 137–49.

[45] Bede, *Historia ecclesiastica* III 25, V 15 (Colgrave and Mynors (1969), 306–9, 506–7).

[46] Bede, *Historia ecclesiastica* III 3 (Colgrave and Mynors (1969), 218–9).

'exiles' and this could have caused the delay in the introduction of the Dionysiac table among the Welsh.

Bibliography

Colgrave, B. and R.A.B. Mynors (1969) *Bede's Ecclesiastical history of the English people*, Oxford.

Corning, C. (2006) *The Celtic and Roman traditions: conflict and consensus in the early medieval church*, New York.

Holford-Strevens, L. (2008) 'Paschal lunar calendars up to Bede,' *Peritia* 20, 165–208.

Krusch, B. (1938) 'Studien zur christlich-mittelalterlichen Chronologie. Die Entstehung unserer heutigen Zeitrechnung,' *Abhandlungen der Preußischen Akademie der Wissenschaften, Jahrgang 1937, phil.-hist. Klasse, Nr. 8*, Berlin.

Lapidge, M. and M. Herren (1979) *Aldhelm: the prose works*, Cambridge.

Mac Airt, S. and G. Mac Niocaill (1983) *The Annals of Ulster (to A.D. 1131)*, Dublin.

Mc Carthy, D.P. (1993) 'Easter principles and a fifth-century lunar cycle used in the British Isles,' *Journal for the History of Astronomy* 24, 204–24.

— (2011) 'On the arrival of the *Latercus* in Ireland,' in I. Warntjes and D. Ó Cróinín, *The Easter controversy of Late Antiquity and the early Middle Ages*, Turnhout, 48–75.

Mc Carthy, D.P. and A. Breen (2003) *The ante-Nicene Christian Pasch: De ratione paschali, the paschal tract of Anatolius, bishop of Laodicea*, Dublin.

Mc Carthy, D.P. and D. Ó Cróinín (1987–8) 'The 'lost' Irish 84-year Easter table rediscovered,' *Peritia* 6–7, 227–42.

Morris, J. (1980) *Nennius: British history and the Welsh annals*, London.

Mosshammer, A.A. (2008) *The Easter computus and the origins of the Christian era*, Oxford.

Nothaft, C.P.E. (2012) *Dating the passion: the life of Jesus and the emergence of scientific chronology (200–1600)*, Leiden.

Ohashi, M. (1999) 'Victor of Capua, De aequinoctio—Criticism of the identification of the work quoted in Bede's Letter to Wicthed by C.W. Jones,' *Journal of the History of Christianity* 53, 123–36 (in Japanese).

— (2011), 'The Easter table of Victorius of Aquitaine in early medieval England,' in I. Warntjes and D. Ó Cróinín, *The Easter controversy of Late Antiquity and the early Middle Ages: its manuscripts, texts, and tables*, Turnhout, 137–49.

Pitra, J.-P. (1852–8) *Spicilegium Solesmense: complectens sanctorum partum scriptorumque ecclesiasticorum anecdota hactenus opera selecta et Graecis orientalibusque et Latinis codicibus*, 4 vols., Paris.

Plummer, C. (1896) *Venerabilis Baedae opera historica*, 2 vols., Oxford.

Sharpe, R. (1997–2001), *A hand list of the Latin writers of Great Britain and Ireland before 1540*, 2 vols., Turnhout.

Stancliffe, C. (2013) 'Dating Wilfrid's death and Stephen's Life,' in N.J. Higham, *Wilfrid: abbot, bishop, saint*, Donington, 17–26.

Walker, G.S.M. (1957) *Sancti Columbani opera*, Dublin.

Wallis, F. (1999) *Bede: The reckoning of time*, Liverpool.

Warntjes, I. (2007) 'The Munich Computus and the 84 (14)-year Easter reckoning,' PRIA 107C, 31–85.

— (2010) *The Munich Computus: text and translation. Irish computistics between Isidore of Seville and the Venerable Bede*, Stuttgart.

CONTACTS I:

IRELAND IN THE INSULAR WORLD

COLIN IRELAND

SOME IRISH CHARACTERISTICS OF THE WHITBY LIFE OF GREGORY THE GREAT[1]

Abstract

The anonymous *Vita Gregorii* produced at Whitby is among the earliest of the hagiographical works to come from Anglo-Saxon England. It is the first *vita* written of Pope Gregory the Great. The traditional dates for its production are between AD 704 and 714. It relates Gregory's works and emphasizes his role as originator of the Christian mission to the Anglo-Saxons centred at Canterbury. In terms of Anglo-Saxon matters it highlights the conversion of King Edwin of Northumbria by Bishop Paulinus. In so doing it avoids mention of the successful Irish mission in Northumbria from Iona, the famous 'synod' that was held in AD 664 at Whitby and, by extension, Bishop Wilfrid and his 'Roman' legacy. It has been described as one of the most 'idiosyncratic' of the Anglo-Saxon *vitae* with 'numerous (and spurious) miracles involving the great pope'. Despite its emphasis on the contribution of Rome and Pope Gregory to the conversion of Anglo-Saxons generally, and Northumbria specifically, many of the *vita*'s episodes and their *topoi* are more typical of Irish hagiography and reveal the Whitby hagiographer's debt to Irish learning and teaching. This paper will examine some of those Irish narrative features.

Keywords

Emperor Trajan, Pope Gregory the Great, anonymous Whitby hagiographer, Abbess Ælfflæd, Eanflæd, King Ælle, King Edwin of Northumbria, Bishop Paulinus, Cuimméne Ailbe, Laidcenn *sapiens*, Ailerán *sapiens*, Theodore, Aldhelm, Willibrord; Deira, Angli; *Vita Gregorii*, Bede's *Historia Ecclesiastica*, Cummian's letter *De controversia paschali*, *Liber de ordine creaturarum*;

[1] I am pleased to contribute this essay to a *Festschrift* honouring Prof. Dáibhí Ó Cróinín who has done so much to encourage cross-cultural research in the early medieval world. I thank Professors Mary Clayton, David Howlett, Pádraig Ó Riain, Jean-Michel Picard, the editors of this volume, and others named in footnotes for their helpful suggestions. I alone am responsible for any shortcomings or errors.

Early medieval Ireland and Europe: chronology, contacts, scholarship, ed. by Pádraic Moran and Immo Warntjes, Studia Traditionis Theologiae, 14 (Turnhout, 2015), pp. 139–78.

 10.1484/M.STT-EB.5.103119

Adomnán's *Vita Columbae* and *De Locis Sanctis*, Tírechán's *Collectanea*, Muirchú's *Vita Patricii*, Infancy Gospel of Thomas; Irish penitential literature; 'etymological narrative', *naturale bonum*, cursing, 'Golden Mouth', 'secret watcher', 'doctor of souls', 'whipped in a dream'.

Introduction

The first Life of Gregory the Great, *Vita Gregorii*, was written by an anonymous member of the monastic community of Whitby sometime in the early 8th century. The English had every reason to celebrate this important pope who was responsible for sending the papal mission to the English which was established at Canterbury in Kent in AD 597.[2] It is appropriate that an Anglo-Saxon should commemorate one of the most famous popes and Church Fathers but surprising, perhaps, that it should be a Northumbrian rather than someone from further south.

The consensus on its time of composition has not changed from the original assessment of its editor and translator, Bertram Colgrave, who argued for a timeframe between AD 704 and 714,[3] that is, during the latter years of the abbacy of Ælfflæd. The author, based on internal evidence, was English, a Northumbrian, and a member of the double monastery at Whitby.[4] No specific identification has ever been proposed for the author and so I refer to our hagiographer as 'Anonymous'. Abbess Ælfflæd (AD 680–714) is one of the few Anglo-Saxon women from whom a written document has survived.[5] Several scholars have hinted at the possibility that our anonymous author could have been a woman.[6]

[2] For a good discussion of relationships between the papacy and the Anglo-Saxons in the wider context of insular Christianity, see Ortenberg (1999), 31–42.

[3] Colgrave (1968), 48. The editor had written an article previous to the edition that contains much of the same information as is found in the introduction: Colgrave (1963).

[4] Colgrave (1968), 45–6.

[5] She wrote a letter *c.*AD 700 to the abbess of Pfalzel near Treves commending a friend. The editor (Colgrave (1968), 40) states that 'her Latin style is somewhat florid and not altogether unlike the style of Aldhelm'; see also Fell (1981), 95.

[6] See, for example, Hollis (1992), 126, but see also chapter 8 of her book (pp. 243–70), 'Rewriting Female Lives: Hild of Whitby and Monastic Women in Bede's *Ecclesiastical History*'. Andrew Breeze (2012) developed this theme most elaborately. He named several critics who hinted at the possibility of a female author and listed several features that he felt suggest female preoccupations: 1) emphasis on identifying and naming Gregory's mother Sylvia; 2) concentration on the physical appearance of the Anglian youths in Rome; 3) emphasis in the Life on Abbess Ælfflæd and her mother

This is, potentially, an important topic but I will not investigate it further in the present paper.

The author's Latin style has been criticized as being 'crabbed, awkward, and ungrammatical even by contemporary standards'.[7] Colgrave noted that the writing lacks the florid qualities of Aldhelm's elaborate style[8] and remarked that 'it would seem that little rhetoric was taught at Whitby in the writer's time'.[9] The Life is not based in form and style on previous lives. For example, it has no dedication which adds to difficulties in identifying its dating and provenance, nor does the author indulge in the typical humility *topos* of writers of hagiography.[10]

While the Life reveals for the first time a great deal about Pope Gregory (AD 590–604), roughly half of the text is taken up with matters concerning King Edwin of Northumbria (AD 616–633), the retrieval of his remains from Hatfield Chase and their translation to Whitby, and his conversion in AD 626/7 by Bishop Paulinus of the Gregorian mission. The identifiable written sources used by the Anonymous are limited in their scope and include a liberal use of the Bible; the writings of Pope Gregory, including the Dialogues, the homilies on Ezekiel and the Gospels, *Moralia in Iob*, and *Regula Pastoralis*; and, to a much lesser extent, the *Liber Pontificalis* and letters of Jerome.[11]

Eanflæd; 4) the story of the woman who made communion bread and the fact that she is quoted; 5) the story of Trajan's concern for a wronged widow and the fact that she is quoted; 6) the story of a divorced woman. I thank Prof. Mary Clayton for directing me to these studies.

[7] Colgrave (1968), 55. David Howlett (1997), 135, agrees that the anonymous author has 'limited Latinity'. He demonstrates, nonetheless, that the Anonymous understood and practiced the biblical style of composition although without the skill and flourish of Aldhelm. The entire work is based on a chiastic structure, as are individual sections. Howlett (1997), 135, reminds us that we must not forget 'the inexperienced audience to which the work is addressed'.

[8] Aldhelm may have learned his Latin style from Máeldub, his Irish teacher as identified by William of Malmesbury; see Orchard (1994), 4–5. Aldhelm's first-hand knowledge of the 7th-century Hiberno-Latin hymn *Altus Prosator* helps demonstrate his familiarity with texts from Iona; see Orchard (1994), 54–60. Michael Lapidge (2010), 147–56, has argued that Aldhelm may have spent time at Iona during the AD 660s. David Howlett (forthcoming) has also argued that Aldhelm knew *Altus Prosator* and may have studied at Iona.

[9] Colgrave (1968), 55.

[10] Contrast, for example, how the earlier anonymous Life of St Cuthbert relied on continental models, especially for the prologue; see Colgrave (1940), 11, 310.

[11] Colgrave (1968), 50–4 and Appendix 168–72. The evidence of the Life cannot be used to argue for a substantial, well-stocked library at Whitby. Subsequent research into the sources of the *Vita Gregorii* have added some continental sources and deleted

Because of the limited identifiable written sources, and due to the unusual characteristics of several of the episodes in the Life, many critics accept that the Anonymous drew heavily on hitherto unidentified oral sources.[12] It is certainly true that many episodes in the *Vita Gregorii* have no parallels in either other Anglo-Latin or continental saints' lives. In fact, Michael Lapidge has characterized the Life as follows:[13] 'This is one of the most idiosyncratic and engaging of all the Anglo-Latin *vitae*, and contains a version of the famous story of Gregory and the English slave boys, as well as numerous (and spurious) miracles involving the great pope.'

It is precisely the idiosyncratic nature of this text that I wish to address in this essay. Many of the unusual episodes in the *Vita Gregorii* have parallels or similarities in 7th-century Irish texts, both in Latin and in Old Irish, that support the notion that the Anonymous worked in a cultural environment heavily imbued with Irish influence. Three of the 7th-century Irish texts from which I will draw examples, Tírechán's *Collectanea* on Patrick, Muirchú's *Vita Patricii*, and Adomnán's *Vita Columbae*, are themselves hagiography. Other Hiberno-Latin texts such as letters by St Columbanus, Cummian's letter *De controversia paschali*, the anonymous *Liber de ordine creaturarum*, and texts by named Irish *sapientes*, can be firmly dated in the 7th century. Some texts cannot be firmly dated, but an estimation of *c.* AD 700 is accepted for them. I have drawn some examples from 8th-century texts, but have kept these to as few as possible.

This Irish influence may have continued to inhere in the ethos of the monastery of Whitby itself, as we know that Abbess Hild and her community supported the Irish at the 'Synod' of Whitby in AD 664.[14] Irish influence may have included the presence at Whitby of Irish members

others. For example, it is now argued that the Anonymous cited once each from Athanasius' Life of Anthony and from Sulpicius Severus' Life of Martin of Tours, but may not have used the *Liber Pontificalis*; see *Fontes Anglo-Saxonici* (http://fontes.english.ox.ac.uk).

[12] In chapter 30 (Colgrave (1968), 130–3), the Anonymous admits that information gathered about Gregory could not come from eye witness reports, or from those who would have heard directly from eye witnesses.

[13] Lapidge (1986), 15.

[14] At the 'Synod' of Whitby in AD 664, Bede noted that Abbess Hild and her community supported the Irish rather than Wilfrid's faction; Bede, *Historia ecclesiastica* III 25 (Colgrave and Mynors (1969), 298): *Hild abbatissa cum suis in parte Scottorum*.

of the community who left no written records,[15] or it may have been absorbed by the anonymous author after a sojourn *in regionibus Scottorum*.[16] I do not present this essay as an example of the source study that can be applied so successfully to most Anglo-Latin or Old English religious texts. But rather, I argue that many of the idiosyncratic features and episodes in *Vita Gregorii* can be explained as the absorption of Irish characteristics and *topoi* by the anonymous author through either oral or literary transmission.

'Golden Mouth'

The application of the term 'Golden Mouth' to Pope Gregory by the anonymous Whitby hagiographer is the first recorded example of it among the English. The term was apparently first applied to John Chrysostom (*c.*AD 347–407) and then, by the fifth century, used by the Greeks to describe favourite orators generally.[17] 'Golden Mouth' is used

[15] Bede provides several examples of Irishmen working at various locations throughout Anglo-Saxon England for whom no other records survive. During the time of Bishop Felix, Fursa and his Irish companions Fáelán, Gobbán, Dícuill, and Ultán, were present in East Anglia; Bede, *Historia ecclesiastica* III 19 (Colgrave and Mynors (1969), 274–7). In the land of the South Saxons an Irishman named Dícuill and five or six brothers had worked at a place called Bosham to convert the pagans previous to Bishop Wilfrid's arrival there; Bede, *Historia ecclesiastica* IV 13 (Colgrave and Mynors (1969), 372–3). For the Irish in Bede's HE, see the unpublished Galway Ph.D. thesis by Sarah McCann.

[16] Both Aldhelm and Bede provide examples of English students who studied in Ireland. Aldhelm corresponded with Wihtfrith and Heahfrith who each spent time in Ireland; Aldhelm, *Epistolae* 3, 5 (ed. by Rudolf Ehwald in MGH Auct. ant. 15, 479–80 (Wihtfrith), 486–94 (Heahfrith)); for discussion and translation see Lapidge and Herren (1979), 139–40, 154–5 (Wihtfrith); 143–6, 160–4 (Heahfrith). Bede (*Historia ecclesiastica* IV 4 (Colgrave and Mynors (1969), 346–9)) tells of the thirty English monks who accompanied Bishop Colmán back to Ireland after the 'Synod' of Whitby, and the English of all social levels who came to Ireland during the bishoprics of Fínán and Colmán (*Historia ecclesiastica* III 27 (Colgrave and Mynors (1969), 312–3)), and of the many English who studied at Ráith Melsigi such as Willibrord between AD 678–690 (*Historia ecclesiastica* V 10–11 (Colgrave and Mynors (1969), 480–1, 484–7)), Ecgberht for most of his adult life (*Historia ecclesiastica* III 27, V 9 (Colgrave and Mynors (1969), 312–5, 474–9)), Wihtberht (*Historia ecclesiastica* V 9 (Colgrave and Mynors (1969), 478–81)), Black and White Hewald (*Historia ecclesiastica* V 10 (Colgrave and Mynors (1969), 480–3)), Æthelhun and Æthelwine (the latter became bishop at Lindsey; *Historia ecclesiastica* III 27 (Colgrave and Mynors (1969), 312–5)), Chad (who became fifth bishop of Mercia; *Historia ecclesiastica* IV 3 (Colgrave and Mynors (1969), 336–47)), and many more.

[17] Colgrave (1968), 155 n 99; Walsh and Ó Cróinín (1988), 82–3 notes to line 190.

as an epithet in the *Vita Gregorii* because of the elegance, skill, and wisdom of Gregory's writing especially, according to the Anonymous, his Homilies. In chapter 24 the author states 'therefore he was called the 'golden-mouthed' by the Romans'.[18] However, it was not the Romans who first applied the term to Gregory, although a Romanizing Northumbrian might wish to have had them do so. Inaccurate statements of this kind have lead commentators to note the shortcomings in the formal training and learned style of the anonymous author.

The first recorded example of 'Golden Mouth' being used to name Gregory comes from the Irish. Cummian's letter of *c.*AD 632, *De controversia paschali*, written to Abbot Ségéne of Iona and a certain hermit named Beccán, defended the 'orthodox' methods of paschal reckoning favoured by Rome after discussing 'no fewer than ten such cycles by name'[19] and, by implication, argued against Iona's continued use of the 84-year paschal cycle.[20] In the context of this *Romani* position, Cummian states:[21] 'What more? I turned to the words of Pope Gregory, bishop of the city of Rome, accepted by all of us and given the name 'Golden Mouth', for although he wrote after everyone, nevertheless he is deservedly to be preferred to all.' It should be noted that Gregory is mentioned by Cummian as pope and bishop of Rome, 'accepted by all of us' and, although most recent of the Church Fathers, 'he is deservedly to be preferred to all'. These statements leave no doubt of the esteem accorded Pope Gregory from an early date by the Irish *Romani*.[22]

The English, as already noted, honoured Pope Gregory because he established the mission from Rome to the Anglo-Saxon kingdoms. Critics argue that the 'cult' of Gregory among the Anglo-Saxons began early and gained strength. Bede, in his *Historia ecclesiastica*, records Gregory's

[18] Anonymous *Vita Gregorii* 24 (Colgrave (1968), 116–9 and 155 n 99): *ut a gente Romana* [...] *os aureum appellatur.*

[19] Walsh and Cróinín (1988), 16.

[20] Of the three persons named in the letter only Ségéne, fifth abbot of Iona, AD 623–652, can be firmly identified. Both Beccán and Cummian (Cuimmíne/Cuimméne) have various possible identities. The most likely identity for Cummian is Cuimmíne Fota *sapiens* (†AD 662) of Clonfert (Cluain Ferta Brénnain), Co. Galway; see Walsh and Ó Cróinín (1988), 12–5. For a sense of Cummian's skill in Latin writing, see Howlett (1995), 91–102. For more on Cuimmíne Fota, see Ireland (1996), 65–7.

[21] Cummian, *De controversia paschali* ll. 190–2 (Walsh and Ó Cróinín (1988), 82–3): *Quid plura? Ad Gregorii papae urbis Romae epi<scopi, a nobis in>commune suscepti et oris aurei appellationi donati, uerba <me> conuerti. Qui etsi post omnes scripsit, tamen est merito omnibus preferendus.*

[22] Ó Néill (1984), 287.

correspondence with Bishop Augustine and Abbot Mellitus of Canterbury and with King Æthelberht of Kent.[23] Colgrave noted that at least three churches, Canterbury, York, and Whitby, had altars dedicated to Gregory by Bede's time.[24] After the decision at the 'Synod' of Whitby in AD 664 King Oswiu of Northumbria and King Ecgberht of Kent wrote to the pope requesting an archbishop for Canterbury. Pope Vitalian wrote back (*c.*AD 668) to King Oswiu and praised him for his efforts in bringing the faith to his subjects and sent relics of the saints, including some of Gregory's.[25] When Theodore and Hadrian arrived at Canterbury as a result of King Oswiu's request to the pope, Theodore set about cultivating a cult of Gregory according to Alan Thacker.[26] Aldhelm, in his *De Virginitate*, would be the first known Anglo-Saxon scholar to recognize the special role of Gregory for the English.[27] On the Continent, *c.*AD 700, two Gregorian feasts are entered in Willibrord's Calendar, commemorating his deposition and *ordinatio*.[28] But we must not lose sight of the Irish training and learning in the backgrounds of these last two named Anglo-Saxon ecclesiasts. As the 8th century progressed the 'cult' of St Gregory grew stronger among the Anglo-Saxons.[29]

What can be said of the establishment of an English 'cult' of Pope Gregory the Great in the 7th century must be compared with the recognition and appreciation by Irish scholars and clerics of the great pope

23 Bede, *Historia ecclesiastica* I 27, 29–32 (Colgrave and Mynors (1969), 78–103, 104–15). The Anonymous seems unaware of these Gregorian letters that Bede is able to quote only a few decades later, relying on the authority and help of Abbot Albinus of Canterbury, educated by Theodore and Hadrian, and on the priest Nothhelm, who searched the archives in Rome and acted as intermediary between Bede and Albinus (Bede, *Historia ecclesiastica* praefatio (Colgrave and Mynors (1969), 2–5)).

24 Colgrave (1968), 19, 44.

25 Bede, *Historia ecclesiastica* III 29 (Colgrave and Mynors (1969), 320–1).

26 Thacker (1998), 75. Against this claim it should be noted how little of Gregory's writings figure in biblical commentaries generated at the school run by Theodore and Hadrian; see Bischoff and Lapidge (1994).

27 Aldhelm, *De virginitate* (ed. by Rudolf Ehwald in MGH Auct. ant. 15, 314, 322); for discussion and translation see Lapidge and Herren (1979), 70, 108, 125, 131; Thacker (1998), 76.

28 Wilson (1918), fol. 35b, 5, 23–4, 26 (March 12, deposition; March 29, ordination); Thacker (1998), 77–8.

29 See, for example, Meyvaert (1964). Michael Richter (1984), 99–114, has argued that Bede adopted the word *Angli* as a general designation for the English from Pope Gregory. Erin Thomas A. Dailey (2010), 195–207, has argued that one of the purposes of the Anonymous was to create the notion of a *gens Anglorum* unified through baptism and the church.

in that same century.[30] The earliest example we have of the recognition of Pope Gregory by an Irish scholar is the letter of Columbanus to Gregory himself, written probably *c.*AD 603. Columbanus argued that if Gregory were to prefer the Easter calculation methods of Victorius of Aquitaine then he must oppose Jerome who favoured Anatolius, and 'anyone impugning the authority of St. Jerome will be a heretic or reprobate in the eyes of the Western Churches'.[31] Although Columbanus addresses Gregory as 'the fairest Ornament of the Roman Church',[32] it is clear that he is not afraid to challenge him, as bishop of Rome, with a contrary opinion.[33] At the same time Columbanus praises Gregory's *Regula Pastoralis*, which he has read, and requests a copy of the Homilies on Ezekiel.[34] A few decades later we have the reference of Cummian *c.*AD 632, cited above, to Pope Gregory as 'Golden Mouth'. Cummian's respectful tone makes it clear that Gregory's prestige had grown substantially among the Irish *Romani*.[35] One of the texts attributed to the *sapiens* Laidcenn mac Baíth Bannaig of Clonfert-Mulloe (Cluain Ferta Mo-lua), Co. Laois (†AD 661), is an epitome of Gregory's own *Moralia in Iob* and is referred to as *Egloga de moralibus in Iob*.[36] Another *sapiens*, Ailerán of Clonard (Cluain Iraird), Co. Meath (†AD 665), wrote *Interpretatio mystica progenitorum Domini Iesu Christi*.[37] The most recent editor, Aidan Breen, has shown that Gregory is an important source for Ailerán.[38] The editor of the anonymous 7th-century Irish text *Liber de ordine creaturarum* (*c.*AD 680) also argues that Gregory's writings

30 I wish to thank Dr Anthony Harvey for his assistance in helping me identify references to Gregory through the Archive of Celtic-Latin Literature.

31 Columbanus, *Epistola* I 5 (Walker (1957), 8–9): *quod contra sancti Hieronymi auctoritatem veniens apud occidentis ecclesias hereticus seu respuendus erit*. For an exposition of Columbanus' Latin style, see Howlett (1995), 82–91.

32 Columbanus, *Epistola* I 1 (Walker (1957), 2–3): *Romanae pulcherrimo Ecclesiae Decori*.

33 In the Anonymous's *Vita Gregorii* 28 (Colgrave (1968), 124–5, 159–61 n 120) we are given an anecdote where Gregory champions Jerome over a previous pope. See the discussion in Sims-Williams (1990), 188–9.

34 Columbanus, *Epistola* I 9 (Walker (1957), 10–1).

35 Pádraig Ó Néill (1984), 287 *et passim*, argued this point in greater detail.

36 Kenney (1929), 278–9 (§106); Lapidge and Sharpe (1985), 80 (§293). See also, Ireland (1996), 64–5 and David Ganz's article in the present volume.

37 Kenney (1929), 279–80 (§107); Lapidge and Sharpe (1985), 82 (§299); Ireland (1996), 67.

38 Breen (1995), 111, 160–1, 178.

are an important source.[39] The works of Gregory were known in the 7th century at the monastery of Iona, from which so much of Northumbria was successfully evangelized.[40] Adomnán, ninth abbot of Iona (AD 679–704), used Gregory's Dialogues as a source in both the *Vita Columbae*[41] and *De locis sanctis*[42], the latter came to be known throughout Northumbria through the efforts of King Aldfrith.[43] Gregory's *Homilia in Evangelia* are cited in vernacular, or mixed Latin and Old Irish, texts like the Cambrai Homily (*c.*AD 700).[44] As in Anglo-Saxon England, Gregory's importance grew in Ireland after the 7th century and can be seen in 8th-century hagiography and such works as the *Collectio canonum hibernensis* (*c.*AD 725).[45]

Etymological narratives

One of the most frequently discussed episodes in the Whitby Life is the story of the English youths in Rome who are noticed by Gregory and become the focus of his desire to evangelize the English. The narrative evolves based on etymological play on the words for the race of Angles, their King Ælle, and his kingdom Deira.[46] This story is elaborated by Bede and critics tend to interpret their differing versions as products of

[39] Díaz y Díaz (1972), 34–5, 140–1, 188–9; Lapidge and Sharpe (1985), 98 (§342). Marina Smyth (2003–4) has argued that this treatise was written in Ireland between AD 655 and 680 and she has shown that Bede knew the work. For an English translation, see Smyth (2011).

[40] Clancy and Márkus (1995), 219; Charles-Edwards (2010); Ritari (2010); Sharman (2010).

[41] Herbert (1988), 137; Anderson and Anderson (1991), lxviii; O'Loughlin (1994), 41; Charles-Edwards (2010), 208–9, 215–6; Ritari (2010), 279–81; Sharman (2010), 292–4.

[42] O'Loughlin (1994), 41.

[43] Bede, *Historia ecclesiastica* V 15 (Colgrave and Mynors (1969), 504–9).

[44] Ó Néill (1981), 139–40; Herbert (2011), 182.

[45] For 8th-century hagiography, see Herbert (2011); for the *Collectio*, see Davies (2002).

[46] Howlett (1997), 144, pointed out the Anonymous's 'fondness for puns' and notes some examples of his word play. 'Etymology' is, in some ways, an inadequate term to describe these processes of medieval word play since modern philology and historical linguistics define a stricter, narrower range of meaning for the term. Early medieval scholars applied a metaphorical interpretation to words and phrases that manipulated the polysemy within a language, as well as across languages. It is this metaphorical interpretation based on the polysemic nature of language that we are dealing with here.

the oral tradition.[47] Variants within the narrative by the Anonymous appear to support the notion of oral transmission of the story. The Anonymous tells us of the English youths seen by Gregory that 'some say they were beautiful boys, while others say that they were curly-haired, handsome youths'.[48] When Gregory asked them what race they belonged to they answered, "The people we belong to are called Angles [*Anguli*].'— 'Angels [*Angeli*] of God', he [Gregory] replied. Then he asked further, 'What is the name of the king of that people?' They said, 'Ælli [Ælle]', whereupon he said, 'Alleluia, God's praise must be heard there'. Then he asked the name of their own tribe, to which they answered, 'Deire [Deira]', and he replied, 'They shall flee from the wrath [*de ira*] of God to the faith."[49] These exotic, fair-skinned people were, of course, Angles from Deira, the southern portion of Northumbria, and their king in the years before Gregory became pope was Ælle (*c.*AD 560–588/590). Gregory's meeting with the English youths struck him as a great opportunity and he determined to go on mission himself to the English but that was not to be. However, once he became pope, Gregory organized the papal mission to Anglo-Saxon England that was to send Augustine, Mellitus, and Laurentius to Canterbury.[50]

[47] Bede, *Historia ecclesiastica* II 1 (Colgrave and Mynors (1969), 132–5). The existence of multiforms, while acknowledged as typical of oral traditions, is not limited to them and can be found in literate societies. The editor of the anonymous Life (Colgrave (1968), 56–9) argued that Bede did not know the *Vita Gregorii* firsthand but it seems hard to credit that argument; see counter arguments in Richter (1984), 101–2. Bede almost certainly had firsthand knowledge of Whitby's traditions and texts since he had been ordained deacon (*c.*AD 692) and priest (*c.*AD 703) by John of Beverly (*Historia ecclesiastica* V 24 (Colgrave and Mynors (1969), 566–7)) who was one of five trained at Whitby who went on to hold bishoprics elsewhere in Anglo-Saxon England (*Historia ecclesiastica* IV 23 (Colgrave and Mynors (1969), 408–11)).

[48] Anonymous *Vita Gregorii* 9 (Colgrave (1968), 90–1): *Quos quidam pulchros fuisse pueros dicunt et quidam vero crispos iuvenes et decoros.*

[49] Anonymous *Vita Gregorii* 9 (Colgrave (1968), 90–1): *"Anguli dicuntur, illi de quibus sumus", ille dixit, "Angeli Dei." Deinde dixit, "Rex gentis illius, quomodo nominatur?" Et dixerunt, "Aelli." Et ille ait, "Alleluia. Laus enim Dei esse debet illic." Tribus quoque illius nomen de qua erant proprię requisivit. Et dixerunt, "Deirę." Et ille dixit, "De ira Dei confugientes ad fidem.* Other etymological plays on words are found in the anonymous *Vita Gregorii* 10, 12–14 (Colgrave (1968), 90–3, 94–7). Michael Richter (1984), 102, argues that this etymological narrative may well have originated with Gregory himself. The etymologizing of personal and place names has a long tradition in patristic and other church writings as, for example, in Jerome's *Liber interpretationis Hebraicorum nominum* (ed. by Paul de Lagarde in CCSL 72, 57–161) or in Ailerán's *Interpretatio mystica et moralis progenitorvm Domini Iesv Christi* (ed. by Breen (1995)).

[50] As pointed out by the editor (Colgrave (1968), 92–3, 146–7 n 50), the Anonymous does not seem to be aware, as Bede was, that there were two missions sent by

The Anonymous creates an 'etymological narrative' based on word play about Gregory's desire to depart Rome for Britain. Once Gregory had set his mind on evangelizing the English, he pleaded with the pope to be able to depart Rome and go on mission. The pope reluctantly granted him permission to go but the Romans themselves were distraught at the thought of losing Gregory and taunted the pope for allowing Gregory to leave. Although Gregory had already begun his journey, the pope sent an emissary to stop Gregory and bring him back to Rome. After a three day journey, through holy insight, Gregory stopped to rest in his travels. When a locust (*locusta*) alighted on him as he sat reading Gregory realized that it was a divine message telling him to 'stay in the place' (*sta in loco*).[51] Both the story about the English youths and the anecdote about Gregory stopping on his journey reflect types of 'etymological narratives' that can be found in the Irish tradition.

Word play with names and their meanings, for both personal and place names, has a long tradition in the Middle Ages and the Anglo-Saxons participated in both Latin and Old English language texts.[52] This is most frequently seen in word play based on the meanings of biblical names, but the Anglo-Saxons learned to apply this method in vernacular names as well, frequently giving explanations with exegetical purposes.[53] The Anonymous is interested in attempting exegetical word play with the names Angli, Ælle, and Edwin.[54]

Paronomasia of all kinds is common in the Irish literary tradition, in whatever language or period, and may involve word play such as parody, puns based on homonymy and synonymy, or philosophical, or

Gregory, the first (AD 597) including Augustine and Laurentius, and the second (AD 601) with Mellitus, accompanied by Laurentius who had returned to the Continent to report on progress and then came back as part of the second mission. Paulinus was part of this second mission; Bede, *Historia ecclesiastica* I 29 (Colgrave and Mynors (1969), 104–7).

51 Anonymous *Vita Gregorii* 10 (Colgrave (1968), 92–3). The editor (Colgrave (1968), 146 n 48) points out that the original phrase was probably *loco sta*, with *loco* being a locative. He uses this as another opportunity to criticize the Anonymous's Latinity.

52 See, for example, Robinson (1968a). I thank Prof. Mary Clayton for supplying me with a copy of this article. See also Robinson (1968b).

53 A good example is found in texts about St Guthlac; see Robinson (1968a), 43–50.

54 Anonymous *Vita Gregorii* 13–14 (Colgrave (1968), 94–7). However, David Howlett (1997), 145, says of the Anonymous that 'the meditations on the spiritual significance of the names Angli, Ælle, and Edwin in chapters 13 and 14 have little to commend them'.

interpretative, etymology.[55] Irish love of paronomasia helps explain the early reception of Isidore's *Etymologiae* in Ireland.[56] Etymological narrative plays a productive and frequent role in Irish literature and can be seen in Old and Middle Irish texts such as 'Cormac's Glossary' (*Sanas Cormaic*),[57] the metrical *Dindsenchas* ('Place Lore'),[58] and the 'Fitness of Names' (*Cóir Anmann*).[59] This short list points out only the obvious examples of Irish literary genres that employ etymologies to build narratives and is far from exhaustive. It disguises the frequency with which etymological narratives appear as episodes in all genres of early Irish literature. As Mark Scowcroft pointed out about Irish narratives: 'What is noteworthy [...] is the way words and names inspire *narrative* ideas in Ireland where Isidore and his followers would prefer analysis and exposition.'[60]

We find examples of the etymologizing of names in 7th-century Irish hagiography[61] that show how prevalent it was, and how it was seen as necessary to the full exposition of a person through names. At one level, in other words, it can follow Isidorean practice and emphasize 'analysis and exposition'. In the 2nd preface of the *Vita Columbae* Adomnán pointed out that Columba, father and founder of monasteries, had the same name as the prophet Jonah (*Iona*). And he notes that, although they are pronounced differently in the three languages, what is pronounced as *iona* in Hebrew, and *peristera* in Greek, is called *columba* in Latin and they all mean the same thing.[62] This multi-lingual exposition, of course, allows Adomnán to begin to indulge his sense of narrative and

55 Word play based on etymology has been common throughout European literary tradition. See, for example, Curtius (1953), 495–500 ('Etymology as a Category of Thought').

56 Hillgarth (1984).

57 Meyer (1912). For some helpful background, see Russell (1988); Russell (1996).

58 Gwynn (1903–35).

59 Arbuthnot (2005–7). Robinson (1968a), 39, pointed out the importance of this Irish text in support of his arguments.

60 Scowcroft (1995), 124. On pp. 124–30 of the same publication, he lists 'etymological narrative' as one of the most important types of abstract narrative in the early Irish literary tradition. For an insightful discussion of how early Irish glossators use paronomasia productively for the interpretation of texts, see Davies (1996), 13–9.

61 The 7th-century Irish *vitae* most frequently cited in the present study are: Adomnán's *Vita Columbae*, *c.*AD 688–704; Tírechán's *Collectanea* of Patrick, *c.*AD 670–693; and Muirchú's *Vita Patricii*, *c.*AD 680–695. I have given a broad time range for each work here, although it can be argued that recent consensus has been tending towards the later dates in each of these ranges.

62 Adomnán, *Vita Columbae* 2nd preface (Anderson and Anderson (1991), 2–5).

exegesis and he points out that a bird, in the form of a dove, descended upon the only son of the eternal Father and that a dove is understood to signify the Holy Spirit.[63]

In the hagiography of St Patrick both Tírechán and Muirchú cite the 'four names of Patrick', giving the meanings of the names and the circumstances under which Patrick was known by each name.[64] Both attribute their source to an earlier hagiographer, Bishop Ultán moccu Chonchobair (†*c.*AD 657) of Ard Breccáin in Co. Meath. There are minor differences in the accounts of Tírechán and Muirchú even though they claim to have the same source, but their pattern is to give each of the four names and its meaning. In both cases one of the names attributed to Patrick during his captivity in Ireland is Cothirthiacus 'because he served four households of druids; and one of them bought him, whose name was Milúch moccu Bóin, the druid, and he [Patrick] served him seven years'.[65] What is interesting here is that we can already see the core of an etymological narrative being formed in the way the name Cothirthiacus is presented to us. It is being etymologized, without explicitly saying so, as Old Irish *cethir* ('four') and *tech* ('house'). We can see the incipient narrative being developed that Patrick served four households of druids at some point in his captivity. One of those druids is explicitly named and, in a good example of intertextuality, occurs in other narratives about Patrick.[66]

In an article on what he calls 'creative' etymology in medieval Irish hagiography, Rolf Baumgarten argued for two instances in Adomnán's *Vita Columbae.*[67] The first example involves a visit by Columba to the monastery at Terryglass where the keys to the church are lost and the saint heard the murmuring of the embarrassed monks within.[68] When the saint approached the locked doors he declared that the Lord could open doors without keys for his servants and the locks were suddenly

[63] Adomnán, *Vita Columbae* 2nd preface (Anderson and Anderson (1991), 4–5).

[64] Mac Eoin (2002).

[65] Muirchú, *Vita Patricii* praefatio (Bieler (1979), 62–3): *quia seruiuit quattuor domibus magorum; et emit illum ab illis unus, cui nomen erat Milúch Mocuboin magus, et seruiuit illi septem annis.* Cf. Tírechán, *Collectanea* 3.1 (Bieler (1979), 124–5).

[66] The druid is Miliucc [Milúch] moccu Bóin and is named again in Muirchú's *Vita Patricii* I 11(10).2; I 11(10).7 and in Tírechán's *Collectanea* 16.6; 49.1 (Bieler (1979), 78–9 (Muirchú), 136–7, 162–3 (Tírechán)); cf. Howlet (2006), 62–5. The name occurs again in a 9th-century vernacular Life of Partrick; Mulchrone (1939), 9–13.

[67] Baumgarten (2004).

[68] Adomnán, *Vita Columbae* II 36 (Anderson and Anderson (1991), 146–9).

opened. The Irish name of the monastery is *Tír dá Glas* ('land of two streams') and is translated as such in the chapter heading (*ager duorum riuorum*) and in the text (*rus duorum riuulorum*). Baumgarten argues that the creative etymologizing is found in the Irish form of the name because *glas*, in addition to meaning 'stream', also means 'lock; bolt', and it is the second meaning that is being played on in this narrative.[69]

In the second example by Adomnán, a monk named Lugaid Laithir (*Lugaidus Laitirus*) was to sail from Iona to Ireland using one of the saint's ships.[70] He found on the ship a milk-skin (*uter lactarius*) which he placed in the sea under large stones to soften. When he told Columba his plans, the saint informed him that the skin would be missing because he knew that the tide would carry it away, but it would also bring it back. Lugaid had to make his journey without the milk-skin, but the tide returned the milk-skin to its owner as the saint had foreseen. Baumgarten argues that Latin *lactarius*, the Latinized cognomen *Laitirus*, its Irish form *Laithir*, and the Irish *lacht* ('milk') and Welsh *laith* ('milk') are the basis for another multilingual etymological narrative.[71]

A vernacular example of an etymological episode comes at the end of *Táin Bó Fraích* ('The Cattle Raid of Fróech'), a prose narrative of *c.*AD 700.[72] The latter part of the story tells how the hero Fróech had to go to the Continent with the Ulster hero Conall Cernach to retrieve special faerie cows that had been stolen from him. As they return to Ireland with the recaptured cattle, one of the party, Bicne mac Lóegaire, died thus giving his name to Inber mBicne ('Bicne's river mouth') at Bennchor (Bangor, Co. Down). The cattle are driven across the river mouth where it empties into the sea and then we have the strange line:[73] *Iss and ro·lásat a n-adarca díb, conid de atá Trácht mBennchoir* ('it is there they [the cattle] threw their horns from them, so that hence it is called the Strand of Bennchor [Bangor]'). This seeming *non-sequitur* in the narrative makes sense only as an etymological play on words. The verb *ro·lásat* is from the suppletive perfective form of the verb *fo·ceird* ('throws, casts'). Its verbal noun is *cor* ('act of throwing or casting'). *Adarc* is the usual word for animal horn, but *benn*, which normally means 'peak,

[69] Baumgarten (2004), 68–72.

[70] Adomnán, *Vita Columbae* II 38 (Anderson and Anderson (1991), 152–3).

[71] Baumgarten (2004), 72–3.

[72] The editor (Meid (1967), xxv) dated this text on linguistic data to between AD 700 and 750. James Carney (1955), 26–7, had argued for a wider range of dates, AD 680–775, based on internal evidence and philological data.

[73] *Táin Bó Fraích* ll. 382–3 (Meid (1967), 16).

summit, point', can also refer to an animal's horns. So the redactor has etymologized Bennchor as '(the place of) horn throwing'. It would appear that a monk from Bangor, a monastery famed for producing both Latin and vernacular literature, has found a way to work his foundation into the narrative.

These examples from 7th-century Irish hagiography and from Old Irish prose narratives show that 'etymological narrative' was an active part of the literary culture *in regionibus Scottorum* and in the insular world that came under their influence. It is most logical to look to the Irish to understand where the Anonymous learned the tradition.

Baptizing (virtuous) pagans

One of the most famous episodes from the anonymous *Vita Gregorii* is the baptism of the soul of the long dead Roman Emperor Trajan (AD 98–117) by the tears of Gregory.[74] One day while crossing the Forum Gregory learned of a deed performed by Emperor Trajan that struck him as more like the deed of a Christian than a pagan. As Trajan was leading his army in haste out of the city, a widow approached him and asked him to help her get recompense from the men who had killed her son. Trajan promised to look into the matter when he returned from dealing with the enemy, but the widow implored him again, reminding him that he might not return from battle. So Trajan made the guilty men compensate the widow for her son's death then and there. The story reminded Gregory of the words of the Bible: 'Judge the fatherless, plead for the widow. Come now and let us reason together, saith the Lord.'[75] Gregory was so impressed with this story about Trajan that 'he went to St. Peter's Church and wept floods of tears, as was his custom, until he gained at last by divine revelation the assurance that his prayers were answered, seeing that he had never presumed to ask this for any other pagan'.[76]

[74] Anonymous *Vita Gregorii* 29 (Colgrave (1968), 126–7): *sancti Gregorii lacrimis animam Traiani imperatoris refrigeratam vel baptizatam*. For a discussion of 'baptism by tears' among the Anglo-Saxons, see O'Loughlin and Conrad-O'Briain (1993).

[75] Is 1:17–18. The Anonymous subsequently refers to this quote from Isaiah as the 'words of Christ' (*Christum loquentum*). Since Isaiah is a major prophet it can be interpreted that he foreshadows Christ, but Christ is not the immediate source of the quote.

[76] Anonymous *Vita Gregorii* 29 (Colgrave (1968), 128–9): *ingrediens ad sanctum Petrum solita direxit lacrimarum fluenta usque dum promeruit sibi divinitus revelatum fuisse exauditum, atque ut numquam de altero illud presumpsisset pagano.*

This story in this interesting chapter has two aspects that deserve discussion. The first is how important baptism is to the practice of the early church, and the second is the appropriateness and desirability of baptizing worthy pagans, in some cases, even retrospectively.[77]

The Anonymous stated earlier in the chapter 'for without baptism none will ever see God'.[78] Yet this anecdote makes it clear that other fluids, rather than only holy water from the baptismal font, can be effective in baptism. The editor, in a footnote, discusses other possible fluids, such as tears or blood, that can be substituted in appropriate circumstances.[79] He noted a famous instance, cited by Bede, from the history of Roman Britain in which a soldier who refused to execute Britain's first martyr, St Alban, was himself beheaded along with the saint and was said to have been baptized by his own blood and rewarded with heaven.[80]

There are also examples of baptism by blood from 8th-century Old Irish vernacular texts that suggest that such traditions may have been extant in 7th-century Ireland, although I have not been able to identify specific 7th-century examples. In the vernacular poems by Blathmac mac Con Brettan, which are dated to *c.*AD 750–770 by their editor, Christ's blood, when he is crucified, is said to have baptized both Adam, whose head was buried beneath the place where the cross was planted, and the soldier who pierced Christ's side with the lance.[81] The tradition of apocryphal literature is much richer in early Ireland than among the Anglo-Saxons and helps account for the existence of some unorthodox episodes in a wide variety of Irish narratives.[82]

[77] For a discussion of the importance of baptism to an early Irish hagiographer, see O'Loughlin (2002). For the importance of baptism in the early Middle Ages, see Angenendt (1984); for retrospective baptism in both continental and insular contexts, see also Rob Meens's article in this volume.

[78] Anonymous *Vita Gregorii* 29 (Colgrave (1968), 126–7): *nemo enim sine babtismo Deum videbit umquam.*

[79] Colgrave (1968), 163 n 123.

[80] Bede, *Historia ecclesiastica* I 7 (Colgrave and Mynors (1969), 34–5). Bede attributes Venantius Fortunatus (†*c.*AD 600–609), bishop of Poitiers, as his source for the St Alban story.

[81] Carney (1964), xiv (for dating), §§56–8 (for baptism by blood), 123 notes to lines 227–8 (for tradition that Adam's head had been buried in the exact spot where the crucifixion took place). For a translation of a text that deals with this tradition of Adam's remains and their burial, see Herbert and McNamara (1989), 16 (§§51–3).

[82] For a brief discussion of apocrypha in Ireland from the 7th through the 9th centuries, see McNamara (1975), 7–9; for a poem on Adam's head of the 10th or 11th century, McNamara (1975), 23 (§5); and for an apocryphal work about Longinus,

There is a highly stylized poem, referred to as a *retoiric*, of the early 8th century, if not earlier, that portrays the Ulster hero, King Conchobar, lamenting the fact that he was not present at the crucifixion to protect and fight for Christ. As the editor notes in his commentary: 'The poem describes Conchobar's conversion from being a pagan king, who would resort instinctively to the force of the sword, to being a Christian believer.'[83] The events of the Ulster Cycle of heroic tales dealing with King Conchobar, Cú Chulainn, and the heroes of the *Cráeb Ruad* ('Red Branch'), are typically portrayed as taking place at the time of Christ.[84] Later prose narratives, one containing the *retoiric*, describe Conchobar as flying into a rage upon learning of Christ's crucifixion and dying when an old wound reopens. The blood from his re-opened wound is said to baptize Conchobar as he dies.[85]

At least one example of an unusual baptism comes from 7th-century Ireland. In Tírechán's *Collectanea*, an episode relates that as Patrick was passing through a certain area a sick woman who was pregnant was brought to him and he baptized the woman's son in her womb and 'the woman's liquid served as the son's baptismal water'.[86] The woman was buried at a nearby church.

Tírechán also provides a rather startling example of the conversion and baptism of a long dead pagan. While travelling in Ulster, apparently in Co. Tyrone, Patrick and his companions came across a huge grave and his companions told Patrick that they did not believe anyone could be so large. Patrick told his companions that they could see who occupied the grave if they wanted, and they agreed that they wished to see. Patrick implored the Lord to open the grave and a huge man arose from the grave and said to Patrick: "Thanks be to you, o holy man, that you have raised me even for one hour from many pains"[87] and he wept and asked to accompany Patrick and his companions. Patrick refused his request

McNamara (1975), 81 (§69). For a discussion of apocryphal material that applies to hagiography used in this essay, see O'Leary (1996).

83 Corthals (1989), 51.

84 See discussions in Kelleher (1971); and further Dumville (1977–9); as well as Mc Carthy (2008), 278–9, 282.

85 Meyer (1906), 14–5 (Ms 23 N 10), 16–7 (*Liber Flavus Fergusiorum*); Corthals (1989), 42, 52–3. The theme of Conchobar as a pre-conversion believer is discussed by Cronan (2007), 148–54. I owe this latter reference to Prof. Mary Clayton.

86 Tírechán, *Collectanea* 44.1 (Bieler (1979), 158–9): *aqua babtismi filii ipsa est aqua commonis mulieris.*

87 Tírechán, *Collectanea* 40.4 (Bieler (1979), 154–5): "*Bene sit tibi, o uir sancte, quod suscitasti me etiam una hora a doloribus multis.*"

because normal men would be afraid of him, but he told the giant to believe in God and receive baptism and he would not have to return to his torment. But first Patrick asked the giant who he was. The giant replied: "I am the son of the son of Cass son of Glas; I was the swineherd of Luga[i]r king of Hirota [Iruaith?]. The warrior band of the sons of Macc Con killed me in the reign of Coirpre Nie Fer."[88] After giving this personal information the giant 'was baptized, and confessed God, and fell silent, and was laid again in his grave'.[89] While this example of converting a long-dead pagan is not motivated by the good deeds of the pagan himself, as was the case with Gregory and Trajan, it does show that some Irish considered a saint capable of converting and baptizing pagans long after their deaths.

The early Irish were concerned with pagans who lived good lives, and the concept of the 'natural good' (*naturale bonum*) was alive and well among them from an early period. Adomnán cites two examples in the *Vita Columbae*.[90] The first tale is told as an example of Columba's ability to prophesy a future event. Once when visiting the island of Skye the saint struck the ground with his staff and declared:[91] "My children, strange to tell, today in this place, on this plot of ground, a certain pagan old man, who has preserved natural goodness throughout his whole life, will be baptized, and will die, and will be buried." A short time later a ship arrived carrying a feeble old man, Artbranán, who was lifted from the ship and set down before the saint. Through an interpreter he received the word of God, believed, and was baptized. He presently died and was buried in that place as Columba had prophesied. And in an example of *dindsenchas*, Adomnán relates that the stream beside his grave was known as *dobur Artbranáin* to the present day.[92]

Another example relates that once when Columba was travelling near Loch Ness, the saint declared to his companions that they must

[88] Tírechán, *Collectanea* 40.7 (Bieler (1979), 154–5): *'Ego sum Macc Maicc Cais Maic Glais, qui fui subulcus Lugir* ríg *Hirotæ. Iugulauit me* fian maicc *Maicc Con in regno Coirpri Nioth Fer.'* The ancient heroes of Ireland were often considered to have been of enormous size, as was Conchobar in at least one version of his death tale; see Meyer (1906), 18–9.

[89] Tírechán, *Collectanea* 40.8 (Bieler (1979), 154–5): *Et babtitzatus est et confessionem Dei fecit et resticuit et positus est iterum in sepulcro suo.*

[90] For a fuller discussion, see O'Sullivan (2010).

[91] Adomnán, *Vita Columbae* I 33 (Anderson and Anderson (1991), 62–3): *'Mirum dictu Ó filioli hodie in hac huius loci terrula quidam gentilis senex, naturale per totam bonum custodiens uitam, et babtizabitur et morietur et sepelietur.'*

[92] Adomnán, *Vita Columbae* I 33 (Anderson and Anderson (1991), 62–3).

hasten toward the angels who had been sent to conduct the soul of a pagan. The angels would be awaiting their arrival so that they could minister baptism to the pagan Emchath before he died because he had 'preserved natural goodness through his whole life, into extreme old age'.[93] The saint hurried ahead of his companions to meet Emchath who received the word of God gladly and was baptized before departing to meet the Lord. Emchath's son Virolec and his household also believed and were baptized.

The stories of Trajan, as told by the Anonymous, and of Artbranán and Emchath, as told by Adomnán, demonstrate that there was a belief in 7th-century Ireland and 8th-century Britain in the 'natural good' and that pagans who had not been raised as Christians could be worthy of baptism and the rewards of heaven.[94]

Pagans might also have the perspicacity to honour Saint Patrick and, hence, be enlisted into the ranks of the church. Two examples from Muirchú's *Vita Patricii* (*c.*AD 695) involve productive encounters, the first with a druid and the second with two professional praise poets.

When Patrick was summoned to the pagan court in the presence of King Lóegaire the druids urged their people not to honour Patrick when he arrived. However, when Patrick came 'there was only one man who, with the help of the Lord, refused to obey the command of the druids, that is Ercc, son of Daig [Ercc mac Dego], whose relics are now worshipped in the city called Slane [Sláine]. He stood up, and Patrick blessed him, and he believed in the eternal God'.[95] The pagan druid, Ercc mac Dego, voluntarily submitted himself to Patrick against the orders of his fellow druids, and was blessed and converted by Patrick. As stated by Muirchú, his relics are now kept at Slane, in Co. Meath, and these details are borne out by the annal entry for AD 513 that gives the

[93] Adomnán, *Vita Columbae* III 14 (Anderson and Anderson (1991), 200–1): *ut ipsum naturale bonum per totam uitam usque ad extremam senestutem.*

[94] For further discussions of the 'natural good', see Donahue (1949–51); Ó Corráin, Breatnach, and Breen (1984), 385–6, 428–9; Corthals (1989) where the concept of *naturale bonum* is implied by Conchobar's conversion; Scowcroft (2003), 147 and notes; and for a discussion of the interest among the Anglo-Saxons and the Irish in their pre-Christian ancestors, see Cronan (2007).

[95] Muirchú, *Vita Patricii* I 17(16).3 (Bieler (1979), 88–9): *sed unus tantum a Domino adiutus qui noluit oboedire dictis magorum, hoc est Ercc filius Dego, cuius nunc reliquiae adorantur in illa ciuitate quae uocatur Slane, surrexit et benedixit eum Patricius et credidit Deo aeterno*; see also Howlett (2006), 76 ll. 13–9.

obit of Bishop Ercc of Sláine.[96] So although Muirchú does not explicitly say so, we must assume that the druid Ercc, having been converted and baptized, went on to gain the status of bishop at Sláine.

On another occasion when Patrick and his retinue came to King Lóegaire's court, it happened to be Easter and, significantly, a professional poet and his pupil rose before Patrick to honour him and were subsequently converted. Muirchú relates:[97] 'As he [Patrick] entered the banquet hall of Tara, none of them all rose in order to welcome him, except one man only, Dubthach maccu Lug[a]ir, an excellent poet. With him was then in that place a young poet named Fíacc, who afterwards became a renowned bishop, whose relics are worshipped in Sléibte.' As we see, Dubthach's pupil Fiacc Finn Sléibte became the founding bishop at Sletty [Sléibte], and it was Bishop Áed of Sletty (†AD 700) who commissioned the Life of Patrick from Muirchú.[98] So Muirchú was, in fact, relating part of the foundation legend of the church that he was working for as he wrote the Life of Patrick.

The excellent poet, Dubthach maccu Lugair, who stood up to honour Patrick at King Lóegaire's court, plays an important role in the aetiological legends about the syncretism of native Irish law with Christian doctrine as narrated in the preface to the *Senchas Már*.[99] The episode is replete with implications for the church's arguments about capital punishment[100] and with the implicit comparison of the pre-Christian Irish with the Jews of the Old Testament.[101] All of which show the Irish portraying their pagan ancestors as standing on the cusp of the new Christian dispensation, many of them worthy to be included immediately. It cannot be shown that the Anonymous borrowed directly from any specific Irish example, but the precedent was well established in the in-

[96] See, for example, the Annals of Ulster *s.a.* AD 513 (Mac Airt and Mac Niocaill (1983), 513). Charles-Edwards (2006), 87, notes that this information is recorded in the Annals of Ulster, in the Annals of Tigernach, and in the *Chronicon Scotorum*.

[97] Muirchú, *Vita Patricii* I 19(18).3 (Bieler (1979), 92–3): *Adueniente ergo eo in caenacolum Temoriae nemo de omnibus ad aduentum eius surrexit praetor unum tantum, id est Dubthoch macccu Lugir, poetam optimum, apud quem tunc temporis ibi erat quidam adoliscens poeta nomine Feec, qui postea mirabilis episcopus fuit, cuius reliquiae adorantur hi Sleibti*; see also Howlett (2006), 80 ll. 10–5.

[98] Muirchú, *Vita Patricii* praefatio (Bieler (1979), 62–3); see also Howlett (2006), 40–1.

[99] Quite a critical literature has developed on the episodes involving Dubthach in the preface to the *Senchas Már*. See McCone (1986); Carey (1990); Carey (1994).

[100] Bracken (1995).

[101] Scowcroft (2003).

sular Christian world for a worthy pagan, like the Emperor Trajan, to be baptized, even posthumously, by the saints.

Dealing with rivals

Among the most idiosyncratic of miracles performed by Gregory has to do with how he dealt with a successor who was denigrating his memory. Gregory's successor in the papacy was said to have been envious of Gregory's fame among the people because he had made provision for those he had converted. Pope Sabinianus (AD 604–606), who is never explicitly named by the Anonymous, was not willing or able to provide for the multitudes of Rome and, therefore, did not enjoy a good reputation among them. Sabinianus, apparently out of jealousy, spoke disparagingly of Gregory which caused Gregory to return, as a revenant, to remonstrate with Sabinianus.[102] The Anonymous relates that 'the saint [Gregory] appeared to him [Sabinianus] and is said to have asked him in far from gentle tones why he had judged his motives so wrongly when he had done it for the Lord's sake alone. Since Gregory was unable to silence him by his words, on the third occasion he kicked the man on the head. His successor died in a few days from the pain of the blow.'[103] The chapter ends in this way, without any explanation of how or why a saint should act so as to cause the death of anyone.

Daniel Binchy, basing his comments on observations of early Irish hagiography made by Charles Plummer, has stated that the 'Irish *Heiligensage* is based on Irish *Heldensage*'.[104] Several narratives from 7th-century Irish hagiography have examples of the saint's curse resulting in the death of someone who transgresses the saint's command or challenges his authority.

Adomnán relates the story of the young Columba who, while studying in Leinster with his teacher Gemmán, was present when 'a certain cruel man, a pitiless oppressor of the innocent'[105] killed a young girl with

[102] For the historical background to this story, see Colgrave (1968), 161 n 121.

[103] Anonymous *Vita Gregorii* 28 (Colgrave (1968), 126–7): *[a sancto Gregorio adsumptorum] ei apparuisse, non leniter adlocutus dicitur cur ista de se sic iudicasset in eo quod tantum pro Domino faciebat. Cumque eius non adquievit sermonibus, tertia vice eum adloquens, pede suo percussit in caput. Cuius dolore percussionis in paucis diebus defunctus est.*

[104] Binchy (1982), 167; Binchy was commenting on evidence described by Plummer (1910), i cxxix–clxxxviii.

[105] Adomnán, *Vita Columbae* II 25 (Anderson and Anderson (1991), 130–1): *homo quidam innocuorum inmitis persequutor crudilis.*

a spear at the feet of Gemmán and Columba. The young girl had run to Gemmán seeking protection. In anguish Gemmán cried out, asking how long such crimes and dishonour against God could go unavenged? At once the young Columba pronounced: "In the same hour in which the soul of the girl whom he has slain ascends to heaven, let the soul of her slayer descend to hell."[106] The killer fell dead on the spot, and Columba's fame spread throughout Ireland for exacting this vengeance.

Muirchú, in the *Vita Patricii*, relates a similar story in which a challenge to the saint's authority is met with death for the challenger. Patrick was summoned to the presence of King Lóegaire at his pagan court in Tara and the druids discouraged anyone from honouring Patrick as he arrived. The druid Lochru 'provoked the holy man and dared to revile the catholic faith with haughty words'.[107] Patrick said, as Peter had said of Simon: "may this impious man, who blasphemes thy name, now be cast out and quickly perish".[108] Lochru was lifted into the air and fell down to earth dashing his brains out on a stone in the presence of the pagans.

Likewise, Tírechán relates in the *Collectanea* how Patrick was baptizing near the River Moy in Co. Mayo and the local druids decided to oppose him. 'And behold, Patrick stood up and raised his left hand to God in heaven and cursed the (chief) druid, and he dropped dead in the midst of his druids, and he was consumed by fire before the eyes of all as a sign of punishment.'[109] One of the characteristics we see in this episode is that, while the right hand is used to bless, the saint uses his left hand to curse.

One of the most unusual examples of a holy person challenging rivals comes from vernacular poetry of *c.*AD 700, the date suggested by its

[106] Adomnán, *Vita Columbae* II 25 (Anderson and Anderson (1991), 130–1): '*Eadem hora qua interfectae ab eo filiae anima ascendit ad caelos, anima ipsius interfectoris discendat ad inferos.*' This incident is compared by Adomnán to the death of Ananias in the presence of Peter; see Act 5:5.

[107] Muirchú, *Vita Patricii* I 17(16).4 (Bieler (1979), 88–9): *procax erat in conspectu sancti audiens detrachere fidei catholicae tumulentis uerbis*; see also Howlett (2006), 76–7 ll. 22–3.

[108] Muirchú, *Vita Patricii* I 17(16).5 (Bieler (1979), 88–9): '*hic impius qui blasfemat nomen tuum eleuetur nunc foras et cito moriatur*'; see also Howlett (2006), 76–7 ll. 31–2. Clare Stancliffe (1992), 91, reminds us that this episode as related by Muirchú has an apocryphal text as an exemplar.

[109] Tírechán, *Collectanea* 42.5–6 (Bieler (1979), 156–7): *Et ecce uir sanctus surrexit Patricius et eleuauit manum sinistram Deo caeli et maledixit magum, et cedidit mortuus in medio magorum eius, et exustus est ante faciem omnium in uindictae signum.*

editor,[110] and is based on the apocryphal Infancy Gospel of Thomas.[111] In this poem the child Jesus is portrayed as being precocious and very inventive but when a little boy destroyed the play-things that the child Jesus had made for himself from mud and water he was cursed by Jesus[112] and 'collapsed like a withered twig'.[113] In a somewhat more drastic example, another little boy annoyed the young Jesus who said: 'May it not be a going and a coming, the journey you have made.'[114] The boy suddenly collapsed and died. Needless to say, the family of the dead child was upset and insisted that Joseph should take his son and leave the village. When queried by Joseph about the deaths caused by the curses the child Jesus replied: 'Anyone who is innocent does not die from judgements. It is only the wicked that the curse pursues.'[115]

These words put in the mouth of the child Jesus summarize the outlook of these early texts that express the values of a secular heroic age for a Christian audience. They seem to say that you have nothing to fear from these representatives of an omnipotent Lord so long as you do not challenge or transgress their authority. And again we see that the Anonymous had abundant precedence in the Irish tradition for stories of saints dealing rather brutally with rivals.

Secret watcher

Sometimes the saint, while communing with God in some extraordinary way, is witnessed by another member of the community. Occasionally the saint finds himself in circumstances where he voluntarily tells his companions what has been divinely revealed to him. But on other occasions, the saint is observed clandestinely or surreptitiously in circumstances where the saint desires privacy. Once the saint is aware of

[110] Carney (1964), xviii n 29, xix.

[111] Infancy Gospel of Thomas 46 (McNamara (1975), 52–3); see also Herbert and McNamara (1989), 44–7 (§14). This particular apocryphon does not appear to have been known in Anglo-Saxon England; see Biggs (2007), 23–5.

[112] Jesus said to the boy: 'may you be as a little branch that falls before its fruit' (*ro-bé amail chroebnatain do-thuit re n-a mes*); Carney (1964), 92–3 (§9).

[113] *Fo-cairt in mac tar a chenn amail chepán crín*; Carney (1964), 92–3 (§10).

[114] *Níb techt tuidecht, in fecht ro-feras;* Carney (1964), 92–3 (§12). This line has been translated as 'May the journey which you have made be one of no return' by Herbert and McNamara (1989), 45 (§12).

[115] *Nech bas endac, ol Ísu, do bráthaib ní bá, is in miscadach lenas in mallacht namá*; Carney (1964), 94–5 (§16).

the secret watcher he will reprimand him. In nearly all cases he will forbid the person who has observed him, whether secretly or not, to reveal what he has witnessed until after the saint's death. As we will see, this device is most thoroughly developed by Adomnán in book three of the *Vita Columbae.*

In chapter 26 of the Life, the Anonymous relates an anecdote about Gregory diligently engaged in writing his famous homilies on Ezekiel. We are told that a certain member of Gregory's household who was very intimate with him saw a white dove, symbol of the Spirit of God,[116] resting upon the saint as he worked and communed. Gregory was very angry with the household member because the watcher had approached him while he was preoccupied and had seen the evidence of his special communion with God. Gregory 'instructed the man never to make this known to anyone during his lifetime, for fear that, through this clear sign of his renown in heaven, his earthly renown might be spread abroad'.[117] As we shall see, many of the features of this anecdote are paralleled in Admonán's Life of Columba.

In book 3 of Adomnán's *Vita Columbae* there are several instances of Columba being observed by members of his community in circumstances where the saint communes with angels or the Holy Spirit in the presence of a brilliant, divine light.[118] In several of these cases we are told the name of the person who has observed the saint in this hallowed state. In some cases the saint voluntarily relates his experience to those present, but at other times, when he wants privacy, he is observed by a secret watcher. In the latter case the saint will reprimand the secret watcher, but in all cases he will impose the injunction that the watchers not reveal what they have observed so long as the saint lives.

Book 3 chapter 6[119] of the *Vita Columbae* relates the example of Aidan mac Libir being present with Columba when the saint saw angels at war against adversaries over the soul of a pilgrim. Columba requested that Aidan not reveal any of what he had seen during the saint's lifetime.

[116] Note how Adomnán in the 2nd preface to the *Vita Columbae* emphasized the meaning of Columba's name (i.e. 'dove') and how it symbolizes the Holy Spirit, discussed above in the section on 'Etymological narrative'.

[117] Anonymous *Vita Gregorii* 26 (Colgrave (1968), 122–3): *precepit ne quandiu ipse viveret in carne, id alicui indicaret, ne scilicet aperto celestis signo claritatis, fama extolli foris videretur humana.*

[118] See further Ritari (2010) and Sharman (2010).

[119] Adomnán, *Vita Columbae* III 6 (Anderson and Anderson (1991), 190–1).

The immediately following chapter 7[120] provides the two reasons why Columba always forbade those who observed him in these states to reveal what they had seen during his lifetime. Columba once revealed to a pilgrim who was visiting Iona the death of a man known to the pilgrim and from his own province. But, we are told, many secret mysteries known to Columba were never allowed by the saint to reach the knowledge of men.[121] Two reasons are given for keeping these special instances of divine communion from the knowledge of men: 1) to avoid boasting, and 2) not to invite questioning of the saint by intolerable crowds. We saw above, in the case of Gregory, the desire to avoid boasting and having the saint's fame spread among men.

Chapter 16 of book 3[122] of the *Vita Columbae* provides the fullest example of the 'secret watcher' with all the details outlined at the beginning of this section. One day on the island of Iona Columba declared to the assembled brothers that he wanted to be alone and admonished that no one should follow him. But a certain 'cunning spy' (*callidus explorator*)[123] secretly took another path and crept up a hill to observe Columba and learn why the saint wished to be alone. The secret watcher saw the saint at prayer with his arms outstretched and his eyes turned towards heaven when suddenly angels (visible to human eyes) came and stood around the saint communing with him. The angels, however, quickly departed as if aware that they were being watched. When Columba returned to the monastery he asked reprovingly who among the brothers was guilty of a transgression. The secret watcher, realizing that his transgression was known to the saint, begged Columba's forgiveness in the presence of the other brothers. Columba took the secret watcher aside and demanded that he not reveal to anyone what he had seen as long as the saint lived. Upon the saint's death, the brother revealed to others what he had observed when Columba communed with the angels and became the primary disseminator of the story. Also, in another example of *dindsenchas*, the place where Columba communed became known afterwards as *cnoc angel* ('hill of angels').

[120] Adomnán, *Vita Columbae* III 7 (Anderson and Anderson (1991), 192–3).

[121] This tendency for Columba to keep esoteric knowledge and secret mysteries from the masses is also recorded in an 8th-century vernacular text about the saint; see Carey (2002), 54–71.

[122] Adomnán, *Vita Columbae* III 16 (Anderson and Anderson (1991), 204–7).

[123] Adomnán, *Vita Columbae* III 16 (Anderson and Anderson (1991), 204–5).

In chapter 19[124] of the same book, it is related how Virgno [Fergnae], who would become fourth abbot of Iona (†AD 623), went alone to the church to pray one night when Columba also entered the same church soon afterwards. But, once the saint had entered, the church suddenly filled with such brilliant light that Virgno had to look away to protect his eyes and tried to conceal himself. The light was as brilliant as the midday sun. The next morning Columba called Virgno to him and commended him for looking away, otherwise he would have been blinded. Virgno was told by Columba never to reveal during the saint's lifetime what had occurred in the church that night. Adomnán related that he had heard the story from the priest Commán who was Virgno's nephew (sister's son), and Virgno had himself related the experience directly to Commán.

A certain Colcu mac Áedo Draigniche came to the door of the church one night and stopped to pray, as related in chapter 20 of book 3,[125] when suddenly the church filled with heavenly light which then vanished. Unbeknownst to Colcu Columba was at the same time inside the church praying. Next morning Columba called Colcu to him and reprimanded him and ordered him not to reveal what he had seen of the heavenly light as long as the saint lived.

The immediately following chapter 21[126] relates how Columba admonished Berchán, a pupil of the saint, not to come to the saint's lodgings that night as he was in the habit of doing. Berchán came anyway, despite having been told not to, and tried to spy on the saint through the keyhole in anticipation of seeing some heavenly sight. Instead, the lodgings filled with brilliant light and Berchán was forced to turn away because of the brightness and fled to protect himself. Next morning Columba called Berchán to him and reprimanded him for spying, informing him that only through Columba's intercession had he been spared from blindness or even death. Berchán performed penance as recommended by Columba when he admonished his spying pupil.

The 'secret watcher' device is also found in Northumbrian hagiography dealing with St Cuthbert, in both the anonymous Life (AD 698–705)[127] and in the later reworking in Bede's prose Life (*c.*AD 720).[128] I have discussed these episodes in the context of 'penance and prayer in

[124] Adomnán, *Vita Columbae* III 19 (Anderson and Anderson (1991), 208–11).

[125] Adomnán, *Vita Columbae* III 20 (Anderson and Anderson (1991), 212–3).

[126] Adomnán, *Vita Columbae* III 21 (Anderson and Anderson (1991), 212–5).

[127] Anonymous *Vita Sancti Cuthberti* II 3 (Colgrave (1940), 78–83).

[128] Bede, *Vita Sancti Cuthberti* 10 (Colgrave (1940), 188–91).

water', another example of Irish influence in Northumbrian hagiography.[129] In this episode Cuthbert is called away from Melrose to Coldingham by Abbess Æbbe. While at Coldingham Cuthbert does not relax his habitual practices and goes alone at night to the seashore to pray and keep his vigils while immersed in the waves. In both the anonymous and in Bede's prose Life a 'secret watcher' surreptitiously follows Cuthbert to observe his nocturnal immersions in water as he prays, chants, and keeps vigil. The secret watcher, realizing that he has transgressed against the saint, falls ill and begs forgiveness of the saint. Cuthbert reveals that he was aware of being watched and grants forgiveness as long as the secret watcher does not reveal what he has seen while the saint remains alive. Needless to say, the secret watcher becomes the source for knowledge of this episode in Cuthbert's Life.

Thus we see three Northumbrian examples of the 'secret watcher' device, the anonymous hagiographer of Gregory from Whitby, the anonymous hagiographer of Cuthbert from Lindisfarne, and Bede, all share features in common with the *topos* of the 'secret watcher' developed most thoroughly by Adomnán in the *Vita Columbae.*

Doctor of souls

The notion of a spiritual teacher being a doctor of the soul is a metaphor that is repeated several times in the Whitby Life of Gregory. It is a metaphor that appears early in Irish religious texts and especially in penitential literature where penance is often described as medicine for the soul.[130] Sin and transgression are seen as illness or wounds of the soul and penance, along with religious counselling, offers healing medicine prescribed by the spiritual advisor. This extended metaphor arose early in church history as suggested by a quotation attributed to Jerome[131] and cited early in a text called the Bigotian Penitential:[132] 'Let the power of

[129] Ireland (1997), 61–3, where I also argued that details in Bede's version of 'penance and prayer in water' are closer to Irish examples than those related by Cuthbert's anonymous hagiographer.

[130] For the role of penance as medicine in the scheme of conversion for an early Irish hagiographer, see O'Loughlin (2002), 135.

[131] The quotation attributed to Jerome has not been specifically identified in his works; McNeill and Gamer (1938), 148.

[132] Bigotian Penitential 1 (Bieler (1963), 198–9): *Tanto maior potentia medici quanto magis creuit morbus egroti.* This particular penitential has been dated to the

the physician become greater in the degree in which the fever of the sick man increases.' The succeeding text extends the comparison between the methods of the physician of the body and the application of penance for the individual.[133]

In chapter 22 of the *Vita Gregorii*, the Anonymous describes two magicians who were enlisted by a wealthy Roman to harm Gregory. The magicians' intentions were discovered and the magicians struck blind for their misdeeds. They were eventually converted and baptized and placed in charge of church funds for the poor so that they became 'righteous healers of souls (*medici animarum*) for the Lord'.[134]

Gregory was not only a 'doctor of souls' (*medicus animarum*) but, as the Anonymous tells us in chapter 23, he proved to be an effective doctor of the body. Gregory healed and converted a king, presumably of the Lombards,[135] who had earlier threatened the safety of Rome but was dissuaded by Gregory's powers of persuasion. When the king fell ill Gregory recognized that the king should return to the milky diet of his youth in the Alps and the king recovered his health. Thus Gregory, through his eloquence and knowledge, proved to be both a doctor of souls and of the body.[136]

Furthermore, Gregory's writings could be portrayed as medicine for souls, extending the metaphor beyond the immediate words and deeds of the spiritual worker to the writings themselves and their effects on subsequent generations. In chapter 27, the Anonymous declares that Gregory's work in 'expounding the story of the blessed Job in his *Moralia*'[137] worked against human vices and offered medicine for souls (*contra vitia humanorum medicamina animarum*).[138]

first half of the 8th century; see Lapidge and Sharpe (1985), 157 (§614). However, it may be earlier; see Kenney (1929), 241–2; Follett (2006), 67–9.

133 This use of the doctor/medicine metaphor for penance was pointed out by Davies (1989), 51.

134 Anonymous *Vita Gregorii* 22 (Colgrave (1968), 114–5): *perfectos pro Domino medicos animarum*.

135 Anonymous *Vita Gregorii* 23 (Colgrave (1968), 114–5). The Anonymous here admits to not knowing the name or origins of the king in question, but other historical records make it clear that an incident in AD 593 involving King Agilulf of the Lombards is being discussed; see Colgrave (1968), 154 n 94.

136 For a fuller discussion, see Butler (2011).

137 Anonymous *Vita Gregorii* 27 (Colgrave (1968), 122–3): *quę beatum Iob exponendo, dictis Moralibus*.

138 Anonymous *Vita Gregorii* 27 (Colgrave (1968), 122–3).

The writing of penitential literature began early in Ireland and the Penitential of St Columbanus (†AD 615) is among the earliest.[139] In the preface to the B section, which is addressed to the clergy, the metaphor of the 'doctor of souls' is elaborated and the work of providing spiritual guidance through penitential practice is compared to the work of a physician, a doctor of the body. The argument is that just as physicians offer diverse medicines depending on the various physical problems in the body, so should 'spiritual doctors' (*spirituales medici*) treat with diverse cures the 'wounds of souls' (*animarum uulnera*).[140]

The 7th-century Irish penitential by Cummean[141] has as part of its subtitle 'Here begins the Prologue on the Medicine for the Salvation of Souls',[142] where it is clear that penance is considered a spiritual medicine. The Ambrosian Penitential, whose origins may be either British or Irish, also adopts the metaphor of penance serving as the medication to heal spiritual wounds (*spiritualium uulnerum medicamenta*).[143] Another 7th-century Irish text, the anonymous *Liber de ordine creaturarum* (pre-AD 680), states that those who commit mortal sins and do not apply the 'medicine of penance' (*poenitentiae medicamentum*)[144] will be sentenced to eternal punishment. An interesting point about this latter reference is that *De ordine creaturarum* is not a penitential like the other Irish sources cited but rather a work on cosmography, yet the metaphor of penance as medicine is repeated naturally.

The metaphor of a spiritual advisor as a 'doctor of the soul' and penance and spiritual counselling as 'medicine for the soul' did not originate with the Irish. It has an earlier and more widespread pedigree. But it was consistently maintained by the Irish from an early period and the frequency of the metaphor used in the *Vita Gregorii* helps support the argument that the Anonymous worked in an atmosphere where Irish learning and training prevailed.

139 For a discussion of the relative chronology of the various sections of the penitential by Columbanus, see Charles-Edwards (1997).

140 Columbanus, *Penitentiale* section B, preface (Bieler (1963), 98–9).

141 This penitential seems to have been known among the Anglo-Saxons; Frantzen (1983), 130–7.

142 Cummean, *Penitentiale* (Bieler (1963), 108–9): *Incipit prologus de medicinae salutaris animarum*.

143 *Paenitentiale Ambrosianum* I. 2 (Körntgen (1993), 258). Although often assigned a 9th-century date, Körntgen (1993), 7–35 has argued that the *Paenitentiale Ambrosianum* should be dated to a period before Cummean's. See also Charles-Edwards (1997), 218 n 4. I thank Prof. Mary Clayton for calling this penitential to my attention.

144 *De ordine creaturarum* XIII 3 (Díaz y Díaz (1972), 180–1).

Whipped in a dream

Another literary motif found frequently in religious writings that originated well before the Irish began using it, is the motif of being whipped in a dream as a means of urging a person on to complete a divinely assigned task. Sometimes the whipping, although described as occurring in a dream, leaves physical marks on the body of the whipped victim, who is subsequently able to use those marks as proof of the veracity of the dream which convinces others to comply with the requests of the person who experienced the dream. The dreamer frequently does not react to the demands of the dream until the third occurrence. Some of the motifs and *topoi* used by the Anonymous are found in the works of earlier Church Fathers and hagiographers on the Continent.[145] But these same motifs can also be identified in Irish texts that preceded the *Vita Gregorii* and show that the Anonymous and the Irish hagiographers worked in the same intellectual milieu. Previous evidence suggests that the Anonymous was more likely to have encountered these shared motifs and *topoi* through Irish sources rather than directly from the Continent. The motif of being whipped or scourged in a dream is such an example.

Chapters 18 and 19 of the *Vita Gregorii* relate the circumstances of how the bones of King Edwin of Northumbria (AD 616–633) came to be venerated at Whitby. A certain man (*quidam*) appeared in a dream to a priest named Trimma, who was in a monastery of the 'South English' (*Sudranglorum*),[146] telling him to go to Hatfield Chase to get the bones of King Edwin and bring them back to Whitby (*Streunesalae*).[147] This happened twice and the priest ignored them knowing that dreams had deceived many in the past.

[145] Colgrave (1968), 151 n 74. Specific examples cited by Colgrave appear in the following discussion.

[146] It is interesting that we are given details of the name of the priest Trimma and, later in the narrative, the name of the *ceorl* Teoful who helped Trimma identify the location of Edwin's remains at a battle site near Hatfield Chase. Yet we are given no details as to the location of Trimma's monastery other than of the 'South English', which to the editor meant anywhere south of the River Humber; see Colgrave (1968), 102, 150 n 69. It seems possible that the reader is intended to interpret this vague southern location as being Canterbury, the site of the Gregorian mission to the Anglo-Saxons. Trimma's lack of familiarity with the location of Hatfield Chase which is in Yorkshire and his reliance upon the knowledge of Teoful from Lindsey reflect his ignorance of the northern regions and emphasize his southern origins.

[147] Anonymous *Vita Gregorii* 18 (Colgrave (1968), 102–3).

On the third time the man appeared to Trimma in a dream he rebuked the priest harshly and used a whip (*flagellum*) saying: "Have I not twice shown you what you must do and you have taken no notice? Now show me whether you intend to obey or disobey me."[148] Trimma then set off to look for a *ceorl* named Teoful who was to help in identifying the location of Edwin's relics. They only found what they were looking for on their second attempt at digging.[149] They brought the bones to Whitby where they were buried at the Church of St Peter to the south of the altar which was dedicated to St Peter. The east of the altar was dedicated to St Gregory.[150] The Anonymous makes clear that Edwin's bones were placed in the church together with the bones of other kings,[151] which must refer to those of King Oswiu (AD 642–670), husband of Eanflæd and father of Abbess Ælfflæd.[152]

The motif of being whipped in a dream is recorded in texts that preceded Christianity in Ireland and among the Anglo-Saxons. The editor lists several instances in a footnote,[153] among them is an example cited by Eusebius (AD 263–339) in his *Historia ecclesiastica* where a heretical bishop, Natalius, is scourged all night long by angels.[154] When Natalius had a change of heart about his heretical ideas and wanted to rejoin the church he showed the strokes of the lashes on his body to others in his efforts to be allowed back into communion with them. In another example,

[148] Anonymous *Vita Gregorii* 19 (Colgrave (1968), 102–4): *'Nonne bis indicavi tibi quid debes facere et neglexisti? Proba modo si adhuc inoboediens an oboedians mihi esse volueris.'*

[149] Tírechán, *Collectanea* 16.8–9 (Bieler (1979), 136–7), relates an anecdote about a certain Bruscus who, as a revenant, appeared in a dream three times to a certain holy man complaining of his loneliness in his solitary burial at his church. After the third time the holy man had this dream he went and dug up Bruscus' bones and reburied them at the monastery and the holy man never dreamed of Bruscus again. I thank Dr Shane Lordan for calling my attention to the importance of this episode and much more besides.

[150] Anonymous *Vita Gregorii* 19 (Colgrave (1968), 104–5). When Pope Vitalian wrote to King Oswiu (*c.*AD 668) with the intention of sending Hadrian and Theodore as teachers he included relics of Pope Gregory; Bede, *Historia ecclesiastica* III 29 (Colgrave and Mynors (1969), 320–1). Some of these relics must have been present at each of the three altars dedicated to Gregory at Canterbury, York, and Whitby.

[151] Anonymous *Vita Gregorii* 19 (Colgrave (1968), 104): *sancta ossa cum ceteris conduntur regibus nostris.*

[152] Bede, *Historia ecclesiastica* III 24 (Colgrave and Mynors (1969), 292–3).

[153] Colgrave (1968), 151 n 74.

[154] Eusebius, *Historia ecclesiastica* V 28 (ed. by Eduard Schwartz and Theodor Mommsen in GCS 9, 503–5). For a translation by Lake (1926), 518–21.

Jerome (AD 347–420) relates in *Epistola* 22, that he was himself scourged in a dream by the Divine Judge for his love of heathen literature.[155] In an example not recorded until after the *Vita Gregorii* was written, but describing events of the early 7th century, Bede relates that Laurentius of the Gregorian mission to the Anglo-Saxons was scourged in a dream by St Peter because he considered returning to Gaul due to lack of success. When Laurentius showed King Eadbald of Kent the marks on his body from the whip, the king accepted the faith and was baptized thus helping ensure the conversion of his kingdom and success for Laurentius.[156]

Colgrave also noted an example from Adomnán's *Vita Columbae* which should be elaborated here. In book 3 chapter 5 Adomnán relates that when Columba was living on the island of Hinba[157] one night 'in a trance of the mind' (*in extasi mentis*) an angel carrying a glass book visited him on three successive occasions.[158] He was urged to read the book which commanded him to ordain Aidan [Áedán] mac Gabráin king, but Columba favoured Aidan's brother Iógenán. Because of the saint's hesitation to comply the angel 'suddenly stretched out his hand and struck the holy man with a scourge, the livid scar from which remained on his side all the days of his life'.[159]

The episode related above was derived by Adomnán from the writings of the seventh abbot of Iona, Cuimméne Ailbe (AD 657–669).[160] Book 3 chapter 5 contains the one section of the *Vita Columbae* which

[155] Jerome, *Epistola* 22.30 (ed. by Isidor Hilberg in CSEL 54, 189–91). For a translation see Wright (1933), 124–9. The *Epistolae* are the one text by Jerome for which it can be shown that the Anonymous probably had firsthand knowledge.

[156] Bede, *Historia ecclesiastica* II 6 (Colgrave and Mynors (1969), 154–7). Bede's story is repeated in the Anglo-Saxon Chronicles *s.a.* 616, but the Anonymous seems to know nothing about this story, nor anything about the characters of the Gregorian mission to the Anglo-Saxons beyond the details related about Paulinus.

[157] Although this island is the site of a monastery and is mentioned several times in the *Vita Columbae* its location has never been confirmed.

[158] Adomnán, *Vita Columbae* III 5 (Anderson and Anderson (1991), 188–9).

[159] Adomnán, *Vita Columbae* III 5 (Anderson and Anderson (1991), 188–9): *subito angelus extendens manum sanctum percussit flagillo, cuius liuorosum in eius latere uestigium omnibus suae diebus permansit uitae*. Bede's telling of the Vision of Fursa, which derived directly from an Irish *libellus*, involves visions of rewards and punishments and Fursa is burned by fires he caused himself and 'he bore for the rest of his life the marks of the burns which he had suffered while a disembodied spirit; they were visible to all on his shoulder and his jaw' (*omni uitae suae tempore signum incendii, quod in anima petulit, uisibile cunctis in humero maxillaque portauit*); Bede, *Historia ecclesiastica* III 19 (Colgrave and Mynors (1969), 274–5).

[160] Anderson and Anderson (1991), 188–91 and n 214.

clearly derives directly from Cuimméne's earlier work on Columba. There Columba warns Aidan and his descendants of their obligations to the saint and his successors; Columba says: "the scourge that I have endured from an angel on your account will be turned by the hand of God to a great disgrace upon them".[161] This passage refers to the scourging in the dream sequence related by Adomnán above and was composed by Cuimméne Ailbe several decades before Adomnán worked.[162]

This last section could have been expanded into a discussion of dream visions reflecting an Irish cultural milieu recorded by English ecclesiasts rather than concentrating on the single motif of being 'whipped in a dream'. Simply by examining Bede's *Historia ecclesiastica* one can find several examples that, if not derived from Irish sources, are about Irishmen or suggest Irish influence. For example, Bede devotes a longish chapter to the vision of the Irishman Fursa,[163] a similar vision story is told about Dryhthelm and Bede's source for the story is Hæmgisl, who retired to live a hermit's life in Ireland,[164] Boisil of Melrose appeared in dreams to a monk in Ráith Melsigi in Ireland in order to encourage Ecgberht to undertake the conversion of Iona to the Roman Easter,[165] and, finally, the Irish monk Adamnanus [Adomnán] was able to foretell the destruction of the monastery at Coldingham due to their lax practices.[166] There is abundant evidence to suggest that the Anonymous worked in a similarly Irish-influenced environment.

Conclusion

The quality and degree of formal training acquired by the Anonymous at Whitby has been questioned. The editor and subsequent researchers

[161] Adomnán, *Vita Columbae* III 5 (Anderson and Anderson (1991), 190–1): *'flagellum quod causa tui ab angelo sustenui per manum dei super eos in magnum flagitium uertetur.'*

[162] In a 9th-century vernacular text called the Sickbed of Cú Chulainn 8 (Dillon (1953), 3), Cú Chulainn falls into a sleep and in a dream (*res* 'vision') two faerie woman come toward him and begin striking him with whips (*echflesc*). When he awakens he remains speechless in his sickbed for a year.

[163] Bede, *Historia ecclesiastica* III 19 (Colgrave and Mynors (1969), 268–77).

[164] Bede, *Historia ecclesiastica* V 12 (Colgrave and Mynors (1969), 488–99).

[165] Bede, *Historia ecclesiastica* V 9 (Colgrave and Mynors (1969), 474–81). Bede, interestingly, gives here the correct etymology for Colum Chille, the Irish name of St Columba; see Colgrave and Mynors (1969), 478–9.

[166] Bede, *Historia ecclesiastica* IV 25 (Colgrave and Mynors (1969), 420–7).

of the *Vita Gregorii* have shown that the written sources used by the Anonymous are limited, for the most part, to the Bible and to works by Gregory himself. Based on identifiable literary sources in the Life, the library at Whitby could not have been well stocked. On the other hand, motifs and *topoi* common to 7th-century Irish writings are frequent in the Life by the Anonymous. Internal evidence and the Anonymous's own statements, most notably found in chapters 3 and 30, support arguments that knowledge of Irish motifs and their influences were most likely transmitted through oral rather than written sources.

The Anonymous's sympathies are Roman. The Life emphasizes the achievements of Pope Gregory who sent a mission to the Anglo-Saxons, includes Bishop Paulinus, a missionary of the second wave of that papal mission who converted King Edwin, the second most important person in the Life, and the first Northumbrian king to be converted and baptized. Having established the Anonymous's Roman credentials, it is surprising that the 'Synod' of Whitby of AD 664 which is pivotal in Stephan's Life of Bishop Wilfrid and in Bede's Ecclesiastical History is not mentioned, even in passing, by the Anonymous. The decision at the 'Synod' of Whitby guaranteed Northumbria's Roman future. The synod's omission means that the successful Irish mission to Northumbria from Iona, and its impressive list of participants, plays no role in the Life. But, likewise, neither do any of the Roman protagonists, such as Bishop Wilfrid, garner any mention in the *Vita Gregorii*. Even Abbess Hild, who founded Whitby, makes no appearance. These omissions must have been deliberate.[167]

If we accept that the Anonymous relied primarily on oral rather than written sources, it is precisely stories about characters such as Hild, Wilfrid, and Oswiu that we would expect to be transmitted and recorded. The two persons from Whitby who are named by the Anonymous are the current Abbess Ælfflæd and her mother Eanflæd. Some commentators have stressed the fact that Edwin, whose bones were transported to Whitby, was the father of Eanflæd and, therefore, the grandfather of Abbess Ælfflæd.[168] The Deiran royal line represented by Edwin effectively came to an end in terms of Northumbrian power with his death

[167] The larger purpose behind the Anonymous's Life of Gregory is too big a topic to broach here. However, it should be noted that any thorough investigation must query the obvious omissions cited above. In fact, it can be argued that deliberate silence about specific topics or persons is a narrative strategy employed in hagiography.

[168] Thacker (1995), 105–7; Dailey (2010), 204.

in AD 633.[169] Any argument that privileges the Deiran royal line and its relationships with Eanflæd and Ælfflæd[170] must overlook the fact that King Oswiu's bones had already been buried at Whitby before Edwin's were; and Eanflæd was Oswiu's wife, and Ælfflæd was Oswiu's daughter. Both Eanflæd and Ælfflæd had decades of working relationships with Hild who was also of Deiran descent. Furthermore, Bede makes the specific point that King Oswald (AD 634–642), brother of King Oswiu and successor of King Edwin, was related to both the Bernician and Deiran royal lines and through his efforts helped unite the two kingdoms into one people.[171] Abbess Ælfflæd was directly related to every Northumbria king during her lifetime (AD 654–714): her father Oswiu (AD 642–670), her brother Ecgfrith (AD 670–685), her half-brother Aldfrith (AD 685–704), and her nephew Osred (AD 705–716).

The Anonymous's purpose in writing the Life advances a Roman viewpoint that leaves out the Wilfridian party's role in its promotion. The narrative is full of Irish literary motifs and *topoi* that have been absorbed and transmitted by the Anonymous. But there had always been plenty of Irish *Romani* present in the insular cultural milieu that shaped the Anonymous's world view.

Bibliography

Anderson, A.O. and M. O. Anderson (1991) *Adomnán's Life of Columba*, Oxford.

Angenendt, A. (1984) *Kaiserherrschaft und Königstaufe: Kaiser, Könige und Päpste als geistliche Patrone in der abendländischen Missionsgeschichte*, Berlin.

Arbuthnot, S. (2005–7) *Cóir Anmann: a Late Middle Irish treatise on personal names*, 2 vols., London.

Baumgarten, R. (2004) 'Creative medieval etymology and Irish hagiography (Lasair, Columba, Senán),' *Ériu* 54, 49–78.

Bieler, L. (1963) *The Irish penitentials*, Dublin.

[169] Yorke (1990), 169 and Table 9 p 76. Oswiu ensured the lack of rivalry from the Deiran line with the elimination of Oswine in AD 651; Bede, *Historia ecclesiastica* III 14 (Colgrave and Mynors (1969), 254–61).

[170] For example, Thacker (1992), 143, refers to Whitby as the '*Eigenkloster* of the Deiran royal line'; Daily (2010), 204, argues that the Anonymous 'seems to have had a political agenda, since the middle chapters made the effort to praise members of Ælfflæd's family'. Edwin is the praised member of Ælfflæd's family in those middle chapters.

[171] Bede, *Historia ecclesiastica* III 6 (Colgrave and Mynors (1969), 230–1).

— (1979) *The Patrician texts in the Book of Armagh*, Dublin.
Biggs, F.M. (2007) *Sources of Anglo-Saxon culture: the Apocrypha*, Kalamazoo.
Binchy, D.A. (1982) 'A pre-Christian survival in mediaeval Irish hagiography,' in D. Whitelock, R. McKitterick, and D. Dumville, *Ireland in early mediaeval Europe*, Cambridge, 165–78.
Bischoff, B. and M. Lapidge (1994) *Biblical commentaries from the Canterbury school of Theodore and Hadrian*, Cambridge.
Bracken, D. (1995) 'Immortality and capital punishment: Patristic concepts in Irish law,' *Peritia* 9, 167–86.
Breen, A. (1995) *Ailerani interpretatio mystica et moralis progenitorum Domini Iesu Christi*, Blackrock.
Breeze, A. (2012) 'Did a woman write the Whitby Life of St Gregory?,' *Northern History* 49, 345–50.
Butler, B. (2011) 'Doctor of souls, doctor of the body: Whitby *Vita Gregorii* 23 and its exegetical context,' in E. Mullins and D. Scully, *Listen, o isles, unto me: studies in medieval word and image in honour of Jennifer O'Reilly*, Cork, 168–80.
Carey, J. (1990) 'The two laws of Dubthach's judgment,' *Cambridge Medieval Celtic Studies* 19, 1–18.
— (1994) 'An edition of the pseudo-historical prologue to the *Senchas Már*,' *Ériu* 45, 1–32.
— (2002) 'The Lough Foyle colloquy texts: *Immacaldam Choluim Chille 7 ind Óglaig oc Carraig Eolairg* and *Immacaldam in Druad Brain 7 inna Banfátho Febuil ós Loch Febuil*,' *Ériu* 52, 53–87.
Carney, J. (1955) *Studies in Irish literature and history*, Dublin.
— (1964) *The poems of Blathmac son of Cú Brettan together with the Irish Gospel of Thomas and a poem on the Virgin Mary*, Dublin.
Charles-Edwards, T.M. (1997) 'The penitential of Columbanus,' in M. Lapidge, *Columbanus: studies on the Latin writings*, Woodbridge, 217–39.
— (2006) *The Chronicle of Ireland*, Liverpool.
— (2010) 'The structure and purpose of Adomnán's *Vita Columbae*,' in J.M. Wooding, *Adomnán of Iona: theologian, lawmaker, peacemaker*, Dublin, 205–18.
Clancy, T.O. and G. Márkus (1995) *Iona: the earliest poetry of a Celtic monastery*, Edinburgh.
Colgrave, B. (1940) *Two Lives of Saint Cuthbert: a Life by an anonymous monk of Lindisfarne and Bede's prose Life*, Cambridge.
— (1963) 'The earliest Life of St Gregory the Great, written by a Whitby monk,' in N.K. Chadwick, *Celt and Saxon: studies in the early British border*, Cambridge, 119–37.
— (1968) *The earliest Life of Gregory the Great, by an anonymous monk of Whitby*, Cambridge.

Colgrave, B. and R.A.B. Mynors (1969) *Bede's Ecclesiastical History of the English People*, Oxford.

Corthals, J. (1989) 'The *retoiric* in *Aided Chonchobuir*,' *Ériu* 40, 41–59.

Cronan, D. (2007) '"Beowulf", the Gaels, and the recovery of the pre-Conversion past,' *Anglo-Saxon* 1, 137–80.

Curtius, E.R. (1953) *European literature and the Latin Middle Ages*, trans. by W.R. Trask, New York.

Dailey, E.T.A. (2010) 'The *Vita Gregorii* and ethnogenesis in Anglo-Saxon Britain,' *Northern History* 47, 195–207.

Davies, L.M. (2002) 'The "mouth of gold": Gregorian texts in the *Collectio Canonum Hibernensis*,' in P. Ní Chatháin and M. Richter, *Ireland and Europe in the early Middle Ages: texts and transmission/Irland und Europa im früheren Mittelalter: Texte und Überlieferung*, Dublin, 249–67.

Davies, M.T. (1996) 'Protocols of reading in early Irish literature: notes on some notes to *Orgain Denna Ríg* and *Amra Coluim Cille*,' *Cambrian Medieval Celtic Studies* 32, 1–23.

Davies, W. (1989) 'The place of healing in early Irish society,' in D. Ó Corráin, L. Breatnach, and K. McCone, *Sages, saints and storytellers. Celtic studies in honour of Professor James Carney*, Maynooth, 43–55.

Díaz y Díaz, M.C. (1972) *Liber de ordine creaturarum*, Santiago de Compostela.

Dillon, M. (1953) *Serglige Con Culainn*, Dublin.

Donahue, C. (1949–51) 'Beowulf, Ireland and the natural good,' *Traditio* 7, 263–77.

Dumville, D. (1977–9) 'Ulster heroes in the early Irish annals: a caveat,' *Éigse* 17, 47–54.

Fell, C.E. (1981) 'Hild, abbess of Streonæshalch,' in H. Bekker-Nielsen, *Hagiography and medieval literature: a symposium*, Odense, 76–99.

Follet, W. (2006) Céli Dé *in Ireland: monastic writing and identity in the early Middle Ages*, Woodbridge.

Frantzen, A. (1983) *The literature of penance in Anglo-Saxon England*, New Brunswick.

Gwynn, E.J. (1903–35) *The Metrical Dindshenchas*, 5 vols., Dublin.

Herbert, M. (1988) *Iona, Kells, and Derry: the history and hagiography of the monastic* familia *of Columba*, Oxford.

— (2011) 'The representation of Gregory the Great in Irish sources of the pre-Viking era,' in E. Mullins and D. Scully, *Listen, o isles, unto me: studies in medieval word and image in honour of Jennifer O'Reilly*, Cork, 181–90.

Herbert, M. and M. McNamara (1989) *Irish biblical Apocrypha: selected texts in translation*, Edinburgh.

Hillgarth, J.N. (1984) 'Ireland and Spain in the seventh century,' *Peritia* 3, 1–16.

Hollis, Stephanie (1992) *Anglo-Saxon women and the church: sharing a common fate*, Woodbridge.

Howlett, D. (1995) *The Celtic Latin tradition of biblical style*, Blackrock.

— (1997) *British books in biblical style*, Dublin.

— (2006) *Muirchú Moccu Macthéni's 'Vita Sancti Patricii' Life of Saint Patrick*, Dublin.

— (forthcoming) 'The *Altus prosator* of Virgilius Maro Grammaticus,' in E. Purcell, P. MacCotter, J. Nyhan, and J. Sheehan, *Clerics, kings, and Vikings: essays on medieval Ireland*, Dublin.

Ireland, C. (1996) 'Aldfrith of Northumbria and the learning of a *sapiens*,' in K.A. Klar, E.E. Sweetser and C. Thomas, *A Celtic florilegium: studies in memory of Brendan O Hehir*, Lawrence, 63–77.

— (1997) 'Penance and prayer in water: an Irish practice in Northumbrian hagiography,' *Cambrian Medieval Celtic Studies* 34, 51–66.

Kelleher, J.V. (1971) 'The *Táin* and the Annals,' *Ériu* 22, 107–27.

Kenney, J.F. (1929) *Sources for the early history of Ireland: ecclesiastical*, New York, repr. Dublin 1979.

Körntgen, L. (1993) *Studien zu den Quellen der frühmittelalterlichen Bußbücher*, Sigmaringen.

Lake, K. (1926) *Eusebius: the Ecclesiastical History, vol. 1*, London.

Lapidge, M. (1986) 'Chapter 1: The Anglo-Latin background,' in S.B. Greenfield and D.G. Calder, *A new critical history of Old English literature*, New York, 5–37.

— (2010) 'Aldhelm and the "Epinal-Erfurt Glossary",' in K. Barker with N. Brooks, *Aldhelm and Sherborne: essays to celebrate the founding of the bishopric*, Oxford, 129–63.

Lapidge, M. and M. Herren (1979) *Aldhelm: the prose works*, Ipswich.

Lapidge, M. and R. Sharpe (1985) *A bibliography of Celtic-Latin literature 400–1200*, Dublin.

Mac Airt, S. and G. Mac Niocaill (1983) *The Annals of Ulster*, Dublin.

Mac Eoin, G. (2002) 'The four names of St Patrick,' in M. Richter and J.M. Picard, *Ogma: essays in Celtic Studies in honour of Próinséas Ní Chatháin*, Dublin, 300–11.

Mc Carthy, D.P. (2008) *The Irish Annals: their genesis, evolution and history* Dublin.

McCone, K. (1986) 'Dubthach maccu Lugair and a matter of life and death in the pseudo-historical prologue to the *Senchas Már*,' *Peritia* 5, 1–35.

McNamara, M. (1975) *The Apocrypha in the Irish Church*, Dublin.

McNeill, J.T. and H.M. Gamer (1938) *Medieval handbooks of penance*, New York.

Meyer, K. (1906) *The death-tales of the Ulster heroes*, Dublin.

— (1912) '*Sanas Cormaic,* an Old-Irish glossary,' in O.J. Bergin, R.I. Best, K. Meyer, and J.G. O'Keeffe, *Anecdota from Irish manuscripts, vol. 4*, Halle.

Meyvaert, P. (1964) 'Bede and Gregory the Great,' *Jarrow Lectures* 7, Jarrow.

Mulchrone, K. (1939) *Bethu Phátraic: the Tripartite Life of Patrick*, Dublin.

Ó Corráin, D., L. Breatnach, and A. Breen (1984) 'The laws of the Irish,' *Peritia* 3, 382–438.

O'Leary, A. (1996) 'An Irish aprocryphal apostle: Muirchú's portrayal of Saint Patrick,' *Harvard Theological Review* 89, 287–301.

O'Loughlin, T. (1994) 'The library of Iona in the late seventh century: the evidence from Adomnán's *De Locis Sanctis*,' *Ériu* 45, 33–52.

– (2002) 'Muirchú's theology of conversion in his *Vita Patricii*,' in M. Atherton, *Celts and Christians: new approaches to the religious traditions of Britain and Ireland*, Cardiff, 124–45.

O'Loughlin, T. and H. Conrad-O'Briain (1993) 'The "baptism of tears" in early Anglo-Saxon sources,' *Anglo-Saxon England* 22, 65–83.

Ó Néill, P. (1981) 'The background to the *Cambrai Homily*,' *Ériu* 32, 137–48.

— (1984) '*Romani* influences on seventh-century Hiberno-Latin literature,' in P. Ní Chatháin and M. Richter, *Irland und Europa. Die Kirche im Frühmittelalter*, Stuttgart, 280–90.

Orchard, A. (1994) *The poetic art of Aldhelm*, Cambridge.

Ortenberg, V. (1999) 'The Anglo-Saxon church and the papacy,' in C.H. Lawrence, *The English church and the papacy in the Middle Ages*, Stroud, 29–62.

O'Sullivan, T. (2010) 'The anti-Pelagian motif of the "Naturally Good" pagan in Adomnán's *Vita Columbae*,' in J.M. Wooding, *Adomnán of Iona: theologian, lawmaker, peacemaker*, Dublin, 253–73.

Plummer, C. (1910) *Vitae Sanctorum Hiberniae*, 2 vols., Oxford, repr. Dublin 1997.

Richter, M. (1984) 'Bede's *Angli*: Angles or English?,' *Peritia* 3, 99–114.

Ritari, K. (2010) 'Heavenly apparitions and heavenly life in Adomnán's *Vita Columbae*,' in J.M. Wooding, *Adomnán of Iona: theologian, lawmaker, peacemaker*, Dublin, 274–88.

Robinson, F.C. (1968a) 'The significance of names in Old English Literature,' *Anglia* 86, 14–58.

— (1968b) 'Some uses of name-meanings in Old English poetry,' *Neuphilologische Mitteilungen* 69, 161–71.

Russell, P. (1988) 'The sounds of a silence: the growth of Cormac's Glossary,' *Cambridge Medieval Celtic Studies* 15, 1–30.

— (1996) '*Dúil Dromma Cetta* and Cormac's Glossary,' *Études Celtiques* 32, 147–74.

Scowcroft, R.M. (1995) 'Abstract narrative in Ireland,' *Ériu* 46, 121–58.

— (2003) '*Recht Fáide* and its gloss in the pseudo-historical prologue to the *Senchus Már*,' *Ériu* 53, 141–50.

Sharman, S. (2010) 'Visions of divine light in the writings of Adomnán and Bede,' in J.M. Wooding, *Adomnán of Iona: theologian, lawmaker, peacemaker*, Dublin, 289–302.

Sims-Williams, P. (1990) *Religion and literature in Western England 600–800*, Cambridge.

Smyth, M. (2003–4) 'The date and origin of *Liber de ordine creaturarum*,' *Peritia* 17–8, 1–39.

— (2011) 'The seventh-century Hiberno-Latin treatise *Liber de ordine creaturarum*: a translation,' *Journal of Medieval Latin* 21, 137–222.

Stancliffe, C. (1992) 'The miracle stories in seventh-century Irish saints' lives,' in J. Fontaine and J.N. Hillgarth, *Le septième siècle: changements et continuités / The seventh century: change and continuity*, London, 87–112.

Thacker, A. (1992) 'Monks, preaching and pastoral care in England,' in J. Blair and R. Sharpe, *Pastoral care before the parish*, Leicester, 137–70.

— (1998) 'Memorializing Gregory the Great: the origin and transmission of a papal cult in the seventh and early eighth centuries,' *Early Medieval Europe* 7, 59–84.

Walker, G.S.M. (1957) *Sancti Columbani opera*, Dublin.

Walsh, M. and D. Ó Cróinín (1988) *Cummian's letter* De controversia paschali, *together with a related Irish computistical tract* De ratione conputandi, Toronto.

Wilson, H.A. (1918) *The Calendar of St. Willibrord*, London.

Wright, F.A. (1933) *Select letters of St. Jerome*, London.

Yorke, B. (1990) *Kings and kingdoms of early Anglo-Saxon England*, London.

ANTHONY HARVEY

CAMBRO-ROMANCE? CELTIC BRITAIN'S COUNTERPART TO HIBERNO-LATIN

Abstract

This contribution raises a double question about the Latin that was written by literate Celts in Britain in the early Middle Ages:[1] to what extent does their output correspond to the Latin of their monastic contemporaries in Ireland? And is it appropriate to call it Cambro-Romance? The second issue turns upon the extent to which, following the demise of Roman rule in Britain, Latin may have continued as a language of active communication there. This is a long-standing question but, in presenting a systematic analysis of those entries so far published in the *Dictionary of Medieval Latin from Celtic Sources* that codify the vocabulary of British-Latin authors, the paper is able to arrive at a better-substantiated answer than has been possible hitherto: this suggests that the language in fact enjoyed a surprisingly deep and tenacious hold on early medieval Celtic Britain, enduring for many centuries. Turning then to the first issue, the contribution compares this scenario with the situation in Ireland. The contrast is found to be striking, and the implications are explored.

[1] Insofar as this paper does not focus primarily upon Ireland or the Irish it may appear to sit ill with the title of the volume (the piece was originally commissioned by Professor Dafydd Johnston as an address for delivery to the Centre for Advanced Welsh and Celtic Studies, Aberystwyth, in October 2011, an opportunity for which I am most grateful). However, Dáibhí Ó Cróinín's scholarly, literary, and cultural interests have always been famously resistant to Procrustean limitation, and I note that other contributors too have cheerfully transgressed the expected boundaries of the book. In my own case, the decision to respond to the editors' kind invitation with this particular offering was prompted precisely by the fact that, hearing of my experiments with spoken versions of it, Professor Ó Cróinín had expressed an interest in the topic that was as keen and enquiring as it was well-informed and stimulating. I am grateful to Dr Pádraic Moran for his editorial help.

Early medieval Ireland and Europe: chronology, contacts, scholarship, ed. by Pádraic Moran and Immo Warntjes, Studia Traditionis Theologiae, 14 (Turnhout, 2015), pp. 179–202.

 10.1484/M.STT-EB.5.103120

Keywords
Latin; the DMLCS project; Gerald of Wales, Caradog of Llancarfan, Sulien's family, Asser, Gildas, St Patrick; the colloquy *De raris fabulis*, the term Welsh, the Welsh laws.

Introduction

There is a question-mark in the title of this paper, but I hesitated about where to place it. Ideally there would have been two, one applying to 'Cambro-Romance' and one to the term 'counterpart'; but that would have offended against all convention. The point is that I am raising a double question about the Latin that was written by literate Celts in Britain in the early Middle Ages: to what extent does their output correspond to the Latin of their monastic contemporaries in Ireland?[2] And, whether it corresponds or not, is it appropriate to call it Cambro-Romance? That term is itself shorthand, twice over. I am using 'Romance' in the sense intended when one refers to French, Portuguese, Catalan, Romanian, etc. as Romance languages, namely organic, regional descendants of Latin. As for the 'Cambro-', that too is shorthand and, I admit, slightly misleading: where is Cambria? For my purposes it would be arbitrary to restrict the domain either geographically to Wales within its modern boundaries or, for that matter, in terms of persons to authors who necessarily spoke Welsh as their first language. For insisting that the writing must have been done within the borders of today's Wales would exclude both St Patrick and, probably, Gildas; and leaving them out would deprive the latinity we shall be examining of its traditional external and internal reference points respectively. It might also involve omitting, from centuries later, the colloquy *De raris fabulis*, with its glosses in what is surely best described simply as Bristol Channel Brythonic. As we shall see, that colloquy is a key text. As for requiring that a writer must have been a native speaker of Welsh, that would cause problems because such a characteristic is not always easy to determine when the medium of the writing is Latin. It would also beg a serious question, which we shall encounter at the end. And the requirement would in any case be a shame because it would probably knock out one of the most notorious wordsmiths in the whole of insular latinity, namely Giraldus Kambrensis.

[2] Still fairly definitive as a fully documented inventory of surviving early medieval Celtic-Latin output is Lapidge and Sharpe (1985).

In short, then, my criterion for a work to be considered is that it should have been written by an author in or from that part of the former Roman Britain that, at the time in question, was not yet English-speaking. The geographical domain therefore contracts over the period with which we are dealing, from potentially the whole island as far north as Pictland at the time of the demise of Roman rule, down to more or less the territory of modern Wales and Cornwall (and, in principle, Cumbria and Strathclyde) by the time the Normans had become firmly established on the scene.

This paper is based upon material drawn from the published, first constituent volume of the *Dictionary of Medieval Latin from Celtic Sources* (DMLCS).[3] As words beginning with the letters I to Z are still being researched for the project at the time of writing, it will be understood that almost all the examples produced here necessarily belong to the first half of the alphabet. However, while the results are to that extent provisional, the reader may be assured that there is no reason to suspect them of having been skewed in any particular way in consequence.

Welsh law texts attributed to Hywel Dda

For reasons that I hope will become apparent I wish to begin at the end of the period with which the DMLCS project deals, and work backwards. The least venerable, then, of the British-Latin texts that we have captured on our database,[4] and from which we have extracted words that were still genuinely new at the time they were written, are the five Latin recensions of the Welsh laws attributed to king Hywel Dda ('Hywel the Good'); these date from the 13th century to the end of the 14th.[5] Vocabulary added to Celtic latinity by these texts includes

[3] Harvey and Power (2005), henceforth NCLCL. It is to be hoped that our honorand, as a highly effective Chair of DMLCS since 2004 and a member of its Editorial Board since 1991, and having had close personal ties with the project almost since its inception, will see the current offering as an appropriate example of the scholarly fruit that the venture, under his leadership, is now in a position to bear.

[4] The most recent publication of the project's full-text, searchable database of sources has been *Royal Irish Academy Archive of Celtic-Latin Literature*, second (developed and expanded) edition, online at www.brepolis.net (created by A. Harvey and A. Malthouse in 2010; referenced as ACLL). ACLL uses the same numeration as Lapidge and Sharpe (1985) for each of the texts it contains.

[5] The recensions in question are Lapidge and Sharpe (1985)/ACLL items A149–A153; Lapidge and Sharpe (1985), 49, contains a bibliography of scholarship on them

loans from Old English such as **acra** (for a determinate area of plough-land, an acre) and, probably under Norman influence (since it is found in Domesday Book), the verb <**forisfacere**> ('to commit an offence').[6] The word **aratura** (compare Old French **areure** as well as Classical Latin **arare**) is used elsewhere for the task of ploughing, but in these Cambro-Latin texts to refer to the land so ploughed. And the Late Latin word **comminister** ('a fellow-minister'), whose pan-European sense was an ecclesiastical one only, is broadened out in this material to designate a secular fellow-servant or fellow-office-bearer in the royal court.

Those examples are of vocabulary that, globally speaking, was already current, but that only entered the lexicon of Celtic latinity through the Welsh laws. In contrast, items that seem to have been brought into Latin of any kind for the first time by those texts include <**appropinare**> ('to give one to drink'); an adjective **baculosus** ('having a crozier', that is as a mark of ecclesiastical rank); **benefictus** (an adjective applied to a book, in the sense of definitive, or well set out); **candelarius** to designate a candle-bearer; possibly **cauilla** (compare Old French **cheville** as well as Classical Latin **clauicula**) in the sense of an ankle; **commodatarius** for a tenant, or one who hires; **conquestor** in the sense of a complainant at law, or plaintiff; **debitarius** to designate someone who has a legal entitlement; and **exconcludere**, a compound meaning 'to confine or conclude' (in terms of the law). And the Latin texts of the Welsh laws seem to have been among the first anywhere to use the verb **ferrare** ('to shoe'; that is, a horse).

Furthermore the ubiquitous post-Classical noun **desertum**, with its general meaning of an uninhabited wilderness or wasteland of the kind much sought after by hermits, is in this Welsh legal usage de-spir-

to 1985, which needs controlling (particularly in regard to conclusions as to dating) by the inclusion of subsequent works such as Russell (2011).

6 These and all other lexemes mentioned in this article are given in the forms under which they have been alphabetized and dealt with in NCLCL; therefore, closer identifications of the works in which they appear, the editions from which these were digitally captured, the location of the words' occurrences therein, details of etymologies, meanings, etc. are in each case most handily pursued further by consulting NCLCL in the first instance. The words may be viewed in their settings in the original texts by means of appropriate electronic word-searches conducted on ACLL; to do this, wild-cards will of course be required, since the actual occurrences will usually be in grammatical shapes (oblique cases of nouns, finite forms of verbs, etc.) that differ from the citation-forms that—as is indicated by the **bold font**—are used as headwords in NCLCL, in other dictionaries, and for reference in the present essay. Angle-brackets enclose citation-forms that have had to be normalized orthographically to fit their etymologies or the likely shape of hitherto undiscovered instances.

itualized and qualified with the genitive *regis* so as to refer simply to land at the king's disposal, being uncultivated. (In this sense it can also be used metaphorically, and rather crudely, of an unmarried female!) A particularly interesting point to note is how the well-known, pan-European, but (surprisingly) post-Classical word **hostilitas** comes to be deployed in a new way in these texts ascribed to Hywel Dda. This constitutes a fine example of how a word in a corpus such as ours can prove to have been given a precise technical sense in addition to whatever more obvious meanings are familiar from other sources; for, in Welsh legal usage, the term **hostilitas** corresponds to the concept of *galanas*, and so gets used to refer to the formal declaration of a blood feud, as well as to the feud itself. By extension from that, the word can also designate, precisely, whatever is the cause of the blood feud: for example, in one instance we find it explicitly defined as *hominem interficere*, thus, in this case, referring to homicide. If one may say so—speaking up for the craft of lexicography here—it is worth pointing out that this example constitutes a nice illustration of why dictionary work such as that of DMLCS is required: without it, historians or other researchers could gain the impression of having understood a passage of medieval Latin, while in fact missing the central concept: they would see the word **hostilitas** in the text, assume that it simply meant non-specific enmity of some kind, translate it that way, observe that it seemed to make perfect sense in the context when so translated, and move contentedly on, while all the time its key significance had escaped them.

Giraldus Kambrensis

It will have been noticed that none of the words extracted from the legal texts are, in origin, latinizations of Welsh words. Instead, where their roots do not lie within Classical Latin itself (and they do whenever not noted otherwise here), they tend to derive from Old French. That tendency—the use of foreign rather than of indigenous resources when those of Latin were perceived to be wanting—forms part of a pattern that proves to continue throughout all of the texts with which the DMLCS project has worked: it might be expected that the principal source for new vocabulary would turn out to be the underlying Celtic vernaculars of the respective regions, but this is spectacularly not the case. In the thousands of articles written for the project's *Dictionary* so far (and not counting proper names) a Gaelic etymology has been posited for fewer than thirty headwords, and a Welsh origin for less than a dozen.[7] In the case of Hiberno-Latin I see this finding as the other side of the coin to the marked readiness on the part of Irish authors to experiment with Latin from within its own resources: they were doing this experimentation from the vantage point of their own language, and were therefore reluctant to involve that language itself in the games that they played.[8] Foreign tongues such as Greek and even Hebrew could be and often were pressed into service, but not their own, because this was serving as the metalanguage.[9] In British Celtic areas, though the vernacular-averse result was the same, the reason was probably different, and to this we shall turn at the end. In the meantime, let us move back in time from the Cambro-Latin law texts to a really substantial author, the first of the named ones so far treated thoroughly by DMLCS that we encounter when moving in this anti-chronological direction. This is of course the notorious Giraldus Kambrensis, or Gerald of Wales: half-Welsh, half-Norman churchman, adventurer, raconteur, polemicist, and thorn in the side of his contemporaries (to say nothing of his successors) on an international scale.[10] That said, he was also a keenly observant recorder of contemporary events and their agents; and he should be given credit as well for an ability to empathize if not sympathize with both sides in a conflict, and for a willingness to be the fall-guy in many of his own anecdotes.

Gerald's writings date from between AD 1188 and the early 1220s and, similarly to what we noted with the Cambro-Latin law texts, many of the coinings that we find therein are grammatically straightforward extrapolations from existing, standard Latin words. Thus, for example, it is Gerald who added to the medieval wordstore the verbs **ablambere** from Classical **ab** plus **lambere** meaning 'to lick off', **aduidere** from Classical **ad** plus **uidere** for 'to observe or catch sight of', and **brumescere** from the standard noun **bruma** in the sense of 'to be wintry or cold'. It was Gerald who gave the world such slightly Hisperic-looking adaptations as that of the Classical adverb **delicate** into the form

[7] On some of these Celtic-based coinings, and the likely reasons for them, see Harvey (2011), 68–9, as well as the present contribution's references (pp. 194–5 below) to **corbum** and **colornaticus** specifically.

[8] For details of the some of the games see Harvey (forthcoming).

[9] Harvey (2011), *passim*.

[10] Gerald's works are inventoried, along with details of editions, etc., in Lapidge and Sharpe (1985) as items A52–A75.

delicaciter with the sense of delicately or elegantly, of the established verb **fricare** into a noun **fricamen** for a grinding together or rasping, and of the standard adjective **herbosus** into a noun **herbositas** so as to mean an abundance of grass. Again, Gerald is adept at applying diminutives: from the Classical noun **aduersarius** he generates a diminutive **aduersariunculus** with the pejorative sense of petty opponent; from standard **anguilla** he gives us **anguillula** for a little eel; Gerald refers to a small division or section of a book as a **distinctiuncula**, from the established noun **distinctio**; and he coins an accusative *glomellum* as the diminutive of Classical **glomus** so as to refer to a little ball (in the specific instance, a ball of thread). He is very fond of adding the Greek prefix ἀρχι- to Classical Latin words, coining such macaronic compounds as **archisigillarius** (for the keeper of the Great Seal of the kingdom of England) and **archiaduersarius** (for arch-enemy, a term which—somewhat unsurprisingly—Gerald uses many times).

Those items, though apparently newly minted by Gerald, are all Classical enough in shape. Being who, where, and when he was, though, his writings are naturally larded with clearly post-Classical terminology that, loosely speaking, is feudal or to do with property. This includes **arpentum**, with which we should compare Classical Latin **arepennis** but also French **arpent**, famous as one of the words which has come through to that modern language from Gaulish and which designates a particular measure of land; **baronia** ('a barony, or estate held in baronial tenure'); **feodare** ('to bring into subordination by granting land in fee, or 'enfeoff''); **excambium** ('property given in exchange or compensation'); and **homagium** and **hominium** ('acts of homage, as to a feudal superior'). It is in such items that we begin to detect Norman influences creeping into the etymologies.

Gerald also served as a broad channel into our corpus for the administrative and/or legal Latin terms of the day; thus it is from him that it received **bedellus** ('an official or agent, a beadle'; compare Old French **bedel** and Old English **bydel**); **cancellaria** for the office of a chancellor; **citatorius**, an adjective meaning concerned with a summons; **litterae comminatoriae** ('threatening letters'); and <**deratiocinare**> and <**derationare**>, meaning 'to claim title' and 'to establish a right' respectively (with the latter term compare Old French **deraisnier**). Gerald uses what in the context is a sarcastically macaronic, deliberately hyperlearned term **falsigraphus** to designate a writer of falsehoods.

When it comes to ecclesiastical and monastic terminology, the non-English Latin of Britain owes to Gerald the adoption of the designations

archileuita (from—again—Greek ἀρχι-, plus the biblical term Levite) for an archdeacon; **cardinalis** in the sense of a cardinal (in Classical Latin it had been an adjective only, referring to something that served as a hinge or pivot); **cathedraliter** for having diocesan status, whether applied to a church (and so meaning a cathedral) or an individual (in which case he was either a bishop or, as it could be, a professor); **celleraria** for the office of a cellarer; **coabbas**, a term for a fellow-abbot, employed by Gerald as possibly the first non-Englishman to do so in Britain since the 6th-century Gildas, who however had used the distinctive form *conabbas*;[11] **cucul(l)atus**, literally hooded or cowled, used as a noun metonymically to mean a monk; **effunerarius** in the sense of a funerary attendant or undertaker; **episcopalia** to designate a bishop's robes; and **hospitalaris** to refer to one serving as guest-master.

Gerald uses most of these words merely (as he might himself have said) **clericaliter**—that is, as befits or in the manner of a cleric. Though he sometimes deploys them in somewhat aberrant senses (such as **curialitas** for courtesy, rather than as the office-title of a municipal councillor, which was its Late Latin meaning), there is usually nothing particularly original in the shape of them, except when he indulges in his not very subtle wordplay so as to make a point: examples include **demonachus**, which he coins as an opposite of the ubiquitous Late Latin word **monachus** so meaning a non-monk, with obvious play on **d(a)emoniacus** ('devilish, or possessed by an evil spirit'); or when he takes Late Latin **exhonorare**, meaning 'to despise or treat with contempt', and uses instead a form **ex(h)onerare**, influenced by (or perhaps with play on) Classical Latin **exonerare**, so giving it the precise sense of 'to deprive of specific honour(s)'. A possibly accidental example of this type of coining by Gerald would appear to be his **colideus**, built from Irish *céile Dé* ('companion of God') but influenced by Classical Latin **colere** ('to worship') and so meaning a hermit or anchorite subject to strict rule, namely a Culdee (the English term comes of course from the same Gaelic original).

It is when Gerald turns to matters of what we would nowadays call natural history that he really comes into his own in terms of generating new vocabulary. His interest in trees gives us the adjective **alburneus** for made of auburn, which is a kind of wood; **aralus** for a maple and **castanus** for a sweet-chestnut tree; and **alnetum** for an alder-grove, that last example exploiting the Classical Latin suffix **-etum** as a way of

[11] See pp. 191–3 below on Gildas and his works.

forming collective plurals of kinds of tree. Among freshly-minted bird names we owe to Gerald **aureolus** as a name for, perhaps, the golden oriole or the yellowhammer; and **aurifrisius**, an existing Latin word for gold-embroidered cloth which he has inventively diverted to designate the osprey because he sees it as the etymology of the Old French word for that bird, **orfrai** (in fact the latter comes from Classical Latin **ossifraga** ('the bone-breaker')). **Bisia** is what Gerald calls the common name (*uulgare uocabulum*, whatever exactly that means) for some kind of large goose. He uses **cercella** for teal (relatinized from Old French **cercelle**, since that is itself derived from Classical Latin **querquedula**); **gruta** to designate the grouse; **hobelus** as the hobby, a kind of small falcon (Old French **hobel**); and **gyrofalco** from Old French **gerfaucon** ('a gerfalcon'), about which Gerald speculates explicitly that the etymology may be *a gyro faciendo* ('from describing circles'), or else *in gyrum falcando* ('mowing down in a circle'), the verb there itself having been back-formed by Gerald from Classical Latin **falcatus**. Before (or perhaps not before!) moving on to kinds of fish, we should note that Gerald's word for a barnacle goose is **bernaca**, with which we may compare Welsh **brennig** ('limpets') as well as Old French **bernaque**.

In classifying denizens of the genuinely marine world Gerald distinguishes **bricius**, which is some kind of trout or similar, perhaps the char (compare Irish **breac**); **catus**, perhaps the shad; **gardio**, maybe the chub (compare Old French **gardon**); and **glassanus**, perhaps the pollan, but again some kind of trout or similar fish, and again with Gerald's name for it derived from an Irish word (in this case **glasán**, which nowadays can mean a whiting). He coins the phrase **conchosi pisciculi** for shellfish, with an associated adjective **conchilis** ('as of a mollusc'), both words of course generated from Classical **concha**. Not to be excluded at this point is Gerald's splendid phrase for the muddy foreshore where such creatures might be found, **marina glis** (compare Old French **glise**).

In addition, and inevitably given his career and the circles he moved in, Gerald is interested in military affairs. Thus it is through him that entry to the non-English corpus of British medieval latinity seems to have been gained by such specialized terms as **castellarium**, an old but surprisingly rare word for a fortification; **constabularius**, meaning a constable in the sense of a military officer commanding; and **excuba** for a guard or sentry (Gerald also uses the well-established Late Latin term **excubator** in this sense). The noun **desubitatio**, a word for a sudden action or attack, may actually be a coining of his own. He uses a fourth-declension noun **conductus**, which in Late Latin meant a contraction, in the quite different sense of guidance or safe-conduct. And, though **fossatum** is a Late Latin term that could already have significations as diverse as royal quarters and a trench, it is Gerald who brings it into our corpus and makes it his own, in senses ranging from a rath (the sort of circular earthwork typical of Celtic Ireland) to a ditch defending an Irish monastic settlement or an Irish settlement of Viking origin, to a trench constituting a tactical impediment to a linear advance, to an earthwork forming part of the outermost defence of a Norman fortification, whether in Ireland, in Wales, or in England.

Caradog of Llancarfan

Thus far Gerald: how much we should have missed if we had omitted him! Moving back from him we come to Caradog of Llancarfan, who died in AD 1150. In his Life of St Cadog we find the interesting Cambro-Latin coining **aequoralis**;[12] this should be compared with the Classical Latin noun **aequor** and contrasted with the standard adjectival derivative of that, namely **aequoreus**. Its general signification is, of course, simply marine, and that would seem to be how it is used in the Life of St Teilo, a text, preserved in the famous Book of Llandaf, that was originally composed between AD 1095 and 1128 and thus antedated Caradog.[13] The latter, however, in what seems to be the only other use of it that is extant, gives **aequoralis** the more precise meaning of seaward, since he applies it to Flat Holm in order to distinguish its location from that of Barry Island (both being off the coast of Glamorgan). Another term used by Caradog in a sense that seems appealingly precise is **britannigena**, which means one of Celtic British ancestry or living in Britain—if this word had gone on to be anglicized it might have been possible to use it in place of the rather over-long explanatory preamble with which the present paper begins! As it is, though, the noun in question seems to be extant in only one other place (namely the anonymous 12th-century Life of St Cyngar),[14] and so may well be a coining of Caradog's own making. A third example of Caradog's offering to the Latin language of a neatly precise term—though in this case no one else ever

[12] On Caradog see Lapidge and Sharpe (1985), 16–7; his works are Lapidge and Sharpe (1985)/ACLL texts A37–A38.

[13] The *Uita S. Teiliaui* is Lapidge and Sharpe (1985)/ACLL text A93.

[14] The *Uita S. Cungari* is Lapidge and Sharpe (1985)/ACLL text A116.

took it up—is the noun <**collectionarius**>, which he has compounded from the Classical prefix **con-** combined with **lectio** and an agentive suffix, or else with the already-formed Late Latin **lectionarius**, so as to designate a fellow-pupil or classmate (the English word **colleague** is of course an exactly analogous, but French-based calque).

Sulien's family

Moving back another few decades brings us to the celebrated writings of Sulien's family at Llanbardarn Fawr. These have an altogether higher stature within the Cambro-Latin tradition, and their more studied style goes along with this. The great Rhygyfarch,[15] dying just before the end of the 11th century, had introduced through his *carmina* the classy Hellenism **adelphus** in the sense of a brother (in Classical Latin this had only been found in the title of plays, and only Frithegod of Canterbury seems to have used it in Britain before him). Rhygyfarch it is, too, in his canonical Life of St David, who, wishing to calque the Welsh epithet **dyfrwr** in which the Saint rejoiced as one who drank only water, diverted for the purpose the Classical adjective **aquilentus**, which had originally simply meant watery. Again, Rhygyfarch imparts to his work a further Classical ring by using for chief, or head, the word **cephal**, first borrowed from Greek κεφαλή and used in the literal sense by Aldhelm of Malmesbury.[16] In the same meaning Rhygyfarch also uses what is apparently his own, etymologically cryptic coining **bragmaticus** and, in the abstract sense of headship or primacy, the clearly related noun **bragminatio**. To describe the twisting or swirling around of smoke he uses the rather high-flown verb <**circumgyrare**>, as does Gerald following him; while Greek comes into the picture again in Rhygyfarch's constant use of *agius* (from ἅγιος ('holy')) with the quasi-titular meaning of Saint, placed after the name (the match with such Welsh-language titles as *Dewi sant* for St David is thus a perfect one). In short, Rhygyfarch leaves us with the impression of one who wished to raise the register in Cambro-Latin writing. In this he followed a trend that was set in the middle of the 11th century and

[15] Rhygyfarch's works are captured on ACLL as texts A31 and A100 (*sic*; in Lapidge and Sharpe (1985) the latter has been confused with text A32).

[16] The use of specific words even by non-Celtic Latin authors such as Aldhelm, which is consequently not captured in ACLL, can nevertheless be tracked down using many of the same procedures (see n 6 above) by employing Brepols' so-called 'cross-database search-tool' at www.brepolis.net.

taken to Hisperic lengths by Owain in the two *carmina* preserved in Cambridge, Corpus Christi College, 139.[17] In these, we find the Hebrew word **ben** used for a son (exploiting the opportunity to play on the composer's name, which he spelled *Euben*); the word **fornifer** derived from Greek φερνόφορος ('dowry-bearing'), influenced by the Classical Latin suffix **-fer** and metonymically meaning one bearing or conveying a boon of learning (in other words, a scribe—himself!). Owain also retrieves from as far back as Gildas the epithet **ambrones** ('greedy ones'), and applies it (as he had done) to the enemies of the British Celts, in this case to the English of Northumbria.[18]

Asser

Asser, the interesting Welsh turncoat (if that is what he was) and biographer of King Alfred, died in the year AD 893.[19] In a usage subsequently adopted by Domesday Book, Petrus Cantor, and the Cambro-Latin laws ascribed to Hywel Dda, but seemingly by no one else until Erasmus of Rotterdam, Asser coined, from Classical Latin **accipiter**, the word **accipitrarius** for a keeper of hawks, or falconer. In a similar vein he seems to have given to the Latin language for the first time the noun **canicularius** for a keeper of hounds. Asser is responsible for the noun **enauigatio** to mean a voyaging off or about; the diminutive **foliuncula** for a little leaf (in the example, a leaf of vellum); and **gronnosus** for marshy. That adjective is derived from **gronna** or **grunna**, a bog or swamp, which is a noun of unknown etymology, seemingly having been coined by the Irish author Cogitosus in the 7th century and gone on to be one of the very few medieval Latin words whose use was widespread among Celtic authors generally but which was more or less unknown to other schools (as such, it is almost diagnostic for Celtic authorship of a text).[20] Astonishingly, as far as extant attestations go Asser seems also to have been the first person anywhere to use the adverb **anglice** for 'in the English language', though it duly went on to be used by all the other

17 Owain's *carmina* are Lapidge and Sharpe (1985)/ACLL texts A35–A36.

18 Owain does this in a prose passage associated with the *Historia Brittonum* (and captured as part of ACLL text A36A).

19 Asser's work *De rebus gestis Aelfredi regis* is Lapidge and Sharpe (1985)/ACLL text A30.

20 Cogitosus' famous *Uita S. Brigitae* is Lapidge and Sharpe (1985)/ACLL text B302.

authors already mentioned and of course became the standard term in 2nd-millennium latinity.

So, if we may sum up so far by characterizing Gerald as macaronic and imaginative, Caradog as precise, Rhygyfarch as stylish, and Owain as pretentious, we may say that Asser was winning in his word-coining, since his neologisms had a much higher take-up rate among later authors than did those of the others. Of course, the nature and transmission of the texts in which they were embedded will have been a vital factor too.

Gildas

Pressing on back in our chronology, unfortunately we fall into an enormous hole at this point! Apart from Moucan's *Oratio*,[21] preserved in an 8th-century Mercian manuscript, we have nothing at all by a named British-Celtic author until we encounter the great Gildas in the 6th century. So much may or may not have happened in this gap of at least three and a half centuries that any conclusions we are tempted to draw about the development of the tradition during that time must be largely speculative. Working with what we have, though, which is the only thing we can do, we find Gildas coining the words **aethralis** for coming from or in the heavens, the noun **bilustrum** for a period of ten years, the diminutive **cauernicula** for a small cavity or recess, **circio** for the north-west (from the standard wind-name **circius**), *clustellum* (for ***claustellum**) for a bolt, lock, or prison cell; and **commessor**, from the standard elements **con-** plus **messor**, to mean figuratively a fellow-reaper (see Luke 10:2), but with ironic rhetorical play on **comesor** ('a glutton'). Gildas makes a compound **condebitores** so as to mean joint or mutual debtors, and also uses the result metaphorically to designate fellow-sinners or allies. He coins the phrase **conuolatus palpebrarum** to mean blinking ('a coming-together-rapidly of the eyelids'), as well as the noun **depressor** to signify an oppressor; and a verb **fulcimentare** ('to support or prop up'). Gildas is responsible for making from a Classical adjective a noun **coruscus** (or perhaps **coruscum**; oblique cases only are attested) to designate radiance or brightness, a usage subsequently picked up by the Irish *Hisperica famina*. And of course it is from Gildas that we get—but only in the ablative plural—the two famous nautical words *curucis* and *cyulis*, the first (exceptionally for the British Latin tradition) being a word of insular

[21] This is Lapidge and Sharpe (1985) text A29 (not yet captured for ACLL).

Celtic etymology, referring to curraghs or coracles (compare Welsh **corwg** and Irish **curach**), and the second, *cyulis*, meaning warships or their complements and representing the first ever loan into Latin of an English word (the modern form of which is, of course, **keel**). For a fellow-bishop Gildas uses the obvious and widespread Late Latin noun **coepiscopus**, but with his distinctive retention of the nasal in the prefix, so as to give *conepiscopus* (it will be recalled that we saw him doing this earlier, in his form *conabbas*).

If all of these words look somewhat familiar to early medievalists it is because the Gildasian work in which they are first found, the polemic *De excidio Britanniae*, went on to have such vast influence in subsequent centuries that any insular Latin author throughout the Middle Ages, whether Celtic, Anglo-Saxon, or Norman, and whether located in Britain, Ireland, Brittany, or further afield, would be sure to include quotations or at least obvious echoes from it in his own work.[22] To take Gildas' two nautical coinings that I mentioned just now, for example, we see that both of them went on to be used as active items of vocabulary by such later writers. Within Celtic latinity, *curucis* was employed twice—but both times in the ablative plural, the only form that Gildas gives—by Adomnán in his Life of St Columba (Colum Cille), in distant Iona, at the turn of the 8th century;[23] while the 'keel' word appears several times in the *Historia Brittonum* and was also used once, around the year AD 880, by the Breton-Latin author Wrdisten, abbot of Landévennec, in his Life of St Winwaloe (Guénolé).[24] In the latter, the relevant form is the ablative plural *cyulis*, this again being exactly that coined by Gildas.

Now, because of his (at times) high-flown style, Gildas is sometimes regarded as the father of hispericism, a term already used a couple of times in this paper. Strictly speaking it should be used only to refer to the language of the so-called *Hisperica famina*, those quasi-poetic, 7th-century, almost certainly Hiberno-Latin exercises in the description of everyday scenes using deliberately obscure vocabulary.[25] However, going

[22] As well as the tract *De excidio* we have from Gildas' pen what is now a fragmentary *Epistola*; the two items are Lapidge and Sharpe (1985)/ACLL texts A27 and A28 respectively.

[23] This *Uita S. Columbae* is Lapidge and Sharpe (1985)/ACLL text B305.

[24] This *Uita S. Uinualoei* is Lapidge and Sharpe (1985) text D827; the narrative prose part is numbered D827 TXT A as captured on ACLL.

[25] See Harvey (forthcoming); the four recensions of the *Hisperica famina* are Lapidge and Sharpe (1985)/ACLL texts B325–B328; Lapidge and Sharpe (1985), 93–4, also provide an inventory (to 1985) of secondary literature on these texts.

slightly against the modern scholarly grain, in the DMLCS project it has been considered valid and more useful to regard also as 'Hisperic' the vocabulary of the equally 7th-century Irishman Virgilius Maro Grammaticus—and indeed of other Celtic-Latin writers later and elsewhere, such as the Breton Lios Monocus in the 9th century and, more than occasionally, Sedulius Scottus at the Carolingian court—whenever this vocabulary of theirs is characterized by being 'deliberately arcane or affectedly learned' (that being the exposition of the label 'hisp.' as applied to the relevant lexemes in the DMLCS *Dictionary*).[26] Now, such 'Hisperic' works do draw upon and recycle the vocabulary of Gildas—for example, the D-text of the *Hisperica famina* themselves uses the word **tithicus**, a Gildasian adjective for marine. But, as has hopefully become clear from the other examples of his vocabulary just given, Gildas himself was hardly using such words in a deliberately arcane sense. Rather, he is marshalling for the purposes of his brave, denunciatory plea for reformation in church and society all the resources of his training in Latin rhetoric. The truly remarkable thing is that, in Britain in the AD 500s, he achieves this to a level that the most exacting Roman Classical standards of earlier centuries could barely have faulted.

Patrick

One century back from Gildas is St Patrick.[27] Though he perpetrates some mild vulgarisms, such as the conversion of some Classical deponent verbs to such corresponding active forms as <**aggredere**> ('to undertake'), **exhortare** ('to encourage'), and **fruere** ('to enjoy'), Patrick is remarkably restrained as far as semantic coinings go. The most interesting is his use of **hiberionaci** as a name for the Irish people, since this reflects a direct borrowing from the Gaelic of his time of the word that, to this day, means of course the same thing, namely—to cite it in the singular—**Éireannach**. Patrick does give us the term <**chrismare**> ('to anoint with chrism'); perhaps by association with Classical **efficere** he does produce a verb **effitiari** so as to oppose standard **infitiari** and so

[26] See NCLCL, xvii. The works of the three named authors are catalogued as Lapidge and Sharpe (1985) items B295–B297, D829, and C672–686 respectively; on Virgilius and his vocabulary see most recently Harvey (2014).

[27] St Patrick's works are Lapidge and Sharpe (1985)/ACLL texts A25–A26; on these and their probable historical and social context see Kelly (2011) and the other layers of www.confessio.ie (created by A. Harvey and F. Fischer).

mean to make an affirmation or declaration when it is the Holy Spirit doing so; and he does coin the etymologically mysterious **exagaelliae** to denote the figurative legacy or bequest that he will leave to his followers. But there is little else.

Now with the exception of Gerald the present writer, at least, does not gain the impression from any of the medieval authors we have examined that they were struggling to fill gaps within their Latin vocabulary in order to express themselves. Rather, any Latin coinings they made were for rhetorical reasons, to enhance the power of that expression. That is an important distinction and, as we shall see, it contrasts markedly with the situation in early medieval Ireland: its implication is that the British were the inheritors of an unbroken, still functioning Latin tradition that already contained within it, at least latently, all the semantic resources they might require. But first let us test the hypothesis. If it is right, it should mean that a British-Latin work that is fairly obviously designed to teach specific Latin vocabulary to students of British Celtic background will be found to concentrate on areas of life that are technical, specialized, and perhaps post-Roman, so as to be of semantic help even to participants in what was a living Latin tradition.

De raris fabulis

Such a work is the colloquy *De raris fabulis*, perhaps originally composed in the 9th century: let us see what coinings are introduced apparently for the first time in the course of it.[28] Many of these words are glossed in the Bristol Channel Brythonic that I mentioned before and, looking at the items involved, we notice first of all a prominent group of equestrian terms. These include **antel(l)a** (compare Late Latin **antilena**) for a horse's breast-plate (though it is actually glossed *postoloin* ('a crupper (strap)')); **corbum** (compare Welsh **corf**) for the pommel of a saddle, or saddle-bow; **bullo**, probably another term for a breast-plate since it is glossed *bronnced*; and a few further, unidentified items of a horse's tack such as **glomerarium**,[29] glossed *hloimol*, and **appetitorium**, which from

[28] The colloquy is Lapidge and Sharpe (1985)/ACLL text A85; to the relevant literature listed in Lapidge and Sharpe (1985), 31, should be added Falileyev and Russell (2003) and the further references given there.

[29] Following my presentation of this material at a lecture in University College Cork, John Barry kindly drew my attention to Pliny the Elder's use of a clearly related word, **glomeratio**, to refer to the fluid action of high-stepping horses (Caius Plinius

its Latin shape as well as its gloss, *gurtharet*, ought to mean a 'striver' (whatever precisely that might imply). Then there are words for tools and implements, such as **artauus** ('a dagger'), found also in the 9th-century *Historia Brittonum* and, around the year AD 1100, in Cornwall in the sense of a penknife; **baxus**, glossed *creman* ('a sickle'); **foratorium**, itself glossing *rostrum* and defined with the vernacular *gilb* for an awl or hole-punch; and **cupanum**, with which we should compare Classical Latin **cupa** (though probably not Welsh **cwpan**), for a cup, goblet, or perhaps the contents thereof.

That last example borders on the culinary, which introduces another prominent group of words in the colloquy: here, **fornilium** means brushwood for building a fire (it is glossed *munutolau*, and we should compare Late Latin **furnale** and French **fournilles** as well as Classical Latin **fornax** and **furnus**). The form **cipus** (compare Classical **caepa** ('an onion') and **cippus** ('a stump')) refers guessably enough to a leek or other edible plant of the Allium genus, as is proved by its gloss *cennin*. The word that I believe we should read **colornaticus** (so as to see an etymology resembling Welsh **celwrn** ('a pail or pitcher') plus the adjectival suffix **-edig**) seems to mean, by metonomy, cream, since it is glossed with the word *barr* (literally 'top' or 'summit'), which would then be analogous to the Irish use of vernacular **úachtar** for that dairy product. **Fordalium**, glossed *lefet*, would seem to refer to some kind of edible herb or vegetable (perhaps compare Late Latin **faratalia**), while **hordinaceus panis** is the colloquy's phrase for barley-bread, as opposed to the wheaten sort (the Classical noun **hordeum** has been combined with the adjectival suffix **-aceus** and the whole then influenced by **ordinatio**). And finally there is the pan-Celtic lexeme **ba(t)tutus** or **baptutus**, meaning 'churned' (of milk), thus specifying buttermilk or, in the feminine form **babtuta** that is found in the colloquy, butter itself, since there it appears to be glossed *emmenin*.

What is striking about these sets of vocabulary is surely their highly practical nature. They are just the kinds of items that even students being brought up within a Latinate environment might be considered likely not yet to know, but to be in need of. The dairying terms, in particular, are ones that even a Roman would never have been acquainted with, simply because the products involved are essentially foreign to the warm, sunny,

Secundus, *Naturalis historia* 8.166; the etymology indicates that the horses' conformation was bunched up into a ball). Assuming that the item referred to in the colloquy was designed to induce the gait in question, Dr Kate Younger has suggested to me that it may have been a sort of standing martingale.

olive-oil-based Mediterranean world, while being almost stereotypically central to the cattle-owning Celt. So these coinings are specialized ones; but there is nothing of the high register about them, and no high-flown, pretentious, or philosophical-sounding terminology. And in general in the course of this paper, as we have peeled away the successive layers of additional vocabulary from British-Celtic Latin by looking further and further back in time (and correspondingly outwards in area), what we have seen is a sparser and sparser ratio of new words to established ones. In other words, the longer ago, the less innovative—perhaps because the more assured. The contrast with Ireland in this regard is instructive, so I propose to explore that for the remainder of my contribution.

Comparison with Ireland

In Ireland, after Norman influence began, we find borrowings, calquings and the generation of new words from within Latin's own resources proceeding at much the same rate as in Britain—and this is not surprising, considering that by that stage there was a substantial overlap in the personnel involved (Gerald of Wales is the lynchpin, of course, with his extensive network of contacts in both islands among the Norman élites of both church and state, with his writings dealing with Ireland just as much as with Wales, and with their wide circulation and subsequent influence in both territories). But three or four centuries earlier, at the Carolingian court, we find mainly John Scottus Eriugena, but other Irishmen too, being even more inventive in their coinings of new Latin words. In fact, fully five percent of the articles that we have published in our *Lexicon* are estimated to be for headwords that the DMLCS corpus attests first or indeed exclusively in the works of Eriugena; and that excludes variations by him on Classical vocabulary and his semantically innovative use of Late Latin items.[30] But two hundred years earlier still, in the 7th century, and within the island of Ireland, Hibernian writers were already busy coining new Latin vocabulary from existing Latin sources in seemingly unprecedented ways. Elsewhere I have identified three distinct and well developed methodologies that they used to do this, one based on a technique that I have christened disunderstanding, one on the use of virtual punctuation, and one on puns and other word-

[30] Eriugena's works are catalogued as Lapidge and Sharpe (1985) items C695–C713; for examples of his coinings see Harvey (2013), 99.

play.[31] But all of this prompts the question: why were they doing it? A response should surely begin by stressing the unlikelihood of its being a mere coincidence that, to the early medieval Irish, Latin was an entirely foreign language, which they had had to learn from books. (Ireland not having been in the Roman Empire, they had no alternative; and they were in fact the first nation to attempt this task.) But the result was that they had lexical gaps to fill: probably not even all of the real Virgil was available in Ireland, to say nothing of any of the other classics. In fact, not all of the Latin vocabulary that they needed was at the disposal of the Irish learned classes at any time in the early Middle Ages. So they were quick to take existing Latin words that they did know and extrapolate from them. But, given that the Irish were at their most experimental in the early part of their Latinate history, this is therefore somewhat different from what we have just found among the British Celts, where the further back we go the more conservative with words they seem to be.

Now, I have the impression from working with my fellow editors of territorial dictionaries of medieval Latin from across Europe that the British pattern resembles the one also found among authors who were native speakers of Romance languages: the rate of lexical innovation increased as the centuries passed. Should we not then logically conclude that the reason is the same: the British did not need to build up their Latin at an early stage by extrapolation, as the Irish did, because they already knew it thoroughly well? Of course such a conclusion should not be too surprising: there were, of course, varying degrees of romanization within the Roman Empire but, if we look at it in a binary fashion and put things bluntly, the British had been in it and the Irish had not. May this not to a large extent account for the difference?

After all, the surviving Hiberno-Latin tradition is self-consciously aware that its commencement marked a new beginning in Ireland. Presenting itself as having begun with St Patrick's mission (whether it really did or not is another matter), it sees itself as part and parcel of the introduction of Christianity to the island. The hagiographical strand of that tradition, always one of its strongest components, can be seen to have been born of the will to come to terms with and describe—and thus to define—what had been taking place and changing as a result of the labours of evangelists and church organizers during the previous couple of centuries. And then to take that process one step further. It is in that context that Muirchú Maccu Machthéni in his 7th-century Life

[31] Harvey (forthcoming).

of St Patrick meticulously latinizes—and, given the context, is surely therefore trying to cope with and tame—utterances that had reached him in an Irish-language medium.[32] Given his theme, that medium was an ex-druidic, and therefore still a potentially dangerous one; in explicit contrast with it, Muirchú is at pains to show who he was, and who he thought he was, within a self-consciously *Roman* Christian strand of Hiberno-latinity. But really he protests too much: his work is riddled with Hibernicisms, and the pagan past is something he is still clearly trying to exorcize, as he helps to build a Christian future.[33]

Now contrast that with Gildas. He was writing at least five generations earlier but, located in Britain, being a Roman and a Christian is already for him so much a given that it is in fact the prevailing decline from these that he bewails in the society around him. For Gildas it is the past that is golden (making a paradox of the fact that, in the event, his work was to shape the future so much).[34] And, of course, probably more than a hundred years had already elapsed since the official Roman withdrawal when he wrote his Latin;[35] that Latin is still polished and educated, so how much better still must standards of education and literacy presumably have been in the larger island when the imperial apparatus was still intact. Let us go back into the previous century, to St Patrick. Here we have someone who really was kidnapped at sixteen and taken as a slave to a hostile country. In his *Confessio*, he himself bewails the fact that he 'did not learn as others did, who drank in equally well both the law and the sacred writings, and never had to change their way of speaking since childhood, but always grew better and better at it'.[36] He says that one can easily see from his writings the standard of the instruction and learning that he has had and, as if on cue, it was standard practice until less than a generation ago to agree that St Patrick's writings did indeed give an impression of artlessness and general syntactic break-

[32] Muirchú's *Uita S. Patricii* is Lapidge and Sharpe (1985)/ACLL text B303.

[33] For a contextual discussion see Dawson (2011); an analysis of Muirchú's work from a lexical point of view, prepared by the present writer, is currently with editors.

[34] Still relevant in this context are the various contributions to Lapidge and Dumville (1984); these are evaluated in a review published as Harvey (1986).

[35] According to Sims-Williams (1990), 223, 'we may have to reckon that Gildas may have written at any period between *c.*500 and *c.*560'; to the relevant scholarship cited by Sims-Williams should be added Herren (1990).

[36] *non didici sicut et ceteri, qui optime itaque iura et sacras litteras utraque pari modo combiberunt et sermones illorum ex infantia numquam mutarunt, sed magis ad perfectum semper addiderunt* (*Confessio* 9, ed. by Bieler (1952), i 61; trans. by McCarthy at www.confessio.ie/etexts/confessio_english).

down. However, in a key intervention by David Howlett the argument was then advanced that, on the contrary, St Patrick's own protestations of rusticity and lack of erudition were deliberately ironic and intended to shame the *domini cati rhetorici* back home.[37] Importantly, Howlett's vindication of Patrick's writing did not depend primarily upon the numerical theories of composition for which that scholar has since become noted (and, frequently, criticized),[38] but rather upon his demonstration that the *Confessio* shows its author to be well capable of using *clausulae*, cursus rhythms, rhetorical argument, and every shade of biblical citation from direct quotation to allusion by context. I also note, for what it is worth, that it is since the appearance of Howlett's article that a sea-change has come over the accepted view of St Patrick's writings. No one now speaks of Patrick's 'spluttering incoherence' or the like;[39] but the fact is that, until Howlett wrote, they did. I do not think there are any other reasons for the change, so this means that even Howlett's opponents have tacitly accepted his arguments in at least that case, whether they are aware of having done so or not. This is a point that he has himself modestly not made; but I think he would be justified in doing so. At all events, if he is even approximately correct then we can forget all about incoherence, lack of fluency and inability to conduct a sustained argument in Latin on the part of St Patrick. But in that case, how much more polished must have been the Latin of 5th-century romanized Britons whose education had not been interrupted as Patrick's was. Further back still, in the days of the empire, it must have been even better; so that as we pursue back into time the tradition of writing Latin among the medieval British Celts, we do not sense that we are approaching any sort of starting-point, as in Ireland. Instead, in a spectrum ranging from stylish writers like Pelagius down to the scrappy private notes of the Vindolanda tablets,[40] the language merges seamlessly with the various registers of Roman imperial Latin from which it was in the process of evolving.

[37] Howlett (1989), *passim*.

[38] See most fundamentally Howlett (1995) and, most relevantly to the corpus of texts being discussed in the present paper, Howlett (1998); the criticism alluded to is exemplified in a review of the latter by McKee and McKee (2000).

[39] The phrase is that of Hood (1978), 18.

[40] Pelagius' works are Lapidge and Sharpe (1985) texts A2–A20 (the first of these, the monumental *Expositiones xiii epistolarum Pauli*, having duly been captured on ACLL). The Vindolanda tablets will be catalogued as text A287a in the planned second edition of Lapidge and Sharpe (1985).

Conclusion

Now, to conclude: what should we call that emerging Latinate tradition? As is well known, the term that the English language uses for its senior neighbour-tongue in the island of Britain and the speakers thereof, namely **Welsh**, unfortunately tends to carry as part of its inherited semantic load the concept of 'members of a despised nation different from one's own'. With or without the slur, but with a probably associated informality, use of this etymon is actually quite widespread among the Germanic and Slavic peoples of Europe when referring to others:[41] thus in the colloquial German of North Rhine-Westphalia the adjective **welsch** refers to the adjacent *Walloons* of Belgium, while in at least part of Austria it designates Italians; and in Chur, capital of the Swiss canton of Graubünden, the district of *Welschdörfli*, with its distinctive (and perhaps originally slightly patronizing) diminutive termination, was so named by the surrounding German-speakers because of the foreignness—to them—of its inhabitants, these being users of a tongue that is today the country's fourth national language. At what is by now, at least, a more official level, the Polish word for Italy is **Włochy,** and in English the name **Wallachia** is only slightly obsolete in its reference to a region lying along the north bank of the river Danube; while, to return to Switzerland, the French-speaking cantons in the west of the country are known to German-speakers as the *Welschland*. But what else have all the peoples designated by the etymon (or living in the areas indicated by it) in common with one another? The answer is that they are all native speakers of languages that are directly descended from Latin. That is the full meaning of Romance, and one can see why I used it—albeit with a question-mark—in the title of this paper. If all its cognates apply to mother-language Romance speakers, why should we necessarily make an exception of the English word **Welsh**?[42] The implication of not doing so

[41] I owe the examples given here to personal knowledge kindly shared at various times by Roman Bleier, Franz Fischer, Patricia Ronan, Brian Scott, Gilbert Stucky, Anna Zajko, and particularly (following my presentation of this material to a seminar of Cambridge University's *Department of Anglo-Saxon, Norse and Celtic*) Debbie Bryce. The latter has also been most helpful with comments and criticisms, as has my colleague Jane Power.

[42] A famous essay by Tolkien (1963) seems still to be widely followed (for example, by various Internet sites) in its suggestion that the linguistic component of our etymon's semantic load can refer to speakers of Celtic as well as of Latinate dialects. However, the single example of the English word **Welsh** appears alone to be responsible for this view, since the numerous further examples of the etymon supplied even by

would appear to be that when the Anglo-Saxons first began to arrive in the east of Britain, they perceived at least the significant figures among the indigenous people they encountered there to be characterized not by their Celtic speech, but by their living use of Latin. However, in my opinion the lexical evidence amassed by the DMLCS project suggests that just such a possibility should be taken seriously into account.[43]

Bibliography

Bieler, L. (1952) *Libri epistolarum Sancti Patricii episcopi*, 2 vols., Dublin.

Dawson, E. (2011) 'Pillars of conversion in Muirchú and Tírechán: two case studies,' www.confessio.ie/more/article_dawson.

Falileyev, A. and P. Russell (2003) 'The dry-point glosses in *Oxoniensis Posterior*,' in P. Russell, *Yr Hen Iaith: Studies in early Welsh*, Aberystwyth, 95–101.

Harvey, A. (1986) Review of Lapidge and Dumville (1984), *Journal of Ecclesiastical History* 37, 485–6.

— (1991) 'The Cambridge Juvencus glosses: evidence of Hiberno-Welsh literary interaction?,' in P.S. Ureland and G. Broderick, *Language contact in the British Isles*, Tübingen, 181–98.

— (2011) 'Lexical influences on the medieval Latin of the Celts,' in M. Pérez González and E. Pérez Rodríguez, *Influencias léxicas de otras lenguas en el latín medieval*, León, 65–77.

— (2013) 'The non-Classical vocabulary of Celtic-Latin literature: an overview,' in M. Garrison, A. Orbán, and M. Mostert, *Spoken and written Latin: relations between Latin and the vernacular languages in the earlier Middle Ages*, Turnhout, 87–100.

sources that echo the suggestion would appear, at least ultimately, all to have Romance-language referents.

[43] The question of how long my putative 'community Romance' may then have survived, at some level and in some circles, in British Celtic areas is a matter of ongoing debate, in the context of which I have benefited particularly from fruitful discussion with Peter Household. One can arguably countenance a post-Norman date for its final demise—beyond the chronological range of the DMLCS project, and thus a matter primarily for others to investigate! In the meantime, some circumstantial evidence for its longevity may be thought to have been provided by Harvey (1991) since, though the argumentation there is subjected to a searching examination in the long and detailed 'Introduction' (pp. 1–75) to McKee (2000), my conclusion (Harvey (1991), 195) about the presence of spoken Latin as 'an everyday, not just liturgical, language in at least one international house in ninth- to tenth-century Wales' would appear to remain unscathed.

— (2014) 'Linguistic method in his literary madness? The word-coinings of Virgilius Maro Grammaticus,' in E. Roma and D. Stifter, *Linguistic and philological studies in early Irish*, Lewiston, 79–104.

— (forthcoming) 'Blood, dust and cucumbers: constructing the world of Hisperic latinity,' in E. Purcell et al., *Medieval Ireland: clerics, kings, and Vikings*, Dublin.

Harvey, A. and J. Power (2005) *The non-Classical lexicon of Celtic latinity, 1: Letters A–H*, Turnhout (referenced as NCLCL).

Herren, M.W. (1990) 'Gildas and early British monasticism,' in A. Bammesberger and A. Wollmann, *Britain 400–600: language and history*, Heidelberg, 65–78.

Hood, A. (1978) *St Patrick: his writings and Muirchu's Life*, Chichester.

Howlett, D. (1989) 'Ex saliva scripturae meae,' in D. Ó Corráin, L. Breatnach, and K. McCone, *Sages, saints and storytellers: Celtic studies in honour of Professor James Carney*, Maynooth, 86–101.

— (1995) *The Celtic Latin tradition of biblical style*, Blackrock.

— (1998) *Cambro-Latin compositions: their competence and craftsmanship*, Dublin.

Kelly, D. (2011) 'St Patrick's writings: *Confessio* and *Epistula*,' www.confessio.ie/more/article_kelly.

Lapidge, M. and D. Dumville (1984) *Gildas: new approaches*, Woodbridge.

Lapidge, M. and R. Sharpe (1985) *A bibliography of Celtic-Latin literature 400–1200*, Dublin.

McKee, H. (2000) *The Cambridge Juvencus manuscript glossed in Latin, Old Welsh, and Old Irish: text and commentary*, Aberystwyth.

McKee, H. and J. McKee (2000) Review of Howlett (1998), *Cambrian Medieval Celtic Studies* 39, 79–80.

Russell, P. (2011) *Welsh law in medieval Anglesey: British Library Harleian MS 1796 (Latin C)*, Cambridge.

Sims-Williams, P. (1990) 'Dating the transition to neo-Brittonic: phonology and history, 400–600,' A. Bammesberger and A. Wollmann, *Britain 400–600: language and history*, Heidelberg, 217–61.

Tolkien, J.R.R. (1963) 'English and Welsh,' in H. Lewis, *Angles and Britons: O'Donnell lectures*, Cardiff, 1–41.

PAUL RUSSELL

BEYOND JUVENCUS: AN IRISH CONTEXT FOR SOME OLD WELSH GLOSSING?

Abstract

Starting from the Old Irish input into the glossing of the Welsh Juvencus manuscript, it is argued that there are hints that some of the Old Welsh glossing on another manuscript, St Dunstan's Classbook, may have been created in an Irish-influenced context.

Keywords

Juvencus, Ovid; Old Welsh, Old Irish; glosses.

It has long been observed that the glossing in the Cambridge Juvencus manuscript (Cambridge, University Library, Ff.4.42), though predominantly in Latin, contains a proportion of glosses in Old Welsh and Old Irish.[1] Most interesting of all is the small group of glosses which seems to represent a less than perfect translation of Old Irish glosses into Old Welsh. While long thought of as errors, I have argued that they are important evidence for translation of glosses from Irish into Welsh: 'the fact that in one way or another they have 'failed' is what allows us to see them for what they are, and we are left to wonder how many more of the Old Welsh glosses in this manuscript are the successful product of this kind of gloss-translation'.[2] For those who seek to understand the nature of vernacular glossing in Latin manuscripts, the Juvencus manuscript is crucial: in addition to the evidence for translation from Old Irish into Old Welsh, the fact that the manuscript was copied, glossed, and more generally

[1] For a facsimile of this manuscript, see McKee (2000b); for a detailed edition of the text, see McKee (2000a); and for discussion of the glossing and commentary, see Lapidge (1982), 111–3; Harvey (1991); McKee (2000c); and Russell (2012), 206–14.

[2] Russell (2012), 212.

Early medieval Ireland and Europe: chronology, contacts, scholarship, ed. by Pádraic Moran and Immo Warntjes, Studia Traditionis Theologiae, 14 (Turnhout, 2015), pp. 203–14.

 10.1484/M.STT-EB.5.103121

commented upon by six different scribes highlights the cumulative nature of the glossing process; had only a fair copy of this manuscript had survived, we would have no clue to the complex layers of glossing which have gone into the making of the manuscript text. In some respects, though, I would suggest that this manuscript has no more or less complex a transmission than many others; it simply allows us to see the complexity.

The Juvencus manuscript is only one of a number of manuscripts which provides evidence for the translation of glosses. Pierre-Yves Lambert has discussed this phenomenon in a number of continental manuscripts, mainly those containing Old Breton glosses which can be shown to be closely related to, and in part dependent on, glossing in other vernaculars.[3] In some cases, such as the Juvencus manuscript, there is a significant Irish contribution. In what follows, I want to consider the possibility that there are hints of an Irish context to the glossing of another Welsh manuscript.

Oxford, Bodleian Library, Auct. F.4.32 (saec. ix) is a compilation of several sections, many of which have a Celtic connection, probably compiled in Glastonbury in the second half of the 10th century; the sections are as follows:[4]

1r–9v	Eutyches, *Ars de uerbo*; glossed in Old Breton;
10r–18v	Old English homily added later;
19r–36v	*Liber Commonei* ('The Book of Commoneus') is probably the oldest part of the manuscript (perhaps early 9th century), described as 'the patriarch of all Welsh books known' by Bradshaw.[5] Its wide range of unusual texts, including especially rare evidence for knowledge of Greek, contains various sub-sections, including a text on weights and measures glossed in Latin and Old Welsh;
37r–47r	Ovid, *Ars Amatoria* I; glossed in Latin and Old Welsh.

It has been suggested by Breen that the *Liber Commonei* has Irish links but for our purposes the last section is most relevant.[6] Folios 37r–47r

3 See, for example, Lambert (1982); Lambert (1989); Lambert (1990a); Lambert (1990b).

4 For a facsimile, see Hunt (1961); for discussion of the manuscript, see Bodden (1979), Budny (1992); digital images of the manuscript are available at http://image.ox.ac.uk/show?collection=bodleian&manuscript=msauctf432.

5 Letter from Bradshaw quoted by Ellis (1880), 426.

6 Breen (1992).

contain the oldest surviving copy of Ovid's *Ars Amatoria*, Book I, and as such has been of great interest to classical scholars; other aspects of the text have attracted the interest of medievalists.[7] The text (and glossing) was copied by four scribes:[8]

Scribe A: 37r1–42r18 (ll. 1–379), but also copying glosses in the first part of scribe B's stint;
Scribe B: 42r19–46r end (ll. 380–704);
Scribe C: 46v (ll. 705–46);
Scribe D: 47r (ll. 747–72) (perhaps St Dunstan[9]).

Two sections of the text, 37r1–42r28 (ll. 1–389) and 45r33–v26 (ll. 620–52), are glossed in Latin and Old Welsh with occasional marginal commentary in Latin. Most glossing (apart from three glosses on 37r) and commentary seems to have been copied with the exemplar, and no distinction can be made in terms of ink between the Latin and Old Welsh glosses; it appears then that the Old Welsh was copied along with the Latin from an earlier exemplar. Overall, there are approximately 479 Latin glosses and 81 Old Welsh.[10]

As has been demonstrated by Lambert, comparison of different glossed copies of the same text can be illuminating; he has shown that there are glosses shared between different manuscripts of Priscian's *Institutiones* and of the works of Bede and Orosius, and of the *Collectio Canonum Hibernensis*, and McKee has argued that the distribution of glosses in the Cambridge Juvencus is probably the outcome of a process of cumulative glossing.[11] It appears that something similar can be found among the manuscripts of Ovid's *Ars Amatoria*; a comparison of some

[7] Cf., for example, Hexter (1986).

[8] In what follows, folio and line references to the manuscript are given, followed by line references to the standard edition of Ovid, *Ars Amatoria* (Kenney (1995); cf. also Ramírez de Verger (2003)). For the division of hands, I follow Charles-Edwards (2012), 400–1; Charles-Edwards (2013), 644–5, following a suggestion of Conway (1997); for the older view that 37r–46v was the work of one scribe, see, for example, Budny (1992), 115. For a new edition of this text and further discussion, see Russel (forthcoming).

[9] On this hand as St Dunstan's, see Budny (1992), 104, 141–2.

[10] For studies of the Old Welsh glosses in this manuscript, see Stokes (1860–1), 234–7; Rhŷs (1873), 230v5; Williams (1929–30); Williams (1932–3); most of them are collected in Loth (1884) and Falileyev (2000).

[11] See Lambert (1982); Lambert (1990), 342–59; Lambert (2005); McKee (2000b), 43–75; McKee (2000c), 12–20.

of the early glossed manuscripts of Ovid's love poetry shows that it is probable that the glossing has accumulated in the process of successive copying. The simple fact that scribe A of the Ovid was copying both text and glosses is suggestive of glosses travelling through the manuscript tradition. Moreover, it is clear too that the Old Welsh glossing simply represents the final stage of the accumulation of glosses in this manuscript.[12] In two instances in particular we can see that, probably in the archetype of our manuscript, the Latin gloss must have already been in place when the Old Welsh gloss was added and that the latter has been displaced: at 38r4 (l. 73) *miseris patruelibus* is glossed above in Latin by the explanatory gloss *fili aegypti* ('the sons of Aegyptus') but in the right margin an Old Welsh gloss, *dir arpeteticion ceintiru* ('the wretched cousins'), referring to the same lemma has also been added.[13] While the Latin gloss is providing explanation, the Old Welsh gloss is simply translating the main text but could not have been added interlinearly as the space was already occupied by the Latin gloss. At 38r33 (l. 102) *cum* is glossed *donec uel cant* where *cant* ('since') offers an alternative (signposted by *uel*) and correct rendering of *cum* thought by the Latin glossator to mean 'until'.[14] The point is that the Latin gloss had to be in place for the Welsh glossator to react against it.

Furthermore, a comparison of the glosses in our manuscript (henceforth indicated by the siglum O) with those found in St Gall, Stiftsbib-

[12] That is apart from three glosses added on the first page (37r) in a later hand and a darker ink.

[13] The preposition *di* ('to', combined with the definite article) is used by the glossator to mark the case of the Latin as dative; on this technique, see Lambert (1987), 285–6; Lambert (1990c), 17–8.

[14] This gloss seems to have been accident prone. It is not to be found in Zeuss (1853); nor in Loth (1884); nor in Falileyev (2000). Henry Bradshaw, Cambridge University librarian, transcribed it in his notes on this text gathered in Cambridge, University Library, Add. 6425, 556r–572r (at 557r (an alphabetical index of the Old Welsh glosses), 560r (item 22 in a transcription of text and glosses), 568r (listed as a conjunction in an index of parts of speech), 570r (alphabetical list of Old Welsh words), 571r (list of Old Welsh words in textual order), 572r (*ditto*)), but it is not found in Stokes's discussion (Stokes (1860–1), 235). However, the note on the previous gloss seems garbled: it runs as follows (Stokes (1860–1), 234–5): '*termisceticion* gl. solicitos. 'Primos solicitos fæcisti Romule ludos'. This gloss is omitted by Zeuss. Cf. the modern *terfysgu* 'to raise a tumult'.' *Termisceticion* was not omitted by Zeuss and it is likely that somewhere in the printing process a line of type fell out between 'ludos' and 'This gloss' (the latter sentence probably intended to refer to *cant*); subsequently Stokes may have added the note about *terfysgu* at proof stage (as was his wont) without noting the omission. On the relationship between Stokes and Bradshaw and Stokes's editing processes, see Russell (2011). As far as I can tell, the gloss was first recorded in print by Dumville (1992), 73, 76.

liothek, 821, 94–6 (saec. xi; containing *Ars Amatoria* I, ll. 1–230 only; henceforth S)[15] and in London, British Library, Add. 14086, 3r1–15v28 (*c*.1100; henceforth A) suggests that there is a number of glosses in common;[16] some may be trivial and created independently, but others however are likely to be the result of glosses being recopied alongside the main text and/or copied over from one manuscript to another as part of the process of collation. Glosses shared by all three manuscripts include (Old Welsh glosses are in bold):[17]

38r28 (l. 97)	*cultissima*: glossed *ornatus* OA, *ornatissima* S;
39v3 (l. 183)	*natales*: glossed ***litolaidou*** ('festal') O, *dies* A, *dies festales* S.

Glosses shared with one or other of the manuscripts include:

37r12 (l. 12)	*contudit*: glossed *domuit* OA;
37v8 (l. 41)	*loris*: glossed *habenis* OS;
38r11 (l. 80)	*arguto*: glossed ***in ir guorunhetic*** ('noisy') O, *stridenti* S;
38r27 (l. 96)	*timia*: glossed *flos uel proprium* O, *flos dulci apibus* A; l. 110 *mouent*: glossed *cogitant* OS;
39r10 (l. 153)	*dimissa*: glossed ***amlais*** ('loose') O, *prolixa* S;
39r18 (l. 161)	*tabellam*: glossed *fabillam* O, .i. *flabello* A;
39v31 (l. 211)	*quid*: glossed *parthe* O, *.i. cur o parthe* A;
40r16 (l. 231)	*possitis teneris*: glossed *hominibus habitantibus* O, *in communibus hominibus* A;
40v19 (l. 270)	*plagas*: glossed *retia* O, *.i. retia* A.

In these cases, it is possible to argue that the parallel glosses are more than coincidental; for example, *domuit* is by no means an obvious gloss on *contudit* but it is accurate in the context, and the same case can be made for some of the others. It is also noteworthy that in some case the gloss in O is in Old Welsh and so, if we are to accept that there is a link, we have to assume translation. That, of course, is difficult to demon-

[15] St Gall, Stiftsbibliothek, 821 is readily available online at: www.e-codices.unifr.ch/en/list/one/csg/0821.

[16] These are not the only manuscripts which merit consideration in this respect but will suffice for the present purposes. On A, see Boutemy (1936); Boutemy (1937).

[17] I leave aside simple identificatory glosses where, for example, a pronoun is identified as referring to a particular individual.

strate in these instances, but there is one case where a much stronger case can be made. At 41r16–19 (ll. 303, 305, and 306) three lines begin with *quid tibi*, the first meaning 'for what?', the second and third 'what?'.[18] In an attempt by the glossator to distinguish the senses of *quid*, the first is glossed by Old Welsh *padiu*, the second by Old Welsh *pui*, and the third is left unglossed. It is a feature of the glossing in this manuscript that much of it is designed to focus on features which are unique to Latin verse and especially to make distinctions between homonyms which only arise in Latin verse, and this is a case in point. Now at the corresponding place in MS A (8r4–6) the first *quid* is glossed by *prodest* to indicate that *quid tibi* means in this case 'what does it benefit you?'.[19] The gloss in MS A is written with the conventional abbreviations for *pro* and *est* and this may be significant for our understanding of the Old Welsh gloss. The best study of the senses of *padiu* (later *pyddew*) is that of Caerwyn Williams;[20] he concludes that the core sense of the word is 'to whom is' (used in both an interrogative and a relative sense) but that the Old Welsh instance from the Ovid manuscript is an outlier which does not fit the usage of the other attestations; interestingly he suggests that the Ovid example might be understood as *beth a dycia* ('what does it avail?'), but that is in effect a reading back from the Latin.[21] I propose that in fact *padiu* is a Welsh rendering of the abbreviated form of *prodest* as in MS A with the abbreviation for *pro* being read as *pa* and the *est* abbreviation rendered as Old Welsh *iu* (later *yw*; 'is'); it is a moot point whether it should be called a 'translation' rather than a 'transcription', though it is rare for Latin abbreviations to be rendered into Welsh. However, it might be relevant for what follows that reading Latin abbreviations into the vernacular is what regularly happens in Old Irish, e.g. *s̄* read as *acht*. For the moment, however, the point is that this is a pretty clear example of a Latin gloss being rendered in Welsh and thus it leaves the door open for some of the other Old Welsh glosses (where

[18] Note that these are not the readings of the standard edition (Kenney (1995), 133–4) which reads *quo* [...] *quid tibi* [...] *quid totiens*, and it is likely that our text has been created through several eye-skips. It might be argued that such a text might be in greater need of glossing so as to recover some sense from it.

[19] Another manuscript, London, British Library, Add. 49368 (*olim* Holkham 322; saec. xiii), 81r1–88r37, shares the gloss *prodest* with A, but has added *est* above the *quid* on l. 305, as if to make the distinction crystal clear.

[20] Williams (1969–70), 221–3, especially 229; cf. also Evans (1964), 77–8.

[21] Williams (1969–70), 229.

there are corresponding Latin glosses in another manuscript) likewise to be translations from Latin.

So far, it emerges that the Ovid manuscript shares a number of features with other Latin manuscripts glossed in vernacular Celtic languages: the glosses are layered and may be the product of collation and cross-copying of glosses (the latter being likely with MS A which belongs to a different branch of the main tradition);[22] furthermore, there is at least a possibility that some of the glosses have been translated from Latin into Old Welsh. There is nothing particularly surprising about any of this. What I wish to go on to suggest is that there may be another feature which this MS has in common with at least one of the others.

It has already been noted that the latest stratum of glossing is in Old Welsh. We can in addition identify a layer of Latin glossing which almost certainly took place in a Celtic context where Celtic languages were being spoken. At 42r10 (l. 371), where Ovid is arguing that one way for a lover to pick up a high-born lady (*domina*) is first to get her maid-servant (*ancilla*) on side so she will talk to her mistress about him: in that line *de te narret* ('let her (*sc.* the maid-servant) talk about you') is provided with an expanding gloss *contra illam ancella* which is to be understood as supplying the subject, *ancilla*, and to whom she is talking, her mistress. The use of *contra* after a verb of saying is familiar in the Latin of Celtic-speaking countries, corresponding as it does to the use of Welsh *wrth*, Irish *fri* ('to'), with verbs of saying and speaking. A second instance has already been recognized by David Dumville:[23] at 39v20 (l. 200) *stabit pro signis* ('it (*sc. ius* 'legitimate law') will stand before the standards') is glossed by *frangere bellum ante se* ('war breaks before it') which can be compared with Old Irish *maidid* (*in cath*) *re* X *for* Y (lit. '(the battle) breaks before X upon Y' meaning 'X defeats Y'); we can also contrast the transitive usage of *brissid* X *for* Y (lit. 'X breaks upon Y' again meaning 'X defeats Y') which is paralleled in Welsh by *torri ar*.[24] On the other hand, Dumville notes that there seems to be no Welsh parallel to the impersonal idiom of *maidid cath*. Dumville concludes as follows:[25]

> 'The fact that the impersonal construction is attested in Latin in both Ireland and Wales gives pause for thought. We have no reason to argue

[22] On the manuscript tradition of Ovid's love poetry, see Kenney (1962).

[23] Dumville (1982–3), 286–8; and for other Latin examples, cf. also Dumville (1975–6) and Löfstedt (1980–1).

[24] See Dumville (1982–3), 287 for Welsh examples.

[25] Dumville (1982–3), 288.

> that the Welsh example derives from an Irish exemplar or is the work of an Irishman in Wales. In default of a parallel Brittonic vernacular construction, we must consider the possibility that this Latin usage was common Celtic Latin dependent ultimately on an Irish vernacular idiom.'

The arguments presented here give some grounds for thinking that there could have been some Irish involvement. While the *contra illam* example could equally well be of Irish or Welsh origin, the impersonal *maidid cath* is much more likely to be Irish than Welsh.

A further instance may point in the same direction: at 39v22 (l. 202) *Latio* ('Latium', the areas around Rome, Lazio) is glossed by Old Welsh *litau* ('Brittany', later *Llydaw*).[26] Again, if we turn to Irish, Irish *Letha* is used to refer to both Brittany and Latium, and sometimes in a confused fashion;[27] for example, in Fiacc's Hymn, l. 10, *conidfarcaib la German andes i ndeisciurt Letha* ('so that he left him with German [i.e. St Germanus] southwards in the southern part of Letha' where *Letha* refers to a part of Gaul) is glossed *.i. Latium quae Italia dicitur eo quod latuit Saturnus fugens Iouem; sed tamen Germanus [erat] in Gallia, ut Beda dicit* ('*Latium* which is what Italy is called because Saturn 'hid' there in flight from Jupiter; however, Germanus was in Gaul, as Bede says').[28] However, as in the previous case, there is a more marginal Welsh example: in the genealogies the adjective *letewic* is used to refer to Aeneas, *Eneas letewic o Lydaw*.[29] The implication of the genealogy is that we have to do with Brittany as suggested by *o Lydaw*, but the adjective associated with Aeneas is suggestive of the same kind of confusion, or perhaps double use, found in Irish.

These examples are tantalising and suggestive, but I would submit that, if they were encountered in the Juvencus manuscript, no one would hesitate to posit Irish influence, perhaps by way of translation of a gloss *letha* into Old Welsh *litau*. Furthermore, if we do think that the *maidid cath for* X idiom is more likely to reflect Irish input, then the Irish contribution may run more deeply as this is found in a relatively late stratum of the Latin glossing. All of this is suggestive but nothing

[26] For discussion, see Koch (1986), 17–9, here 17: 'the name which came to mean in Welsh and Irish, to designate 'Brittany', and also, through confused pedantry, 'Latium''; cf. also Koch (1991), 20–1; Evans (2008), 28 n 99.

[27] See *DIL*, *s.v.* 'Letha'.

[28] Stokes and Strachan (1901–3), ii 311–2 (my translation of the gloss); note that the gloss is referring to the etymology of *Latium* provided in Virgil, *Aeneid* VIII 322–3.

[29] *Bonedd y Saint* 19 (ed. Bartrum (1966), 57).

more. However, since we know that the Juvencus manuscript had a significant Irish input in its creation, a further step can be suggested.

The gloss *dir arpeteticion ceintiru* on *miseris patruelibus* (38r4 (l. 73)) was discussed above in the context of an Old Welsh gloss being relegated to the margins since a Latin gloss occupied the interlinear space above the lemma. It was noted by Thomas Charles-Edwards some time ago that the form *ceintiru* is southern Welsh in form.[30] It may therefore provide a clue to the provenance of the manuscript (or the glossator). That the manuscript ended up in Glastonbury no more than a century later would make a southern Welsh provenance plausible simply on geographical grounds. There is, however, a further hint to be gleaned from another gloss: at 39v8 (l. 188) *in cunis* is glossed by *mapbrethinnou* ('swaddling clothes') which should be compared with the gloss in the Juvencus manuscript (5v3) where *conabula* (referring to the swaddling clothes of the infant Jesus) is glossed by *mapbrith .i. onnou*.[31] This gloss is spelt slightly differently and has clearly been miscopied perhaps by misreading a descender from the line above as *.i.* But the striking fact is that these are the only two attestations in Welsh of this compound and it would be tempting to think that there is a connection. We know that both manuscripts are southern Welsh productions though it may be premature to speculate as to whether they are products of the same scriptorium, especially since the scripts are so different.[32] However, there is one final point to be made: when one considers the productivity and use of the prefixed *map-* meaning 'baby-, junior-, child-, etc.' in Welsh there are relatively few medieval examples; the following are all the pre-1500 attestations in *Geiriadur Prifysgol Cymru*: *mabddysg* ('early learning'), *mabiaith* ('chatter'), *mablan* ('grave'), *mablygad* ('pupil (of the eye)'), *mabsant* ('patron saint'), and *mabwraig* ('young girl').[33] For the present purposes, we may leave aside *mablan* and *mabsant* where the semantics seem rather different. By contrast, Old Irish compounds in *mac-* are relatively frequent.[34] Nicolas Jacobs has recently made a similar point

[30] Charles-Edwards (1973–4).

[31] McKee (2000b), 144–5, 528.

[32] On the Juvencus manuscript, see McKee (2000b), 27–39; McKee (2000c), 20–2.

[33] See *GPC*, *s.vv.* Of these, *mablygad* (with its Breton cognate *mabiagad*) is particularly striking as it is difficult to escape the thought that this is modelled on Old Irish *mac imblissen* ('pupil (of the eye)', lit. 'son of an iris (of the eye)'). It is also worth adding that *macbrat*, a parallel to *mapbrethinnou*, is attested in Irish but all the examples are late and so the parallel should not be pressed.

[34] See *DIL*, *s.v.* '1 macc IV'.

about 'loose compounds' containing Welsh *map*, in particular *mab llen* ('student') in relation to Irish *mac léi(g)enn*:[35]

> 'In general the idiom seems better developed and better exemplified in Irish than in Welsh, and while to suggest that the idiom itself is borrowed from Irish might be to carry speculation too far, it is likely, given the associated expressions containing *léi(g)enn* '(sacred) learning', that *mab llen* at least is a loose compound formed under Irish influence.'

The point that such forms are contextually much more embedded in Irish than in Welsh is well taken and applies to the prefixed forms as well. If so, it is arguable again that such a gloss (and indeed some of the other glossing practice in the Ovid manuscript) would be best understood as a product of a bilingual Irish-Welsh glossing context such as that posited for the Juvencus manuscript.

The proposal that there may be an Irish context to the glossing in the Welsh Ovid manuscript remains speculative. However, if a connection can be made between the Ovid and the Juvencus in terms perhaps of a shared rare gloss, then cumulatively the evidence is suggestive, and we may be able to discern yet another strand, however faint, of the transmission of learning and scribes across the Irish Sea in the 9th century.

Bibliography

Bartrum, P.C. (1966) *Early Welsh genealogical tracts*, Cardiff.

Bodden, M.-C. (1979) 'A study of the Anglo-Saxon classbook Bodley, Auct. F.4.32, along with a close study of its second gathering, an 11th-century Old English homily on the finding of the true cross,' unpublished Ph.D. thesis, University of Toronto.

Boutemy, A. (1936) 'Un manuscrit inconnu de l'*Ars Amatoria* d'Ovide au British Museum,' *Revue des études latines* 14, 271–3.

— (1937) 'Une copie de l'*Ars Amatoria* au British Museum,' *Revue des études latines* 15, 92–102.

Breen, A. (1992) 'The liturgical material in MS Oxford, Bodleian Library, Auct. F.4.32,' *Archiv für Liturgiewissenschaft* 34, 121–53.

[35] Jacobs (2013), 108–9; cf. also Charles-Edwards (2013), 603–4, 607. That *map lyen* is also attested in Cornish need not be a counter-argument as it is perfectly reasonable to assume that, if such a form could be taken over into Welsh, it could likewise be taken up in Cornish and Breton or be borrowed from one Brittonic language to another.

Budny, M. (1992) '"St Dunstan's Classbook" and its frontispiece: Dunstan's portrait and autograph,' in N. Ramsay, M. Sparks, and T. Tatton-Brown, *St Dunstan: his life, times and cult*, Woodbridge, 103–42.

Charles-Edwards, T.M. (1973–4) '*Nei*, *keifn*, and *kefynderw*,' *Bulletin of the Board of Celtic Studies* 25, 386–8.

— (2012) 'The use of the book in Wales, *c*.400–1100,' in R. Gameson, *The Cambridge history of the book in Britain, vol. I:* c.*400–1100*, Cambridge, 389–405.

— (2013) *Wales and the Britons 350–1064*, Oxford.

Conway, G. (1997) 'Towards a cultural context for the eleventh-century Llanbadarn manuscripts,' *Ceredigion* 13, 9–28.

Dumville, D.N. (1975–6) 'An Irish idiom Latinised,' *Éigse* 16, 183–6.

— (1982–3) 'Notes on Celtic Latin,' *Bulletin of the Board of Celtic Studies* 30, 283–8.

— (1992) 'A *Thesaurus Palaeoanglicus*? The Celtic experience,' in R. Derolez, *Anglo-Saxon glossography*, Brussels, 61–76.

Ellis, R. (1880) 'De *Artis Amatoriae* Ovidianae codice Oxoniensi,' *Hermes* 15, 425–32.

Evans, N. (2008) 'Royal succession of kingship among the Picts,' *Innes Review* 59, 1–48.

Evans, D.S. (1964) *A grammar of Middle Welsh*, Dublin.

Falileyev, A. (2000) *An etymological glossary of Old Welsh*, Tübingen.

Harvey, A. (1991) 'The Cambridge Juvencus glosses – evidence of Hiberno-Welsh interaction,' in P. Sture Ureland and G. Broderick, *Proceedings of the eighth international symposium on language contact in Europe, Douglas, Isle of Man, 1988*, Tübingen, 181–98.

Hexter, R.J. (1986) *Ovid and medieval schooling: studies in medieval school commentaries on Ovid's* Ars Amatoria, Epistulae ex Ponto, *and* Epistulae Heroidum, München.

Hunt, R.W. (1961) *Saint Dunstan's classbook from Glastonbury*, Amsterdam.

Jacobs, N. (2013) 'Irish influence on mediaeval Welsh vocabulary: the case of the gnomic poems,' in Liam Mac Amhlaigh and Brian Ó Curnáin, *Ilteangach, Ilseiftiúil. Féilsgribhinn in ómós do Nicholas Williams. A Festschrift for Nicholas Williams*, Dublin, 97–120.

Kenney, E.J. (1962) 'The manuscript tradition of Ovid's *Amores*, *Ars Amatoria*, and *Remedia Amoris*,' *Classical Quarterly NS* 12, 1–31.

— (1995) *P. Ovidi Nasonis Amores, Medicamina faciei femineae, Ars amatoria, Remedia amoris*, revised ed., Oxford.

Koch, J.T. (1986) 'New thoughts on *Albion*, *Iernē* and the Pretanic Isles,' *Proceedings of the Harvard Celtic Colloquium* 6, 1–28.

— (1991) '*Ériu*, *Alba*, and *Letha*: when was a language ancestral to Gaelic first spoken in Ireland?,' *Emania* 9, 17–27.

Lambert, P.-Y. (1982) 'Les gloses du manuscrit BN Lat. 10290,' *Études celtiques* 19, 173–213.

— (1987) 'Les gloses grammaticales brittoniques,' *Études celtiques* 24, 285–308.

— (1989) 'Gloses en vieux-breton: 1– 5,' *Études celtiques* 26, 81–93.

— (1990a) 'Gloses en vieux-breton: 6– 9,' *Études celtiques* 27, 337–61.

— (1990b) 'Old Irish *gláośnáthe* "linea, norma",' *Celtica* 21, 235–9.

— (1990c) 'La typologie de gloses en vieux-breton,' *Britannica Monastica* 1, 13–20.

— (2005) 'Les gloses en vieux-breton aux écrits scientifiques de Bède, dans le manuscrit Angers 477,' in S. Lebecq, M. Perrin, and O. Szerwiniack, *Bède le Vénérable entre tradition et postérité*, Lille, 309–19.

Lapidge, M. (1982) 'The study of Latin texts in Anglo-Saxon England: I. The evidence of Latin glosses,' in Nicholas Brooks, *Latin and the vernacular languages in early medieval Britain*, Leicester, 99–140.

Löfstedt, B. (1980–1) '*Fregit bellum ante Cassibellaunum*,' *Éigse* 18, 181.

Loth, J. (1884) *Vocabulaire vieux-breton*, Paris, repr. 1970, 1982.

McKee, H. (2000a) *The Cambridge Juvencus manuscript glossed in Latin, Old Welsh and Old Irish. Text and commentary*, Aberystwyth.

— (2000b) *Juvencus Codex Cantabrigiensis Ff.4.22. A ninth-century manuscript glossed in Welsh, Irish and Latin. Facsimile*, Aberystwyth.

— (2000c) 'Scribes and glosses from Dark Age Wales: the Cambridge Juvencus manuscript,' *Cambrian Medieval Celtic Studies* 39, 1–22.

Ramírez de Verger, A. (2003) *P. Ovidius Naso, Carmina amatoria: Amores, Medicamina faciei femineae, Ars amatoria, Remedia amoris*, Leipzig.

Rhŷs, J. (1873) 'Die kymrischen Glossen zu Oxford,' *Beiträge zur vergleichenden Sprachforschung* 7, 228–39.

Russell, P. (2011) 'Grilling in Calcutta: Whitley Stokes, Henry Bradshaw, and Old Welsh in Cambridge,' in P. Russell and E.L. Boyle, *The Tripartite life of Whitley Stokes (1830–1909)*, Dublin, 144–60.

— (2012) '*An habes linguam Latinam? Non tam bene sapio*: views of multilingualism from the early-medieval West,' in A. Mullen and P. James, *Multilingualism in the Greco-Roman worlds*, Cambridge, 193–224.

— (forthcoming) *Reading Ovid in medieval Wales*, Columbus.

Stokes, W. (1860–1) 'Cambrica: 2. The Old-Welsh glosses at Oxford,' *Transactions of the Philological Society*, 234–7 (corr. 292–3).

Stokes, W. and J. Strachan (1901–3) *Thesaurus Palaeohibernicus: a collection of Old-Irish glosses, scholia, prose and verse*, 2 vols., Cambridge.

Williams, I. (1929–30) 'Glosau Rhydychen,' *Bulletin of the Board of Celtic Studies* 5, 1–8.

— (1932–3) 'Glosau Rhydychen a Chaergrawnt,' *Bulletin of the Board of Celtic Studies* 6, 112–5.

Williams, J.E.C. (1969–70) '*difod, diw, pyddiw*,' *Bulletin of the Board of Celtic Studies* 23, 217–33.

Zeuss, J.K. (1853) *Grammatica celtica*, Leipzig, 2nd edition Berlin 1871.

PIERRE-YVES LAMBERT

PRETIUM BENEDICTIONIS

Abstract

An Old Welsh gloss and a Hiberno-Latin text (*Collectio Canonum Hibernensis* 63.1) refer to *pretium benedictionis*, a kind of tip which a customer would give to a craftsman when his work is done. This was meant to ensure that the artefact had not been invested with any evil intention on the part of the producer. Accordingly, the craftsman was asked to give the artefact his blessing. This *pretium benedictionis* corresponds to *duilchinne* in Old Irish law (cf. *Cóic conara fuigill*, H §89). At a time when magic could be suspected in every craft, such a blessing was used as a sort of exorcism.

Keywords

blessing, price of building a church, salary of craftsmen; *dúilchinne*, *forlóg*, *opartu* / *apartu*; Old Irish.

On the occasion of this homage, I am glad to offer to Dáibhí this discussion about a (very special) Celtic benediction.

Old Welsh glosses on the tract *De ponderis et mensuris*[1]

A long section of this commentary is concerned with the price of sparrows according to the Gospels. In one of his first sermons, Jesus speaks about 'Divine Providence', which knows the fate of every creature, even of the small birds which used to be offered in sacrifice, and which were sold at the entrance to the temple at Jerusalem. But the words of Jesus

[1] See a detailed analysis and commentary in Lambert (2003), especially 126–32: 'Gloss 77: *dupondeus* and the price of sparrows'.

Early medieval Ireland and Europe: chronology, contacts, scholarship, ed. by Pádraic Moran and Immo Warntjes, Studia Traditionis Theologiae, 14 (Turnhout, 2015), pp. 215–23.

 10.1484/M.STT-EB.5.103122

have been transmitted in two different versions. Matthew 10:29 says: *Nonne duo passeres asse veneunt, et unus ex illis non cadet super terram sine Patre vestro*! ('Can you not buy two sparrows for a penny? And yet not one falls to the ground without your Father knowing.'[2]) But Luke 12:6 gives the following: *Nonne quinque passeres veneunt dipondio* [or *dupondio*]? *Et unus ex illis non est in oblivione coram Deo*! ('Can you not buy five sparrows for two pennies? And yet not one is forgotten in God's sight!')

This difference in prices has been the object of many comments. A *dupondius* is worth two *asses*, so that the same *dupondius* would have been the price of four sparrows according to Matthew, and of five according to Luke. Matthew and Luke refer both to very small amounts of money, represented by the smallest available coins: *as* and *dupondius* (two asses, or half a *sestertius*). The disparity between the two prices is also tiny when compared with the sum mentioned in the Edict of Diocletian (AD 224), where the price of a sparrow amounts to almost 13 asses.[3]

Let us now come to the Old Welsh commentary on this difference of price:[4]

> *ir pimhet eterin diguormechís Lucas, hegit hunnoid* in pretium benedictionis *hoid hoitou hou bein(t) atar. ha beinn(t) cihunn* reliqua

> 'The fifth bird which Luke has added, this one goes for the price of a blessing for ever and ever—if they (really) are birds which are of the same sort *et cetera*.'

The solution proposed by the glossator consists in supposing that in the purchase mentioned by Luke there is an additional bird (the payment being regularly fixed as one *dupondius* for four birds), and that this fifth bird represents the counterpart of 'a blessing for ever and ever'. The successive steps would be: 1) The purchaser buys four sparrows for two asses. 2) When handing over the coins, the purchaser expresses a blessing. 3) The seller thanks him by giving him an additional bird, a sort of bonus. One could, however, argue that the blessing is uttered by the seller himself, as an expression of his satisfaction. Nevertheless, the use of the word *pretium* would rather indicate an additional purchase, or

2 Translations are from the Jerusalem Bible.

3 Exactly: 16 *denarii*, i.e. 128 asses for 10 sparrows.

4 Ed. Lambert (2003), 112 (gl. 77). The translation is mine.

exchange: so that the fifth bird seems to me to be given in exchange for a blessing, and not as a token of a blessing. The other attestation of the expression *pretium benedictionis* will confirm this view.

In the rest of his commentary, the Old Welsh glossator tries another explanation, by supposing that the *as* had a lesser value at the time when Matthew's Gospel was written—the same idea of a deflation occurs also in Hiberno-Latin commentaries.[5]

Concerning the use of *pretium benedictionis* in the case of purchase, it is possible that the corresponding Old Irish expression was *forlóg* ('additional price'), a word used in the *Additamenta* to the Patrician biographies by Muirchú and Tírechán in the Book of Armagh. This word occurs in a passage concerning the purchase of Óchter Achid by Cummén, or, more exactly, of the reimbursement to his wife of the share representing her dowry. The dowry (*séuit*) is paid in the form of three ounces of silver, plus various jewellery in gold or silver, sheep and pigs for the value of an ounce, and a valuable item which is a mantle, exchanged with a brown horse, then with an ounce of silver, *and luid in chumal sin du forlóg Ochtir Achid* ('that *cumal* went to the additional price of Óchter Achid').[6]

Collectio Canonum Hibernensis

Another occurrence of *pretium benedictionis* is found in the *Collectio Canonum Hibernensis*, in a quotation of the *Hibernenses* (= *Canones Hibernenses*). This belongs to book 63, *De artificio artificium:*[7]

> *Hibernenses dicunt: Si quis artifex opus inertis faciat, et ferramenta usque ad dimidium quaesiverit, dimidium pretium habebit, sin vero, tertiam partem aedificii sui accipiet, ut sit tertia pars operariis, tertia cibo et ferramentis, unde judices habebunt, hoc est, judex ab artificibus et judex a praesidentibus ecclesiae vel castelli, et quantumcumque voluerit, secundum operationem judicabunt, non secundum utilitatem, postea autem artifex habebit pretium benedictionis. Sic judicabuntur et alia dona. Qui vero noluerit secundum hoc concilium facere, fiat excommunis, et nemo eam accipiet, et in morte carebit communione.*

[5] See glosses in London, British Library, Harley 1802, f 28a and quotations in the *Bibelwerk*, both edited in Lambert (2003), 129 and 128–9 respectively.

[6] *Additamenta* 11 (ed. and trans. Bieler (1979), 174–5).

[7] *Collectio Canonum Hibernensis* 63 (ed. Wasserschleben (1885), 230).

This difficult text cannot be understood without the help of Old Irish texts. An extract from Old Irish law in Dublin, Trinity College, 1336 (*olim* H.3.17) deals with prices for the construction of ecclesiastical buildings, *durthach, damliacc, cloicthech.*[8] It has already been commented on by G. Petrie and E. O'Curry.[9] We find there the same kind of tripartition:[10]

> *Log na ndurtaige do rer dligid sin,* ⁊ *a trian do eladain* ⁊ *a trian da adbur* ⁊ *a trian do biud* ⁊ *do frithcnam* ⁊ *do gobnib.*
>
> 'This is the price of the oratory according to law, and a third of it goes to the art [that is, to the builder], and a third to material, and a third to food and to attendance and to smiths.'

The correspondence with the Latin text is not entirely satisfactory. According to the *Hibernenses*, two cases are to be distinguished, the first one when 'the architect does the work of a person without competence' (*artifex opus inertis facit*) and the second one, when he does not. In the second case, we find a real tripartition: a third of the payment goes to the architect (*artifex*), another third to the workers (*operariis,* corresponding to *frithgnam*), and the last third is for the food and for the iron tools (*cibo et ferramentis*). The Latin text has apparently omitted the material, *adbar,* which is replaced by *operarii.* But in the following sentence of the Old Irish text, we find that the part given to the smiths may be subject to some variation, according to their real contribution to the building.

How can we understand *opus inertis*? In my opinion, this is not a contemptuous assessment of the work of the architect. It refers to the work of the unqualified, but not to the work of common workers, which are later mentioned as *operarii.* Here, the architect seems to have no other competence than architecture, and particularly not the competence of a smith, since he had to seek for the iron tools (*ferramenta quaesivit*). *Quaesivit* implies that he has purchased these iron tools from other people. It is then comprehensible that he should receive more than the ordinary remuneration of an architect, having replaced the smith. What is implied by *usque ad dimidium,* I cannot really explain, it seems to anticipate the following clause *dimidium praetium habebit.*

8 Binchy (1978), vi 2099.23–2100.10.

9 Petrie (1845), 364–6; O'Curry (1873), iii 48–9.

10 Binchy (1978), vi 2099.29–30; trans. by O'Curry (1873), iii 48–9.

In the following sentence, we have a sort of ellipsis, *judices* [...] *quantumcumque voluerit judicabunt* ('the judges will decide whatever the amount of payment he wanted to receive', that is, they will decide in due course what he will receive as his remuneration). I have not found in the Old Irish laws an exact match for this sentence. The Latin text, anyway, is rather clear: it distinguishes between two types of judges, the judge specialized in the determination of architect fees—this *judex ab artificibus* is chosen among the architects, and could correspond to the *ollam suad saeir* ('chief expert wright') or the *breitheam bes tualaing fuigell frisind aes dána* ('judge who is competent to decide over artisans');[11] he has to reach a decision in agreement with another judge, 'a judge appointed by the dignitaries of the church or of the fort' (*judex a praesidentibus ecclesiae vel castelli*). This judge certainly represents the interests of the purchaser, either lay or ecclesiastical.

The final aim of these proceedings is to reach an agreement with the architect, so that he finally receives *pretium benedictionis*. This last step is clearly seen as the final settlement of a dispute. What remains to be said is that 'other trades' (*alia dona = ind dána aili*, though a sort of Hiberno-Latinism) will be judged the same way. And the conclusion is the customary sanction of ecclesiastical decisions: whoever does not follow this will be excommunicated.

We can now propose a translation:

> 'The *Canones Hibernenses* say: 'If the architect does the work of an unqualified man, and purchases the iron tools up to the half (?), he will have the half of the sum, otherwise, he will receive one third of the price of the new building, in such way that a(nother) third will go to the labourers, and a third for food and iron tools. From where will they take their judges? The answer is, a judge taken amongst the architects and a judge taken amongst the chiefs of the church or of the fort, and whatever the sum he asks for, they will decide his salary not according to suitability (of the building), but according to his real work; and then, the architect will receive a *pretium benedictionis* (the price of his blessing); and other arts will be regulated the same way. Whoever refuses to act according to this decision (read *consilium*), let him be excommunicated, and nobody will receive him (read *eum*), and he will die deprived of Holy Communion."

[11] Binchy (1978), v 1612.27 and 1613.38; both from *Uraicecht Becc* (ed. Binchy (1978), v 1590.1–1618.40; see Breatnach (2005), 315–8).

The blessing of the craftsman in Old Irish law

One of the paths of procedure discussed in *Cóic conara fuigill* ('The five paths of procedure') is called *cert* ('equity'). This is about the execution of contracts. When products or services are to be paid for, we might have some doubts about their just price, either because the price is exaggerated or because the service or the product purchased is not of the expected quality. But the tract introduces an additional payment, *dúilcinne cecha h-aicce* ('the supplementary payment for every artefact'):[12]

> ⁊ *duilcinne gacha haice .i. duil cintech dlegar do tabairt ar gach n-aici .i. dechmad gacha dula duilcinne* ⁊ *a thabairt sidhen a mbiudh* ⁊ *a lind.* ⁊ *is cutruma caithit itir degsaor* ⁊ *drochsaor, uair is cutruma is etir leo a mbennacht do tabairt.* ⁊ *iar n-ic loigidecht[a] na haice dlegur a ici son.* ⁊ *nochan-fuil eraic orra gengu-tugat in duilcinne imach, acht na-tabrait in lucht ele a mbennachta arin aice, noco-tugthar in dulcinne doib.*

> '*dúilcinne cecha h-aicce*, a (special) payment for every artefact, means something that should be given for every artefact: the *dúilcinne* represents a tenth of the value of the product, and it is delivered in food and drink; it is consumed both by the good and the bad craftsman, because both are equally able to give their blessing. Payment of *duilcinne* takes place only after payment of the artefact: and there is no *éraic* to be paid by them (the purchasers) if they refuse to pay *dúilchinne*: but the other part will simply not give their blessing on the artefact, as long as *dúilcinne* is not paid.'

Here is the commentary of Thurneysen:[13]

> '*Dūilchinne, dūilginne* f. war ursprünglich der Lohn, der für das Verfertigen eines Gerätes (oder sonst eine Leistung) gegeben wurde; so in den alten Glossen, in *AL* [Hancock et al. (1865–1901)] V, 266.10 f. und auch in unserm Haupttext. Aber das Wort hat dann eine besondere Bedeutung angenommen. Die Verfertiger des Gerätes müssen ihren Segen über es sprechen, damit es nicht schaden kann (cf. *AL* I, 132.5); für diesen Segen erhalten sie ein Zehntel des Wertes des Gerätes an Speise und Trank (*AL* V, 98.9), das ist die *dūilchinne* in speziellem Sinn. Nach unserm Abschnitt muss aber die *dūilchinne* nicht gegeben

[12] *Cóic conara fuigill*, version H, §89 (ed. Thurneysen (1926), 48–9; the translation is mine). A useful commentary on this text is available in Archan (2007).

[13] Thurneysen (1926), 72 §44.

werden: wenn ich den Schluss richtig verstehe, dann nicht, wenn auf diesen Segen verzichtet wird. Über die Buße, die auf der Verweigerung des Segens steht, wenn er verlangt wird, s. die Stellen unter *abarta AL* VI 3 und D'Arbois de Jubainville, *Ét. sur le Droit Celt.* II. 75, 118.'

The reference to *Ancient Laws*, i 132, is to an extract of *Cethairṡlicht Athgabála* where we also find that when craftsmen refused to give their blessing to the product, they were liable to pay a fine equal to a seventh of the price, called *oparta* or *aparta*.[14]

Other important texts referring to *dúilchinne* are *Uraicecht Becc*[15] and *Heptads*.[16] Here is the extract of *Uraicecht Becc*:[17]

Duilghine caca hoic(di) .i. rofitir in duil cinnteach is coir as gach oigdi ⁊ *dechmadh cacha dula a duilgine a mbiud* ⁊ *im linn,* ⁊ *a leth d'aes dana* ⁊ *a leth d'aes borb-eladan, ar daig co tucad a mbendachtain fora n-oigdib.*

'*Dúilchine* of every artefact: he knows the exact element which should be that of every artefact, and the *dúilchine* is made of a tenth of every element, in food and drink, a half goes to the men of art, and a half to the men of vulgar arts, so that they give their blessing on their products.'

This *dúilchinne* applies to every art (*sic judicabuntur et alia dona*) according to the *Collectio Canonum Hibernensis* cited above; we may quote in parallel the *Aibidil Cuigni maic hEmoin*, where we find the sentence *cach dán a duilgine* ('every art is entitled to its *dúilchinne*').[18]

O'Mulconry's Glossary

Thanks to our editor, Pádraic Moran, I can add a reference to O'Mulconry's Glossary, which gives an equivalent of *dúilchinne*: *fobrithe idem et dúilchinne* ('*Fobrithe* ('sub-award'), the same as *dúlchinne*

14 Binchy (1978), ii 352.25–422.36, v 1897.16–1904.16, etc.; see Breatnach (2005), 286–7.

15 Hancock et al. (1865–1901), v 98; cf. Binchy (1978), v 1614.1.

16 Hancock et al. (1865–1901), v 266 = Binchy (1978), i 40.10.

17 Binchy (1978), v 1614.1–4 (from the Book of Ballymote—Dublin, Royal Irish Academy, 23 P 12); cf. Binchy (1978), vi 2330.23–26 (from the Yellow Book of Lecan—Dublin, Trinity College, 1318); the translation is mine.

18 Meyer (1905–7), 227.

('remuneration')').[19] According to Moran,[20] this entry is out of alphabetical sequence in a run of headwords beginning *Fa-*. The entry is also missing from the shorter version, OM². It seems therefore to be an extension of the previous entry, *fáebur a fabro* ('*Fáebar* ('blade'), from [Latin] *faber* ('smith')').[21] This would indicate that *fobrithe* was understood as connected with Latin *faber* ('smith'). The etymology of *fobrithe* has probably nothing to do with *fáebor* ('blade'), and both of them have no connection with Latin *faber*, but this entry was interesting as a witness to the exemplarity of smithery amongst crafts.

Conclusion

Today, a customer may show his satisfaction by giving a tip (French *pourboire* would show that this could be for something to drink). But *dúilchine* is much more than a tip, since it is considered as corresponding to the price of a blessing—the blessing of the producer. The purchaser himself asks for this blessing. As Thurneysen rightly wrote in the quote reproduced above, purchasers might have imagined that the artefacts were possibly harmful—as if they conveyed with them not only the fingerprints of the producer, but also his (hostile) intentions and whatever he may have intended to achieve when he was working. A blessing was needed to exorcise the artefact, because every craftsman (and not only the smith) might have used magical powers. For this reason, the purchaser was led to ask for a blessing from the producer himself, in order that he publicly annulled any bad spell he might have attached to the artefact during its fabrication.

Though the situations where *pretium benedictionis* occurs might be seen as very different (the selling of sparrows, the building of a church, or the delivering of an artefact), it seems that in every case, a blessing takes place when the transaction comes to an end. Asking for it as well as accepting to deliver it were both manifesting the good will of the partners: with such attitudes they were renouncing any further claim. This blessing is clearly a sort of exorcism, exorcising in the first place the man who utters it. It is different from a blessing of thanks, such as Breton

19 O'Mulconry's Glossary 483 (ed. Stokes (1898–1900), 258).

20 Personal communication.

21 O'Mulconry's Glossary 482 (ed. Stokes (1898–1900), 258).

Doue r'ho pennigo ('God bless you'), uttered by thankful beggars, or Welsh *Bendith Duw ytt* ('the blessing of God to you').[22]

Bibliography

Archan, C. (2007) *Les chemins du jugement, procédure et science du droit dans l'Irlande médiévale*, Paris.

Bieler, L. (1979) *The Patrician texts in the Book of Armagh*, Dublin.

Binchy, D.A. (1978) *Corpus Iuris Hibernici*, 6 vols., Dublin.

Breatnach, L. (2005) *A companion to the Corpus Iuris Hibernici*, Dublin.

Hancock, W.M. et al. (1865–1901) *Ancient laws and institutes of Ireland*, 6 vols., Dublin.

Jones, T. (1992) *Ystoryaeu Seint Greal. Rhan I: Y Keis*, Cardiff.

Lambert, P.-Y. (2003) 'The Old Welsh glosses on weights and measures,' in P. Russell, *Yr Hen Iaith, Studies in Early Welsh*, Aberystwyth, 103–34.

Meyer, K. (1905–7) 'Das Alphabet des Cuigne mac Emoin,' in *Archiv für celtische Lexikographie* 3, 226–30.

O'Curry, E. (1873) *On the manners and customs of the ancient Irish*, 3 vols., London.

Petrie, G. (1845) *Inquiry into the origin of the round towers in Ireland*, Dublin.

Stokes, W. (1898–1900) 'O'Mulconry's glossary,' *Archiv für celtische Lexikographie* 1, 232–324, 473–81, 629.

Thurneysen, R. (1926) 'Cōic conara fuigill, die fünf Wege zum Urteil. Ein altirischer Rechtstext,' *Abhandlungen der Preussischen Akademie der Wissenschaften*, Jahrgang 1925; repr. in R. Thurneysen, *Gesammelte Schriften*, 3 vols, ed. by P. de Bernado Stempel and R. Ködderitzsch (Tübingen, 1995), iii 1–87.

Wasserschleben, H. (1885) *Die irische Kanonensammlung*, 2nd ed., Leipzig.

[22] *Ystoryaeu Seint Greal* l. 3010 (ed. Jones (1992), 85).

DAVID HOWLETT

TWO IRISH JOKES

Abstract

The essay considers by editing, translating, and analysing two famous Irish jokes, first a celebrated exchange between the philosopher Iohannes Scottus Eriugena and the Emperor Charles the Bald, and second the Bamberg Cryptogram. From four sources, one poem by Theodulf of Orleans and three prose accounts by William of Malmesbury, Gerald de Barri, and Matthew Paris, the first joke can be understood to function in five distinct ways. The second part of this paper considers two works by Dubthach mac Máel-Tuile, a colophon and the Bamberg Cryptogram, a letter from Suadbar to Colgu explaining the code of the cryptogram, a colophon by Nandharius, scribe of the letter, a poem by a Welsh priest named Cyfeiliog using Dubthach's code, and an account of scholarly needle in insular Latin literature. The Appendix by Colin Ireland discusses the Irish names in Suadbar's letter.

Keywords

Alcuin, Aldfrith king of Northumbria, Aldhelm of Malmesbury and Sherborne, Cadac Andreas, Cadfan king of Anglesey, Caunchobrach, Cellanus of *Peronna Scottorum*, Charles the Bald, Charles the Great, Colgu, Columban of Bangor and Bobbio, Conchen or Cyngen ap Cadell ap Brochfael king of Powys, Cummian, Cyfeiliog, Dominnach, Dubthach mac Máel-Tuile, Fergus, Gerald de Barri's *De principis instructione liber*, Gildas' *De excidio Brittanniae*, Iohannes Scottus Eriugena, Maglocunus Venedotiae or Maelgwn Gwynedd, Maildub of Malmesbury, Martial Epigrams X xlviii and XIV lxxxvii, Martinus Hibernensis, Matthew Paris' *Chronica maiora*, Merfyn Frych king of Gwynedd, Nandharius, Patrick's *Confessio*, Priscian's *Periegesis* and Grammar, Sedulius Scottus, Suadbar, Theodulf of Orleans, Virgilius Maro Grammaticus of Iona's *Altus Prosator*, *Epistole*, and *Epitome*, William of Malmesbury's *Gesta pontificum Anglorum*; Bamberg, Staatsbibliothek, HJ IV 11 (Class. 6), Brussels, Bibliothèque royale de Belgique / Koninklijke Bibliotheek van België, 9565–66, Laon, Bibliothèque

Early medieval Ireland and Europe: chronology, contacts, scholarship, ed. by Pádraic Moran and Immo Warntjes, Studia Traditionis Theologiae, 14 (Turnhout, 2015), pp. 225–64.

 10.1484/M.STT-EB.5.103123

municipale, 444, Leiden, Universiteitsbibliotheek, Voss. lat. F. 67; alliteration, alphanumeric code, *annominatio*, computus, cryptanalysis, cryptography, *cursus* rhythms, *gematria*, Greek, Latin, *mensa*, rhyme, *Scottus*, *sottus*, *tabula*.

Inter sottum et Scottum

For one of the oldest Irish jokes, set in the 9th century, we have four sources, the first of the early 9th century, the second of the early 12th century, the third of the early 13th, the fourth of the mid-13th.

The first source is a satirical attack by the Carolingian poet Theodulf of Orleans (†AD 821) on an Irishman Cadac Andreas ('Battling Andrew'):[1]

> Hic poenasue dabit fugietue simillimus Austro,
> Utque sit hic aliud, nil nisi Scottus erit.
> Cui si litterulam, quae est ordine tertia, tollas —
> (Inque secunda suo nomine forte sedet:
> Quae sonat in 'caelo' prima, et quae in 'scando' secunda,
> Tertia in 'ascensu', quarta in 'amicitiis';
> Quam satis offendit; pro qua te, littera salui,
> Utitur) — haud dubium quod sonat, hoc et erit.

> 'This man shall pay his penalty or flee like the south wind; however different he may try to be, he will be nothing if not a *Scottus*. If you take away therefrom the letter which is third in the alphabet — (and which happens to stand second in that his designation: the one that in *caelo* sounds first, and which in *scando* comes second, third in *ascensu*, fourth in *amicitiis*; which he stumbles upon often enough; in place of which he presses into service the letter standing for *saluus*) — then, without doubt, what he says he will also be!'

> In other words, if from the term *Scottus* ('Irishman') you remove the letter *c*, then you get Battling Andrew's pronunciation of the word.

Dr Harvey has explained clearly and elegantly that in the 9th century Irishmen pronounced the Latin letter *C* in all positions in the Classical fashion as *K*, but although Franks continued to pronounce it that way before back vowels *A*, *O*, and *U*, they had begun to pronounce it before front vowels *AE*, *E*, *I*, *OE*, and *Y* as *S*. Battling Andrew relied not upon

[1] Harvey (2002), 20.

the learning for which other Irish scholars were famous, but upon patronage: *caelum scandit ascensu amicitiarum* ('he ascends to heaven by a ladder of patronage', as the letter *C* ascends in order in the four words). In an attempt to ingratiate himself among the Franks he adopted their pronunciation of *C* before front vowels, but mistakenly extended it to inappropriate contexts, making himself, a *Scottus*, seem a *sottus*, and providing the background for a famous remark.

I have arranged the texts of the three passages that follow *per cola et commata* ('by clauses and phrases'), marking rhythms of the *cursus* with acute and grave accents and rhymes with italics.

William of Malmesbury, the greatest English historian after Bede, published in AD 1125 his *Gesta pontificum Anglorum*, in which he wrote:[2]

> Huius [sc. Elfredi] tempore uenit Ángliam Iohànnes Scóttus
> uir perspicacis ingenii et múltae facúndiae
> qui dudum relicta patria Frantiam ad Karolum Cáluum trans*ierat*
> a quo magna dignatione susceptus familiarium pártium hàbebátur
> transigebatque cum eo tam séria quam ióc*a*
> indiuiduusque comes et mensae et cubícul*i érat*.
> Multae facetiae ingenuíque lepóris
> quorum exempla hódieque cónstan*t*
> ut sunt *i*st*a*.
> Assederat ad mensam contra regem ad aliam tábulae pártem.
> Procedéntibus pó*culis*
> consumptísque fér*culis*
> Karolus frontem hilarior póst quaedam ál*ia*
> cum uidisset Iohannem quíddam fecísse
> quod Gallicanam comitátem offéndere*t*
> urbane incrépuit et díx*it*
> 'Quid distat inter sóttum et Scót*tum*?'
> Retulit ille sollemne conuitium in auctórem et respónd*it*
> 'Tábula tán*tum*.'
> Quid hoc dícto facéti*us*?
> Interrogauerat rex de morum differé*nt*i *st*úd*io*.
> Respondit Iohannes de loci distá*nte* *sp*át*io*.
> Nec uero réx commótus es*t*
> quod miraculo sciéntiae ipsìus cápt*us*
> aduersus magistrum nec dicto insúrgere uélle*t*
> sic enim eum usitáte uocába*t*.

[2] William of Malmesbury, *Gesta pontificum Anglorum* V 240 (ed. Winterbottom (2007), 586). The translation is mine, here and throughout.

'In his [Alfred's] time John the Scot came to England,
a man of perspicacious intellect and of great eloquence,
who with his fatherland left behind formerly had gone over to France to Charles the Bald,
by whom, received with great regard, he was held as a familiar of his partisans,
and he used to carry on transactions with him, serious as well as jocose,
and he was an inseparable companion both of the table and of the private chamber.
Many remarks witty and of innate cleverness,
of which examples survive even today,
as these are.
He had sat at table opposite the king at the other part of the table.
With cups proceeding
and courses consumed
Charles rather happy in countenance after certain other things,
when he saw that John had done something
that would offend Gallic refinement
he reproved urbanely and said
'What distinguishes [lit. 'stands apart'] between a sot and a Scot?'
That man returned the solemn reproach on to its author and answered
'Only a table. '
What wittier than this saying?
The king had asked about a different pursuit of customs.
John replied about a distinguishing space of a place.
In truth the king was neither moved to anger
(because captivated by the miracle of the learning of the same man)
nor did he wish to rise up because of the saying [or 'in a word'] against the master
(for so he used to call him in everyday usage).'

The Cambro-Norman Gerald de Barri, sometime tutor to King John, published about AD 1217 *De principis instructione liber*, in which he wrote:[3]

Karolus Magnus [...] preceptorem habebat hic uirum éruditíssim*um*
de borealibus Maioris Britannie fínibus òriúnd*um*
quem secum assidue ne ullo tempore correctore carebat círcumducéba*t*
scilicet Alquinum dé quo légitur
quod cum ad cenam aliquando coram rége sed*éret*
mensa solum ínterpósita

3 Gerald de Barri, *De principis instructione liber* I 11 (ed. Warner (1891), 42).

rex inter edendum hec illi resolutus in iocum lúdicro díx*erit*
'Quid distat inter Scótum et sót*um*?'
uocabulorum alludens annóminatióne*m*.
Cui Alquinus tale facetum quidem et eodem schemate periculosum támen et exásperans
nisi mansuetudinem príncipis nóss*et*
responsum ded*it*
'Tábula tánt*um*.'

'Charles the Great [...] used to have as preceptor a most erudite man
arisen from the northern confines of Greater Britain,
whom he used assiduously to lead about with him lest at any time he would lack a corrector,
understand Alcuin, about whom it is read,
with only a table placed between,
the king while eating said these things to that man relaxed into a joke in a witticism,
'What distinguishes between a Scot and a sot?'
alluding to the alliteration of the words,
to whom Alcuin gave such a response, witty indeed and in the same fashion, yet perilous and exasperating,
unless he knew the clemency of the prince,
'Only a table.''

Matthew Paris, the finest English historian after William of Malmesbury, ended his *Chronica maiora* at AD 1259. I have marked diction different from William's with boldface, word order different from William's with underline, and omissions from William's text with three dots.[4]

Eodem anno [AD 884] uenit **in** Angliam **magister** Iohannes **nátione** Scótus
uir perspicacis ingenii et [...] facúndie **sìngulàris.**
Hic dudum relicta patria **ad partes Gallicanas** transiens Karolum Cáluum **ádiit**
atque in magna **ab eo** dignatióne suscéptus [...]
indiuiduus comes **ei fuerat** et ménse et cubículi.
Huius autem ingenii et scientie magnitudo ac leporis [...] exempla **usque** hódie **mánent** [...]
Assederat **namque** ad mensam **ante** regem **ex oppósito dìe quádam**
ubi consumptis ferculis poculis**que** **díscurr**éntibus
Karolus fronte hilárior **èst effectus.**

4 Matthew Paris, *Chronica maiora s.a.* 883 (ed. Luard (1872), i 415–6).

Rex denique cum magistrum Iohannem uidisset quíddam **egísse**
quod comitatem Gallicanam offéndere **uìderétur**
increpauit **eum sátis** urbàne **dícens**
'**Iohannes** quid distat inter Scótum et sótum?'
Ille **respóndit et dìxit régi**
'**Mensa** tantum.'
Sicque magister Iohannes solenne conuitium **rétulit** ìn auctórem.
Quid hoc **respónso** facétius?
Interrogauerat **namque** de morum differénti stúdio
et respondit Iohannes de loci distánte spátio.
Nec uero rex **uerbis eíus** commótus est
sed potius ipsum cum assessoribus suis commóuit ad cachínnum.

'In the same year [AD 884] there came into England master John, by nation a Scot,
a man of perspicacious intellect [...] and singular eloquence.
This man, with his fatherland left behind formerly, going over to Gallic regions, went to Charles the Bald,
and received by him in great regard [...]
was to him an inseparable companion both of the table and of the private chamber.
The greatness, however, of his intellect and learning and examples of cleverness remain till today [...] .
For he had sat at table before the king on the opposite side on a certain day,
when with courses consumed and cups circulating,
Charles was made rather happy in countenance.
The king finally, when he saw master John had done something
that might be seen to offend Gallic refinement
reproved him urbanely enough, saying,
'John, what distinguishes [lit. 'stands apart'] between a Scot and a sot?'
That man responded and said to the king,
'Only a table.'
And so master John returned the solemn reproach on to its author.
What wittier than this response?
For he had asked about a different pursuit of customs,
and John responded about a distinguishing space of a place.
And in truth the king was not moved to anger by his words,
but rather he [John] moved the same man with his own men seated with him to laughter.

William, Gerald, and Matthew all composed their narratives carefully. The third account, Matthew's, is a revision of William's, notable for varied diction, principally *mensa* for *tabula*. As Matthew says nothing new about either the composition or the working of the joke, we may set his derived version aside. The second account, Gerald's, is also a revision of William's, but with more important changes. As Gerald held a low opinion of the English[5] but thought even less of the Irish[6], he may have transferred William's story from Charles the Bald (AD 823–877) and Iohannes Scottus Eriugena (†AD 877) to Charles the Great (AD ?742–814) and Alcuin (AD 735–804) to avoid celebrating an Irish hero. He appears to have noticed only the alliteration of *sotum* and *Scotum*, which he calls *annominationem*, and only one way to understand the joke, a cheeky and potentially dangerous response to the emperor, though the joke loses even that single dimension if the responder is, like Alcuin, not Irish. So we may set Gerald's version aside as well, relying more securely upon the testimony of William as the earliest writer, the finest historian, and the best narrator of the three.

Let us consider first the rhythm and the sound of the exchange:

> Quid distat inter ***sóttum*** et ***Scóttum***?
> **Tábula tán***tum*.

This exchange that involves two men is composed on duple ratio 2:1. It consists of two lines, the emperor's question containing ten syllables and the Irishman's answer containing five. Both question and answer exhibit the rhythm of a *cursus planus* /xx/x. Both question and answer alliterate internally, ***sottum et Scottum***, and ***tabula tantum***, and both rhyme, *Scottum* and *tantum*. From this we infer that Matthew's *mensa*, which destroys the alliteration of the answer and leaves it one syllable short, cannot have been the original reading.

William demonstrates better than Gerald an explicit understanding that the joke works in two ways. In the first way, the words *quid distat inter*, construed as a question about morals and habits, 'what is the difference between a sot and a Scot?', 'what distinguishes a sot and a Scot?', invite an expected answer about morals and habits, *tabula tantum* ('only a table'), implying that a man with no self-control approaches a table as an Irishman and leaves it as a drunk, a conclusion offensive to the Irishman. In the second way, the words *quid distat inter*, construed as a question about space, 'what stands between a sot and a Scot?', elicit an

5 Davies (1920), 93–4, 128, 202.

6 Dimock (1867), 164–71, 181.

unexpected answer implying, since John is a Scot, that the emperor is a sot, a conclusion offensive to the emperor.

The joke works further in a third way. What distinguishes *sottus* from *Scottus* orthographically is the letter *C*, the sound of which, pronounced in the fashion of Cadac Andreas, makes *sottum* and *Scottum* homophones, in which case there is no difference at all between a sot and a Scot, a conclusion offensive to the Irishman.

The joke works also in a fourth way. John's contemporary Martinus Hibernensis (†AD 875) owned what is now Laon, Bibliothèque municipale, 444, a Graeco-Latin glossary that contains more than 15,000 Greek lemmata. John was not merely competent but fluent in Greek, able to translate the Celestial Hierarchy of Pseudo-Denys the Areopagite from Greek and to compose his own verse in Greek. He knew well that the shape of the Latin letter *C* is identical with the shape of the Greek lunate sigma. In the Classical Latin poetry of Martial (?AD 40–101) in Epigram X xlviii 6

septem sigma capit, sex sumus, adde Lupum

and Epigram XIV lxxxvii (*Stibadia*) 1

accipe lunata scriptum testudine sigma
octo capit, ueniat quisquis amicus erit

the word *sigma* designates 'a semicircular couch for reclining at table', which brings us by a different route back to the context of the joke, an encounter across a table.

The joke works in a fifth way. If one construes the word *sottus* as 'fool', 'simpleton', and the word *tabula* as 'table', specifically a table of computistic numbers, what distinguishes a sot from a Scot is mathematical competence. From the end of the 6th century and the beginning of the 7th to the 9th and long after Irish scholars were famous throughout Europe as mathematicians, as teachers of computus, and as setters and solvers of *problemata mathematica*, cryptograms, and intellectual puzzles.[7]

[7] For Hiberno-Latin computistic texts see Lapidge and Sharpe (1985), 77–8, 89–92, 194, 198, 202–3 (§§288–9, 315, 317–19, 321–4, 720, 732, 752). For editions of two 7th-century Hiberno-Latin mathematical poems see Howlett (forthcoming). For editions of two 7th-century Hiberno-Latin poems about the numbers of the Eusebian Canons see Howlett (2010b); Howlett (2013). For editions of two 9th-century Hiberno-Latin *problemata mathematica* see Howlett (2010a). For an edition of a 10th-cen-

The polyvalence of this joke is a playful reflex, a ramification of a symptom deeply rooted in early Irish intellectual life. It is like the desire to understand and accommodate discrepant points of view of different grammarians, revealed in the library of Hiberno-Latin grammars and in the parodies of Virgilius Maro Grammaticus.[8] It is like the intent to understand not only the computational cycle sanctioned officially at Rome, but also ten different computational cycles, expressed in Cummian's *Epistola de controuersia paschali*[9] and referred to in the 7th-century poem *De ratione temporum, Annus solis continetur quatuor temporibus.*[10] It is like the convention of recording varied interpretations in exegetical compositions[11] and contradictory regulations in the *Collectio Canonum Hibernensis.*[12] It is like the presentation in the *Versus de annis a principio, Deus a quo facta fuit huius mundi machina*, a poem that dates itself in three ways to the year AD 645, of three independent but related traditions, the biblical, the classical, and the Irish, on parallel and equal footing.[13] This polyvalent joke is a celebration of wit, but without a single victim, instead with surprising and varied targets, a monument to a richly inclusive frame of mind.

Dubthach, Suadbar, and the Bamberg Cryptogram[14]

The *Bibliography of Celtic-Latin Literature* attributes to the 9th-century Hiberno-Latin author Dubthach mac Máel-Tuile two texts. One is

tury Hiberno-Latin text about rules for a game of *tafel* that teaches the numbers of the Eusebian Canons see Howlett (2013). For an edition of the 10th-century Bamberg Cryptogram see 'Dubthach, Suadbar, and the Bamberg Cryptogram' below.

8 For Hiberno-Latin grammatical texts see Lapidge and Sharpe (1985), 81–2, 86–7, 94–6, 175–7, 179–80, 197–8, 202 (§§295–8, 306, 331–4, 337, 663–5, 670, 681–4, 731, 750–1), and Law (1982); Law (1995).

9 Cummian, *De controversia paschali* ll. 204–270 (ed. and trans. Walsh and Ó Cróinín (1988), 82–7).

10 Howlett (forthcoming).

11 See the sub-series *Scriptores Celtigenae* within CCSL: 82 (1997), 108E (1996), 108F (2003); and within CCCM: 173 (2000).

12 See the edition and translation by Dr Roy Flechner (forthcoming).

13 Howlett (1996b), 1–6.

14 I owe thanks to our honorand for his characteristic generosity in supplying me with a 'reader's pack', his collection of materials for study of the cryptogram, to Dr Anthony Harvey for advice about matters of Celtic philology, and to Drs Andrew Breeze and Tomás Kalmar. Particular debts are acknowledged in the appropriate places.

a colophon to a manuscript of the *Periegesis* and Grammar of Priscian (Leiden, Universiteitsbibliotheek, VLF 67, 7v):[15]

<table>
<tr><td colspan="2">Finit Perigesis Prisciani.
Dubthach hos uersus transcripsit tempore paruo
   indulge lector qui mala scripta uides</td></tr>
<tr><td>tertio idus Apriles</td><td>tribus degitis</td></tr>
<tr><td>tertio anno decenno[uenalis] cicli</td><td>tribus instrumentis penna
   membrano atramento</td></tr>
<tr><td>tertia decima luna incipiente</td><td>Trinitate auxiliatrice</td></tr>
<tr><td>tertia hora post meridiem.</td><td></td></tr>
</table>

<table>
<tr><td colspan="2">'The *Periegesis* of Priscian ends.
Dubthach transcribed these verses in a short time—
   indulge, reader, who see bad things written—</td></tr>
<tr><td>on the third of the Ides of April,</td><td>with three fingers,</td></tr>
<tr><td>in the third year of the nineteen-year cycle,</td><td>with three instruments,
   pen, membrane, ink,</td></tr>
<tr><td>with the thirteenth moon beginning,</td><td>with the Trinity as helper,</td></tr>
<tr><td>in the third hour past midday.'</td><td></td></tr>
</table>

The third line begins with the first of seven words for 'three': *tertio, tribus, tertio, tribus, tertia decima, Trinitate, tertia*. The first *tertio* is the thirteenth word, after which the third word is *tribus* |, between which and | *tertio* there are three syllables. Between *tertio* | and | *tribus instrumentis* there are three words. After *tribus instrumentis* | Dubthach lists three instruments, *penna, membrano, atramento*. Between the first *tertio* | and | *tertia decima* there are thirteen words, and between *tribus* | and | *tertia decima* there are thirteen syllables. Between *tertia* | *decima* and | *Trinitate* there are three words, and from | *tertia decima* to | *Trinitate* there are thirteen syllables. From the last *tertia* | to the end there are three words. The words for 'three' contain the letter *T* thirteen times. From the beginning of the couplet to | *decennouenalis* there are nineteen words. There are also twelve alliterating syllables, five on *te-*, *tempore, tertio, tertio, tertia, tertia*, and seven on *tr-*, *transcripsit, tribus, tribus, instrumentis, atramento, Trinitate, auxiliatrice*.[16]

Dubthach completed his work at 3pm on the third of the Ides of April, Maundy Thursday, Thursday in Holy Week, 11 April AD 838.

[15] Lapidge and Sharpe (1985), 181 (§688); Lindsay (1910), 36; MGH Poetae 3, 685.

[16] I owe this observation to Dr Tomás Kalmar.

Copying the *Periegesis* and Grammar of Priscian and composing an elegiac couplet demonstrate Dubthach's understanding of the foundations of the linguistic arts of the *triuium*. The rest of the colophon demonstrates his understanding of computus, the foundation of the numerical sciences of the *quadruuium*.

Like many Hiberno-Latin writers from the 5th century onward Dubthach was well informed about the tradition in Hebrew, Greek, and Latin of reckoning the numerical values of letters of the alphabet.[17] From *Dubthach* | to the end of the elegiac couplet there are 65 letters, coincident with the alphanumeric value in the twenty-three-letter Latin alphabet of DUBTHACH, 4+20+2+19+8+1+3+8 or 65. From *Dubthach* | to the *A* | of *Apriles* inclusive there are 76 letters, coincident with the alphanumeric value of APRILES, 1+15+17+9+11+5+18 or 76. From | *Dubthach* to *meridiem* | there are nine phrases and 276 letters and spaces between words, equal to the number of months and the number of days from the Annunciation, celebrated on 25 March, to the Nativity, celebrated on 25 December.[18]

Dubthach's other extant work is usually known as the Bamberg Cryptogram:

IB E IZ IB E IΓ. IZ E KA. Γ IΔ IΓ Γ H IΓ. IH A IA K IΘ E IB.[19]

This text survives in Brussels, Bibliothèque royale de Belgique / Koninklijke Bibliotheek van België, 9565–66 on folio 13r, and in Bamberg, Staatsbibliothek, HJ IV 11 (Class. 6).[20] In the latter manuscript it is embedded in a letter written to his master Colgu by another Hiberno-Latin author who signs himself here with his Irish name as Suadbar, though we may know him otherwise as Sedulius Scottus.[21] Dubthach's text is short, four words, eight syllables, and 22 letters. Suadbar's composition, in providing a context for the cryptogram, allows us to see a relationship between Brittonic kings, intellectual rivalries between Irishmen and Welshmen and among Irishmen themselves at a Welsh

[17] For *gematria* in ancient and insular literatures see Howlett (2005a), *passim*; Howlett (2006a), *passim*; Howlett (2006b), 100–2.

[18] For other examples in insular literature see Howlett (1997a), 294 n 59; Howlett (2000), 84, 89, 95, 159–60, 192.

[19] Lapidge and Sharpe (1985), 181 (no. 687).

[20] For a transcript of the former see Derolez (1954), 97. For a facsimile of the latter see Ó Cróinín (1993), 52.

[21] Ó Cróinín (1993), 47–50.

court, and knowledge of computus, cryptography, cryptanalysis, *gematria*, and Greek among Hiberno-Latin writers. Suadbar's composition is so wonderfully dense that its artifice can hardly be shown in a single presentation, yet it is so unified that it can hardly be unpicked for separate analyses. The text of Suadbar's letter that follows is based upon the Bamberg manuscript, arranged here *per cola et commata* ('by clauses and phrases'), with capital letters and punctuation marks in boldface representing features of the manuscript, with italics suggesting rhymes, and with rhythms of the *cursus* marked by acute and grave accents: *planus*, *régis demísit*; *tardus*, *scriptúram dinóscere*; *uelox*, *intellígere pòtuísse*; *medius*, *désignáuimus*; *trispondiacus*, *uírum non latébunt*.[22] The arrangement in lines is mine, distinct from that in the Bamberg manuscript, but putatively authorial, for reasons that will become apparent in the analysis. The first column on the left contains Roman numerals that function both as cardinal numbers and as line numbers. From the evidence of the colophon, in which the scribe spells his name *Dubthach*, I have normalized to that form the variants of the Bamberg manuscript, *Dubtach*, *Dubthachi*, and *Dubthace*, retained double *t* in *Scottorum*, *Brittonum*, and *littera*, and for *e-caudata* and flattened *e* retained the Classical diphthong *ae*.

i	A	a	**H**aec est inscriptio quam Dubthach in arce Mermin Brittannorum régis demísit **.** ad probandos Scottórum sapié*ntes* **.**	A	i
ii	B	b	se ipsum excellentissimum ómnium Scottórum **.** Brittonúmque opínan*s* **.**	B	ii
iii	Γ	c	scilicet putans nullum Scóttigenárum **.** quanto magis Brittonum doctorum in praesentia Mermin regis istam scriptúram perlégere **.** atque intellígere pòtuíss*e* **.**	Γ	iii
iiii	Δ	d	**S**ed nos Caunchobrach **.** Fergus **.** et Dominnach **.** et Suadbar **.** opitulante Deo illa scriptúra non látuit **.** per an- nalem Graecórum libéllum **.** atque alpha- beti eandem inscriptionem ínuestigá*ntes* **.**	Δ	iiii

[22] For accounts of the tradition of composing rhythmic prose see Howlett (1995a), 21–9; Howlett (1997a), 22–30; Howlett (1997b), 53–116.

u	E	e	IB E IZ IB E IΓ. IZ E KA. Γ IΔ I Γ Γ H I Γ IH A IA K IΘ E IB.	E	u
ui	S	f	Istius scripturae tális est sénsu*s* .	S	ui
uii	Z	g	Mermin rex Cónchen salútem .	Z	uii
uiii	H	h	Si ergo uolueris istam scriptúram dinósce*re*	H	uiii
uiiii	Θ	i	perspicaci mente praescriptam Graecorum annalis compoti seriem Latinasque sequentes litteras post ipsa Graeca eleménta ordinátas . ánimaduértito	Θ	uiiii
x	I	k	átque cognóscito . Latinas litteras subsequentes Graecis elementis praedicéntibus cònuení*re* .	I	x
xi	IA	l	sicut in praescriptis lineis désignáu*imus*	K	xx
xii	IB	m	Cum ergo .IB. Graecas uidelicet litteras in praefata Dubthachi scriptura aspiciéndo uidéris .	Λ	xxx
xiii	IΓ	n	respice Graecarum litterarum sériem àntescrípta*m* .	M	xl
xiiii	IΔ	o	atque in illa serie .IB. Graeca uidelicet elementa . tuum uírum non latébu*nt* .	N	l
xu	IE	p	et quia duodecimum eaedem litterae óptinent *lócum* .	Ξ	lx
xui	IS	q	necesse est ut duodecimam Latini alphabeti M lítteram désigne*nt* .	O	lxx
xuii	IZ	r	Item quia .E. in ipsa Graeci calculi serie quintum póssidet *lócum* .	Π	lxxx
xuiii	IH	s	recte quintam Latini alphabeti .E. litteram ésse designátam .	O	xc
xuiiii	IΘ	t	atque ita per caetera decurrens totum sensum ipsius uel similis | descriptiónis intéllig*es* .	P	c
xx	K	u	Notum autem sit tuae prudentiae optime Colgu . nosterque doctíssime magíster .	C	cc
xxi	KA	x	quod non quasi tibi ignoranti istam expositiúnculam transmítt*imus* .	T	ccc
xxii	KB	y	sed supplíciter pósc*imus* .	Y	cccc

xxiii	KΓ	z	ut istam explanationem ignorantibus et simplicioribus nostris Scottigenis fratribus trans Brittannicum mare nauigare uolentibus per tuam beniuolam caritátem insínu*es* .	Φ	d
xxiiii	KΔ		**ne** forte in praesentia Mermin gloriosi Brittonum regis illam inscriptionem non intelligéntes erubésca*nt* .	X	dc
xxu	KE		**N**os autem coram Déo testámur .	Ψ	dcc
xxui	K		quod nec caúsa elàtiónis . aut tumidae inflatiónis quod ábsit . istam uobis transmittimus éxpositióne*m* .	Ω	dccc
xxuii	KZ		sed istam latebram uestram sanctitatem latere fraterno amore nón passi sú*mus* .	+	dcccc
xxuiii	KH		**O**mnes in Xpisto fratres gaudete . Valete .		
xxuiiii	KΘ		IH K A Δ B A IZ. IH Γ IZ Θ IE IH Θ IΘ.		
xxx	Λ		**H**ic erras Dubthache in tuis nótulis scríbens .H. pro Θ. uel pro .E. uel pro aspirátionis nóta .		
xxxi	ΛA		quae nec secundum Brittannicam linguam in ipso término bène sóna*t*.		

IΓ A IΓ Δ H A IZ Θ K IH IH A Z A KA B I Δ IΓ IΔ A IΓ Θ IB IΔ Γ IΔ IΓ IH Γ IZ Θ IE IH E IZ A IΘ Θ IH IΘ A I B A IZ Θ IΘ H IB E IΘ Θ I A IB

15 .xiimum. 16 .xiimum. latini alphabetum literam designent. 26 quod inflationis absit.

I 1 This is an inscription that Dubthach in the fortress of Merfin king of the Britons sent out for testing wise Scots [i.e. 'Irishmen'],

2 supposing himself to be most excellent of all Scots and Britons,

3 thinking, understand, that none of the learned men of the Scots-born – how much more of the Britons – in the presence of Merfin the king could read through and understand this writing.

II 4 But with us, Caunchobrach, Fergus and Dominnach and Suadbar, investigating the same inscription, with God supporting, by means of the computus [lit. 'calendrical book'] and the little book of the alphabet of the Greeks, that writing did not lie hidden.

III 5 MERMEN. REX. CONCHN. SALUTEM.

IIII 6 Of this writing such is the sense.

V 7 Merfin king to Conchen [sends] greeting.

VI 8 If therefore you should wish to know this writing,

9 with a perspicacious mind turn your attention to the series of the calendrical book of the computus of the Greeks forewritten [i.e. the first two columns to the left of the text] and the Latin letters following ordered after the same Greek letters [i.e. the third column to the left of the text],

10 and understand that the Latin letters following after agree with [lit. 'come together with'] the foretelling Greek letters,

11 just as we have designated in the lines forewritten [i.e. to the left].

VII 12 When therefore, it is plain to see, you will have seen, looking at the Greek letters IB in the foresaid writing of Dubthach,

13 look back at the series of Greek letters written before,

14 and in that series the Greek letters, it is plain to see, will not hide your man,

15 and because the same letters occupy the twelfth place,

16 it is necessary that they designate the twelfth letter of the Latin alphabet, M.

VIII 17 In the same way because E in the same series of Greek calculus possesses the fifth place,

18 you will understand rightly that the fifth letter of the Latin alphabet is designated,

19 and so running through the others [you will understand] the whole sense of this or a similar inscription.

VIIII 20 It should be known to your prudence, best Colgu, and our most learned master,

21 that not as if to you being ignorant are we sending this little exposition,

22 but we humbly request

23 that this explanation to our Scots-born brothers, ignorant and more simple, wishing to ship

24 across the British sea, through your well-wishing charity you might insinuate, lest by chance in the presence of Merfin the glorious king of the Britons, not understanding that inscription, they might blush.

X 25 We, however, before God bear witness

26 that not because of elation or tumid swelling with pride – may which be absent – are we sending to you this exposition,

27 but from fraternal love we have not suffered this secret to lie hidden to your holiness.

XI 28 All brothers in Christ, rejoice. Farewell.

XII 29 SUADBAR SCRIPSIT. Suadbar wrote.

XIII 30 Here you err, Dubthach, in your little notes, writing H [the Greek letter eta] for Θ [the Greek letter theta, as numeral for 9 the equivalent of the ninth Latin letter I] or for [Latin] E or for a note of aspiration [i.e. Latin H],

31 which according to the Brittonic language does not sound well in that position.

NANDHARIUS SAGAX BONO ANIMO CONSCRIPSERAT ISTAM ARITHMETIKAM
Nandharius the sagacious with a good mind had written this arithmetic.

Let us begin by observing the parallel and chiastic arrangement of every element of Suadbar's letter. Note the chiastic aspect of the frame of the letter, Roman numerals in the first column on the left and the last column on the right, numbers in Greek alphanumeric notation in the second column on the left and Greek letters as numbers in the penultimate column on the right, with the text in the middle. Perception of this balance may have inspired the continental scribe to add his cyptogrammatic colophon at the bottom, enhancing the pattern. In the text that follows letters and numbers to the left and indented spaces show which clauses and phrases are paired with which, italics marking parallel and chiastic diction.

I
A *Haec* est *inscriptio* quam Dubthach
B *in arce Mermin* Brittannorum *regis* demisit
C ad probandos Scottorum *sapientes*
D se ipsum excellentissimum *omnium Scottorum Brittonumque*
E *opinans*
F scilicet
E' *putans*
D' *nullum Scottigenarum quanto magis Brittonum*
C' *doctorum*
B' *in praesentia Mermin regis*
A' *istam scripturam* perlegere atque intelligere potuisse
II
A Sed *nos Caunchobrach Fergus et Dominnach et Suadbar*
B1 opitulante Deo
B2 *illa scriptura*
C non latuit
B'1 per annalem Graecorum libellum atque alphabeti
B'2 *eandem inscriptionem*
A' *inuestigantes*
III–IIII–V
A IB E IZ IB E IΓ. IZ E KA. Γ IΔ IΓ Γ H IΓ. IH A IA K IΘ E IB.
B Istius scripturae talis est sensus
A' Mermin rex Conchen salutem
VI–VII–VIII
A Si ergo *uolueris* istam scripturam *dinoscere*
B1 perspicaci mente *praescriptam* Graecorum annalis compoti seriem
B2 *Latinasque sequentes litteras* post ipsa *Graeca elementa* ordinatas
B3 *animaduertito*
B4 atque
B3' *cognoscito*
B2' *Latinas litteras subsequentes Graecis elementis* praedicentibus conuenire
B1' sicut in *praescriptis* lineis designauimus

B'1 Cum ergo *IB*
B'2 *Graecas* uidelicet *litteras* in *praefata* Dubthachi *scriptura*
B'3 a*spic*iendo
B'4 uideris
B'3' re*spic*e
B'2' *Graecarum litterarum* seriem *antescriptam*
B'1' *atque* in illa serie *IB Graeca* uidelicet elementa tuum uirum non latebunt
B''1 et quia *duodecimum* eaedem litterae optinent *locum*
B''1' *necesse* est ut *duodecimam Latini alphabeti* M *litteram designent*
B'''1 *Item quia E* in ipsa *Graeci* calculi serie *quintum* possidet *locum*
B'''1' *recte quintam Latini* alphabeti *E litteram* esse *designatam*
A' atque ita per caetera decurrens totum sensum ipsius uel similis descriptionis *intelliges*

VIIII–X
A *Notum* autem *sit*
B *tuae prudentiae* optime Colgu nosterque doctissime magister
C1 quod non quasi *tibi*
C2 *ignoranti*
C3 *istam expositiunculam*
C4 *transmittimus*
C5 sed *suppliciter*
C4' *poscimus*
C3' ut *istam explanationem*
C2' *ignorantibus* et simplicioribus nostris Scottigenis fratribus trans Brittannicum mare nauigare uolentibus
C1' per *tuam* beniuolam caritatem insinues
C3'' ne forte in praesentia Mermin gloriosi Brittonum regis *illam inscriptionem*
C2'' *non intelligentes* erubescant
C4'' *Nos* autem coram Deo *testamur*
C5' quod *nec causa elationis aut tumidae inflationis* quod absit istam uobis
C4'' *transmittimus*
C3''' *expositionem*
B' sed istam latebram *uestram sanctitatem*
A' *latere* fraterno amore *non* passi sumus

XI
A Omnes in Xpisto fratres gaudete

A' Valete

XII

IH K A Δ B A IZ. IH Γ IZ Θ IE IH Θ I Θ.

XIII

A Hic erras Dubthache in tuis notulis scribens H pro Θ uel pro E uel pro aspirationis nota

A' quae nec secundum Brittannicam linguam in ipso termino bene sonat

With the text presented thus, some phenomena that puzzled earlier scholars can be explained. In sentence II line 4 the centre of the 23 words is *scriptura*, preceded and followed by phrases that explain how the cryptogram was solved, preceded by the ablative absolute *Deo opitulante* and followed by an account of the source resorted to, the sentence beginning and ending with *nos ... inuestigantes*, understood as an accusative absolute.[23]

Derolez wrote of sentence III line 5 'the mistake *Conchn* is corrected in the note addressed to Dubthach',[24] but we shall consider below indications that Dubthach did not err.

Though Derolez inferred from the empty space caused by erasure in sentence VII line 14 that the text is damaged here,[25] it is sound.

In sentence VIII line 18 the construction is an accusative and infinitive dependent on *intelliges* in the following line.

The entire text is grammatically and syntactically faultless and completely rhythmical, every line ending with a good *cursus* rhythm.

Dubthach's cryptogram is the salutation of a letter from Merfin to Cyngen, both identifiable. Merfyn Frych ('Merfyn the Freckled'), son of Gwriad ab Elidir and Esyllt ferch Cynan, ruled the kingdom of Gwynedd in northwestern Wales from AD 825 until his death in 844. Descended through his mother from Maglocunus, the tyrant attacked by Gildas in *De Excidio Brittanniae* in AD 540, Merfin was the first member of the second dynasty of Gwynedd, father of Rhodri Mawr.[26] During Merfin's reign Nennius published, probably in Gwynedd, the

[23] For another accusative absolute in insular Latin literature see Howlett (2000), 53–5.

[24] Derolez (1954), 99.

[25] Derolez (1954), 98.

[26] Powicke and Fryde (1961), 47.

Historia Brittonum in AD 829–830.[27] As Merfin's wife was Nest, sister of Cyngen ap Cadell ap Brochfael, the letter is addressed to his brother-in-law, who ruled the kingdom of Powys in eastern Wales from AD 808 until his death during a pilgrimage to Rome in AD 854 or 855.[28] Cyngen was responsible for the longest extant Cambro-Latin inscription, on the pillar of Elise, once a cross, in Llandysilio-yn-Iâl, from which cross Valle Crucis took its name.[29] The name recurs, belonging to another man, *Cjncenn filius Grípiud*, in the earliest of the memoranda from Llandeilo Fawr in Carmarthenshire, written into the Gospels in Lichfield, Cathedral Library, 1, about AD 820–840.[30]

Suadbar, providing many indications that he understood the structure of Dubthach's compositions, offers a form of homage by incorporating elements of those works into his own composition. He understood in Dubthach's colophon the importance of the number 3, arranging his own sentence I in three lines. In sentence II he lists three sources for deciphering the cryptogram: the help of God, the calendrical book of the Greeks, and the little book of the alphabet of the Greeks. The section about Dubthach's cryptogram, beginning at sentence III, contains three sentences, III–IIII–V. The section about cryptanalysis contains three sentences, VI–VII–VIII. The address to Suadbar's master Colgu contains three sentences, VIIII, X, XI. Suadbar uses the name *Dubthach* three times, the word *inscriptio* three times, and the word *alphabetum* three times.

Suadbar understood also in Dubthach's colophon the importance of the number 13. His entire letter contains thirteen sentences, of which the thirteenth is addressed to Dubthach himself. The account of the cryptogram in sentences III–IIII–V contains thirteen words. The dactylic hexameter in sentence XI line 28 contains thirteen syllables.

As Dubthach's cryptogram contains four words, Suadbar incorporated the number 4 into his own composition, naming himself as the fourth of the travelling companions Caunchobrach, Fergus, Dominnach, and Suadbar. His own signature contains four syllables. He refers to *Scotti* and *Scottigenae* four times, to *Brittones* and *Brittanni* four times, and to *Mermin* four times. He uses *Latinus* four times and

[27] For analysis see Howlett (1995a), 333–5; Howlett (1998a), 69–83; Howlett (2005a), 45–52.

[28] Derolez (1954), 99; Powicke and Fryde (1961), 47.

[29] Howlett (1998a), 27–32.

[30] Howlett (2005a), 52–4.

Graecus eight times (4×2). Including the Roman numerals in the first and last columns, the Greek numbers and letters of the second and penultimate columns, the Latin alphabet of the third column, and the words of the letter proper, there are exactly CCCCXXXXIIII (444) words in the entire composition.[31]

Dubthach's cryptogram contains 22 letters; Suadbar's line 22 contains 22 letters and with line 23 22 words.[32]

Other indications of scrupulous attention to detail include Suadbar's line 12, which, considering the Greek letters IB as the alphanumeric representation of 12, contains twelve words. In accordance with sound pedagogical procedure and conformity with the basic principles of statement and restatement in biblical style Suadbar writes the numeral *IB* twice and refers twice to the ordinal place of the letter *M* as *duodecimus* and twice to the ordinal place of the letter *E* as *quintus*. Having shown how to decipher the first two letters of the cryptogram, *ME*, he stops, as *per caetera decurrens totum sensum ipsius uel similis descriptionis intelliges.*

Sentence X begins *Nos autem coram Deo testamur*, which contains ten syllables. The letter proper occupies 27 lines, coincident with the 27 Greek symbols for numerals in the penultimate column on the right. After line 27 follows the verse sentence *Omnes in Xpisto fratres gaudete*, which contains 27 letters. The entire letter occupies 31 lines, coincident with the 31 lines of Roman numerals and their representations in Greek alphanumeric symbols in the first two columns on the left. From | xxx Λ *Hic erras Dubthache* to *in ipso termino bene sonat* | 30–31 there are 31 words.

Suadbar manifestly understood Dubthach's practice of *gematria* in the colophon, for he reproduced it in the letter. In sentence I line 1 from *Dubthach* | to | *se ipsum* [i.e. *Dubthach*] there are 65 letters, coincident with the alphanumeric value of DUBTHACH. There is a further form of homage in that Suadbar, while declining to follow Dubthach's orthography, still calculates *gematria* according to Dubthach's usage.

[31] For other examples of the number 444 in insular compositions see Howlett (1996a), 132–5; Howlett (2000), 84: The year AD 444 is recorded in Irish tradition as the date of Patrick's foundation of Armagh, in Welsh tradition as *Annus* I of the *Annales Cambriae*, and in Scottish tradition as the year in which King Ungus met Saint Regulus at Rig Monaid with the relics of Saint Andrew, marked at the 444th word of the text in which it is discussed.

[32] The number 22 is important as the number of things God created in Genesis 1, the number of letters in the Hebrew alphabet, the number of books in the Hebrew Bible, the number of generations from Adam to Israel, the number of syllables in the Greek text of Christ's creation of the universe in John 1:3, and the number of letters in the Latin text of the same passage, 22–2–22.

From the beginning of the letter the 64th word is IB E IZ IB E IΓ |, coincident with the alphanumeric value of MERMEN, 12+5+17+12+5+13 or 64. Between *Mermin* | 1 and | *Mermin* 7 there are also 64 words. Between *in arce Mermin* | 1 and | *in praesentia Mermin* 3 there are 64 syllables. From MERMEN | REX 5 to *Mermin* | *rex* 7 there are 64 letters. From the beginning to IB E IZ IB E IΓ IZ E KA *Mermen rex* | there are 444 letters, which reminds us of the 444 words of the entire composition.

From | *Istius* 6 to *Conchen* | there are 54 letters and spaces between words, coincident with the alphanumeric value of CONCHN, 3+14+13+3+8+13 or 54. Here again Suadbar calculates the *gematria* according to Dubthach's orthography that he criticizes.

In Suadbar's own *gematria* there are in sentence VIIII lines 20 and 21, from | *Colgu* to *tibi* [i.e. *Colgu*] | 55 letters, coincident with the alphanumeric value of COLGU, 3+14+11+7+20 or 55. More astonishing is that from | *Haec est inscriptio* at the beginning of the letter to the end of line 3, just before | *Sed nos Caunchobrach Fergus et Dominnach et Suadbar* there are 283 letters, which, with the three Roman numerals in the first column, the three Greek letters in the second column, the three Latin letters in the third column, the three Greek letters in the penultimate column, and the three Roman numerals in the last column, together 15, total 298, coincident with the alphanumeric value of CAUNCHOBRACH, 3+1+20+13+3+14+2+17+1+3+8, FERGUS, 6+5+17+7+20+18, DOMINNACH, 4+14+12+9+13+13+1+3+8, and SUADBAR, 18+20+1+4+2+1+17, 85+73+77+63 or 298.

For the name of the king of Gwynedd Dubthach used the traditional spelling *Mermen*, but Suadbar preferred the current pronunciation spelling *Mermin*, similar to modern Welsh *Merfyn*.[33] For the name of the king of Powys Dubthach used the spelling CONCHN, but Suadbar rendered this as *Conchen* and accused Dubthach of error, *Hic erras Dubthache*. Let us suppose that Dubthach had good reasons for writing as he did and imagine what they might have been. First, he may have adopted the spelling *Conchn* to maintain an impression of equality between the kings by spelling their names with six letters each, the syllables of the former beginning *me* – *me*, those of the latter beginning *c* – *c*, and both names ending *-en*. Second, he may have understood a convention of Romano-British epigraphy, illustrated in the earliest monuments, from the first century AD onward, by which one could make a

[33] Dr Harvey reminds me that the third consonant, regardless of whether it was spelled with *M* or *F*, was always pronounced /v/.

single carved letter do double duty for two adjacent identical letters.[34] In the memorial for Titus Flaminius, for example, erected probably before AD 61, we read [D]IVVAVINIETAQVAPROHIBENTVBI | TA[R] TARADITIS, which is a line of dactylic hexameter verse, DI VVA VINI ET AQVA PROHIBENT VBI TARTARA ADITIS ('the gods restrain from the grape of wine and from water when you enter Tartarus') with a single *A* carved for both the last letter of TARTARA and the first of ADITIS. So Dubthach may have intended Greek H eta to represent both Latin *H* and Greek eta, transliterated as Latin *E*. In this latter consideration he shares the practice of the Hiberno-Latin scribe Ferdomnach of Armagh, who in his colophon in the Book of Armagh wrote sometime between AD 807 and 845 |-HPHΔH for *herede*.[35] Third, Dubthach may have known of the cross Cyngen commissioned Conmarch to carve in memory of his great-grandfather Elise. On that monument the king's name recurs six times spelled CONCENN.[36] This form is similar to that of the name *Cjncenn filius Grípiud* found, as mentioned above, in the first of the memoranda from Llandeilo Fawr inserted into the Gospels of Lichfield, Cathedral Library, 1.[37] Fourth, if Dubthach spelled the king's name as CONCHN, i.e. CONCHEN, but pronounced it as *Congen*, he may even have pressed the letter *H* into triple duty, not only as Latin *H* and Latin *E*, but Latin *H* as softening the unvoiced sound represented by the preceding letter *C* to the voiced sound represented by letter *G*.[38] For all of this good contemporary 9th-century evidence suggests that Dubthach was a well trained and well informed scholar, to whose work we can see varied responses.

The first response is that of the four Irish scholars at Merfin's court. They may have perceived Dubthach as an arrogant man whose pretensions they would deflate by asking their master Colgu to share the key to his cryptogram with everyone who might follow them, an act Nora Chadwick described as 'a delightful bit of patriotic cheating'.[39] Suadbar's negative criticism of Dubthach's cryptogram may be countered, leaving

[34] Howlett (2005a), 8–10.

[35] Howlett (2005a), 76–7.

[36] Howlett (1998a), 27–32.

[37] Howlett (1999), 60–2.

[38] Though in the fairly standard first-millennium spelling-system used for all Celtic languages *CH* designated the voiceless fricative /c/, traces remain in both British and Gaelic documents of earlier orthographical experimentation, including the use of *CH* for /g/. See Harvey (1991), n 36.

[39] Chadwick (1958), 96.

us with an impression of a man who wrote correctly. But in any case the positive incorporation of elements of Dubthach's compositions into Suadbar's own magisterial work suggests that deep called unto deep.

A second response is the use of Dubthach's cryptographic system in a note added to the Cambro-Latin manuscript of Juvencus (Cambridge, University Library, Ff.4.42). The manuscript was written by a scribe named *Núadu*, either an Irishman or a Welshman with an Irish name, working at a scriptorium in Wales probably after about AD 850.[40] The cryptogram was composed by a Welshman named Cyfeiliog, who spelled his name *Cemelliauc*, and copied, probably by someone else, on the right side of the upper margin of folio 36r:

ΓεΙβεΙαΙαθακΓΙεΙζκδΙΓΙΗΙεΙΓΙΗΙεΙΗΙεθΙθΙζΗεΓ [...]
ΓαεΙΓθΙθΙζδΙβsζαΙθΙζεΙΗsθΙζΙβΙθεΙζΙδΙζαΙθΙεΙεΙζ[Ι]δ[...]
ΙβΙθΙζ

Helen McKee presents it thus:[41]

ΓεΙβεΙαΙαθακΓ ΙεΙζκδΙΓΙΗ ΙεΙΗΙεθΙθΙζ
ΗεΓ [...] ΙαεΙΓθΙθΙζ
δΙβsΙζαΙθΙζεΙΗsθΙζΙβθΙθεΙζ
ΙδΙζαΙθε ΙεΙζ[Ι]δΙβε [...] ΙβΙθΙζ

Cemelliauc prudens prespiter	Cyfeilliog the learned priest
Hec [...] leniter [ ]	this without any trouble.
D*eu*m fratres firmiter	To God, brothers, constantly,
Orate pro me [...]mtr	Pray for me [ ].

Of the final *mtr* she states:[42]

> 'Rhys proposed *premiter* here. The final three letters of the word, ib iq iz (= **m t r**) are still legible, but the part of the folio bearing the rest has almost entirely disintegrated. I do not think, however, that the damaged Greek letters begin ιε (= **p**); an iota (which by itself would equal Latin **k**) is definitely visible, and it seems to be followed by either a Γ or an Η (that is, Latin **c** or **h**, or – in combination with the iota – **s** or **n**).'

40 McKee (2000b), 9–12. For a facsimile see McKee (2000a). The Welsh form of the name, *Nud*, recurs in Evans (1893), 414 (index).

41 McKee (2000b), 27–9.

42 McKee (2000b), 27 n 141.

Let us pay attention to phenomena the cryptographer infixed into his text to help us to restore it. Cyfeiliog manifestly composed a quatrain of octosyllabic verse with three lifts in each line, two of them alliterating: *pru-* – *pre-* 1 and *fra-* – *fir-* 3. The first three lines rhyme on *-iter*. The word missing from line 2 should begin with *L*, contain four syllables, and mean something like 'wrote'. This implies that *hec*, if it is an accusative object, cannot be 'this'; it must be neuter plural 'these'. *Deum* cannot be correct, as it would leave line 3 one syllable short. The part of the word missing from line 4 should begin *prom-*, alliterating with *pro me*; rhyme with *firmiter* demands that it end *-miter*. So with boldface marking alliteration and italics marking rhyme, let us read:

	W	S	L
C*e*mélliauc **prúdens** **pr*é***sp*iter*	3	8	26
h*e*c **lí**teráuit **l*é***n*iter*.	3	8	19
D[*ó*minu]m **frá**tr*e*s **fír***miter*	3	8	17
*o*ráte **pr*ó* m*e*** **pró***miter*.	4	8	18
	13	32	80

'Cyfeiliog the prudent priest
wrote these letters with smooth sound.
To God, brothers, steadfastly
pray for me righteously.'

The name *Cemelliauc*, read here with synizesis of the *I*, recurs in the *Liber Landauensis* as *Cimelliauc*.[43] As the name is rare, one is tempted to identify our cryptographer with a man mentioned in the Parker MS of the Anglo-Saxon Chronicle *s.a.* 914:[44]

Her on þysum geare com micel sciphere hider ofer suþan of Lidwiccum
7 twegen eorlas mid, Ohtor 7 Hroald [...]
7 gefengon Cameleac biscop on Ircingafelda
7 lædon hine mid him to scipum
7 þa aliesde Eadweard cyning hine eft mid .xl. pundum.

'Here in this year came a great ship-army hither from the south, from the Bretons,
and two earls with it, Ohtor and Hroald [...]

[43] Evans (1893), 251.

[44] Bately (1986), 65.

and they seized Cyfeiliog the bishop in Archenfield
and they led him with them to the ships
and then Edward the king [the Elder] ransomed him again with forty pounds.'

All words in the poem other than the name are recorded in Classical, Late, and Insular Latin. The last, *probiter*, is recorded in Late Latin, formed from Classical Latin *probus* + *-iter*, written here with *M* by a man accustomed to intervocalic lenition.[45] The eighty letters are coincident with the alphanumeric value of CEMELLIAUC, 3+5+12+5+11+11+9+1+20+3 or 80. Omission of *I* and *E* from the last word, which destroys rhyme and *gematria* alike, suggests that Cyfeiliog composed the cryptogram, maybe to counter the opinion, perhaps shared by Dubthach and Suadbar, implied by the words *quanto magis Brittonum* in the letter. Cyfeiliog, however, did not write this defective copy.

A third response is recognition of the pattern of the frame of the letter by the 10th-century continental scribe Nandharius, who extended the pattern by adding his cryptographic colophon at the bottom of the folio.

The response of Suadbar to Dubthach fits into a long tradition of scholarly needle in Insular Latin literature that began with the attack on the *domini cati rethorici* in the apology in Patrick's *Confessio*,[46] where in apparent self-depreciation Patrick subtly displays his skills as a forensic rhetor, using for the only time in his composition Ciceronian *clausulae*, and relying not only upon his hearers' and readers' recognition of his quotations and allusions but upon their knowledge of the unquoted contexts of those quotations and allusions to condemn those who had attacked him.

It continues in *De excidio Brittanniae* chapter 33, in which Gildas, attacking the Five Tyrants, rounds last on the greatest, Maglocunus Venedotiae (Maelgwn Gwynedd), who must once have been an intimate colleague and friend, describing him as wallowing *in tam uetusto scelerum atramento ueluti madidus uino de Sodomitana uite expresso* ('in such ancient ink of sins, as if drenched with wine expressed from a Sodomitic vine'). One might alternatively render *madidus* as 'drunk with', or 'steeped in', *uite* as 'shoot' or 'cane', and *expresso* as 'squeezed from'. As

[45] Compare in the *Orationes Moucani* 1.15 and 9.28 (Howlett (1995a), 195, 210): *Eli Eli laba sabacthani*. Compare also ogam QRIMITIR; McManus (1997), 4.6, 4.9, 5.14, 5.18–19, 6.24–25, 6.28, 6.30. I owe thanks to Dr Harvey for drawing my attention to this analogue.

[46] Howlett (1994), 56–61, 95–103.

there is no doubt about the implication of *Sodomitana*, one infers that Gildas accused the king of committing buggery and fellatio.

Maelgwn's great-great-grandson, Cadfan king of Anglesey, was also apparently a bit of a lad. Cadfan's father Iago died in AD 615, his son and successor Cadwallon in AD 634, his grandson Cadwaladr, traditional founder of Llangadwaladr in Anglesey, in AD 664. Cadfan is commemorated in an inscription of the last third of the 7th century in the parish church of Llangadwaladr:[47]

+ CATAMANUS REX	Cadfan the king,
SAPIENTISIMUS	most wise,
OPINATISIMUS	most highly esteemed
OMNIUM REGUM	of all kings.

One may doubt whether this king of Anglesey deserved the double superlatives, especially as the epithet *sapiens* was applied not to his ancestor, but to Gildas, who had attacked him. As Gildas had in his criticism of Maglocunus applied the words *regum omnium Regi* to God, the epigraphist's application of the words *sapientisimus omnium regum* to Cadfan is not only a reversal, but a deliberate misappropriation, one aspect of the provocative outrageousness of this inscription.

Professor Charles Thomas has drawn attention to two large letters *A*, suggesting *aures*, shaped like ass's ears, and alluding to the story of Midas in Ovid, *Metamorphoses* XI. One can hardly fail to notice that in the word *rex* the letter *E* lacks its central member, which is actually attached as a fifth member of the letter *X* thrust into the centre of *E*. Again in the word *regum* the letter *E* lacks its central member, which is actually attached to the top bar of insular *G* (ʒ) thrust into the centre of *E*. The only author known to the present writer who refers to letters copulating is Plautus, who at the beginning of Act I of *Pseudolus* makes Pseudolus Seruus, trying to read a note to Calidorus Adulescens, say *ut opinor quaerunt litterae hae sibi liberos: alia aliam scandit* ('as I think, these letters are seeking children for themselves: one is mounting another'). One may suppose that a reason for the double superlatives is to supply a string of identical letters in adjacent lines, suggesting body parts, descending from the cross +:

C for *caput* ('head') or *crines* ('hair'), *S* for *summa pars* ('highest part'), two *A*s for *aures* ('ears'), two *O*s for *oculi* ('eyes'), *P* for *palatum* ('palate')

47 Howlett (1998a), 21–2; Howlett (2005a), 35–8.

or *pharynx* ('throat'), *I* for *iugulum* ('collar bone'), *N* for *nexus* ('grasping', 'entwining'), the topmost *N* in the middle of *manus* ('hand'), *T* for *thorax* ('chest'), *I* for *intestina* ('guts'), with *U* above for *umbilicus* ('navel'), *S* for *sexus* ('sex') topped by *manus* ('hand'), *I* for *inguen* ('groin'), *MU* for *membra ulteriora* ('lower members', 'legs'), *S* for *sub* ('below'). A picture of a man emerges, lying on his back with an erect penis in his hand.[48] Professor Thomas has suggested that this slur on the royal house of Gwynedd was perpetrated by an Irish priest named Issiu. If so, the insult went undetected, as the stone survives in the church to this day.

The earliest Hiberno-Latin writer whose works have descended to us under his own name is Columban of Bangor, founder of Annegray, Luxeuil, and Bobbio. In AD 600 he wrote a letter in which he refers to and quotes Gildas, *Epistola I*, addressed to Gregory the Great. The letter, about calculation of the date of Easter, is a pyrotechnic display of linguistic competence, forensic argument, and wit, to demonstrate to the pope Columban's superiority as both Latinist and debater.[49]

The earliest extant Hiberno-Latin letter written in Ireland was composed in AD 633 from Cummian to Ségéne abbot of Iona and Béccán the hermit to persuade them to adopt the Roman system of calculating the date of Easter. His Valediction is another pyrotechnic display of computistic and linguistic competence, forensic argument, and wit, in which the syntax of an elaborately wrought sentence reduces to *bicipi labii uestri forcipe* [...] *tangite* [...] *preputium* ('with the two-part forceps of your lip [...] touch [...] the foreskin').[50] This is a shocking challenge to Ségéne and Béccán either to convict Cummian of error or to change their minds about calculating the date of Easter. Doing neither will convict them as something disreputable.

From the beginnings of the Hiberno-Latin tradition there were at least three distinct centres: first, from AD 431 the Palladian mission; second, traditionally from AD 432 the Patrician mission; third, from about AD 550 the monastery of Bangor. From the first may have issued the Bishops' Synod;[51] from the second certainly issued the *Epistola ad milites Corotici*, the *Confessio*, and the Hymn of Saint Secundinus or Saint Sechnall's Hymn, *Audite omnes amantes Deum*;[52] from the third issued

48 For full analysis see Thomas (1998), 162–8; Thomas (2002).

49 Howlett (1995a), 82–91.

50 Howlett (1995a), 98–101; Howlett (1995b), 3–6.

51 Howlett (1998b), 238–53.

52 Howlett (1994), 138–52.

the early works of Columban and the Antiphonary of Bangor.[53] All these writers strove to write Latin in a high register that conformed in orthography, diction, and syntax with the literary norms of Classical and Late Latin. Four years after the death of Isidore bishop of Seville his successor Braulio published in AD 640 Isidore's *Etymologiae*, which became a source for a Hiberno-Latin poem, the *Versus de annis a principio, Deus a quo facta fuit huius mundi machina*, that dates itself in three ways to AD 645.[54] A Hiberno-Latin manuscript of the *Etymologiae* dates itself to AD 655,[55] and an anonymous Hiberno-Latin computist quotes the *Etymologiae* in the Oxford Computus that dates itself to AD 658.[56] As with the works of Isidore came knowledge of the way 7th-century Spaniards wrote Vulgar Latin that was evolving into Spanish, there was from the central third of the 7th century another model of Latinity than the pure book-learned language written previously. This latter Hibero-Latin model provides examples of phenomena that used to be considered specifically Hiberno-Latin.[57] As Isidore had stated in *Etymologiae* IX 1.6-7 that there were four forms of Latin, *Priscam*, *Latinam*, *Romanam*, and *Mixtam*, the 7th-century author of the Old-Irish *Auraicept na n-éces* stated in a bout of literary one-up-manship that there were five forms of Irish.[58] In his *Epitome* and *Epistole* Virgilius Maro Grammaticus, a James Joyce of the 7th century, the most imaginative of Hiberno-Latin grammarians, parodied the striving of his fellows for a single standard normative Latinity, affirming in *Epitoma I* that there are twelve forms of Latinity, instructing his readers about a word for 'fire' in each of the twelve forms, even supplying models of declension.[59] Virgilius also signed himself as author of the Hiberno-Latin cosmological poem *Altus Prosator*.[60]

The first Anglo-Latin author, Aldhelm abbot of Malmesbury and later bishop of Sherborne, wrote a Letter to Heahfrith, probably AD 672, in which he tried to dissuade Heahfrith from studying in Ireland by parodying the allegedly bogus learning of the Irish and extolling the merits of the school of Archbishop Theodore and Abbot Hadrian at Canter-

53 Walker (1957); Warren (1893–5).

54 Howlett (1996b), 1–6.

55 Carley (1991).

56 Howlett (2010c), 268–79.

57 Howlett (2005b), 44–60.

58 Calder (1917), 16.

59 Howlett (1996b), 50–7.

60 Howlett (1996b), 54–7. See also Howlett (2014).

bury.[61] At the beginning of the letter Aldhelm quotes the *Altus Prosator*, and at the end he parodies the words of *Epistola II De Pronomine*:

> Verumtamen ne in illud Glengi incedam, quod cuidam conflictum fugienti dicere fidenter ausus est: gurgo inquit fugax fambulo dignus est, pauca tibi tui negotii necessaria de pronomine profabor

by turning them into a travesty of Irish Latin verse, a jingling heptasyllabic couplet

> ut uersidicus ait digna:
> Fiat fante Glingio
> gurgo fugax fambulo

before concluding with proper dactylic hexameters and an elegiac couplet in the approved Canterbury style. The point was to depreciate the Irish tradition by alluding to the most accomplished cosmological poet at the beginning and the most imaginative grammarian at the end, both in the person of Aldhelm's former tutor Virgilius.[62]

This Letter to Heahfrith elicited a response in the form of a Letter to Aldhelm from the Hiberno-Latin poet Cellanus of *Peronna Scottorum* in Picardy, feint praise that hides a devastating attack on Aldhelm's Latinity and his manhood.[63] Cellán's letter consists almost entirely of Aldhelmian diction. As Aldhelm had occasionally misunderstood from glossaries the meanings of words, Cellán deliberately re-used Aldhelm's misprised diction, and he repeatedly converted masculine and neuter nouns into feminine forms, as if to imply that Aldhelm's Latin was ignorant and pretentious and his demeanour effeminate. He began his Salutation *Domino lectricibus ditato studiis* ('To the lord enriched by studies appropriate to female readers'), and he ended it *in tota et tuta Trinitate salutem*. As Aldhelm had been taught by the Irishman Maildub at Malmesbury and by the Irishman Virgilius Maro Grammaticus at Iona, and as he was godfather to Aldfrith of Northumbria, whose reputation as an Irish author survived into the 12th century,[64] it is reasonable to suppose that he understood at least some Irish. One may then hear in Latin *tota* Irish *toth* ('the female

61 Howlett (1996a), 105–24.

62 For the suggestion that Aldhelm had studied at Iona under Virgilius, see Lapidge (2010), 129–63.

63 Howlett (1995a), 108–13.

64 Ireland (1999).

pudenda'), in Latin *tuta* Irish *túatae* ('boorish', 'ignorant'), in Latin *Trinitate* Irish *tríanach* ('tripartite'), so that Cellán could say at the same time in Latin 'in the whole and safe Trinity salvation' and in Irish 'a tripartite ignorant twat'. In the last sentence of the letter proper Cellán wrote:

> Sed si peregrini triste reficere uis corculum
> paucos transmitte sermunculos illius pulcherrimae labiae tuae
> de cuius fonte purissimo dulces diriuati riui multorum possint reficere mentes.
>
> 'But if you wish to refresh the sad little heart of a pilgrim
> send over a few sermonettes from your most beautiful labia
> from the most pure fountain of which sweet streams led off [or 'artificial conduits diverted'] might refresh the minds of many.'

The implication of 'tripartite ignorant twat' may be that Aldhelm is sexually passive in his mouth, his rectum, and his *labia*, a noun that Cellán has transgendered from a Classical neuter to a feminine form. One can suppose that none of this was lost on Aldhelm, who replied in the language of a wrist-flipping queen:

> **Mi**ror quod **me** tantil*lum* homuncu*lum*
> de **f**amoso et **f**lorigero **F**rancorum rure
> uestrae **fru**nitae **fra**ternitatis **ind**ustria **int**erpellat
>
> 'I am amazed that me, such a very little manlet,
> from the famous and flower-bearing countryside of the Franks
> the industry of your learned brotherhood should solicit [or 'accost'].'

We see in all these exchanges serious debate about matters of great political and ecclesiastical import, suffused with personal animosities, expressed sometimes in provocative and outrageous innuendo, but always with learning, wit, style, and panache. Into such a context fit the relations between Merfin and Cyngen, between Merfin and Dubthach, between the Welsh and the Irish, and between Dubthach and the four Irish travellers, Cauncobrach, Fergus, Dominnach, and Suadbar, and their master Colgu, also between Dubthach and Suadbar and those who read and copied their work, like the cryptographers Cyfeiliog and Nandharius. Dubthach's little four-word cryptogram has produced widespread and varied reflexes, not least the sparkling little jewel Suadbar made of his explanatory letter.

APPENDIX: 'THE IRISH NAMES IN SUADBAR'S LETTER' BY COLIN IRELAND

Suadbar's letter to a certain Colgu, in which he solves the riddle of the cryptogram set by Dubthach mac Máele Tuile at the court of King Mermin [Merfyn] of the Britons, is a prime example of the Irish love of paronomasia. This preoccupation with word play is also shown in the frequent use of nicknames and appellatives. The tendency to play on personal names is notable among personnel in the early Irish church. For example, two of St Patrick's early hagiographers, Tírechán and Muirchú, both record four names for Patrick, and each hagiographer claims to have found these four names in the writings of Ultán, an even earlier hagiographer.[65] St Columba of Iona is widely known by his gaelicised name Colum Cille ('dove of the church'), derived from his Latin name in religion, but his Irish given name was Crimthann.[66] Adomnán, one of Columba's successors at Iona, referred to himself frequently as *homunculus* in a clear example of using a nickname or an appellative.[67]

Four Irishmen are named in the Bamberg Cryptogram letter: Caunchobrach, Fergus, Dominnach, and Suadbar.[68] Two of these names, Caunchobrach and Dominnach, are unusual and may have been adjectival epithets, perhaps based on actual names. Of these four, only Fergus and Suadbar have been recorded as personal names and only Fergus occurs with any frequency. It has long been assumed that this Fergus named in Suadbar's letter is the same person named in two poems by Sedulius Scottus almost certainly written on the Continent.[69] John Contreni suggested that a certain *Fregus* (sic) *Grammaticus* is, in fact, this same Fergus mentioned in the two poems by Sedulius,[70] and this identification has been accepted and expanded by Michael Lapidge and

65 Muirchú, *Vita Patricii* prologus (Bieler (1979), 62–3); Tírechán, *Collectanea* 3.1 (Bieler (1979), 124–5). See also Mac Eoin (2002).

66 Anderson and Anderson (1991), xxix.

67 Márkus (2010), 151, 157–63.

68 Reeves (1857) submitted a report to the Royal Irish Academy in which he discussed a charter from Honau of AD 810 signed by Irish bishops which included the names Suathar, Caincomrihc, Erdomnach. Subsequently Wilsdorf (1975), 8–9, suggested those three names were equivalent to Suadbar, Caunchobrach, and Dominnach; but Eberl (1982), 226–8, corrected that mistaken impression as being chronologically impossible.

69 Chadwick (1958), 101–2 (*carmina* 34 and 35); MGH Poetae 3, 1199–200.

70 Contreni (1978), 89–90, 92.

Richard Sharpe under the name Electus Scottigena.[71] A certain Fergus is named in a poem, along with Finnian and Ailerán, which celebrates the accomplishments of the monastery at Clonard, Co. Meath, and implies that the Continent is desirous of their learning. Dáibhí Ó Cróinín has suggested that Sedulius Scottus composed the poem.[72] If his suggestion is accepted, it implies that Fergus came from Clonard.

While the rarer name Suadbar is also found in early records as a personal name, neither Dominnach nor Caunchobrach appears, to my knowledge, anywhere in the Irish tradition as given names, and both are more likely to have been 'nicknames' or epithets based on adjectives or adjectival forms that may have played on forms of the given names of the individuals. The forms in which these nicknames have been preserved by continental scribes, however, are unlikely to be the forms that the Irish would have themselves used and written. A caveat must be offered for the suggestions that follow. As M.A. O'Brien, the renowned scholar of genealogy and onomastics, noted, 'isolated treatment of individual names is to a large extent mere guesswork'.[73] O'Brien's warning is particularly apt in the context of the names associated with the Bamberg Cryptogram because the background is so vague. The following suggested nickname forms attempt to remain as close to those recorded in manuscript as possible.[74]

Dominnach has the appearance of an adjective based on another Old Irish adjective *domain* ('deep, profound, thoughtful') with the additional adjectival ending *-ach* added. Thus *domainach* would mean something like 'the deep one, the thoughtful one', entirely appropriate as an epithet for a wandering Irish scholar. Dominnach may be a mis-transcription of the minims used by an earlier scribe, in this case interpreting the three minim strokes of an Irish open *a* followed by *i*, as *in*. In a commonly used word, one might expect to see syncope of the middle syllable of this three-syllable word resulting in a form like

[71] Lapidge and Sharpe (1985), 192–3 (§§714–6).

[72] Ó Cróinín (1993), 49; for more on the poem, see Howlett (1995a), 129–31; Howlett (1996b), 6–7; Lapidge and Sharpe (1985), 198 (§733).

[73] O'Brien (1973), 217. A helpful article for understanding these name forms is Russell (2001).

[74] None of the Irish names in Suadbar's letter is given Latin inflexional endings as frequently happened in Hiberno-Latin texts; see Harvey (1999), 59–62. Latin inflexional endings are most commonly recorded on Irish names where oblique case endings would be used.

domnach.[75] The fact that syncope did not occur supports the notion that this was an invented nickname or epithet and was not in common use.

Caunchobrach, at first appearance, looks like an adjective based on the Old Irish name Conchobar (i.e. Conchobar + *ach* > Conchobrach 'someone who is Conchobar-like'), but the spelling *caun* of the first syllable seems to exclude that explanation. The first syllable would look more natural if spelled *cuan*, but that complicates the problem because either vowel can be lengthened to create different meanings for the element. While assuming a metathesis from *cuan* makes sense phonologically for Irish, we are still left with making semantic sense of the name.[76] The semantic puzzle can be solved by assuming that the forms of the name have been obscured by continental scribes who have misconstrued the number of minims and added an extra one. If we assume that *caun* was intended as the prefix *caín* ('fine, good, fair') we solve the puzzle, at least on a superficial level.[77]

The second half of the name presents further ambiguities. Formally it looks like *coba*(i)r + *ach*, but *cobar* can mean 'desiring'[78] and *cobair* means 'help, assistance'. Whether or not the *r* was palatal or non-palatal in Old Irish would not be consistently shown in the orthography. Note that we get syncope of the third of four syllables in this reconstruction, i.e. *caín* + *coba(i)r* + *ach*. Thus a nickname Caínchobrach could mean 'finely desiring one' (based on *cobar*) or 'gently helpful one' (based on *cobair*). Either makes sense as an epithet, and one could imagine either form being applied to a wandering Irish scholar journeying to the schools of the Continent.

Suadbar, although found as a given name in early records, is not common. For example, it is not found in either the *Corpus genealogiarum*

[75] These wandering Irish scholars may well have been playing on a word like *domnach* 'Sunday; church', an element in the fairly common ecclesiastical name Ferdomnach.

[76] Personal names have been recorded with the forms Cúán (O'Brien (1962), 575–6) and Cuan (Ó Riain (1985), 238). But how they would relate to *coba*(i)r + *ach* is not clear.

[77] Caínchomrac ('gentle encounter' or 'gentle contention') is an example of an ecclesiastical name that contains this element. A certain Caínchomrac, bishop of the Déisi, served as Dublitir's confessor (*anmchara*) at Finglas: Gwynn and Purton (1911–2), 130 (§7); and Mac Airt and Mac Niocaill (1983), 246–7 (*s.a.*AD 791). A Caínchomrac mac Siadail, steward of Kildare, died in AD 835 (Mac Airt and Mac Niocaill (1983), 292–3); and a Caínchomrac, bishop and superior of Lugbad, died in AD 903 (Mac Airt and Mac Niocaill (1983), 352–3).

[78] This noun is the second element in such recorded names as Conchobar (*cú* ('hound') + *cobar*) and Ólchobar (*ól* ('drink') + *cobar*).

Hiberniae[79] or in the *Corpus genealogiarum sanctorum Hiberniae.*[80] The name Suadbar, in the form Soadbar, is recorded for a bishop at the date 26 June in the Martyrologies of Tallaght,[81] Gorman,[82] and Donegal.[83] In the Annals of the Four Masters at the year AD 889 an anchorite named Suadbar is listed as having died at Inishnag, Co. Kilkenny.[84] The earliest datable recording of the name Suadbar is on the guarantor list of the *Cáin Adomnáin* at Birr in AD 697 where a Suadbar of Inis Teimle signed.[85] In research on the location of Inis Teimle, Máirín Ní Dhonnchadha identified this Suadbar, through genealogical material preserved in the Book of Leinster, as an abbot who was involved in the politics of south Leinster and equated Suadbar of Inis Teimle with the bishop mentioned in the three genealogies at 26 June.[86]

Dáibhí Ó Cróinín has suggested that the Suadbar who composed the letter and solved the cryptogram was the person the world has come to know as Sedulius Scottus,[87] one of the Irish scholars, along with Johannes Scottus Ériugena, to demonstrate a knowledge of Greek. The obvious writing skills and cleverness at word play that Suadbar displayed in his letter and his, at least rudimentary, knowledge of Greek supports this suggestion.[88] The presence of a certain Fergus in this group of four at the Welsh court and the mention of a Fergus in poems attributed to Sedulius adds circumstantial evidence that this equation may be correct.[89]

79 O'Brien (1962). I would like to thank Dr Jürgen Uhlich for helpful discussions about the name Suadbar/Soadbar.

80 Ó Riain (1985).

81 Best and Lawlor (1931), 52. The compilation of this martyrology is dated to the period *c.*AD 826 to 833 and is, therefore, earlier than the period assumed for our Irish scholars who solved Dubthach's cryptogram.

82 Stokes (1895), 124–5. In this case Soadbar is referred to as *súi epscoip* ('sage of a bishop').

83 Todd and Reeves (1864), 180–1.

84 Annals of the Four Masters *s.a.* 889 (O'Donovan (1848–51), i 542–3).

85 *Cáin Adomnáin* 10 (Ní Dhonnchadha (1982), 180, 188).

86 Ní Dhonnchadha (2002), 452–3.

87 Ó Cróinín (1993), 49–50.

88 See, for example, Herren (2010), 514. I would like to thank Anthony Harvey of the *Dictionary of Medieval Latin from Celtic Sources* for providing me with information, through references in Latin vocabulary used by Sedulius, supporting his familiarity with the basics of Greek. (See also Michael Herren's contribution in this volume.)

89 It should be noted that James Carney (1956), 242, argued that none of Sedulius' extant writings provides any firm evidence that he was ever in Wales. On the other hand, in a recent study Richard Sharpe (2010), 23, was at least willing to entertain the equation of Suadbar with Sedulius.

The Dubthach who created the cryptogram deciphered by Suadbar is usually assumed to be Dubthach mac Máele Tuile described as *doctissimus Latinorum totius Europę* ('most learned of the Latinists of all Europe') who died in AD 869.[90] There is no indication of his place of origin in Ireland. The letter by Suadbar is intended by him and his companions for their teacher (*magister*) Colgu back in Ireland whom, presumably, they had only recently left. They are asking that Colgu prepare any of their 'brothers' who might be planning to follow in their footsteps for the challenge of deciphering Dubthach's cryptogram should they pass through the Welsh court on their journey to the Continent.

The *floruit* for Sedulius Scottus is imprecise and extends from sometime in the AD 840s, which coincides roughly with the date of Suadbar's letter about Dubthach, to around AD 860 or 874.[91] Using the widest possible dates of AD 840–874 as a *floruit* for Sedulius and his circle, which takes in the *obit* of Dubthach at AD 869, we can search the annals for a possible Colgu to whom Suadbar and his companions refer in the letter.

One, who is almost certainly too early, is Colgu mac Fedaig, anchorite, who died in AD 843, but no location is given.[92] Another Colgu, whose dates fall more certainly within the expected range, is Colgu mac Cellaig, superior (*princeps*) of Cell Tuama, who died in AD 851.[93] Two abbots of Monasterboice, Colgu and Áed, both died in the year AD 866.[94] A fourth person mentioned in the annals who falls within the time frame for the circle of Sedulius is Colgu mac Máele Tuile, priest, anchorite, and abbot of Cluain Chonaire Tómáin, who died in AD 871.[95] The location is pre-

[90] Mac Airt and Mac Niocail (1983), 324–5; Lapidge and Sharpe (1985), 181 (§§687–8). We have no idea whether Dubthach died on the Continent or returned to Ireland.

[91] Kenney (1929), 555.

[92] Annals of Ulster *s.a.* 843 (Mac Airt and Mac Niocail (1983), 302–3).

[93] Annals of Ulster *s.a.* 851 (Mac Airt and Mac Niocail (1983), 310–1). The location may refer to Cell Tómae in what is now Co. Westmeath near Fore. This position of superior may well have been hereditary as a Cellach mac Echdach *princeps* of Cell Tuama (Tómae) died in AD 813 (Annals of Ulster *s.a.* 813 (Mac Airt and Mac Niocail (1983), 268–9)).

[94] Annals of Ulster *s.a.* 866 (Mac Airt and Mac Niocail (1983), 320–1). It has not been possible to identify anything about either of these two abbots.

[95] Annals of Ulster *s.a.* 871 (Mac Airt and Mac Niocail (1983), 328–9): *Colgu mac Máele Tuile, sacerdos ⁊ ancorita, abbas Cluana Conaire Tommaen, quieuit* ('Colgu son of Mael Tuile, priest, anchorite and abbot of Cluain Chonaire Tómáin, rested'). If this site was near Cloncurry, Co. Kildare, there is no certainty of its relations with the far more famous Clonard. Colgu may have retired there as anchorite.

sumed to be near Cloncurry, Co. Kildare, about ten miles from Clonard. This Colgu shares a patronymic with Dubthach and they died within two years of each other, suggesting that they may have been close in age and had the same father. If that is the case, and this particular Colgu was the *magister* of Suadbar and his companions, family connections between Colgu and Dubthach as well as professional and intellectual pride would have compelled these wandering scholars to send their letter deciphering Dubthach's cryptogram to Colgu back in Ireland.

Bibliography

Anderson, A.O. and M. O. Anderson (1991) *Adomnán's Life of Columba*, Oxford.

Bately, J. (1986) *The Anglo-Saxon Chronicle, vol. 3: MS A*, Cambridge.

Best, R.I. and H.J. Lawlor (1931) *The Martyrology of Tallaght*, London.

Bieler, L. (1979) *The Patrician texts in the Book of Armagh*, Dublin.

Calder, G. (1917) *Auraicept na n-éces, the scholar's primer*, Edinburgh, repr. Dublin 1995.

Carley, J.P. and A. Dooley (1991) 'An early Irish fragment of Isidore of Seville's *Etymologiae*,' in L.J. Abrams and J.P. Carley, *The archaeology and history of Glastonbury Abbey*, Woodbridge, 135–61.

Carney, J. (1956) 'Sedulius Scottus,' in R. McNally, *Old Ireland*, Dublin, 228–50.

Chadwick, N.K. (1958) 'Early culture and learning in North Wales,' in N. Chadwick, K. Hughes, C. Brooke, and K. Jackson, *Studies in the Early British Church*, 29–120.

Contreni, J.J. (1978) *The cathedral school of Laon from 850 to 930: its manuscripts and masters*, Munich.

Davies, W.S. (1920) '*Giraldus Cambrensis: De Invectionibus*,' *Y Cymmrodor* 30.

Eberl, I. (1982) 'Das Iren-Kloster Honau und seine Regel,' in M. Richter and P. Ní Chatháin, *Die Iren und Europa im früheren Mittelalter*, Tübingen, 219–38.

Derolez, R. (1954) *Runica Manuscripta: the English tradition*, Brugge.

Dimock, J.F. (1867) *Giraldi Cambrensis opera, vol. 5: Topographia Hibernica. Expugnatio Hibernica*, London.

Evans, J.G. (1893) *The text of the Book of Llan Dâv, reproduced from the Gwysaney Manuscript*, Oxford.

Gwynn, E.J. and W.J. Purton (1911–2) 'The monastery of Tallaght,' *PRIA* 29C, 115–79.

Harvey, A. (1991) 'Retrieving the pronunciation of early insular Celtic scribes: the case of Dorbbéne,' *Celtica* 22, 48–63.

— (1999) 'Some observations on Celtic-Latin name formation,' in J. Carey, J.T. Koch, and P.-Y. Lambert, *Ildánach, Ildírech: a Festschrift for Proinsias Mac Cana*, Andover, 53–62.
— (2002) "Battling Andrew' and the West-Brit syndrome twelve hundred years ago,' *Classics Ireland* 9, 19–27.
Herren, M.W. (2010) 'The study of Greek in Ireland in the early Middle Ages,' in *L'irlanda e gli irlandesi nell'alto medioevo*, Spoleto, 511–32.
Howlett, D.R. (1994) *'Liber Epistolarum Sancti Patricii Episcopi': The Book of Letters of Saint Patrick the Bishop*, Dublin.
— (1995a) *The Celtic Latin tradition of biblical style*, Dublin.
— (1995b) 'Five experiments in textual reconstruction and analysis,' *Peritia* 9, 3–6.
— (1996a) *The English origins of Old French literature*, Dublin.
— (1996b) 'Seven studies in seventh-century texts,' *Peritia* 10, 1–70.
— (1997a) *British books in biblical style*, Dublin.
— (1997b) 'Insular Latin writers' rhythms,' *Peritia* 11, 53–116.
— (1998a) *Cambro-Latin compositions: their competence and craftsmanship*, Dublin.
— (1998b) '*Synodus Prima Sancti Patricii*: an exercise in textual reconstruction,' *Peritia* 12, 238–53.
— (1999) *Sealed from within: self-authenticating insular charters*, Dublin.
— (2000) *Caledonian craftsmanship: the Scottish Latin tradition*, Dublin.
— (2005a) *Insular inscriptions*, Dublin.
— (2005b) 'Hibero-Latin, Hiberno-Latin, and the Irish foundation legend,' *Peritia* 19, 44–60.
— (2006a) *Muirchú moccu Macthéni's 'Vita Sancti Patricii', Life of Saint Patrick*, Dublin.
— (2006b) 'Gematria, number, and name in Anglo-Norman,' *French Studies Bulletin* 27, 90–2.
— (2010a) 'Two mathematical poets,' *Peritia* 21, 151–7.
— (2010b) 'Hiberno-Latin poems on the Eusebian Canons,' *Peritia* 21, 162–71.
— (2010c) 'Computus in Hiberno-Latin literature,' in I. Warntjes and D. Ó Cróinín, *Computus and its cultural context in the Latin West, AD 300–1200*, Turnhout, 259–323.
— (2013) *'Alea Euangelii,'* in J. Elfassi, C. Lanéry, and A.-M. Turcan-Verkerk, *'Amicorum Societas'. Mélanges offerts à François Dolbeau pour son 65e anniversaire*, Firenze, 335–59.
— (2014) 'The *Altus Prosator* of Virgilius Maro Grammaticus,' in E. Purcell, P. MacCotter, J. Nyhan, and J. Sheehan, *Medieval Ireland: clerics, kings, and Vikings*, Dublin.
— (forthcoming) 'Two additions to the Hiberno-Latin canon,' in I. Warntjes and D. Ó Cróinín, *Proceedings of the 3rd International Conference on the Science of Computus in Ireland and Europe, Galway, 2010*.

Ireland, C.A. (1999) *Old Irish wisdom attributed to Aldfrith of Northumbria: an edition of Bríathra Flainn Fhína maic Ossu*, Tempe.

Kenney, J.F. (1929) *The sources for the early history of Ireland: ecclessiastical*, New York, repr. Dublin 1979.

Lapidge, M. (2010) 'Aldhelm and the "Epinal-Erfurt Glossary",' in K. Barker and N. Brooks, *Aldhelm and Sherborne*, Oxford, 129–63.

Lapidge, M. and R. Sharpe (1985) *A bibliography of Celtic-Latin literature 400–1200*, Dublin.

Law, V. (1982) *The insular Latin grammarians*, Woodbridge.

— (1995) *Wisdom, authority and grammar in the seventh century: decoding Virgilius Maro Grammaticus*, Cambridge.

Lindsay, W.M. (1910) *Early Irish minuscule script*, Oxford, repr. Hildesheim 1971.

Luard, H.R. (1872–83) *Matthæi Parisiensis monachi Sancti Albani Chronica majora*, 7 vols., London.

Mac Airt, S. and G. Mac Niocaill (1983) *The Annals of Ulster (to A.D. 1131)*, Dublin.

Mac Eoin, G. (2002) 'The four names of St Patrick,' in M. Richter and J.-M. Picard, *Ogma: essays in Celtic Studies in honour of Próinséas Ní Chatháin*, Dublin, 300–11.

Márkus, G. (2010) '*Adiutor Laborantium* – a poem by Adomnán?,' in J.M. Wooding, *Adomnán of Iona: theologian, lawmaker, peacemaker*, Dublin, 145–61.

McKee, H. (2000a) *Juvencus Codex Cantabrigiensis Ff.4.42*, Aberystwyth.

— (2000b) *The Cambridge Juvencus manuscript glossed in Latin, Old Welsh, and Old Irish: text and commentary*, Cambridge.

McManus, D. (1997) *A guide to Ogam*, Maynooth.

Ní Dhonnchadha, M. (1982) 'The guarantor list of Cáin Adomnáin, 697,' *Peritia* 1, 178–215.

— (2002) 'Inis Teimle, between Uí Chennselaig and the Déissi,' *Peritia* 16, 451–8.

O'Brien, M.A. (1962) *Corpus genealogiarum Hiberniae*, Dublin.

— (1973) 'Old Irish personal names: 'Rhŷs Lecture'—Notes, 1957,' ed. by R. Baumgarten, *Celtica* 10, 211–36.

Ó Cróinín, D. (1993) 'The Irish as mediators of antique culture on the Continent,' in P.L. Butzer and D. Lohrmann, *Science in Western and Eastern civilization in Carolingian times*, Basel, 41–52.

O'Donovan, J. (1848–51) *Annála Ríoghachta Éireann: Annals of the Kingdom of Ireland by the Four Masters*, 7 vols., Dublin.

Ó Riain, P. (1985) *Corpus genealogiarum sanctorum Hiberniae*, Dublin.

Powicke, F.M. and E.B. Fryde (1961) *Handbook of British chronology*, 2nd ed., London.

Reeves, W. (1857) 'On the Irish abbey of Honau, on the Rhine,' *PRIA* 6, 452–61.

Russell, P. (2001) 'Patterns of hypocorism in early Irish hagiography,' in J. Carey, M. Herbert, and P. Ó Riain, *Studies in Irish hagiography: saints and scholars*, Dublin, 237–49.

Sharpe, R. (2010) 'Books from Ireland, fifth to ninth centuries,' *Peritia* 21, 1–55.

Stokes, W. (1895) *Félire Húi Gormáin, The Martyrology of Gorman*, London.

Thomas, C. (1998) *Christian Celts: messages and images*, Stroud.

— (2002) *Whispering reeds or the Anglesey Catamanus Stone stript bare*, Oxford.

Todd, J.H. and W. Reeves (1864) *The Martyrology of Donegal: a calendar of the saints of Ireland*, Dublin.

Walker, G.S.M. (1957) *Sancti Columbani opera*, Dublin.

Walsh, M. and D. Ó Cróinín (1988) *Cummian's letter* De controversia paschali, *together with a related Irish computistical tract* De ratione conputandi, Toronto.

Warner, G.F. (1891) *Giraldi Cambrensis opera, vol. 8: De principis instructione liber*, London.

Warren, F.E. (1893–5) *The Antiphonary of Bangor*, 2 vols., London.

Wilsdorf, C. (1975) 'Le 'monasterium Scottorum' de Honau et la famille des ducs d'Alsace au VIIIe siècle. Vestiges d'un cartulaire perdue,' *Francia* 3, 1–87.

Winterbottom, M. (2007) *William of Malmesbury, Gesta pontificum Anglorum*, Oxford.

PÁDRAIG P. Ó NÉILL

ANGLO-IRISH INTERACTIONS IN A LITURGICAL CALENDAR FROM CAMBRIDGE, CORPUS CHRISTI COLLEGE LIBRARY, 405

Abstract

This article presents an edition of a hitherto unpublished liturgical calendar composed in Ireland *c.*AD 1200 (now part II of Cambridge, Corpus Christi College Library, 405), together with an investigation of its origins and provenance as suggested by certain commemorations which it contains. The calendar is also examined for the evidence which it provides of Anglo-Irish ecclesiastical interactions in the late 12th and early 13th century.

Keywords

Abingdon, Ferns, Kilbarrymedan, Waterford, Winchester; Albinus O'Molloy (Ailbe Ó Maelmuaid), Faritius, Malchus (Máel Ísu Úa hAinmire), Peter fitz John Le Poer, St Barrmedinus, St Moling, St Mullins, St Olaf, St Vincent of Saragossa; *Historia Ecclesie Abbendonensis*, Life of St Abbán, Martyrology of Gormán.

Tá clú agus cáil ar an Ollamh Dáibhí Ó Cróinín as ucht a chuid scoláireachta i gcúrsaí ríomhaíochta, ach ní hé sin bun agus barr a chuid saíochta. Ina theannta sin tá raidhse alt foilsithe aige leis na blianta ar ábhair éagsúla a bhaineann le staidéar na Meánaoiseanna. Thaispeáin sé go háirithe conas is féidir úsáid éifeachtach a dhéanamh d'fhéilirí eaglasta mar fhoinsí eolais ar theagmhálacha idir Gaeil agus Sasanaigh i dtréimhse na Sean-Ghaeilge. Ar ndóigh is ó ré na Normannach a thagann an féilire atá á phlé anseo agam ach, más ea féin, tá súil agam go bhfeileann sé don ócáid speisialta seo i gceiliúradh scoláire a bhfuil dearcadh leathan ar stair na hÉireann aige.

Early medieval Ireland and Europe: chronology, contacts, scholarship, ed. by Pádraic Moran and Immo Warntjes, Studia Traditionis Theologiae, 14 (Turnhout, 2015), pp. 265–98.

 10.1484/M.STT-EB.5.103124

Introduction

The calendar edited here for the first time occupies folios 11r–16v (pp. 23–34) of Cambridge, Corpus Christi College, 405. It is the second booklet (volume II) in a manuscript compiled in the early 14th century, comprising documents ecclesiastical and secular connected mainly with the Waterford area.[1] Exactly how the manuscript reached the Corpus Library is not clear. For what it is worth, a note in Samuel Savage Lewis's (Corpus librarian from 1870 to 1896) personal copy of James Nasmith's catalogue of that library states that the present manuscript came 'probably from the library of Bale Bishop of Ossory'.[2] Bale (†1563) was a well-known collector of manuscripts for Matthew Parker, archbishop of Canterbury, so it is conceivable that he obtained MS 405 in Ireland and passed it on to Parker. From Canterbury it would then have come to the Corpus Library as part of Parker's famous bequest of 1574. It was certainly there by 1600, since a catalogue of the library's holdings published by Thomas James in that year lists a manuscript (no. 70) whose contents match those of MS 405.[3]

Date

The calendar itself (hereafter referred to with the siglum 'W') dates more than a century earlier than the manuscript in which it is now bound. A *terminus post quem* of AD 1165 is indicated by an entry in the main hand for Thomas à Beckett who died in that year (Dec 29). Negative evidence for a *terminus ante quem* of *c.*AD 1220 is indicated by the complete absence in W of a series of notable commemorations which begin to appear in Anglo-Irish calendars about this time,[4] such as Wulfstan of Worcester (canonization AD 1203, translation July AD 1220), Thomas

[1] For a description, see James (1909–12), ii 277–88; and the revised online version at http://parkerweb.stanford.edu. I am grateful to the Master and Fellows of Corpus Christi College, Cambridge, for permission to publish the contents of the calendar. My thanks to the sub-librarians of the Parker Library, Gill Cannell and Suzanne Paul, for their help and hospitality.

[2] Nasmith (1777), 381. Lewis's copy is now at the Corpus Library.

[3] James (1600), 75. The manuscript was subsequently renumbered as G.4 (as attested in the catalogue of Stanley (1722), 20–1), before eventually receiving its present numbering from Nasmith.

[4] These entries are all found in the Martyrology of Christ Church, Dublin, as additions made in the first half of the 13th century; see Ó Riain (2008), 16.

à Beckett (translation July AD 1220), Laurence O'Toole (canonization AD 1225, translation AD 1226), Francis of Assisi (canonization AD 1228, translation AD 1230), Anthony of Padua (canonization AD 1232), and Edmund of Canterbury (canonization AD 1246).[5] Also consonant with a date around the turn of the 13th century is the evidence of W's script, an early liturgical Gothic; while other palaeographical features such as the layout of its pages with writing above the top ruled line[6] and the absence of a cross bow in the Tironian '7' point more generally to the earlier part of that century.

Codicology

W's three bifolia form a discrete section within MS 405. Its leaves are much thicker and more stained than those of the preceding and following booklets and, even in their present cropped state, of slightly larger dimensions (145×219mm, 148×219mm, 148×218mm, 148×218mm, 146×219mm, and 146×220mm as against 145×215mm, the norm for the rest of the manuscript).[7] Some wear in the lower sections of the first and final recto (especially evident in the coloured letters; cf. the entries in red of the lower section of *Plate 1* in the Appendix) suggests that W may have circulated as an independent booklet before being incorporated into MS 405.[8] Likewise, damage to the final leaf, in the form of two holes and a tear (which seems to postdate the writing of the main text), is more likely to have occurred when it lacked the protection afforded by the covers of a larger manuscript. Ruling in plummet marks the horizontal lines (30–33 per page) while five prick marks on the top left of each page guide the ruling of the four vertical columns on the left side containing the chronological data (in a sequence of red, black, green and red ink). On the final page (f 16v), two of the four chronological

5 A marginal obit, probably entered contemporaneously with the event it notes, the death of Peter Fitzjohn Le Poer in AD 1327, provides an absolute *terminus ante quem*; see below pp. 278–9.

6 A practice that was then going out of fashion (in favour of writing below the top ruled line); see Ker (1960), 13–6.

7 An exception is the final leaf of the calendar which has been cropped on the left verso margin (with some loss of letters in the first column of numbers/dates), in order to make it fit the dimensions of the leaf immediately following, the first of the third booklet. In general both the upper and the left margins have been cropped by the binder.

8 Though it could conceivably have been the first gathering of a psalter.

columns (the first and third) are empty, except for a single entry in the second column. The fifth column of each page contains the commemorative entries, the focus of the present paper.

Scribes and scripts

The hands of three scribes can be discerned in W. The main scribe copied virtually all of the text, employing a Gothic script of oval aspect, with some compression of minims. The bottoms of the minims, which are merely rounded off (often crudely) with an upward turn of the pen (see, for example, *Plate 1*, line 7, in the Appendix), while typical of early Gothic also suggest a lower grade of writing. For most entries the scribe employed an ink that varies from dark brown to black. He also used: (1) red and green ink (usually in combination) for the initial decorated *KĿ* (*Kalendae*) at the beginning of each month; (2) green ink for the calendrical date (Roman style) preceding each entry; (3) red for the computistical dates of the first column; and (4) either red or green to highlight 48 entries, of which 39 are in red and 9 in green (Matthew, Mark, Moling, John the Baptist, Peter and Paul, Mary Magdalen (see *Plate 2*, line 24), Virgin Mary, Exaltation of the Cross, Michael the Archangel). A second scribe wrote the three entries in red for May 1, 3, and 6, in a larger, thicker, and rounder hand than the main scribe, employing the ampersand instead of the Tironian '7' favoured by the latter. A third scribe, somewhat later than his predecessors, filled lacunae in the text in a distinctive light brown ink. Thus, he supplied entries for Finbarr (July 4; see *Plate 2*, line 6, in the Appendix), Bartholomew (Aug 24), Meiccnisse (Sept 3), All Saints (Nov 1), and All Souls (Nov 2). He also marked the Vigils of St Lawrence (Aug 9), Mary's Assumption (Aug 14), Matthew (Sept 20), and Christmas Day (Dec 24), as well as noting the Octave of the Assumption (Aug 22). On the margin he supplied seventeen identifications of *dies mala* (from the prognostic 'Egyptian days') for the months of April to December, which had been left incomplete by the main scribe, and entered the words *O sapientia* after the entry for Ignatius (Dec 17). His hand is larger and much less oval than that of the main scribe, and often uses a characteristic contraction mark shaped like a slanting '7' rather than the horizontal or upward-sloping mark employed by the former.

Contents

In layout, component parts, and liturgical contents, W is typical of its genre. The generalized description of such calendars given by Rebecca Rushforth in her survey of twenty-seven English witnesses from before AD 1100 could apply no less to the present one:[9]

> 'Typically there is one page for each month. Basic information about the month, for example how many days it has and its Latin name [...] is written at the top of the page. There is one line for each day of the month, and down the left-hand side is recorded the date in Roman notation. Typically the 'kl' abbreviation for *kalendae* on the first day of the month was written in large letters, perhaps in coloured ink and decorated. Also down the left-hand side there are probably letters to ascertain on which day of the week each date falls in any given year, letters to calculate the phase of the moon on each day, and perhaps other such technical material. Sometimes all these columns of letters were distinguished by the use of coloured inks. [...] Saints' names were written in the genitive against the date to which they refer, sometimes just in the form (for example) 'Felicis' but sometimes with the type of feast—perhaps an 'ordinatio', 'translatio', 'passio', or 'depositio'—and the type of saint—for example confessor, martyr, virgin, abbot, or bishop—specified. An important feast might be marked as such by the use of coloured inks. [...] Information about astronomical signs and natural occurrences like the solstices and equinoxes was also written in this central space.'

While W rarely defines 'the type of feast' being commemorated (other than a few notices of *translatio* and *commemoratio*), it almost always gives 'the type of saint'. And in keeping with its liturgical character it defines a hierarchy of commemoration among these saints, one indicated visually by the use of black, red, and green in ascending order of importance. At the same time W reflects the *horror uacui* characteristic of the martyrological genre, providing at least one saint each for most days, in contrast to 'regular' liturgical calendars which commemorate only those feastdays of special interest to their particular community. In the same spirit of inclusiveness W occasionally has double entries for a single day. For example, the entry for Sept 10 has the conjoined commemoration of *Sanctorum Finneani et Ateluoldi confessorum*, where the first is an Irish saint and the second Anglo-Saxon. This hybridity is symptomatic of W,

[9] Rushforth (2008), 3.

which seems to reflect a concern with balancing native Irish and 'imported' Anglo-Norman cults. Altogether, it contains the names of more than sixty Irish saints. Some of these were already present in continental martyrologies, whence they might have found their way into W, but the majority are saints who enjoyed a strictly Irish cult. In the broadest sense they attest to the new state of affairs in Ireland after the Norman Conquest (AD 1170), a period during which the Anglo-Norman church, as it gradually appropriated native foundations, began to incorporate local Irish saints into its liturgical repertoire; correspondingly, certain native churches under direct Norman control adopted cults associated with the new ecclesiastical order. For example, as Pádraig Ó Riain has argued, the Anglo-Norman foundation of canons regular at Christ Church, Dublin, maintained a martyrology that 'received a new layer of additions in the AD 1160s, consisting of over thirty native feasts, many of which reflected the spread within Ireland of houses of the regular canons'.[10]

Origins and provenance

On this subject three entries offer significant clues. The first is a commemoration of St Moling (June 17), an Irish saint said to have flourished in the second half of the seventh century, who enjoyed a considerable cult in both the Midlands and the Southeast, and is well represented in Irish martyrologies. What makes this entry striking is that it is written in green (for another example see *Plate 2*, line 24, in the Appendix), signifying the highest grade of commemoration; indeed, of the nine entries in the calendar so coloured, his is the only Irish name. Pádraig Ó Riain has drawn attention to the visual aggrandizement of Moling's name in another contemporary Irish production, the Martyrology of Turin, composed *c.* AD 1175–1240, where the entry is written in majuscule (though not coloured). In that particular case he would attribute the special treatment of Moling to the origins of the martyrology at the Anglo-Norman convent of Augustinian nuns at Lismullin (Co. Meath), whose very name reflects the Midlands cult of that saint.[11]

However, it is unlikely that the same origins can be posited for W, which lacks any mention of saints with cults in the Midlands. Instead,

10 Ó Riain (2008), 14.

11 Ó Riain (2002), 127–30.

it is worth considering the other region where Moling's cult enjoyed great popularity, the Southeast, particularly the Wexford/Carlow area. Within this quadrant lay Moling's main foundation at St Mullins on the banks of the river Barrow in south Carlow. On the opposite side of the river lay Uí Cheinselaig territory which, while venerating its own tutelary saints (notably, Maedóc and Abbán), held Moling in high regard, to judge by the evidence of contemporary hagiography from that region. Thus, the Life of Abbán, composed probably at Ferns in the early 13th century, lists Moling as one the three great saints of Leinster, while both the Life of Maedóc (of Ferns) and the Life of Moling present the latter as succeeding the former as bishop of Ferns.[12] It seems reasonable to posit that W's exceptionally prominent marking of Moling's feastday reflects its origins in south Leinster, perhaps at St Mullins.

What makes the hypothesis of south Leinster origins more likely is a second piece of evidence in W which commemorates, not an Irish saint, but a 4th-century Spanish martyr, St Vincent of Saragossa. As might be expected, the cult of Vincent belonged in the first instance to Spain where he gained the title of national protomartyr (†AD 304) for his witness to the faith during the persecution of Diocletian. Outside of Spain Vincent did not enjoy any special attention—beyond inclusion in the martyrologies (including two 12th-century Irish ones, the Martyrology of Drummond and the Martyrology of Christ Church Cathedral).[13] So it comes as a surprise to find that the present calendar not only has an entry for his feastday in red (Jan 22; see *Plate 1*, line 24, in the Appendix), the colour for marking feasts of the second highest grade, but also commemorates his octave (Jan 29; see *Plate 1*, line 31, in the Appendix). The octave, a celebration of a feast prolonged for eight days, was originally reserved for the most important feastdays, such as Easter and Pentecost. By the 13th century the practice had spread to mere saints, though such octaves did not normally enjoy the privileged status of those connected with the life of Christ and consequently were usually limited to a particular diocese, religious order or foundation.[14] It is to this latter category that the octave for St Vincent belongs.

12 *Vita Sancti Abbani* 2 (ed. Plummer (1910), i 3–4); *Vita Sancti Maedoc* 58 (ed. Plummer (1910), ii 162); *Vita Sancti Moling* 8 (ed. Plummer (1910), ii 193).

13 The Martyrology of Drummond and the Martyrology of Christ Church Cathedral are ed. by Ó Riain (2002) and (2008), respectively.

14 An exception is St Agnes, the commemoration of whose octave (Jan 28) was already widespread in pre-Conquest England. Agnes's feastday (Jan 21) and octave also occur in W, but significantly neither is accorded the special status indicated by red ink.

Remarkably, the Vincentian octave was observed not in Spain but in England,[15] specifically at Abingdon, a Benedictine monastery in the south of England. By the early 12th century Abingdon had amassed a formidable collection of relics. A catalogue made in AD 1116 at the behest of its abbot, Faritius, an avid collector, indicates that they ranged in variety from a small piece of a nail used for Christ's crucifixion to cuttings from St Peter's beard and St Mary Magdalene's hair, as well as the arm, thighbone, shoulder-blade, and rib of St Vincent.[16] Oddly enough, it was these latter relics, despite competition from their more venerable antecedents, which were singled out for special veneration at Abingdon. According to the earliest 'official history' of the monastery, *Historia ecclesiae Abbendonensis* (composed in the 12th century by an author who had evidently lived through Faritius' abbacy), Vincent's relics were 'sought out by [Faritius] [...] and tended with resourceful vigilance by the brethren then living here [*sc.* at Abingdon] [...] because of the remedy of the support of so great a witness [to the faith]'.[17] The same passage in the *Historia* also notes that '[m]ore than any of his predecessors, he [Faritius] raised to particular magnificence the solemn day of St Vincent'.[18] Just how far Faritius' heortological zeal for Vincent's cult extended is revealed in another work closely associated with Abingdon, *De abbatibus Abbendonie*,[19] which relates that the abbot elevated Vincent's commemoration to a feast 'in copes', a level second only to the six most solemn feasts of the year that included Christmas and Easter.[20] A feast of such solemnity would entail an octave, albeit one confined to Abingdon and its dependencies. Significantly, a late 13th-century calendar from Abingdon commemorates Vincent's main feastday on January 22 (*Sancti Vincentii martiris*) with blue ink and for January 29 marks the octave (*Octave Sancti Vincentii*) in red.[21]

[15] Two pre-AD 1100 English calendars edited by Rushforth (2008), Table I (January), enter the notice of his feastday in majuscule, though not in coloured ink, and neither calendar accords him an octave.

[16] *Historia ecclesiae Abbendonensis* 226–228 (ed. and trans. Hudson (2002–7), ii 220–4).

[17] As we learn from the *Historia ecclesiae Abbendonensis* 56 (Hudson (2002–7), ii 70–1).

[18] *Historia ecclesiae Abbendonensis* 56 (Hudson (2002–7), ii 70–1).

[19] In its surviving form perhaps from the early 13th century, though it may contain a core going back to the mid-12th century; see Hudson (2002–7), ii xxi–xxiii.

[20] See Hudson (2002–7), ii civ–cvi; the passage in question is *De abbatibus Abbendonie* (ed. Stevenson (1858), ii 287).

[21] The calendar is found in Cambridge, University Library, Kk.1.22, 1v–7v (ed. Wormald (1939), 15–30: 19).

All of which raises the question of how this special commemoration of a relatively obscure (at least for Ireland) and highly localized cult found its way from Abingdon into an Irish calendar. The answer would seem to be found in the strange complementary relationship, first established by Pádraig Ó Riain,[22] between two roughly contemporary works, one from Ireland, the other from England, namely, the Life of St Abbán and the *Historia Ecclesie Abbendonensis*, respectively. The Life relates that while on his way to Rome Abbán stopped over in the south of England where by means of a miracle he converted the local king and subsequently built a church *in ciuitatem que dicitur Abbaindun vel Dun Abbain* ('in the town which is called 'Abingdon' or 'the residence of Abban'').[23] For its part the *Historia* (Recension B)[24] confirms that Abingdon monastery was founded by a devout Irish monk named Abben (Lat. *Abbennus*) from whom it acquired its name (Lat. *Abbendon*) with the addition of a vernacular suffix, *dun*, denoting either Irish *dún* ('a dwelling') or English *dun* ('a hill'): *Secundum enim idioma Hibernensium, ut ex relatione modernorum accepimus, Abbendon mansio Abenni interpretatur; secundum uero idioma Anglorum Abbendun mons Abenni uulgariter nuncupatur* ('For we have learned from our contemporaries that, according to the language of the Irish, Abingdon is interpreted 'house of Aben'; but according to the language of the English, Abingdon commonly means 'the hill of Aben'').[25] The agreement of these two works, Irish and English, that Abingdon was founded by the Irish saint Abbán and the recourse to the same pseudo-etymology based on his name (in its Irish form) as proof points to collusion between the two in developing a shared onomastic legend about the origins of Abingdon.[26] On the English side, Abingdon presumably stood to gain some prestige from having as reputed founder a holy man from a country which in an earlier period enjoyed a reputation for sanctity—similar kinds of claims for Irish connections were being made at this time by rival monasteries in the south of England such as Glastonbury and Malmesbury.[27] On the Irish side, the Abbán legend helped to counter accusations about the

[22] Ó Riain (1986), who first made the connection.

[23] *Vita Sancti Abbani* 16 (Plummer (1910), i 10–2: 12). The translation is mine.

[24] Dated by Hudson (2002–7), i xxxvii, to 'the second quarter or perhaps the middle of the thirteenth century'.

[25] *Historia ecclesiae Abbendonensis* B2 (Hudson (2002–7), i 234–5).

[26] According to Ó Riain (1986), 161, 'Abingdon's 'mythical founder' is almost certain to have been originally dreamt up in Ireland'.

[27] See Lapidge (1993), 434–6.

degeneracy of the contemporary Irish church, such as were being leveled by 12th-century Anglo-Norman ecclesiastics, notably Gerald of Wales.[28]

According to the author of the *Historia*, the community of Abingdon learned about its alleged Irish origins in conversations with contemporary informants (*ex relatione modernorum*),[29] who were, one would have to presume, Irishmen.[30] Although these informants are not identified, a particular candidate has been suggested, the Irish ecclesiastic Albinus O'Molloy (Ailbe Ua Máel Muaid), abbot of the Cistercian house of Baltinglass (Co. Wicklow) and subsequently bishop of Ferns (*c.* AD 1186–1223). As first pointed out by Ó Riain, the evidence of state papers and a monastic chronicle indicate that Albinus was no stranger to the south of England. Following the same line of enquiry, Richard Sharpe proposed a specific occasion for the exchange, a stay at Abingdon by the archbishop of Dublin, Laurence O'Toole (Lorcán Ua Tuathail), who spent three weeks there in AD 1180, and whose entourage may have included Albinus.[31] Understandably, both scholars focused on the Irish contribution to Abingdon's history, but our present interest lies in the possibility of a *quid pro quo*, that Abingdon gave the Irish party something in return, arguably its special cult of St Vincent, bolstered perhaps with a donation of relics. Albinus is as likely to have been the agent for this putative transaction as for the 'Irish etymology' of Abingdon.

Indeed, two aspects of his background would recommend him as a likely candidate for the role of promoting an 'English' cult in Ireland. First, for an Irishman he had remarkably close ties to the English church and crown, making frequent visits to England, as well as passing through on his way to Rome under the king's protection. He knew King John personally and had officiated at the coronation of his predecessor, Richard I, while also sharing in the deliberations of the first council of that monarch.[32] Moreover, as a Cistercian abbot, he consecrated the chapel at the abbey of Waverley, the mother-house of the English Cistercians; he acted as suffragan in the diocese of Winchester; and he was made a member of the cathedral priory (Benedictine) of St Swithun's,

[28] Gerald of Wales, *Topographia Hibernie* 3 (ed. O'Meara (1949), 169–70; trans. O'Meara (1982), 112–4).

[29] *Historia ecclesiae Abbendonensis* B2 (Hudson (2002–7), i 234–5).

[30] As first argued by Ó Riain (1986), 160.

[31] Sharpe (1991), 352–3. See also Hudson (2002–7), i xliii. Lawrence's stay at Abingdon will have occurred before November 14, the date of his death at Eu (Normandy) in that year.

[32] See Cullen (1898), 233–5.

Winchester.[33] Secondly, he seems to have taken a personal interest in matters liturgical. Such activity, of course, goes with the episcopal office, but Albinus evidently relished the role, to judge by the number of times that the chroniclers portray him performing particular liturgical ceremonies. Thus, we find him dedicating a cemetery at the Cistercian Abbey of Duiske (AD 1207); assisting in the ritual attending Richard I's coronation at Westminster (AD 1189); dedicating a chapel at Waverley (AD 1201), and years later (AD 1214) at the same abbey consecrating the five altars of its great church as well as anointing all its crucifixes and blessing the cemetery reserved for those who had died while under recent interdiction.[34] Whether visiting Waverley or Winchester, or on his way to London or Rome, Albinus would have passed close to Abingdon and had numerous opportunities to stop there and visit the community with its thesaurus of relics. Once back in Ireland he would have commanded the authority, both as episcopal administrator and liturgical expert, to promote Vincent's cult in the diocese of Ferns and south Leinster.[35]

Nor is the presence in W of a cult of Vincent newly propagated by the diocese of Ferns in any way at odds with the proposition (based on the special status accorded St Moling) that W's exemplar came from St Mullins.[36] St Mullins had been a major ecclesiastical centre in its own right during the early Irish period, but by *c.* AD 1160 its lands (at least in part) had become subject to the Augustinian canons at Ferns, the episcopal seat of the diocese of the same name.[37] Relations between Ferns and St Mullins were close in the 13th century, as argued above from the evidence in the Lives of the south Leinster Irish saints composed about that time. And although St Mullins was now subordinate to its neighbour, the cult of its patron (Moling) continued to thrive. Thus the evidence in W for these two cults is quite compatible with a single time and place, an ecclesiastical centre in south Leinster that lay within the

33 See Marie Therese Flanagan *s.v.* 'Ó Maelmuaid, Ailbe' in *ODNB* 41, 789–90.

34 See *Annales Monasterii de Waverleia s.a.* 1201, 1214 (ed. Luard (1865), 253, 282).

35 Sharpe (1991), 380, has drawn attention to the fact that Irish bishops (at least by the 14th century) could mandate the celebration of certain saints throughout their dioceses.

36 See above, p 271.

37 See Flanagan (2005), 286–7.

area of influence of the diocese of Ferns, probably St Mullins, during the episcopacy of Albinus.[38]

A different location, however, has been proposed for W by Dónal O'Connor.[39] His starting-point is a set of saints especially venerated at pre-Norman Old Minister in Winchester that are shared by W and the Martyrology of Gormán (MG), a work assembled at Knock Abbey, Co. Louth, *c.*AD 1170. Emphasizing the rarity of some of these commemorations (e.g. Edburga and Judoc) outside of Winchester, he argued for the likelihood of some direct, personal, influence to explain their presence in these two Irish works. For that role he suggested Malchus (Máel-Ísu Úa hAinmire), a native of Waterford, who was educated at Winchester, became a Benedictine monk there, and subsequently returned to Waterford (AD 1096) as the first bishop of the city's Ostmen. Malchus spent much of his time at Lismore, Co. Waterford, where, O'Connor argues, he introduced a Winchester-style calendar whose direct influence is evident in W.[40] The presence of the same Winchester commemorations in MG he would explain as the result of Malchus' influence on Malachy of Armagh (Máel-Máedóc Úa Morgair) whom he mentored at Lismore (from *c.*AD 1122–32). Malachy later became the leader of the reform movement, in which role he consecrated Knock Abbey (AD 1148), the place where MG was composed by his protégé, Abbot Máel Muire Úa Gormáin.

But if W were actually produced in Waterford, one would expect—based on the assumption of its propinquity to the alleged source, Bishop Malchus' calendar—a fuller and more accurate complement of Winchester entries than MG. That, however, is not the case. By comparison with MG, W lacks the feasts of Alphege the Elder (Mar 12), Hedda (July 7), and Grimbald (July 8), as well as one of the two feasts for Edburga (June 15), while giving the wrong dates for both the translation (Sept 5 instead of Sept 4) and deposition (Dec 2 instead of Dec 3) of Birinus. Such evidence leads one to suspect that the underlying source for these Winchester entries should be sought not in W but rather in MG. Indeed, a plausible explanation of how MG came to have such a trove of Winchester commemorations has been offered by Pádraig Ó Riain who argues that its primary source was the well-known continental Marty-

[38] Significantly, W commemorates the feastday of Maedóc, the patron of Ferns, with an entry in red (on Jan 31), along with Melanfid, a Co. Waterford saint.

[39] O'Connor (2006).

[40] O'Connor (2006), 57.

rology of Usuard (MU), but in a version of the latter compiled at Winchester. He suggests that this Winchester MU was brought to Ireland by Flann Úa Gormáin of Armagh who had spent many years studying in England and who may have been closely related to Máel Muire Úa Gormáin, the author of MG.[41]

Another weakness of the hypothesis of Waterford origins for W is that its complement of Irish names reveals no predilection for saints traditionally associated with that region. Admittedly, it commemorates four Irish saints with Waterford connections, Máelanfaid of Dairinis (Jan 31), Brocán of Mothel (July 8), Declán of Ardmore (July 24), and Karthage (Carthach) of Lismore (May 14), the latter two of whom were the patron saints of their respective dioceses.[42] However, three of these names are marked in black ink, the register for normal feastdays; and the exception, Máelanfaid (in red; see *Plate 1*, line 33, in the Appendix, though the name is now almost indecipherable), is the second of two names for January 31, the first of which is Maedóc, the patron of Ferns, whose position at the head of the entry suggests his priority. Nor does the presence of these Waterford saints signify any special local cult since all four are commemorated in the Martyrology of Óengus and thus had already acquired 'national' profiles. Significantly, Waterford saints with more localized cults such as Cormán of Lismore (Jan 4), Molaisre of Kilmolash (Jan 17), Bríg of Killbrige (Jan 21), and Gormgal of Ardailen (Aug 5),[43] are strikingly absent from W.

Yet even if Waterford origins for W on the basis of its Winchester commemorations are ruled out, there remains another piece of local evidence to consider, one that can hardly be ignored since it is an entry in red. Under July 29 is found the commemoration of St Olaf, king and martyr (†AD 1030), whose cult was especially strong in towns settled by the Scandinavians of Britain and Ireland.[44] Given the setting of south Leinster proposed above for W's origins, his presence would seem to point to a Hiberno-Norse town in that general area. Of the two obvious candidates, Wexford and Waterford, the latter seems more likely given

[41] Ó Riain (2006), 165–7.

[42] Perhaps also Factne (Aug 14), bishop of Ros Ailithir, Co. Cork, who, if the Martyrology of Cashel is to be believed, had been *Abbas de Dar inis Moelanfaidh in regione Desiorum in Momonia*; see Ó Riain (2002), 180.

[43] Although not from Waterford, his relics were venerated at Lismore; see Ó Riain (2002), 164–5.

[44] See Dickins (1937–45); Dickins (1944). Ó Riain (2002), 130, notes that Olaf's feast was added to the Martyrology of Christ Church, Dublin.

that it had a church dedicated to Olaf.[45] However, there is an odd twist to the evidence: the Olaf entry is a later addition, albeit supplied by the main scribe. It was squeezed in on the right margin in a compressed form with arbitrary abbreviating of *Sancti* as *S* and *martiris* as a simple *m* (see *Plate 2*, line 31, in the Appendix). The convenient explanation for this state of affairs is that Olaf's name was omitted in the first round of copying because the entry would have required the scribe to change from black to red ink. This hypothesis would seem to be confirmed by several instances where the main scribe left a dedicated space blank pending an entry (for an apostle) in red—which he then forgot to supply.[46] But in the present instance the scribe did not leave the space for July 29 blank. Instead, he initially filled it with an entry in black ink for the two Roman martyrs, Felix and Simplicius, the universal commemoration for that day, generously spread across most of the page in a manner clearly indicating that he did not envisage any further names. From this one might hypothesize that Olaf's feastday did not mean anything special to the scribe; more importantly, one would have to conclude that the exemplar of W did not contain an entry for Olaf. Granted this line of argument, how then do we explain the fact that he subsequently supplied Olaf's name in a prominent colour? This apparently contradictory behavior suggests some kind of extraneous prompting of the main scribe, presumably after the first round of entries in black, by someone solicitous of Olaf's cult. That would suggest that although based on an exemplar from the Ferns diocese, W was modified for use in the diocese of Waterford (city).

What makes this scenario more plausible is the evidence from two entries supplied somewhat later that point to Waterford provenance for W at that time. The first is the addition by scribe 3 (13th century?) to the original entry for July 4 (St Martin's translation) of the words *Sancti Finbarri episcopi et confessoris* (see *Plate 2*, line 6, in the Appendix). The latter name refers not to the celebrated Finnbar of Cork (Sept 25), but to a saint associated with Inis Doimle (now known as Great Island), situated a few miles downriver from Waterford City. His commemoration in W presumably reflects the influence of a local cult. The second addition is an obit entered on the right margin adjacent to the liturgical commemorations for April 22 and 23, which records in a contemporary

[45] See Barry, Cleary, and Hurley (1997), 19, 191–2.

[46] For example, May 1 (Philip and James) and August 24 (Bartholomew), both of which as apostles would almost certainly have merited a coloured entry. Significantly, both entries were supplied in red by a later scribe.

hand the death of Peter fitz John Le Poer in AD 1327: *Obitus Petri filii Johannis Le poer anno domini .M°.CCC°.XXVIJ.* The Le Poers were a prominent Anglo-Norman family of Co. Waterford with their *caput* at Dunhill (Donoil) in the eastern part of the county. As we learn from the Annals of Friar John Clyn, Peter died fighting against Maurice fitz Thomas of Desmond, the result of a longstanding feud between these two powerful Anglo-Norman families.[47] His premature death would have been a major blow to the Le Poer dynasty, since he was not only the son of John, the reigning baron of Donoil, but also his heir. The chronological precision of Peter's obit suggests that the event was of immediate interest to the writer; while its location in an ecclesiastical calendar presumably reflects a desire to ensure that his death would be commemorated liturgically on the corresponding feastday. Thus interpreted, the entry would suggest that W was still being used as a liturgical calendar *c.*AD 1327 by an ecclesiastic with close ties to the Le Poers of Dunhill.

It so happens that adjacent to Dunhill lies the parish of Kilbarrymedan whose main church in medieval times was located near the present village of Kill, about six kilometers west of the Le Poer castle.[48] Although it does not merit an entry in Gwynn and Hadcock's inventory of medieval religious houses in Ireland,[49] Kilbarrymedan church was an important ecclesiastical center in the early Irish period. Indeed, Patrick Power has argued that it may originally have been the seat of a small diocese.[50] More to the point, he notes that although located geographically in the diocese of Lismore, Kilbarrymedan was see-land to the diocese of Waterford,[51] an association which would explain the special commemoration of St Olaf in W. What makes the proposed association of W with Kilbarrymedan more likely is that the latter place-name figures in the

47 Friar John Clyn, *Annales Hiberniae s.a.* 1328 (ed. and trans. Williams (2007), 188–91): *Item 11 Kal: ejusdem mensis et anni, occiditur Petrus Poer filius et heres baronis de Donhulle cum aliis de cognomina suo circa 12 per familiam domini Mauricii filii Thome.* ('**Item**, on 11 Kal of the same month and year [Tuesday 21 April], Peter Poer, son and heir of the baron of Dunohill was killed with around twelve others of his *cognomine*, by the *familia* of lord Maurice Fitz Thomas.') The discrepancy between Clyn's date (AD 1328) and that of W (AD 1327) may reflect a different method of dating in Clyn's source; see Williams (2007), 36.

48 On the surviving remains of the church, see Moore (1999), 177 (no. 1366).

49 Gwynn and Hadcock (1970).

50 Power (1937), 194: 'This fact [*sc.* that it was see-land of Waterford], as well as its former headship of a Deanery, suggests that the place was originally the seat of a bishop'.

51 On the disposition of see-land in Anglo-Norman Munster, see MacCotter (2000).

third booklet of MS 405 (volume III), the one immediately following W. This booklet of liturgical contents contains (*inter alia*) a series of nine readings for an office of a certain Barrmedinus, a saint otherwise unknown.[52] As argued by Richard Sharpe, 'Barrmedinus is a saint derived from the place-name Kilbarrymedan (Cell Bairre Mittíne), a local manifestation of St. Finnbarr, reflecting perhaps the local devotion of a compiler from Co. Waterford'.[53] The conjoining of this booklet (with its local Waterford associations) and W within a manuscript compiled by the early 14th century suggests that by this date (and perhaps earlier) the calendar was located in Waterford, perhaps in Kilbarrymedan.

To sum up: As suggested by its original liturgical contents, W was based on an exemplar originating in south Leinster, in a location within the area of influence of the diocese of Ferns, probably St Mullins. Despite its origins in this area, the calendar seems to have been intended for use in the diocese of Waterford, judging by the addition of the Olaf commemoration in red by the main scribe. W was almost certainly located in Co. Waterford about a century after being copied, as suggested by its careful record of the death of Peter Le Poer (AD 1327). While this obit points to a general location near the Le Poer *caput* at Dunhill, the readings from the purported Life of Barrmedinus in the section of MS 405 following W make a more precise location within the parish of Kilbarrymedan plausible. Broadly speaking, in its blend of saints, native Irish and non-Irish, W bears witness to Anglo-Irish ecclesiastical interactions in southeast Ireland during the decades after the Norman Conquest. More specifically, in its double commemoration of St Vincent it confirms a remarkable instance of such interactions, the special link between the English monastery of Abingdon and the diocese of Ferns that was evidently forged by Bishop Albinus.

Edition

The aim of the present edition is to present the calendar's liturgical contents in their original form as copied by scribe 1. Accordingly, the later entries of scribes 2 and 3 are omitted, though recorded in the footnotes.

52 See Lapidge and Sharpe (1985), 145 (§571), who date the putative Life of Barrmedinus underlying these lessons to AD 1208.

53 Sharpe (1991), 373. I am indebted to Dr Kevin Murray for onomastic advice on the place name Kilbarrymedan, which he would analyze as 'the Church of Barra of Mitíne'.

In keeping with the liturgical focus of the edition, the four parallel columns of chronological and computistical data, entered respectively in red, black, green, and red ink to the left of the main entries, are omitted. For ease of reference the dates of the month in the modern dating system are supplied in square brackets, as well as the manuscript foliation of the calendar. Missing letters are supplied in angled brackets. For the sake of consistency proper names are invariably capitalized, though not always so represented in the manuscript, and their spellings have been emended in cases where retaining the original form would cause misunderstanding. A sequence of asterisks on a line indicates an original entry that was erased (see under Aug 28–30). Common abbreviations for *abbatis*, *apostoli*, *confessoris*, *episcopi*, *martiris/martirum*, *octauas/octaue*, *pape*, *presbyteri*, *translatio*, and *uirginis* have been silently expanded. Likewise, the Tironian note (7) and the ampersand have been silently expanded to *et*. All entries that appear in the manuscript in red ink (thirty four occurrences) are italicized, while those in green ink (nine) are represented by bold font.

[fol. 11r]

Prima dies mensis et septimus truncat ut ensis.
Januarius habet dies xxxi lunam xxx.

[1] *Circumcissio Domini* *Dies Mala*
[2] *Octauas Sancti Stephani*
[3] *Octauas Sancti Iohannis Apostoli*
[4] *Octauas sanctorum innocentium*
[5] Sancti Simeonis monachi et confessoris
[6] *Ephiphania Domini*
[7] Sancti cleri diaconi et confessores
[8] Sancti Luciani martiri
[9] Sancti Iudoci translatio
[10] Sancti Pauli primi heremite
[11] Sancte Columbe uirginis
[12] Sancti Archadii martiris
[13] Octauas Ephiphanie et Sancti Hilari confessoris
[14] Sancti Felicis impinsis
[15] Sancti Mauri abbatis
[16] Sancti Marcelli pape
[17] Sancti Antonii monachi
[18] Sancte Prisce uirguinis Sol in aquarium

[19] Sanctorum Mari et Marthe
[20] Sanctorum Fabiani et Sebastiani martirum
[21] Sancte Agnetis uirguinis
[22] *Sancti Uincentii martiris*
[23] Sancte Emerentiane uirginis
[24] Sancti Babilli episcopi et confessoris
[25] *Conuersio Sancti Pauli ad fidem*
[26] Sancti Policarpi episcopi et martiris
[27] <S>ancti Iohannis Crissostomi[54]
[28] Octauas Sancte Agnetis
[29] Sancti Uincentii octauas[55]
[30] Sancte Baithildis regine
[31] *Sanctorum Medoc et Melanfid*[56]

[fol. 11v]

Quarta subiit mortem prosternit tertia fortem
Februarius habet dies xxviii lunam xxix.
[1] Sancte Brigide uirginis
[2] Purificatio Sancte Marie uirginis
[3] Sancte Uuarburge uirginis
[4] Sancti Auentini episcopi *Dies Mala*
[5] <S>ancte Agathe uirginis
[6] <S>anctorum Uedesti et Amandi confessorum
[7] <S>ancti Moysetis episcopi et confessoris
[8] <S>ancti Samsonis martiris
[9] <S>ancte Eufrosie uirginis
[10] <S>ancte Scolastice uirginis
[11] <S>ancti Desiderii episcopi
[12] <S>ancte Eulalie uirginis
[13] Sancti Lucinii
[14] <S>ancti Ualentinii martiris
[15] <S>ancti Blassii episcopi et martiris
[16] Sancte Iuliane uirguinis
[17] <S>ancti Fintani confessoris
[18] Sancti Simeonis episcopi

54 Here and in later entries the initial 'S' is missing, perhaps because the scribe anticipated that a rubricated version would be added later.

55 Discussed above, pp. 271–2.

56 Discussed above, p 277.

[19] Sancti Gabini martiris
[20] Sancti Galli presbyteri[57]
[21] Sanctorum martirum lxx et ix
[22] *Cathedra Sancti Petri apostoli*
[23] Sancti Policarpi presbyteri
[24] **Sancti Mathie apostoli** *locus bissexti*
[25] Sanctorum Uictoris et Uictorini martirum
[26] Sancti Felici martiris *Dies Mala*
[27] Sancti Iuliani martiris
[28] Sancti Ruphi martiris

[fol. 12r]

Primus mandentem dirumpit quarta bibentem
Martius habet dies xxxi lunam xxx.
[1] Sancti Dauid episcopi et confessoris *Dies Mala*
[2] Sancti Ceaddi confessoris
[3] Sancti Marini martiris
[4] Sancti Lucii pape
[5] Sancti Kerani confessoris[58]
[6] Sancti Iulani episcopi
[7] Sanctarum Perpetue et Felicitatis
[8] Sancti Senani confessoris
[9] Sanctorum .xl. martirum
[10] Sanctorum Uiti et Modesti[59]
[11] Sancti Gordiani martiris[60]
[12] *Sancti Gregorii pape*
[13] Sancti Mochemoc confessoris
[14] Sancti Petri martiris[61]
[15] Sancti Longuini militis
[16] Sancte Eugenie uirginis

[57] Gall's feast is usually on Oct 16 (the date of his death), but the present entry accords with certain ancient martyrologies which probably commemorate an early translation feast, as suggested by Farmer (2004), 199.

[58] MS 'c' with contraction mark.

[59] Usually celebrated on June 15—as found below in W on that date.

[60] Usually celebrated on May 10—as found below in W on that date.

[61] The 47/48 martyrs at Rome who were converts of Peter are normally commemorated on this date; perhaps Peter's name was entered by mistake.

[17] *Sancti Patricii episcopi*[62]
[18] Sancti Eaduardi[63] regis et martiris *Sol in arietem*
[19] Sancti Lactani confessoris
[20] Sancti Guthberti episcopi
[21] *Sancti Benedicti abbatis*
[22] Sancti Affrosidii episcopi
[23] Sancti Theodori presbyteri
[24] Sancti Moctai confessoris
[25] *Annuntiatio Sancte Marie*
[26] Sancti Castoli martiris
[27] *Resurrectio Domini*
[28] Sanctorum Prisci et Malchi *Dies Mala*
[29] Sancti Uictorini martiris
[30] Sancti Quirini martiris
[31] Sancte <B>albine uirguinis

[fol. 12v]

Denus et undenus est mortis uulnere plenus
Aprilis habet dies xxx lunam xxix.
[1] Sancti Uenantii martiris
[2] Sancte Marie Egiptiace
[3] Sancte Agapis uirguinis
[4] Sancti Ambrosi episcopi et confessoris
[5] Sancte Herinis uirguinis
[6] Sancti Sixti martiris
[7] Sancti Finani confessoris
[8] Sancti Perpetui confessoris
[9] Sancti Procorii diaconi
[10] Sancti Appollonii presbyteri[64]
[11] Sancti Leonis pape
[12] Sancti Iulii presbyteri
[13] Sancte Eufemie uirginis
[14] Sanctorum Tiburtii, Ualeriani
[15] Sancti Ruadani confessoris
[16] Sanctorum decem et uiii martirum
[17] Sancti Petri diaconi et martiris

62 MS 'epi' with bar through the shaft of 'p'.

63 MS 'Eadmundi'.

64 'Dies Mala' added on the margin by scribe 3.

[18] Sancti Lasreani abbatis
[19] Sancti Ealphegii episcopi
[20] Sancti Uictoris presbyteri[65]
[21] Sancti Simeonis episcopi et martiris
[22] Sancti Gaii presbyteri et martiris[66]
[23] Sancti Georgii martiris
[24] Sancti Melliti episcopi et confessoris
[25] **Sancti Marci euangeliste**
[26] Sancti Anacleti martiris
[27] Sancti Anastasii pape
[28] Sancti Uitalis martiris
[29] Sancti Agapiti martiris
[30] Sancti Ronani confessoris

[fol. 13r]

Tertius occidit et septimus ora relidit
Maius habet dies xxxi lunam xxx.
[1][67]
[2] Sancti Athanasii episcopi
[3][68]
[4] Sancti Quiriaci martiris
[5] Sancti Niceti episcopi
[6][69]
[7] Sancti Iohannis episcopi
[8] Sancti Uictoris[70] martiris
[9] Sancti Gregorii episcopi
[10] Sanctorum Gordiani et Epimachi[71]
[11] Sancti Mamerti episcopi

65 'Dies Mala' added on the margin by scribe 3.

66 Immediately after this entry on the right margin of the same line and the line underneath is the entry 'Obitus Petri filii Johannis Le poer anno domini .M°.CCC°. XXVIJ'; see pp. 278–9, above.

67 For this date scribe 2 supplied (in red) the entry 'Sanctorum apostolorum Pilippi et Iacobi'.

68 For this date scribe 2 supplied (in red) the entry 'Inuentio Sancte crucis'; and scribe 3 added 'Dies Mala' on the right margin.

69 For this date scribe 2 supplied (in red) the entry 'Sancti Iohannis apostoli ante portam'.

70 MS 'Uictoriis'.

71 MS 'Epimathi'.

[12] Sanctorum Nerei Achillei atque Appulei[72]
[13] Sancti Muti presbyteri
[14] Sancti Karthagii episcopi et confessoris
[15] Sancti Ysiodori martiris
[16] Sancti Brendini abbatis
[17] Sancti Torpetis martiris
[18] Sanctorum Medani et Domnani confessorum Sol in geminos
[19] Sancti Dunstani episcopi
[20] Sancte Basille uirguinis
[21] Sancti Secundini martiris
[22] Sanctorum Casti et Modesti
[23] Sancti Desiderii episcopi
[24] Sancti Donatii martiris
[25] Sancti Urbani martiris <et> papae
[26] Sancti Augustini archiepiscopi Anglorum[73]
[27] Sancti Iulii martiris
[28] Sancti Germani episcopi et confessoris
[29] Sancti Maximi episcopi
[30] Sancti Felicis presbyteri
[31] Sancte Petronille uirginis

[fol. 13v]

Denus pallesit quindenus federa nescit
Iunius h<abe>t[74] *dies xxx lunam xxix.*

[1] Sancti Nicomedis martiris
[2]
[3] Sancti Comgeni episcopi et confessoris
[4] Sancti Quirini
[5] Sancti Bonefaci episcopi
[6] Sancti Philippi diaconi
[7] Sancti Pauli episcopi
[8] Sancti[75] Medardi episcopi
[9] Sancti Columbe confessoris
[10] Sancti Censurii episcopi[76]

72 The third member of this trio may be an error for 'Pancratii'.

73 'Dies Mala' added on the margin by scribe 3.

74 MS 'ht' without the contraction mark.

75 In addition to the normal contraction mark above 'ci' there is another above 'S'.

76 'Dies Mala' added on the margin by scribe 3.

[11] *Sancti Barnabe Apostoli*
[12] Sanctorum Basilidis, Quirini
[13] Sancte Felicule uirguinis et martiris
[14] Sancte Felicule[77]
[15] Sanctorum Uiti et Modesti
[16] Sanctorum Ciricii et Uilite matris eius[78]
[17] **Sancti Moling confessoris**
[18] Sanctorum Marcii et Marcelliani
[19] Sanctorum Geruassi et Protassi
[20] Sancti Nouati confessoris
[21] Sancti Leufredii confessoris
[22] Sancti Albani confessoris
[23] Sancte Etheldride uirguinis *Vigilia*
[24] **Na<ti>uitas Sancti Iohannis Baptiste**
[25] Sancti Moluoc confessoris
[26] Sanctorum Iohannis et Pauli martirum
[27] Sancti Benigni confessoris
[28] Sancti[79] Leonis pape *Vigilia*
[29] **S***anctorum apostolorum Petri et Pauli*
[30] Commemoratio Sancti Pauli

[fol. 14r]

Tredecimus mactat Iuli denus labefactat
Iulius habet dies xxxi lunam xxx.
[1] Octauas Sancti Iohannis
[2] Sancti Suithuni episcopi
[3] Sancti Tome translatio[80]
[4] Sancti Martini translatio.[81]
[5] Sancti Domitii martiris
[6] Octaue apostolorum
[7] Sanctorum Claudi, Nicostrati[82]
[8] Sancti Brocani confessoris
[9] Sancti Brictii episcopi et confessoris

77 Apparently a duplication of the previous entry.
78 'Dies Mala' added on the margin by scribe 3.
79 MS 'Sancte'.
80 This refers to Thomas the Apostle.
81 Immediately after, 'Sancti Finbarri episcopi et confessoris' added by scribe 3.
82 This commemoration belongs to the previous day.

[10] Sanctorum septem fratrum *Dies Mala*
[11] Sancti Benedicti translatio
[12] Sancti Ermagorii episcopi
[13] Sancti Musiloc confessoris
[14] Sancti Berach episcopi et confessoris
[15] Sancti Suithuni episcopi
[16] Sancti Eustachii episcopi
[17] Sancti Kenelini regis et martiris
[18] Sancte Eadburge uirginis
[19] Sanctarum uiduarum[83] Iuste[84] et Rufine
[20] *Sancte Margarite uirguinis*
[21] Sancte Praxedis uirginis
[22] Sanct**e Marie Magdalenis**[85] *Dies Mala*
[23] Sancti Appollinaris martiris
[24] Sancti Declani episcopi et confessoris
[25] *Sancti Iacobi apostoli*
[26] Sancti Herasti episcopi
[27] Sanctorum septem dormientium
[28] Sancti Pantaleonis martiris
[29] Sanctorum Felicis Simplicii martirum. *Sancti Olaui regis et martiris*[86]
[30] Sanctorum Abdon et Senen
[31] Sancti Germani episcopi et confessoris

[fol. 14v]

Prima necat fortem perditque secunda cohortem
Augustus habet dies xxxi lunam xxix.
[1] Ad uincula Sancti Petri[87]
[2] Sancti Stephani protomartiris
[3] Inuentio Sancti Stephani
[4] Sancti Mulo[88] confessoris

[83] MS 'uuduinum'. Evidently the scribe misread in his exemplar the opening minims 'ui' as 'uu' and 'ar' as 'in'.

[84] MS 'Fuste'.

[85] The scribe mechanically began the entry with 'Scī' in black, and subsequently changed 'ī' to 'e' by adding a loop in green.

[86] Discussed on pp. 16–7, above.

[87] 'Dies Mala' added on the margin by scribe 3.

[88] Evidently, Molua (of Clonfertmulloe) is intended.

[5] Sancti Osualdi regis et martiris
[6] Sancti Sixti martiris
[7] Sancti Donati episcopi et martiris
[8] Sancti Cirani[89] martiris
[9] Sancti Romani episcopi[90]
[10] Passio Sancti Laurentii martiris
[11] Sancti Tiburtii martiris
[12] Sancti Lasriani confessoris
[13] Sancti Momedoc[91] confessoris
[14] Sancti Factne confessoris[92]
[15] Sancte Marie in assumpsione
[16] Sancti Arnulfi episcopi et confessoris
[17] Sancti Laurentii octauas
[18] Sancti Agapiti martiris
[19] Sancti Mocte confessoris
[20] Sancti Filiberti abbatis
[21] Sancti Priuati episcopi et confessoris
[22] Sanctorum Timothei et Simphoriani martirum[93]
[23] Sancti Eugenii episcopi et confessoris
[24][94]
[25] Sancti Micheani confessoris
[26] Sancti Alexandri martiris
[27] Sancti Rufi martiris
[28] ******************[95]

89 Probably 'Cyriani' who, with several others martyrs, is commemorated on this date.

90 'Vigilia' added on the margin by scribe 3.

91 MS 'memodoc'.

92 'Vigilia' added on the margin by scribe 3.

93 'Octaua Sancte Marie' added by scribe 3.

94 'Sancti Bartholomei apostoli' entered by scribe 3 on the original blank line.

95 The original three entries for August 28–30 were erased; traces of letters for all three days are still visible (including the final word 'bap' (with suprascript abbreviation mark) for 'Baptisti' on August 29 and the initial word 'Sancti' for August 30). Traditionally, these would have been the feasts of Augustine of Hippo (August 28), the beheading of John the Baptist (Aug 29) and Felix and Adauctus (August 30). However, since the latter was incorrectly entered under August 31 (traditionally, the feast of St Paulinus), it appears that the previous entries were off by a day, a slip which probably led to their erasure.

[29] *****************[96]

[30] *****************

[31] Sanctorum Felicissimi et Audacti martirum.[97]

[fol. 15r]

Tercia cum dena clamat sis integra uena

September habet dies xxx lunam xxx.

[1] Sancti Egidii abbatis

[2] Sanctorum confessorum inpiensi, et Lomnani et Colmani[98]

[3][99]

[4] Sancti Ultani confessoris

[5] Sancti Bertini abbatis et confessoris

[6] Sancte Columbe uirguinis

[7] Sanctorum martirum Euursi et Iohannis

[8] **Natiuitas Sancte Marie uirginis**

[9] Sancti Ciarani confessoris et abbatis

[10] Sanctorum Finneani et Ateluoldi confessorum

[11] Sanctorum Prothi et Iacincti martirum

[12] Sancti Eilbe[100] episcopi et confessoris

[13] Sancti Degani episcopi et confessoris

[14] **E***xaltatio sancte crucis*

[15] Sancti Nicomedis martiris

[16] Sancte Eufemie uirginis

[17] Sancti Lamberti episcopi et martiris

[18] Sancti Ferreoli martiris

[19] Sancti Signi episcopi et confessoris

[20] Sancti Eologi pape et martiris[101]

[21] *Sancti Mathei apostoli*[102]

[22] Sancti Mauricii sociorumque eius

96 August 29 has an entry, 'Decollacio sancti Johannis', in a later cursive hand (14th century?).

97 'Dies Mala' added on the margin by scribe 3.

98 The two Irish saints Lomnanus (recte 'Lonanus') and Colmanus are usually conjoined with Meicnisse, all three under Sept 3; see Ó Riain (2008), 148.

99 'Sancti Meiccnisse confessoris' entered on the original blank space by scribe 3, and 'Dies Mala' added on the margin by the same hand.

100 St Ailbe.

101 'Vigilia' added on the margin by scribe 3.

102 'Dies Mala' added on the margin by scribe 3.

[23] Sancti Ada<m>n<a>ni[103] confessoris
[24] *Conceptio Sancti Iohannis Baptiste*
[25] Sancti Barre confessoris
[26] Sancti Colmani abbatis et confessoris
[27] Sanctorum Cosme et Damiani
[28] Sancti Experini martiris[104]
[29] **Sancti Michaelis Archangeli**
[30] Sancti Ieronimi presbyteri et confessoris

[fol. 15v]

Tertius et denus est sicut mors alienus
October habet dies xxxi lunam xxx.
[1] Sanctorum Remegii et Germani confessorum[105]
[2] Sancti Leodogari episcopi et martiris[106]
[3] Sanctorum Dionisi et Candidi martirum[107]
[4] Sanctorum Marci et Marciani,[108] et Cipriani martirum
[5] Sancti Appollinaris martiris
[6] Sancte Fidis uirguinis et martiris
[7] Sancti Marcii papae et confessoris, et Marcelli martiris
[8] Sanctorum Demetri et Semsonis martirum
[9] Sanctorum Rustici Dionisi et Eleutherii martirum
[10] Sancti Paulini confessoris
[11] Sancti Cainneche[109] confessoris
[12] Sancti Mobi confessoris
[13] Sancti Comgani confessoris
[14] Sancti Calisti pape et confessoris
[15] Sanctorum martirum quiquaginta
[16] Sanctorum Colmani et Regula confessorum
[17] Sancte Etheldride uirguinis
[18] Sancti Luci euangeliste, et Sancti Iusti martiris

103 MS 'Adanni'.

104 Perhaps an error for 'Exsuperius'.

105 This entry had to be squeezed in on the same line as the rubric giving the number of solar and lunar days in October, perhaps the result of skipping a line. It commemorates the two saints' translation rather than their separate feastdays (*dies natalis*).

106 'M<artiris>' corrected from 'C<onfessoris>' by the original scribe.

107 'Dies Mala' added on the margin by scribe 3.

108 MS 'Mansi' and 'Mansiani'.

109 MS 'cammabe'.

[19] Sanctorum Thelomei et Luci martirum
[20] Sanctarum .lxi. milium uirginum et martirum
[21] Sancti Munne confessoris
[22] Sancti Philippi episcopi et martiris
[23] Sancti Daluachi confessoris
[24] Sancti Martini abbatis
[25] Sanctorum Crispini et Crispiniani martirum
[26] Sancti Amandi episcopi et confessoris
[27] Sanctorum confessorum Ercani, Abbani, Odrani
[28][110]
[29] Sancti Narcissi[111] episcopi
[30] Sancti Germani episcopi
[31] Sancti Quintini martiris

[fol. 16r]

Scorpius est quintus et tertius est nece tinctus
Nouember habet dies xxx lunam xxx.

[1][112]
[2]
[3] Sancti Corcunutain episcopi
[4] Sancti Bristani episcopi et confessoris
[5] Sancti Colmani confessoris *Dies Mala*
[6] Sancti Felicis martiris; et sanctorum .x. martirum
[7] Sancti Uuldeboldi[113] episcopi confessoris
[8] Sanctorum quatuor coronatorum[114]
[9] Sancti Theodori martiris
[10] Sancti Edani confessoris[115]
[11] Sancti Martini episcopi et confessoris

110 Since the apostles Simon and Jude are normally commemorated on this day, it seems likely that the space was left blank in anticipation of a coloured entry that was never provided.

111 MS 'Marcissi'.

112 Scribe 3 supplied the entries 'Sollennitas omnium sanctorum', for this day, and, for the next day, 'Commemoratio omnium fidelium defunctorum'. The spaces for both days were originally blank.

113 St Willibrord.

114 Namely, Sancti Severus, Severianus, Carpophorus, and Victorinus.

115 Aed Mac Bricc of the Uí Néill. There is a gap between his name and his title of confessor. Perhaps 'episcopi' was originally meant to be entered, a title accorded him by MG; see Stokes (1895), 214–5.

[12] Sancti Cummini episcopi
[13] Sancti Bricci episcopi et confessoris
[14] Sanctorum Colmani et Garbani[116] confessorum
[15] Sancti Machin confessoris[117]
[16] Sancti Macudis episcopi et confessoris[118]
[17] Sancti Amani episcopi et confessoris
[18] Sancti Martini octauas
[19] Sancti Marinii episcopi et confessoris
[20] Sancti Eadmundi regis et martiris
[21] Sancti Rufi confessoris
[22] Sancte Cecilie uirguinis et martiris
[23] *Sancti Clementis pape et martiris*[119]
[24] Sancti Crissogoni martiris
[25] *Sancte Katerine uirginis et martiris*
[26] Sancti Lini pape et martiris
[27] Sancti Maximi episcopi
[28] Sancti Ruphi martiris[120]
[29] Sancti Brendini confessoris *Vigilia*
[30] *Sancti Andree Apostoli*

[fol. 16v]

Septimus exsanguis uirosus denus ut angis
December habet dies xxxi lunam xxx.

[1] Sanctorum Crisanti et Darie
[2] Sancti Birini confessoris[121]
[3]
[4] Translacio Sancti Benedicti[122]

116 For 'Gabrani', who is also commemorated on this day in MG.

117 Perhaps a corruption of 'Mogain', a commemoration found in MG, though there identified as a virgin rather than confessor; see Stokes (1895), 218–9.

118 The Breton saint Machutus (*alias*, Maclovius, Malo), who is usually commemorated on Nov 15. There is a pronounced gap in the manuscript between the saint's two titles.

119 Uncharacteristically for scribe 1, this entry and the one for Nov 25 use the ampersand instead of Tironian '7'.

120 'Dies Mala' added on the margin by scribe 3.

121 His feastday was Dec 3, which may explain the space left blank for that date in anticipation of a rubricated entry.

122 This event is commemorated on this date in English calendars, but on June 4 in MG; see Stokes (1895), 134–5.

[5] Sancte Crispine uirguinis
[6] *Sancti Nicholai episcopi*[123]
[7] Sancti Andree apostoli octauas[124]
[8] *Conceptio Sancte Marie uirginis*
[9] Sancti Cipriani abbatis
[10] Sancte Eulalie uirginis
[11] Sancti Damasi pape
[12] Sancti Finneani abbatis
[13] Sancte Lucie uirguinis
[14] Sancti Nicassi episcopi
[15] Sancti Maximi abbatis[125]
[16] Sancte Barbare uirginis[126]
[17] Sancti Ignacii episcopi et martiris[127]
[18] Sancti Flannani confessoris
[19] Sancte Samthinne uirginis
[20] Sancti Iuli martiris
[21] *Sancti Thome apostoli*
[22] Sanctorum xxx. martirum[128]
[23] Sancte Uictorie uirguinis et martiris
[24] Sancti Mucho[129] confessoris Vigilia[130]
[25] *Natiuitas Domini nostri Iesu Christi*
[26] *Sancti Stephani protomartiris*
[27] *Sancti Iohannis apostoli et euangeliste*
[28] *Sanctorum Innocentium*
[29] *Sancti Thome archiepiscopi et martiris*
[30] Sancti Sabini episcopi
[31] *Sancti Siluestri pape*

123 Letters erased between 'Nicolai' and 'episcopi', probably 'archi-'.

124 'Dies Mala' added on the margin by scribe 3.

125 'Dies Mala' added on the margin by scribe 3.

126 'Dies Mala' added on the margin by scribe 3.

127 'O sapientia' added on the margin by scribe 3.

128 'Dies Mala' added on the margin by scribe 3.

129 For 'Mochua'.

130 Although written in black ink, the hand is that of scribe 1.

APPENDIX

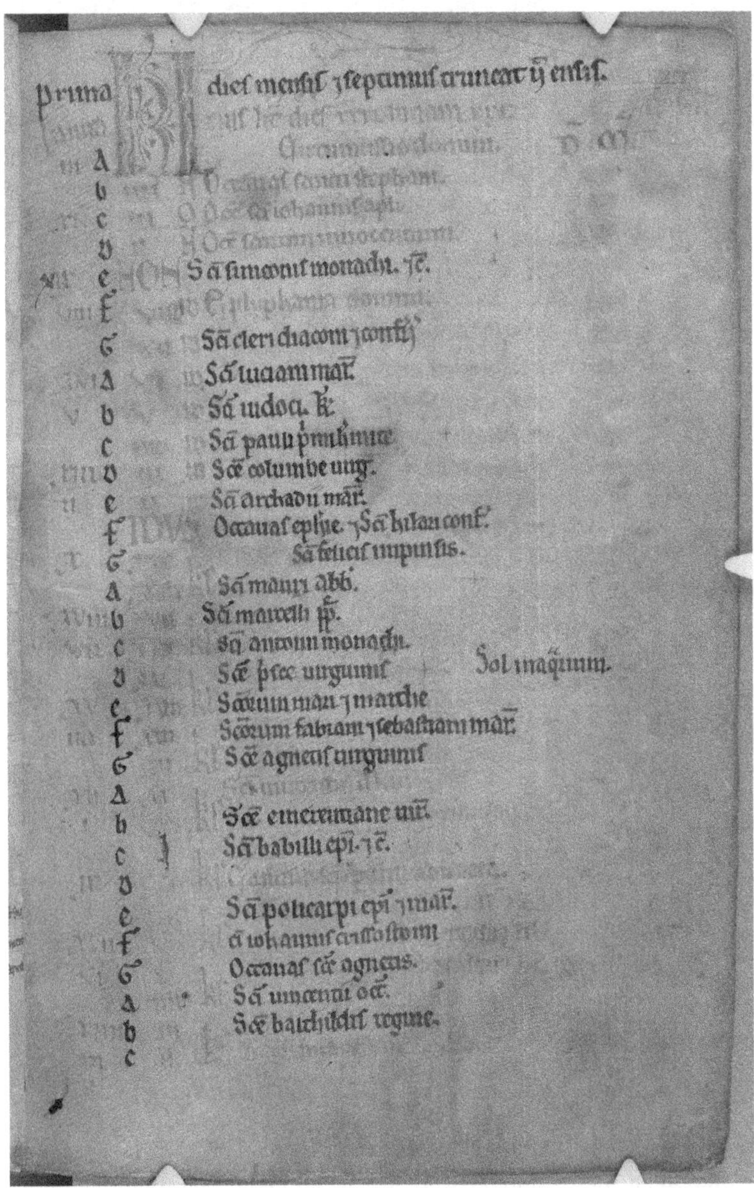

Plate 1 Cambridge, Corpus Christi College Library, 405, 11r (January page); cf. the edition pp. 281–2 above. (Reproduced with permission from the Master and Fellows of Corpus Christi College, Cambridge.)

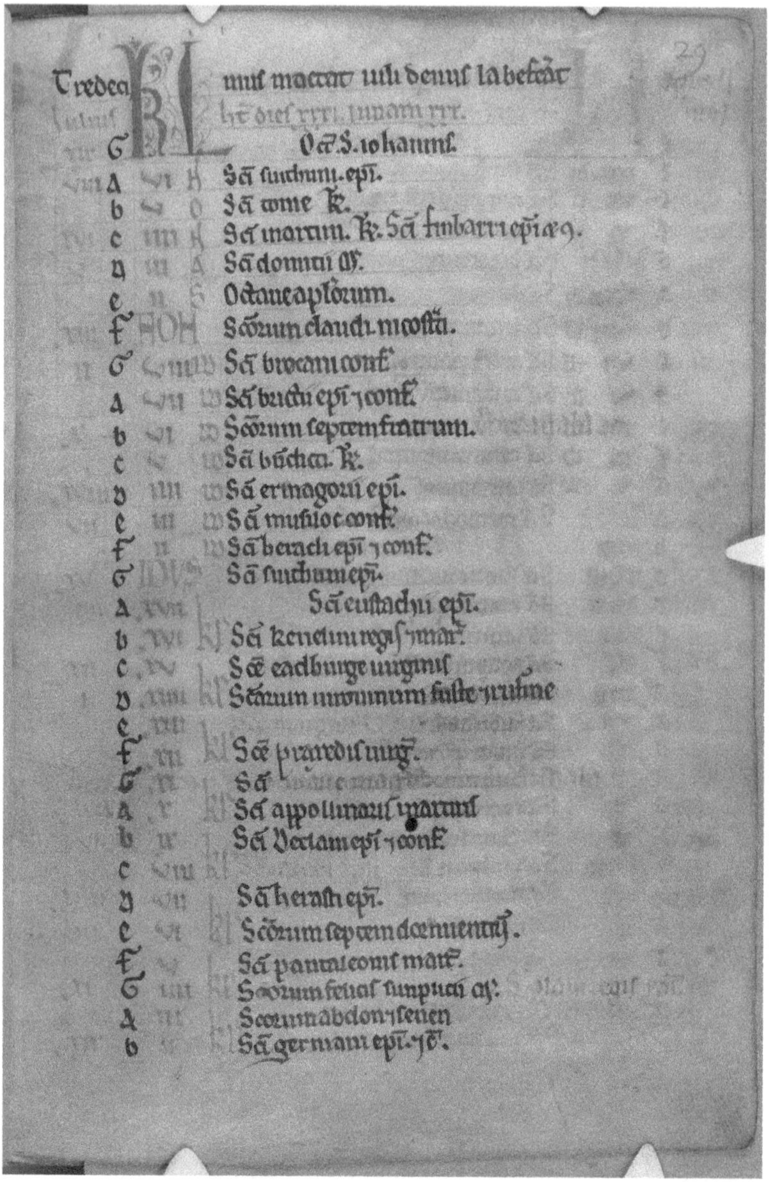

Plate 2 Cambridge, Corpus Christi College Library, 405, 14r (July page); cf. the edition pp. 287–8 above. (Reproduced with permission from the Master and Fellows of Corpus Christi College, Cambridge.)

Bibliography

Barry, T., R.M. Cleary, and M.F. Hurley (1997) *Late Viking Age and Medieval Waterford: excavations 1986–1992*, Waterford.

Cullen, J.B. (1898) 'The Pembroke tombs: Westminster Abbey II,' *Irish Ecclesiastical Record, fourth series* 4, 226–36.

Dickins, B. (1937–45) 'The cult of S. Olave in the British Isles,' *Saga-Book of the Viking Society* 12, 53–80.

— (1944) 'St. Olave and the British Isles,' *The Norseman* 2, no. 5.

Farmer, D.H. (2004) *The Oxford dictionary of saints*, Oxford.

Flanagan, M.T. (2005) *Irish royal charters: texts and contexts*, Oxford.

Gwynn, A. and R.N. Hadcock (1970) *Medieval religious houses: Ireland*, Harlow, repr. Blackrock 1988.

Hudson, J. (2002–7) *Historia ecclesiae Abbendonensis: the History of the Church of Abingdon*, 2 vols., Oxford.

James, M.R. (1909–12) *A descriptive catalogue of the manuscripts in the library of Corpus Christi College Cambridge*, 2 vols., Cambridge.

James, T. (1600) *Ecloga Oxonio-Cantabrigiensis tribute in libros duos, quorum prior continent catalogum confusum librorum manuscriptorum in illustrissimis bibliothecis, duarum florentissimarum Academiarum, Oxoniae et Cantabrigiae*, London.

Ker, N.R. (1960) 'From "Above Top Line" to "Below Top Line": a change in scribal practice,' *Celtica* 5, 13–6.

Lapidge, M. (1993) 'The cult of St Indract at Glastonbury,' in M. Lapidge, *Anglo-Latin Literature 900–1066*, London, 419–52.

Lapidge, M. and R. Sharpe (1985) *A bibliography of Celtic-Latin literature 400–1200*, Dublin.

Luard, H.R. (1865) *Annales Monasticii, vol. II*, London.

MacCotter, P. (2000) 'The see-lands of the diocese of Ardfert: an essay in reconstruction,' *Peritia* 14, 161–204.

Moore, M. (1999) *Archaeological inventory of County Waterford*, Dublin.

Nasmith, J. (1777) *Catalogus librorum manuscriptorum quos Collegio Corporis Christi et B. Mariae Virginis in Academia Cantabrigiensis legauit Reverendissimus in Christo Pater Matthaeus Parker, Archiepiscopus Cantuariensis*, Cambridge.

O'Connor, D. (2006) 'Bishop Malchus: his arrival in Lismore, and the Winchester saints in a Waterford Calendar,' *Decies* 62, 49–63.

O'Meara, J.J. (1949) 'Giraldus Cambrensis *In topographia Hibernie*: text of the first recension,' *PRIA* 52C, 113–78.

— (1982) *Gerald of Wales: the History and Topography of Ireland*, Harmondsworth.

Ó Riain, P. (1986) 'St Abbán: the genesis of an Irish Saint's Life,' in D.E. Evans, J.G. Griffith, and E.M. Jope, *Proceedings of the Seventh International Congress of Celtic Studies*, Oxford, 159–70.

— (2002) *Four Irish martyrologies: Drummond, Turin, Cashel, York*, London.

— (2006) *Feastdays of the saints: a history of Irish martyrologies*, Brussels.

— (2008) *A martyrology of four cities: Metz, Cologne, Dublin, Lund*, London.

Plummer, C. (1910) *Vitae sanctorum Hiberniae*, 2 vols., Oxford.

Power, P. (1937) *Waterford & Lismore: a compendious history of the United Dioceses*, Cork.

Rushforth, R. (2008) *Saints in English Kalendars before A.D. 1100*, London.

Sharpe, R. (1991) *Medieval Irish Saints' Lives: an introduction to the Vitae sanctorum Hiberniae*, Oxford.

Stanley, W. (1722) *Catalogus librorum manuscriptorum in Bibliotheca Collegii Corporis Christi in Cantabrigia quos legavit Matthaeus Parkerus Archiepiscopus Cantuariensis*, London.

Stevenson, J. (1858) *Chronicon monasterii de Abingdon*, 2 vols., London.

Stokes, W. (1895) *Félire húi gormáin. The martyrology of Gorman*, London.

Williams, B. (2007) *The Annals of Ireland by Friar John Clyn*, Dublin.

Wormald, F. (1939) *English Benedictine Kalendars after A.D. 1100, vol. 1: Abbotsbury–Durham*, London.

CONTACTS II:

CONTINENTAL INFLUENCES IN IRELAND

DONNCHADH Ó CORRÁIN

ÁUI, ÚI, UÍ: A PALAEOGRAPHICAL PROBLEM?

Abstract

Irish *úa* ('grandson, descendant'), especially important in the formation of lineage names and surnames, has many forms in Old and Middle Irish, and what is taken to be its abbreviation *h.* has been expanded in many different ways by scholars. This is an enquiry into some of its forms and into a palaeographical problem about the origin of the abbreviation. The conclusion is that *h.* derives from Tironian *a*.

Keywords

Ogam AVI, AVII; *Áui, áuë, úa*; Early Old Irish forms; Tironian *a*; genealogies; Dublin, Trinity College, 1298 (*olim* H.2.7).

The Irish word *úa* ('grandson, descendant') may appear to be a word without problems, but its abbreviation in medieval manuscripts is, to say the least, curious and unexamined. In the spirit of enquiry that is so conspicuously his, I offer this little lucubration for the amusement of a fine historian and a good and generous friend.

The following examples are mostly dated, and written *plene* in early texts:[1]

[1] The nom. sg. *hūaë*, cited in *DIL s.v. úa*, is alas mistaken: the MS (Book of Leinster (Dublin, Trinity College, 1339 (*olim* H.2.18)), 49) reads *h.* Meyer (1912a), 12 (§ 6a), 16 (§ 22c), carefully indicates his expansion in italic, missed by the lexicographer. Best, Bergin, O'Brien, and O'Sullivan (1954–83), i 243, has h*ua*, as one expects.

Early medieval Ireland and Europe: chronology, contacts, scholarship, ed. by Pádraic Moran and Immo Warntjes, Studia Traditionis Theologiae, 14 (Turnhout, 2015), pp. 301–9.

 10.1484/M.STT-EB.5.103125

nom. sg.: *haue* gl. *nepos*, Sg. 29a10;[2] *aue muiredaich* (Poem V from Codex S. Pauli);[3] *Duncath aue Ronain iugulatus*, AU 647.2;[4] *Colman auę Oirc*, AU 701.2; *Eladach aui* (sic) *Maeluidhir*, AU 738.4; *oa Suanaich*, AU 763.2; *Ailill aua Duncadha rex Connacht*, AU 764.8; *huę Miannaigh abbas sruithi Cluana M. Nois*, AU 768.3; *Encorach huę Doadain abbas Glinne Da Locha*, AU 769.4.
nom. dual: *Da auę Cheallaigh Cualand*, AU 744.6.
voc. sg. fem.: *auë Bresail maic Déin slán seiss a Brigit* ('Hail Brigit');[5] *A húa engach athemas* (*Saltair na Rann*).[6]
gen. sg.: *Mors Dunchado hui Ronain*, AU 670.6; *Iugulatio Airmedaigh hui Guaire*, AU 675.2; *Mors Colmain aui Suibni*, AU 707.7; *Mors Flaind Sinnae aui Collę*, AU 732.1; ⁊ *occisio Coibdenaigh filii Flainn hui Chongaile*, AU 734.3; *Dub Da Crich m. aui Cellaigh m. Triein, Fiangalach h. Maele Aithcen, Conall h. Aithecdai; ceithir meic Flainn aui Conghaile, Eladach aui Maeluidhir* ⁊ *ceteri multi*, AU 738.4; *Mors Sothcathaigh aui Maele Toili*, AU 738.8; *Mors hui Becce abbatis Fobair*, AU 770.15; *Mors Flainn hui Do Chuę abbatis Innsi Cain Degha*, AU 771.1; *Mors Dathail episcopi, scribae,* ⁊ *ancoritę, hui Duibleni*, AU 817.1; *Lex aui Suanaich*, AU 748.8; *Mors aui Cuirc Cille Daro*, AU 750.7; ⁊ *co tuc giallu hUi Ruairc*, AU 955.3.
nom. pl.: *maicc* ⁊ *háui reliqua .i. is follus issin maigin sin téte aitherrechtaigthe Ní ashire oldáta m*aicc ⁊ *aui reliqua*, Sg. 30b12;[7] ⁊ *manserunt hUi Neill*, AU 770.8; *Laigin* ⁊ *Oi Neill*, AU 841.4; ⁊ *coru giallsat hUi Cernaig*, AU 822.3; *Longport oc Linn Duachaill asar orta tuatha* ⁊ *cealla Tethbai. Longport oc Duiblinn as-rorta Laigin* ⁊ *Oi Neill etir tuatha* ⁊ *cealla co rice Sliabh Bledhma*, AU 841.4.

acc. pl.: *Sendom*nach *la Au. Er*cæ, Book of Armagh (Dublin, Trinity College, 52), 19ra24 (*Notulae*);[8] *la Auu Censelich*, Book of

[2] Stokes and Strachan (1901–3), ii 80. (Sg. refers throughout to the Old Irish glosses on the Priscian manuscript, St Gall, Stiftsbibliothek, 904; reference is by page and column, followed by sequence number.)

[3] Stokes and Strachan (1901–3), ii 295.10.

[4] AU refers to the Annals of Ulster, ed. Mac Airt and Mac Niocaill (1983), by year and entry number.

[5] Meyer (1912a), 18 (§26); Best, Bergin, O'Brien, and O'Sullivan (1954–83), i 246 (*codex unicus*).

[6] Stokes (1883), 88, line 6006 (in reference to Michal); Meyer (1914), 939–58: 946 (§ 124).

[7] Stokes and Strachan (1901–3), ii 82.29–31.

[8] Bieler (1979), 182 (§42).

Armagh (Dublin, Trinity College, 52), 18rb11 (*Additamenta*);[9] *iter Auu Maine* 7 *Ua Fiachrach*, AU 743.5; *hiter Uu Ailello* 7 *Gailengo*, AU 743.6; *fri Uu Ailello*[10].
gen. pl.: *regis Oa Failghe*, AU 741.9; *ri Ardda Oa Cinn Faeladh*, AU 749.5; *hOirt hEchu mac Neill meic Trichim gialla Conaille Muirthemni i nInis na nGiall* 7 *propter hoc occisus est Eochu rex hUae Trichim apud Conaille*, Dublin, Trinity College, 1298 (*olim* H.2.7), 157;[11] *co Dumacha Óa nAilello*[12].
dat. pl.: *.i. cotchen diachoibnius .i. do maccaib* 7 *auib*, Sg. 28a20;[13] *dia Uibh Liathain*, AU 732.7; *dia Uib Fidgenti*, AU 744.4; *o Auib Cremhtainn*, AU 757.3; *Corbetrige .i. Cruibte mac Cosgaib meic Cruinnd de Corco hE de Auib Bodamnai*, Dublin, Trinity College, 1298 (*olim* H.2.7), 162; *decollatus est o Auib Echach*, AU 878.3; *do guin o hUib Echoch*, AU 914.2; *i nOib Muredaig* (gloss to Broccán's Hymn)[14].

Old forms written *plene* are attested in genealogical texts preserved in late manuscripts. Early genealogies of the Déissi that may date from *c.*AD 700 preserve the Early Old Irish nom. pl. *Aui*:[15]

> .iii. familie .i. Daurgabul a quo Dub De Muge 7 Aes Torra .ii. Corc. Dulnech a q*u*o Aui Orci. Aed Tusech.

The parallel passage in the 12th-century Book of Leinster reads:[16]

> Treae fa*m*ilie .i. Daurgabail a q*u*o Dub De Moge et Aes Torra *du*ae Corc, Duinech a quo h*Ui* Orci. Aed Toesech.

The early genealogies of the Uí Brigte of the Déissi have the following corrupt passages:

9 Stokes and Strachan (1901–3), ii 241.6.

10 Stokes (1887), i 94, line 13 = Mulchrone (1939), 58, line 1051.

11 Written *c.*AD 1350 by Lúcás Ó Dalláin.

12 Stokes (1887), i 98, line 1 = Mulchrone (1939), 60, line 1091.

13 Stokes and Strachan (1901–3), ii 78.27–8.

14 Stokes and Strachan (1901–3), ii 342.20.

15 Dublin, Trinity College, 1298 (*olim* H.2.7), 83a36–b4.

16 Dublin, Trinity College, 1339 (*olim* H.2.18), 328d56 (O'Brien (1962), 401).

> G*enelach* h*ua* mBrigdi so. Corm*a*c Fin*n* m. Coibdeanaich m. Dubchraidi m. Maeluidir m. Cilli*ne* m. Corm*aic* m. En*na* m. Caelbad m. Theachtaich m. Ailealla. Tri męic amaili aui mBrigde. Aui Tigernaich Fear Deilithi.[17]

> Ceithri m*eic* Brigti ingini Dubt[h]aig do Ultaib: Ros, Feidlimid, Clár a quo Ui Clair. Is e a carnd fuil i nEdarbiu. [...] *Tres* familie hUa mBrigte. Aui Thigernaig [text loss].[18]

We can confidently restore: *Tres familiae Auë Brigte: Aui Thigernaich* [text missing].

Again, in early Munster genealogies older forms are preserved *plene*:

> Da m*a*c Gerrai*n*: Conall Find, Conall Cloen. Aui Gerrain h*oc est* Aes Aicthith Mingti.[19]

> Corc Lossat de Araid Tire gegui*n* Bebrae Fiac[h]rach Tortchothis; is ind as-rith crich hUe Cathbath Tire o Ḟirt Morai*n*d co Sliab nEblinne.[20]

> Is he inso aes dana Ethne hUat[h]che. Corbroth mac Englae m*ei*c Nuadat a rath Eochach meic Luchta. Bruth de Cheniul Cuirb aui Nuadat. Is de Brodrige la hEli.[21]

[17] Book of Lecan (Dublin, Royal Irish Academy, 23 P 2; facsimile ed. Mulchrone (1937)), 101ra1. Book of Ballymote (Dublin, Royal Irish Academy, 23 P 12; facsimile ed. Atkinson (1887)), 149re44, has the reading: *m. Familie h. in* Brigdi *ui* Tig*er*naich. Cp. Book of Leinster (Dublin, Trinity College, 1339 (*olim* H.2.18)), 328a33 (O'Brien (1962), 397). *Fear Deilithi* belongs to the beginning of the next genealogy.

[18] Dublin, Trinity College, 1298 (*olim* H.2.7), 82a27–b10. Variants in the Book of Leinster (Dublin, Trinity College, 1339 (*olim* H.2.18)), 328a40, are 'C*h*láre' (for 'Clair') and 'Etarba' (for 'nEdarbiu').

[19] Dublin, Trinity College, 1298 (*olim* H.2.7), 86.27–29. The parallels are Oxford, Bodleian Library, Rawlinson B. 502, 155a33 (O'Brien (1962), 259) = Book of Lecan (Dublin, Royal Irish Academy, 23 P 2), 112rc13 = Book of Ballymote (Dublin, Royal Irish Academy, 23 P 12), 197ra5 = 200b21. Book of Ballymote (Dublin, Royal Irish Academy, 23 P 12), 197ra5, reads very correctly (if modernized): Da m*ac* Gęrain: *Con*all Clæn ⁊ *Con*all Fi*n*d. Hui Gęran h*oc est* Aes Ac*h*aig Mi*n*gthi.

[20] Dublin, Trinity College, 1298 (*olim* H.2.7), 132c22. The parallel witnesses are Oxford, Bodleian Library, Rawlinson B. 502, 151a25 (O'Brien (1962), 222) = Book of Lecan (Dublin, Royal Irish Academy, 23 P 2), 217rb42 = Book of Ballymote (Dublin, Royal Irish Academy, 23 P 12), 176e22. For *hUe* all read *h*.

[21] Dublin, Trinity College, 1298 (*olim* H.2.7), 157.10.

Coel ingen Maini de Orbraigiu ben Oengusa Builgg. Is f*o*rræ hilocht aincleir ho Cheniul Mani. Is de do-bert-si Laegaire mac Crimthaind, ar is a siur ro bai lais. Is de Carrac Laegaire. Is de tolongeth Cenel Mane a Cleir. Is de Fert Coelae hi Taulaig. Is de séntai cach fer Ceniu[i]l Nath I 7 ni*con* sena nach fer Ceniuil Mani. Crothru *con*-gab duini 7 Catta dia ta Ros Catte di ingin (ingin) in sin Conaill Chluin. .iii. m*ei*c Indnaiscai m*a*ccu Luigde oc Cin*n* Chaille .iii. manaich Mo [C]hoemoc Leith. .iii. duma .iii. n-aue mBirnn hi Femun oc Inde[o]in Derc. .iii. n-aue mBirnn oc Tig Gailleni for Luaisc hi chlas a Sid Nesain anair airm hi tutet Loesc is and ad-ranac[h]t.[22]

Corco Muchit. [...] Cethri m*ei*c Me Dochith m*ei*c Fergusa m*ei*c Briu[i]n m*ei*c Echach Muinbethan. Cano Mauc*h*cot. Mathene. Methorse a siur *coic* m*ei*c Corco Muchit. Aui Conbici, Aui Decci, Aui Dego, Aui Thalain, Aui Chuirb.[23]

Again, it is evident from the genealogies that the forms of *áuë*, *úa*, etc. are more diverse than the forms in the 12th-century manuscripts indicate. Here, by way of illustration, is a diplomatic transcript of some passages from Oxford, Bodleian Library, Laud Misc. 610:[24]

Cinaet*h* a q*u*o hoí mamáin 7 hoi mothlacháin 7 húi mugrón 7 hói gartnȩn 7 huí uíttitén.
Diarmait a q*u*o muintȩr cȩnnetig, hoi chairellain 7 hu muredaig 7 corrán a q*u*o m*uin*t*er* chorrán.
Flaithb*er*tach a q*u*o huí dubdai 7 húi baígill 7 hoe merleich 7 hói dublaích.
Longsech a q*u*o hoí chathalan 7 hui mail brȩsail 7 hoí murcȩrtaig.
Dub indreȩcht a q*u*o hui doblec*h*an 7 hoí thanaide 7 hoi lathrai.
Brogan a q*u*o hui bræslain.
Mael finne a q*u*o hui mail finne.
Drucan a q*u*o hui eochathan 7 hoí longsig.
Furudran a q*u*o hoi gottáin 7 hói muredaig 7 hoi branacán 7 cumuscach a q*u*o huí chuind 7 hu muȩrȩgaid.

22 Dublin, Trinity College, 1298 (*olim* H.2.7), 160.7.

23 Dublin, Trinity College, 1298 (*olim* H.2.7), 185a27–b6.

24 It is not always clear whether what I represent as length-marks are really such or whether they are diacritics marking minims. Only capitals (i.e. larger letters) in the MS are printed as capitals here.

Longsech a quo huí maelan.
Cumascach a q*u*o cland focartaig .i. hói lainn 7 hoi c*h*inaith 7 hoi maíl maill 7 hui dubacáin.
Dondchad ní fil huad.[25]

Tręmpan im*morru* oenm*a*c acai fælcú.
Is huad hui maíl moc*h*ęrge 7 oí duibli 7 oe duibgillai 7 oi dinęrtaig 7 oe murnechán 7 hoí dobráin 7 oi dubain[26]

Aed m*a*c Fęrg*us*a .uii. m*ei*c lais .i. loegaire, taután, uanaind, comán, breccán, lannan, ubban.
O loegaire tellac*h* cinæda .i. oe branacain, óé gan, óe mail maige, óe cathalan 7 tellach muræda*igh* .i. óe loingsechain, oe enaisc, oe bercdai, óe scuiri, oe mail fin*n*, hóe lannacain, oe firaiste.
Oe t*h*uatain .i. oe bruatair, oe murcad*h*a, oe beoailb.
O uanainn .i. munt*er* melláin.
O co*m*mai*n* .i. oe didnaid.
O brecán .i. o airisnig.
O hubban .i. cland duban hi con*nacht*aibh.
O loegaire .i. oé chollai.[27]

Two things appear to be indicated by the foregoing examples from the genealogies: older forms *áuë*, *áui* are commonly written out in full without prefixed *h-* in some older texts and the forms of that word are diverse, perhaps dialectal, in the well-preserved texts in Oxford, Bodleian Library, Laud Misc. 610.

We now come to the problem of the use of *h.* as a *nota* or abbreviation for *áuë* in all its forms, singular and plural, and how this could have come about. There is little agreement among editors of texts. They handle the abbreviation in different and inconsistent ways. Regardless of the forms in the text, Stokes, in both of his great editions of the Martyrology of Óengus, indexes alphabetically under *H* in the form

[25] Oxford, Bodleian Library, Laud Misc. 610, 76va1–21 (ed. Meyer (1912b), 296.1–18).

[26] Oxford, Bodleian Library, Laud Misc. 610, 77rb23–27 (ed. Meyer (1912b), 298.15–17).

[27] Oxford, Bodleian Library, Laud Misc. 610, 77va28–b7 (ed. Meyer (1912b), 299.1–10).

Húi.[28] Toirdhealbhach Ó Raithbheartaigh prints *H.* throughout except when he is in error or when the word is written *plene* in the manuscript: *Hua, Ua* (§§32, 35, 44, 179 [pp. 142, 143, 146, 184–7]); *O, I, Hi* (§§14, 28, 33–4, 58, 61, 74, 86, 111, 117, 133, 142, 163, 168, 174, 177–9, 182, 184 [pp. 137, 140, 142–3, 150, 150, 153, 156, 160, 161, 166, 168, 178, 180, 183, 183–7, 189–90, 192–4]); *Uib* (§§55, 129, 170, 178 × 2 [pp. 149, 165, 183–4]); *Aib, Ib, Haib* (§§178 [pp. 183–4], 184 [pp. 192–4]); *Huib* (§§179 × 2 [pp. 184–7], 182 [p 190], 184 [p 194]); *Uí Neill* (§148 [p 171]) is an error for *Ua Neill.*[29] In his epoch-making *Corpus genealogiarum Hiberniae* (1962), M.A. O'Brien renders MS *h.* in the nominative plural as H*ūi* throughout, regardless of the putative date of the text. The following are examples of how he treats text written *plene*: *la Hū Bairrche Tīre* (49.24); *la Huu Failge* (84.2); *fri Hū Maine* (153.22); *Do Hūib Briūin* (49.23); *la Hūib Nēill* (137.41); *ata nesom do hŪib Nēill* (147.4); *ata nessom de lochaib de hŪib Néill* (153.32); *De hŪib Cairpri* (204.20); *De hŪib Duach* (222.23); *de hŪib Cuirp* (229.1); *de hŪib Cathbath* (258.12); *do Hūib Echach* (278.3); *De hŪib Ambrit* (301.24); *De hŪib Angáin* (304.24); *De Hūib Luchta in so sís* (312.9). O'Brien avoids Stokes's problem of index order: he indexes under the name, not the generic prefix, but he religiously retains the form *Hūi* throughout his index. How are we to account for these forms?

In the first place, *h* is not organic. The etymology of *áuë, áui*, etc. is certain. It comes from **aw-io-* (cognate with Latin *auus*, Old Norse *áe*). It derives from *awo-*, originally an adult male relative other than one's father. In Latin *auus* points backwards to 'grandfather', and secondarily 'ancestor'; in Irish it points forward to 'grandson', and secondarily 'descendant'.[30] The ogam forms, AVI, AVII (gen.) are well attested, both in form and meaning.[31] The diphthong is retained before *-i-*, and does not coalesce with the following vowel. It later becomes a monophthong, presumably in Middle

[28] Stokes (1880); Stokes (1905). For example, in Stokes (1880), the in-text forms *ind huaib fælain, inhuib fælan* (p clxxxiii), *hi tuaisciurt* h*uafoelain* (p cxlvi), *in úib fælan amuig laigen* (p lxxxviii), *ciuitas eius inuib fælan* (p xcix), *in* huib *foelan* (p cxxx), *o lathrach briuin inúib foelan* (p cxli), etc. appear in the index as *Húi Faeláin.*

[29] Ó Raithbheartaigh (1932), 133–95; Book of Lecan (Dublin, Royal Irish Academy, 23 P 2), 177rb1–183rd51.

[30] Vendryes, Bachellery, and Lambert (1959–), A-103–4, U-1.

[31] Macalister (1945–9), i §§3, 7, 19.1, 37, 40, 43, 63.1, 66, 124, 142, 162, 177, 185, 189, 230, 270, 275, 282, 288, 378 (AVI); 30, 46, 378 (AVVI); McManus (1991), *passim*; Ziegler (1994), 132.

Irish.[32] The letter *h*, so often prefixed to the word in its various forms, is not Irish at all. It is taken over from Late Latin and is mute, without phonetic value in Old Irish. It is often prefixed to words beginning in *ua*, *ui* (and to other short words, e.g. *i*, *a*, *ó*, *ed*, *uisse*, *uile*, *ic(c)*, *ires*) probably to indicate that they are not Latin and should not be so pronounced.[33] How are we to explain how a silent and exotic *h* came to be the commonest representation of *áue* in all its many forms in almost all medieval Irish manuscripts?

It seems that what appears as *h.* is quite different in origin, belonging to the period when *áuë*, *áui* were the current forms, and represents a scribal development based on the letter *a* in the Tironian *notae*. Tironian *a* takes two forms: the first resembles a majuscule lambda (Λ), the second a minuscule *h*.[34] The second is in question here. Tironian *notae* were, of course, known to the early Irish scholars, and they may have observed the *notae* for Latin *auus* and *aui*, both based on the second form,[35] and may have been inspired by them, but this is not a necessary condition. Thus what appears to be the Latin letter *h* is simply the Tironian tachygraph *h.*, understood to be a first-letter abbreviation for *áuë*, *áui*, etc. Later, when its origin was forgotten, scribes confused it, to a degree, with the Latin-derived mute *h* commonly placed before vowel-initial short words in Old Irish. Hence the *plene* forms with *h* cited above. But these are by no means the commonest forms in the best and oldest texts.

If this hypothesis is well founded, there are some consequences for editors. The abbreviation is to be expanded as a*ui*, A*ui* etc. in Early Old Irish, when it was a genuine abbreviation. Thereafter, *h.* becomes a *nota* pure and simple, a symbol, and should be expanded without intial *h*, in whatever form editors consider to be contemporary with the text. If editors wish readers to know what they have done, the whole word should be printed in italic. Forms written *plene* with initial *h*- should, of course, be printed as they are in the manuscript. For example, 'Gilla cellaic*h* m*a*c co*m*altai*n* huichlerich do ma*r*bad a cath et*er* hú fiachrach 7 hú mane' could appear in the edited text as 'Gilla Cellaic*h* m*a*c Co*m*altai*n* hUī Chlērich do ma*r*bad a cath et*er* hÚ Fiachrach 7 hÚ Mane'.[36] The use of lower-case *h*, as a convention, may serve to indicate that it is non-organic and mute.

[32] Pedersen (1909–13), i 55 (§37.4).

[33] Thurneysen (1909), 17–8 (§23); Thurneysen (1946), 19–20 (§25).

[34] Kopp (1817–29), i 74 (§94).

[35] Kopp (1817–29), i 239 (§282); ii 39 (descriptions and drawings).

[36] Best and Mac Neill (1933), f 20rb9–13; Mac Airt (1951), 176 (*s.a.* 1004.2).

Bibliography

Atkinson, R. (1887) *The Book of Ballymote, a collection of pieces (prose and verse) in the Irish language, compiled about the beginning of the fifteenth century*, Dublin.
Best, R.I. and E. Mac Neill (1933) *The Annals of Inisfallen reproduced in facsimile from the original manuscript*, Dublin.
Best, R.I., O.J. Bergin, M.A. O'Brien, and A. O'Sullivan (1954–83) *Book of Leinster*, 6 vols., Dublin.
Bieler, L. (1979) *The Patrician texts in the Book of Armagh*, Dublin.
Kopp, U.F. (1817–29) *Palaeographia critica*, 4 vols., Mannheim.
Mac Airt, S. (1951) *The Annals of Inisfallen*, Dublin.
Mac Airt, S. and G. Mac Niocaill (1983) *The Annals of Ulster (to A.D. 1131)*, Dublin.
Macalister, R.A.S. (1945–9) *Corpus inscriptionum insularum celticarum*, 2 vols., Dublin.
McManus, D. (1991) *A guide to ogam*, Maynooth.
Meyer, K. (1912a) *Hail Brigit: an Old-Irish poem on the Hill of Allen*, Halle.
— (1912b) 'The Laud genealogies and tribal histories,' *Zeitschrift für celtische Philologie* 8, 292–338.
— (1914) 'Zur keltischen Wortkunde VI,' *Sitzungsberichte des Königlich-Preussischen Akademie der Wissenschaften, phil.-hist. Klasse*, 939–58.
Mulchrone, K. (1937) *The Book of Lecan. Leabhar Mór Mhic Fhir Bhisigh Leacain*, Dublin.
— (1939) *Bethu Phátraic*, Dublin.
O'Brien, M.A. (1962) *Corpus genealogiarum Hiberniae*, Dublin.
Ó Raithbheartaigh, T. (1932) *Genealogical tracts I*, Dublin.
Pedersen, H. (1909–13) *Vergleichende Grammatik der keltischen Sprachen*, 2 vols., Göttingen.
Stokes, W. (1880) *On the Calendar of Oengus*, Dublin.
— (1883) *Saltair na rann*, Oxford.
— (1887) *The tripartite life of Patrick*, 2 vols., London.
— (1905) *Félire Óengusso céli Dé; the Martyrology of Oengus the Culdee*, London.
Stokes, W. and J. Strachan (1901–3) *Thesaurus palaeohibernicus: a collection of Old-Irish glosses, scholia, prose, and verse*, 2 vols., Cambridge.
Thurneysen, R. (1909) *Handbuch des Alt-Irischen*, Heidelberg.
— (1946) *A grammar of Old Irish*, Dublin.
Vendryes, J., E. Bachellery, and P.-Y. Lambert (1959–) *Lexique étymologique de l'irlandais ancien*, Dublin.
Ziegler, S. (1994) *Die Sprache der altirischen Ogam-Inschriften*, Göttingen.

HAYLEY HUMPHREY

BATHED IN MYSTERY: IDENTIFYING THE 'BATHING OF THE CHRIST CHILD' SCENE ON AN IRISH HIGH CROSS

Abstract

The uppermost panel on the high cross of Camus, Co. Derry, displays a scene which has yet to be satisfactorily identified by previous scholars. Based on iconographic comparisons with continental depictions of the Nativity and similarities with a panel on the Broken Cross at Kells, Co. Meath, this article will suggest a new identification for the panel as the 'Bathing of the Christ Child'.

Keywords

Camus, Kells; bathing, baptism, nativity, Salome, infancy cycle; high cross, iconography.

Introduction

Attempting to identify accurately the scenes depicted in the figural panels on the Irish high crosses is perhaps one of the most perilous tasks in the study of medieval Irish art. No texts exist to verify potential identifications of the scenes, and comparisons with biblical stories are often inconclusive, as there is a disconnect between what one reads, what one envisions in one's own mind, and what one sees portrayed on the high crosses. The inherent biases of historians and art historians further complicate matters, as each person will undoubtedly focus on different elements in a given panel, and can thus interpret the same evidence in a variety of ways. However, this is perhaps the only way that we can ever truly understand the purpose and message of these monuments, and it is important to re-examine previous identifications of figural scenes in an attempt at reaching a consensus. With this goal in mind, this article

Early medieval Ireland and Europe: chronology, contacts, scholarship, ed. by Pádraic Moran and Immo Warntjes, Studia Traditionis Theologiae, 14 (Turnhout, 2015), pp. 311–27.

 10.1484/M.STT-EB.5.103126

will re-examine a panel on the high cross at Camus, Co. Derry, in order to suggest a new identification of the scene depicted. Based on iconographic comparisons with continental depictions of the 'Bathing of the Christ Child' scene, as well as similarities discovered with a panel on the Broken Cross at Kells, Co. Meath, this article will suggest that the Camus panel could be identified as the 'Bathing of the Christ Child'.

Origins of the bathing scene: the midwife motif

Before attempting to identify the 'Bathing of the Christ Child' scene on the Irish high crosses, it is important to understand the origins and artistic development of this scene. The 'Bathing of the Christ Child' (also referred to as the 'Washing of the Christ Child') appeared regularly in depictions of the Nativity in both eastern and western art from the 8th century on, despite the fact that it has no textual basis and is not mentioned in canonical or apocryphal accounts of Christ's birth.[1] Iconographically speaking, depictions of Christ's first bath usually feature two midwives,[2] one standing on either side of the Christ child, who appears partially submerged in a chalice-shaped basin. The midwife on the left of the scene is often shown in a kneeling or seated position, and she reaches towards the Christ child in the basin; the midwife on the right of the scene is usually shown standing, as she pours water into the basin from a large jug or bottle.

Although the bathing motif itself has no textual basis, the story and identity of the two midwives are accounted for in the Apocrypha. The Protoevangelium of James and the Evangelium Pseudo-Matthew describe two midwives who were present during the birth of Christ: Zelomi, who believes in the Virgin birth, and Salome, who fails to believe and insists on a tactile examination of the Virgin to verify her virginity.[3] As a result of her disbelief in the Virgin birth, Salome is punished: according

[1] Kitzinger (1963), 100; Harbison (1992), i 239–40; Nordhagen (1961), 334.

[2] Nordhagen (1961), 334, identifies the standard layout of the scene as depicting 'one midwife holding the Child, and the other pouring water into the basin'. However, only a single midwife appears on the Vicopisano and Fieschi Morgan reliquaries, both dated to the 9th century. In these cases, the solo midwife appears on the left of the Christ child. For further discussion of the single midwife on the Vicopisano and Fieschi Morgan reliquaries, see Schiller (1971), i 65; Thunø (2002), 73.

[3] Pseudo-Matthew provides names for both midwives, and identifies the believing midwife as Zelomi and the doubting midwife as Salome. The Protoevangelium of James also names the doubting midwife Salome, but does not provide a name for the

to the Protoevangelium of James, her hand 'falleth away in fire', while in Pseudo-Matthew her hand withers before her eyes.[4] Her hand is restored only after she asks forgiveness and, on the advice of an angel, reaches her damaged hand towards the Christ child and touches him.[5]

The motif of doubting Salome appears in artistic renderings of the Nativity as early as the 6th century. She is generally depicted kneeling in front of the Christ child, who lies in the crib, or in front of the reclining Virgin, and is shown proffering her withered hand.[6] But beginning in the 8th century, the kneeling Salome theme was gradually phased out due to the 'crudeness' of the story, and was eventually replaced by the bathing theme.[7] The amalgamation of kneeling Salome and the bathing motif is evident in a mosaic in John VII's oratory (AD 705–707) in Old St Peter's Basilica, where the Nativity image includes both Salome kneeling at the crib and two midwives washing the Christ child in a basin.[8] The

believing midwife. See James (1924), 74, 46–7. Salome the midwife is not the same Salome who danced for the head of John the Baptist.

4 See James (1924), 47 for the quote and 74 for a description of her withering hand.

5 Pseudo-Matthew states (James (1924), 74): 'Joseph was gone to find midwives and brought Zelomi and Salome. Zelomi believed, Salome was incredulous, and her hand withered and was healed by touching the swaddling cloth.' The Protoevangelium of James states (James (1924), 46-7): 'And the midwife went forth of the cave and Salome met her. And she said to her: Salome, Salome, a new sight have I to tell thee. A virgin hath brought forth, which her nature alloweth not. And Salome said: As the Lord my God liveth, if I make not trial and prove her nature I will not believe that a virgin hath brought forth. And the midwife went in and said unto Mary: Order thyself, for there is no small contention arisen concerning thee. And Salome made trial and cried out and said: Woe unto mine iniquity and mine unbelief, because I have tempted the living God, and lo, my hand hath fallen away from me in fire. [...] And lo, an angel of the Lord appeared, saying unto her: Salome, Salome, the Lord hath harkened to thee: bring thine hand near unto the young child and take him up, and there shall be unto thee salvation and joy.'

6 6th-century examples of the kneeling Salome motif include the Throne of Maximian, an ivory plaque from Manchester, and an ivory plaque in the British Museum. In the early images, only Salome is shown; Zelomi does not appear and the angel is rarely shown. See Nordhagen (1961), 333; Schiller (1971), i 64.

7 Nordhagen (1961), 333 n 7, states that 'Salome at the Crib became extremely rare after the early middle ages' due to the 'crudeness' of the subject. Schiller (1971), i 64–5, states that the kneeling Salome motif was 'sharply repudiated by western doctors of the church' and argues that 'the bathing scene was regarded as a variation upon the offensive theme of the midwife'.

8 Nordhagen (1961), 333; Kitzinger (1963), 100; Harbison (1992), i 240; Osbourne (1981), 86. Only a portion of the Bathing image from the oratory of John VII survives, which is now preserved in the Vatican grottoes. For further discussion, see van Dijk (1995), 52–8, 146–53. A fresco in S. Maria di Castelseprio also shows both kneeling Salome at the Crib and the Bathing, but the date of this example is uncertain;

consolidation of kneeling Salome and the Bathing is most evident in an 8th century fresco in San Valentino in Rome, where Salome is not only shown kneeling and extending her damaged arm towards Christ in the crib, but she is also explicitly identified as one of the two female figures bathing the Christ child.[9] The inscription on this image sets a precedent for identifying one of the figures bathing the Child as Salome, with the logical inference being that the second female bather represents Zelomi.

The incorporation of Salome into the bathing scene during the 8th century marked a crucial turning point in the development of the motif, as in subsequent centuries, the Bathing continues to be a key theme in depictions of the Nativity, while the figure of the kneeling Salome rarely appears. During the 9th century, only the Bathing appears in a number of different examples, including three reliquaries (Pope Paschal's cross from the Sancta Sanctorum objects and the Vicopisano and Pliska reliquaries) and a fresco in San Vincenzo al Volturno.[10] On Paschal's cross (*Plate 1* in the Appendix), the Pliska reliquary (*Plate 2* in the Appendix) and the San Vincenzo al Volturno fresco, two midwives appear, one on either side of the Child. The midwife on the left is shown seated or kneeling and reaches towards the Child, while the midwife on the right pours water into the basin from a bottle or jug. On the Vicopisano reliquary (*Plate 3* in the Appendix), only a single midwife is positioned on the left of Christ. Rather than including a second midwife to the right of Christ, the seated figure of Joseph appears facing the Child.[11] In the first three examples, the basin is chalice-shaped, consisting of a rounded bowl with a stemmed base, while the basin on the Vicopisano reliquary consists of only a rounded bowl, without a stemmed base.

see Leveto (1990), 393–4 for a further discussion of the dating of the Castelseprio image and a description of the Nativity scene.

[9] Osbourne (1981), 84; Nordhagen (1961), 334; Schiller (1971), i 64–5.

[10] These examples have been singled out for discussion here because they are iconographically similar to the Irish scenes. The Bathing also appears in manuscripts from this period (such as the Utrecht Psalter and the Sacramentary of Drogo) and on the Fieschi Morgan reliquary. See Harbison (1992), i 240, and Schiller (1971), i 64–5, for a complete list of Bathing scenes and an analysis of their iconography.

[11] In addition to the two midwives flanking Christ on Paschal's cross, Harbison (1992), i 240, has suggested that a third smaller figure on the right may represent Salome (rather than one of the attending figures). However, based on the appearance of Joseph on the Vicopisano and Fieschi Morgan reliquaries and the similar gestures of these two figures with the third figure on Paschal's cross, it seems more likely that the additional figure on Paschal's cross represents Joseph, and that one of the attendant figures represents Salome.

The 'Bathing of the Christ Child' on the Irish high crosses: the Broken Cross at Kells and Camus

Although Salome kneeling at the crib has never been identified on any of the Irish high crosses, a panel on the Broken Cross at Kells has been identified as the 'Bathing of the Christ Child'. On the east face of cross, the fourth panel from the bottom features four figures (*Plate 4* in the Appendix). Only the upper body of the second figure from the right is shown, and the figure is placed immediately above a large, circular object which has 'splaying vertical fluting' extending from its base to the bottom of the scene.[12] Peter Harbison has suggested that this rounded object may represent the basin or bathtub in which the Christ Child is being washed, and although it does not share the chalice-shape of the basins described above, similar vertical striations do appear on the basin depicted in the oratory of John VII.[13] On either side of Christ, a standing figure appears to pour water from a jug directly into the basin; Harbison identifies the figure on the right as Zelomi, but it is unclear which figure represents Salome, as there is a fourth figure at the extreme left of the panel which extends a long, thin object towards the head and shoulders of the figure immediately to its right.[14] Harbison believes that the figure immediately to the left of Christ is most likely Salome, and suggests that this figure may be holding its arm up to the Christ Child's face (although this is not immediately clear). However, he argues that the figure on the extreme left may also be Salome, with the long, thin object representing her withered hand, or alternatively, that this figure may represent the angel.[15]

Although the panel on the Broken Cross at Kells is the only one to have been identified as the 'Bathing of the Christ Child' by previous scholars, there is another panel on the cross at Camus which appears to share some iconographic similarities with the Kells panel. The uppermost panel on the east face of the Camus cross depicts three human figures (*Plate 5* in the Appendix). Like the Kells panel, there is a half-figure at the center of the Camus scene, which appears directly above a large, rounded object, which may represent a basin. The central figure is flanked on either side by single attendant figures; the standing figure

12 Harbison (1992), i 102.

13 Harbison (1992), i 240.

14 Harbison (1992), i 102, 240.

15 Harbison (1992), i 102.

on the left of the scene appears to extend a long, thin object towards the shoulder of the central figure, in a gesture similar to the figure on the extreme left of the Kells panel, while the figure on the right of the central figure places its hands lower, nearly touching the edge of the rounded object. It is unclear whether the right-hand figure holds anything in its hands, but as the hands appear so close to the edge of the possible basin, it is possible that the figure may be holding a jug, in a gesture similar to the right-hand figure in the Kells scene. The Camus panel has received a number of identifications, including the 'Marriage Feast at Cana', the 'Last Supper' and the 'Multiplication of the Loaves and Fishes'.[16]

The identification of the Camus panel as the 'Multiplication of the Loaves and Fishes' is primarily based on perceived visual similarities with another cross in the Ulster group, the high cross of Arboe, Co. Tyrone (*Plate 6* in the Appendix). On the west face of the Arboe cross, the third panel from the bottom has been identified as the Multiplication by previous scholars. Like the Camus panel, a central half-figure appears above a rounded structure at the center of the scene; this structure has been identified as a dish or basket containing the fish that were multiplied. Harbison has suggested that fish may also be detected above the rounded structure in the Camus scene;[17] however, due to the current physical condition of the Camus cross, it is unclear whether any fish can be detected.

Although the shape of the rounded structure and the central half-figure are similar, these appear to be the only real similarities between the Arboe and Camus panels, as the treatment of the figures and the composition of the scenes do not appear to be related. The Arboe panel features five figures, rather than the three present in the Camus panel, and none of the Arboe figures are shown reaching towards the central figure like the two attendant Camus figures. The figures on either side of the central figure in the upper register of the Arboe panel are also shown as half-figures, rather than full standing figures like those on Camus, while two additional figures crouch below on either side of the rounded structure. The central figure in the Arboe scene holds a long,

[16] Anthony Weir suggested that the panel may represent the Wedding at Cana or the Last Supper (Weir (1980), 122), while Arthur Kingsley Porter, Ann Hamlin, and Malgorzata D'Aughton identify it as the Multiplication (Porter (1931), 116–117; Hamlin (1982), 73; D'Aughton (2004), 16). Harbison has included a question mark in his own identification of the panel, and includes the qualifier that this scene 'probably' represents the Multiplication, allowing for reinterpretations (Harbison (1992), i 31).

[17] Harbison (1992), i 17–8, 256.

pointed object, but there is no such object held by the central Camus figure.[18] While there are similarities between the centralized figures in both panels, the differences between these panels are more striking. The fact that the Arboe panel features five figures rather than three, the lack of standing figures, the addition of a pointed object held by the central figure, and the absence of the 'reaching' gesture makes it unlikely that the Arboe panel depicts the same scene as the Camus panel. The similarities between the Camus and Kells panels are much more striking. The central rounded structure in both could be identified as the basin in which the half-figure of Christ is washed, and although the Camus basin does not possess the vertical striations of the Kells basin, this does not eliminate its identification as a basin, as the inclusion of vertical ribbing was atypical.[19]

Although the Camus basin cannot be identified as chalice-shaped because no stem or base is visible, it does closely resemble the basin on the Vicopisano reliquary, which is also shown without a stem. The number of figures in the Camus panel (three, including Christ) is also standard for representations of the Bathing, and the flanking position of the standing figures, one on either side of the basin, is typical. Finally, the reaching gesture of the left-hand figure in both the Kells and Camus scenes suggests that both figures could potentially be identified as Salome extending her withered hand towards Christ, a gesture which is notably absent from the Arboe scene.

Further support for identification of the Bathing Scene: the 'Baptism of Christ' panel

The Bathing was traditionally depicted as part of the Nativity scene. Curiously, the 'Nativity of Christ' has never been identified on any of

[18] I have suggested elsewhere (Humphrey (2011), 71–3) that the appearance of the long, pointed object coupled with the rounded structure may suggest that this panel could be identified as the 'Circumcision of Christ', with the central figure representing the priest holding the scalpel (represented by the pointed object) and the rounded structure representing the cot or manger in which the Christ Child was placed for the procedure. The iconography of the Arboe panel is iconographically and compositionally much closer to a panel on the cross at Clones, Co. Monaghan, which may also represent the Circumcision.

[19] Harbison (1992), i 240, cites the oratory of John VII and an example in the Armenian Tetraevangelium No. 362 G from Etchmiadzin (dated to AD 1057) as containing vertical striations on the basins. As discussed above, the typical form was the chalice-shaped basin.

the extant high crosses, despite the appearance of other scenes from the Infancy of Christ. However, there is another panel on both the Kells and Camus crosses that may support the identification of the bathing scenes—the 'Baptism of Christ'.

The biblical accounts of Jesus' baptism state that this event happened when Jesus was an adult, so it may seem unusual to compare a scene from Christ's adulthood with one from his childhood.[20] However, depictions of the Baptism were often included as the final scene in 'Infancy of Christ' cycles, and it is not unusual to see Christ depicted as a beardless youth in Baptism scenes.[21] For example, the Pliska, Vicopisano, and Paschalian reliquaries each include the 'Baptism of Christ' as the culmination of the Infancy cycle. Although the position and iconography of Baptism scenes on the Irish high crosses vary, there are a number of examples where the Baptism is shown in close proximity to panels showing the 'Infancy of Christ' cycle, and it is possible to interpret the Baptism as an Infancy scene on these crosses.[22] The appearance of the Baptism near the Bathing on the Kells and Camus crosses would thus be thematically consistent.

The theological messages of the Bathing and the Baptism are also related—both scenes feature an act of cleansing (physical and spiritual), and both center on Christ's dual human and divine nature. Ernst Kitzinger argues that the bathing motif is dogmatically questionable, as the Child and his mother were both pure, and as such, the infant Christ would not require the ritual cleansing.[23] And yet by showing a divine being submitting to this human ritual, the focus becomes his dual human

[20] Mt 3:13–17; Mk 1:9–11; Lk 3:21.

[21] According to Thunø, the Baptism was included in the Infancy cycle because it was associated with the concept of regeneration through the Virgin's womb. The Baptism scene was not exclusive to Infancy cycles, however, and could be included in other cycles from the 'Life of Christ'. In addition, Christ is not always shown as a youth. For example, he is shown as a bearded adult in the Baptism scenes found in John VII's oratory and the 6th-century Pontian catacomb. See Thunø (2002), 47–51, particularly 50. For a further discussion of the typological differences in Baptism scenes, see Schiller (1971), i 127–43; Harbison (1992), i 250–2.

[22] For example, on the crosses of Killary, Galloon, and Armagh, the Baptism appears next to Infancy scenes such as the 'Adoration of the Magi' and the 'Annunciation to the Shepherds'.

[23] Kitzinger (1963), 103–4 n 38 and 39, cites several patristic sources relating to the topic of Jesus and Mary's purity, including John Chrysostom and Irenaeus (for example, *Adversos haereticos* IV 55.2: *purus pure puram aperiens vulvam quam ipse puram fecit*).

and divine nature, made manifest through the Incarnation.[24] Similarly, Jesus describes his baptism as 'an act of obedience and submission to the Law of his race'.[25] Gertrud Schiller summarizes the theological relationship between the Bathing and the Baptism by stating: 'not only does [the Bathing] now refer to Christ's acceptance of human nature but [it] also looks forward to the Baptism, in which the Son of God shows himself subject to human order'.[26]

Not only do the theological messages of the Baptism and the Bathing overlap, but the iconography and compositional layout of these scenes are related. Both scenes show Christ immersed in water, and the chalice-shape of the basin in the Bathing was intended to recall a baptismal font.[27] On the three reliquaries that depict both the Bathing and the Baptism (the Pliska, Vicopisano, and Paschalian reliquaries), the compositional parallels are clear: John the Baptist is always shown to the left of Christ, and he reaches towards Jesus in a gesture similar to that of Salome in the bathing scenes. The Kells and Camus crosses also exhibit compositional similarities between the Bathing and Baptism panels. On Kells, four figures are shown in the Bathing, two to the left of Christ (who is immersed in the basin) and one to the right. Similarly, the Kells Baptism features four figures, two to the left of Christ (who is immersed in the river Jordan) and one to the right. Both the Camus Baptism and Bathing panels feature three figures each, rather than four, but the layout of the figures in both panels is similar. In the Baptism scene, Christ appears at the center of the scene and is flanked on either side by a figure (John the Baptist to the left, and the smaller figure of an

[24] The concept of Christ's dual nature was expressly defined in AD 451 at the Council of Chalcedon, and placed into the credal formulation (Tanner (1990), 86): *ante saecula quidem de Patre genitum secundum deitatem, in novissimis autem diebus eundem propter nos et propter salutem nostram ex Maria virgine Dei genetrice secundum humanitatem, unum eundemque Christum Filium dominum unigenitum, in duabus naturis inconfuse, immutabiliter, indivise, inseparabiliter agnoscendum* ('begotten before the ages from the Father as regards his divinity, and in the last days the same for us and for our salvation from Mary, the virgin God-bearer, as regards his humanity; one and the same Christ, Son, Lord, only-begotten, acknowledged in two natures which undergo no confusion, no change, no separation.') See also Rubin (2009), 48.

[25] Schiller (1971), i 127. For the biblical account of Christ's baptism, see Mt 3:13–17; Mk 1:9–11; Lk 3:21.

[26] Schiller (1971), i 65.

[27] For further discussion of the iconographic parallels between the Bathing scene basins and baptismal fonts, particularly in 12th-century French and Spanish depictions, see Arad (2003), 22–7.

angel to the right). Similarly, the Bathing scene features the centralized figure of Christ, flanked by an attendant figure on either side.

Conclusions

Although it is difficult to confirm the identification of the panel on the Camus cross with absolute certainty, it is plausible that it may represent the 'Bathing of the Christ Child', based on the evidence presented here. The appearance of the Bathing scene on the Broken Cross at Kells sets a precedent for depicting the scene on the Irish high crosses, and means that the motif was known in Ireland during the time that the crosses were constructed. The iconography of the Camus scene is similar to the Kells panel, as well as to continental depictions of the bathing scene, and because of these iconographic similarities, it seems appropriate to suggest a similar identification. The appearance of the 'Baptism of Christ' on both the Kells and Camus crosses may provide additional evidence for the identification of the Bathing scene, as both the Bathing and the Baptism can be considered 'Infancy of Christ' scenes. The theological and compositional relationship between the Bathing and the Baptism may further support the identification of the panels presented here.

APPENDIX

Plate 1 Pope Paschal's enameled reliquary cross, *c.*AD 817–24 (Musei Vaticani). Photo: Vatican Museums.

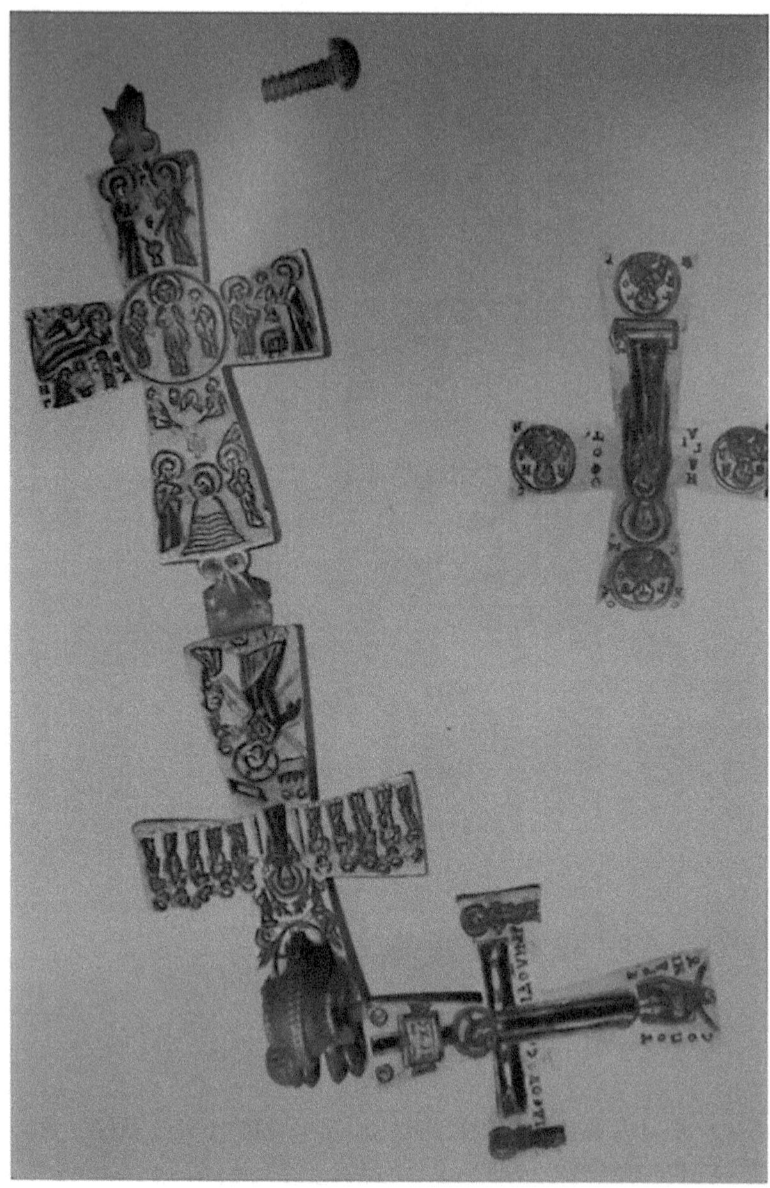

Plate 2 Pliska reliquary cross (Archaeological Museum, Sofia). Photo reproduced from Thunø (2002), Pl. VI.

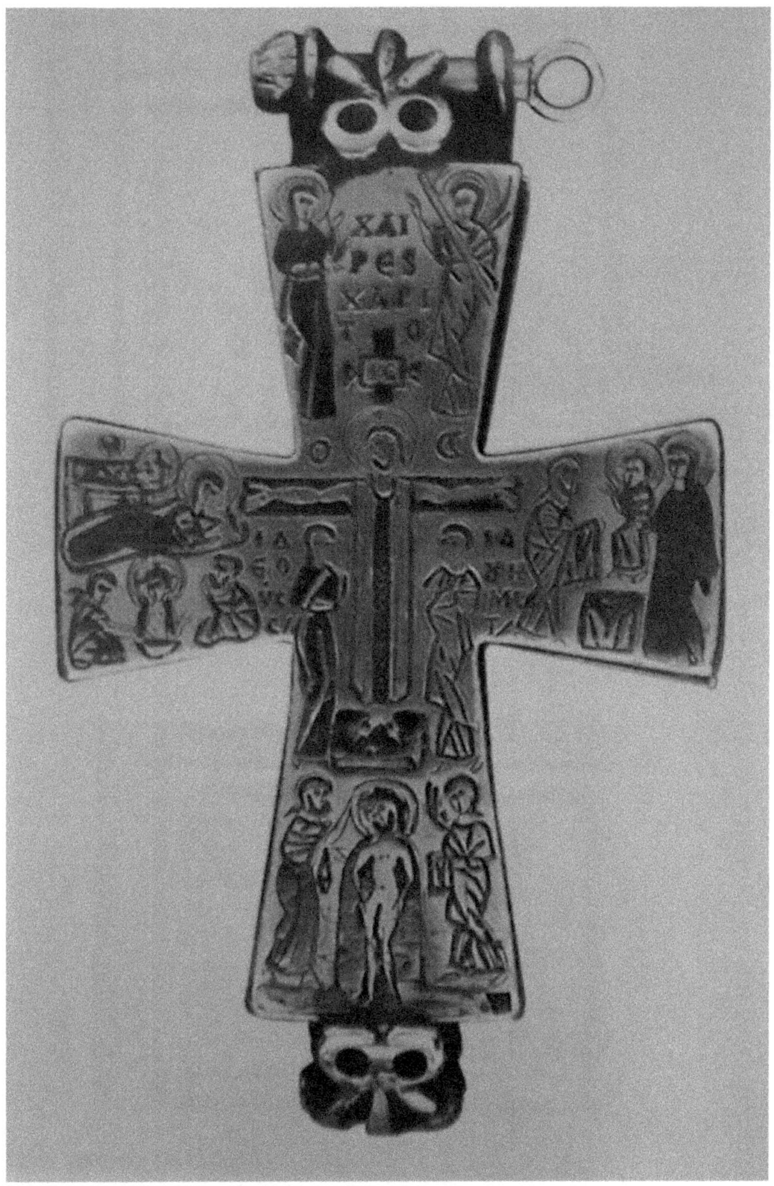

Plate 3 Vicopisano reliquary cross (Pieve di S. Maria e S. Giovanni, Pisa). Photo reproduced from Thunø (2002), fig. 5.

Plate 4a Broken Cross (Kells, Co. Meath), East face. © National Monuments Service. Department of Arts, Heritage and the Gaeltacht.

Plate 4b Broken Cross (Kells, Co. Meath), East face. © National Monuments Service. Department of Arts, Heritage and the Gaeltacht.

Plate 5 Camus (Co. Derry), East face. Photo courtesy of Alfie Hunter.

Plate 6 Arboe (Co. Tyrone), West face. Photo from Department of the Environment for Northern Ireland.

Bibliography

Arad, L. (2003) 'The Bath and the Baptism of Christ: a theological and liturgical link in Romanesque Art,' *Miscel·lània litúrgica catalana* 11, 21–44.

D'Aughton, M. (2004) 'The Kells Market Cross: Epiphany sequence reconsidered,' *Archaeology Ireland* 18, 16–9.

Hamlin, A. (1982) '*Dignatio Diei Dominici*: an element in the iconography of the Irish crosses,' in D. Whitelock, R. McKitterick, and D. Dumville, *Ireland in early medieval Europe: studies in memory of Kathleen Hughes*, Cambridge, 69–75.

Harbison, P. (1992) *The high crosses of Ireland: an iconographical and photographic survey*, 3 vols., Bonn.

Humphrey, H. (2011) *Representations of the Virgin Mary on Irish high crosses: icons, narratives and symbols of power*, unpub. Ph.D. dissertation, National University of Ireland, Galway.

James, M.R. (1924) *The Apocryphal New Testament*, Oxford.

Kitzinger, E. (1963) 'Hellenistic heritage in Byzantine art,' *Dumbarton Oaks Papers* 17, 97–115.

Leveto, P. (1990) 'The Marian theme of frescoes in S. Maria at Castelseprio,' *The Art Bulletin* 72, 393–413.

Nordhagen, P.J. (1961) 'The origin of the washing of the child in the Nativity scene,' *Byzantinische Zeitschrift* 54, 333–7.

Osbourne, J. (1981) 'Early medieval wall-paintings in the catacomb of San Valentino, Rome,' *Papers of the British School at Rome* 49, 82–90.

Porter, A.K. (1931) *The crosses and culture of Ireland*, New Haven.

Rubin, M. (2009) *Mother of God: a history of the Virgin Mary*, London.

Schiller, G. (1971) *Iconography of Christian art*, 2 vols., trans. Janet Seligman, London.

Tanner, N.P. (1990) *Decrees of the Ecumenical councils*, Washington.

Thunø, E. (2002) *Image and relic: mediating the sacred in early medieval Rome*, Rome.

van Dijk, A. (1995) *The oratory of Pope John VII (705–707) in Old St. Peter's*, Ph.D. dissertation, Johns Hopkins University.

Weir, A. (1980) *Early Ireland: a field guide*, Belfast.

PETER HARBISON

TUOTILO—ST GALL'S *UOMO UNIVERSALE*: RECONSIDERING HIS ARTISTIC OUTPUT

Abstract

Two Carolingian ivory panels decorating the covers of the *Evangelium Longum* (St Gall, Stiftsbibliothek, 53) have been attributed to an all-round craftsman named Tuotilo, and are generally dated to around AD 900 because abbot Salomo is credited with having commissioned them during the mid-AD 890s. But, because the figures of *Earth* and *Ocean* carved on one of the panels are comparable to some counterparts on Crucifixion ivories from the lifetime of the Emperor Charles the Bald (AD 843–877), this paper suggests that the St Gall figures should be derived from them and from a contemporary manuscript, and ought possibly to be dated a decade or more earlier. At the same time, around AD 880, Tuotilo may also have been decorating the walls of the monastic church with frescoes containing New Testament scenes analogous to those found on Irish high crosses, both of which presumably go back to a common pattern-book source in an atelier of Charles the Bald. Tuotilo may well have been trained in the imperial workshops in the AD 870s, and could subsequently have conformed to a pan-European pattern of artists/craftsmen abandoning them upon the collapse of artistic patronage after the emperor's death, and going to various other places including Ireland, but also possibly as far away as the court at Constantinople, where their iconography could have contributed to the illumination of the great 9th-century Byzantine manuscript of the Homilies of Gregory Nazianzen (Paris, Bibliothèque nationale de France, Gr. 510).

Keywords

St Gall, Metz; Tuotilo, Charles the Bald, Notker Balbulus, Ekkehard IV, Moengal/Marcellus, Abbots Grimald, Hartmut, and Salomo, Gregory Nazianzen; Irish high crosses, *Earth* and *Ocean,* frescoes, ivories.

Early medieval Ireland and Europe: chronology, contacts, scholarship, ed. by Pádraic Moran and Immo Warntjes, Studia Traditionis Theologiae, 14 (Turnhout, 2015), pp. 329–42.

 10.1484/M.STT-EB.5.103127

Tuotilo was a very gifted artist/craftsman who lived in the Swiss monastery of St Gall some eleven hundred years ago. Because of the Irish connections of this foundation, I had wondered whether the man's name could possibly have been originally an Irish one, such as that of Tuathal, found on a memorial stone at Clonmacnois.[1] In seeking an answer to such ponderings, I turned to Dáibhí Ó Cróinín—the one *samildánach* who knew all about the Irish scholars abroad in the medieval period. Because I had compared the name-ending with that of Tassilo, the duke of Bavaria famous for his chalice,[2] Dáibhí, in his usual kind and helpful way, consulted with a Bavarian colleague who said that *-ilo* was simply a diminutive form, which made the name more likely to be continental rather than Irish. But Dáibhí, in his light-hearted fashion, commented to me that it was a nice idea, and deserved to be right!

Another contributor to this volume, Anthony Harvey, has kindly provided me with the requisite indications that the Bavarian scholar's hint that Tuotilo was non-Irish was, indeed, correct.[3] He pointed out to me that, while Irish names when latinized were declined in the second declension, Notker Balbulus in his *Vita Sancti Galli metrica*[4] declined the name Tuotilo in the third declension—*Tuotilonem*—in the continental fashion.

It is a pity that we have to strike out the name of such a talented man as Tuotilo from amongst the ranks of medieval Irish artists and *literati* on the Continent, but we can at least content ourselves with the thought that he was taught the seven liberal arts, including music,[5] by an eminent Irishman named Moengal, otherwise known as Marcellus. Among his fellow pupils were the above-named Notker Balbulus (*c.*AD 840–912), a poet who described Tuotilo as 'the brightest of the bunch' in Anthony Harvey's inspired translation of *inter eos plane iuvenis acutissimus*.[6] This would suggest that the pair knew each other when (comparatively) young—presumably in St Gall—and probably sometime in the AD 860s or thereabouts.

1 Petrie (1872), i 25, Fig. 35 with Pl. XIV. I subsequently discovered that my musings were preceded by [Anon.] (1936), who actually gave Tuotilo the name Tuathal!

2 Haseloff (1951).

3 Compare Harvey (1999).

4 Notker Balbulus, *Vita Sancti Galli metrica* praefatio (ed. by Karl Strecker in MGH Poetae 4, 1095).

5 Duft (1991), 57.

6 Notker Balbulus, *Vita Sancti Galli metrica* praefatio (MGH Poetae 4, 1096). The translation was via personal communication.

Ekkehard IV, the author of the first continuation of the *Casus Sancti Galli* written around AD 1030,[7] describes the 'stellar trio' of Tuotilo, Notker, and one Ratpert as being of 'but one heart and one soul', and extols Tuotilo's talents as follows:[8]

> *celaturae elegans et picturae artifex, musicus sicut et socii eius; sed in omnium genere fidium et fistularum prae omnibus. Nam et filios nobelium in loco ab abbate destinato fidibus edocuit.* [...] *concinnandi in utraque lingua potens* [...] *versus et melodias facere praepotens.*
>
> 'He was a master of sculpturing and painting, like his companions a musician, but superior to all in every kind of string and wind instrument; indeed, he instructed the sons of nobility in playing the strings in a room specified by the abbot for the purpose. [...] He was well versed in poetry in both languages, [...] and he was a masterful creator of verses and melodies.'

Among his tropes was one entitled *Hodie cantandus est nobis puer* which was composed for Christmas, and his metal/goldsmithing work included a cross, a Marian altar, an *antependium* with *Christ in Glory* for Mainz, and an evangelist lectern for a church in Konstanz—in one of which, it is said, the Virgin guided his hand![9] His multiple talents led Christoph Eggenberger to give him the title of *uomo universale*, a term which only became common many centuries after his day.[10]

Ekkehard also mentions *duas tabulas eburneas*,[11] which have been interpreted as a diptych once owned by Charlemagne, one part of which was given to Tuotilo to carve on one face.[12] Goldschmidt[13] believed that

7 Ekkehard IV, *Casus Sancti Galli* 3 (ed. by Ildephons von Arx in MGH SS 2, 94). My thanks to Anthony Harvey for having provided me with this reference. See also Duft (1991).

8 Ekkehard IV, *Casus Sancti Galli* 3 (MGH SS 2, 94); translation by Duft (1991), 59. See von Schlosser (1891), 180–5 for a summary of the 19th-century discussion about the credibility of Ekkehard's description of Tuotilo. Some, sycophantically, thought that he was the greatest craftsman of the Carolingian period—and a predecessor to Leonardo da Vinci, no less—but von Schlosser and others doubted Ekkehard's veracity, as his words were written more than a century after Tuotilo's death.

9 Eggenberger *s.v.* 'Tuotilo' in *LM* 8, 1095.

10 Eggenberger (1991), 98.

11 Reference to Ekkehard IV, *Casus Sancti Galli* 1 (MGH SS 2, 88–9). Eggenberger *s.v.* 'Tuotilo' in *LM* 8, 1095.

12 See also Eggenberger (1991), 98.

13 Goldschmidt (1914–8), i 80–1, no. 163a,b with Taf. LXXV–LXXVI.

Tuotilo carved both of the faces that we see today and considered that they had in fact twice already formed a diptych before being pressed into their present service as centrepieces for the front and back covers of St Gall, Stiftsbibliothek, 53—which gets its name *Evangelium Longum* because its tall format was dictated by the height of the pre-existing ivory panels.[14] This manuscript had been commissioned by Abbot Salomo, it is thought sometime around AD 893–895,[15] so the ivories can scarcely have been carved any later than that, to which Goldschmidt added 'only a little earlier', as he dated them to the end of the 9th century (which could conceivably be construed as including the years around AD 880 suggested here).

While the main themes of the two plaques are *Christ in Glory* (as in the Mainz *antependium* above) and *The Ascension of the Virgin into Heaven* respectively (*Plates 1–2* in the Appendix), what makes them stand out from the content of other Carolingian ivories is the representation of Saint Gall with a bear, an animal which, to this day, is the symbol of the town of Sankt Gallen. But what had first attracted my attention to this pair of plaques was the presence on one of them of the late antique figures of *Earth* and *Ocean*[16] which are also present on Irish high crosses. It was, indeed, while writing a footnote to the text of an article on this very subject for the latest number of the *Journal of the Royal Society of Antiquaries of Ireland*[17] that I had turned to Dáibhí for advice on the nature of the Tuotilo name. It was also that footnote, however, that set my mind thinking about the date of these two ivories, which is normally given as being around AD 900, as Abbot Salomo is said to have commissioned Tuotilo to carve them around the mid-AD 890s for the *Evangelium Longum*, and presumably also because documentary sources record Tuotilo's presence at St Gall between AD 895 and 912, the year in or before which he is presumed to have died. But such a dating, proposed by most of the leading specialists in the field

14 Eggenberger *s.v.* 'Tuotilo' in *LM* 8, 1095; Berschin (1991), 74, caption to Ill. 23. St Gall, Stiftsbibliothek, 53 may be viewed online at www.e-codices.unifr.ch/en/list/one/csg/0053.

15 Eggenberger *s.v.* 'Tuotilo' in *LM* 8, 1095.

16 These are cosmic symbols which, according to von Schlosser (1891), 154–5, were earlier represented on a round table made specially for Charlemagne.

17 Harbison (2012).

(Goldschmidt,[18] Steenbock,[19] Fillitz,[20] Gaborit-Chopin,[21] and Marguerite Menz-Vonder Mühll,[22] among others), places the *Earth* and *Ocean* figures a quarter of a century later than most of the other Carolingian examples—in the fragmentary Sacramentary of Metz of *c.*AD 870[23] and on a number of Crucifixion ivories, such as those in the Victoria and Albert Museum in London which, in the latest evaluation by Paul Williamson,[24] would be ascribed roughly to the last decade and a half of the life of the Carolingian Emperor Charles the Bald (AD 843–877). This ascription finds support in the date *ante quem* of AD 875, when Charles gave to Pope John VIII a throne decorated with ivories which contained a figure of *Earth* analogous to those on the Crucifixion ivories,[25] and probably carved somewhere in northern France around the AD 860s. Some of the closer parallels for the St Gall *Ocean* figure, however, are found on two ivories which, like Tuotilo's, were dated by Goldschmidt to the end of the 9th century.[26] Being associated with his Liuthard group which, too, has links with northern France, this pair also hark back to works of the time of Charles the Bald, yet need not necessarily be associated directly with Tuotilo's ivories which are not connected with the Liuthard group. Both of these are *Crucifixion* ivories, whereas the St Gall panel features *Earth* and *Ocean* not with a *Crucifixion*, but with *Christ in Glory*, which finds its best parallel

[18] Goldschmidt (1914–8), i 80.

[19] Steenbock (1965), 98–100, no. 23 with Abb. 36–37.

[20] Fillitz (1969), 162, no. 99. My thanks to the late Marline von Stockhausen for having presented me with a copy of this book and the one mentioned in the previous footnote.

[21] Gaborit-Chopin (1978), 78 with 192–3, no. 72. She considers the *Earth* and *Ocean* figures to have been rather awkwardly carved.

[22] Menz-Vonder Mühll (1981). She points out that a fold on the knee of the St Gall *Gaia/Earth* finds its best parallel in an ivory dating from the time of Charlemagne (p 410), and that the figures of *Earth* and *Ocean* re-appear in the 11th-century manuscript Hildesheim, Dombibliothek, 18, 174r (p 399)—whose figure of *Ocean* closely resembles that on the St Gall ivory, both probably going back to the court school of Charles the Bald. My thanks to Sybille Schneiders of Freiburg for having provided me with a copy of the Menz-Vonder Mühll article.

[23] Facsimile edition by Mütherich (1972).

[24] Williamson (2010), nos. 44–5, and 49.

[25] See in particular Weitzmann (1971), 224–5 with Tav. XXXIX,2; he presumed that the corresponding figure of *Ocean* had been lost.

[26] Goldschmidt (1914–8), i 28, no. 44 with Taf. XXI (in the National Museum in Munich) and 54, no. 100 with Taf. XLVII (formerly in the Martin Le Roy Collection in Paris).

in a manuscript, where the wings of the Cherubim find a close comparison in the aforementioned Metz Sacramentary, thought to have been hurriedly commenced to celebrate the marriage of Charles to his second wife, Richildis, in January AD 870. Goldschmidt and others cited above also point out similarities between the figures on the ivory plaques and those of the Codex Aureus from St Emmeram (Munich, Bayerische Staatsbibliothek, Clm 14000), which is also dated to around the year AD 870.[27]

So why, then, should we continue to be dazzled by the years AD 895–912 as the approximate period of creation of our two plaques? These are, after all, merely two of the dates when Tuotilo is actually recorded as being at St Gall towards the end of his life. We know that the ivories themselves were already in existence when the *Evangelium Longum* was initiated, allegedly around AD 893/895. We know, furthermore, that Tuotilo must have been in St Gall when he recited some of his tropes in the presence of the Emperor Charles the Fat during the imperial visitation to the monastery in AD 883.[28] Steenbock considers it unlikely that the ivories were carved before that year.[29] But why? The iconographical and stylistic features of the plaques are sufficiently close to the other *Earth* and *Ocean* figures found on ivories and in the Metz Sacramentary of the later years of Charles the Bald that Peter Lasko—who, nevertheless, also dated the St Gall plaques to around AD 900—could afford to suggest that Tuotilo might well have received his training at the court of Charles the Bald in the late AD 870s.[30] But could we go back even further than that? Paul Williamson ascribes two of the *Earth* and *Ocean* plaques to the AD 860s[31] during the lifetime of Lothair II, king of Lotharingia, and suggests that they originated in Lothair's capital at Metz, after which Goldschmidt named his Younger Metz Group of Ivories[32] which encompass most of those bearing the figures of *Earth* and *Ocean*. In this connection, it is interesting to note that Ekkehard IV, writing very much later, around AD 1030, says that Tuotilo visited Metz (date

27 Compare Mütherich and Gaehde (1976), Pl. 38.

28 Duft (1991), 59. Even if the ivories were created during the AD 890s, rather than in the period around AD 880 as suggested here, it would not affect the discussion below on Tuotilo's earlier career prior to AD 883.

29 Steenbock (1965), 99.

30 Lasko (1972), 71.

31 Williamson (2010), nos. 44–5.

32 Goldschmidt (1914–8), i nos. 81–119.

unspecified),[33] and one wonders whether he could have been re-visiting the area where he first went as a young man from St Gall to start learning his craft as an ivory carver? Lothair's workshop probably declined after his death in AD 869, when his kingdom was taken over by his uncle Charles the Bald, who must have brought some of Lothair's expert craftsmen with him to his, as yet unlocalized, court somewhere in northern France, where he would appear to have continued the style of the Metz workshops. One possible explanation of the presence of *Earth* and *Ocean* on the St Gall plaques is, therefore, to suggest that Tuotilo may have left the Metz workshops when they began to decline, and returned to St Gall.

Another somewhat more likely possibility, however, is that Tuotilo may have either moved from Metz to Charles's court or actually started his artistic career at the latter, possibly some time around or after AD 870, when he may have been in his twenties or thirties. It seems improbable that he would have carved the St Gall ivories while there because, as a young—albeit multi-talented—all-rounder, he would scarcely have been allowed to carve valuable older ivories brought from St Gall which went back to the time of Charlemagne. But, at Charles's court, he could have perfected his carving craft, learned to paint and goldsmith, and could even have enhanced his poetic skills beyond what Moengal/Marcellus had already taught him—perhaps under the tutelage of the great Irish neo-platonist poet and philosopher, Johannes Scotus Eriugena, who was a close friend of the emperor's.[34] The similarities in style and content between the Swiss ivories and the products of Charles the Bald's workshops, mentioned above, might argue in favour of Tuotilo having left his fellow artists before the emperor died, to go and carve the ivories on his own at St Gall in the fashion that he had recently learned. But why would Tuotilo want to depart from the court workshops when they were at their height, and where he could participate in what was probably the most exciting artistic centre anywhere in Europe at the time?

There remains a third option as to why he may have returned to St Gall, which I consider to be the most likely one. Peter Lasko noted that, with the death of Charles the Bald in AD 877, 'the Carolingian dynasty lost its last great patron of the arts',[35] and I surmise that

[33] Ekkehard IV, *Casus Sancti Galli,* 3 (MGH SS 2, 100). Eggenberger *s.v.* 'Tuotilo' in *LM* 8, 1095.

[34] See the (apocryphal?) story about the emperor and Johannes Scotus dining together, as told in Ó Cróinín (1995), 227.

[35] Lasko (1972), 69.

Tuotilo was among those artists and craftsmen who, having become redundant and been left stranded as a result, now moved eastwards in search of work to places where their talents would have been appreciated. It was Peter Lasko, again, who suggested that Corvey and Fulda may have received some of them,[36] and Tuotilo would clearly have been welcomed back to St Gall, where he would have quickly felt at home again because of the cultural flourishing already manifest during the reign of abbot Grimald (AD 841–872). In Harbison (2012), I have suggested that the same lack of work may have caused the exodus of some (wood) carvers to Ireland (possibly at the suggestion of Johannes Scotus), where the figures of *Earth* and *Ocean* which they had brought with them were duly incorporated into the iconography of some of the Irish high crosses.

It is noteworthy that the carved panels on these Irish crosses[37] share a considerable number of New Testament scenes with a roughly contemporary set of long-vanished frescoes whose *tituli* are generally recognized as having once adorned a church in St Gall.[38] It had been built under Abbot Gozbert (AD 816–837), but its walls must have remained plain until the frescoes were added half a century later under his fourth successor, Hartmut (AD 872–883). The second half of the latter abbot's reign tallies precisely with the period when, as suggested above, Tuotilo may have been coming home to St Gall after the demise of Charles the Bald in late October AD 877. Rather than accepting the view that the frescoes were executed by an unknown artist, or by Reichenau painters who had earlier decorated Otmar's church in Grimald's time, as von Euw suggested,[39] should we not—in the scenario presented here—ascribe them to Tuotilo, who was, after all, highly

[36] Lasko (1972), 78.

[37] See Harbison (1992).

[38] These *tituli*, poetic Latin lines and couplets acting as brief captions to explain the content of biblical pictures painted above them, were copied onto folios 48v to 50v of Zürich, Zentralbibliothek, C 78 (available online at: www.e-codices.unifr.ch/en/list/one/zbz/C0078); they are edited by Ernst Dümmler in MGH Poetae 2, 480–2; see also Sennhauser (1988), for a copy of which I am grateful to Gisula Bönhof, Aarau.

[39] von Euw (2008), 95. If the Reichenau painters were decorating the Otmar church during Grimald's abbacy, the question may be asked as to why did they not do the frescoes in Gozbert's church at the same time? In his two valuable volumes, Anton von Euw accepts Salomo's commissioning of the ivory carvings for the *Evangelium Longum*, and also suggests (p 149) that Tuotilo may have been involved in decorating manuscripts as well, particularly the Evangeliary Einsiedeln, Stiftsbibliothek, 17 (405) (available online at: www.e-codices.unifr.ch/en/list/one/sbe/0017).

praised by Ekkehard IV as a master painter? Hartmut would presumably have been delighted to welcome back a multi-talented artist coming in all likelihood from the imperial workshops, whose training in painting and iconography would have made him the ideal man to decorate the church walls after they had lain bare for so long. As was presumably also the case with the Irish high cross carvings, the fresco compositions probably go back to iconographical pattern-books preserved in the schools of Charles the Bald. Because *Earth* and *Ocean* are not mentioned in the recorded *tituli*, we cannot say whether or not they featured among the frescoes, but what we do know—or presume that we know—is that Tuotilo did at least carve the two figures on one of the ivory panels, which he may well have completed at around the same time, possibly not too many years after leaving the late emperor's employ around AD 877 while the imperial workshop's details were still fresh in his mind, rather than some twenty years later after the memory of them may have dimmed when he was perhaps already in his fifties, or even sixties.

To suggest a date for the pair of ivories within a year or two of AD 880 would see Tuotilo fitting into a pan-European pattern of an exodus of artists and craftsmen abandoning the court workshops when imperial Carolingian patronage had virtually ceased after the death of Charles the Bald in October AD 877. Some (probably wood) carvers seem to have gone to Ireland to contribute to the creation of the country's great scripture crosses which, as mentioned above, also feature *Earth* and *Ocean*, and at least one of which (the Cross of the Scriptures at Clonmacnois, on which Dáibhí has worked) can be dated to no earlier than AD 879. Other craftsmen, Peter Lasko suggested,[40] went to Fulda and Corvey to carry on their work there. Those with iconographical pattern-books may, surprisingly, have decided to go even farther afield to the only other European imperial court—at Constantinople—there to offer their material to assist in the creation of the most richly illustrated of all 9th-century Byzantine manuscripts, the Homilies of Gregory Nazianzen (Paris, Bibliothèque nationale de France, Gr. 510), which contains interesting parallels with scenes on the Irish high crosses,[41] and probably also with those in the long-vanished frescoes in the church of St Gall. This

[40] Lasko (1972), 78.

[41] This notion was first mooted in Harbison (2011), 143.

codex, which Brubaker[42] has dated to between late AD 879 and 882, thus dovetails in very neatly with the period when, as argued above, Tuotilo was probably making his first major contributions to the artistic life of St Gall.[43]

[42] Brubaker (1999), 6.

[43] Since completing this article, two relevant works have come to my notice which were not originally available to me. The first is Duft and Schnyder (1984), where, on p 84, the question is posed as to whether the triple-zone design of the ivories mirrored that used in the long-lost frescoes painted on to the east wall of Gozbert's church under Hartmut, though before he became abbot in AD 872. It was, however, suggested above that the frescoes were painted at a somewhat later stage, sometime during the abbacy of Hartmut before he resigned in AD 883. Any similarity there may have been between frescoes and ivories could possibly be explained by the suggestion that Tuotilo may have executed both. The second is Tremp (2013), 41, which says that the two Tuotilo ivories were given to St Gall in AD 893/4 by Hatto I, archbishop of Mainz, as part of the estate left by the Emperor Charlemagne. Even if this means that Tuotilo did not carve the two tablets before that date, it does not invalidate the remainder of the argument put forward here that Tuotilo was involved in a workshop associated with Charles the Bald, and that he may well have painted the frescoes in the Gozbert church executed under Hartmut.

APPENDIX

Plate 1 Front cover of St Gall, Stiftsbibliothek, 53. (Reproduced with permission.)

Plate 2 Back cover of St Gall, Stiftsbibliothek, 53. (Reproduced with permission.)

Bibliography

[Anon.] (1936) 'From the hill tops,' *The Catholic Bulletin* 26, 731.

Berschin, W. (1991) 'The medieval culture of penmanship in the Abbey of St Gall,' in J.C. King and W. Vogler, *The culture of the Abbey of St Gall: an overview*, Stuttgart, 69–80.

Brubaker, L. (1999) *Vision and meaning in ninth-century Byzantium. Image as exegesis in the Homilies of Gregory Nazianzen*, Cambridge.

Duft, J. (1991) 'The contribution of the Abbey of St Gall to sacred music,' in J.C. King and W. Vogler, *The culture of the Abbey of St Gall: an overview*, Stuttgart, 57–67.

Duft, J. and R. Schnyder (1984) *Die Elfenbein-Einbände der Stiftsbibliothek St Gallen*, Beuron.

Eggenberger, C. (1991) 'The art of the book in St Gall,' in J.C. King and W. Vogler, *The culture of the Abbey of St Gall: an overview*, Stuttgart, 93–118.

Fillitz, H. (1969) *Das Mittelalter I*, Berlin.

Gaborit-Chopin, D. (1978) *Elfenbeinkunst im Mittelalter*, Berlin.

Goldschmidt, A. (1914–8) *Die Elfenbeinskulpturen aus der Zeit der karolingischen und sächsischen Kaiser, VIII.–XI. Jahrhundert*, 2 vols., Berlin, repr. 1969.

Harbison, P. (1992) *The high crosses of Ireland*, 3 vols., Bonn.

— (2011) 'An Irish stroke of European genius: Irish high crosses and the Emperor Charles the Bald,' in C. Hourihane, *Insular & Anglo-Saxon art and thought in the early medieval period*, Princeton, 133–48.

— (2012) '*Earth* and *Ocean* on Irish high crosses,' *Journal of the Royal Society of Antiquaries of Ireland* 140, 83–7.

Harvey, A. (1999) 'Some observations on Celtic-Latin name formation,' in J. Carey, J.T. Koch, and P.-Y. Lambert, *Ildánach Ildírech, A Festschrift for Proinsias Mac Cana*, Andover, 53–62.

Haseloff, G. (1951) *Der Tassilo Kelch*, München.

Lasko, P. (1972) *Ars Sacra 800–1200*, Harmondsworth.

Menz-Vonder Mühll, M. (1981) 'Die St. Galler Elfenbeine um 900,' *Frühmittelalterliche Studien* 15, 387–434.

Mütherich, F. (1972) *Sakramentar von Metz. Fragment MS Lat. 1141*, Graz.

Mütherich, F. and J.E. Gaehde (1976) *Carolingian Painting*, New York.

Ó Cróinín, D. (1995) *Early medieval Ireland, 400–1200*, London.

Petrie, G. (1872) *Christian inscriptions in the Irish language*, 2 vols., ed. M. Stokes, London.

Sennhauser, H.R. (1988) *Das Münster des Abtes Gozbert (816–837) und seine Ausmalung unter Hartmut*, St. Gallen.

Steenbock, F. (1965) *Der kirchliche Prachteinband im frühen Mittelalter von den Anfängen bis zum Beginn der Gotik*, Berlin.

Tremp, E. (2013) 'Karl der Grosse als rex philosophus,' in M. Riek, J. Goll, and G. Descoeudres, *Die Zeit Karls des Grossen in der Schweiz*, Sulgen, 38–45.

von Euw, A. (2008) *Die St. Galler Buchkunst vom 8. bis zum Ende des 11. Jahrhunderts*, St. Gallen.

von Schlosser, J. (1891) 'Beiträge zur Kunstgeschichte aus den Schriftquellen des frühen Mittelalters,' *Sitzungsberichte der Kaiserlichen Akademie der Wissenschaften zu Wien, philosophisch-historischen Classe* 123, 2. Abh.

Weitzmann, K. (1971) 'The iconography of the Carolingian ivories of the throne,' in M. Maccarrone et al., *La cattedra lignea di S. Pietro in Vaticano*, Vatican City, 217–45.

Williamson, P. (2010) *Victoria and Albert Museum. Medieval ivory carvings, early Christian to Romanesque*, London.

JACOPO BISAGNI

FLUTES, PIPES, OR BAGPIPES? OBSERVATIONS ON THE TERMINOLOGY OF WOODWIND INSTRUMENTS IN OLD AND MIDDLE IRISH

Abstract

Old and Middle Irish sources offer a rich array of terms referring to woodwind instruments. However, terms like *buinne*, *cúisech*, *cuisle*, *fetán*, *pípa*, etc. are variously translated as 'flute', 'whistle', 'pipe', 'bagpipe', and the like, seemingly without much consideration for the organological reality underlying these lexical items. This article will look at the linguistic and textual evidence relating to some of these terms, with the aim of achieving a more precise identification of the musical instruments in question.

Keywords

woodwinds, *fetán*, *cúisech*, *cuisle(nn)*, *buinne*, *psalterium*, cithara, flute, whistle, (reed-)pipe(s), bagpipes, harp; *Tech Midchúarta*, Mac Díchoíme, *Epistula ad Dardanum*; archaeomusicology, medieval organology, iconography, Irish high crosses, Cross of Muiredach.

Introduction

It is a well-known fact that no Irish written musical record exists prior to the 12th-century.[1] It is for this reason that, as eloquently put by Ann Buckley, 'it has become a commonplace to introduce this topic with a litany of apologetic negatives, expressions of regret for what is lost and what may once have existed as evidence for the practice of music in medieval Ireland'.[2] Nonetheless, once we have accepted the idea that we shall probably never know which melodies were played and sung in early

1 Cf. Buckley (2000), 165; Buckley (2005), 782–3.

2 Buckley (1995), 13.

Early medieval Ireland and Europe: chronology, contacts, scholarship, ed. by Pádraic Moran and Immo Warntjes, Studia Traditionis Theologiae, 14 (Turnhout, 2015), pp. 343–94.

 10.1484/M.STT-EB.5.103128

medieval Ireland, it is equally true that the evidence for other aspects of medieval Irish music is in fact quite plentiful.

In a nutshell, if we want to know anything at all about music in Ireland before *c.*AD 1200, we must rely on evidence of three kinds: (1) archaeological (usually consisting in the recovery of musical instruments or parts thereof); (2) iconographic (i.e. depictions of musical instruments and musicians); (3) textual (musical terminology found in Old and Middle Irish sources, anecdotal description of musical performances, etc.). Given that the first is rather scarce (at least for the period under scrutiny here, approximately AD 600–1200), and the second often poses considerable interpretative problems, it is clear that the third type will necessarily have an important role to play in this context.

While textual evidence has been explored in some detail in respect to stringed instruments by virtue of the prominent place which they occupied in medieval Irish society (as well as in narrative literature),[3] the same cannot be said for woodwinds. The present article is meant to be a contribution towards the fulfilment of this *desideratum*, with a particular focus on the terminology pertaining to this class of musical instruments.

Woodwinds

Before discussing the terminology of woodwinds in Old and Middle Irish sources, it will be useful to provide some basic information concerning this type of instrument.

In modern organological taxonomy, woodwinds are essentially flutes and reed instruments.[4] From a purely mechanical point of view, the sound of flutes is produced by an airflow which is directed against a sharp edge, while in reed instruments, the airflow is forced through a vibrating resonator, i.e. the reed. Ancient, medieval, and many traditional instruments typically use single or double reeds. In the former, the airflow triggers a rapid vibration of a single blade against a larger component. In double reeds, instead, the airflow moves through two

[3] E.g. Rimmer (1977); Buckley (1978); Sayers (1988); Buckley (2005), 750–1, 757–62.

[4] More precisely, the instruments which I will discuss in this article are edge-blown and reed aerophones, according to the well-known Hornbostel-Sachs classification of musical instruments (cf. von Hornbostel and Sachs (1914), 583–8; cf. also Baines (1967), 25–7). For more details on the classification of flutes, see Veenstra (1964).

tightly-bound blades which, if subject to a certain air pressure, start vibrating against each other.[5]

While double reeds certainly existed in Graeco-Roman Antiquity,[6] there is on the contrary lack of evidence that they were used at all in Western Europe during the early Middle Ages. It is usually posited that double reeds were re-introduced in Western Europe through contact with the Middle East at some stage during the high or even late Middle Ages:[7] a convenient *terminus ante quem* is provided by the unambiguous depiction of double reeds on folios 10r and 399r of the 14th-century German manuscript Heidelberg, Universitätsbibliothek, Pal. germ. 848 (the famous Codex Manesse).[8] It is also believed that the bore (i.e. the interior chamber of woodwinds) was predominantly cylindrical during the early Middle Ages, while the use of conical bores may be a somewhat later development.[9] The same applies to side-blown or transverse flutes, which seem to have come to Europe through contacts with Asia around the 11th or 12th century.[10] Thus, in the lack of evidence to the contrary, a working hypothesis which can be formulated for pre-Norman Ireland is that woodwinds may have belonged to three main categories: (1) duct flutes, where a 'block' (sometimes called 'fipple') creates a narrow passage for the airflow, which is directed against a sharp edge;[11] (2)

[5] For more details, see Baines (1967), 29–32, 76–90; Campbell, Greated, and Myers (2004), 75–82, 116–21.

[6] Descriptions of (double?) reeds can be found in the writings of Theophrastus (*Historia Plantarum* IV 2.1–7, ed. and trans. Hort (1916)) and Pliny the Elder (*Naturalis Historia* XVI 169–172, ed. and trans. Rackham (1940)); cf. also Baines (1967), 198–9; West (1992), 83–4; Mathiesen (1999), 198–218; Moore (2012), 36–41.

[7] Cf. Campbell, Greated, and Myers (2004), 83; Montagu (2007), 75–6; Cabiran (2010), 26, 29.

[8] This manuscript is readily available online at http://digi.ub.uni-heidelberg.de/diglit/cpg848.

[9] Munrow (1976), 8; Montagu (2007), 78. Graeco-Roman reed-pipes normally had cylindrical bores (cf. West (1992), 83), although one should note the combination of double reed and conical bore which characterizes the *calamaula* depicted on a Roman inscription (dated to the 1st or 2nd century AD) preserved in the Museo Nazionale Atestino at Este, in North Italy (cf. Gioielli (1999); Guizzi (2001–2); I owe these references to Paolo Simonazzi). It is also worth mentioning here a possible Irish exception: the 7th-century 'horn' discovered in 1791 in Bekan, Co. Mayo, has a long conical bore (193 cm), and may have been played with a reed (cf. O'Dwyer (2004), 111, 132–9). It is now hard to tell whether this instrument was played with a single or a double reed (if indeed it was a reed instrument): conical pipes with single reeds are rare, but not unattested; cf., e.g. Baines (1960), 87–9.

[10] Cf. Baines (1967), 222; West (1992), 113; Montagu (2007), 60–1.

[11] Cf. Baines (1967), 221; Montagu (2007), 53–4.

panpipes, formed by a series of end-blown flutes of different length tied together or drilled in the same block of wood;[12] (3) reed-pipes which, as we have seen, were most likely cylindrical and fitted with single reeds.

This last category offers many possible variants: a musician may play just one reed pipe, or, as it is often the case, two or three pipes may be played simultaneously. In some cases the same notes are played on both pipes, like in the North African *zummara*. In other cases, different notes are played at the same time: for instance, one of the pipes may play a single note, giving a drone, like in the Sardinian *benas* (*Plate 1*), while other instruments may have the potential for more complex polyphonic techniques (e.g. the Sardinian *launeddas*, or the Graeco-Roman *aulos/tibia*).[13]

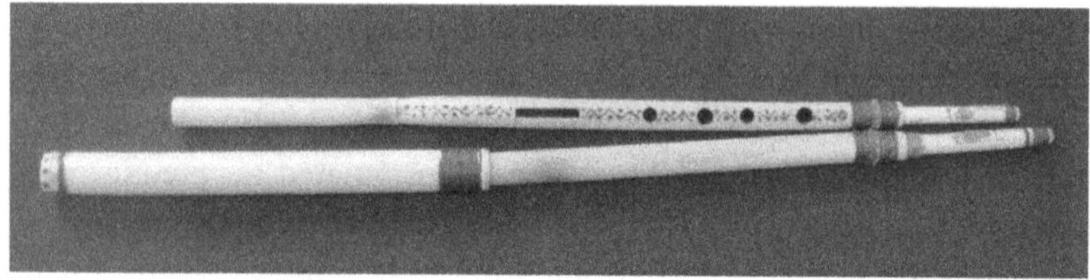

Plate 1 Sardinian *benas*, fitted with single reeds.

Some of these organological types are actually attested in the Irish archaeological record: in particular, wooden and bone whistles were found in Dublin in 13th-century sites.[14] Unfortunately, no reed-pipes have yet emerged from archaeological excavations in Ireland, but there is considerable comparative evidence from continental Europe. For instance, single and double pipes were found in 1975 at Charavines, on the shores of the Lac de Paladru, in south-eastern France.[15] Early medieval cylindrical reed-pipes (made of wood and bone) were also discovered

[12] Cf. Baines (1967), 223–4; West (1992), 109–12.

[13] For the various possible combinations of reed-pipes, see Baines (1967), 194–208. For a description of the *zummara*, see Baines (1960), 33–6. For thorough descriptions of the *launeddas* and other Sardinian reed instruments, see Bentzon (1969); Spanu (1994). For the different types of Greek *aulos*/Roman *tibia* and their functioning, see West (1992), 89–94; Mathiesen (1999), 177–222; Hagel (2010), 327–64.

[14] Cf. Buckley (1990), 45, 51; Buckley (2000), 173; Buckley (2005), 775.

[15] Cf. Bec (1992), 22; Homo-Lechner (1993); Cabiran and Dieu (2003); Cabiran (2010), 25–6.

in the Netherlands and Hungary.[16] Given the considerable diffusion of such instruments throughout early medieval Europe and their relative organological uniformity, it is reasonable to assume that analogous woodwinds also existed in pre-Norman Ireland.[17]

Research questions and methodology

Numerous mentions of musical instruments broadly identifiable as woodwinds occur in Old and Middle Irish sources; however, as I have pointed out in the introduction, while this terminology has attracted some scholarly interest,[18] it has never been thoroughly analyzed, and a number of important research questions remain open. Some of them are purely organological: for instance, can the study of terminology reveal anything about the actual shape, functioning, and playing technique of these instruments? Can we obtain even more information by investigating the possible relationship between Irish terms and designations found in contemporary Hiberno-Latin writings, or in literatures produced outside Ireland? Moreover, what is the relationship between the linguistic evidence and the actual material objects discovered by archaeologists or depicted in early Irish art? In broader terms, could a linguistic and textual approach help us understand which social connotations were ascribed to specific types of musical instruments and the musicians who played them? And finally, could this kind of study facilitate the

16 Crane (1972), 44 (§432.1), 45 (§433.1), 46 (§434.1); in the same context, cf. also Buckley (1990), 45–6. Some of these reed instruments may have been part of hornpipes, bladder-pipes, or bagpipes (cf. the following note and Zloch (2006)).

17 It is worth mentioning here that a bagpipe could of course be obtained simply by fitting one or several reed-pipes into a skin-bag (cf. Collinson (1975), 1). However, there is no direct evidence for the existence of bagpipes in pre-Norman Ireland, and even in continental Europe bagpipes began to appear regularly in iconography only from the high Middle Ages onwards (cf. Collinson (1975), 76–7; Donnelly (2001), 1–2, 5–6; Matte (2010), 9). The existence of bagpipes in ancient Rome has been inferred largely on the basis of quasi-*hapax legomena* like *utricularius* (Suetonius, *De vita Caesarum* 54 (Nero), ed. Ihm (1908), 258) and *ascaules* (Martial, *Epigrammata* X 3.8, ed. Shackleton Bailey (1990), 316), which apparently meant 'bagpiper'. Such terms are, however, both rare and controversial (cf. Baines (1960), 63–7; Collinson (1975), 42–7; West (1992), 107–9). As to the early Middle Ages, evidence is basically non-existent (cf. Baines (1960), 67–8); for the problem of the bagpipe-like instrument named *chorus*, mentioned in the Pseudo-Jerome *Epistula ad Dardanum*, see *infra*, pp. 374–82.

18 Cf., e.g. Herbert (1976), 21–30; Buckley (1990), 23–4; Buckley (2005), 749, 751–3.

reconstruction of aspects of the acoustic landscape—or 'soundscape'—of early medieval Ireland?

As already mentioned in the introduction, if we want to try to answer any of these questions we must certainly rely on archaeology and iconography, but also on linguistics and philology. As Ann Buckley conveniently summarized, medieval Irish literature 'abounds in allusions to musicians, instruments and occasions of music-making, and reveals a rich and detailed vocabulary to describe all manner of sounds. The Irish soundscape is well attested also in poetry and, not unrelatedly, the range of linguistic terminology and elaborate description in respect of 'musical' (and non-'musical') timbres, forms and instruments is considerable and varied'.[19]

Although not very common, a linguistic approach to medieval organology is not unprecedented: of particular importance is, for instance, the innovative research carried out by the Romance philologist Pierre Bec concerning the medieval Romance terminology of bowed instruments and bagpipes.[20] (My own approach in this paper owes much to his methods.)

If we want to obtain a coherent understanding of the textual evidence available to us for what concerns medieval Irish woodwinds, I suggest we should proceed as follows. To begin with, all Old and Middle Irish terms pertaining to woodwinds must be collected (i.e. names of instruments and terms used to designate or describe their sound, as well as the musicians who played them). Thankfully, this work is nowadays much facilitated by the availability of searchable on-line resources such as the *Electronic Dictionary of the Irish Language* (*eDIL*).[21]

[19] Buckley (1995), 14; cf. also Buckley (1990), 13–4.

[20] Bec (1992); Bec (1996). In his works, Pierre Bec defines his methodology as 'philologie organologique'; in particular, in his book dedicated to the medieval Romance designations of the bagpipe, he provides an illuminating description of his methodological approach, which is worth citing here (Bec (1996), 13): 'Cette enquête sur la cornemuse et ses désignations [...] correspond [...] à une double approche de l'instrument: d'une part, une étude linguistique, philologique et littéraire [...], les désignations d'instruments de musique, actuels ou révolus, n'étant qu'un aspect particulier d'une problématique plus générale qui intéresse le linguiste en tant que tel (plan du signifiant); mais aussi, parallèlement, en partant des signifiants, une approche organologique portant sur ces mêmes instruments [...]: leur typologie [...], leur spécificité acoustique, leur technique de jeu, leur présence dans les textes (théoriques et littéraires), leur impact socio-culturel, leur hiérarchie dans les représentations iconographiques et éventuellement dans l'ensemble de l'*instrumentarium* d'une époque donnée (plan du signifié)' (the same programmatic statement can be found in Bec (1992), 8–9).

[21] A very useful repertoire of relevant sources can moreover be found in Fletcher (2001), and, although outdated in its conclusions, Eugene O'Curry's *On the manners and customs of the Ancient Irish* (O'Curry (1873)) remains fundamental as a collection of interesting Old and Middle Irish passages pertaining to music and musical instruments.

It will then be necessary to provide a reliable and up-to-date account of the etymology of these terms,[22] as well as a contextual analysis of all their occurrences in texts dating from the Old and Middle Irish period. In particular, three types of occurrences are likely to yield the most interesting data from the organological point of view:

(1) First of all, the names of instruments and musicians often appear in lists, a fact which also applies to continental medieval literatures.[23] In the absence of texts providing us with an explicit classification of the Irish *instrumentarium*,[24] lists of instrumental designations may at least offer some indirect evidence for medieval taxonomic principles,[25] which of course do not necessarily correspond to modern forms of classification (even our category of 'woodwinds' may well have been completely irrelevant in medieval Ireland).

[22] The existing secondary literature is unfortunately not exempt from mistakes and misunderstandings in this field: cf., for instance, the erroneous derivation of Irish *fetán* from Latin *fistula* in Buckley (1990), 14.

[23] Lists occur especially when an author wishes to convey impressions of completeness: for instance, the (often unrealistic) presence of all sorts of musical instruments at a royal court can become a symbol of a king's power, the mention of numerous instruments played by the same individual signifies the high level of that musician's artistic accomplishments, etc. For numerous examples of instrumental lists in various medieval literary traditions, as well as for an analysis of the reasons for this phenomenon, see Bec (1992), 45–8, 119–51.

[24] I am here referring to actual categorizations of the *instruments* themselves, rather than social hierarchies of *musicians* such as the one found in the *Tech Midchúarta*, on which see below, pp. 361–3.

[25] Medieval Irish *literati* were undoubtedly familiar with the 'subdivision of music' (*diuisio musicae*) found in Isidore, *Etymologiae* III 20–22 (ed. Lindsay (1911), i; cf. also the English translation in Barney, Lewis, Beach, and Berghof (2006), 96–8), according to which music is subdivided into three categories: *harmonica* (music produced by the human voice), *organica* (music made with all types of wind instruments), and *rythmica* (music produced by string instruments and percussions). As one may expect, Isidore's taxonomy owes much to classical and late antique musical theory, such as the classification adopted by Cassiodorus (*tensibilia*, i.e. string instruments, *inflatilia*, i.e. wind instruments, *percussionalia*, i.e. percussions; cf. Cassiodorus, *Institutiones* II 5.6, ed. Mynors (1937), 144). However, it is unclear whether such writings had any major impact outside the ecclesiastic milieu, e.g. among secular musicians. There is no direct evidence that the dichotomy between loud (*haut*) and soft (*bas*) instruments ever had in pre-Norman Ireland a role comparable to that which it had in medieval France (on these notions, cf. Bowles (1954); Bowles (1958); Charles-Dominique (2006), 23–41). On the relative and culture-related nature of organological taxonomies, see Kartomi (1990), 3–15.

(2) Any passage providing a description of the sound of an instrument, or any information concerning the actual playing technique and/or performance practices will obviously have to be considered carefully.

(3) Finally, the most precious witness of all will of course be any text providing an actual description of a musical instrument, in terms of shape, structure, functioning etc. Unfortunately, as we shall see, textual evidence of this kind is exceedingly rare in early Irish literature.

A number of potential difficulties associated with this methodological approach also need to be acknowledged and discussed. First of all, it is important to keep in mind that etymology, however important, may sometimes be completely irrelevant for the identification of a 'real-world' extra-linguistic referent synchronically designated by a given lexeme: in other words, etymology may be neither the only nor the best way to understand which specific object was designated by a certain term at a particular stage of the history of the Irish language.[26]

The next problem affects all research dealing with ancient and medieval terminology of musical instruments. As pointed out by Pierre Bec, given that pre-modern terminology of musical instruments was generally far from being uniform or standardized (and it is most likely that Ireland was no different in this respect), such terms are almost invariably characterized by a high degree of *polysemy* and *polymorphism*:[27] the

[26] This methodological principle has been stated in very clear terms by Liam Breatnach (1996), 76, in the context of a discussion of the origins and meaning of the Old Irish term *file* ('poet'): 'an elementary principle which seems to have been overlooked is that the Indo-European etymology of an OIr. word is not the same as a definition of its meaning in OIr., and it is worth recalling here the careful distinction drawn by Thurneysen ((1921), 66) between an original etymological meaning [of the word *file*] 'seer' and the actual meaning in the historical period of 'educated and learned poet''. This same problem has also been addressed by Pierre Bec (1992), 17, in the specific context of medieval organology: 'l'évolution des signifiants [...] n'est jamais absolument parallèle à celle des signifiés. L'instrument évolue, devient autre et peut garder le même nom'.

[27] Cf. Bec (1992), 28–34; Bec (1996), 30–2. Bec points out how these phenomena were due, in some cases at least, to the presence of conflicting terminologies: in particular, the Latin terminology inherited from classical and Late Antiquity may have co-existed with local vernacular terms (cf. Bec (1992), 32: 'il y a une différence fondamentale entre la terminologie latine et la terminologie 'populaire': la première est plus vague, plus emblématique, plus polysémique aussi, la seconde plus technique et plus précise. Au surplus, la terminologie populaire [...] est en relation avec la *pratique* musicale, alors que la terminologie savante en latin l'est beaucoup plus avec la *théorie*').

former notion refers to the fact that one term may have been applied to a variety of instruments, while the latter involves the opposite process, whereby the same instrument may have been designated by several different names.

In addition to this, naming practices and conventions may have differed from place to place, and may have also changed over time. Finally, we cannot exclude that some authors may not have been interested in providing accurate descriptions of contemporary instruments, while some others may have been simply ignorant as to music and organology (as we shall see, this last problem also directly concerns iconography).

Fetán, *cúisech*, *cuisle*(*nn*)

It is obviously impossible to give a full account of all Old and Middle Irish terms pertaining to woodwinds in this relatively short contribution. Thus, I have chosen to present here some of the evidence available for three terms which offer much material for discussion: *fetán*, *cúisech*, and *cuisle*(*nn*).

Before looking at these terms one by one, it is worth noting on a more general level that, at least within the confines of Western Europe, broad cross-cultural tendencies can be observed in respect to the linguistic designation of musical instruments, and sometimes the designating criteria (Bec's 'critères dénominatifs') remain semantically transparent for several generations of speakers of a given language. For example, some names may refer to the acoustic quality of an instrument (e.g. English *whistle*, Italian *pianoforte*); some other names refer to the shape or structure of an instrument (e.g. English *bagpipe*, French *flûte à bec*); in some cases (somewhat less frequently) names are based on the material out of which the instrument is made (e.g. English *woodwind* or *brass*, Occitan *cabreta/chabreta* ('bagpipe', but literally 'little goat')).[28] On the contrary, some terms may be purely traditional and no longer etymologically transparent (cf. English *guitar*, ultimately deriving from Lat. *cithara* < Gr. κιθάρα).

[28] Cf. Bec (1992), 51–8; Bec (1996), 32–3. Occitan *cabreta/chabreta* is especially interesting, since here we can see how different criteria of designation may co-exist and interact: while the practice of referring to the bagpipe as 'little goat' (already attested in medieval France) was probably motivated by the actual animal skin out of which the bag is usually made, the term may have also been understood as an allusion to the sound of the instrument (cf. Bec (1996), 44–9).

The term *fetán* seems to belong to the former category, i.e. nouns whose designating criterion remains semantically transparent. *Fetán* (translated as 'musical pipe' in *DIL*[29]) is simply a diminutive of *fet*, an Old Irish term most likely deriving from Proto-Celtic **winto-* < PIE **$h_2$weh$_1$-nt-o-* (the same Indo-European form which underlies Latin *uentus* and English *wind*).[30] Interestingly, *fet* was used in the Saint Gall Priscian glosses as a translation of Latin *sibili hominum*,[31] suggesting that this term designated a hissing or whistling sound. This is confirmed by numerous occurrences in early Irish literature, where *fet* can designate, for instance, the hissing of snakes, a decoy signal used by fishermen,[32] the tweeting of birds,[33] the soughing of wind,[34] and even the sound of a sword cleaving the air.[35]

[29] *DIL s.v. fetán*.

[30] Cf. McCone (1996), 63, 107; Isaac (2007), 66; de Vaan (2008), 662–3; Matasović (2009), 423. For a different but less convincing etymology, see de Bernardo Stempel (1999), 273 n 107.

[31] Ed. Stokes and Strachan (1901–3), ii 50.33 [3a7].

[32] The last two designations are found in the following entry from O'Mulconry's Glossary (ed. Stokes (1898–1900), 259 (§527); cf. also www.asnc.cam.ac.uk/irish glossaries at OM[1] §532): *Fet .i. quia euitat* [probably for *inuitat*] [*.i.*] *dooccurethar* [for *do·cuirethar*] *.i. is bes dond nathruig, foceird fit isin tracht frissin n-escmogin* [probably for *escongain*], ⁊ *is femen a cenél sin uile,* ⁊ *dotheit docum na nathrach cotalaig,* ⁊ *focerdat ind iascaire fit friusom condagaibett* ('*Fet*, because *inuitat*, i.e. 'it invites', i.e. it is a habit for the snake, it casts a hissing/whistling sound on the strand towards the eel (?), and all of that kind is female, and it goes towards the snake to lie with it; and the fishermen cast whistles to them in order to catch them'; many thanks to Pádraic Moran for letting me use his unpublished working translation of this passage). This curious entry seems to be a conflation of information on the viper (*uipera*) and the moray eel (*murena*), ultimately derived from Ambrose, *Hexameron* V 7.18 (ed. by Karl Schenkl in CSEL 32,1, 153) and Isidore, *Etymologiae* XII 6.43 (Lindsay (1911), ii): all the elements mentioned in O'Mulconry's Glossary can be found in these two sources, including the reference to the alluring whistle used by snakes and fishermen. It is particularly interesting that the word used by both Ambrose and Isidore to refer to this sound is Lat. *sibilus*, which, as we have seen, is translated as OIr. *fet* also in the Saint Gall glosses.

[33] This attribution is found, for instance, in a quatrain attested in the *Lebor Brecc* (ed. in Meyer (1919), 66 (§151)), whose last line describes as follows the sound of a blackbird (*lon*): *is bind boc síthamail th' fet* ('your whistling is sweet, gentle, peaceful'; my translation).

[34] Cf. *fet gaíthe* ('whistling of wind') in the Middle Irish *Aígidecht Aithirni* ('The Guesting of Athirne', ed. Meyer (1914), 4–5).

[35] This sense is found, for instance, in a quatrain of *Cath Cairnd Chonaill* where Diarmait mac Áeda Sláni's sword is praised with the words *is for rígaib fo·cheird feit* ('it is on kings that [Diarmait's sword] makes a whistling sound'; ed. Stokes (1901), 214–5); for more examples, cf. *DIL s.v. fet*, col. F-99.42–4.

Given that the term *fet* was used in both Old and Middle Irish to designate this type of sound, it is most likely that the semantic link between *fet* and its lexicalized diminutive *fetán* would have been transparent, thereby helping to maintain a close linguistic association between the instrument named *fetán* and its sound: in other words, we can reasonably assume that the name *fetán* would have been exclusively or predominantly attributed to musical instruments capable of producing a *fet*.[36]

As rightly pointed out by Ann Buckley, the terminology of sounds in early Irish sources is non-specific, and is regulated by 'cognitive codes now out of our reach. References are descriptive rather than analytical, and usually emotive, metaphorical—but rarely technical or systematic'.[37] Nonetheless, the presence of extra-linguistic referents among the sounds designated by means of the term *fet* (i.e. the sound of birds, swords moving through the air, wind blowing, human whistling, etc.) allows us to conclude that *fetán* was probably used in most cases as the name of a flute rather than a reed-pipe. This view may receive some support from the fact that the *fetán* is described as *fogur-binn* ('sweet-sounding') in this passage from *Acallam na Senórach*:[38]

> *in ceol sirrechtach síde* ⁊ *an timpan téitbhinn* ⁊ *an fedán fogurbinn*
>
> 'the beguiling music of the *síd* and the sweet-stringed dulcimer and the sweet, melodious pipes'

Interestingly, *prima facie* the association with the 'sweet-stringed *timpán*' in this passage would seem to associate the *fetán* with a fairly high social status.[39] However, other texts indicate the contrary. In a Middle Irish gloss to *Uraicecht Becc*, a legal tract on status, players of *fetán* are listed among various practitioners of *fo-dána* ('base arts' or 'subordinate professions'), that is performers whose honour-price depends on that of their patrons.[40] Moreover, the term *fetánach* is used as a downright insult in

[36] The meaning 'pipe' or 'tube', listed in *DIL s.v. fetán*, is then clearly secondary and derivative (a flute being a tube-like object).

[37] Buckley (1995), 15.

[38] *Acallam na Senórach* ll. 1717–20 (ed. Stokes (1900), 49; trans. Dooley and Roe (1999), 53 (as we have seen, *fedán* should rather be translated as 'flute' here)).

[39] For the *timpán*, see Buckley (1978); Buckley (2005), 750–1. For the high social status enjoyed by the players of string instruments (especially harpists) in medieval Ireland, cf., e.g., Kelly (1988), 64–5; Buckley (2000), 170–1.

[40] The passage reads as follows (ed. Atkinson et al. (1868–1901), v 108 = Binchy (1978), vi 2281.30; cf. also Fletcher (2001), 148, 493–4; the main text of *Uraicecht Becc* is

a satirical quatrain recently edited by Roisin McLaughlin.[41] Thus, while things probably varied according to time and place, it is likely that players of *fetán* had a relatively low social status, undoubtedly lower than the position enjoyed by harpists: as we shall see, this condition probably applied to players of wind instruments in general.

Now, if on the one hand we can argue fairly confidently that *fetán* meant 'flute' or 'whistle', on the other hand its exact relationship to the term *cúisech*, which could also have meant 'flute', is far from being clear.

According to the *Lexique étymologique de l'irlandais ancien*,[42] the etymology of *cúisech* is unknown, but I suggest to understand this term as an adjective derived from *cúas* ('hollow, cavity'): *cúisech* would thus have originally meant something like 'hollowed (object)'.[43] Whereas the semantic development from 'hollowed object' to 'flute/(musical) pipe' is obvious enough,[44] the phonological and morphological details are less straightforward.

The alternance between palatal and non-palatal quality in the final consonant of the nominal base (*cúas* : *cúisech*) is not particularly worrying, given that considerable analogical confusion originated from the existence of pairs like *gábud* : *gáibthech*, where the palatalization visible in the adjective is regular (*gábud* < **gābitu-*, therefore *gáibthech*

here in bold face): ***āes ciuil*** *.i. crōnānaig* ⁊ ***airfidid*** *.i. fedānaig* ('musicians, i.e. performers of *crónán* and minstrels, i.e. players of *fetán*'). On *Uraicecht Becc*, see Kelly (1988), 64, 267, and Breatnach (2005), 315–8. In the *Uraicecht Becc* the only entertainer who has his own honour-price is the harper (cf. Kelly (1988), 64). The dichotomy between high-status harpers and lower kinds of entertainers (belonging to the *fo-dána*) seems to correspond broadly to the continental opposition between *musici* and *histriones/ ioculatores* (cf. Marchesin (2000), 96–8).

41 The quatrain reads (ed. and trans. McLaughlin (2008), 154–5 (§50)): *A fetánaig, / a chornaire, a chléraige, / a fis fon tír, / a chris cen scín, a scélaige*. ('You piper, / you horn-player, you wandering musician, / you enquiry throughout the land, / you belt without a knife, you storyteller'; as we have seen, though, *fetánach* is likely to mean 'flute-player' rather than 'piper'.)

42 Vendryes et al. (1959–) [hereafter *LEIA*], C-279, *s.v. cúisech*.

43 Cf. Russell (1990), 93: 'In general terms, [in *-ach/-ech* adjectives] the meaning of the derivative is determined by the meaning of the base. Nominally-derived bases normally mean 'having X' etc.' Thus, if indeed *cúisech* < *cúas* + *-ech*, the original meaning was 'having a cavity'. Notice that *-cúisech* and *fetchúisech* are actually recorded by Russell in his list of adjectives in *-ach/-ech* (cf. Russell (1990), 205).

44 This semantic *rapprochement* is also supported by the actual occurrence of *cúas* in a description of *fetáin* in *Togail na Tebe* l. 2225 (ed. and trans. Calder (1922), 142–3): *fetāna cūas-mōra cēolbindi* ('great-hollowed sweet-noted whistles').

< _*gābit-ākos_ or _*gābit-ikos_):[45] eventually, this situation produced historically 'irregular' fluctuations such as _delgu_ : _delgnach/delgnech_.[46]

The difference in the vocalism of the first syllable of the base and its adjective (_-úa-_ : _-ú-_) is more puzzling. One may wonder whether this phenomenon could be related to the fluctuation between _úa_ and _ú_ recorded in _DIL_ for the noun _cúasal_ ('hollow, cavity'),[47] this being perhaps due to the apparent confusion between the nominative and dative in the forms of _cúas_.[48] However, the fact that _**cúaisech_ is never attested makes this explanation difficult to accept. Given that the earliest attestations of _cúisech_ seem to occur in texts not older than the Early Middle Irish phase (i.e. in the 10th-century _Cath Almaine_ and in _Esnada Tige Buchet_[49]), _cúisech_ may reflect the Middle Irish sporadic raising of _ó_ to _ú_ between _c-_ and a palatal consonant observable in OIr. _cóis_ ('cause'), _cóic_ ('five') > MIr. _cúis_, _cúig_,[50] in which case we could posit an OIr. form _*cóisech_.[51] Here, the difference in vocalism between the adjective and its base could simply be due to the well-known fluctuation between _ó_ and _úa_ in Old Irish: while the exact circumstances under which _ó_ changed to _úa_ are still somewhat unclear, it has been pointed out by McCone that 'it would be tempting to suppose that this breaking, like that of _é_ to _ía_, originally occurred before a non-palatal consonant but, if so, there had already been considerable analogical confusion both ways by the time of Old Irish'.[52] Given that an adjective _cúasach_ ('hollow, having cavities') is also attested,[53] it is possible to imagine a situation where the two co-existing variants _cúasach/*cóisech_ > _cúisech_ (where the distribution of _úa/ó_ may have been originally conditioned by the quality of the following _s_)

[45] The block to palatalization constituted by the presence of _ā_ before the relevant consonant is removed whenever the palatal vowel following the consonant is liable to syncope (cf. McCone (1996), 117).

[46] Cf. Russell (1990), 97–8, 100.

[47] Cf. _DIL s.v. cúasal_.

[48] Cf. _DIL s.v. cúas_.

[49] For _Cath Almaine_, see below, pp. 336–7; for the occurrence of the term _cúisech_ in _Esnada Tige Buchet_, see Stokes (1904), 36 (§16).

[50] Cf. Breatnach (1994), 233 (§3.10).

[51] If not due to a scribal error, this spelling may actually be attested in Dublin, Royal Irish Academy, Stowe D iv 2, 52v, in the story 'King Eochaid has horse's ears' (ed. and trans. Meyer (1903), 47: MS _fetchoisig_, most likely standing for _fetchōisig_), on which see below, pp. 367–70.

[52] McCone (1996), 134.

[53] Cf. _DIL s.v._ 1 _cúasach_.

eventually generate a semantic distinction, the latter being lexicalized with the specific meaning of '(musical) pipe'.[54]

If this etymology is right, the term *cúisech* originally designated a tube- or pipe-like object: obviously, such a shape-based designation could have applied basically to any kind of wind instrument, and for this reason it is extremely difficult to associate *cúisech* with a specific instrumental type. Interestingly, in the *Dindshenchas* poem known as 'The Fair of Carmun', which presents an idealized account of an ancient royal *óenach*, the *cúisech* is associated with high-status instruments and musicians:[55]

> *Is iad a ada olla / stuic cruitti cuirn chróes-tholla, / cúisig timpaig cen tríamna, / filid ⁊ fáen-chlíara.*
>
> 'These are the Fair's great privileges: / trumpets, fiddles, hollow-throated horns, / pipers, timpanists unwearied, / poets and meek musicians.'

In another stanza from the same poem, *pipaí* ('pipes') and *cuslennaig* ('players of *cuislenn*'; on which see below, pp. 358–70), have a clearly much lower social status:[56]

[54] The fact that *cúisech* appears to behave as a feminine *ā*-stem suggests that the lexicalization may have proceeded from a collocation where the adjective qualified a feminine noun, such as, for instance, **cráeb chóisech* ('hollow branch'), or the like.

[55] 'The Fair of Carmun' (ed. and trans. Gwynn (1903–35), iii 18–9); *cruitti* should rather be translated as 'harpers'; moreover, Gwynn translates *cúisig* as 'pipers', but I am not aware of any other text that would support such an interpretation: thus, this term is much more likely to refer here to the instrument named *cúisech*, rather than to its players (indeed, terms for both musicians and instruments are employed in this stanza). As we have just seen, it is hard to tell whether *cúisech* meant 'flute' or '(reed-)pipe' (or whether in fact this was intended as a generic term, akin to English 'wind instruments' or 'woodwinds'). For a discussion of this passage from the *Dindshenchas*, cf. O'Sullivan (2004), 80–3.

[56] 'The Fair of Carmun' (Gwynn (1903–35), iii 20); Gwynn's translation of *cuslennaig* as 'bag-pipers' is questionable. Interestingly, this passage appears to contain the earliest attestation of the term *píp(a)* (> Modern Irish *píob*), which is of course a loan-word (cf. Herbert (1976), 27), as indicated by its initial *p*. This term belongs to a long series of terms designating pipes and bagpipes in various European languages (English and French *pipe*, Northern Italian *piva*, German *(Sack)pfeife*, etc.), all ultimately derived from Vulgar Latin/Proto-Romance **pīpa*, a noun formed from the Latin verbs *pīpāre* and *pīpīre* ('to chirp, to peep'): the term would have originally referred to a 'chirping instrument', thus most likely a flute; it later became a much wider cover term for woodwinds, as well as for various objects characterized by a long narrow cavity (cf. Bec (1996), 82–9; *LEIA* P-9). Interestingly, the Modern Irish form *píob* points to a pronunciation /pīb(ə)/ for Middle Irish *píp(a)*: the voicing of the intervocalic *p* of Vulgar Latin **pīpa* suggests that the term may have reached Ireland via Wales (either

> *Pípai, fidli, fir cengail, / cnámfhir 7 cuslennaig, / slúag étig engach égair / béccaig 7 búridaig.*
>
> 'Pipes, fiddles, gleemen, / bones-players and bag-pipers, / a crowd hideous, noisy, profane, / shriekers and shouters.'

Thus, whichever instrument the term *cúisech* may refer to in this poem, it would seem to be played by musicians of fairly high standing. However, the inherently vague semantic nature of the term *cúisech* makes it impossible to provide a definitive answer on this matter. Indeed, to complicate the picture even further, in Middle Irish texts the term *fet* is occasionally prefixed to *cúisech* in order to create what appears to be a more specific instrumental designation: *fet-chúisech* ('whistling pipe'). For instance, in the 10th-century story edited by Kuno Meyer with the title 'King Eochaid has horse's ears' (see below, pp. 367–70), the young nobleman Mac Díchoíme, son of the brother of Eochaid, king of Uí Failgi, entertains the royal household with *fetchoisig* 7 *timpānacht*, i.e. 'by playing the whistling pipe and the *timpán*'.[57]

Is this the same instrument also designated by the term *fetán* or not? This is hard to tell, but the composition with *fet* suggests at least that we may be dealing once again with a term referring to some kind of flute. As

through British Latin **pīpa* = /pība/, or directly from Welsh *pib*); we could then speculate that the term may have come to Ireland from Britain together with the import of a new instrument, which, considering the time of composition of 'The Fair of Carmun' (11th century), may well be the bagpipe (for a discussion of Middle Irish *pípa*, cf. also Donnelly (2001), 1–5).

[57] 'King Eochaid has horse's ears' (ed. Meyer (1903), 47); the translation here is my own, while Meyer's (on p 50) reads 'by piping and timpan-playing'. The term seems to refer here to the playing of the instrument, rather than to the instrument itself. The same occasionally applies to the term *cúisech* (not in composition with *fet*); cf. the poem on the beheading of John the Baptist by Mog Ruith (ed. and trans. Scarre (1910), 174 (§8)): *Do[g]nīdh Neiptis, ceōl fa bloidh, cúiseach bind asa bēalaibh* ('Neiptis used to make—a famous music!—sweet piping from her lips'); cf. the similar phrasing at p 180 (§34); it is actually unclear whether the term *cúisech* refers here to the music made with that instrument, or whether it is intended as an implicit comparison between Neiptis' whistling (or singing?) and the music usually made on a *cúisech*. This passage corresponds to a section of the Lebor Brecc homily (Dublin, Royal Irish Academy, 23 P 16, 188b) on the Passion of John the Baptist (*Pais Eoin Bauptaist*) where ll. 889–90 (ed. Atkinson (1887), 66) we find a description of the various arts practised by the two daughters of Herodias, here named as Saluisa and Neptis; the latter, in particular, is expert *oc ambrán* [sic] 7 *oc luindiucc* 7 *oc féthcusib* [sic] 7 *ciúil examail ar-chena* ('at singing, and playing tunes, and whistle-playing, and other types of music too'; my translation).

we shall see, this seems to be confirmed by a number of passages where *cúisech* appears in opposition to *cuisle(nn)*.

This last term occurs very frequently in Old and Middle Irish texts, and I believe that an interdisciplinary approach combining philology, iconography, and ethnomusicology can bring us closer to the identification of the instrumental type which was most commonly designated as *cuisle(nn)*.

This noun is characterized by allomorphism between *cuisle*, inflected as an *n*-stem, and *cuislenn*, inflected as an *ā*-stem. Karin Stüber has argued (convincingly, in my opinion) that the term was originally an *ā*-stem which later adopted the *n*-stem inflection, a view which is especially based on the fact that the term already occurs as nom. sg. *cuislen* in the Old Irish glosses on Philargyrius.[58] In the following pages I will then treat *cuislenn* as the older form, and *cuisle* as a Middle Irish derivative.[59]

In 1860, Whitley Stokes suggested to understand this term (which also means 'vein, blood-vessel, pulse') as a loanword from Latin *pulsus*.[60] This etymology is somewhat cautiously accepted in *LEIA*:[61] 'On doit certainement accepter l'emprunt au lat. *pulsus* au moins pour une partie des sens, car il est possible que deux mots se soient ici confondus.'

Now, while it would in fact be relative unproblematic to derive *cuislenn* from *pulsus* from the semantic point of view ('pulse' > 'vein, blood-vessel' > 'tube-like object' > '(musical) pipe'), this etymology is however highly questionable in terms of its phonology and morphology. In particular, it is unclear how the palatal cluster *-sl-* would result from

[58] Cf. Stüber (1998), 180 (Stüber's argument overturns what is maintained in *LEIA* C-279, *s.v. cuisle*: 'f. th. à nas., plus tard aussi *cuislen* f. th. en *-ā*'). In the Philargyrius glosses (Stokes and Strachan (1901–3), ii 48.17; cf. also 363.16, where the manuscript presents the garbled reading *cüis lenus*), *cuislen* occurs as a translation of Lat. *stipula*, from Virgil, *Eclogue* III 25–27 (ed. Geymonat (1973), 13; trans. Day Lewis (1999), 11): *cantando tu illum? aut umquam tibi fistula cera / vincta fuit? non tu in triviis, indocte, solebas / stridenti miserum stipula disperdere carmen?* ('*You* beat him at music? Have you ever owned a set / of reed-pipes waxed together? You amateur, puffing a scrannel / tune on a squeaky straw at the crossroads is more your mark!') Thus, *cuislen* was here identified by the glossator as the appropriate term for a humble, rustic wind instrument (a 'squeaky straw'!).

[59] Although *cuislen* (with single *-n*) is the spelling found in the Philargyrius glosses, the unlenited quality of the nasal must be assumed on the basis of Mac Neill's Law: I will therefore consistently write this term as *cuislenn* (as it is indeed more often attested) rather than *cuislen*.

[60] Cf. Stokes (1860), 47: 'Cuisle is a fem. stem in *n*, and perhaps derived (by the frequent change of *p* into *c*) from Lat. pulsus.'

[61] *LEIA* C-280, *s.v. cuisle*.

the obviously non-palatalising environment of Lat. *pulsus*; the inflectional class of *cuislenn* would also be puzzling in this context, irrespective of whether one considers it as an original *n*- or *ā*-stem.[62]

I would like to suggest here an alternative etymology. First of all, the lack of assimilation of *-sl-* to *-ll-* indicates that this word was created/introduced in Celtic after the Proto-Celtic phase,[63] or, alternatively, that the consonantal cluster in *cuislenn* may be the outcome either of Irish syncope or of a metathesis *-ls-* > *-sl-*. If we proceed on the basis of this last working hypothesis, *cuislenn* could be the regular outcome of Proto-Irish forms like **kulsinā/*kulsīnā* or **kolsinā/*kolsīnā*. The former seems particularly appropriate, given that we could recognize in **kulsinā/*kulsīnā* an ultimate reflex of the zero-grade of PIE **keh*$_2$*ul-* ('stalk, stem (of a plant)') (i.e. **kh*$_2$*ul-* > Proto-Celtic **kul-*).[64] A suffix *-īnā* forming denominative nouns is attested in Celtic (cf. OIr. *buiden* ('(armed) company') < **budīnā*);[65] **kuls-īnā* could then be based on a noun formed with an *s*-suffix, i.e. **kul-s-o-s* or **kul-s-ā*.[66] We would then have a regular development **kul-s-īnā* > **kuls'ina* > **kuls'ena* > **kuls'en* > OIr. *cuislenn* (by metathesis + MacNeill's Law) > MIr. *cuisle*

[62] Although some Latin loanwords are inflected as *ā*-stems 'even where they have a different flexion in Latin' (Thurneysen (1946), 574 (§925)), analogical pressure is usually the likely cause for the shift (cf. *croch*, fem. *ā*-stem in spite of being from Lat. *crux*, probably due to analogy on nouns like *cloch* ('stone'), as suggested by Thurneysen (1946), 574 (§925)). Moreover, the ending *-enn* in *cuislenn* would in any case remain unexplained.

[63] For Proto-Celtic *-sl-* > *-ll-*, cf. McCone (1994), 68 (§3.5); Schrijver (1995), 433; McCone (1996), 46.

[64] Cf. Schrijver (1991), 268–9; Matasović (2009), 196. PIE **keh*$_2$*ul-* > Proto-Celtic **kawlā* survives in OIr. *cúal* ('faggot, bundle of sticks') and *cúalne* > *cúaille* ('stake, pole') (singulative of *cúal*; cf. de Bernardo Stempel (1999), 364).

[65] Cf. *LEIA* B-114, *s.v. buiden*; de Bernardo Stempel (1999), 459.

[66] The zero-grade of the root is not particularly problematic, in view of forms such as **b*^{h}*r-s-o-s* > OIr. *barr* ('top, end') (cf. de Bernardo Stempel (1999), 260 n 4). As for intervocalic *-ls-*, according to Pedersen (1909–13), i 429, this cluster assimilated to *-ll-* 'in sehr alter Zeit'; however, he did not provide any example of this sound change from Celtic, and Jackson (1953), 540 (§127), pointed out that 'good examples are lacking from British'. In the lack of clear evidence pointing to the contrary, it is possible that *-ls-* did not, in fact, assimilate in Celtic (for the preservation of this cluster—perhaps due to analogy—in several Greek forms, cf. Sihler (1995), 218 (§229)). In forms like *mell* ('error') < **melsos*, the final *-ll* could be the result of a simplification of the post-apocope cluster *-ls*, inadmissible in auslaut in Old Irish (the geminated spelling would then simply indicate the unlenited nature of the liquid). It is worth noting that the outcome of both **kul-s-o-s* and **kul-s-ā* would have been indistinguishable from *coll* ('hazel-tree') < Primitive Irish **kollah* < Proto-Celtic **koslos* (on which cf. McCone (1996), 46; Matasović (2009), 218) after the Irish apocope (**kulsos*, **kulsā* > **kulsah*, **kulsa* > **kols* > *coll*).

(by transfer to *n*-stems).[67] Although some aspects of this derivation are necessarily *ad hoc*, **kulsīnā* is nevertheless attractive from the semantic point of view, given that reeds and simple reed-pipes are indeed often made from the stalk of certain plants.[68] If this etymology is correct, then the meanings 'vein' and 'pulse' must be secondary ('pipe made from a stalk' > 'pipe-like object' > 'vein, blood-vessel' > 'pulse').

In any case, it is most likely that the designating motivation underlying *cuislenn* would have been no longer transparent in Old Irish (unlike the already discussed *fetán*): for this reason, even this new etymology of *cuislenn* does not reveal much about the specific instrumental type which was designated by this term during the period AD 600–1200. Early Irish literature, however, provides us with relatively abundant evidence concerning this musical instrument and the musicians who played it: in particular, several Old and Middle Irish texts inform us on the social status of the *cuislennaig* ('players of *cuislenn*').

In a description of the physical (and consequently social) collocation of individuals of various ranks and conditions within a royal hall, the 8th-century legal tract *Críth Gablach* prescribes the relatively low status of the *cuislennaig* by placing them in the south-east corner of the hall, together with other low-ranking entertainers (horn-players and acrobats), and further away from the king than the *cruitti* ('harpers').[69]

[67] An alternative explanation may entail a derivation of *cuislenn* from an adjective **kul-s-i-no-s/-nā*, possibly based on a hypothetical *i*-stem **kul-s-i-* (cf. de Bernardo Stempel (1999), 459).

[68] Several interesting typological parallels can be found in Latin, Romance, and Old Irish: for instance, the name of the above-mentioned Sardinian instrument known as *benas* derives from Lat. *auēnās* (acc. pl.), literally meaning 'oats' (the stalk of this plant can be easily fashioned into a pipe; cf. Spanu (1994), 132–3); indeed, *auēna* can already be found in the sense of 'reed-pipe' in Latin literature (most famously in Virgil, *Eclogue* I 2); cf. also the use of Lat. *stipula* ('stalk, straw') mentioned at n 58 above. Moreover, OIr. *buinne* ('sprig, stalk, sapling') is used twice in the Old Irish glosses to translate Latin terms for woodwinds: *tibia* (literally 'shin-bone') at Stokes and Strachan (1901–3), i 577.19 (Wb. 12c41), and *cicuta* (literally 'hemlock') at Stokes and Strachan (1901–3), ii 46.24 (Philargyrius).

[69] Cf. *Críth Gablach* 46 (ed. Binchy (1941), 23; my translation): *cu[i]slennaig, cornairi, clesamnaig i n-airthiur foitsi* ('players of *cuislenn*, horn-players, acrobats in the south-east'). Significantly, on the other side of the hall (i.e. in the north-eastern corner), in a position corresponding symmetrically to that of the entertainers, we find forfeited hostages in fetters. The placement of *cuislennaig* together with horn-players and acrobats matches perfectly (with the addition of players of *pípaí*) a Middle Irish gloss to a quotation from an Old Irish legal tract found in Dublin, Trinity College, 1337 (*olim* H.3.18), 874 (ed. and trans. Fletcher (2001), 152, 496): *Daernemid tra .i. fodana na graid si tuas 7 comeneclainni iat 7 na pipairedha 7 na clesamnaigh 7 na cornaireda 7 na cuislennaig* ('These are the base, that is, inferior professions, and they are entitled

A similar seating arrangement can be found in the short Old Irish tract on status *Lánellach tigi rích ocus ruirech*, where the *cuislennaig* are placed together with horn-players and charioteers.[70] In a similar context, players of *cuislenn* are also mentioned among various other performers in a series of Middle Irish texts describing the *Tech Midchúarta*, the ancient banqueting hall of Tara. In these texts, the banqueting hall effectively becomes an idealized allegorical representation of the structure of medieval Irish society, social ranks being indicated by the combination of two factors, i.e. the seating arrangement in the hall and the cut of meat assigned to each individual.[71] The texts which are most relevant in the present context are: (1) the poem *Suidigud Tige Midchúarta*;[72] (2) a diagram representing the seating-plans of the *Tech Midchúarta*;[73] (3) a section of the *Dindshenchas* poem *Temair toga na tulach*.[74]

to the same amount of honour-price as the pipers and the jugglers/tricksters/acrobats and the horn players and the *cuisle* players'); cf. the above-mentioned inclusion of the *fetánaig* among practitioners of the *fo-dána* ('inferior professions').

[70] Cf. *Lánellach tigi rích ocus ruirech* 14 (ed. and trans. O Daly (1962), 83–4): *Ar-sesatar cornairi áraith cuslennaich airthiur* ('The horn-blowers, charioteers, and flute-players sat in the front part (of the house)'; O Daly's translation of *cuslennaich* as 'flute-players' must of course be taken *cum grano salis*, and *airthiur* can also mean 'in the east').

[71] The complex relationship between the texts belonging to the *Tech Midchúarta* tradition has been recently reassessed in Downey (2010). For an overview of various medieval traditions (including the Irish) where the dining table functions as a symbolic representation of human society, cf. Montanari (2012), 217–37. Cf. also Herbert (1976), 27–8; Sayers (1988), 373–4; Buckley (1995), 36–8; Buckley (2000), 170–1; O'Sullivan (2004), 88–95.

[72] The poem is found in four manuscripts: (1) Dublin, Trinity College, 1339 (Book of Leinster), 29b; (2) Dublin, Trinity College, 1318 (Yellow Book of Lecan), cols. 245.37–247.4; (3) London, British Library, Egerton 1782, 45v–46r; (4) Dublin, Royal Irish Academy, B iv 2, 130v–132r. I have used the edition of the poem from the Yellow Book of Lecan, found in Petrie (1839), 199–204, and the diplomatic edition from the Book of Leinster, found in Best, Bergin, and O'Brien (1954–67), 117–20 ll. 3702–89. For more details, cf. Fletcher (2001), 469–70, 593–4; Downey (2010), 8–9.

[73] Two copies of the diagram exist, differing from each other in many details: (1) Dublin, Trinity College, 1339 (Book of Leinster), 29a (ed. Petrie (1839), 205–11, reproduced in Plate 8; Best, Bergin, and O'Brien (1954–67), 116); (2) Dublin, Trinity College, 1318 (Yellow Book of Lecan), cols. 243–4 (reproduced in Petrie (1839), Plate 9). For more details, cf. Fletcher (2001), 467–9, 592–3; Downey (2010), 16–8.

[74] This poem is labelled 'Temair III' in Gwynn's edition (Gwynn (1903–35), i 14–45). The relevant section of the poem (ll. 149–80) consists of eight quatrains listing the guests who attend the *Tech Midchúarta* of Tara (Gwynn (1903–35), i 24–7; cf. also Fletcher (2001), 197, 521; Downey (2010), 19–24).

In the poem *Suidigud Tige Midchúarta*, the quatrain mentioning the players of *cuislenn* reads as follows:[75]

> *Cuslennaig féil fidchellaig / i n-airidiu airthir / is colptha cóir cia firt gleis / fora meis scuirther*
>
> 'Good players of *cuislenn*, chess-players, / in the eastern *airide*. / A proper shank is given for their skill, / is put for them on their dish.'

First of all, it is worth noticing the correspondence between the eastern placement of the *cuislennaig* in this poem and the analogous collocation found in the Old Irish poem *Lánellach tigi rích ocus ruirech*:[76] this suggests that the Middle Irish *Tech Midchúarta* tradition may present partial re-elaborations of earlier texts. In other quatrains of the same poem, the same portion which is here assigned to *cuislennaig* and chess-players (*colptha*, i.e. 'shank')[77] is given to jugglers (*clessamnaig*) and buffoons (*fuirseóiri*),[78] and also to the druid and the *aire déso* ('lord of vassalry').[79] While *prima facie* it may seem surprising that humble entertainers receive the same portion as a lord, things become clearer if we look at the diagrams showing the actual seating plans: in both manuscript versions of the diagram, guests are seated in four rows, two on each side of the fire which is in the middle of the hall. As pointed out by Máirín O Daly, low-ranking individuals are mostly placed in the inner rows, so that, being nearer to the fire, they 'were liable in stormy weather to suffer from their proximity to the smoke-hole above the fire'.[80] Thus, while in the

[75] *Suidigud Tige Midchúarta* ll. 3762–5 (Book of Leinster copy, ed. Best, Bergin, and O'Brien (1954–67), 119; trans. (slightly adapted) from Petrie (1839), 202–3). The term *airide* seems to refer to a group of seats.

[76] Cf. n 69 above.

[77] In his discussion of the distribution of portions in the *Tech Midchúarta*, Fergus Kelly (1997), 358, writes: 'The most important guests are entitled to the best cuts [of pork], such as the *loarg* 'haunch' or the *lónchrúachait* 'tenderloin steak'. Those of somewhat lower status get the *colpthae* 'shank' or the *leschrúachait*, which is probably to be identified with the centre-cut loin steak. Low-ranking persons get such inferior cuts as the *milgetan* 'belly', the *dronn* 'chine', or *remur n-imda* 'shoulder fat'.'

[78] The quatrain mentioning jugglers and buffoons is not found in the Book of Leinster version of the poem.

[79] Cf. Kelly (1988), 27: 'The law-texts distinguish a number of grades of lord, and differ slightly in their arrangement of them. There is, however, agreement in placing the *aire déso* at the bottom of the list. He is clearly the typical lord—his title simply means 'lord of vassalry' (*déis*).'

[80] O Daly (1962), 82 (also cited in Downey (2010), 18).

Book of Leinster version of the diagram a shank is equally assigned to *cuislennaig*, chess-players (*fidchellaig*), jugglers (*clessa[m]naig*), seers (*fádi*), druids (*druid*), conjurers (*commilid*[81]), lords of vassalry (*airi desa*) and poets of the fifth grade (*doss*[82]), these categories are nonetheless set apart by their seating position: the first three categories sit in the inner rows, while the remaining five sit in the outer rows, being of higher rank.[83]

The *dindshenchas* poem *Temair toga na tulach* does not contradict this arrangement:[84]

> *Drúth, fidchellach, fuirseóir fáen, / cuislendach, clesamnach cláen, / colpa a cuit feóla iar fír, / in tan tigdís i tech ríg.*
>
> 'Jester, chess-player, sprawling buffoon, / piper, cheating juggler, / the shank was their share of meat in truth, / when they came into the king's house.'

In a nutshell, whenever we find a mention of the *cuislennaig*, both legal tracts and texts belonging to the *Tech Midchúarta* tradition agree in classifying this category of musicians among low-ranking entertainers.[85] It seems then worth asking why that was the case: could it be that the low status attributed to the *cuislennaig* was a direct consequence of some specific feature of their instrument, or of its playing technique?

Interestingly, in several different cultural and historical contexts, a distinctive feature which is often associated with players of wind

[81] Cf. *DIL s.v.* 2 *comal.*

[82] Cf. *DIL s.v.* 2 *dos.*

[83] A similar situation can be found in the Yellow Book of Lecan version of the diagram: among those who receive a *colptha*, players of *cuislenn*, chess-players, and buffoons (*fuirseoire*) sit in the inner rows, while seers, druids, conjurers sit in the outer rows (poets of the fifth grade and lords of vassalry receive here different cuts of meat).

[84] *Temair toga na tulach* ll. 165–8 (ed. and trans. Gwynn (1903–35), i 26–7; nobody else receives the shank in this poem). Cf. also the interesting discussion of the terms *caisleóir* and *bonnaire* (occurring at ll. 170–1) in Downey (2010), 22–3. (I wish to thank Clodagh Downey for providing me with her unpublished notes on the term *buinnire*.)

[85] In both versions of the diagram, among entertainers sitting in the inner rows only the *braigetóiri* ('farters') receive a cut of meat of quality clearly lower than the shank (i.e. *remur n-imda* ('shoulder fat')). Of course, practices may have occasionally varied, as pointed out by Fergus Kelly (1988), 64 n 198: '*Bretha Nemed déidenach* (*CIH* 1117.41 = *Ériu* 13 (1942) 23.2) disagrees with *U[raicecht] B[ecc]* in including the piper among the professionals who have their own honour-price (*eneclann*)'.

instruments, especially if reed-sounded, is the facial distortion caused by the need to blow air into them at a high pressure: this is especially prominent in the case of folk reed-pipes, which are often played with the technique known as 'circular breath', whereby the musician creates a small air reservoir in the mouth by puffing out his or her cheeks, as this allows to blow air into the instrument while at the same time breathing in new air through the nose (the result of this being a potentially endless uninterrupted sound—very much like what happens in a bagpipe).[86] Such a facial distortion has sometimes been perceived as grotesque and undesirable: in particular, according to a well-known classical story, Athena threw away the wind instrument she had just invented, after seeing in the water a reflection of her own distorted face.[87] To give yet another example, in 17th-century France the perceived ugly appearance of musicians who played mouth-blown bagpipes eventually drove pipemakers to introduce a new system, whereby the bag of the instrument was inflated by means of a bellows placed under the player's arm.[88]

Given the well-known medieval Irish tendency to correlate physique and rank (especially in regard to kingship),[89] it is not unreasonable to think that the puffed-out cheeks of a piper may have been regarded as indicators of low status. Some early Irish texts seem to support this view:

[86] Cf., e.g., Montagu (2007), 75; Moore (2012), 42–5.

[87] Cf., e.g., Ovid, *Fasti* VI 697–702 (ed. and trans. Frazer (1931), 372–3): *prima, terebrato per rara foramina buxo, / ut daret, effeci, tibia longa sonos. / uox placuit: faciem liquidis referentibus undis / uidi uirgineas intumuisse genas. / 'ars mihi non tanti est; ualeas, mea tibia' dixi: / excipit abiectam caespite ripa suo* ('I [Athena] was the first, by piercing boxwood with holes wide apart, to produce the music of the long flute. The sound was pleasing; but in the water that reflected my face I saw my virgin cheeks puffed up. 'I value not the art so high; farewell, my flute!' said I, and threw it away; it fell on the turf of the river-bank'; the Latin term *tibia*, here translated as 'flute', is more likely to correspond to Greek *aulos*, a reed instrument).

[88] Cf. Borjon de Scellery (1672), 5 (my translation): *comme il falloit soufler pour joüer de cet Instrument, & que cette fatigue estoit accompagnée d'une tres-mauvaise grace, afin de le rendre autant commode qu'agreable, on a trouvé le secret dépuis 40 ou 50 années, d'y ajoûter un souflet que l'on a emprunté des orgues, par le moyen duquel on le remplit d'autant d'air que l'on veut* ('since blowing was necessary to play this instrument, and given that this effort was accompanied by a very bad appearance, in order to make its playing comfortable as well as pleasant, the secret has been known for forty or fifty years, which consists in adding a bellows, borrowed from organs, by means of which the instrument can be filled with air as much as one wants'). Cf. also Charles-Dominique (2006), 186.

[89] Cf. Kelly (1988), 19: 'A king is expected to have a perfect body, free from blemish or disability. The sagas provide a number of instances of a king losing his kingship through some disfigurement'; cf. also Kelly (1988), 94: 'Physical disabilities may also limit a person's legal capacity or responsibility'.

in the legal tract *Miadślechtae* it is stated, in respect to the entertainer referred to as *réimm* ('contortionist'), that 'every man who brings distortion on his body and face is not entitled to honour-price, because he goes out of his proper form before hosts and crowds'.[90] Moreover, a passage found in both the *Irish Triads* and *Bretha Nemed Toísech* specifies 'three things which confer status on a *crossán* ('jester'): distending his cheek, distending his bag, distending his belly'.[91] It is perhaps not a coincidence, then, that players of triple pipes are often represented with prominent puffed-out cheeks in medieval Irish art.[92]

If the distended cheeks of the performer were indeed at least one of the reasons why the *cuislennach* was considered as a low-ranking entertainer, this element may suggest that the term *cuislenn* predominantly designated a reed instrument. This supposition receives some support from a number of Middle Irish texts which present interesting organological hints.

In a story found in the Fragmentary Annals of Ireland, the king Fergal mac Maíle Dúin decides to test his two sons, who had come to visit him, by spying on their behaviour during the night. While the younger son, Níall, spends the night with nobility and restraint, listening to *cruitireacht ciúin bind* ('sweet, quiet harp playing') and songs of praise to the Lord, the elder son, Áed, is entertained in a rather different fashion:[93]

> *Rá bhattur fuirseoiri ⁊ cainteadha ⁊ eachlacha ⁊ oblóiri ⁊ bachlaigh ag beceadhoig ⁊ acc buireadhaigh ann. Dream ag ól, ⁊ dream 'na ccodladh, ⁊ dream og sgeathraigh, dream occ cusleannaigh, dream oc featcuisigh. Timpanaigh ⁊ cruithiri og seanmaimh; dream og imarbhaghadh ⁊ oc reasbagaibh.*

[90] *Miadślechtae* (ed. Atkinson et al. (1868–1901), iv 354; trans. from Fletcher (2001), 497): *nach fer dobeir remmad fo corp ⁊ a enech ni dligh dire uair teit asa richt ar beluib slúagh ⁊ sochaidhe.* On *Miadślechtae*, cf. Kelly (1988), 267; Breatnach (2005), 264–5).

[91] Triads of Ireland 116 (ed. Meyer (1906), 16 (= Binchy (1978), vi 2220.2); trans. from Kelly (1988), 64–5; cf. also Fletcher (2001), 157, 460, 500; Harrison (1988), 300–1): *Tréde neimthigedar crossán: rige óile, rige théighe, rige bronn.* It is unclear what the word 'bag' means here: Fergus Kelly (1988), 65 n 203, has suggested that '*tíag* 'bag' (Latin *theca*) may refer to the inflated bladder brandished by the jester, or possibly to his testicles—he may distend his scrotum for comic effect'.

[92] Cf., e.g. Buckley (1990), 46; Ramsey (2002), 29, 34; Buckley (2008), 26–8, 37.

[93] Fragmentary Annals of Ireland §177 [AD 721] (ed. and trans. (slightly adapted) from Radner (1978), 60–1; Radner translated the term *timpanaigh* as 'drummers'; the *timpán* was, however, a string instrument (cf. n 39 above)). This story is also discussed in Buckley (1995), 46–7.

'There were buffoons and satirists and horseboys and jugglers and oafs, roaring and bellowing there. Some were drinking, some sleeping, some vomiting, some piping, some whistling. *Timpán*-players and harpers were playing; a group was boasting and arguing.'

Rather than being the realistic depiction of a musical performance, the list of musicians found in this passage is probably rather aimed at conveying an impression of loud noise and chaos: many kinds of instruments and sounds can be here heard simultaneously, without any order or sense.[94] However, by compiling this list, the author also provided us implicitly with a series of instrumental categories. In particular, it is clear that both wind and string instruments are played at the feast. Within the former category, the terms *cusleannaigh* and *featcuisigh* (here used as verbal nouns, cf. p 357 above) represent a minimal example of contrastive taxonomy:[95] in other words, they are likely to refer to the playing of different instruments and, as a consequence, perhaps also to different types of sound. Given that, as we have seen, *fet-chúisech* almost certainly designated some kind of flute, it is tempting to take this terminological opposition as an additional indication that, conversely, the *cuislenn* may have been a reed-pipe.

The same opposition can be found in the 10th-century *Cath Almaine*, the story of the battle of Allen which occurs, like the previous source, in the Fragmentary Annals of Ireland. The night before the battle, King Fergal asks Donn Bó (a Connachta man of great nobility and skill, loved and respected by all the people of Ireland) to entertain the troops:[96]

'Déna airfideadh dúin, a Doinnbó, fo bith as tú as deach airfidhidh fail i nEirinn, .i. i cúisigh agas i cuisleandoibh ⁊ i cruitibh ⁊ randaibh ⁊ raidseachoibh ⁊ righshgealaibh Eireann, ⁊ isin madin si imbarach do beramne cath do Laignib.'

"Entertain us, Donn Bó, for you are the best musician in Ireland, with flutes and piping, and with harps and poems and talk and royal stories of Ireland, and tomorrow morning we give battle to the Laigin."

94 The literary *topos* of the 'instrumental series' as a means of evoking 'l'euphorie collective d'une grande fête' is discussed in Bec (1992), 70–3.

95 I borrow this notion from Pierre Bec's 'typologie contrastive' (cf. Bec (1992), 297–304).

96 Fragmentary Annals of Ireland §178 [AD 722] (Radner (1978), 68–71; cf. also Ó Riain (1978), 5 §6).

The completeness of Donn Bó's artistic accomplishments is here shown by the accumulation of instruments and other forms of entertainment. What is especially interesting in the present context, though, is that once again *cúisig* and *cuislenna* clearly belong to two distinct categories. At this point, one may legitimately wonder whether we could posit a terminological dichotomy reflecting a basic instrumental taxonomy whereby the *fetán*/(*fet*)*c*(*h*)*úisech* ('flute, whistle') was distinguished from the *cuislenn* ('reed-pipe').

Some further indications in favour of this interpretation can be found in a Middle Irish text which has attracted very little scholarly interest so far, in spite of being unusually rich in organological details: the already-mentioned story of Mac Díchoíme, which is found, to my knowledge, in a single manuscript, i.e. Dublin, Royal Irish Academy, D iv 2, 52va–53vb. The story was edited in two separate articles: the first half was published by Kuno Meyer in 1903 with an English translation, while the second half was edited and translated into German by Rudolf Thurneysen in 1933; both editors agreed in dating this text to the 10th century.[97]

The part of the tale edited by Meyer centres on the young nobleman (and able musician) Óengus Mac Díchoíme, who falls into a wasting sickness caused by the heavy secret that he must keep: indeed, he has come to discover that his uncle Eochaid, king of Uí Fáilge, has horses' ears (a blemish which, if revealed, would make Eochaid unsuitable for kingship). One day, while crossing a desolate moor, Mac Díchoíme falls upon his face: three streams of blood flow from his lips and nostrils, so that the secret flows out of him, and he is immediately cured. After a year, while crossing the same moor, Mac Díchoíme finds out that three saplings have grown from the three streams of blood. Some time after that, a famous harper, who was travelling from Munster to come and see King Eochaid, overhears the three saplings talking to each other, saying: 'Eochaid, the man of the shield, has two horses' ears'. As one may expect, the harper later reveals the secret in front of the king's court, but, curiously enough, the people of Uí Fáilge decide not to reject their king, and the king spares the harper's life. Mac Díchoíme then makes a double pipe (*cuislenn dégabail*) from the three saplings, and later becomes king after Eochaid's death. Significantly, this part of the tale closes with the important remark that 'though he had become king he did not part

97 The section of the story edited by Meyer was also discussed, re-edited, and translated into Italian in Bolelli (1950), 43–73.

from his pipe',[98] suggesting that this was perceived as an unusual behaviour (after all, as we have seen, *cuislennaig* had a low social status).

In the part of the story published by Thurneysen, Mac Díchoíme, who in the meantime has become a good and just king, never parts from his pipe (here interchangeably referred to as *cuisle(nn)* or *buinne dégabail*), which possesses magical virtues (it can be heard from a great distance, and animals which hear its sound triple the amount of milk that they yield).[99] One day, however, he kidnaps a girl who was a servant of 'the old Brigit', daughter of Domma (*Sen-Brigid ingen Domma*), and refuses to release her. The old Brigit then begs Saint Brigit to help her recover the girl: thus, the saint cunningly asks the king to liberate the girl, or, alternatively, to give her his double pipe, secretly knowing that Mac Díchoíme will not survive nine days without his beloved musical instrument. Of course, everything happens as foretold: the king dies of anguish, so that Saint Brigit obtains both the girl and the pipe. At this point, we come to the most interesting section of the text, that is a description of the pipe and its destiny:[100]

> *Is [s]i tra cathbuadach noem-Brigdi in chuissle sin Meic Dichoeme, do·ronadh don run. At·berat araile dano conad buinne tregabail do·ronadh donaib chuislennaib tredaib, ro·fassatar triasin run. Coros·raind Brigit Cille Dara: benn dia bennaibh na cuislinne do Shen-Brigit ingin Domma ina hainech ⁊ ina sarugud, benn aile do Mac Tail dia hanmcarait Brigdi. In tresbenn dana ⁊ cois na cuisslinne sin Meic Dichoeme fo·rfaccaib Brighit aicce feisin. Conidh i in sin cathbuadach boi fri hidhacht ⁊ fri hadhart noem-Brigde, in tan do·luid a dochum richidh; ⁊ is amlaid boi: a cathbuadach 'na laim oc eitsecht tri comurtha a grad n-epscoip; ar ni mó is bachall ind oencendach crom oldass an debennach diriuch cenn.*

'Thus, this pipe of Mac Díchoíme, which had been made from the secret, is Saint Brigit's 'victorious one'. Some others, then, say that it was a three-forked pipe that was made from the three saplings which had grown on account of the secret. And Brigit of Kildare separated them: [she gave] one of the pipes of the *cuislenn* to the old Brigit, daughter of

[98] 'King Eochaid has Horse's Ears' (ed. and trans. Meyer (1903), 50, 54): *gabais īar sin rīghe i ndegaid Eochach ⁊ cīa rogab rīge, nī roscar fria chuisslind.*

[99] A similar increase in milk-yield in relation to music can be found in *Longes mac nUislenn*; cf. Kelly (1997), 39.

[100] 'Die Flöte von Mac Dīchoeme' 13 (ed. Thurneysen (1933), 120; the translation is mine).

Domma, the second pipe to Mac Tail, confessor of Brigit. Then, as for the third pipe and the foot of that *cuisle* of Mac Díchoíme, Brigit kept that for herself. So, this is 'the victorious one' which was there at the point of death and on the death-bed of Saint Brigit, when she went to the Kingdom [of Heaven], and it is so that it happened: her 'victorious one' in her hand when she died, as a mark of her rank of bishop; for the single-headed crooked staff is no greater a crosier than the double-pointed straight one.'

Undoubtedly this is one of the most detailed descriptions of a woodwind instrument to be found in an early Irish text.[101] Interestingly, this passage is introduced as a sort of 'textual variant' apparently driven by the wish to rationalize a potentially puzzling aspect of the story: since three saplings had grown from Mac Díchoíme's blood, the compiler seems to wonder why he should have made a *double* pipe out of them, whereas a *triple* pipe would provide a much more logical solution. While on the one hand it would be easy to dismiss this as an example of somewhat pedantic aetiology, on the other hand this passage presents a number of striking features.

First of all, Saint Brigit's use of the third pipe as a crosier does not pose any problem from the organological point of view. Many medieval Irish crosiers have survived and have been studied by archaeologists and art historians: one of their most notable characteristics is that they tend to be considerably shorter than their contemporary continental counterparts. One of the longest, the Kells Crosier (also known as British Museum Crosier), only measures approximately 130 cm, and many Irish crosiers are in fact even shorter.[102] This length is perfectly compatible with reed-pipes found in some living musical traditions: in some types of Sardinian *launeddas* the drone-pipe (called *tumbu*) can be as long as 150 cm, and the drone-pipe of the Egyptian *arghul* can also reach a considerable length.[103]

[101] To my knowledge, this passage has not attracted much scholarly interest, apart from a brief discussion in Ramsey (2002), 31.

[102] Cf. Johnson (2000), 118: 'Irish crosiers were of two lengths, the shorter of which measured approximately 1m, as evidenced by a crosier found in the River Bann in Co. Antrim. The longer crosiers are represented by two other complete specimens both of which measure approximately 1.3m in length (the British Museum crosier and the Prosperous crosier).'

[103] For the *launeddas*, cf. Spanu (1994), 141; for the *arghul*, cf. Braun (2002), 219–20.

This passage is most interesting especially by virtue of its detailed terminology. The term *buinne/cuisle(nn) tregabail*, literally meaning 'three-forked pipe', clearly refers here to the instrument as a whole, while *benn* (a term whose broad semantic range shows that it referred to any pointed shape)[104] indicates a single pipe, i.e. a single component of the instrument. This *cuislenn* appears to be constituted by three detachable pipes, thus supporting the typological comparison with instruments such as the above-mentioned *launeddas*. Moreover, one of the most intriguing terms pertains to the component that Brigit keeps for herself, described as *in tresbenn ocus cois na cuislinne* ('the third pipe and the 'foot' of the *cuislenn*'). What does the 'foot' refer to? As indicated in *DIL*,[105] *cos* can mean 'stem, support, handle, shaft of various objects'; we may then wonder whether this term could designate here some kind of stand on which the instrument was placed: after all, a vertical stand can be seen supporting a long single pipe played by one of the musicians accompanying King David in London, British Library, Cotton Tiberius C VI (Tiberius Psalter, an 11th-century manuscript from Winchester), 30v. This interpretation, however, seems problematic: first of all, representations of such a stand seem exceedingly rare in medieval iconography (indeed, the one visible in the Tiberius Psalter is the only example that I am aware of); moreover, in the passage from the story of Mac Díchoíme, the 'foot' seems to be an integral component of the part of the instrument which eventually becomes Brigit's crosier. This piece is clearly described as *debennach diriuch*, that is it has two pointed ends, and it is straight. Although this is impossible to prove, the term *cos* might refer here to a detachable component, possibly used to lengthen one of the pipes: indeed, the longest pipe (usually the drone) of the already mentioned *arghul*, *benas*, and *launeddas* is never made in one piece, but the desired length is rather obtained by addition of a detachable piece which lowers the pipe's pitch (clearly visible in *Plate 1* above).[106]

[104] Cf. *DIL s.v. benn*, providing meanings such as 'mountain, peak, point, pinnacle, corner, horn, point (of various forked and pointed objects)' etc.

[105] *DIL s.v. cos.*

[106] Alternatively, the *cos* might designate a detachable section in which the reed was inserted, similar to the system used in the Graeco-Roman *aulos*; cf. West (1992), 85: 'The stem of the mouthpiece reed fitted into a bulbous section of the pipe. Vase-paintings often show two of these bulbs, one socketed into the other, or occasionally, as it appears, even three. In other instances the instrument has continuous straight outlines but is crossed by bands at the corresponding places, indicating joints between separate pieces.'

The problem of iconography and the *Epistula ad Dardanum*

Although the interpretation of the organological details may be speculative, the rich technical terminology found in this passage from the story of Mac Díchoíme suggests at least that its author may have possessed some knowledge of the shape and structure of a *cuislenn*. After all, triple reed-pipes are attested not only from living musical traditions (e.g. the *launeddas*), but they also feature in medieval manuscript iconography: for instance, in Glasgow, University Library, Hunter 229 (U.3.2) (a 12th-century manuscript from northern England also known as Hunterian Psalter), 21v, we see David playing the harp, accompanied by musicians; at the bottom of the page, two young boys (perhaps students of music)[107] play woodwinds: one seems to play a sort of rudimentary bagpipe, or a bladder-pipe, while the other plays what appears to be a set of triple pipes. A famous realistic depiction of '*launeddas*-like' triple pipes can moreover be found in the 13th-century Escorial copy of the *Cantigas de Santa Maria* (El Escorial, Real Biblioteca, B.I.2 ('codex E'), 79r).

As is well known, depictions of players of triple pipes also occur on early medieval monuments in both Ireland and Gaelic Scotland, for instance on the Cross of the Scriptures at Clonmacnoise, Muiredach's Cross at Monasterboice, St Martin's Cross on Iona, or the cross slab of Ardchattan (Argyll). This fact poses a number of fundamental but challenging questions: what is the relationship between the textual evidence presented above and such iconographic evidence? Can we find a precise correspondence between linguistic designations and the instruments depicted on the Gaelic crosses? Can we take these images as reliable representations of real musical instruments played, say, in 9th- or 10th-century Ireland and Scotland?

The main reason why it is so difficult to provide convincing answers to these questions is of course that the use of iconography as a basis for medieval organology presents many problems of its own. First of all, it is essentially impossible to know whether these depictions relied upon the artists' direct acquaintance with actual instruments, or whether they were in fact copied from models and exemplars which are no longer extant (not to mention the possibility that they may have been based on pure fantasy). Quite clearly, this problem bears directly on the legitimacy of iconography as a source of organological data. A concrete example of

[107] For an analysis of this scene as a representation of musical instruction, cf. Marchesin (2000), 93–4 (she interprets the 'triple pipe' as a syrinx).

this is the representation of a siren playing a set of triple pipes found in a 12th- or 13th-century English bestiary (Oxford, Bodleian Library, Bodley 602, 10r):[108] the instrument itself is fairly detailed, and its organology is realistic; the puffed-out cheeks of the siren (who is accompanied by two other sirens, one playing the harp, and one possibly singing) add further plausibility to the representation (see *Plate 2*). An almost identical scene can be found in a 13th- or 14th-century bestiary contained in the miscellaneous codex Oxford, Bodleian Library, Douce 88, 138v (see *Plate 3*): although much cruder in its execution, this image matches perfectly the one in Bodley 602, to the point that it may well have been directly copied from it (or from a very similar common exemplar). However, the two images differ as to one important detail: the woodwind instrument visible in Douce 88 is a double pipe. If, for argument's sake, Bodley 602 had not survived, we may have been misled into considering the image in Douce 88 as the depiction—however careless—of a real instrument, while in fact this set of double pipes is in all likelihood nothing other than the result of the work of an inaccurate copyist.

[108] For a brief discussion of this image cf. Buckley (1991), 180–2. The fact that the three sirens are respectively represented as singing, playing pipes, and playing the harp, is not fortuitous, as this configuration is found in several late antique and early medieval sources, such as Isidore's *Etymologiae* XI 3.30 (Linday (1911), ii; Barney, Lewis, Beach, and Berghof (2006), 245): *Sirenas tres fingunt fuisse ex parte virgines, ex parte volucres, habentes alas et ungulas: quarum una voce, altera tibiis, tertia lyra canebant. Quae inlectos navigantes sub cantu in naufragium trahebant.* ('People imagine three Sirens who were part maidens, part birds, having wings and talons; one of them would make music with her voice, the second with a flute, and the third with a lyre. They would draw sailors, enticed by the song, into shipwreck.') In turn, Isidore's account derives from a passage in Servius' commentary on Vergil; cf. Holford-Strevens (2006), 24. As noted in Leach (2006), 197–8, the musical activities of the three sirens correspond perfectly to the traditional threefold division of *musica instrumentalis*, as found in Isidore's *Etymologiae* III 19 (Lindsay (1911), i; Barney, Lewis, Beach, and Berghof (2006), 96): *Ad omnem autem sonum, quae materies cantilenarum est, triformem constat esse naturam. Prima est harmonica, quae ex vocum cantibus constat. Secunda organica, quae ex flatu consistit. Tertia rhythmica, quae pulsu digitorum numeros recipit. Nam aut voce editur sonus, sicut per fauces, aut flatu, sicut per tubam vel tibiam, aut pulsu, sicut per citharam, aut per quodlibet aliud, quod percutiendo canorum est.* ('It is accepted that all sound that is the material of song has three forms by its nature. The first division is the *harmonicus*, which consists of vocal song. The second division is the *organicus*, which is composed of blowing. The third is the rhythmic, which takes its measures from the plucking of fingers. For sound is emitted either by the voice, as through the throat, or by blowing, as through a trumpet or a flute, or by plucking, as with the cithara, or any other sort of instrument that is melodious when plucked.') Thus, the hybridity of the sirens consists not only in their woman/bird nature, but also in the 'mismatch between positive musical features (attractive song, singer, and sound) and negative ethical features (sweetness as a form of gluttony or lechery)'; Leach (2006), 187.

Plate 2 Oxford, Bodleian Library, Bodley 602, 10r. (Reproduced with permission.)

Plate 3 Oxford, Bodleian Library, Douce 88, 138v. (Reproduced with permission.)

Perhaps even more importantly, several scholars have argued that the instruments found in medieval iconography should not be *necessarily* or *automatically* understood as direct or indirect reproductions of organological realities: in particular, their nature and function may vary from case to case, and may be partially or exclusively symbolic, especially in the light of the plainly biblical and Christian context in which they are often found.[109] Indeed, much has been written over the past century con-

[109] Cf. Buckley (1990), 14–5: '[In medieval Irish art] musical instruments are usually depicted as one element of a scene in religious carvings: not for the purpose of

cerning the exegetical interest shown by late antique and medieval writers for the symbolic meaning of the musical instruments mentioned in the Bible (especially in the Psalms): allegorical interpretations of musical instruments can be found, for instance, in the writings of Augustine, Jerome, Cassiodorus, and Isidore; it is more than likely that religious iconography would have been strongly influenced by these *auctoritates*.

One text which undoubtedly had a deep and long-lasting impact on the visual representation of biblical instruments is a short letter falsely attributed to Jerome, known as *Epistula ad Dardanum de diversis generibus musicorum*. In the *Epistula*, the anonymous author provides fanciful organological descriptions and allegorical interpretations of the musical instruments mentioned in the Bible. This text, or excerpts from it, survives in no less than sixty-one copies dating from the 9th century onwards,[110] many of which are accompanied by drawings and diagrams attempting to visualize the biblical instruments. The extraordinary number of extant copies is a clear indication of the wide diffusion of the *Epistula* throughout medieval Europe; regrettably, in spite of the text's obvious importance, no modern critical edition is yet available. The version found in a 10th-century manuscript preserved in Munich was edited by Reinhold Hammerstein in 1959,[111] but this copy is often at variance with the version edited in the *Patrologia Latina* (PL), which was ultimately based

conveying information of a musicological nature but to preach the Christian message, portraying scenes of adoration and ritual of which music was a component. As in the case of literary references the purpose was not to convey accurate depictions of instruments; many illustrations are stylized, unrealistic copies of foreign works of art (e.g. manuscript illuminations, carvings) whose details may well have been ill-understood by native craftsmen, and even at times by the makers of the original. Musical instruments are particularly vulnerable to inaccurate artistic representation.' Cf. also McKinnon (1968), 15: 'when an artist illustrates the psalms which mention instruments it is not immediately apparent whether his intent is allegorical or literal. He depicts men playing instruments whether he means simply to represent ancient Israelites playing instruments or whether he means to represent these instrumentalists as symbols of Christian mystical instrument-playing.' Marchesin (2000), 25–6, proposes a classification of medieval depictions of musical instruments into three broad types: (1) more or less accurate copies from earlier depictions; (2) more or less imaginary 'reconstructions' of ancient biblical instruments; (3) depictions based on real-life contemporary instruments.

[110] Cf. Lambert (1969–72), iiiA 108 (no. 323); McNamara (1986), 55 = McNamara (2000), 215; Markovits (2003), 445. The earliest copy is found in the mid-9th-century manuscript Angers, Bibliothèque municipale, 18 (14), 12v–13r (cf. van Schaik (1992), 71–2). For a discussion of the influence which the *Epistula* had on medieval iconography of musical instruments, cf. especially Page (1977).

[111] Cf. Hammerstein (1959); the manuscript in question is Munich, Bayerische Staatsbibliothek, Clm 14523, 49v–52r (available online at: http://daten.digitale-sammlungen.de/~db/bsb00002112/images/index.html).

on an edition published in the early 18th-century by the Maurist scholar Jean Martianay.[112] Most scholars consider the *Epistula* as a Carolingian composition of uncertain provenance: a convenient *terminus ante quem* for its composition is given by the fact that Rabanus Maurus seems to have used it as a source for his work *De Universo*, written around AD 843 (if the *Epistula* was not based on Rabanus' text, as believed by Hammerstein—but, as we shall see, there is strong evidence against this view).[113]

The possibility that the *Epistula* influenced the representation of musical instruments in early Irish art has been taken into account by Ann Buckley, who, in particular, wrote the following in respect to the occurrence of triangular and quadrangular chordophones on medieval Irish crosses and pillars:[114]

> 'their lack of specificity in detail suggests comparison with the panoply of representations of David's biblical instrument, and illustrations in sources of the so-called Dardanus letter. In other words, they were never intended to represent contemporary stringed instruments, or indeed any particular organological type: rather they conform to another kind of typology, that of Late Antique and Early Christian iconography of David of the Old Testament, the sacred Other, preserving a distance from the contemporary world and from activities of secular musicians.'

Most interestingly, in his brief discussion of the *Epistula ad Dardanum*, Martin McNamara pointed out that

> 'there is a long citation from it (agreeing verbatim with the text printed in Migne) in the St Gall manuscript of the Irish *Eclogae tractatorum in Psalterium* (late 8th-century), containing a description of the organ, and carrying AG. (presumably Agustinus) as marginal ascription. Substantially the same text on the organ is found in the Irish 'Bibelwerk' (likewise late 8th-century), where it is ascribed to ORIG. presumably

112 Cf. PL 30, 213–5; Migne here reproduced the edition by Domenico Vallarsi contained in *Sancti Eusebii Hieronymi Stridonensis Presbyteri Opera* (Verona, 1734–1742; 2nd ed.: Venice, 1766–1772); this was in turn based on the edition prepared by Jean Martianay for his *Sancti Eusebii Hieronymi Stridonensis Presbyteri Opera* (Paris, 1693–1706). It is not clear which manuscript(s) Martianay used for his edition of the *Epistula*; however, a 10th-century copy which appears to be quite close to the Martianay/PL edition is found in Paris, Bibliothèque nationale de France, Lat. 1781, 249v–250v. I hope to be able to present a more detailed account of this copy in a future publication.

113 Cf. Hammerstein (1959), 117–8; Seebass (1973), 141–4; Page (1977), 301–3; van Schaik (1992), 64–5; Marchesin (2000), 25–6.

114 Buckley (1991), 165.

> Origen [...]. This evidence tells against Rabanus' authorship of the work and the presumed Carolingian date of composition. The same letter is the source of some of the glosses in [Vatican, Biblioteca Apostolica,] Pal. lat. 68 [...], a fact which obliges us to push the date of composition back further still.'[115]

The remarkable Irish affiliations of the *Epistula* pose a serious question as to whether we could consider this text as the product of Irish exegesis, or perhaps as a Carolingian re-elaboration of earlier material of Irish provenance. I believe strong support to this view can be found by analyzing the section of the *Epistula* dealing with the biblical instrument named *sambuca* (apparently a wind instrument of some kind).

Here is the relevant passage as presented in Hammerstein's edition, which I have integrated with variants and additions from the version published in PL (in square brackets);[116] the passage is followed by my own tentative translation (which occasionally follows the readings of the PL version):

> *Sambuca itaque etiam apud peritissimos Hebreorum ignota res est. Antiquis autem temporibus apud Caldeos fuisse repperitur. Sicut scriptum est: 'cum audieritis uocem tubae, fistulae, citharae, et sambucae'. 'Buca' uero tuba apud Hebreos, deinde per diminutionem bucina dicitur. 'Sam' autem sol apud Hebreos interpretatur, unde dicitur 'Samson sol eorum'. Propter hoc 'sambuca' apud eos scribitur, quia multa* [PL: *multi*] *corticem alicuius arboris putant esse, et per sobilitatem* [PL: *soliditatem*] *mellis lignei ac nobilitatem* [PL: *ac uenti mutabilitatem*] *quasi in modum tubae de ramis arboris moueri potest.* [PL adds here: *ideo sambuca dicitur, quia aestatis tempore fieri potest, et usque ad frigoris tempus durare potest.*] *Arescit enim secundum communem consuetudinem, tipus eorum qui in bonis suis* [PL: *in bonis operibus*] *Dominum laudant, et in tempore frigoris, id est in tempore tribulationis et persecutionis, eum laudare non possunt, propter infidelem uitam abundantiae* [PL: *propter infidelitatem uitae et abundantiam*] *diuitiarum suarum.*

[115] McNamara (1986), 54–5 = McNamara (2000), 215–6. The passage from the *Eclogae* mentioned by McNamara is in St Gall, Stiftsbibliothek, 261, 148 (material on the biblical musical instruments can also be found at pp. 149–50; the MS is available online at: http://www.e-codices.unifr.ch/en/list/one/csg/0261); the passage from the 'Bibelwerk' is in Munich, Bayerische Staatsbibliothek, Clm 14276, 34r–v (available online at: http://daten.digitale-sammlungen.de/~db/0004/bsb00046658/images/index.html). Against Rabanus' authorship of the *Epistula* (or sections thereof) cf. also Robbins Bittermann (1929), 399 n 1; Dekkers (1995), 221 (§633) (openly agreeing with McNamara).

[116] *Epistula ad Dardanum* (Hammerstein (1959), 129; PL 30, 214–5).

'The *sambuca* is also unknown among the most learned of the Hebrews [or perhaps: 'the most learned on Hebrew things'?], but it can be found to have existed in ancient times among the Chaldeans. Thus it is written: 'As soon as you hear the sound of the trumpet, flute, lyre, and *sambuca*' [Daniel 3:5]. Indeed, *buca* in Hebrew means 'trumpet', and the term *bucina* is its diminutive. And *sam* in Hebrew means 'sun', and from this is said 'Samson, i.e. their sun'. This is why, then, *sambuca* is written by them, because many believe it to be the bark of a certain tree, and it can be produced (?) from the branches of this tree thanks to the solidity and flexibility of [its] pliable wood (?),[117] almost in the manner of a trumpet. [*PL*: For this reason it is called *sambuca*, because it can be made in summer-time, and it can last until the cold season.[118]] Indeed, it dries up according to the common custom, [and it is] an allegory of those who praise the Lord in their good [times?], and cannot praise Him in the cold season, i.e. in the time of tribulation and persecution, because of their faithless life and the abundance of their wealth.'

This passage contains of course numerous textual problems which cannot be discussed here. Nonetheless, it is clear that the core of this allegory is based on the (pseudo-)etymology of *sambuca* from Hebrew *sam* ('sun'), allegedly the same element found in the name of Samson.

This etymology ultimately derives from Jerome's Hebrew Names, where we read:[119]

Samson 'sol eorum' uel 'solis fortitudo'.

'Samson, [i.e.] 'their sun' or 'the sun's strength'.'

The same explanation of the name Samson can also be found in Augustine's *Enarrationes in Psalmos*[120] and Isidore's *Etymologiae*.[121] Even

[117] I tentatively take the Latin here to be a corruption of *per soliditatem mollis ligni ac mutabilitatem*.

[118] This passage about summer-time is found in PL but is completely absent from the Munich copy, where it may have been omitted due to homoeoteleuton, given that both this and the previous sentence end with the same verb *potest* (I owe this observation to Mark Stansbury).

[119] Jerome, *Liber interpretationis Hebraicorum nominum* (ed. by Paul de Lagarde in CCSL 72, 33); cf. also ibidem (CCSL 72, 78): *Samson 'sol eorum'*.

[120] Augustine, *Enarrationes in Psalmos* 80 §14 (ed. by Eligius Dekkers and Johannes Fraipont in CCSL 39, 1129): *unde Samson noster, qui etiam interpretatur 'sol ipsorum'*.

[121] Isidore, *Etymologiae* VII 6.56 (Lindsay (1911), i): *Samson 'sol eorum' uel 'solis fortitudo'*.

more explicit references to the Hebrew word for 'sun' actually occur in several other entries of Jerome's Hebrew Names, where the term variously spelt as *samis*, *sames*, *semsi* does indeed correspond to Hebrew *šameš* ('sun').[122] This term was known in 7th- and 8th-century Ireland (most likely through the intermediary of Jerome and/or Isidore), as shown by its occurrence in Hiberno-Latin computistical writing: for instance, in the Munich Computus *simpsia*, indicated as the Hebrew term for 'sun', is clearly a corruption of Jerome's *semsi*;[123] the same term (spelt *simsia*) can moreover be found in *De ratione conputandi* and in the computistical glosses contained in Angers, Bibliothèque municipale, 477 (461).[124]

Notice that in the Irish computi, as well as in Jerome, the Hebrew word is always disyllabic. On the contrary, the *Epistula* only mentions monosyllabic *sam*. Now, the exact same form occurs in a list of words meaning 'sun' in various languages (just like in the Munich Computus), found in the exegetical tract on Genesis contained in Paris, Bibliothèque nationale de France, Lat. 11561, 65vb (belonging to the Irish Reference Bible tradition, according to Bischoff):

> *Sam in Eb*raico, *eleos in Greco, panib*[us?] *in philosophia, Feb*us *apud Syrus, Tytan aput Aegyptius, sol aput Latinos.*
>
> '[The sun is called] *sam* in Hebrew, *eleos* in Greek, *panibus* in philosophy, *Febus* among the Syrians, *Tytan* among the Egyptians, *sol* among the Latins.'[125]

Perhaps even more interestingly, the 'Hebrew' form *sam* can be found in *Sanas Cormaic*, together with the above-mentioned traditional etymology of the name Samson. Significantly, the short form *sam* is here used

122 Jerome, *Liber interpretationis Hebraicorum nominum* (CCSL 72, 25, 30, 36, 41); cf. also Thiel (1973), 149.

123 Munich Computus 37 (ed. Warntjes (2010), 100): *Sol dictus est* [...] *gamse in Hebreo uel simpsia, elios in Graeco, panath cum philosophis, foebe cum Syris, titan cum Chaldeis.*

124 *De ratione conputandi* 1 (ed. in Walsh and Ó Cróinín (1988), 115–6; see the apparatus for the Angers gloss and more examples); the Angers gloss also in Warntjes (2010), 100 (apparatus); cf. also Howlett (1997), 127.

125 A transcription of this passage can be found in Bischoff (1976), 102; the translation is mine. Cf. also Thiel (1973), 31 n 113.

to etymologize the Old Irish word for 'summer', *samrad* (which can also occur simply as *sam* in Old Irish):[126]

> *Samrad .i. sam* quasi *Ebra sól* quasi *Lait*in. *un*de *d*icitur *'Sam*h*son sol eo*rum*'. samrad di*diu *.i. riad rithes grian. is and is mou doaitne a sollsi* 7 *a hairde.*
>
> '*Samrad*, i.e. almost as *sam* in Hebrew, *sol* in Latin ['sun']; from this it is said 'Samson, i.e. their sun'. *Samrad* ['summer'], thus, i.e. the course that the sun runs; it is then that its light shines more, and its height is greater.'

It seems then reasonable to assume that the Hebrew form often cited by Jerome as *samis/sames/semsi* was shortened to *sam* in Irish sources such as *Sanas Cormaic* precisely in order to obtain a closer match with Old Irish *samrad* (this modification may of course have been facilitated by a segmentation of *Samson* into *Sam-son*). This etymologizing technique has been well described by Pádraic Moran in an article on Hebrew in medieval Irish glossaries; for example, Moran shows how Irish *bás* ('death') was explained in O'Mulconry's Glossary as if matching perfectly a Hebrew word of analogous meaning. The relevant entry in the Irish glossary reads as follows:[127]

> *Bás ebraice, tribulatio uel angustiae uel mors latine.*
>
> '*Bás*, 'death', in Hebrew, 'affliction' or 'difficulties' or 'death' in Latin.'

The Hebrew word occurring in Jerome's Hebrew Names is actually *bosra*,[128] but, as Moran pointed out, 'the compiler [of O'Mulconry's Glossary] not only jettisons the final syllable of the Hebrew word, but exacerbates its significance from acute ('anguish or difficulties') to terminal ('death')'.[129]

[126] Transcribed from Dublin, Royal Irish Academy, 23 P 16 (*Lebor Brecc*), 271b (available at: www.isos.dias.ie; my translation); cf. also Stokes (1862), 40; Meyer (1913), 101 (§1154).

[127] O'Mulconry's Glossary 129 (ed. Stokes (1898–1900), 240; my translation).

[128] Jerome, *Liber interpretationis Hebraicorum nominum* (CCSL 72, 3): *Bosra in tribulatione uel angustia*; ibidem (CCSL 72, 49): *Bosra in tribulatione.*

[129] Moran (2010), 13.

Needless to say, this process is in essence identical to the modification of *sames* (and variants thereof) into *sam* so that the Hebrew form may correspond to Irish *sam(rad)*.

In this context, it is also highly significant that, at least according to the *Patrologia Latina* version of the *Epistula ad Dardanum*, the musical instrument in question is said to be called *sambuca* precisely 'because it can be made in summer-time' (*quia aestatis tempore fieri potest*): the rationale behind such a pseudo-etymology can then be recognized much more clearly if this whole explanation is assumed to rely on an implicit equivalence between 'Hebrew' *sam* ('sun') and Irish *sam(rad)* ('summer').

On balance, the textual affiliations pointed out by McNamara, combined with the remarkably 'Irish' etymology of *sambuca*, strongly suggest that the *Epistula* was written either in Ireland, or by a continental compiler who relied at least in part on sources of Irish provenance.[130]

Given that speculation concerning the shape and allegorical meaning of the musical instruments mentioned in the Bible may have been part of Irish exegesis already in the 8th century, we may now try and look at the representation of instruments on the Irish high crosses under a different light. For example, in the *Epistula*, the *psalterium* is described as follows:[131]

> *Psalterium* [...] *non quasi in modum cytharae sed quasi in modum clipei quadrati confirmatur*[132] *cum cordis, sicut scriptum est: 'In psalterio X cordarum psallite illi* [PL: *psallam tibi*]*'* [Ps 143:9]. [...] *Psalterium itaque cum X cordis, ecclesia cum X uerbis legis contrariis contra omnem heresim* [PL: *cum decem uerbis legis contritis contra omnem haeresim*], *quadrata per quattuor Euangelia intellegitur* [PL: *potest intelligi*].

130 A text such as the *Epistula* can be understood as growing out of the existing explanations on biblical instruments contained in Hiberno-Latin exegetical commentaries (especially to the Psalms); cf. for example the subtle distinction between *psalterium* and *cithara* in the Introduction to the Psalter from the Irish Reference Bible (cf. McNamara (1973), 297), or the mention of *saltirium*, *cithara*, *tympanum*, *chorus*, *organum*, and *cimbali* in a passage from the '*Catena* on the Psalms' found in Vatican, Biblioteca Apostolica, Pal. lat. 68 (cf. McNamara (1973), 283). In turn, these early medieval accounts would have been based on patristic sources such as the *Expositio Psalmorum* by Cassiodorus (cf., e.g., praefatio, cap. 4 (ed. by Marcus Adriaen in CCSL 97); for further references, cf. van Schaik (1992), 71, 153–4; Marchesin (2000), 31 n 54 and 55, 124 n 32).

131 *Epistula ad Dardanum* (Hammerstein (1959), 127; PL 30, 215; my translation).

132 Manuscript variants cited in Hammerstein (1959), 127, present here remarkably different readings (*formatur* and *in modum quadrati formati*). The form *confirmatur* attested in the Munich MS could then be emended to *conformatur*, in which case this passage would mean: 'The psaltery [...] is not shaped in the manner of a *cythara*, but rather more like a square shield with strings'.

> 'It is confirmed that the psaltery [...] [is made] not in the manner of a *cythara*, but rather more like a square shield with strings, as it is written: 'On the ten-stringed psaltery make music to Him'. [...] Therefore, the ten-stringed psaltery can be understood [to symbolize] the church, with Ten Pronouncements of the Law that oppose every heresy, and square-shaped by virtue of the four Gospels.'

A square *psalterium* is indeed represented on the earliest witness containing material related to the *Epistula*, a mid-9th-century manuscript preserved in Angers (Angers, Bibliothèque municipale, 18 (14), 13r), as well as in other copies of the same text. Therefore, as pointed out above, the *Epistula ad Dardanum* (or a text of similar nature), rather than real contemporary instruments, could be the main source underlying the depiction of quadrangular string instruments on some Irish high crosses, such as the crosses of Castledermot, Ullard etc.[133]

Likewise, the triangular chordophones played by King David, represented on monuments such as Muiredach's Cross at Monasterboice (see *Plate 4*), corresponds to the biblical *cythara*, also described in the *Epistula*:[134]

> *Cythara* [...] *propriae consuetudinis apud Hebraeos quae cum chordis XXIIII quasi in modum deltae litterae sicut peritissimi tradunt, utique componitur* [...]. *Cythara autem de qua sermo est, ecclesiam spiritaliter* [PL: *ecclesia est spiritualiter*] *quae cum XXIIII seniorum dogmatibus trinam formam habens quasi in modum deltae litterae per fidem sanctae Trinitatis manifestissimo* [PL: *manifestissime sine dubio*] *utique significat, et per manus Petri apostolici* [PL: *per manus uiri Petri apostoli*] *qui praedicator illius est, in diuersos modulos Veteris et Noui Testamenti, aliter in littera, aliter in sensu figuraliter concitatur* [PL: *concutitur*].

> 'The *cythara* is indeed formed according to the custom proper to the Hebrew, with twenty-four strings, as if in the shape of a letter delta,

[133] Cf. the detailed discussions in, e.g., Buckley (1990), 15–23 (see esp. p 18); Buckley (1991), 141–5, 164–5. For a description of the crosses of Castledermot and Ullard in particular, cf. Harbison (1992), i 37–41 (§§36–7), 183–4 (§231); cf. also ibidem, pp. 213–4 for a brief account of the representation of David as harper on the Irish high crosses, mentioning the parallel with the Angers manuscript. Interesting parallels between early Irish depictions of David playing the harp and the Angers manuscript had also been pointed out in Henry (1960–1), 29–30, 32. For a list of manuscript examples of the *psalterium quadratum*, cf. Seebass (1973), 47–50.

[134] *Epistula ad Dardanum* (Hammerstein (1959), 125; PL 30, 214; my translation).

> as most learned [authors] relate.[135] […] The *cythara* in question spiritually signifies the church, with the doctrine of the twenty-four Elders, and having three-fold shape by virtue of the faith in the holy Trinity, and it is made to resound by the hands of the Apostle Peter, who is the preacher of that faith, according to the different interpretative modes of the Old and New Testament, sometimes according to the literal sense, sometimes according to the figurative sense.'

That the depiction of David on the east face of Muiredach's Cross owes much to traditional iconographic models is demonstrated by the presence of a bird, symbolising divine inspiration or the Word of God, perched upon the king's instrument: the same motif can be found on the Irish shrine of Saint Máedoc (where David's instrument is however much richer in realistic organological details),[136] and also in several English and continental manuscripts, such as Cambridge, Trinity College, B.5.26 (an 11th-century manuscript from Canterbury), 1r, or Cambridge, University Library, Ff.1.23 (the Cambridge Psalter, an 11th-century manuscript from Winchcombe), 4v.[137] Rather than being interested in fixing in stone a realistic representation of a medieval Irish harp, it is quite clear that the sculptor of the Last Judgement scene on Muiredach's Cross (or whoever designed its iconographic contents) was primarily concerned with providing a coherent and spiritually instructive visualization of Christian motifs, whose foundations can be found in the Bible as well as in exegetical works.

Indeed, the scene corresponds perfectly to the description of the Last Judgement in Matthew 25:31–46, where Christ separates 'the sheep from the goats': to his right, the blessed souls who will go to Heaven; to his left, the cursed ones who will fall into the eternal flames of Hell. In this context, the presence of the figure of David is justified by the fact that the biblical king corresponds allegorically to Jesus Christ according to both the literal sense—as both came from the same stock, the *stirps*

135 The theme of the *cythara* (or sometimes the *psalterium*) shaped like the letter *delta* is an exegetical *topos* found, for example, in the writings of Cassiodorus, who attributed this piece of information—perhaps mistakenly—to Jerome (cf. the detailed discussion of the origins and development of this theme in van Schaik (1992), 70–6, 152). The same theme can be found in a passage from the Hiberno-Latin Introduction to the Psalter in the Irish Reference Bible (Munich, Bayerische Staatsbibliothek, Clm 14276, 98v); cf. McNamara (1973), 297 = McNamara (2000), 140–1. For additional examples of the *delta*-shaped instrument, cf. Seebass (1973), 50–3.

136 Cf. Rimmer (1977), 26.

137 Cf. Marchesin (2000), 50. The theme of the bird perched on David's harp is discussed in Buckley (1991), 145–6, 166; Buckley (2008), 25. For the possibility that this iconographic motif may have been influenced also by classical models, cf. Roe (1949), 55–6.

Jesse—and the figurative sense (David constitutes the prefiguration of Christ himself, being the one who foretold the coming of the Lord in the Psalms, hence the traditional formula *Dauid rex et propheta*).[138]

Plate 4 The Last Judgement scene on Muiredach's Cross (Monasterboice).

The whole scene can thus be said to encompass visually the whole history of Salvation: the Old and the New Testament, the Crucifixion and the Last Judgement, Heaven and Hell. Moreover, in agreement with the above-mentioned passage from Matthew's Gospel, the figures are clearly organized on the basis of a strong right/left dynamic, especially marked by: (1) the opposition between the inward look of the blessed souls, oriented towards Jesus, and the outward movement of the damned souls, who are driven away from him; (2) the appearance of the bird standing on Christ's head (presumably the Holy Spirit), with its wing open in a welcoming gesture directed to its right-hand side.

In view of the carefully structured symbolic coherence of this scene, I am inclined to concur with the interpretation suggested by Ann Buckley and other scholars, according to which the presence of a player of triple pipes standing to the left of Christ may possess a negative or even

[138] For more details on the representation of David as *figura Christi,* cf. van Schaik (1992), 96–8; Marchesin (2000), 21–2, 74, 136.

demonic connotation (a symbolic association which, after all, is repeatedly found across numerous European cultures);[139] the Monasterboice piper (who, it should be noted, sits just beside a devil with a fork) would thus constitute an evil mirror-image of David the harper, who is instead accompanied by celestial musicians (one playing a wind instrument, unfortunately difficult to identify, and at least two singers).

Some explicit representations of the opposition between heavenly music and music of the Devil, or between sacred and profane music, are indeed known from medieval iconography: a famous example can be found in Cambridge, St John's College, B.18 (the so-called Psalterium Triplex, a 12th-century manuscript possibly from Rheims), 1r (see *Plate 5*).[140] What is particularly interesting about this image is that, while the superior panel contains some of the most typical instruments associated with divine harmony (e.g. the bells, the organ, the harp, the monochord, etc.), the inferior panel presents in accompaniment to various forms of 'disorderly behaviour' (such as dancing and making acrobatic moves) also a very realistic musical instrument: a rebec. Far from being a speculative biblical instrument, in 12th-century France the rebec would have

[139] Cf. Rimmer (1977), 20; Buckley (1991), 190–1; Ramsey (2002), 31–3 (in Buckley (2008), 26, we find a different interpretation of the Monasterboice triple piper: 'since he faces Christ he is presumably one of the Just and a member of the musical ensemble'; however, I find this argument much less convincing). The profane, sinister or demonic connotations often attributed to pipes and bagpipes are discussed in detail from an anthropological point of view in Charles-Dominique (2006), 113–93, especially 171–89; cf. also Bec (1996), 27–30; Charles-Dominique (2010). The specific contents of the symbolic meaning attributed to the triple pipes may of course vary from one monument to another: what applies to the Last Judgement scene on Muiredach's Cross is not necessarily relevant to other high crosses in Ireland or Scotland. Nonetheless, it is striking that on several monuments the pipes appear together with, or perhaps in opposition to, the harp or the lyre. For instance, as pointed out in Ramsey (2002), 33, on the Cross of the Scriptures at Clonmacnoise a player of triple pipes is placed on a side panel of the shaft, while 'the panel on the opposite side has David playing a stringed instrument', so that this juxtaposition may represent a 'symbolic pair', such as the dichotomy between good and evil, sacred and profane, Christian and pagan, etc. (cf. also Buckley (1990), 17; Buckley (2008), 28); on the (possibly 10th-century) Lethendy Slab (Perthshire), a harpist and a player of triple pipes face each other (cf. Fisher and Greenhill (1974), 239–40; Buckley (1991), 159–60), and it is not clear whether the scene should be interpreted as if the two musicians were actually playing together, or whether they should be seen as standing in opposition to each other as purely symbolic figures (possibly the embodiment of sacred and profane music respectively?).

[140] For a detailed discussion of this image, cf. Marchesin (2000), 95–8.

been an instrument of fairly recent adoption,[141] and is here clearly associated with profane music for dancing and secular entertainment.

Plate 5 Cambridge, St John's College, B.18, 1r. (Reproduced by permission of the Master and Fellows of St John's College, Cambridge.)

[141] Bowed instruments seem to have been introduced into western Europe through contact with the Arab world, perhaps around the 11th century; cf. Bec (1992), 18–22, 278–80.

This example makes it clear, thus, that purely symbolic instruments based on textual authorities such as the *Epistula ad Dardanum* can co-exist with realistic and organologically accurate representations within the same iconographic context.[142]

Examples of this phenomenon may be easily multiplied. For instance, we could consider the depiction of David and his four accompanying musicians in the 11th-century Polirone Psalter (Mantua, Biblioteca Comunale, 340, 1v):[143] as pointed out by Christopher Page, while one of the musicians is represented in the act of playing an entirely realistic rebec, another one can be seen to be blowing into a sort of rudimentary bagpipe which matches perfectly the description of the biblical *chorus* found in the *Epistula ad Dardanum*.[144]

To mention yet another example of reliable organology found in an otherwise conventional iconographic context, some scholars have noted a remarkable similarity between, on the one hand, the horns played by two clerics visible on the right-hand side of the full-page depiction of King David and his musicians in the 8th-century Anglo-Saxon Vespasian Psalter (London, British Library, Cotton Vespasian A I, 30v), and, on the other hand, the early medieval horn found in 1956 in the river Erne (Co. Fermanagh).[145]

Given that the triple pipes sculpted on the Irish high crosses do not correspond to any of the instruments described in exegetical tracts like the *Epistula*,[146] it is at least possible that their source may rather have

[142] This can of course happen in texts too: as pointed out by Bec (1992), 83, 'le lettré médiéval écrivant sur la musique, ou l'utilisant à des fins littéraires, est en quelques sorte partagé entre une terminologie antiquisante (ou biblique), [...] et, d'autre part, un monde organologique contemporain qui est celui de son entourage immédiat et concret, inconnu des Anciens'.

[143] For an in-depth iconographic analysis of the traditional representation of David in the Polirone Psalter and other manuscripts, cf. Walther (2010). For the representation of David in early Irish art, cf. Roe (1949), especially 54–9.

[144] Page (1977), 307–8; cf. *Epistula ad Dardanum* (Hammerstein (1959), 131).

[145] Cf. Waterman (1969); Purser (2002); O'Dwyer (2004), 103–7, 109–11.

[146] The only possible exception to this is the description of the *tuba*; cf. *Epistula ad Dardanum* (Hammerstein (1959), 122), where it is said that *tribus fistulis aereis in capite angusto inspiratur* ('it is blown through three bronze pipes in [its] narrow head'). However, the next sentence of this passage specifies that *in capite lato per iiii vociductas aereas, quae per aereum fundamentum ceteras voces producunt* ('[it is blown] in [its] broad head through four bronze resonating ducts, which produce other sounds through a bronze base (?)'). Moreover, the depictions of the *tuba* which can be seen in the various illustrated copies of the *Epistula* look very different from the usual medieval iconography of the triple pipes.

been real instrumental practice. This view may receive some support from the close match between these instruments and the *cuislenn tregabail* from the roughly contemporary story of Mac Díchoíme. After all, if it is true that the pipes on the high crosses were meant to constitute a symbol of profane or diabolic music, we can then reasonably assume that the artists would have most likely chosen an instrument actually employed in the context of lowly secular entertainment, one perhaps even frowned upon by the ecclesiastical order (the above-mentioned story of the two sons of King Fergal mac Maíle Dúin is an obvious case in point).[147] In this context, it seems particularly significant that the final action of Saint Brigit in the story of Mac Díchoíme consists precisely in making the *cuislenn* unusable for music by breaking it into three pieces, one of which is later 'Christianized' by being turned into a crosier.[148]

Conclusion

In conclusion, it may be useful to present a brief summary of some of the main points discussed in this contribution. In particular, I hope to have shown that:

(1) in Old and Middle Irish the term *fetán* most likely referred to a flute;

(2) the Old/Middle Irish term *cuisle(nn)* may have derived from Proto-Irish **kulsīnā* (roughly meaning '[instrument made from the] stalk of a plant'), and probably designated reed-pipes (more specifically double and triple reed-pipes, in the case of the story of Mac Díchoíme);

(3) the term *cúisech* could be etymologically related to *cúas* ('cavity'), and seems to have originated as a fairly general cover-term for 'pipes' in general (thus including both flutes and reed-pipes), although its frequent occurrence in opposition to *cuisle(nn)* might indicate that it came to be used more frequently in reference to flutes (as suggested also by the existence of the compound *fetchúisech* ('whistling pipe'));

[147] For a brief discussion concerning 'the Irish Church's candid detestation for the men of art', cf. O'Sullivan (2004), 38–9.

[148] It may be worth mentioning here also the story of the anchorite Cornán, player of *cuislenn*, who receives a clear refusal from Saint Máel Rúain of Tallaght when proposing to play a tune for him ('The Monastery of Tallaght' 10 (ed. Gwynn and Purton (1911–2), 131)); the story is briefly discussed in Buckley (1995), 48.

(4) as shown by Old and Middle Irish legal tracts, as well as by texts belonging to the *Tech Midchúarta* tradition, professional players of woodwinds were in most cases associated with a fairly low social status (although Middle Irish narrative texts occasionally present high-status woodwind players);
(5) the so-called *Epistula ad Dardanum* was probably written in 8th-century Ireland, or may at least be a Carolingian composition based on earlier sources of Irish provenance;[149]
(6) the representation of musical instruments in early Irish art probably owes much to exegetical texts (such as the *Epistula*) describing the nature and symbolic meaning of the instruments mentioned in the Bible; nonetheless, such text-based iconographic *topoi* can be shown to co-exist occasionally with depictions which, on the contrary, almost certainly rely on real contemporary musical practices. In particular, the triple pipes which occur on several Irish and Scottish monuments (e.g. the high crosses of Monasterboice and Clonmacnoise) may be examples of the latter iconographic type, and may have been intended—at least in some cases—as symbols of profane or even diabolic music;
(7) the similarity between the sculpted triple pipes and the *cuislenn* described in the story of Mac Díchoíme is at least suggestive that they may in fact be one and the same musical instrument; if this is indeed the case, we might have here a precious one-to-one match between the artistic interpretation of a real-world musical object and (one of) its linguistic signifier(s), i.e. *buinne/cuisle(nn) tregabail* ('three-forked pipe').

In more general terms, although I am aware that in the present article I have only been able to scratch the surface of a complex and infinitely rich domain of investigation, and although some of the above conclusions may still be seen as somewhat speculative, I am nonetheless convinced that an approach integrating historical linguistics, textual analysis, archaeology, iconography, organology, and ethnomusicology, can lead us to a better understanding of music and musical instruments in pre-Norman Ireland. Given the complete lack of contemporary musical written sources, it is obvious that we shall never know what music was played on a double or a triple pipe in an early medieval Irish royal hall. However, a

[149] Additional evidence for the Irish origin of the *Epistula ad Dardanum* will be presented in a separate publication.

thorough multi-disciplinary analysis of the available evidence may enable us to hear at least a faint distant echo of this otherwise lost musical world.

Bibliography

Atkinson, R. (1887) *The Passions and Homilies from Leabhar Breac: text, translation and glossary*, Dublin.

Atkinson, R., W.N. Hancock, W.M. Hennessy, T. O'Mahony, A.G. Richey (1865–1901) *Ancient laws and institutes of Ireland*, 6 vols., Dublin.

Baines, A. (1960) *Bagpipes*, Oxford.

Baines, A. (1967) *Woodwind instruments and their history*, 3rd ed., London.

Barney, S., W. Lewis, J. Beach, and O. Berghof (2006) *The Etymologies of Isidore of Seville*, Cambridge.

Bec, P. (1992) *Vièles ou violes? Variations philologiques et musicales autour des instruments à archet du moyen âge*, Paris.

— (1996) *La cornemuse: sens et histoire de ses désignations*, Toulouse.

Bentzon, A.F.W. (1969) *The launeddas: a Sardinian folk music instrument*, 2 vols., Copenhagen.

Best, R.I., O. Bergin, and M.A. O'Brien (1954–67) *Book of Leinster, formerly Lebar na Núachongbála*, 5 vols., Dublin.

Binchy, D.A. (1941) *Críth Gablach*, Dublin.

— (1978) *Corpus Iuris Hibernici*, 6 vols., Dublin.

Bischoff, B. (1976) 'Turning-points in the history of Latin exegesis in the early Middle Ages,' in M. McNamara, *Biblical Studies: the medieval Irish contribution*, Dublin, 74–160.

Bolelli, T. (1950) *Due studi irlandesi: Preistoria della poesia irlandese — La leggenda del re dalle orecchie di cavallo in Irlanda*, Pisa.

Borjon de Scellery, C.-E. (1672) *Traité de la Musette*, Lyon.

Bowles, E.A. (1954) 'Haut and bas: the grouping of musical instruments in the Middle Ages,' *Musica Disciplina* 8, 115–40.

— (1958) 'La hiérarchie des instruments de musique dans l'Europe féodale,' *Revue de musicologie* 42, 155–69.

Braun, J. (2002) *Music in ancient Israel/Palestine*, Grand Rapids.

Breatnach, L. (1994) 'An Mheán-Ghaeilge,' in K. McCone, D. McManus, C. Ó Háinle, N. Williams, and L. Breatnach, *Stair na Gaeilge*, Maynooth, 221–333.

— (1996) 'Poets and poetry,' in K. McCone and K. Simms, *Progress in Medieval Irish Studies*, Maynooth, 65–77.

— (2005) *A companion to the Corpus Iuris Hibernici*, Dublin.

Buckley, A. (1978) 'What was the tiompán? A problem in ethnohistorical organology: evidence in Irish literature,' *Jahrbuch für musikalische Volks- und Völkerkunde* 9, 53–88.

— (1990) 'Musical instruments in Ireland from the ninth to the fourteenth centuries: a review of the organological evidence,' in G. Gillen and H. White, *Irish Musical Studies 1: Musicology in Ireland*, Dublin, 13–57.

— (1991) 'Music-related imagery on early Christian insular sculpture: identification, context, function,' *Imago Musicae* 8, 135–99.

— (1995) "And his voice swelled like a terrible thunderstorm…'—Music and symbolic sound in medieval Irish society,' in G. Gillen and H. White, *Irish Musical Studies 3: music and Irish cultural history*, Dublin, 13–76.

— (2000) 'Music and musicians in medieval Irish society,' *Early Music* 28, 165–90.

— (2005) 'Music in Ireland to c. 1500,' in D. Ó Cróinín, *A new history of Ireland: I. Prehistoric and Early Ireland*, Oxford, 744–813.

— (2008) 'Musical monuments from medieval Meath,' *Records of Meath Archaeological and Historical Society* 19, 23–42.

Buhle, E. (1903) *Die musikalischen Instrumente in den Miniaturen des frühen Mittelalters: I. Die Blasinstrumente*, Leipzig.

Cabiran, P.-A. (2010) 'Muses & cornemuses…,' in D. Loddo and C. Ribouillault, *Un monde qui bourdonne*, Cordes, 25–32.

Cabiran, P.-A. and L. Dieu (2003) 'A la découverte des muses médiévales,' *Histoire médiévale* 45 (http://articles.instrumentsmedievaux.org/cab dieumuses.pdf).

Calder, G. (1922) *Togail na Tebe*, Cambridge.

Campbell, M., C. Greated, and A. Myers (2004) *Musical instruments: history, technology & performance of instruments of western music*, Oxford.

Charles-Dominique, L. (2006) *Musiques savantes, musiques populaires: les symboliques du sonore en France 1200–1750*, Paris.

— (2010) "Sémio-logiques' de la cornemuse,' in D. Loddo and C. Ribouillault, *Un monde qui bourdonne (Actes du colloques de Gaillac, décembre 2008)*, Cordes, 131–50.

Collinson, F. M. (1975) *The bagpipe*, London.

Crane, F. (1972) *Extant medieval musical instruments: a provisional catalogue by type*, Iowa City.

Day Lewis, C. (1999) *Virgil: the Eclogues and the Georgics*, Oxford.

de Bernardo Stempel, P. (1999) *Nominale Wortbildung des älteren Irischen*, Tübingen.

de Vaan, M. (2008) *Etymological dictionary of Latin and the other Italic languages*, Leiden.

Dekkers, E. (1995) *Clauis patrum latinorum*, 3rd ed., Turnhout.

Donnelly, S. (2001) *The early history of piping in Ireland*, Dublin.

Dooley, A. and H. Roe (1999) *Tales of the Elders of Ireland*, Oxford.

Downey, C. (2010) '*Dindshenchas* and the *Tech Midchúarta*,' *Ériu* 60, 1–35.

Fisher, I. and F.A. Greenhill (1974) 'Two unrecorded carved stones at Tower of Lethendy, Perthshire,' *Proceedings of the Society of Antiquaries of Scotland* 104, 238–41.

Fletcher, A.J. (2001) *Drama and the performing arts in pre-Cromwellian Ireland*, Cambridge.

Frazer, J. (1931) *Ovid. Fasti*, Cambridge.

Geymonat, M. (1973) *P. Vergili Maronis opera*, Turin.

Gioielli, M. (1999) 'La 'calamaula' di Eutichiano,' *Utriculus* 8.4, 44–5.

Guizzi, F. (2001–2) 'The oboe of Quintus Appeus Eutychianus: a rare representation of a Roman single conical reed-pipe,' *Imago Musicae* 18–19, 121–54.

Gwynn, E. (1903–35) *The Metrical Dindshenchas*, 5 vols., Dublin.

Gwynn, E. and W. Purton (1911–2) 'The monastery of Tallaght,' *PRIA* 29C, 115–79.

Hagel, S. (2010) *Ancient Greek music*, Cambridge.

Hammerstein, R. (1959) 'Instrumenta Hieronymi,' *Archiv für Musikwissenschaft* 16, 117–34.

Harbison, P. (1992) *The high crosses of Ireland: an iconographic and photographic survey*, 3 vols., Bonn.

Harrison, A. (1988) 'Tricksters and entertainers in the Irish tradition,' in G.W. MacLennan, *Proceedings of the First North American Congress of Celtic Studies*, Ottawa, 293–307.

Henry, F. (1960–1) 'Remarks on the decoration of three Irish psalters,' *PRIA* 61C, 23–40.

Herbert, M. (1976) 'Ár nUirlisí Ceoil,' in P. Ó Fiannachta, *Léachtaí Cholm Cille VII: an Ceol i Litríocht na Gaeilge*, Maynooth, 21–30.

Holford-Strevens, L. (2006) 'Sirens in Antiquity and the Middle Ages,' in L.P. Austern and I. Naroditskaya, *Music of the sirens*, Bloomington.

Homo-Lechner, C. (1993) 'Les instruments de musique,' in M. Colardelle and E. Verdel, *Les habitats du lac de Paladru (Isère) dans leur environnement – La formation d'un terroir au XI*[e] *siècle*, Paris, 259–62.

Hort, A.F. (1916) *Theophrastus. Enquiry into plants*, 2 vols., Cambridge.

Howlett, D. (1997) 'Israelite learning in insular Latin,' *Peritia* 11, 117–52.

Ihm, M. (1907) *C. Suetoni Tranquilli De vita Caesarum libri VIII*, Leipzig.

Isaac, G. (2007) *Studies in Celtic sound changes and their chronology*, Innsbruck.

Jackson, K. (1953) *Language and history in Early Britain*, Edinburgh.

Johnson, R. (2000) 'On the dating of some early-medieval Irish crosiers,' *Medieval Archaeology* 44, 115–58.

Kartomi, M.J. (1990) *On concepts and classifications of musical instruments*, Chicago.

Kelly, F. (1988) *A guide to Early Irish Law*, Dublin.

— (1997) *Early Irish farming*, Dublin.

Lambert, B. (1969–72) *Bibliotheca Hieronymiana manuscripta: la tradition manuscrite des œuvres de Saint Jérôme*, 4 vols., Steenbrugge.

Leach, E.E. (2006) '"The little pipe sings sweetly while the fowler deceives the bird': sirens in the later Middle Ages,' *Music and Letters* 87, 187–211.

Lindsay, W.M. (1911) *Isidori Hispalensis episcopi etymologiarum sive originum libri XX*, 2 vols., Oxford.

Marchesin, I. (2000) *L'image organum: la representation de la musique dans les psautiers médiévaux 800–1200*, Turnhout.

Markovitz, M. (2003) *Die Orgel im Altertum*, Leiden.

Matasović, R. (2009) *Etymological dictionary of Proto-Celtic*, Leiden.

Mathiesen, T.J. (1999) *Apollo's lyre: Greek music and music theory in Antiquity and the Middle Ages*, Lincoln.

Matte, J.-L. (2010) 'Le bourdon d'épaule, histoire et géographie,' in D. Loddo and C. Ribouillault, *Un monde qui bourdonne*, Cordes, 9–24.

McCone, K. (1994) 'An tSean-Ghaeilge agus a Réamhstair,' in K. McCone, D. McManus, C. Ó Háinle, N. Williams, and L. Breatnach, *Stair na Gaeilge*, Maynooth, 61–219.

— (1996) *Towards a relative chronology of ancient and medieval Celtic sound change*, Maynooth.

McKinnon, J.W. (1969) 'Musical instruments in medieval Psalm commentaries and Psalters,' *Journal of the American Musicological Society* 21, 3–20.

McLaughlin, R. (2008) *Early Irish satire*, Dublin.

McNamara, M. (1973) 'Psalter-text and Psalter study in the Early Irish Church (A.D. 600–1200),' *PRIA* 73C, 201–98.

— (1986) *Glossa in Psalmos: the Hiberno-Latin gloss on the Psalms of Codex Palatinus Latinus 68*, Città del Vaticano.

— (2000) *The Psalms in the Early Irish Church*, Sheffield.

Meyer, K. (1903) 'Stories and songs from Irish manuscripts: VII. King Eochaid has horse's ears,' *Otia Merseiana* 3, 46–54.

— (1906) *The Triads of Ireland*, London.

— (1913) *Sanas Cormaic*, Dublin.

— (1914) 'The Guesting of Athirne,' *Ériu* 7, 1–9.

— (1919) *Bruchstücke der älteren Lyrik Irlands*, Berlin.

Montagu, J. (2007) *Origins and development of musical instruments*, Lanham.

Montanari, M. (2012) *Gusti del medioevo: i prodotti, la cucina, la tavola*, Rome.

Moore, T. J. (2012) *Music in Roman comedy*, Cambridge.

Moran, P. (2010) 'Hebrew in early Irish glossaries,' *Cambrian Medieval Celtic Studies* 60, 1–21.

Munrow, D. (1976) *Instruments of the Middle Ages and Renaissance*, London.

Mynors, R.A.B. (1937) *Cassiodori Senatoris Institutiones*, Oxford.

O'Curry, E. (1873) *On the manners and customs of the Ancient Irish*, 3 vols., London.

O Daly, M. (1962) 'Lānellach Tigi Rīch 7 Ruirech,' *Ériu* 19, 81–6.

O'Dwyer, S. (2004) *Prehistoric music of Ireland*, Stroud.
Ó Riain, P. (1978) *Cath Almaine*, Dublin.
O'Sullivan, C.M. (2004) *Hospitality in medieval Ireland, 900–1500*, Dublin.
Page, C. (1977) 'Biblical instruments in medieval manuscript illustration,' *Early Music* 5, 299–309.
Pedersen, H. (1909–13) *Vergleichende Grammatik der keltischen Sprachen*, 2 vols., Göttingen.
Petrie, G. (1839) 'On the history and antiquities of Tara Hill,' *Transactions of the Royal Irish Academy* 18, 25–232.
Purser, J. (2002) 'Reconstructing the River Erne Horn,' *Ulster Journal of Archaeology* 61, 17–25.
Rackham, H. (1961) *Pliny, Natural History*, 10 vols., Cambridge.
Radner, J.N. (1978) *Fragmentary Annals of Ireland*, Dublin.
Ramsey, G. (2002) 'The triple pipes on Irish high crosses: identification and interpretation,' *Ulster Journal of Archaeology* 61, 26–36.
Rimmer, J. (1977) *The Irish harp/Cláirseach na hÉireann*, 2nd ed., Cork.
Robbins Bittermann, H. (1929) 'The organ in the early Middle Ages,' *Speculum* 4, 390–410.
Roe, H.M. (1949) 'The 'David Cycle' in Early Irish art,' *The Journal of the Royal Society of Antiquaries of Ireland* 79, 39–59.
Ross, A. (1998) ''Harps of their owne sorte'? A reassessment of Pictish chordophone depictions,' *Cambrian Medieval Celtic Studies* 36, 37–60.
Russell, P. (1990) *Celtic word formation: the velar suffixes*, Dublin.
Sayers, W. (1988) 'The bound and the binding: the lyre in early Ireland,' in G.W. MacLennan, *Proceedings of the First North American Congress of Celtic Studies*, Ottawa, 365–85.
Scarre, A.M. (1910) 'The Beheading of John the Baptist by Mog Ruith,' *Ériu* 4, 173–81.
Schrijver, P. (1991) *The reflexes of the Proto-Indo-European laryngeals in Latin*, Amsterdam.
— (1995) *Studies in British Celtic historical phonology*, Amsterdam.
Seebass, T. (1973) *Musikdarstellung und Psalterillustration im früheren Mittelalter*, 2 vols., Bern.
Shackleton Bailey, D.R. (1990) *M. Valerii Martialis epigrammata*, Stuttgart.
Sihler, A. L. (1995) *New comparative grammar of Greek and Latin*, New York.
Spanu, G.N. (1994) *Sonos: strumenti della musica popolare sarda*, Nuoro.
Stokes, W. (1860) *Irish glosses: a medieval tract on Latin declension*, Dublin.
— (1862) *Three Irish glossaries*, London.
— (1898–1900) 'O'Mulconry's Glossary,' *Archiv für celtische Lexicographie* 1, 232–324, 473–81.
— (1900) 'Acallamh na Senórach,' in W. Stokes and E. Windisch, *Irische Texte mit Übersetzungen und Wörterbuch* 1, Leipzig.

— (1901) 'The Battle of Carn Conaill,' *Zeitschrift für celtische Philologie* 3, 203–19, 572–3.

— (1904) 'The songs of Buchet's house,' *Revue Celtique* 25, 18–39, 225–7.

Stokes, W. and J. Strachan (1901–3) *Thesaurus palaeohibernicus: a collection of Old-Irish glosses, scholia, prose and verse*, 2 vols., Cambridge.

Stüber, K. (1998) *The historical morphology of n-stems in Celtic*, Maynooth.

Thiel, M. (1973) *Grundlagen und Gestalt der Hebräischkenntnisse des frühen Mittelalters*, Spoleto.

Thurneysen, R. (1921) *Die irische Helden- und Königsage bis zum siebzehnten Jahrhundert*, Halle.

— (1933) 'Die Flöte von Mac Dīchoeme,' *Zeitschrift für celtische Philologie* 19, 117–24.

van Schaik, M. (1992) *The harp in the Middle Ages: the symbolism of a musical instrument*, Amsterdam.

Veenstra, A. (1964) 'The classification of the flute,' *Galpin Society Journal* 17, 54–63.

Vendryes, J., E. Bachellery, P.-Y. Lambert (1959–) *Lexique étymologique de l'irlandais ancien*, Dublin.

von Hornbostel, E. and C. Sachs (1914) 'Systematik der Musikinstrumente,' *Zeitschrift für Ethnologie* 46, 553–90; trans. A. Baines and K.P. Wachsmann, 'Classification of musical instruments,' *Galpin Society Journal* 14 (1961), 3–29.

Walsh, M. and D. Ó Cróinín (1988) *Cummian's letter De controuersia paschali, together with a related Irish computistical tract De ratione conputandi*, Toronto.

Walther, S. (2010) 'David rex et propheta: der Polirone-Psalter und die norditalienische David-Tradition von der Spätantike bis ins 11. Jahrhundert,' *Germanistik in der Schweiz* 7, 77–101.

Warntjes, I. (2010) *The Munich Computus: text and translation. Irish computistics between Isidore of Seville and the Venerable Bede and its reception in Carolingian times*, Stuttgart.

Waterman, D.M. (1969) 'An early medieval horn from the River Erne,' *Ulster Journal of Archaeology* 32, 101–4.

West, M.L. (1992) *Ancient Greek music*, Oxford.

Zloch, M. (2006) 'Rohrblattinstrumente mit rechteckigem bis flachrundem Querschnitt—archaische Regionalform oder „Europäer"?,' in E. Hickmann, A. Both, and R. Eichmann, *Studien zur Musikarchäologie V*, Rahden, 49–58.

LEOFRANC HOLFORD-STREVENS

THE HARP THAT ONCE THROUGH AULUS' HALLS

Abstract

Dáibhí Ó Cróinín's association of the debate in Virgilius Maro Grammaticus on the vocative of *ego* with that in Aulus Gellius on the vocative of *egregius* is confirmed by other echoes of the *Noctes Atticae* in the *Epitomae* and *Epistolae*. The work must therefore be added to the classical texts that were known in early medieval Ireland.

Keywords

Aulus Gellius, Virgilius Maro Grammaticus; Ireland.

The background

No-one who has had the pleasure of attending the *International Conference on the Science of Computus in Ireland and Europe* organized every two years in Galway by Dáibhí Ó Cróinín will need to be told of his erudition, enthusiasm, and friendliness; nor are his serendipity in discovering new sources and his readiness to challenge orthodoxy and to venture on new ideas unknown to readers of his many publications on early Irish history, chronology, computistics, and palaeography. It is, not unfittingly, a suggestion of his own that inspires my contribution to his well-deserved *Festschrift*, and a title humorously invented by himself that I give to it; if I can show that the suggestion is well founded, I shall have established that Aulus Gellius, the Roman miscellanist of the 2nd century AD, was known to an Irish author of the 7th, Virgilius Maro Grammaticus. I say 'an Irish author', for Virgilius' nationality ought by now no longer to be in doubt; to the arguments particularly of Dáibhí and

Early medieval Ireland and Europe: chronology, contacts, scholarship, ed. by Pádraic Moran and Immo Warntjes, Studia Traditionis Theologiae, 14 (Turnhout, 2015), pp. 395–404.

 10.1484/M.STT-EB.5.103129

Herren,[1] we may add not only his references to computists,[2] which in principle might have pointed to Spain or North Africa, but the doctrine that the imperative has a first person in the plural but not the singular,[3] which suits neither Latin (spoken in those two regions), in which it has no first-person forms at all, nor Hebrew (the other verb-initial language introduced by way of emendation elsewhere),[4] in which it has none even of the third, but is largely true of Old Irish despite the exceptions noted by Thurneysen.[5]

The vocative of *ego*

In the second of Virgilius' *Epistolae* we learn of an academic dispute between two of the main characters in his reminiscences, Terrentius and Galbungus:[6]

[1] Ó Cróinín (2003); Herren (1979); Herren (1995) (refuting the suggestion by Bischoff (1988) that Virgilius was a Spanish Jew; cf. Richter (1999), 167 and n 28).

[2] Virgilius Maro, *Epitomae* 8.183–5; 12.81–2; *Epistolae* 2.179–80 (ed. Löfstedt (2003), 195, 243, 31).

[3] Virgilius Maro, *Epitomae* 7.46–55 (Löfstedt (2003), 175).

[4] Virgilius Maro, *Epitomae* 5.3–4 (Löfstedt (2003), 137–8). Virgilius addresses the complaint that priority has been accorded in the Latin-speaking world to the noun, *cum* [here the witnesses offer variously *in hibonorum*, *inhiborum*, *iniborum*, and *in horum*] *eloqutione et conpossitione primatum tenere aestimatur uerbum*; Huemer (1886), 180, in the name-index of his Teubner text, emended *Hibonorum* to *Hebreorum*, but Sittl (1889), 71, reviewing Huemer's earlier edition of the *Epitomae*, preferred *Hibernorum*, which is less drastic. I cannot make syntax of Herren's interpretation in (1979), 56, 'the good men of Hy', i.e. the Irish community on Iona; Dáibhí's suggestion (Ó Cróinín (1989), 13 n 2 = (2003), 191 n 2) of reading *hiberbatonicorum*, meaning *grammaticorum*, 'as in the seventh-century Irish *Anonymus ad Cuimnanum*' would settle the author's nationality for good.

[5] Thurneysen (1946), 374–5 (§586). At *Epitomae* 8.24, if Löfstedt (2003), 185, is right to read *Conacti* instead of *Coacti*, we clearly have a pseudo-etymological spelling; but coming just after the preceding *coactio*, the strange form invites us to look for a motivation, which I can find only in a hit at the Connachta.

[6] Virgilius Maro, *Epistolae* 2.70–4 (Löfstedt (2003), 26–7). The two combatants, said at *Epistolae* 1.16–8 (Löfstedt (2003), 8) to have been the leading scholarchs of Virgilius' day and mentioned by him more frequently than anyone else except his master Aeneas (who resolves the dispute), bear names that suggest a rivalry between Gael and Teuton (settled by a Roman), for Ter(r)entius is the standard translation of Toirdhealbhach, while Galbungus has the air of Latinized Frankish, though there is no authentic root **galb* to which the patronymic suffix *-ung* might be attached; however, Dáibhí suggests (personal communication) that the name conceals an Irish pun on 'Beating the Foreigner', from *Gall* + *bongid* ('strikes'), nor unlike the *Galli* remarked on below is he presented as an ignorant alien. At *Epistolae* 2.44–6 *Et iterum Galbungus*

> *Verum Galbungus et Terrentius quattuordecim diebus totidemque noctibus in contentionibus mansisse refferuntur tali, ut, si 'ego' uocatiuum casum haberet aut non haberet, ex omnibus doctorum ueterum traditionibus approbarent.*

Whether *ego* has a vocative was a well-worn topic amongst Latin grammarians (the Greeks denied that case to ἐγώ);[7] but our honorand was reminded of a dispute in Aulus Gellius' *Noctes Atticae* XIV 5:[8]

> *Defessus ego quondam diutina commentatione, laxandi leuandique animi gratia in Agrippae campo deambulabam.*[9] *Atque ibi duos forte grammaticos conspicatus non parui in urbe Roma nominis, certationi eorum acerrimae adfui, cum alter in casu uocatiuo 'uir egregi' dicendum contenderet, alter 'uir egregie'.*[10]

The two swapped arguments for a good long time,[11] finally wearing out Gellius' patience:[12]

> *Sed cum ille paulisper oppositu horum uocabulorum commotus reticuisset, et mox tamen se conlegisset, eandemque illam quam definierat regulam retineret et propugnaret* [...] *eaque inter eos contentio longius duceretur, non arbitratus ego operae pretium esse eadem istaec diutius audire, clamantes conpugnantes illos reliqui.*

This chapter impressed itself on the 11th-century anthologist who put together chapters from Gellius and Valerius Maximus,[13] and the 12th-

quidam [read *quidem*] *ueteranus in Indiae partibus constitutus* (Löfstedt (2003), 25) are we to suppose a hit at missionaries?

7 For the Latin grammarians see *Ps.-Remmii Palaemonis Regulae* II 4 (ed. Rosellini (2001), 41–3 with commentary pp. 122–3); for the Greeks see Holford-Strevens (2003a), n 10.

8 Aulus Gellius, *Noctes Atticae* XIV 5.1 (ed. Marshall (1968), ii 439). Ó Cróinín (1995), 212 n 85.

9 The *Campus Agrippae* was near the modern *Fontana di Trevi.*

10 On this question, see Holford-Strevens (2003), 178–9 n 34.

11 But not authorities, which Gellius values higher than arguments (Holford-Strevens (2003), 178–9).

12 Aulus Gellius, *Noctes Atticae* XIV 5.5 (ed. Marshall (1968), ii 440).

13 This *Florilegium Valerio-Gellianum* is preserved in MSS Cambridge, Trinity College, R.16.34 (982) (R.16.34) (Salisbury Cathedral, *c.*1100), 1r–22v (part only); Bremen, Staats- und Universitätsbibliothek, msc 0041 (western Germany, saec. xii[1]), pp. 1–68, 70–80 (part only); Vatican, Biblioteca Apostolica, Vat. lat. 3307 (French, s.

century scribe who appended it (plus two snippets from book 15) to Guy d'Amiens's narrative poem on the Norman Conquest, *Carmen de Hastingae proelio*, in what is now the concluding booklet of MS Brussels, Bibliothèque royale de Belgique / Koninklijke Bibliotheek van België, 10615–729, 230vb;[14] it would therefore not be difficult to believe that it also impressed itself on Virgilius, whose ear might have been struck by the initial *eg*.[15] In view of this, it seems worthwhile to seek other possible reflections of the *Noctes Atticae* in Virgilius' works.[16]

Personal reminiscences

Most medieval grammarians, like those of Antiquity and our own times, stick grimly to their subject, the only personal note being struck in epistles dedicatory prefixed to their treatises. The *Epitomae* and *Epistolae* of Virgilius Maro Grammaticus are different, being open to personal reminiscence. In this, they resemble the *Noctes Atticae*, not indeed a work of grammar but a miscellany, yet nevertheless with much grammatical content, in both the broad ancient and the narrow modern sense, often presented in anecdotal form. *Epitomae* 7 and 11 both begin *memini*,[17] a word with which Gellius several times introduces learned discussions; in *Noctes Atticae* XIX 10 it is even the first word.[18] In *Epitomae* 7 the

xii); Paris, Bibliothèque nationale de France, Lat. 4952 (French, saec. xii), 136v–203r; Paris, Bibliothèque nationale de France, Nouvelle acquisition latine 1777 (Italian, *c.*1382), 1r–25v (selective); Florence, Biblioteca Marucelliana, C 220 (Florence, saec. xv), 26r–75v (Gellius only); extracts in Bonn, Universitäts- und Landesbibliothek, S. 218 (Maria Laach, saec. xii in MS of saec. xi from Sankt Maximin, Trier), 25r, 41v. See Valentini (1910); Schullian (1937); Falmagne (2001), 249.

14 On the MS see Barlow (1999), xix–xx with partial illustration of the excerpt on p xcii; Holford-Strevens (2004), 269–70.

15 The fourteen-day-and-night debate is of course his own embellishment, than which he was to go one better at *Epistolae* 3.238–79 (Löfstedt (2003), 48–9) with the fifteen-day-and-night debate between Regulus the Cappadocian and Sedulus the Roman that all but saw swords drawn.

16 Although the choice of Terrentius as the name of a grammarian may seem an allusion to the greatest of Roman scholars M. Terentius Varro, it was not from Gellius that Virgilius could have learnt he bore that *nomen*, despite the quotation at *Noctes Atticae* XI 1.4 (Marshall (1968), ii 338) of a passage in which Varro, as was his wont, used it in an example. Gellius does, however, mention Terentius Scaurus, *diui Hadriani temporibus grammaticus uel nobilissimus* (*Noctes Atticae* XI 15.3 (Marshall (1968), ii 351)).

17 Virgilius Maro, *Epitomae* 7.1; 11.1 (Löfstedt (2003), 171, 225).

18 Aulus Gellius, *Noctes Atticae* XIX 10.1 (Marshall (1968), ii 576).

verb is followed by *me cum essem adulescentulus scolaribus studîs deditus quodam interfuisse die*;[19] this recalls *adulescentulus cum etiamtum in scholis essemus* in Gellius, who more than once refers to his student self as *adulescentulus*, but also recalls a philosophical discussion with the words *His quondam ego acriter atque contente pro suis utrimque decretis propugnantibus, cum essemus una omnes Ostiae cum Fauorino, interfui*, and in another chapter beginning with *adulescentulus* gives an account of *illa quodam die sermocinatio* on a grammatical question.[20]

In some of these anecdotes Gellius, in person, asks for information; so does Virgilius.[21] One reminiscence, introduced by *Memini*, is of seeking instruction *a quodam Lupo, Christiano uiro Atheniensi in ratione uerborum satis experto*; earlier in the same letter a disputant is described as *uir ammodum ingenio acutus atque eloquentia satis floridus*.[22] Such parenthetic sketches are characteristic of Gellius, e.g. *Herodem Atticum, consularem uirum ingenioque amoeno et Graeca facundia celebrem* and *T. Castricius* [...] *summa uir auctoritate grauitateque et a diuo Hadriano in mores atque litteras spectatus*.[23]

In one place Virgilius interrupts his grammatical instruction to report wise words uttered by his beloved teacher Aeneas, which he introduces with the words *Et quia ipsius Aeneae mentio incedit* [recte *incidit*];[24] Gellius, too, offers the 'And while we are on the subject' digression (e.g. *Et quoniam facta litui mentio est*) and the self-interpolatory reminiscence, not least of his own beloved teacher Favorinus.[25]

Other echoes

Naturally it is not suggested that Virgilius wrote with a copy of Gellius open before him on his desk; rather, that he had read him in the past and that certain things had stuck in his mind. When in the second and third epistles he speaks of *Gallus noster, nostrorum maxime Gallorum*,

19 Virgilius Maro, *Epitomae* 7.1–2 (Löfstedt (2003), 171).

20 Aulus Gellius, *Noctes Atticae* XVI 1.1; XVIII 1.2; XIX 8.1–2 (Marshall (1968), ii 474, 537, 569).

21 E.g. Virgilius Maro, *Epistolae* 1.160–80; 3.340–52,378–97 (Löfstedt (2003), 14–5, 52–3, 54).

22 Virgilius Maro, *Epistola* 3.340–1,257–8 (Löfstedt (2003), 52, 49).

23 Aulus Gellius, *Noctes Atticae* IX 2.1; XIII 22.1 (Marshall (1968), i 278, ii 408).

24 Virgilius Maro, *Epitomae* 5.187–218 (Löfstedt (2003), 149–51).

25 Aulus Gellius, *Noctes Atticae* V 8.8; I 3.27; III 3.6 (Marshall (1968), i 198, 46, 137).

Gallorum nostrorum,[26] one can hardly not think of the words attributed by Gellius to Favorinus of Arelate, who, living in Rome, begins an account of local wind-names with the words *nostri namque Galli*, meaning 'the Gauls from whom I come'.[27] A 7th-century Irishman cannot have used it in that sense; on the face of it the expression means 'the Gauls amongst us', for the word was still occasionally applied to the inhabitants of *Gallia* even if they were Franks,[28] but the Irish reader would have recognized these *Galli* as *gaill*, foreigners, such as might be encountered at Rath Melsigi,[29] especially as on all three occasions they are cited for aberrant usages.[30]

By now we have good reason to suppose that the resemblance between the two works is not accidental; it is therefore not unreasonable to suggest echoes of Gellius elsewhere in Virgilius' work that might not seem conclusive in isolation. In his first letter we are instructed:[31]

> *Sic 'tibi' si scribis datiuo casu pronominis finiti, posteriorem syllabam tibi, si uero imperatiuo modo actiui illus uerbi scripseris, quod est 'tibio', priorem syllabam acuere debes. 'Tibio' autem hunc sensum habet: 'citarizo'; 'tibia' enim quoddam cantandi genus est.*

Absurd as the accentuation *tibí* and the invention of *tibio* are,[32] this is not the only place where Virgilius extends to pairs of inflected forms the accentual distinction made by Roman grammarians between an

[26] Virgilius Maro, *Epistolae* 2.255; 3.207–8,211 (Löfstedt (2003), 34, 46, 47).

[27] Aulus Gellius, *Noctes Atticae* II 22.20 (Marshall (1968), i 112). For Favorinus' Gaulish ethnicity see above all Philostratus, Lives of the Sophists I 8.489 (Kayser (1870–1), ii 9). He was honoured at length by his compatriot Legré (1900), and is now commemorated at Arles by a *rue Favorin*.

[28] Jonas, *Vita Columbani* I 15 (ed. by Bruno Krusch in MGH SS rer. Germ. 37, 178): *tegumenta manuum, quae Galli wantos uocant*.

[29] See Ó Cróinín (1984).

[30] That none of these usages can be associated with any particular nation makes no difference: the misplaced enclitic of *solemque lunam* for *solem lunamque* can be found here and there throughout post-classical Latinity; the first-conjugation verb *scripsero scripserare* is pure fantasy; nor is *canno* for *cano* characteristic of England or Francia. (According to Krusch and Levison's apparatus in MGH SS rer. Merov. 1.1, 157, l. 16 n p; 158, ll. 11 n z, 13 n 1; 208, l. 7 n y, 7th- and 8th-century Merovingian scribes occasionally spell *cannones* and *cannonicus* in Gregory of Tours' history, but never import the geminate into *canis* or *cano*.) See too Herren (1979), 49 n 131.

[31] Virgilius Maro, *Epistolae* 1.199–203 (Löfstedt (2003), 16).

[32] There is of course no such verb as *tibio tibire tibiui tibitum*; if there were a verb derived from *tibia* it would be *tibio tibiare tibiaui tibiatum*, with long *i* in the first syllable contrasting with the short *i* of the pronoun.

inflected form and an indeclinable;[33] but there was a precedent in Nigidius Figulus' already obsolete differentiation cited by Gellius between *Valéri* genetive and *Váleri* vocative:[34]

> *P. Nigidii uerba sunt ex commentariorum grammaticorum uicesimo quarto, hominis in disciplinis doctrinarum omnium praecellentis: 'Deinde' inquit 'uoculatio qui poterit seruari, si non sciemus in nominibus, ut Valeri, utrum interrogandi an uocandi sint? Nam interrogandi secunda syllaba superiore tonost quam prima, deinde nouissima deicitur; at in casu uocandi summo tonost prima, deinde gradatim descendunt.' Sic quidem Nigidius dici praecipit. Sed si quis nunc Valerium appellans in casu uocandi secundum id praeceptum Nigidii acuerit primam, non aberit quin rideatur. Summum autem tonum προσῳδίαν acutam dicit, et quem accentum nos dicimus, uoculationem appellat, et casum interrogandi eum dicit quem nunc nos genetiuum dicimus.*

The *tibia*, moreover—that is to say the Greek aulos, mistranslated 'flute' by the organologically challenged, but in fact a double-reed wind instrument usually paired treble and bass—is mentioned in three chapters of the *Noctes Atticae*:[35] it accompanies Spartan and Lydian armies on the march, and Gaius Gracchus has a slave who employs a pitch-pipe to calm him down when he becomes carried away by his oratory; its music brings relief to sufferers from sciatica and cures the bite of adders; it falls out of favour in Athens after Alcibiades is disgusted by the ugly faces he is obliged to pull while playing it. The Latin verb for playing an instrument, which Gellius naturally uses, is *canere*, also 'to sing'; Virgilius surely exploits this when he mischievously, rather than ignorantly, defines the *tibia* as a kind of singing.

In another letter Virgilius discusses the alternative names for frequentative verbs such as *uictito*, meaning *magis ac magis uinco*.[36] There is no such verb as *uĭctito* from *uinco* on record, but there is a verb *uīctito*

[33] At *Epitomae* 3.91–101 (Löfstedt (2003), 121–2) Virgilius first invents the noun–verb distinctions *sédes* 'seat' ~ *sedés* 'thou sittest', *réges* 'kings' ~ *regés* 'thou wilt rule', then cites the standard doctrine that *pone* is accented on the first syllable when it is the singular imperative 'put' and the second when it is the adverb or preposition 'behind'. Immediately after treating of the two forms *tibi*, Virgilius invents an adverb *estó*, meaning 'rightly' or 'perhaps', to be contrasted with the future imperative singular *ésto*.

[34] Aulus Gellius, *Noctes Atticae* XIII 26.1–3 (Marshall (1968), ii 417–8).

[35] Aulus Gellius, *Noctes Atticae* I 11; IV 13; XV 17 (Marshall (1968) i 50–60, 179–80, ii 462–3).

[36] Virgilius Maro, *Epistolae* 3.168–75 (Löfstedt (2003), 45).

from *uiuo*, meaning 'I live in a particular way', usually 'I live off' something. It occurs eight times in Plautus, once in Terence, and four times in Gellius, who not only makes frequent use of frequentative verbs but devotes a whole chapter to them.[37] Might Virgilius be adapting Gellius to his own purposes?

Virgilius' assertion that *plebs* denotes the boneheaded and cowardly idle rich, *populus* the strong in brawn or brain,[38] is of course nonsense, but he might have got the idea of distinguishing them from Gellius, who correctly states that *plebs* excludes, but *populus* includes, the patricians.[39] However, I dare not press this point, less because Gellius uses the apparently older nominative *plebes*[40]—after all, Virgilius himself can produce a nominative *plebis*[41]—than because another distinction, also incorrect and scarcely less absurd (*plebs* excludes, *populus* includes, the *seniores*), is drawn in Isidore's *Etymologiae*, a work that Virgilius is known to have read.[42]

Nevertheless, I submit that sufficient evidence has been produced to confirm Dáibhí's suggestion that Virgilius knew Gellius. To be sure we have no evidence outside the *Epitomae* and *Epistolae* that the *Noctes Atticae* were known in early medieval Ireland, but neither have we evidence that Macrobius' *Saturnalia* were known save for the excerpting of the *Disputatio Chori et Praetextati*.[43] That of course does not mean that manuscripts of either author were generally available; there may indeed have been only one copy of each in all Ireland, but as we have no evidence that there were others, so we have no evidence that there were not. At all events, the evidence for Gellius in Ireland is at least as strong as that for Gellius in pre-Conquest England, which is no more than a possible allusion in Aldhelm.[44] Our honorand may therefore be congratulated on yet another discovery.

[37] Aulus Gellius, *Noctes Atticae* IX 6 (Marshall (1985), i 285).

[38] Virgilius Maro, *Epitomae* 4.208–15 (Löfstedt (2003), 129).

[39] Aulus Gellius, *Noctes Atticae* X 20.5 (Marshall (1968), i 324).

[40] Besides *plebs plebis* in the third declension, the word is also found in the fifth declension, *plebes pleb(e)i*, whence the frequent *tribunus plebi* and *plebi scitum*.

[41] Virgilius Maro, *Epitomae* 5.280 (Löfstedt (2003), 155).

[42] Isidore, *Etymologiae* IX 4.5–6 (ed. Lindsay (1911), i unpaginated). See Herren (1979), 45–6.

[43] I argue for an Irish origin in my edition of that text, to be published in the Proceedings of the 2010 Galway conference. On evidence for Latin texts in Ireland see Sharpe (2010).

[44] Aldhelm writes to King Geruntius (*Epistola ad Geruntium*, ed. by Rudolf Ehwald in MGH Auct. ant. 15, 483): *quia et eorum barones et hostes exercitu superato sub corona vendere solebant*. If *eorum barones* means *seruos suos*, as indicated in the Brit-

Addendum

Howlett (forthcoming), kindly shared with me by its author, combining the arguments of Stevenson (1999), that the poem, which she shows to share features with Virgilius, was composed on Iona, and of Lapidge (2010), that Aldhelm studied there, will suggest that his teacher was none other than Virgilius. In that case, if Aldhelm did indeed allude to Gellius, he may have used Virgilius' own copy.

Bibliography

Barlow, F. (1999), *The* Carmen de Hastingae Proelio *of Guy Bishop of Amiens*, Oxford.

Bischoff, B. (1988), 'Die "zweite Latinität" des Virgilius Maro Grammaticus und seine jüdische Herkunft,' *Mittellateinisches Jahrbuch* 23, 11–6.

Falmagne, T. (2001) *Un texte en contexte: les Flores paradisi et le milieu culturel de Villers-en-Brabant dans la première moitié du XIIIe siècle*, Turnhout.

Herren, M.W. (1979) 'Some new light on the life of Virgilius Maro Grammaticus,' *PRIA* 79C, 27–71.

— (1995) 'Virgil the Grammarian: a Spanish Jew in Ireland?,' *Peritia* 9, 51–71.

Holford-Strevens, L.A. (2003) *Aulus Gellius: an Antonine scholar and his achievement*, Oxford.

— (2003a) Review of M. Rosellini, *Ps. Remmii Palaemonis regulae*, *Bryn Mawr Classical Review* 2003.03.24 (http://bmcr.brynmawr.edu/2003/2003-03-24.html).

— (2004) '*Recht as een Palmen-Bohm* and other facets of Gellius' medieval and humanistic reception,' in L.A. Holford-Strevens and A. Vardi, *The worlds of Aulus Gellius*, Oxford, 249–81.

Howlett, D. (forthcoming) 'The *Altus prosator* of Virgilius Maro Grammaticus,' in E. Purcell, P. MacCotter, J. Nyhan, and J. Sheehan, *Clerics, kings, and Vikings: essays on medieval Ireland*, Dublin.

Huemer, J. (1886) *Virgilii Maronis Grammatici opera*, Leipzig.

Kayser, C.L. (1870–1) *Flauii Philostrati opera*, 2 vols., Leipzig.

ish Academy's *Dictionary of Medieval Latin from British Sources* i 183 *s.v.* 'baro', this conflates *Noctes Atticae* VI 4 (Marshall (1968), i 230), on slaves sold wearing caps, with Festus, *De uerborum significatu, s.v.* 'sub corona' (Lindsay (1913), 400). At Lapidge and Herren (1979), 157 Herren, following Ehwald's reference in MGH Auct. ant. 15, 483 to Isidore, *Etymologiae* IX 4.31 (Lindsay (1911), i unpaginated), where *barones* is equivalent to *mercennarii* ('hired hands'), renders 'the enemy and their mercenaries': but why should mercenaries be mentioned first, or at all?

Lapidge, M. (2010) 'Aldhelm and the "Epinal-Erfurt Glossary",' in K. Barker, *Aldhelm and Sherborne: essays to celebrate the founding of the bishopric*, Oxford, 129–63.

Lapidge, M. and M. Herren (1979) *Aldhelm: The prose works*, Cambridge, repr. Woodbridge 2009.

Legré, L. (1900) *Un philosophe provençal au temps des Antonins: Favorin d'Arles. Sa vie — ses œuvres — ses contemporains*, Marseille.

Lindsay, W.M. (1911) *Isidori Hispalensis episcopi etymologiarum sive originum libri XX*, 2 vols., Oxford.

— (1913) *Sextus Pompeius Festus de uerborum significatu quae supersunt cum Pauli epitome*, Leipzig.

Löfstedt, B. (2003) *Virgilius Maro Grammaticus: Opera omnia*, Munich.

Marshall, P.K. (1968) *A. Gellii Noctes Atticae*, 2 vols., Oxford.

Ó Cróinín, D. (1984) 'Rath Melsigi, Willibrord, and the earliest Echternach manuscripts,' *Peritia* 3, 17–49 (with appendix by Thomas Fanning), repr. in Ó Cróinín (2003), 145–72.

— (1989) 'The date, provenance and earliest use of the works of Virgilius Maro Grammaticus,' in G. Bernt, F. Rädle, and G. Silagi, *Tradition und Wertung. Festschrift Franz Brunhölzl*, Sigmaringen, 13–22, repr. in Ó Cróinín (2003), 191–200.

— (1995) *Early medieval Ireland, 400–1200*, London.

— (2003) *Early Irish history and chronology*, Dublin.

Richter, M. (1999) *Ireland and her neighbours in the seventh century*, Dublin.

Rosellini, M. (2001) *Ps. Remmii Palaemonis regulae*, Hildesheim.

Schullian, D.M. (1937) 'The anthology of Valerius Maximus and A. Gellius,' *Classical Philology* 32, 70–2.

Sharpe, R. (2010) 'Books from Ireland, fifth to ninth centuries,' *Peritia* 21, 1–55.

Sittl, K. (1889) Review of Johann Huemer, *Virgilii Maronis Grammatici opera* and idem, 'Die Epitomae des Grammatikers Virgilius Maro nach dem Fragmentum Vindobonense 19556', *Jahresbericht über die Fortschritte der klassischen Altertumswissenschaft* 59, 71–3.

Stevenson, J. (1999) 'Altus Prosator,' *Celtica* 23, 326–78.

Thurneysen, R. (1946) *A grammar of Old Irish*, trans. D.A. Binchy and O. Bergin, Dublin.

Valentini, R. (1910) 'Di un'antologia Valerio-Gelliana del sec. XII,' *Classici e neolatini* 6 (1910), 251–77.

THOMAS O'LOUGHLIN

THE SO-CALLED *CAPITULA* FOR THE BOOK OF THE APOCALYPSE IN THE BOOK OF ARMAGH (DUBLIN, TRINITY COLLEGE, 52) AND LATIN EXEGESIS

Abstract

In the Book of Armagh, on f 159v, we find a lozenge of text which suggests a division system for the text of the New Testament's Book of the Apocalypse. This short text, which is also found in the Metz Bible, identifies fourteen moments in the Apocalypse in a manner very similar to the way a set of *capitula* identifies passages within a text while dividing it into sections—and this text has traditionally been studied as one more set of textual divisions for this biblical book. However, closer examination of the text, combined with a comparison with other sets of *capitula* from biblical codices and summaries in exegetical handbooks suggest this text neither sections the book efficiently nor does it provide an introduction to its content. Rather, the numbered list of items proceeds visually through the book, offering the reader a guide to imagining the visions directly while knowing the narrative account of those visions is to be found in the biblical book's text.

Keywords

Apocalypse, Book of Revelations, New Testament, Bible, *Vetus Latina*, Vulgate; Book of Armagh, *Codex Fuldensis*, Metz Bible; Isidore; *capitula*, division systems, exegesis, sectioning, summaries, *tituli*, visions.

Introduction

How any text was divided into parts constitutes an act of basic interpretation of that text because it indicates one manner in which it was understood. This is all the more important when the text was consulted as an authority: now the division system may have shaped its reception,

Early medieval Ireland and Europe: chronology, contacts, scholarship, ed. by Pádraic Moran and Immo Warntjes, Studia Traditionis Theologiae, 14 (Turnhout, 2015), pp. 405–23.

 10.1484/M.STT-EB.5.103130

providing a guide to its contents, its purpose, and its uses.[1] Moreover, how any division system was used within a particular codex may offer us an insight into how that text was appreciated in the manuscript's milieu: a dated and localized detail of exegetical practice. Such codices also constitute part of the reception history both of the text (as a division system) and of the division system itself (as an exegetical artefact). So in this paper I shall focus my work on a division system as it is found in the biblical book the Apocalypse of John, and in just one codex: the Book of Armagh, produced in Armagh in 807.[2]

The division of any work by an editor is an act of interpretation, and in the case of a biblical book it constitutes a work of exegesis by creating fundamental parameters for the reader. Yet this is an area that has received limited attention from historians of exegesis, and has been pursued largely by those seeking to establish links between manuscripts of particular works in the course of producing modern editions.[3] In such research into the links between manuscripts, the division system, as an intellectual artefact, is irrelevant because there is a universally accepted system of referencing which can accommodate any set of divisions imposed on the text,[4] and the only residual importance relates to how codices are gathered into families such that another aspect of the history of the Vulgate is revealed.[5]

However, if our concern is not the history of the Vulgate as a text, but the history of a particular region's biblical exegesis, then the variety of division systems must become an object of study in its own right.

[1] See O'Loughlin (2007a), where the importance of studying these systems is explored within a more general framework.

[2] Dublin, Trinity College, 52 (available online at: www.confessio.ie); see Lapidge and Sharpe (1985), 103–5, 137, 141 (§§354–60, 526, 538–9); and Gryson (1999–2004), i 92–3 (§61).

[3] See, for example, the survey of the division systems of the Apocalypse in Gryson (2000–3), 62–77, which builds upon de Bruyne (1914), 392–9 and 553–5; and the edition of Wordsworth and White (1905), 410–8 (*Capitula in Apocalypsin Iohannis*). It is Wordsworth and White's text of the Book of the Apocalypse that will be used here, but always compared with that of Weber (1994).

[4] Indeed, it will be the accepted division system into chapters and verses that will be used for locating points in the biblical text in the paper.

[5] It was with this task in mind that de Bruyne produced his *Sommaires* (1914) where he identified (p 398) the division system being examined here as extant in two manuscripts: Dublin, Trinity College, 52, 159v and Metz, Bibliothèque municipale, 7 (see *CLA* 6, 26 (no. 786), and Gryson (1999–2004), i 217–8 (no. 145)) which dates from the period of 8th–9th century (this manuscript was destroyed in 1944 but a complete set of photographs is in existence). For an example of how division systems were used in producing the critical edition of the Vulgate, see, for example, Quentin (1926), 71–133; O'Loughlin (1999a), 207–43, 325–33.

How they were used is yet another element in the history of exegesis, alongside commentaries, introductions, and homilies on the biblical text. Such division systems may cover several biblical books (such as the systems we find that are related to the Eusebian Apparatus and cover the four Gospels),[6] particular bodies of scriptural material (such as division systems relating to the Pauline corpus),[7] or simply individual books (as that for the Apocalypse in the Book of Armagh).[8]

The particular system under examination is interesting for the history of the exegesis of the Apocalypse for several reasons. First, it is found in just two manuscripts—both roughly contemporary—and so offers a distinct perspective from other division systems which often have much in common. Second, in the Book of Armagh it is a clearly identified item of biblical information in that (a) it is given an entire page to itself in the manuscript (f 159v), although there is far less text than would fill a page; and (b) it was laid out in a special display format as a lozenge of text[9] which indicated that it was considered by the scribe to be significant and, for him at least, valuable. Third, the content of the division system both (a) in its prose style and (b) in its coverage of the biblical text is radically different to other surviving systems for the Apocalypse. Fourth, we know from the presence of another exegetical aid located in the text of the Apocalypse—a plan of the New Jerusalem—that those who produced this manuscript had a particular interest in this biblical book.[10] Fifth, this is a codex whose date and origin are beyond dispute—it was produced in Armagh in 807[11]—and, therefore, we can locate with certainty the intellectual milieu where this division system was valued, although we should note that we can say little with certainty about either the state of Apocalypse exegesis in that milieu, except in general terms.[12]

[6] See O'Loughlin (1999b) and (2010).

[7] See Willard (1971).

[8] The text of the Book of Armagh used here will that that of the diplomatic edition by Gwynn (1913); the text of the division system is found on f 159v of the manuscript, p 314 of the edition.

[9] The significance of the lozenge shape within insular manuscripts has been studied by Richardson (2002) (the '*capitula*' lozenge is reproduced on Pl. 12 of this article); and see two earlier articles by Richardson (1984) and (1996). In view of Richardson's work on this theme, I shall say no more about it here. Gryson (2000–3), 17, has noted that the text 'est précédé [...] de la capitulation [...] curieusement disposée en forme de losange'.

[10] See O'Loughlin (2000).

[11] See Sharpe (1983).

[12] For a survey of the role of the Apocalypse-derived imagery of the New Jerusalem at the end of the 8th century in Ireland, see O'Loughlin (1999c). How the

The text

The text of the division system reads:[13]

i Apocalipsis Ihesu Christi quam dedit illi Deus.
ii Iohannis septem[14] aeclessiis quae sunt in assia.
iii ego iohannis frater uester et socius in tribulatione.
iiii anguelo ephessi aeclessiae scribe.
u post haec uidi et ecce hostium apertum in caelo.
ui et uidi cum aperuerit[15] unum de sigillis.
uii ubi primus anguelus tuba cecinit.
uiii et apertum est templum Dei quod est in caelo et apparuit arca testamenti eius.
uiiii et stetit super harenam maris et uidi de mari bestiam discendentem.[16]
x et post haec uidi et apertum est templum tabernaculi testimonii sancti in caelo[17] et septem[18] angueli[19] effudent.

Apocalypse was used later in the 9th century by Eriugena is a more tractable problem, but we cannot infer from the nature of his later work on the Continent that he is a witness to concerns at home at the time of the composition of the Book of Armagh; see O'Loughlin (2002).

13 Dublin, Trinity College, 52, 159v (ed. Gwynn (1913), 314). In this transcription spelling has been retained as in the manuscript (a normalized spelling can be found in de Bruyne (1914), 398); however, in contrast with Gwynn, correct word divisions have been introduced as it is clear that where spaces were omitted by the scribe, this was due to his need to fit lines within his lozenge-shaped outline; the *nomina sacra* are silently expanded, as are common suspensions and contractions.

14 The numeral *uii* is used in the manuscript.

15 Metz has *aperuisset*.

16 Metz has *ascendentem* which is the reading of Apoc 12:18.

17 In the manuscript it is clear that this phrase ends with the suspension for *sunt*; however, given the impossibility of this reading (*et apertum est templum tabernaculi testimonii sancti in caelo sunt*) both Wordsworth and White (1905), 415, and Gwynn (1913), 314, printed the abbreviation without further comment; there is no corresponding word in Metz. Pádraic Moran has suggested to me that *sed* is syntactically possible. We could imagine this sequence: (1) *et* was replaced by the Vulgate expression *sed et* (found on nearly 300 occasions in the Vulgate); (2) *sed* was then abbreviated; (3) another copyist found that this use of *sed et* was incorrect (*sed et* is used on forty occasions in the Vulgate New Testament but not once in the Apocalypse), but less he miss out something, inserted the abbreviation for *sunt*. However we seek to explain it, it remains a puzzle.

18 The numeral *uii* is used in the manuscript.

19 Metz adds *fialas suas* after *angeli*.

xi post haec uidi alium anguelum discendentem de caelo habentem potestatem magnam.
xii et uidi caelum apertum et equum album et qui sedebat super eum uocatur fidelis et uerus.
xiii et uidi caelum nouum et terram nouam.
xiiii et ostendit mihi flumen aquae uiuae splendidum.

Reading the text it is apparent that unlike most sets of *capitula*, there is no element here that is descriptive of the text it divides. For example, in several codices the *capitulum* for the section beginning Apocalypse 19:11 reads *De iusto iudicio et uastatione incolarum meretricis*,[20] following a formula found in most sets of *capitula*. Our text, by contrast, uses a biblical lemma—item *xii* in the text above—that assumes the reader enters directly into the world of the text's author. Second, the text is almost entirely a collection of biblical lemmata. Third, it seems to fail as a division system because the units of text vary so much in size: some are but a few verses long, others cover several of our chapters. And lastly, it appears as if one is to read it as a single piece of prose rather than use it as a contents, reference list. On the other hand, against the last two points, the presence of the numerals in the left-hand margin indicate that it is to be read as a list.[21]

Sources and analysis[22]

1. The first item (*apocalypsis Iesu Christi quam dedit illi Deus*) is the opening words of Apocalypse 1:1. The text is identical with that of the Vulgate, while Armagh's text reads *dedit illi Dominus* using the *nomen sacrum* 'dns'. Such a small discrepancy is only significant in showing that the scribe did not see a need to check, and then presumably harmonize, one text with another.
2. *Iohannes septem ecclesiis quae sunt in Asia* is Apocalypse 1:4. This is identical with the Vulgate text (and so also with Armagh). In

[20] See 'Series A' in de Bruyne (1914), 396; Gryson (2000–3), 63; and Wordsworth and White (1905), 417 (where it is attributed to Apoc 20:1).

[21] The numbers are also present in the Metz Bible; we cannot know whether or not the numbering is original to the set or was added by someone using the set of lemmata as *capitula*.

[22] In these analytic sections, the standard Vulgate orthography will be used in rendering the Book of Armagh (e.g., *hostium* for *ostium* will be ignored) as this facilitates comparisons.

Armagh *Asia* is spelled in the same way, *assia*, in both the lozenge and the book.

3. *Ego Iohannes frater uester et socius in tribulatione* is Apocalypse 1:9. However, here the text departs from the Vulgate (including Armagh) in that it reads *socius* instead of *particeps*. *Socius* is found in some texts influenced by the *Vetus Latina*.
4. *Angelo Ephesi ecclesiae scribe* is Apocalypse 2:1. This is identical with the Vulgate text, including that in the Book of Armagh.
5. *Post haec uidi et ecce ostium apertum in caelo* is Apocalypse 4:1. This is identical with the Vulgate text, while that in the Book of Armagh has the pleonasm: *apertum est*. Contrariwise, the Metz list has *apertum est*.
6. *Et uidi cum aperuerit unum de sigillis* is a somewhat garbled quotation of Apocalypse 6:1. The Vulgate reads: *et uidi quod aperuisset agnus unum de septem signaculis*, which has five points of difference with our text: (1) *cum* replacing *quod* (Metz reads *quum*); (2) *aperuerit* instead of *aperuisset* (Metz has *aperuisset*); (3) the omission of *agnus*; (4) *septem*; and (5) *sigillis* replacing *signaculis*. Moreover, our text differs from the text of the Apocalypse in the Book of Armagh: *et uidi quod aperuisset agnus unum de septem sigillis*—only in this last word does Armagh agree with the list against the Vulgate. Several of these differences can be explained by harmonization in memory of a common phrase in the Apocalypse: at the opening of the remaining six seals (Apocalypse 6:3, 6:5, 6:7, 6:9, 6:12, and 8:1) we have this phrase *et cum aperuisset sigillum*.[23] This would explain the presence of *cum* instead of *quod*, and of *sigillis* instead of *signaculis* (and from the apparatus to Wordsworth and White it is clear that this was a common substitution as we can see, for example, in the Book of Armagh). The omissions of *agnus* and *septem* are more difficult to understand if we think of these lemmata as *capitula*. The omission of *agnus* is perplexing given the identification of this lamb with the Christ; in this case who it is that opens the seal is of greater significance than the fact that the seal is opened. Is this omission a scribal error, or is the image of whom it was who opened the seals so well known as to need no mention? Moreover, if we think of this

[23] In the case of the second, third, fourth, sixth, and seventh seal the Vulgate places the number after *sigillum*, and before the word in the case of the fifth. The Apocalypse text in Armagh follows the Vulgate except that it places the numeral before *sigillum* in the case of both the fifth and the seventh seals.

list as *capitula*, the omission of *septem* is a major fault: one is not introduced to a section of the book, but only to a single scene. Lastly, we come to the replacement of the pluperfect subjunctive (*aperuisset*) with the perfect subjunctive (*aperuerit*) which represents only a minor change in meaning.[24] This text apart, there is no evidence in either the apparatus to the Vulgate nor in the archives of the *Vetus Latina Institut*[25] for such a change: the simplest explanation is that it is a blunder by the scribe of Armagh. However, why this particular form? It is possible that it is a combination from memory of Apocalypse 3:20: *ecce sto ad ostium et pulso si quis audierit uocem meam et aperuerit ianuam*.

However, taken together, these variations do not constitute evidence for the influence of any other source than that witnessed in the Vulgate form of the Apocalypse.

7. *Ubi primus angelus tuba cecinit* is Apocalypse 8:7 as found in Wordsworth and White,[26] and the text of the Book of Armagh.
8. *Et apertum est templum Dei quod est in caelo et apparuit arca testamenti eius* is Apocalypse 11:19. It departs from the Vulgate, including the text in the Book of Armagh, in two ways. First, it adds *quod est* to the phrase *templum Dei in caelo* which indicates contact with a *Vetus Latina* text of the Apocalypse either directly or through an intermediate author. But we should note that in the Metz Bible *quod est* is omitted, which is most likely explained by Metz harmonizing with the Vulgate. Second, the Vulgate reads *et uisa est arca*, but that has been changed to *apparuit* in the list—in both Metz and Armagh copies; and there are no other witnesses for such an alteration. However, we should not attach too much significance to this change as *apparuit* is used on many occasions in the Vulgate (e.g. 1 John 1:2) with the sense 'it was revealed' to us as observers; and anyone familiar with the Scriptures could have made the substitution in memory without hesitation.
9. *Et stetit super harenam maris et uidi de mari bestiam discendentem* is Apocalypse 12:18–13:1.[27] There are two differences here between the edition of the Vulgate and our text. The Wordsworth

[24] I am indebted to Pádraic Moran for his help on this point.

[25] Consulted using the CD-ROM edition produced by Brepols from the cards held in the workroom in Beuron.

[26] Note that the 1994 edition of the Vulgate omits *angelus*.

[27] The Metz codex had *steti* rather than *stetit*, but this is simply a blunder.

and White edition reads *de mare*, but this departure is of no significance as a great many Vulgate codices, including the Book of Armagh, read *de mari*. Indeed, if Wordsworth and White had available to them the evidence assembled by the *Vetus Latina Institut* they would have, in all likelihood, let the decision go the other way, i.e. put *mari* in the text and relegated *mare* to the apparatus as a very frequent reading.

The other difference, not found in the list in Metz, is more amazing: the Vulgate, including the text in the Book of Armagh, reads: *et uidi de mare/mari bestiam ascendentem*. This seems obvious; indeed, if something is coming out of the water, it can only *come up* out of the water. One could not observe, even in a vision, an animal going down out of the water, yet that is what our text reads! The Armagh reading *discendentem* (note the spelling—which we meet again in item 11) can only be explained as a slip of attention, such as that which in English might confuse 'imflammable' with 'inflammable' or, in any language, an omission of the negative particle which reverses the whole meaning of a sentence. The same blunder can be seen in some copies of Bede's *Explanatio Apocalypsis* at 6.3.1.[28] The probable cause of this blunder is that the word *descendentem* is used on five occasions in the Apocalypse and may have been, as is said in English, 'rattling around in his head'.[29]

10. *Et post haec uidi et apertum est templum tabernaculi testimonii sancti in caelo et septem angeli effudent* is a combination of two elements: first, it is a quotation of Apocalypse 15:5 and then a summary paraphrase of Apocalypse 16:1–17.

In the Vulgate, Apocalypse 15:5 reads: *Et post haec uidi et ecce apertum est templum tabernaculi testimonii in caelo*; the text in the Book of Armagh only differs from this in that it omits *testimonii*. Our text omits *ecce*, and this is an omission that is found in several codices. More significant is its addition of *sancti* after *testimonii* in the list, which is a variation that is not found elsewhere. In some *Vetus Latina* texts *sancti* is added immediately after *tabernaculi*, the noun it qualifies, and in a few other *Vetus Latina* texts, and some citations of such texts, the word *martyri* is added after *testimonii*. The presence of *sancti* in our text is probably a witness to contact of some sort with those *Vetus Latina* traditions.

[28] Bede, *Explanatio Apocalypsis* 6.3.1 (ed. by Roger Gryson in CCSL 121A).

[29] The word *descendentem* is used in Apoc 10:1, 18:1, 20:1, 21:2, 21:10.

The second element, the phrase *et septem angeli effudent* (or as we find in Metz: *et septem angeli fialas suas effuderunt*), is the first example of our text summarizing the content of a section of the Apocalypse rather than simply quoting the book.[30] However, even here the phrase resembles Apocalypse 16:1 and then the repeated phrase (in Apocalypse 16:2–17) of *et [angelus] secundus effudit fialam suam*, etc. The reader is expected to know that after seeing the vision of the temple opened in heaven, there is a vision of angels, seven of them one after another, who pour out their bowls of wrath upon the earth.

11. *Post haec uidi alium angelum discendentem de caelo habentem potestatem magnam* is Apocalypse 18:1 exactly as in the Vulgate, including Armagh. The spelling *disendentem* (for *descendentem*) we have already met above, and is identical with the spelling of the word in the text of the Book of Armagh.
12. *Et uidi caelum apertum et equum album et qui sedebat super eum uocatur fidelis et uerus* is Apocalypse 19:11, but differs from the Vulgate in two details. The Vulgate, including the Book of Armagh, reads: *Et uidi caelum apertum et ecce equus albus*. The difference in our text can be explained by combining in memory the image of the opened heaven and what is seen there: a white horse—we have a memory of a vision rather than a memory of a line of text. In such a memory of an image, the use of *ecce* is redundant.

    The second difference concerns the final phrase: *uocatur fidelis et uerus*, which is a *Vetus Latina* reading. The Vulgate reads *uocabatur fidelis et uerax uocatur*, while the Book of Armagh reads: *super eum fidelis et uerax uocatur*. In the list in Metz we find *uocabatur fidelis et uerax* which may be another case (like item 8 above) where Metz harmonized with the Vulgate.
13. *Et uidi caelum nouum et terram nouam* is Apocalypse 21:1 exactly as found in the Vulgate including the Book of Armagh.
14. *Et ostendit mihi flumen aquae uiuae splendidum* is Apocalypse 22:1 and differs from the Vulgate, including the text of Armagh, in only one respect: it has *flumen* rather than *fluuium*. *Flumen* represents the *Vetus Latina* version of this verse.

[30] The word *effudent* is ungrammatical. It can probably be explained by reference to the seven uses in the Apocalypse of the phrase *[angelus] effudit fialam suam* (e.g. at Apoc 16:2).

From this analysis three points stand out. First, that with the exception of three words (*et septem angeli effudent*) this entire text is made up of biblical phrases: the text is providing its own explanation by way of being excerpted rather than a commentator imposing his words on the text. Second, it was compiled in some place where the *Vetus Latina* was in common use, or else a text with a high-level of *Vetus Latina* contamination. Third, as is also the case with the New Jerusalem map, the compiler of Armagh did not notice the inconsistency between the book's text and the text embedded in items of apparatus. On this basis I consider our text to be a witness to the *Vetus Latina* rather than the Vulgate.

From this we can draw an immediate conclusion: this set of phrases should not just be seen as simply an haphazard introductory element to a biblical book in this codex, but as a separate work worthy of consideration on its own, for which we have only two witnesses. So what sort of work is it?

Comparison with other division systems

The essential feature of series of *capitula* as division systems is that they provide a summary of contents to enable the reader to find a particular portion of text more conveniently than by searching the text with the eye until the right place is found, while at the same time giving an overview of a book's significant contents. Considered from this perspective, this list is a failure. We see this, firstly, through a direct numerical comparison of the number of sections of text it identifies. Our text identifies 14 sections, whereas the series of *capitula* in Wordsworth and White, for example, break the text into 25 sections,[31] 38 sections, 39 sections, and 49 sections. These numbers become even more startling when we consider that items 1 (Apocalypse 1:1) and 2 (Apocalypse 1:4) in our list are really no more than the title of the book and do not help us find anything, while the third item (Apocalypse 1:9) follows on only four verses later and 'describes' a section of barely twelve verses. (This would be fine if the whole text was treated with this density of guidance as to content, but this is exceptional.) Therefore, it could be argued that there are, in fact, only twelve divisions of the text; and this means that one must also search at least two of our chapters for any particular piece of text. Even then one is only provided with opening lines of the sequence

[31] This particular set is examined in the next section of this article.

of visions rather than content descriptions. Second, while the compiler of the Book of Armagh evidently valued this text and so presented it in a special display format on a page of its own, it did not affect his own presentation of the text of the Apocalypse where the biblical text is broken into sections using display script and *diminuendo*.[32] The text of the Apocalypse is broken into many short sections, very often by the device of placing *et* in the margin in display script (this happens on 61 occasions): it is clear that the scribe wanted the reader to be able to use these to locate themselves within the biblical text. While the points in the text highlighted in our text are all so highlighted, this cannot be seen as the influence of our text but simply the coincidence of what our text considers significant with that which others also considered significant (but those others noted a great many other points besides). So if our text does not fit the category of *capitula*, what is it?

The most obvious comparison to our text is the set of twenty-five divisions found in a number of biblical codices, the earliest of which is the *Codex Fuldensis* which brings us into the world of Latin biblical scholarship of the mid-6th century.[33] As with our text, this set of division points is made up virtually entirely of biblical lemmata. When we read them in parallel (as outlined in *Figure 1*), our text's purpose comes into view.

Reading these in parallel it is clear that they are independent of one another as texts, but equally that they derive from a similar agenda and stimulus. Both can be seen as synopses of the Apocalypse which list *seriatim* the visions of the John. Each is an aide-mémoir to the whole book that proceeds *visually* through the text: John saw this, and then he saw that, and then he saw something else. The reader is expected not to use these as a finding tool for a passage in the book, but by reading though these lemmata to recall visually the various scenes: as John the Seer saw and described, so you now see the vision in your own imagination. And, just as the book is a written record of the visions, so this list is a synopsis of the contents by recalling those visions in their opening or most memorable scenes.

[32] This lack of correspondence between the list and the divisions of the text was noted by Gwynn (1913), cxxix.

[33] Fulda, Landesbibliothek, Bonifatianus 1; see Fischer (1985), 377; Wordsworth and White (1905), 410–8, identified this set of '*capitula*' in three of the codices, including Fulda, upon which they based their edition, and called it as 'FKU'; in de Bruyne (1914), 398, it is called 'B [B2] (Fr)', and in Gryson (2000–3), 68–70, it is called 'Series B'. (The other manuscripts are London, British Library, Add. 10546 [K] and London, British Library, Add. 11852 [U].)

Apoc	Fulda text	Armagh text
1:1		*Apocalypsis Iesu Christi quam dedit illi Deus*
1:4	*Iohannes septem ecclesiis quae sunt in Asia*	*Iohannes septem ecclesiis quae sunt in Asia*
1:9		*Ego Iohannes frater uester et socius in tribulatione*
1:19–2:1	*Scribe ergo quae uidisti et quae sunt et quae oportet fieri post haec et sacramentum septem stellarum*	
		Angelo Ephesi ecclesiae scribe
4:1	*Post haec uidi et ecce osteum apertum in caelo*	*Post haec uidi et ecce ostium apertum in caelo*
5:1	*Et uidi in dextera sedentis super thronum librum scriptum*	
6:1	*Et uidi quod aperuisset agnus unum de septem sigillis*	*Et uidi cum aperuerit unum de sigillis*
7:1	*Post haec quottuor angelos stantes super quottuor angulos terrae*	
7:9	*Post haec uidi turbam magnam quam dinumerare nemo poterat*	
8:1	*Et cum aperuisset sigillum septimum factum est silentium in caelo*	
8:7		*Ubi primus angelus tuba cecinit*
10:1	*Et uidi alium angelum fortem descendentem de caelo amictum nube*	
10:8	*Et uox quam audiui de caelo iterum loquentem mecum*	
11:15	*Et septimus angelus tuba cecinit et factae sunt uoces magnae in caelo dicentes*	
11:19	*Et apertum est templum Dei in caelo et uisa est arca testamenti eius in templo eius*	*Et apertum est templum Dei quod est in caelo et apparuit arca testamenti eius*
12:7	*Et factum est proelium in caelo: Micahel et angeli eius proeliabantur cum dracone*	
12:18		*Et stetit super harenam maris et uidi de mari bestiam [ascendentem]*

Apoc	Fulda text	Armagh text
13:11	*Et uidi aliam bestiam ascendentem de terra et habebat cornua duo*	
14:1	*Et uidi et ecce agnus stabat super montem Sion et cum illo centum quadraginta quattuor milia*	
15:5	*Post haec uidi et ecce apertum est templum tabernaculi testimonii in caelo*	*Et post haec uidi et apertum est templum tabernaculi testimonii sancti in caelo* *et septem angeli effudent*
17:1	*Et uenit unus de septem angelis qui habebant septem plagas et locutus est mecum dicens*	
18:1	*Post haec uidi alium angelum descendentem de caelo habentem potestatem magnam et terra inluminata est a gloria eius*	*Post haec uidi alium angelum descendentem de caelo habentem potestatem magnam*
19:1	*Post haec audiui quasi uocem magnam turbarum multarum in caelo dicentium alleluia*	
19:11	*Et uidi caelum apertum et ecce equus albus et qui sedebat super eum uocabatur fidelis et uerax*	*Et uidi caelum apertum et equum album et qui sedebat super eum uocatur fidelis et uerus*
20:5–6	*Haec est resurrectio prima beatus et sanctus qui habet partem in resurrectione prima*	
21:1		*Et uidi caelum nouum et terram nouam*
21:9	*Et uenit unus de septem angelis habentibus fialas plenas septem plagis nouissimis*	
22:1	*Et ostendit mihi flumen aquae uiuae splendidum tamquam chrystallum*	*Et ostendit mihi flumen aquae uiuae splendidum*
22:6	*Et dixit mihi haec uerba fidelissima et uera sunt*	
22:16	*Ego Iesus misi angelum meum testificari uobis haec in ecclesiis*	

Figure 1 *Codex Fuldensis* divisions and Book of Armagh *capitula* compared

These two works do not serve to introduce the book by telling the reader about it, rather they seek to put the reader in direct contact with the visions which are re-presented from the reader's memory. Hence the appropriateness of using the lemmata that mark the openings of what the compiler of our text believed to be the key visions, rather than using descriptive phrases such as one find in lists of *capitula*. *Tituli* and *capitula* form, as has often been pointed out, a metatext to the scriptural work to which they relate and serve to formalize a teacher's understanding of the purpose, nature, and content of the biblical book.[34] And in so far as these vision-lists are texts about a text, they can be classed as metatexts; but this categorization should not obscure their creators' distinctive method. Each lemma recalls an image to consciousness for the reader (for example, each reader's image of 'the white horse'; cf. Apocalypse 19:11), but what is brought to mind is the actual vision-image, not an item in a biblical book. For this hermeneutic alone, these texts deserve remembrance within exegetical history. As such, we should stop classing them with *capitula* and have a separate category: 'vision lists'.

Exegetical considerations

The contrast between our text and that of a set of *capitula* has been examined, but to appreciate the manner in which texts in the *Codex Fuldensis*, the Metz Bible, or the Book of Armagh serve as synoptic introductions to what is conveyed in the Apocalypse, it is worth comparing them with a readily recognizable introduction to this biblical book. A suitable comparison can be found in the introduction to the Apocalypse by Isidore in his *Prooemia*.[35] This work is slightly later than that contained in the *Codex Fuldensis*, and, while we cannot know how its date relates to the other vision-list, it is a work from a broadly similar theological milieu. In the *Prooemia* Isidore's treatment of the Apocalypse is distinctive: not only in that in this case, alone among his introductions to the biblical books, he concentrates on supplying an item-by-item summary of the book's contents to the exclusion of contextualization. Moreover, just as it is apparent from his work that he imagines the Apocalypse as the *coda* to the whole body of the Scriptures, so he wants his description of the Apocalypse to

[34] See, for example, Stansbury (1999), 65.

[35] Isidore, *In libros ueteris et noui testamenti prooemia*, *De Apocalypsi* 106–9 (PL 83, 178–80).

be a *coda* to his own book. It is because Isidore chooses to give an item-by-item synopsis that I have chosen it for examination as illustrating clearly these different relationships to the biblical text (see *Figure 2*).

Isidore, *In libros ueteris et noui testamenti prooemia, De Apocalypsi* 106–9 (PL 83, 178–80)	**Reference points in the Apocalypse**
[106] *Ioannes, postquam scribere septem iubetur ecclesiis,*	The theme is introduced at 1:4 (and that John is ordered to write is at 1:7); the activity of writing the letters covers 2:1–3:22.
aspicit filium hominis sedentem in throno,	4:2; the identification that the one sitting is the Son of Man is an interpretation based on 1:12.
et uiginti quatuor seniores,	4:4
et quatuor animalia procedentia ante thronum	4:6
in dextera quoque sedentis librum septem sigillis signatum	5:1
in quo bellum, egestas, mors, clamor interfectorum, finis quoque mundi notatur et saeculi.	This is an interpretation of the contents of the 'second seal'—6:3–4; the 'third seal'—6:5–6; the 'fourth seal'—6:7–9; and the 'fifth seal'—6:9–11 (the shouting of those killed) and 6:12–6 (the end of all).
[107] *Describit deinde duodena millia seruorum Dei,*	7:5–8; but this is misleading in that it is 12,000 from 12 tribes, i.e. 144,000, that is the total number of the 'servants of God' (this designation of the saved is based on 7:3).
qui signantur in frontibus;	7:5
ibi septem angeli tubis canunt	8:2
sequenti grandine et igne cum sanguine in terra.	8:7
Tertia quoque pars terrae ibi comburitur,	8:7
et tertia pars maris sanguis efficitur;	8:9
astraque ipsa rutilantia tertiam fulgoris partem amittunt;	Cf. 8:12
ibi de fumo putei locustae producuntur daemoniorum,	9:2–3; the identification with the demons is based on 9:11.
accipientes potestatem laedendi qui non sunt agni cruore signati.	9:4–5

[108] *Praeterea comedit Euangelista librum Testamenti oris praedicatione suauissimum, et operis difficultate amarum.*	10:9–10; the identification of the John of the Apocalypse with the evangelist was a commonplace.[36]
Metiturque coeleste templum,	11:1
describitque uerba uiginti quatuor seniorum,	11:16–8
et arcam Testamenti,	11:19
ac mulierem amictum sole,	12:1
pugnamque in coelis Michaelis cum dracone,	12:7
ruinamque draconis.	12:8
Conspicit praeterea et Antichristi figuram,	13:1; the identification of the beast in 13:1 with the figure of the Antichrist is an exegetical projection common within the tradition of interpreting the Apocalypse.[37]
habentem capita regni septem,	13:1; the link with kingdoms is based on 17:9.
et cornua potestatis,	13:1; the link with power is based on 17:12.
et numerum hominis.[38]	13:18
[109] *Narrat inter haec et canticum Testamenti nouum,*	12:10–2
speculaturque angelos gestantes pateras,	16:1–21
cernitque similiter interitum bestiae,	17:1–18
et beatitudinem eorum qui corporis sui uestimenta absque carnis uoluptate munda seruauerunt.	19:7 and 19:14 read in conjunction; the notion that the purity of the saints is a function of their avoidance of carnal pleasure is an interpretation that reflects Isidore's spirituality; the link between the pure group and those with beatitude is based on 22:14.

36 Isidore makes this explicit in *Etymologiae* VI 2.49 (ed. by Oroz Reta and Marcos Casquero (1982-3), i 576): *Apocalypsin librum Iohannes euangelista scripsit eo tempore, quo ob euangelii praedicationem in insulam Pathmon traditur relegatus.*

37 The figure of the Antichrist appears nowhere in the Apocalypse; it is found only in the letters of John (i.e. 1 Jn 2:18, 2:22, 4:3, 4:7, and in 2 Jn 7). On the origins of the identification, see Jenks (1991).

38 The PL text reads *et numerum nominis*; however, this is a misprint, for the biblical text reads *numerus enim hominis est* (Apoc 13:18).

Exsequitur deinde interitum meretricis Babyloniae,	18:1–24; the reference to the whore is derived from 19:2.
et nuptias agni,	19:6–9
aduentum iudicii,	19:11
interitumque Antichristi,	19:20; continuing the interpretation of 'the beast' used in 13:1.
et sempiternam punitionem diaboli.	20:10; but linking back to 20:1–3.
Ad ultimum memorat resurrectionem mortuorum,	20:4–6 in conjunction with 20:11–5.
coelique nouitatem, et terrae,	21:1
descriptionemque Ierusalem,	21:2 and 10–26.
flumen etiam baptismi mundum	22:1; there is no reference to baptism or the baptized in Apoc, but this identification of the river with baptism was a commonplace.[39]
Lignumque uitae Dominum Iesum Christum.	22:2; and, again, the identification of this tree with Jesus is a commonplace within the tradition.

Figure 2 Isidore's synopsis of the Book of the Apocalypse

Isidore's aim is to provide a summary guide to what one reads in the book, whereas the vision-lists aim to recall the visions recorded in the book directly to memory. Isidore wants the reader to remember what is pointed out in the book and, therefore, the summary does not quote the text at any point but rather summarizes what he considers to be the significant points. Moreover, his summary is itself a brief commentary on the Apocalypse not only in that it offers identifications of various images, reflecting the dominant strands of Apocalypse interpretation (for example, the beast of Apocalypse 13 with the Antichrist, the tree of life with the Christ), but in that his whole text is an interpretation of the book's purpose: John has written the letters as ordered and presented the great battle of the heavenly and diabolical forces which result in the latter's defeat, while the victory of the celestial forces opens on to the risen life of the New Jerusalem. No such agenda is presented for the book in the vision-lists; rather they serve to enable the reader to encounter the visions directly.

[39] See O'Loughlin (2007b), 34–6.

Conclusions

The need to provide summaries, synopses, guides, aids to memory for the biblical books was well acknowledged by the mid-5th century (e.g. Eucherius of Lyons) and many authors sought to provide these aids to readers (e.g. Cassiodorus).[40] In several codices, including the Book of Armagh, we have attempts to help the reader of the Apocalypse. However, when we compare these with either summaries in the form of *capitula* or exegetical introductions, we find that they differ in both form (as lemmata) and hermeneutic (they do not point to the book, but seek to recall the images, recorded in the book, to memory). As such, they need to be viewed as vision-lists. Moreover, setting out the list as a separate visual item in the Book of Armagh invited the reader to interact directly the list's contents, without the intermediary of the book's text.

This leaves us with three questions. First, is there any direct link between these vision-lists and sequences of actual representations in art of the Apocalypse—other than both the lists and the representations derive from a common text?[41] Second, what does the presence of the list, laid out as a lozenge in Armagh, tell us about how its compiler envisaged this list (and, indeed, the New Jerusalem map) being used? Third, while the vision-lists examined here come from different authors, they show a common intellectual inspiration: are there other 'summaries' that behave in a similar way?

Bibliography

de Bruyne, D. (1914) *Sommaires, rubriques et divisions de la Bible latin*, Namur.

Fischer, B. (1985) *Lateinische Bibelhandschriften im frühen Mittelalter*, Freiburg.

Gryson, R. (1999–2004) *Altlateinische Handschriften. Manuscrits vieux latins: répertoire descriptif*, 2 vols., Freiburg.

— (2000–3) *Apocalypsis Johannis*, Freiburg.

Gwynn, J. (1913) *Liber Ardmachanus/The Book of Armagh, edited with introduction and appendices*, Dublin.

Jenks, G.C. (1991) *The origins and early development of the Antichrist myth*, Berlin.

Lapidge, M. and R. Sharpe (1985) *A bibliography of Celtic-Latin literature*, Dublin.

40 See O'Loughlin (2004).

41 I am grateful to Prof. Tommy Wasserman for this question.

O'Loughlin, T. (1999a) *Teachers and code-breakers: the Latin Genesis tradition, 430–800*, Turnhout.

— (1999b) 'The Eusebian apparatus in some Vulgate Gospel books,' *Peritia* 13, 1–92.

— (1999c) 'Distant islands: the topography of holiness in the *Nauigatio sancti Brendani*,' in M. Glasscoe, *The medieval mystical tradition: England, Ireland and Wales*, Woodbridge, 1–20.

— (2000) 'The plan of the New Jerusalem in the Book of Armagh,' *Cambrian Medieval Celtic Studies* 39, 23–38.

— (2002) 'Imagery of the New Jerusalem in the *Periphyseon* and Eriugena's Irish background,' in J. McEvoy and M. Dunne, *History and eschatology in John Scottus Eriugena and his time*, Leuven, 245–59.

— (2004) 'Early medieval introductions to the Holy Book: adjuncts or hermeneutic?,' in R.N. Swanson, *The church and the book: papers read at the 2000 summer meeting and the 2001 winter meeting of the Ecclesiastical History Society*, Woodbridge, 22–31.

— (2007a) 'Division systems for the Gospels: the case of the Stowe St John (Dublin, RIA, D.ii.3),' *Scriptorium* 61, 150–64.

— (2007b) *Adomnán and the holy places: the perceptions of an insular monk on the locations of the biblical drama*, London.

— (2010) 'Harmonizing the truth: Eusebius and the problem of the four Gospels,' *Traditio* 65, 1–29.

Oroz Reta, J. and M.-A. Marcos Casquero (1982–3) *San Isidoro De Sevilla, Etimologías*, 2 vols., Madrid.

Quentin, H. (1926) *Biblia sacra iuxta latinam vulgatam versionem ad codicum fidem. Librum Genesis*, Rome.

Richardson, H. (1984) 'Number and symbol in early Christian Irish art,' *Journal of the Royal Society of Antiquaries of Ireland* 114, 28–47.

— (1996) 'Lozenge and logos,' *Archaeology Ireland* 10, 24–5.

— (2002) 'Biblical imagery and the heavenly Jerusalem in the Book of Armagh and the Book of Kells,' in P. Ní Chatháin and M. Richter, *Ireland and Europe in the early Middle Ages: texts and transmission*, Dublin, 205–14.

Sharpe, R. (1983) 'Palaeographical considerations in the study of the Patrician documents in the Book of Armagh,' *Scriptorium* 36, 3–28.

Stansbury, M. (1999) 'Early medieval biblical commentaries, their writers and readers,' *Frümittelalterliche Studien* 33, 49–82.

Weber, R. et al. (1994) *Biblia sacra iuxta vulgatam versionem*, 4th revised ed., Stuttgart.

Willard, L.C. (1971) *A critical study of the Euthalian apparatus*, Ann Arbor.

Wordsworth, J. and J.H. White (1905) *Nouum Testamentum Domini nostri Iesu Christi latine*, Oxford.

JEAN-MICHEL PICARD

VIR APOSTOLICUS: ST PETER AND THE CLAIM OF APOSTOLICITY IN EARLY MEDIEVAL IRELAND

Abstract

The use of the expression *vir apostolicus* in hagiographical texts written in early medieval Ireland is explained in the context of the claims of apostolicity made by the early Christian churches in continental Europe. Hagiographers from different communities in Ireland appear to have been aware of the significance of the term and of the stakes involved. The success of the Armagh scholars in imposing a vision of their patron saint as the 'apostle' of Ireland was the result of a long and ingenious process, using elements of rhetoric found in early Christian writers of the previous centuries.

Keywords

Armagh, Iona, Rome; Patrick, Palladius, Columba, St Peter; early Christian church, apostolicity, martyrs, relics; Hiberno-Latin; Patristics, Irish hagiography.

Introduction

The question of the apostolicity of the Western European churches, especially the Gallic churches, has a long history, more recently outlined by Pierre Riché, Richard Landes, Alain Dierkens and further developed by Samantha Kahn-Herrick[1]. For the early Middle Ages, Pierre Riché was able to show that the attribution of ecclesiastical foundations to an apostle or a disciple of St Peter could be linked on the one hand to the

[1] Riché (1993), 3–9; Landes (1995), 3–22, 214–84; Dierkens (2006), 24–37; Kahn-Herrick (2007); Kahn-Herrick (2010), 235–70; Kahn-Herrick (2012), 129–38; Kahn-Herrick (2013).

Early medieval Ireland and Europe: chronology, contacts, scholarship, ed. by Pádraic Moran and Immo Warntjes, Studia Traditionis Theologiae, 14 (Turnhout, 2015), pp. 425–40.

 10.1484/M.STT-EB.5.103131

expansion of papal power and on the other hand to the Roman policy of the Carolingians. Such claims could be entertained for Gaul or other provinces of the Roman Empire, where Christianity could be traced back to the second century, but certainly not for Ireland, where the first Christian churches were constituted more than two hundred years later. However ideological and political rivalry has its own logic and by the 7th century some Irish churches were seeking pre-eminence by claiming a direct link to St Peter.

Columbanus and the model of the early church

The first manifestations of Irish interest in St Peter and apostolicity date from the beginning of the 7th century, arising from interaction with the new Roman mission in England and increased contacts with the Continent. Medieval Irish scholars were well aware of rivalries and diversity within the Christian church. They had access to the writings of Origen, Pelagius, and Theodore of Mopsuestia and they also knew about the different methods of computing Easter. When Columbanus reached Italy in AD 612, not only was Arianism still flourishing in Lombardy, but there were also major dissensions among the Catholics. The authority of the pope was far from being accepted and Boniface IV was considered by the dissident Lombard bishops as a heretic and an obstacle to the unity of the catholic church. The letter written by Columbanus to Pope Boniface in AD 613 is an appeal for strong leadership and for an attitude of goodwill in order to bring about concord within the church. The position of the Irish among the European churches is clearly stated:[2]

> *Nos enim sanctorum Petri et Pauli et omnium discipulorum diuinum canonem spiritu sancto scribentium discipuli sumus, toti Iberni, ultimi habitatores mundi, nihil extra euangelicam et apostolicam doctrinam recipientes; nullus hereticus, nullus Iudaeus, nullus schismaticus fuit; sed fides catholica, sicut a uobis primum, sanctorum uidelicet apostolorum successoribus, tradita est, inconcussa tenetur.*

'For all we Irish, inhabitants of the world's edge, are disciples of Saints Peter and Paul and of all the disciples who wrote the sacred canon by the Holy Ghost, and we accept nothing outside the evangelical and apostolic teaching; none has been a heretic, none a Jew, none a schismatic;

[2] Columbanus, *Epistola* V 3 (ed. and trans. Walker (1957), 38–9).

but the catholic faith, as it was first delivered by you, who are the successors of the holy apostles, is maintained unbroken.'

Columbanus does not mention the names of Patrick or Palladius or Auxilius or Iserninus, but he refers to the early evangelisation of Ireland by men sent by the popes, successors of St Peter. The kind of apostolicity which Columbanus claimed for the Irish churches was not a new idea.

From the very beginnings of the church, the number of apostles had been in expansion. After Judas' death, it was ruled that the man chosen to replace him as the twelfth apostle should be a follower of Jesus throughout his ministry, from the time of his baptism by John until the day of his ascension:[3]

> *Oportet ergo ex his viris qui nobiscum congregati sunt in omni tempore quo intravit et exivit inter nos Dominus Iesus, incipiens a baptismate Iohannis usque in diem qua adsumptus est a nobis testem resurrectionis eius nobiscum fieri unum ex istis* [...] *et dederunt sortes eis et cecidit sors super Matthiam et adnumeratus est cum undecim apostolis.*

> 'So, among the men who have been our companions during the whole time when the Lord Jesus lived with us, from the baptism by John until the day he was taken up, we must choose one of them to be a witness to his resurrection [...] and they drew lots and the lot fell upon Matthias and he was numbered with the eleven apostles.'

In addition, according to St Luke's Gospel, Christ had also sent seventy-two disciples to spread the good news around the world:[4]

> *Post haec autem designavit Dominus et alios septuaginta duos et misit illos binos ante faciem suam in omnem civitatem et locum quo erat ipse venturus.*

> 'After these things, the Lord appointed seventy-two other [disciples] and sent them two by two ahead of him to every city and place where he would go.'

Paul was soon added to the number of the apostles. To distinguish other founder members of Christianity from these apostles, the early church

[3] Act 1:21–26. The translation is mine, here and throughout if not stated otherwise.

[4] Lk 10:1.

writers used the term *uir apostolicus*. This was the term used to refer to the evangelists Mark and Luke, or for disciples of the apostles such as Polycarp, Papias, Irenaeus, or Clement. The Church Fathers constantly refer to *apostoli et uiri apostolici*, a set phrase which is especially frequent in Jerome, and would later become a favourite of Bede's. The expression had been used first by Tertullian at the beginning of the 3rd century in the context of the fight against heretical churches. The only churches who could claim to be orthodox were those who could prove a regular succession of bishops beginning with a disciple of the apostles or 'apostolic men', that is men who were companions of the apostles:[5]

> *Edant ergo origines ecclesiarum suarum, euoluant ordinem episcoporum suorum, ita per successionem ab initio decurrentem ut primus ille episcopus aliquem ex apostolis uel apostolicis uiris, qui tamen cum apostolis perseuerauerit, habuerit auctorem et antecessorem.*
>
> 'Let them show the origins of their church; let them unroll the list of their bishops, running from the beginning in this order of succession where the first bishop had as his sponsor or predecessor one of the Apostles or an apostolic man who constantly remained with the Apostles.'

However, when the debate became heated, the distinction between the two categories could become blurred. For example, defending the writings of Origen against Jerome at the end of the 4th century, Rufinus of Aquilea argues that Clement, disciple and successor of Peter, is not only an 'apostolic man' but nearly an apostle (*paene apostolus*) since he wrote down the sayings of the apostles:[6]

> [*Clemens*] *apostolicus uir, immo pene apostolus (nam ea scribit quae apostoli dicunt), cui Paulus apostolus testimonium dedit dicens: 'Cum Clemente et ceteris adiutoribus meis, quorum nomina sunt in libro uitae'.*
>
> [Clement], an apostolic man, or rather almost an apostle (for he wrote what apostles say), to whom Paul the Apostle bore his testimony, saying: 'With Clement and my other fellow workers, whose names are written in the book of life'.

5 Tertullian, *De praescriptione haereticorum* 32 (ed. by Raymond-François Refoulé in CCSL 1, 212).

6 Rufinus, *De adulteratione librorum Origenis* 3 (ed. by Manlio Simonetti in CCSL 20, 10).

7th-century Irish developments

Shortly after AD 604, Laurence, archbishop of Canterbury, sent a letter addressed to all abbots and bishops of Ireland, urging them to follow the customs of the universal church, especially in the calculation of the date of Easter. The letter may have boosted the confidence of a party of reformers in the Irish church who had started promoting Roman customs and papal policies and are referred to in legal and exegetical documents originating from Ireland as *Romani*. As Pádraig Ó Néill has shown, the *Romani* 'were ardent believers in the unique position of Peter and the doctrine of Petrine supremacy'.[7] It may not be fortuitous that, at around the same time, St Patrick seems to have acquired apostolic status. Long before his cult was taken over by Armagh, it was well established in the area of his early mission, namely on the northern east coast of Ireland, in modern counties Down and Antrim. The relics of his body were still in Saul, near Downpatrick, and the earliest known hymn in his honour can be attributed to Colmán Elo, who came from the nearby area of Connor.[8] According to the Annals of Ulster, Colmán died in AD 611 and the hymn *Audite omnes amantes* probably dates from the first decade of the 7th century.[9] The picture of the holy man presented by Colmán is quite different from that found in later hagiographical texts, where the power of Patrick over pagan lords and druids is emphasized. Instead, it is more akin to the image of the saint found in his own writings—the *Confessio* and the Letter to the Soldiers of Coroticus—where suffering, hard work, humility, and trust in God are the important elements.[10] However, the purpose of the hymn is to proclaim the position of Patrick as one of the apostles. The first and last stanzas highlight the central theme: Patrick is equal to the apostles and will sit enthroned with them on doomsday:[11]

Audite omnes amantes Deum sancta mereta
uiri in Christo beati Patrici episcupi
quomodo bonum ob actum similatur angelis
perfectamque propter uitam aequatur apostolis.

7 Ó Néill (1984), 285.

8 Doherty (1991), 88–92.

9 Annals of Ulster *s.a.* 611 (ed. Mac Airt and Mac Niocaill (1983), 106). For the date of the *Audite omnes amantes*, see Curran (1984), 36–8.

10 The *Confessio* and the *Epistola ad milites Corotici* are ed. by Bieler (1993), 56–102.

11 Colmán Elo, *Audite omnes amantes* ll. 1–4 and 89–92 (ed. Bieler (1953), 119, 122).

[...]
Zona Domini praecinctus diebus ac noctibus
sine intermisione Deum orat Dominum
cuius ingentis laboris percepturus praemium
cum apostolis regnabit sanctus super Israel.

'Hear ye all, lovers of God, the holy merits
Of the man blessed in Christ, Patrick the bishop,
How for his good ways he is likened to the angels,
And because of his perfect life is deemed equal to the Apostles
[...]
Girt with the Lord's girdle day and night,
He prays unceasingly to God the Lord.
He will receive the reward for his immense labor
A holy man, he will reign with the Apostles over Israel.'

Stanza 3 makes him an equal of Peter:[12]

Constans in Dei timore et fide inmobilis
super quem aedificatur ut Petrus aecclesia
cuiusque apostolatum a Deo sortitus est
in cuius porte aduersum inferni non praeualent.

'Constant in the fear of God and steadfast in his faith
Upon whom the church is built as on Peter;
And his Apostleship has he received from God
The gates of Hell will not prevail against him.'

Stanza 6 emphasizes the apostolic nature of his deeds:[13]

Fidelis Dei minister insignisque nuntius
apostolicum exemplum formamque praebet bonis
qui tam uerbis quam et factis plebi praedicat Dei
ut quem dictis non conuertit actu prouocet bono.

'God's faithful minister and His distinguished envoy,
He gives the good an Apostolic example and model,
As he preaches to God's people in words as well as in deeds,
So that him whom he does not convert with words, he inspires with good conduct.'

[12] Colmán Elo, *Audite omnes amantes* ll. 9–13 (Bieler (1953), 119).

[13] Colmán Elo, *Audite omnes amantes* ll. 21–24 (Bieler (1953), 120).

This is again repeated at the end of the hymn, in stanza 21, where Patrick is described as the vicar of Christ on earth appointed by the Lord himself:[14]

> *Xpistus illum sibi elegit in terris uicarium*
> *qui de gemimo captiuos liberat seruitio*
> *plerosque de seruitute quos redemit hominum*
> *innumeros de zaboli absoluit dominio.*

> 'Christ chose him to be His vicar on earth.
> He frees captives from a two-fold servitude:
> The great numbers he liberates from men's bondage,
> These countless ones he frees from the yoke of the devil.'

The claim for apostolicity made in the *Audite omnes* is not based on historical arguments, as on the Continent in subsequent centuries, but on the nature of the saint's apostolic mission, directly linked to Christ and providing the faithful with the same protection as that offered by the prince of the apostles.

In the next generation the scholars of Armagh were to build on this claim by adding two major arguments which would secure their primacy among Irish churches: the performance of apostolic miracles by the saint and the power of Roman relics.

The importance of relics had already been stressed by Columbanus in his Letter to Pope Boniface: Rome and the pope owed their fame to the chair of St Peter and were extremely lucky to have the relics of Peter and Paul, which brought them authority and made them illustrious throughout the world:[15]

> *Nos enim, ut ante dixi, deuincti sumus cathedrae sancti Petri; licet enim Roma magna est et uulgata, per istam cathedram tantum apud nos est magna et clara* [...] *in duobus illis feruentissimis Dei Spiritus equis, Petro uidelicet et Paulo apostolis, quorum cara pignora uos felices fecerunt.* [...] *Ex tunc uos magni estis et clari, et Roma ipsa nobilior et clarior est; et si dici potest, propter Christi geminos apostolos* [...] *uos prope caelestes estis, et Roma orbis terrarum caput est ecclesiarum.*

> 'As for us, as we have said before, we are bound to St Peter's chair. For, though Rome be great and famous, among us it is only on that chair that

[14] Colmán Elo, *Audite omnes amantes* ll. 81–84 (Bieler (1953), 122).

[15] Columbanus, *Epistola* V 11 (Walker (1957), 48). The translation is mine.

> her greatness and her fame depend [...] and on those two fiery steeds of God's Spirit, I mean the apostles Peter and Paul, whose dear relics have made you blessed. [...] From that time you are great and famous and Rome itself is nobler and more famed; and if it may be said, it is for the sake of the twin apostles of Christ [...] that you find yourself near to the heavenlies and that Rome is the head of the churches of the world.'

A similar point is found in the letter sent in AD 632 by Cummian to Ségéne, abbot of Iona, to convince him and the traditional party in Ireland to adopt the Roman Easter. The letter ends on the concrete vision of Catholic unity as experienced in Rome by a group of Irish emissaries who saw Christians from Asia Minor, Egypt, Greece, taking part together in the same Easter mass in the basilica of St Peter in Rome:[16]

> *Et in uno hospicio cum Greco et Hebreo, Scitha et Aegiptiaco in aecclesia sancti Petri simul in Pascha, in quo mense integro disiuncti sumus, fuerunt. Et ante sancta sic testati sunt nostris, dicentes: 'Per totum orbem terrarum hoc Pascha, ut scimus, celebratur.' Et nos in reliquiis sanctorum martyrum et scripturis quas attulerunt probauimus inesse uirtutem Dei. Uidimus oculis nostris puellam caecam omnino ad has reliquias oculos aperientem, et paraliticum ambulantem, et multa demonia eiecta.*

> 'And they were in one lodging in the church of St Peter with a Greek, a Hebrew, a Scythian and an Egyptian at the same time at Easter, in which we differed by a whole month. And so they testified to us before the holy relics, saying: 'As far as we know, this Easter is celebrated throughout the whole world.' And we have tested that the miraculous power of God is in the relics of the holy martyrs and in the writings they brought back. We saw with our own eyes a totally blind girl opening her eyes at these relics, and a paralytic walking and many demons cast out.'

Here, divine approval is confirmed by the superior power of the Roman relics, through which major miracles, especially the healing of a blind girl, were performed in front of the own eyes of the writer and his Irish companions.

We must turn toward contemporary Irish exegesis to understand the significance of such miracles. The final chapters of the treatise *De mirabilibus sacrae scripturae*, written *c.*AD 650, deal with the miraculous power of St Peter. Like Christ, Peter has the power to cure paralytics

[16] Cummian, *De ratione paschali* ll. 281–286 (ed. and trans. Walsh and Ó Cróinín (1988), 94–5).

and to raise people from the dead, but also to punish those who are seen as enemies of God or who transgress the rules of the Christian church. These miracles are signs of his apostolic authority (*apostolica auctoritas*) and his apostolic power (*apostolica uirtus*):[17]

> *Caput xvii. Virtus Petri*
> *Ecce quanta est apostolica uirtus in Christo, sanum Ananiam dum Petrus arguit per sermonis tantum imperium morte ligauit; et Tabitham mortis uinculo ligatam, eadem imperii potestate dissoluit. Ideoque prius Ananias et Saphira in conspectu ecclesiae cito mortui sunt, ut apostolica auctoritas quanta esset ostenderetur.*

> 'Chapter 17. Peter's miraculous power
> Here is the greatness of the apostolic power in Christ: when Peter bound to death the healthy Ananias, condemned through the great authority of his speech and when, by the same power of authority, he freed Tabitha from the chains of death. This is also why Ananias and Saphira have to die suddenly in front of the Christian community, so that the greatness of apostolic authority can be shown.'

When the community of Iona tried to counter the pretensions of Armagh at the end of the 7th century, they also presented their patron saint as a *uir apostolicus*, precisely on account of the evangelical miracles performed by Columba.[18] In his *Vita Columbae*, Adomnán gives a clear interpretation of the episode of the rising from the dead of a young boy:[19]

> *Cum hac sancti honorabili uoce anima ad corpus rediit defunctusque apertis reuixit oculis; cuius manum tenens apostolicus homo erexit, et in statione stabiliens secum domum egresus deducit, et parentibus rediuiuum adsignauit.*[...] *Hoc noster Columba cum Elia et Eliseo profetis habeat sibi commone uirtutis miraculum, et cum Petro et Paulo et Joanne apostolis partem honoris similem in defunctorum resuscitatione, et inter utrosque hoc est profetarum et apostolorum coetus, honorificam caelestis patriae sedem homo profeticus et apostolicus aeternalem, cum Christo qui regnat cum patre in unitate spiritus sancti per omnia saecula saeculorum.*

[17] *De mirabilibus sacrae scripturae* III 17 (PL 35, 2200).

[18] The same terminology was used by Sulpicius Severus in the *Vita Martini* I 7.7 (ed. Fontaine (1968), 268). On the use of the term *apostolicus* in the context of evangelical miracles, see Fontaine's commentary to this chapter ibidem, 631–3.

[19] Adomnán, *Vita Columbae* II 32 (ed. Anderson and Anderson (1961), 398). The translation is mine.

'At the saint's glorious word, the soul returned to the body and the dead boy opened his eyes and lived again. The apostolic man took hold of the boy's hand, raised him to his feet and, steadying him, lead him out of the house. He gave the boy, now restored to life, back to his parents. [...] One must recognise that in this miracle of power our saint Columba is seen to share with the prophets Elijah and Elisha and with the Apostles Peter and Paul and John the rare distinction of raising the dead to life. He has a seat of everlasting glory in the heavenly homeland as a prophetic and apostolic man among the companies of prophets and the apostles, with Christ who reigns with the Father in the unity of the Holy Ghost, for ever and ever.'

Armagh

However, Adomnán does not push the apostolic agenda and, in any case, Iona's riposte came too late. Armagh had already secured two important elements to support their claim: the adhesion of the Roman party and above all the relics of Peter and Paul.[20]

The Armagh dossier seems to have been completed in the AD 680s and the main arguments are found in the *Liber Angeli*, the *Collectanea* of Tírechán and the *Vita Patricii* written by Muirchú. Like Adomnán, Muirchú develops the miracle argument. Patrick is equal to Peter in standing against Loeguire's druids just as the apostle stood against Simon the magician.[21] Patrick is also the only one to share with Stephen, the first martyr and disciple of the apostles, the miraculous vision of heaven opened before his eyes:[22]

Dominici et apostolici uiri Patricii, cuius mentionem facimus, quoddam miraculum mirifice gestum in carne adhuc stanti quod ei et Stephano poene tantum contigisse legitur, breui retexam relatu.

'I shall briefly relate a miracle of the godly and apostolic man Patrick, of whom we are speaking, something that miraculously happened to him when he was alive. This, as far as I know, has been written about him and Stephen only.'

20 On the significance of these relics, see Picard (1999), 44–52.

21 Muirchú, *Vita Patricii* I 17 (Bieler (1979), 88): *sanctus Patricius ut quondam Petrus de Simone cum quadam potentia et magno clamore confidenter ad Dominum dixit.*

22 Muirchú, *Vita Patricii* I 28 (ed. and trans. Bieler (1979), 100–1).

Patrick is also granted by the angel the same privilege as the apostles, that of being a judge with Christ at the last judgement:[23]

> *Quarta petitio, ut Hibernenses omnes in die iudicii a te iudicentur—sicut dicitur ad apostolos 'Et uos sedentes iudicabitis duodecim tribus Israel'— ut eos quibus apostolus fuisti iudices.*
>
> 'The fourth request: that all the Irish on the day of judgement shall be judged by you—as it is said to the Apostles: 'And you shall sit and judge the twelve tribes of Israel'—so that you may judge those whose apostle you have been.'

The second argument is developed by Tírechán. Patrick's apostolic status is confirmed by his ownership of the relics of Peter and Paul. These relics were used for the foundation of churches set up by Patrick's disciples and were kept at Armagh in Tírechán own time:[24]

> *et in Duin Sebuirgi sedit supra petram, quae petra Patricii usque nunc, et ordinauit ibi Olcanum sanctum episcopum, quem nutriuit Patricius et dedit illi partem de reliquiis Petri et Pauli et aliorum, et uelum quod custodiuit reliquias;* [...] *et scripsit illi librum psalmorum, quem uidi, et portauit ab illo partem de reliquís Petri et Pauli, Laurentii et Stefani quae sunt in Machi.*
>
> 'and in Dún Sobairche, he sat on a rock which is called Patrick's rock until now, and there he consecrated as holy bishop Olcán, whom Patrick had educated, and he gave him a portion of the relics of Peter and Paul and others, and a veil to protect the relics; [...] And he wrote for him a book of the Psalms, which I have seen, and he [= Sachellus] received from him a portion of the relics of Peter and Paul, Lawrence and Stephen, which are in Armagh.'

Tírechán omits to mention that Armagh's major difficulty was that they did not have the body of Patrick, which was still in Saul or in Downpatrick. However, the relics of Peter were far more important, since they provided a direct link with the very foundation of the Christian church.

23 Muirchú, *Vita Patricii* II 6 (Bieler (1979), 116–7).

24 Tírechán, *Collectanea* 48.3 and prelude to the *Collectanea* (ed. Bieler (1979), 160 and 122). The translation is mine.

The claim for apostolic status and supremacy over the other Irish churches is fully voiced in the *Liber Angeli*:[25]

> *Patricio sancto episcopo summus Domini anguelus debitam reuerentiam cathedrae suae apostolicae honoremque proprium sui heredis ab omnibus Scotis traditum sapienter a Deo sibi dictauit.* [...] *De speciali reuerantia Airdd Machae et honore praesulis eiusdem urbis dicamus. Ista quippe ciuitas summa et libera a Deo est constituta et ab anguelo Dei et ab apostolico uiro sancto Patricio episcopo specialiter dedicata. Preest ergo quodam preuilegio omnibus aeclessis ac monasteriis cunctorum Hibernensium uel superna auctoritate summi pontificis illius fundatoris. Nihilhominus uenerari debet honore summorum martyrum Petri et Pauli, Stefani, Laurendi et caeterorum.*
>
> 'The supreme angel of the Lord, taught by God, announced to holy bishop Patrick the reverence due to his apostolic see and the due honour of his heir to be rendered by all the Irish. [...] Let us speak now of the special reverence for Armagh and of the honour for the bishop of the same city. Now this city has been established by God and by the apostolic man, the holy bishop Patrick. It therefore has precedence, by a certain privilege and by the heavenly authority of the supreme bishop its founder, over all churches and monasteries of all the Irish. Further more it ought to be venerated in honour of the principal martyrs Peter, Paul, Stephen, Lawrence and the others.'

By the next century the process is complete. In the Book of Armagh (AD 807), the notes added to Tírechán's text conflate the stories of Patrick and Palladius. Patrick is sent on his mission to Ireland by the pope, direct successor of St Peter:[26]

> *Tertio decimo anno Teothosii imperatoris a Celestino episcopo papa Romae Patricius episcopus ad doctrinam Scottorum mittitur, qui Celestinus quadragesimus quintus episcopus a Petro apostolo in urbe Roma.*
>
> 'In the thirteenth year of the emperor Theodosius, bishop Patricius is sent by bishop Celestine, the pope of Rome, for the teaching of the Irish. This Celestine was the forty fifth bishop, beginning from Peter the Apostle in the City of Rome.'

25 *Liber Angeli* prologue; 17 (ed. Bieler (1979), 184, 186). The translation is mine.

26 *Notae suppletoriae ad Tirechanum* 56 (ed. Bieler (1979), 164). The translation is mine.

In subsequent centuries, hagiographers no longer have to make a case. The phrase *Patricius apostolus* is currently used in the *Vita Tertia Patricii* and *Vita Quarta Patricii*, and Patrick will remain not just the national apostle but a saint with the same status and power as the apostles of the early church:[27]

> *Ipse enim dux noster a Domino, ipse pastor noster, ipse iudex noster, ipse pater noster, ipse apostolus noster, quem nobis misit dominus noster Jesus Christus.*
>
> 'For he is our leader appointed by the Lord, he is our shepherd, he is our judge, he is our father, he is our apostle, who was sent to us by our Lord Jesus Christ.'

Conclusion

In a famous broadcast, Dáibhí Ó Cróinín denounced the Armagh dossier concerning Patrick as 'a deliberate pack of lies' and 'a demonstrable pack of lies'.[28] The same accusation was levelled in the 11th century by Benedict, abbot of San Michele della Chiusa, against Adémar of Chabannes who had been active in promoting the cult of Martial, founder of the church of Limoges, as an apostle of Christ. Benedict lost his case at the Council of Limoges in AD 1031 and, from then on, Martial was venerated as *Martialis Apostolus Christi*. However, modern scholarship has shown how the dossier of Saint Martial of Limoges was tampered with and that Adémar himself had forged documents to further the cause of his patron saint.[29] Establishing the apostolicity of Martial involved the rewriting of annals, the creation of a new liturgy for the saint, the refurbishment of reliquaries and church buildings and, above all, the writing of a saint's Life that would insure a wider impact in neighbouring regions and further afield. The *Vita Prolixior Martialis*, written between AD 1025 and 1030, is a propaganda document where Adémar reworks the elements of earlier Lives in order to emphasize the direct links between Christ and Martial.[30] On a verbal level, he

27 *Vita Tertia Patricii* (ed. Bieler (1971), 189). The translation is mine.

28 RTÉ One Television, 'Patrick: the Renegade Saint,' *Would you Believe*, 8 April 2012.

29 See above, n 1.

30 Adémar's *Vita Prolixior Martialis* is ed. by Surius (1618).

systematically replaces the terms *praesul* and *confessor* by *apostolus*. The case of Saint Martial is exemplary, precisely because the deception and forgery of documents were denounced by contemporaries, but it was not an exception. Other churches on the Continent were involved in similar claims and, in all these cases, hagiography played a major role in establishing the apostolicity of the saint. Notable examples are the abbeys of St Denis, near Paris, and Mozac, near Clermont-Ferrand. At St Denis, the claim of apostolicity corresponds to the time of the abbey's expansion when closer links with the royal power were formed. Two Lives were written then to support this claim: a *Vita secunda Dionysii* in the AD 820s and a Life written in AD 835–840 by Hilduin, disciple of Alcuin, where the Dionysius of Paris was assimilated to Dionysius the Areopagite, the alleged disciple of St Paul in Athens.[31] Like St Denis, Mozac is associated with the Carolingians. The expansion of the monastery in the AD 840s corresponds to the patronage of Pepin II of Aquitaine, who ordered the relics of Saint Austremoine, first bishop of Clermont, to be transferred to Mozac in 848.[32] A saint's Life was written for the occasion (*Vita prima Austremonii*), followed shortly by a second Life, written before AD 900 (*Vita Austremonii secunda*), both claiming that Austremoine was one of the seventy-two disciples of Christ.[33] The techniques used by the hagiographers were similar: conflation or association with other saints (as in the case of Patrick and Palladius), deliberate shift in chronology to place the saint at an earlier period and emphasis on the links with Rome and St Peter.[34] The rewriting of the Lives of early bishops of Gaul dates from the Carolingian period (*Vita antiquior Martialis*, *c.*AD 850; *Vita prima Austremonii*, *c.*AD 850; *Vita secunda Dionysii*, *c.*AD 820; *Vita Dionysii auct. Hilduino*, AD 835–840). It would appear that, as in other fields of scholarship and church politics, the Irish were ahead of the game in developing a rhetoric of apostolicity to boost the status of a church with ambitions of pre-eminence and strong royal patronage.

31 The *Vita secunda Dionysii* is ed. by the Bollandists in *Acta Sanctorum Octobris, tome II*, 792–4 (Oct. 4); Hilduin's *Vita sancti Dionysii* in PL 106, 13–50.

32 See Levillain (1904).

33 The two *Vitae* are ed. by the Bollandists in *Acta Sanctorum Novembris, tome I*, 49–61 (Nov. 1). Cf. Dierkens (2005), 73–80; Dierkens (2006), 28–9.

34 Sot (2001), 173–9.

Bibliography

Anderson, A.O. and M.O. Anderson (1961) *Adomnán's Life of Columba*, Edinburgh.

Bieler, L. (1952) *Libri epistolarum Sancti Patricii episcopi*, Dublin, repr. 1993.

— (1953) 'The hymn of St. Secundinus,' *PRIA* 55C, 117–27, repr. in L. Bieler, *Ireland and the culture of early medieval Europe*, ed. by R. Sharpe, London 1987, IX.

— (1971) *Four Latin Lives of St. Patrick*, Dublin.

— (1979) *The Patrician texts from the Book of Armagh*, Dublin.

Curran, M. (1984) *The Antiphonary of Bangor*, Dublin.

Dierkens, A. (2005) 'Une abbaye médiévale face à son passé: Saint Pierre de Mozac, du IXe au XIIe siècle,' in N. Bouter, *Écrire son histoire: les communautés régulières face à leur passé*, Saint-Étienne, 71–105.

— (2006) 'Martial, Sernin, Trophime et les autres: à propos des évangélisateurs et des apôtres en Gaule,' in C. Andrault-Schmitt, *Saint-Martial de Limoges – Ambition politique et production culturelle (X^e^–XIIIe siècles)*, Limoges, 24–37.

Doherty, C. (1991) 'The cult of St Patrick and the politics of Armagh in the seventh century,' in J.-M. Picard, *Ireland and Northern France AD 600–850*, Dublin, 53–94.

Fontaine, J. (1968) *Sulpice Sévère, Vie de saint Martin*, Paris.

Kahn-Herrick, S. (2007) *Imagining the sacred past: hagiography and power in early Normandy*, Cambridge.

— (2010) 'Studying apostolic hagiography: the case of Fronto of Périgueux, disciple of Christ,' *Speculum* 85, 235–70.

— (2012) 'Le pouvoir du passé apostolique,' in E. Bozoky, *Hagiographie, idéologie et politique au Moyen Âge en Occident*, Turnhout, 129–38.

— (2013) 'Apostolic founding bishops and their rivals,' in C. Bousquet and Y. Maurey, *Espace sacré, mémoire sacrée: les saints-évêques et leurs villes*, Turnhout, forthcoming.

Landes, R.A. (1995) *Relics, apocalypse and the deceits of history: Ademar of Chabannes, 989–1034*, Cambridge.

Levillain, L. (1904) 'La translation des reliques de saint Austremoine à Mozac et le diplôme de Pépin II d'Aquitaine,' *Le Moyen Âge* 8, 281–337.

Mac Airt, S. and G. Mac Niocaill (1983) *The Annals of Ulster (to A.D. 1131)*, Dublin.

Ó Néill, P. (1984) 'Romani influences on seventh-century Hiberno-Latin literature,' in P. Ní Chatháin and M. Richter, *Irland und Europa. Die Kirche im Frühmittelalter*, Stuttgart, 280–90.

Picard, J.-M. (1999) 'Le culte des reliques en Irlande (VIIe–IXe siècle),' in E. Bozoky and A.M. Helvétius, *Les reliques: objets, cultes, symboles*, Turnhout, 39–55.

Riché, P. (1993) 'Discours du Président', *Annuaire-Bulletin de la Société de l'Histoire de France. Années 1991–1992*, Paris, 3–9.

Sot, M. (2001) 'La Rome antique dans l'hagiographie épiscopale en Gaule,' in P. Zerbi, *Roma antica nel Medioevo: mito, rappresentazioni, sopravvivenze nella 'Respublica Christiana' dei secoli IX–XIII*, Milan, 163–88.

Walker, G.S.M. (1957) *Sancti Columbani opera*, Dublin, repr. 1970.

Walsh, M. and D. Ó Cróinín (1988) *Cummian's letter* De controversia paschali *together with a related Irish computistical tract* De ratione conputandi, Toronto.

MICHAEL CLARKE

THE *LEABHAR GABHÁLA* AND CAROLINGIAN ORIGIN LEGENDS

Abstract

The Irish *Leabhar Gabhála* is poised between several different literary modes: conduit of ancient traditions, bogus charter of national identity, by-product of commentary on Latin cosmography and world history. Attempts to explain the themes and purposes of its earlier sections (Tracts I and II) usually focus on parallels between the story of the ancestors of the Irish and that of the Hebrews of the Old Testament. This article attempts to situate the work in the context of Carolingian global and national histories, focussing on the theme of the origins of each nation in the westward wanderings of fugitives from the classical heartlands of the eastern Mediterranean or western Asia. It is argued that the narrative of the travels of the ancesters of the Goídil (Irish) involves an implicit parallel with the travels of the ancestors of Romans, Franks, and British from the fall of Troy. The paper proposes that this parallel may have been prominent in a lost Latin version of the *Leabhar Gabhála* of which parts are preserved as embedded quotations in hagiographical texts.

Keywords

Leabhar Gabhála; origin legends, Carolingian historiography, hagiography, mythology, scholia; Picts; Fénius Farsaid, Lucan, Virgil.

Introduction

Surveying the texts that are most prominent in overviews of medieval Irish literature, one might assume that the medieval *literati* were almost exclusively interested in Ireland itself: the backward look and the inward gaze. Despite the labours of a small number of scholars, among whom Dáibhí Ó Cróinín has taken a leading role, this assumption has too seldom been challenged. A dispassionate assessment shows that the

Early medieval Ireland and Europe: chronology, contacts, scholarship, ed. by Pádraic Moran and Immo Warntjes, Studia Traditionis Theologiae, 14 (Turnhout, 2015), pp. 441–79.

 10.1484/M.STT-EB.5.103132

literati were concerned at least equally with the wider world, a study pursued in relation to cosmography, biblical Antiquity, and gentile history both pagan and Christian.[1] Nor were the two projects separable from each other. A concern with the interplay between inward and outward perspectives is most appparent in literary design: to take two celebrated examples, *Saltair na Rann* absorbs the Christian story into vernacular poetics by enacting the narrative of salvation in sustained Irish syllabic verse, while *Táin Bó Cuailnge* and *Togail Troí* alongside each other give Ireland a pagan heroic past to rival the Trojan War and also integrate Graeco-Roman antiquity into the cycles of Irish narrative.[2] In such texts the encounter between vernacular and Latinate discourses is the springboard for creative synthesis and mutual enrichment.

This encounter takes a simpler form in texts that simply set the two worlds alongside each other in tabular mode. There is a thematic kinship between the glossaries, with their bold correlations between the elements of Irish and those of the 'three sacred languages',[3] and the historical texts that set up systematic correspondences between events in Ireland and simultaneous events close to the centre of the world in the eastern Mediterranean. This is vividly evoked by the synchronisms, where an Irish scholar essentially takes the Chronicle of Eusebius–Jerome, where the histories of world nations are tabulated in parallel columns, and adds an extra column for events at the corresponding points of Irish history.[4] The precision of these correspondences becomes a thing of beauty in poetry like Gilla Coemáin's *Annalád anall uile*,[5] and is worked out piecemeal in the Annals.[6] There, indeed, the confrontation often seems to be realized through a switch of language as well as subject-matter, as in this typical example from the Oxford, Bodleian Library, Rawlinson B 502 text of the Annals of Tigernach:[7]

[1] I have discussed this at greater length in Clarke (2011).

[2] Miles (2011); Poppe and Schlüter (2011); essays in O'Connor (2014).

[3] Moran (2010); Moran (2012); Russell (1988).

[4] For the classic example of the Laud Synchronisms see Meyer (1913); further texts in Mac Carthy (1892), 278–317. Cf. Jaski (2009), 68–72.

[5] Edition by Smith (2007), 188–210; further discussion by Tristram (1985), 172–5; Smith (2002); Clarke (2009), 245–6. The Ireland-centred synchronisms of this poem are the converse of those followed in *A rí richid réidig dam* (Book of Leinster, ed. in Best et al. (1954–83), iii 574–87), where Irish correspondences are introduced piecemeal into a sequence determined by the central events of world history.

[6] See Mc Carthy (2007), esp. 118–52.

[7] Stokes (1895–6), 405. Unless otherwise stated, all translations in this article are my own.

> *Marcus Antonius Niger victus ab Augusto in Alaxandria sese propria manu interfecit ⁊ Cleopatra uxor eius serpentis morsu in sinistra tacta exanimata est. Hoc anno cepit regnare in Emain Conchobar mac Nessa, qui regnavit annis .lx. Ro rannad Hériu iársin isin cóic, iar n-árcain Conare Móir mac Etarsceóil hi mBrudin Dá Dergga, etir Conchobur mac Nessa ocus Coirpre Nia fer ⁊ Tigernach Tétbannach ⁊ Dedad mac Sin ⁊ Ailill mac Mágag.*
>
> 'Marcus Antonius Niger, defeated by Augustus, killed himself by his own hand in Alexandria, and Cleopatra his wife was done to death, touched by a serpent's bite in the left hand. In this year Conchobar son of Nes began to reign in Emain; he reigned for 60 years. Ireland was divided into five, after the slaughter of Conare Mór son of Etarscél in the Hostel of the Da Derga, between Conchobar son of Nes and Cairbre Nia fer and Tigernach Tétbannach and Dedad son of Sen and Ailill son of Mága.'

The section about Antony and Cleopatra is derived from Orosius,[8] the division of the kingdom linked to the events at Da Derga's Hostel is embedded in indigenous lore of kingship and perhaps refers directly to the text *Togail Bruidne Da Derga*. In the linking sentence the phrase *cepit regnare* is odd Latin, and we might detect behind it an Irish original, as **ro gab rige i nEmain Conchobar mac Nessa*. But in the manuscript there is no distinction of script or layout to mark these switches between languages; the relationship between the two perspectives remains unspecified, at least until the coming of Christianity through St Patrick,[9] and the gulf can be crossed only by picturing the simultaneities in the mind's eye.

The *Leabhar Gabhála* and its purposes

Precisely this gap is negotiated by the 'synthetic pseudohistory' of national origins, preserved most systematically in the *Leabhar Gabhála*[10]

[8] Orosius VI 19.18.

[9] Stokes (1895–6), 30, 32, 121.

[10] Texts from the *Leabhar Gabhála* discussed in this paper are cited from the edition of Macalister (1938–56), which remains the best available touchstone despite its manifest shortcomings. Given Macalister's confusing presentation, it is useful to cross-refer to the version in the so-called Book of Leinster, which is the only single version that can easily be read as an integral unity, using the diplomatic edition (Best et al. (1954–83), i 1–55), with the invaluable translation by John Carey (in Carey and Koch (2003), 226–71; for the status of the Book of Leinster version in the overall

but present in variant versions in many associated verse and prose texts, of which one of the earliest and most important is *Can a mbunadus na nGaedel*, ascribed to Mael Muru Othna (†AD 887).[11] After many generations of study, the themes and purposes of these works remain puzzling. What caste or generation of *literati* was responsible for their articulation? Did the elements originate in different learned centres at different times, to be worked up into narratives now lost that were subsequently welded into new unities by later generations who perhaps misunderstood the genre or genuineness of their materials? Or does the whole scheme originate in a single creative programme designed to produce a bogus narrative of national origins, a pseudohistory in the most extravagant sense of the term?

So far as I know, answers to these questions remain in the realm of guesswork; but in the scholarship there is a consensus that the overarching purpose of the legend is to give the Irish a past and an identity commensurate with those of the Hebrews of the Old Testament. Scowcroft expresses it well:[12]

> 'The purpose [of the *Leabhar Gabhála*] was [...] to find a place for Ireland in the biblical history of the world, for her inhabitants among the descendants of Noah, and for her many nations and dynasties in an immense genealogical scheme that subsumed their pedigrees and claims under those of the Tara kingship. Essential to these efforts were the standard authorities on chronology, geography, history, ethnography and language, who had already brought the Old Testament, classical scholarship, and early medieval thought into some sort of harmony.'

This sense of global context is declared by the opening words of the text—*In principio fecit Deus celum et terram*—and the national story begins with the creation of the world and Noah's Flood; from his three sons descend all nations who settle the three continents, and among

tradition see Scowcroft (1988), 7–8, with Schlüter (2010), 36–44). In working on this difficult text I have drawn much on the published studies by John Carey (1993), (1994), (2005), (2010), Mark Scowcroft (1987), (1988), (2009), and Bart Jaski (2003), (2006), (2009).

[11] The only edition with commentary is that by Todd (1848), 220–71; updated text in Best et al. (1954–83), iii 133b–5a; see also Carey (2010); Scowcroft (1988), 8–9. Carey (1993), 5 n 10, points out that Gilla Coemáin's *Gaedel glas ó tát Gaídil* (see Macalister (1938–56), ii 90 (no. XIII)) depends directly on *Can a mbunadus*.

[12] Scowcroft (1987), 13–4, 20; cf. van Hamel (1915), 177–8; Carey (1993), 2–3; Carey (2005), 32–8.

these is a descendant of Japheth, Fénius Farsaid, chieftain (*toísech*) of Scythia, who is responsible for the invention of the Irish language out of the confusion of Babel and in Egypt fathers a son, Nél, by Scotta daughter of Pharaoh, before going home to Scythia where his son Noenual succeeded him. After many generations his descendants in Egypt themselves return to Scythia and ultimately give rise to the ancestors of the Irish, who will be called Scotti (Irish *Scuit*) after their Egyptian ancestress, an etymology apparently supplanting or complementing the more obvious-seeming idea that Scotti are named after their Scythian origins;[13] they travel over many lands and oceans before they turn their eyes to this western island. The story criss-crosses the story of the Hebrews, with exile in Egypt followed by a journey which seems irresistibly to suggest that Ireland is equivalent to the Promised Land. The sense of parallelism between Irish and Hebrew journeys is neatly encapsulated within the biblical narrative of *Saltair na Rann* itself, where the story of Gáedel Glas and his departure from Egypt is inserted into the main narrative of the Hebrews' captivity before the exodus under Moses.[14]

Although the enmeshing of Irish origins with the Genesis story is clearly a key element of the programme of the *Leabhar Gabhála* wanderings, it is not a sufficient explanation on its own, if only because it was conventional in the early Middle Ages for any nation's origins to be contextualized in that way, following or imitating the schemes set out by Isidore in the racial histories of the ninth book of the Etymologies.[15] More important, there are no obvious biblical echoes in the part of the story that comes after Fénius' return to Scythia, and it demands a different kind of explanation. This part of the narrative makes up much of the bulk of the earlier sections of the work, Tract I and the last part of Tract II in the conventional terminology.[16] When Nél and Scotta's Egyptian descendants arrive back in Scythia they seize the kingship (as by now it is called) from their cousins the descendants of Noenual, and for many generations there is strife and killing between the two sides of the fam-

[13] Scowcroft (1988), 17 n 44; cf. van Hamel (1915), 173–8. Compare how Nennius allows the obviously eponymous Britus/Brutus to sit alongside the claim that the island is named after Brutus the Roman consul (Nennius, *Historia Brittonum* (ed. by Theodor Mommsen in MGH Auct. ant. 13, 147.7)).

[14] *Saltair na Rann* ll. 3993–4012 in Greene (n.d.), noted by Scowcroft (1988), 10 n 25.

[15] For *comparanda* to the Irish materials see e.g. Ó Cróinín (1983), 1–11; Tristram (1985), esp. 180–93; see further below, pp. 458–65, and cf. in general Geary (2002).

[16] Scowcroft (1987), 101–15; Scowcroft (2009), 6–7.

ily. At length Agnoman, from the Egyptian branch, kills his cousin for the kingship and is subsequently exiled with his people. From Scythia they sail up the Caspian Sea, which in this period was understood to connect with the Ocean;[17] they are beguiled by the music of the sirens, but Caicher the druid uses Ulysses's trick to plug their ears with wax;[18] the wind drives them out into the Ocean and they nearly die of thirst there; they fall on the promontory of the Rhipaean mountains in the north, where they find a well of wine, drink from it and sleep three days and four nights; Caicher prophesies that one day their descendants will reach Ireland. Via the Maeotic marshes they go into the Mediterranean by Crete and Sicily and thus at length to Spain, which they conquer in three battles. There, in Brigantia, Íth son of Breogon sees Ireland one winter's day from his father's tower. Íth goes to Ireland, where the Tuatha Dé Danann allow him to judge and, jealous of his just judgments, they kill him; to avenge him come the sons of Míl, Íth's nephew, who take Ireland and become the ancestors of the Goídil of historical reality. In what follows I will explore this earlier part of the *Leabhar Gabhála* legend as an example of an international pattern in pseudohistorical narrative in the early Middle Ages: a pattern which characterizes the nation as originating in the classical heartlands of the eastern Mediterranean and western Asia and thus makes its origins analogous to but distinct from those of Rome. We will see that a decisive part in the creative process was played by the comparison and confrontation between national origin legends that went on in the international climate of Carolingian intellectualism, and that much of the logic of the Irish origin legend took shape against that background.

Leabhar Gabhála: the problem of unity

When did the composition of the *Leabhar Gabhála* begin?[19] Elements at least of this lore are present in the very early poems preserved in the Lagin genealogies of Oxford, Bodleian Library, Rawlinson B 502, perhaps as early as the 7th century,[20] and in *Scél Tuáin meic Chairill*,

[17] Orosius I 2.48–49; see Merrills (2005), 90.

[18] This lore is also found in Gilla in Chomded's chronological poem: see Best et al. (1956–83), iii 143b ll. 32–3, with Miles (2011), 48–9.

[19] Useful summary of the evidence by Carey (1993), 3–7.

[20] O'Brien (1962), 1–9; see Carey (2005), 32–6.

composed not later than the beginning of the Middle Irish period.[21] We can be confident that the significant elements of the narrative existed before the composition of the *Historia Brittonum*, which was compiled, according to David Dumville's authoritative analysis, in Wales about AD 830.[22] The account in the *Historia* is composite, and combines elements from at least two distinct sources: the series of successive occupations of Ireland, culminating in the coming of *tres filii militis Hispaniae* to Ireland, and the account attributed to the most learned of the Irish, *peritissimi Scottorum*, concerning the wanderings of a noble from Scythia, *vir nobilis de Scythia*.[23] This Scythian is evidently the figure named in *Auraicept na nÉces* and subsequent Irish texts as Fénius Farsaid.[24] The presence in the *Historia* of proper names originating as misunderstood Irish phrases, like Damhoctor for *dam ochtair* 'a company of eight people' and *builc* corresponding the Fir Bolg, suggests that parts of his narrative have originated in an Irish-language source and that this source was concerned with a parallelism between the 'group of eight' who came to Ireland and the eight human inhabitants of the Ark.[25] By extension, it is likely that the 'three sons of a Spanish soldier' are an attempt by the author of the *Historia* to make sense of some other, underlying phrase in Latin or Irish, which is independently reflected in the *Leabhar Gabhála* account of the sons of Míl.[26]

We can thus be confident that elements at least of the origin legend were well formed in the pre-Carolingian period; but it is only in texts composed in Irish a little later that it can be seen taking on the unity of form that characterizes the *Leabhar Gabhála* proper. When, why, or by whom the synthesis was carried out we can only guess;[27] but the resulting

21 Carey (1984).

22 Dumville's analysis of the text and its origins is conveniently summarized in Dumville (1994). The authoritative edition remains that of Mommsen in MGH Auct. ant. 13, 111–222.

23 Nennius, *Historia Brittonum* (MGH Auct. ant. 13, 156.15).

24 *Auraicept na nÉces* ll. 1–46, 104–177 (ed. Calder (1917), 2–4, 8–14); for the earlier core text of the corresponding sections see Ahlqvist (1983), 47 (§§1.1–1.11).

25 Scowcroft (1988), 22–4; Jaski (2009), 48–50.

26 *Miles Hispaniae* is odd Latin if it simply means 'a Spanish soldier', and the *Historia* offers no parallels for this genitive of country of origin; it makes sense best as a Latinization of something encountered as an Irish phrase. On *builc*, *Damhoctor*, and *miles Hispaniae* see already van Hamel (1915), 157–9, shrewdly suspicious about the mechanics of the transmission.

27 Cf. the elegant discussion by Scowcroft (1987), 90–6; and for a more baldly-stated model of the composition process cf. van Hamel (1915), 193–6.

literary artefacts are extraordinarily difficult to intepret, because they unite things that in our own cultural world belong in different and irreconcileable categories. On the one hand we have what seem to be survivals from or reminiscences of authentic Irish traditions; on the other we have motifs, names and incidents derived from learned Latin texts and commentary upon them, specifically the etymologizing of personal names and placenames.[28] It is not problematic that fragments of authentic pre-Christian myth might survive in medieval Irish tradition, nor that glossed readings of late antique Latin texts can generate vernacular narratives: both processes are quite credible and well paralleled internationally. What remains more puzzling that the two phenomena are fused in a single narrative with no obvious sense of disjuncture, so that in the absence of external clues we cannot guess at the origins or antiquity of any one element of the whole. Open a standard anthology of Irish poetry, and near the beginning we will probably find the words that the *Leabhar Gabhála* attributes to Amairgen son of Míl when he set foot on the shore of Ireland:[29] *Am gáeth i mmuir, Am tond trethan i tír, Am fuaim mara, Am dam secht ndírend* — 'I am a wind on the sea, I am a sea-wave upon the land, I am a sound of the sea, I am a stag of seven combats'. Perhaps this is a survival from a lost vernacular narrative cycle; perhaps it is an archaising fantasy, an attempt to create fake rhythmical *roscad* by recasting a prosodic pattern that Middle Irish saga uses for speeches of heroic vaunting,[30] while deploying the extravagant metaphorical resources that were familiar to the audience from the marked and decorated language of passages like the messenger scenes of *Táin Bó Cuailnge*.[31] No less, it may be a recreation in Irish of an originally Latin or Latinate discourse that happens not to survive in its own right.[32] No reading is possible without an implicit choice between such alternatives.

This problem of sources and unity offers grave challenges to any attempt to read the legend *in toto*. Let me illustrate this from a well-known

[28] Scowcroft (1988), 12–3.

[29] For the Book of Leinster version see Best et al. (1954–83), i 12b ll. 39–42.

[30] See van Hamel (1915), 180, adducing *Compert Con Culainn* 7 (van Hamel (1933), 6–8).

[31] Compare the Book of Leinster version of *Táin Bó Cuailnge* ll. 4396–8 in O'Rahilly (1967), 121, with translation p 257.

[32] The diction and imagery often correspond closely to the learned kennings in the *Immaccallam in Dá Thuarad*, a poetic dialogue with especially close connections to Latinate educational culture: see e.g. §§20–38, 90–105 in Stokes (1905), with discussions by Wright (2013); Clarke (2013).

example in the poem of Mael Muru. Describing the arrival of the sons of Míl on the south coast of Ireland, the poet tells how Donn dies at the moment of arrival:[33]

Ro gab Dond cosin leith aile
iar n-urd innaiss,
ba marb ic ascnam cen chomais
descert hIrraiss.

Co tuarcbad carn le lia a cheneoil
as lir lethach
sentreb tontech conid Tech Duinn
de congarar.

Ba hésin a hedacht adbul
dia chlaind chetaich
cucum dom tic tissaid uili
iarbar n-écaib.

> 'Donn went on the other side in progressive order; he died as he was sailing, without strength, to the south of Irrus. There was raised for him a cairn, with the stone of his race, above the broad sea: an ancient dwelling, a house of the waves, which is called the House of Donn. This was his mighty legacy to his abundant descendants: 'To me, to my house, let them all come after their deaths'.'

Donn's is no ordinary death: but what is the 'legacy', *étacht*, to which his prediction refers? Clues come from elsewhere in the literature: the learned text *Airne Fíngein* mentions *Tech Duind frisndálait mairb* ('The house of Donn to which the dead gather'),[34] and many have been drawn to see Donn as a euhemerized pagan divinity, even a Celtic god of the dead.[35] If so, one can assume that this tradition has been superficially

[33] Best et al. (1954–83), iii 134b ll. 7–13.

[34] Vendryes (1953), 257.

[35] John Carey has argued (2010) that there are two groupings among the sons of Míl: first Íth, Donn, and Amairgen, who go back to ancient and possibly Indo-European tradition, and then a long series of 'two-dimensional ancestor figures' (p 327). He associates Donn and Amairgen with other Indo-European stories of pairs of founding brothers, and finally suggests that Íth personifies the fatness of the land—he recognizes the qualities of the land, its richness, and the Tuatha Dé Danann see him as a threat (cf. *Audacht Morainn* 32 in Kelly (1976), 12–5). Carey does not seek to explain how such traditions could have become seamlessly integrated into material of such a different

Christianized in the Old Irish poem *Reicne Fothaid Canainne,* where Donn seems to be identified as a demon who tortures the soul of a pagan after death,[36] and likewise in the more complex lore of the prose *Dindshenchas*, which recounts that according to the pagans (*do reir na ngennti*) the souls of sinners visit Tech Duinn before going to Hell 'and give their blessing [...] to the soul of Donn', while the righteous only see it from a distance.[37] This notion of pagan survival is made all the more enticing by the notion that Donn's death might originally have been understood in terms of human sacrifice, and by the identification (first securely attested in relatively recent times) of Tech Duinn with the eminence now known as Bull Rock beyond the mouth of the Kenmare River, in which there is a dark passage eerily suggesting an entrance to the Underworld.[38]

In its original context, however, this poem is embedded among lore of an utterly different kind. It has long been known that parts at least of the lore of the sons of Míl are linked to a passage in the description of Ireland in Orosius' History against the Pagans, one of the principal repositories of world history and geography in early medieval Europe:[39]

> *Hibernia insula inter Britanniam et Hispaniam sita longiore ab africo in boream spatio porrigitur. Huius partes priores intentae Cantabrico oceano Brigantiam Gallaeciae civitatem ab africo sibi in circium occurrentem spatioso intervallo procul spectant et ab eo praecipue promonturio ubi Scenae fluminis ostium est et Velabri Lucenique consistunt.*
>
> 'The island of Ireland lies between Britain and Spain, its longer side running from the south-west to the north-east. Its closer parts, especially from the promontory where the mouth of the river Scena is found and the Velabri and the Luceni live, look south-west across a great expanse of the Cantabrian ocean towards the Gallaecian city of Brigantia which faces it, looking north-west.'

kind, plainly derived from commentary on learned Latin texts. For earlier studies of the house of Donn see for example Meyer (1919); Mac Cana (2011), 222–4.

36 *Reicne Fothaid Canainne* 48 (ed. Meyer (1910), 16).

37 Gwynn (1903–35), iv 310–1. The onomastic lore of Tech Duinn is found in the *Liber Hymnorum* in a gloss to Fiacc's Hymn, Stokes and Strachan (1901–3), ii 316 (noted by van Hamel (1915), 167).

38 See Hogan (1910), *s.v.* 'tech duinn'; Mac Carthaigh (1966–7), 51–5. I thank Máirín Ní Dhonnchadha for this reference.

39 Orosius I 2.39.

This passage, added to the nearby mention of the tall tower (*pharus*) at Brigantia which looks towards Britain,[40] and presumably bostered by Isidore's addition to Orosius' etymology linking Hibernia to Hiberia, that is Spain,[41] motivates the origin legend that represents the coming of the Goídil as a journey from Spain to Ireland.[42] Breogon—invented eponym of Brigantia—looks across from his tower and sees Ireland for the first time, and this sighting that leads to the coming of the sons of Míl. Here is the account in the poem of Mael Muru:[43]

Brigantia ainm na cathrach
na cét n-airech;
Tor mBregoin a ssaide in subach
forsa suided.

Sairtuaid as Tur atchess Hériu
do iath Lumnig;
fescur gemrid fosfuair Ith
mac Bregoin buidnig.

'Brigantia is the name of the city of the hundred chieftains; Bregon's Tower, that is the cheerful seat on which he sat. North-east from the tower was Ériu seen, towards the land of Lumnech; on a winter evening Íth discovered it, the son of Bregon of the companies.'

This is very close to Orosius' original words; and it is striking that the verbal logic of the Latin sources is also preserved in the earliest surviving prose reference to the legend, in O'Mulconry's Glossary, probably composed in the late 7th or early 8th centuries.[44] This text etymologizes Ériu as a derivative of Hiberia, Spain, on the grounds that the two countries are close to each other and the invasion came from there: *ar is di is nessam 7 is ese ro gabad* ('because to there it is closest and from there it was taken').[45]

40 Orosius I 2.33.

41 Isidore, *Etymologiae* XIV 6.6. (All citations from Isidore are from the edition of Lindsay (1911).)

42 Cf. Baumgarten (1984); Scowcroft (1988), 14–5.

43 Text from the Book of Leinster (Best et al. (1954–83), iii 134a ll. 24–7).

44 MacNeill (1930–2).

45 O'Mulconry's Glossary §416 in Stokes (1900), 254.

Still denser lines of connection can be traced in the following lines of Mael Muru's poem. The landing was at Inber Scéne, the mouth of Orosius' river *Scena*; but something new is introduced in association with this place:[46]

Ic Inbiur Scene ro scuirset—
scél cen dúnad—
sruth dían dermar inros fothraic
Fíal ben Lugdach.

'At Inber Scéne they landed (a tale without completion), the rapid mighty stream in which Fíal wife of Lugaid bathed.'

The story referred to here is told more fully in the prose of *Leabhar Gabhála* proper, in the recension represented by the Book of Leinster version:[47]

No fothraic Lugaid mac Itha i lLoch Luigdech. Ros fothraic dano Fial ben Luigdech sind abaind téit assin loch. Luid a fer chucci nocht co n-accassa ferda a fir, co n-erbailt ar náre. Unde Loch Luigdech ⁊ Fíal ⁊ Inber Féle nominantur.

'Lugaid son of Íth washed himself in Loch Luigdech. Lugaid's wife Fial, however, washed herself in the river which flows from the lake. Her husband went to her naked, so that she saw his private parts and died of shame. From which Loch Luigdech and Fial and Inber Féile are named.'

Following so close on the Orosian *Scena,* the resemblance of the genitive forms *Luigdech* and *Féile* to Orosius' *Luceni* and *Velabri* cannot be coincidental. We must conclude that the narrative began as an aetiological explanation of the names known from Orosius, and then took on an independent life of its own within the *Leabhar Gabhála* tradition. Yet *before* the extended narratives took their known form, this textually based aetiology had become seamlessly fused with the story of Tech Duinn, which as we saw begs to be read as a survival from earlier traditions originating in the remoter antiquity of Irish traditions—unless, of course, that story itself was developed in the *scriptorium* in interaction with another textual source that happens not to have been identified by modern scholars.

46 Best et al. (1954–83), iii 134b ll. 14–5.

47 Best et al. (1954–83), i 13a ll. 6–11; Macalister (1938–56), v 60 (§419). Translation adapted slightly from Carey and Koch (2003), 266.

Carolingian Gloss Commentary

This evidence for textual commentary as the springboard for pseudo-historical narrative finds close correspondences in a number of glosses in surviving manuscripts from Carolingian libraries on the Continent of Europe, in which *peregrini* of Irish origin (or their peers) can be seen matching lore of the *Leabhar Gabhála* type to the very passages of Latin authors on which that lore was originally built. The most remarkable example is a manuscript of Orosius, dated between AD 850 and 900, whose glosses have been studied by Olivier Szerwiniack.[48] The manuscript is glossed heavily and with wide classical learning, and among this the words discussed above, *ubi Scenae fluminis ostium est et Velabri Lucenique consistunt*, carry the following annotations:[49]

> Scene] id <est> Fele quae prius dictum *est.*
> Velabri] a flumine *vel* Velabri; nam *vel* aber—niger—intellegitur.
> Luceni] id de nomine viri, *vel* de nomine fluminis qui dicitur Lugid *vel* Lugdech di ut stagnum Lugdech, quae.

Although the wording of the glosses is obscurely abbreviated, they allow us to see that Orosius' three names—Scena, Velabri, Luceni—are being matched to the story of Fíal wife of Lugaid. When Scene is identified with *Fele,* the original point may have been (as Szerwiniack suggests) that the glossator takes *Fele* as an abstract noun *féile* ('modesty'), derived from the adjective *fial* ('modest'); and *Velabri* is apparently broken up into *vel-aber* taken as an equivalent to *Inber Féle.* Similarly *Luceni,* though for Orosius it is clearly a tribal name, has here been linked to the story of Lugaid and the lake. Although the details are conjectural, it is clear that the glossator preserves a record of a series of linkages by which Orosius' names of tribes and places generated the names now preserved in the *Leabhar Gabhála*—with the added twist that the glossator or his readers can now use that narrative to elucidate Orosius anew.

These Orosius glosses also include an extract from Isidore's *Etymologiae,* in which Isidore explains that the Scotti are named from a word

48 Szerwiniack (1992–3, 2007); discussion, Szerwiniack (1995). Szerwiniack identifies the manuscript Vatican, Biblioteca Apostolica, Reg. lat. 1650 as a copy made at Reims in the second half of the 9th century on the basis of earlier materials imperfectly understood by the copyist or compiler, hence the numerous obscurities and misspellings.

49 Szerwiniack (1992–3, 2007), 68, with commentary 127–8; Szerwiniack (1995), 211–2.

in their own language that refers to their painted bodies, *a picto corpore*, 'because they are marked by iron points with ink in the pricking of various patterns'.[50] A copy of the *Etymologiae* itself, produced at Laon not later than AD 850 and associated with the circle of Irish *peregrini* there dominated by Martinus Hiberniensis, carries a further gloss on this passage:[51]

> *Haec aethimologia Pictis magis convenit, quia Scottus* [*leg. Scotti*?] *a Scotta enim Pharaonis filia Scotti nominati sunt.*
>
> 'This etymology suits the Picts better, because the Scotti are named indeed after Scotta the daughter of Pharaoh.'

This combination of text and gloss is closely reflected in a Latin passage at the beginning of the *Míniugud* version of the *Leabhar Gabhála*:[52]

> *Scoti autem a Scota, filia regis Egipti Pharaonis, sunt dicti, que fuit Nelii uxor. Phoeni autem a Foenio Fariseo dicuntur. Scoti autem idem et Picti a picto corpore quasi scissi, eo quod aculeis ferreis cum atramento variarum figurarum stigmate adnotentur.*
>
> 'The Scoti are named after Scota, the daughter of Pharaoh king of Egypt, who was the wife of Nelius. The Féni are named after Fénius Farsaid. The Scoti—the same as the Picts—[are named] from their body-painting as if *scissi* [= incised], because they are marked by iron points with ink in the pricking of various patterns.'

Rolf Baumgarten ingeniously argued that this implies an additional Irish-language etymology, taking *Scotti* as equivalent to *scottai*, past participle of *scothaid* ('cuts').[53] Although this remains speculative, the

[50] Isidore, *Etymologiae* IX 2.103; the gloss is at Orosius I 2.81. See Szerwiniack (1992–3, 2007), 68; Szerwiniack (1995), 210.

[51] Laon, Bibliothèque municipale, 447, 89ra, cited and discussed by Contreni (1989). Contreni compares a gloss in Munich, Bayerische Staatsbibliothek, Clm 6411, 24v, taking *Scotti* from the same Scotta daughter of Pharaoh and calling her a *meretrix*, for which Contreni conjectures the link *Scotta—Scortum*; and the same Munich MS has a note on the river Slane in Leinster with the town Chedni beside it, *quod nos cellam interpretamur a viro quodam*. Although Contreni's reconstruction of the background in this case must remain doubtful, it is significant that the focus here is again on the origins of placenames, and that this lore is attributed to *nos*, 'ourselves'—presumably the Irish *peregrini* gathered around the glossator himself.

[52] For the text see Macalister (1938–56), i 64; the version in the Book of Lecan (Dublin, Royal Irish Academy, 23 P 2) is on f 16v, col. 2.

[53] Baumgarten (1983).

correspondences show that the Irish passage is closely related to the glossed text of Isidore. Further, the three etymologies correspond exactly to lines in the poem of Mael Muru discussed earlier,[54] though it is impossible to tell whether the prose depends on the verse, or vice versa, or indeed whether both depend on a third source that is not to hand.

In sum, the only straightforward explanation of these glosses is that they preserve the record of an early stage in the invention or elaboration of Irish pseudohistory on the basis of a reading of Irish-related material in Latin texts. Possibly they originated as part of a body of *scholia* made in Ireland; possibly, in a more confused transmission, they are the work of Irish *peregrini* who reapplied existing Irish pseudohistory when working on the Latin texts during their time on the Continent. It is remarkable that a third example of this process of reception and renewal, preserved elsewhere in the *Leabhar Gabhála* tradition, concerns a closely-related topic: the origin and naming of the Picts of Scotland in relation to tattooing. The starting point appears to be two references in Vergil to Scythian tribes, *picti Agathyrsi* and *pictosque Gelonos*.[55] On the former, the extended version of Servius' Vergilian commentary compares the 'painted Agathyrsi' with a British tribe, *gens in Britannia*, noting that the latter are tattooed, *stigmata habentes*, but that the Agathyrsi are *picti* only in the vaguer sense of 'beautiful'.[56] Associated information is developed in two Irish-associated bodies of Carolingian *scholia*.[57] In the *Brevis expositio*, the two *picti* tribes of Scythia are directly compared with each other,[58] and in the Bern *scholia* proper the Geloni are associated with the Picts of Scotland under their Irish-language name:[59]

> *Pictos, quos alii dicunt 'Cruithnecdiu' sed false. Pictosque Gelonos, qui stigma habent. Sunt autem Thraces a Gelono Herculis et Chaoniae Nymphae filio dicti.*
>
> "The painted ones', whom others call *Cruithnecdiu*, though incorrectly. 'And the painted Geloni', those who have tattooing. Indeed the Thracians are named after Gelonus, son of Hercules and the nymph Chaonia.'

[54] See Best et al. (1954–83), iii 133b ll. 46–7.

[55] Vergil, *Aeneid* IV 146; *Georgica* II 115.

[56] Servius Auctus at Vergil, *Aeneid* IV 146 in Thilo and Hagen (1881–1902), i 490.

[57] On these *scholia* and their interrrelationships see most recently Miles (2011), 28–33.

[58] *Pictosque Gelonos, stigmata habentes populi Scythiae, ut pictique Agathyrsi* (*Brevis Expositio* on Vergil, *Georgica* II 115, in Thilo and Hagen (1881–1902), iii.2 293).

[59] Text from Hagen (1867), 225–6.

The first part of this implies that the identification between Picts and Cruithnecdiu was current in the scholiast's world, even if he himself disbelieves it. There is another link with the Irish legend in a further manuscript source, Laon, Bibliothèque municipale, 468, compiled under the guidance of Martinus Hiberniensis of Laon. Here in a Vergilian glossary the Geloni are listed as *populus Scythiae stigmata habentes* with the marginal note *.i. picturas ut Scoti.* The annotator has seen the tattooing or body-painting of the Picts as a custom with parallels in Ireland, presumably referring implicitly to the Isidorean passage with which the whole sequence began. One suspects a further link between the British name Alba and Isidore's claim that the Scythians are known as Albani because they are born with white hair,[60] though this is not explicit in the surviving *scholia*.

Within this body of fluctuating information, the point about descent from Gelonus son of Hercules somehow fed the *Leabhar Gabhála* tradition. The origin of the Picts of Scotland is given as follows in the version in the Book of Ballymote:[61]

> *A tīr Tracia tāncatar Cruithnig, .i. clanda Geloin mac Ercoil iadside. Agathirsi a n-anmand.*
>
> 'From the land of Thrace came the Cruithnig, viz. they are family of Gelonus son of Hercules. Their name is Agathirsi.'

This apparently descends from a version of the Vergilian *scholia* that identified the Picts squarely with the Geloni and Agathyrsi—a match held together, presumably, by the coincidence of the epithet *picti* itself and the shared tattooing practices of the peoples in question. Just as with Orosius' names in Ireland, this bare onomastic information becomes part of a developed narrative of Pictish origins in the *Leabhar Gabhála* and the Irish Nennius, to which we will return later in this article.

Such examples show clearly that the *literati* developed pseudohistorical narratives partly on the basis of place-names in learned Latin sources, and that versions of this lore were current among Carolingian scholars, who were aware to some extent of the linkages from narrative to source text. This internationalizing perspective on the origin legend begs to be associated with the deepening of national identities and international rivalries that characterized the intellectualism of that period. Elsewhere

60 Isidore, *Eymologiae* IX 2.65, noted by Jaski (2009), 56; cf. Scowcroft (1988), 18–9.

61 Macalister (1938–56), v 178 (§496).

in the Carolingian manuscript heritage there are striking parallels for glosses on Latin authors as a conduit for transmission or creation of lore about the pasts of the barbarian nations. For example, the Bern *scholia* on the Roman poet Lucan include extraordinary information on the ancient Gauls, including the varieties of human sacrifice offered respectively to Teutates, Hesus, and Taranis.[62] This example is isolated and mysterious; but it is possible to see more of the developments undergone by such lore through a parallel case, the account of the Saxons given in a mid-9th-century hagiographical text, the *Translatio S. Alexandri* of Rudolf of Fulda.[63] This text offers a strange mixture of sheer inaccuracy and authentic-sounding survivals: it begins with the extraordinary claim that the Saxons came from Britain, apparently a muddle based on the contemporary presence there of *Saxones,* but goes on to describe their pagan customs in precise terms that suggest detailed use of authentic sources. Some of the details—human sacrifice, worship of Mercury, divination by the whinnying of horses—are lifted directly from Tacitus' *Germania* and Einhard's Life of Charlemagne,[64] showing that the scholars mined ancient and recent Latin texts for information about the remote past of the peoples of their own world. But other details cannot be pinned to a known source: above all, the famous account of how the Saxons vacillated between paganism and Christianity and returned to their old cults:[65]

> *Truncum quoque ligni non parvae magnitudinis in altum erectum sub divo colebant, patria eum lingua Irminsul appellantes, quod latine dicitur universalis columna, quasi sustinens omnia.*

> 'They also worshipped a sizeable stump of wood, set up in the open air, which they called in their own language Irminsul, which in Latin means *universalis columna*, as if supporting all things.'

62 *Scholion* at Lucan I 445 in the *Commenta Lucani* from Bern, Burgerbibliothek, 370, 15v; see Usener (1869), 39. On the origins of these commentaries see Werner (1994).

63 Rudolf of Fulda's *Translatio S. Alexandri* is ed. by Georg Heinrich Pertz in MGH SS 2, 637–81; on the borrowings from the *Germania* and the *Vita Karoli* of Einhard, already noted by Pertz in his edition, see Innes (2000), 238; McKitterick (2004), 42. On Latin historiography as a model for the Carolingians see McKitterick (2004), 28–59, 174–217 *passim*.

64 Tacitus, *Germania* 4; Einhard, *Vita Karoli* 7 (ed. by Otto Holder-Egger in MGH SS rer. Germ. 25, 9).

65 Rudolf of Fulda, *Translatio S. Alexandri* 3 (MGH SS 2, 676).

Just as with the House of Donn in the legend of the Sons of Míl, we are left puzzling over a detail that *sounds* like the record of indigenous pagan tradition, adrift among borrowings from the Latin learning of the *scriptorium*. Considered piecemeal, these records may seem merely to look backward to the past of the writer's own forebears; but the investigation of 'ethnic pasts' of this kind is an implicitly comparative and internationalizing activity. This wider context is well exemplified by the historical sections of the Verona Miscellany, made in north Italy in first half of the 9th century, a compilation of materials for a universalising history from the Old Testament world to the peoples of the compilers' own time.[66]

The Carolingian themes of the wanderings of the Goídil

Seen in relation to such explorations, the *Leabhar Gabhála* narrative does not merely give the Irish a context among the nations descended from Noah; it shows Irish identity being worked out among the nascent ethnographies of Carolingian Europe. In this light, the wanderings of the Goídil take on new resonances if traced on to the graphic counterpart of Orosius' account of nations and peoples, the T-O map in Isidore's *Etymologiae* (as illustrated in *Plate 1*):

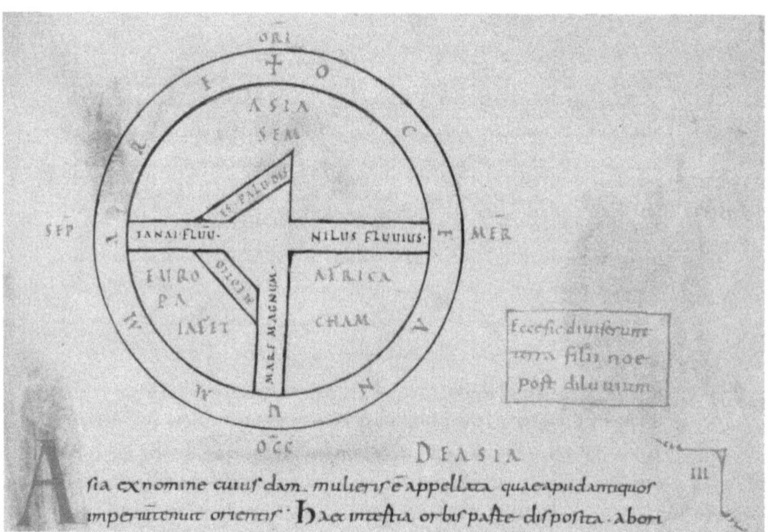

Plate 1 Isidore's T-O map from St Gall, Stiftsbibliothek, 236, p 89. (Reproduced with permission.)

[66] See McKitterick (2004), 52–9.

From Fénius Farsaid onward, the wanderings of the ancestors take them over each waterway and land-mass in the scheme: Irish identity is traced through all the basic outlines of the world,[67] just as the projects of translation and correlation discussed at the outset of this essay assimilate Irish literature and history to the edifice of world-knowledge.

Building on this, it is possible to associate the story of the Goídil with the pattern of a pseudohistorical origin narrative which is attested many times over among the new nations of the early Middle Ages, inserting the nation in question into the grand narrative of world history centred on the eastern Mediterranean—Rome, Athens, Jerusalem. Typologically, such narratives can be seen as an attempt to make sense of marginality by tracing a tangible relationship to the centre: but in detail they differ from each other profoundly. There are two abiding schemes, which are not easily reconciled. The first depicts the people in question as newcomers from a remote and mysterious land in the unknowable beyond, most famously Scandza, the *officina gentium* or *vagina nationum* ('factory of peoples', 'womb of nations') described by Jordanes in the *Getica* and later incorporated by Paul the Deacon in the *Historia Langobardorum*.[68] An important influence on this kind of origin legend is the (so-called) Frankish Table of Nations, which is preserved in Carolingian manuscripts but was probably composed in Ostrogothic Italy in the AD 520s and modified in Francia in the early 8th century.[69] Here the Germanic nations are said to descend from three brothers, whose names vary but are earliest attested as Erminus, Inguo, and Istio, and who seem to have begun as eponymous ancestors derived from the names of three tribes listed in Tacitus' *Germania*: Ingvaeones, Herminones, Istaevones.[70] From these descend painfully transparent eponymous ancestors, of which the most important for us are the sons of Hissicon: Brittus, Francus, Romanus, Albanus. The second scheme asserts that the ancestor of the nation was a fugitive from the classical heartlands of the south-eastern Mediterranean; as we will see, he is typically esacaping from the fall of Troy, and thus associated with Aeneas either by shared story-pattern or literal kinship, with the clear implication (never, so far as I know, stated openly in any surviving early medieval source)

[67] Gerberding (1987), 24–9, makes a similar point about the Frankish origin legend in the *Liber Historiae Francorum*, on which see further below.

[68] Jordanes, *Getica* I 4.25; Paul the Deacon, *Historia Langobardorum* I 1–2 (ed. Capo (1992), 12–4). See Goffart (1988), esp. 20–3, 87–96, 382–8.

[69] Goffart (1983).

[70] Tacitus, *Germania* 2.

that his descendants are on a par with the Romans in the antiquity and dignity of their line. Although the scheme based on the three brothers appears in the *Leabhar Gabhála*,[71] I suggest that the narratives based on Troy may provide the key to understanding the Scythian ancestry of the Goídil.

The 'Trojan fugitive' story has a long history, first attested as one of a series of explanations of Gaulish origins recorded in the late 4th century by Ammianus Marcellinus.[72] Ammianus claims to draw on the now lost work of Timagenes of Alexandria: this was presumably the universal history entitled On Kings, which was a compilation of dynastic history and disguised myth and may even have overlapped in substance or subject-matter with the heroic songs that Ammianus says were sung by the Gaulish bards about their forebears, *fortia virorum illustrium facta heroicis composita versibus*.[73] According to Ammianus some say that the Gauls are *aborigines*, indigenous first inhabitants of their land; some say that they are descended from Dorians who settled alongside the ocean having left Greece following 'the earlier Hercules', whose role as a founder of far-flung nations appears elsewhere in late antique sources. The druids hold that they are partly indigenous and partly made up of newcomers fleeing from storms and inundations in distant lands across the Rhine; others say that a small number fleeing the Greeks after the fall of Troy occupied regions that then were empty; others hold that they descend from the more famous Hercules, who fathered them on his journey back from defeating Geryon and Tauriscus, tyrants of Spain and Gaul;[74] and Ammianus' list culminates (*a Phocaea vero*)[75] with the story that a people from Phocaea in Asia Minor, fleeing the tyranny of the Persian empire, divided into groups of which one settled Velia in Lucania and the other Massilia (modern Marseilles)—a story consistent with the famous narrative attributed originally to Aristotle,[76] in which the Pho-

71 See Macalister (1938–56), I 22–5, 156–7, 166–7: the forms of the names imply that this version is derived from or closely akin to that in the *Historia Brittonum* (MGH Auct. ant. 13, 149).

72 Ammianus Marcellinus, *Res gestae* XV 9.2–7 (ed. Galletier (2002), 135–6).

73 Ammianus Marcellinus, *Res gestae* XV 9.8 (Galletier (2002), 136–7).

74 Ammianus Marcellinus, *Res gestae* XV 9.6 (Galletier (2002), 136). Compare the longer account of the same story in Diodorus Siculus, Historical Library V 24: see Carey and Koch (2003), 37–8.

75 Ammianus Marcellinus, *Res gestae* XV 9.7 (Galletier (2002), 457). Does *vero* here simply mark the culmination of the rhetorical period, or does it imply that Ammianus considers this to be the true version?

76 See Rankin (1987), 35–8.

caean stranger is chosen by the indigenous king's daughter who offers him drink in a cup,[77] suggestive of the 'draught of sovereignty' familiar from later traditions in Ireland and elsewhere. Throughout this series runs the theme of fusion between indigenous descent, usually vested in the female line, and the mediating force of the male stranger who is involved in the grand narrative of Greek and Roman origins in the eastern Mediterranean. Whether he is a fugitive from the Trojan War, a Greek founder-hero, or a victim of Persian tyranny, the narrative explains how this people are linked to the Mediterranean centre of the world.

It can only be guessed where Ammianus' information originates, how much of it deserves to be called Celtic, to what extent its classical content may be due to the Hellenized Massilians who were most likely their informants.[78] More important for our purposes is its later reception of Ammianus' narrative. The monastic library at Fulda held manuscripts of Tacitus' *Germania*[79] and Ammianus Marcellinus—both, as it happens, the manuscripts from which all modern editions descend;[80] and this makes it at least possible that the passage discussed above was available to be imitated or emulated, at least as far back as the famous campaign of manuscript-collecting said to have been undertaken under Charlemagne's personal direction.[81] We cannot be certain that a

[77] Athenaeus, *Deipnosophistae* XIII 576; Justin, *Historiae Philippicae* XLIII 3; see Carey and Koch (2003), 38–9.

[78] Wood (2006) and Barlow (1995) gather evidence to support the view that the later Frankish stories of the Trojan origins of the Franks may go back to politically driven pseudohistory from as early as the 4th century AD. This includes Sidonius Apollinaris' mention of a link between the people of Clermont and the Trojans (*Epistola* VII 7.2; cf. *Epistola* II 2.19) and the ancient Burgundians' claim to Roman origins (Ammianus Marcellinus, *Res gestae* XXVIII 5.11), along with the *gratiarum actio* addressed to Constantine, in which the people of Autun are said to have been brothers to the Romans (*Panegyrici Latini* V 3.1 in Mynors (1964)), though this latter may refer only to metaphorical brotherhood.

[79] On the Jasi manuscript see Reynolds (1983), 410–1; marginal corrections have been attributed to Heiric of Auxerre or one of his circle (McKitterick (2004), 42). The principal evidence for early medieval reading of this or a related manuscript is its use by Rudolf of Fulda in the *Translatio S. Alexandri* (see p 457 above).

[80] For Ammianus Marcellinus at Fulda see Reynolds (1983), 6–8; Bischoff (1994), 149–51; McKitterick (2004), 39–42, 190.

[81] For a survey of Carolingian library-building see Bullough (1991), 1–38. Since the Carolingian campaign of manuscript-collecting included imports from across the Alps (Bischoff (1994), 134–60), we have no way of telling whether texts like Ammianus Marcellinus were available north of the Alps in the earlier AD 700s, when the Chronicle of Fredegarius was composed. It therefore remains an economical hypothesis that the Frankish origin legend was originally composed much earlier, perhaps even before the collapse of Imperial Roman hegemony.

given manuscript attested for a Carolingian library was there a century beforehand; but it is certainly telling that it is in historical works from Francia that the 'Trojan fugitive' story resurfaces.[82] For these historians, the variant versions of this legend-type do not necessarily demand a choice: just as Ammianus presents the variant versions alongside each other, so Freculph simply sets the story of the Trojan origins of the Franks alongside the version from Jordanes:[83] *Alii vero affirmant eos de Scanza insula, quae vagina gentium est, exordium habuisse, de qua Gothi et caeterae nationes Theotiscae exierunt* ('Other men insist that [the Franks] had their origins on the isle of Scandza, the womb of nations, from which the Goths and other *nationes theodiscae* came'). However, it seems that for purposes of propaganda and national self-presentation the Trojan story early became the dominant account.

The key text is the Chronicle of Fredegarius.[84] This work was composed as early as the mid-7th century and copied 'about a generation later', but all but one of the manuscripts are of later date, implying that Fredegarius 'came into his own rather suddenly in the Carolingian age'.[85] The Chronicle begins with a summary of world protohistory beginning with the sons of Noah and their descendants, among them the Phrygians and Trojans (*Trociane, Frigiiae*) sprung from Japhet.[86] The overall structure of the work is prescribed by the sequence of Old Testament events and the chronicles of Jerome and others, just as with the *Leabhar Gabhála*; but when it reaches the Trojan War period, it explains that after the sack of the city two groups of Trojans went into exile, led by their king, Frigas. One group did mercenary service under the Macedonians and became absorbed into their people—and thus into the ancestors of

[82] It remains possible that the theme was first developed in a much earlier phase of historiographical development, perhaps the lost *Historia Gothorum* of Cassiodorus, which influenced Jordanes and thus the subsequent Germanic historiographers (cf. Barlow (1995); Goffart (1988), 21–42). For the political importance of the myth for self-assertion in the Carolingian period see Innes (2000).

[83] Freculph, *Chronicon* I 2.17 (PL 106, 967, discussed by Innes (2000), 233).

[84] The text is edited by Bruno Krusch in MGH SS rer. Merov. 2, 1–193. On Fredegarius see Wallace-Hadrill (1962), 71–94; Collins (2007); and on the relationship between Fredegarius and the *Liber Historia Francorum* see Gerberding (1987), 11–30; Graus (1989), 32–5.

[85] Wallace-Hadrill (1962), 72.

[86] Mentioned at Fredegarius, *Chronicon* I 5 (MGH SS rer. Merov. 2, 21); main narrative at Fredegarius, *Chronicon* II 4 (MGH SS rer. Merov. 2, 45–6).

Alexander, a future holder of world-kingship. Another group became the Franks:[87]

> *Nam et illa alia pars, quae de Frigia progressa est, ab Olexo per fraude decepti, tamen non captivati, nisi exinde eiecti, per multis regionibus pervacantis cum uxores et liberos, electum a se regi Francione nomen, per quem Franci vocantur. In postremum, eo quod fortissimus ipse Francio in bellum fuisse fertur, et multo tempore cum plurimis gentibus pugnam gerens, partem Asiae vastans, in Eurupam dirigens, inter Renum vel Danuvium et mare consedit.*
>
> 'For that other group, which travelled out of Phrygia, deceived dishonestly by Ulysses, but nonetheless not taken captive, although expelled from there, went wandering through many regions with their wives and children; and a name was chosen by them from their king Francio, through whom they were called Franci. Finally, because Francio himself is said to have been most brave in war, and held combat for a long time with many peoples, laying waste part of Asia, then directing the journey to Europe, he settled between the Rhine and the Danube and the sea.'

After Francio's death few of these Franci were left, and they appointed leaders (*duces*, later taken as 'dukes') from among their number. Always they refused to be ruled by others, and when Pompey subjugated them but they continued to resist: in this, as Fredegarius says, they resembled their cousins the Macedonians (*qui ex eadem generatione fuerunt*).[88] A third group separated off with a leader called Torquatus or Torcoth; they settled in the Danube area between the Ocean and Thrace, and became the Turks.[89] Later Fredegarius points out that the first king of the Latins was a fugitive from Troy, and therefore another relative (*ex ipso genere et Frigas*); there was one kingdom of Latini and one of Frigi, which presumably means the people of Aeneas, so that Aeneas and Frigas could be said to be *germani*.[90] Later a variant version of this story is given, with the important detail that they began to build a new city near the Rhine recalling old Troy (*civitatem ad*

[87] Fredegarius, *Chronicon* II 4–5 (MGH SS rer. Merov. 2, 45–6).

[88] Fredegarius, *Chronicon* II 6 (MGH SS rer. Merov. 2, 46).

[89] Fredegarius, *Chronicon* II 6 (MGH SS rer. Merov. 2, 46); Graus (1989) discusses this, citing on p 34.

[90] Fredegarius, *Chronicon* II 8 (MGH SS rer. Merov. 2, 47).

instar Trogiae nominis),[91] but it was never finished, and their westward journey continued.

Distinct but clearly related traditions are found in a number of pre-Carolingian sources, suggesting that Fredegarius' version emerged from a tradition that flourished early in the emergence of Frankish identity.[92] In the 7th-century Cosmography of Aethicus Ister, Romulus, seen as a savage usurper, goes to Troy where Francus and Vassus remain as survivors of the royal line after its sack by the Greeks.[93] He defeats them and returns to Italy; they make an alliance with the Albanians, and after further wars they flee to eastern Germania and the Maeotic marshes, and there found a city called Sichambria, after words meaning 'sword' and 'bow'.[94] Another variant version comes at the start of the Neustrasian *Liber Historiae Francorum,* which was widely used as a document of Frankish identity in the Carolingian period and after.[95] It too begins at Troy, but with a difference.[96] Aeneas is king of Troy, a fierce aggressor who has conquered the surrounding lands; the kings of the Greeks rise up against him and besiege the city for ten years; after the sack Aeneas goes to Italy to find people to fight, but the remnant of the Trojans wander further. They reach the shores of the Tanais and go thence to the Maeotic marshes and the lands of the Pannonians; there, as in Aethicus Ister, they built the city Sicambria. At the same time the Alani rebel against the emperor Valentinian, and hide in the Maeotic marshes; Valentinian offers a reward to whoever will penetrate the marshes to subdue them; when the Trojans do so, Valentinian names them *Francos* because in the 'Attic language' *francus* has the same meaning as Latin

[91] Fredegarius, *Chronicon* III 2 (MGH SS rer. Merov. 2, 93). Gerberding (1987), 16–7, proposes that this section is by a different author.

[92] Curiously, both Aethicus' and Fredegarius' *second* account attribute their knowledge of the early kings of the Franks to Jerome. If this is not coincidental, does it suggest shared dependence on a single pseudonymous source?

[93] Aethicus Ister, *Cosmographia* 102–103a (ed. Herren (2011), 202–5). The question of the Irish affinities of this work is beyond the scope of the present paper.

[94] Herren (2011), 310, cites evidence from much later sources to support this as a genuine etymology. However, Gerberding points out that Sigambri as a tribal name occurs in Claudian's *De Consulatu Stilichonis* I 222 with the mention of a bow: is this coincidental, or does it suggest the origins of the explanation?

[95] *Liber Historiae Francorum* = *Gesta Francorum*, Version A, ed. by Bruno Krusch MGH SS rer. Merov. 2, 241–328.

[96] See MGH SS rer. Merov. 2, 241–4; useful translation by Gerberding (1987), 173–4. Gerberding has a full but inconclusive discussion of the purpose or origins of the Trojan legend of the Franks (pp 17–30); see also Barlow (1995); Innes (2000), esp. 248 n 52; and for an overall assessment of the work cf. McKitterick (2004), 14–22.

ferus ('fierce'), 'from the hardness or bravery of their hearts'. Later these Franks refuse to pay tribute to the Romans; this leads to war and they move to Germania to settle, taking kings like other peoples. In a further twist, several Carolingian and later copies of Fredegarius contain an extra section at the account of the Trojan war:[97] this is headed *De Origine Francorum* and attributes itself to Dares Phrygius, the supposed eye-witness chronicler of the Trojan War.[98] This adds further information akin to that given by Aethicus Ister, with an unexplained reference to one Pherecides, who was evidently a character in the text from which the account was originally excerpted.[99] His son Frigio is a mighty aggressor and conquers Dalmatia; he fathers Francus and Vassus, and like the sons of Oedipus in the Theban story they seize the kingship from each other by turns and go savagely to war.

As Wallace-Hadrill showed, the divergence between these various accounts is sufficient to show that none is directly derived from another, and they must derive independently from a cluster of traditions of unguessable antiquity.[100] However, there is also a striking parallelism with the same Latin sources of authority that we saw for the Irish texts. Elements of the story chime significantly with the scanty information on Frankish origins given by Isidore, who says that there are two theories for the origin of their name: either they are called after one of their own leaders (*a quodam proprio duce*) or after the fierceness of their customs (*a feritate morum*).[101] The first irresistibly suggests the name of Francus, the second corresponds to the story of Valentinian's naming of them in the *Liber Historiae Francorum*; and it is remarkable for our purposes that this passage of Isidore is immediately followed by his accounts of the name of the Britons and then of the Scotti as discussed above, whose relationship with the Irish origin legend is guaranteed by the evidence of the glosses. In terms of these intertextual relationships, the parallels with the Irish origin-legend seem too close to be a mere matter of vague typology.

[97] This section is inserted at Fredegarius, *Chronicon* II 3 (MGH SS rer. Merov. 2, 193–200).

[98] Cf. Collins (2007), 83–8.

[99] Fredegarius, *Chronicon* II 3 (MGH SS rer. Merov. 2, 199): *Adeo ad Pherecides indolem prepropere revertamur.* Just as Pherecides is referred to as if previously mentioned, so his son Frigio is referred to as *alium Frigionem,* as if an ancestor of the same name has already been referred to. This can only mean that the passage has been copied from a longer account.

[100] Wallace-Hadrill (1962), 81–2; cf. Gerberding (1987), 17–20.

[101] Isidore, *Etymologiae* IX 2.101.

Brutus and the British

Parallel to the story of Francus is that of Brutus, ancestor of the British. The story is first attested in the *Historia Brittonum*, and latterly picked up and recast by Geoffrey of Monmouth, Wace, and authors of other Anglo-Norman chronicles and romances.[102] Here Aeneas, leader of the Trojan exiles in Italy, finds that the wife of his son Ascanius is pregnant. He arranges for a sage (*magus*) to examine her; the sage says that this is a boy-child who will be called 'a son of death, because he will kill his father and his mother and will be *exosus omnibus hominibus*, accursed or hated among all men'.[103] In return Ascanius kills the *magus*, but the boy, Brutus, kills his mother when she dies in childbirth, and goes on to kill his father by mistake with an arrow. He is sent into exile and goes first to Greece, whence he is expelled because of his descent from the hated Aeneas; he goes on to Gaul and founds the city of Turnis (modern Tours), and finally goes to Britain and there becomes the founder of the British race. It is more than likely that this account took shape alongside with or in emulation of the Frankish story discussed above.[104] Comparing Brutus with Francus, however, a significant difference emerges. Francus' Trojan ancestry puts him on a par with the Romans in the ancient status of his origins, but his story is one of implacable hostility to the Romans and refusal to submit to their rule. Brutus, on the other hand, is himself a scion of the line of Aeneas, making his people the cousins of the Romans themselves. Does this conception originate as an attempt to outdo the Franks—to declare that the British are authentic members of the Roman empire, in contrast to the barbarian newcomers in continental Francia? Here we can only speculate: but the implication remains that these origin narratives are parallel examples of a single pattern in ethnogenetic pseudohistory, driven by an implicit parallelism with Roman origins.

In this context it begins to make more sense that the wanderings of the Irish from Scythia to Inber Scéne might have taken shape by following the same paradigm, emulating or attempting to trump the claims to cultural centrality of Franci and the British,[105] or indeed the

[102] Geoffrey of Monmouth, *De gestis Britonum* I 6–22 (ed. Reeve and Wright (2007), 6–31); Wace, *Roman de Brut* ll. 1–1250 (convenient edition with translation in Weiss (1999), 1–33); for Wace's dependence on Geoffrey see Wright (1988), xi–cxiv; cf. Weiss (1999), xviii.

[103] Nennius, *Historia Brittonum* (MGH Auct. ant. 13, 150.16–20).

[104] Argued by Dumville (1994), 407–10.

[105] First suggested by van Hamel (1915), 144; cf. Wright (2012), 166.

Anglo-Saxon English who supplanted them and borrowed their legends.[106] Consider again the origin legend of the Goídil as recounted in the *Leabhar Gabhála*. There, the starting-point is dynastic strife in Scythia. Fénius Farsaid has two sons, Noenual who takes the chieftainship after his death in Scythia and Gáedel Glas, born in Egypt to Pharaoh's daughter, whose great-grandson Éber Scot returns with his father to Scythia and wrests the chieftainship from the sons of Noenual. Strife and kinslaying between the rival sides of the family are repeated over several generations, until eventually the descendants of Gáedel Glas are driven into exile and from them, ultimately, spring the sons of Míl who occupy Ireland.[107] In both cases the ancestor's origins lie towards the eastern extremity of the world of Graeco-Roman antiquity; his name is an obvious eponym of the nation he will found in the north; and he is driven into exile as the result of kinslaying. It is also suggestive that a pivotal stage of the Frankish wanderings is located in the Maeotic marshes, which are represented as a diagonal-running waterway in the Isidorean T-O map illustrated above as *Plate 1*. In the *Leabhar Gabhála* the ancestors of the Goídil also spent time there, and *na Gaethlaige Meotecda* were the birthplace of Éber Glúnfind.[108] The episode figures among Gilla Coemáin's synchronisms:[109]

Ochtmoga blíadan dia és
ba rí in talman Tutanés;
is 'na ré ro gabsat tair
Gáedil isna Gáethlaigib.

'Eighty years after him
Tautanes was king of the earth:
it is in his era that
the Goídil settled in the Maeotic Marshes in the east.'

[106] The Germanic-speaking English seem never to have been distanced from the Brutus legend despite their obviously different ancestry.

[107] Following Scowcroft's terminology, I summarize the narrative as found in the Recension a and *Míniugud* versions (Macalister (1938–56), ii 9–32) and the poem *Gaedel Glas ó tát Gaídil* attributed to Gilla Coemáin (Macalister (1938–56), ii 91–106), with Carey's translation corresponding to the Book of Leinster copy (Carey and Koch (2003), 228–35 (§§14–30)).

[108] See e.g. Macalister (1938–56), ii 22–3, and the corresponding verse in Gilla Coemáin's *Gaedel Glas ó tát Gaídil* (Macalister (1938–56), ii 102–3 §§30–31). The sojourn in the Marshes figures already in the poem of Mael Muru, though the lines in question were omitted in the Book of Leinster copy (see Best et al. (1954–83), iii 134a l. 20 with n 1).

[109] Text and translation from Smith (2007), 194 (§16).

The quatrain following specifies that this coincided with the sack of Troy and the battle of Moytura: is it significant that the Irish trace this part of their path across the world-map long before the Frankish ancestors do so in their own origin legend? Here as elsewhere both narratives beg to be read in terms of rivalry and one-upmanship between nations, with claim and counter-claim revolving around the war of Troy and, implicitly, around the fundamental primacy of the origin-legend of the Romans themselves.

Given these multiple levels of correspondence and cross-echo, it is plausible to conclude that this part of the *Leabhar Gabhála* sequence originated in, or was influenced by, the same kind of Carolingian myth-making that gave rise to the narratives of Frankish and British origins. This suspicion is corroborated by a remarkable fourth *comparandum* that appears within the *Leabhar Gabhála* tradition: the origin narrative of the Picts of north Britain. The *Historia Brittonum* states simply that the Picts arrived via the Orkneys and invaded a part of Britain;[110] but Bede asserts that they came from Scythia,[111] and this evidently underlies the Irish tradition above that gives them Thracian origins as descendants of Gelonus son of Hercules, associated with the *picti Geloni* of Vergil. This origin-legend takes more elaborate form in certain versions of the *Leabhar Gabhála* and the Irish translation of the *Historia Brittonum*:[112] much of this is concerned with explaining the Pictish custom of matrilineal succession, but it also articulates another variant on the theme of exile in response to family violence. When the Picts or Cruithnecdiu came from Thrace, they were led by six brothers, fleeing because Policornus king of Thrace had wooed their sister but refused her bride-price; they went to the land of the Franks and there too the king tried to take their sister, so they came to Ireland, where they fought as mercenaries and were given women; thus they settled in the north of Britain and lived there ever since. In the *Lebor Bretnach,* the Irish recasting of the *Historia Brittonum,* the account includes the poem *Cruithnig cid dosfarclam*, which is closely similar in phrasing and themes to Mael Muru's *Can a mbunadus.*[113] Although the *Historia Brittonum* itself clearly plays a central role as a conduit for the transmission of the legends of Scotti,

[110] Nennius, *Historia Brittonum* (MGH Auct. ant. 13, 154).

[111] Bede, *Historia Ecclesiastica* I 1 (ed. Plummer (1896), i 11).

[112] See Macalister (1938–56), v 278–81 (§§493–4), with further texts and analysis by Mac Eoin (1964).

[113] See *Lebor Bretnach* 6–7 (in van Hamel (1932), 8–14, with Mac Eoin (1964)).

Brittones, and Picti, the Frankish paradigm seems to lie behind them and motivate them all.

The *Vita Cadroe*

Just as with the Saxon lore in the *Translatio S. Alexandri* discussed above, a number of versions of the Irish origin-legend are preserved in Latin hagiography, in the form of accounts of the national background of the saint. Attested examples are relatively late, notably the *Vita S. Abbani Abbatis*[114] and the Life of St Brendan, *Legenda Brandani*, quoted among sources for the legend in John of Fordun's 14th-century Latin Chronicle of the Scottish People.[115] Fortuitously, however, part of a remarkable version survives in the *Vita Cadroe*,[116] the Life of the 10th-century *peregrinus* Cadroe, which was composed near Metz around AD 1000 and must therefore reflect an early stage of the monumental compilation of the *Leabhar Gabhála*. It includes many authentic Irish placenames alongside names derived from Isidore, especially his chapter on islands,[117] and in the prologue, the author defends his account of Irish origins by advising potential critics to read the texts, presumably in Latin: *Legat potius historias, ut nos vera dixisse cognoscat* ('let him rather read the histories, so that he will learn that we have spoken the truth'). The *Vita* opens with a narrative of the origin of the Scotti which clearly originated in such an external source, as its florid style contrasts

[114] *Vita S. Abbani Abbatis* 1 (ed. Plummer (1910), i 3): *Scoti vero a Scota, matre eiusdem gentis, dicuntur, qui fuit filia regis Egypti. Quomodo de Egypto ipsa venit in Hiberniam, causa brevitatis omittimus, quia satis invenitur de illa in libris qui narrant quomodo in primis temporibus habitata est Hibernia.* ('The Scoti are so called after Scota, the mother of that race, who was the daughter of the king of Egypt. As to how she came from Egypt to Ireland, we will omit this for the sake of brevity, since enough is to be found concerning her in the books which recount how Ireland was inhabited in the early times.') See Ó Riain (1983), 159–70, suggesting an Anglo-Norman context for this.

[115] There exists no more recent edition of John of Fordun than that of Skene (1872), but the passages here discussed are presented and discussed by Broun (1999), 33–81; see also Jaski (2009), 60–2. A narrative largely derived from this informs Walter Bower's *Scottichronicon* I 9–18; see MacQueen (1993), 26–45.

[116] The text survives because it was printed by Colgan (1645), 494–507. Dumville (2001), 172–3, argues that it was composed at Metz in the AD 980s, not long after Cathróe's death about 945. Along with Dumville's study I have benefited from the studies by Ó Riain (2008), (2009) and Jaski (2006), (2009). I follow the section numbers used by Ó Riain, which are not the same as Colgan's, though he follows Colgan's text.

[117] Isidore, *Etymologiae* XIV 6; see Ó Riain (2009), 39–40, with Ó Riain (2008) for the Irish place-names.

markedly with the conventional plainness of the rest of the *Vita*. Some of the details, notably the tradition that the first landing of the Goídil was in the north not the south of Ireland, are akin to a variant version of the origin legend assigned to the *Cín Dromma Snechta* and preserved in fragmentary form in the Book of Leinster and the Book of Lecan,[118] so it is reasonable to guess that the source was akin to an item in that corpus. In this version, the ancestors of the Irish are of Greek stock, *lingua et cultu nationeque Graeci*,[119] and they travel from Asia Minor via Greece itself through the Mediterranean and over the ocean to Ireland, whence they expand via Iona into Scotland, the main focus of the narrative's interest. The explanation given for the naming of this land as Scotia is unmistakeably familiar:[120]

> *Sicque totam terram suo nomine Chorischiam nominatum, post cuiusdam Lacedaemonii Aeneae filium nomine Nelum, seu Niulum, qui princeps eorum fuerat, et olim Aegyptiam coniugem bello meruerat, ex vocabulo coniugis, patrio sermone depravato, Scotiam vocaverunt.*

> 'The land had previously been named Chorischia after their own name; but after the son of a certain Spartan Aeneas, who was called Nelus or Niulus, who was their prince, and formerly had gained an Egyptian wife in war, they called it Scotia.'

Clearly this family group is a version of Fénius Farsaid, Nél his son, and his wife Pharaoh's daughter Scotta, familiar from the *Leabhar Gabhála,* with the curious but easily explicable shift that the aetiology is here associated with Scotland rather than Ireland proper. As we have seen, the lore of Scotta daughter of Pharaoh is attested in Carolingian glosses on Isidore; the gloss survivals have another curious reflex in the *Vita*, where the ancestors land in Ireland at a mountain called *Cruachan Feli, montem Hiberniae.*[121] Dumville has argued that this is a form of Cruachán Aighle, the old name of Croagh Patrick which has a variant form in

[118] Hull (1933); cf. Carey (2005), 37–8.

[119] *Vita Cadroe* 1 (ed. Ó Riain (2008), 35–6). Cf. Hull (1983), 156–7 and other sources collected by Jaski (2003); Jaski (2009). The theme of Greek origins is best known from Mael Muru's poem *Can a mbunadus*, and it recurs in O'Mulconry's Glossary (ed. Stokes (1900), 232–4; cf. Jaski (2003), 12): *Scoti de Graecis originem duxerunt, sic et linguam.* ('The Irish drew their origin from the Greeks, and in just the same way their language.')

[120] *Vita Cadroe* 6 (Ó Riain (2009), 41–2).

[121] *Vita Cadroe* 5 (Ó Riain (2009), 40–1).

the *Historia Brittonum* as Cruachan Eile;[122] but the simplification of the *-gl-* cluster is difficult to explain at this date,[123] and I suggest that the name here is influenced by (or based upon) the element *Fele* found in *Inber Fele,* the location of the southern landing by the sons of Míl recounted in the mainstream tradition and referenced in the 9th-century glosses to Orosius discussed above. Given these contextual associations, it seems clear that the exemplar of the *Vita* version was close to the early articulations in whatever versions were current among the Carolingian scholars on the Continent, whether or not it ever circulated within Ireland itself.

But there is an added puzzle. How does Fénius correspond to Aeneas?[124] There can be no reasonable doubt that Fénius is the original form,[125] and it is possible to posit a transmission akin to the effects of listening to the corresponding passage of Mael Muru *Can a mbunadus* without background knowledge to recognize that there is a lenited *f* at the start of the name:[126]

Féni ó Fhaenius asambertar,
clú cen dochta,
Gaedil ó Gaediul Glas garta,
Scuitt o Scotta.

'The Féni are named after Fénius,
fame without niggardliness
the Gaedil are called after Gáedel Glas,
the Scuitt after Scotta.'

Whether or not this suggestion is fanciful, the effect of naming Fénius as Aeneas plainly contributes to the parallelism with Roman origins suggested above: he becomes explicitly paralleled with the founder of Rome, and to be 'a Spartan Aeneas' is in a sense for the Irish to be identified with what was best of both Greece and Rome. However, within this section of the *Vita* there is a remarkable passage of rhetorically

122 See Nennius, *Historia Brittonum* 54 (MGH Auct. ant. 13, 197.5), with Dumville (2001), 175 n 16; cf. Dumville (1993), 224 n 47.

123 Ó Riain (2008), 15.

124 With the argument that follows compare Jaski (2006), 26–8, who sees the shift from Fénius to Aeneas in terms of error rather than creative allusion.

125 Scowcroft (1988), 13 n 33: 'Despite its latinate look it is a masculine u-stem of common type, based on a word for the Irish used particularly in legal and other contexts.'

126 Text from Best et al. (1956–83), iii 133b ll. 46–7.

heightened Latin that may give us a clue to the logic of the implicit parallel. As the ancestors travel through the Mediterranean, a storm arises and the great force of the wind drives them onto the Italian coast, sending them into despair and confusion:[127]

> *Quid enim facerent? Sol occultaverat, luna et astra profusa caligine damnaverant diem. Nusquam erat terra, hiems horrida caelestibus, ut ita credas, terrenas miscuerat undis, ut, antiquo redeunte, Chaos omnia crederes miscuisse.*
>
> 'What could they do? The sun had hidden [itself], the moon and the stars had destroyed the day by the onpouring of mist. Nowhere was the land; terrible storm had (if you would believe it) mixed earthly with celestial waves, so that (with the return of the ancient state) you would believe that Chaos had thrown everything into confusion.'

As the account continues, the intertextual logic reveals itself:

> *Ablata erat miseris spes vivendi: quis enim tanta eorum non horreat pericula? Nam neque Aeneas aut Ulisses, quos historiae tradunt plurima pertulisse, tanta perferre potuerunt.*
>
> 'The hope of survival was taken away from those miserable ones; who indeed would not be terrified by such great dangers? For not even Aeneas or Ulysses, who the histories say endured the most evil things, would have been able to endure the like of this.'

Here it is explicit that the wanderings of the Irish are like those of the wandering heroes of classical legend. The parallel with Ulysses recalls the motif in the mainstream *Leabhar Gabhála* narrative, where the ancestors sail past the Sirens and on the advice of Caicher the druid they put wax in their ears, just as Ulysses had asked his men to do in the same situation. Here, however, the parallel with Aeneas is the more potent one, and plainly the description of their despair at the storm chimes with the passage of the *Aeneid* in which Aeneas despairs at the storm that Juno raises to prevent him from landing in Italy.[128]

The strangely-worded reference to Chaos and the 'return of the ancient state' (*antiquo redeunte*) points the way to an unexpected

[127] *Vita Cadroe* 3 (Ó Riain (2009), 37).

[128] Vergil, *Aeneid* I 81–123.

textual borrowing from elsewhere in Latin epic. In the exordium of his *Pharsalia*, the epic of the Civil War of the Romans, Lucan evokes the collapse and disorder of the war as a figure of the final collapse of the physical universe at the end of time:[129]

> *Sic, cum conpage soluta*
> *saecula tot mundi suprema coegerit hora,*
> ***antiquum** repetens iterum **chaos,** omnia **mixtis***
> *sidera sideribus concurrent, ignea pontum*
> *astra petent, tellus extendere litora nolet*
> *excutietque fretum, fratri contraria Phoebe*
> *ibit et obliquum bigas agitare per orbem*
> *indignata diem poscet sibi, totaque discors*
> *machina divolsi turbabit foedera mundi.*

> 'Even so, when the framework of the world is dissolved and the final hour, closing so many ages, reverts to primeval chaos, then all the constellations will clash in confusion, the fiery stars will drop into the sea, and earth, refusing to spread her shores out flat, will shake off the ocean; the moon will move in opposition to her brother, and claim to rule the day, disdaining to drive her chariot along her slanting orbit; and the whole distracted fabric of the shattered firmament will overthrow its laws.'

I do not know why the author of the *Vita* borrowed a phrase from this passage, but Lucan's poetry was certainly studied in the Carolingian schools,[130] and it is also possible that this passage was transmitted as an excerpt a *florilegium*—perhaps in a cosmological context similar to that in which Isidore quotes another of Lucan's storm-descriptions,[131] or in a collection of such passages akin to that surviving in Macrobius' *Saturnalia*.[132] Whatever the exact route of transmission and remodelling, the image shows clearly that the pseudohistorical wanderings of the Irish are being carefully correlated with those of Aeneas, and that the theme

[129] Lucan, *Bellum Civile* I 72–80 (trans. Duff (1928), 9).

[130] Werner (1994); McKitterick (2004), 44.

[131] Lucan, *Bellum Civile* V 623–6 (Duff (1928) 286–7), cited by Isidore in *De natura rerum* 40.3 (ed. and trans. Fontaine (1960), 308–9) in a discussion of the extent and limits of the ocean.

[132] Macrobius, *Saturnalia* V 6.3–7.1 (ed. Kaster (2011), ii 268–79). Is it a mere idle coincidence that the Orosius manuscript with the *Leabhar Gabhála* glosses also transmits a substantial chunk of the *Saturnalia*? See Szerwiniack (1992–3, 2007), 5.

was developed before the compilation of the surviving Middle Irish version of *Leabhar Gabhála*.

There is a further intriguing link between this passage and the other great expression of Irish pseudohistorical self-invention: the Ulster Cycle. In an entirely different context, Brent Miles has identified the influence of this same passage of Lucan in *Táin Bó Cuailnge*, in the series of rhetorical images that punctuate the build-up to the climax of the final encounter between the Ulstermen and the enemy army.[133] The decapitated head of Sualtaim, Cú Chulainn's father, cries out prophesying the coming battle, and Conchobar responds:[134]

> *'Romór bic in núall sa', bar Conchobor, 'dáig nem úasaind ⁊ talam ísaind ⁊ muir immaind immácúaird, acht munu tháeth in firmimint cona frossaib rétland bar dunadgnúis in talman ná mono máe in talam assa thalamchumscugud ná mono thí in fhairge eithrech ochorgorm for tulmoing in bethad, dobér-sa cach bó cach ben díb cá lias ⁊ cá machad, co'aitte ⁊ co'adbai fadessin ar mbúaid chatha ⁊ chomlaind ⁊ chomraic.'*

> "That cry was a little too loud', said Conchobor, 'for the sky above us, the earth beneath us and the sea in circumference around us, but unless the firmament with its showers of stars fall upon the surface of the earth, or earth burst in an earthquake, or unless the finny, blue-bordered sea come over the surface of the world, I will bring back every cow to its pen and enclosure, and every woman to her own abode and dwelling, after victory in battle and combat and contest."

Is it a coincidence that a single image from Latin epic, otherwise relatively obscure, informs or influences two such different passages in the cycles of Irish pseudohistory? It would be impossible to prove otherwise: but this linkage between the imaginative resources deployed in the *Táin* and the *Leabhar Gabhála* at least suggests a kinship between the development of the two narrative cycles. It remains anyone's guess whether this is because the same caste of *literati* was responsible for both parts of the project of inscribing the Irish story in the grand narratives of world history, or whether it is simply a byproduct of the fact that the early medieval bookshelf in Ireland and Francia alike held a smaller and more selective body of texts and excerpts that sometimes appears to be the

[133] Miles (2009), 72. See more generally Miles (2011), 145–244 *passim*.

[134] Book of Leinster text of *Táin Bó Cuailnge* ll. 4041–7 in O'Rahilly (1967), 112, with translation p 247.

case when we hunt for sources and exemplars in the very different libraries that we rely on today. Either way, it serves as a strong indication that the slice of *Leabhar Gabhála* text that survives in the *Vita Cadroe* is derived from an extended text in sophisticated literary Latin, which articulated a close parallelism between the origins of the Irish and those of the Romans and probably the Franks and British as well. It is an attractive possibility that the Latin passage at the beginning of the *Míniugud* version of the *Leabhar Gabhála*, where we find an account of the wonders of Ireland along with the cluster of etymologies from Orosius and Isidore discussed above, might ultimately be derived from the same source. Cumulatively, then, these fragments of the Latin articulation of the Irish origin-legend bear witness to what must in its time have been a daring and creative assertion of national identity on the world stage.

Bibliography

Ahlqvist, A. (1983) *The early Irish linguist: an edition of the canonical part of* Auraicept na nÉces, Helsinki.

Barlow, J. (1995) 'Gregory of Tours and the myth of the Trojan origin of the Franks,' *Frühmittelalterliche Studien* 29, 86–95.

Baumgarten, R. (1983) 'A Hiberno-Isidorean etymology,' *Peritia* 2, 225–8.

— (1984) 'The geographical orientation of Ireland in Isidore and Orosius,' *Peritia* 3, 189–203.

Best, R.I. et al. (1954–83) *The Book of Leinster*, 6 vols., Dublin.

Bischoff, B. (1994) *Manuscripts and libraries in the age of Charlemagne*, trans. by M. Gorman, Cambridge.

Broun, D. (1999) *The Irish identity of the kingdom of the Scots in the twelfth and thirteenth centuries*, Cambridge.

Bullough, D. (1991) 'Roman books and the Carolingian *renovatio*,' in D. Bullough, *Carolingian renewal: sources and heritage*, Manchester, 1–38 (rev. version of article first published in *Studies in Church History* 14 (1977), 23–50).

Calder, G. (1917) *Auraicept na nÉces*, Edinburgh.

Capo, L. (1992) *Paolo Diacono, Storia dei Longobardi*, Milano.

Carey, J. (1984) 'Scél Tuáin meic Chairill,' *Ériu* 35, 93–111.

— (1993) *A new introduction to Lebor Gabála Érenn*, London.

— (1994) *The Irish national origin-legend: synthetic pseudo-history*, Cambridge.

— (2005) '*Lebor Gabála* and the legendary history of Ireland,' in H. Fulton, *Medieval Celtic literature and society*, Dublin, 32–48.

— (2007) *Ireland and the Grail*, Aberystwyth.

— (2010) 'Donn, Amairgen, Íth and the prehistory of Irish pseudohistory,' *Journal of Indo-European Studies* 38, 319–42.
Carey, J. and J.T. Koch (2003) *The Celtic Heroic Age*, 4th ed., Aberystwyth.
Clarke, M. (2009) 'An Irish Achilles and a Greek Cú Chulainn,' in R. Ó hUiginn and B. Ó Catháin, *Ulidia 2: Proceedings of the Second International Conference on the Ulster Cycle of Tales*, Maynooth, 238–51.
— (2011) 'Translation and transformation: a case study from medieval Irish and English,' in M. Clarke and K.M. Shields, *Translating emotion*, Oxford, 27–46.
— (2013) 'Linguistic education and literary creativity in early medieval Ireland,' *Cahiers de l'Institut de Linguistique et des Sciences du Langage* 38, 39–71.
Colgan, J. (1645) *Acta Sanctorum veteris ac majoris Scotiae seu Hiberniae* [...] *sanctorum insulae*, Louvain.
Collins, R. (2007) *Die Fredegar-Chroniken*, Hannover.
Contreni, J. (1989) 'The Egyptian origins of the Irish: two ninth-century notes,' in K. Wittstadt, *St. Kilian: 1300 Jahre Martyrium der Frankenapostel*, Würzburg, 51–4.
Dumville, D. (1993) *Saint Patrick AD 493–1993*, Woodbridge.
— (1994) '*Historia Brittonum*: an insular history from the Carolingian age,' in A. Scharer and G. Scheibelreiter, *Historiographie im frühen Mittelalter*, München, 406–34.
— (2001) 'St Cathróe of Metz and the hagiography of exoticism,' in J. Carey et al., *Studies in Irish hagiography: saints and scholars*, Dublin, 172–88.
Enright, M. (1995) *Lady with a mead cup: ritual, prophecy and lordship from La Tène to the Viking Age*, Dublin.
Evans, N. (2010) *The present and the past in medieval Irish chronicles*, Cambridge.
Galletier, É. (2002) *Ammien Marcellin, Histoires, Livres XIV–XVI*, 2nd ed., Paris.
Geary, P. (2002) *The myth of nations: the medieval origins of Europe*, Princeton.
Gerberding, R.A. (1987) *The rise of the Carolingians and the Liber Historiae Francorum*, Oxford.
Goffart, W. (1983) 'The supposedly "Frankish" table of nations: an edition and study,' *Frühmittelalterliche Studien* 17 (1983), 98–130, repr. in W. Goffart, *Rome's fall and after*, London 1990, 133–65.
— (1988) *The narrators of Barbarian history (AD 550–800): Jordanes, Gregory of Tours, Bede and Paul the Deacon*, Princeton.
Graus, F. (1989) 'Troja und trojanische Herkunft im Mittelalter,' in W. Ergräber, *Kontinuität und Transformation der Antike im Mittelalter*, Sigmaringen, 26–43.
Greene, D. (n.d.) Typescript and translation of *Saltair na Rann*, available at www.celt.dias.ie.

Gwynn, E. (1903–1935) *The metrical Dindshenchas*, 5 vols., Dublin.
Hagen, H. (1867) *Scholia Bernensia ad Vergili Bucolica atque Georgica*, Leipzig.
Herren, M.W. (2011) *The Cosmography of Aethicus Ister*, Turnhout.
Hogan, E. (1910) *Onomasticon Goedelicum*, Dublin.
Hull, V. (1933) 'The Milesian Invasion of Ireland,' *Zeitschrift für celtische Philologie* 19, 155–60.
Innes, M. (2000) 'Teutons or Trojans? The Carolingians and the Germanic past,' in Y. Hen and M. Innes, *The uses of the past in the early Middle Ages*, Cambridge, 227–49.
Jaski, B. (2003) 'We are of the Greeks in our origin: new light on the Irish national origin-legend,' *Cambrian Medieval Celtic Studies* 46, 1–53.
— (2006) 'Aeneas and Fénius: a classical case of mistaken identity,' in R. Corradini et al., *Texts and identities in the early Middle Ages*, Wien, 17–33.
— (2009) 'The Irish origin legend: seven unexplored sources,' in J. Carey, *Lebor Gabála Érenn: textual history and pseudohistory*, London, 48–75.
Kaster, R.A. (2011) *Macrobius, Saturnalia*, 3 vols., Cambridge.
Kelly, F. (1976) *Audacht Morainn*, Dublin.
Lindsay, W.M. (1911) *Isidori Hispalensis Episcopi etymologiarum siue originum libri XX*, 2 vols., Oxford.
Macalister, R.A.S. (1938–56) *Lebor Gabála Érenn: the book of the taking of Ireland*, 5 vols., London.
Mac Cana, P. (2011) *The cult of the sacred centre*, Dublin.
Mac Carthaigh, M. (1966–7) 'Dursey Island and some placenames,' *Dinnseanchas* 2, 51–5.
Mac Carthy, B. (1892) *The Codex Palatino-Vaticanus No. 830*, Dublin.
Mac Eoin, G. (1964) 'On the Irish legend of the origin of the Picts,' *Studia Hibernica* 4, 138–54.
Mac Neill, E. (1930–2) '*De origine Scotticae linguae*,' *Ériu* 11, 112–29.
Mc Carthy, D.P. (2007) *The Irish annals: their genesis, evolution and history*, Dublin.
McKitterick, R. (2004) *History and memory in the Carolingian world*, Cambridge.
Merrills, A.H. (2005) *History and geography in Late Antiquity*, Cambridge.
Meyer, K. (1910) *Fianaigecht*, Dublin.
— (1913) 'The Laud Synchronisms,' *Zeitschrift für celtische Philologie* 9, 471–85.
— (1919) 'Der irische Totengott und die Toteninsel,' *Sitzungsberichte der Preussischen Akademie der Wissenschaften* 32, 537–46.
Miles, B. (2009) 'The literary set piece and the *imitatio* of Latin epic in the Cattle Raid of Cooley,' in R. Ó hUiginn and B. Ó Catháin, *Ulidia 2: Proceedings of the Second International Conference on the Ulster Cycle of Tales*, Maynooth, 66–80.
— (2011) *Heroic saga and classical epic in medieval Ireland*, Cambridge.

Moran, P. (2010) 'Hebrew in early Irish glossaries,' *Cambrian Medieval Celtic Studies* 60, 1–21.

— (2012) 'Greek in early medieval Ireland,' in A. Mullen and P. James, *Multilingualism in the Graeco-Roman worlds*, Cambridge, 172–92.

Mynors, R.A.B. (1964) *XII panegyrici latini*, Oxford.

O'Brien, M.A. (1962) *Corpus genealogiarum Hiberniae*, Dublin.

O'Connor, R. (2013) *The Destruction of Da Derga's Hostel: kingship and narrative artistry in a medieval Irish saga*, Oxford.

— (2014) *Classical literature and learning in medieval Ireland*, Cambridge.

Ó Cróinín, D. (1983) *Sex Aetates Mundi*, Dublin.

O'Rahilly, C. (1967) *Táin Bó Cuailnge from the Book of Leinster*, Dublin.

— (1976) *Táin Bó Cuailnge Recension I*, Dublin.

Ó Riain, P. (1983) 'St. Abbán: the genesis of an Irish saint's life,' in D.E. Evans et al., *Proceedings of the Seventh International Congress of Celtic Studies*, Oxford.

— (2008) 'An *Vita Cadroe,* an *Leabhar Gabhála* agus Corcaigh,' *Journal of the Cork Historical and Archaeological Society* 113, 9–19.

— (2009) '*Scottorum origines fabulosae*: the Metz version of *Lebor Gabála Érenn*,' in J. Carey, *Lebor Gabála Érenn: textual history and pseudohistory*, London, 33–47.

Plummer, C. (1896) *Venerabilis Baedae opera historica*, 2 vols., Oxford.

— (1910) *Vitae Sanctorum Hiberniae*, 2 vols., Oxford.

Poppe, E. and D. Schlüter (2011), 'Greece, Ireland, Ulster and Troy: of hybrid nations and heroes,' in W.M. Hoofnagle and W.R. Keller, *Other nations: the hybridization of insular mythology and identity*, Heidelberg, 127–44.

Rankin, D. (1987) *Celts and the classical world*, London.

Reeve, M. and N. Wright (2007) *Geoffrey of Monmouth, The history of the kings of Britain*, Woodbridge.

Reynolds, L.D. (1983) *Texts and transmission: a survey of the Latin classics*, Oxford.

Russell, P. (1988) 'The sounds of a silence: the growth of Cormac's Glossary,' *Cambridge Medieval Celtic Studies* 15, 1–30.

Schlüter, D. (2010) *History or fable? The Book of Leinster as a document of cultural memory in twelfth-century Ireland*, Münster.

Scowcroft, R.M. (1987) '*Leabhar Gabhála* Part I: the growth of the text,' *Ériu* 38, 81–140.

— (1988) '*Leabhar Gabhála* Part II: the growth of the tradition,' *Ériu* 39, 1–66.

— (2009) 'Medieval recensions of the *Lebor Gabála*,' in J. Carey, *Lebor Gabála Érenn: textual history and pseudohistory*, London, 1–20.

Smith, P. (2002) 'Early Irish historical verse: the evolution of a genre,' in P. Ní Chatháin and M. Richter, *Ireland and Europe in the early middle Ages: texts and transmission / Irland und Europa im früheren Mittelalter: Texte und Überlieferung*, Dublin, 326–41.

— (2007) *Three historical poems ascribed to Gilla Coemáin*, Münster.
Stokes, W. (1895–6) 'The Annals of Tigernach', *Revue celtique* 16 (1895), 374–419; 17 (1896) 6–33, 119–263; reprinted (1993), with same pagination as W. Stokes, *The Annals of Tigernach*, Llanerch.
— (1900) 'O'Mulconry's Glossary,' *Archiv für celtische Lexicographie* 1, 232–324, 473–81.
— (1905) 'The colloquy of the two sages,' *Revue celtique* 26, 4–64.
Stokes, W. and J. Strachan (1901–3) *Thesaurus Palaeohibernicus*, 2 vols., Cambridge.
Szerwiniack, O. (1992–3, 2007) 'Un commentaire hiberno-latin des deux premiers livres d'Orose, Histoire contre les païens,' *Archivum Latinitatis Medii Aevi* 51, 5–137; 65, 165–207.
— (1995) 'D'Orose au *LGÉ*,' *Études celtiques* 31, 205–17.
Thilo, G. and H. Hagen (1881–1902) *Servii Grammatici qui feruntur in Vergilii Carmina Commentarii*, 3 vols., Leipzig.
Todd, J.T. (1848) *The Irish version of the Historia Brittonum of Nennius*, Dublin.
Tristram, H.L.C. (1985) *Sex aetates mundi: Die Weltzeitalter bei den Angelsachsen und den Iren — Untersuchungen und Texte*, Heidelberg.
Usener, H. (1869) *M. Annaei Lucani commenta Bernensia*, Leipzig.
van Hamel, A.G. (1915) 'On *Lebor Gabála*,' *Zeitschrift für celtische Philologie* 10, 97–197.
— (1932) *Lebor Bretnach, the Irish version of the Historia Brittonum ascribed to Nennius*, Dublin.
— (1933) *Compert Con Culainn and other stories*, Dublin.
Vendryes, J. (1953) *Airne Fíngein*, Dublin.
Wallace-Hadrill, J. M. (1962) *The long-haired kings and other studies in Frankish history*, London.
Weiss, J. (1999) *Wace's Roman de Brut: text and translation*, Exeter.
Werner, S. (1994) 'On the history of the *Commenta Bernensia* and the *Adnotationes super Lucanum*,' *Harvard Studies in Classical Philology* 96, 343–68.
Wood, I. (2006) 'Defining the Franks,' in F.X. Noble, *From "Roman" provinces to medieval kingdoms*, London, 110–19.
Wright, C.D. (2012) '*Genesis A* ad litteram,' in M. Fox and M. Sharma, *Old English literature and the Old Testament*, Toronto, 121–71.
— (2013) 'From monks' jokes to sages' wisdom: *Immaccallam in Dá Thuarad* and the *Ioca Monachorum*,' in M. Garrison, A.P. Orbán, and P. Mostert, *Spoken and written language: relations between Latin and the vernacular languages in the earlier Middle Ages*, Turnhout, 199–225.
Wright, N. (1988) *The 'Historia Regum Britanniae' of Geoffrey of Monmouth II: the first variant version*, Woodbridge.

PÁDRAIC MORAN

GREEK DIALECTOLOGY AND THE IRISH ORIGIN STORY

Abstract

O'Mulconry's Glossary (*De origine scoticae linguae*), an Irish etymological tract dating from around the late 7th or early 8th centuries, makes the striking claim that the Irish language derives from Greek, and specifically from the Attic, Doric, and Aeolic dialects. This article explores the cultural background to this assertion. It first addresses the question of why these dialects are mentioned to the exclusion of Ionic or koine Greek. It then surveys the sources for Greek that were potentially available in the early medieval West, to determine how much if anything the compilers could have known about Greek dialects. Finally, the broader significance of Greek origins is explored, drawing parallels between Irish and Roman origin stories.

Keywords

O'Mulconry's Glossary, St Gall glosses, *Auraicept na nÉces*, *Lebor Gabála*; Greek, Greek dialects, digamma; Priscian, Macrobius, Diomedes, Varro, Evander.

Early medieval Ireland and Europe: chronology, contacts, scholarship, ed. by Pádraic Moran and Immo Warntjes, Studia Traditionis Theologiae, 14 (Turnhout, 2015), pp. 481–512.

 10.1484/M.STT-EB.5.103133

Introduction

The *curieuse préface latine*, so characterized by Paul Grosjean,[1] of O'Mulconry's Glossary (OM) makes a bold assertion about the origins of the Irish language and race:[2]

> *Incipit discreptio de origine scoticae linguæ quam congregauerunt religiosi uiri, adiunctis nominibus ex Hebricano Hironimi et tractationibus, i.e. Ambrosi ⁊ Cassiani ⁊ Augustini ⁊ Eisiodori Virgili Prisciani Commiani Ciceronis, necnon per literas Grecorum, i.e. Atticae Doricae Eolicae lingæ, quia Scoti de Grecis originem duxerunt, sic et lingam.*
>
> 'Here begins an account of the origin of the Irish language which religious men compiled, having combined Jerome's Hebrew Names and [other] discussions, i.e. by Ambrose and Cassian and Augustine and Isidore, Virgil, Priscian, Commianus, Cicero, and also using Greek writings, i.e. in the Attic, Doric and Aeolic language, because the Irish derive their origin from the Greeks, and thus too their language.'

The text, dated to the late 7th or early 8th centuries, is a collection of *c.* 874 etymologies for Irish words.[3] In the absence of contrary evidence we may assume that the preface was composed at the same time.[4] Whatever about the claims for the Latin and Hebrew origins of Irish, striking in themselves,[5] the preface is most remarkable for its statements about Greek. The Irish connection to Greece was not only genealogical, but

[1] Grosjean (1961), 393: 'Depuis que le texte en a été imprimé par Whitley Stokes, voici soixante ans, il ne semble pas que les amateurs de gloses se soient du tout intéréssés à la curieuse préface latine du glossaire irlandais dit d'O'Mulconry [...] Il faudrait remonter aux sources de ce glossaire, excellent sujet de thèse ou de dissertation.' I suspect these words were somewhere in the back of our honorand's mind when he first suggested I explore Irish glossaries as a Ph.D. topic. I am very grateful to Anders Ahlqvist, Franck Cinato, Michael Clarke, Alessandro Garcea, Edward Herring, Pierre-Yves Lambert, and Paul Russell for comments and corrections on this article.

[2] O'Mulconry's Glossary is ed. by Stokes (1898–1900); see also the *Early Irish Glossaries Database* (*EIGD*) www.asnc.cam.ac.uk/irishglossaries. I am currently preparing a new edition. Variants (see *EIGD* for sigla): discreptio] discreps\ł t/io OM[4]; adiunctis] adiunsis MSS; Cassiani] casiani OM[4]; duxerunt] OM[3], dixerunt OM[1], OM[4]. The translation is mine.

[3] See Mac Neill (1930–2).

[4] Grosjean (1961), 393: 'A quelque date que remontent les citations irlandaises, le latin de ces brèves lignes paraît d'assez haute époque.' An analysis of all of the named sources awaits an exhaustive study.

[5] On Hebrew in the glossaries, see Moran (2010).

linguistic too, and furthermore traceable to specific, named regional varieties.

The claim to an origin for Irish in Greeks dialects is supported explicitly by one entry only in the main text: OM 160: *Briathor insce apud Eoles.* ('*Bríathor*, 'word' in Aeolic.') This short statement can be traced to a passage in Priscian where he explains that the Aeolians pronounced the letter digamma (ϝ) before ρ as though β, giving the example βρήτωρ for ϝρήτωρ.[6] The glossary entry blurs the distinction between 'speaker' ([β]ρήτωρ) and 'speech' ([β]ρήτρα) to create an association with Irish *bríathor* ('word').[7]

The assertions in the preface raise a number of queries. Firstly, why these three dialects in particular? Ionic is conspicuously absent. And Isidore tells us, for example, that there were in fact five Greek dialects, counting koine or common Greek as the fifth.[8] Secondly, did the glossary author really know anything about ancient dialects of Greek?[9] And finally, why Greek at all? What was the broader significance of this idea in the context of contemporary discourses on Irish origins?

How many Greek dialects?

Before evaluating our glossator's knowledge of Greek dialects, it may be useful to sketch out the linguistic reality which he was purporting to describe. Immediately we stumble over an imprecision of terminology. While a distinction between 'dialect' and 'language' is commonplace in non-technical language, for sociolinguists the dividing line between these two is much less clear. When can a dialect be called a language? Mutual intelligibility as a criterion for classification of dialects cannot be applied consistently: many Italian dialects, for example, are not at all comprehensible to speakers from other parts of that country;[10] on the other hand, speakers of Danish, Norwegian, and Swedish can all

6 Priscian, *Institutiones grammaticae* I 23 (ed. by Martin Hertz in Keil (1855–80), ii 18.5–7; cf. ibidem, ii 19.16–25); discussed in Moran (2012), 183–4; Russell (2012), 27–9. Citations from Keil (1855–80) are hereafter abbreviated *GL*.

7 The Irish word, if we accept a 7th-century date for the text, would originally have had the closer form *brēthor*.

8 Isidore, *Etymologiae* IX 1.4–5 (ed. Lindsay (1911), i).

9 I assume one author here for present purposes, although a process of compilation may potentially have involved several individuals over an extended period.

10 See Morpurgo Davies (1987), 154–5.

understand each other rather well, despite their speech being classified as different languages.

The difficulty of separating dialect from language is in fact reflected in the terminology employed in both Greek and Latin. In Greek, γλῶττα/γλῶσσα,[11] φωνή, and διάλεκτος are used interchangeably to refer to Greek dialects and foreign languages; the last begins to assume its narrower, more specialized sense only sometime after Aristotle, though the exact chronology is unclear.[12] Similarly, the Latin terms *lingua*, *loquela*, *oratio*, *verbum*, *vox* can refer to varieties of speech within wide parameters.[13]

The absence of lexical distinctions in Latin between languages and language varieties explains the apparent contradiction in OM's preface, where the term *lingua* does service both for the Greek language and for Greek dialects.

As a working definition, we can take 'dialect' to refer to the speech variety of a specific geographic area. Ancient Greek sources assign regional speech varieties to specific cities, whether the language of regional stereotypes in Attic comedy or exotic words collected in Hellenistic glossaries.[14] As far as broader groupings of dialects are concerned, any efforts to identify commonalities would have been hampered not only by the linguistic complexity on the ground, but also by the absence of descriptive grammars (before the Hellenistic period at least) and the lack of any systematic evidence before the development of modern epigraphy.[15] Instead, a broader classification of dialects emerged from an existing genealogical framework. A tripartite division grouped local varieties according to the descendants of the eponymous Dorus (Dorians), Ion (Ionians), and Aeolus (Aeolians).[16] Hesiod provides the earliest record of this scheme:[17]

[11] Itself a dialectal shibboleth, the former being characteristic of Attic and Boeotian.

[12] Morpurgo Davies (1987), 161

[13] See, for example, the entries for these words in Lewis and Short (1879), *s.vv.*

[14] Hainsworth (1967), 66, 70.

[15] Hainsworth (1967), 75–6.

[16] Hainsworth (1967), 64–8.

[17] Hesiod, *Φυναικῶν κατάλογος siue Ἠοῖαι*, frag. 9 (ed. Merkelbach and West (1967), 7). Xouthos is the ancestor of the Ionians through his son Ion. It is tempting to identify a survival of the early tripartite tradition in Pliny, *Historia naturalis* VI 2.7 (ed. and trans. Rackham (1961), ii 342–3): *quo in omni tractu proditur tres tantum gentes Graecas iure dici, Doricam, Ionicam, Aeolicam, ceteras barbarorum esse* ('It is reported that in all this region there are only three races that can rightly be designated, Greek, the Dorian, the Ionian and the Aeolian, all the rest being tribes of barbarians'). Here, however, he describes the colonies of the Black Sea, none of which were Athenian.

> Ἕλληνος δ' ἐγένοντο φιλοπτολέμου βασιλῆος
> Δῶρός τε Ξοῦθός τε καὶ Αἴολος ἱππιοχάρμης.
>
> 'From Hellen the warrior king sprang
> Doros and Xouthos and Aiolos lover of horses.'

The Athenians were originally identified with the Ionians, as noted, for example by Cicero:[18]

> *Quamquam quis ignorat qui modo umquam mediocriter res istas scire curavit, quin tria Graecorum genera sint vere? quorum uni sunt Athenienses, quae gens Ionum habebatur, Aeolis alteri, Doris tertii nominabantur.*
>
> 'And yet who that has ever felt even a moderate desire to know about these things is ignorant that there are really three divisions of the Greek race? Of these the Athenians are one; they are considered to be of the Ionian race. The second are called Aeolians, the third Dorians.'

However, as a result of Athens' dominance in political, commercial, and cultural affairs, Attic was assigned the status of an independent dialect as early as the mid-3rd century BC.[19] Quintilian, for example, follows the four-dialect model:[20]

> *Σαρδισμός quoque appellatur quaedam mixta ex varia ratione linguarum oratio, ut si Atticis Dorica et Aeolica Iadicis confundas.*
>
> 'There is also what is called *Sardismos*, a style made up of a mixture of several kinds of language, for example a confusion of Attic with Doric, Aeolic with Ionic.'

Nonetheless, the separation of Attic and Ionic was never absolute. Strabo's extended discussion on dialect divisions on the one hand acknowledges the four-dialect model, but on the other persists in identifying Attic with Ionic:[21]

[18] Cicero, *Pro Flacco* 27 (ed. and trans. Lord (1959), 434–5).

[19] Hainsworth (1967), 67: 'it is a tribute to the predominance of Attic in literature and commerce and to the national arrogance of its speakers'.

[20] Quintilian, *Institutio oratoria* VIII 3.59 (ed. and trans. Russell (2002), iii 374–5).

[21] Strabo, *Geographica* VIII 1.2 (ed. and trans. Jones (1917–33), iv 4–5). Strabo goes on to equate Doric and Aeolic, which Hainsworth (1967), 68, explains as 'a

τούτων δ' αὐτῶν τεττάρων οὐσῶν τὴν μὲν Ἰάδα τῇ παλαιᾷ Ἀτθίδι τὴν αὐτὴν φαμέν (καὶ γὰρ Ἴωνες ἐκαλοῦντο οἱ τότε Ἀττικοί, καὶ ἐκεῖθέν εἰσιν οἱ τὴν Ἀσίαν ἐ ποικήσαντες Ἴωνες καὶ χρησάμενοι τῇ νῦν λεγομένῃ γλώττῃ Ἰάδι).

'But though the dialects themselves are four in number, we may say that the Ionic is the same as the ancient Attic, for the Attic people of ancient times were called Ionians, and from that stock sprang those Ionians who colonized Asia and used what is now called the Ionic speech.'

Finally, a fifth dialect was added to the model, with the emergence of a new supra-regional standard, koine or 'common' Greek. In conformance with the overwhelmingly synchronic approach to language variation by ancient commentators, this variety was categorized not as a derivative (from Attic, mainly, with some admixture of other forms) but as a separate dialect (ἡ κοινὴ διάλεκτος). The earliest reference to koine in either Latin or Greek sources may possibly be in Quintilian, who, though he refers at one point to four dialects (cited above), also relates an anecdote about P. Licinius Crassus (consul, 131 BC) who mastered five forms of the Greek language.[22] By late antiquity, the enumeration of five dialects had become commonplace. Servius, for example, writes as much,[23] as does Isidore, whose account is somewhat idiosyncratic:[24]

concession to symmetry'. Modern scholarship recognizes Attic-Ionic as a single dialect group on account of shared language features; the association in Strabo, however, appears to be ethnographic rather than linguistic. The Attic-Ionic association (though not Doric-Aeolic) also finds expression in Greek grammatical tracts; see Hainsworth (1967), 68.

22 Quintilian, *Institutio oratoria* XI 2.50 (Russell (2002), v 84–5); subject to varied interpretation: see Morpurgo Davies (1987), 163–4.

23 Servius, *Commentarius in Vergilii Aeneidos libros*, on *Aeneid* III 122 (ed. Thilo and Hagen (1878–1902), i 365.18): *quinque Graecae sunt linguae, Aeolica, Iaca, Dorica, Attica, communis* ('there are five Greek dialects: Aeolic, Ionian, Doric, Attic, common'). *Iaca* is coined after Greek Ἰακή ('Ionic'); the term evidently caused difficulties for copyists, with *ionica, actica* and *antica* registered as manuscript variants.

24 Isidore, *Etymologiae* IX 1.4–5 (Lindsay (1911), i; trans. Barney et al. (2006), 191; Barney et al.'s translation of the apparently corrupt passage marked with editorial crosses is rather loose.) Compare citations below (pp. 489–90) from Diomedes and Eriugena. Isidore's location of Doric in Egypt and Syria is geographically puzzling as well as apparently anachronistic (if we take his use of the present tense to imply that this dialect was still spoken). Arévalo in PL 82, col. 327a (note b) proposed to emend *Syri* to *Siculi*, transposing the Doric speakers to Sicily. This offers at least some historical plausibility: Syracuse, for example, was founded by Doric-speaking Corinthians. I have found no comment on this point in Fontaine (1959–83) or Reydellet (1984).

> *Graeca autem lingua inter ceteras gentium clarior habetur. Est enim et Latinis et omnibus linguis sonantior: cuius varietas in quinque partibus discernitur. Quarum prima dicitur κοινή, id est mixta, sive communis quam omnes utuntur. Secunda Attica, videlicet Atheniensis, qua usi sunt omnes Graeciae auctores. Tertia Dorica, quam habent Aegyptii et Syri. Quarta Ionica, quinta Aeolica, †quas Αἰολιστὶ locutos dixerunt.† Et sunt in observatione Graecae linguae eiusmodi certa discrimina; sermo enim eorum ita est dispertitus.*
>
> 'Greek is considered more illustrious than the other nations' languages, for it is more sonorous than Latin or any other language. We can distinguish five varieties of Greek. The first of these is called κοινή, that is, 'mixed' or 'common', which everyone uses. The second is Attic (*Atticus*), namely the Greek of Athens (*Atheniensis*), which all the authors of Greece used. The third is Doric, which the Egyptians and the Syrians employ. The fourth, Ionic; the fifth, Aeolic, which they say the Eolisti spoke. In examining the Greek language we find settled differences of this kind, because their speaking communities were dispersed in this way.'

But, shortly after, he too acknowledges the genealogical identity of Attic and Ionic speakers:[25]

> *Cecropi Atheniensium regi successit Cranaus, cuius filia Atthis nomen et regionis et gentis dedit. Et ex ea Attici cognominati, qui sunt Athenienses. Ion, vir fortis, ex suo nomine eosdem Athenienses vocavit Iones.*
>
> 'Cranaus succeeded to Cecrops, king of the Athenians; his daughter Atthis gave her name to the region and the nation. Also from her the Attic people were named, and they are the Athenians. Ion was a powerful man, and he called those same Athenians 'Ionians', from his own name.'

Isidore was certainly a key source for OM,[26] and so its departure from his presentation of five dialects is all the more striking. It should be noted, of course, that OM does not claim that its list of dialects (Attic, Doric, and Aeolic) is exhaustive. The three in question may have been chosen to lend the assertion a rhetorical specificity, for example. Even so, the three-dialect model in OM is not incompatible with the older tradition. Attic and Ionic were originally conflated and elements of this single identity persisted in the scholarly tradition, whether in Strabo or in Isidore's own

[25] Isidore, *Etymologiae* IX 2.76–77 (Lindsay (1911), i; Barney et al. (2006), 196).

[26] See Moran (2012), 180–1.

remarks on Attic and Ionic genealogy (the latter undoubtedly the key influence). The motivation to omit koine is more difficult to explain, although we can note at this point that it accords with the older tradition.

An alternative approach would be to consider the possibility that the author of OM's preface was not following any inherited schema at all. Instead his ideas about Greek dialects may well have been formed on the basis of scattered fragments of information, found in a multiplicity of authors and lacking any overall coherence. If this model is more applicable to our glossary compiler's state of knowledge, we need not look for specific authorities, but instead search out the textual sources that could have provided some dialectal information and might plausibly have been available. I explore this alternative approach in the discussion that follows.

Knowledge and use of dialects

Against a backdrop where the knowledge of Greek in the early Middle Ages was extremely scant,[27] with Ireland as no exception,[28] it would seem reasonable to assume that knowledge of Greek dialects was either non-existent or extremely limited. Neither of the two major Carolingian Greek–Latin glossaries contain, as far as I can find, any Greek terms identified as dialectal.[29] The same applies to the collection of bilingual classroom materials referred to as *hermeneumata*.[30] Late Latin grammars present a slightly more promising quarry, and particularly those by Greek-speaking authors whose works offered some comparative analysis of both languages. Even so, the presentation of dialectal information is sometimes unexpected. Diomedes describes the standard five dialects more in stylistic terms than as purely linguistic varieties:[31]

27 Berschin (1988) is still the principal survey.

28 See most recently Moran (2012); Moran (2011); Herren (2010); Russell (2000); Howlett (1998).

29 The Philoxenus and Cyrillus Glossaries published in Goetz (1888–1923), ii; on which see Dionisotti (1988).

30 Edited in Goetz (1888–1923), iii and now in Dickey (2012). See also Dionisotti (1982).

31 Diomedes, *Ars grammatica* (*GL* i 440.1–26; the translation is mine). Kaster (1988), 270–2, dates his text to after the middle of the 4th century. His place of origin is unknown, though his name is obviously Greek, as is that of his dedicatee Athanasius. Law (1982), 20, notes the use of Diomedes in the Hiberno-Latin grammars of Malsachanus and Clemens and the *Anonymus ad Cuimnanum*.

de qualitate locutionum:
quinque sunt linguae Graecorum, Ias Doris Atthis Aeolis coene. iuxta has igitur quinque linguas et Latina uerba conprehensa colliguntur hoc modo. Ias relictis propriis utitur <similibus qua>si propriis nominibus ac uersatur in omnibus tropis. Doris in singulis partibus orationis nunc adiectioni nunc breuitati studens barbarismos facit [qui barbarismi metaplasmi appellantur], quos cum sibi uindicauerint docti, metaplasmos appellant, ut 'Teucrum mirantur inertia corda' pro Teucrorum, et 'aggere moerorum' et 'aulai medio'. Atthis, quae breuitati studet, admittit soloecismos, quos cum docti fecerint, non soloecismi sed schemata logu appellantur, ut est 'nuda genu' et 'urbem quam statuo uestra est'. ibi enim nudum genu habens debuit dicere et urbs quam statuo uestra est. sed seruiens schemati quod appellatur Hellenismos tres partes orationis redegit in duas usus per Atticismon. Aeolis ultra modum copiosa est et amat per circuitum uerba protendere et periphrasi res explicare ac per hoc πλεονάζει; cuius uitium schema dianoeas appellatur. coene communis est, in qua omnes idem sentimus.

'On the quality of expressions:
The Greeks have five dialects: Ionic, Doric, Attic, Aeolic, koine. Accordingly, after the manner of these five dialects, all Latin words are also grouped in the same way. Ionic, having abandoned proper nouns, uses similar words [?] like they were proper nouns and concerns itself with every figurative use of words. Doric produces barbarisms in every single part of speech, sometimes favouring an extension, sometimes a shortening (these barbarisms are called metaplasms). When scholars have claimed authority for these, they call them metaplasms, as in 'the ignorant hearts of the Trojans [*Teucrum*] were amazed', instead of *Teucrorum* [*Aeneid* IX 55]; and 'with a mass of walls [*moerorum*]' [for *murorum*; *Aen.* X 144] and 'in the middle of the room [*aulai*]' [for *aulae*; *Aen.* III 354]. Attic, which favours shortening, includes solecisms, which, whenever scholars have produced them, are not called solecisms but figures of speech, as in *nuda genu* ('bare in knee') [*Aen.* I 320] and *urbem quam statuo vestra est* ('the city which I found is yours') [*Aen.* I 573]. For in those examples *nudum genu habens* should be said and *urbs quam statuo vestra est*. But favouring a figure of speech called Hellenism, it reduces three parts of speech to two usages, in the manner of Atticism. Aeolic is exceedingly prolific and loves to set out words in a roundabout way and to explain things by periphrasis, and accordingly it is said [in Greek] to be pleonastic. This fault is called the figure of speech *dianoea*. Koine is the common variety, in which we all understand the same thing.'

Diomedes distinguishes Greek dialects here not on the basis of phonology or morphology, as we might expect, but using the terminology of faults and figures found, for example, in the third and final book of Donatus' *Ars maior*.[32] I have not found any similar exposition in other texts, and what application a reader might have for this information is unclear. Nonetheless, the passage in question does appear to have been read closely in an Irish milieu. Diomedes here unusually refers to the dialects by their Greek names (Ἰάς, Δωρίς, Ἀτθίς, Αἰολίς),[33] and this appears to be the source for Eriugena in his commentary on Martianus Capella:[34]

> *PRAE SE FERENTES: id est unusquisque ferebat signum suae linguae. Omnis enim lingua suum signum habet apud Grecos; Atis habet suum, Doris suum, Eoles suum, Ias suum, Coene suum.*
>
> 'CARRYING BEFORE THEM: That is, each of them carried the symbol of their own language. For every dialect in Greek has its own symbol: Attic has its own, Doric its own, Aeolic its own, Ionic its own, koine its own.'

Scraps of information of a more specific nature can be found scattered throughout the corpus of Latin grammars. Charisius, for example, cites τοῦ Ἀγρίππα ('of Agrippa') as an Attic variant of τοῦ Ἀγρίππου, in his discussion of Greek declension in Latin.[35] Diomedes elsewhere discusses the dual number as a special category of Greek grammar not found in Latin, and notes the fluctuation of dual and plural forms in Attic and in Homer.[36] However, by far the most common focus for discussion of Greek dialect is the Greek letter digamma (ϝ). Donatus, with typical economy, mentions digamma merely as a name for the Latin semivowel [w] represented in writing as *u* before another *u*—his examples are *seruus, uulgus*.[37] But other grammarians supply the additional information that

[32] Donatus, *Ars maior* III (ed. Holtz (1981), 653–74).

[33] I have not found any other use of the term *Ias* (for Ἰάς) in Latin sources.

[34] John Scotus Eriugena, *Annotationes in Marcianum* 213.17 (ed. Lutz (1939), 110.1–3; the translation is mine). It is probably coincidental that the first three dialects mentioned by Eriugena correspond to those listed in OM, and in the same order.

[35] Charisius, *Ars grammatica* I (ed. Barwick (1925), 84.14–18; the translation is mine); see Buck (1955), 87–8 (§105.2).

[36] Diomedes, *Ars grammatica* (*GL* i 334–5) (if I understand this passage correctly).

[37] He compares this to *u* in the sequence *qu-* plus vowel; Donatus, *Ars maior* I 2 (Holtz (1981), 604.5–7).

digamma is associated specifically with Aeolic Greek.[38] The Donatus commentaries attributed to Sergius (or Servius), *De littera*, etc. (on *Ars maior*, book I) and *Explanationes in artes Donati*, provide some more detailed discussion.[39] Sergius notes that Aeolic digamma gives words a certain 'thick' pronunciation and can be subtracted without loss of sense.[40] He illustrates this with the by-form *Velena/Elena*, but castigates Donatus for his example *uulgus*, for which no corresponding form ***ulgus* exists:[41]

> *est autem [haec] digammos dicta Graecorum <lingua>, quod character eius ex duabus gammis fit. Aeolenses enim Graeci quibusdam sermonibus, ut pinguescant, istam digammon adponunt, ut pro Elena dicant Velena. sed hic Donatus arguitur, quod apud Graecos digammos hanc legem habet, ut u detracta nihil absit nomini, ut si de Velena tollamus digammon, remanet tamen integrum nomen, ut Elena; his uero nominibus si detrahatur u, integrum deperit nomen, ut si de uulgus tollamus unum u et remaneat ulgus, quod non dicitur.*

> 'This is called digamma in the Greek language, because its shape comes from two gammas. The Aeolian Greeks add digamma on to certain words so that they acquire a 'thick' pronunication, as when they say *Velena* for *Elena*. But here Donatus posits, because in Greek digamma has this rule, that a noun still remains intact after *u* is taken away, just as if we were to take digamma from *Velena* to make *Elena*; but if *u* is taken away from these nouns [sc. *seruus, uulgus*], the intact noun is undone, as though we took one *u* from *uulgus* leaving *ulgus*, which is not said.'

[38] For example, Cledonius, *Ars grammatica* (*GL* v 27.21): *hoc ab Aeolicis processit*; Pompeius, *Commentum artis Donati* (*GL* v 105.3–4): *apud istos Aeolicos est una littera quae appellatur digammos, quasi duo gamma superposita.*

[39] Sergius, *De littera, de syllaba, de pedibus, de accentibus, de distinctione* (*GL* iv 475–85); Sergius, *Explanationes in artes Donati* (*GL* iv 486–565). See Law (1982), 17; Holtz (1981), 233–4.

[40] 'Thick' is my translation for *pinguis* and related words (e.g. *pinguesco*), which occur here. The Greek categories of stop consonant were ψιλή ('bare') (voiceless unaspirated, π τ κ), δασεῖα ('hairy, thick') (voiceless aspirated, φ θ χ), μέση ('middle') (voiced unaspirated, β δ γ). In Latin, *tenuis* and *media* correspond to the first and last of these; *pinguis* ('fatty, rich, thick') seems to be a rendering of the second, leaving *aspiratio* to refer exclusively to the sound of the letter *h*. It may be, therefore, that the author associated digamma with an aspirated sound like [w^h] or [hw]; alternatively, the spelling *benetos* in the *Expanationes* passage below suggests [β].

[41] Sergius, *De littera, de syllaba, de pedibus, de accentibus, de distinctione* (*GL* iv 476.14–22; the translation is mine).

The *Explanationes* provide more detail still. This passage below gives information on the relationship of Aeolic to other dialects, noting that digamma in Aeolic corresponds to aspiration in other dialects word-initially, and is omitted in other positions.[42] It tells us that initial aspiration in Greek was originally marked with a half-*H*: this is the archaic form of the Greek *spiritus asper* (ʿ), originally a modification of the Greek letter eta (H) with the right vertical stroke omitted. The observation that digamma corresponds to aspiration word-initially is historically broadly true, although the digamma is not in fact limited to Aeolic, but occurs in all dialects apart from Attic-Ionic and Lesbian.[43] This passage also criticizes Donatus for comparing the Greek phenomenon to Latin, and again specifically for his example *uulgus*, though on slightly different grounds to those above. If his analogy between digamma and Latin consonantal *u* were to hold, it is argued, we should expect to find in Latin a similar variation between *u*- and *h*-, and therefore a Latin by-form ***hulgus*.

> *nam Graeci [Aeoli] hunc crassiorem sonum, <quem> facit u littera, cum consonans est, non habent, sed pro Venetis Henetos dicunt; Daos dicunt, quos nos Dauos dicimus. ergo apud nos hoc facit u littera, quod facit apud Aeolicos digammos. illi scribunt Enetos et superinponunt digammon, quae est tali figura, quali est apud nos F, et pronuntiant benetos, quo modo et in adspiratione cum nos habemus h, illi aliud signum [significationis] habent, cuius figura talis est, ut est dimidium H. et apud Latinos tunc quidem efficit u littera, quod apud Graecos digammos, quando loco ponitur consonantis. Donatus unam rem ueram posuit, unam falsam. ueram praeposuit, cum huius litterae redderet rationem: dixit enim tunc est digammos u, cum illic ponitur loco consonantis, ubi erat adspiratio, et falsa subiecit exempla: uulgus ait et uulnus, quasi possit dici hulgus et hulnus. debuit ergo dicere Venetos, quoniam detracta u facit Henetos, et Dauus.*

42 Sergius, *Explanationes in artes Donati* I (*GL* iv 521.13–26). For this reason, I take the first mention of Aeolians in the text as an error. *Davos* or *Davus* is a stereotypical slave's name in Roman comedy, taken over from Greek Δᾶϝος (Attic-Ionic Δᾶος). Its mention at the end seems incoherent (perhaps originally a gloss?), as the completed analogy would require an impossible form *Dahus* (like *Henetos* for *Venetos*).

43 See, e.g., Sihler (1995), 182–4 (§§187–188). Pompeius' commentary on Donatus draws on both of these passages, though without discussing Greek aspiration (*GL* v 105.3–29). I have not been able to locate an ancient grammatical source which states that the form of Latin *F* derives from digamma. Had this been merely assumed, it would be surprising not to find some acknowledgement of the fact that the sound values of digamma [w] and Latin *f* were quite different. Perhaps, in that case, the formal similarity was regarded as coincidental?

'For the Greeks do not have this harsher (*crassior*) sound which the letter *u* makes when it is a consonant, but they say *Heneti* for *Veneti*. They call *Daus* those men we call *Dauus*. So for us this letter *u* makes the sound which digamma makes for the Aeolians. They write *Eneti* and insert digamma before it (which has the same shape as *F* for us) and pronounce it *beneti*; in the same way as we have *h* for aspiration, they have another sign whose shape is the same as half-*H*. And then in Latin the letter *u* does what digamma does in Greek when it is put in place of a consonant. Donatus made one true and one false statement. He made a true statement when he gave the function of the letter: he said indeed that digamma is *u* when it is put in place of a consonant, where there used to be aspiration. But he supplied bad examples: he said *uulgus* and *uulnus*, as though you could say *hulgus* and *hulnus*. He ought to have said *Veneti*, since with the *V* taken away it makes *Heneti*, and [to have said] *Dauus*.'

Whereas the first of these two passages supplied some information about a characteristic feature of Aeolic (that it employed the letter digamma, having a similar pronunciation to Latin consonantal *u*), the latter expands on this to reveal something about the relationship of Aeolic to other Greek dialects (they have a sound corresponding to Latin *h* occurring in the same place, and written with a special half-*H* sign in Greek). Notably, however, the purpose of both passages is not to elaborate on Greek dialects *per se*, but only to supply such information as may serve as comparanda for Latin descriptive grammar. The scope is therefore very restricted, and for that reason very little dialectal information is to be found.

If the encounters with Greek dialects in grammatical sources discussed so far are extremely limited, we find a somewhat broader engagement in two other works that draw explicitly on the Greek grammatical tradition, and on Apollonius Dyscolus in particular. The first is the treatise *De uerborum Graeci Latinique differentiis uel societatibus* by Macrobius (early 5th century), no longer fully extant but excerpted by a Iohannes identified as John Scotus (Eriugena) in Paris, Bibliothèque nationale de France, Lat. 7186 (saec. IX$^{2/2}$).[44] The focus of the tract is scholarly rather than didactic, and accordingly Macrobius makes a number of passing references to Greek dialects:[45]

[44] Macrobius, *De differentiis et societatibus Graeci Latinique verbi* (ed. de Paolis (1990); see xix–xxviii on sources). Although Macrobius' title indicates that he aimed to produce a comparative study, Eriugena's excerpts are focused almost exclusively on the Greek language.

[45] I give some linguistic commentary in passing, drawing mainly on Buck (1955) and Sihler (1995).

Attic: 1) Macrobius tells us that εἰκάζω ('I liken to') has the unusual Attic imperfect ᾔκαζον (for εἴκαζον elsewhere).[46] 2) Imperfects ἐβουλόμην ('I was wishing') and ἐδυνάμην ('I was able') have double-augment forms ἠβουλόμην and ἠδυνάμην according to *Attica licentia*.[47] 3) The future perfect, e.g. πεποιήσομαι ('I will have done'), γεγράψομαι ('I will have written'), is called 'Attic' (presumably regarded as an Attic innovation).[48]
Ionic: Macrobius claims that the variation between aspirated and unaspirated initial consonants (e.g. τρέφω ('I nurture'), fut. θρέψω, or conversely θρίξ ('hair'), gen. τριχός) shows the influence of Ionic pronunciation, as they were inclined to add or remove aspiration as they pleased.[49]
Doric: 1) Future forms π<ε>ινάσω ('I will be hungry') and διψάσω ('I will be thirsty') (for πεινήσω, διψήσω).[50] 2) Doric future formation in -σέω.[51] 3) A distinction of accent separates imperfect ἔτρεχον ('I was running') from ἐτρέχον ('they were running') where other dialects have ambiguous ἔτρεχον.[52] 4) Doric infinitive ὁρῆν ('to see, look') (for Attic ὁρᾶν).[53] **Aeolic:** Digamma is Aeolic.[54]
Misc. (all comments on 'moveable' *nu*): In Aeolic final -α in λεγόμεθα ('we discuss') and similar words becomes -ε and attracts ('moveable')

[46] Macrobius, *De differentiis et societatibus Graeci Latinique verbi* (de Paolis (1990), 41.3–4); supported in Liddell and Scott (1940), *s.v.*

[47] Macrobius, *De differentiis et societatibus Graeci Latinique verbi* (de Paolis (1990), 43.19–22); see Sihler (1995), 486 (§442.1).

[48] Macrobius, *De differentiis et societatibus Graeci Latinique verbi* (de Paolis (1990), 73.21–24). I have not found any corroboration of this as a specifically Attic feature (cf. e.g. Sihler (1995), 579 (§521)).

[49] Macrobius, *De differentiis et societatibus Graeci Latinique verbi* (de Paolis (1990), 63.3–6): *quibus libido est aspirationem modo addere, modo demere*. What seemed apparently arbitrary to Macrobius is now explained as Grassmann's law, by which the first of two originally voiced aspirated stops is dissimilated (Sihler (1995), 142–4 (§138)). Perhaps his remark is connected to the early loss of initial aspiration in Ionic (see Buck (1955), 52–3 (§57)).

[50] Macrobius, *De differentiis et societatibus Graeci Latinique verbi* (de Paolis (1990), 61.4–6); presumably preserving inherited ᾱ, which changed to η in Attic-Ionic.

[51] Macrobius, *De differentiis et societatibus Graeci Latinique verbi* (de Paolis (1990), 67.8–11); see Buck (1955), 115 (§141).

[52] Macrobius, *De differentiis et societatibus Graeci Latinique verbi* (de Paolis (1990), 93.4–8); see Buck (1995), 85 (§103).

[53] Macrobius, *De differentiis et societatibus Graeci Latinique verbi* (de Paolis (1990), 129.18–20); both from ὁράειν; see Buck (1995), 37 (§41.1).

[54] Macrobius, *De differentiis et societatibus Graeci Latinique verbi* (de Paolis (1990), 51.22–52.2).

ν.[55] In Doric the reverse occurs (-εν becomes -α). Likewise, Ionic makes pluperfect ᾔδειν ('I had known') into ᾔδεα.[56]

The dialectal information available in Macrobius would represent a very significant advance, in quantitative terms at least, on that found in the Donatus commentary tradition. The context here is comparative, as before, but now the languages are treated more on equal terms: Macrobius does not limit himself to those aspects of Greek that answer to Latin, but presents a fuller exposition of both languages, aiming to record their similarities systematically.[57] Whereas Donatus was fundamentally a pedagogical text, the scope of Macrobius' discussion is less narrowly practical and more exploratory. This explains why he records many more dialectal forms. Nonetheless, no more than for the Donatus commentaries above, the forms he records in passing are not representative of Greek dialects in general, but merely happen to be relevant to the discussion at hand.

Similarly embedded in the Greek grammatical tradition is Priscian, who declares in the preface to his *magnum opus* that he sets out to write a new Latin grammar based on Greek models.[58] Priscian's debt is especially clear in the final two books (17–18) of the *Institutiones* (*c.*AD 527), where he provides the first account of Latin syntax, after Apollonius' treatise on Greek syntax.[59] While the availability in Ireland of Macrobius is uncertain,[60] the St Gall manuscript of Priscian has copious glosses in Old Irish, some dating perhaps to the 7th century,[61] and it is generally

[55] Macrobius, *De differentiis et societatibus Graeci Latinique verbi* (de Paolis (1990), 91.9–3).

[56] Macrobius, *De differentiis et societatibus Graeci Latinique verbi* (de Paolis (1990), 91.13–15). Sihler (1995), 578–9 (§520), treats the Ionic form as original, the -ειν ending particular to later Attic.

[57] That is, in the original text, as far as we can tell. Eriugena was clearly mining Macrobius as a source for Greek grammar, and so his abridgement omits much of the discussion on Latin.

[58] Priscian, *Institutiones grammaticae* preface (*GL* ii 1.8–10; the translation is mine): *quid enim Herodiani artibus certius, quid Apollonii scrupulosis quaestionibus enucleatius possit inueniri?* ('What could be more reliable than the works of Herodian? What could be found to be more revealing than the exhaustive enquiries of Apollonius?')

[59] The first of Priscian's two books on syntax is now translated in Baratin et al. (2010).

[60] See Law (1982), 28.

[61] St Gall, Stiftsbibliothek, 904 (AD 851); images available online at http://www.e-codices.unifr.ch/en/list/one/csg/0904. On the date of the manuscript see Ó Néill (2000); on the date of the glosses see Strachan (1903); Lambert (1996).

held that it was written in Ireland.[62] Priscian frequently provides a comparative analysis of Latin and Greek, citing Greek dialectal forms where these offer closer analogies.[63]

Attic: Books 1–16: 1) Attic has -ττ- for -σσ- elsewhere.[64] 2) The diphthong οι in Attic is shortened before η, as reflected in Latin *poēta* from Greek ποιητής.[65] 3) Latin shortens final -ως in Greek words to *-us*, just as Attic has Ἀνδρόγεος for Ἀνδρόγεως.[66] 4) The form *Androgeo* in *Aeneid* VI 20 is an Attic genitive.[67] 5) Attic has a future perfect τετύψομαι ('I will have struck').[68] 6) It adds emphatic -γε to pronouns ἔγωγε ('I'), ἔμοιγε ('to me').[69] Books 17–18: Attic is extremely prominent in Priscian's section on syntax: there are three references in book 17, but 147 in the final book 18.

Ionic: Like Macrobius, Priscian cites Ionic in relation to aspiration in a sequence of consonants, citing Ionic κύθρα for χύτρα ('pot') and ἐνθαῦτα for ἐνταῦθα ('here') as a parallel for Latin *triumphus* = θρίαμβος.[70]

Doric: 1) Latin pronouns *tu* and *te* resemble Doric τύ and τέ rather than σύ and σέ in other dialects.[71] 2) Latin has *Aiax* from Αἴας

[62] All of the glosses are published at www.stgallpriscian.ie, incorporating the earlier, partial edition of Hofman (1996). On its origin, see Hofman (2000), 260–2, and, for a contrary position, Dumville (1997), 23–7, 34–6, 51–2.

[63] On Greek in Priscian, see now Conduché (2012), especially 259–99 on dialectology. Regrettably, as this thesis came to my attention directly before submitting this article, I was unable to incorporate its analysis here.

[64] Priscian, *Institutiones grammaticae* I 31 (*GL* ii 24.11); see Buck (1955), 69–70 (§81).

[65] Priscian, *Institutiones grammaticae* I 53 (*GL* ii 40.1–2); see Buck (1955), 32 (§31).

[66] Priscian, *Institutiones grammaticae* VI 13 (*GL* ii 255.12–13). The latter in fact, and not the former, would appear to be characteristic of 'Attic declension'; see Sihler (1995), 256 (§259.1a).

[67] Priscian, *Institutiones grammaticae* VII 13 (*GL* ii 297.5–6); see previous note on Attic declension.

[68] Priscian, *Institutiones grammaticae* VIII 38 (*GL* ii 405.15–17); compare Macrobius above on Attic future perfects.

[69] Priscian, *Institutiones grammaticae* XII 25 (*GL* ii 592.12–15); hardly Attic?

[70] Priscian, *Institutiones grammaticae* VIII 98 (*GL* ii 446.12–17). The last word was discussed by several Greek grammarians; see Liddell and Scott (1940), *s.v.*

[71] Priscian, *Institutiones grammaticae* I 31 (*GL* ii 24.10); see Buck (1955), 97–8 (§118).

('Ajax'), just as Doric has ὄρνιξ for ὄρνις ('bird').[72] 3) Greek ει is normally *ī* in Latin, though *Typhoëa* ('Typhoean') (Τυφωεῖα) in *Aeneid* I 665 shows Doric -ε- for -ει-.[73] 4) Doric sometimes has αι for ει.[74] 5) ου becomes ω in Doric and Aeolic (e.g. βῶς for βοῦς).[75] 6) -ευς becomes -ης in Doric and hence Latin: Ἀχιλλεύς *Achillēs*, Οὐλιξεύς *Vlixēs*, etc.[76] 7) Doric has the by-forms ἐμοῦς for ἐμοῦ ('of me'), σοῦς for σοῦ ('of you'), οὗς for οὗ ('of him').[77]

Aeolic: In common with other Latin grammarians, Priscian characterizes digamma as Aeolic.[78] He notes that it is found in place of aspiration in other dialects,[79] and that it sometimes changes to *b*.[80] Latinists 'follow the Aeolians' by changing *o* to *e* (e.g. *pes* for πός = πούς ('foot')),[81] or by replacing various vowels with short *u*,[82] or long vowels with *ae*,[83] or in the treatment of diphthongs,[84] or of ει,[85] or in marking hiatus with *u*.[86] There are also similarities between Latin and Aeolic in the accentuation of prepositions.[87]

72 Priscian, *Institutiones grammaticae* I 41 (*GL* ii 32.16); see Buck (1955), 116 (§142a).

73 Priscian, *Institutiones grammaticae* I 54 (*GL* ii 41.6–8); see perhaps Buck (1955), 31 (§28)?

74 Priscian, *Institutiones grammaticae* II 49 (*GL* ii 74.17–21); see Buck (1955), 105 (§134.1).

75 Priscian, *Institutiones grammaticae* VI 69 (*GL* ii 253.20–21); see Buck (1955), 34 (§37.1).

76 Priscian, *Institutiones grammaticae* VI 92 (*GL* ii 276.4); see perhaps Buck (1955), 95 (§111.4)?

77 Priscian, *Institutiones grammaticae* XIII 4 (*GL* iii 2.30–3.1); see Buck (1955), 97 (§118.3).

78 Priscian, *Institutiones grammaticae* I 6, 12, 20–21, 22, 36 (*GL* ii 7.17–18, 11.5–6, 15.1–16, 16.19, 35.13–17).

79 Priscian, *Institutiones grammaticae* I 22, 22; XIII 25 (*GL* ii 17.6–9; iii 16.18–20).

80 Priscian, *Institutiones grammaticae* I 23, 25 (*GL* ii 18.5–7, 19.18–20), the source for OM160, discussed p 483 above. See Buck (1955), 47, 50–2 (§§51, 55).

81 Priscian, *Institutiones grammaticae* I 34 (*GL* ii 26.17–20).

82 Priscian, *Institutiones grammaticae* I 36 (*GL* ii 27.24–28.4, with a mention of υ in Aeolic metre at 28.14–16).

83 Priscian, *Institutiones grammaticae* I 51 (*GL* ii 38.4–6).

84 Priscian, *Institutiones grammaticae* I 53 (*GL* ii 39.19–22); cf. Priscian's *Partitiones* (ed. Passalacqua (1999), 58.6–8).

85 Priscian, *Institutiones grammaticae* I 54; II 48 (*GL* ii 40.10–12, 74.3–4).

86 Priscian, *Institutiones grammaticae* VI 69 (*GL* ii 253.16–20); citing *ouis* ('sheep') compared to Aeolic ὄϝις and other examples.

87 Priscian, *Institutiones grammaticae* XIV 6 (*GL* iii 27.5–8,16–20).

The aims of Priscian's work in many ways echo those outlined for Macrobius above. Although ostensibly writing a grammar of Latin, his comparative focus is emphasized right from the beginning. Like Macrobius, Priscian's objectives are scholarly and discursive rather than narrowly didactic, and the fact that he treats Latin grammar in its entirety (unlike Macrobius, who focuses on the verb), and writes at considerable length, gives him ample scope to include discussion of Greek dialectal forms in passing. But once again we must recognise the absence of any systematic presentation of dialects, which ultimately are used to serve an argument on comparative grammar. Greek dialectal forms which do not relate to this topic, however significant they may be for Greek dialectology as a whole, are passed over.

The dialect references in Priscian collected above are subject to frequent glosses in the St Gall manuscript, showing at least that those sections were closely read by Irish scholars. Some of the glosses indicate that Latin terms for Greek dialects may have been assimilated into Irish. Where Priscian notes *Androgeo Virgilius in VI genetiuum posuit Atticum*, the glossator clarifies *Atticum* as meaning *fo rīaguil n-atacdai* ('according to the Attic rule'). This clarifies to the reader that the name *Androgeo* is to be understood as an Atticism, having a genitive ending unusual in Latin. (The gloss occurs over the word *Atticum* perhaps to avoid confusing the dialect name here with the familiar personal name Atticus.[88]) When Priscian discusses the Greek future perfect, another gloss emphasizes *.i. la atacu insin* ('that belongs to Attic [speakers]').[89] The word *Dorice* is once glossed *in doracdid insin* ('that is, in the Doric fashion'), presumably clarifying the word as an adverb.[90] *Aeolica* (MS *Eolica*) is similarly glossed *eolensta*,[91] and the phrase *solent Aeolis* (MS *Eolis*) *sequentes uel in digamma* [...] *conuertere aspirationem* is translated

[88] Priscian, *Institutiones grammaticae* VII 13 (*GL* ii 297.5); Sg. 118a37 r (= *Thes.* 118a2). (I use Sg. to refer to the online edition at www.stgallpriscian.ie, incorporating Hofman (1996). This refers to the page, column, and line on which the gloss occurs, with an additional letter tracking the sequence of glosses on each page. *Thes.* refers to the standard edition of Old Irish glosses in Stokes and Strachan (1901–3), cited by page and column, with a number sequencing Irish glosses only.)

[89] Priscian, *Institutiones grammaticae* VIII 38 (*GL* ii 405.17); Sg. 147a35 t (= *Thes.* 147a8).

[90] Priscian, *Institutiones grammaticae* XIII 4 (*GL* iii 3.1); Sg. 204b30 x (= *Thes.* 204b9).

[91] Priscian, *Institutiones grammaticae* II 35 (*GL* ii 65.16); Sg. 31b25 ss (= *Thes.* 31b18). Hofman (1996), ii 154, suggests that this gloss may 'distinguish the adj. 'eolica' from the frequently occurring subst. 'eoles''.

air do-soat eoldai tinfed in digaim ('for the Aeolians convert aspiration into digamma').[92] According to *DIL s.vv. Atacdae, Doracdid, eolda, eolensta*, these Irish loanwords are either *hapax legomena* or very rare, and we may therefore infer that they were either once-off coinages (nonce words) or part of a technical jargon used by scholars with specialist interests. By contrast, the Irish term *digaimm* for *digamma* occurs nine times throughout the glosses, suggesting that this word had a broader currency.[93] It probably reflects a more general awareness of the Greek letter name deriving from the tradition of elementary Latin instruction, where Donatus remained the key text.

One of the marginal sigla on the St Gall Priscian that remains to be explained fully is the symbol Γ with suspension mark overhead, presumably representing the Greek letter gamma.[94] This occurs at least 13 times in the manuscript, and was interpreted by Hofman in his edition as a suspension for Latin *graeca*.[95] We may well question why so *few* occurrences of this, given the enormous quantity of Greek material in the text, and a common thread is indeed hard to divine. It may be significant that some of these mark passages where Greek dialects are discussed. For example, a section where Priscian remarks on correspondences between *s* and *ss* in various words in Latin, Attic, and Doric is bookended by two Γ sigla with additional linking marks against each line.[96] Priscian in this passage says that the Latin pronoun *tu* is closer to Doric τύ than the σύ of other dialects, a statement that could equally apply to the Irish cognate *tú*. On the facing page, another pair of linked Γ marks is found against notes on correspondences between Latin and Aeolic in respect

[92] Priscian, *Institutiones grammaticae* XIII 25 (*GL* iii 16.19–20); Sg. 209b8 m (= *Thes.* 209b8). The sense of the Latin may not have been clear, to judge from grammatical glosses identifying the case forms of *Eolis* (*accusativus*, Sg. 209b8 k) and *sequentes* (nom. *latini*, Sg. 209b8 l).

[93] Sg. 5b27 z (= *Thes.* 5b7), 7b31 ee (= *Thes.* 7b16), 7b33 ii (= *Thes.* 7b17), 7b34 mm (= *Thes.* 7b18), 9b14 bb (= *Thes.* 9b10), 14a15 m (= *Thes.* 14a6), 17a23 l (= *Thes.* 17a3a), 17a31 r (= *Thes.* 17a5), 209b8 m (= *Thes.* 209b8). See Russell (2012).

[94] Greek letters frequently do service for Latin elsewhere, apparently in an arbitrary way. See, for example, the rubrics *de λιττερα* (St Gall, Stiftsbibliothek, 904, 3a), *expλïcvιτ λïβer prï/μvs de λιττερα* (St Gall, Stiftsbibliothek, 904, 20b), *INcipiτ λiβeρ .ii. de syλλaβa* (St Gall, Stiftsbibliothek, 904, 21a).

[95] Sg. 12a6 g, 13b26 w, 13b31 y, 13b36 z, 14a13 h, 14a22 p, 67b42 aa, 70a1 b, 75a3 d, 101a25 k, 146b10 n, 187b41, 219b13 c.

[96] Priscian, *Institutiones grammaticae* I 31 (*GL* ii 24.8–13); St Gall, Stiftsbibliothek, 904, 12a1–6.

of short *u*.[97] Although not all of the passages marked with Γ seem to discuss dialects, its occurrence on the passages mentioned above may indicate that dialect was one particular topic of focus.

The material collected above would indicate that a very small amount of information relating to Greek dialects could have been found throughout the Latin grammatical tradition (relating almost entirely to the letter *digamma*), supplemented substantially by Macrobius on the Greek and Latin verbs and Priscian's *Institutiones*. Although the former may not have been available in Ireland (notwithstanding it being used by Eriugena on the Continent), the latter was clearly studied intensively. In general, the information on dialects contained in these tracts is presented in an unstructured and often parenthetical way, and furthermore limits itself to material deemed relevant for the comparative study of Latin and Greek. For that reason, a modern reader who expected to find some elementary information on Greek dialects would be surprised to find no mention of some of the more obvious dialectal differences—Attic-Ionic η for ᾱ in other dialects, for example.[98] But the practical utility of the information available is scarcely the point. Even a comprehensive manual of dialectal features would hardly have been of much use given the lack of more basic resources for the study of the Greek language, its often corrupt state in the manuscripts, and the fact that very few continuous literary texts were available to study. We must conclude, therefore, that the interest displayed in Greek dialects was fundamentally of a scholarly nature and in the spirit of pursuing knowledge for its own sake. This is significant for how we view the scope and focus of the early Irish intellectual tradition.

Cultural significance of Greek dialects: Rome

Priscian is particularly notable for emphasizing a direct dependence of Latin on Aeolic, repeatedly employing the verb *sequi* ('to follow') in this regard: *in quo Aeolis sequimur*,[99] *Aeolis secuti hoc facimus*,[100] *quamquam antiqui Romanorum Aeolis sequentes*,[101] *in quo Aeolis*

[97] Priscian, *Institutiones grammaticae* I 36 (*GL* ii 27.24–28.4); St Gall, Stiftsbibliothek, 904, 13b26–31.

[98] See e.g. Horrocks (2010), 24–6, for a convenient list.

[99] Priscian, *Institutiones grammaticae* I 34 (*GL* ii 26.19).

[100] Priscian, *Institutiones grammaticae* I 36 (*GL* ii 27.25).

[101] Priscian, *Institutiones grammaticae* I 46 (*GL* ii 35.15).

sequimur,[102] *in hoc quoque Aeolis sequimur,*[103] *et in priore sequimur Aeolis,*[104] *in nominatiuo quoque* [...] *illos sequimur,*[105] *solent Aeolis sequentes.*[106] Priscian's assertion that Latin follows Aeolic is congruent with a tradition going back at least to Varro's *De lingua latina*, completed probably before 43 BC. Much like OM later does for Irish, Varro sets out of hundred of etymologies for Latin words, deriving very many from Greek.[107] From a modern viewpoint, these can be categorized into three groups. First, there are correspondences between Latin and Greek that reflect a shared linguistic inheritance from Indo-European.[108] Second, some of Varro's associations reflect genuine borrowings from Greek into Latin.[109] And third, there are pairs which are phonetically similar, but superficially so: in other words, for which modern linguistics does not support any historical relationship.[110] Varro does not set out his etymological principles in the extant parts of his text,[111] but in any case his assumptions about the Greek origins of Latin words would have been reasonably congruent with other writers of the same period.[112]

[102] Priscian, *Institutiones grammaticae* I 51 (*GL* ii 38.6–7).

[103] Priscian, *Institutiones grammaticae* I 53 (*GL* ii 39.21).

[104] Priscian, *Institutiones grammaticae* I 54 (*GL* ii 40.11).

[105] Priscian, *Institutiones grammaticae* I 69 (*GL* ii 253.19–20).

[106] *GL* iii 16.19. On Aeolism in Priscian, see also Maltby (2009), 242–4.

[107] A electronic search for words beginning *graec-* in Varro's *De lingua latina* in the Cross Database Searchtool (CDS) available at clt.brepolis.net yields an indicative figure of 119.

[108] E.g. Varro's comparison, in *De lingua latina*, of Latin *ager* ('field') and Greek ἀγρός (V 34; ed. Kent (1938), i 32); *sus*/ὗς ('swine'), *bos*/βοῦς ('cow'), *taurus*/ταῦρος ('bull'), *ovis*/ὄϊς ('sheep') (V 96; Kent (1938), i 92); *domus* 'house'/πρόδομος ('front room') (V 160; Kent (1938), i 150); *dies* ('day')/Δία ('Zeus') (VI 4; Kent (1938), i 174); *nox*/νύξ ('night'), *uesper*/ἑσπέρα ('evening') (VI 6; Kent (1938), i 178); *menses*/μῆνες ('months') (VI 10; Kent (1938), i 182); *aevum*/αἰων ('period of time') (VI 11; Kent (1938), i 182); *dico* ('I say')/δεικνύω ('I show') (VI 61; Kent (1938), i 228); etc.

[109] E.g. Varro, *De lingua latina* V 78 (Kent (1938), i 74–6): *polypus, hippopotamios* [*sic*], *crocodilos* from πολύπους, ἱπποπόταμος, κροκόδειλος, etc.

[110] E.g. Varro, *De lingua latina* V 182 (Kent (1938), i 168): *stips* ('donation')/στοιβή ('pile'); Varro, *De lingua latina* VI 96 (Kent (1938), i 262): *errare* ('to stray')/ἔρρειν ('to perish'), *stringere* ('to scrape')/στλεγγίς ('scraper'); etc. Although I have not quantified all the examples, the first two categories seem by far the largest.

[111] See Amsler (1989), 24–31. It is possible that books 2–4 of *De lingua latina*, which may originally have been a separate treatise on etymology, did outline some formal principles, but these are now lost.

[112] See Stevens (2007), 121–7.

Occasionally, Varro draws Latin etymologies from Greek dialects specifically. He offers the suggestion (among others) that Latin *ver* ('spring') could derive from Ionic ἤρ (ἔαρ in other dialects) ('spring').[113] He also mentions also that *orchitis*, a kind of olive, derives from Attic ὄρχις μορία ('the sacred olive berry').[114] But Aeolic receives most attention:[115]

Is si quamvis deorsum in terra, unde sumi pote, puteus; nisi potius quod Aeolis dicebant ut πύταμον sic πύτεον a potu, non ut nunc φρέαρ.

'If [this moisture] is in the ground no matter how far down, in a place from which it *pote* 'can' be taken, it is a *puteus* 'well'; unless rather because the Aeolians used to say, like πύταμος [for ποταμός 'river'], so also πύτεος 'well' [for ποτέος 'drinkable'], from *potus* 'act of drinking', and not φρέαρ 'well' as they do now.'[116]

Lepus, quod Sicu<li, ut Aeo >lis quidam Graeci, dicunt λέποριν: a Roma quod orti Siculi, ut annales veteres nostri dicunt, fortasse hinc illuc tulerunt et hic reliquerunt id nomen.

'*Lepus* 'hare', because the Sicilians, like certain Aeolian Greeks, say λέπορις. Inasmuch as the Sicilians originated from Rome, as our old *Annals* say, perhaps they carried the word from here to Sicily, but also left it here behind them.'[117]

Malum, quod Graeci Aeolis dicunt μᾶλον.

'*Malum* 'apple', because the Aeolian Greeks call it μᾶλον.'[118]

113 Varro, *De lingua latina* VI 9 (Kent (1938), i 180).

114 Varro, *De lingua latina* V 108 (Kent (1938), i 104).

115 I have found no reference to Doric. On Varro's treatment of Aeolic and the conceptual relationship between Latin and Greek, see Garcea and Lomanto (2004), 43–50.

116 Varro, *De lingua latina* V 25 (Kent (1938), i 24–5). Kent's translation here is quite loose and I enclose his expansions in square brackets. Paul Russell points out to me that *nisi potius* looks suspicious taken as 'unless rather', and suggests that the phrase could have originated as a scribe recording a variant on the previous word *puteus*.

117 Varro, *De lingua latina* V 101 (Kent (1938), i 96). Note that the text here is corrupt, and I reproduce Kent's emendation. Liddell and Scott (1940) records λέπορις (*s.v.*) as a word found only in Varro. Dionysius of Halicarnassus, *Antiquitates Romanae* I 22 (ed. Carey (1960), i 68) writes that the Sicels emigrated southwards from the area around Rome. Assuming that the emendation is correct, Varro may imply here that they had already by that time acquired words from the Aeolian dialect.

118 Varro, *De lingua latina* V 102 (Kent (1938), i 96–7).

> *Dos, si nuptiarum causa data; haec Graece δωτίνη: ita enim hoc Siculi. Ab eodem donum: nam Graece ut Aeolis δόνειον, et ut alii δόμα et ut Attici δόσιν.*

> '*Dos* 'dower', if it is given for the purpose of a marriage; this in Greek is δωτίνη, for thus the Sicilians call it. From the same comes *donum* 'gift'; for in Greek it is δόνειον with the Aeolians, and δόμα as others say it, and δόσιν of the Athenians.'[119]

The sources of Varro's dialectal information are not known. He may have relied on Greek grammatical tracts or the *viva voce* teaching of dialectologists active in Rome.[120] There may also have been some familiarity with Greek dialectal forms outside of literary and intellectual circles, among Romans who interacted with citizens of Magna Graecia, for example, historically Ionic or Doric speakers.[121] But from the outset, we can observe that Varro fuses linguistic observation with origin legend, a pattern to be continually repeated. His very first etymology from Greek is immediately associated with Evander, the founding hero of Rome:[122]

> *Terminus* [...] *hoc Graeci quod τέρμονα. Pote vel illinc; Euander enim, qui venit in Palatium, e Graecia Arcas.*

> '*Terminus* 'boundary' [...] this is what the Greeks call τέρμων. Perhaps it comes from that word: for Evander, who came to the Palatine, was an Arcadian from Greece.'

Evander's story is well known from Livy,[123] Dionysius of Halicarnassus,[124] and in particular Virgil, who imbues the hero with a literary persona in *Aeneid* books 8 and 11. A refugee from Arcadia, he gave the Palatine Hill its name (either from Pallanteum in Arcadia or from the name of his son Pallas or variations thereon), instituted the Lupercalia (connected with Arcadian cult of Lycaean Pan) and was associated with the Roman cult of

[119] Varro, *De lingua latina* V 175 (Kent (1938), i 164–5).

[120] E.g. Philoxenus of Alexandria, see Theodorides (1976).

[121] See Weiss (2009), 480, for details.

[122] Varro, *De lingua latina* V 20 (Kent (1938), i 20). The classic study is Bayet (1920); see Cornell (1995), 68–9; Delcourt (2001).

[123] Livy, *Ub urbe condita* I 5, 7 (ed. Ogilvie (1974), 8–9, 10–1). Livy's statement that Evander brought writing to Rome seems to reflect another, possibly earlier, strand of the Latin origin story.

[124] Dionysius of Halicarnassus, *Antiquitates Romanae* I 31–33 (ed. and trans. Carey (1960), i 98–109).

Hercules. As an Arcadian, Evander's dialect would have been categorized, according to the ancient scheme, as Aeolic. See, for example, Strabo:[125]

> ἐλείφθη δ' ἐν τῇ Πελοποννήσῳ τὰ δύο ἔθνη, τό τε Αἰολικὸν καὶ τὸ Δωρικόν. ὅσοι μὲν οὖν ἧττον τοῖς Δωριεῦσιν ἐπεπλέκοντο — καθάπερ συνέβη τοῖς τε Ἀρκάσι καὶ τοῖς Ἠλείοις [...] οὗτοι αἰολιστὶ διελέχθησαν, οἱ δ' ἄλλοι μικτῇ τινι ἐχρήσαντο ἐξ ἀμφοῖν, οἱ μὲν μᾶλλον οἱ δ' ἧττον αἰολίζοντες.
>
> 'and so there were left in the Peloponnesus only the two tribes, the Aeolian and the Dorian. Now all the peoples who had less intercourse with the Dorians — as was the case with the Arcadians and with the Eleians [...] these peoples, I say, spoke the Aeolic dialect, whereas the rest used a sort of mixture of the two, some leaning more to the Aeolic and some less.'

The association of Aeolic and Latin was echoed in Dionysius and subsequently Quintilian:

> Ῥωμαῖοι δὲ φωνὴν μὲν οὔτ' ἄκρως βάρβαρον οὔτ' ἀπηρτισμένως Ἑλλάδα φθέγγονται, μικτὴν δέ τινα ἐξ ἀμφοῖν, ἧς ἐστιν ἡ πλείων Αἰολίς.
>
> 'The language spoken by the Romans is neither utterly barbarous nor absolutely Greek, but a mixture, as it were, of both, the greater part of which is Aeolic.'[126]
>
> *Continet autem in se multam eruditionem, sive ex Graecis orta tractemus, quae sunt plurima praecipueque Aeolica ratione, cui est sermo noster simillimus, declinata.*
>
> '[Etymology] involves much erudition, whether we have to deal with words coming from the Greek, which are very numerous and are chiefly derived from Aeolic (this is the dialect which our language most closely resembles).'[127]

The ideological impetus for these ideas has been variously interpreted. One view would see the Romans' claim to Greek roots as an attempt to appropriate Greece's more prestigious intellectual, literary, and artistic culture. The extent to which the rapacious Roman elite of this period

[125] Strabo, *Geographica* VIII 1.2 (ed. and trans. Jones (1917–33), iv 6–9).

[126] Dionysius of Halicarnassus, *Antiquitates Romanae* I 90 (Cary (1960), i 308–9).

[127] Quintilian, *Institutio oratoria* I 6.31 (Russell (2001), i 174–5).

had a deficit of self-confidence may perhaps be debated.[128] In any case, the arrival of Rome as a new force to be reckoned with in the Hellenistic world and the attested presence of Greek grammarians as slaves and freedmen or travelling teachers in the city provides a background in which Greek thinkers were forced to come to terms with their new masters. The ethnographic and linguistic theorising that took place in Republican Rome, in other words, can be seen as originating not from Romans looking out, but from Greeks looking in. Whatever their origin, such expressions of kinship between Romans and Greeks could have been ideologically expedient in the expanding western power's claims to political legitimacy in the east.[129]

Cultural significance of Greek dialects: Ireland

Various Irish sources dating from around the 7th century AD and after attest to similar preoccupations with reconciling native identity (ethnic difference) to prestigious external cultures, worked out both in kinship narratives and in theories of language origin. *Auraicept na nÉces* ('the Scholars' Handbook') contains one of the best known (and possibly earliest, dated to the late 7th century), taking biblical history as its framework.[130] Fénius Farsaid, a descendant of Japhet, son of Noah, was present at the Tower of Babel at the time of the division of languages. In the aftermath, Fénius was charged by 'the school' (*in scol*) to synthesize a new language from 'what was best then of every language and what was widest and finest',[131] and he gave this new tongue to his relative Goídel, from whom the Irish language (*Goídelc*) took its name.[132]

[128] Farrell (2001), 28–51, undermines the literary topos that the Latin language was inferior to Greek.

[129] See Erskine (2001).

[130] The earliest 'canonical part' of *Auraicept na nÉces* is ed. and trans. in Ahlqvist (1982), 47–53; the fuller commentary in Calder (1917).

[131] *Auraicept na nÉces* 1.13 (Ahlqvist (1982), 48). The translation 'widest' here for *leithiu* seems quaint; *DIL s.v. lethan* 'wide', however, records the extended senses 'more comprehensive, of wider application'. This description of Irish mirrors the etymology for *latinitas* offered by Virgilius Maro Grammaticus, *Epitomae* 1.3 (ed. Polara and Caruso (1979), 4.46–7): *ex latitudine ipsius linguae constat fuisse derivatum*; echoed in Clemens Scottus, *Ars grammatica* (ed. Tolkiehn (1928), 23.8); Murethach, *In Donati artem maiorem* II (ed. by Holtz in CCCM 40, 46.25–47.30). We might also compare Diomedes' remark that Aeolic is *ultra modum copiosa* (*GL* i 440.23, cited in full above p 489).

[132] For recent discussion, see Clarke (2013), 48–51.

In contrast to the simplicity of the narrative just presented, the entirety of genealogies and origin legends represented in the monumental *Lebor Gabála* and some related texts presents a dense thicket of inconsistent and often contradictory detail. Bart Jaski has argued that while the different recensions of the *Lebor Gabála* (compiled *c.*AD 975–1075) present the Irish race as descending from either of Japhet's sons Gomer (ancestor of the Galatians) or Magog (ancestor of the Scythians), there are vestiges in various other sources of an alternative tradition tracing Irish origins to the Greeks.[133] Leaving aside for the moment the prologue of OM, some of the material collected by Jaski may be noted briefly here. The *Auraicept* states that Goídel is a descendant of Agnoman 'of the Greeks'.[134] The short genealogical tract titled *Diluvium factum est* by Jaski identifies Agnoman as a grandson of Javan (Iauan), ancestor of the Ionians, and may also imply that all the island-dwellers of Europe were descendants of Javan.[135] Fénius has been shown by John Carey to have been based on the prototype Fenech in the *Liber Antiquitatum Biblicarum*, the latter also a son of Javan;[136] Fénius, furthermore, is described in passing as Greek in the later *Auraicept* commentary.[137] The Harleian recension of the *Historia Brittonum* (AD 829–830) traces Alanus, an ancestor of all of the European peoples, to Javan.[138] The poem *Can a mbunadus na nGaedel* ('Whence the origin of the Gaels?'), attributed to Máel Muru (†AD 887), declares *do Grecaib dún conar mbunud, conar ndligud* ('we are of the Greeks in our origin, in our laws').[139] Jaski suggests that the early dates of several of these sources suggest that an older tradition of Greek origins for the Irish race was gradually deprecated during the development of the Irish origin tracts, and came to be effaced almost entirely in the more or less canonical tradition of the *Lebor Gabála*.[140]

Jaski also draws attention to some linguistic comparisons with Greek in the *Auraicept*.[141] It states, for example, that ogam has no semivowels

[133] Jaski (2000).

[134] *Auraicept na nÉces* 1.11 (Ahlqvist (1982), 47).

[135] Jaski (2003), 15–23, with a partial edition of the text.

[136] Carey (1990).

[137] *Auraicept na nÉces* 513–516 (Calder (1917), 38); see Jaski (2003), 9–12.

[138] Jaski (2003), 27–31.

[139] *Can a mbunadus na nGaedel* 31–32 (ed. Todd (1848), 220–71: 224); trans. Jaski (2003), 12.

[140] Jaski (2003), 46–7.

[141] Jaski (2003), 10.

just as there are none in Greek.[142] Its five-fold division of Irish mirrors the five dialects of Greek as found, for example, in Isidore. In particular, the description of the fifth variety of Irish (*gnathbérla fogni do cach o ilcenela* ('the common language that serves everyone from many kindreds')) mirrors closely Isidore's definition of koine ('the 'mixed' or 'common', which everyone uses').[143] Jaski further suggests that Ionian may have been omitted from the list of Greek dialects in OM because of the genealogical association between the Irish and Javan, perhaps implying that the Irish and Ionian languages were considered interchangeable.[144]

Whether the genealogical references collected by Jaski amount to a coherent origin narrative or just a tendency to attribute Greekness in a much looser way, they attest to a high degree of prestige associated with Greek culture in early medieval Ireland. OM, however, is quite unlike any of the other sources mentioned here. It does not merely assert a connection between Irish and Greek, it seeks to demonstrate one by enumerating nearly 200 Irish words with putative Greek etymologies. In this respect it is directly analogous to the work of Varro in the Latin tradition. As with Varro, whether linguistic speculation gave rise to genealogical tradition or vice versa is impossible to prove, but it must be noted that in both traditions the linguistic texts are among the earliest extant sources, and so the possibility of language enquiry stimulating origin legend must remain open.

The enumeration of Greek dialects in the preface to OM may have had a merely rhetorical purpose, adding specificity in order to strengthen the claim. We have seen that only one etymology actually justifies it, drawing an Irish word from Aeolic. The source in that case is Priscian and that should not be surprising: firstly because Priscian was certainly the intermediary through which the Aeolism first elaborated in Varro was transmitted, and secondly because his text provides far more scraps of information on Aeolic than any other in circulation. Priscian was clearly the model for a comparative study of Greek—OM does for Irish what he did for Latin—and his method implicitly involved dialectal study. The naming of Greek dialects in OM's preface may therefore be

[142] *Auraicept na nÉces* 1.16 (Ahlqvist (1982), 48). This assertion seems to make no sense, given that semivowels are manifestly abundant in both languages. (Semivowels in the ancient classification correspond to continuants in modern terminology: e.g. *f, l, m, n, r, s, x*.)

[143] *Auraicept na nÉces* 201 (Calder (1917), 16); Isidore, *Etymologiae* IX 1.4–5 (Lindsay (1911), i); cited in full p 487 above.

[144] Jaski (2003), 12.

regarded less as a genealogical assertion, and more a declaration of affiliation to the tradition of Graeco-Roman linguistic scholarship and its methods.

Conclusion

The first question regarding the preface to O'Mulconry's Glossary raised at the start of this piece was concerned with its specification of three dialects (Attic, Doric, Aeolic) as the matrices for Irish, to the exclusion of Ionic and koine. The division of Greek dialects in antiquity was based on genealogical tradition rather than linguistic analysis. Under Athenian influence, the oldest schema (Ionic, Doric, Aeolic) was adapted to make room for Attic. This dialect had originally been categorized as Ionic, and the two continued to be closely associated (see Strabo in relation to dialect, Isidore on genealogy). Another reason for conflating Ionic with Attic, or simply ignoring it altogether, was its almost complete absence from the Latin grammatical tracts that gave any access at all to Greek dialectal features. (The contrast is particularly stark in Priscian, who barely mentions Ionic, but emphasizes the significance of Aeolic in several places and refers to Attic 150 times in his final two books on syntax.) If we take it that OM's list of dialects was informed by a close study of Priscian and not the encyclopaedic tradition represented in Isidore or similar sources, this would also explain the absence of koine: Priscian, with the conservative and antiquarian focus typical of a late antique grammarian, does not mention koine at all.

In relation to the question of the broader significance of Greek and Greek dialects, we have seen that the Irish claim to Greek roots, both linguistic and genealogical, in OM mirrors Roman assertions some seven centuries earlier. The parallels are not superficial. Greek culture had a symbolic prestige for both, and these ideas were developed at a time when each explored their cultural identities as part of a process of accommodation to external influences. The Romans sought to explain their connection to the Hellenistic world, while the Irish wished to reconcile native tradition with the foreign influence of Christian and late antique textual culture. Constructions of cultural affiliation were expressed in terms both genealogical and linguistic, both involving the appropriation of external traditions. The genealogical approach adapted foreign origin stories: the Evander story emanating from Greece and the genealogical schema of the Old Testament, respectively. The linguistic model made use of older grammatical traditions. It is significant that these traditions were Greek in origin. For Varro and his contemporaries, Greek grammatical texts provided both a model to follow and a stimulus for comparison. The fact that Priscian declares his affiliation to the Greek tradition and draws on Greek materials, including the study of dialects, far more than any other Latin grammarian, provided a similar stimulus in Ireland.

Bibliography

Ahlqvist, A. (1982) *The early Irish linguist: an edition of the canonical part of the Auraicept na nÉces*, Helsinki.

Amsler, M. (1989) *Etymology and grammatical discourse in Late Antiquity and the early Middle Ages*, Amsterdam.

Baratin, M. et al. (2010) *Priscien. Grammaire livre XVII — Syntaxe, 1. Texte latin, traduction introduite et annotée par le Groupe Ars Grammatica*, Paris.

Barney, S.A., W.J. Lewis, J.A. Beach, and O. Berghof (2006) *The Etymologies of Isidore of Seville*, Cambridge.

Barwick, K. (1925) *Flavii Sosipatrii Charisii artis grammaticae libri V*, Leipzig.

Bayet, J. (1920) 'Les origines de l'arcadisme romain,' *Mélanges d'archéologie et d'histoire* 38, 63–143.

Berschin, W. (1988) *Greek letters and the Latin Middle Ages: from Jerome to Nicholas of Cusa*, trans. J.C. Frakes, Washington.

Buck, C.D. (1955) *The Greek dialects: grammar, selected inscriptions, glossary*, Chicago.

Calder, G. (1917) *Auraicept na n-Éces, the scholars' primer*, Edinburgh.

Carey, J. (1990) 'The ancestry of Fenius Farsaid,' *Celtica* 21, 104–12.

Cary, E. (1960) *The Roman Antiquities of Dionysius of Halicarnassus, vol. 1.*, Cambridge.

Clarke, M. (2013) 'Linguistic education and literary creativity in medieval Ireland,' *Cahiers de l'Institut de Linguistique et des Sciences du Langage* 38, 39–71.

Conduché, C. (2012) 'Les exemples grecs des *Institutions grammaticales*, héritages et doctrines', unpublished Ph.D. thesis, Université de Lille 3.

Cornell, T. (1995) *The beginnings of Rome: Italy and Rome from the Bronze Age to the Punic Wars (c. 1000–264 B.C.)*, London.

Delcourt, A. (2001) 'Évandre à Rome: réflexions autour de quatre interprétations de la légende,' *Latomus* 60, 829–63.

de Paolis, P. (1990) *De verborum Graeci et Latini differentiis vel societatibus excerpta*, Urbino.

Dickey, E. (2012) *The colloquia of the Hermeneumata Pseudodositheana. Volume 1: Colloquia Monacensia-Einsidlensia, Leidense-Stephani, and Stephani*, Cambridge.

Dionisotti, A.C. (1982) 'From Ausonius' schooldays? A schoolbook and its relatives,' *Journal of Roman Studies* 72, 83–125.

— (1988) 'Greek grammars and dictionaries in Carolingian Europe,' in M.W. Herren, *The sacred nectar of the Greeks: the study of Greek in the west in the early Middle Ages*, London, 1–56.

Dumville, D.N. (1997) *Three men in a boat: scribe, language, and culture in the church of Viking-age Europe*, Cambridge.

Erskine, A. (2003) *Troy between Greece and Rome: local tradition and imperial power*, Oxford.

Farrell, J. (2001) *Latin language and Latin culture from ancient to modern times*, Cambridge.

Fontaine, J. (1959–83) *Isidore de Séville et la culture classique dans l'Espagne wisigothique*, 3 vols., Paris.

Garcea, A. and V. Lomanto (2004) 'Gellius and Fronto on loanwords and literary models,' in L. Holford-Strevens and A. Vardi, *The worlds of Aulus Gellius*, Oxford, 41–64.

Goetz, G. (1888–1923) *Corpus glossariorum latinorum*, 7 vols., Leipzig.

Grosjean, P. (1961) 'Quelques remarques sur Virgile le grammairien,' in J.A. Watt, J.B. Morrall, and F.X. Martin, *Medieval studies presented to Aubrey Gwynn SJ*, Dublin, 393–408.

Hainsworth, J.B. (1967) 'Greek views of Greek dialectology,' *Transactions of the Philological Society* 66, 62–76.

Herren, M.W. (2010) 'The study of Greek in Ireland in the early Middle Ages,' in *L'Irlanda e gli Irlandesi nell'alto medioevo*, Spoleto, 511–28.

Hofman, R. (1996) *The Sankt Gall Priscian commentary*, 2 vols., Münster.

— (2000) 'The Irish tradition of Priscian,' in M. de Nonno, P. de Paolis, and L. Holtz, *Manuscripts and tradition of grammatical texts from Antiquity to the Renaissance*, 2 vols., Cassino, 257–88.

Holtz, L. (1981) *Donat et la tradition de l'enseignement grammatical*, Paris.

Horrocks, G. (2010) *Greek: a history of the language and its speakers*, 2nd ed., Oxford.

Howlett, D. (1998) 'Hellenic learning in insular Latin: an essay on supported claims,' *Peritia* 12, 54–8.

Jaski, B. (2003) ''We are of the Greeks in our origin': new perspectives on the Irish origin legend,' *Cambrian Medieval Celtic Studies* 46, 1–53.

Jones, H.L. (1917–33) *The Geography of Strabo*, 8 vols., Cambridge.

Kaster, R. (1988) *Guardians of language: the grammarian and society in Late Antiquity*, Berkeley.

Keil, H. (1855–80) *Grammatici latini*, 6 vols., Leipzig.

Kent, R.G. (1938) *Varro on the Latin language*, 2 vols., Cambridge.

Lambert, P.-Y. (1996) 'Les différents strates de gloses dans le ms. de Saint-Gall no. 904 (Priscien),' in P. Ní Chatháin and M. Richter, *Irland und Europa im früheren Mittelalter: Bildung und Literatur / Ireland and Europe in the early Middle Ages: learning and literature*, Stuttgart, 187–94.
Law, V. (1982) *The insular Latin grammarians*, Woodbridge.
Lewis, C.T. and C. Short (1879) *A Latin dictionary, founded on Andrews' edition of Freund's Latin dictionary*, Oxford.
Liddell, H.G and R. Scott (1940) *A Greek–English lexicon*, rev. by H.S. Jones, Oxford.
Lindsay, W.M. (1911) *Isidori Hispalensis episcopi etymologiarum sive originum libri XX*, 2 vols., Oxford.
Lord, L.E. (1959) *Cicero. The speeches. In Catilinam I–IV. Pro Murena. Pro Sulla. Pro Flacco*, Cambridge.
Lutz, C.E. (1939) *Iohannis Scotti annotationes in Marcianum*, Cambridge.
Mac Neill, E. (1930–2) 'De origine scoticae linguae,' *Ériu* 11, 112–29.
Maltby, R. (1993) 'Varro's attitude to Latin derivations from Greek,' *Papers of the Leeds International Latin Seminar* 7, 47–60.
— (2009) 'Priscian's etymologies: sources, functions and theoretical basis: '*Graeci, quibus in omni doctrinae auctoribus utimur*',' in M. Baratin, B. Colombat, and L. Holtz, *Priscien: transmission et refondation de la grammaire de l'antiquité aux modernes*, Turnhout, 239–46.
Merkelbach, R. and M.L. West (1967) *Fragmenta Hesiodea*, Oxford.
Moran, P. (2010) 'Hebrew in early Irish glossaries,' *Cambrian Medieval Celtic Studies* 60, 1–21.
— (2011) 'A living speech? The pronunciation of Greek in early medieval Ireland,' *Ériu* 61, 29–57.
— (2012) 'Greek in early medieval Ireland,' in A. Mullen and P. James, *Multilingualism in the Graeco-Roman worlds*, Cambridge, 172–92.
Morpurgo Davies, A. (1987) 'The Greek notion of dialect,' *Verbum* 10, 7–27, repr. in T. Harrison, *Greeks and barbarians*, Edinburgh 2001, 151–71.
Ogilvie, R.M. (1974) *Titi Livi Ab Urbe Condita, vol. 1*, Oxford.
Ó Néill, P.P. (2000) 'Irish observance of the Three Lents and the date of the St. Gall Priscian (MS 904),' *Ériu* 51, 159–80.
Passalaqua, M. (1999) *Opuscula vol. II. Institutio de nomine et pronomine et verbo. Partitiones duodecim versuum Aeneidos principalium*, Rome.
Polara, G. and L. Caruso (1979) *Virgilio Marone grammatico: epitomi ed epistole*, Naples.
Rackham, H. (1961) *Pliny, Natural History*, Cambridge.
Reydellet, M. (1984) *Isidore de Séville, Étymologies, livre IX: les langues et les groupes sociaux*, Paris.
Russell, D.A. (2002) *Quintillian. The orator's education*, 5 vols., Cambridge.

Russell, P. (2000) '*Graece... Latine*: Graeco-Latin glossaries in early medieval Ireland,' *Peritia* 14, 406–20.

— (2012) '*Fern do frestol na .u. consaine*: perceptions of sound laws, sound change, and linguistic borrowing among the medieval Irish,' in P. Probert and A. Willi, *Laws and rules in Indo-European*, Oxford, 17–30.

Sihler, A.L. (1995) *New comparative grammar of Greek and Latin*, Oxford.

Stevens, B. (2007) 'Latin as a dialect of Greek,' *The Classical Journal* 102, 115–44.

Stokes, W. (1898–1900) 'O'Mulconry's Glossary,' *Archiv für celtische Lexikographie* 1, 232–324, 473–81, 629.

Stokes, W. and J. Strachan (1901–3) *Thesaurus palaeohibernicus: a collection of Old-Irish glosses, scholia, prose and verse*, 2 vols., Cambridge.

Strachan, J. (1903) 'On the language of the St Gall glosses,' *Zeitschrift für celtische Philologie* 4, 470–92.

Theodorides, C. (1976) *Die Fragmente des Grammatikers Philoxenos*, Berlin.

Thilo, G. and H. Hagen (1878–1902) *Servii Grammatici qui feruntur in Vergilii carmina commentarii*, 3 vols., Leipzig.

Todd, J.H. (1848) *The Irish version of the Historia Britonum of Nennius*, Dublin.

Tolkiehn, J. (1928) *Clementis ars grammatica*, Leipzig.

Weiss, M. (2009) *Outline of the historical and comparative grammar of Latin*, New York.

CONTACTS III:

IRISH INFLUENCES ON THE CONTINENT

MICHAEL W. HERREN

SEDULIUS SCOTTUS AND THE KNOWLEDGE OF GREEK

Abstract

This article examines the evidence for Sedulius Scottus' knowledge of the Greek language and evaluates it in comparison to that possessed by his contemporary, John Scottus. The following categories are assessed: (1) the use of Greek in Latin poetry; (2) skill as a scribe of the Greek Psalter and as glossator of the Sibylline Oracles preserved in Paris, Bibliothèque de l'Arsenal, 8407; (3) the glossing of Greek grammatical and rhetorical terms in his commentary on Priscian's *Institutiones grammaticae*. The results of the investigation do not support the claim frequently made that Sedulius played a role in the interlinear translation of 9th-century Irish manuscripts of the Greek Gospels, the Psalter, and Epistles of Paul.

Keywords

Sedulius Scottus, John Scottus, Fergus, Marcus; Greek Psalter, Sibylline Oracles, Lactantius' *Divinae Institutiones*; Leiden, Universiteitsbibliotheek, BPL 67, Leiden, Universiteitsbibliotheek, VLF 67, Oxford, Bodleian Library, Auct. T.1.26, Paris, Bibliothèque de l'Arsenal, 8407.

Introduction

The subject of the Irish knowledge of Greek in the early Middle Ages (7th to 9th centuries) has been rehearsed many times.[1] The topic has created a sharp division into 'believers' and 'deniers', with a range of opinion in between. The two groups are, in fact, a subset of the sectarian controversy between irophiles and irophobes: those who believe that the Irish were

[1] Most recently Moran (2012); Herren (2010). For an excellent overview of the entire history of the study of Greek in the West, see Berschin (1988).

Early medieval Ireland and Europe: chronology, contacts, scholarship, ed. by Pádraic Moran and Immo Warntjes, Studia Traditionis Theologiae, 14 (Turnhout, 2015), pp. 515–35.

 10.1484/M.STT-EB.5.103134

the saviours of civilization in the dark ages and those who think that they kept the ages dark. The two factions initiated their strife in the 7th century and continue it unabated to the present day. In the matter of Greek learning, much of the debate has focussed on what knowledge of a language actually means. Deniers point to the fact that Classical Greek texts were not copied in Ireland and translations of any type of work in Greek are very rare, while believers cling to tips of icebergs and protest that much more evidence lies beneath the surface. Progress has been retarded precisely because each new contestant appeals to a static body of evidence (the Fahan Mura stone, the Schaffhausen Lord's Prayer, etc.).[2] However, over the last forty years new batches of evidence have come on stream: the *Hisperica famina* and their associated poems, the biblical glosses of John Scottus, and most recently the Old Irish–Latin glossaries, specifically O'Mulconry and Cormac.[3] These last, of course, have long been known, but until they were recently studied for their yields of *graeca*,[4] they were confined to the cloister of Old Irish philology. One should also not forget the potential importance of the discovery of the biblical glosses (with *graeca*) of the Canterbury school,[5] as we know that Irish students were in attendance there.[6]

One point on which deniers have nothing to say: John Scottus Eriugena ('John the Irishman born in Ireland') knew Greek. He translated several important and very difficult Greek patristic texts; he used his knowledge of Greek to comment on texts; he even wrote a limited amount of Greek poetry. Scholars have identified errors in his translations,[7] and his Greek poetry shows mistakes of scansion and a deficient grasp of lexical register. But no scholar in the West for two centuries before and four centuries afterwards had a patch on him. He stood virtually alone[8] as the only western scholar whose knowledge of

[2] For a catalogue of these monuments see Howlett (1988).

[3] *Hisperica famina*, ed. Herren (1974–87); John Scottus, Biblical Glosses, ed. Contreni and Ó Néill (1997); O'Mulconry's Glossary, ed. Stokes (1898–1900); Cormac's Glossary, ed. Meyer (1912).

[4] See especially Moran (2011); Russell (1988); Russell (2000).

[5] Bischoff and Lapidge (1994).

[6] See Aldhelm, *Epistula* 5 (ed. by Rudolf Ehwald in MGH Auct. ant. 15, 493), referring to the Irish students as *molosorum catasta ringente* ('a snarling pack of hounds').

[7] The most comprehensive study of John's Greek remains Jeauneau (1979).

[8] One must allow, however, for the translation of the works of Pseudo Dionysius by Hilduin of St Denis (†AD 840). A comparison of his translation of *Epistola IX* with that by Eriugena shows the former to be superior in some respects; see Pépin (1986).

Greek embraced sufficient syntax to enable the construing of whole texts. However, the irosceptics pose the question: where did he acquire his knowledge?[9] The question is a reasonable one, given that so much of the evidence for early medieval Irish learning is contained in continental manuscripts. However, current research is bringing to light at least some of the sources of lexical information available in pre-Carolingian Ireland—enough, I think, to argue that John Scottus could have begun his Greek studies in his home country.[10]

John Scottus may have been only one of two western scholars who had a proven capacity to translate difficult Greek texts such as the *Dionysiaca*. But could there not have been others who had the ability to work with easier material, say, the Greek New Testament? We know, for example, that the Venerable Bede had painstakingly acquired such a facility by the time he was working on the *Retractatio* to his Commentary on the Acts of the Apostles.[11] Moreover, there is a solid case that Christian of Stavelot (9th century) also used a Greek version when writing his Commentary on Matthew.[12] A possibility that comes immediately to mind is Sedulius Scottus, John Scottus' contemporary and compatriot, who also flourished on the Continent. It is certain that Sedulius wrote out a copy of the Greek Psalter, and finished it with an autograph subscription in Greek.[13] He also wrote a noted commentary on Priscian's *Institutiones grammaticae*,[14] in which he commented on Greek terms and cited biblical passages in Greek.

An intriguing aspect of Irish activity on the Continent during the Carolingian Renaissance is the attention given to the works of Priscian, especially the *Institutiones grammaticae.* Numerous 9th-century manuscripts contain full or partial commentaries to the *Institutiones*, or glossaries based on them.[15] Several have been identified as Irish: one each

[9] Among the most pronounced irosceptics regarding Greek was Mario Esposito; e.g. Esposito (1912), 679–80: 'and lastly, it is utterly wrong to assert that he [John Scottus] obtained his knowledge of Greek in an Irish school'.

[10] The Graeco-Latin glossary of Pseudo-Cyril is one resource now established to have been known in Ireland before AD 800 and used by John Scottus; see Herren (2010), 516–8, 523.

[11] Dionisotti (1982).

[12] On Christian of Stavelot see Berschin (1988), 130–2.

[13] See below pp. 521 (subscription), 524–5.

[14] Sedulius Scottus' Commentary on Priscian's *Institutiones grammaticae* is ed. by Löfstedt in CCCM 40C, 57–84.

[15] Passalacqua (1978).

by Sedulius Scottus and John Scottus,[16] the extensive anonymous commentaries of St Gall, Stiftsbibliothek, 904[17] and Karlsruhe, Badische Landesbibliothek, Aug. CXXXII, the interlinear anonymous commentary in Leiden, Universiteitsbibliotheek, BPL 67,[18] and the fragment in Milan, Biblioteca Ambrosiana, A 138 sup. Priscian's grammar was an important source of Greek words and quotations of Greek authors. The presence of such a large Greek element must have presented a formidable obstacle to all but the most intrepid students. Commentators included the great Alcuin, but it is noteworthy that his commentary avoids dealing with it.[19] By contrast, all of the Irish Priscian commentaries of the 9th century deal extensively with Priscian's *graeca*.[20] I shall return to Sedulius' engagement with *graeca* in Priscian below. Here I should like to interject the suggestion that such intense engagement with a particular work is not generated *ex nihilo*. Priscian must have been studied in Ireland in the centuries that preceded the Carolingian period. Recent work has uncovered new evidence from O'Mulconry's Glossary that Priscian's *chef d'oeuvre* was studied there by the 8th century.[21]

How does one evaluate the level of Sedulius' knowledge of Greek? Let us consider the following *testimonia*: (1) use of Greek in his Latin poems and allusions to his love of Greek; (2) a tiny fragment of a poem (?) written in Greek, with the inscription 'Sedulius to Fergus', plus the autograph scribal colophon in the Psalter; (3) use of Greek in grammatical and biblical commentaries; (4) abilities as a scribe in copying out the Psalter, and, more particularly, the formatting of the text of the Sibylline Oracles. This last matter is especially important, as it raises the question of whether Sedulius translated independently or used a ready-made translation.

16 Luhtala and Dutton (1994).

17 See the partial edition and translation by Hofman (1996). A complete transcription is now available online at www.stgallpriscian.ie; the manuscript may be viewed at www.e-codices.unifr.ch/en/list/one/csg/0904.

18 Parts of Leiden, Universiteitsbibliotheek, BPL 67 may be viewed at: http://socrates.leidenuniv.nl.

19 O'Donnell (1976), 222–3.

20 For a close study of a sample of Old Irish glosses to *graeca* in St Gall, Stiftsbibliothek, 904, see Ahlqvist (1988). Byrne (1984), xix–xx, suggests that the manuscript was written in Ireland and brought to the Continent by Sedulius.

21 Moran (2012), 184. On the antiquity of the Irish glosses that surface in St Gall, Stiftsbibliothek, 904, see Strachan (1903), 470–1; Lambert (1996).

Latin poems

First, the Latin poems. Like many Carolingian poets, Sedulius employs Greek words, including one or two quite rare ones, in his published Latin poetry. He prefers the archaic (Hellenized) *gnosco* to the latinate *nosco*. But this of itself proves little. The classical poets also used Greek words, sometimes even Greek constructions. The fondness for Greek vocabulary and neologisms based on Greek increases in the Late Latin and early medieval period,[22] and is pronounced in Anglo-Latin poetry and prose.[23] But there is nothing in Sedulius' poetry that resembles the macaronic verse of Ausonius, such as we find in the verse epistle to Paulus (no. 27.6, ed. Green (1991), pp. 198–200), nor—and here is the rub—is there anything to compare with the continuous Greek verse of his contemporary John Scottus. John filled his Latin poetry with verses and groups of verses written entirely in Greek. He also wrote a number of short poems entirely in Greek, proving that he possessed at least a rudimentary grasp of the language, even if the prosody was shaky.[24] To this day, nothing points up a person's grasp of a foreign language quite so well as a written composition in that language.

One poem by Sedulius, however, refers not only to a love of Greek, but to a penchant for writing Greek verses. This is no. II.vii in Traube's edition.[25] The poem is the seventh in a series of poems addressed to his patron Bishop Hartgar. Hartgar's name occurs in Greek characters at line 154. This poem of 160 lines, with its reminiscences of Vergil's *Aeneid* and *Georgics*,[26] describes the poet's sadness at the departure of his patron to Rome. At lines 11–16, the poet writes:

Ast ego maestificus tristabar Musicus Orpheus,
Euridice liquit me quia sponsa mea.
Sed cum florigeri micuerunt tempora veris,
Dulcisonis cecinit Calliope modulis;
Aedibus in nostris melliflua carmina promsit
Graecula graecizans ore sonora modos.

[22] Prinz (1971).

[23] Lapidge (1975).

[24] For an evaluation of the Greek in John's poetry see Herren (1993), 46–50.

[25] Traube's edition can be found in MGH Poetae 3, 173. (Translations are mine.) This is published as no. 7 in the edition by Meyers in CCCM 117, 15.

[26] For the Vergilian echoes see Meyers' edition *ad loc.*

'But I, the musician Orpheus, was sad and downcast
Because my bride Euridice had left me.
But since the season of flowering spring was aglow,
Calliope sang with dulcet modulations;
She brought forth honeyed songs in our house
A Greek, singing Greek metres sonorously from her lips.'

For a poet to state that his muse sang songs to him in Greek could mean that the poet himself was composing verses in Greek. But it might also point to something less ambitious, namely, composing or inventing on a Greek theme in Latin. The statement is too ambiguous to admit of a sure interpretation.

Sedulius to Fergus

Did Sedulius write verses in Greek? To date, no entire verse written in Greek has been identified as the work of Sedulius. Yet I think that it can be shown that Sedulius attempted to write at least one Greek verse. Some time ago Bernhard Bischoff published a fragmentary Greek verse which he assigned to the Irishman Fergus on the basis of his reading of the manuscript attribution. This Fergus was also responsible either as scribe or as author of a Greek glossary contained in Valenciennes, Bibliothèque municipale, 81 (74).[27] In any case, an inscription is found in the 9th-century manuscript Paris, Bibliothèque nationale de France, Lat. 10307, 246v, which reads as follows, according to Bischoff:[28]

Versus Ferg....sc(ott...?)
uel COΦE
... ΛIXNON ... E. E. ΛΑΜΠΡΟΝ

The page concerned is much rubbed and extremely difficult to read. However, after spending some hours with it under relatively good light, I was able to make out some more letters in the places where Bischoff indicated erasure:

[27] Valenciennes, Bibliothèque municipale, 81 (74) is available online at: http://bookline-03.valenciennes.fr/bib/fondsvirtuels/microfilms/accueil.asp.

[28] Bischoff (1951), 267 n 107.

Vers ... ferg ... dic ... y ** oc sco
uel CΟΦΕ
CΟΦΙΑC ... ΛΙΧΝΟΝ ... ΛΑΜΠΡΟΝ

Where I have placed two asterisks stands a character that is very like the ligatured *lambda–iota* used in Sedulius' subscription to his Psalter on f 55r of Paris, Bibliothèque de l'Arsenal, 8407:

CΗΔΥ*ΛΙ*ΟΣ CΚΟΤΤΟΣ ΕΓΟ ΕΓΡΑΨΑ

I therefore reconstruct the inscription as follows:

Vers<um> Ferg<o> dic<tauit> <Sed>ylioc Sco<ttus>
uel CΟΦΕ
CΟΦΙΑC ... ΛΙΧΝΟΝ ... ΛΑΜΠΡΟΝ

'Sedulius Scottus wrote (this) verse to Fergus:
Glowing lamp of learning' [gloss over ΛΑΜΠΡΟΝ: 'or O wise man']

In this restoration we now have at least one fragment of Greek composition by Sedulius (additional to the well-known colophon), and this directed to a Fergus, who can reasonably be supposed to be the *Magister Fergus* of the Valenciennes glossary and one of the authors of the Bamberg Cryptogram.[29] That Sedulius was in contact with an Irish scholar named Fergus is beyond dispute. This is shown by the mention of Fergus in a poem addressed to a group of Irish scholars and by a separate poem addressed expressly to Fergus. In the first poem (no. II.xxxiv), Sedulius writes:[30]

Egregios fratres, Fergum Blandumque saluta,
Marcum, Beuchellem, cartula, dulce sonans

'O parchment, bearing sweet sounds, greet your distinguished brethren: Fergus, Blandus, Marcus, and Beuchel.'

At the end of the poem, these four are described as *quadrigae domini* ('four-horsed teams of the Lord', or 'chariots of the Lord') and *Scottensis*

[29] Valenciennes glossary: Bischoff (1951), 267 n 109; Bamberg Cryptogram: Kenney (1966), 556 (no. 363) and Howlett's contribution in the present volume.

[30] MGH Poetae 3, 199–200.

lumina gentis ('lights of the Irish people'). This last metaphor clearly parallels the light-image of the Greek verse addressed to Fergus: ΣΟΦΙΑΣ … ΛΙΧΝΟΝ … ΛΑΜΠΡΟΝ ('shining light of learning'). Another poem (no. II.xxxv) fascinates because it expands the prosopography of Fergus.[31] We learn from it that Fergus distinguished himself by writing poems to Charles the Bald. Unfortunately, the poems alluded to do not survive.

Biblical commentaries

It is also important to note that Sedulius addressed a certain Marcus, one of the *quadrigae Domini*.

> *Marce, precor, fidei scuto meritisque beatis*
> *Pellito vulniferas hostis, amice, minas.*

> 'Marcus, I pray, with the shield of faith and holy merit
> Ward off the threatening wounds of the enemy, friend.'

Who, precisely, was this Marcus? We know the name as one of a group of scholars responsible for planning and copying three Irish bilingual biblical manuscripts (the St Gall Gospels (MS 48), the Basel Psalter, and the Codex Boernerianus Pauline Epistles);[32] as an Irish bishop resident in St Gall;[33] as an Irish-educated British bishop, who settled as an anchorite in Soissons.[34] It is by no means impossible that a single individual, not three, is involved.

I think it very likely that the scribe and the anchorite at Soissons were the same person. There is certainly no difficulty with chronology. The Irish biblical bilinguals, on the basis of the names of living persons mentioned in the glosses, were written originally in the time of John Scottus and Sedulius, i.e. between AD 850 and 870.[35] The extant manuscripts, all of which were at St Gall during the Middle Ages, are copies

[31] MGH Poetae 3, 200. More on Fergus's career can be gleaned from Contreni (1982), 767–8.

[32] Kaczynski (1988), 23.

[33] Kaczynski (1988), 23.

[34] Kenney (1966), 593.

[35] Bischoff (1981), 46.

written not much later, according to Bischoff.[36] We know that Marcus was at Soissons when Heiric was there, i.e. in the early AD 860s.[37] Heiric, of course, was a pupil of John Scottus, who was also at Soissons in the time of Abbot Wulfad.[38] If Sedulius is writing to Marcus at Soissons and addressing the other members of the *quadrigae* in the same poetic epistle, then it may be the case that the writer has been separated from his old circle of Irish friends. As Düchting notes in his discussion of II.xxxiv,[39] the mentions of an enemy and a viper in the poem may not be simply conventional metonomies of Satan, but refer to some contemporary danger. Is Sedulius concerned that his old friends might be infected by the 'heresies' of John, whom he does not name? We shall never know, but the poem seems useful for marking a separation between Sedulius and his Irish circle and the relocation of that circle in the western kingdom of Charles the Bald. The poems to King Charles by Fergus, to which Sedulius alludes in II.xxxv, serve as a reminder that there is a geographical distance between Sedulius and his old friend.[40]

Two members of Sedulius's *quadriga*, Fergus and Marcus, are named in the margins of two Irish bilingual biblical texts:[41] Basel, Universitätsbibliothek, A VII 3 (Psalms), 23r (Marcellus);[42] and Dresden, Staats- und Universitätsbibliothek, A 145 b (the Codex Boernerianus with Pauline Epistles, damaged), 82v, 94r (Fergus), 30v, 32v, 39r, 43v, 44v, 45r, 48r, 48v, 64r, 66v, 77r, 89r (Μαρ[κος]), 111v (Μαρκος μοναχος).[43] To this group of codicologically and palaeographically similar manuscripts is added

36 Bischoff (1977), 46.

37 Contreni (1978), 145.

38 Contreni (1978), 145; see also Herren (1993), 3.

39 Düchting (1968), 121.

40 It is possible that the poems may reveal a rivalry between two schools that is also reflected in the marginalia of three bilingual biblical manuscripts assigned to the 'Circle of Sedulius'. On the juxtaposition of names in the margins with biblical passages that imply criticism of the individuals named see Herren (1996), 316.

41 The references to 'Μαρ' in St Gall, Stiftsbibliothek, 48 (four Gospels), pp. 256 and 359, may refer rather to Martianus Capella (compare marginal notes 'Felix Capella' and 'Martian' at pp. 222 and 294 respectively). There is a marginal reference to Sedulius on p 377, however. Manuscript images online at www.e-codices.unifr.ch/en/list/one/csg/0048.

42 Manuscript images online at www.e-codices.unifr.ch/en/list/one/ubb/A-VII-0003.

43 Zimmer (1881), xxxiv. Manuscript images online at http://digital.slub-dresden.de/id274591448. See also facsimile of Reichardt (1909).

Bern, Burgerbibliothek, 363, a collection of classical texts and excerpts.[44] However, the autograph Psalter of Sedulius (Paris, Bibliothèque de l'Arsenal, 8407)[45] must be separated from the other biblical manuscripts of the 'Circle'.[46] Whoever was responsible for the interlinear translation of the biblical bilinguals—and I have argued elsewhere for John Scottus in this capacity in connection with St Gall, Stiftsbibliothek, 48[47]—had the ability to adjust an existing Latin translation of the biblical works concerned to the demands of Greek syntax, and modify it where necessary. The interlinear translations, therefore, while retaining as far as possible the text of the mixed Vulgate, are completely literal. They translate the Greek word for word in the exact order of the Greek text. Whoever carried out this task was qualified to undertake independent translations from the Greek. Because of their divergences from the known Vulgate and Old Latin versions, they cannot be classified.

Sedulius' Psalter

The Psalter of Sedulius (Paris, Bibliothèque de l'Arsenal, 8407) provides no evidence of a similar capacity. The text of the Psalms is entirely in Greek, with Latin used only in the *tituli*. There is practically no glossing. Nonetheless, Sedulius' talents as a Greek scribe were highly remarkable. In a small sample of collation of his text against the Septuagint, I noted the following: (1) Word separation is almost invariably correct. This, in itself, is an exceptional achievement for a westerner copying Greek; Martin of Laon, for example, had considerable difficulty with it. (2) Greek letters are never confused. It was common, for example, for western scribes to confuse alpha, delta, and lambda, or kappa and chi. This type of mistake does not occur in Sedulius. (3) The distinction between the long and short vowels *eta* and *epsilon*, *omega* and *omicron*, is scrupulously observed. (4) Sedulius, using a curious overhead dotting system, correctly preserves the primary and the secondary accents of Greek words, although he occasionally neglects to mark some words. The only

44 Bischoff (1981), 45; for a full study, see Contreni (1982).

45 Manuscript images online at http://gallica.bnf.fr/ark:/12148/btv1b55000821o.

46 The concept of 'the Circle of Sedulius' goes back to Ludwig Traube's fundamental study (1891). It remains current to this day. It should be noted that none of these manuscripts is written in the hand of Sedulius, as can be shown by a comparison with his Psalter.

47 Herren (1989).

faults to be noted are not really faults at all. First of all, Sedulius occasionally deviates from the printed Septuagint with readings that are not incorrect, but are simply established variant readings. Secondly, Sedulius rather frequently employs spellings that reflect Late Greek rather than classical pronunciation, especially of the iotacistic variety.

All of this points to two conclusions: (1) Sedulius possessed an exemplar of the Psalms written in clear Greek characters, doubtless in biblical uncial. The exemplar almost certainly contained marks of word separation as well as accents. The systematic use of these two features in Greek manuscripts is rare for the period; thus it is possible that a Greek scribe resident in the West supplied them. (2) Sedulius had thorough training in writing Greek. Though the insular character of his script is clearly observable, the writing is fluent and easily legible, revealing a practised hand.

However, when we turn to the appendix of the manuscript, a quite different situation obtains. The Psalms are followed by a group of biblical *cantica* in Greek followed by the Lord's Prayer and Nicene Creed (Paris, Bibliothèque de l'Arsenal, 8407, 55v–64r). These are all accompanied by facing-page Latin translations, which are ready-made. However, it is the attempt to copy the Greek text of the Lactantian Sibylline Oracles (Paris, Bibliothèque de l'Arsenal, 8407, 64v–66v), where Sedulius reveals his inability to think past his exemplar. To be sure, the 'Oracles' present challenges absent in the Psalms, especially as they are written in a Classical Greek with occasional archaic features. Generally speaking, Sedulius manages the writing of the Greek relatively well. The marking of word separation is generally accurate, and accents, when marked at all, are correct—it is noteworthy that here circumflex accents are distinguished from acute and grave. The Latin translation in the facing right column is very literal, indeed word-for-word. However, the translation is not by Sedulius. It is a ready-made interpretation that was made in Late Antiquity, which accompanied the Greek text of the Oracles in Lactantius' *Divinae institutiones* found in Bologna, Biblioteca Universitaria, 701 (saec. V, in uncial script).[48]

There are signs, however, that Sedulius does not know what to do with his exemplar. At a couple of places, he seems to misinterpret *signes de renvoi* and inserts glossing material into the text at inappropriate places. Six lines down from the beginning of the Oracles marked only by *Orpheus dicit* (Paris, Bibliothèque de l'Arsenal, 8407, 64v) he breaks the order of his bilingual text and writes across the page:

[48] Bischoff (1966), 150–1. See *CLA* 3, 2 (no. 280).

> CIOΥC. deos. non ΘΕΟΥΣ. et consilium non ΒΟΥΛΗΝ sed ΒΟΥΛΙΑΝ appellabant.
>
> 'They call 'gods' CIOΥC not ΘΕΟΥΣ, and 'counsel' not ΒΟΥΛΗΝ, but ΒΟΥΛΙΑΝ.'

Apart from the disruptive positioning of the inserted line, the gloss it contains is irrelevant to the passage that has preceded it. The gloss provides a Greek etymology for Σιβύλλα (*Sibylla*). It is likely that it was originally meant to accompany a lost title (*Oracula Sibyllina* or the like). Note that the only indication of change from Greek prayers to the Oracles is the bald *Orpheus dicit*. In any case, the gloss itself is an excerpt from a longer *scholion* ascribed to Varro in the citation by Lactantius, *Divinae institutiones* I 6.7. Variants of the *scholion* are given by Servius, Jerome, Philargyrius, Isidore,[49] and John Scottus in the Paris version of the *Annotationes in Marcianum* (9.22).[50] Because the excerpt corresponds word for word (allowing for the miscopying of ΒΟΥΛΙΑΝ for ΒΟΥΛΛΑΝ) to the Varro citation in Lactantius, it is all but certain that the *scholion*—and indeed both the Greek and the Latin texts—derive from a copy of the *Divinae institutiones* that contained the Latin translation.

Another example of a gloss running across the page and interrupting the flow of the text is the following (Paris, Bibliothèque de l'Arsenal, 8407, 65r):

> Ericthonius dictus est ΑΠΟ ΤΗC ΕΡΙΔΟC ΚΑΙ ΧΘΟΝΟC id est ex certamine et terra.
>
> 'Erichthonius was named from ἔρις and χθών, that is, from Strife and Earth.'

Once again, the placement is inexplicable, as there is no mention of Erichthonius in the lines immediately above or below. Again, the *Divinae institutiones* of Lactantius (I 17.13) is the direct source, as the Sedulian gloss echoes Lactantius word for word, excepting that Lactantius' *humo* has been replaced by *terra*.

49 Details in Maltby (1991), 565.

50 *Annotationes in Marcianum* 9.22 (ed. Lutz (1939), 16).

More intelligent placement is found two lines below the Erichthonius *scholion* cited above. This contains the famous etymology of ΑΝΘΡΩΠΟC:

ΑΝΘΡΩΠΟΝ idest hominem greci appellant quod sussum [*sic*] spectet

'The Greek call a human ἄνθρωπος because he looks upwards.'

ΑΝΘΡΩΠΟC (nom.) occurs in the line below of the Oracles text, where the Greek appears to be garbled. The etymology is found in Isidore, *Etymologiae* XI 1.5 (with slight variants),[51] but the direct source, again, is Lactantius. What is disconcerting about these intrusions into the text is that they are presented visually as text, not gloss. Indeed, all of the examples cited are introduced by exaggerated majuscules. One can only conclude that if the cross-page glosses cited here stood in Sedulius' exemplar in the same places as in the Arsenal manuscript, Sedulius was unable to identify them as extraneous to the text. If they were written in the exemplar as marginal glosses, then Sedulius imported two of the three into the wrong places.

One *scholion* might be argued to be the result of Sedulius' initiative, i.e. not imported from his exemplar (Paris, Bibliothèque de l'Arsenal, 8407, 65r). Tucked in after the last (short) line of the Oracles text cited below and written in minuscules, the following note is clearly meant to be viewed as a gloss: *Hermes qui et Trismegestus et Mercurius dicitur.* Let us look at the text that it accompanies:

ΕΠΙ.ΠΛΑΝΑ.ΠΑΝΤΑ.ΤΑ.Α.ΕCΤΙΝ
.Α.ΠΕΡΑΦΡΟΝΕC.ΑΝΔΡΕC.ΕΥΡΕΥΜΩΣΙΝ
ΚΑΤΑ. ΗΜΑΡ

and the translation in the facing column:

Quia errores omnia haec sunt
quae stulti uiri scrutantur
secundum cor

'And all these things are errors
which unreasoning men search for
next to their heart'

[51] Isidore, *Etymologiae* XI 1.5 (ed. Lindsay (1911), ii).

Despite the help of the facing-column Latin translation, which translates KATA HMAP with *secundum cor*, Sedulius mistook HMAP (ἧμαρ ('liver')) for the god's name EPMHC (Ἑρμῆς). In the gloss tradition, Hermes is associated with the firmament (*herma*), speech (*sermo*), and interpretation ('hermeneutics'), but not the liver.[52] I suspect, then, that the *scholion* is original. The reference to *Trismegistus*, however, is probably owed to Isidore, *Etymologiae* VIII 11.49.[53]

One matter is now established. There is no basis for connecting the Psalter of Sedulius with the other three 9th-century Irish biblical manuscripts attributed so often to 'the Circle of Sedulius'. The attribution has persisted because of Traube's erroneous grouping of them on palaeographical grounds[54] and J.F. Kenney's mistaken assertion that Sedulius' Psalter was a bilingual.[55] The industrious Canadian scholar, on whom all continue to rely, must not have visited the Bibliothèque de l'Arsenal in Paris, or seen a photograph of MS 8407, or he would have learned that the section with the Psalms contains only the Greek text. On the other hand, the appendix that follows the Psalms contains a collection of prayers in facing-page Greek and Latin versions and facing-column Greek and Latin versions of the Sibylline Oracles, of which the Greek was transmitted by Lactantius. However, even there Kenney was in error, for he states: 'All in Greek with Latin interlinear translation.'[56] All of the Latin translations of the appendix are either in facing-page or facing-column format. Thus, there is nothing to support the assertion that Sedulius employed the interlinear format in any part of the *graeca* in Paris, Bibliothèque de l'Arsenal, 8407. By employing the facing-page format for the *cantica* and facing-page format for the Oracles, he departed from the interlinear format used in the three extant Irish bilingual books attributed to his activity, namely, the Basel Psalter (Basel, Univer-

52 Maltby (1991), 274. It should be noted that an early type of Greek physical allegory identified gods with parts of the body, including innards. Thus Metrodorus of Lampsacus 'the Elder' (late 5th century BC?) equated Demeter with the liver, Dionysus with the spleen, Apollo with the gall. Cf. Diels (1912), 414 (no. 48, fr. 4). It is not impossible that this type of allegorizing was applied to Hermes with reinforcement from etymology (Hermes from HMAP). However, I have not been able to find this exact identification.

53 Lindsay (1911), i.

54 On Traube's mistake see especially Berschin (1988), 13–4.

55 Kenney (1966), 557 (no. 364 iii). Unhappily, Kenney's error has been repeated by almost everyone who wrote about the Psalter, and has been used to connect Sedulius' autograph Greek text with the three Irish interlinear Bible texts.

56 Kenney (1966), 557 (no. 364 iii).

sitätsbibliothek, A VII 3), the Codex Boernerianus text of the Pauline Epistles (Dresden, Staats- und Universitätsbibliothek, A 145 b), and the Gospels of St Gall, Stiftsbibliothek, 48. As shown above, a ready-made translation for the Oracles was available in his exemplar, and the Greek prayers were extracted almost entirely from biblical passages, for which Latin versions would have been to hand. Thus, it is impossible to assess Sedulius' skill as a translator of Greek from the autograph copy of the Psalms that we possess.

This raises the question of what may have been Sedulius' role, if any, in the work of translating the Greek in the interlinear bilinguals. It is not possible to say that he participated in the design of those books, which involved word-for-word interlinear translation as opposed to the use of facing-page or facing-column translations in the *non*-Psalter portions of Sedulius' autograph. It is interesting to note, however, that a scholar known to favour the interlinear format was John Scottus. John left samples of translations of passages from Classical Greek works in the margins of his glossed copy of Priscian, Leiden, Universiteitsbibliotheek, BPL 67 (the so-called Dubthach Priscian). These are word-for-word interlinear translations.[57] This, of itself, does not prove that John Scottus was the architect of the 'biblical translation project'. However, there seems now to be at least a basis for questioning the validity of the long-held belief in 'the manuscripts of the Circle of Sedulius'. What unite the three biblical interlinears are their hands and codicology, the fact that all were at one time at St Gall,[58] and the repetition of certain Irish names in the margins of the manuscripts.

In Priscianum

Let us now examine Sedulius' *In Priscianum* for what it can tell us about its author as a scholar of Greek. The largest portion of the commentary is preserved in a single manuscript, Leiden, Universiteitsbibliotheek, VLF 67 (saec. IX), 9r–16v.[59] Some *scholia* from the beginning are also found in Leiden, Universiteitsbibliotheek, BPL 67 and Oxford, Bodle-

57 Herren (1998), 195–6; see also plates 1–3.

58 Kaczynski (1988), 84–6.

59 Kenney (1966), 556 (no. 364), appears to have conflated two separate Leiden MSS containing Priscian commentaries: Leiden, Universiteitsbibliotheek, VLF 67, which has the Sedulian Commentary on *Institutiones*, and Leiden, Universiteitsbibliotheek, BPL 67, which has only some Sedulian *scholia* at the beginning. The latter is the

ian Library, Auct. T.1.26. It is very probable that the commentary was composed after Sedulius had written out the Arsenal text of the Psalms, as he quotes from Psalm 143 word for word from his own text (Paris, Bibliothèque de l'Arsenal, 8407, 53r).[60] The commentary as we have it is not extensive, and it is impossible to decide whether we have a series of fragments from a longer commentary, or if Sedulius simply wrote *scholia* to passages that interested him. The scribe of Leiden, Universiteitsbibliotheek, VLF 67 may have suspected the latter alternative. He prefaced the commentary on book 1 (f 11r) with the words: *Incipit commentariolum eiusdem Sedulii Scotti in quaedam dicta Presciani grammatici* ('Here begins the the little commentary of the same Sedulius Scottus on certain sayings of Priscian the Grammarian'). In any case, examples that survive show Sedulius' mastery of several Greek rhetorical and philosophical terms.

Sedulius devotes much attention to Priscian's prefatory letter, *Iuliano consuli et patricio*. At 1.5[61] he demonstrates the use of the *schema* ἐπεξήγησις,[62] *id est explanatio dicti superioris, ut sit talis ordo*: *in quibus erroribus Greca ars, uetustissima uidilicet grammatica ars, arguitur peccasse* ('ἐπεξήγησις, that is, an explanation of the previous term, so that the order might be such: 'into which errors the Greek art', that is, the most venerable art of grammar, 'is said to have fallen"). The schema, here introduced by *uidilicet*, is used simply to explain that the *Greca ars* is the *ars gramatica*. Similarly, a few lines below, commenting on the same sentence he writes: *Et nota, quod μετωνυμικῶς artem grammaticam peccasse dicat, cum ipsi potius grammatici peccauerunt, rem quae animo et intellectu continetur pro ipsis continentibus personis ponens.* ('And note that he says metonymically that the art of grammar erred, whereas it was the Greek grammarians themselves who erred, substituting a thing which is contained in the mind and understanding for the very persons who contain it'). Sedulius knows the Greek word for metonymy (Latin *translatio*) and knows how to apply it. Ingeniously, he uses the same sentence of Priscian to demonstrate epexegesis (*explanatio*) and metonymy (*translatio*), and gives the Greek names for them.

copy of Priscian written by Dubthach (in AD 838), with some *scholia* added by i[1] (John Scottus). It is easy to see how the two were conflated, but the mistake is unfortunate.

60 Noted in Löfstedt (1977), xvii.

61 Priscian, *Institutiones grammaticae*, ed. by Keil (1857–80), ii 1.

62 The word was printed by Löfstedt (1977), 59, in Greek type; the MS has *efexegesis*. Löfstedt transliterates throughout.

Conclusion

For scholars of the intellectual history of the Middle Ages, Sedulius' discussion of grammatical terms having philosophical implications will prove interesting. Whereas the 9th-century commentary on Priscian is largely grammatical, 12th-century commentators used Priscian as their starting point for 'speculative grammar'.[63] Sedulius began the construction of a bridge between the two ages with his discussion of the terms ἔννοια (*notitio*) and οὐσιώδης (*substantialis*), relating the first term to accident or property, the second to substance.[64] While an admixture of rhetoric and grammar can be found in many grammarians, the application of dialectic to grammar appears to be innovative, at least in the Latin tradition.[65] Further study of Sedulius' and John Scottus' commentaries on Priscian, coupled with a closer examination of the Priscian commentary in St Gall, Stiftsbibliothek, 904 should result in a larger group of these Greek dialectical terms and possibly point to their source.

Beyond these few Greek terms there is little else in the principal manuscript of Sedulius' Priscian commentary to show his facility in that language. The *excerpta* given in Leiden, Universiteitsbibliotheek, VLF 67, 15r–v[66] provide an explanation of ὁ αὐτός: *ὁ quod est articulus praepositiuus, αὐτός uero pronomen relatiuum* ('ὁ which is an article that precedes (a noun), while αὐτός is a relative pronoun'). In the same *scholion* he states more accurately: *Item ὅστις, quod interpretatur qui, subiuntiuus articulus est cum nomine infinito* ('Likewise ὅστις, which is translated as *qui*, is an article that is coupled with an indefinite (?) noun'). The same fragment also contains the first line of Psalm 143 cited from Sedulius' Psalter, used to illustrate a rule of Greek accentuation: *Εὐλογητὸς Κύριος ὁ θεός μου; ubi nanque ὁ graui accentu pronuntiatum ad subsequentem dictionem, quae est θεός, quasi in unius dictionis compaginem conglutinatur* ("Blessed be the Lord my God', where ὁ is pronounced with a grave accent to the following word, which is θεός, as if joined in a union of a single word'). This last is completely accurate. It

63 See e.g. Peter Helias, *Summa super Priscianum* (ed. Reilly (1993)).

64 Löfstedt (1977), 67.

65 See Law (1997), 144–5. Law attributes this innovation to a common source used by the *scotti peregrini*. For an appreciative study of Sedulius' originality as a grammarian see Luhtala (1993).

66 Ed. by Löfstedt in CCCM 40C, 83–4.

seems likely that Sedulius had access to parts of a Greek grammar adjusted to the needs of Latin readers.[67]

It is difficult using the evidence cited here to provide a comprehensive evaluation of Sedulius' knowledge of Greek. The Irish scholar expressed his love of Greek, claims to have written Greek verses (of which we have only two or three words), could write a fluent Greek script, and apparently had access to a Greek grammar and lexical resources. If we could be sure that he played a role in composing the interlinear translation in the three Irish bilingual biblical texts discussed above, we would be much more certain of his competence. However, we have reviewed evidence that undermines confidence that an achievement of that level was within his gift. This study corroborates Mario Esposito's evaluation of Sedulius' Greek: 'His knowledge of the language [...] is by no means as extensive or accurate as that possessed by his contemporary Johannes Scottus.'[68] That having been said, Sedulius Scottus was a brilliant intellect, a polyglot whose activity ranged across poetry, grammar, political philosophy, the study of the Scriptures, and study of the Roman classics. It is surely time for a new evaluation of the man and his accomplishments.[69] None has been undertaken since Sigmund Hellmann's pioneering work of 1906.[70]

Bibliography

Ahlqvist, A. (1988) 'Notes on the Greek materials in the St. Gall Priscian (Codex 904),' in M.W. Herren, *The sacred nectar of the Greeks: the study of Greek in the West in the early Middle Ages*, London, 195–214.

Berschin, W. (1988) *Greek letters in the Latin Middle Ages*, tr. J.C. Frakes, Washington.

Bischoff, B. (1951) 'Das griechische Element in der abendländischen Bildung des Mittelalters,' *Byzantinische Zeitschrift* 44, 26–55, repr. in B. Bischoff, *Mittelalterliche Studien: ausgewählte Aufsätze zur Schriftkunde und Literaturgeschichte, vol. 2*, Stuttgart 1967, 246–75.

[67] See Dionisotti (1988), 25–6. Dionisotti points out the existence of a fragment of Herodian's grammar with Latin interlinear gloss in the Corbie Priscian commentary (Paris, Bibliothèque nationale de France, Lat. 7501).

[68] Esposito (1912), 678.

[69] I am certain that our distinguished honoree, as one who has done so much to encourage the study of Ireland's Latin tradition, will agree.

[70] Hellmann (1906).

— (1966) 'Die lateinischen Übersetzungen und Bearbeitungen aus den Oracula Sibyllina,' in B. Bischoff, *Mittelalterliche Studien: ausgewählte Aufsätze zur Schriftkunde und Literaturgeschichte, vol. 1*, Stuttgart, 150–71.

— (1977) 'Irische Schreiber im Karolingerreich,' in R. Roques, *Jean Scot Erigène et l'histoire de la philosophie*, Paris, 47–58, repr. in B. Bischoff, *Mittelalterliche Studien: ausgewählte Aufsätze zur Schriftkunde und Literaturgeschichte, vol. 3*, Stuttgart 1981, 39–54.

Bischoff, B. and M. Lapidge (1994) *Biblical commentaries from the Canterbury school of Theodore and Hadrian*, Cambridge.

Byrne, F.J. (1984) 'Introduction', in T. Ó Neill, *The Irish hand*, Mountrath, xi–xxviii.

Contreni, J.J. (1978) *The cathedral school of Laon from 850 to 930: its manuscripts and masters*, München.

— (1982) 'The Irish in the Western Carolingian Empire (according to James F. Kenney and Bern, Burgerbibliothek 363),' in H. Löwe, *Die Iren und Europa im früheren Mittelalter*, 2 vols., Stuttgart, 758–98.

Contreni, J.J. and P.P. Ó Neill (1997) *Glossae divinae historiae: the biblical glosses of John Scottus Eriugena*, Florence.

Diels, H. (1912) *Fragmente der Vorsokratiker, vol. 1*, 3rd ed., Berlin.

Dionisotti, A.C. (1982) 'On Bede, grammars, and Greek,' *Revue Bénédictine* 42, 111–41.

— (1988) 'Greek grammars and dictionaries in Carolingian Europe,' in M.W. Herren, *The sacred nectar of the Greeks: the study of Greek in the West in the early Middle Ages*, London, 1–56.

Düchting, R. (1968) *Sedulius Scottus: seine Dichtungen*, München.

Esposito, M. (1912) 'Greek in Ireland during the Middle Ages,' *Studies: an Irish quarterly review* 1, 665–83, repr. in M. Esposito, *Latin learning in mediaeval Ireland*, ed. by M. Lapidge, London 1988, IX.

Green, R.P.H. (1991) *The works of Ausonius*, Oxford.

Hellmann, S. (1906) *Sedulius Scottus*, München.

Herren, M.W. (1974–87) *Hisperica famina*, 2 vols., Toronto.

— (1989) 'St. Gall 48: a copy of Eriugena's glossed Greek Gospels,' in G. Bernt et al., *Tradition und Wertung: Festschrift für Franz Brunhölzl*, Sigmaringen, 97–105.

— (1993) *Iohannis Scotti Eriugenae Carmina*, Dublin 1993.

— (1996) 'John Scottus and the biblical manuscripts attributed to the circle of Sedulius,' in G. van Riel, C. Steel, and J. McEvoy, *Iohannes Scottus Eriugena, the Bible and hermeneutics*, Leuven, 303–20.

— (1998) 'The humanism of John Scottus,' in C. Leonardi, *Gli umanesimi medievali: atti del II Congresso dell' 'Internationales Mittellateinerkomitee', Firenze, Certosa del Galluzzo, 11–15 settembre 1993*, Florence, 191–9.

— (2010) 'The study of Greek in Ireland in the early Middle Ages,' in *L'irlanda e gli irlandesi nell'alto medioevo*, Spoleto, 511–32.

Hofman, R. (1996) *The Sankt Gall Priscian commentary*, 2 vols., Münster.

Howlett, D. (1988) 'Hellenic learning in insular Latin: an essay on supported claims,' *Peritia* 12, 24–53.

Jeauneau, E. (1979) 'Jean Scot Érigène et le grec,' *Archivum Latinitatis Medii Aevi* 41, 5–50.

Kaczynski, B.M. (1988) *Greek in the Carolingian age: the St. Gall manuscripts*, Cambridge.

Kenney, J.F. (1966) *The sources for the early history of Ireland: 1. Ecclesiastical*, revised by L. Bieler, New York.

Keil, H. (1857–80) *Grammatici latini*, 6 vols., Leipzig.

Lambert, P.-Y. (1996) 'Les différents strates de gloses dans le ms. de Saint-Gall no. 904 (Priscien),' in P. Ní Chatháin and M. Richter, *Irland und Europa im früheren Mittelalter: Bildung und Literatur / Ireland and Europe in the early Middle Ages: learning and literature*, Stuttgart, 187–94.

Lapidge, M. (1975) 'The hermeneutic style in tenth-century Anglo-Latin literature,' *Anglo-Saxon England* 4, 67–111, repr. in M. Lapidge, *Anglo-Latin literature 900–1066*, London 1993, 105–49.

Law, V. (1997) *Grammar and grammarians in the Middle Ages*, London.

Lindsay, W.M. (1911) *Isidori Hispalensis episcopi etymologiarum sive originum libri XX*, 2 vols., Oxford.

Löfstedt, B. (1977) *Sedulius Scottus. In Donati artem minorem. In Priscianum. In Eutychem*, CCCM 40C, Turnhout.

Luhtala, A. (1993) 'Syntax and dialectic in Carolingian commentaries on Priscian's *Institutiones grammaticae*,' in V. Law, *History of linguistic thought in the early Middle Ages*, Amsterdam, 145–91.

Luhtala, A. and P.E. Dutton (1994) 'Eriugena in Priscianum,' *Mediaeval Studies* 56, 153–63.

Lutz, C.E. (1939) *Iohannis Scotti Annotationes in Marcianum*, Cambridge.

Maltby, R. (1991) *Lexicon of ancient Latin etymologies*, Leeds.

Meyer, K. (1912) 'Sanas Cormaic: an Old-Irish glossary compiled by Cormac Úa Cuilennáin, king-bishop of Cashel in the tenth century,' *Anecdota from Irish Manuscripts* 4, i–ix, 1–128.

Moran, P. (2011) 'A living speech? The pronunciation of Greek in early medieval Ireland,' *Ériu* 61, 29–57.

— (2012) 'Greek in early medieval Ireland,' in A. Mullen and P. James, *Multilingualism in the Graeco-Roman worlds*, Cambridge, 172–92.

O'Donnell, J.R. (1976) 'Alcuin's Priscian,' in J.J. O'Meara and B. Naumann, *Latin script and letters A.D. 400–900: Festschrift presented to Ludwig Bieler on the occasion of his 70th birthday*, Leiden, 222–35.

Passalacqua, M. (1978) *I codici di Prisciano*, Roma.

Pépin, J. (1986) 'Jean Scot Érigène, traducteur de Denys: l'exemple de la *Lettre IX*,' in G.-H. Allard, *Jean Scot Écrivain: Actes du IVe colloque international Montréal, 28 août–2 septembre 1983*, Montréal, 129–41.

Prinz, O. (1971) 'Zum Einfluss des griechischen auf den Wortschatz des Mittelalters,' in J. Autenrieth and F. Brunhölzl, *Festschrift Bernhard Bischoff zu seinem 65. Geburtstag*, Stuttgart, 1–15.

Reichardt, A. (1909) *Der Codex Boernerianus. Der Briefe des Apostels Paulus*, Leipzig.

Reilly, L. (1993) *Peter Helias, Summa super Priscianum*, 2 vols., Toronto.

Russell, P. (1988) 'The sounds of silence: the growth of Cormac's Glossary,' *Cambridge Medieval Celtic Studies* 15, 1–30.

— (2000) 'Graeco-Latin glossaries in early medieval Ireland,' *Peritia* 14, 406–20.

Stokes, W. (1898–1900) 'O'Mulconry's glossary,' *Archiv für celtische Lexikographie* 1, 232–324, 473–81, 629.

Strachan, J. (1903) 'On the language of the St. Gall Glosses,' *Zeitschrift für celtische Philologie* 4, 470–92.

Traube, L. (1891) 'O Roma nobilis: philologische Untersuchungen aus dem Mittelalter,' *Abhandlungen der Bayerischen Akademie der Wissenschaften* 19, 299–395.

Zimmer, H. (1881) *Glossae hibernicae e codicibus Wirziburgensi Carolisruhensibus aliis adjuvante academiae regiae Berolinensis liberalitate*, Berlin.

JEAN RITTMUELLER

CONSTRUE MARKS, A CONTRACTION MARK, AND AN EMBEDDED OLD IRISH GLOSS IN A HIBERNO-LATIN HOMILY ON THE OCTAVE OF EASTER

Abstract

Vatican, Biblioteca Apostolica, Reg. lat. 49, a late 10th-century Breton-Latin manuscript, is a miscellany of Latin religious texts that may have served as a preacher's source book. Half of its 56 texts were copied or adapted from Hiberno-Latin works. The Vatican manuscript's homily on the Octave of Easter contains an apparent Old Irish gloss, originally interlinear. Once its language was misidentified and its meaning misunderstood at some point in the manuscript tradition, the gloss was changed into a two-word Latin noun phrase and made part of the Latin text. The phrase, however, makes no sense in its Latin sentence, nor does the noun exist in any Latin dictionary. The Vatican scribe added construe marks to clarify the main elements of the relative clause in which the phrase is found. This paper provides a photograph and transcription of the passage in the manuscript, discusses the purpose of the construe marks, identifies the Old Irish word, and explains why it was an appropriate choice for the Latin word it was intended to interpret.

Keywords

Bible commentary, *Catechesis Celtica*, exegesis, homily; Hiberno-Latin, Old Irish gloss; construe marks; penitence, salvation; satisfaction.

Introduction[1]

Vatican, Biblioteca Apostolica, Reg. lat. 49 is a late 10th-century Breton-Latin manuscript copied by a scribe who identified himself as Guil-

[1] A version of this paper was presented at the Fourteenth International Congress of Celtic Studies, Maynooth, 2011. I am grateful to those who made helpful comments

Early medieval Ireland and Europe: chronology, contacts, scholarship, ed. by Pádraic Moran and Immo Warntjes, Studia Traditionis Theologiae, 14 (Turnhout, 2015), pp. 537–76.

 10.1484/M.STT-EB.5.103135

helm.[2] This collection of 56 Latin religious texts may have served as a preacher's source book.[3] Half of the texts are said to be patristic or Carolingian in origin.[4] The other half have close relationships with known Hiberno-Latin exegetical and homiletic works and are thought to date to the 9th or 10th century.[5] The Latin homily on the Octave of Easter (or Low Sunday) with its simple heading *Secundum Iohannem* is such a work—a single copy, replete with themes and expressions found in both Irish-language and Latin texts composed by Irish authors.[6] It may have an additional tie to Ireland, for it seems to preserve an Old Irish gloss, originally interlinear, but later embedded into the text, corrupted, reformed as a Latin phrase, and then treated as part of the homily.

The first part of this article describes the features of this homily that bolster the case for its Irish origin. The second part lays out the elements of the passage—the meaning of the contraction *sc̄i*, the construe marks, the Latin noun phrase *tinanci sui*—that, considered together, lead to a progressive resolution of problems that meet in a single relative clause. (A photograph and transcription of the passage in question accompany previous editors' suggested emendations.)

and suggestions. The photograph of Reg. lat. 49 is reproduced here by kind permission of the Biblioteca Apostolica Vaticana, with all rights reserved.

[2] Vatican, Biblioteca Apostolica, Reg. lat. 49, 53rb: *Guilhelm scripsit hunc librum., Deo gratias.* On the date of the manuscript, McNamara summarizes Boyle's conclusion sent in a letter that the 'ubiquitous' cedilla 'definitely' dates the MS to the 'late tenth century'; see McNamara (1994), 197–8.

[3] Wilmart (1933), 33; McNamara (1990), 291.

[4] McNamara (1994), 191–3.

[5] McNamara (1994), 191. Wilmart (1933) published editions of the fourteen texts that he judged to be Irish in origin, naming them *les catéchèses celtiques* (p 29). They are identified throughout this paper as *CC*. See O'Loughlin (2001), 22–3; Lapidge and Sharpe (1985), 268 (§974). Grosjean (1936), 136, suggested that they might be the product of the Irish Céli Dé movement in the 8th and 9th centuries although he admitted that this period was not yet well enough known to permit firm conclusions; Follett (2006), 162–3, concluded that 'nothing has come to light in the internal evidence or the manuscript tradition that might support Grosjean's supposition'.

[6] Homily 26R (Vatican, Biblioteca Apostolica, Reg. lat. 49, 32va1–35vb13) = *CC* 4 (Wilmart (1933), 47–58). Other texts of this manuscript mentioned in the present paper include: Homily 17R (Vatican, Biblioteca Apostolica, Reg. lat. 49, 18va11–20ra16) = *CC* 2 (Wilmart (1933), 39–44); Homily 34R (Vatican, Biblioteca Apostolica, Reg. lat. 49, 43vb24–45rb21) = *CC* 6 (Wilmart (1933), 65–71); Homily 39R (Vatican, Biblioteca Apostolica, Reg. lat. 49, 24ra28–25ra5) = *CC* 8 (Wilmart (1933), 79–82). Item numbers with an R suffix belong to the numbering system I have adopted for the edition of this manuscript in preparation. Previous numbering systems by Wilmart (1937), 112–7; McNally (n.d.); Rittmueller (1992–3); and McNamara (1994) are not cited in this paper.

On the homily's Irish origin

This homily's linguistic, liturgical, ecclesiastical, scholarly, and exegetical expressions characterize it as the work of an Irish author.[7]

Linguistic evidence

Linguistically, it has at least three Latin calques on OIr. expressions: *dicit contra* for OIr. *asbeir fri* ('he says to'), *ad dextera/dextralis* for OIr. *dess* ('on the right'), and a usage with ordinals that calques an OIr. usage, in which, for example, *quartus* means 'one of four'.

1. *Dicit contra aliquem/loquitur contra aliquem* ('he says to someone') is a calque on OIr. *asbeir fris* ('he says to him') and is a standard usage in Hiberno-Latin texts.[8] In contrast, Cl. Lat. *dicit contra eum* means 'he speaks in opposition to him' and continues to have this sense with verbs of speaking.[9] Chr. Lat. expresses 'he says to him' by replacing Cl. Lat. dative with *ad* + accusative, e.g. *dicere ad eum*.[10] Homily 26R has five instances of *dicit contra/loquitur contra* ('he says to'):
   (1) Vatican, Biblioteca Apostolica, Reg. lat. 49, 32va20–1 (*CC* 4; Wilmart (1933), 47.14):[11]
   quia locutus est contra Moisen
   'because he said to Moses'
   (2) Vatican, Biblioteca Apostolica, Reg. lat. 49, 32vb21 (*CC* 4; Wilmart (1933), 48.46):
   dicens contra illos
   'saying to them'
   (3) Vatican, Biblioteca Apostolica, Reg. lat. 49, 34vb8–9 (*CC* 4; Wilmart (1933), 55.77):
   ut dixit Christus contra mulierem quae sanata est

7 In making this case, I have added to evidence already identified in the following studies: Grosjean (1936); Stancliffe (1982); Ó Laoghaire (1987); McNamara (1990); Wright (1993); McNamara (1994).

8 Herren (1976), 121.

9 Plater and White (1926), 85 (§111.7.a.7 *contra*).

10 Plater and White (1926), 83 (§111.7.a.1 *ad*).

11 The translations of Homily 26R's citations of non-Vulgate and other untranslated Latin texts are mine. My translations of Homily 26R's Vulgate quotations are adapted from the Douay-Rheims edition.

'as Christ said to the woman who was healed'

(4) Vatican, Biblioteca Apostolica, Reg. lat. 49, 34vb17–8 (*CC* 4; Wilmart (1933), 55.84–5):
postquam dixit Christus contra se
'after Christ said to him'

(5) Vatican, Biblioteca Apostolica, Reg. lat. 49, 34vb21–2 (*CC* 4; Wilmart (1933), 55.89):
donec postea dixit contra Tomas
'until he said to Thomas afterwards'

2. Directions that substitute *dexter/dextralis* for *auster* ('south'), and *sinister/sinistralis* for *aquilo* ('north') render OIr. *dess*, which means both 'right' and 'south', and *túaid*, which means both 'left' and 'north'.[12] Löfstedt is not familiar with the meanings 'southern' for *dextralis* and 'northern' for *sinistralis* 'ausserhalb des keltischen Lateins'.[13] Apocalypse 21:13 is the basis for the homily's description of the celestial city's twelve gates, three in the east, three in the north, three in the south, and three in the west:

(6) *ab oriente portae tres, et ab aquilone portae tres, et ab austro portae tres, et ab occasu portae tres*
'in the east three gates, and in the north three gates, and in the south three gates, and in the west three gates'

Instead of the biblical *ab austro* ('in the south'), however, the homilist writes *ad dextera* (lit. 'to the right'):

(7) Vatican, Biblioteca Apostolica, Reg. lat. 49, 35ra15–7 (*CC* 4; Wilmart (1933), 56.14–5):
Item uidit XII hostias ciuitatis .i. III ab oriente et III ab occidente et III ad dextera et III ab aquilone.
'Likewise, he saw the city's twelve entrances, that is, three in the east and three in the west and three to the south and three in the north.'

Later, when expressing what each triad of doors symbolizes:

(8) Vatican, Biblioteca Apostolica, Reg. lat. 49, 35rb24–5,31–2 (*CC* 4; Wilmart (1933), 57.53, 57–8):
Item III dextrales ianuae [...] *Iohannes est dux istarum III ianuarum in parte dextrali .i. in plaga ardoris et lucis et solis.*

[12] Stancliffe (1982), 24; *DIL s.v. dess* 'right (as opposed to left)', *dessel* 'direction of the sun; right-hand course', *túaid* 'north, in the north', *túath* 'northern; left, on the left'.

[13] Löfstedt (1965), 133 n 1.

'Likewise the three southern doors [...] John is the keeper of those three doors in the southern part, that is, in the zone of heat and light and sun.'

(9) Vatican, Biblioteca Apostolica, Reg. lat. 49, 35va12–4 (*CC* 4; Wilmart (1933), 58.74–5):

Item III aliae sinistrales ianuae ciuitatis caeli .i. babtismum, poenitentia, martirium.

'Likewise, the three other northern doors of city of heaven, that is, baptism, penitence, martyrdom.'

In each instance, *dexter/dextralis* and *sinister/sinistralis* should be translated using the Hiberno-Latin meaning of 'south/southern' and 'north/northern', rather than the literal meaning of 'right/ right-hand' and 'left/left-hand'.

3. Homily 26R has two Latin examples of the distinctive Irish usage for the ordinal—the sense 'one of'. Like the OIr. ordinals *tress, cethramad*, for example, *tertius* and *quartus* can have the traditional meanings 'third' and 'fourth', but context may instead demand the meaning 'one of three' and 'one of four':[14]

(10) Vatican, Biblioteca Apostolica, Reg. lat. 49, 32vb36–40 (*CC* 4; Wilmart (1933), 48.59–62):

Ipsa est tertia caro quae sanctissima fuit in mundo: .i. Caro Christi, quae fuit sine macula peccati; .ii. Caro Mariae, quae consecrata est de conceptione Christi; .iii. Caro Iohannis, qui dormiebat super pectus Christi.

'His [John's] flesh is itself one of the three holiest in the world: i. the flesh of Christ, which was without the spot of sin; ii. the flesh of Mary, which was made holy as a result of her conception of Christ; iii. the flesh of John, who used to sleep on Christ's breast.'

(11) Vatican, Biblioteca Apostolica, Reg. lat. 49, 33ra8–13 (*CC* 4; Wilmart (1933), 49.67–71):

Ipse ergo est IIII euangelista qui narrauit natiuitatem Christi secundum humanitatem et babtismum et praedicationem et uirtutes et passionem et sepulturam et resurrectionem et osten<ta>tiones apostolis post resurrectionem per XL dies usque ad ascentionem in caelum.

[14] Grosjean (1936), 125; McNamara (1994), 188, 213; *DIL s.v. tress* 'third, one of three', *cethramad* 'fourth, one of four'.

'Therefore, he is himself one of the four evangelists who reported the birth of Christ according to his humanity and his baptism and his preaching and his works of power and his suffering and burial and resurrection and appearance to the apostles after the resurrection through the forty days until his ascension to heaven.'

Irish liturgical usage

Liturgically, the homily adopts the Irish usage for two terms, *refectio* and *Pascha modicum*.

1. The primary meaning of *refectio* in both Cl. Lat. and Chr. Lat. is the same. The *Oxford Latin Dictionary* and *Dictionnaire Latin-Français des auteurs Chrétiens* provide similar meanings:[15] 1. 'the act of repairing, restoration', 2. 'the process of recouping one's strength'; 1. 'action de se refaire (par le sommeil)', 'action de se restaurer, repas'. In the OIr. glosses, *airtach* is used to translate forms of *reficere* that have this sense of repair and physical restoration.[16] The 'well-established' secondary meaning for *airtach* in both 'secular and religious' contexts, writes McNamara, is 'act of celebrating; festival, ceremony'.[17] In the *Leabhar Breac* (Dublin, Royal Irish Academy, 23 P 16) homily on St Michael, the Irish translator's use of *erd(d)ach* to render *refectio* shows that both *refectio* and *airtach* had acquired this meaning by the Middle Irish period. McNamara believes that a more specific religious meaning for both the Latin and Irish words—'liturgical celebration'—is appropriate for the *Leabhar Breac* homily:

   (12) *Leabhar Breac* (Dublin, Royal Irish Academy, 23 P 16, 73b5–15):
   Feast of St Michael: *Tres uero refectiones sunt quae in omnibus festiuitatibus sanctorum agi debent* [...] *Primae (!) refectio est ymnorum diuinorum psalmorumque celebratio lectionisque*

[15] Glare (1996), 1593; Blaise (1954), 704.

[16] McNamara (1994), 189; *DIL s.v. airtach* 'act of refreshing, restoring'. Cf. Wb. [glosses in Würzburg, Universitätsbibliothek, M.p.th.f.12] 32a23 (Philemon 1:20; Stokes and Strachan (1901–3), i 704): *Refice viscera mea in Domino* i.e. *is irtach dom a airitiusom* ('Refresh my bowels in the Lord', i.e. 'To receive him is a refreshment for me'); Ml. [glosses in Milan, Biblioteca Ambrosiana, C301] 118c7 (Ps 101; Stokes and Strachan (1901–3), i 400): *reficiendi* i.e. *ertaig*.

[17] *DIL s.v. airtach*.

diuinae praedicatio [...] *Sacunda (!) refectio est communicatio et participatio corp<or>is <et> sanguinis Domini nostri Iesu Christi* [...] *Tertia refectio est egenorum paaperum (!) cibo et potu et uestitii retributio.*

'But there are three <liturgical> celebrations that are to be performed at all the saints' feasts [...] The first celebration is the performance of the divine hymns and psalms and the preaching of the *lectio diuina* [...] The second celebration is the communication and participation in the body and the blood of our Lord Jesus Christ [...] The third celebration is the recompense of the destitute poor with food and drink and clothing.'

(13) *Passions and Homilies from the Leabhar Breac* (hereafter *PHLB*) 16, ll. 6370–4:[18]

Feast of St Michael: *Tri herdaige dlegar do denum i sollamnaib na noem ⁊ na fhíren; is e in cetna erddach, celebrad ⁊ procept brethri Dé; is e imorro in t-erddach tanaise, edpairt chuirp Crist meic Dé bíí ⁊ a fhola, de chind in phopuil Cristaide; is e in tres erddach, biad ⁊ étach do thabhairt do bochtaib ⁊ do aidelcnechaib in mor choimded na ndúla.*

'Three <liturgical> celebrations are required to be performed at the feasts of the saints and the righteous: the first celebration is the performance and preaching of the word of God; the second celebration, moreover, is the offering of the body of Christ, the Son of God, and his blood on behalf of the Christian people; the third celebration is the giving of food and clothing to the poor and to the needy of the great Lord of the elements.'

McNamara identifies a second, similar passage, 'reproduced, in Irish only', in the third *Leabhar Breac* narrative of Christ's passion, in which he also takes *erdach* to mean 'liturgical celebration':

(14) *PHLB* 19, ll. 3600–6:[19]

O tri modaib tra ordaigther in sollamain-sea do anoir: is e in cetna herdach, celebrad ⁊ procept brethri Dé; is e in t-erdach tánaise, almsana do tharbairt i n-anoir in chomded, do sheirc ⁊ trocaire for na bochtaib; is e tra in tres erdach, in n-oifriund, a ndéntar hídpairt chuirp Crist ⁊ a fhola tar chend na firén.

[18] Ed. by Atkinson (1887), 218; trans. adapted from p 456.

[19] Ed. by Atkinson (1887), 141; trans. adapted from p 390.

Ocus cid mor dliges cech sollamain a herdach 7 a hanoir o na modaib-si, is in mor-mo dliges in sollamain-si.
'This feast is directed to be honoured in three ways: the first <liturgical> celebration is the reading and preaching of the word of God; the second <liturgical> celebration consists in giving alms in honour of the Lord, through love and mercy shown to the poor; the third <liturgical> celebration consists in the Mass, in which is made the offering of the body of Christ and of his blood on behalf of the righteous. And though each feast fully deserves its <liturgical> celebration and honour in these three ways, still more does this feast.'

He also identifies a passage in Homily 26R that uses *refectio* in the same sense:

(15) Vatican, Biblioteca Apostolica, Reg. lat. 49, 32va19–23 (*CC* 4; Wilmart (1933), 57.13–6):
Iste dies et Pasca magnum nec minor in honore quia locutus est contra Moisen ut nullus faceret opera in ista ebdomada Pascae nisi quod pertineret ad orandum Dominum et refectionem solemnitatis.
'This day <that is, the Small Easter> and the Great Easter <are> not less in honour because he <that is, God> said to Moses that no one should work in this week of the Passover unless it had to do with praying to the Lord and with the <liturgical> celebration of the feast.'

McNamara emphasizes that 'this secondary meaning of the word *refectio* <'act of celebrating; festival, ceremony'> does not appear to be registered in the lexica of the Latin language'. He concludes that this distinctive sense of *refectio* is Irish in origin.

2. 'Easter' and 'the Octave of Easter' are called *Pascha*/*Pascha magnum* and *Pascha modicum*/*Pascha minus* ('Easter/Great Easter' and 'Small Easter/Lesser Easter'). Tírechán's mention of *pasca magnum* is the basis for Grosjean's suggestion that its opposite, *pascha minus* or *pascha modicum*, also dates to the end of the 7th century, when Tírechán was writing.[20] The Irish equivalents *in*

[20] Grosjean (1936), 119. Tírechán, *Collectanea* 3.27(4) (ed. Bieler (1979), 146), writes that Bishop Cethiacus customarily celebrated mass in Corcu Sai *in pasca magno*. (Grosjean reads *in pasca maiore*.) For the date of the text and Tírechán's *floruit* see Bieler (1979), 5, 42.

Cásc mór and *min Chásc*, notes McNamara, 'are common' from at least the 9th century.[21] Both Latin terms appear in Homily 26R:

(16) Vatican, Biblioteca Apostolica, Reg. lat. 49, 32va13–20 (*CC* 4; Wilmart (1933), 47.9–14):

Utebantur panem infermentatum sine amaritudine usque ad finem VIII dierum .i. a Pasca magno usque ad modicum. Immolatur nunc corpus Christi et sanguis eius in ista ebdomada a resurrectione usque ad Pasca modicum post expultionem ueteris fermenti peccati Adae ab humano genere in Pasca resurrectionis, id est, iste dies et Pasca magnum nec minor in honore.

'They used unleavened bread, which lacked the sourness <of old leaven>, until the end of the eight days, that is, from the Great Easter to the Small <Easter>. Now the body of Christ and his blood is sacrificed in this week from the resurrection until the Small Easter, after the expulsion of the old leaven of Adam's sin from the human race in the Easter of the resurrection; that is, this day and the Great Easter are not less in honour.'

(17) Vatican, Biblioteca Apostolica, Reg. lat. 49, 32vb1–3 (*CC* 4; Wilmart (1933), 48.30–1):

Qua causa Tomae ostendit <se> Christus <et> apostolis die Pascae modici in domu clausa in Hierusalem?

'For what reason did Christ show <himself> to Thomas <and> to the apostles on the day of the Small Easter in the locked house in Jerusalem?'

A third mention of Easter also refers to the *Pascha magnum* and *Pascha modicum*, but omits the two adjectives:

(18) Vatican, Biblioteca Apostolica, Reg. lat. 49, 33ra18–20 (*CC* 4; Wilmart (1933), 49.73–6):

POST DIES VIII ITERUM, reliqua [John 20:26]. *Ita intigri sunt isti VIII dies si a medio diei usque ad alium medium numeretur unusquisque dies quia intiger est numerus VIII dierum a medio diei Saturni ante Pasca resurrectionis Christi usque ad medium Pascae quod est hodie.*

[21] McNamara (1994), 190, 213; McNamara (1990), 322. Both designations in Irish are found in the 9th-century Old Irish life of Brigid: *Bethu Brigte* 21 (ed. Ó hAodha (1978), 7): *o Chaisc Móir co Minchdáisc*; mention of *minchásc* in *Bethu Brigte* 28 (Ó hAodha (1978), 9): *co Minchaisc*; and *Bethu Brigte* 29 (Ó hAodha (1978), 9): *Dia Lúain Minchasc*; allusion to the two Easters in *Bethu Brigte* 24, 25, 26 (Ó hAodha (1978), 8–9): *eter di Cháisc*. A discussion of the language and date of this Life are in Ó hAodha (1978), xxv–xxvii.

> 'AFTER EIGHT DAYS AGAIN, etc. In this way are those eight days complete if each day is counted from the middle of the day until the middle of another day because the number of eight days is complete from the middle of the Saturday before the Easter of Christ's resurrection until the middle of the Easter that is today.'

Ecclesiastical and monastic terminology

Ecclesiastical and monastic terminology is the next category in which the homily adopts Irish usage. These terms include *gradus angelorum* ('orders of angels') and its opposite *exercitus daemonum* ('army of demons'), *princeps* (rather than *abbas* ('abbot')), *familia* ('inhabitants'), and *filius uitae* ('son of life').

1. Vatican, Biblioteca Apostolica, Reg. lat. 49 has five examples of *gradus angelorum*, *gradus caeli*, and *gradus caelestes* ('the orders of angels, the orders of heaven, the celestial orders'), two in Homily 26R:
   (19) Vatican, Biblioteca Apostolica, Reg. lat. 49, 34rb27–8 (*CC* 4; Wilmart (1933), 53.31):
   quia in pace creati sunt gradus angelorum in paradiso caelesti
   'because in peace were the orders of angels in the celestial paradise created'
   (20) Vatican, Biblioteca Apostolica, Reg. lat. 49, 35va37 (*CC* 4; Wilmart (1933), 58.94):
   conregnabunt cum gradibus caeli
   'they will rule together with the orders of heaven'
   (21) Vatican, Biblioteca Apostolica, Reg. lat. 49, 19vb38–40 (*CC* 2 [Item 17R]; Wilmart (1933), 40.61–2):
   lux .i. IX gradus caeli, a qua luce separauit Deus tenebras .i. Demones iecit de paradiso propter superbiam eorum.
   'the light, that is, the nine orders of heaven, from which light God separated the shadows; that is, He threw the demons from paradise because of their pride.'
   (22) Vatican, Biblioteca Apostolica, Reg. lat. 49, 44rb19–22 (*CC* 6 [Item 34R]; Wilmart (1933), 67.62–3, 65–6):
   in qua caeli domu mansiones multae sunt .i. IX ordines angelorum [...] unusquisque gradus tantum alio praecellens quantum proprius est Trinitati

'in which home of heaven there are many mansions, that is, the nine ranks of angels [...] each order surpassing the other only to the extent that it is nearer to the Trinity'

(23) Vatican, Biblioteca Apostolica, Reg. lat. 49, 24vb16–7 (*CC* 8 [Item 39R]; Wilmart (1933), 82.97):

Hic gradus caelestes imperantur per Spiritum aperire portas caeli.

'Here the celestial orders are ordered by the Spirit to open the gates of heaven.'

Grosjean cites numerous instances of the same terminology in the Irish sections of *Passions and Homilies from the Leabhar Breac*. McNamara concurs in the frequency of these expressions in both Latin and the vernacular Irish texts.[22]

2. The designation of the celestial orders as *gradus caelorum* has its opposite term *exercitus daemonum*, which Grosjean believes has 'une saveur irlandaise'.[23] Homily 26R has two examples:

(24) Vatican, Biblioteca Apostolica, Reg. lat. 49, 33rb17–18; 35va33 (*CC* 4; Wilmart (1933), 50.101; 58.90):

cum exercitu daemonum

'with the army of demons'

Found in Irish as *slóg/slúag/léigión/drong demne/demna/demun* ('army, host/legion/throng of devils'), the phrase appears in many religious texts.[24]

3. The word *familia* in Hiberno-Latin has the same semantic range as OIr. *muinter*.[25] It can mean 'household (including servants)' in the Cl. Lat. sense, but also 'adherents', or ' the disciples of a saint collectively', or 'a religious community or monastery', or 'inhabit-

[22] Grosjean (1936), 121; McNamara (1994), 190. Cf. *PHLB* 30, l. 1443 (Atkinson (1887), 81): *noí ngrád nime*; *PHLB* 21, l. 1939 (Atkinson (1887), 95): *noi ngrad nime*; *PHLB* 19, l. 3651 (Atkinson (1887), 143): *noi ṅgrad nime*; *PHLB* 15, l. 6176 (Atkinson (1887), 213): *nói ngrad nime*; *PHLB* 36, l. 8346 (Atkinson (1887), 273): *nói ngrad nime.*

[23] Grosjean (1936), 122.

[24] Instances from the *Passions and Homilies from the Leabhar Breac* include: *PHLB* 33, l. 7237 (Atkinson (1887), 243): *in slog demun*; *PHLB* 36, l. 8176 (Atkinson (1887), 269, 509): *a oirfitid na ṅdemna ṅdubsa, a frescisiu in tslóig dórcha* ('sport of these black demons, expectation of the darksome host'); *PHLB* 20, l. 3913 (Atkinson (1887), 150): *na huli légión na ṅdemnu*; *PHLB* 36, l. 8261 (Atkinson (1887), 271, 512): *hi nglaccaib na ndrong ṅdemnachsa* ('at the hands of these devilish throngs'); *PHLB* 36, l. 8288 (Atkinson (1887), 272, 513): *la drungu démnu* ('among the demon throngs').

[25] Grosjean (1936), 121; McNamara (1994), 190.

ants'.[26] In Homily 26R Christ has appeared to his *familia*, whose primary meaning is 'adherents', but whose secondary meaning, 'religious community', its audience must also have understood:

(25) Vatican, Biblioteca Apostolica, Reg. lat. 49, 33ra29–31 (*CC* 4; Wilmart (1933), 49.82–3):
Sicut apparuit Christus nunc familiae suae octauo diae post resurrectionem in domu clausa clauibus in Hierusalem
'Just as Christ appeared now to his adherents on the eighth day after the resurrection in a house locked with keys in Jerusalem'

The Irish phrase *muinter nime* 7 *talman* 7 *ifirn* (and its Hib. Lat. equivalent, *familia caeli et terrae et inferni*) is translated 'the inhabitants of heaven and earth and hell' in *DIL*, but is more accurately understood as 'household of heaven and earth and hell', that is, all people, living and dead:[27]

(26) Vatican, Biblioteca Apostolica, Reg. lat. 49, 32va4–5 (*CC* 4; Wilmart (1933), 47.3):
eo quod uenerabilis est hic dies cum familia caeli et terrae
'because the household of heaven and of earth considers this a day to be honoured'

The *familia* of heaven is itself divided into three smaller *familiae*, the angels, the patriarchs, and the apostles, who guard each gate to the celestial city:

(27) Vatican, Biblioteca Apostolica, Reg. lat. 49, 35ra18–24 (*CC* 4; Wilmart (1933), 56.15–20):

[26] Cl. Lat. *familia*: 'household' including 'all persons subject to the control of one man, whether relations, freedmen, or slaves'. It can also mean 'a body of persons closely associated by blood or affinity' or 'school of philosophy', or it is the legal term for 'estate (consisting of the household and household property)', according to the *Oxford Latin Dictionary* (Glare (1996), 675). *DIL s.v. muinter*: 'In general sense a community or group of persons connected by some common bond, hence esp. (a) a family or household (including servants), corresponding to Lat. *familia* [...] (b) in wider sense, followers, adherents, party, attendant troops [...] (c) often of the disciples of a saint collectively, a religious community or monastery [...] (d) of inhabitants, etc. *muntar nime*, Wb. 21d1; *i n-óentu muintire nime*, Wb. 9c28 (cf. *PHLB* lines 4357, 6520); *eter muntir nime et talman* (= *quae in caelis sive quae in terris sunt*), Wb. 26d5; *hí figuir noe montar nimæ* (= the nine celestial hierarchies), *Thes.* ii 254.10 (Stowe Miss. 65b); *na teora muntera .i. munter nime* 7 *talman* 7 *ifirn*, *Trip.* 118.19; *Righ na tri muinnter, RC* 28, 322 § 49; *muinter na catrach*, *FB* 82.'

[27] *muinter nime ocus talman*: *PHLB* ll. 3606, 4357, 4654, 5514, 7067 (Atkinson (1887), 141, 162, 170, 194, 223); *muinter nime*: *PHLB* ll. 6210, 6256, 6520, 8075 (Atkinson (1887), 214, 215, 238, 266); *muinter ifirn*: *PHLB* l. 8175 (Atkinson (1887), 269).

Et uidit XII apostolos et XII patriarchas custodientes ciuitatem, III angelos et III patriarchas et III apostolos in unaquaque parte ciuitatis, quia hae sunt III familiae quibus commendatum est aperire regnum celorum sanctis omnibus in die iudicii et quibus iterum commendatum est claudere regnum Dei in fine saeculi contra daemones et peccatores.

'And he saw the twelve apostles and the twelve patriarchs guarding the city, three angels and three patriarchs and three apostles in each part of the city, because these are the three households that have been charged with opening the kingdom of heaven to all the saints on the day of judgment and that again have been entrusted with closing the kingdom of God at the end of the world against the demons and sinners.'

A variant is the phrase *uiri caeli et terrae*/*fir nimi, fir thalman* ('the people of heaven, the people of the earth'), of which Homily 26R has two examples:[28]

(28) Vatican, Biblioteca Apostolica, Reg. lat. 49, 33rb31–3 (*CC* 4; Wilmart (1933), 50.104–5):

et possidebit pacem sempiternam, quae erit inter uiros caeli et terrae post iudicium

'and he will possess eternal peace, which there will be among the people of heaven and earth after the judgment'

(29) Vatican, Biblioteca Apostolica, Reg. lat. 49, 34rb38–9 (*CC* 4; Wilmart (1933), 54.39–40):

Ipsa est quam uoluit Christus fieri cum apostolis et reparare iterum inter uiros caeli et terrae.

'It is the very <peace> that Christ wanted to happen with the apostles and to restore again among the people of heaven and earth.'

4. *Princeps* frequently replaces *abbas* in Hiberno-Latin texts. It is the Hib. Lat. equivalent of Irish *airchinnech*.[29] Homily 26R uses *princeps* in this sense three times:

(30) Vatican, Biblioteca Apostolica, Reg. lat. 49, 33vb5–9 (*CC* 4; Wilmart (1933), 51.152–5):

[28] Martyrology of Tallaght (ed. Best and Lawlor (1931), 102): *Fir nimi, fir thalman*; and cited by Grosjean (1936), 121.

[29] Hughes (1966), 126; Stancliffe (1982), 24; McNamara (1994), 213. Grosjean (1936), 122, writes that the *princeps monachorum* is the *airchinnech* (abbot) with his *manaig*, that is, the chief and his vassals.

Ipse est uir cum honeribus omnis princeps cum monachis multis et inmundis sub sua potestate quia etiam si sit sanctus peribit cum monachis nisi uituperauerit uitia illorum ut Dominus per profetam dicit contra omnes principes et doctores et contra omnes potentes.

'The man with burdens is himself every chief with his many and impure monks in his power because even if he should be holy, he will perish with his monks unless he has censured their vices, as the Lord says through the prophet to all the chiefs and to teachers and to all the men in power.'

(31) Vatican, Biblioteca Apostolica, Reg. lat. 49, 33vb15–6 (*CC* 4; Wilmart (1933), 51.160):

Si uero annuntiauerit princeps monachis

'But if the chief has made known to his monks'

Grosjean believes, furthermore, that the occurrence of *monachus* in Hiberno-Latin texts refers not to a monk in the normal sense, but to the *manach*, the lay occupant of the monastic establishment, described by Grosjean as 'paysans, vassaux soumis à un chef (sur des biens ecclésiastiques)'.[30] Still, context will determine whether a given writer intends the audience to understand that *monachus* means *manach* or 'monk'.

5. The phrases *filius mortis/mac báis* and *filius uitae/mac bethad* designate 'a son of death, a wicked man' versus 'a son of life, a righteous man' (the latter often used of 'a professed religious').[31] An early Hib. Lat. example is in the Commentary on the Catholic Epistles attributed to Pseudo-Hilary and dated to the early 8th century.[32] Another example in the Tripartite Life, dated between AD 895–901, uses the phrase *cin peceth* ('without sin') to gloss *mac bethoth*.[33] The earliest Irish example is in the *Apgitir Crábaid*, dated either to the beginning of the 7th century if by Colmán mac

30 Grosjean (1936), 122.

31 *DIL s.v. mac*. Cf. Grosjean (1936), 120, and McNamara (1994), 188.

32 Pseudo-Hilarius, *Expositio in septem epistulas catholicas* 2 Pet 3.1 (ed. by Robert McNally in CCSL 108B, 51–124: 105): *Hucusque filios perditionis increpat. Nunc filios uitae alloquitur.* ('Up to this point he rebukes the sons of ruin. Now he speaks to the sons of life.') See bibliography at Lapidge and Sharpe (1984), 99 (§B346).

33 Tripartite Life of St Patrick l. 20 (ed. Stokes (1887), i 84); glosses on the Tripartite Life from Dublin, Trinity College, 1337 (*olim* H.3.18), 524 (Stokes (1887), i lii).

Béognae (†AD 611) or to the early 8th if an early *Céli Dé* text.[34] Homily 26R has one instance of *filius uitae* and a variant expression *filius benedictionis*:

(32) Vatican, Biblioteca Apostolica, Reg. lat. 49, 33va20–1 (*CC* 4; Wilmart (1933), 50–1.133–4):
Ipsa est uia quae ducit filios uitae ad regnum.
'It is the very path that leads the sons of life to the kingdom.'

(33) Vatican, Biblioteca Apostolica, Reg. lat. 49, 35rb24–7 (*CC* 4; Wilmart (1933), 57.53–4):
Item III dextrales ianuae, per quas ueniunt filii benedictionis in ciuitate caeli .i. uirginitas et paenitentia et matrimonium.
'Likewise, the three right-hand doors, through which the sons of blessing come into the city of heaven, that is, virginity and penitence and marriage.'

Irish scholarly and exegetical terminology

Scholarly and exegetical terminology with an Irish background includes the words *sapiens*, *aliter*, *uetus lex/nouus lex*, plus a cognomen for John (*Iohannes super pectus*). The enumerative style is also a marked rhetorical feature.

1. In citing authorities, Hiberno-Latin writers often mention *sapiens*, 'a formal term for a scholar (Irish *suí*) used in the Irish annals', a title that describes men expert in 'the Latin language and theological studies'.[35] The context of Homily 26R indicates *sapiens* is to be understood as a biblical scholar:

(34) Vatican, Biblioteca Apostolica, Reg. lat. 49, 35vb4–5 (*CC* 4; Wilmart (1933), 58.99–100):
et ideo putant sapientes diem iudicii in tempore Pascae
'and therefore the biblical scholars think that the day of judgment <will be> at Easter'

[34] *Apgitir Chrábaid* 22, 30 (ed. Hull (1968), 72, 74): *Cethoir trebairi inda mac mbethad* [...] *Is ed in so immefolngai duine dend-í bes mac báis combi mac bethad, dend-í bes mac dorchai combi mac solse.* ('The four safeguards of the 'sons of Life' [...] This it is that causes a person to be a 'son of Life' from being a 'son of Death' [and] to be a 'son of Light' from being a 'son of Darkness'.') Hull (1968), 52, surmises that *Apgitir Chrábaid* is a 'composite text which was probably compiled sometime in the first half of the 8th century during the early period of the Culdee movement'; Ó Néill (1987), 203 and 215, however, argues for an early 7th century date.

[35] Wright (1993), 23 n 91; Hughes (1958), 247.

2. Or, they will list 'alternative interpretations with *aliter* or *alii dicunt*', as does Homily 26R:[36]
   (35) Vatican, Biblioteca Apostolica, Reg. lat. 49, 33va31–2 (*CC* 4; Wilmart (1933), 51.141–2):
   Aliter haec sunt duo limina huius ianuae, amor Dei et proximi.
   'In another interpretation, these are the two cross-pieces of this door, the love of God and of neighbour.'
3. With respect to exegetical terminology Grosjean mentions that the expression *uetus lex* has 'une saveur irlandaise' to the extent that it is 'si indissolublement unis' in the thought of the religious writers that a single Irish word (*fetarlicce*) was made from it:[37]
   (36) Vatican, Biblioteca Apostolica, Reg. lat. 49, 33rb4–5 (*CC* 4; Wilmart (1933), 49.90–1):
   Figuratus est item iste numerus per circumcisionem, quae fuit in ueteri lege VIII diae.
   'Likewise, that number was symbolized by circumcision, which in the old law was on the eighth day.'
   (37) Vatican, Biblioteca Apostolica, Reg. lat. 49, 34ra33–5 (*CC* 4; Wilmart (1933), 53.5–7):
   Hae sunt duae stationes quae reputantur sanctis in aeclesia Dei sequendo Christum [...] *Figuratae sunt in ueteri lege hae* II^{as} *stationes.*
   'These are the two stations that are counted as holy acts in the church of God by following Christ [...] These two stations have been symbolized in the old law.'
   (38) Vatican, Biblioteca Apostolica, Reg. lat. 49, 35ra35–6 (*CC* 4; Wilmart (1933), 56.30–1):
   Item XII patriarchae quos uidit Iohannes in foribus ciuitatis, hi sunt doctores qui custodiunt ueteris legis <praecepta>.
   'Likewise, the twelve patriarchs whom John saw in the entrances of the city, these are the teachers who guard the <precepts> of the old law.'

   The expression *noua lex* also occurs:
   (39) Vatican, Biblioteca Apostolica, Reg. lat. 49, 35ra36–7 (*CC* 4; Wilmart (1933), 56.31–2):

[36] Wright (1993), 13.

[37] Grosjean (1936), 120. *DIL s.v. fetarlaic*: 'OIr. *fetarlicce*, from *(in) uetere lege*; later *fetarlaic(c)*'.

Item XII apostoli quos uidit Iohannes, hi sunt praeceptores qui seruant nouam legem.
'Likewise, the twelve apostles whom John saw, these are the authorities who protect the new law.'

4. At least one biblical figure receives a designation that, although borrowed from the Bible, is characteristic of Hiberno-Latin and Irish writing. The Irish cognomen for St John, *Iohannes super pectus*, has its basis in two verses in John:

(40) John 13:23:
Erat ergo recumbens unus ex discipulis eius in sinu Iesu, quem diligebat Iesus.
'Now there was leaning back on Jesus' breast one of his disciples, whom Jesus loved.'

(41) John 21:20:
Conuersus Petrus uidit illum discipulum quem diligebat Iesus, sequentem, qui et recubuit in cena super pectus eius et dixit: Domine, quis est qui tradet te?
'Turning around, Peter saw following them the disciple whom Jesus loved, who also had leaned back on his breast at supper and said: 'Lord, who is it that will betray you?''

St John is called *Eoin Bruinne* ('John of the Breast') in Irish writing.[38] The cognomen *Iohannes super pectus* occurs in numerous Latin texts with Irish affiliations:

(42) Pseudo-Hieronimus, *Expositio quatuor euangeliorum* [*Resc. 1*]:[39]
De diuinitate Ioannes dicit, 'In principio erat Uerbum' [John 1:1]. *Iste iacebat super pectus Iesu, et scientia diuinitatis, quae fuerat in pectore Iesu, ascendit Ioanni de coniunctione duorum pectorum.*
'Of <Jesus'> divinity, John says: "In the beginning was the Word". He used to lean on Jesus' breast, and the knowledge of his divinity, which was in Jesus' breast, climbed up to from the union of their two breasts.'

(43) Pseudo-Isidorus, *De ortu et obitu patriarcharum* 48.1:[40]

[38] McNamara (1994), 213. Cf. *Beatha Eoin Bruinne* (ed. Mac Niocaill (1953–4)).

[39] Pseudo-Hieronimus, *Expositio quatuor euangeliorum* [*Resc. 1*] (saec. VII^{ex}) (PL 30, 588–9). See Lapidge and Sharpe (1985), 97–8 (§341).

[40] Pseudo-Isidorus, *De ortu et obitu patriarcharum* 48.1 (saec. VIII^{2}) (ed. by Carracedo Fraga in CCSL 108E, 63–4). See Lapidge and Sharpe (1985), 209 (§780).

Iohannis [...] *a Domino electus et in tantum dilectus, ut in cena recumberet super pectus Domini*
'John [...] chosen by the Lord and so beloved that at supper he leaned back on the Lord's breast'

(44) *Commentarium in Iohannem* (Wien, Österreichische Nationalbibliothek, Lat. 997, 67r):[41]
Et de Iohanne dicitur: 'Iactabat super pectus Iesu' [John 21:20], *et scientia diuinitatis quae uiuit in pectore Iesu ascendit in anima Iohannis.*
'And about John it is said: 'He cast himself on Jesus' breast', and the knowledge of divinity that lives in Jesus' breast climbed up into John's soul.'

(45) *Commentarius in Apocalypsin* prologus:[42]
Sed cur promeruit, ut ipse scriberet? Quia primum super pectus Domini recumbens spiritalia ab eius ore trahebat, oportuit ut post ascensionem ab ipso caelestes et spiritales sumeret visiones.
'But why did he <that is, John> deserve to write <the apocalypse>? First, because, when leaning back on the Lord's breast, he used to draw spiritual things from his <Lord's> mouth, it was proper that after the ascension he should receive heavenly and spiritual visions from the Lord himself.'

The designation occurs twice in Homily 26R:

(46) Vatican, Biblioteca Apostolica, Reg. lat. 49, 32vb34–6 (*CC* 4; Wilmart (1933), 48.57–9):
POST DIES VIII ITERUM ERANT DISCIPULI INTUS ET TOMAS CUM EIS [John 20:26]. *Iohannes discipulus Christi narrat hoc factum, qui dormiebat super pectus Christi in epulis.*
'AFTER EIGHT DAYS HIS DISCIPLES WERE AGAIN INSIDE, AND THOMAS WITH THEM. John, a disciple of Christ, who slept upon Christ's breast at the feast, relates this deed.'

(47) Vatican, Biblioteca Apostolica, Reg. lat. 49, 32vb40 (*CC* 4; Wilmart (1933), 48.61–2):
caro Iohannis, qui dormiebat super pectus Christi
'the flesh of John, who used to sleep upon Christ's breast'

[41] The manuscript is saec. VIII/IX; the passage is ed. by Kelly in CCSL 108C, 105. See Lapidge and Sharpe (1985), 208 (§774).

[42] *Commentarius in Apocalypsin* (saec. VIII/IX) (ed. by Lo Menzo Rapisarda in PL Supplementum 4, 1851). See Lapidge and Sharpe (1985), 209 (§781).

5. The enumerative style is a persistent feature of Homily 26R.[43] There are the triads, beginning with a variation of the three-fold martyrdom, where the homilist substitutes baptism for the white martyrdom, which Clare Stancliffe concludes is the 'daily martyrdom of the ascetic life':[44]

(48) Vatican, Biblioteca Apostolica, Reg. lat. 49, 35ra28–35 (*CC* 4; Wilmart (1933), 56.24–8):
Quibus lapidibus comparantur actus sanctorum quando per martiria probantur et per plures necessitates: aliis actibus probatis per babtismum, aliis per iacintha martiria, aliis per rubra martiria ensium persecutor<is> pro amore Dei uel per sanguinem pudoris dando confessionem ductoribus animarum.
'The acts of the saints are compared to these stones when they are tested through martyrdom and through many exigencies: to some acts that have been tested through baptism, to others through the sapphire martyrdoms, to others through the red martyrdoms of the persecutor's swords for the love of God or through the blood of shame by giving a confession to the helmsmen of souls.'

There are the four triple doors leading into the kingdom of heaven—faith, hope, charity; virginity, penitence, marriage;[45] deed, word, thought;[46] baptism, penitence, martyrdom:

(49) Vatican, Biblioteca Apostolica, Reg. lat. 49, 35rb16–7 (*CC* 4; Wilmart (1933), 57.47):
Hae sunt III ianuae ab oriente .i. fides, spes, caritas.
'These are the three doors in the east, that is, faith, hope, love.'

(50) Vatican, Biblioteca Apostolica, Reg. lat. 49, 35rb24–7 (*CC* 4; Wilmart (1933), 57.53–4):
Item III dextrales ianuae per quas ueniunt filii benedictionis in ciuitate caeli .i. uirginitas et paenitentia et matrimonium.

[43] Wright (1993), 49–105.

[44] Stancliffe (1982), 44; Wright (2000), 149–50. If baptism, Homily 26R's replacement for the white martyrdom of the ascetic life, is a shorthand for the baptism of tears, emblematic of the penitent heart, one would expect it to replace the blue martyrdom of the penitent.

[45] See Wright (2000), 153.

[46] Sims-Williams (1978), 78–111, esp. 85–6.

'Likewise, the three southern doors, through which the sons of blessedness come into the city of heaven, that is, virginity and penitence and marriage.'

(51) Vatican, Biblioteca Apostolica, Reg. lat. 49, 35rb36–35va1 (*CC* 4; Wilmart (1933), 57.62–5):
Item ciuitatis III ianuae quae sunt ab occasu, per quas ueniunt sancti in ciuitatem caeli. Hae sunt opus et uerbum et cogitatio. Haec est ianua excelsissima et optima earum .i. opus si fuerit poenitentiale quia in ipso perficiuntur cogitationes et uerba.
'Likewise, the three gates of the city that are in the west, through which the saints come into the city of heaven. These are deed and word and thought. This is the highest and best of them, that is, the deed if it is penitential because in it thoughts and words are perfected.'

(52) Vatican, Biblioteca Apostolica, Reg. lat. 49, 35va12–19,30–31 (*CC* 4; Wilmart (1933), 58.74–9,87–9):
Item III aliae sinistrales ianuae ciuitatis caeli .i. babtismum, poenitentia, martirium. Ipsa sinistra ianua earum optima est .i. babtismum, ut Christus dicit: 'Nisi quis renatus fuerit ex aqua et Spiritu sancto, non', reliqua [John 3:5]. *Item pro babtismo reputatur penitentia, ut est: 'Lacrimae paenitentiae pro babtismate reputantur'. Item martirium pro babtismo reputatur sanctis* [...] *Istae sunt III ianuae per quas maxime superatur diabolus .i. babtismum et penitentia et martirium.*
'Likewise, the three other, northern, doors of the city of heaven, that is, baptism, penitence, martyrdom. The left-hand door is itself the best of these, that is, baptism, as Christ says: 'Unless a man has been born again of water and the holy Spirit, <he can>not', etc. Likewise, penitence is reckoned as a baptism, as it is: 'The tears of baptism are reckoned as baptism'. Likewise, martyrdom is reckoned to the saints as baptism [...] These are the three doors through which the devil is especially defeated, that is, baptism and penitence and martyrdom.'

There is the earth divided into three parts among the sons of Noah, who are later understood spiritually as the sons of Christ, the spiritual Noah, and are identified as virgins, penitents, and married couples:

(53) Vatican, Biblioteca Apostolica, Reg. lat. 49, 33rb14–5 (*CC* 4; Wilmart (1933), 50.98–9):

Et diuisa est terra in III partes inter III filios Noe, quod conuenit misterio generis humani.
'And the earth was divided into three parts among the three sons of Noah, and this <division> applies to the mystery of the human race.'

(54) Vatican, Biblioteca Apostolica, Reg. lat. 49, 33rb23–6 (*CC* 4; Wilmart (1933), 50.104–7):
Et diuidetur positio caelestis quam deseruerunt apostatae angeli, id est demones, inter III filios Noe spiritualis, id est Christi, id est inter uirgines et penitentes et coniugales.
'And the celestial setting that the apostate angels, that is, the demons, deserted is divided among the sons of the spiritual Noah, that is, of Christ, that is, among the virgins and penitents and married couples.'

There are the four kinds of peace—between God and men, between angels and men, between bodies and souls, between neighbours:

(55) Vatican, Biblioteca Apostolica, Reg. lat. 49, 34rb18–20 (*CC* 4; Wilmart (1933), 53.23–5):
Quia sunt IIII modi pacis qui efficiuntur per Christum .i. pax inter Deum et homines, inter angelos et homines, inter corpora et animas, inter utrosque proximos.
'Because there are four kinds of peace that are brought about through Christ, that is, the peace between God and men, between angels and men, between bodies and souls, between two neighbours.'

There are the five people who cannot enter through the narrow door, mentioned in Matthew 7:13–14:

(56) Vatican, Biblioteca Apostolica, Reg. lat. 49, 33vb2–4 (*CC* 4; Wilmart (1933), 51.150–1):
Sunt V uiri qui non possunt intrare per hanc ianuam: uir cum oneribus, uir cum cicatricibus, uir crassus, uir humilis ualde, uir altus ualde.
'There are five men who cannot enter through this door: the man with burdens, the man with scars, the fat man, the exceptionally small man, the exceptionally tall man.'

There are the six benefits of peace. Although the homilist identifies Augustine as the author of the list, the *Collectio Canonum Hibernensis* is its actual verbatim source:[47]

(57) Vatican, Biblioteca Apostolica, Reg. lat. 49, 34rb20–4 (*CC* 4; Wilmart (1933), 53.25–8):

Sunt VI utilitates quas efficit pax hominibus, ut Agustinus dicit: 'In pace multa continentur, dilectio proximi, agnitio Dei, contemptus mundi, uisitatio angelorum, serenitas praesentium, meditatio futurorum.'

'There are six benefits that peace brings to pass for men, as Augustine says: 'In peace many things are included, love of neighbour, knowledge of God, contempt of the world, the visitation of angels, the serenity concerning present-day events, thinking about things that will happen."

The eight days of Easter are symbolized by the eight souls in the ark, the eight days of the Passover, the eight books of the New Testament,[48] the eight Beatitudes of the Gospel, the eight ages from the beginning of the world, the eight periods of the present life, the eight principal vices:

(58) Vatican, Biblioteca Apostolica, Reg. lat. 49, 33ra21–3 (*CC* 4; Wilmart (1933), 49.77–8):

Figurate sunt nunc isti VIII dies in 'VIII animabus' quae fuerunt in 'arca Noe' [1 Peter 3:20], *quae liberatae sunt de diluuio.*

'These eight days have already been symbolized in the 'eight souls' who were in 'Noah's ark', who were delivered from the flood.'

[47] *Collectio Canonum Hibernensis* XXI 8 (ed. Wasserschleben (1885), 64): *De his, qui per pacem habentur.* See Lapidge and Sharpe (1985), 157 (§612). *CCH* cites *Hieronimus* as the source of its definition, and Wasserschleben suggests comparing it with Jerome's *Commentariorum in epistolam ad Ephesios libri tres* III 6.24 (AD 467–590) (PL 26, 588), but the passages are not close.

[48] Cf. *PHLB* 31 (On the Octave of Easter; Atkinson (1887), 468; the translation is mine): *Haec lectio sensum habet spiritualem, ad Christum et ad ecclesiam pertinentem. Mystice ergo, octo dies octo libri sunt Noui Testamenti, qui nomine dierum nuncupantur, quia sicut corporali lumine nostram (sic!) corpus illuminatur, ita spirituali lumine nostra anima ad domini mandata dirigitur, Christo dicente: 'Si quis ambulauerit in die, non offendit.'* [John 11:9] ('This lection has a spiritual sense, which applies to Christ and to the penitent church. Mystically, therefore, the eight days <are> the eight books of the New Testament, which are named from the names of the days, because just as our body is illuminated by a bodily light, so our soul is directed to the commandments of the Lord by a spiritual light, as Christ says: 'If a man walks in the day, he does not stumble."')

(59) Vatican, Biblioteca Apostolica, Reg. lat. 49, 33ra23–4 (*CC* 4; Wilmart (1933), 49.79):
Figurate sunt <isti VIII dies> in VIII diebus Pascae, quod imperauit Deus Moisi in Egipto.
'<These eight days> were symbolized in the eight days of the Passover, which God ordered Moses <to institute> in Egypt.'

(60) Vatican, Biblioteca Apostolica, Reg. lat. 49, 33ra25–6 (*CC* 4; Wilmart (1933), 49.80):
Significant nunc isti VIII dies VIII libros Noui Testamenti.
'These eight days now signify the eight books of the New Testament.'

(61) Vatican, Biblioteca Apostolica, Reg. lat. 49, 33ra26–7 (*CC* 4; Wilmart (1933), 49.80–1):
Significant nunc isti VIII dies [...] *VIII beatitudines euangelii.*
'These eight days now signify [...] the eight beatitudes of the gospel.'

(62) Vatican, Biblioteca Apostolica, Reg. lat. 49, 33rb19–20 (*CC* 4; Wilmart (1933), 50.102):
qui impleuerit VIII beatitudines euangelii
'the one who fulfilled the eight beatitudes of the gospel'

(63) Vatican, Biblioteca Apostolica, Reg. lat. 49, 33rb27–30 (*CC* 4; Wilmart (1933), 50.107–9):
in arca aeclesiae .i. in domu clausa contra demones et uitia, ubi implentur VIII beatitudines euangelii et VIII orationes dominicae et VIII libri Noui Testamenti
'in the ark of the church, that is, in the house locked against demons and vices, where the eight beatitudes of the gospel and the eight petitions of the Lord's prayer and the eight books of the New Testament are fulfilled'

(64) Vatican, Biblioteca Apostolica, Reg. lat. 49, 33ra27–9 (*CC* 4; Wilmart (1933), 49.81–2):
Significant item VIII tempora quae numerantur a principio mundi usque ad fidem.
'Likewise, they signify the eight periods of time that are counted from the beginning of the world up to the end.'

(65) Vatican, Biblioteca Apostolica, Reg. lat. 49, 35ra1–4 (*CC* 4; Wilmart (1933), 56.1–3):
Item isti VIII dies Pascae significant VIII tempora uitae praesentis a principio mundi usque ad iudicium quia sub forma ebdomadis constituit Deus hunc mundum.

'Likewise, these eight days of Easter signify the eight periods of the present life from the beginning of the world until the judgment because God constituted this world using the week as its pattern.'

(66) Vatican, Biblioteca Apostolica, Reg. lat. 49, 33rb11 (*CC* 4; Wilmart (1933), 49.96):
legem circumcisionis VIII principalium uitiorum
'the law of circumcision of the eight principle vices'

(67) Vatican, Biblioteca Apostolica, Reg. lat. 49, 33rb30–1 (*CC* 4; Wilmart (1933), 50.110):
circumcisio spiritualis VIII principalium uitiorum
'the spiritual circumcision of the eight principle vices'

Theological issues

With respect to theological issues in Homily 26R, Grosjean mentions 'une indication très clair' of the belief in guardian angels, 'très répandue et très profonde':[49]

(68) Vatican, Biblioteca Apostolica, Reg. lat. 49, 35ra39–b4 (*CC* 4; Wilmart (1933), 56–7.32–6):
Item 'XII angeli' [Apoc 21:12] *quos uidit Iohannes, hi sunt ministri et custodes aeclesiae catholicae, ut psalmista dicit: 'Quoniam angelis suis mandauit de te ut custodiant te', reliqua* [Ps 90:11], *quia custodiunt angeli caeli animam uniuscuiusque hominis a die natiuitatis sue usque ad diem quando exierit de corpore suo.*
'Likewise, 'the twelve angels' whom John saw, these are the ministers and guardians of the catholic church, as the psalmist says: 'For he has given his angels charge over you to keep you', etc., because the angels of heaven guard the soul of each man from the day of his birth until the day when it has left his body.'

Stancliffe mentions 'the great stress' Homily 26R lays 'upon the efficacy of penance', which belongs to the practices and beliefs that are 'peculiarly those of the Irish or other Celtic churches'.[50] Penitence and penance are referenced eight times in connection with Thomas, the locked house, the types of men who cannot enter heaven through the narrow door of penitence, Noah, the

[49] Grosjean (1936), 129.

[50] Stancliffe (1982), 24.

three gates in the wall encircling heaven, and the elements of faith.

In his first mention of penitence, the homilist suggests that because Thomas had done penance in the days between the two Easters for doubting Christ's resurrection, Jesus forgave him and allowed him to put his hand into his side:

(69) Vatican, Biblioteca Apostolica, Reg. lat. 49, 32va30–6 (*CC* 4; Wilmart (1933), 47.22–6):

Hic est dies in quo misit 'Tomas manum' suam 'in latus' Christi [cf. John 20:27] *super uestigium 'lanceae militis' Longini, qui 'latus' Christi iugulauit quando fuit in cruce* [cf. John 19:34]. *Et indulsit Christus sibi hoc factum per paenitentiam quam fecit donec uidit deitatem per humanitatem et donec miles fuit Deo postea praedicando <in> nomine Dei et uerbo et opere.*

'This is the day on which 'Thomas' placed his 'hand into' Christ's 'side' over the track of the 'lance of the soldier' Longinus, who slit Christ's 'side' when he was on the cross. And Christ permitted him <i.e. Thomas> this action through the penance that he did up to the time he saw the divine nature through the humanity and up to the time he was a soldier for God afterwards by preaching <in> God's name in both word and deed.'

The locked house is the church, which is shut to all unrepentant sinners, but whose narrow door of penitence is open to sinners who have reached it by taking the steep path, comprised, in part, of penitence:

(70) Vatican, Biblioteca Apostolica, Reg. lat. 49, 33va1,6,9–15,17–21 (*CC* 4; Wilmart (1933), 50–1.118–9,122–34):

Domus clausa, in qua uenit Christus ad apostolos [...] *conuenit domui aeclesiae* [...] *ut non ueniat in illam qui fuerit extra in malitia sua, in uoluntatibus, et in peccatis et in uitiis suis, nisi uenerit per angustam ianuam penitentiae, ut legitur in euangelio: 'Intrate per angustam portam* [...] *Quam angusta porta et arcta est uia quae ducit ad uitam, et pauci sunt qui inueniunt eam'* [Mt 7:13–14] [...] *Ipsa est ergo arcta uia uel ascensa contemptio uoluntatum et penitentia peccatorum et amor inimicorum et indulgentia unicuique qui tibi fecit malum. Ipsa est uia quae ducit filios uitae ad regnum.*

'The locked house, in which Christ came to the apostles [...] applies to the house of the church [...] so that he may not come into that <church> who was outside in his malice, in his inclinations, both in his sins and in his vices, unless he comes through the narrow door of penitence, as it is read in the gospel: 'Enter through the narrow gate [...] How narrow the gate and close is the road that leads to life, and there are few who find it.' [...] Therefore, the close or steep road is itself the contempt of desires and the penitence of sinners and the love of one's enemies and indulgence for each person who has done you wrong. It is the very path that leads the sons of life to the kingdom.'

In a second interpretation of the narrow door, the man guilty of the eight deadly sins and the man who despairs cannot enter heaven unless they have done penance:

(71) Vatican, Biblioteca Apostolica, Reg. lat. 49, 33vb2–3,21–6, 34ra1–8 (*CC* 4; Wilmart (1933), 51–2.150–1,165–8,178–84): *Sunt V uiri qui non possunt intrare per hanc ianuam: uir cum oneribus, uir cum cicatricibus, uir crassus, uir humilis ualde, uir altus ualde* [...] *Ipse uero est uir cum cicatricibus quem lacerant VIII principalia uitia .i. gula et fornicatio, ira et cupiditas, accidia et tristitia, superbia et iactantia. Si unum de his uitiis habuerit aliquis, non potest saluus esse in caelo nisi penitentiam diligenter fecerit* [...] *Ipse est uir humilis <ualde> qui non intrat per ianuam .i. qui non fidem <habet> et in quo fit disperatio, quae pessima est omnium peccatorum, ut dicitur: 'Disperatio peior est omni peccato', quia non oportet hominem disperationem habere per quodcumque peccatum <quod> commisserit si penitentiam egerit eo quod dicit Christus: 'Omne peccatum et blasfemia' remittuntur 'hominibus'* [Mt 12:31], *sed tantum per penitentiam. Item dicit: 'Penitentiam agite', reliqua* [Mt 4:17].

'There are five men who cannot enter through this door: the man with burdens, the man with scars, the fat man, the exceptionally short man, the exceptionally tall man [...] He is himself the man with scars whom the eight principle vices tear apart, that is, gluttony and fornication, anger and greed, sloth and sadness, pride and boasting. If someone has one of these vices, he cannot be safe in heaven unless he has carefully performed his penance [...] He is himself an <extremely> short man who does not enter through the door, that is, he who does not <have> faith and in whom despair happens, which is the worst of all sins, as it is said: 'Despair is worse than every sin' because it is not proper that a man have despair through whatever sin he has committed if he has done penance, because Christ says: 'Every sin and blasphemy are forgiven to men', but only through penitence. Likewise he says: 'Do penance', etc.'

The penitents are one of the three groups identified as the 'sons of the spiritual Noah', who inhabit the place in heaven abandoned by the fallen angels (see citation 54, above). When examining the eight days of Easter in light of the last judgment, the homilist counts penitence among three of the four sets of triple doors that permit entrance to heaven. The southern set of doors, that is, virginity, penitence, and marriage, welcomes the children of blessedness (50). The saints enter through the western set of doors, that is, through deed, word, and thought (51). The best of the doors is deed if it is a penitential act because one's promise and intention are fully realized in the penitential act. The three northern doors are baptism, penitence, and martyrdom, which defeat the devil (52). Baptism is the most important door, but penitence, which is a baptism of tears, and martyrdom are also counted as baptism. In a credal formula defining the elements of faith, baptism and penitence are again mentioned together, this time as the two things necessary for the forgiveness of sins. This belongs to the passage examined more fully in the second part of this article:[51]

(72) Vatican, Biblioteca Apostolica, Reg. lat. 49, 34va31–4 (*CC* 4; Wilmart (1933), 54.64–6):
Ipsa est ergo fides sancta credere [...] *indulgentiam peccatorum per babtismum et penitentiam.*
'The holy faith itself is to believe in [...] the remission of sins through baptism and penitence.'

The emphasis on the need for penitence to receive forgiveness of sins and entry to heaven cannot by itself prove that Homily 26R is a product of the Irish church. However, the linguistic, liturgical, ecclesiastical, and exegetical usages in the Latin text that mirror those originating in the Irish language or found in Irish-language texts, considered together with the penitential theme, are strong foundational reasons supporting this homily's Irish origin.

51 See pp. 565–74 below.

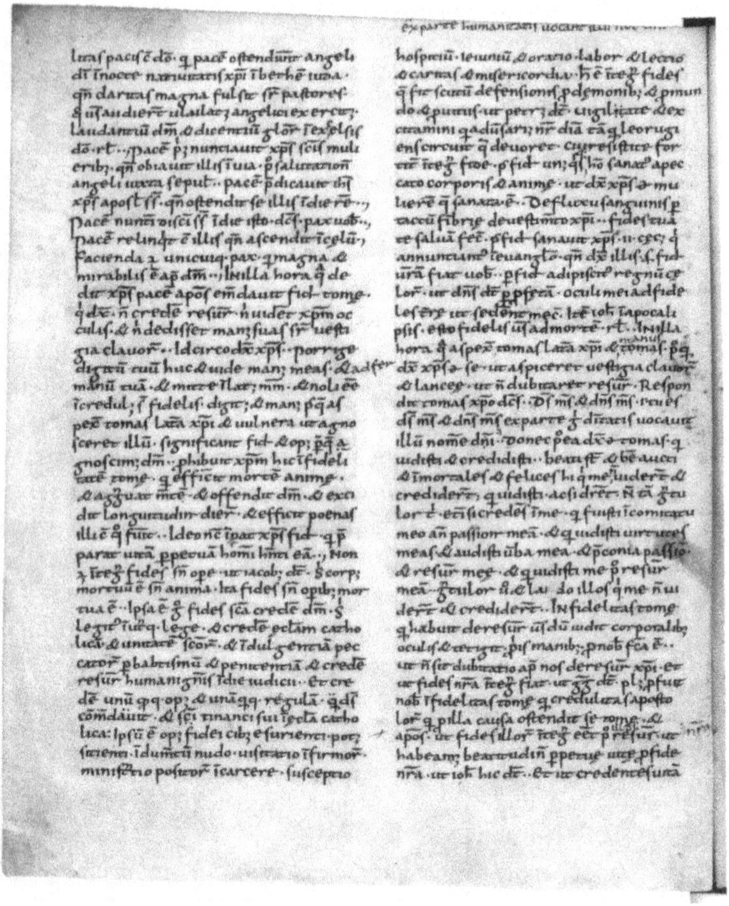

Plate 1 Biblioteca Apostolica Vaticana, Reg. lat. 49, 34v. ()

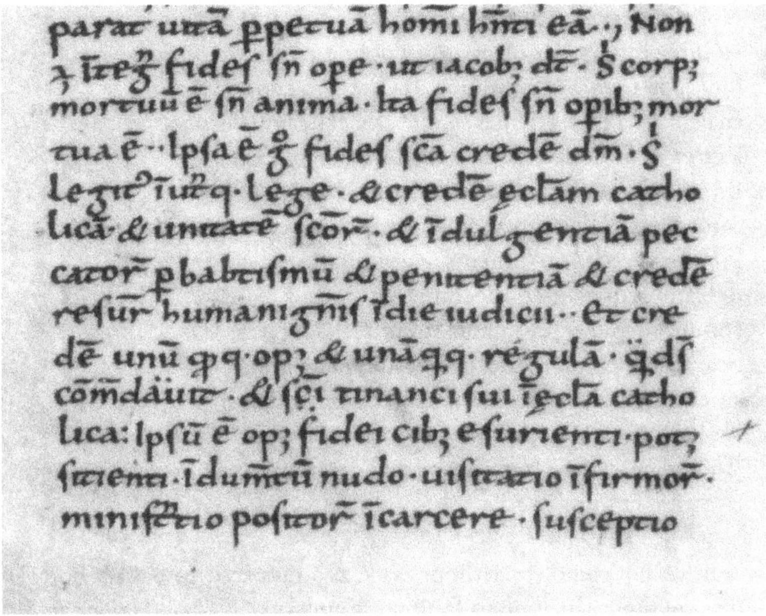

Plate 2 Biblioteca Apostolica Vaticana, Reg. lat. 49, 34va28–40. (©2014 Biblioteca Apostolica Vaticana)

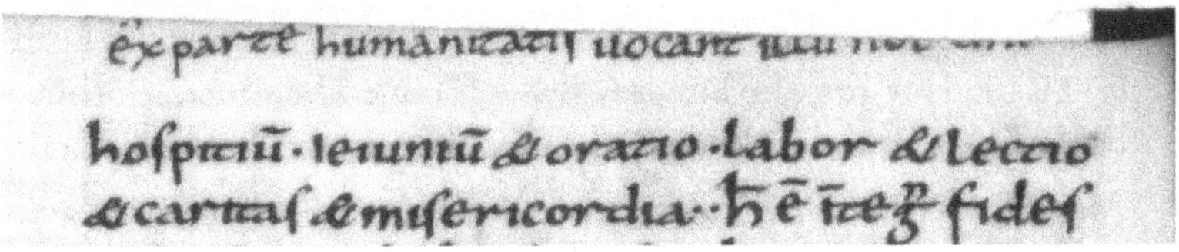

Plate 3 Biblioteca Apostolica Vaticana, Reg. lat. 49, 34vb1–2. (©2014 Biblioteca Apostolica Vaticana)

Analysis of the glossed passage

The manuscript reading

The alleged embedded OIr. gloss appears in a three-part passage that discusses the relationship between faith and works (see *Plates 1–3*):[52]

[52] Vatican, Biblioteca Apostolica, Reg. lat. 49, 34va28–b2 (*CC* 4; Wilmart (1933), 54.62–72).

Non
est in*tegra* fides s*ine* op*ere*. ut iacob*us* d*ic*it. Si*cut* corp*us*
mortuu*m* e*st* s*ine* anima. Ita fides s*ine* op*er*ib*us* mor
tua e*st*..Ipsa e*st er*go fides s*anct*a cred*ere* d*eu*m. Si*cut*
legit*ur* i*n* utraq*ue* lege. et cred*ere* aecl*esi*am catho
lic*am*. et unitate*m* s*anct*or*um*. et i*n*dulgentia*m* pec
cator*um* *per* babtismu*m* et penitentia*m* et cred*ere*
resur*rectionem* humani *gener*is i*n* die iudicii. Et cre
d*ere* unu*m*q*uod*q*ue* op*us* et una*m*q*uam*q*ue* regula*m*. q̈*uam* d*eus*
co*m*me*n*dàüit. et sc̄i tinanci sui i*n* aecle*sia* catho
lica: Ipsu*m* e*st* op*us* fidei cib*us* esurienti. pot*us*
sitienti. i*n*dum*en*tu*m* nudo. uisitatio i*n*firmor*um*.
ministr*a*tio positor*um in* carcere. susceptio
[f 34vb] hospitiu*m* [*recte* hospitum]. ieiuniu*m* et oratio. labor et lectio
et caritas et misericordia.

'Faith is not complete without work, as James says: 'Just as the body is dead without the soul, so faith without works is dead' [James 2:26]. The holy faith itself is to believe in God, just as it is read in each law, and to believe in the catholic church and the unity of the saints and the remission of sins through baptism and penitence and to believe in the resurrection of the human race on the day of judgment and to believe in every single work and in every single rule *q̈(uam) d(eu)s co(m) m(en)dàüit et sc̄i tinanci sui* in the catholic church. The work of faith itself is food for one who hungers, drink for one who thirsts, clothing for the naked man, visitation of the sick, the ministry of those placed in prison, the reception of guests [cf. Matthew 25:35–36], fasting and prayer, labour and *lectio*, and charity and mercy.'

This passage opens with the statement that faith is not complete without work and cites James 2:26 for support (Vatican, Biblioteca Apostolica, Reg. lat. 49, 34va28–30):

(74) *Non est integra fides sine opere, ut Iacobus dicit: 'Sicut corpus mortuum est sine anima, ita fides sine operibus mortua est'.*

The homilist next defines the requirements of a holy faith by listing items from a credal statement. These include belief in God, in the catholic church, in the unity of saints, in the forgiveness of sins through baptism and penitence, in the resurrection of the human race on the day of judgment. Two additional items that are not traditional parts of a credal formula include the belief in each work and each rule that God has established. The end of this sentence (*et sc̄i tinanci sui ī ęcla catholica*) contains the crux phrase *tinanci sui* and requires closer examination before providing a translation:

> (75) *Ipsa est ergo fides sancta credere Deum, sicut legitur in utraque lege, et credere aeclesiam catholicam et unitatem sanctorum et indulgentiam peccatorum per babtismum et penitentiam et credere* [35] *resurrectionem humani generis in die iudicii et credere unumquodque opus et unamquamque regulam quae Deus commendauit.* ***et sc̄i tinanci sui in aeclesia catholica.***

The third section of this meditation on the makeup of *integra fides* [...] *fides sancta* clarifies the meaning of *opus* (l. 36) as *opus fidei*, which has two basic aspects: the six duties described by Christ in Matthew 25:35–36 (providing food for the hungry, drink for the thirsty, clothing for the naked, visitation of the sick, ministry to prisoners, reception of guests) and six additional duties that are the special province of the religious life (fasting, prayer, physical labour, reading, charity, and mercy):

> (76) *Ipsum est opus fidei cibus esurienti, potus sitienti, indumentum nudo, uisitatio infirmorum, ministratio positorum in carcere, susceptio* [f 34vb] *hospitum* [*emend.* Ó Laoghaire (1987), 149; MS *hospitium*], *ieiunium et oratio, labor et lectio et caritas et misericordia.*

Regarding the *crux* in section two (75), the two previous editors of this homily conclude that the end of the sentence in question is corrupt, and a third scholar recognizes that *tinanci sui* (l. 37) might be a corruption of an Irish word.

Passage as edited by Wilmart[53]

> (77) *Ipsa est ergo fides sancta* [...] *credere unumquodque opus et* [Wilmart *est*] *unamquamque regulam quam deus commendauit,* ***et sancti tinanci sui in aeclesia catholica.***

[53] *CC* 4; Wilmart (1933), 54.64–9.

Wilmart does not emend the text, but he does discuss the phrase *tinanci sui* in a footnote. Although written clearly in the codex, it is the result of some error, he writes.[54] Perhaps, *tinanci sui* is a mistake for *tenencia sua* or *tenencia sunt*. He speculates that *tenencia* might mean *induciis* or *securitate*, but he translates neither the phrase nor his suggested equivalents. Pádraic Moran suggests that 'by matching *tenencia* to abl. *induciis* and *securitate*, Wilmart clearly has abl. *tenentia* in mind, not the Classical nom./acc. pl. participle. This is the medieval abstract noun behind English 'tenancy'. *Tenencia* would then mean 'tenancy, holding, possession' (sing.), and would have no Classical equivalent. I would interpret his equivalent terms as intended to convey similar ideas of rightful occupation, that is, *securitas* ('security (i.e. of tenure)'), *indutiae* ('freeholding').'[55]

Based on Wilmart's suggested emendation of *tinanci sui* as (1) *tenencia sua* or (2) *tenencia sunt*, and on Moran's clarification of Wilmart's meaning, and after correcting Wilmart's transcription error (*opus est* should read *opus et*), I translate the passage as follows:

> 'Therefore, the holy faith itself [...] is to believe in every single work <of faith> and every single rule[56] <of conduct> that God has established, (1) **and the saints <are> in the catholic church as in their own freehold tenancy**', OR '(2) **and the saints are in the catholic church as in a freehold tenancy**.'

This is apparently to be understood in the sense that 'the saints—those who embrace the holy faith as just defined—live in the catholic church as freehold tenants, that is, for life'. As a final suggestion, Wilmart poses the possibility that *tinanci sui* is a mistake for Greek *tenaci ui*, but offers no translation or further explanation.

[54] *CC* 4; Wilmart (1933), 54 n 6: 'Sic clare in cod. illa scripta sunt, ex aliquo vitio; fortasse, *tinanci* pro *tenencia*, idest (vulgariter) induciis seu securitate, atque *sui* pro *sua* vel *sunt*; sed alia similiter modica commoditate coniceres, v. gr. *tenaci ui*.'

[55] Personal correspondence, 5 Dec 2013.

[56] For *regula* I adopt the sense 'rule of conduct' suggested by Pádraig Ó Néill at the 2011 Celtic Congress session in preference to my previous definition 'monastic rule'.

Passage as edited by McNally[57]

(78) *Ipsa est ergo fides sancta* [...] *credere unumquodque opus et unamquamque regulam quam Deus commendauit* ***et sancti tinancis ui<xerunt> in aeclesia catholica.***

McNally sees a probable corruption, recognizes that *et sancti* [...] *catholica*, as edited, does not belong as another complement of *ipsa fides sancta*, and realizes a finite verb is required for this part of the sentence. He adopts Wilmart's expansion of *sc̄i* as *sancti* but divides the manuscript reading *tinanci sui* as *tinancis ui<xerunt>*, without providing a translation. Since he does not identify what word is meant by *tinancis* or its possible function in the sentence, perhaps he had *tenaces*, nom./acc. pl. of adj. *tenax* ('steadfast') in mind. His intended meaning seems to be something like:

> 'Therefore, the holy faith itself [...] is to believe in every single work and every single rule that God has established, **and the saints have lived steadfastly in the catholic church.**'

Emendation of tinanci sui *suggested by Ó Laoghaire*[58]

(79) *Ipsa est ergo fides sancta* [...] *credere unumquodque opus et unamquamque regulam quam Deus commendauit* ***et sancti tánaise in aeclesia catholica.***

Ó Laoghaire in 1987 speculated that *tinanci sui* might be a corruption of an Irish word, which he takes to be not a gloss, but part of the text. Since the sense of the passage 'seems to be belief in or obedience to God's laws and those of his holy successors or heirs', Ó Laoghaire suggests *tinanci sui* 'is a latinisation, and corrupt at that, of *tánaise*, referring perhaps immediately to the pope as the vicar of Christ'—God's *tánaise in aeclesia catholica*.[59]

Although he does not translate the passage, his intended meaning seems to be:

[57] *Catechesis Celtica: Vat. Reg. lat. 49* (unpublished draft edition by McNally (n.d.), 236, l. 273 (no. 37)).

[58] Ó Laoghaire (1987), 161.

[59] Ó Laoghaire (1987), 161.

'Therefore, the holy faith itself [...] is to believe every single work and every single rule that God **and his holy second-in-command** have established **in the catholic church.**'

If this is what Ó Laoghaire has in mind, *sancti* should be emended to *sanctus*. Alternatively, the phrase *sancti tánaisi* ('holy lieutenants') is a plausible emendation.

The three scholars, then, differ on the general meaning of the passage. Wilmart apparently emphasizes that those who follow the tenets of the holy faith are saints who dwell in the catholic church forever, as if freehold tenants. McNally appears to stress that the saints lived steadfast lives in the catholic church. Ó Laoghaire clarifies that the definition of faith is to believe in the works and in the laws of God and of his holy successor(s).

The contraction sc̄i and the construe marks

The first question to ask about this passage is not 'What is *tinanci sui*?', but 'What is the correct expansion of the contraction *sc̄i*?'. The two previous editors of this homily conclude that the sentence in question is corrupt, and one scholar recognizes that *tinanci sui* might be a corruption of an Irish word, but none questions Wilmart's expansion of *sc̄i* as *sancti*. Furthermore, none of these scholars mentions the trio of double-dot construe marks placed above *q̧* (*quam*) and *cōm̄dauit* (*commendauit*) and under heavily abbreviated *sc̄i*:

(80) *Ipsa est ergo fides sancta* [...] *credere unumquodque opus et unamquamque regulam. q ds comdauit. et sci tinanci sui in aeclesia catholica.*

The construer, seeing the potential for misinterpretation, alerts the reader (1) that relative pronoun *quam* is a direct object governed by *commendauit*, (2) that *quam* is also governed by *sc̄i*, (3) that *sc̄i* is therefore not the normal contraction for *sancti*, but through its construed association with *quam* and fully inflected *commendauit*, linked to it by *et*, should be read as a perf. 3rd sg. verb, i.e. *sanctificauit*. On the relationship of the apparent noun phrase, *tinanci sui*, to *sc̄i*, which precedes it, the construer is silent. So far, then, the Vatican text, as expanded, reads:

(81) Ipsa est ergo fides sancta [...] credere unumquodque opus et unamquamque regulam q̈*uam* **D***eus* **co***m***mendäuit et** **s***a***nçt***ificauit* **tinanci sui** in aeclesia catholica.

> 'Therefore, the holy faith itself is [...] to believe in every single work <of faith> and every single rule <of conduct> **that God has established and has made holy *tinanci sui*** in the catholic church.'

The phrase *tinanci sui* makes no sense in its Latin sentence. If a nom. pl. masc. subject, it governs no verb. As a gen. sg. masc./neut., it could modify *catholica aeclesia*, but neither *tinancus/tinancum* nor their variants are found in other Latin texts or dictionaries.

What then was the original function and meaning of *tinanci sui* in this sentence? The position of this phrase after *sanctificauit* suggests that *tinanci sui* may have served initially as an interlinear gloss over *sanctificauit*. Since the phrase, as it stands, is nonsense, perhaps *tinanci sui* is a corruption of a phrase in a different language. Perhaps it was originally an interlinear Irish gloss that became embedded in the body of the Latin homily through a scribal lapse. A third scribe, not recognizing its language nor its meaning, changed the now embedded gloss into a two-word Latin noun phrase.

The glossator seems to be answering this unspoken question: 'When the homilist says that part of the holy faith is [...] to believe in every single work and rule that God [...] has sanctified in the catholic church, what does he mean?' Found first in the African Fathers, Tertullian (*c.*AD 160–220) and Cyprian (†AD 257), *sanctifico* is a compound of *sanctus* + *facio* and means 'to make holy or treat as holy, to sanctify, consecrate, dedicate'.[60] Additional definitions go beyond the literal in determining the exact meaning of 'holy'.[61] In its meaning 'to render justified' Cyprian and the Vulgate join it to *baptizo*. In the Vulgate's Old Testament and Jewish context it means 'to consecrate', 'to offer in sacrifice', 'to raise to a state of legal purity'. In the present context, acceptable translations for this excerpt would then be: (1) 'every single work and every single rule that God [...] has made holy'; (2) 'every single work and every single rule that God [...] has justified, that is, made righteous', and (3) 'every single work and every single rule that God [...] has raised to a state of legal purity'.

[60] Lewis and Short (1879), 1625 (*s.v. sanctifico*).

[61] *Dictionnaire Latin-Français des auteurs Chrétiens s.v. sanctifico* (Blaise (1954), 736A) — 'tr., 1. sanctifier, rendre saint, justifié (ἁγιάζω): *baptizari et sanctificari*, CYPR. *Ep.* 69, 8'; '*s. baptizatos, Ep.* 69, 10; *sed abluti estis, sed sanctificati estis, sed iustificati estis*, 1 Cor. 6, 11' —'4. consacrer, offrir en sacrifice: Ex. 13, 2; Deut. 22, 29; Leu. 22, 14. — 5. élever à l'état de pureté légal: Ex. 19, 10; *si enim sanguis hircorum... inquinatos sanctificat*, Hebr. 9, 13 — || purifier: *regeneratio nostra... ab omnibus inquinamentis sanctificata*, TERT. *Carn. Chr.* 20.'

If the glossator was interested in translating *sanctificauit* literally with an Irish gloss, he could have used the word typically found in the glosses: *noíbaid* ('he makes righteous, sanctifies; hallows; consecrates').[62] The vn. *noíbad* renders *sanctificatio*; the adj. *noíb* translates *sanctus*. This is not the word found in our text, however. If *tinanci sui* is a corrupted Irish gloss on *sanctificauit*, what Irish word is meant? Rather than simply a translation, it appears to be an interpretation of the Latin verb, explaining how God has made each work of faith and each rule of conduct holy.

Tincisin, or its by-form *tincisiu*, the vn. of OIr. *do-incai*, MIr. *tincaid*, may be the word originally written over *sanctificauit*. Its literal meaning is 'act of looking at', but it also has two legal definitions: 'act of offering (to repay)', and the act of sick maintenance (*othrus*) that the defendant provides 'at the victim's own house'.[63] (Binchy notes that the 'legal mean-

[62] *DIL s.v. noíbaid*: '(vb.) 'makes righteous, sanctifies; hallows; consecrates''. Cf. *PHLB* 11, ll. 5086–7 (Atkinson (1887), 183, Latin at p 431; the translation mine): *nach at anmand uaisle* [...] *noemait* [...] *nech ico'n choimdid/non nomina sed opera sanctificant* ('not names but works make holy'); *PHLB* 35, l. 7824 (Atkinson (1887), 259, Latin at p 495; the translation mine): *sanctificetur nomen tuum/noemthar th'ainm* ('May your name be made holy'). *DIL s.v. noíbad*: '(vn.), 'gl. *sanctificatio*''. Cf. Wb. 25b2 (1 Th 4:3; Stokes and Strachan (1901–3), i 659): *Haec est enim uoluntas Dei, sanctificatio uestra/.i. ishé inso innoíbad* ('For this is the will of God, your sanctification, i.e. This is the sanctification'); Wb. 3b31 (Rm 6:22; Stokes and Strachan (1901–3), i 512): *habetis fructum uestrum in sanctificationem/.i. bid hinoibad dúibsi ón* ('You have your fruit unto sanctification, i.e. That will be unto sanctification for you'). *DIL s.v. noíb*: 'Of persons holy; of things sacred, consecrated'. Inflected adj. after a noun, but indeclinable before proper names, where it means saint. 'In Glosses it renders Lat. sanctus'. Cf. Wb. 16a21 (2 Cor 7:1): perficientes sanctificationem in timore Dei/corrop noíb for n-anim in homun daé ('perfecting holiness in the fear of God, i.e. so that your soul be holy in fear of God').

[63] *DIL s.v. tincisin*. For the use of *tincisin* in the context of sick maintenance, see *Bretha Crólige* 18, gloss 5 (ed. Binchy (1934–8a), 16): *masa gradh is dir do thincisin corigi a tech* ('if he is of a rank for whom attendance to his house [for sick maintenance] is proper'). Also a commentary in Dublin, Royal Irish Academy, 23 Q 6, 44b, on the operation of *othrus* required as a result of wilful injury (*Bretha Crólige* 7 (Binchy (1934–8b), 89–90)): *Na huile daine reisa foglaither tre comraiti no tre anfot fergi dethbiri 7 indetbiri, is loghacht a tinchisin doib goruigi a tech*. ('All persons to whom injury is done through wilfulness, or through negligence [which is the result] of anger, justified or unjustified, they [the injured parties] are to get their attendance fee [sent] to them to their house.') And as a result of injury through negligence (*Bretha Crólige* 7 (Binchy (1934–8b), 90)): *cebe fogail eitgid treisi ferfaighther cned orra, is loghacht a thinchisin doib goruigi a tech* ('[E]ven if it be through wanton [i.e. non-wilful] damage that injury is inflicted on them, it is their attendance fee [that is sent] to them in their house'). '[T]he technical meaning of *tincisin* 'attendance' when used with reference to injuries' is to have the defendant supply 'the materials of *othrus*', i.e. 'food and physician', to the victim in his own house, according to Binchy (1934–8b), 125–6.

ing' of *tincisin* 'seems to vary in different contexts'.[64]) The verb *do-incai* has a literal meaning 'looks, gazes (at)', and an extended meaning found not just in epic literature, but especially in legal texts: 'sees to; responds to, deals with, satisfies (a claim, summons, challenge, attack, obligation, foe, etc.)'.[65] *DIL* includes one example from a religious text—the Milan glosses—of the literal meaning of *do-incai*, but the word in its legal sense 'to satisfy a claim or obligation' is a meaning that most aptly interprets the homilist's statement here:[66]

> 'The holy faith itself is [...] to believe in every single work <of faith> and every single rule <of conduct> that God has established and has made holy in the catholic church **by satisfying a claim.**'

The meaning of *tincisin* in this homily, then, is not connected with *othrus*, but rather with the act of satisfying a claim or obligation, of paying a debt. Jaroslav Pelikan writes that Tertullian had 'spoken of penance as a way of 'making satisfaction to the Lord', and the term 'satisfaction' had become standard' as it applied to penance.[67] With this sense, *tincisin* and *do-incai* evoke the language found in penitential literature, in which acts of penance 'make satisfaction for sins committed', both 'by amendment of conduct', but also, when another party is involved, 'by the reparation of injury caused'.[68] The two earliest Irish penitentials, *Penitentialis Vinniani*, dating to the 6th century, and the *Synodus I S. Patricii*, perhaps also from the 6th century, likewise require both amendment of conduct through penitential acts and material reparations when another party is involved.[69]

In the current glossed sentence, however, it is God who makes each work of faith and rule of conduct righteous in the universal church through, in the glossator's word, *tincisin*—paying what is owed. Why is God paying what is owed, how is he paying it, and to whom? This single word, *tincisin*, takes us from one requirement of human penance—satis-

64 Binchy (1934–8b), 125 n 1.

65 *DIL s.v. do-incai.*

66 Although other instances of *tincisin/tincisiu* or *do-incai/tincaid* used in vernacular religious texts as the meaning for or interpretation of *sanctifico* may exist, they have yet to be identified.

67 Pelikan (1978), 143.

68 Connolly (1995), 136.

69 *Penitentialis Vinniani* 1, 5, 9, 22, 23, 25, 28, 30, 35, 36 (ed. Bieler (1975), 74–95); *Synodus I S. Patricii* 15, 16 (ed. Bieler (1975), 54–9).

fying a material claim—to the entirely separate realm of Christ's saving work on the cross. *Deus* here must refer not just to God, but to God in Christ. Since Christ, both divine and sinless, did not need to pay claims for his own sins, his death instead satisfied all claims against sinful mankind. Even the works of faith and the rules of conduct that God had established in his church needed to be justified by Christ's death because, being carried out now by sinful men, they were no longer perfect. Christ's death settled all debts, thereby purifying everything done in his name.

The glossator's brief comment only hints at the fuller meaning. It would not be until Anselm of Canterbury (AD 1033–1109) in *Cur Deus homo*, when speaking 'of what was required as a consequence of human sin', formally incorporated and deepened the penitential language of satisfaction into his analysis of what Christ's death achieved. Although 'the satisfaction offered in penance was a natural analogy', writes Pelikan, it was nevertheless 'inadequate because [...] man was giving God only what he owed him'. Since Christ's death, on the other hand, offered a satisfaction of 'infinite worth, redemption on the cross could be seen as the one supreme act of penitential satisfaction. 'Satisfaction', then, was another term for 'sacrifice', and Christ's sacrificial act of penance made even human acts of satisfaction worthy, since of themselves they were not.'[70]

Before Anselm's formal formulation, however, the Irish glossator and perhaps other insular theologians were using the penitential language of satisfaction to hint at how Christ's saving work made both works of faith and rules of conduct righteous.

In sum, the construe marks over *q(uam)* and *co(m)m(en)dauit* and under *sc̄i* (i.e. *sanctificauit*, not *sancti*) identify *quam* as the direct object of *commendauit* and *sanctificauit*. The Irish word later corrupted into the unintelligible Latin phrase, *tinanci sui*, may be OIr. vn. *tincisin* (byform *tincisiu*), originally placed over *sanctificauit* as a gloss. It became embedded as part of the text at some stage in the transmission of the homily. Miswriting it as *tincisui*, a later (non-Irish?) scribe mistook final *-sin* or *-siu* as *-sui*, which is, writes Moran, 'basically just a corruption of three minims'.[71] The same or another scribed added the syllable *-an-* to the word, either mistakenly as 'a sort of dittography', suggests Moran, or

[70] Anselm, *Cur Deus homo* I 20 (ed. Schmitt (1928–61), ii 86–7) as referenced and discussed by Pelikan (1978), 143.

[71] Personal correspondence, 5 Dec 2013.

consciously in order to make sense of the form in his exemplar. The word was divided into *tinanci sui* at this point or later. The Irish gloss is an interpretation of *sanctificauit* rather than a literal translation. It uses the legal language of satisfying a claim to explain how God—in Christ—has purified each work of faith and rule of conduct. A next step in explaining why the glossator has joined *tincisin* with *sanctificauit* would be to examine Irish religious writings that describe Christ's saving work by analyzing the language of atonement used by authenticated and alleged Irish religious writers to see whether any uses the language of a claim satisfied to explain the meaning of Christ's crucifixion.

Bibliography

Atkinson, R. (1887) *The passions and the homilies from Leabhar Breac: text, translation, and glossary*, Dublin.

Best, R. I. and H. J. Lawlor (1931) *Martyrology of Tallaght*, London.

Bieler, L. (1975) *Irish penitentials*, Dublin.

— (1979) *The Patrician texts in the Book of Armagh*, Dublin.

Binchy, D.A. (1934–8a) '*Bretha Crólige*,' *Ériu* 12, 1–77.

— (1934–8b) 'Sick maintenance in Irish law,' *Ériu* 12, 78–134.

Blaise, A. (1954) *Dictionnaire Latin-Français des auteurs Chrétiens*, Turnhout.

Connolly, H. (1995) *The Irish penitentials and their significance for the sacrament of penance today*, Dublin.

Follett, W. (2006) *Céli Dé in Ireland: monastic writing and identity in the early Middle Ages*, Woodbridge.

Glare, P.G.W. (1996) *Oxford Latin Dictionary*, Oxford.

Grosjean, P. (1936) 'À propos du manuscrit 49 de la Reine Christine,' *Analecta Bollandiana* 54, 113–36.

Herren, M.W. (1976) 'The pseudonymous tradition in Hiberno-Latin: an introduction,' in J.J. O'Meara and B. Naumann, *Latin script and letters, A.D. 400–900*, Leiden, 121–31.

Hughes, K. (1958) 'The distribution of Irish scriptoria and centres of learning from 730 to 1111,' in N.K. Chadwick, *Studies in the early British church*, Cambridge, 243–72.

— (1966) *The church in early Irish society*, London.

Hull, V. (1968), 'Apgitir Chrábaid: the alphabet of piety,' *Celtica* 8, 44–89.

Lapidge, M. and R. Sharpe (1985) *A bibliography of Celtic-Latin literature 400–1200*, Dublin.

Lewis, C.T. and C. Short (1879) *A Latin dictionary*, Oxford.

Löfstedt, B. (1965) *Der hibernolateinische Grammatiker Malsachanus*, Uppsala.

Mac Niocaill, G. (1953–4) 'Beatha Eoin Bruinne,' *Éigse* 7, 248–53.
McNamara, M. (1990) 'The Irish affiliations of the *Catechesis Celtica*,' *Celtica* 21, 291–333.
— (1994) 'Sources and affiliations of the *Catechesis Celtica* (MS Vat. Reg. Lat. 49),' *Sacris Erudiri* 34, 185–237.
McNally, R.E. (n.d.) *Catechesis Celtica: Vat. Reg. lat. 49*, unpublished typescript.
Ó hAodha, D. (1978) *Bethu Brigte*, Dublin.
Ó Laoghaire, D. (1987) 'Irish elements in the *Catechesis Celtica*,' in P. Ní Chatháin and M. Richter, *Ireland and Christendom: the Bible and the missions*, Stuttgart, 146–64.
O'Loughlin, T. (2001) 'Irish preaching before the end of the ninth century: assessing the extent of our evidence', in A.J. Fletcher and R. Gillespie, *Irish preaching 700–1700*, Dublin, 18–39.
Ó Néill, P. (1987) 'The date and authorship of *Apgitir Chrábaid*: some internal evidence,' in P. Ní Chatháin and M. Richter, *Irland und die Christenheit: Bibelstudien und Mission*, Stuttgart, 203–15.
Pelikan, J. (1978) *The growth of medieval theology (600–1300)*, Chicago.
Plater, W.E. and H.J. White (1926) *A grammar of the Vulgate*, Oxford.
Rittmueller, J. (1992–3) 'MS Vat. Reg. Lat. 49 reviewed: a new description and a table of textual parallels with the *Liber questionum in euangeliis*,' *Sacris Erudiri* 33, 259–305.
Schmitt, F.S. (1928–61) *Sancti Anselmi opera omnia*, Seckau.
Sims-Williams, P. (1978) 'Thought, word, and deed: an Irish triad,' *Ériu* 29, 78–111.
Stancliffe, C. (1982) 'Red, white and blue martyrdom,' in D. Whitelock et al., *Ireland in Early Mediaeval Europe: studies in memory of Kathleen Hughes*, Cambridge, 21–46.
Stokes, W. (1887) *The Tripartite Life of St. Patrick*, 2 vols., London.
Stokes, W. and J. Strachan (1901–3) *Thesaurus palaeohibernicus: a collection of Old-Irish glosses, scholia, prose and verse*, 2 vols., Cambridge.
Wasserschleben, H. (1885) *Die irische Kanonensammlung*, 2nd ed., Leipzig.
Wilmart, A. (1933) 'Reg. lat. 49: Catéchèses celtiques,' in A. Wilmart, *Analecta Reginensia*, Vatican, 29–112.
— (1937) *Codices Reginenses Latini I: codices 1–250*, Vatican.
Wright, C.D. (1993) *The Irish tradition in Old English literature*, Cambridge.
— (2000) 'Bischoff's theory of Irish exegesis and the Genesis commentary in Munich clm 6302: a critique of a critique,' *Journal of Medieval Latin* 10, 115–75.

ROB MEENS

WITH ONE FOOT IN THE FONT: THE FAILED BAPTISM OF THE FRISIAN KING RADBOD AND THE 8TH-CENTURY DISCUSSION ABOUT THE FATE OF UNBAPTIZED FOREFATHERS

Abstract

This contribution tries to outline a context for the well-known story of the Frisian King Radbod withdrawing from the baptismal font when hearing that his ancestors would not receive the same privilege. This story is transmitted in the *Vita Wulframni*, a text that has been regarded as a forgery. Following a summary of Stéphane Lebecq's analysis of the *Vita*, the story about Radbod's failed baptism can be shown to belong to a part of this text that was composed by the Frisian monk Ovo in the AD 740s. As such, it is a central document in the debate about the fate of pagan ancestors vibrant at precisely this time, with Boniface and the Irish bishop Clemens being the best-known protagonists. The anecdote was not written to deny Willibrord his pride of place in the Christianization of Frisia, but rather to corroborate Boniface's point of view with Willibrord's authority. There is some indication suggesting that Willibrord himself had a different opinion in this question, a crucial element in the process of Christianization.

Keywords

Radbod, Boniface, Clemens, Bede, Adomnán, St Wandrille, Theodore of Canterbury, Patrick, Columba, Trajan, Willibrord, Wulfram of Sens; Frisians; Palagianism, baptism, Christianization, paganism, ancestors, burial, churches.

Introduction

Alcuin described Radbod, 'king of the Frisians', as a major opponent of Willibrord, the Anglo-Saxon missionary of noble, possibly even royal, descent who set out from the Irish monastery of Rath Melsigi to convert

Early medieval Ireland and Europe: chronology, contacts, scholarship, ed. by Pádraic Moran and Immo Warntjes, Studia Traditionis Theologiae, 14 (Turnhout, 2015), pp. 577–96.

 10.1484/M.STT-EB.5.103136

the Frisians.[1] Radbod was a man with a heart of stone, who became infuriated when he discovered that Willibrord had desecrated a holy well devoted to the god Fosite on the island of Helgoland.[2] We need not follow Alcuin in all details here. It can be questioned, for example, whether Radbod was actually 'king of the Frisians' as Alcuin says, a statement eagerly adopted by modern historians. Perhaps he was just 'a king of Frisians' and as such comparable to some Frankish aristocrats active in the same region.[3]

Radbod was clearly involved in Frankish politics. He married his daughter Theudesinda to Grimoald, son of the Frankish mayor of the palace Pippin II. In the political turmoil following the murder of this Grimoald in AD 714 and the death of Pippin later that year, Radbod allied himself with the Neustrian mayor of the palace Ragamfred.[4] He was, therefore, an important player in high Frankish politics in the early 8th century. We may also question whether he was such a fervent opponent of Christianity, since he allowed Willibrord to travel and preach in his kingdom. It is, moreover, not implausible that his daughter Theudesinda had been baptized when marrying Grimoald.[5] Yet, Alcuin describes him as a fervent pagan and most other sources of the period do likewise. The most famous portrayal of Radbod as an uncompromising pagan comes from the *Vita Wulframni*, the Life of Archbishop Wulfram of Sens composed in the monastery of Saint Wandrille at the end of the 8th or in the early 9th century. This source relates how Wulfram nearly succeeded in converting the Frisian king. The text runs as follows:[6]

> *Praefatus autem princeps Rathbodus, cum ad percipiendum baptisma inbueretur, percunctabatur a sancto episcopo Vulframno, iuramentis eum per nomen Domini astringens, ubi maior esset numerus regum et principum seu nobilium gentis Fresionum, in illa videlicet caelesti regione, quam, si crederet et baptizaretur, percepturum se promittebat, an in ea, quam dicebat tartaream dampnationem. Tunc beatus Vulframnus: 'Noli errare, inclite princeps, apud Deum certus est suorum numerus electorum.*

1 Ó Cróinín (1984); Ó Cróinín (2007).

2 Alcuin, *Vita Willibrordi* 9, 11 (ed. by Wilhelm Levison in MGH SS rer. Merov. 7, 123, 125); on Radbod as Willibrord's main adversary, see Berschin (1991), 127–9.

3 van Egmond (2005).

4 Fouracre (2000), 53, 61; Fischer (2012), 51–3.

5 Angenendt (1998), 81.

6 *Vita Wulframni* 9 (ed. by Wilhelm Levison, MGH SS rer. Merov. 5, 661–73: 668); the translation is mine, here and throughout.

> *Nam praedecessores tui principes gentis Fresionum, qui sine baptismi sacramento recesserunt, certum est dampnationis suscepisse sententiam; qui vero abhinc crediderit et baptizatus fuerit, cum Christo gaudebit in aeternum.' Haec audiens dux incredulus – nam ad fontem processerat – et, ut fertur, pedem a fonte retraxit, dicens, non se carere posse consortio praedecessorum suorum principum Fresionum et cum parvo pauperum numero residere in illo caelesti regno.*

> 'When the named King Radbod was to be immersed in order to receive baptism from the holy Bishop Wulfram, he hesitated and asked him (Wulfram), meanwhile binding him through an oath in the name of the Lord, where the greater part of the kings, princes, and nobles of the Frisian people were: in the celestial realm that Wulfram had promised him to be shown if he believed and would be baptized, or in that region that he called the Tartarus of damnation. Whereupon the blessed Wulfram responded: 'Don't be mistaken, glorious prince, there is a certain amount of the elect with God. For it is certain that your predecessors as princes of the people of the Frisians, who have departed without the sacrament of baptism, have received a sentence of damnation. But he who from this moment believes and is baptized, will enjoy eternal bliss with Christ.' When the still pagan duke—pagan, because he was still on his way to the baptismal font—heard this, he, as they tell, withdrew his foot from the font declaring that he could not go without the company of his predecessors, the princes of the Frisians, to reside with a small number of the poor in that celestial kingdom.'

Many modern scholars of this period have remarked on this famous anecdote.[7] Interestingly, others pass over it in silence.[8] This remarkable discrepancy is probably the result of a different assessment of the authenticity of the story. Already Wilhelm Levison, who edited Wulfram's Life for the *Monumenta Germaniae Historica* in 1910, expressed severe doubts about its reliability as a historical source. 'Itaque pleraque quae narrantur aut pro fabulis aut pro dubiis habenda sunt', was his judgement.[9] Levison was critical because of the chronological problems presented by the text. The most striking example of this is the date of

[7] See e.g. Fletcher (1997), 239; Brown (2003), 417; Lynch (1998), 72; Dumézil (2005), 172; Blair (2005), 58; Charles-Edwards (2000), 199 (although presenting a garbled version of the story); Smith (2005), 228; Weiler (1989), 78; Scheibelreiter (1999), 481.

[8] Palmer (2009); Innes (2007); Wickham (2009); Noble and Smith (2008); Blok, Prevenier et al. (1981).

[9] MGH SS rer. Merov. 5, 659.

the failed baptismal rite. According to the *Vita*, this event took place not long before the death of Radbod in AD 718. Yet, the *Gesta* of the abbots of St Wandrille inform us that Wulfram had died before AD 704, as his body was translated by Abbot Bainus of Fontenelle (St Wandrille) in that year. The date given for Wulfram's death in the *Vita* (AD 720) is therefore clearly mistaken.

Historians have dealt with the question of the reliability of this story in three different ways. Some present the anecdote as historical fact without further qualification.[10] Others have simply ignored it completely.[11] A third group of historians consider the story itself unreliable, but maintain that its theme, the insecurity about the fate of pagan forefathers, is a reflection of real issues involved in the early stages of Christianization. Characteristic for this approach is the succinct phrase by Lutz von Padberg:[12] 'Mag diese pittoreske Szene auch der Phantasie des Hagiographen entstammen, so spiegelt sie doch tatsächliche Missionserfahrungen der Übergangsepoche.' A fourth approach is to regard the story as a way in which Wulfram and Radbod were remembered at the time of composition of the *Vita*.[13] If the story does reflect authentic experiences in the missionary field, this raises the question why no other historical or hagiographical source refers to this. The aim of this paper is to provide the background for the emergence of the story about Radbod's failed baptism by demonstrating that the theme of the fate of unbaptized forefathers was a real issue in the AD 740s in a couple of texts related to mission and conversion. This 8th-century debate forms the context for the story in the Life of Wulfram.

Authenticity and context

For this paper, the question of the authenticity of the story is, therefore, of secondary importance. Yet, some remarks about this vexed question are necessary in order to get a better understanding of the text and its background. Recently, Ian Wood and Stéphane Lebecq have rekindled the debate on its authenticity and I will begin by outlining their

10 See Dumézil (2005), 172; Blair (2005), 58; Smith (2005), 228; Weiler (1989), 78; Scheibelreiter (1999), 481.

11 See n 8.

12 von Padberg (2003), 123; van Eijnatten and van Lieburg (2005), 74.

13 Brown (2003), 417.

arguments. Ian Wood sees the *Vita Wulframni* mainly as a response by the monks of St Wandrille to the composition of the *Vita Willibrordi* by Alcuin. The text is designed not only to demonstrate the pre-eminence of Wulfram over Willibrord, but also to promote a different conception of mission. For the author of the *Vita Wulframni*, miracles are of primary importance, whereas Alcuin instead stresses the role of preaching. According to Wood, the *Vita Wulframni* was written as a reaction to the *Vita Willibrordi* because the monks of St Wandrille wanted to highlight their contribution to the Frisian mission. For this purpose, they were not hesitant in formulating 'totally fraudulent assertions', although the *Vita* may also contain 'a record of genuine events'. Wood does not explicitly address the question of the authenticity of the story of Radbod's failed baptism, but by pointing to similar concerns about the fate of forefathers raised elsewhere, he suggests that the story had at least some link with problems encountered in the missionary field. Wood considers the reference to the faith of Clovis's forefathers in the letter of Avitus of Vienne sent on the occasion of his baptism as a close parallel.[14]

Stéphane Lebecq, although acknowledging the indisputable problems that the text presents, has fervently defended the *Vita Wulframni* as a reliable source for the history of early medieval Frisia. The monastery of St Wandrille was in contact with this region and some of the details mentioned in the *Vita* have clear parallels with Frisian evidence. Lebecq furthermore provides an explanation for the blatant inconsistencies in the text, which have seriously prejudiced historians' judgment of the text's reliability. The author, for example, calls himself Jonas (of Bobbio), the 7th-century biographer of St Vedastus and St Columbanus, and pretends to dedicate the work to abbot Bainus, abbot of St Wandrille in the early years of the 8th-century, while in other parts of the text references to two later abbots of that monastery can be found: Wando (AD 716–719 and 742–747/754) and Austrulf (AD 747–753).[15] The text as transmitted must therefore postdate AD 747, which makes a dedication to Bainus not only impossible but also suspiciously preposterous. According to Lebecq, these inconsistencies result from a somewhat clumsily amalgamation of already existing smaller dossiers. A brief biographical text was probably composed on the occasion of the elevation of Wulfram's remains in AD 704. Anecdotes mainly concerned with Frisian

[14] Wood (1991), 12–4; Wood (2001), 92–4 ('may include a record of genuine events'); Wood (2005), 720 ('totally fraudulent assertions') and 726–7; see Avitus of Vienne, *Epistula* 46 (ed. by Rudolf Peiper in MGH Auct. ant. 6,2, 75–6).

[15] Lebecq (2000), 432–3.

issues were reported and possibly written down by the monk Ovo, one of the Frisian boys saved by Wulfram and then brought to the monastery of St Wandrille. Two miracle stories are closely related to Abbot Wando and were probably recorded by him or under his direction.[16] These then were put together in the late 8th or early 9th century. Such a genesis of the *Vita* may perhaps seem overly complicated, but it explains well the incoherence of the text as a whole; certainly, the chronological discrepancies can better be squared by this interpretation than by the assumption the *Vita* forms a coherent composition to compete with Alcuin's carefully balanced account of Willibrord's activities, unless we regard the monks of St Wandrille incapable of writing a structured narrative.

Moreover, the short anecdotes concerning Frisia show exceptional features when compared to the rest of the *Vita*. Three chapters in the *Vita*, for example, deal with the tradition of human sacrifices among the Frisians.[17] According to these, young boys were chosen by lot and then offered to the gods, either by hanging or drowning. Sacrifice by drowning especially is peculiar and corresponds well with the Frisian landscape dominated by wetlands and the sea. Such descriptions do not, or only partly, rely on hagiographical *topoi*; rather, they show parallels with the sacrificial procedures related in other sources from Frisia, such as the *Vita Willibrordi* or the *Lex Frisionum*, but clearly do not derive from these.[18]

The *Vita* as such can therefore be dated to the end of the 8th or the early 9th century, but its components, in Lebecq's reconstruction, were composed earlier. Lebecq suspects that Wando might have been involved in the recording process of Ovo's oral testimonies, which form the basis of the Frisian *couleur locale* of the *Vita*. Both Wando and Ovo died around the middle of the 8th century. If Lebecq is correct, and I see no reason for questioning his reconstruction, then the story about the failed baptism of Radbod was probably recorded in St Wandrille in the AD 740s when Ovo would have been in his old age. Since the *Vita* refers to Ovo's talents as a scribe (*in arte scriptoria eruditus*), it is even possible that Ovo himself composed the anecdotes in question, reflecting his own experiences.[19]

Lebecq thus dates the anecdote about Wulfram and Radbod to the AD 740s. This date could be corroborated by further evidence for a

16 Lebecq (2000), 440–1.

17 *Vita Wulframni* 6–8 (MGH SS rer. Merov. 5, 665–7).

18 Lebecq (2007).

19 On Ovo's talents as a scribe, see *Vita Wulframni* 7 (MGH SS rer. Merov. 5, 666). The parts probably written by him are translated in Lebecq (2011a).

contemporary discussion of the fate of unbaptized forefathers. Some scholars have argued that the crucial question raised in the story of Radbod's failed baptism—i.e. why are we saved by the grace of baptism while our ancestors are not?—must have been of major concern in many missionary contexts. Yet, the *Vita Wulframni* seems to be the only Saint's Life in which this issue is addressed. Comparison with the other major Anglo-Saxon missionary, Boniface, however, demonstrates that the issue was of some concern to him and to other contemporaries. First, there is Pope Gregory III's reply to an earlier letter of Boniface which has not survived. In his papal letter of AD 732, the pope discusses several issues related to baptism. He asks Boniface to baptize again in the name of the Trinity those who have received baptism from 'pagans'. Furthermore, Boniface was to (re)baptize those who are uncertain whether they have received baptism. Those baptized by a priest who sacrificed to Jupiter or who participated in pagan sacrificial meals should also undergo another baptism. These papal demands raise a number of questions: Who are these pagans baptizing heathens? Does the pope here refer to Christians who had not received proper baptism themselves and should therefore technically be treated as pagans? Did this cause such a confusion that people were uncertain about their state as Christians? Were pagans possibly imitating baptismal ceremonies for specific reasons? There are no definite answers to these questions. Still, it is obvious that Boniface, at this time, encountered a number of problematical baptismal issues.[20]

In the same letter a question is raised which is closely related to the central issue of the story of Wulfram and Radbod. Gregory here responds to Boniface's initial question whether one may bring liturgical offerings for the deceased. Gregory allows this only for the deceased who are real Christians (*vere christianis*). A priest may do so, but only for them, not for those who are impious, even when the latter were Christian, the pope specified.[21] The term *impios* in this context is ambiguous. It seems to refer to 'unbelievers', whether (formally) Christian or pagan. Pope Gregory III here seems to respond to a desire of recent converts to make liturgical offerings for unbelievers. We may assume that some of these unbelievers are to be identified with their deceased pagan ancestors.[22]

[20] Boniface Letters 28 (ed. by Michael Tangl in MGH Epp. sel. 1, 50–1).

[21] Boniface Letters 28 (MGH Epp. sel. 1, 50–1).

[22] As supposed by Clay (2010), 386, who also relates this letter to the story about Radbod's failed baptism.

That Boniface was confronted with precisely this issue and that other contemporaries of a certain religious authority came to different conclusions, is evident from his conflict with the Irish Bishop Clemens. This Clemens proved to be a fervent adversary of the Anglo-Saxon archbishop. He is often mentioned in the same breath as the Frankish Bishop Aldebert and they were both condemned by the same Roman Synod of AD 745.[23] Yet, we need to distinguish carefully between these two charismatic men. Clemens is accused by Boniface of following several unorthodox views and embracing uncanonical practices. Although the accusations of heresy levelled against Clemens may simply reflect heretical stereotypes, the Irishman may still have acted non-conformist.[24] One of the accusations involves Clemens teaching the doctrine that Christ had descended into Hell and liberated everyone there, believers and unbelievers (*credulos et incredulos*) alike, the worshippers of God and the idolaters (*laudatores Dei simul et cultores idulorum*).[25] This suggests that Clemens held a more favourable view on the salvation of those who had not had a chance to embrace Christianity in their lifetime. The Roman synod, when summarizing Clemens's case, chose exactly the same ambiguous term for describing the unbelievers that Pope Gregory III had used in his Letter to Boniface discussed above: *impios*. This indicates that Gregory's letter and Clemens's teaching possibly dealt with a similar problem, i.e. the salvation of pagan forefathers.

Another text that has recently been associated with Boniface addresses the same question. The text in question is a short sermon, known as *Rogamus vos*, which has traditionally been attributed to Augustine of Canterbury.[26] Michael Glatthaar has recently demonstrated that there is no firm basis for this attribution and has shown that the sole manuscript witness of this text is closely associated with Boniface and his mission. This manuscript, Vatican, Biblioteca Apostolica, Pal. lat. 577, contains a collection of texts that can, more or less directly, be associated with the 'apostle of the Germans'. According to Glatthaar, the connection with Boniface was so close that we may dub this collection the *Sententiae Bonifatianae Palatinae*.[27] It includes the

[23] On Boniface's two opponents, see de Jong (2005); Innes (2008); Meeder (2011).

[24] For the influence of heretical stereotypes, see Zeddies (1995); the links with Irish traditions are stressed by Meeder (2011).

[25] Roman Synod of AD 745 (ed. by Albert Werminghoff in MGH Conc. 2,1, 40).

[26] Machielsen (1961), 504–5.

[27] Glatthaar (2004), 455–502; the argument is accepted by Mostert (2013), 115–9.

famous list of problematic religious observances that is known as the *Indiculus superstitionum*, the so-called Old-Saxon baptismal formula, and the texts of the *Concilium Germanicum* (AD 742) and the Council of Estinnes (AD 743). The short sermon *Rogamus vos* deals with the question of why the remedies for salvation (*salutis remedia*) were preached so late. Why did Christ arrive so late in this world and let so many thousands of people perish? The fact that the sermon strongly argues against the validity of such a question indicates that it was actually directed against Clemens and his followers, who, as we have seen, also worried about the salvation of the souls of those who died before Christian doctrine was known.[28] That such questions must have been particularly prominent in a missionary context may be obvious, but it needs to be stressed that without someone like Clemens who actually explicitly formulated such concerns, these were generally suppressed or remained unarticulated.

An influential penitential handbook that probably was known to Boniface contains a couple of sentences that also deal in a very rigorous way with pagan ancestors. This penitential is attributed to Theodore of Canterbury, whose teachings indeed form the basis of this text. Actually, the *Iudicia Theodori* are known from five textual traditions of which the *Discipulus Umbrensium* version together with the *Canones Gregorii* were the best known.[29] The *Discipulus Umbrensium* version was probably composed in the late 7th or early 8th century, as it features in the canon law collection known as the *Collectio Vetus Gallica*, redacted at Corbie *c.*AD 725–750.[30] Boniface was in close contact with the monks of Corbie and particularly with Abbot Grimo, who is the most plausible candidate as redactor of the *Collectio Vetus Gallica*.[31] Theodore's penitential contains the following two sentences:[32]

[28] A connection between the sermon and Clemens's preaching is suggested by Glatthaar (2004), 488–9.

[29] For these traditions, see Kottje *s.v.* 'Paenitentiale Theodori' in *HRG* 3, 1413–6.

[30] Mordek (1975), 86.

[31] For Boniface's contact with Grimo, see Glatthaar (2004), 215, 386–9; see also Meens (2007), 220–1.

[32] *Paenitentiale Theodori, Discipulus Umbrensium*-version (U) II 1, 4–5 (ed. Finsterwalder (1929), 312; I added some punctuation); cf. *P. Theodori Canones Gregorii* 149–150 (ed. Finsterwalder (1929), 267); *P. Theodori Capitula Dacheriana* 98 (ed. Finsterwalder (1929), 247); *P. Theodori Canones Cottoniani* 56–58 (ed. Finsterwalder (1929), 274); *P. Theodori Canones Basilienses*, 71a–b, 89 (ed. Asbach (1975), Anhang, 85 and 87); see also Meens (2012), 128; Meens (2014), 90–6; and the comments in Blair (2005), 236.

> *In ecclesia in qua mortuorum cadavera infidelium sepeliuntur, sanctificare altare non licet sed si apta videtur ad consecrandum inde evulsa et rasis vel lotis lignis eius reaedificatur.*
> *Si autem consecratum prius fuit, missas in eo caelebrare licet si relegiosi ibi sepulti sunt. Si vero paganus sit, mundare et iactare foras melius est.*
>
> 'One should not consecrate the altar in a church in which the bodies of unbelievers (*infidelium*) are buried, but if the altar seems well suited for consecration, the bodies should be removed and it can be re-established after the planks are scoured and washed.
> But if it has already been consecrated, Mass may be celebrated in it when the people buried there are *relegiosi*. But if it concerns a pagan it is better to clean it and to throw [the remains] out.'

These enigmatic sentences can be interpreted as reflecting a desire among recent converts to have their ancestors buried in consecrated churches (or to build churches on their graves). It is obvious that Theodore took an uncompromising stand against such practices, a position that is in line with Boniface's views, who, before going to the Continent, had close links with Theodore's successor Berhtwald.[33] The same opinion is expressed in the story of Radbod's failed baptism.

Clemens's background

The story about the failed baptism of Radbod, therefore, though unique in hagiographical literature, can be set in the context of a group of texts all known and used in the northern Frankish region which concentrate on the salvation of pagan ancestors. This theme seems to have been a major issue of dispute between Boniface and the Irish Bishop Clemens. Clemens took a more lenient stance in this debate, while Boniface denied any possibility for pagan ancestors to be saved. We may wonder whether Clemens's approach was singular, or whether he represented a wider movement. Sven Meeder recently suggested that Clemens might have been influenced by Pelagianism, which would explain the accusation of asserting 'horrible' ideas on predestination levelled against Clemens at the Roman Synod of AD 745.[34] His Irish background could, of course, have provoked such claims, as Pelagianism was strongly associated with

33 Yorke (2007), 32.

34 Roman Synod of AD 745 (MGH Conc. 2,1, 40); Meeder (2011), 277–9.

the British Isles, partly thanks to Bede's treatment of this issue in his recent *Historia ecclesiastica*.[35]

If we look at the religious culture of Clemens's native Ireland, it becomes apparent that his positive attitude towards the pagan past had its roots there. Quite a few Irish texts speak of pagan ancestors with an exemplary life though uninfluenced by Christianity. Moreover, some texts claim that Irish men believed in the Christian God even before Patrick spread the word on the island.[36] Adomnán, in his *Vita Columbae* written in the late 7th century, relates how the saint miraculously foresaw the arrival of a man who had preserved natural goodness (*naturale bonum*) throughout his entire life without having been baptized, and therefore uninfluenced by Christianity, or so the story implies. When this man, Artbranán, heard the word of God from the holy man, he agreed to be baptized by Columba and died almost immediately thereafter.[37] Later in the same text, a similar story is narrated.[38] These episodes have been interpreted as evidence of persistent Pelagianism in the Irish church.[39] Yet, both episodes stress the importance of baptism, even for someone who had preserved natural goodness throughout his life. Rather than reading these stories as statements of Pelagianism, they should be taken as expressions of the pervading force of divine grace which makes a naturally good person receive baptism before encountering death.[40] They do show, however, 'a conciliatory attitude towards paganism'.[41]

The same can be observed in the late 7th-century Life of Patrick by Muirchú. When Patrick returned to Ireland, he met a certain Dichu, who became the first Irishman to convert to Christianity. According to Muirchú, before meeting Patrick he had already been 'from nature a good man, although a pagan'.[42] Tírechán, the other late 7th-century biographer of Patrick, went even further. In his *Collectanea*, in which he as-

35 Bede raised the issue particularly by his quote from the letter of Pope-elect John to the northern Irish clergy in *Historia ecclesiastica* II 19 (ed. and trans. Colgrave and Mynors (1992), 200–3); see Ó Cróinín (1985).

36 McCone (1991), 72–5.

37 Adomnán, *Vita Columbae* I 33 (ed. and trans. Anderson and Anderson (1991), 62–3).

38 Adomnán, *Vita Columbae* III 14 (Anderson and Anderson (1991), 200–3).

39 Herren and Brown (2002), 95.

40 O'Sullivan (2010).

41 Charles-Edwards (2000), 200.

42 Muirchú, *Vita S. Patricii* I 11(10) (ed. and trans. Bieler (1979), 78–9): *cuiusdam uiri natura boni licet gentilis*.

sembled a lot of information about the saint in order to support the material claims of the church of Armagh, he relates how the saint revived a deceased pagan man and baptized him before he was returned into his grave.[43] We can imagine that such posthumous baptisms appealed to newly converted Christians worrying about their ancestors' salvation.

Thus, a conciliatory attitude towards paganism seems to have existed in Ireland, resulting in three stories in which a naturally good pagan is finally baptized before passing away. In one case even a pagan man is resurrected and received baptism before being returned to his grave. These stories all date from the end of the 7th century, a period when, we may surmise, Clemens, who was active on the Continent in the early AD 740s, spent his youth in Ireland. Even if Clemens was younger than this, he certainly must have been active in Ireland in the early 8th century at the latest. We must therefore conclude that Clemens appears to have grown up in an environment supportive of the idea of retrospective baptism of the deceased.

But not only in Ireland do we find traces of such discussions in hagiographical sources. In early 8th-century Northumbria, an anonymous monk or nun composed a Life of Pope Gregory the Great.[44] This text contains an intriguing chapter concerning the posthumous baptism of the Roman Emperor Trajan by Pope Gregory. When walking through the Forum of Trajan in Rome, Gregory learned the anecdote of the Roman emperor stopping on his way to do battle to oversee justice for a widow whose son had been killed. Because the killers were unwilling to pay compensation, the emperor made them do so. This Christian act done by a pagan emperor moved Gregory so greatly that he went to St Peter's church and wept 'floods of tears' for the emperor. By these tears, Trajan's soul was 'refreshed' and baptized (*refrigeratam vel baptizatam*). The author seems to expect some criticism for his choice of the term *baptizare* here, but he stressed that without baptism no one is able to see God.[45] The author of this Life, probably a monk of the monastery of Whitby, has been criticized for his lack of theological sophistication, but he seems to have been aware of the critique which the story could potentially generate.[46] He insisted on the importance of baptism and it

[43] Tírechán, *Collectanea* 40 (ed. and trans. Bieler (1979), 154–5).

[44] The *Vita Gregorii* and its account of the baptism of the Roman Emperor Trajan are also discussed in Colin Ireland's contribution elsewhere in this volume.

[45] The anonymous Life of Gregory 29 (ed. and trans. Colgrave (1968), 126–9).

[46] For the criticism levelled against the author, see, e.g., Marenbon (2012), 46: 'From a theological point of view, there is almost everything wrong with this story.'

appears that he wanted to make the story of the pagan Emperor Trajan being saved acceptable by introducing the act of baptism. There are no indications that the author knew the Irish Lives we just discussed, but it is hardly a coincidence that the theme of the salvation of a just pagan by baptism appears in Northumbria, a region closely linked to the Irish church. This evidence demonstrates that there was a lively debate on such issues in these regions, which made the Whitby author choose his words carefully. Such a discussion might be linked to persistent forms of Pelagianism in the British Isles, but the relevance of such a topic in a recently converted region is easy understood without any Pelagian influence.[47]

Clemens Willibrordus

The debate about the fate of pagan ancestors, of which we find traces in the Irish and Northumbrian hagiographical literature of the late 7th and early 8th century, provides the general background for Clemens's opinion on this matter. In the AD 740s, this debate was one of the central themes in the dispute between Boniface and Clemens, who cherished a much more positive view of the salvation of pagans than Boniface did. The story about the failed baptism should be considered as contemporary evidence of this dispute. It agrees fully with Boniface's position: there is no salvation without baptism. A possible connection to an overarching debate on predestination is suggested by the text's insistence on the well-defined number of those eligible for salvation, thus expressed in Wulfram's words: *certus est suorum numerus electorum* ('there is a certain amount of the elect with God').[48] The author here cites Bede's commentary on the Gospel of Luke; Bede himself, it will be remembered, considered Pelagianism an imminent threat to the church of his time.[49]

The story about Radbod's failed baptism therefore represents Boniface's position in the struggle with Clemens. Michael Glatthaar has recently argued in favour of a connection between the Irish opponent of Boniface and Willibrord, Northumbrian missionary and former

[47] For Pelagianism, see Herren and Brown (2002), *passim*.

[48] *Vita Wulframni* 9 (MGH SS rer. Merov. 5, 668).

[49] Bede, *In Lucae Evangelium Expositio* II 5 (ed. by David Hurst in CCSL 120, 115); on Bede's views on Pelagianism, see Herren and Brown (2002), 97–8; Holder (2005).

companion of Boniface.[50] There exists no firm evidence for a relation between the two except for Clemens's name. Willibrord had received that very name from Pope Sergius and though not uncommon, the fact that Clemens bore the same name might suggest a connection between the two. Moreover, although the geography of Clemens's activity is difficult to establish with certainty, the fact that Carloman was deemed responsible for the capture of Clemens, we can infer that Austrasia was the territory of his mission, which was also the region where Willibrord was active.[51] A connection between the two men therefore can neither be proven nor rejected.

If Glatthaar is right in his assessment of the relationship between Clemens and Willibrord, this would shed new light on the relation of the *Vita Wulframni* to Willibrord. Ian Wood argued that the *Vita Wulframni* was composed as a reply to Alcuin's *Vita Willibrordi*. This may be true for its final composition, but it cannot explain the reference to Willibrord in the episode of Radbod's failed baptism, if this indeed originated in the AD 740s, decades before Alcuin started to work on the *Vita Willibrordi*. In the anecdote under discussion here, Willibrord plays a prominent role. He is summoned by Radbod as the teacher on the Frisian people (*doctor praefatae gentis*) in order to discuss the conversion of the Frisian king with Wulfram. Radbod, however, kept arguing with the bishop, apparently not interested in becoming Christian. According to the anecdote, Willibrord said the following when receiving Radbod's summon:[52] "Why should your duke who spurns the preaching of our brother the saintly Bishop Wulfram, be inclined to follow my advice? For tonight in a dream I have seen him bound in fiery chains. Therefore, it is certain that he is already undergoing eternal damnation." When on his way to Radbod, Willibrord received the news that the Frisian leader had died without baptism, and thus his vision was substantiated.

Wood argues that Willibrord's role in the Christianization of the Frisians was so well known that the author of the *Vita Wulframni*, although presenting Wulfram and Willibrord as competitors, could not simply pass over the Anglo-Saxon missionary in silence.[53] Yet, the text

[50] Glatthaar (2004), 152, 523.

[51] For Clemens's connection to Austrasia, see Meeder (2011), 266.

[52] *Vita Wulframni* 9 (MGH SS rer. Merov. 5, 668): *'Quia praedicationem sancti fratris nostri Vulframni pontificis dux vester audire contempsit, meis quoque qualiter obsecundabit edictis? Nam hac nocte vidi illum in visu catena religatum ignea. Unde certum fore constat, dampnationem illum iam subisse aeternam.'*

[53] Wood (2001), 93.

does not seem to indicate any rivalry between the two men, it rather stresses their cooperation: 'together with the blessed Wulfram, who agreed [with him] in his religious teaching'.[54] Willibrord fully endorses Wulfram's theological position. Perhaps this is the crucial message that the story wants to bring across: Wulfram's position, which so neatly concurs with that of Boniface in the dispute with Clemens, was fully vindicated by Willibrord. Willibrord had died in AD 739. This chronology suggests that after his death, reference to his authority was used to substantiate a claim that featured in a dispute of the AD 740s between another Clemens, perhaps a (self-acclaimed) follower of Willibrord, and Boniface.

We know that Willibrord and Boniface had been at loggerheads, which Willibald, in his *Vita Bonifatii*, describes as a beautiful and harmonious form of discord.[55] There are indications that Willibrord considered a conciliatory approach to the Christian mission, based on compromise and assimilation, most fruitful, whereas Boniface was a more uncompromising character.[56] Archaeological evidence suggest that *de facto* posthumous Christianization of ancestors happened, as for example in the Rhineland near Alzey, where a church was built on top of a pre-Christian burial site.[57] Moreover, archaeological records from the early medieval period indicate that in missionary regions in the Low Countries and Germany, graves were frequently opened shortly after burial, presumably by relatives of the deceased.[58] In some cases gold-foil crosses seem to have been deposited in such reopened graves, which suggests a form of posthumous Christianization.[59] Formerly, such violations of graves were considered grave robberies, but more recently archaeologists interpret them as forms of ancestor worship or as an on-going relationship between the dead and the living.[60] Boniface would probably have objected to such forms of behaviour, but they seem nevertheless to have frequently occurred in many regions, also in Willibrord's area of activ-

[54] *Vita Wulframni* 9 (MGH SS rer. Merov. 5, 668): *simul cum beato Vulframno, in doctrina suae religionis concordante.*

[55] Willibald, *Vita Bonifatii* 5 (ed. by Wilhelm Levison in MGH SS rer. Germ. 57, 25): *spiritalis inter eos orta est contentio et consona pulchrae discretionis facta dissensio.*

[56] For Willibrord's possibly more accommodating attitude, see Meens (2000); Meens (2014), 102–6.

[57] Geary (1994), 36–8.

[58] van Haperen (2010), 3.

[59] van Haperen (2010), 15.

[60] van Haperen (2010).

ity. In this context, the story about the failed baptism of Radbod may very well be regarded as an appropriation of Willibrord's authority in a conflict over his 'religious inheritance'. The St Wandrille author of the text sided with Boniface and added Willibrord's authority to counter the views of Clemens and his followers. Willibrord may have disagreed with Boniface on this subject given his inclination for a more compromising approach in religious matters. As a native of Northumbria, he may have known the story of Trajan's posthumous baptism. Also, he spent twelve years in Ireland, where, as we have seen, texts were written towards the end of the 7th century with a decidedly positive view of pagan ancestors. Whether Willibrord had access to these texts cannot be determined, but the *Vitae* probably reflect attitudes and discussions current in Irish and Northumbrian ecclesiastical circles at that time. It is hardly conceivable that Willibrord was not aware of such tendencies, especially since the issues in question were of primary importance for his missionary work.

Conclusion

The well-known story of the Frisian King Radbod withdrawing his foot from the font when supposed to be baptized by Bishop Wulfram of Sens is only rarely regarded as historically trustworthy. More often it is considered an imaginary episode; its relevance, in this reading, lies in its depiction of sincere hopes and fears by those involved in the process of Christianization. If we follow Lebecq's persuasive reconstruction of the genesis of the *Vita Wulframni*, we can date this specific story to the AD 740s. In those years, Boniface had serious disputes with an Irish bishop named Clemens who was active in Austrasia. One of the main issues of controversy was the question of the fate of pagans who had remained ignorant of Christian doctrine. Clemens, whose views are only known through the defamation by Boniface and the papacy, seems to have been more positive concerning the fate of pagan ancestors than the uncompromising Boniface. The theme of the naturally good pagan to be found in Irish hagiographical texts of the end of the 7th century can explain Clemens's positive approach. The story about Radbod's failed baptism should be seen as a text supporting the views of Boniface *cum suis*. It argues against a possible salvation for pagan ancestors and stresses the need for baptism. The discussion between Clemens and Boniface may also reflect an earlier dispute between Boniface and Willibrord. This at least would explain why Willibrord, besides Wulfram, plays such a central role in the Radbod story. Willibrord's authority is claimed here in order to corroborate the Bonifatian view on the condemnation of pagan ancestors. This need not have been Willibrord's own opinion and there are some indications to the contrary. Boniface's strict attitude in such matters may have been an exception in the more general process of Christianization. If so, this would explain why we have only this single testimony to what must have been a central question. Other missionaries seem to have been less outspoken on the subject than Boniface was and thus seem to have given their new converts more comfort in dealing with their pagan ancestors in ways they considered appropriate.

Bibliography

Anderson, A.O. and M.O. Anderson (1991) *Adomnán's Life of Columba*, Oxford.

Angenendt, A. (1998) *Die Geschichte des Bistums Münster, Bd. 1: Mission bis Millennium, 313–1000*, Münster.

Asbach, F.B. (1975) *Das* Poenitentiale Remense *und der sogen.* Excarpsus Cummeani*: Überlieferung, Quellen und Entwicklung zweier kontinentaler Bußbücher aus der 1. Hälfte des 8. Jahrhunderts*, Regensburg.

Berschin, W. (1991) *Biographie und Epochenstil im lateinischen Mittelalter, Bd. 3: Die karolingische Biographie 750–920 n. Chr.*, Stuttgart.

Bieler, L. (1979) *The Patrician texts in the Book of Armagh*, Dublin.

Blair, J. (2005) *The church in Anglo-Saxon society*, Oxford.

Blok, D., W. Prevenier et al. (1981) *Algemene Geschiedenis der Nederlanden 1: Middeleeuwen*, Bussum.

Brown, P. (2003) *The rise of western Christendom: triumph and diversity A.D. 200–1000*, 2nd edition, Malden.

Charles-Edwards, T.M. (1995) 'The penitential of Theodore and the Iudicia Theodori,' in M. Lapidge, *Archbishop Theodore: commemorative studies on his life and influence*, Cambridge, 141–74.

— (2000) *Early Christian Ireland*, Cambridge.

Clay, J.-H. (2010) *In the shadow of death. Saint Boniface and the conversion of Hessia, 721–54*, Turnhout.

Colgrave, B. (1968) *The earliest Life of Gregory the Great by an anonymous monk of Whitby*, Laurence.

Colgrave, B. and R.A.B. Mynors (1992) *Bede's Ecclesiastical History of the English People*, rev. ed., Oxford.

de Jong, M. (2005) 'Bonifatius: een angelsaksische priestermonnik en het Frankische hof,' *Millennium* 19, 5–23.

Dumézil, B. (2005) *Les racines chrétiennes de l'Europe. Conversion et liberté dans les royaumes barbares Ve–VIIIe siècle*, Paris.

Finsterwalder, P.W. (1929) *Die* Canones Theodori Cantuariensis *und ihre Überlieferungsformen*, Weimar.

Fischer, A. (2012) *Karl Martell. Der Beginn karolingischer Herrschaft*, Stuttgart.

Flechner, R. (2003–4) 'The making of the canons of Theodore,' *Peritia* 17–8, 121–43.

Fletcher, R. (1997) *The conversion of Europe: from paganism to Christianity*, London.

Fouracre, P. (2000) *The age of Charles Martel*, Harlow.

Geary, P. (1994) 'The uses of archaeological sources for religious and cultural history,' in P. Geary, *Living with the dead in the Middle Ages*, Ithaca, 30–45.

Glatthaar, M. (2004) *Bonifatius und das Sakrileg. Zur politischen Dimension eines Rechtsbegriffs*, Frankfurt.

Herren, M.W. and S.A. Brown (2002) *Christ in Celtic Christianity. Britain and Ireland from the fifth to the tenth century*, Woodbridge.

Holder, A. (2005) 'The anti-pelagian character of Bede's Commentary on the Song of Songs,' in C. Leonardi and G. Orlandi, *Biblical studies in the early Middle Ages*, Florence, 91–103.

Innes, M. (2007) *Introduction to early medieval Western Europe, 300–900: the sword, the plough and the book*, London.

— (2008) '"Immune from heresy": defining the boundaries of Carolingian Christianity,' in P. Fouracre and D. Ganz, *Frankland: the Franks and the world of the early Middle Ages. Essays in honour of Dame Jinty Nelson*, Manchester, 101–25.

Lebecq, S. (2000) 'Vulfran, Willibrord et la mission de Frise: pour une relecture de la *Vita Vulframni*,' in M. Polfer, *L'évangélisation des régions entre Meuse et Moselle et la fondation de l'abbaye d'Echternach (Ve–IXe siècle)*, Luxemburg, 431–51, repr. in Lebecq (2011), 75–93.

— (2007) 'Paganisme et rites sacrificiels chez les Frisons des VIIe–VIIIe siècles,' in F. Felten, J. Jarnut, and L.E. von Padberg, *Bonifatius – Leben und Nachwirken. Die Gestaltung des christlichen Europas im Frühmittelalter*, Mainz, 111–20.

— (2011) *Hommes, mers et terres du Nord au début du Moyen Âge I: peuples, cultures, territoires*, Villeneuve d'Ascq.

— (2011a) 'Traduction du prologue et des chapitres 6 à 10 de le *Vie de Vulfran* du pseudo-Jonas, moine de Fontenelle,' in Lebecq (2011), 95–101.

Lynch, J. (1998) *Christianizing kinship: ritual sponsorship in Anglo-Saxon England*, Ithaca.

Machielsen, L. (1961) 'Fragments patristiques non-identifiés du ms. Vat. Pal. 577,' *Sacris Erudiri* 12, 488–539.

Marenbon, J. (2012) 'A problem of paganism,' in C. Steel, J. Marenbon, and W. Verbeke, *Paganism in the Middle Ages: threat and fascination*, Leuven, 39–54.

McCone, K. (1991) *Pagan past and Christian present in early Irish literature*, Maynooth.

Meeder, S. (2011) 'Boniface and the Irish heresy of Clemens,' *Church History* 80, 251–80.

Meens, R. (2000) 'Christentum und Heidentum aus der Sicht Willibrords? Überlegungen zum *Paenitentiale Oxoniense II*,' in M. Polfer, *L'évangélisation des régions entre Meuse et Moselle et la fondation de l'abbaye d'Echternach (V^e–IXe siècle)*, Luxemburg, 417–28.

— (2007) 'Aspekte der Christianisierung des Volkes,' in F.J. Felten, J. Jarnut, and L.E. von Padberg, *Bonifatius – Leben und Nachwirken. Die Gestaltung des christlichen Europas im Frühmittelalter*, Mainz, 211–29.

— (2012) 'Exil, Buße und sozialer Tod. Ausschließungsmechanismen in den frühmittelalterlichen Bußbüchern,' in C. Garnier and J. Schnocks, *Sterben über den Tod hinaus. Politische, soziale und religiöse Ausgrenzung in vormodernen Gesellschaften*, Würzburg, 117–31.

— (2014) *Penance in medieval Europe, 600–1200*, Cambridge.

Mordek, H. (1975) *Kirchenrecht und Reform im Frankenreich. Die Collectio Vetus Gallica, die älteste systematische Kanonessammlung des fränkischen Gallien. Studien und Edition*, Berlin.

Mostert, M. (2013) 'Communicating the faith: the circle of Boniface, Germanic vernaculars, and Frisian and Saxon converts,' *Amsterdamer Beiträge zur älteren Germanistik* 70, 87–130.

Noble, T. and J. Smith (2008) *The Cambridge history of Christianity, vol. 3: early medieval Christianities, c.600–c.1100*, Cambridge.

Ó Cróinín, D. (1984) 'Rath Melsigi, Willibrord, and the earliest Echternach manuscripts,' *Peritia* 3, 17–49, repr. in Ó Cróinín (2003), 145–72.

— (1985) '"New heresy for old". Pelagianism in Ireland and the papal letter of 640,' *Speculum* 60, 505–16, repr. in Ó Cróinín (2003), 87–98.

— (2003) *Early Irish history and chronology*, Dublin.

— (2007) *The kings depart: the prosopography of Anglo-Saxon royal exile in the sixth and seventh centuries*, Cambridge.

O'Sullivan, T. (2010) 'The anti-Pelagian motif of the 'naturally good' pagan in Adomnán's *Vita Columbae*,' in J. Wooding et al., *Adomnán of Iona: theologian, lawmaker, peacemaker*, Dublin, 253–73.

Palmer, J. (2009) *Anglo-Saxons in a Frankish world, 690–900*, Turnhout.

Scheibelreiter, G. (1999) *Die barbarische Gesellschaft. Mentalitätsgeschichte der europäischen Achsenzeit 5.–8. Jahrhundert*, Darmstadt.

Smith, J. (2005) *Europe after Rome: a new cultural history 500–1000*, Oxford.

van Egmond, W. (2005) 'Radbod van de Friezen, een aristocraat in de periferie,' *Millennium* 19, 24–43.

van Eijnatten, J. and F. van Lieburg (2005) *Nederlandse religiegeschiedenis*, Hilversum.

van Haperen, M. (2010) 'Rest in pieces: an interpretive model of early medieval 'grave robbery',' *Medieval and Modern Matters* 1, 1–36.

von Padberg, L.E. (2003) *Die Inszenierung religiöser Konfrontationen. Theorie der Missionspredigt im frühen Mittelalter*, Stuttgart.

Weiler, A. (1989) *Willibrords Missie. Christendom en cultuur in de zevende en achtste eeuw. Met een vertaling van de voornaamste literaire bronnen door P. Bange*, Hilversum.

Wickham, C. (2009) *The inheritance of Rome: a history of Europe from 400 to 1000*, London.

Wood, I. (1991) 'Saint Wandrille and its hagiography,' in I. Wood and G.A. Loud, *Church and chronicle in the Middle Ages*, London, 1–14.

— (2001) *The missionary life: saints and the evangelization of Europe, 400–1050*, Harlow.

— (2005) 'Christianisation and the dissemination of Christian teaching,' in P. Fouracre, *The new Cambridge medieval history, vol. 1: c.500–c.700*, Cambridge, 710–34.

Yorke, B. (2007) 'The insular background to Boniface's continental career,' in F.J. Felten, J. Jarnut, L.E. von Padberg, *Bonifatius – Leben und Nachwirken. Die Gestaltung des christlichen Europas im Frühmittelalter*, Mainz, 23–37.

Zeddies, N. (1995) 'Bonifatius und zwei nützliche Rebellen: die Häretiker Aldebert und Clemens,' in M.T. Fögen, *Ordnung und Aufruhr im Mittelalter: historische und juristische Studien zur Rebellion*, Frankfurt, 217–63.

DAVID GANZ

THE EARLIEST MANUSCRIPT OF LATHCEN'S *ECLOGAE MORALIUM GREGORII* AND THE DATING OF IRISH CURSIVE MINUSCULE SCRIPT

Abstract

This paper gives a description of the fragments of Lathcen's *Eclogae Moralium* in Düsseldorf, New York, and Essen/Werden, a collation of the unedited portions of text, and a discussion of the script and the date of the fragments. There is a list and brief description of all early Irish cursive minuscule manuscripts.

Keywords

Lathcen, Adomnán, Gregory the Great, Wealdhere, Paulinus of Nola; Bobbio, Echternach, Werden; palaeography, cursive minuscule; Book of Durrow, Book of Armagh; Julian Brown.

Introduction

Among the fragments in the Universitäts- und Landesbibliothek in Düsseldorf are ten pieces of vellum which can be assembled to form seven leaves which contain four portions (Fragments 1–4 in the following) of Lathcen's *Eclogae Moralium*,[1] the work of Lathcen of Clonfert whose death is recorded in the Annals of Ulster, Tigernach, and Inisfallen for AD 661,[2] in the 9th-century Martyrology of Oengus, and in a

[1] The present shelf mark is Düsseldorf, Universitäts- und Landesbibliothek, K I B 212, 1r–4v; see Zechiel-Eckes (2003), 24–6 and plate 2. I thank Marcus Vaillant, the keeper of manuscripts, for supplying me with superb digital images of these fragments, which are reproduced in the Appendix, with kind permission from the Universitäts- und Landesbibliothek Düsseldorf.

[2] Annals of Ulster *s.a.* 661 (ed. Mac Airt and Mac Niocaill (1983), 132–3); Annals of Tigernach *s.a.* [AU 660] (ed. Stokes (1991), 156); Annals of Inisfallen *s.a.* [661] (ed. Mac Airt (1988), 94–5); see also Charles-Edwards (2006), 188.

Early medieval Ireland and Europe: chronology, contacts, scholarship, ed. by Pádraic Moran and Immo Warntjes, Studia Traditionis Theologiae, 14 (Turnhout, 2015), pp. 597–624.

 10.1484/M.STT-EB.5.103137

genealogical text in Dublin, Trinity College, 1336 (*olim* H.3.17).[3] Two further fragments (5–6) from the same manuscript contain a unique version of the Commentary on Job by Philippus, the student of Jerome who died about AD 455. Both texts are copied in two columns of some 45 lines, in a cursive minuscule script. There is no ruling. The fragments were first recorded by Lowe in his *Codices Latini Antiquiores*.[4] Fragment 1 consists of two separate pieces of parchment, the text runs across both for 34 lines, but one fragment preserves the top line of the original page and the other the bottom line. The smaller fragment preserves the centre of the original bifolium. Fragment 2 has a complete column of text and some four letters of the second column. Fragment 3 consists of two pieces of a single column, each with eight lines of text. The text continues from the upper to the lower piece, but they have been cut so that they do not fit together. Fragment 4 contains the upper part of a page, with two columns of text, and the inner margin and pricking holes of the outer margin. The top outer corner is rounded, as in many early Irish manuscripts. The two leaves Fragment 5 has the inner columns and two or three letters of the outer column of a bifolium, Fragment 6 consists of two pieces which fit together to give most of the inner column and all of the outer column, lacking the top and bottom.

Two further fragments of this manuscript are a leaf in Columbia, University Library, Plimpton 54, which came from a private collection in Germany,[5] and a leaf in the Propsteiarchiv in Werden, which I have not seen, but which by its text must be the leaf following Düsseldorf Fragment 3.[6] All came from the monastery of Werden where the Düsseldorf leaves

[3] Martyrology of Oengus 12 Jan (ed. Stokes (1905), 35). A good discussion of the sources relating to Laidcen can be found in Grosjean (1955), 92–6. Elizabeth Okasha and Katherine Forsyth publish a slab from Toureen Peacaun, County Tipperary (no. 16) which bears the names of Cummene and Ladcen both of whom died in AD 661; see Okasha and Forsyth (2001), 253–4.

[4] *CLA* 8, 46 (no. 1185).

[5] This leaf may be viewed on Digital Scriptorium at: http://ucblibrary4.berkeley.edu:8088/xtf22/search?smode=basic;rmode=digscript;text=lathcen;docsPerPage=1;startDoc=1;fullview=yes. I am very grateful to Consuelo Dutschke for allowing me to work with it.

[6] The Werden leaf was discovered in 1991 as the cover of an account book. I am grateful to the archivist, Franz Josef Schmitt, for confirming that the shelf mark is Fragment Nr. 1. There is a plate of one side of the Werden leaf in Schütz (2009), 71. I am most grateful to Dr Julia Schneider, Librarian of the Medieval Institute of the University of Notre Dame, for sending me a scan of this plate as the volume is not in any UK library.

were reused in the later Middle Ages.[7] Fragment 1r has in the left hand margin *Computationes Officii Granarii* and below *Officii Fabrice*, Fragment 2v has been inverted and overwritten with a large *B* and *Officiorum Parvorum Granarii* with other entries canceled and *Fabrice* in the last line. Above this are two lines in a very crude cursive and between the lines of Lathcen are several lines in a tiny script with the date AD 1434. Fragment 4 bears the note *Cellerariae A 1432 B*, Fragment 6r (with Philippus) is labeled *Computationes Officii Branarii Officii Fabrice Officiorum Parvorum Granarii* with a large *B*, Fragment 5v has *Cripte Prioratus Pomerii, Firmarie, Granarii* Structura B and the Werden leaf in inscribed Porta D. Fragment 4r is inscribed in each column, the right column upside down, suggesting that the leaf may have been a wrapper. On Fragment 1r there seems to be the offset of Gothic textualis script. The complete text of Lathcen, copied in this 2 column format, would have required some 60 folia; since the manuscript also included a unique version of the text of Philippus it presumably had at least 100 folia. It is hard to find early instances of a manuscript with copies of two commentaries on the same book of the Bible.

Most of the extant manuscripts of the text of Lathcen were listed by Adriaen in his edition.[8]

St Petersburg, Rossijskaja Nacional'naja Biblioteka, F v I 7 (Northern France, end of the 8th century, later at Corbie).[9]

Laon, Bibliothèque municipale, 50 (Northern France, end of the 8th century, copied from an insular exemplar, later at Laon).[10]

Karlsruhe, Badische Landesbibliothek, Aug. perg. 134 (Reichenau, saec. IX ¾).[11]

Freiburg, Universitätsbibliothek, Fragment 59 (France, saec. IX ⅔).[12]

Vienna, Österreichische Nationalbibliothek, 921 (Salzburg, AD 836–859).[13]

7 Werden was founded around AD 799. The question of how the Lathcen text reached the abbey remains unclear, though Barker-Benfield (1991), 55, notes that the founder was recorded has having brought books from York to Utrecht in AD 773, quoting the *Vita S. Liudegeri* I 12 and noting the Lathcen fragments on p 53. Cf. Gerchow (1999), citing these fragments on p 55.

8 CCSL 73, VI. The Freiburg fragment is not listed; see now Castaldi (2008).

9 *CLA* 11, 7 (no. 1604); Bischoff (1998–2004), ii 78 (no. 2305).

10 *CLA* 6, 18–9 (no. 763). Bischoff (1998–2004), ii 21–2 (no. 2053).

11 Bischoff (1998–2004), i 347 (no. 1657).

12 Bischoff (1998–2004), i 274 (no. 1302).

13 Bischoff (1980), 158–9.

Ljublijana, Narodna in univerzitetna knjižnica, 6 (North-eastern France, saec. IX ex.).[14]

Cambridge, Pembroke College, 88 (France, from Bury St Edmunds, saec. X).[15]

Munich, Bayerische Staatsbibliothek, Clm 16053 (from St Nicholas Passau, saec. XI).

Laon, Bibliothèque municipale, 46 (Cuissy where the text is ascribed to Isidore, saec. XIII).

Admont, Stiftsbibliothek, 408 (listed in the 14th-century Admont catalogues, saec. XII in.).

The text of the fragments

Adriaen had collated the text of Düsseldorf Fragment 4, the text of the remaining Düsseldorf fragments was identified by Zechiel-Eckes. I have identified the passages on the Columbia and Werden leaves.

Fragment 1r: Lathcen, *Eclogae Moralium* 7.55–8.15 (CCSL 73, 70–3); *Explicit li vii. Incip liber viii* in column 1.

Fragment 1v: Lathcen, *Eclogae Moralium* 8.18–41 (CCSL 73, 73–6); two columns and three letters at the base of the second column, 45 lines.

Fragment 2r: Lathcen, *Eclogae Moralium* 11.23–30 (CCSL 73, 114–6); one column of 44 lines and the last four or five letters of the preceding column.

Fragment 2v: Lathcen, *Eclogae Moralium* 11.30–36 (CCSL 73, 116–7); one column of 44 lines and the first three or four letters of the following column.

Fragment 3r: Lathcen, *Eclogae Moralium* 11.19–23 (CCSL 73, 113–4).

Fragment 3v: Lathcen, *Eclogae Moralium* 11.39–41 (CCSL 73, 118).

Werden leaf recto: Lathcen, *Eclogae Moralium* 11.59–67 (CCSL 73, 121–3); in two columns of 41 lines.

Fragment 4r: Lathcen, *Eclogae Moralium* 17.1–16 (CCSL 73, 207–9);[16] the text opens *In nomine sancta trinitatis Incipit liber Xviii* with a diminuendo on the first word *Verbis*; two columns with 39 lines.

14 Bischoff (1998–2004), i 421 (no. 2031).

15 Bischoff (1998–2004), i 183 describes the script as 'französische Schrift unter insularem Einfluss'.

16 A black and white photograph of the recto is Plate 1 of Gattermann (1989); a colour photograph, printed upside down, is Seibt (1990), 39.

Fragment 4v: Lathcen, *Eclogae Moralium* 17.16–34 (CCSL 73, 209–12, using this fragment); two columns with 41 lines.

Columbia, University Library, Plimpton 54, recto: Lathcen, *Eclogae Moralium* 20.21–55 (CCSL 73, 240–2).

Columbia, University Library, Plimpton 54, verso: Lathcen, *Eclogae Moralium* 20.55–213 (CCSL 73, 242–5).

Zechiel-Eckes, who identified the text of Phillippus, noted that it does not seem possible to establish whether that text preceded or followed the text of Lathcen.[17]

At Lathcen, *Eclogae Moralium* 7.37.57 (CCSL 73, 71), the fragments share the distinctive readings of Laon 50. In general they are closest to the St Petersburg manuscript. But the manuscript from which these fragments came cannot have been the exemplar for either manuscript. In some passages the text of these fragments is closer to Gregory's *Moralia* than any other witness. I record the variants in bold type, using the line numbers of Adriaen's CCSL edition; 'om.' indicates that the previous word is omitted.

Düsseldorf Fragment 1r (Lathcen, *Eclogae Moralium* 7.55–8.15):

CCSL 73, 70:

l. 243: *veritatis sermonibus,* ***et*** *cum*; l. 245: *aperte* om.

CCSL 73, 71:

l. 246: *repraehensabilia*; l. 249: ***aeloquium***; l. 250: *est enim genus inoportunum vanae iam loquaquitatis quod utique studit aetiam recta increpare. Et iram ut ex certamine ostendatur exagitare* (as Laon 50 and Pembroke 88); l. 256: *ex cuius* (as St Petersburg); l. 258: *et unde usque ad iustititae increpationis audaciam pervenitur protinus innotuit cum subiuncxit* (as Laon 50 and Pembroke 88); l. 259: *est* om.; (book 8) l. 1: ***super***; l. 2: *conti****g****escunt* (closer to Gregory's *conticescunt*) ***unde*** *sequitur.*

CCSL 73, 72:

l. 5: *praebite*; l. 6: ***inlatas*** [...] *Tripido*; l. 7: *praesus* [...] ***ipse***; l. 10: ***Neque suis***; l. 11: ***adsequi***; l. 16: *non* om.; l. 20: *non* om.; l. 23: ***a*** *mea*; l. 23: ***stultitia***; l. 24: *concupiscentia* for *conscientia*; l. 31: *itaque ipsa* (as Gregory); l. 32: *Invigelat*; l. 35: *augmen****tum***.

CCSL 73, 73:

l. 37: ***mercinari***; l. 39: *perigrinationem*; l. 43: *serv****us***; *est* om.; l. 44: *oper****is***; *requiem* om.; l. 46 *praestulatur* (as St Petersburg); l. 48: *cum usque et* om.; l. 56: ***aelecti*** *querunt*; l. 57: ***noctesque***; l. 58: *tenebrat.*

[17] Zechiel-Eckes (2003), 25.

Düsseldorf Fragment 1v (Lathcen, *Eclogae Moralium* 8.18–8.41):

CCSL 73, 73:

l. 66: *consulante.*

CCSL 73, 74:

l. 68: *et* om.; l. 69: *aetiam seducta*; l. 70: *iungit*; ***Sequitur***; l. 76: ***Sequitur***; l. 78: *autem* om.; l. 81: *sunt* om.; l. 83: *disperavi*; l. 86: *transiuntem quia* ***et***; l. 87: *misericodias*; l. 92: *recta* ***bona*** *opera exuti.*

CCSL 73, 75:

l. 111: ***Hoc est qui***; l. 119: ***cognoscitur***; l. 120: ***agnitio***; l. 127: ***unde*** *sequitur.*

CCSL 73, 76:

l. 130: ***inpugnet***; l. 132: ***Confitebor***; l. 133: *Intus contra me* (as Gregory).

Düsseldorf Fragment 3r (Lathcen, *Eclogae Moralium* 11.19–23):

CCSL 73, 113:

l. 111: *ideo* om.; l. 113: ***proficit,*** *quisque aeterna* (om. *ideo*); l. 117: ***sint***; l. 119: *Baltheum*; l. 120: *baltheum desolvit* (as St Petersburg); l. 121: ***videantur***; *elationem castitatis* (om. *culpam*) *eis* (om. *in*).

CCSL 73, 114:

l. 123: *desolvit* (as Karlsruhe).

Düsseldorf Fragment 2r (Lathcen, *Eclogae Moralium* 11.23–30):

CCSL 73, 114:

l. 138: ***enim*** *veracium*; l. 139: ***Priorum***; l. 142: ***commutatur***; l. 144: *suos dixisse* (as Karlsruhe); l. 147: ***dispectionem*** (as St Petersburg); l. 148: ***relevat***; l. 150: *opraessi profunda.*

CCSL 73, 115:

l. 154: *a credentibus* (as Gregory); l. 157: *umbram* ***ergo***; l. 164: *subversas*; l. 166: *direlinquit*; l. 170 ***commutat***; l. 176: *mollerentur* (as St Petersburg); l. 177: ***credulitati***; l. 178: *omnium* ***consistere.***

Düsseldorf Fragment 2v (Lathcen, *Eclogae Moralium* 11.30–36):

CCSL 73, 116:

l. 185: *posset*; l. 188: ***dispicit***; l. 189: *et* ***interloquentem***; l. 192: *per prophetiae* (*spiritum* om.); l. 194: ***adsistentia***; l. 200: *unde subditur* (*apte* om. as Karlsruhe); l. 201: *aliquis.*

Düsseldorf Fragment 3v (Lathcen, *Eclogae Moralium* 11.39–41):

CCSL 73, 118:

l. 249: *autem* ***placere***; l. 250: *hoc* (*in eis* om.) *iudicat*; l. 251: *famularis*; l. 253: ***quonam***; l. 254: ***vidistis***; l. 255: *repraehensibiles.*

Werden leaf recto (Lathcen, *Eclogae Moralium* 11.59–67):

CCSL 73, 121:

Dilectum for *delictum* throughout; l. 361: ***cogitatione sola***; l. 364: *me inimicum tuum* om.; l. 365: *qui.*

CCSL 73, 122:

l. 366: ***requessit***; l. 367: *ait ergo* (as Karlsruhe); l. 368: *quia si cut*; l. 369: ***privaris***; l. 370: *quoque* om. (as Karlsruhe); l. 375: *alto cicidit*; l. 377: *esse* om.; l. 378: ***etiam***; l. 379: ***unde*** *sequitur.*

CCSL 73, 123:

l. 411: *sanctus vir* (as Gregory); l. 414: ***habuit*** (as St Petersburg and Karlsruhe); l. 421: ***qui.***

Düsseldorf Fragment 4 (Lathcen, *Eclogae Moralium* 17.1–34) was collated by Adriaen in CCSL 73, 206–12. Most of the readings recorded by Adriaen are unique, some are shared with the Karlsruhe manuscript.

Columbia leaf recto (Lathcen, *Eclogae Moralium* 20.21–55):

CCSL 73, 240:

l. 75: ***sequi*** before *Filii stultorum*; l. 76: ***poenitus*** (*et-proverbium* om.); l. 82: *dispectior* (as St Petersburg).

CCSL 73, 241:

l. 83: *quando*; l. 84: ***abuminabiles***; l. 90: ***Faretram***; l. 97: *elegit*; l. 107: ***obpraesserunt*** (as St Petersburg); l. 110: ***inlabitur feret.***

CCSL 73, 242: l. 117: *dilegit.*

Columbia leaf verso (Lathcen, *Eclogae Moralium* 20.55–72):

CCSL 73, 242: l. 140: ***nobis*** for *nubes.*

CCSL 73, 243: l. 150: *perfuratur*; l. 162: ***adsimilatus*** (as St Petersburg); l. 163: *favellae cineris* (*et* om.); l. 164: ***dispiciuntur*** (as St Petersburg); l. 172: ***defferi*** (as St Petersburg).

CCSL 73, 244:

l. 177: *sancto viro* (as Gregory); l. 179: *aperte* (as Gregory); l. 188: *est domus* (as Karlsruhe); l. 194: *consumptionem* (as Gregory).

Since the text was composed in Ireland, the orthography of these fragments may be closer to the author's usage than that found in other manuscripts.

The script

Capital letters

The capital letters are all simple, without any marked thickening of the stroke. A very distinctive *A* with a curved bow and the final stroke prolonged above the bow on Fragment 2v. Capital *A* is like *a cc* in *ad* Fragment 1r. Initial *B* has open bow Fragment 3r. Capital *C* encloses the following letter. *D* with a vertical shaft sometimes with a pronounced loop. *E* with the upper curve turning back and a large lower bow. The tongue of *E* is extended slanting down at an angle to form the bow of *t* in capital *Et*, *L* curving below the letter Fragment 1v. *N* with open triangles at the top of the ascender Fragment 1v. *Q* with a large oval bow. On Fragment 1r the very large *Q* has a pronounced wedge at the top of the shaft, the end of the upper curve of the bow rests on top of it, smaller versions are found on the other leaves. *S* descends to the next line with a deep v-shaped fork Fragment 3v. The capitals on the Columbia leaf are smaller than those in Düsseldorf.

Minuscule letter forms[18]

a has several forms: flat topped, uncial, and with the second stroke rising up to a point; *c* rises above the line of writing; *d* is curved, but sometimes has a long s-shaped ascender like the Greek small delta; high *e* is found in ligature as is the reversed *e* like a theta; *g* always has a closed loop; the shaft of *h* is remarkably short; when *i* is the second letter in a ligature, it is prolonged below the base line; *l* in ligature straight, but on its own sometimes at start of a word it has a marked bowl; the final minim of final *m* is prolonged below the base line; the bow of *p* is open; the cross stroke of *r* at the end of a word rises; *z* is found on the verso of Columbia leaf column 1; the cross strokes of *g* and *t* rise to the right; in *-bus* and *-tur* the *u* is written above the line; *nunc* with uncial *N*; *fi*-ligature resembling an *x*; *fi-*, *si-*, *ti*-ligatures, and a distinctive *st*-ligature in which the top of *s* descends into the *t*; *mo*-ligature with the looped *o* on Fragment 4r–v; *ci*-ligature; high *u* in *iustus bona* with *a* hanging from *n*; in the word *Praesenti* in the top line of Fragment 1v column 1 *ti* hangs from *n*; *m* hangs from *u*; *nt*-ligature. The aspect of the script is characterized by the curves of high *c* and *e*, the delta shaped *d*, the high *f*, the head of *s*, long *i*, and the long *t* in a *ti*-ligature, resulting in a fluid appearance.

[18] My terminology owes much to Lindsay (1922).

Abbreviations

Insular *autem*; reversed *c* for *con*; insular abbreviation for *est*, *pro*; *sequi* and *sqr* for sequitur; *q* with a stroke through the shaft for *que*; *p* with hook for *per* Fragment 1r, 1v column 2.

Fragment 4v is perhaps by a second scribe with smaller capitals.

On Fragment 1r *militia* is written with a diminuendo, as are *Verbis* on Fragment 4r and *Ecce* on Fragment 4v.

In the fragments of Lathcen the biblical text is set off by three dots and an enlarged letter, and indicated by a diple in the outer margin.

The text of Philippus on Fragment 5v uses small insular half uncial script for the first ten lines of the left hand column, with a capital *R*. This change of script is unrelated to the text, and shows that Irish scribes were able to write several grades of script, and to vary the script they wrote.

Comparison with other texts written in insular cursive script

On what basis can we assign a date to these fragments? They are written in a fluid cursive minuscule script with distinctive ligatures and abbreviations. The letter forms and ligatures of insular cursive originate in the ligatures of New Roman Cursive,[19] and were presumably used to copy letters and charters in the insular world.[20] Insular cursive is also used for pocket Gospel books presumably copied for private use. In an article published in 1913 Lindsay noted the distinctive features of Irish cursive minuscule: 'In Irish minuscule the writing is crowded, the laws of syllable-division between the lines are ignored, subscript (and suprascript) letters are common, abbreviation symbols are especially frequent.'[21] Lindsay noted the presence of specific letter forms: cursive *I*,

[19] I note a similar *ti*-ligature in the 5th-century copy of the Grammar of Probus in Naples, Biblioteca Nazionale, 2, 110r, and it is used in the Ravenna papyri, as are the theta-shaped *e* and the looped *o*; see Tjader (1954), 104, 106.

[20] No such documents have survived from Ireland, but the letter of Bishop Wealdhere of London (London, British Library, Cotton Augustus II 18, dated to AD 704) is in a cursive minuscule. The script of the letter is discussed by Chaplais (1978) with a plate of the letter. Note the comment of O'Sullivan (2005), 514, on this letter: 'Such hands cannot at present be distinguished as Irish or Anglo-Saxon.'

[21] Lindsay (1913), 307.

i-longa after *r* and *t*, *ti* and subscript *o*, a cursive *e* turning to the left, high backed *a* and a Greek minuscule delta form of *d*.[22]

Surviving specimens of Irish cursive minuscule script display a slanted pen-angle which produces sharply pointed minims and descenders. Julian Brown gives the fullest discussion of the minuscule, though he did not mention these leaves.[23] Brown listed the significant details of his 'Phase I': looped ascenders, especially on straight *d*, reversed form of *e* in ligatures, and a narrow loop or near loop on the descender of *g*.[24] He considered instances such as the cursive minuscule of the Vatican Paulinus as 'an informal, natural version of the more stately script found in Echternach, Durham and A II 10'.[25]

The Wealdhere letter establishes that the *ti-* and *tio-*ligatures, the *a* with the right hand stroke rising to a point, high *c* and *e* when in ligature with a following letter, *m* with an elongated final minim and *s* with a deep fork, all found in Irish cursive minuscule, were in use in AD 704. It may be that the Naples manuscripts from Bobbio are of a similar date; they are the work of several scribes writing cursive minuscule. The distinctive letter forms can be found in the glossed copy of the Pauline Epistles in Cambridge, Trinity College, B.10.5 (with London, British Library, Cotton Vitellius C VIII, 85r–90v) which Brown thought the work of an Irish scribe working in Northumbria.[26] Elsewhere they are found when a scribe briefly writes in a lower grade of script as in the copy of the canons of St Blasien in Cologne, Dombibliothek, 213, the work of an accomplished scribe who frequently copied the last three lines of a page in a minuscule, sometimes a calligraphic cursive minuscule which uses the *ti-* and *tio-*ligatures, the reversed 8-shaped *e* and the looped *o* in ligatures after *m* and *n*.[27] Simple early insular cursive script is found on folio 124r of the Book of Durrow, to copy the Hebrew names in the following Gospel: *a* is open, curved and straight forms of *d*, high *e* in

22 Lindsay (1913), 306.

23 Lindsay (1910) is more concerned with a full listing of abbreviations than with features of script, though he does note the presence of different scribes in the manuscripts he describes.

24 Brown (1993), 212–3. Brown's schema offered orientation rather than a map; cf. Crick (1997), 63.

25 Brown and Mackay (1988), 17.

26 Brown (1993), 218; cf. Bishop (1964–8).

27 The manuscript may be viewed at: www.ceec.uni-koeln.de. The letter forms listed may be found on 39r and 127r.

en- and *er-*ligatures and the *u* written above the line. One of the earliest examples of insular cursive is found in Durham, Cathedral Library, A.II.10, 3v where the last ten lines are copied in a lower grade of script which uses the looped *o* and the *ti*-ligature; ascenders have prominent wedges, and the curve first stroke of *d* and *q* curls to the left; *A* is uncial; the ascender of *h* bends to the left as in the more formal half uncial.[28] But this cursive is a slower and more mannered script than in the Naples manuscripts, the Wealdhere letter, or the Lathcen fragments. The letter forms may occasionally be found in the script used for the chapters and prefaces in the Echternach Gospels.[29] An equally calligraphic cursive minuscule is found in the work of one of the scribes of the Vatican manuscript of Paulinus of Nola.[30] All of these instances may be dated around *c.*AD 700. Brown distinguished this Northumbrian type from the Southumbrian minuscule used by St Boniface and the scribe of the Spangenberg Servius fragment.

Brown seems to have regarded the *ti*-ligatures and the use of pendant *a* or *i* as the hallmarks of his 'Phase I', so that despite the great discipline and regularity of the text scripts in the Book of Armagh and one of the hands in the Book of Mulling he considered both those manuscripts to be in 'Phase I' minuscule. Brown's 'Phase II' minuscule, which he described as simpler and lighter, the lightness obtained by the use of a thinner pen, a preference for letter forms which are simple, discretion in the use of ligatures and abbreviations, did not affect Ireland.[31] He saw no features of Irish 'Phase I' cursive which offered clues to an earlier or a later date. But his published treatment of Irish minuscule manuscripts is summary and reveals his bafflement at the lack of any evident development.

The two datable insular minuscule manuscripts are the Antiphonary of Bangor[32] dated between AD 680 and 691, and the manuscript of the Life of St Columba by Adomnán, copied in an elegant set minuscule by

28 *CLA* 2, 9 (no. 147), dated by Brown (1993), 191: 'probably before 664'.

29 *mo* in ligature on 13v; *ti* on 14v, 15v, 17r, 74r, 113r, 114r, 174v; reversed *e* on 111r; and *a* hanging from the previous letter on 112r and 174r.

30 The manuscript (Vatican, Biblioteca Apostolica, Pal. lat. 235, 4r–29v) has been fully digitized for the Bibliotheca Laureshamensis digital website: http://bibliotheca-laureshamensis-digital.de/bav/bav_pal_lat_235. It was reproduced in facsimile by Brown and Mackay (1988).

31 Brown (1993), 217. Dumville (1999), 63, allows for the existence of a 'Gaelic Phase II'.

32 Milan, Biblioteca Ambrosiana, C 5 inf.; *CLA* 3, 12 (no. 311), with a full facsimile by Warren (1893). There are more cursive letters at line ends and at the bottoms of pages.

Dorbéne, abbot of Iona before his death in AD 713, with a more cursive passage on page 108.[33] Neither has script particularly close to the cursive minuscule of the Lathcen fragments. Some of the additions in the Calendar of St Willibrord dating to the first half of the 8th century show cursive features, the high *e* and the *ti-* and *tio*-ligatures.[34] The cursive colophon of Vergilius on f 45v of Paris, Bibliothèque nationale de France, lat. 9382[35] (Jeremiah, Ezechiel, Daniel, Minor Prophets) was probably copied at Echternach, where a Vergilius wrote charters between AD 709 and 722, but of the characteristic letter forms it only uses the high *e* in ligature, looped *g*, and an *a* with the second stroke rising to a point as the final letter. The only clearly datable example of insular minuscule displaying the letter forms which Lindsay and Brown regarded as characteristic is the Wealdhere letter.

The remarkable continuity of letter forms and ligatures found in the very small number of Irish cursive minuscule manuscripts caused Julian Brown to formulate the problem of dating:

> 'If, as I believe, there was a continuous tradition of Phase I minuscule in Ireland between the second half of the seventh and the first half of the ninth century, if simplified minuscule was not confined to the latter half of the same period, and if both types are sometimes found in the same manuscript, then the scope for refined dating and localization of Irish books by their handwriting alone would seem to be restricted.'[36]

Cursive minuscule could be written in a free and clumsy way, as in the work of the first scribe in the Book of Mulling, or in a highly compressed and disciplined way, as in the Book of Armagh.

Comparable slanting script to that of the Lathcen fragments, with the distinctive high *c* and *e* and the *ti-* and *tio*-ligatures are found in:

Naples, Biblioteca Nazionale, lat. 2 part 1, 1r–42v:[37] Jerome, Gennadius, *Quodvultdeus*, Augustine's *De haeresibus*, *De diversis quaestionibus*

[33] Schaffhausen, Stadtbibliothek, Generalia 1; *CLA* 7, 45 (no. 998). A digitized facsimile can be accessed at: http://www.e-codices.unifr.ch/en/sbs/0001.

[34] Paris, Bibliothèque nationale de France, Lat. 10837; *CLA* 5, 26 (no. 606), with full facsimile by Wilson (1918). Cursive minuscule entries with *ti*-ligatures can be found on f 37r–v.

[35] *CLA* 5, 18 (no. 577).

[36] Brown (1993), 219.

[37] *CLA* 3, 36 (no. 391).

ad simplicianum, Gennadius' *Liber ecclesiasticorum dogmatum*;[38] long lines of varying number probably written at Bobbio; reversed *e* in Gennadius, the tail of *g* is open, *ti*-ligature, very 'small Irish minuscule of excellent quality'[39]; the scribes do not use the looped *o*.

Naples, Biblioteca Nazionale, lat. 2 part 2, 42bisr–75v:[40] Servius, Sergius, Victorinus, Priscianus' *De laude Anastasii*, *Carmen de Iona*, Hieronymus' *Epistula 109*, Eutyches' *Ars de verbo*, Faustus' *Homilia*, Caesarius' *Homiliae*, Augustinus; two columns by several hands; *g* very seldom loops; 57r is Plate 1 in Lindsay's 'Early Irish cursive script', showing a change of hand;[41] open *a*, curved *d*, *ti*- and *ri*-ligatures; 74r–v has *ti*-ligature in the sermon of Caesarius.

A vey tiny cursive minuscule is found in:

Naples, Biblioteca Nazionale, IV A 8, 1r–39v:[42] Charisius, Servius' *De centum metris*; two columns of 56 to 70 lines; tiny upright 'Phase I'-minuscule, high *c*, straight and curved *d*, reversed *e*, *ti*-ligature; the hand on f 8r–v closer Bobbio.[43]

Brown thought these Naples manuscripts were datable to the 7th/8th century, Lowe to the end of the 8th. Mirella Ferrari, in her unpublished Lyell lectures on Bobbio, favours the earlier dating.

Paris, Bibliothèque nationale de France, Lat. 10399, 35r–36v:[44] Paschal texts, pseudo-Theophilius, Gaudentius, pseudo-Anatolius; two columns *c*.35 lines;[45] three dots for punctuation; letter forms: pointed *a*, long *e vero veritas*, closed *g*, final minim of *m*, prolonged open *p*, *ti*-ligature; the script is more cursive on 36r (Augustine and pseudo-Athanasius), less elaborate than Lathcen, lacks high *c*; these leaves are dated by Ó Cróinín to around AD 700.[46]

38 I rely on Beer (1910–3), ii, for a list of the contents of this manuscript, which deserves further study.

39 Brown (1993), 215. Beer (1910–3), ii, has plates of 31r–v, 33v, 35v, 37v, and 41r–v.

40 *CLA* 3, 37 (no. 394).

41 Lindsay (1910); Bick (1908), plates III–VI show 45v (Servius) as *Tafel III* and 62r as *Tafel V*. There are further plates in Cipolla (1907), and Beer (1910–3), ii, has plates of 53r–v, 57r–v, 61r–v, 68v, 69v, 49v, 54, 47v, 55r–v, 74v, 43r–v, and 67v.

42 *CLA* 3, 39 (no. 400).

43 Plates can be found in *Archivio paleografico italiano* 2 (1884), 63–5.

44 *CLA* 5, 20 (no. 585).

45 Ó Cróinín (1999), 92.

46 Ó Cróinín (1989), 142–3.

Paris, Bibliothèque nationale de France, Lat. 10400, 109r–110v[47] and Paris, Bibliothèque nationale de France, Lat. 11411, 124r–125v:[48] Eutyches; two columns (sometimes more for word lists), 39 lines visible; Irish minuscule, enlarged elaborate *Et*, straight and curved *d*, *e* with bow reversed, *g* with exaggerated cross bar extended to right, the bow of *g* is sometimes looped, pronounced wedges on the ascenders of *b*, *d*, *h*, *l*, final minim of *m* curves below baseline, *ti*-ligatures; the capital *Et* and *q* are similar to the Lathcen fragments; the text apparently has Old Irish glosses.[49]

Basel, Universitätsbibliothek, F III 15d:[50] Isidore Iunior's *De vitiis*, Consentius' *De barbarismis*; copied in two columns of 34 to 41 lines; very expert rapid cursive, *mo*- and *ti*-ligatures, high *e* but no reversed *e*, *g* is never looped, the first scribe on 1r column 1 uses several forms of *a*, straight and curved *d*, the second scribe uses open *a*, the capitals are distinct, *p* is open at the top, *S* is uncial; the appearance of the script is more angular than Lathcen, using bold wedges and short minim strokes;[51] Brown wrote of 'a wedged variety of cursive' and compared it to the work of the second scribe in Kassel, Universitätsbibliothek, Fol. theol. 22.[52]

Kassel, Universitätsbibliothek, Fol. theol. 22:[53] Hieronymus' *In prophetas minores*; two columns, 42 to 56 lines; 'Phase 1'-minuscule to 24v, loops on the top of ascenders, high *c* and *e*, low fork on *s*, *ti*-ligatures, 25r–38v is written in a simpler script in which hollow wedges replace loop on *l*, *P* is forked and open, very high *e*, and a marked wedge on the ascenders of *h* and *l*, capital *E* is wide, capital *S* is uncial.

Paris, Bibliothèque nationale de France, Lat. 9538: Augustinus' *De trinitate* XI–XV; has high *c* and reversed *e* but very different triangular *A* with long stroke at the left, loops on *d* but wedges on *b*, *h*, *l*, *fi*- and *ti*-ligature, suprascript *u*, elaborate flourishing on final leaf (55v); script is

47 A black and white microfilm of the manuscript may be viewed at: gallica.bnf.fr/ark:/12148/btv1b9066770w.

48 *CLA* 5, 24 (no. 599).

49 Stokes and Strachan (1901–3), ii 42.

50 *CLA* 7, 3 (no. 847). The manuscript may be viewed at: www.e-codices.unifr.ch/en/list/one/ubb/F-III-0015b.

51 There are three plates of 1r, 9r, and 15v in Aris and Pütz (2010), *Tafeln 6*, *7*, and *8*. Cf. Spilling (1982).

52 Brown (1993), 217.

53 *CLA* 8, 33 (no. 1135). The manuscript may be viewed at: orka.bibliothek.uni-kassel.de/viewer/image/1328187128694/2.

by the scribe of 1r–47v of Paris, Bibliothèque nationale de France, Lat. 9526: Hieronymus' *In Isaiam*;[54] the script has a more pointed appearance than the Lathcen fragments.

Longleat House, Library of the Marquis of Bath, NMR 10589:[55] Isidore's *Etymologiae*; two columns of 36 lines; clumsy foot serifs, high shoulder of *r*, dip of last minim of *m* and *n*, second stroke of *a* long, tall *c* and *e* with high bow as conservative features, *D* uncial, shoulder of *r* bends very low, run-overs, *s* minuscule, cross stroke of *t* rises, marked wedges on the ascenders of *b* and *l*, *c* rising above following letter; dated by Carley and by *CLA* *c.*AD 680–700.[56]

Vatican, Biblioteca Apostolica, Pal. lat. 235, 4r–29v:[57] Paulinus Nolanus; the work of Scribe B includes letter forms found in the Lathcen fragments; pointed *a* last line of 17v col. 1, a theta shaped reversed *e* 16r, *g* with closed curve 23v, looped *o* in ligature *no* 17v col. 2, 18v, 20v col. 1, open *p*, *s* with low fork, ascending cross stroke of *t* in the *ti*-ligature 8r col. 1, 23v col. 2; some sections are elaborately flourished; Brown dated the main text to between AD 700 and 737.[58]

Two Irish pocket Gospel books use cursive minuscule.

Dublin, Trinity College, 59 (Book of Dimma):[59] The scribe of p 7 (Gospel of Mark)[60] and p 31[61] uses the *mi*-, *ni*-, and *ti*-ligatures but writes a very uneven script, with poorly formed letters and no clear baseline. The scribe of p 75 (Gospel of Luke)[62] is also untidy using *mi*- and *ni*-ligatures, the reversed *e*.

Dublin, Trinity College, 60 (Book of Mulling):[63] high *e* and *c*, *ro*- and *ti*-ligature 18r[64]; dated to the end of the 8th century by Lowe, accepted by McGurk.[65]

54 Both manuscripts may be viewed in colour at: gallica.bnf.fr.

55 Bischoff and Brown (1985), 297 (no. 1873).

56 Carley and Dooley (1991), 144.

57 *CLA* 1, 26 (no. 87). The manuscript has been fully digitized for the Bibliotheca Laureshamense site: http://bibliotheca-laureshamensis-digital.de/bav/bav_pal_lat_235. It was reproduced in facsimile by Brown and Mackay (1988).

58 Brown and Mackay (1988), 26.

59 *CLA* 2, 44 (no. 275); McGurk (1987), plates 4–6.

60 McGurk (1987), plate 5.

61 *CLA* 2, 44 (no. 275).

62 McGurk (1987), plate 6.

63 *CLA* 2, 44 (no. 276).

64 McGurk (1987), plate 3.

65 *CLA* 2, 44 (no. 276); McGurk (1987), 166.

Turin, Biblioteca Nazionale Universitaria, F IV 1:[66] Theodore of Mopsuestia's *In Psalmos*; 2 columns, 38–59 lines; curved *d*, high *er*-ligature, the bow of *g* open, *n* with pendant *a*, *p* open, cross strokes of *t* and *g* rise to the right, *na*-, *mi*-, and *ti*-ligatures, run overs, many abbreviations; 'Phase I'-cursive written in a compressed way; ascribed to Ireland in *CLA* and by Brown.[67]

A much more set minuscule is found in:

St Omer, Bibliothèque d'agglomération, 342:[68] *Glossae super Amos*; dated saec. vii ex. by Parkes and Brown,[69] no doubt copied in Ireland. The gloss is chiefly in a set minuscule with a line in a more cursive script in the second column.

Milan, Biblioteca Ambrosiana, F 60 sup.:[70] *Excerpta ex patribus*; 2 columns, 33 lines; wider spacing, many abbreviations, 'rough set minuscule with cursive tendencies'; round and straight *d*, simple flat topped *g*, wedge on ascenders, high *er*; no published plate shows a *ti*-ligature; the script is more angular than the Lathcen fragments and the initials are thickened; a more cursive script is found on fols. 47r–49v, 55r–57v, and 58r–v;[71] probably copied in Ireland.[72]

Thinner and more angular minuscule, closer to the script of the Book of Armagh, is found in:

Paris, Bibliothèque nationale de France, Lat. 10400, 107r–v:[73] Bede's *In Apocalypsin*; copied after AD 716; has the *tio*- and *ti*-ligatures, and looped *o* in ligature; there is no loop on *g*, and *d* is never curved; *et* is written with the *t* formed by bringing the upper curve of *e* down vertically to cross the horizontal tongue of *e*; very angular appearance.

Würzburg, Universitätsbibliothek, M.p.misc.f.28:[74] *Grammatica* (an unedited Irish commentary on Donatus); 2 columns of 39 lines; wedges on *b* and *l*, loop on *d*, reversed *e*, high *e* and high *c*, curve on final minim of *m*, curving cross stroke of *t*, *ti*-ligature, punctuation by single dots; the enlarged initials are very different to those in the Lathcen fragments; *A*

[66] *CLA* 4, 14 (no. 452) (fasc. 5 and 6 of that manuscript).

[67] Brown (1993), 216.

[68] *CLA* 6, 37 (no. 828).

[69] Parkes (1992), plate 9 and p 177; Brown (1993), 218.

[70] *CLA* 3, 21 (no. 336). The description is from Brown (1993), 218.

[71] *CLA* 3, 21 (no. 337).

[72] Brown (1993), 218.

[73] *CLA* 5, 24 (no. 598).

[74] *CLA* 9, 46 (no. 1399).

has a triangular shape, *e* is wider than it is high, *q* has a wide angular bow, *s* is generally round; the fragment in Jena (*CLA* 8, no. 1227) is by the same hand and probably a part of this manuscript; the general appearance is much more upright than the Lathcen fragments; Spilling dated these fragments to the end of the 8th century.[75]

Dublin, Trinity College, 52 (Book of Armagh):[76] parts of this manuscript may be dated to AD 807; it is the work of at least three scribes who use the *fi*- and *ti*-ligatures, the reversed *e*, *h*, *m*, and *n* with pendant *a* or *i*, the looped *o* (*homo* 175v col. 1), occasionally the low forked *s* and a similar large *Et*;[77] the Z-shaped *t* may be a late feature; at the ends of sections there are elaborate calligraphic flourished colophons with more cursive ligatures.

Milan, Biblioteca Ambrosiana, C 301 inf.:[78] Theodore of Mopsuestia's *In Psalmos*; 2 columns of 37 lines;[79] the script is a distinct variety of cursive in which the looped *o* in ligature is very small, the reversed *e* is slanting, there are unique forms of *tio*-ligature, *p* open, *g* swings to right; signed by the scribe Diarmait; thought to date from the early 9th century.[80]

A very clumsy and perhaps early Irish minuscule is found in:

Vatican, Biblioteca Apostolica, Vat. lat. 491 + Florence, Biblioteca Medicea Laurenziana, Ashburnham 60:[81] Ambrosiaster's *In epistolis Pauli*; 27–31 long lines; punctuation uses 2 dots and comma, many abbreviations, 3-shaped *g*; script is an uncalligraphic and debased Irish minuscule.

Zürich, Staatsarchiv, A.G.19 no. XII:[82] glossed leaf of Ezechiel with glosses in columns on either side; it is the script of the glosses which is the most cursive minuscule.

75 Spilling, (1984), 879. The five leaves may be viewed on the Libri Sancti Kiliani Digtal website: http://vb.uni-wuerzburg.de/ub/mpmiscf28/ueber.html.

76 *CLA* 2, 42 (no. 270).

77 Sharpe (1982). The Patrician documents on fols. 2r–24v of the Book of Armagh have been digitized by the Royal Irish Academy at: www.confessio.ie, showing the work of Ferdomnach 20r–24v and scribe A. In addition, Gwynn (1913) included plates of 53v (Plate II), 102r (Plate III), 127r (Plate IV), 170v (Plate V), and 175v (Plate VI).

78 *CLA* 3, 17 (no. 326).

79 There is a full facsimile by Best (1936).

80 Brown (1993), 218.

81 *CLA* 1, 3 (no. 5b).

82 *CLA* 7, 47 (no. 1008).

Conclusion

The Echternach Gospels and the Cologne St Blasien canonical collection show that insular scribes knew the distinctive letter forms of minuscule cursive, though the script was most commonly used for grammar and exegesis. It was clearly a lower grade than the script of large Gospel books and some liturgical texts. It was rapid and economical of space: all of the examples I have listed have at least 35 lines to the column. The pocket Gospel books were for personal use, and the Book of Dimna is written in a less formal and less tidy script. This was always the risk presented by cursive minuscule script: a less accomplished scribe could write uneven lines and ill balanced letters. In the Lathcen fragments that risk is mastered, despite the lack of ruling there is a clear sense of the line of writing, and the strokes move from thick to thin so as to create variation. Curves predominate, the verve of the script derives from the curves of *s*, *d*, and the *ti*-ligature, with g and final m creating curves below the base line. Letters touch so that words and not letters are the unit. Though the features of Irish cursive minuscule noted by Lindsay and Brown remained in use from the late 7th to the mid-9th centuries, the fluid script of the Lathcen fragments is closest to the script of the Naples manuscripts from Bobbio and the script of the Paris computistica fragment. Both of these comparanda have been dated to around 700. They share many of the distinctive letter forms, ligatures and abbreviations. So the Lathcen fragments could also date from the early 7th century: in that case they would be the earliest surviving copy of a substantial Latin text composed in Ireland.

APPENDIX

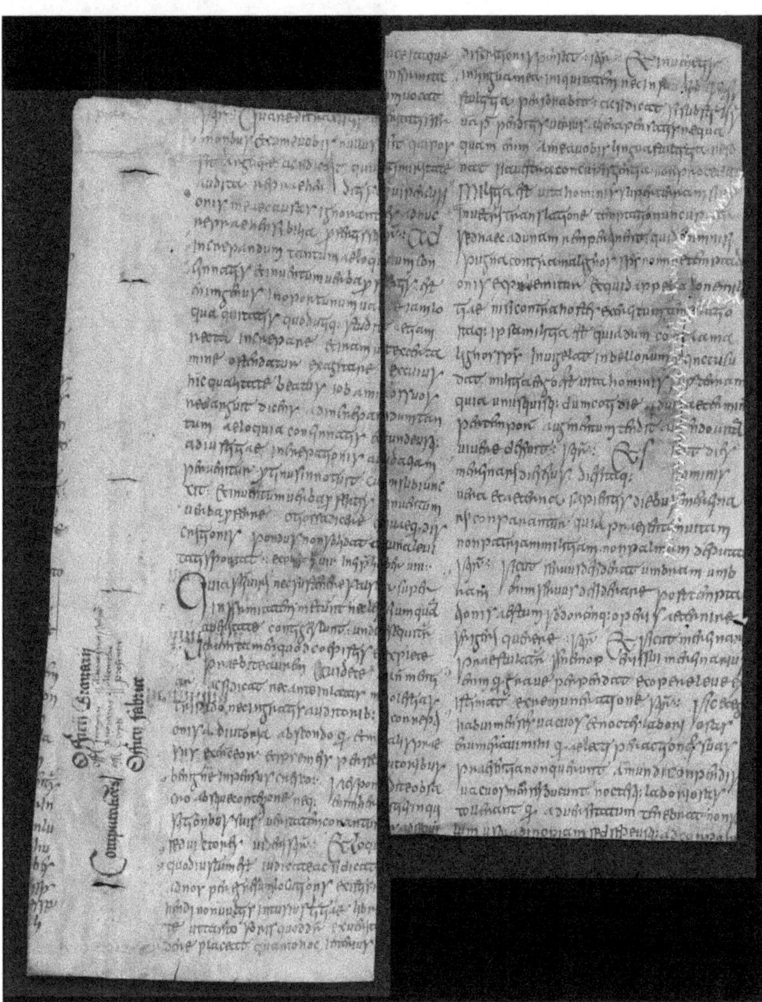

Plate 1 Düsseldorf, Universitäts- und Landesbibliothek, K I B 212, 1r. (Die Handschrift ist Leihgabe der Stadt Düsseldorf an die Universitäts- und Landesbibliothek Düsseldorf.)

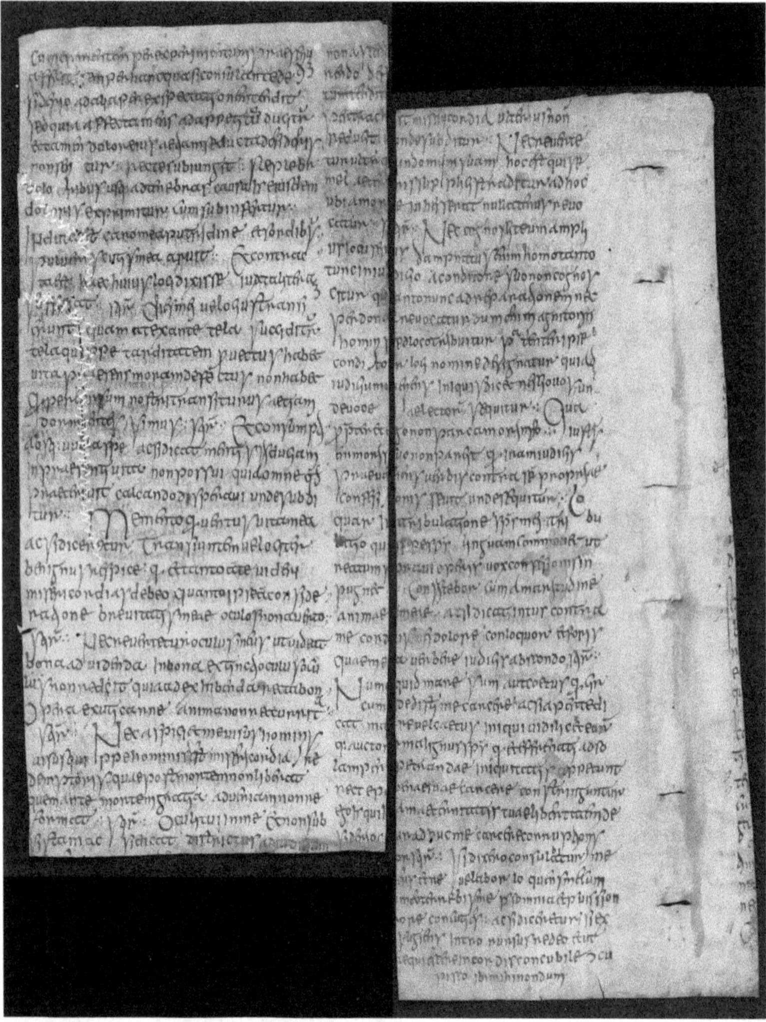

Plate 2 Düsseldorf, Universitäts- und Landesbibliothek, K I B 212, 1v. (Die Handschrift ist Leihgabe der Stadt Düsseldorf an die Universitäts- und Landesbibliothek Düsseldorf.)

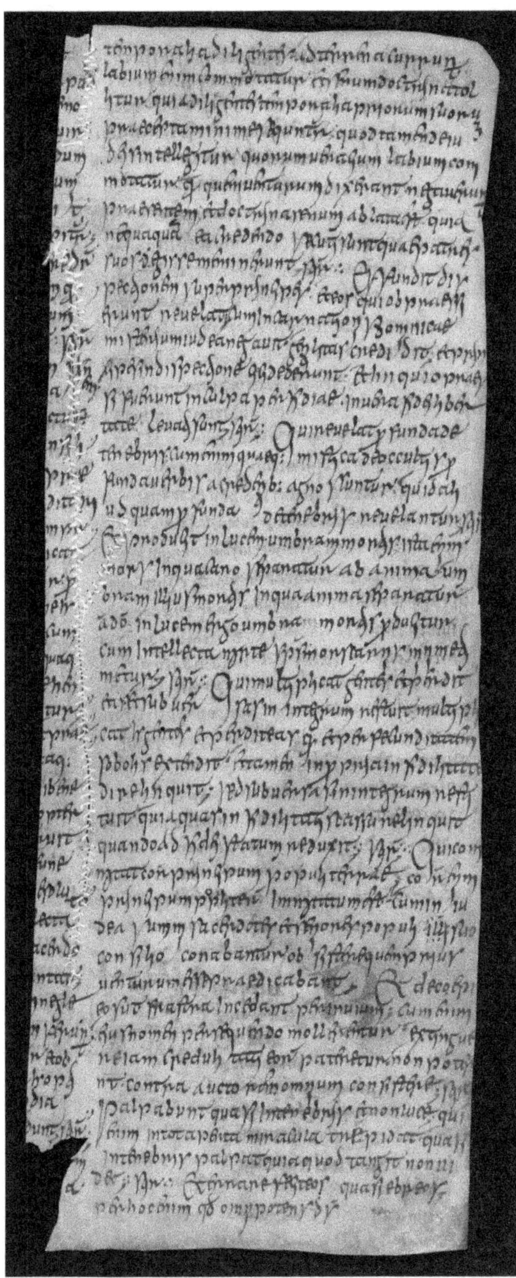

Plate 3 Düsseldorf, Universitäts- und Landesbibliothek, K I B 212, 2r. (Die Handschrift ist Leihgabe der Stadt Düsseldorf an die Universitäts- und Landesbibliothek Düsseldorf.)

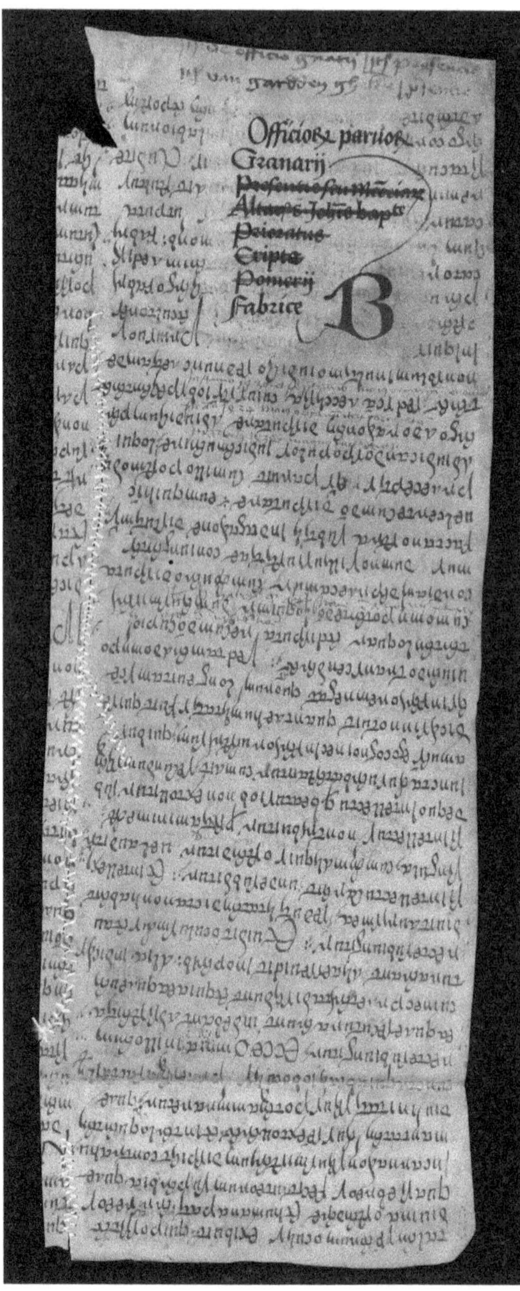

Plate 4 Düsseldorf, Universitäts- und Landesbibliothek, K I B 212, 2v. (Die Handschrift ist Leihgabe der Stadt Düsseldorf an die Universitäts- und Landesbibliothek Düsseldorf.)

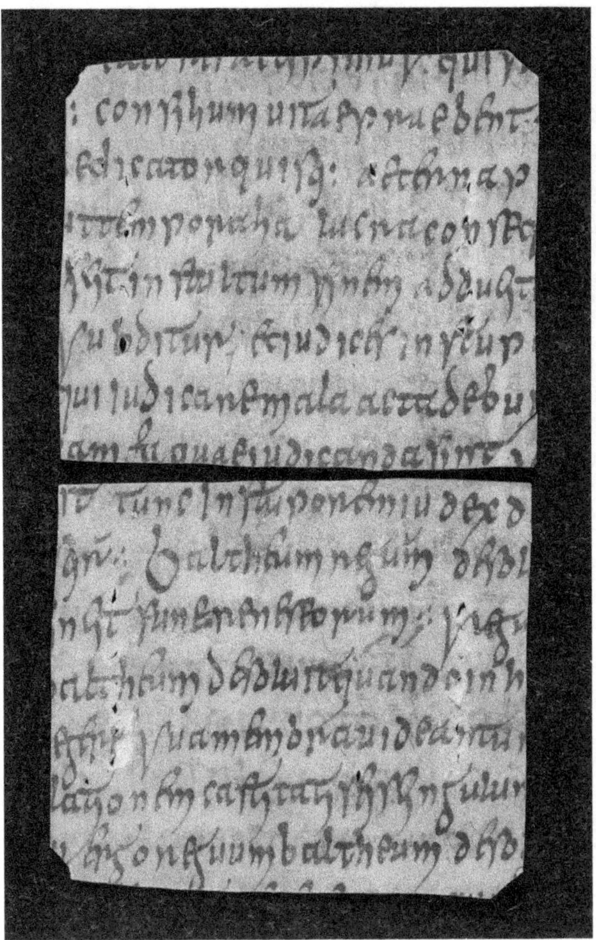

Plate 5 Düsseldorf, Universitäts- und Landesbibliothek, K I B 212, 3r. (Die Handschrift ist Leihgabe der Stadt Düsseldorf an die Universitäts- und Landesbibliothek Düsseldorf.)

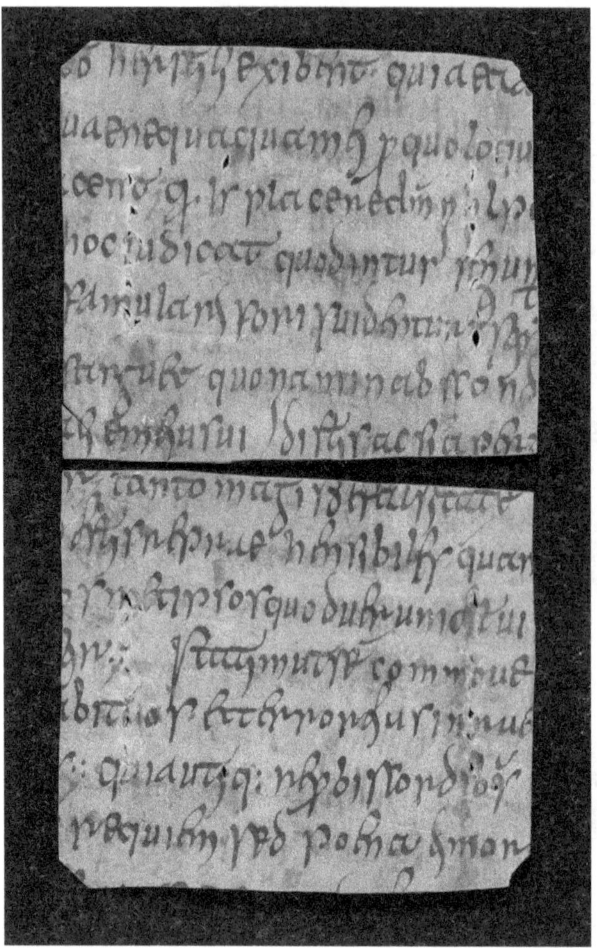

Plate 6 Düsseldorf, Universitäts- und Landesbibliothek, K I B 212, 3v. (Die Handschrift ist Leihgabe der Stadt Düsseldorf an die Universitäts- und Landesbibliothek Düsseldorf.)

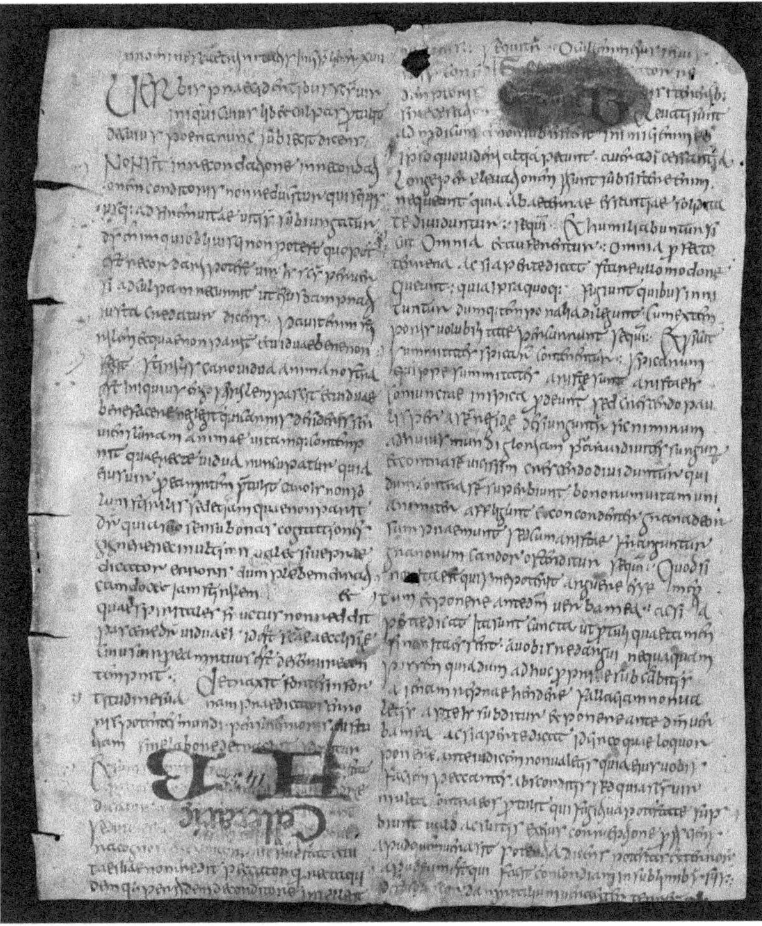

Plate 7 Düsseldorf, Universitäts- und Landesbibliothek, K I B 212, 4r. (Die Handschrift ist Leihgabe der Stadt Düsseldorf an die Universitäts- und Landesbibliothek Düsseldorf.)

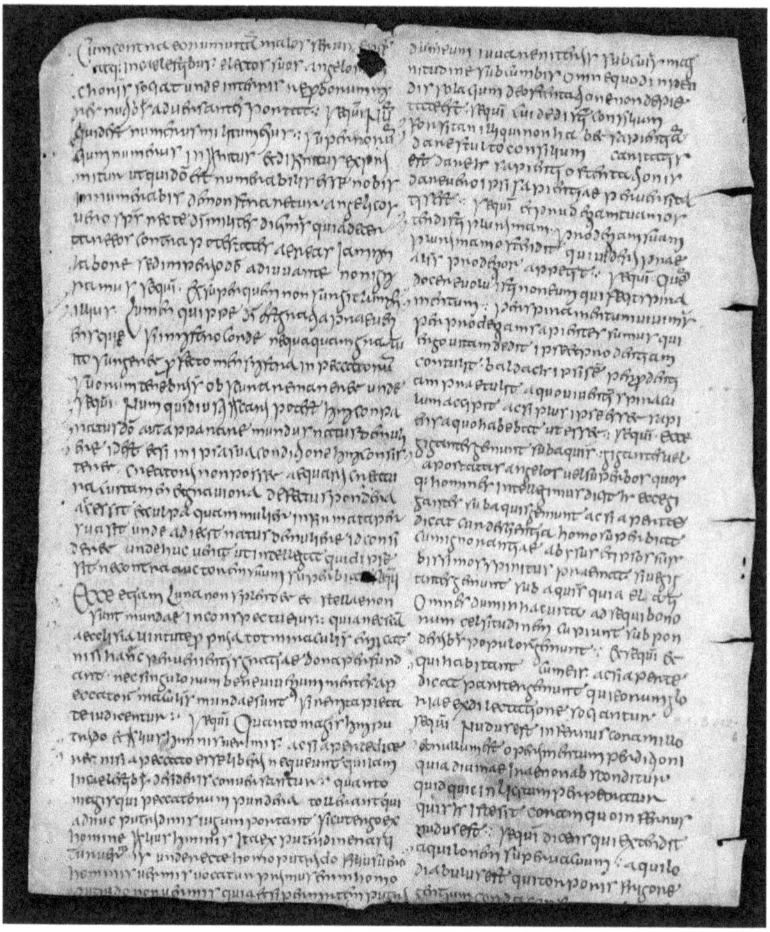

Plate 8 Düsseldorf, Universitäts- und Landesbibliothek, K I B 212, 4v. (Die Handschrift ist Leihgabe der Stadt Düsseldorf an die Universitäts- und Landesbibliothek Düsseldorf.)

Bibliography

Aris, M.-A. and R. Pütz (2010) *Bibliotheca Fuldensis*, Fulda.

Barker-Benfield, B. (1991) 'The Werden 'Heptateuch',' *Anglo-Saxon England* 20, 43–64.

Beer, R. (1910–3) *Monumenta palaeographica Vindobonensia: Denkmäler der Schreibkunst aus der Handschriftensammlung des habsburg-lothringischen Erzhauses*, 2 vols., Leipzig.

Best, R.I. (1936) *The commentary on the psalms with glosses in Old-Irish preserved in the Ambrosiana Library*, Dublin.

Bick, J. (1908) 'Wiener Palimpseste,' *Sitzungsberichte der Kaiserlichen Akademie der Wissenschaften in Wien, phil.-hist. Klasse* 159, Nr. 7.

Bischoff, B. (1980) *Die südostdeutschen Schreibschulen und Bibliotheken in der Karolingerzeit, Bd. 2: Die vorwiegend österreichischen Diözesen*, Wiesbaden.

— (1998–2004) *Katalog der festländischen Handschriften des neunten Jahrhunderts (mit Ausnahme der wisigothischen)*, 2 vols., Wiesbaden.

Bischoff, B. and V. Brown (1985) 'Addenda to Codices Latini Antiquiores,' *Medieval Studies* 47, 317–66.

Bishop, T.A.M. (1964–8) 'Pelagius in Trinity College B.10.5,' *Transactions of the Cambridge Bibliographical Society* 4, 70–7.

Brown, T.J. (1993) 'The Irish element in the insular system of scripts to circa A. D. 850,' in Janet Bately, Michelle Brown, and Jane Roberts, *A palaeographer's view: selected writings of Julian Brown*, London, 201–19.

Brown, T.J. and T.W. Mackay (1988) *Codex Vaticanus Palatinus Latinus 235: an early insular manuscript of Paulinus of Nola Carmina*, Turnhout.

Carley J. P. and Dooley, A. (1991) 'An early Irish fragment of Isidore of Seville's *Etymologiae*,' in L. Abrams and J. P. Carley, *The archaeology and history of Glastonbury Abbey: essays in honour of the ninetieth birthday of C.A. Raleigh Radford*, Woodbridge, 135–61.

Castaldi, L. (2008) 'Lathcen,' in P. Chiesa and L. Castaldi, *La trasmissione dei testi latini del Medioevo, vol. 3*, Firenze, 374–87.

Chaplais, P. (1978) 'The letter from Bishop Wealdhere of London to Archbishop Brihtwold of Canterbury: the earliest original 'letter close' extant in the West,' in M. B. Parkes and A G. Watson, *Medieval scribes, manuscripts and libraries: essays presented to N. R. Ker*, London, 3–23.

Charles-Edwards, T.M. (2006) *The Chronicle of Ireland*, Liverpool.

Cipolla, C. (1907) *Codici Bobbiesi dell Biblioteca Nazionale Universitaria di Torino*, Milan.

Crick, J. (1997) 'The case for a West Saxon minuscule,' *Anglo-Saxon England* 26, 63–79.

Dumville, D. (1999) *A palaeographer's review: the insular system of scripts in the early Middle Ages*, Osaka.

Gattermann, G. (1989) *Kostbarkeiten aus der Universitätsbibliothek Düsseldorf: mittelalterliche Handschriften und alte Drucke*, Wiesbaden.

Gerchow, J. (1999) 'Liudger, Werden und die Angelsachsen,' in J. Gerchow, *Das Jahrtausend der Mönche: Klosterwelt Werden 799–1803*, Köln, 49–58.

Grosjean, P. (1955) 'Sur quelques exégètes irlandais du VIIe siècle,' *Sacris Erudiri* 7, 67–98.

Gwynn, J. (1913) *Liber Ardmachanus: the Book of Armagh*, Dublin.

Lindsay, W.M. (1910) *Early Irish minuscule script*, Oxford.

— (1913) 'Irish cursive script,' *Zeitschrift für celtische Philologie* 9, 301–8.

— (1922) 'The letters in early Latin minuscule (till *c.*850),' *Palaeographia Latina* 1, 7–66.

Mac Airt, S. (1988) *The Annals of Inisfallen (MS. Rawlinson B. 503)*, Dublin.

Mac Airt, S. and G. Mac Niocaill, *The Annals of Ulster (to A.D. 1131)*, Dublin.

McGurk, P. (1987) 'The Gospel book in Celtic lands before AD 850: contents and arrangement,' in P. Ní Chatháin and M. Richter, *Irland und die Christenheit: Bibelstudien und Mission*, Stuttgart, 165–89.

Ó Cróinín, D. (1989) 'Early Echternach manuscript fragments with Old Irish glosses,' in G. Kiesel and J. Schroeder, *Willibrord, Apostel der Niederlande, Gründer der Abtei Echternach*, Luxembourg, 135–43 and plates.

— (1999) 'The Old Irish and Old English glosses in Echternach manuscripts,' in M.C. Ferrari, J. Schroeder, and H. Trauffler, *Die Abtei Echternach 698–1998*, Luxembourg, 85–101.

Okasha, E. and K. Forsyth (2001) *Early Christian inscriptions of Munster: a corpus of the inscribed stones*, Cork.

O'Sullivan, W. (2005) 'Manuscripts and palaeography,' in D. Ó Cróinín, *A new history of Ireland, vol. I: Prehistoric and Early Ireland*, Oxford, 511–48.

Parkes, M.B. (1992) *Pause and effect: an introduction to the history of punctuation in the West*, Aldershot.

Schütz, R.L. (2009) *Heiliger Liudger: Zeuge des Glaubens, 742–809. Gedenkschrift zum 1200. Todestag*, Bochum.

Seibt F. (1990) *Vergessene Zeiten: Mittelalter im Ruhrgebiet*, 2 vols., Essen.

Sharpe, R. (1982) 'Palaeographical considerations in the study of the Patrician documents in the Book of Armagh,' *Scriptorium* 36, 3–28.

Spilling, H. (1984) 'Irische Handschriftenüberlieferung in Fulda, Mainz und Würzburg,' in H. Löwe, *Die Iren und Europa im frühen Mittelalter*, Stuttgart, 876–902.

Stokes, W. (1905) *Félire Óengusso Céli Dé – The Martyrology of Oengus the Culdee*, London.

— (1993) *The Annals of Tigernach, vol. 1*, Felinfach.

Stokes, W. and J. Strachan (1901–3) *Thesaurus palaeohibernicus: a collection of Old Irish glosses; scholia, prose, and verse*, 2 vols., Cambridge.

Tjäder, J.-O. (1954) *Die nichtliterarischen lateinischen Papyri Italiens aus der Zeit 445–700*, Lund.

Warren, F.E. (1893) *The Antiphonary of Bangor*, London.

Wilson, H.A. (1918) *The Calendar of St. Willibrord from MS Paris. Lat. 10837*, London.

Zechiel-Eckes, K. (2003) *Katalog der frühmittelalterlichen Fragmente der Universitäts- und Landesbibliothek Düsseldorf: vom beginnenden achten bis zum ausgehenden neunten Jahrhundert*, Wiesbaden.

MARK STANSBURY

THE 'PRIVATE' BOOKS OF THE BOBBIO CATALOGUE

Abstract

In the first three hundred years of its history, the library at the monastery founded by Columbanus at Bobbio recorded books held in common, books held by individual monks, and books donated. By examining the books held by individual monks we can identify the books associated with elementary monastic education and duties within the monastery.

Keywords

Bobbio; Columbanus; manuscripts, medieval library catalogues; monastic education.

Introduction

The library of Bobbio was one of the best known in the Middle Ages. And since the 19th century it has been the site of discoveries, real and imagined, that have shaped our view of what medieval libraries were like—especially their relationships with the classical past. As the custodians of such a valuable resource, the monks of Bobbio kept records of the books they owned. Unlike most library inventories, however, the earliest one from Bobbio seems to record both books held in common and books in the possession of individual monks. By taking a closer look at how books were owned and stored in the monastery we can then see what our inventory can tell us about the interests of these monks and their lives in the monastery. In order to do this, there are two sorts of evidence we can use. First, a set of ownership notices in manuscripts belonging to the monastery and second an inventory of the library's contents done either

Early medieval Ireland and Europe: chronology, contacts, scholarship, ed. by Pádraic Moran and Immo Warntjes, Studia Traditionis Theologiae, 14 (Turnhout, 2015), pp. 625–41.

 10.1484/M.STT-EB.5.103138

in the late 9th or 10th century. This inventory was copied by Cantelli and printed by Muratori in 1741, then by Becker in 1885, who numbered the codices, by Tosi in 1985, who re-numbered them, then by Zironi in 2004, who returned to Becker's numbering. In addition, the catalogue done in 1461 is also significant because when the books were being catalogued ex-libris notices (*Liber Sancti Columbani de Bobio*) were added to the manuscripts as well as numbers corresponding to the catalogue listing.[1]

De arca notices

The earliest evidence of personal book ownership at the monastery is found in three of the library's older manuscripts.

The first, Milan, Biblioteca Ambrosiana, S 45 sup., is a half-uncial manuscript, dated by Lowe to the 7th century, of Jerome's commentary on Isaiah.[2] This is one of the famous Bobbio palimpsests, with Jerome's text written over Ulfila's. At the bottom of page 2 in uncial is the inscription *L(i)b(er) de arca domno Atalani*.[3] Athala was Columbanus' successor as abbot of Bobbio and died around AD 626.

The second, Vatican, Biblioteca Apostolica, Vat. lat. 5758, is an uncial manuscript of Augustine's sermons dated by Lowe to the 6th or 7th century.[4] On page 1, in what Lowe describes as 7th-century uncial, is the entry *Liber de arca dom(ini) Bobuleni*.[5] Bobulenus was the fourth abbot and died some time after AD 652.

The third, Turin, Archivio di Stato, IB. II. 27 (*olim* IB. VI. 28), is an uncial manuscript of Lactantius, Hilary, Origen, and others, dated by Lowe to the 6th or 7th century.[6] On folio 1v above the decorative border enclosing the title is the uncial inscription *Libros Ragnap(er)to pr(e)sb(i)t(er) ex suo ingenio* and underneath *De arca dom(ini) Uorgusti abba(t)i(s)*. Vorgustus is otherwise unknown, but the name would probably be either Irish or Welsh. A verb is missing and the relationship of the two lines is also unclear: perhaps we are meant to supply *scripsit* or

1 Peyron (1824), 1–68.

2 *CLA* 3, 29 (no. 365).

3 The *t* has elements of the typical minuscule beginning of the cross-stroke.

4 *CLA* 1, 12 (no. 36).

5 *CLA* 1, 12 (no. 36).

6 *CLA* 4, 10 (no. 438); Bischoff (1984), 250 especially n 15; Cipolla (1907), 89–93 and Tavv. 29–31.

something similar, which would give: 'Ragnaperto the priest [wrote] the books by his own skill [which are] from the chest of the lord abbot Vorgustus.' Whatever part Ragnaperto played in the book's history, however, the salient point is that the abbot Vorgustus, like Athalanus and Bobulenus, had an *arca* in which his books were kept.

This use of *arca* as a place for keeping books is unusual. *Armarium* is much more common and indicates a free-standing cupboard like the one in the mosaic of St Lawrence in the mausoleum of Galla Placidia in Ravenna. *Arca* is a storage place on the ground, a box or chest, like the chest (or chests) in which Hugo Grotius escaped from Loevestein Castle.[7] The ship that Noah built is also an *arca*, as is the Ark of the Covenant (*arca foederis*).[8] Although we do find a few references to *arca* as a storage place for books—Pomponius Porphyrius' commentary on Horace,[9] Rufinus' translation of Origen's sermons on Exodus,[10] and Aldhelm's riddle in the 7th century, whose solution is *arca libraria*[11]—these references are few, while examples with *armarium* could be multiplied at will, beginning with the jurists cited in Justinian's code. Indeed, the usage of *arca* is unusual enough that Michael Lapidge argues, based on the Aldhelm riddle cited above, that the book chest was the normal form of keeping books in Anglo-Saxon libraries.[12]

That this was also the method employed at Bobbio is supported by the *Regula magistri*. In chapter 17 pertaining to the storage of the tools

7 Butler (1826), 119–20.

8 Gen 5:14; Jos 3:15–6.

9 Pomponius Porphyrius, *Commentum in artem poeticam* l. 332 (ed. Holder (1894), 355): *Et leui seruanda cupresso: Libri enim, qui aut cedro inlinuntur, aut arca cupress<e>a inclusi sunt, a tineis non uexantur.* Porphyrius taught in Rome during the early 3rd century.

10 This also makes the connection between the Ark of the Covenant and the chest for books. Origen's Homily on Exodus translated by Rufinus IX 4 (ed. Baehrens (1920), 244): *Habeat et arcam testamenti, in qua sint tabulae legis, ut 'in lege Dei meditetur die ac nocte' et memoria eius arca et bibliotheca efficiatur librorum Dei, quia et propheta beatos dicit eos, qui memoria tenent mandata eius, ut faciant ea.*

11 Aldhelm, *De arca libraria* (Riddle 89, ed. by Rudolf Ehwald in MGH Auct. ant. 15, 138):

Nunc mea divinis complentur viscera verbis
Totaque sacratos gestant praecordia biblos;
At tamen ex isdem nequeo cognoscere quicquam:
Infelix fato fraudabor munere tali,
Dum tollunt dirae librorum lumina Parcae.

12 Lapidge (2006), 61–2.

and other property of the monastery, the belongings of the abbot are mentioned as being kept in an *arca*:[13]

> *Simul etiam et ipse frater consignatas habeat cutes et spungias calciariorum, facitergia, mappas uel sabana. Simul etiam et arcam cum rebus abbatis uel arcas diuersarum decadum cum rebus fratrum cum clusuris praepositorum.*
>
> 'Likewise also let the same brother [who oversees the *ferramenta*] have under his control the skins and sponges for the shoes, the towels, napkins, and cloths. Likewise also the chest [*arca*] with the belongings of the abbot and the chests with the belongings of the various groups of brothers with locks for the superiors.'

And again in chapter 81, the rule says that the *arcae* of the brothers are to be located in the *uestarium* of the monastery.[14]

In 7th-century Bobbio, then, these marks of ownership and the evidence from the *Regula magistri* allow us to argue that the monastery's abbots had books that were kept separate from others' as their property. If we follow the evidence of the *Regula magistri* further, then we may also argue that individual monks may also have kept books among their own belongings. It is also interesting to note that even though these manuscripts remained at Bobbio until the 17th century, no subsequent inventory mentions these marks of ownership.

The 10th-century catalogue

The second period for which we have evidence comes from the inventory of the library's holdings carried out during the 9th or 10th century. The text was located by Muratori in 1714 when he visited the library of Bobbio[15] and he commissioned a copy to be made by Cantelli. The printers of volume 3 of the *Antiquitates* then worked from Cantelli's copy, which today is in the Archivio Muratoriano of the Biblioteca Estense in Mod-

[13] *Regula magistri* 17.10–11 (ed. and trans. de Vogüé (1964–5), ii 86). De Vogüé notes the comparison with 81.9–11 (see next note), where the abbot's *arca* has disappeared but the single *arca* for a dozen has remained.

[14] *Regula magistri* 81.9–10 (de Vogüé (1964–5), ii 332): *Quas omnes res per singulas decadas singulae arcae contineant, tenentibus ex eis clauem praepositis suis. Quae arcae in uestario ponantur, ubi et ferramenta monasterii et omnes res positae sunt.*

[15] Esposito (1931), 337.

ena.[16] The manuscript that Cantelli copied was then lost, perhaps when the library was dissolved in 1803. Muratori's printed inventory was then reprinted several times, most notably by Becker in his *Catalogi bibliothecarum antiqui*.[17] Then one hundred years after Becker, Michele Tosi returned to Cantelli's transcription and in 1985 re-edited and published the inventory. As a result, Muratori's 666 codices grew to 690. Zironi in 2004 then returned to Becker.[18]

Muratori dated the catalogue to the 10th century, though does not give a reason for doing so. This has largely been accepted, though Bernhard Bischoff follows Mario Esposito in arguing for a date at the end of the 9th century.[19] Esposito's argument is based on Gottlieb's misdating of the manuscripts described in the inventory. It is clear that when Cantelli transcribed the manuscript it was difficult to read, a fact that is often remarked on in the 1461 catalogue,[20] and he made a practice of approximating the size of the lacunae by putting one dot in his transcription for each missing letter, and occasionally he was able to look closer and read what he had first omitted. We also know that there seem to have been two sections in the inventory, as the remark 'Da un'altra parte della pergamena' makes clear.[21] And also, if we accept Tosi's reconstruction, that it relied on an earlier inventory.

The inventory of manuscripts is divided into two main sections: the first lists codices classified according to contents, the second lists codices according to ownership or location.

As you can see from the pie chart (*Figure 1*), about three-fourths of the monastery's holdings have no personal association and thus appear to be in common, while in the second part of the list we have groups of books associated with seven persons (presumably monks):

[16] Modena, Biblioteca Estense, Archivio Muratoriano, Filza 23, fasc. 3a.

[17] Becker (1885).

[18] I have followed Tosi's catalogue, which does not differ materially for our purposes.

[19] Bischoff (1971), 230; Esposito (1931), 338–43. See also Gottlieb (1887).

[20] Phrases such as *in littera longobarda difficili ad legendum* (Peyron (1824), 45 (no. 165)) occur several times, though always with the script *litterae longobardae*, so it is perhaps the script and not the condition of the manuscript that caused the difficulty.

[21] Tosi (1985), 522.

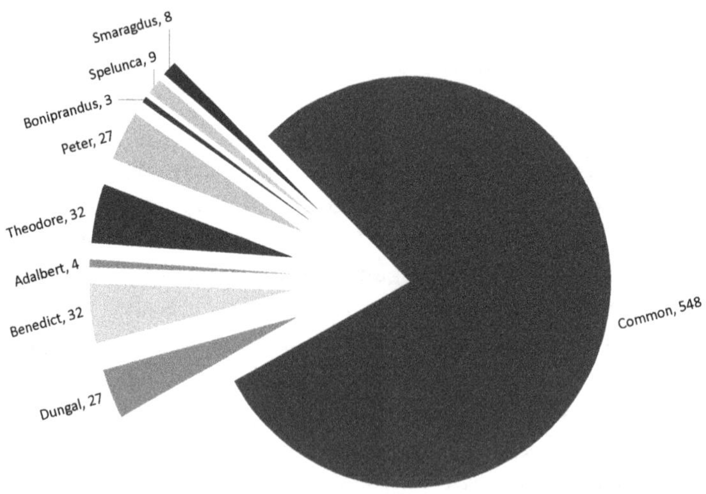

Figure 1 Bobbio manuscripts according to owner.

> [27] Dúngal: *Item de libris quos Dunghalus pręcipuus Scottorum obtulit beatissimo Columbano*
> [32] Benedict: *De libris benedicti presbyteri. Breuis recordationis de libris uenerabilis Benedicti [presbyteri]*
> [4] Adalbert: *De fratre Adalberto*
> [32] Theodore: *Breue de libris Theodori presbyteri*
> [27] Peter: *Item de libris Petri presbyteri*
> [3] Boniprandus: *De libris Boniprandi*
> [8] Smaragdus: *De libris fratris Smaragdi*
> and one place, the *Spelunca*.

In all of these cases but one, they are described as the books of a person, presumably in the monastery.

Three are *presbyteri*, two are *fratres*, and one simply named. This also corresponds to different numbers of books: Dúngal and the three *presbyteri* have 27 or 32 codices associated with their names, while the two *fratres* have four and eight, and Boniprandus has three.

The books of the *fratres* and Boniprandus

If we look first at the two people with the fewest books, we see that they both have a similar collection: they both have a copy of the apocryphal (or parabiblical) Infancy Gospel,[22] then an administrative text (Boniprandus has the Rule of Benedict, Adalbert has Bishop Halitgar of Cambrai's collection of Canons), while Boniprandus has a book on computus and Adalbert an antiphonary and a psalter. Perhaps the reason that Boniprandus is not called a *frater* is that he has newly entered the monastery and is still in a probationary period. This would mean, then, that Adalbert would be a step more advanced in his monastic studies, and Smaragdus a step beyond Adalbert. If this picture is accurate, then we can get an idea of the course of reading a monk might go through: beginning with knowledge of ecclesiastical time-reckoning, the Rule, and an Infancy Gospel, which would then be supplemented by a written Psalter and liturgy, as well as a selection of canons. We see in Smaragdus the replacement of the Infancy Gospel with the four canonical Gospels, an intense interest in Augustine's theological works—*De uera religione*, the *Soliloquies*, and *De magistro*—as well as the study of the arts of music, arithmetic, and grammar with prosody.

The books of Dúngal and the three priests

This leaves us with the books of Dúngal and the three *presbyteri*, Benedict, Theodore, and Peter. Benedict and Theodore have exactly the same number of codices (32) and Peter has the same number as Dúngal (27).

Dúngal and his books have been extensively written about by Mario Esposito,[23] Mirella Ferrari,[24] Bernhard Bischoff,[25] and Jean Vezin,[26] so I will simply make two points here.

First, the notice of his books is unlike the others in that it mentions books he gave (*obtulit*) to the monastery. Bischoff and Vezin have

22 See James (1927) and McNamara et al. (2002).

23 Esposito (1931).

24 Ferrari (1972).

25 Bischoff (1971). Corrections in Dúngal's hand can be seen in Milan, Biblioteca Ambrosiana, C 74 sup., 28r. Bischoff argues that Dúngal's hand is also to be seen in the insular corrections of the *codex oblongus* of Lucretius (Leiden, Universiteitsbibliotheek, VLF 30, 30r–v).

26 Vezin (1982).

identified these manuscripts as coming from Northern France in the area of St-Denis, where Dúngal and Alcuin were friends.[27] Thus we are left with the question whether Dúngal brought these manuscripts with him to Pavia and then to Bobbio, where he bequeathed them to the library, or whether, once at Pavia or Bobbio, he used his connections with Northern France to commission the copies. (Vezin argues that the books could not have been produced in Italy.[28]) Although we cannot be sure whether he brought or commissioned the books, the position of this list in the catalogue and the verb *obtulit* indicate that, however they got to the monastery, the books were seen as belonging to Dúngal and in his power to dispose of as he wished.

For the second point I have my colleagues Jacopo Bisagni and Pádraic Moran to thank. One of the books that Dúngal is listed as giving is *librum quendam latine scotticae linguae*, which may be identified with O'Mulconry's Glossary. This is the earliest Old Irish–Latin glossary and the beginning of the Latin preface, *Incipit discreptio de origine scoticae linguae*, contains the same unusual adjective to describe Irish (*scotica*) as the catalogue entry.[29]

Let us now turn to the manuscripts of the three priests. *Figure 2* in Appendix II provides an overview of the individuals' books to give you an idea of numbers. Because those who compiled the inventories were interested in physical manuscripts more than the works they contained, the contents of the manuscripts is often not carefully recorded. I have listed the individual contents of the 125 manuscripts and divided them into categories. These categories are meant to be a guide to the contents and to facilitate a comparison of interests among the priests. To arrive at the categories I made a list of the works from the catalogue and then grouped them into:

1. Biblical works, i.e. texts of books of the Bible.
2. Exegesis, i.e. commentaries on books of the Bible.
3. Liturgy, i.e. books specifically designed for liturgical use.
4. Theology, i.e. texts concerning theological questions.
5. Administration, i.e. texts concerning the administration of the monastery such as rules and canon collections.

[27] Bischoff (1971) 411; Vezin (1982) 127, 137.

[28] Vezin (1982) 144.

[29] Ed. by Stokes (1898–1900). For further information and bibliography on O'Mulconry's Glossary, see www.asnc.cam.ac.uk/irishglossaries.

6. Language, i.e. texts concerning language learning and teaching.
7. Poetry, i.e. poetical works.
8. Reference, which is a catch-all category, whose name might as well be 'miscellaneous'.

In what follows, I have not pursued the identity of the individual texts much further.

If we begin by looking at the first two categories, biblical and exegetical works in *Figure 3* in Appendix II, the different interests of the priests become apparent: Benedict is very interested in the Gospels and also in the Pauline Epistles. Theodore's interests seem less advanced, while Peter's interests are focused exclusively in the Psalms, and his collection includes the three codices of Cassiodorus' Psalm Commentary. All of the priests have at least one copy of the Psalms, while Peter has two and Theodore has a glossed copy, perhaps indicative of his educational level.

If we turn to the next two categories, liturgical and monastic works in *Figure 4* in Appendix II, Benedict's interest seems a bit more advanced, though he has the same collection of canons that the *fratres* do. Theodore seems enormously interested in liturgy, and we may wonder whether all of these books could have been intended for personal use. In addition, he also has the largest collection of *vitae*. We might be tempted to ask whether Theodore was in charge of some liturgical function. Peter seems to have the least interest, with the least number of liturgical books. All three of the priests have a basic collection of a missal and collection of canons.

Although the three priests have a smaller number of codices dealing with questions of language (*Figure 5* in Appendix II), many of them are florilegia. Benedict seems to have the smallest collection of works, while Theodore has the greatest variety. Both Theodore and Peter seem to share an interest in dialectic and rhetoric. Interestingly, all of the priests have copies of *Donatus minor* and *maior*, as well as at least one collection of Priscian.

My miscellaneous category and theology show that all three priests have *prognostica*, that Theodore is especially interested in arithmetic, and that Peter seems to have the most ambitious collection, including five works by Augustine. Benedict's collection is, by comparison, small.

Finally, all of the priests have works of poetry, and all have works by Prudentius. Benedict has by far the most ambitious collection of poetical works, while Peter has just Prudentius.

To sum up then:

Benedict seems to have been interested in the Gospels and Pauline Epistles as well as poetry, but not in language.

Theodore seems to have been interested in liturgy, dialectic, rhetoric, language, and arithmetic, but not in biblical or exegetical works.

Peter seems to have been interested in the Psalms, dialectic, rhetoric, the works of Augustine, but not liturgy or poetry.

Now all these results must be taken with a grain of salt for several reasons, perhaps the most important of which is that these monks would presumably have had access to the large common store of books as well.

Conclusion

The study of these catalogue entries allows us to reach the following conclusions:

In the 7th century the abbot's books seem to have been kept separately in a chest and that this situation seems to correspond to the one described in the *Regula magistri*. This may also have been the case for monks.

The example of Dúngal shows that in the 9th century individuals seem to have been able to accumulate books over which they had control, though it is unclear whether these are books brought with him from St-Denis or commissioned while at Bobbio.

From the three smallest collections (Boniprandus and the two *fratres*) we can get an idea of how the study done by novice monks progressed and see the importance of parabiblical texts in introducing elementary concepts of the Gospels. Interestingly, these débutants seem not to have florilegia.

Aside from the interests outlined above, all of the priests have the following books:

Psalter
Missal
Canons
Priscian
Donatus
Prognostica (Theodore and Peter have Augustine *Dialectica*)
Prudentius (Benedict and Theodore have Juvencus)

Inevitably, perhaps, this exercise raises more questions than it answers. Why do we have books associated with so few monks? Would they alone had private books? Were these books stored in *arcae* as well? Were they 'loaned' for temporary use from the books held in common? Were they purchased or commissioned by their owners?

As suggestive as these questions are, they will have to wait for another day—and perhaps another catalogue. Until then, however, the Bobbio inventory can, perhaps, give us some indication of the interests of some of the monastery's brothers in the 9th century.

APPENDICES

Appendix I: Structure of the 1461 catalogue

First section: authors and genres

Item de libr(is) [Hieronymi] (27–91)
Item de Eusebij lib(ris) (92–102)
Item de Hilarij [libris] (103–106)
Item de beati Gregorij papae Lib(ris) (107–130)
Item de beati Ambrosij lib(ris) (131–150)
Item de Origenis lib(ris) (151–158)
De Lib(ris) Cipriani (159–164)
Item de Ysidori lib(ris) (165–186)
Item de Canonib(us) (187–204)
Item de lib(ris) diuersoru(m) autoru(m) (205–274)
Item de libris incertis (275–305)
Item de uita et passionibus s(an)c(t)oru(m). (306–495)

Second section: particular books

Item de lib(ris) quos Dunghalus pręcipuus Scottoru(m) obtulit beatissimo Columbano. (496–522)

Da un'altra parte della pergamena (523–690)
De libris Benedi(ct)i pr(es)b(yte)ri (543–574)
De fratre Adalberto (575–578)
Breue de libris Theodori pr(es)b(yte)ri (579–610)
Item de libris Petri pr(es)b(yte)ri (611–637)

[De libris] quos non reperimus, sed [habemus] (638–663 or 690?)
De lib(ris) Boniprandi (663–665)
Ad Speluncam (666–674)
Item de libris fratris Smaragdi (675–682)
Item de libris (683–690)

Appendix II: Details of books with named owners

Boniprandus (3 MSS)	**Adalbertus frater (4 MSS)**	**Smaragdus frater (8 MSS)**
Infantia Saluatoris	Infantia Saluatoris	Euangelium plenarium
	Psalterium	Soliloquiorum Augustini
	Antiphonarium plenarium	Eiusdem de uera religione
Regula S. Benedicti (Taur. G VII 18)	Canones quos excerpsit Alitgarius episcopus	Liber Augustini de magistro
Liber computi (Ambr. D 30 inf.)		Liber Augustini de musica
		Quędam pars de arithmetica Boetij (Taur. F IV 1 fasc. 3)
		Liber Prisciani maior
		Liber Bedae de metris

Figure 2 Books of the non-priests.

Genre	**Works**	**MSS**
Biblical	9 (5 OT, 4 NT)	9
Exegetical	19 (9 OT, 10 NT)	20
Liturgical	18	17
Theological	12	8
Monastic and administrative	22	22
Language	46	19
Poetry	12	8
Reference	25	22

Figure 3 Priests: genres.

Benedict (9 MSS)	Theodore (3 MSS)	Peter (7 MSS)
Psalterium	Psalterium glosatum	Cassiodorus, Expositio in Psalterium (Ambr. D 519 inf.; Ambr. B 22 inf.; Ambr. B 23 inf. *Collura*)
Chrysostom, Homelia de Euangeliis	Anon., In Apocalypsin (Taur. G V 3)	Einhard, De Psalmis
Anon., Liber super Mathaeum	Eucherius, De situ Hierusalem	Psalterium
Anon., Liber super Mathaeum	Anon., Epistola de Melchidedech (Taur. G V 3)	Psalterium
Anon., Liber super Marcum	Eucherius, Quaestiones in vet. & nov. test.	Bede, De titulis Psalmorum
Anon., Liber super Lucam		
Anon., Liber super Iohannem		
Anon., Liber super Iohannem		
Liber epistolarum Pauli		

Figure 4 Priests: biblical and exegetical works.

Benedict (10 MSS)	Theodore (19 MSS)	Peter (7 MSS)
Missale plenum	4 × Missale	Missale
2 × Missale paruum	2 × Homeliae (Gregory and Bede)	Anthiphonarium
Liber hymnorum in quo conpotum	Gregory, Diurnum (Ambr. I 2 sup. *Collura*)	Missale collectarium
Liber collectanearum	De predicationibus	Regula canonica
Canones Alithgarij episcopi	De decimis et expositione missae	2 × Libellum canonum
De regula Sancti Benedicti	Regula canonica	Liber canonum
Isidore, Liber officiorum	3 × Liber sinodorum	
Junilius, De diuina lege	Benedict, Regula (Taur. G VII 18)	

Benedict (10 MSS)	Theodore (19 MSS)	Peter (7 MSS)
Rufinus, De vita patrum (Ambr. F 84 sup. *Collura*)	De ordine eccelsię	
	Jonas? De vita Sancti Columbani	
	Anon.? De vita Sancti Gutberti	
	De collatione abbatis Cheremonis	
	2 × Martyrologium (Bede and Jerome)	

Figure 5 Priests: liturgical and monastic works.

Benedict (4 MSS)	Theodore (5 MSS)	Peter (6 MSS)
Priscianus Maior (= Institutiones?)	Glosis librum	Pomerius, Opus incertum
Priscianus, De accentibus	Priscian, Maior (= Institutiones?)	Opera incerta
Priscianus, De metris	Donatus, Maior	Donatus, Maior
Priscianus, Alia opuscula	Donatus, Minor	Donatus, Minor
Donatus, Opus incertum	Glosis super Donatum	Donatus, Opuscula
Anon., Tractatus super Donatum	Isidore, Opus incertum	Eutyches, Opus incertum (Ambr. B 71 sup.)
Donatus, Opus incertum	Servius, Opus incertum	Priscian, Minor
Bede, Opus incertum	Sergius, Opus incertum	Caper, Opus incertum
Opus incertum	Maximus, Opus incertum	Agroecius, Opus incertum
	Victor, Opus incertum	Alcuin, Opus incertum
	Opus incertum	Alcuin, Rhetorica Karoli et Albini
	Priscian, Minor	Apuleius, Periermenia
	Bede, Opus incertum	Opera incerta
	Clement, Opus incertum	Augustine, Dialectica
	Eutichys, Opus incertum	
	Alia opuscula	

Benedict (4 MSS)	Theodore (5 MSS)	Peter (6 MSS)
	Alcuin, Rhetorica	
	Karoli et Albini	
	Martianus, Dialectica	
	Augustinus, Dialectica	
	Apuleius, Dialectica	
	Isidore, Dialectica	

Figure 6 Priests: works on language.

Benedict (5 MSS)	Theodore (5 MSS)	Peter (8 MSS)
Julian, Liber prognosticorum (Ambr. P 40 sup. *Collura*)	Julianus, Prognostica (Taur. G V 3)	Einhard, Orationes quę specialiter dicuntur
Victor, Liber conpoti (Ambr. H 150 inf. *Collura*)	Isidore, Chronica	Liber prognosticorum
Jerome, Opera diuersa	Macrobius, De arithmetica	Martianus, De nuptiis philologie et Mercurij
Einhard, Opus incertum	Dionysius, De arithmetica	Ausonius, Opus incertum
Augustine, De quantitate animae	Anatolius, De arithmetica	Fulgentius, Mictologia
	Victorius, De arithmetica	Cicero, De senectute
	Bede, De arithmetica	Macrobius, Expositio in somnio Scipionis
	Colmanus, De arithmetica	Boethius, De musica
	Anon., De arithmetica	Augustine, Enchiridion
	Boethius, De consolatione philosophiae	Augustine, De magistro
	Chrysostom, De reparatione lapsorum (Ambr. R 42 sup.)	Augustine, De ordine
	Chrysostom, De aliis (Ambr. R 42 sup.)	Augustine, De achademica
	Albinus, De Trinitate	Augustine, De uera religione

Figure 7 Priests: reference and theology.

Benedict (5 MSS)	Theodore (2 MSS)	Peter (1 MS)
Vergilius, Opus incertum	Cato, Liber	Prudentius, Liber plenarium (Ambr. D 36 sup.)
Sergius, Super Vergilium	Sedulius, Opus incertum	
Anon., Versus Apostolorum	Juuencus, Opus incertum	
Prudentius, Psychomachia	Prosper, Opus incertum	
Juuencus, Opus incertum	Prudentius, Opus incertum	
	Anon., Opus incertum	

Figure 8 Priests: poetry.

Bibliography

Baehrens, W.A. (1920) *Origenes Werke, Bd. 6: Homilien zum Hexateuch in Rufins Übersetzung, Teil 1: Die Homilien zu Genesis, Exodus und Leviticus*, Leipzig.

Becker, G. (1885) *Catalogi bibliothecarum antiqui*, Bonn.

Bischoff, B. (1971) 'Die Bibliothek im Dienste der Schule,' in *La scuola nell'occidente latino dell'alto medioevo*, Spoleto, 385–415, repr. in B. Bischoff, *Mittelalterliche Studien, Bd. 3*, Stuttgart 1981, 213–33.

— (1984) *Paläographie des römischen Altertums und des abendländischen Mittelalters*, Berlin.

Butler, C. (1826) *The life of Hugo Grotius*, London.

Cipolla, C. (1907) *Codici Bobbiesi della Biblioteca Nazionale Universitaria di Torino*, Milan.

de Vogüé, A. (1964–5) *La règle du maître*, 3 vols., Paris.

Esposito, M. (1931) 'The ancient Bobbio catalogue,' *Journal of Theological Studies* 32, 337–44.

Ferrari, M. (1972) 'In Papia conveniant ad Dungalum,' *Italia medioevale e umanistica* 15, 1–52.

Gottlieb, T. (1887) 'Über Handschriften aus Bobbio,' *Zentralblatt für Bibliothekswesen* 4, 442–63.

Holder, A. (1894) *Pomponi Porphyrionis commentum in Horatium Flaccum*, Leipzig.

James, M.R. (1927) *Latin infancy Gospels*, Cambridge.

Lapidge, M. (2006) *The Anglo-Saxon library*, Oxford.

McNamara, M. et al. (2002) *Apocrypha Hiberniae I: Evangelia infantae*, 2 vols., Turnhout.

Muratori, L. (1740) *Antiquitates Italiae medii ævi, vol. 3*, Milan.

Peyron, A. (1824) *De bibliotheca Bobiensi commentatio in Cicero, Orationum pro Scauro, pro Tullio et Clodium fragmenta inedita*, Stuttgart.

Stokes, W. (1898–1900) 'O'Mulconry's Glossary,' *Archiv für celtische Lexicographie* 1, 232–324, 473–81.

Tosi, M. (1985) 'Il governo abbaziale di Gerberto a Bobbio,' in M. Tosi, *Gerberto: scienza, storia e mito. Atti del Gerberti Symposium (Bobbio 25–27 Iuglio 1983)*, Bobbio, 71–234.

Vezin, J. (1982) 'Observations sur l'origine des manuscrits légués par Dungal à Bobbio,' *Münchener Beiträge zur Mediävistik und Renaissance-Forschung* 32, 125–44.

Zironi, A. (2004) *Il monasterio longobardo di Bobbio. Crocevia di uomini, manoscritti e culture*, Spoleto.

SCHOLARSHIP

RICHARD SHARPE

SEÁN Ó CLÉIRIGH AND HIS MANUSCRIPTS

Abstract

Seán Ó Cléirigh (†1846) was fifth in descent from Cú Choigcríche Ó Cléirigh (†1665), one of the Four Masters, and in 1817 he brought to Dublin five manuscripts in the hand of or in one case merely owned by his ancestor and sold them. During the 1840s different stories circulated about this transaction, put on record by Eugene O'Curry and John O'Donovan, and this paper draws together the evidence that shows, for the first time, that Ó Cléirigh sold manuscripts to three different buyers, Edward O'Reilly, William Monck Mason, and Patrick Lynch. All survive, but one was split into parts at the time of the sales. The increase in prices during the 1830s and 1840s appears to have led Seán Ó Cléirigh to argue that these manuscripts had not been sold but merely lent to Edward O'Reilly.

Keywords

Cú Choigcríche Ó Cléirigh (†1665), Patrick Lynch (1757–1818), Edward O'Reilly (1765–1830), William Monck Mason (1775–1859), John O'Donovan (1806–1861), Fr Paul Walsh (1885–1941); Four Masters; Irish manuscripts, Irish manuscript sales; Dublin, National Library of Ireland, G 50, Dublin, National Library of Ireland, G 131, Dublin, Royal Irish Academy, 23 D 17 (cat. 790), Dublin, Royal Irish Academy, 23 K 32 (cat. 617), Dublin, Royal Irish Academy, 23 N 28 (cat. 137), Dublin, Royal Irish Academy, 23 P 24 (cat. 138), Dublin, Trinity College, 1398.

Four manuscripts in the handwriting of one of the Four Masters, Peregrinus O'Clery, better known by his Irish name Cú Choigcríche Ó Cléirigh (who probably died in 1665), were brought to Dublin in 1817 by his descendant Seán Ó Cléirigh, of Tullavally, Co. Cavan, who sold

Early medieval Ireland and Europe: chronology, contacts, scholarship, ed. by Pádraic Moran and Immo Warntjes, Studia Traditionis Theologiae, 14 (Turnhout, 2015), pp. 645–70.

 10.1484/M.STT-EB.5.103139

them.[1] There is a fifth said to have belonged to Cú Choigcríche. All survive, though one is now divided into two parts with some loss.[2] They are properly the subject of palaeographical examination.[3] This paper, however, will be concerned only with the episode of their sale in 1817 and perspectives on it over the following decades. The story was first put on the public record by John O'Donovan in 1844 in his book *The genealogies, tribes, and customs of Hy-Fiachrach*.[4] The family origin of the manuscripts was referred to in the introduction to O'Donovan's edition of the Annals of the Four Masters, first published in 1851.[5] And in 1861 Eugene O'Curry, in his widely read *Lectures*, adds some colour while drawing on the same evidence as O'Donovan.[6] In the first of these published works O'Donovan quoted a letter dated 12 February 1842, addressed to him by Seán Ó Cléirigh's son, John O'Clery, in which he said that his father had lent the books to Edward O'Reilly but did not recover them before O'Reilly's death. He also said that, when the sale catalogue of O'Reilly's books was published in 1830, Seán Ó Cléirigh had made an affidavit to the effect that 'he merely lent, but did not sell them to Mr O'Reilly', but this failed to prevent their sale at auction on 30 November 1830. More than ten years later Ó Cléirigh was actively concerned to let people know that he felt he had been cheated by O'Reilly.

This story was known to O'Curry before O'Donovan put it into print, but I have seen no actual evidence to confirm the account that Ó Cléirigh had stated his claim as early as November 1830. Young John O'Clery's version gained currency, and it seems that one reason for this was that it reflected the bad faith of Edward O'Reilly, whose reputation had sunk very quickly after his death. In 1845, however, John O'Donovan changed his opinion in this matter, believing that he had found evidence to prove that O'Reilly had actually paid Ó Cléirigh for the books. The evidence comes from one of his letters, surviving with

[1] My thanks to Pádraig Breatnach and Nollaig Ó Muraíle for their advice on the draft of this paper and to Aoibheann Nic Dhonnchadha for guiding me to her published work (n 29).

[2] These were first listed by Walsh (1935a), 259–61. The same hand is found correcting and annotating in the autograph manuscripts of the Annals of the Four Masters. See further Mac Cárthaigh (2009).

[3] Breatnach (2013).

[4] O'Donovan (1844), 397.

[5] O'Donovan (1851), i xxvii–xxviii. The discussion occurs at the same point in both editions.

[6] O'Curry (1861), 178–9.

some manuscript bits and pieces given by him to the library of Trinity College. O'Donovan's correspondence, collected and annotated, would make for fascinating reading, but such an edition would be no small task.[7] The truth in this case may never be known, but the story is not without interest as reflecting on several important figures in the emergence of Irish scholarship between the 1810s and the 1840s. It must also be recognized that over the same period the market in Irish manuscripts changed beyond recognition, and the prices that manuscripts might fetch in 1820 and in 1845 were very different. This change might have materially affected Seán Ó Cléirigh's memory and his son's interest in the manuscripts.

Earlier than any published comment in this matter are the two catalogues of Edward O'Reilly's manuscripts, the first drawn up by himself in 1825 (Dublin, Royal Irish Academy, 23 H 1 (cat. 1287)), the other being the printed sale catalogue based upon it in 1830. For twenty years and more O'Reilly had been able to make some sort of a living out of what passed for Irish scholarship in the early years of the 19th century. He did not prosper and frequently needed to borrow money. When he died, on 26 August 1830, his chief asset was his library of some hundreds of printed books and more than two hundred manuscripts. They were auctioned in Dublin on 30 November 1830, and a good deal is known about the sale. We are here concerned with four entries in the sale catalogue:[8]

18 *A Small Quarto Paper Book,* MS. containing only 36 written pages; but it is of *great value*, as it contains, perhaps the best copies extant of the famous Topographical Poems of John O'Dugan, and Giolla na

[7] With O'Donovan the letters he wrote are often more interesting than the letters he received, but the latter form a necessary complement to understanding his subject-matter, his engagement with others interested in Irish language, texts, antiquities, and place-names, and his influence on their work. He retained an archive of in-letters, which appears in the sale of his library, 1867 O'Donovan 1086: 'Letters—The late Dr O'Donovan's extensive Correspondence for a number of years'. The collection was bought from Mrs O'Donovan privately by Dr J.H. Todd. Much of this is now Dublin, Royal Irish Academy, 23 O 39 / JOD / 1–395, which comprises many more than 395 letters; the earliest letters date from 1830 (from M.J. O'Reilly), but it is not clear how selective O'Donovan was in what he kept. Finding his out-letters depends on what has happened to the papers of those with whom he corresponded. The personal letters form an important extension of his official letters written in the course of his work for the Ordnance Survey, whose publication proceeds in the hands of Michael Herity.

[8] 1830 O'Reilly (sale catalogues are referenced here throughout by year of sale, name of owner, and item number where relevant). Much space is devoted to this in a forthcoming work (see n 63).

Naomh O'Huidhrin: the former died, AD 1372, and the latter 1420. The hand-writing is said to be that of Peregrine O'Clery, one of the compilers of the Annals of the Four Masters. No doubt can be entertained that this is a most excellent copy: it contains by far a greater number of verses than any copy Mr E. O'Reilly ever saw in any library, private or public. This book contains some other ancient and Topographical Poems, one of which was written by Teige mor O'Higgin, who lived at the latter end of the 12th-century.

Now Dublin, Royal Irish Academy, 23 N 28 (cat. 137), written by Cú Choigcríche Ó Cléirigh.[9]

112 *A Paper Book*, 164 *pages, large Folio*, MS. copied by Mr E. O'R. This Book is perhaps the most interesting of all the Irish productions in Literature of the latter Ages, excepting the Annals of the Four Masters: it is a History of the Life of *Aodh ruadh*, or Red Hugh O'Donnell, Prince of Tirconnell; written by O'Clery, one of the Four Masters, and Secretary to Red Hugh. This is perhaps the only copy of this Work extant.

Now Dublin, Royal Irish Academy, 23 P 9 (cat. 139), copied by Edward O'Reilly, probably in 1818, on paper with watermark 1794. In Charles Sharpe's copy of the printed sale catalogue, now in the Royal Irish Academy, the attribution is altered to read: 'written by Lughaidh, father of Cucogry, one of the 4 M'.

113 *A Paper Book*, 261 *pages, Quarto*, MS. beautifully written. This is the original Copy of the *Leabhar Gabhala*, or Book of Invasions, by the O'Clerys, and is of the greatest value and importance to the Irish Historian, as it contains all the most authentic Chronicles in Verse, on which the leading facts of Ancient Irish History are founded.

Now Dublin, Royal Irish Academy, 23 K 32 (cat. 617), written by Cú Choigcríche Ó Cléirigh. O'Reilly's handwritten catalogue includes these words: 'The book is in the handwriting of Cucoigcriche (or Peregrinus) O'Clery, one of the compilers of this work, and of the Annals of the Four Masters, and is

[9] Another copy of the topographical poems, also written by Cú Choigcríche Ó Cléirigh, is now Dublin, Royal Irish Academy, Stowe C ii 1 (cat. 1084), dated 1661 ('cat.' refers to catalogue numbers in Mulchrone et al. (1926–1970)); this subsequently belonged to Ruaidhrí Ó Flaithbheartaigh (1629–1716) and Charles O'Conor (1710–1791).

still preserved in the original binding'; he goes on to itemize the contents at length (Dublin, Royal Irish Academy, 23 H 1, pp. 190–9).

114 *A Paper Book*, 284 *pages*, *Quarto*, MS. beautifully written by O'Clery. It contains a very large collection of Genealogical Tables of the principal Families of Ireland: there are also large Pedigrees of the leading Families of the early English Invaders — Several Poems are also introduced, as authority for the facts related. Mr O'R. considered this Book to contain the most valuable collection of Pedigrees he had ever seen in the Irish Language.

Now Dublin, Royal Irish Academy, 23 D 17 (cat. 790), written by Cú Choigcríche Ó Cléirigh. O'Reilly's handwritten catalogue says 'in the handwriting of Cucoigcriche O'Clery' (Dublin, Royal Irish Academy, 23 H 1, p 199). The will of Cú Choigcríche Ó Cléirigh, dated 8 February 1664 [i.e. 1665], is pasted to p 271 of the manuscript (O'Curry (1861), 560–2; Walsh (1936), 87). The whole manuscript was transcribed and printed by Pender (1951).

The wording here follows O'Reilly's own descriptions, in which no mention is made of Seán Ó Cléirigh. O'Reilly rarely revealed his sources. The sale catalogue was issued by Charles Sharpe soon after 2 November 1830, and the sale took place on 30 November. All four of these manuscripts were bought for the Royal Irish Academy by George Petrie. The prices he paid for **18**, **113**, and **114** were respectively £3, £3 7s 0d, and £6. Even **112**, avowedly a modern copy, fetched £3 7s 0d.[10] If news of these prices reached Seán Ó Cléirigh, he may have begun already to feel aggrieved.

In the case of **112**, the catalogue falls into absurdity, suggesting that a modern transcript by O'Reilly himself may be 'perhaps the only copy of this Work extant'. Already in 1820 O'Reilly had published the explanation in his *Irish Writers*, where he misattributed *Beatha Aodha Ruaidh Uí Dhomhnaill*, the work of Lughaidh Ó Cléirigh (*c.*1580–*c.*1630?), to the scribe Cú Choigcríche Ó Cléirigh, adding: 'The original copy of this work is in the library of William Monck Mason, Esq., and a transcript of it in the collection of the Assistant Secretary, who has now nearly

[10] The prices are from the auctioneer's copy in the Royal Irish Academy. In two cases a different price was entered in copies of the printed catalogue, now in TCD, by Myles John O'Reilly, who recorded £2 7s 0d for **113** (£1 less than in the hammer copy) and £3 17s 6d for **112** (10s more). The auctioneer's copy ought to be reliable.

translated into English, with an intent to publish, this invaluable piece of Irish history'.[11] The exemplar appeared in the sale room in London when William Monck Mason's manuscripts were sold:[12]

> 556 Life of Aodh, *anglice* Hugh, roe O'Donnell, chief of Tirconnell, by Cucoigchriche (Peregrinus) O'Clery, *circa* 1620, small 4to, *morocco extra, gilt, by Mackenzie*, pp. 170.
>
> *** The original of this composition. (See O'Reilly's Writers, p. cxc.) The O'Clery by whom this work was composed was one of the Four Masters by whom the Annals of Ireland were compiled. It is a masterpiece of Irish calligraphy.

On this occasion the price was £21; an agent did the bidding in London, and the buyer was J.H. Todd for the Royal Irish Academy. The manuscript is now Dublin, Royal Irish Academy, 23 P 24 (cat. 138), written by Cú Choigcríche Ó Cléirigh. Long before the original was acquired by the Academy, however, Eugene O'Curry pasted a note into O'Reilly's own descriptive catalogue of his manuscripts. This note reads:[13]

> This Life of Red Hugh O'Donnell was written [*composed*] by Lugaidh O'Clery, and the original, or a copy of it, by Peregrine O'Clery was brought to Dublin about the year 1824 by John O'Clery [*Seán Ó Cléirigh*], the direct descendant of Peregrine, who now holds an humble situation in the Gas Works on the Rings End Road, and who lent the Book to Edward O'Reilly, who after making this, not accurate, copy of it sold it to Mr William Monck Mason, without the consent of O'Clery, and without giving him any part of the proceeds of the sale. This account I have from John O'Clery himself, who is now in about the 67th year of his age. This 10th August 1843. Eugene O'Curry.

O'Reilly is accused of selling what was not his to sell and keeping the proceeds. O'Curry says he had this from Seán Ó Cléirigh himself. It is a not-entirely-accurate representation of what was said by Seán Ó Clé-

[11] O'Reilly (1820), cxc. O'Reilly was himself the Assistant Secretary of the Society. The translation by O'Reilly appeared in the first part of the sale, that is, not among the Irish manuscripts; it sold as lot 277 and is now Dublin, Royal Irish Academy, 24 D 14 (cat. 140). It has a first series number (10/5), so it was acquired by the Academy no later than 1844, but I cannot prove that it was bought at the O'Reilly sale in 1830.

[12] 1858 Monck Mason 556.

[13] Dublin, Royal Irish Academy, 23 H 1 (cat. 1287), facing p 190. Editorial clarifications are in square brackets.

irigh, as we shall see, but it ties in with what O'Curry himself wrote, probably just a little earlier, in his description of **112** in the Academy catalogue:[14]

> The autograph original was brought to Dublin about twenty-four years ago, along with the Book of Invasions [**113**], and the Book of Pedigrees of the O'Clerys' [**114**], by Mr John O'Clery, who says that he lent them all to the late Edward O'Reilly, that O'Reilly without his, Clery's, authority sold the first to William Monk Mason Esqr and that the others were sold at the sale of his library after his death.

The date 1824, which is contradicted by what O'Reilly had already stated in print in his *Irish Writers*, is perhaps an erroneous echo of 'about twenty-four years ago', which, from 1843, would point to 1819. Whether it is correct remains to be seen.

There is a further complication. The thirty-six pages of the topographical poems as described by O'Reilly [**18**] bear the folio-numbers 132–150, leading Kathleen Mulchrone to observe that they are 'but a fragment of a larger manuscript'.[15] In 1935 Fr Paul Walsh added Dublin, National Library of Ireland, G 131 to the tally of manuscripts in the handwriting of Cú Choigcríche, 'according to the experts'.[16] What he did not say is that this book represents folios 1–123 of the same manuscript from which O'Reilly retained the topographical poems.[17] It reached the National Library as part of the Phillipps purchase, and it was previously Phillipps 17082. Phillipps acquired it from the agent Parker, who paid £15 for it in 1858 at the auction of the manuscripts of William Monck Mason. In this case the London auctioneers did not know that they were offering another manuscript in Cú Choigcríche Ó Cléirigh's hand. It appears in the sale catalogue in these words:

> **555** A Collection of ancient Compositions in prose and verse, transcribed about the latter end of the 16th or beginning of the 17th century, small 4to, *morocco extra, gilt, by Mackenzie*, pp. 246.

[14] Eugene O'Curry's First Series catalogue, covering manuscripts in the Academy before the Hodges & Smith purchase in 1844, compiled 1842–1844, now Dublin, Royal Irish Academy, 67 E 9–11 (cat. 1301–3).

[15] Mulchrone et al. (1926–70), iv 395.

[16] Walsh (1935b), 66; Walsh (1935a), 260, where the identification of the scribe is attributed to 'the official catalogue of the newly acquired Phillipps manuscripts'.

[17] Ní Shéaghdha and Ó Macháin (1961–96), iv 51–2.

> ⁂ This volume contains 56 pieces and is all throughout admirable for the perfection of its penmanship. It had unfortunately suffered somewhat in its condition from constant usage, but has been most skilfully repaired.

There is a possibility here that, if O'Curry were correct in saying that O'Reilly had sold the Life of Aodh Ruadh to Monck Mason, he may also have decided to divide this manuscript, separating Dublin, National Library of Ireland, G 131 from Dublin, Royal Irish Academy, 23 N 28, and to sell the major part to Monck Mason, who had it richly bound.[18] If O'Curry had known about this act of book-breaking, he would surely have berated O'Reilly for mutilating such a monument of the Master. It would perhaps not be the only case of his dividing a manuscript for sale.[19] Still, it is not certain that Monck Mason bought from O'Reilly. For that we rely on statements from Seán Ó Cléirigh.

A more direct source is the letter from Seán Ó Cléirigh's young son, John O'Clery, to John O'Donovan, dated 12 February 1842, which O'Donovan quoted, and which mentions not four but five manuscripts:[20]

> Cucogry left his books to his sons Dermod and Shane. Cairbre, son of Dermod, had them in his possession, and left them to his son Cosnamha, who left them to his son Patrick, through whom they came into the possession of his son John, my father. By an accidental fire, which occurred in the house of my grandfather, a great part of Cucogry's manuscripts was materially injured. The only ones which escaped damage were the following:—The Book of Pedigrees [**114**], the Book of Invasions [**113**], the Life of Red Hugh O'Donnell [exemplar of **112**], the Amhra Choluim Chille [**14**], and Triallam timcheall na Fodhla [**18**], which were brought to Dublin by my father in 1817. He *lent* these

[18] The sale catalogue mentions the binding in 'morocco extra, gilt' in respect of four items, lots 555 and 556, quoted here, and lots 557 and 558, now Dublin, National Library of Ireland, G 129 and G 130.

[19] The case of Dublin, National Library of Ireland, G 2 and G 3, which were nos. 10 and 11 in his collection, has divided opinion. O'Sullivan (1968), 118, inferred from O'Reilly's saying that no. 11 had been 'lately rebound in green vellum' that he was himself responsible for their division. Ní Shéaghdha (Ní Shéaghdha and Ó Macháin (1961–96), i 12) inferred from the darkened outer pages that the two parts had been separate for a considerable time before O'Reilly bound them, still separate. It is fortunate that they did not and have not parted company.

[20] O'Donovan (1844), 397. I have not found the original letter. John O'Clery is reported to have been born in 1823 (Clery (1943–5), 124); O'Curry (1861), 178, calling him the last recognized descendant of Cú Choigcríche, tells us that he 'died quite a young man in Dublin about four years ago' [i.e. ?1857].

> books to the late Mr Edward O'Reilly, *but did not bargain for or sell them* to him. He never got them back, however, as he did not know of Mr. O'Reilly's illness until he heard of his death, and saw that he had included these very books in his catalogue, except the Life of Hugh Roe, which, it appears, he had disposed of to Mr Monck Mason, who resided at that time in Harcourt-street, and this he had done without letting my father know any thing about it. My father, on hearing of his books being thus advertised for sale, made an affidavit that he merely lent, but did not sell them to Mr. O'Reilly. Notwithstanding this, however, his executor, the Rev. Eugene O'Reilly of Navan proceeded with the sale of them, and it was under these circumstances that they came by purchase, at O'Reilly's auction, into the possession of the Royal Irish Academy.[21] But although they could not perhaps be placed in better hands, or any where that they would be taken better care of, as far as their preservation is concerned, yet by all the laws of strict justice, they are as much my father's property, even at this moment, as if the Royal Irish Academy had never paid one farthing for them. Little did Cucogry think that these very books, on which he set so high a value, as is seen by his own Will, would ever, by such means, pass out of the hands of his descendants. My father has still a copy, which he made himself, of the Book of Pedigrees, and he has also some of the very books which belonged to Cucogry.

The genealogical setting here has attracted attention in the past, but I propose to pass it over for the time being. The last clause is tantalizing, yet books owned by Cú Choigcríche Ó Cléirigh have generally proved unrecognizable. There is one exception: John O'Clery here mentions a fifth manuscript, which has been identified with another item in the O'Reilly sale catalogue by Nessa Ní Shéaghdha:[22]

> 14 *A Paper Book, Quarto size, consisting of* 142 *pages,* MS. It wants a few leaves at the beginning, and something at the latter end; but it still contains so much, and of such quality, as to render it extremely curious and interesting. It appears to be written about 150 years, but it contains

[21] The Reverend Eugene O'Reilly (1768–1852) was one of the first graduates of St Patrick's College, Maynooth, in 1797 and served for more than fifty years, first as curate and schoolmaster, and from 1827 as parish priest in Navan, where he was responsible for the building of St Mary's Church. He is named as a subscriber to O'Reilly's *Irish–English Dictionary* (Dublin, 1817), but I have not seen other evidence that he was Edward O'Reilly's executor. The small collection of letters to Edward O'Reilly now in Dublin, University College Archives, IE UCDA LA7, includes some from Eugene O'Reilly and some from Edward's son Patrick attending his cousin's school in Navan.

[22] Ní Shéaghdha and Ó Macháin (1961–96), ii 66–7.

> copies of Ancient Composition, originally written by Dallan Forgaill, in the 6th century. It contains a perfect copy of the *Amhra Coluim Cille*, which is a thing extremely *rare*, but the History of the Bards, and the cause of their expulsion into Ulster, which is prefixed to the *Amhra*, wants two or three leaves in the beginning: it likewise contains the *Elegy of St Seanan*. This is an *extremely curious* and *scarce* poem; it is the *only* copy that Mr E. O'Reilly ever met with. These two elegies are written in the Fenian dialect, and is accompanied by a copious Gloss, interlined. There is a preface prefixed, shewing the cause of writing the poem; the remainder of the book is on religious subjects.
>
> Now Dublin, National Library of Ireland, G 50 with O'Reilly's book-plate (f iiiv) and the entry from the catalogue pasted on the front cover. The writing dates from the 17th century. The buyers in 1830 were Messrs Hodges & Smith, who paid £1 1s 0d. They resold to Sir Thomas Phillipps, in whose collection it was MS 10276. It came to the National Library of Ireland as part of the Phillipps purchase.

Discussing the poem *Amhra Choluim Cille*, O'Reilly refers to various manuscripts, saying that he himself had 'a perfect copy, written on paper, which was once the property of Cucoigcriche O'Clery, one of the persons employed in the compilation of the annals of the Four Masters'.[23] He does not say that it was written by Cú Choigcríche but that it was owned by him: its appearance in John O'Clery's letter therefore suggests that this too came to O'Reilly from Seán Ó Cléirigh, even if the scribe was not Cú Choigcríche himself.[24]

John O'Clery's letter is elusive on the matter of time. Between 1817, when the books were brought to Dublin, and 1830, when O'Reilly died, we are not told when Seán Ó Cléirigh is supposed to have lent them to O'Reilly, but it is carefully implied that the loan was unexpectedly overtaken by O'Reilly's illness and death. The inclusion of the books in the 1825 catalogue is enough to rebut this, throwing the notion of loan into question. Up to this point, all we have seen on the record about Seán Ó Cléirigh's transaction with Edward O'Reilly is based on Ó Cléirigh's statements. In 1844 O'Donovan printed the claim as though he accepted its veracity.

23 O'Reilly (1820), xxxix.

24 Professor Breatnach judges the script of this manuscript to be not Cú Choigcríche's hand.

In 1845, however, O'Donovan came upon other evidence which made him change his mind. He set out this and more in a revealing letter written to J.H. Todd, fellow and librarian of Trinity College, which I present in its entirety. The letter quotes two papers that are germane to our purpose, which are discussed after the letter. Other points of interest arising are commented on in footnotes. O'Donovan wrote:[25]

8 Ne<w>comen Place
July 1st 1845

Revd Dear Sir,

I send you the extracts from the Book of Fermoy and some papers in the handwriting of Haliday and O'Reilly.[26] These are in a very shattered condition, but should be preserved as memorials of those people who did all in their power to preserve the native language. I also send the MS transcribed in Ulster in 1679. It contains very curious poems in good preservation.[27] The last is unfortunately broken: it is the address of Carroll O'Daly to the daughter of Sir Murragh Kavanagh.

[25] Dublin, Trinity College, 1398/72. The letter was treated as MS 1398, no. 1, in Abbott and Gwynn (1921), 262, but the contents of the box have been renumbered. I use \ / to show words added above the line. All interpolations in brackets are O'Donovan's own.

[26] The items sent are now Dublin, Trinity College, 1398/1 ('Extracts from the Book of Fermoy to illustrate the meanings of old Irish words') and 1398/2 ('Extracts from the Book of Fermoy'). The first was written for Michael Casey, the second is in Casey's own hand, and there is a note on it by O'Donovan: 'This is the handwriting of the late Michael [*read* Michael Casey] of Cnoc Firinne near Ballingarry in the County of Limerick. He was an herb doctor in Dublin in his old age, and discovered a cure for the gout in some old Medical Irish MS.' In his *Irish Grammar*, O'Donovan (1845), lxxx–viii, says of the same piece: 'The latter of these manuscripts is in the handwriting of old Mr Casey, formerly of Myler's Alley, Dublin, and was purchased for the Author by his friend, Myles John O'Reilly, Esq., of the Heath House, in the Queen's County, at the sale of the manuscripts of the late Edward O'Reilly, author of the Irish Dictionary.' Dublin, Trinity College, 1398/1 had appeared in the sale of O'Reilly's manuscripts as no. 88, 1398/2 as no. 90. The papers in the writing of William Haliday may be Dublin, Trinity College, 1398/51 ('Tenses of Irish Verbs'), on which John O'Donovan has written: 'These collections made by Haliday for his Grammar and Dictionary were found among the MSS of the late Edward O'Reilly of Harold's Cross, author of the Irish Dictionary, who died in 1830. J. O'Donovan'. The box contains nothing manifestly in the hand of Edward O'Reilly. Most of the papers are short glossaries in various hands that may represent notes gathered for his dictionary. How they came to O'Donovan is not apparent. An interesting item is a single leaf with a poem composed in honour of O'Reilly and his dictionary by Fr Paul O'Brien of Maynooth (Dublin, Trinity College, 1398/55), as it appeared in the second edition (1821).

[27] This manuscript is now Dublin, Trinity College, 1399 (H.5.28), written in 1679. It was used by O'Donovan as a source for Ulster Irish in his grammar (O'Donovan (1845), lxxxviii). Abbott and Gwynn (1921), 263, merged this sentence with what is

In looking over some papers in the hand-writing of Edward O'Reilly I found the following memorandum written in \bad/ Irish, which appears to me to prove that he bought the MS. from John Clery which the latter denies:

"This little book was written by Michael O'Clery, or one of his colabourers (for I know the handwriting) in the house of the friars \of St Francis/ at Donegal: for it was from a man of the race of this friar \O'Clery's/ family I ~~got~~ \bought/ (~~*fuaras*~~) \(*cheanais*)/ the book for a pound and a half of money (*airgiott*), and many other small articles that I do not here mention. John O'Clery is the name of the man, a poor labourer (*sclábhuidhe*) who sold the book to me in as dirty and naked a condition as \was/ the poor man himself. Of four brothers this John is the second oldest; they are the sons of Patrick O'Clery and Anna O \Ny/ Gowan or Smith of Tullabally in the parish of Drung, barony of Tullygarvey and county of Cavan. At the time of his death two years since, this Patrick was four score and one \81/ years of age. The following is the pedigree of the aforesaid Patrick, viz. Patrick, son of Cuconnaught, son of Carbry, son of Lewis, son of Cuconnaught, son of Dermot, son of Cucogry, son of Cuconnaught, son of Dermot, son of Dermot of the Three Schools. Carbry the grandfather of the above Patrick followed the adherents of Capt Manus O'Donnell ~~of~~ from Ballyshannon in Tirconnell to the county of Mayo, and after the war he took a farm near the mountain Nephin, whence his children removed to Knock Bennis in the county of Leitrim, whence Patrick moved and settled at Tullabally aforesaid, where his children now are. John is 37 years of age. These sons (of Patrick) had a great deal of the writings of their ancestors. John brought three other books with him to this city and sold them. Edmond O'Reilly [i.e. Edward was only his literary name JO'D] bought one of them, viz. the Life of O'Donnell, chief of Donegal, and William Monk Mason bought the two other books, viz. the Book of the Invasions of Ireland, and another book, in which there are many poems on the History of Ireland. Written by me in the Record Tower the 18th of January 1818 and my own age will be sixty years next St Patrick's day."

On a smaller piece of paper I find the following memorandum in the same hand and in \very/ bad Irish:

"John O'Clery, son of Patrick of Tullabally, in the parish of Drung, barony of Tullagarvey and county of Cavan, brought this book to Dublin in the winter of 1817, and, in January 1818, I bought it from him. This John is the second of four other sons, viz. Cuconnaught, the eldest, John the next to him, and Patrick and Thomas are the other two,

said later in the letter, supposing that O'Reilly had bought this from Seán Ó Cléirigh as written by one of the Four Masters, but there is no connexion whatever.

and Anna Ny-Gowan Smith is the mother of these sons of Patrick son of Cuconnaught, son of Carbry, son of Lewy, son of Cuconnaught, son of Cuconnaught, son of Cucogry, son of Dermot, son of Cleire, son of Dermot of the Three Schools."

These memoranda were written by Edward O'Reilly for his own use; and I can hardly believe he would have written them if he had not bought the MS. They clash most strangely with the account printed in the Hy-Fiachrach, p. 397. I am satisfied that he is wrong in the line of pedigree, and that he penned it from memory (for it does not agree with any authority, written or traditional); but I can hardly think that he would have left such memoranda to witness a falsehood after his death. If he left them written for such a purpose he must remain a long time in purgatory, even though he died a great penitent and a most orthodox and pious Catholic.

I thought it proper to send you translations of these memoranda for though I am not responsible for the truth of the passage in the Hy-Fiachrach, p. 397, still it is too bad that the memory \character/ of O'Reilly should be stigmatized by any thing looking \so/ like a falsehood; and I think that these memoranda should be inserted in one of those books in the Royal Irish Academy.

I also send you the original MS. of the grammar, shattered as it is by the printer, to see if you might be tempted to preserve it.[28]

I find I lent the sheets of the Med. MS. 1414 to Curry to compare it with some MS. in the Academy of which he thought it might be a part. Get them from him. The single leaf I now send will show you the size.[29]

The quotation from Irenaeus I found in Ledwich's Antiquities of Ireland, second edition, p. 325, where he writes, "To which I add that its copiousness arises from its corruption, and so does its harmony; for in

[28] Now Dublin, Trinity College, 1400 (H. 5. 29). John O'Donovan's *Grammar of the Irish Language* had only recently been printed by M. H. Gill at the University Press and published by Hodges & Smith in 1845.

[29] The reference is to Dublin, Trinity College, 1398/7 (H. 5. 27), a vellum leaf, 'which, according to O'D's letter [printed here] seems to have formed part of a medical manuscript lent by him to O'Curry' (Abbott and Gwynn (1921), 263). The fragment begins part way through chapter 40 and continues through chapters 41–53 of Eóin Ó Callannáin's translation, dated 1414, of Arnaldus de Villanova, *Speculum medicine*. O'Donovan (1851), iv 817n, himself refers to it in a note on the Annals of the Four Masters *s.a.* 1414: 'In a fragment of an old medical Irish manuscript, in the Library of Trinity College, Dublin, [H. 5. 27], the exact date of his death is given.' The 15th-century leaf is described by Aoibheann Nic Dhonnchadha at the website of Irish Script on Screen (www.isos.dias.ie). This leaf was separated by O'Donovan from the various fragments loaned to O'Curry, which are now among the latter's manuscripts at Maynooth, Russell Library, C 110, 1–14 (Ó Fiannachta (1966), 127–8). Dr Nic Dhonnchadha has not identified any further fragment from this source in the Academy, and it is not clear now what O'Curry had in mind.

the fourth and fifth centuries, and much earlier, it is branded by the (12) ancients with the harshest expressions for its barbarism." In a note (12) he ~~says~~ has: "Irenaei adv. haeres. Lib. 1. Non esse fastidio rudem hunc & incultum transalpini sermonis horrorem. Pacat Panegyr. Sermonis Celtici squamam. Sid. Apollin. l. 3 ep. 3."[30]

I think by looking to the second edition of Ledwich you will be able to correct this without any assistance from me. I hope Ledwich has not misquoted. He shows a great nack of suppressing and garbling, but I can hardly think that he would fabricate such a quotation as the one in question.

I have not got Whitelaw and Walsh's History of Dublin. I do not think it necessary to give the page in which it describes the Irish Quack doctor of Myler's Alley.[31] The old doctor himself used to quote it regularly in the Newspapers as a kind of diploma for curing Irish men with Irish herbs.[32] I suppose it would take me a week to find it out. It is a specimen of the Irish topographical writing of the day by which every thing was overdrawn. The \Irish/ writers of the last century and of the beginning of the present had little or no love for true truth, but exhibited a great tendency to hunching and tell white lies! We find the authors of this Big History of Dublin assert gravely that ould Doctor Casey, the last \specimen/ of the Iberno-Celtic Druid-doctors, had two hundred volumes on vellum on ancient Irish Medical science and Pharmacopoeia!

Your obedient servant,
John O'Donovan

On this basis O'Donovan's note in the introduction to the Annals of the Four Masters and O'Curry's statement in his *Lectures* modify the stance taken in *Hy Fiachrach* in 1844. Indeed, O'Curry wrote a retrac-

30 The passage quoted may be found in Ledwich (1790), 84, and in the enlarged second edition (1804), 325–6. It follows the comment: 'There is not one Irish MSS extant older than the 11th century, long after metaphysics and such trifling sort of learning had been successfully studied there. To which I add.' The footnote is correctly cited, and Ledwich's references can be found in Irenaeus's *Contra haereses* I 3, Pacatus's *Panegyricus* 1.3, and Sidonius's *Epistulae* III 3.2. The passage continues: 'and a native writer, about the year 700, calls it a vile tongue', citing the preface to Adomnán's *Vita S. Columbae* from Ussher's *Sylloge* (1632), 42.

31 Warburton, Whitelaw, and Walsh (1818), ii 760–1, tell of the old 'doctor' and his seventy-three manuscripts on vellum, but he is named only in the Appendix, lxxxiii. The reason for this mention of Michael Casey is that O'Donovan sent to Dr Todd two pieces derived from the Book of Fermoy that had come from Casey (above, n 26).

32 In *Freeman's Journal*, Monday, 13 February 1826, a front-page advertisement for Michael Casey's gout ointment includes the comment: 'Please to refer to Mr Warburton's, &c., History of Dublin, 2d vol, page 760, appendix 83, for further particulars'.

tion next to his catalogue description quoted above: 'I have (since writing the above) discovered a different account of this book transaction in the handwriting of Edward (or Edmund as he writes himself) O'Reilly himself. EC 1846'. The alternative names Edward and Edmund point to the first paper copied by O'Donovan as O'Curry's source. These papers have not come to light but they were enough to persuade O'Donovan and O'Curry that O'Reilly had paid Seán Ó Cléirigh for his manuscripts. The corollary is that Ó Cléirigh was not telling the truth when he claimed otherwise through his son's letter in 1842. Neither revealed the full story.

Before we accept what O'Donovan says at face value, we may pause to reflect. In the first paper, the writer refers to O'Reilly in the third person, presumably in the form Éamonn Ó Raghallaigh to judge from O'Donovan's rendering it in English as Edmond and commenting that Edward was merely his literary name. Two lines later, he says 'written by me'. Would a writer using the first person refer to himself in the third person? Probably not. Moreover, the writer says that O'Reilly bought the Life of Aodh Ruadh Ó Domhnaill while Monck Mason bought 'the two other books', namely the Book of Invasions and a volume of historical poetry. This conflicts with what we know from the sale catalogues, which show that Monck Mason owned the Life of Aodh Ruadh Ó Domhnaill (**556**, of which O'Reilly had a transcript, **112**), while O'Reilly owned *Leabhar Gabhála* (**113**). What the paper refers to as a book 'in which there are many poems on the History of Ireland' sounds like Dublin, National Library of Ireland, G 131 rather than Dublin, Royal Irish Academy, 23 N 28, two parts of a manuscript that we know was divided between Monck Mason (**555**) and O'Reilly (**18**). It is difficult to believe that O'Reilly would make such obvious mistakes. The memorandum begins by saying 'This little book', and by elimination we can say what it was. Of the four manuscripts under consideration, it ought to be the Book of Pedigrees (**114**), now Dublin, Royal Irish Academy, 23 D 17 (cat. 790), which John O'Clery named as one of those acquired by O'Reilly from his father. Although purchased by Petrie for the Academy at the sale of O'Reilly's books, it has a notice at the front saying that it had belonged to Patrick Lynch (†1818) and was now the property of Patrick Vincent FitzPatrick (1792–1865). This notice was almost certainly written between May and October 1818.[33] The writer of bad Irish dates his

[33] The notice is printed in the RIA catalogue (Mulchrone et al. (1926–1970), xx 2503), and it is also given by Pender (1951), xiv–xvi, who, perplexed by the dates of the owners, questioned whether the book could have reached the Academy as early as 1830 (Pender (1951), xi): 'I have been unable to discover any evidence either in support or in

memorandum, 18 January 1818, in the Record Tower, adding: 'and my own age will be sixty years next St Patrick's day'. Now, Edward O'Reilly's date of birth was 6 December 1765.[34] Patrick Lynch, however, was born on 17 March, and by his own reckoning here the year was 1758.[35] From about 1815 to his death he was Clerk for Indexing in the Record Tower at Dublin Castle.[36] O'Donovan has not recognized the handwriting correctly, but his judgement on the language was doubtless fair. O'Reilly started to learn Irish as an adult, and O'Donovan was used to scoffing at his mistakes; Lynch was a native speaker from Co. Clare, but he was not at ease in writing Irish.[37]

The second paper, apparently in worse Irish, tells us nothing more, and, without sight of the original to be assured that both were written by the same hand, we can do nothing with it.

That first paper, however, makes a huge difference to the story. For a start, it tells us that 30 shillings was the price paid by Lynch for the Book of Pedigrees, which he bought from Seán Ó Cléirigh. Lynch

refutation of the apparently now well-established tradition that the MS was acquired by purchase for the Academy at the dispersal of O'Reilly's library in 1830.' The solution to his difficulty must be read between the lines. FitzPatrick writes in complimentary terms about Lynch, as if he were recently dead (though he misdates his death to 1817); he introduces himself as 'Patrick Vincent FitzPatrick (eldest son of Hugh FitzPatrick of Capel Street in the city of Dublin, Bookseller)'. Hugh FitzPatrick died on 23 October 1818, and I think we must suppose that he was alive when this was written and that the book had come into his son's hands by way of trade, following Lynch's death on 10 May 1818. McCabe (2009) records that at this period Patrick was engaged in the family business. The young man was 'ignorant of the Irish language', as he himself says (Dublin, Royal Irish Academy, 23 D 17, f iiir), and the book was no doubt soon resold to O'Reilly. What is most surprising about the note is its reference to Lynch's work in 'the Public Record Office in Dublin Castle', the earliest instance I have seen of this name.

34 So stated in a letter to Myles John O'Reilly, 7 April 1830 (Dublin, Trinity College, 3407, 81v), brought to light by de Brún and Herbert (1986), xv n 39.

35 The date is given, almost certainly on Lynch's own authority, by Robert Walsh in what Séamus Ua Casaide has called 'an obscure footnote' (Ua Casaide (1912), 47–8): 'P. Lynch was born near Quin, in the county of Clare, on St Patrick's day, 1757. It is the practice in Ireland to call the child by the name of the saint whose day is next at hand, and he was called Patrick.' He was quoting from Warburton, Whitelaw, and Walsh (1818), ii 936n; the large second volume was all the work of Dr Robert Walsh (1772–1852), who had direct contact with Lynch himself. The year is stated as 1754 by Dowling (1931), 464, but his source was the same passage in Walsh.

36 Ua Casaide (1912), 58.

37 Theophilus O'Flanagan, writing to John MacNamara, 20 March 1809, about translating Keating, says (London, British Library, Add. 43376, 353): 'Halliday's want of acquaintance with the native idiom disqualifies him, while Lynch's less than supercial (*sic*) knowledge of the written language leaves him no authority to judge.'

presents Ó Cléirigh as selling, and he names three separate buyers. Lynch has muddled what they bought, and he does not tell us how much Ó Cléirigh got for the other three manuscripts. The paper does not, as O'Donovan supposed, prove that O'Reilly had paid Ó Cléirigh for the books he got. Indeed it does not eliminate the possibility that O'Reilly borrowed the books. But it leads one to think rather that Ó Cléirigh had three buyers for four books, one of which was divided into two. Lynch bought one, and allowing for the division O'Reilly took two and Monck Mason took two. The expectation would be that both of them paid Ó Cléirigh, though at what rate we cannot guess. It is not necessarily significant that the copy of *Ambra Choluim Cille* is not mentioned. The story that it was O'Reilly who sold one of the books to Monck Mason and kept the money comes only from Ó Cléirigh, and it comes only long after the event. It leaves out Patrick Lynch, who had died on 10 May 1818. The Book of Pedigrees then passed through the hands of Patrick Vincent Fitzpatrick. In 1825 it was certainly in O'Reilly's possession, though he appears already to have made excerpts from it.[38] In 1823 it was available to Seán Ó Cléirigh, who made a transcript from it, presumably by arrangement with the current owner. This copy, referred to at the end of John O'Clery's letter, was still in his father's possession in 1842.[39] At the time of O'Reilly's sale in 1830, therefore, three of the four manuscripts and a copy of the fourth were all in his collection, and so too was the fifth, mentioned only by John O'Clery.

It is possible that Ó Cléirigh was aware of this. In the 1820s and 1830s we find him acting as a scribe, and he may have maintained contact with people interested in manuscripts. In 1832 Owen Connellan handled a copy of *Iomarbháigh na bhFileadh*, written by Seán Ó Cléirigh in 1825, which had already come into the possession of Lord George Hill. He added a note to say that the scribe was fifth in descent from one of the Four

[38] The manuscript itself was no. 114 in O'Reilly's catalogue, but no. 184 is described as 'very full Pedigrees of the O'Donells, O'Neills, and other great Tribes of Ulster, copied by E. O'R. from P. O'Clery's Book, one of the Four Masters, also one of the hereditary Senachies of the House of O'Donell'; the copy is now Dublin, Royal Irish Academy, 23 G 6 (cat. 680), which passed through the hands of M.J. O'Reilly and Messrs Hodges & Smith before reaching the Academy in 1844. The manuscript itself contains no mention of the source in Pereginus O'Clery's book, obviously something known to O'Reilly himself.

[39] This is now Dublin, Royal Irish Academy, 23 P 4 (cat. 975). The manuscript was bound for the Academy in 1853.

Masters.[40] The earliest manuscript in his hand is dated 1821, the latest not before 1838.[41] Now, unless evidence can be found to show that Ó Cléirigh actually made the affidavit in November 1830, referred to by his son years afterwards—a son who was no more than a child at that date—there is some likelihood that he began to tell his side of the story only rather later and perhaps near to 1842, when we first find mention of it in writing.

There is no room to doubt whether Seán Ó Cléirigh was descended from Cú Choigcríche Ó Cléirigh, who made his will in February 1664/5, and little room to doubt the identity of the testator and the scribe. The manuscripts in which this hand is found make a strong case for his being identified as one of the Four Masters.[42] The descendant brought with him to Dublin several manuscripts that had been written by his ancestor more than a hundred and fifty years earlier. O'Donovan's published account adds the detail that Seán Ó Cléirigh's father died in 1816, which suggests that Seán remained at Tullavally until then, moving to Dublin and bringing the books just a year or so after he came into possession of them.[43] Lynch's account of the family clearly parallels what O'Donovan had from John O'Clery, but Lynch has added errors and reduced the detail.[44] O'Clery's story (quoted above, p 653) that the family had had more manuscripts before a fire in the time of Seán's father Pádraig is

[40] Now Cork, Boole Library (University College, Cork), 1 (Ó Conchúir (1991), 1–6; accessible via Irish Script on Screen). The date 1832 derives from Monck Mason's mention of the manuscript among those listed in a review of J. Reid, *Bibliotheca Scoto-Celtica* (Mason (1832), 635). A colophon (p 203) gives the pedigree of the manuscript, copied from an exemplar of 1798, which was copied from one of 1722, which was copied from one made by Mícheál Ó Cléirigh in 1627.

[41] Dublin, Royal Irish Academy, 24 I 19 (cat. 1205), written in 1821. Two others, written on paper watermarked 1824–36, are now Dublin, Royal Irish Academy, 23 G 12 and 23 G 13 (cat. 12–13), were bought by Hodges and Smith and sold by them to the Academy in 1844 (Hodges & Smith Collection 201, 202). Dublin, Royal Irish Academy, 23 O 1 (cat. 65) dates from the 1820s (and also has the name of John O'Clery Junr at p 95), 23 M 5 (cat. 66) from 1838, 23 O 36 (cat. 567) not before 1838.

[42] The case was tested and accepted by Breatnach (1996), 14–5. He finds the hand explicitly associated with the name in Brussels, Bibliothèque royale de Belgique/Koninklijke Bibliotheek van België, 2542–3.

[43] O'Donovan (1844), 396–7. It is compatible with Lynch's memorandum of 1818 (above, p 657), which says that Seán's father Pádraig died two years before.

[44] Lynch (above, p 656–7) has two extra generations between Cú Choigcríche's son Diarmaid and his son Cairbre, which appears to be simple error. He presents the family's migration in a simple sequence from Tirconnel into Co. Mayo, from there to 'Knock Bennis' (Co. Leitrim, but not identified as a townland), and from there to Tullavally, Co. Cavan. O'Donovan (1844), 396–7, covers the same ground with more detail and complexity.

worth noting.[45] There is other evidence that Cú Choigcríche was in possession of old books.[46] Seán knew from his ancestor's will, pasted into the Book of Pedigrees, that Cú Choigcríche had bequeathed to his sons Diarmaid and Seán his dearest possession, his books.[47] 20th-century scholarship has devoted more space to his family-tree than to the story of his books, which—one must believe—had come down the family to him. The line of descent is attested quite simply. We have already seen (above, p 653) that John O'Clery, Seán's son, wrote to O'Donovan in 1842, saying:

> Cucogry left his books to his sons Dermod and Shane. Cairbre, son of Dermod, had them in his possession, and left them to his son Cosnamha, who left them to his son Patrick, through whom they came into the possession of his son John, my father.

Seán Ó Cléirigh died on 28 December 1846, and a contemporary notice of his death has been traced which presents the same line in reverse:[48]

> On Monday, 28th December, 1846, at 10 Hamilton-row, Dublin, John O'Clery, the representative of the branch of his name, aged 72 years. He was the son of Patrick, son of Cosnamhach, son of Cairbre, son of Diarmid, son of Cucogry O'Clery, one of the Four Masters, who died in 1664.

The last date was no doubt derived from Cú Choigcríche's will, taking no account of Lady Day reckoning. This matches the generations

45 Lynch (above, p 656) does not mention the fire but says: 'These sons (of Patrick) had a great deal of the writings of their ancestors', as if many had passed to Seán's generation, whereas O'Clery (above, p 652) says that his father brought to Dublin all those not damaged by the fire.

46 Breatnach (1996), 15, discovered mention of 'some of the old books required for this task' in Cú Choigcríche's hands in the prologue, preserved only in the shorter recension, to the Ó Cléirigh martyrology, *Naomhsheanchas naomh Inse Fáil* (Brussels, Bibliothèque royale de Belgique/Koninklijke Bibliotheek van België, 4639, 2r).

47 O'Donovan (1844), 396; O'Curry (1861), 560; Pender (1951), xvii–xviii; Breatnach (1996), 14.

48 The brief notice of his death was found by Fr John Brady in the *Drogheda Argus*, 16 January 1847, and communicated to Colm Ó Lochlainn, who printed it (Ó Lochlainn (1941–2), 135). Such a notice may have appeared in other newspapers. The statement that he was aged 72 implies a date of birth in 1774; O'Curry said that he was aged 66 in August 1843, implying a date of birth in 1777 or 1778 (above, p 651); Lynch says that he was aged 37 in January 1818 (above, p 657), implying that he was born in 1780. It was not unusual for someone to age a little faster than the calendar.

numbered from 43 to 48 in the line set out by John O'Donovan, who also provides some dates.[49] What has proved controversial is the next step back to the father of Cú Choigcríche Ó Cléirigh, the annalist. O'Donovan said that his father was Lughaidh, and so did Seán Ó Cléirigh himself, in 1838, in his own line of descent: 'Seán Ó Cléirigh mac Padraicc mic Cosnamhaidh mic Cairbre mic Diarmada mic Cucoiccriche do éug 1664 mic Lughaidh mic Mic Con'.[50] Fr Paul Walsh refuted this claim with authoritative evidence that Cú Choigcríche's father was named Diarmaid.[51] And he repeated the point several times, finding it difficult to counteract the influence of O'Donovan's statements.[52] He found no source naming him Lughaidh earlier than Seán Ó Cléirigh himself.[53] It is not hard to see that this was motivated by desire to extend

49 O'Donovan (1844), 395–7.

50 Dublin, Royal Irish Academy, 23 M 5 (cat. 66), p 247; quoted by Kathleen Mulchrone in Mulchrone et al. (1926–70), ii 396–7, in the description of Dublin, Royal Irish Academy, 23 P 26 (cat. 138); Walsh (1935b), 65. It is not apparent when 23 M 5 came to the Academy. Seán also gives his pedigree in Dublin, Royal Irish Academy, 23 G 13 (cat. 13), p 184, which may be a little earlier to judge from the watermarks; though it would appear to have been still in Seán's hands in 1836, it was soon acquired by Messrs Hodges & Smith, being acquired by the Academy from them in 1843–1844 (while Ó Cléirigh was still living) as Hodges & Smith 202.

51 The authors' preface to the Annals of the Four Masters is missing from the copy that lies behind O'Donovan's edition but survives in the other autograph copy (unknown to O'Donovan), now Dublin, University College, A 13, pp. xxiii–xxiv; it was printed by Walsh (1916), 17–24, and reprinted in Walsh (1933), 75. Here the Master is named 'Cúcoigcríche mac Diarmata Uí Clérigh a contae Dhúin na nGall'. Walsh would later cite the poem composed by Cú Choigcríche Ó Cléirigh mac Diarmada following the death in 1662 of Máire, daughter of Aodh Ó Domhnaill (Dublin, National Library of Ireland, G 167, p 284 (*recte* 292)), which establishes that the annalist was still alive within a few years of the testator's making his will (Walsh (1935a), 262; Walsh (1935b), 64). This manuscript, written by Semus Mhaguidhir, 1727, had belonged to J.H. Todd and appears in the sale of his manuscripts (1869 Todd 1438). The scribe-annalist-testator must not be confused with Cú Choigcríche mac Diarmada maic Taidhg Caimm, his great-grandfather, one of whose books is mentioned among the annalistic sources used by the Four Masters (O'Donovan (1851), i lxvi; O'Donovan (1844), 83, 395).

52 Having printed the source in 1916 (repr. 1918 and 1933), Walsh recurs to the subject in Walsh (1932); Walsh (1934); Walsh (1935a), 261–2; Walsh (1935b); Walsh (1936); Walsh (1937), in which he cites six previous statements. On the controversy surrounding his final statement, see Ó Muraíle in Walsh (2003), 19–21. The 1958 general index to the RIA Catalogue (Mulchrone et al. (1926–1970), index ii, 1025), still separated Cú Choigcríche mac Diarmada from the ghostly Cu Choigcríche mac Luighdheach.

53 Walsh (1935b), 66. The implication is surely that O'Donovan was following Seán Ó Cléirigh. Unknown to Walsh is Charles Sharpe's alteration in the sale catalogue (noted above, p 648), which almost certainly dates from 1830. This is no authority.

the pedigree of family-learning backwards to include Lughaidh Ó Cléirigh, author of the *Beatha Aodha Ruaidh*, which was among the family manuscripts of Seán Ó Cléirigh.[54]

It is impossible now to establish what Seán Ó Cléirigh knew about the Four Masters and their work at the time of bringing these manuscripts from Co. Cavan to Dublin. This is dated to the same year by both John O'Clery and Patrick Lynch, 1817, which we may take as secure.[55] Lynch says the winter of 1817, and by January 1818 he had bought the manuscripts. It makes little difference whether by 'winter' he meant a year or so before the time of writing or a month or so. The manuscripts so bought were cited in O'Reilly's hands, or in one case in Monck Mason's hands, in O'Reilly's *Irish Writers*, which he wrote during 1819 and 1820.[56] The sale to Monck Mason had taken place, therefore, within the same time-frame as the sales to Lynch and O'Reilly. We know that in 1818 and 1819 O'Reilly sold a number of manuscripts, some to Monck Mason, some to James Hardiman.[57] He sold because he needed the money. Choosing between John O'Clery's claim that O'Reilly sold *Beatha Aodha Ruaidh* to Monck Mason and Lynch's implication that Ó Cléirigh himself had sold books to several buyers may rest secure on Lynch's lack of any axe to grind. By this date the reputation of the Four Masters

[54] O'Reilly (above, p 650 and n 11) made the connexion a stronger one by claiming Cú Choigcríche as the author of the Life.

[55] See above pp. 652, 656, 659–60.

[56] So, for example, O'Reilly (1820), xciii, refers to a copy of Tadhg Mór Ó hUiginn's poem *Gach én mar a adhbha*: 'A copy of this poem, in the handwriting of Cucoigcriche (*Peregrinus*) O'Clery, one of the Four Masters, is in the collection of the Assistant Secretary.' He refers to Dublin, Royal Irish Academy, 23 N 28 (cat. 137), p 34, which was no. 18 in his collection (above, pp. 647–8). The two topographical poems in the same manuscript are also referred to: 'a complete copy, in the hand-writing of Cucoigcriche O'Clery, one of the Four Masters, is in the collection of the Assistant Secretary'; 'a very valuable copy of this poem, in the hand-writing of Cucoigcriche O'Clery' (O'Reilly (1820), c, cxix). His copy of 'the Book of Invasions by the O'Clerys' is mentioned frequently but less precisely. For the Life of Aodh Ruadh, which he had sold to Monck Mason, see above, pp. 649–50. As for the manuscript of *Amhra Choluim Cille*, we have quoted above (p 653–4 and n 23) his statement that it was 'once the property of Cucoigcriche O'Clery' (O'Reilly (1820), xxxix).

[57] Two important manuscripts apparently sold to William Monck Mason by O'Reilly are now London, British Library, Egerton 1781 and 1782 (1858 Monck Mason 552, 553). A larger number of books passed through O'Reilly's hands into those of James Hardiman around 1819, and the transaction appears to have precipitated a falling out between them.

was well established, though few had studied any of their works.[58] If the family already identified Cú Choigcríche as one of them, we may wonder whether Seán Ó Cléirigh would have parted with the books so quickly or so cheaply. On the other hand, if they were to him simply old manuscripts that had come down the family—the survivors of a fire at his father's house—he may have been glad to take 30 shillings apiece for them, if all were thought as valuable as the Book of Pedigrees. In 1830, if we believe his son, he was aware that the manuscripts in O'Reilly's hands were auctioned, and he may have known what prices they fetched. This was the beginning of a period of rising prices. And in the 1830s and 1840s the Annals of the Four Masters was widely promoted. A copy in the handwriting of Mícheál Ó Cléirigh fetched £53 at auction in 1831, a price, it should be said, far ahead of the ordinary market.[59] It was in the 1830s that O'Donovan was first engaged to copy and translate the Annals.[60] Two printed editions were marketed from 1844.[61] On this basis the particular value of Seán Ó Cléirigh's manuscripts might be expected to have increased faster than the average in a rising market.

The crucial difference was the entry into the market of buyers with money. Why people with money started to buy and what they were looking for are not questions susceptible to tidy answers, but the change in the market was good for the preservation of Irish manuscripts.[62] Some individuals made money out of the change, but the most money was made by the Dublin firm, Messrs Hodges & Smith, who assembled a collection of more than two hundred manuscripts at, we can be sure, low prices

[58] O'Reilly (1820), clxxxvi–cxc, devotes pages to the Annals of the Four Masters and cites them frequently elsewhere. In the catalogue of his own books he eulogizes the work (Dublin, Royal Irish Academy, 23 H 1 (cat. 1287), 163–4), while the 1830 sale catalogue (1830 O'Reilly) against the same item, no. 104, says: 'The great value of the Annals of the Four Masters is well known to every Irish Antiquary', and elsewhere he refers to Mícheál Ó Cléirigh as 'Chief of the Four Masters' (no. 165).

[59] 1831 Cooper 37. The manuscript is now Dublin, Royal Irish Academy, 23 P 6–7 (cat. 687–8). Prices were pushed up by the presence of John Cochran, a London dealer, who bought for Sir Thomas Phillipps.

[60] O'Donovan's work on the Annals was at first sponsored by Myles John O'Reilly. A letter from O'Donovan to O'Reilly, dated 8 May 1833, reports completion of one volume of the translation (Ó Maolfabhail (1991), 98). When O'Reilly withdrew, George Smith took over, and in 1838 O'Donovan's translation could be read in the shop of Messrs Hodges & Smith. The poet Thomas Moore took the opportunity (Russell (1853–6), vii 238, 300).

[61] Cunningham (2006).

[62] A broader view of these questions is taken in *Irish manuscript sales: markets, collectors, libraries* (forthcoming).

and sold them to the Royal Irish Academy for the phenomenal sum of 1250 guineas. A comparison between the sale of Edward O'Reilly's manuscripts at auction in 1830 and the Hodges & Smith purchase in 1844 reveals that the prices paid had, on average, gone up ninefold. The Academy was also the buyer when, a few years later, Sir William Betham sold his collection, formed, like that of Hodges & Smith, with a view to profit. Manuscripts of very different types were sold together, overriding the particular tastes and interests of different buyers. The market was rising but without clear discrimination as to value.

Against this background the story of Seán Ó Cléirigh's manuscripts is an interesting one. He had sold too early, and he lived long enough to realize that he might have done much better. He was no doubt aggrieved, he complained that he was cheated, and his complaint was talked about in the 1840s by various people with an interest in manuscripts. Traces of this discussion were written down, so that we can follow what was said. It turned into a question of credibility, even of integrity, and some people were ready to question the integrity of well-known participants in this market. In the end, O'Donovan justified O'Reilly, while unaware that his source was Lynch, and he even thought the memoranda he had translated for Todd 'should be inserted in one of those books in the Royal Irish Academy'.

Bibliography

1830 O'Reilly: *Bibliotheca Hibernica. Catalogue of the library of the late Edward O'Reilly, Esq. of Harold's-Cross, Author of the Irish–English Dictionary, &c., embracing a fine Collection of Printed Books, on Irish history, Irish language, and other matters connected with Ireland* [...] *together with a unique collection of important and valuable Irish Manuscripts, in fine preservation, which are to be sold by auction, by order of the executors, at the large sale-room, No. 33, Anglesea-Street, Dublin, on Tuesday, November 30, 1830, and following days* [...] *Charles Sharpe, Auctioneer*, Dublin.

1831 Cooper: *Catalogue of the valuable and extensive library of the late Austin Cooper, Esq., FSA, consisting of a choice collection of books* [...] *together with a valuable collection on the history and antiquities of Ireland, many very rare English and Irish manuscripts* [...], *&c. to be sold by auction by Edward Maguire* [...], *23 Suffolk Street, on Monday, February 21st, 1831*, Dublin.

1858 Monck Mason: *A Catalogue of the Literary Collections and Original Compositions of William Monck Mason, Esq., in the departments of Irish History and General Philology* [...], *which will be sold by auction by Messrs S. Leigh Sotheby & John Wilkinson* [...], *on Monday, the 29th of March, 1858, and two following days*, London.

1867 O'Donovan: *Catalogue of Books, in various classes, including the library of the late John O'Donovan, LL.D., manuscripts and select works on Irish History and Antiquities* [...], *Cabinet of Irish Antiquities in Bronze, Coins and Medals, a few Paintings* [...], *study furniture and miscellanies, to be sold by auction by J. Fleming Jones* [...], *Thursday, November 7th, and following days*, Dublin.

1869 Todd: *Catalogue of the Valuable Library of the late Rev. James H. Todd, DD, SFTCD* [...], *comprising select biblical literature; the history, antiquities, and language of Ireland;* [...] *and an important collection of Patristic, Irish, and other Manuscripts on vellum and paper; To be sold by auction by John Fleming Jones at his Literary Salerooms, No. 8, D'Olier Street, by order of the excutors, on Monday, November 15th, 1869 and five following days* [...], Dublin.

Abbott, T.K. and E.J. Gwynn (1921) *Catalogue of the Irish manuscripts in the library of Trinity College, Dublin*, Dublin.

Breathnach, P., see Walsh, P.

Breatnach, P.A. (1996) 'The methodology of *seanchas*: the redaction by Cú Choigcríche Ó Cléirigh of the chronicle poem *Leanam croinic clann nDálaigh*,' *Éigse* 29, 1–18.

— (2013) *The Four Masters and their manuscripts: studies in palaeography and text*, Dublin.

Clery, A.B. (1943–5) 'Sean O'Clery of Dublin (1778–1846),' *Irish book lover* 29, 124–8.

Cunningham, B. (2006) '"An honour to the nation": publishing John O'Donovan's edition of the *Annals of the Four Masters*, 1848–56,' in M. Fanning and R. Gillespie, *Print culture and intellectual life in Ireland 1660–1941: essays in honour of Michael Adams*, Dublin, 116–42.

de Brún, P. and M. Herbert (1986) *Catalogue of Irish manuscripts in Cambridge libraries*, Cambridge.

Dowling, P.J. (1931) 'Patrick Lynch, schoolmaster, 1754–1818,' *Studies. An Irish quarterly review* 20, 461–72.

Ledwich, E. (1790) *The antiquities of Ireland*, Dublin.

— (1804) *The antiquities of Ireland*, 2nd revised edition, Dublin.

Mac Cárthaigh, E. (2009) 'Cú Choigcríche Ó Cléirigh (Peregrine O'Clery),' in J. McGuire and J. Quinn, *Dictionary of Irish biography,* Cambridge (http://dib.cambridge.org).

Mason, H.M. (1832) Review of J. Reid, *Bibliotheca Scoto-Celtica*, *The Christian examiner and Church of Ireland magazine, new series* 1, 627–40.

McCabe, D. (2009) 'Fitzpatrick, Patrick Vincent,' in J. McGuire and J. Quinn, *Dictionary of Irish biography*, Cambridge (http://dib.cambridge.org).

Mulchrone, K. et al. (1926–1970) *Catalogue of Irish Manuscripts in the Royal Irish Academy*, 28 fascicules, 2 index vols., Dublin.

Ní Shéaghdha, N. and P. Ó Macháin (1961–96) *Catalogue of Irish manuscripts in the National Library of Ireland*, 13 vols., Dublin.

Ó Conchúir, B. (1991). *Clár lámhscríbhinní Gaeilge Choláiste Ollscoile Chorcaí: cnuasach Uí Mhurchú*, Dublin.

O'Curry, E. (1861) *Lectures on the manuscript materials of ancient Irish history*, Dublin.

O'Donovan, J. (1844) *The genealogies, tribes, and customs of Hy-Fiachrach, commonly called O'Dowda's Country*, Dublin.

— (1845) *A grammar of the Irish language, published for the use of the senior classes in the college of St Columba*, Dublin.

— (1851) *Annála rioghachta Éireann. Annals of the kingdom of Ireland by the Four Masters*, 7 vols., Dublin, 2nd edition 1856.

Ó Fiannachta, P. (1966) 'An O'Donovan source,' *Irish ecclesiastical record, 5th series* 105, 127–8.

Ó Lochlainn, C. (1941–2) 'Cúcoigcríche Ó Cléirigh,' *Irish book lover* 28, 135.

Ó Maolfabhail, A. (1991) 'Éadbhard Ó Raghallaigh, Seán Ó Donnabháin agus an tSuirbhéireacht Ordanáis, 1830–34,' *PRIA* 91C, 73–103.

Ó Muraíle, N. (2002) 'Paul Walsh as editor and explicator of *Beatha Aodha Ruaidh*,' in P. Ó Riain, *Beatha Aodha Ruaidh: historical and literary contexts*, London, 98–123.

O'Reilly, E. (1820) *A chronological account of nearly four hundred Irish writers*, issued as *Transactions of the Iberno-Celtic Society* 1.1.

O'Sullivan, A. (1968) 'Verses on honorific portions,' in J. Carney and D. Green, *Celtic studies: essays in memory of Angus Matheson*, London, 118–23.

Pender, S. (1951) 'The O Clery Book of Genealogies: 23 D 17 (R.I.A.),' *Analecta Hibernica* 18, ix, xi–xxxiii, 1–198.

Russell, J. (1853–6) *Memoirs, journal, and correspondence of Thomas Moore*, 8 vols., London.

Ua Casaidhe, S. (1912) 'Patrick Lynch, secretary to the Dublin Gaelic Society,' *Journal of the Waterford and South-East of Ireland Archaeological Society* 14, 47–61.

Walsh, P. (1916) 'Extracts from the Franciscan manuscript of the Annals of the Four Masters,' *Irisleabhar Muighe Nuadat* (1916), 17–24, repr. in Walsh (1933), 69–85.

— (1932) [as Breathnach, P.] 'The Four Masters,' *Irish book lover* 20, 105 [from *Irish Press*, 21 May 1932], repr. in Walsh (2003), 345–6 (§64.1).

— (1933) *Gleanings from Irish manuscripts*, 2nd edition, Dublin.

— (1934) [as Breathnach, P.] 'The Four Masters,' *Irish book lover* 22, 128–31, repr. in Walsh (2003), 347–50 (§64.2).

— (1935a) 'The O Clerys of Tirconnell,' *Studies. An Irish quarterly review* 24, 244–62, repr. as P. Walsh, *The O Cléirigh family of Tír Connaill, with the O Cléirigh genealogies*, Dublin 1938.

— (1935b) [as Breathnach, P.] 'What we know of Cuchoigcriche O Cleirigh,' *Irish book lover* 23, 60–6.

— (1936) [as Breathnach, P.] 'Will of Cucogry O'Clery,' *Irish book lover* 24, 87, repr. in Walsh (2003), 377 (§69.1).

— (1937) [as Breathnach, P.] 'Peregrine O'Clery,' *Irish book lover* 25, 75–6 [from *Irish Independent*, 13 May 1937], repr. in Walsh (2003), 377–80 (§69.2).

— (2003) *Irish leaders and learning through the ages*, ed. by N. Ó Muraíle, Dublin.

Warburton, J., J. Whitelaw, and R. Walsh (1818) *History of the city of Dublin*, 2 vols., London.

HANS ULRICH SCHMID

OLD WRITINGS ARE NO MYSTERY TO ME… SKALDENSTROPHEN DER *ORKNEYINGA SAGA* UND GEORGE MACKAY BROWN

One quickly realises that those early Orcadians had a horror of old age and slow witherings[1]
(George Mackay Brown)

Abstract

George Mackay Brown (1921–96), one of the most prominent Scottish authors of modern times, frequently applies historical themes in his work, especially in his lyrics. His favourite source, in this respect, is the 13th-century *Orkneyinga Saga*, presumably of Icelandic authorship. It contains the story of Jarl Røgnvaldr Kolsson's pilgrimage to Jerusalem, which shows more features of a *grand tour* and a raid than of a pious expedition. As in most of the traditional Icelandic saga literature, the *Orkneyinga Saga* also contains a considerable number of Lausavísur, a 'loose rhyme' of predominantly eight lines, especially in the direct speech of Jarl Røgnvaldr. George Mackay Brown has transformed 24 of these Old Norse verses into modern poetry. The present article analyzes his methodology, ranging from close adaptation to vague borrowings.

Keywords

George Mackay Brown, Ermengard of Narbonne, Jarl Røgnvaldr; *Orkneyinga Saga*; Old Norse; *Lausavísur*, skaldic poetry.

Die *Orkneyinga Saga*

Im frühen 13. Jahrhundert verfasste ein unbekannter Autor, vermutlich ein Isländer, die *Orkneyinga Saga*,[2] eine Geschichte der Orkaden-Jarle,

1 Brown (1997), 65.

2 Die *Orkneyinga Saga* ist herausgegeben von Nordal (1913–6).

Early medieval Ireland and Europe: chronology, contacts, scholarship, ed. by Pádraic Moran and Immo Warntjes, Studia Traditionis Theologiae, 14 (Turnhout, 2015), pp. 671–94.

 10.1484/M.STT-EB.5.103140

die vom 9. Jahrhundert bis nahe an seine eigene Gegenwart heranreicht. Die Anfänge liegen noch in einer (unhistorischen) mythischen Vorzeit, doch über weite Teile wird von den Taten und Kämpfen der verschiedenen (historischen) Orkney-Jarle berichtet. Die Partien, die von Ereignissen im 12. Jahrhundert handeln, dürften auf mündlicher Tradition basieren und auf Erzählungen von Augenzeugen zurückzuführen sein. Dazu gehört auch der Bericht über die Reise des Jarls Rögnvald Kolsson mit seinem Gefolge nach Jerusalem (Kapitel 85 bis 90). Die Übereinkunft, diese Reise zu unternehmen, wurde in Norwegen getroffen, wohin Jarl Rögnvald von den Orkneys eingeladen worden war. Schon die Heimreise vor dort auf die Orkneys verläuft turbulent. Rögnvald gerät in Stürme und muss auf den Shetland-Inseln notlanden. In dem Zusammenhang werden einige der sagatypischen achtzeiligen *Lausavísur* ('lose Strophen'), die überwiegend die Form des *Dróttkvætt*[3] zeigen, gesprochen (siehe dazu die Bemerkungen zu Text 4a). George Mackay Brown hat einige davon für seinen Gedichtzyklus adaptiert, unterscheidet aber nicht zwischen den Versen der Vorgeschichte und denen, die auf Etappen und im Verlauf der eigentlichen Jerusalem-Reise gesprochen werden.

Im Verlauf dieser Reise, bei einem Zwischenaufenthalt in Narbonne, wird Rögnvald mit seiner Mannschaft an den Hof der jungen Herzogin Ermengard zu einem Festessen geladen. Auf der Stelle verliebt er sich in das Mädchen, was natürlich nicht ohne dichterische Folgen bleibt. Eine seiner Strophen (siehe unten Text 7a) preist Ermengards Schönheit. Einflussreiche Leute am Hof von Narbonne wollen den Jarl zum Bleiben bewegen. Sogar eine Heirat mit der Schönen wird ihm in Aussicht gestellt, aber, so die Saga, 'der Jarl sagte, er wolle seine Fahrt wie geplant fortsetzen und würde auf dem Rückweg wiederkommen' (*Iarl qvaz fara vilia ferþ þa, er hann hafþi etlat, en qvaz koma mundu þar, er hann feri aptr*).[4] In einer Kurzgeschichte von George Mackay Brown mit dem Titel *A Crusader's Christmas*, die auf die Saga zurückgeht, liest sich das ganz anders: *The lady Ermengarde looked through her window one morning to see fifteen Scandinavian ships drifting one after another out of the harbour.*[5]

Nachdem die kleine Flotte Narbonne in Richtung Jerusalem verlassen und unterwegs einige weitere Abenteuer zu bestehen hat (unter an-

[3] Eine knappe Beschreibung dieser klassischen skaldischen Strophenform bei Simek und Pálsson (2007), 66–7. Vgl. auch Uecker (2004), 233–68.

[4] *Orkneyinga Saga* 86 (hg. von Nordal (1913–6), 234; meine Übersetzung, hier und im Weiteren).

[5] George Mackay Brown, *A Crusader's Christmas* (Brown (2010), 48).

derem werden eine Burg erobert und ein sarazenisches Schiff gekapert), gelangt man an Kreta vorbei nach Akkon und schließlich ins Heilige Land. Über den Aufenthalt an den heiligen Stätten erfährt man nur wenig. In der Saga heißt es 'Rögnvald und die Seinen fuhren dann von Akkon weg und besuchten alle jene heiligsten Stätten im Land von Jerusalem. Sie begaben sich alle zum Jordan und wuschen sich dort' (*Þeir Rognvalldr iarl foru þa or Akrsborg, ok sottu alla hina helguzstu stadi a Iorsalalandi. Þeir foru allir til iordanar ok lauguduz þar*).[6] Das ist alles, was man über das Wallfahrer-Programm am Ziel der Reise erfährt. Dem Saga-Autor waren offenbar die Ermengard-Episode, die Eroberungen einer Burg und das Kapern eines großen arabischen Schiffes viel wichtiger als das Ziel der Wallfahrt. Die Rückreise führt über den Kaiserhof von Konstantinopel zurück auf die Orkneys, nach *Hrossey*, das heutige Mainland. Narbonne wurde nicht mehr angesteuert.

George Mackay Brown

George Mackay Brown wurde 1921 als jüngstes von sechs Kindern eines Postboten in Stromness auf Mainland (Orkney) geboren. Den Großteil seines Lebens verbrachte er in dieser kleinen Hafenstadt. Erst im Alter von 34 Jahren—in seiner Jugend litt er unter Tuberkulose—ging er für einige Zeit nach Edinburgh, um Anglistik zu studieren. Er verfasste Gedichte, Dramen und Prosatexte. Seine auf eigenen Wunsch erst postum veröffentlichte Autobiographie mit dem Titel *For the Islands I sing* erschien 1997. Darin schreibt George Mackay Brown über die Faszination, die die mittelalterliche *Orkneyinga Saga* auf ihn ausgeübt hat:[7]

> *I got to know that Orkney possessed a medieval literature, Orkneyinga Saga. Here was another realm of gold. The desert was actually becoming interesting: the oases lay thicker around than I had imagined, and nearer home. If, in my late teens, I had the death wish—and so intensely that it destroyed a part of my lungs, I think—now life might be worth living after all. The smoulder inside me was almost quenched.*
> *I fed deeply on those stories out of Orkneyinga Saga. Besides being magnificent stories in themselves—the rivalry between Earl Thorfinn and Earl Rognvald the First; the feud between Earl Hakon an Earl Magnus; the pilgrimage of Earl Rognvald the Second to Jerusalem, Bayzantium,*

6 *Orkneyinga Saga* 88 (Nordal (1913–6), 254).

7 Brown (1997), 64–5.

Rome; the extraordinary career of the Viking farmer, Sweyn Asleifson, who every winter sat at his fire in Langskaill, Gairsay, with eighty retainers—they are told by a genius. Whoever he was, what he set down was 'pure narrative', from which everything that might interrupt the flow of the story (description, comment, reflection) is excluded. The characters reveal themselves in a few curt words. A murder or a sea-battle is inset with verse—not the kind of poetry you or I are used to, but short intricate webs of alliteration and kennings. Everywhere there are flashes of humour. One quickly realises that those early Orcadians had a horror of old age and slow witherings: better to die young in an siege or sea-battle; best of all to die with a jest in your mouth that men will remember for generations. [...]
I think that, in the writing of narrative, I learned a great deal from Burnt Njal, Grettir, Orkneyinga Saga. It is good, for a certain kind of writing, to use as few words as possible. The structure and form of the saga stories are magnificent. I think I have learned from them the importance of pure shape. But from my mother's side, the Celtic, I delight too in decoration. Look at the intricacies of early Gaelic art. Whether it is desirable to marry 'pure narrative' with elaborate decoration is not for me to say. I write as I must.

Immer wieder nimmt George Mackay Brown in seinen Werken Bezug auf die *Orkneyinga Saga*. Schon in der frühen Veröffentlichung von Gedichten unter dem Titel *The Storm* von 1954 findet sich folgendes Gedicht mit dem Titel *Song to Ermengarde* (Text 1):[8]

The winds embrace you, my lover
And the quiet stars bless,
Noons touch with ardour
And dawns with tenderness
All these are my brothers,
They abide: I fare on.
I shall not see your like again
Beneath the enduring sun.
O mould with me a timeless love:
That we, the time-accursed,
May mock the sad and fleeting hours
And bid death to his worst.
But the hours embrace you, my lover
And the grave seasons bless,
The years touch you with wisdom
And death with gentleness.

[8] George Mackay Brown, *Song to Ermengard* (hg. von Bevan und Murray (2006), 2–3).

Im Folgenden werden einige originale Skaldenstrophen[9] der *Orkneyinga Saga* mit den entsprechenden Gedichten von George Mackay Brown verglichen. Dabei wird zu beobachten sein, was aus den mittelalterlichen Saga-Strophen in die modernen Gedichte übernommen worden ist. Welche Metamorphosen haben die mittelalterlichen *Lausavísur* zu den modernen Gedichten hin durchlaufen?

Lyrische Metamorphosen

Innerhalb der Gedichtsammlung *Winterfold* (1976) findet sich unter dem zusammenfassenden Titel *Kestrel, Roseleaf, Chalice* eine Abfolge von insgesamt 24 Gedichten, die bis auf das erste, in dem der junge Jarl Rögnvald Kolsson stolz seine geistigen und sportlichen Fähigkeiten rühmt, im Zusammenhang mit der von ihm angeführten Jerusalem-Reise stehen. Das—historisch bezeugte—Unternehmen muss eine merkwürdige Mischung aus Raubzug und Wallfahrt gewesen sein. Im 'Reisebericht' der *Orkneyinga Saga* (Kapitel 85 bis 90)[10] sind in guter Saga-Manier insgesamt 38 sogenannte *Lausavísur* ('lose Strophen') eingestreut. Als deren Urheber werden verschiedene Reiseteilnehmer genannt. Die meisten der Verse entfallen auf Jarl Rögnvald selbst, einige auch auf Mitreisende wie den Skalden Ármóðr mit dem Beinamen Jarlsskáls ('Skalde des Jarls'), zwei Isländer namens Eiríkr und Oddi Glúmsson, genannt Lítli ('der Kleine'), und einen weiteren Skalden von den Orkneys, Sigmundr Öngull ('Angelhaken'). In der originalen Saga sind diese Strophen in den Erzählzusammenhang integriert. Möglicherweise sind die Strophen auch älter als die Saga, und die Prosa-Erzählung wurde gewissermaßen 'um sie herum' verfasst. Jedenfalls wird ihr Inhalt nur aus den Kontexten der Erzählung verständlich. George Mackay Brown traf eine Auswahl unter den *Lausavísur* der *Orkneyinga Saga*. Kenntnis der Zusammenhänge, in denen die zugrunde liegenden Verse der alten Saga stehen, konnte er bei seinen Lesern allerdings nicht voraussetzen. Doch darum kann es ihm auch letztlich nicht gegangen sein. Er schuf auf der Grundlage der mittelalterlichen Gedichte moderne Lyrik, die für sich selbst steht. Nach jedem Gedicht nennt George Mackay Brown

[9] Die Skaldenstrophen werden zitiert nach der Ausgabe von Jónsson (1912–5). Im Unterschied zur zitierten Saga-Edition, die die *Lausavísur* natürlich ebenfalls enthält, bietet diese Ausgabe der Strophen einen normalisierten und damit leichter lesbaren altnordischen Text.

[10] *Orkneyinga Saga* 85–90 (Nordal (1913–6), 139–262).

den Namen derjenigen Person aus der Saga, der die jeweilige Strophe dort zugeschrieben wird. Die weiteren epischen Zusammenhänge zu ergänzen, bleibt der Phantasie der Leser überlassen.

In Kapitel 85 der *Orkneyinga Saga* wird die Jerusalem-Reise zwischen Jarl Rögnvald und Eindriði ungi, einem Rückkehrer aus Konstantinopel, der sich später im Verlauf der Reise als wenig kooperativ erweisen wird, verabredet. Der eigentliche Aufbruch erfolgt erst einige Zeit später. Zuvor muss Rögnvald noch auf die Orkneys zurückkehren, um alles Nötige vorzubereiten. Doch schon die Fahrt von Norwegen nach Orkney ist ereignisreich. Man gerät in Seenot und muss einige Zeit auf den Shetland-Inseln zubringen. Einige der Gedichte im Zyklus von George Mackay Brown basieren auf Saga-Strophen, die noch in diesen Zusammenhang vor der eigentlichen Fahrt nach Jerusalem (Kapitel 86 bis 90 der Saga) gehören. Darunter ist auch ein Gedicht, das Brown einer Dienstmagd namens Asa zuschreibt. Das stimmt nicht ganz mit der Darstellung in der Saga überein. Denn dort wird erzählt, dass Jarl Rögnvald mit seiner Mannschaft auf einer der Shetland-Inseln gestrandet sei. Die Schiffbrüchigen finden freundliche Aufnahme bei Inselbewohnern, erhalten trockene Kleidung und können sich am Feuer wärmen. Eine Magd kommt vom Wasserholen zurück, ist aber bei Nacht und Kälte in einen Tümpel gefallen. Sie friert, zittert, klagt und schimpft—auf Gälisch. Die Nordmänner verstehen natürlich nichts, doch der Jarl, polyglott und bei bester Laune, übersetzt die Worte des frierenden Mädchens ins Altnordische. An diesem humorvollen Beispiel lassen sich einige Charakteristika der Verfahrensweise von George Mackay Brown zeigen. Asas gälische Worte werden in der Saga (aus verständlichen Gründen) nicht zitiert, wohl aber Rögnvalds Übersetzung (Text 2a):[11]

Dúsið ér, enn Ása
atatata, liggr i vatni,
hutututu, hvar skal ek sitja,
(heldr er mér kalt) við eldinn?

'Ihr wärmt euch. Aber Asa, atatata, liegt im Wasser, hutututu, wo soll ich sitzen (mir ist fürchterlich kalt) am Feuer?'

[11] *Orkneyinga Saga* 85 (Nordal (1913–6), 219; *Vísa*: Jónsson (1912–5), 481).

Der kurze Vers des Jarls, mit dem er die Klage des Mädchens für seine Leute wiedergibt, weist zweimal Binnenreim auf: *at* in *vatni* stimmt zum zähneklappernden *atatata*, und die Lautfolge *eld* steckt in *held* und *eldinn*. Zumindest als Assonanz kann auch *ús* und *ás* in *Dúsið* und *Ása* gelten.

Bei George Mackay Brown hat *Asa the Servant-girl's Song* folgenden Wortlaut (Text 2b):[12]

D-don't d-dare laugh at me,
N-N-Norsemen.
I want a s-seat at the f-f-fire.
Ice in my b-bones!
I f-fell in a well in the f-fog.
It was water to sweeten your ale.
M-make way, easterling!
That th-thick arm, if you were to wrap it round me,
Might make my teeth quiet.

Browns Gedicht ist also keine bloße Umsetzung der altnordischen Strophe ins Englische. Aber er behält Elemente daraus bei: Mit *D-don't d-dare*, *N-N-Norsemen*, *f-f-fire*, *f-fell*, *f-fog* und *th-thick* imitiert er das Zittern von Asa, das schon der Saga-Vers vorgibt. Anders als im Original wird es aber in die Wörter verlegt (*N-N-N-orsemen*, *f-f-fire* usw.) und nicht durch bedeutungslose Laute (dort *atatata* und *hutututu*) imitiert. In *fell* und *well* läge—sofern das vom Autor beabsichtigt und kein Zufall ist—ebenfalls eine Assonanz im Wortinneren vor. Über das hinaus fügt Brown aber auch noch ein neues (episches) Handlungselement hinzu: Das trotzige Mädchen bittet den Jarl, den es mit dem leicht verächtlichen *easterling* anredet, ihr seinen kräftigen Arm umzulegen und sie zu wärmen. In der Saga-Strophe war davon nicht die Rede.

Die weiteren Gedichte des Zyklus *Kestrel, Roseleaf, Chalice* (nicht alle können hier mit den jeweils zugrunde liegenden Originalen verglichen und besprochen werden) zeigen insgesamt einen unterschiedlichen Grad an Nähe zu den Strophen der Saga. Neben Asas Klage kommt das erste Gedicht des Zyklus, das auch noch nicht im Zusammenhang mit der eigentlichen Jerusalem-Reise steht, dem altnordischen Wortlaut am nächsten. Darin rühmt sich der noch junge Rögnvald (schon in Kapitel

[12] George Mackay Brown, *Asa the Servant-girl's Song* (hg. von Bevan und Murray (2006), 159).

58) seiner vielfachen Fähigkeiten. Im Saga-Original lautet die Strophe (Text 3a):[13]

Tafl em ec ǫrr at efla
íþróttir kannk níu
týnik trauðla rúnum,
tíð er bók ok smiðir,
skríða kank á skíðum
skýt ok rœk, svát nýtir,
hvártveggia kank hyggia
harpslǿtt ok bragþáttu.

'Das Schachspiel bin ich kundig zu spielen. Fähigkeiten habe ich neun: Kaum verliere ich Runen [d.h. ich beherrsche die Runen]. Bekannt sind mir Buch und Schmiedewerk. Schreiten kann ich auf Skiern. Ich schieße und rudere, dass es gefällt. An beidem kann ich mich erfreuen. Harfenspiel und Dichtung.'

Das ist eine vergleichsweise trockene Aufzählung. George Mackay Brown macht daraus *The Accomplishments of an Earl* (Text 3b):[14]

Chessboard, tiltyard, trout-stream
Know my sweet passes.
Old writings are no mystery to me
Nor any modern book.
Ski across winterfold flashes.
Deep curves I make with arrow and oar.
I know the twelve notes of a harp.
At the red forge
My clamorous shadow is sometimes rooted.

Der Aufzählungscharakter der originalen Strophe ist zwar noch deutlich erkennbar, aber Brown fasst vorab zusammen: *Chessboard, tiltyard, trout-stream.* Aus Runen werden *old writings*, aus einfachem *bók* wird *any modern book.* Vor dem Skifahrer öffnet sich eine gleißende Winterlandschaft: *Ski across winterfold flashes.* Dem Kompositum *harpslǿtt* ('Harfenspiel') im Saga-Vers korrespondiert *I know the twelve notes of a harp.* Die beiden Schlusszeilen, die das Bild des Schattens eines Schmiedes im ro-

[13] *Orkneyinga Saga* 58 (Nordal (1913–6), 139; *Vísa*: Jónsson (1912–5), 478).

[14] George Mackay Brown, *The Accomplishments of an Earl* (hg. von Bevan und Murray (2006), 157).

ten Feuerschein der Esse entstehen lassen (*At the red forge / My clamorous shadow is sometimes rooted*) bilden einen Satz und basieren auf dem einen Wort *smiðir.* In 'arrow and oar' liegt eine stabreimartige Alliteration vor.

Was sich für die Arbeitsweise Browns daraus ableiten lässt, ist dieses: Er lässt sich von einzelnen Wörtern der Originalstrophen zu poetischen Formulierungen inspirieren, die in der Phantasie des Lesers geradezu optische Bilder entstehen lassen.

Die Strophe der frierenden Asa und das Selbstlob in Versen lassen die Vorlage noch gut erkennen. Manche der Nachdichtungen von George Mackay Brown sind von den Saga-Versen, von denen sie inspiriert sind, im Wortlaut so weit entfernt, dass sich allenfalls noch punktuelle Berührungspunkte erkennen lassen (gelegentlich ist es gar nicht einfach, die Saga-Strophe zu entdecken, die einem der Gedichte Browns zugrunde liegt). Beispiel dafür ist eine Strophe, in welcher der Jarl seine Seelenruhe demonstriert, während sich sein Schiff gerade in höchster Seenot befindet und kurz davor ist, zu zerschellen (Text 4a):[15]

Hengik hamri kringðan
hanga (réttum) tangar
(Grímnis sylg) á galga
ginnungs brúar linna;
svá hefr glóraddar gladdan
gaglfellis mik þella,
lóns at leik við mínar
lautir, hellis Gauta.

An diese *Vísa* lassen sich exemplarisch formale Merkmale einer *Dróttkvætt*-Strophe zeigen: Jede ungerade Verszeile weist einen Stabreim auf, der in jeweils nachfolgenden geraden Zeile aufgenommen wird (Zeile 1 *Hengik* und *hamri*, dazu in Zeile 2 *hanga*). Jede gerade Zeile enthält darüber hinaus auch einen wortinternen Binnenreim (Zeile 2 *hanga* und *tangar*, Zeile 4 *ginnungs* und *linna*, Zeile 6 *fellis* und *þella* und Zeile 8 *lautir* und *Gauta*). Gattungstypisch sind zudem die eingebauten *Kenningar*, schwer verständliche (man könnte auch sagen extrem manierierte) Umschreibungen für an sich sehr gewöhnliche Dinge. Eine wörtliche Übersetzung der *Vísa* ergibt Folgendes:

'Ich ziehe die mit Hämmern bearbeiteten Schlangen der Brücke des Habichts vom herabhängenden Hänge-Galgen der Zange. Wir ma-

[15] *Orkneyinga Saga* (Nordal (1913–6), 218; *Vísa*: Jónsson (1912–5), 480).

chen Odins-Trunk. Auf diese Weise hat die Föhre der leisen Stimme des Riesen mich (so) froh gemacht, dass ich mit den Tälern der Bucht des Gänsetöters spiele.'

Dadaismus? Nein, denn die Unverständlichkeit resultiert aus der Tatsache, dass einiges in *Kenningar* verklausuliert ist.

Im Klartext heißt die Strophe: 'Ich ziehe die mit Hämmern bearbeiteten Armreife (= Schlangen der Brücke des Habichts, wobei mit Brücke des Habichts der Arm gemeint ist) von der herabhängenden Hand (= Hänge-Galgen der Zange). Ich dichte einen Vers (= Odins Trunk). Auf diese Weise hat die Frau (= Föhre der leisen Stimme des Riesen) mich (so) froh gemacht, dass ich mit meinen Fingern (= Täler der Bucht des Gänsetöters) spiele.' Jarl Rögnvald lässt sich von den Elementen, die um ihn herum toben, nicht beeindrucken, sondern zieht sich, so als geschähe nichts, einen Reif vom Arm, spielt mit seinen Fingern und dichtet gleichzeitig die zitierte hochkomplexe Strophe. Aus diesem geradezu stoischen Verhalten macht George Mackay Brown dieses Gedicht (Text 4b):[16]

I've swallowed mouthfuls of sea.
They gladdened me more
Than the best wine or mead.
The sea sings like a girl over my half-drowned feet.
With shivering mouth
I draw the hammered snake-ring from my finger.
I pledge myself to Our Lady of the Waves.

Nach der Metamorphose ist nur noch die Geste des Ringabziehens (allerdings eines Fingerrings, nicht eines Armreifens wie im Original) geblieben. Doch selbst das wird in einen anderen Sinnzusammenhang gestellt. Bei George Mackay Brown darf man es nicht als Demonstration der Gelassenheit in höchster Not verstehen, sondern als Geste an *Our Lady of the Waves*, deren Schutz sich der Jarl anvertraut. *Our Lady of the Waves* kann niemand anderes sein als die heilige Maria. Schon Jahre zuvor hat Brown ein Gedicht mit diesem Titel[17] verfasst.

Auch in anderen Gedichten des Zyklus erscheinen Figuren und Ereignisse in einem völlig anderen Licht als in der *Orkneyinga Saga*. Jarl

[16] George Mackay Brown, *Mouthfuls of Sea* (Bevan und Murray (2006), 158).

[17] George Mackay Brown, *Our Lady of the Waves* (Bevan und Murray (2006), 44–5). Das Gedicht kann hier nicht voller Länge zitiert werden. Es beginnt *The twenty brothers of Eynhallow / Have made a figure of Our Lady* und endet mit der Bitte an Maria *Guard the plough and the nets / Star of the sea, shine for us.*

Rögnvald ist auf der Rückreise von Norwegen auf der Orkney-Insel Westray gelandet. Er geht mit seinen Männern am Sonntag zur Kirche, als sich sechzehn 'unbewaffnete und kahlköpfige' Männer in seltsamer Kleidung auf die Kirche zu bewegen. Die Männer rätseln, um wen es sich da handeln könnte. Der Jarl kommentiert, was er sieht, in folgender spöttischen Strophe (Text 5a):[18]

Sextán hefik sénar
senn með topp í enni
jarðir, elli firðar,
ormvangs saman ganga.
Þat bǫrum vér vitni,
vestr at hér sé flestar
(sjá liggr út við élum
ey) kollóttar meyjar.

'Sechzehn Frauen habe ich zusammen gehen gesehen, fern vom Alter, mit einem Haarbüschel an der Stirn. Diesen Beweis haben wir erbracht, dass hier im Westen kahl geschorene Frauen sind in riesiger Zahl. Diese Insel ist allen Stürmen ausgesetzt.'

In dem darauf basierenden Gedicht von George Mackay Brown—Titel: *The Westray Monks*—macht sich der Jarl gerade nicht über die weiberähnlichen Gestalten lustig. Es lautet (Text 5b):[19]

Sixteen walkers about the church,
Heads bare as stone,
Long striders, deep-voiced, rough-handed.
'Brother wind, gentle sister raindrops'—
That's what they call this black whirl of storm.
They haven't a sword between them.
Here they come, in procession,
Demure and harmless as girls.

Die Zeile *Brother wind, gentle sister raindrops* ist ein Anklang an den Sonnengesang des heiligen Franziskus von Assisi.[20] Diese Anleihe ist kein Mangel, denn natürlich steht es in der Freiheit des Autors, Mönchen aus

18 *Orkneyinga Saga* (Nordal (1913–6), 182; *Vísa*: Jónsson (1912–5), 479).

19 George Mackay Brown, *The Westray Monks* (hg. von Bevan und Murray (2006), 157).

20 Vgl. Franziskus von Assisi, *Il Cantico di Frate Sole*: *Laudato si, mi signore, per frate vento* [...] *Laudato si, mi signore, per sor aqua.*

der Mitte des 12. Jahrhunderts einen erst später entstandenen Vers in den Mund zu legen. Wichtig ist, dass Brown die Mönche aufgrund ihrer Art zu gehen und zu reden (*Long striders, deep voiced*) als Männer darstellt, nicht—wie der Jarl in der Saga—als seltsame Zwitterwesen. Hinweis auf das benediktinische Lebensprinzip *ora et labora* ist das Attribut *rough-handed*. Dass die Mönche unbewaffnet sind (*They haven't a sword between them*) wird in der Saga nicht in der Strophe, sondern schon vorab erwähnt. Doch auch im englischen Gedicht haben die Mönche etwas Weibliches an sich. Sie sind *demure and harmless as girls*. Das ist allerdings nicht im Spott gesagt, sondern allenfalls befremdet, vielleicht auch bewundernd.

Es ist in dieser Phase des Gedichtzyklus nicht die Intention von George Mackay Brown, Jarl Rögnvald und seine teilweise ebenfalls poetisch aktiven Mitreisenden zu frommen Männern zu stilisieren. Das geschieht erst am Ende des Zyklus. Die Saga berichtet von Belagerungen, Seekämpfen und Brandschatzungen auf dem Weg von den Orkneys nach Jerusalem. George Mackay Brown steigert vielmehr den Zynismus, der in folgender Strophe, die einem Isländer namens *Eiríkr* zugeschrieben wird, zum Ausdruck kommt. Zunächst die Originalstrophe (Text 6a):[21]

Bœir ro brendir
en búendr ræntir
(svá hefr Sveinn hagat)
sex í morgin
gerði hann eim
œrinn þeirra
leigir þar kol
leigumanni.

'Sechs Höfe sind verbrannt, die Bauern ausgeplündert, so hat es Sveinn beliebt heute morgen. Er machte genügend Asche für sie. Jetzt leiht er Kohle dem Pächter.'

Im Gedicht *The Burning of a Welsh Village* wird bei George Mackay Brown daraus (Text 6b):[22]

Brits, did you order cheap kindling?
We poured flame through your walls this morning
Till the sun was a cinder.

[21] *Orkneyinga Saga* 78 (Nordal (1913–6), 200; *Vísa*: Jónsson (1912–5), 509).

[22] George Mackay Brown, *The Burning of a Welsh Village* (hg. von Bevan und Murray (2006), 158).

Stay in the wood, farmers.
We took our pay in advance,
Silver coins from a niche here and there.
Sweyn was your coalman.
Cracked hearthstone, charred rooftree.
No flint, bellows, or fireside talk next winter.

Anders als in der Sagastrophe wendet sich *Eric the Icelander* in diesem Gedicht direkt an die geflohenen Bauern, und zwar mit der zynischen Frage *Brits, did you order cheap kindling?* Zynisch ist auch die Äußerung, man habe den Preis für die hinterlassene Kohle bereits *in advance* kassiert. Sveinn/Sweyn ist bei George Mackay Brown nicht der Anstifter, sondern er wird zum *coalman.* Am Schluss beschwört Brown ein negatives winterliches Genre-Bild herauf, das aber—sinnbildlich für das Dorf—zerstört wird. Es wird im nächsten Winter nicht zu *flint, bellows, or fireside talk* kommen. Dieses negative Winterbild steht im Kontrast zu den *winterfold flashes* in Text 3b. Die 'Wallfahrer' aus dem Norden werden durchaus als das gezeichnet, was sie bei George Mackay Brown—noch!— sind: nichts weiter als Barbaren.

Das Verhältnis des Jarls Rögnvald zur Herzogin Ermengard von Narbonne hat George Mackay Brown, wie das eingangs zitierte Gedicht zeigt, früh beschäftigt. Die *Orkneyinga Saga* weiß Folgendes zu berichten: Im Sommer des Jahres 1151 traf der Jarl mit seiner Begleitung in Narbonne ein. Dort wurde er von der provençalischen Herzogin Ermengard zu einem Festmahl geladen. Beim ersten Zusammentreffen, so heißt es in der Saga, war sie gekleidet *inum beztum kleþum, hafþi laust harit sem meyium et titt at hafa ok hafþi lagt gullhlaþ um enni ser*[23] ('sie hatte die besten Kleider an. Sie trug das Haar nach Art von Mädchen offen und hatte ein Goldband um die Stirn gelegt'). Sie schenkt dem Jarl eigenhändig ein, während andere Mädchen Tanzvorstellungen bieten. Wenn man der Saga weiter glauben darf, setzte sich Ermengard auf Rögnvalds Schoß, und er sprach folgende *Vísa* (Text 7a):[24]

Víst'r at frá berr flestu
Fróða meldrs at góðu
velskúfarða vífa
vǫxtr þinn, Bil en svinna.
skorð lætr hár á herðar

[23] *Orkneyinga Saga* 86 (Nordal (1913–6), 232).

[24] *Orkneyinga Saga* 86 (Nordal (1913–6), 233; *Vísa*: Jónsson (1912–5), 482).

haukvallar sér falla,
(atgjǫrnum rauðk erni
ilka) gult sem silki.

'Das ist gewiss, dass dein Wuchs, kluge Frau, hervor ragt aus den meisten wohlgezierten Frauen. Die Frau lässt das Haar, gelb wie Seide, sich auf die Schultern fallen. Ich habe dem futtergierigen Adler die Füße gerötet.'

Der aus dem Stegreif dichtende Jarl verwendet darin zwei Frauen-*Kenningar*. Die erste ist *Fróða meldrs Bil* ('Bil des Fródi-Mehls'). Das Mehl des Fróði ist Gold.[25] Die *Bil* (eine weibliche Gottheit) des Goldes ist eine (vornehme) Frau. Die zweite Frauen-*Kenning* ist *skorð haukvallar* ('Stütze des Falkenfeldes'). Mit 'Falkenfeld' ist der Arm gemeint, der einen Jagdfalken trägt. Dessen Stütze ist die Frau. Mit dem letzten Satz rühmt sich Rögnvald als tapferen Krieger. Dass Ermengard diese an sie gerichtete Skaldenstrophe—falls sie der Jarl denn wirklich so gesprochen haben sollte—verstanden hat, darf mit Fug bezweifelt werden. Allenfalls hätte sie sie verstanden, wenn er 'Klartext' ohne *Kenningar* gesprochen hätte (von der Tatsache, dass sie kaum des Altnordischen mächtig gewesen sein dürfte, einmal abgesehen).[26] Die Neufassung von George Mackay Brown, überschrieben *Ermengarde of Narbonne*, ist weit weniger deskriptiv als das, was von Rögnvalds Original nach Auflösung der *Kenningar* übrig bleibt (Text 7b):[27]

Your hair, lady
Is long, a bright waterfall.
You move through the warriors
Rich and tall as starlight.
What can I give
For the cup and kisses brought to my mouth?
Nothing.
This red hand, a death-dealer.

[25] Vom Mehl des Fróði, das von zwei Riesinnen in Mühlen auf dem Meeresboden gemahlen wird, handelt der *Grottasöngr*, das altnordische 'Mühlenlied' (hg. von Neckel und Kuhn (1993), 297–301), das zwar nicht in der Edda steht, aber inhaltlich und formal den eddischen Götterliedern nahe steht.

[26] Zu dieser *Vísa* und überhaupt zu den Umständen, unter denen der sich adelige Skalde Rögnvaldr Kolsson am Hof zu Narbonne aufhielt und mit einiger Sicherheit auch mit zeitgenössischen provençalischen Troubadours in Kontakt kam, vgl. von See (2011), 9–13.

[27] George Mackay Brown, *Ermengarde of Narbonne* (hg. von Bevan und Murray (2006), 161).

Wieder entsteht ein Bild: Die hochgewachsene Dame mit dem prächtigen Haar bewegt sich durch die Reihen, also auch vor dem Hintergrund verwegener und finsterer Kriegergestalten. Der Kontrast dieser Umgebung verleiht ihrer Gestalt (*rich and tall as starlight*) noch stärkeren Glanz. Auch Browns moderner lyrischer Earl Rögnvald spielt wie sein altnordisches Vorbild *Rögnvaldr jarl* mit der letzten Verszeile auf seine kriegerischen Taten an. Sie ist aber nicht (selbst-)rühmend, sondern vor dem Hintergrund des zuvor Gesagten eher verzweifelt: Die Hand des Kriegers kann zwar Tod verteilen, aber nichts, was eine angemessene Gegengabe *for the cup and kisses* wäre. Mit alliterierendem *cup and kisses* verwendet Brown hier ein altnordisches Stilmittel, auf das er sonst nur sehr sparsam zurückgreift. Er unterliegt also nicht dem Irrtum mancher Übersetzer altnordischer Verse, die meinen, mit äußerlichen, mehr oder weniger krampfhaften 'Stabreimen' wikingerzeitliches Kolorit heraufbeschwören zu können.[28]

In der bereits erwähnten Erzählung *A Crusader's Christmas* findet sich ein anderes Gedicht (Text 7c), das aber auf dieselbe altnordische Strophe zurückgeht wie Text 7b:[29]

[28] Beispiel dafür wäre die Wiedergabe dieser Strophe in der Übersetzung der Saga in der Sammlung Thule (Baetke (1924), 152):

'Weiber besiegst im Wuchse
Weiß es, die allermeisten
Du, die feingefransten
Frodismehls Bil, seelvoll.
Sie lässt's Haar, goldseidnes,
Sich umbuhln die Schultern,
Falkenschär'ns Stütz, während färben
Fuß grimm'n Aars ich mußte.'

Auch die Übersetzung der *Orkneyinga Saga* in der Reihe der Penguin Classics (Pálsson und Edwards (1981), 166) bietet alliterierende Übersetzungen. Die entsprechende Strophe lautet hier:

'I'll swear, clever sweetheart,
you're a slender delight
to grasp and to cuddle,
my golden locked girl.
Ravenous the hawk, crimson
—clawed, flesh-crammed—
but now, heavily hangs
the silken hair.'

Auch das ist keine Übersetzung, sondern der Versuch einer Nachdichtung, wobei nicht wie im Original zwei Alliterationen auf die ungeraden Verszeilen entfallen und die dritte auf die jeweils nachfolgende gerade, sondern auch umgekehrt verteilt sein können.

[29] George Mackay Brown, *A Crusader's Christmas* (Brown (2010), 47).

Golden one,
Tall one
Moving in perfume and onyx,
Witty one,
You with the shoulders
Lapped in long silken hair,
Listen: because of me
The eagle has a read claw.

Das ist vermutlich eine spätere Version. Sie steht dem altnordischen Text wieder näher als Text 7b: Ermengard wird darin als größer als die anderen Frauen dargestellt (Körpergröße muss im Mittelalter als ein Zeichen von Vornehmheit gegolten haben), und sie ist klug. Der Satz *because of me the eagle has a read claw* basiert fast wörtlich auf *atgjǫrnum rauðk erni ilka* ('ich habe dem futtergierigen Adler die Füße gerötet').

Nicht nur Rögnvald bewunderte die Schönheit Ermengards. Auch dem Skalden Ármóðr in der Begleitung des Jarls muss der Abschied schwer gefallen sein. Das geht aus einer ihm zugeschriebenen Strophe hervor, die überdies einen sehr eindeutigen nachträglichen und unerfüllten Wunsch zum Ausdruck bringt (Text 8a):[30]

Ek mun Ermingerði,
nema annars skǫp verði,
margr elr sút of svinna,
síðan aldri finna.
værak sæll, ef ek svefa,
(sýn væri þat gæfa)
brúðr hefir allfagrt enni
eina nǿtt hjá henni.

'Ich werde Ermengard nie wieder treffen, außer das Schicksal bestimmt es anders. Mancher ist bekümmert aus Liebe zu der Klugen. Ich wäre glücklich, wenn ich eine Nacht bei ihr schlafen könnte (das wäre ein offensichtliches Geschenk). Das Mädchen hat eine wunderschöne Stirn.'

Die altnordische Strophe hebt sich formal deutlich von den meisten übrigen ab. Sie enthält weder Stab- und Binnenreim noch eine *Kenning*,

[30] *Orkneyinga Saga* 86 (Nordal (1913–6), 234; *Vísa*: Jónsson (1912–5), 511). Vgl. zu dieser Strophe ebenfalls von See (2011), 11–3.

sondern zeigt Endreim. George Mackay Brown hat diese Strophe zu einem *Farewell to Narbonne* umgearbeitet (Text 8b):[31]

A gale of beauty—like rosepetals
My breath scattered.
Throw, voyagers, now
A last farewell to Ermengarde.
(The cut-throats on the rowing bench
As well as Armod
Had one wild dream,
To toss and snore in her bed.)
O heart-broken poet—
That gold-and-ivory forehead!

Ermengards Glanz strahlt bis auf das Schiff, auf dem selbst die *cut-throats*, verurteilte Mörder und Galeerensklaven, von Ermengard träumen, also nicht nur der Jarl und der *heart-broken poet*. Den parenthetischen Satz des Originals (*sýn væri þat gæfa*) hat Brown zu einer eingeschobenen Vision ausgebaut, die bei ihm allerdings nicht eindeutig-erotisch, sondern lediglich 'wild' ist: Die rauen Gesellen träumen auf ihren harten Ruderbänken nur von einem weichen Bett, um endlich darin *to toss and snore*.

Die weitere Reise führt nun mit mehreren Zwischenstationen durch das Mittelmeer nach Jerusalem. Anders als Ármóðr hofft Rögnvald auf eine baldige Rückkehr nach Narbonne (doch weder in der Saga noch in der historischen Realität ist es dazu gekommen). Dieser Hoffnung verleiht er in folgender Strophe Ausdruck (Text 9a):[32]

Orð skal Ermingerðar
ítr drengr muna lengi;
brúðr vill rǫkk, at ríðim
ránheim til Jórðánar
en er aptr fara runnar
unnviggs of haf sunnan
rístum heim, at hausti,
hvalfrón til Nerbónar.

[31] George Mackay Brown, *Farewell to Narbonne* (hg. von Bevan und Murray (2006), 161).

[32] *Orkneyinga Saga* 86 (Nordal (1913–6), 234; *Vísa*: Jónsson (1912–5), 482).

> 'Der Mann wird sich lange an Ermengards herrliche Worte erinnern. Die treffliche Frau will, dass wir hin segeln sollen zum Jordan. Aber wenn die Krieger (= des Wogenpferdes Büsche) zurück kommen im Herbst über das Meer von Süden, ritzen wir das Wal-Land heim nach Narbonne.'

George Mackay Browns *Love Song* setzt diese Saga-Strophe so um (Text 9b):[33]

> *The summer mouth of Ermengarde*
> *Commands two things—*
> *A sea of saga-stuff, wreckage, gold,*
> *As far as Jordan,*
> *And later, at leaf-fall,*
> *On patched homing wings*
> *A sun-dark hero.*

Ermengards 'Worten' (*Orð* [...] *Ermingerðar*) entspricht hier *The summer mouth of Ermengarde.* Möglicherweise sind Browns *patched homing wings* angeregt von *unnviggs* ('des Wogenpferdes'). Das würde allerdings voraussetzen, dass seine Gedichte nicht ausschließlich auf englischen Übersetzungen der *Orkneyinga Saga* basieren, sondern dass er auch den altnordischen Originaltext vor Augen hatte. Dem Stabreim *heim–hausti* im Original korrespondiert die Alliteration *later–leaf-fall* bei George Mackay Brown. Der Krieger (*drengr*) in der zweiten Zeile des altnordischen Textes wird am Schluss des englischen Gedichtes zum *sun-dark hero*, zu einem unter der Sonne Palästinas gebräunten Kämpfer.

Im weiteren Verlauf der Reise, so die *Orkneyinga Saga*, leisten Rögnvald und seine Leute einem Dorf Hilfe, dessen Bewohner regelmäßig willkürlich vom Burgherren ausgeplündert werden.[34] Die Burg wird unter Schwierigkeiten und Verlusten erobert. Durch hohe Scheiterhaufen, die dicht an der Mauer angezündet werden, bringt man Stücke der Befestigung zum Bersten. Beim Vordringen in die Burg denkt Rögnvald zurück an Ermengard von Narbonne (Text 10a):[35]

[33] George Mackay Brown, *Love Song* (hg. von Bevan und Murray (2006), 161).

[34] Die Episode hat George Mackay Brown in der Kurzgeschichte *A Crusader's Christmas* verarbeitet.

[35] *Orkneyinga Saga* 87 (Nordal (1913–6), 239–40; *Vísa*: Jónsson (1912–5), 482–3).

Vín bar hvít en hreina
hlaðnipt alindriptar
sýndisk fegrð, er fundumk,
ferðum Ermingerdar.
nú tegask ǫld með eldi
eljunfrækn at sækja,
(ríða snǫrp ór slíðrum
sverð) kastala ferðir.

'Wein brachte die weiße und reine Frau [*hlaðnipt alindriptar* = Göttin der Goldbänder], als wir uns trafen. Ermengards Schönheit zeigte sich vor den Reisenden. Nun ist die tapfere Schar [*eljunfrækn ǫld*] auf dem Weg, um das Burgvolk mit Feuer anzugreifen. Die scharfen Schwerter kommen aus der Scheide.'

In der Saga-Strophe ist nur eingangs von der Farbe Weiß die Rede. Es ist ein Attribut für Ermengard. George Mackay Brown macht die Farben Weiß und Rot (das in der Saga-Strophe nicht vorkommt) zu einer Art von Leitmotiven in dem Gedicht *Love and War* (Text 10b):[36]

White as snow
White as silver
The lady,
A beauty all whiteness,
A kindness
Red as wine.
Another redness, fire
About the castle
A sharp whiteness, swords.

Weiß wie Schnee und Silber ist also in der Erinnerung des Jarls die Herzogin von Narbonne. Dieselbe Farbe sieht er aber auch in den blanken Schwertern, die beim Sturm auf die Burg gezückt sind. Ebenso bringt er die Farbe Rot mit Ermengard in Verbindung und findet sie wieder im Feuerschein der brennenden Burg.

Vom Jerusalem-Aufenthalt selbst wird in der Saga äußerst wenig berichtet (s.o.). Die letzte Zeile der folgenden *Vísa* nimmt bereits Bezug auf die Männer, die schon wieder im Aufbruch begriffen sind (Text 11a):[37]

[36] George Mackay Brown, *Love and War* (hg. von Bevan und Murray (2006), 162).

[37] *Orkneyinga Saga* 88 (Nordal (1913–6), 255–6; *Vísa*: Jónsson (1912–5), 486).

Kross hangir þul þessum
(þjóst skyli lægt) fyr brjósti
flykkisk framm á brekkur
ferð, en palmr meðal herða.

'Ein Kreuz hängt von der Brust dem Dichter und ein Palmzweig zwischen den Schultern. Friede sollte geschlossen werden. Die Schar sammelt sich vorne am Abhang.'

Das entsprechende Gedicht im Zyklus von George Mackay Brown, überschrieben *Jerusalem*, ist deutlich länger, bild- und wortreicher (Text 11b):[38]

We stand here, shriven,
A hundred warmen lustred with penance,
In each hand
Assoiled from murders, whoredoms, thievings now
A leaf of palm.
Footsteps, free and fated, turn
To the fourteen redemptive lingerings
And the hill marked † with this sign.

Während der Jarl in der Saga mit knappen Worten und distanziert das Gesehene mehr andeutet als beschreibt, spricht George Mackay Browns Earl in der Wir-Form, schließt sich also selbst mit ein. Auf der Original-Strophe basiert *a leaf of palm* (zu altnordischem *palmr*) als frommes Zeichen. In der Saga-Strophe dient der Abhang bereits als Sammelpunkt für die Abreise. Bei George Mackay Brown ist es ein mit einem Kreuz markierter Berg, den man sich wohl als den Kalvarienberg vorzustellen hat. Von *penance* und den Sünden, die vergeben worden sind (*murders, whoredoms, thievings*) ist in der Saga nicht die Rede. Dort sind die Pilgerzeichen Kreuz und Palmenzweig äußere Symbole. Bei Brown dagegen endet die Pilgerreise in Ergriffenheit und tief empfundener Reue. In der Saga haben es die Nordmänner offenbar sehr eilig, wieder zurück aufs Meer und nach Konstantinopel, letztlich also die alte Normalität, zu kommen.

Die letzte Strophe des Jarls auf der Reise lautet (Text 12a):[39]

[38] George Mackay Brown, *Jerusalem* (hg. von Bevan und Murray (2006), 164).

[39] *Orkneyinga Saga* 88 (Nordal (1913–6), 258; *Vísa*: Jónsson (1912–5), 486).

Ríðum Ræfils Vakri
rekuma plóg af akri
erjum úrgu barði.
út á Miklagarði.
þiggium þengils mála,
þokum fram i gný stála,
rjóðum gylðz góma,
gerum ríks konungs sóma.

'Lasst uns nach Konstantinopel segeln [*ríða Ræfils Vakri* = reiten Ræfils Wackeren = das Schiff]. Lasst uns den Pflug nicht fernab vom Acker führen, sondern pflügen mit dem nassen Bug. Lasst uns die Belohnung des Königs entgegen nehmen. Lasst uns vorwärts drängen im Kampf (*gný stála* = Lärm der Stahle). Lasst uns rot färben die Gabe des Wolfes. Lasst uns des mächtigen Königs Ehre vollbringen.'

Das heißt: Der Schiffsbug soll das Meer mit Kurs auf Konstantinopel (altnordisch *Míklagarðr*) pflügen. Dort waren bekanntlich skandinavische Waräger die Leibgarde des Kaisers. Der König, für dessen Ehre man 'die Gabe des Wolfes rot färben', das heißt nichts anderes als erneut in blutige Kämpfe ziehen will, ist also nicht etwa Christus, sondern der ganz irdische oströmische Kaiser. Auf dieser Strophe basiert nun das letzte Gedicht *A Mass at Sea* im Zyklus von George Mackay Brown (Text 12b):[40]

We left our shares to rust
On a northern hill,
Exchanged oxen for green and blue tramplers!
Poet, peasant, priest,
One ark of pilgrims
Out of the dragon sea, a seaking
Into the lucencies of Christ.
(Salt furrows we make
Under your headlands, Byzantium.)
Sin darkens the grain-hoard.
We have branded their coasts with rage and lust,
The old dragon-breath.
No end of sorrow, soultroth, still.
Kyrie, Christe, Kyrie eleison
The Golden Harvester
Seeks orient, our swineherd mouths.

[40] George Mackay Brown, *A Mass at Sea* (hg. von Bevan und Murray (2006), 164).

Von einer Messe auf hoher See ist nirgendwo in der *Orkneyinga Saga* die Rede. Was George Mackay Brown aus der alten Strophe übernimmt, ist das Bild vom pflügenden Schiffsbug. Dort heißt es *rekuma plóg af akri* ('lasst uns den Pflug nicht fernab vom Acker führen'). Mit dem Acker ist hier das Meer gemeint. Im Gedicht von Brown findet sich dasselbe Bild wieder: *Salt furrows we make.* Anders als Rögnvald und seine Krieger, die in neue Kämpfe ziehen werden, haben die Jerusalemfahrer bei Brown die Kämpfe hinter sich: *We have branded their coasts with rage and lust, The old dragon-breath.* Auch wenn zeitlebens kein Ende von *sorrow* und *soultroth* zu erwarten ist, bittet Browns Earl—anders als der Jarl der Saga—mit dem Gebetsruf *Kyrie, Christe, Kyrie eleison* um Erbarmen.—Wohl kaum Zufall, sondern gewollt sind in diesem Gedicht die Alliterationen *Poet, peasant, priest, pilgrims* sowie *sorrow, soultroth.*

Zusammenfassung

In sprachlicher Hinsicht versucht George Mackay Brown erst gar nicht, durch Stab- und Binnenreime oder kenningartige Metaphern eine (pseudo-)historische Tonlage zu erzeugen. Altnordische Reminiszenzen wie Alliteration und Binnenreim kommen zwar sporadisch vor, wirken zumeist aber wie selbstverständlich und niemals gekünstelt. Browns Sprache erinnert eher an die von ihm so geschätzte karge Saga-Prosa: *It is good, for a certain kind of writing, to use as few words as possible* (s.o.). In der originalen *Orkneyinga Saga* stehen (wie in vielen isländischen Sagas) die manierierten Skaldenstrophen im extremen Kontrast zu dem ansonsten eher lakonischen Prosatext. Oder anders gesagt: Browns lyrische Bearbeitungen der Saga-Verse stehen stilistisch der Saga-Prosa weitaus näher als den Saga-Strophen. Das heißt nicht, dass die Sprache in seinen Gedichten bildlos wäre. Das Gegenteil ist der Fall: Nur einige Beispiele sind *winterfold flashes* und *clamorous shadow* (Text 3b), *mouthfuls of sea* (Text 4b), *heads bare as stone* (Text 5b), *rich and tall as starlight* (Text 7b), *the summer mouth of Ermengarde* oder *a sea of saga-stuff, wreckage, gold* (Text 9b). Charakteristisch sind auch Wortkompositionen wie *time-accursed* (Text 1), *deep-voiced, rough-handed* (Text 5b) oder *a death-dealer* (Text 7b). Immer wieder versteht es Brown, mit wenigen Worten beim Leser bildliche Assoziationen zu erzeugen.

Inhaltlich gesehen handelt es sich bei Earl Rögnvalds Jerusalem-Fahrt in Browns lyrischer Darstellung um eine Reise zum Glauben, während in der *Orkneyinga Saga* doch sehr eindeutig die unterwegs erlebten Abenteuer im Vordergrund stehen und vom Aufenthalt in Jerusalem fast nicht die Rede ist. Vor allem das fromme Ende der Wallfahrt im Gedichtszyklus des zur katholischen Kirche konvertierten Autors könnte ein Reflex seiner eigener Biographie sein.[41]

George Mackay Browns Gedichte des Zyklus *Kestrel, Roseleaf, Chalice* sind keine Übersetzungen und mit Ausnahme der Asa-Verse (Text 2b) und *The Accomplishments of a Jarl* (Text 3b) auch weit mehr als freie Übertragungen der Originale. Vielfach ist es nur ein einzelnes Wort, eine Fügung oder ein Gedanke einer Saga-Strophe, worauf ein neues Gedicht basiert. Im Fall der Texte 4a/b ist es der Ring bzw. Armreifen, den sich der Jarl als Zeichen seiner Unbekümmertheit während des Unwetters von Arm streift, im Fall der Texte 5a/b sind es die frauenähnlichen Mönchsgestalten. In den Texten 6a/b wird übereinstimmend der Name des Brandstifters (*Sveinn/Sweyn*) genannt. In das englische Gedicht ist—sogar verstärkt—auch der zynische Ton des Originals übernommen. Texte 7a/b/c preisen zwar übereinstimmend Ermengards erhabene Schönheit und ihr langes Haar. Der selbstreflexive Satz Rögnvalds am Ende der Strophe steht in allen drei Texten in einem jeweils anderen Verhältnis zum unmittelbar davor Gesagten. In den Texten 8a/b kommt die Sehnsucht nach Ermengards Bett um Ausdruck, doch im Original ist es der Skalde, der diese Sehnsucht äußert, in Text 8b wird sie der Schiffsmannschaft zugeschrieben. In den Texten 9a/b wird zwar übereinstimmend die Rückkehr von Jerusalem thematisiert. Die Erinnerung an Ermengard und die Vision von der Rückkehr sind ganz unterschiedlich gestaltet: Bei George Mackay Brown sieht sich Rögnvald selbst als sonnenverbrannter *hero* zurückkehren. In der zugrunde liegenden Strophe ist von 'wir' (*rístum* ist 1. Person Plural) die Rede. Text 10b stellt das Adjektiv 'weiß' in unterschiedliche Bezüge. In der *Vísa* kommt es nur einmal vor, und zwar als Attribut zu *vín* ('Wein'). Inhaltlich am weitesten vom Original entfernen sich die beiden letzten zitierten Gedichte von George Mackay Brown. In Text 12a ist zwar von einem Pflug (*plóg*) die Rede, doch wird das Wort im metaphorischen Zusammenhang verwendet: Gemeint ist der Schiffsbug, der das Wasser 'pflügt'. George Mackay Brown greift das Wort mit *shares* auf, stellt dieses aber in einen ganz anderen Zusammenhang: *We left our shares to rust / On a northern hill.* Sein Earl Rögnvald spricht von den zuhause zurückgelassenen, mittlerweile rostenden Pflugscharen, greift allerdings auch die Pflug-Bug-Metapher auf: *Salt furrows we make.*

[41] Vgl. dazu Murray und Murray (2004), 90–5.

In den beiden zuletzt zitierten und besprochenen Gedichten schreibt George Mackay Brown den Reisenden Bekehrungserlebnisse zu, von denen in der Saga überhaupt nicht die Rede ist. Lässt man die Abfolge der Gedichte insgesamt Revue passieren, so zeigt sich, dass sich der Autor von *Kestrel, Roseleaf, Chalice* mehr und mehr von seinen Vorlagen entfernt.

Eine offene Frage wäre, welche Textvorlage(n) George Mackay Brown benützt hat. Verwendete er eine englische Übersetzung der *Orkneyinga Saga* oder ging er—möglicherweise mit Hilfe eines Fachmannes—(auch) vom altnordischen Originaltext aus? Für die zweite Möglichkeit spricht die Tatsache, dass er gelegentlich altnordische Stilmittel wie Stab- und Binnenreim verwendet, allerdings—wie bereits festgestellt—nur in sehr geringem Umfang. Möglicherweise hat George Mackay Brown die gängige Penguin-Übersetzung verwendet, sich von deren Nachdichtungen aber nicht zu alliterierenden pseudo-nordischen Versen verleiten lassen.

Literaturverzeichnis

Baetke, W. (1924) *Die Geschichten von den Orkaden, Dänemark und der Jomsburg*, Jena.

Bevan, A. und B. Murray (2006) *The collected poems of George Mackay Brown*, London.

Brown, G.M. (1997) *For the islands I sing. An autobiography*, London.

— (2010) *Winter tales*, London.

Jónsson, F. (1912–5) *Den Norsk-Islanske Skjaldedigtning 800–1200*, København.

Murray, R. und B. Murray (2004) *Interrogation of silence. The writings of George Mackay Brown*, London.

Neckel, G. und H. Kuhn (1993) *Edda. Die Lieder des Codex regius nebst verwandten Denkmälern, I. Text*, 6. Aufl., Heidelberg.

Nordal, S. (1913–6) *Orkneyinga saga*, København.

Pálsson, H. und P. Edwards (1981) *Orkneyinga Saga. The history of the Earls of Orkney*, London.

Simek, R. und H. Pálsson (2007) *Lexikon der altnordischen Literatur*, Stuttgart.

Uecker, H. (2004) *Geschichte der altnordischen Literatur*, Stuttgart.

von See, K. (2011) *Skalden. Isländische Dichter des Mittelalters*, Heidelberg.

NICHOLAS CAROLAN

'OUT OF THE SMOKE': A. MARTIN FREEMAN'S WEST CORK SONG COLLECTION OF 1913–14

Abstract

An important collection of Irish-language traditional songs (melodies and words) was made by the English collector A. Martin Freeman (1878–1959) in Ballyvourney, Co. Cork, in 1913 and 1914. Published in the *Journal of the Folk-Song Society* in London in the troubled years of 1920–21 but of limited circulation, the collection is little-known, and access to it has been further restricted by Freeman's use of a scientific but difficult phonetic orthography. Freeman's field-notebooks survive in the National Folklore Collection, University College Dublin. This illustrated article outlines Freeman's career in music and his Irish collecting trips, his published Ballyvourney collection and his surviving notebooks. It provides a title and first-line listing of the published collection in standard Irish, and gives direction to digitized online versions of the collection and to online interactive scores of its melodies.

Keywords

A. Martin Freeman, Conny Coughlan/Conchubhar Ó Cochláin; collection of Irish traditional songs; Ballyvourney, Co. Cork; songs in Irish.

One of the most sympathetically gathered and accurately noted collections of Irish-language traditional song was made by A. Martin Freeman, an English enthusiast in his mid-thirties, in the district of Ballyvourney in west Cork a hundred years ago.[1] Although the collection

[1] Dáibhí Ó Cróinín's achievements in the study and publication of history and language—not to mention his novel-writing and television-presenting—will have obscured the fact that he has also edited the Irish- and English-language traditional songs of his west Cork grandmother in a best-selling publication: Ó Cróinín (2000). Other members of the Ó Cróinín family, especially Dáibhí's father Donncha and uncle Seán, have also made distinguished contributions to the collection and publication of Irish

Early medieval Ireland and Europe: chronology, contacts, scholarship, ed. by Pádraic Moran and Immo Warntjes, Studia Traditionis Theologiae, 14 (Turnhout, 2015), pp. 695–715.

 10.1484/M.STT-EB.5.103141

was substantial and was published almost in its entirety within a few years of its making, and was described by an authority fifty years ago as 'incomparably the finest collection published in our time of Irish songs noted from oral tradition',[2] it is little known.

Plate 1 A. Martin Freeman on the Isle of Canna, *c.* 1940s (courtesy Canna House, National Trust for Scotland).

There are several reasons for this obscurity: among them the English residence, if not the nationality, of the collector, and the publication of the collection in London in 1920–21 and in the *Journal of the* [Eng-

folklore and other Irish-language materials. This essay outlines the work of a predecessor in their field, and a fellow historian and Gaelic scholar.

[2] O'Sullivan (1960a), part of the Donal O'Sullivan Collection, National Folklore Collection, University College Dublin [hereafter DOSC, NFC]. This typescript is the original of several somewhat shorter published obituaries of Freeman by O'Sullivan (1960b), (1960c), (1961). O'Sullivan (1893–1973, born in Liverpool of Kerry parents) had been a friend and colleague of Freeman's since at least 1920, and his careful note summarizes Freeman's musical activities. Family and personal information on Freeman had been supplied to O'Sullivan for his obituaries by Freeman's only sister Phoebe Annie Freeman (letter of 11 Jan. 1960 from Sussex, Box 23, DOSC, NFC), and by his solicitors Longhurst & Butler (letter of 30 May 1960 from Surrey, ibid.). An anonymous obituary appeared in *The Irish Times* (8 Jan. 1960, p 5) and Brian Ó Cuív contributed a brief obituary to *Éigse*: Ó Cuív (1959–60). O'Sullivan (1960a) is the source of biographical facts given here unless they are otherwise attributed.

lish] *Folk-Song Society* [hereafter *JFSS*]. This had a small circulation in Ireland, even smaller than that of the contemporary *Journal of the Irish Folk Song Society* (which was also published in London). Suffering from indifferent health and of a retiring disposition, Freeman led the secluded life of a private scholar. Unlike most collectors of Irish-language traditional song of the day, he was not active in the language-revival movement in Ireland but rather belonged to the world of Irish and other cultural organizations in England. His collection received little attention when it appeared in print during the politically and militarily fraught years of 1920 and 1921 in Ireland, and it doubtless shared in the neglect suffered by many Irish-language cultural enterprises among the divisions and disillusionment caused by the Civil War. Although the work was written in English, with translations of the song texts into English, Freeman's choice of a scientific but little-used phonetic simplified-spelling orthography for the presentation of his Irish-language texts[3] (see e.g. *Plates 2, 4, 7*) restricted contemporary access to the songs, and it has remained a barrier to their use ever since.

Nevertheless, a century after its creation, Freeman's west Cork collection retains its importance as a documentation of a significant Irish song tradition with local and regional dimensions, as do his surviving music manuscripts and field-notes from Ballyvourney. This is a tradition which still survives with some vigour, although it has suffered continuing erosion with the spread of English. Songs in the collection have been successfully studied and revived in recent times in their own locality and more have the potential of being brought back into active performance. Access to the original publication of 1920–21 has recently been increased by its digitization as part of the *JFSS* and the addition of the journal to the online database JSTOR (www.jstor.org), which is available by subscription and through libraries. In addition a PDF facsimile of the published collection and interactive music scores of its melodies have been made available online as an extension of this essay at www.itma.ie, the website of the Irish Traditional Music Archive (see Appendix below). It is hoped that this essay will further increase this access for singers and scholars by drawing attention to Freeman's collection and by describing and contextualising it in outline.

Alexander Martin Freeman was born on 7 May 1878 in Upper Tooting, south London, the only son of Hubert Alexander Freeman, an architect, and his wife Sarah Maria Jones. He was educated at Bedford

[3] 'Text' is used here throughout to denote verbal text rather than melodic notation.

Grammar School and Lincoln College, Oxford, but his studies were adversely affected by poor health. A good amateur musician and tenor singer, he had seemingly a private income, and after graduation led a life of 'unremitting study and reflective writing'.[4] In 1908 he married

Plate 2 Facsimile page from the published Freeman collection illustrating his idiosyncratic orthography and his care in recording melodic variants. (Public domain.)

[4] O'Sullivan (1960a). Freeman is described as a journalist in 1929 in the grant of probate for his father ('England & Wales, National Probate Calendar' at www.ancestry.com), but this probably only refers to his occasional music writings.

Adelaide Letitia Peoples (1873–1942) of Moville, Co. Donegal, also known as Harriet Aïda or Ada Peoples.[5] She was a painter[6] and a violinist who played Irish music at London concerts and took part in Irish-language dramas there.[7] Brought into touch with various Irish circles, cultural and linguistic, in London, such as the Irish Literary Society in Hanover Square, Freeman studied Irish under Kuno Meyer at University College London, and acquired a good knowledge of the language, including Old and Middle Irish. His surviving notebooks contain copyings from Old Irish published sources and more extensive gleanings of vocabulary, phraseology, proverbs and song texts copied and clipped from the contemporary Irish-language press from 1911 into the 1920s. His early Irish-language studies also encompassed such standard song collections as Hardiman (1831), Walsh (1847) and the various editions of O'Daly (1849), and miscellaneous Gaelic League publications. Although he was over military age and had bad sight and hearing, Freeman served under canvas in the Royal Army Service Corps during the First World War and was based in Greece, in Salonika. For the entire duration of the Second World War he served as a full-time air-raid warden in London. He was a Council member of the Irish Texts Society there from about 1922 and, having succeeded Robin Flower, was its Chairman from 1945 until his death.[8] Living for over 40 years at 166 Lauderdale Court in Maida Vale, he became something of a recluse after his wife's death in 1942, and died aged 81 in London on 18 December 1959. His books were sold for his sister by Fletchers of Cecil Court, London, and his music papers, including those of his Ballyvourney collection, came into the possession of his long-time friend and colleague Donal O'Sullivan, with whom he had spent holidays in Dublin. These were among O'Sullivan's papers at the time of the latter's death; they now form part of the Donal O'Sullivan Collection, National Folklore Collection, University College Dublin.[9]

[5] The first form of her name is given in the record of their marriage ('All England & Wales [...] Marriage Index, 1837–1915' at www.ancestry.com); the second in O'Sullivan (1960a).

[6] *Irish Independent*, 15 June 1932, p 9, and 12 July 1934, p 8, carry notices of exhibitions.

[7] Breathnach and Ní Mhurchú (1990), 39. Listings of officers in *The Journal of the Irish Folk Song Society* record that she served the Society from 1920 to 1939 as its Hon. Financial Secretary.

[8] *The Irish Times*, 8 Jan. 1960, p 5.

[9] The Donal O'Sullivan Collection was donated to the Department of Irish Folklore, University College Dublin, in 1973 by his widow Jeannie O'Sullivan, and it is

Freeman's intellectual interests were wide, as evidenced by the range of his publications. The earliest of these were literary and archival: *Thomas Love Peacock: a critical study* (London, 1911),[10] followed by *Vanessa and her correspondence with Jonathan Swift: the letters edited for the first time from the originals* (London, 1921). The political debates of the period before the Great War seem to have inspired *Freedom,* a work on the subject of liberty (London, 1913). The transcription and editing of historical sources dominated the latter part of Freeman's life: 'The Annals [of Boyle] in Cotton MS A.XXV' (1929),[11] 'Betha Mhuire Eigiptachda' (1936),[12] *The Compossician Booke of Conought* (Dublin, 1936), and his *magnum opus Annála Connacht: the Annals of Connacht (A.D. 1224–1544)* (1933–34, 1944).[13]

Traditional song was also an abiding interest throughout Freeman's life, and a focus of publication and social involvement. He had an early interest in the songs of William Byrd and Thomas Ravenscroft,[14] and had an association with the Madrigal Society.[15] At the same time he was copying into his music manuscripts English folk melodies of the kind popularized by Cecil Sharp and Irish melodies from the published collections of P.W. Joyce. From 1909 he was noting down London lavender-sellers cries and other traditional pieces, and from 1915 was publishing occasional items in the *JFSS* and giving occasional lectures on folk-music topics.[16] His association with the Society continued until his death, and he belonged to the second wave of the Society's collectors and scholars, such as Lucy Broadwood, Anne Gilchrist and J. Frederick Keel, who regarded their work as more 'scientific' than those of the founding members of 1898.[17] In 1915 in London he was collecting Italian songs from women singers from Rome and Irish songs in English

now in the National Folklore Collection there. Boxes 21–24 of the Collection contain the Freeman materials, with a letter from Freeman to O'Sullivan in Box 5.

[10] Reprinted 1969, 1974, 1976, 1977.

[11] *Revue celtique* 41–44.

[12] *Études celtiques* 1.

[13] Part published in *Revue celtique* 50–51 (1933–34); completed edition published by the Dublin Institute for Advanced Studies in 1944.

[14] Unsourced statements about Freeman's musical activities in this essay are based on his personal music MSS in Box 23, DOSC, NFC.

[15] Freeman (1941), 271.

[16] One lecture seemingly arose from his Ballyvourney trips: he read a paper 'An Irish festival' to a meeting of the Folk-Lore Society in London, 19 May 1915 (*Folk-Lore: Transactions of the Folk-Lore Society* 26, no. 2 (June 1915), 113).

[17] Broadwood (1920).

from a west Clare singer Frank Brewe. Three years later Freeman made a manuscript collection of Serbian traditional songs while in Turkey during his war service.[18] Although he had access to Lucy Broadwood's cylinder phonograph, he seems only to have used it infrequently.[19] After the war he became a member of the Editorial Committee of *JFSS* from 1919 until 1931 and of the Editorial Board of its successor, the *Journal of the English Folk Dance and Song Society*, from 1932 until his death in 1959,[20] and was an occasional contributor to both journals, as he was to the *Journal of the International Folk Music Council*. He was also a member of the Publication Committee of the Irish Folk Song Society from 1920 until its demise in 1939 and made important contributions to its *Journal*. About 1926 seemingly, Freeman made a small collection of Irish-language song texts from named sources, along with stories and vocabulary, on Achill Island, Co. Mayo.[21] He contributed materially from 1927 to 1939 to the editing and translating of the Irish-language texts of Donal O'Sullivan's edition of the Bunting Collection of Irish Folk Music and Songs, and to the editing of its melodies, as published in its *Journal*.[22] During those years he noted down occasional songs and melodies from live performance, but in a desultory fashion. He was a regular visitor for a time to his collector musician friends John Lorne Campbell and Margaret Fay Shaw in the Scottish Hebrides, and they persuaded him to sing six of his Ballyvourney songs onto a wire recorder.[23] He contributed modal analysis to Fay Shaw's important 1955 volume *Folksongs and Folklore of South Uist*;[24] after his death she agreed

[18] MS music book (music and texts) 'Twenty Four Serbian Songs collected in Kara Burun from the Serb Guards at the A.S.C. Supply Depot, in the winter of 1918–1919', Box 23, DOSC, NFC.

[19] One occasion was in 1915 to record the mouth-whistling of Brewe and another in 1921 to record the whistling of a Martin Ahern of west Clare (music MS with marbled paper covers, Box 23, DOSC, NFC). The cylinder of Brewe survives and can be heard on the website of the British Library at https://sounds.bl.uk (search 'Freeman').

[20] He is listed as such in both journals throughout this period.

[21] These are preserved in two MS copybooks 'Aichill' and 'Aichill Irish' (Box 24, DOSC, NFC). They are undated but Mrs Freeman had an 'At Home' exhibition of Achill watercolours in London in 1927 (*Irish Independent*, 1 April 1927, p 6).

[22] *JFSS* 22–29 (1927–1939). O'Sullivan itemizes their joint contributions ('Preface', *JFSS* 22 (1927), vii).

[23] Songs 1, 12, 20, 25, 26, 32: letter from John Lorne Campbell to Donal O'Sullivan, 17 Jan. 1960 (Box 23, DOSC, NFC). Although Campbell-Shaw recordings have been digitized for the online Scottish website www.tobarandualchais.co.uk, the recordings of Freeman are not among them.

[24] London, 2nd ed. Oxford 1977.

with Donal O'Sullivan that Freeman was 'a noble character'.[25] He was still publishing brief, astringent folk-music reviews as late as 1958, the year before his death.[26]

But Freeman's most substantial contribution by far to the publishing and study of traditional song was his work on Irish-language traditional song. In August–September 1913 the Freemans spent a holiday in the Irish-speaking district of Ballyvourney, Co. Cork. Becoming aware of its rich song tradition and conscious that English was making inroads into the district, especially among younger people, he noted down on paper there the words and melodies of a small number of songs,[27] songs which he would collect again in 1914 (see *Plates 3–7*). He found the singers 'singularly good vocalists. They are blessed with just the right amount of 'nasal resonance'; their voices are easy, clear and full and their tone pure; they never exert themselves to sing loud, or pitch their songs too high. Time is of course their slave, not their master, and rhythm is their triumph.'[28] Instrumental music was played only for dancing, not for listening.[29] The couple returned in August 1914 for a purposeful visit of ten weeks, during which Freeman, armed with notebooks printed with music-staves and with a tuning fork in A, noted down the songs which make up his published collection.

He ranged widely among the neighbourhood singers, and was well received by them: the people 'manifested a lively interest in my quest [...] were amazed at my industry and astonished at the result'.[30] But his main source was an illiterate, bilingual farm labourer Conny Cochlan (Conchubhar Ó Cochláin) from Derrynasagart, a 'tuneful and easy singer, never forcing a note' who provided him with about half the songs in his collection, and remembered words omitted from songs collected from others.[31] Cochlan was something over 80 years of age in 1914, but was very active and alert, and had a keen interest in the Irish language. Free-

[25] Letter to O'Sullivan, 3 Jan. 1960 (Box 23, DOSC, NFC).

[26] Freeman (1958).

[27] Blue copybook with paper covers, 16 × 20 cm (Box 23, DOSC, NFC). This is a diary-notebook, the first half of which is headed 'Voyage to Ireland August–September 1913', the second 'Second visit to Ireland August– 1914'. Its few music notations were written in 1913 on hand-ruled music staves on stray pages of the copybook: Freeman had not come prepared to collect music in that year.

[28] *JFFS* 23 (Jan. 1921), xx.

[29] *JFFS* 23 (Jan. 1920), 101.

[30] *JFFS* 25 (Sept. 1921), 334.

[31] *JFSS* 23 (Jan. 1920), xix.

man had begun noting his songs in September 1913, 'when he was [...] in the kitchen of Shanacloon and I was in the room above—only boards between us, and plenty of cracks and holes in them'.[32] In spite of occasional moodiness, Cochlan was soon won over to Freeman's 1914 project: 'When my last days in the country arrived he talked with great pleasure of the amount I had recovered [...] 'There are not', he said, 'any two men in Ireland who could do what you and I have done this *fôr* (August to October)'.'[33] Freeman also published songs from three other of his Ballyvourney singers: Mrs Mary Sweeny (Máirín Ní Shuibhne) of Coolea, who was about 78 and had a store of Jacobite songs, her voice 'very small and feeble but well in tune'; Miss Peg O'Donoghue (Peig Ní Dhonnchadha) of Ballymakeery, who was also about 78 and was 'the best natural musician I met in the district [...] she is infirm, emotional, excitable [...] When singing a complete song she becomes ecstatic'; and 37-year-old Miss Abbey Barrett (Gobnait Baróid) who 'has a good ear and a pleasant, very small voice', and who unlike the others was literate, in Irish and English.[34]

Freeman's song manuscripts survive in several sequences, rough and faircopied. Some contain primarily melodies, others verbal texts.

Song melodies and variants are found in two numbered sequences of manuscripts. The first consists of seven unlabelled copybooks (16 × 20.5 cm) with coloured marbled paper covers, printed with music-staves on alternate pages and dating from 7 August to 2 October 1914.[35] They contain pencil notations of some 108 melodies with the first verse of each underlaid and written in conventional Irish orthography of the period. The name of the singer, the date of performance, and various points of language and musical style are also recorded. Some melodies which gave trouble and led to untidy notations were written in 'clean versions' on a following page. The second melody sequence consists of six copybooks of the same kind, labelled 'Book i–vi'[36] and faircopied in ink, which derive from the rougher first sequence but contain only 70 songs with variants. A process of selection and consolidation had been undertaken. The underlaid verses are now written in a phonetic kind of orthography; the order of melodies is only generally that of the published collection. The subjects

[32] Faircopy music copybook i (Box 21, DOSC, NFC). The parallel with J.M. Synge's famous note-taking of speech idioms in Wicklow is striking.

[33] *JFSS* 25 (Sept. 1921), 334.

[34] 'The Singers', *JFSS* 23 (Jan. 1920), xix–xx.

[35] Box 21, DOSC, NFC.

[36] Ibid.

of the songs are those of Irish-language traditional song in general—love, marriage, death, politics, drinking, comic events, adventures, etc.—with a good and unique admixture of songs on local people and places. Versions of many of the songs are known across Munster, and some further afield.

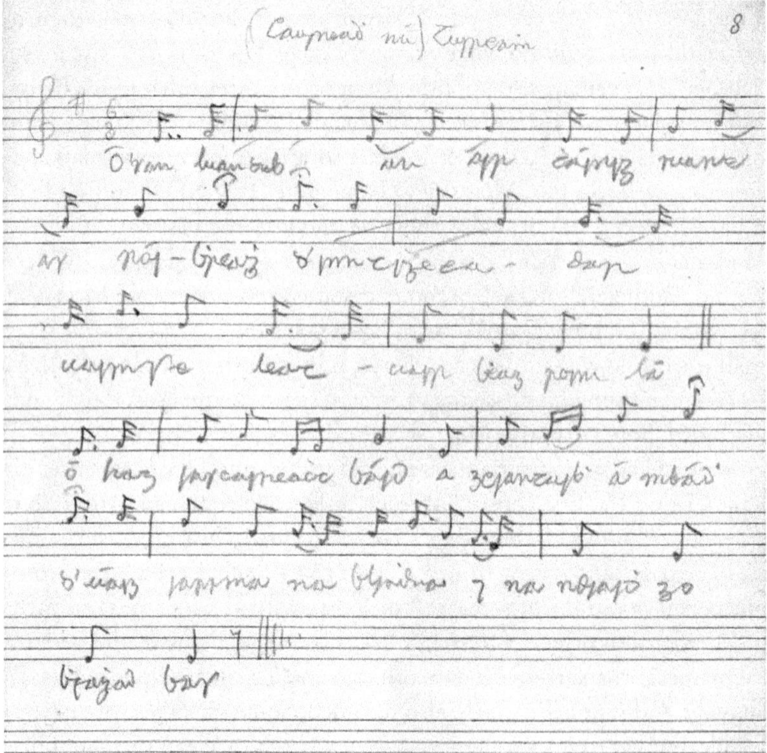

Plate 3 Melody with underlaid verse in conventional orthography as taken down by Freeman in the field (courtesy National Folklore Collection, UCD).

Song texts and variants are found in an individual manuscript and in three later numbered sequences of manuscripts. The individual manuscript, a diary-notebook already mentioned,[37] contains 12 song-texts with the first verses omitted and noted in 1914. The first sequence consists of four brown 'Munster Arms Series' copybooks (16 × 20 cm) with paper covers, undated and labelled 'Rough I–IV',[38] with some 73 texts written in conventional orthography in pencil. In these also the first

[37] See n 28.

[38] Box 22, DOSC, NFC.

Plate 4 Melody with underlaid verse in phonetic orthography as faircopied by Freeman (courtesy National Folklore Collection, UCD).

verse is usually omitted and singers and dates of performance are only sometimes given; the five are clearly companion notebooks which follow on from the melody notebooks. They contain 'variations from F. na S.',[39] variations from different singers, background notes, prayers, and

[39] Doubtless *Fuinn na Smól*, a general collection of Irish-language songs edited by Fr Pádraig Breathnach and issued as a series of inexpensive undated booklets by Browne & Nolan in Dublin about 1913. They contain several pieces collected in west Cork.

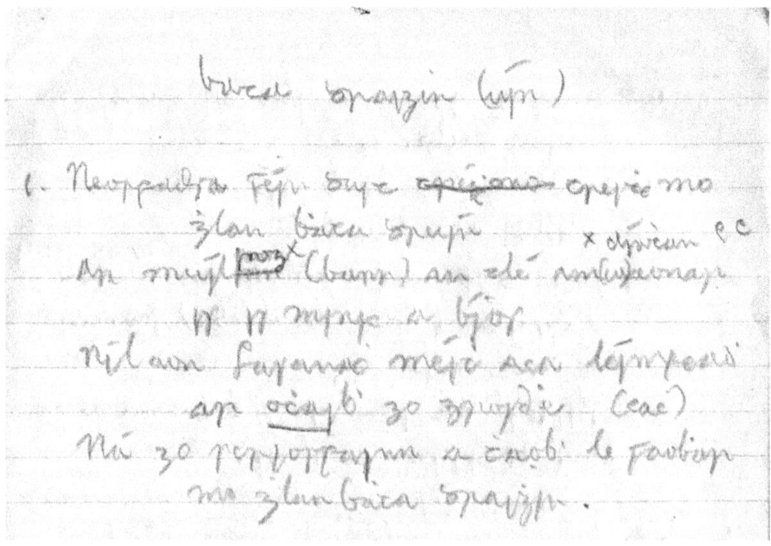

Plate 5 Verse in conventional orthography as taken down by Freeman in the field (courtesy National Folklore Collection, UCD).

Plate 6 Verse in both conventional and phonetic orthography as faircopied by Freeman (courtesy National Folklore Collection, UCD).

a title-list of songs 'Wanted'. The second text sequence consists of nine copybooks of the same kind, undated and labelled 'Abhráin 1–9',[40] written in ink and containing some 88 texts. On the right-hand page of each opening, song texts are written in conventional orthography and on the facing page the same text is 'translated' into a phonetic orthography, a procedure that is abandoned on the last pages which are written only in the latter style. The third text sequence consists of three buff notebooks (18 × 23 cm) with paper covers, labelled 'Words of Ballyvourney

[40] Box 22, DOSC, NFC.

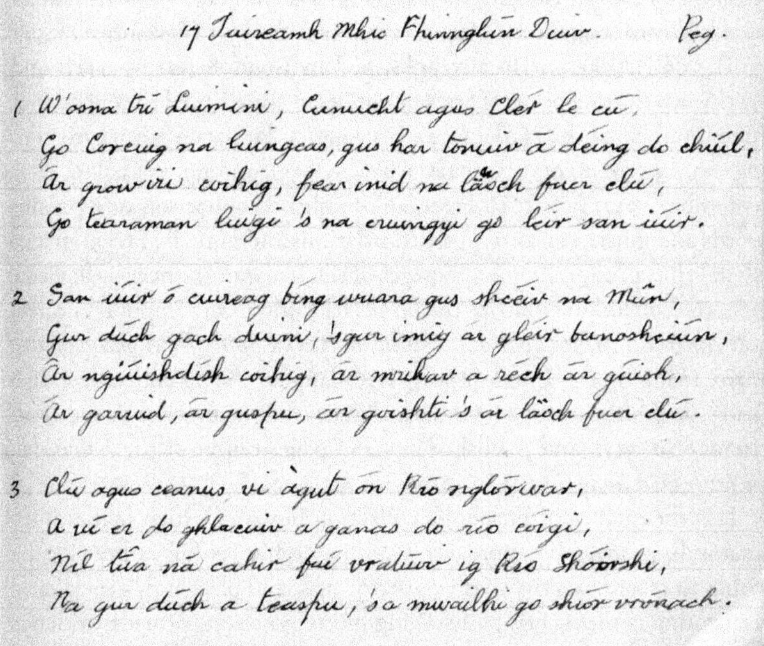

17 Tuireamh Mhic Fhinnghiin Duiv. Peg.

1 W'osna tri Luimini, Cumucht agus Clér le cú,
Go Corcaig na luingeas, gus har tonuiv ā deing do chiúl,
Ar growiri coihig, fear inid na lāoch fuer clú,
Go tearaman luigi 's na cruingyi go leir san iuir.

2 San iuir ó cuireag bing wuara gus sheeiv na Mûn,
Gur duch gach duini, 'sgur imig ar gleir bunoshciun,
Ān ngiuishdish coihig, ār mrikav a réch ār guish,
Ār garrud, ār guspu, ār goishti 's ā lāoch fuer clú.

3 Clú agus ceanus vi àgut ón Rió nglorivar,
a vi er do ghlacuiv a ganas do rio coigi,
Nil tua nā cahir fui vratuiv ig Rio Shóirshi,
Na gur duch a teaspu, 's a mwailhi go shior vronach.

Plate 7 Verses in phonetic orthography as faircopied by Freeman (courtesy National Folklore Collection, UCD).

Songs (Unamended texts)' i–iii,[41] with 87 song texts written in ink and entirely in the phonetic orthography. The order of texts is only generally that of the published collection. A note by Freeman in the second notebook provides a London copying date: 'When I had just written this title, about 10.30 p.m. or so, 8–9–15, an air raid by Zeppelins took place.'

The publication committee of the Folk-Song Society regarded Freeman's collection as 'very valuable' when he offered it to the Society in 1915 for publication, and they intended to publish it in parts, beginning in 1916.[42] War however intervened. While Freeman was on service abroad, Lucy Broadwood, acting editor of the *Journal*, was able to work on preparing the collection for publication and to annotate it 'to a large extent', assisted by Anne Gilchrist, Frank Kidson, Robin Flower, and A.

[41] Ibid.

[42] Broadwood (1920).

Fox-Strangways.[43] On his return in 1919 Freeman resumed work on it—possibly completing the English translations at this stage—and he had revised his third sequence of song-text manuscripts by 3 November 1920.[44]

The collection was finally published in London during 1920 and 1921. With the exception of Society notices, it constituted the entirety of three numbers of the *JFSS*: no. 23 (vol. 6, pt 3, January 1920, xxviii+110 pp.), no. 24 (vol. 6, pt 4, January 1921, [vi]+55), and no. 25 (vol. 6, pt 5, September 1921, [vi]+165). Freeman's published collection of 87 songs (words and music, variants, prose translations and notes by Freeman and others) thus occupies some 370 pages of the *Journal*. In sheer bulk alone then, the collection outstrips the far better known contemporary collection *Amhráin Mhuighe Seóla. Traditional Folk Songs from Galway and Mayo*, made by the London-born Irish-language song collector Edith Drury or Eibhlín Bean Uí Choisdealbha (a fellow-member of the Irish Literary Society), and published as a 160-page volume of the *Journal of the Irish Folk Song Society* in 1919 with 80 songs.[45]

It is the quality of Freeman's collection however which makes it an outstanding one. His approach is ethnographic: as far as possible he wishes to record exactly what was performed, and place it in a social and performing context. His painstaking music notations provide evidence of an acute ear, and an anxiety to record melodic and rhythmic variations, and indicate that Freeman wrote from performance rather than from memory.[46] While he himself seemed to have valued the melodies of the songs more than their texts, and preferred 'folk song' to 'literary stuff',[47] he wished to respect the regard in which his singers held the words and he gave them 'exactly as I heard it from the singers [...] the only form in which I should have consented to their appearance [...] I have printed and translated a number of passages which would be rejected on the grounds of propriety in a popular, published book'.[48] The wish to represent accurately the pronunciation of his singers led him to

43 Ibid.

44 Note on last page of 'Words of Ballyvourney Songs (Unamended texts)', iii. Further changes however appear in the published collection; some are typographical errors in the difficult phonetic orthography.

45 This collection was republished in book form in Costello (1923).

46 Only one melody is noted as not having been written from performance: 'A memory sketch of An Seanduine as it was sung last night (22/9/14) by Murphy of Cluain Drohad' (copybook V, Box 21, DOSC, NFC).

47 'The Words', *JFSS* 23 (Jan. 1920), xiii.

48 Ibid., xiii–xiv. Not all such passages however.

use the form of phonetic orthography already referred to for his texts which, while usefully indicating Ballyvourney pronunciation and dialect features, has ever since remained as an obstacle for those who read standard Irish. Freeman's orthography was his own adaptation of a simplified-spelling system for Irish unsuccessfully promoted from earlier in the century by some Cork revivalists: Dr Osborn J. Bergin, Rev. Dr O'Daly, and especially Seán or Shán Ó Cuív, who wrote a pamphlet advocating the system, and included in it traditional song-texts.[49] The main features of the Ó Cuív system were the use of the Roman alphabet (adding the alien letters *j*, *k*, *q*, *v*, *w*, *x*, *y*, and *z* to the Irish alphabet), and spelling which attempted to imitate exact (Cork) pronunciation. Freeman's sympathetic general ethnographic approach is best seen in his vivid and subtle description of 'An Irish Concert' he attended at harvest-time in a local farmhouse, one of the best descriptions in print of Irish music-making.[50]

Freeman's entire collection was made to a high standard of scholarship, one which immediately won the admiration of his London peers, his colleagues in the Folk-Song Society. But the collection was also made with obvious enjoyment and an empathy with the local Cork singers and their audiences. In response, the Ballyvourney people approved of his enterprise and were amazed at his command of Irish, although they thought him eccentric and were amused at his single-mindedness.[51] He was dryly amused at their amusement. The result of their ten-week collaboration with this unusual Englishman is an exemplary collection of their songs in Irish, many of which might not be now known or available for re-creation were it not for his efforts. We may concur with the expressed sentiments of an anonymous local singer, as recorded in one of his Ballyvourney notebooks: 'Wisha Críost leat go brách and you have it out of the smoke, a Mhister Freeman'.[52]

With thanks to Professor Ríonach uí Ógáin, Director, National Folklore Collection, University College Dublin, for access to the A. Martin Freeman papers and for permission to reproduce images from them, and to Críostóir Mac Cárthaigh, Archivist-Collector, NFC, for various help; to Cathal Goan for advice; to Malcolm Taylor, Librarian, Vaughan

49 Ó Cuív (1907).

50 *JFSS* 23 (Jan. 1920), xxi–xxvii.

51 *JFSS* 25 (Sept. 1921), 333–4.

52 'Rough' copybook II (Box 22, DOSC, NFC).

Williams Memorial Library, London, for advice; to Magda Sagarzazu, Canna House Archivist, Isle of Canna, for photographs of A. Martin Freemann from the John Lorne Campbell Collection, Cana House, National Trust of Scotland; to Dr Cathy Hayes, Administrator, Irish Manuscripts Commission, and Commission members James McGuire, Dr Deirdre McMahon, and Dr Michael Kennedy, for advice; to the staffs of the National Library of Ireland, the Library of the Royal Irish Academy, and the Irish Traditional Music Archive; to Maeve Gebruers, Printed Materials Officer, ITMA, for text scanning and the processing of images; and to Jackie Small, Sound Archivist, ITMA, for the digitization of Freeman's published melodies as interactive music files.

APPENDIX: THE SONGS OF THE FREEMAN COLLECTION

As a general aid to identification and access, the titles and associated first lines of Freeman's published songs are listed here in modern standardized spelling (with the retention of an occasional feature of dialect for metrical and other reasons) and in published order. As an indication of the extent of the collection, the numbers following represent respectively the number of verses in each song and the numbers of lines in each verse as presented by Freeman, but without taking defective lines into account.

As a further aid to access, a PDF facsimile of the published Freeman collection and interactive music scores of its melodies have been made available online as an extension of this essay at www.itma.ie, the website of the Irish Traditional Music Archive (search 'Freeman').

Journal of the Folk-Song Society 23 (vol. 6, part 3), January 1920

1 Habit Shirt ('Do casadh cailín deas orm 'bhí banúil, geanúil, béasach'), 7 × 4
2 I am a Young Fellow ('I am a young fellow that ran out of my land and means'), 11 × 4
3 An Saighdiúirín Singil ('Is saighdiúirín singil mé 'briseadh as garda an rí'), 6 × 4
4 An Seanduine 1 ('Is triúr a bhí agam am' cheangal le hiarlais'), 5 × 4
5 Táimse i mo Chodladh ('Is fada don fhuaim seo ag gluaiseacht eadrainn'), 1 × 8

6 Tráthnóinín Déanach ag Teacht cois Leasa Dom ('Tráthnóinín déanach ag teacht cois leasa dom'), 4 × 8

7 Tráthnóinín Déanach i gCéin ('Tráthnóinín déanach i gcéin cois leasa dom'), 6 × 8

8 A Phádraig, a Stóraigh ('A Phádraig, a stóraigh, ó tá tú go brónach'), 5 × 8

9 An Cailín Deas Rua ('Ar m'aisling aréir dom trím' néalta is mé i mo leaba i mo shuan'), 6 × 4 / second version ('Deineadh aisling aréir dom trím' néal is mé i mo leaba chun suain'), 3 × 4

10 An Bata Draighin ('Neosfadsa féin duit tréithe mo ghlan-bhata draighin'), 4 × 4

11 Loch Léin ('Do shiúlas a lán gan spás i dtosach mo shaoil'), 5 × 4

12 Tadhg Buí ('Nuair a shuím os cionn dí agus cnagaim an clár'), 8 × 4 / second version ('Nuair a shuím chun na dí is gan phingin i mo láimh'), 1 × 4

13 Luan Dubh an Áir ('Ó ins an Luan dubh an áir tháinig suaimhneas róbhreá'), 8 × 4

14 Ar Éirinn Ní Neosfainn Cé hÍ ('Aréir is mé ag aeraíocht ar nóin'), 7 × 8 / second version ('There's a home by the wide Avonmore'), 1 × 4

15 Coill Rois ('Trí Choill Rois im' aonar i ngaorthadh glas aoibhinn'), 5 × 12

16 Maidin Luan Cásca ('Maidin Luan Cásca tríd an mBlárnan soir'), 7 × 8

17 Solas na Ré ('Le solas na ré go déanach dom'), 5 × 8

18 An Chúil Duibh-Ré ('Is dubhach scíosmhar atá an Laoi seo ag gabháil eadraibh siar'), 6 × 4

18a An Rós Geal Dubh 1 ('Ar an aonach má théann tú ag díol do stoic'), 1 × 4 / second version ('Is fada an réim do thug mé féinig ó inné go inniu'), 1 × 4

19 Móra ar Maidin Duit ('Móra agus Muire duit, a spéirbhean chiúin'), 5 × 4 / second version ('Mór ar maidin duit, a spéirbhean chiúin'), 1 × 4

20 Ré-Chnoc Mná Duibhe, *or* Is Fada Dom ar Buaireamh ('Is fada dom ar buaireamh ag cur tuairisc' mo ghrá'), 11 × 4 / second version ('Is fada dom ar buaireamh ag cur tuairisc' mo ghrá'), 1 × 4 / third version ('Is fada dom ar buaireamh ag cur tuairisc' mo ghrá'), 1 × 4

21 Casadh an tSúgáin, *or* An Súisín Bán ('Do casadh cailín deas orm in uaigneas na dtráth'), 8 × 4

22 A Chomharsain a Chroí Istigh, *or* Amhrán na Stagún ('A chomharsain a chroí istigh, ar airíbhse an ní úd?'), 5 × 8
23 Is é Airím ag Mo Mhuintir ('Is é airím ag mo mhuintir á shíor-rá le chéile'), 7 × 4
24 Tráthnóinín Saoire ('Tráthnóinín saoire is mé ar bhuíochtaint na gréine'), 5 × 4
25 Cailín an Chúil Chraobhaigh ('A chailín an chúil chraobhaigh, cad é an taobh ar a luíonn tú?'), 7 × 4
25a Cailín an Chúil Chraobhaigh [no words]
26 Ainnir Dheas Crúite na mBó ('Ar mo thaisteal trí Baile na Múirne'), 7 × 8
27 Cailín Deas Crúite na mBó ('Agus airímse an cailín seo ar shiúl'), 5 × 8
28 Ceo Draíochta ('Ceo draíochta sheol oíche chun fáin mé'), 9 × 8
29 An Ghamhnach ('Lá is mé i nDroichead [na] Bandan'), 9 × 4
30 An tSeanbhean Bhocht ('Maidin aoibhinn shamhraidh dom ar inse cois na Bandan'), 5 × 8
31 An Goirtín Eornan ('Is buachaillín fíor-óg mé, go bhfóire orm Rí na nGrás'), 9 × 4
31a An Goirtín Eornan, *or* Buachaillín Fíor-óg [no words]
32 An Clár Bog Déil ('A shearc is a rúin, is fada liom atá an Domhnach uaim'), 1 × 4 / second version ('Cois na Bríde is gile bímse go súgach sámh'), 8 × 4
33 An Spealadóir ('Cois Abhann Móire is mé ag spealadóireacht lá breá i mo shaol'), 5 × 4
34 Tuireamh Mhic Iníon Duibh ('M'osna trí Luimneach, Connacht agus Cléir [sic] le cumha'), 11 × 4

Journal of the Folk-Song Society 24 (vol. 6, part 4), January 1921

35 Lá Fhéile Pádraig (Lá Fhéile Pádraig i mo shuí 'tigh an tabhairne'), 5 × 8
35a An Cailín Donn ('Ag déanamh smaointe is ea bím liom féinig'), 1 × 8
36 Amhrán an Bháis ('Ar bhóthar Luimnigh is ea do tharla an Bás orm'), 5 × 8
37 Eochaill ('Maidin Domhnaigh is mé ag dul go hEochaill'), 1 × 8
38 Lá dá Rabhas-sa ('Lá dá rabhas-sa i ngleann im' aonar'), 6 × 8
38a An Brianach Óg ('Lá breá gréine is mé ag dul ar aonach'), 3 × 8
39 Aisling Gheal ('Aisling gheal do shlad trím' néal mé'), 5 × 8

40 I nGleann an Chrainn ('I ngleann an chrainn is ann a bhíos-sa'), 4 × 8
41 Fáinnín Geal an Lae [no words]
42 Bean Dubh an Ghleanna ('Tá bó liom ar an sliabh gan éinne beo ina diaidh'), 5 × 8
43 Cad a Dhéanfaidh Sagairt Feasta? ('Cad a dhéanfaidh sagairt feasta gan airgead cléire?'), 5 × 8
44 Éistigh go nInsead Mo Scéal ('Éistigh go n-insead mo scéal agus nach fonn liomsa bréag a aithris'), 5 × 2 + refrain 1 × 2
45 A Dhiarmaid na nAe Istigh ('A Dhiarmaid na n-ae istigh, is náir an scéal duit'), 9 × 8
46 An Staicín Eornan ('Maidin aoibhinn shamhraidh dom cois abhann go nglaonn siad Mealbhrac'), 6 × 8
47 Bó na Leath-Adhairce ('Thíos cois na tuile is ea bheathaíos mo chaora'), 1 × 4 + refrain 1 × 4
48 An Gamhain Geal Bán, *or* Ar Maidin Dé Luain ('Ar maidin Dé Luain is mé ag machnamh'), 7 × 8
49 Nuair d'Éirigh an Ainnir ('Nuair d'éirigh an ainnir ar maidin tar éis phósta'), 3 × 4
50 Aililiú na Gamhna ('Is iníon d'aoire mé féinig gan amhras'), 9 × 4 + refrain 1 × 4
51 Ar Maidin Inné ('Ar maidin inné cois Féile bhíos'), 5 × 8 (incomplete)
52 Níl Sé ina Lá ('Níl sé ina lá, ná ina lá'), 5 × 4 + refrain 1 × 4
53 Seán ó Bharr an Chnoic ('An bfacaíbhse Seán ó bharr an chnoic?'), 1 × 4 + refrain 1 × 1
54 An Cnoicín Fraoigh ('Go deimhin duitse, a Mháire, do thugas searc is grá duit'), 2 × 4

Journal of the Folk-Song Society 25 (vol. 6, part 5), September 1921

55 An Cruimíneach Cam ('Is olc an fear gréasaí an Cruimíneach cam'), 1 × 4
56 An Cailín Donn Deas ('Is bean tú ag baint luachra, mo chailín donn deas'), 6 × 2 + refrain 1 × 2
57 An Crúiscín ('Is fada mé ar an mbaile seo, i mo chónaí ar sráid'), 1 × 5
58 Dá mBeinnse Féinig ('Dá mbeinnse féinig i gCé Phort Láirge'), 5 × 4

59 There was a Lady in Her Father's Garden / The Young and Single Sailor ('There was a lady in her father's garden'), 7 × 4
60 A Dhochtúír Dílis / Uair Bheag roimh Lá ('A dhochtúir dílis, tabhair dom teagasc'), 1 × 8
61 Aréir is Mé im' Aonar ('Aréir is mé im' aonar cois taobh Fleasca an ghaorthaidh'), 6 × 8
62 Lá agus Mé ag Taisteal im' Aonar ('Lá agus mé ag taisteal im' aonar'), 2 × 4
63 Raca Breá mo Chinn ('Maidin aoibhinn fhómhair is mé ag gabháil an ród seo thíos'), 6 × 4
64 Seán Ó Duibhir an Ghleanna ('Éistigh liomsa sealad go neosfad daoibh cér cailleadh'), 1 × 8
65 Éamonn an Chnoic ('Cé hé sin amuigh a bhfuil faobhar ar a ghuth?'), 1 × 4 / second version ('And he says: 'Lady love, won't you come with me now?''), 1 × 4
66 An Páistín Fionn ('Grá le m'anam mo pháistín fionn'), 1 × 4 + refrain 1 × 4
67 An Seanduine 2 / Is Tinn Dubhach an Pósadh Seo ('Is tinn dubhach an pósadh seo, faraoir, a gealladh dom'), 8 × 8
68 Stad, arú a Rógairín, Stad! ('Tráthnóinín déanach i nglaschoill'), 5 × 4 + refrain 1 × 4
69 An Saor ('Do cheapas mar shlí chugam imeacht ó mo mhuintir'), 5 × 8
70 Do Thugas Grá Cléibh Duit ('Do thugas grá cléibh duit, a spéirbhean, ar dtús'), 8 × 8
71 Aréir is Mé ar Mo Bhogadaíl ('Is do tháinig bean ó Chorcaigh chugam, is do thug sí giní óir dom'), 3 × 4
72 Dob Fhonn Liom Scéal ('Dob fhonn liom scéal beag anois do léigheadh dhíbh'), 5 × 8
73 Tráthnóinín Déanach im' Aonar ('Tráthnóinín déanach im' aonar cois Laoi'), 8 × 4
74 An Póiní Beag Buí ('Tá buachaill ar mo eolas, is is brón liom a shlí'), 5 × 4
75 Bearta Crua 1 ('Ar nóin go déanach a ghluaiseas féinig'), 9 × 8
76 An Spéirbhean Cheansa ('Tá spéirbhean cheansa chaoin den cheantar'), 8 × 8
77 Bearta Crua 2 ('Maidin fuar fliuch ag éirí suas dom'), 1 × 8
78 Cnocáinín Aitinn ('Ní Cnoicín Aitinn is ainm don áit seo'), 4 × 8
79 Bímís ag Ól ('Tráthnóinín fómhair ar leataobh an róid'), 4 × 4 + refrain 1 × 4

80 Ar Maidin ar Drúcht ('Ar maidin ar drúcht is mé ag siúl go pras'), 1 × 4
81 Faiche Bhreá Aerach an Cheoil ('Mo shlán ar fad chun mná agus fear san áit seo'), 3 × 8
82 Eibhlín a Rúin ('Do sheolfainn féin na gamhna leat, a Eibhlín a rúin'), 1 × 4
83 Snaidhm an Ghrá ('Is mo ghrá go léir tú, agus Dia do bheatha chugam'), 7 × 4
84 Where are You Going? ('Oh where are you going, my pretty little girl?'), 2 × 4

Bibliography

Breathnach, D., and M. Ní Mhurchú (1990) *Beathaisnéis a Dó, 1882–1982*, Dublin.

Broadwood, L. (1920) 'Preface,' *Journal of the Folk-Song Society* 23, iii.

Costello, E. (1923) *Amhráin Mhuighe Seóla. Traditional folk songs from Galway and Mayo*, Dublin.

Freeman, A.M. (1941) 'Bicentenary of the Madrigal Society,' *The Musical Times* 82, 271.

— (1958) 'Notes on Scottish Gaelic waulking songs by J. L. Campbell,' *Journal of the International Folk Music Council* 10, 106.

Hardiman, J. (1831) *Irish minstrelsy, or bardic remains of Ireland*, 2 vols., London.

Ó Cróinín, D. (2000) *The songs of Elizabeth Cronin, Irish traditional singer: the complete song collection*, Dublin [with 2 CDs].

Ó Cuív, B. (1959–60) [Obituary of A.M. Freeman], *Éigse* 9, 204.

Ó Cuív, S. (1907) *Irish made easy: being lessons, stories, songs, etc., in simplified spelling, with an introduction explaining the reasons for the adoption of this change from the current spelling of Irish*, Dublin.

O'Daly, J. (1849) *The poets and poetry of Munster: a selection of Irish songs by the poets of the last century*, Dublin.

O'Sullivan, D. (1960a) Typescript obituary of 'Mr. A.M. Freeman' (Jan. 1960), Box 23, Donal O'Sullivan Collection, National Folklore Collection, University College Dublin.

— (1960b) [Obituary of A.M. Freeman], *The Times* of London (8 Feb. 1960), 12.

— (1960c) [Obituary of A.M. Freeman], *Journal of the English Folk Dance and Song Society* 9, 60.

— (1961) [Obituary of A.M. Freeman], *Journal of the International Folk Music Council* 13, 94.

Walsh, E. (1847) *Irish popular songs*, Dublin.

MANUSCRIPT INDEX

Lightning Source UK Ltd.
Milton Keynes UK
UKHW020932131222
413854UK00005B/82